THE CULTURES AND GLOBALIZATION SERIES ①

THE CULTURES AND GLOBALIZATION SERIES ①

CONFLICTS AND TENSIONS

Edited by

HELMUT K. ANHEIER AND YUDHISHTHIR RAJ ISAR

SAGE Publications
Los Angeles • London • New Delhi • Singapore

First published 2007

SAGE Publications Ltd
1 Oliver's Yard
55 City Road
London EC1Y 1SP

SAGE Publications Inc.
2455 Teller Road
Thousand Oaks, California 91320

SAGE Publications India Pvt Ltd
B 1/I1 Mohan Cooperative Industrial Area
Mathura Road, Post bag 7
New Delhi 110 044

SAGE Publications Asia-Pacific Pte Ltd
33 Pekin Street #02-01
Far East Square
Singapore 048763

British Library Cataloguing in Publication data

A catalogue record for this book is available from the British Library

ISBN 978 1 4129 3471-8
ISBN 978 1 4129 3472-5 (pbk)

Library of Congress Control Number 2006928698

Typeset by C&M Digitals (P) Ltd., Chennai, India
Printed and bound in Slovenia, by MKT Print d.d.
Printed on paper from sustainable resources

In a sense, globalization began as a cultural phenomenon. The simultaneous availability of information everywhere on the globe was the seed of world-wide developments economically and politically. Strangely perhaps, the economic and political consequences of globalization are not only clearly in evidence but have also been widely studied, whereas few have focused on the cultural consequences of what was originally a cultural phenomenon. *The Cultures and Globalization Series* fills this gap, and for that reason alone it is most welcome.

The financial and general economic consequences of globalization have become a part of our lives, even if they are variegated and in no sense simple. The political consequences of globalization are with us every day, not least through the threat of the world-wide interconnections of terrorism. By contrast, the cultural consequences of globalization are more complex and less visible. Nor are they a set of developments pointing in one direction only. Globalization has now become widely recognized, that is to say the simultaneous extension of relevant cultural spaces and growing significance of more immediate, locally limited sources of cultural identity.

The task of documenting the relations of culture and globalization is thus formidable. It is appropriate that the *Series* editors, Helmut Anheier and Yudhishthir Raj Isar, should have enlisted the support of a large number of authors and advisers to accomplish the task. Professor Anheier himself is no stranger to complexity, as his work on civil society in a variety of countries shows. Professor Isar's background in international cultural policy is equally important to the project's objectives. Thus the project leaders and the authors from diverse parts of the globe guarantee that this *Series* will be about diversity yet usable in many if not all parts of the world.

Such wide utility is strengthened by a methodological feature. The end of ideology has often been stated when in fact ideological politics had a stubborn way of returning. Globalization might be assumed to have consigned ideology finally to the rubbish dumps of history. Yet again we are faced with what has been called, market fundamentalism on the one hand, and with sometimes violent anti-globalization movements on the other. Fortunately there is also the new trend of evidence-based politics, and one may hope that it will prevail. This volume is nothing if not evidence-based. It provides a considerable amount of evidence otherwise unavailable or only accessible in disparate sources. Not the least merit of this *Series* is that it helps find out what is actually happening. There are valuable beginnings of the development of indices of the cultural consequences of globalization. In this way, the volume will contribute to making full use of the opportunities of globalization while not ignoring its threats.

Ralf Dahrendorf
London, 2006

The Cultures and Globalization Series has relied on the support, advice and contributions of numerous individuals and organizations. We endeavor to acknowledge all who have participated in the development and production of this project, and are grateful for the support, advice and encouragement received. The final publication remains the responsibility of the editors.

International Advisory Board

Participants in Consultations held in Paris, New Delhi, New York, Washington, and Barcelona

Alice Abreu, Rob Albro, Jeffrey Alexander, Edith Archambault, Alberta Arthurs, Pat Aufderheide, Sushma Bahl, Ann Baker, Alec Balasescu, Jordi Baltà, Manfred

Bardeleben, Elisenda Belda, Françoise Benhamou, Lluís Bonet, Jozsef Borocz, Tom Bradshaw, Craig Calhoun, Esteve Caramés, Judit Carrera, Miguel Centeno, Joni Maya Cherbo, Tyler Cowen, Diana Crane, Diane Dodd, Zahava Doering, Waddick Doyle, Baykal Eyyubeglu, James Fitzpatrick, Nancy Fuller, Aimee Fullman, Leonore Yaffee Garcia, Sandra Gibson, Bill Gilcher, Salvador Giner, Faye Ginsburg, Mercedes Giovinazzo, William Glade, Xavier Greffe, Narayani Gupta, James Herbert, Bill Ivey, Maria Rosario Jackson, Selim Jahan, Om Prakash Jain, Varun Jain, Arnita Jones, Hagai Katz, Jonathan Katz, Stanley Katz, Inge Kaul, Barbara Kirshenblatt-Gimblett, Adam Klausner, Annamari Laaksonen, Sophia Labadi, Marc Leland, Hui Lu, Bob Lynch, Peter Mandaville, Connie McNeely, Sara Meneses, Tanni Mukhopadhyay, Francesc Muñoz, Mary Ann Newman, Jorge Osterling, Agnieszka Paczynska, Sakiko Fukuda-Parr, Jordi Pascual, Peter Rantasa, Serge Regourd, Greg Richards, David Rieff, Aurea Roldan, Dominique Sagot-Duvauroux, Joan Shigekawa, James Allen Smith, Paul Smith, Kate Stimpson, András Szántó, Nalini Thakur, Stefan Toepler, Heather Townsend, Anne Vena, Shalini Venturelli, Monica Villegas, Ray Wanner, Jean-Pierre Warnier, Janine Wedel, Nancy Weiss, Harrison White, Margaret Wyszomirski, George Yudice.

Additional support

Guest boxes

Sreten Ugričić and Jean-Joseph Boillot.

Research Coordination for Indicator Suites

Tia Morita and Jennifer E. Mosley.

Design and Production of Indicator Suites

Willem Henri Lucas with assistance from David Whitcraft, Levi Richard Brooks and Daniel Tadiarca.

Researchers

Michael Kyle Behen, Lauren Buckland, Karina Danek, Juliet Gharibian, Amber Hawkes, Hagai Katz, Aaron Kofner, Ilona Iskandar, Marcus Lam, Margaret Lee, Luis Medina, Leda Nelson, Aiha Nguyen, Ronaldo Nibbe, Alexander Nino-Ruiz, Cheryl Samson, Lily Song, Swati Solanki.

Artwork

Emilia Birlo

A note from the Artist

> *The images readers will find throughout this volume express an idea I regard as fundamental to the human condition: the human longing for dignity. For this reason, I focused on humans as individuals and not as part of larger groups, let alone masses. I tried to visualize this longing for dignity with images that, increasingly reduced in form and varying in abstraction, are somewhere between ancient cave painting and contemporary urban graffiti. Human dignity is also an ongoing search, and for this reason I tried to make the images express a certain dynamism and optimism.*

Administrative support
Jocelyn Guihama and Laurie Spivak.

Financial Support

We gratefully acknowledge the financial support of the following institutions:

Aventis Foundation
Atlantic Philanthropies
The Bank of Sweden Tercentenary Foundation
Calouste Gulbenkian Foundation
Compagnia di San Paolo
The J. Paul Getty Trust
The Prince Claus Fund for Culture and Development
Bertelsmann Foundation
Shell International Limited
Swedish International Development Agency
UCLA School of Public Affairs

In particular we would like to acknowledge the support of Rui Esgaio (Calouste Gulbenkian Foundation), Els van der Plas (The Prince Claus Fund), Dario Disegni (Compagnia di San Paolo), Dan Brandström, Mats Rolén and Carl-Johan Kleberg (The Bank of Sweden Tercentenary Foundation).

We also wish to recognize the supportive partnership of Forum Cultural Mundial (World Culture Forum), Rio de Janeiro, and its Director-General, Dieter Jaenicke.

Hugo Achugar previously taught at Universidad de la Républica (Uruguay) and Northwestern University, held distinguished visiting appointments at UC Irvine and Dartmouth, and has been the recipient of two Rockefeller Foundation Humanities grants. He is the author of *Ideologías y estructuras narratives en José Donoso (1950–1970)* (1979), *Poesía y sociedad (Uruguay, 1880–1911)* (1986), *La biblioteca en ruinas: reflexiones culturales desde la periferia* (1994) and *Escritos sobre arte, cultura, y literature* (2003).

Laura Adams is an instructor in the sociology department at Princeton University. She has written articles on the globalization of culture in Central Asia and is finishing a book, *The Spectacular State: Culture and National Identity in Uzbekistan*.

Helmut Anheier is Professor of Public Policy and Social Welfare at the University of California, Los Angeles (UCLA), and Director of the Center for Civil Society, and the Center for Globalization and Policy Research at UCLA. He is also a Centennial Professor at the Centre for the Study of Global Governance, London School of Economics (LSE). His work has focused on civil society, the non-profit sector, organizational studies, policy analysis, sociology of culture, and comparative methodology.

Rustom Bharucha is an independent writer, director, and cultural critic based in Kolkata, India. He has written a number of books including: *Theatre and the World*, *The Question of Faith*, *In the Name of the Secular*, *The Politics of Cultural Practice*, *Rajasthan: An Oral History*, and *Another Asia*. Combining cultural theory with theatre practice and activism, he conducts workshops with underprivileged communities on the politics of identity and rights, while intervening in debates relating to international cultural policy.

Emilia Birlo is a visual artist and fashion designer who divides her time between Germany and the United States. Her art can be viewed at www.Milli.Birlo.de and her creations at www.birlos.de.

Jean-Joseph Boillot is Professeur Agrégé de Sciences Economiques et Sociales and has a PhD in Development Economics from the university of Paris-Nanterre. He spent most of the 1980s in India and China as Associate Researcher with an institute attached to the office of the Prime Minister of France. From 1990 to 2005 he was Economic Advisor to the Ministry of Finance on Eastern Europe, Russia, China and India. He is the author of more than 20 books, including *Europe after Enlargement, Economic challenges for EU and India* (Academic Foundation, New Delhi 2005) and many articles.

Ananda Breed is a PhD student of Applied and Social Theatre at the University of Manchester. She has facilitated workshops for the UN Special Session for Children, the UN Third World Water Forum (Osaka, Japan), the City Hall Forum Theatre and Video Initiative (NY), Search for Common Ground (Bukavu, Congo) and the Ministry of Justice (Kigali, Rwanda). Her dissertation will address performance in relation to justice and reconciliation in Rwanda including the Gacaca courts, established theatre companies, and grassroots reconciliation associations. She recently presented her paper 'Theatre as Social Intervention in Post-Genocide Rwanda' at the International Researching Drama and Theatre Education Conference at Exeter University in April 2005.

Amparo Cadavid is professor of Ethics and Communication for Social Change, and a senior research fellow at the Faculty of Communications of the Pontifical Javeriana University, in Bogotá, Colombia, since 2003. She has carried out and published several studies on community and citizen media. She is an expert in the design and application of communication strategies within regional development and peace plans, in zones of high conflict. She has also conducted consultancy and policy advisory work for the REDPRODEPAZ (National Development and Peace Programs Network), the Ministry of Culture and several Development and Peace Programs and citizen media networks in Colombia.

Kathryn A. Carver, a health and human rights lawyer with both a law degree and a degree in epidemiology, is the Executive Director of The Concord Project. The Concord Project undertakes research and action programmes to design successful cross-community organizations and leadership training in divided communities with longstanding animosity. She has led the Technical Assistance Program of the Ryan White Care Act while at John Snow, Inc., a public health consulting company. Previously, she was the Director of the Office of Patient Advocacy of the (U.S.) National Marrow Donor Program. She is the author of many articles on conflict mediation, women's political participation, and the rights of Indian children.

Miguel Angel Centeno is Professor of Sociology and International Affairs at Princeton University and is Director of the Princeton Institute for International and Regional Studies. He is currently working on a book project, *Visualizing Globalization*, as well as an online Historical Atlas of Globalization and the International Networks Archive (www.princeton.edu/~ina).

Georges Corm is Professor at Saint-Joseph University in Beirut and Consultant to several international organizations on issues related to the development of the Arab world and international economic cooperation. His publications and books have focused on international development issues but also on the contemporary history of the Middle East and the relations between the Arab Orient and Europe. He is a member of several scientific councils or trustee boards of non-profit organizations in Europe and the Arab world. His latest book is devoted to a critical examination of the religious revivals in the Moslem and western worlds.

Beverly Crawford teaches Political Economy at the University of California, Berkeley and is Associate Director of UC Berkeley's Institute of European Studies. She is the co-editor of *The Myth of Ethnic Conflict: Politics, Economics and Cultural Violence,* (Berkeley: International and Area Studies, 1998), and *The Convergence of Civilizations: Constructing a Mediterranean Region* (University of Toronto Press, 2006.) She recently served as a co-principal investigator on a Ford Foundation project entitled *Promising Practices in Information Technology Training for Disadvantaged Adults* and is currently working on a three- volume series entitled *Globalization Comes Home: The Impact of Globalization on the United States.*

Franziska Deutsch is a Research Associate and PhD candidate at the School of Humanities and Social Sciences at the International University Bremen, Germany.

Together with Chris Welzel and Ronald Inglehart (2005) she published 'Social Capital, Voluntary Associations and Collective Action: Which Aspects of Social Capital Have the Greatest "Civic" Payoff?' in the *Journal of Civil Society*. Her main research interests cover political participation, political culture, and political and social values.

Janadas Devan is a Singaporean journalist. He was educated at the University of Singapore and Cornell University. His publications include journal articles on culture and politics, as well as articles in newspapers and magazines in Singapore, the United States, Malaysia and elsewhere.

Leo F. Estrada is an Associate Professor of Urban Planning, School of Public Affairs at the University of California, Los Angeles (UCLA). He is a social demographer with a focus on the demographic aspects of ethnic and racial populations, planning for multiple publics and urban revitalization. He has publications on the topic of immigrant adaptation, language access issues and transnational networks.

Aníbal Ford is a Distinguished Professor in the Social Sciences Department at the University of Buenos Aires, where he directed the Communication Studies and Masters of Communication and Culture program. He currently leads research into the visual representations of socio-cultural diversity, for the Secretariat of Science and Technology at the University of Buenos Aires. He has published several books about communications, culture, and information. His latest publications include: *La marca de la bestia. Identificación, Desigualdades e infoentretenimiento en la sociedad contemporánea*; *Resto del mundo: Nuevas mediaciones de las agendas criticas internacionales*, and the fictional *Oxidación.*

Nathan Gardels is editor of National Policy Quarterly, the journal of social and political thought published by Blackwell, as well as the Global Viewpoint service of the *Los Angeles Times* Syndicate/Tribune Media, which has 35 million readers in 15 languages. His latest book is *The Changing Global Order: World Leaders Reflect* (Blackwell, 1997).

Lord Anthony Giddens has taught at the University of Leicester and subsequently at Cambridge, where he was Professor of Sociology. From 1997 to 2003 he was Director of the London School of Economics. He is currently a Life Fellow of King's College, Cambridge. He was made a Life Peer in May 2004. He is a Fellow of the American Academy of Science and the Chinese Academy of Social Sciences and was the BBC Reith Lecturer in 1999. He has had a major impact upon the evolution of New Labour in the UK. He took part in the original Blair–Clinton dialogues from 1997 onwards. He is one of the founders of Polity Press, one of the best known publishers in the social sciences and the humanities.

Alejandro Grimson is Director of the *Instituto de Altos Estudios Sociales* (*Universidad de San Martin*), Buenos Aires, and researcher of the CONICET. He has published books and articles on migration, border zones, and ethnic and national identities, such as: *Argentina and the Southern Cone. Neoliberalism and National Imagination* (with Gabriel Kessler). He participated in different research projects and international seminars with Princeton University, Texas University, Social Science Research Council, and other institutions.

Ronald Inglehart is a professor of political science and program director at the Institute for Social Research at the University of Michigan. He helped found the

Euro-Barometer surveys and directs the World Values Surveys. His research deals with changing belief systems and their impact on social and political change. Author of more than 200 publications, his most recent books are (with Pippa Norris) *Rising Tide: Gender Equality and Cultural Change Around the World* (Cambridge University Press, 2003) and *Sacred and Secular: Religion and Politics Worldwide* (Cambridge University Press, 2004); and (with Christian Welzel) *Modernization, Cultural Change and Democracy: The Human Development Sequence* (Cambridge University Press, 2005). He also edited *Mass Values and Social Change: Findings from the Values Surveys* (Leiden: Brill Publishers, 2003) and *Human Beliefs and Values: A Cross-Cultural Sourcebook based on the 1999-2001 Values Surveys* (Mexico City: Siglo XXI, 2004).

Yudhishthir (Raj) Isar, an anthropologist by training, is Jean Monnet Professor of Cultural Policy Studies at The American University of Paris and also teaches at the *Institut d'Etudes Politiques (Sciences Po).* He is the President of the European Forum for Arts and Heritage (EFAH), a board member of the Institute of International Visual Arts (*inIVA)* and of the Fitzcarraldo Foundation (Turin), Special Advisor to the World Monuments Fund (New York) and the Sanskriti Foundation (New Delhi). Earlier, at UNESCO, he was Executive Secretary of the World Commission on Culture and Development, director of cultural policies and of the International Fund for the Promotion of Culture.

Linda Kaboolian, a sociologist, is a faculty member at the John F. Kennedy School of Government at Harvard University, where she is the Director of the Labor Program and Co-Director of the Executive Program for State and Local Officials. Her areas of specialization are conflict mediation, organizational behaviour, labour policy and educational policy. She is the Co-Principal Investigator of The Concord Project. Her new book, *Win–Win Labor–Management Collaboration in Education* was published in 2006. She is also the co-author of *Working Better Together: A Practical Guide for Union Leaders, Elected Officials and Managers.*

Dragan Klaic is a Permanent Fellow of Felix Meritis (Amsterdam). He teaches Arts and Cultural Policy at the University of Leiden and serves as advisor, editor, researcher and trainer. Klaic has worked as a theatre critic and dramaturge, held professorships at the University of Arts Belgrade and University of Amsterdam and guest professorships in the USA, led the *Theater Instituut Nederland*, co-founded the European Theatre Quarterly *Euromaske*, and served as the President of the European Network of Information Centres for the Performing Arts and of the European Forum for the Arts and Heritage. He was the Moderator of the Reflection Group of the European Cultural Foundation and author of its final report *Europe as a Cultural Project* (2005).

Ronnie D. Lipschutz is Professor of Politics, Co-Director of the Center for Global, International and Regional Studies at the University of California, Santa Cruz. His most recent books are *Globalization, Governmentality and Global Politics: Regulation for the Rest of Us?* (Routledge, 2005) and a text co-authored with Mary Ann Tétreault, *Global Politics as if People Matter* (Rowman and Littlefield, 2005). His areas of research and teaching include international politics, global environmental affairs, US foreign policy, empire and religion, globalization, international regulation, technology and public policy, and film, fiction, and politics.

Willem Henri Lucas (designer) studied at the Academy of Visual Arts in Arnhem in the Netherlands and worked as an intern and apprentice for Max Kisman. From 1990 to 2002 he served as a professor and chair of the Utrecht School of the Arts' Graphic Design department. In 1998 he designed holiday postage stamps for the PTT (Dutch

Post and telecom company). In 2003 and 2004 he won a 'Best Book' award and a nomination from the Art Directors' Club in the Netherlands for his catalogue design and posters series for 'de 4e salon' exhibition for Centraal Museum Utrecht. He teaches at UCLA's D/MA and has done freelance jobs for Ogilvy and Mather. He is working for the Museum of Contemporary Art in Los Angeles where he designed The Painting in Tongues catalogue, and has just finished designing the book *Everythinghappensatonce* on video-artist Euan Macdonald for Kunstverlag Nuremberg, Germany.

Brian Min is a graduate student in political science at the University of California, Los Angeles. He uses formal models and quantitative methods to study the comparative politics of ethnicity and has conducted field research among the Inuit of the Canadian Arctic. He holds a BA from Cornell University and a MPP from Harvard University.

Ahmad S. Moussalli is Professor of Political Science at the American University of Beirut. He was visiting Professor at the Center for Muslim–Christian Understanding at Georgetown University (USA) and University of Copenhagen (Denmark). He is the author of numerous writings, including: *The Islamic Quest for Human Rights, Pluralism, and Democracy*; *Historical Dictionary of Islamic Fundamentalist Movements in the Arab World, Iran and Turkey*; *Human Rights, Pluralism and Democracy in Islam*; *Myths and Realities of Islamic Fundamentalism: Theoretical Aspects and Case Studies*; *Radical Islamic Fundamentalism: The Ideological and Political Discourse of Sayyid Qutb*; *A Theoretical Reading In Islamic Fundamentalism Discourse.*

Barbara J. Nelson, a political scientist, is the Dean of the UCLA School of Public Affairs. She was previously the Vice President of Radcliffe College. Her areas of specialization are conflict mediation in civil society, organizational design, and leadership education. She is the Founder of The Concord Project, and the co-author with Linda Kaboolian and Kathryn A. Carver of *The Concord Handbook: How to Build Social Capital Across Communities.* She is the author of six books including *Leadership and Diversity: A Case Book* (UCLA and the Ford Foundation, 2004) and over sixty articles. Active in community leadership, Dean Nelson is on the Board of Trustees of the United Way of Greater Los Angeles and See Jane, a US organization dedicated to better presentation of girls and women in electronic media for children under 12.

Pippa Norris is the McGuire Lecturer in Comparative Politics at the John F. Kennedy School of Government, Harvard University. Her research compares elections and public opinion, political communications, and gender politics. She has published almost three dozen books, with a related series of volumes for Cambridge University Press including, with Ronald Inglehart, *Rising Tide: Gender Equality and Cultural Change Around the Globe* (2003), and *Sacred and Secular: Religion and Politics Worldwide* (2004, winner of the Virginia Hodgkinson prize from the Independent Sector). Her most recent research is for a new book on *Driving Democracy: Do power-sharing institutions work*? (for Cambridge University Press).

Francis B. Nyamnjoh is Associate Professor and Head of Publications and Dissemination with the Council for the Development of Social Science Research in Africa (CODESRIA). He has taught sociology, anthropology and communication studies at universities in Cameroon, Botswana and South Africa, and has researched and written extensively on Cameroon and Botswana, where he was awarded the 'Senior Arts Researcher of the Year' prize for 2003. His most recent books include *Negotiating an Anglophone Identity* (Brill, 2003), *Rights and the Politics of Recognition in Africa* (Zed Books, 2004), *Africa's Media, Democracy and the Politics of Belonging* (Zed

Books, 2005), *Insiders and Outsiders: Citizenship and Xenophobia in Contemporary Southern Africa* (CODESRIA/ZED Books, 2006).

Silvia Ramos is a social scientist and the area coordinator for minorities, social movements and citizenship at the University Candido Mendes Center for Studies on Public Security and Citizenship, in Rio de Janeiro. Since 2004 she coordinates the project Youth and the Police in partnership with the cultural group Afro Reggae. The experience uses music, art and culture as a means of reducing the barriers between the police and youngsters from slum areas. Silvia Ramos has published *Police Stops, Suspects and Discrimination in the City of Rio de Janeiro* (2005) with Leonarda Musumeci.

Clemencia Rodríguez is Associate Professor at the University of Oklahoma, in the United States. Dr Rodríguez has conducted research since 1984 on citizens' media in different international contexts including Nicaragua, Colombia, Spain, Chile, and among Latino communities in the United States. Dr Rodríguez' publications on citizens' media include *Fissures in the Mediascape: An International Study of Citizens' Media* (2001), 'Citizens' Media and the Voice of the Angel/Poet' (in *Media International Australia,* 2002), 'Civil Society and Citizens' Media: Peace Architects for the New Millennium' (in *Redeveloping Communication for Social Change: Theory, Practice, Power* (ed.) Karin Wilkins 2002), and 'The Bishop and His Star: Citizens' Communication in Southern Chile' (in N. Couldry and J. Curran (eds.) *Contesting Media Power: Alternative Media in a Networked World*, 177–94. Boulder, CO: Rowman and Littlefield).

James Thompson is Professor of Applied and Social Theatre at the University of Manchester and a Director of the Centre for Applied Theatre Research. He is currently the co-director of In Place of War – a major research project funded by the UK's Arts and Humanities Research Council. He was Guest Editor of TDR: the journal of performance studies Social Theatre edition (T183) and is author of *Applied Theatre: Bewilderment and Beyond* (Peter Lang, 2003) and *Digging Up Stories: Applied Theatre, Performance and War* (Manchester University Press, 2005). He is a theatre practitioner and has worked in Brazil, Burkina Faso, Rwanda, Indonesia, Sri Lanka, the UK and USA. He has research interests in Applied Theatre, community-based theatre and theatre and war.

Bassam Tibi, born 1944 in Damascus and educated in Frankfurt, has been, since 1973, Professor of International Relations at the University of Goettingen, Germany and is, since 2004, A.D. White Professor-at-Large at Cornell University. He is author of 26 books in German and 6 monographs in English, including the recent publications: *The Challenge of Fundamentalism: Political Islam and the New World Disorder,* (University of California Press, 1998, updated edition 2002), *Islam between Culture and Politics,* (Palgrave Macmillan, 2001, enlarged 2nd edition 2005). Tibi lectured at more than 30 universities in four continents and co-authored dozens of English books between 1980 and 2006.

Sreten Ugričić is Director of the National Library of Serbia, Belgrade and is the author of seven books (theory and fiction). During 1992–1997, he was a teaching fellow at the Faculty of Philosophy in Priština (Aesthetics and Ethics) and from 1997–2001 he was programme manager at the Soros Fund (Priština, Belgrade, Budapest). He is a member of the Serbian PEN Club, and sits on The European Library Project Executive

Board. He also serves as a member of the Serbia and Montenegro UNESCO Commission as well as member of the Reflection group of the European Cultural Foundation (ECF Amsterdam).

Charles Varner is a graduate student in the department of sociology at Princeton University where he studies processes of stratification and inequality, economic sociology, and urban life. His current work is focused on intergroup contact and threat in multi-ethnic settings.

Dacia Viejo Rose is a PhD student at the University of Cambridge, UK. Her research looks into the reconstruction of cultural heritage after civil wars and the effect this has in building memories, meaning and reconciliation. At Cambridge she has set up the Post-Conflict and Post-Crisis Research Group. She has worked at the United Nations Department of Humanitarian Affairs and at UNESCO where she worked on the Cultural Policies for Development programme and the Cities for Peace Project. Dacia collaborates with a number of NGOs working in areas of cultural heritage preservation and conflict mitigation.

Christian Welzel is Professor of Political Science and Program Coordinator for the Social Sciences at the International University Bremen, Germany. He is a member of the Executive Committee of the World Values Survey Association. His most recent book is *Modernization, Cultural Change and Democracy: The Human Development Sequence* (with Ronald Inglehart, Cambridge University Press, 2005), and he also published numerous articles in the *European Journal of Political Research, Comparative Politics*, *Comparative Sociology, International Journal of Comparative Sociology*, *International Review of Sociology*, *Journal of Civil Society* and others. His main research interests are on cultural change, social values, civil society, democratization, and modernization theory.

Andreas Wimmer is professor of sociology at the University of California, Los Angeles. His research aims to understand the dynamics of nation-state formation, ethnicity making and political conflict from a comparative perspective. He has pursued this theme across several disciplinary fields, focusing on examples from both the developing and the developed world, and pursuing various methodological and analytical strategies: anthropological field research in Mexico and Iraq, network studies in Swiss immigrant neighbourhoods, quantitative cross-national research on wars in the modern world, comparative historical analysis of Swiss, Iraqi, and Mexican nation-state formation, and policy oriented research on the prevention of ethnic conflict.

Diana Wong is currently a freelance researcher residing in Malaysia. She has worked as a sociologist in Germany, Singapore and Malaysia. Her research interests are in the areas of development sociology, migration and religion.

Yunxiang Yan is a professor of Anthropology and co-director of the Center for Chinese Studies at University of California, Los Angeles. He has published two books on social change in rural China and has also published research articles on consumerism, cultural globalization, and state–society relationship.

Boxes

Figures

Illustrations

Tables

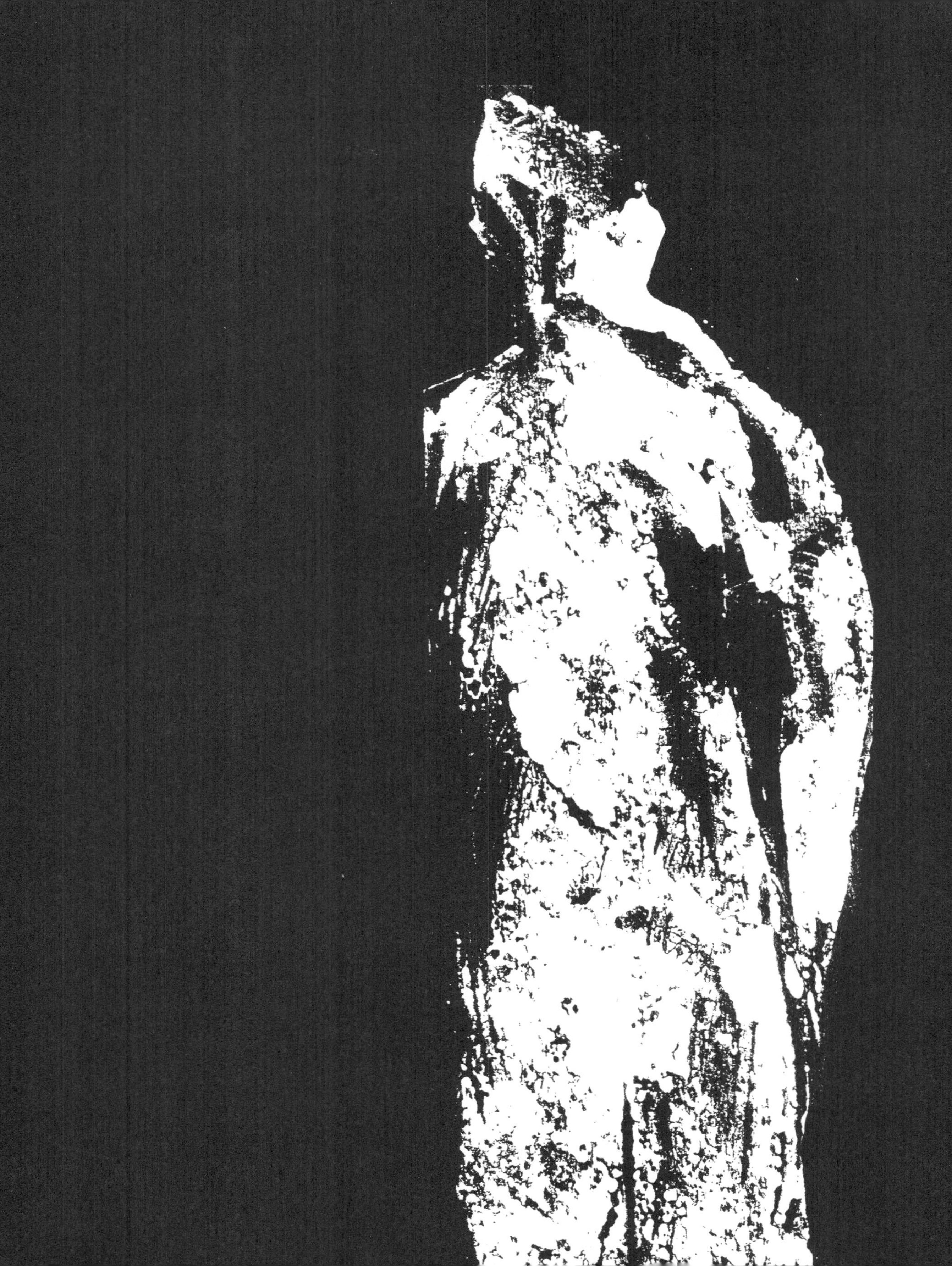

INTRODUCING THE CULTURES AND GLOBALIZATION SERIES

Helmut K. Anheier and Yudhishthir Raj Isar

Why Cultures and Globalization?

The world's cultures are broadly and deeply affected by globalization in ways that are still inadequately documented and understood. These impacts are at once unifying and divisive, liberating and corrosive, homogenizing and diversifying; they have become a truly central contemporary concern. Understandably, the interplay between cultures and globalization crystallizes both positive aspirations and negative anxieties, as it transforms patterns of sameness and difference across the world or modifies the ways in which cultural expression is created, represented, recognized, preserved or renewed (Wieviorka and Ohana 2001). This complex interplay has also contributed to generating new discourses of 'culturalism' that evoke the power of culture in domains as diverse as economic development, the fostering of citizenship and social cohesion, human security and the resolution or prevention of conflict. Yet 'culture and globalization' has become a discursive field that is all too often perceived and thought about – whether in negative or in positive terms – in ways that are simplificatory or illusive.

Clearly, there is a knowledge gap. The *Cultures and Globalization series* is designed to fill this gap, one that – we believe – has already become politically perilous, socially unsustainable and economically constraining. Achieving a better understanding of the relationships between globalization and cultural change is thus of much more than academic interest – it is important for many areas of policy and practice.

That globalization has a profound impact on culture, and that cultures shape globalization, may seem a truism. Yet the two-way interaction involves some of the most vexed and at the same time taken-for-granted questions of our time. It transforms previously stable forms of everyday life and of living together, of identity and belonging; of cultural expression including creative practice and entertainment. Highly diverse and uneven, the impacts of the globalization process on cultural life present unprecedented challenges to many traditional relationships as well, particularly between individuals on the one hand and 'communities', civil society and the nation on the other. What is more, they continue to transform the institutional roles of markets, governments, the non-profit sector and organized citizens' groups and movements.

Analyzing these relationships between globalization processes on the one hand and cultural patterns and developments on the other is the core objective of *Cultures and Globalization*. We seek to draw attention to changes in the world's cultures, and the policy implications they have, by providing an outlet for cutting-edge research, thinking and debate. Our hope is that this book will become a valued reference for the exploration of contemporary cultural issues from different perspectives – in the social sciences, in the arts and the humanities, as well as in policy-making circles – and that it will contribute to building bridges among them. As Fredric Jameson has pointed out:

> *Globalization falls outside the established academic disciplines, as a sign of the emergence of a new kind of social phenomenon ...There is thus something daring and speculative, unprotected, in the approach of scholars and theorists to this unclassifiable topic, which is the intellectual property of no specific field, yet which seems to concern politics in immediate ways, but just as immediately culture and sociology, not to speak of information and the media, or ecology, or consumerism and daily life. Globalization ... is thus the modern or postmodern version of the proverbial elephant, described by its blind observers in so many diverse ways. Yet one can still posit the existence of the elephant in the absence of a single persuasive and dominant theory; nor are blinded questions the most unsatisfactory way to explore this kind of relational and multilevel phenomenon. (Jameson and Miyoshi 1998: xi)*

Globalization affects millions of people across the world, the organizations where they work, and the communities in which they live. People's values and expectations are changing, and their identities and orientations are being transformed in ways that are subtle and fundamental alike, and involve other institutional complexes such as organized religion and civil society more generally, and, of course, politics and the economy. For the first time in human history, communication flows, migration patterns, transnational interpersonal and inter-organizational networks are emerging at such significant scales that they are increasingly achieving global range (Barber 1995; Castells 1996 and 1997; Dicken 2003; Held and McGrew 2000, 2002).

Yet while massive amounts of data exist on the economics of globalization, and have been appropriately interpreted, we face a paucity of information and analysis when it comes to culture. Cultural patterns and changes – including the values, aspirations, meanings, representations and identities they express or suppress, and the ways people appropriate them across the world – remain largely unmeasured and unanalyzed. Moreover, much information is collected but goes unreported and hence does not reach the right audiences in the policy-making arena. There are exceptions, to be sure. For example, European organizations such as ERICarts (with its *Compendium of Cultural Policies and Trends in Europe*, prepared for the Council of Europe), the European Cultural Foundation (with its newly-launched 'LAB for Culture' consortium), or global organizations such as the International Federation of Arts Councils and Culture Agencies (IFACCA) are producing useful new data. And a range of individual researchers are renewing frameworks of analysis (e.g., Mercer 2002) or coming up with new findings (e.g., Ilczuk and Isar 2006). The point remains, however, that comparative research in the field of culture is seriously underdeveloped. In particular, there is a lack of empirical analysis of why globalization matters for culture and why culture matters for globalization, whether nationally or, even more importantly, internationally or globally.

One reason for the neglect at the global level is that the conventional understandings of culture are still connected principally to the sovereign nation-state. However, today, this nexus of culture and nation no longer dominates, as the cultural dimension has become constitutive of collective identity at narrower as well as broader levels. As Paul Gilroy reminds us, the idea of culture 'has been abused by being simplified, instrumentalized, or trivialized, and particularly through being coupled with notions of identity and belonging that are overly fixed or too easily naturalized as exclusively national phenomena' (Gilroy 2004: 6). What is more, cultural processes take place in increasingly 'deterritorialized' transnational, global contexts, many of which are beyond the reach of national policies. Mapping and analyzing this shifting terrain, in all regions of the world, as well as the factors, patterns, processes, and outcomes associated with the 'complex connectivity' (Tomlinson 1999) of globalization, is therefore a main purpose of this Series.

Behind this objective lies the concern, which began to emerge strongly in the 1990s, to provide a more robust evidence base for policy-making in the rapidly changing cultural arena. This concern was crystallized by the World Commission on Culture and Development, whose report entitled *Our Creative Diversity* (World Commission on Culture and Development, 1996), stressed the weakness of the knowledge base as regards to the relationships between culture on the one hand and development on the other. The World Commission's recommendation that UNESCO should prepare a periodic report of worldwide reach in this field was thus the original inspiration for the present endeavor. In the ensuing decade, a number of other influential developments have taken place. UNESCO for its part followed up on the recommendation by preparing and publishing, in 1998 and 2000, two editions of a *World Culture Report* (note the use of the word 'culture' in the singular) devoted respectively to the topics 'Culture, creativity and markets' and 'Cultural diversity, conflict and pluralism'. UNESCO subsequently abandoned this enterprise, creating a vacuum this Series is intended to fill.

It should be noted though, that the UNESCO publication had perforce to keep 'culture' within the nation-state 'container', despite the fact that cultural questions now escape the direct reach of purely national policy-making because the economic and political dimensions, with which they are to varying degrees intertwined, are increasingly organized and played out at the transnational level. UNESCO's reports also had to appear as 'representative' as possible of that intergovernmental organization's nation-state membership and also respond to the imperatives of international cultural diplomacy and politics. They could not be the work of an entirely 'independent team', as called for by the World Commission. The present project is thus the first attempt by an academic consortium to take up the task in total intellectual freedom; and in a spirit of catholicity as regards conceptual frameworks and approaches, with the aim of giving 'voice' to visions and interpretations of the nexus between cultures and globalization and of sharing fresh data about it drawn from as many different world regions as possible.

It is important to stress also that the main focus of this Series is not 'culture and development', as envisaged by the World Commission of the same name, but the relationships between cultures and globalization that came strongly to the fore in the closing years of the twentieth century. By 1998, when the Stockholm Intergovernmental Conference on Cultural Policies for Development mainstreamed many of the key findings and recommendations of the World Commission, the cultural implications of globalization had moved to center stage, often displacing 'development' as the term of reference. Thus the Stockholm Conference called for an international research agenda on precisely the sorts of questions this project now proposes to tackle. The need has been echoed widely in many other policy circles.

Cultures and Globalization thus seeks to rise to a multi-faceted challenge. Prepared by teams of independent researchers and cultural experts, hailing mainly but not exclusively from academia, each edition will focus on a specific set of 'culture and globalization' issues as they are perceived, experienced, analyzed and addressed in different geocultural regions of the world. This inaugural volume is devoted to the complex theme of 'conflict' that is related to or driven by the changing dynamic of cultural sameness and difference vis-à-vis globalization. The next one will tackle the latest issues and developments as regards the cultural economy across the world. The third is likely to explore issues of arts practice and creativity in the arts.

Each volume will also include a major data section that presents a novel form of cultural 'indicators' with the help of state-of-the-art information graphics. We are, of course, aware of the largely underdeveloped state of cultural statistics and, a fortiori, cultural indicators, particularly for cross-national, comparative purposes. Therefore, in a departure from conventional approaches, we will neither seek to list data for indicators by country, nor strive to have a uniform table layout by country; rather we would use 'indicator suites' to present related data and information on specific aspects of the relationships between culture and globalization. A basic premise of this approach, which will be shown in detail in the chapter 'Introducing Cultural Indicator Suites', is that much information on culture and culture-related facets is already 'out there', but that much of this information remains to be systematically assessed, compiled, described, analyzed and presented.

The issues

As Appadurai (1996), Wolton (2003) and others have observed, we are in a time of intense 'culturalism', as cultural difference is consciously mobilized in a politics of recognition and representation, as a political arm, a bulwark or a refuge for both individuals and groups. The terrorist attacks on New York City and Washington DC on September 11, the US invasions of Afghanistan and Iraq, heated debates about the cultural dimensions of migration in Europe, fundamentalist re-assertions in all major religions that are forms of cultural identification rather than spirituality, are among the many events and forces that have turned these articulations of cultural difference into political fault lines. The 'fateful militancy' (Hartman 1997) which culture has achieved in political terms is now high on the policy agenda.

At the same time, immense political pressure from the West on some regions and countries, while it ignores others, is met by a general disillusionment about the largely unmet promises of globalization in the Global South, where the majority of the population lives on less than \$2 a day (Stiglitz 2003). One striking cultural response to such asymmetries has been the rise of 'cultural diversity' as a leading notion in international cultural politics. This is no longer simply the diversity that is a given of the human condition – and the stuff of anthropology – but a normative meta-narrative, deployed as the standard-bearer of a campaign to exclude cultural goods and services from global free trade rules (Isar 2006). In this guise, the term emerged at the turn of the present century, as an alternative to the limited and somewhat negative connotations of the *'exception culturelle'* that France, Canada and other nations had been advocating since the end of the Uruguay Round discussions in the mid-1990s. The discursive maneuver of shifting from 'exception' to 'diversity' as the master concept allowed French international diplomacy to tap into a much broader range of cultural commitments and anxieties across the world. Thus, in UNESCO's 2001 Universal Declaration on Cultural Diversity, Article 8, entitled 'Cultural goods and services: commodities of a unique kind', states:

> *In the face of present-day economic and technological change, opening up vast prospects for creation and innovation, particular attention must be paid to the diversity of the supply of creative work, to due recognition of the rights of authors and artists and to the specificity of cultural goods and services which, as vectors of identity, values and meaning, must not be treated as mere commodities or consumer goods. (2001)*

Recognizing this specificity is also the main purpose of the 'Convention on the protection of the diversity of cultural contents and artistic expressions' adopted by UNESCO in October 2005; it is the sense in which many individuals, non-governmental organizations, cultural activists and government officials deploy the term strategically today.

The principle is laudable. The goal is to foster the dynamism of contemporary cultural production rather than play a preservationist role. Yet this is a 'strategic essentialism' built upon unquestioned, un-deconstructed discourses of nationhood. Precisely because its object is cultural diversity among nations rather than within them, it is less about the negotiation of cultural difference than about the representation of 'cultures' as islands unto themselves, fixed and given (Isar 2006). Yet the key challenge of negotiating difference today is to 'give up notions of cultural purity, and search to uncover the ways in which the meanings and symbols of culture are produced through complex processes of translation, negotiation and enunciation' (Stevenson 2003: 61).

Cultures and globalization: towards a framework

There is a rich and growing body of globalization literature (see Castells 1996; Held and McGrew 2002; Lomborg 2004; Murray, 2006). However, this literature has been focused largely on economic globalization and the spread of the international rule of law, including security issues, and typically devotes one chapter, if that, to cultural trade issues. Only secondarily has it dealt with social-cultural aspects in a broader sense, although the *Global Civil Society Yearbook* (Anheier et al. 2001), and UNDP's *Human Development Report* (2004) and other publications, are beginning to address this imbalance. Specific cultural aspects have been even less acknowledged. Barring some notable exceptions (Appadurai 1996, 2001; various works by Mike Featherstone, particularly 1995; Jameson and Miyoshi 1998; Rao and Walton 2004; Sassen 1998; Tomlinson 1999; Warnier 2004; Wolton 2003), both globalization in the cultural sphere and the relationships between globalization and cultural change remain relatively under-explored. Empirical evidence about them is not being gathered regularly and updated for the purpose of ongoing analysis.

As mentioned earlier, the current destinies of culture have been brought into the international policy debate through a number of publications and the political messages they contained. The process was initiated by UNESCO's World Commission on Culture and Development, which introduced a strong policy link between culture and development. It called for a 'commitment to pluralism' as a middle course between universalism and radical cultural relativism. The notion of a 'constructive pluralism' developed subsequently by UNESCO suggests the active and dynamic coexistence of groups, and incorporates the conditions for a public domain that allows creative contact and transformation. Building on the ground laid by the World Commission on Culture and Development, the *2004 Human Development Report*, sub-titled 'Cultural Liberty in Today's Diverse World', stipulated a close connection between culture, liberty and human development. It suggested that cultural liberty, i.e., the ability to choose one's identity, is important in 'leading a full life'. To some extent the *2004 Human Development Report* was written in the context of concerns about the increasing cultural dominance of the West, in particular the United States, and the exponential growth of identity politics. At the same time, while emphasizing the importance of culture for human development, the Report rejected culture-based theories of development, stressing the plurality of cultural traditions and paths to modernity.

Two aspects of these United Nations publications are worth noting for our purposes. First, they do not test in a systematic manner how different facets or dimensions of globalization relate to cultural development. Cultural fragmentation and modernist homogenization are not just two opposing views of what is happening in the world today but are on the contrary both constitutive of the current reality (Friedman 1996).

Second, these publications, although they stress the importance and the impact of globalization, are rooted in nation-state thinking. The sovereign nation-state remains the default case in grappling with cultural processes and finding solutions to global, transnational problems (Lomborg 2004). Trans-border flows of people and artifacts, which are profoundly cultural, are inadequately addressed. The role of transnational businesses and civil society organizations that span many national and regional boundaries receive scant attention, as does the role of the various international epistemic communities (artists, lawyers, academics, etc.) and committed individuals from different walks of life. This is not to argue, however, that the nation-state is no longer relevant as an organizing framework for cultural belonging and identity, as well as for cultural practice. The point is, rather, that national policy-makers need new tools with which to think the challenges of culture in broader transnational terms.

Our method and framework

As we seek to shift the frame in the ways suggested above, there could be a danger that this volume emerges as little more than a compilation of chapters on loosely connected topics. To counteract this danger, we suggest a set of organizing principles and offer an initial conceptual framework for breaking down the complex relationships between cultures and globalization, and for analyzing the shifting ground on which cultural change is occurring. This framework will inform our editorial policies for the coming years. We will use it to identify and develop our themes, and to set substantive priorities and foci.

The framework will serve three additional purposes: First, for the development of the statistical part of the book, guiding the selection of indicators and the identification of data needs with a view to encouraging evidence-based research and policy analysis; second, by allowing for a systematic exploration of core themes and critical issues, it will help build a permanent 'multilogue' across fields, disciplines, countries and regions. Third, a better conceptual and empirical understanding of how globalization and culture relate to each other can be useful to others in developing policy options and their implications.

Conceptual challenges

To be sure, any attempt at seeking to establish such a framework in the field of cultures and globalization faces many challenges. The initial challenge is that of definition. As a phenomenon, culture is directly or indirectly related to virtually every aspect of the human condition; as a concept, it is even broader and more capacious than 'economy' or 'society.' Kroeber and Kluckhohn's 281 famous definitions of 1952, a classic reference, come to mind immediately; indeed this is not surprising, since within various disciplines – anthropology and sociology in particular – there have been many attempts to stabilize meanings in the interest of a technical vocabulary (Williams 1976). Having entirely escaped academic control in recent decades, however, the notion has become even more protean, especially as cultural difference has come to be consciously mobilized in political ways by individuals and groups.

The word 'culture' is thus the object of a complex terminological tangle. With no single definition generally accepted, differences, overlaps and nuances in meaning complicate rather than facilitate rigor and communication in the field. Various disciplines deal with culture and regard it as their 'terrain', however inclusively or exclusively: anthropology, political science, history, sociology, the law, and, of course, the humanities including cultural studies and art history. These disciplines have become institutionalized as such in the academy, and have come to function as closed intellectual 'silos', as it were, frequently discouraging multidisciplinary approaches and cross-disciplinary dialogue. Within each discipline, we typically find multiple approaches in terms of focus and methodology, such as the split between quantitative and qualitative sociology, or between cultural and social anthropology. For brevity's sake, we will refer to the sum of academic disciplines concerned with culture as the 'cultural disciplines'.

These disciplines present a rich tapestry of approaches, theories and models that sometimes compete, sometimes overlap and conceptually nest one within the other. They frequently span disciplinary boundaries and spill over into other parts of the field. It is neither possible nor necessary to review them further here. This has been done elsewhere. Suffice it to say that these disciplines draw inspiration from many different thinkers, including ancestral figures such as Durkheim (1965), Freud (1961), Gramsci (1971), Marx (1978), Simmel (1983), Weber (1978), or more recent intellectual mentors such as Appadurai (2001), Beck (2000), Bourdieu (1987), (Calhoon, 1994), Castells (1996), Featherstone (1995), Foucault (see Rabinow and Rose 2003), Giddens (1991), Habermas (1987), Hall, (Hall and Du Gay 1996), Hannerz (1992), or Touraine (1997), to mention but a few. Much of the thinking of these scholars is directly relevant to cultures and globalization. Although we cannot offer a systematic review here, we will mention four dominant strands for illustrative purposes, and refer to them more directly over time in the context of specific topics covered in successive volumes in the Series:

- A recurrent theme in the cultural disciplines is the **degree of independence of culture** from the economy, and what form and direction this relationship might take in a globalizing world. This ranges from Marxist notions of economic determinism, to Weberian thinking that attaches greater '*Eigendynamik*' to culture, in particular to the role of ideas, includes Bourdieu's notion of cultural capital as a distinct 'currency' of status-seeking and elite maintenance. This strand of work leads us to address the question of how independent cultural globalization is from other globalization forms and drivers. Does cultural globalization have its own dynamic, relatively independent of economic and political developments?
- Another theme is the **attributed developmental capacity and trajectory of cultures**, and the questions this raises in the context of globalization. This has deep intellectual roots in anthropology and sociology, e.g., the distinction between traditional and modern cultures; Tönnies' (1991) *Gemeinschaft* versus *Gesellschaft* model, or Innis' (1950) distinction between space-binding cultures and time-binding cultures. Assuming that globalization challenges many cultures, and some in fundamental ways in terms of their very survival, what will be their capacity to respond and adapt, in particular in view of the often assumed hegemonic force of American-style consumer culture?
- The **unity (or multiplicity) and impact of modernity** constitutes another theme worth revisiting when examining the relationship between globalization and cultures. Some have suggested that modernity comes in 'packages': some aspects are extrinsic and allow for separation (e.g., modern medicine and Christianity), while others are intrinsic and make separation impossible (modern medicine and notion of causality). Moreover, some cultural aspects have carry-over effects and spill into other life spheres (culture of work into family life), while other cultural patterns may block such movements. There is also a range of perspectives that speaks of 'multiple modernities' (among them Eisenstadt 2000) or 'alternative modernities' (Gaonkar 2001).
- Related to the theme of modernity is the question of identity formation and maintenance in a globalizing world. Conceptualizations of this theme include Appadurai's concepts of global flows and deterrritorialization (1996); García Canclini's understandings of hybridity (1995); Wolton's (2003) notion of 'cultural cohabitation', and what has been called *World Culture Theory* as a reference to the 'compression of the world and the intensification of consciousness of the global whole' (Robertson 1992: 8).

In addition to these themes, there are globalization theories with important implications for our understanding of culture (see Guillen 2001). For example, researchers such as Meyer et al. (1997) argue that a world-culture of institutions such as citizenship, human rights, science and technology, socioeconomic development, education, religion, and management has emerged that penetrates virtually all human endeavor. This increasingly global social organization of rationalized modernity has its logic and purposes built into almost all nation-states, resulting in a world that shows increasing structural *similarities of form* among countries. At the same time, countries differ in the fit between these institutions, their needs and capacities, and therefore produce different cultural, social and economic *outcomes*.

However, with some exceptions, many of the models or ideas listed above, and we could add others, are either not fully testable to begin with or have not yet been explored systematically. Generally, theses and theories tend to be interpreted and reinterpreted, with little verification or further development. While it may be an overgeneralization, it is tempting to conclude that the cultural disciplines tend to add new ideas without discarding old ones, and to create conceptual complexity rather than parsimony. As a result, they display considerable theoretical inertia, and a cacophony of definitions, approaches and theories.

Characteristics

A conceptual framework is neither a theory nor a fully integrated body of knowledge. Rather, it serves as a marker of 'intellectual terrain' by identifying boundaries, major concepts and issues as well as the relations, de facto or hypothesized, among them. Several qualities or characteristics are worth keeping in mind:

- *Parsimony*, i.e., the aim to 'achieve most with least'. Any framework or model produces a picture of the reality that is simpler than reality itself;
- *Significance*, i.e., a framework that identifies the truly critical aspects of a phenomenon and its relationships, and focuses attention on aspects that are neither obvious nor trivial;
- *Combinatorial richness*, i.e., the range of hypotheses that can be generated with the framework, the number of interesting issues, features and relations it helps identify and anticipate; this includes *theoretical fruitfulness*, i.e., the extent to which the framework allows us to explore and develop existing and new insights, models, and theories; and *organizing power*, i.e., the ability of the framework to bring in and integrate new aspects, thereby extending the applicability and range; and, finally,
- *Policy relevance*, i.e., the extent to which a framework leads to insights, options, recommendations and models of interest to policy-makers (e.g., some aspects might be 'interesting' and even theoretically relevant, but have low policy salience).

Prerequisites

The *Series* is unlikely to avoid the problems of definition that are endemic to the cultural disciplines, which are as it were, their conceptual discontents. We do not intend to adopt a single set of omnibus concepts, much less a single lens. We know that the various contributors to this collective endeavor will each work with very different concepts of culture – for the reasons already outlined above. Also, the cultural disciplines, as well as cultural operators, activists and policy-makers, tend to oscillate permanently between variants of the 'ways of life' notions of culture and 'arts and heritage' ones. We nevertheless intend to initiate our work with an agreed understanding of the terms we ourselves shall be using. In other words, we shall offer working definitions for key concepts and also state our methodological approach.

Culture in the broad sense we propose to employ refers to the social construction, articulation and reception of meaning. Culture is the lived and creative experience for individuals **and** a body of artifacts, symbols, texts and objects. Culture involves enactment and representation. It embraces art and art discourse, the symbolic world of meanings, the commodified output of the cultural industries as well as the spontaneous or enacted, organized or unorganized cultural expressions of everyday life, including social relations. It is constitutive of both collective and individual identity. Closely related to culture is the concept of **communication**, which refers to the ways in which meanings, artifacts, beliefs, symbols and messages are transmitted through time and space, as well as processed, recorded, stored, and reproduced. Communication requires media of storage and transmission, institutions that make storage and transmission possible, and media of reception.

Globalization involves the movement of objects (goods, services, finance and other resources, etc.), meanings (language, symbols, knowledge, identities, etc.) and people across regions and intercontinental space. The notion of **cultural globalization** involves three movements (UNDP 2004): flows of investments and knowledge; flows of cultural goods; and flows of people. Cultures or aspects of cultures are globalized to the extent to which they involve the movement of specified objects, systems of meaning and people across national/regional borders and continents. Yet these processes, so closely related to the globalization of communication, the media and the cultural industries, are for one thing inaccessible to the majority of the world's population and actually appear to generate countless counter-affirmations at the level of local reception. Indeed, some analysts such as Warnier (2004) reject the notion of 'cultural globalization' altogether: there are globalized cultural industries, to be sure, but no global culture in the sense of the term as we have defined it above.

Cultural products and values are part of a larger process that involves economic globalization, defined as the functional integration of economic production and distribution processes across multiple national borders (Dicken 1999); the emergence of a global civil society, defined as the socio-sphere of ideas, values, institutions, organizations, networks, and individuals located primarily outside the institutional complexes of family, state, and market and operating beyond the confines of national societies, polities, and economies (Anheier et al. 2001; Kaldor et al. 2003); and international law and the emergence of an international legal system, e.g., the International Court of Justice or the European Court of Justice.

In terms of methodology, the proposed framework is neither self-referential in its intent, i.e., not seen as a closed system; nor does it imply any notion of causality among the concepts specified, nor a strict focus on some 'dependent variable'. Nor does it favor any particular approach, theory or policy. Instead, it is descriptive as well as analytical in the context of seeking to inform theory-building and policy-making in the field. While it is not normative in purpose, this does not mean that we will in any way prevent normative viewpoints and ethical stances from finding their way into these pages; rather, we encourage multiple voices to be heard, and wish to see them engaged in evidence-based debate.

Key understandings

Even though our understanding of the relationships between culture and globalization remains sketchy and uneven, enough has been thought and written on the subject to allow us to extract positions, statements and generic hypotheses that identify, at least initially, key conceptual building blocks and relationships.

A. Context

The world's cultures are being shaped by economic, social and political-legal globalization and vice versa. The strengths and the directions of the reciprocal relationships vary by field, country and region as well as over time. For analytic purposes, we refer to the other globalization processes as context, even though in reality, they are typically concomitant rather than parallel, and occur in different combinations rather than uniformly across time and space.

B. Systems and units of analysis

Culture and globalization are complex, multifaceted concepts, and difficult to reduce to one or two dimensions without conceptual and empirical harm. Like globalization, culture involves social, economic and political aspects, and also the artistic-aesthetic realm. We refer to these dimensions as system, not in the strict sense of system theory, but only to emphasize that different aspects of culture can display considerable dynamics of their own, driven by specific logics, incentives and rewards in terms of recognition, prestige and power (Geertz 1983). Thus, to counteract any reductionist tendencies, we can think of culture as a system of artistic endeavor and realm of creativity, as a social system of meaning and values, as an economic system of production, distribution and consumption, and as a political system of positions of power and influence. Each 'lens' is equally valid and likely brings up different questions, leading to different insights and implications.

The relationship between cultures and globalization is not only multifaceted from a systemic perspective; in each case, it also involves different units of analysis such as individuals, organizations, professions, institutional patterns, communities, societies, as well as nation-states. The different units, in turn, may be interrelated and affect each other over time. In making observations, and in reaching conclusions about these relationships, it is important to specify the units of analysis involved. Importantly, however, given the objectives of the *Series*, we generally also put emphasis on units other than nation-states, national cultures or countries. This would involve in particular units like organizations, communities, and actual networks among individuals as well as virtual networks like the Internet.

C. Structures and processes

Within the context of globalization and for the different units of analysis, we can address the two major conceptual blocks we regard as the central substantive concern of the project (i) cultural identities, patterns and structures; and (ii) cultural processes, communication and flows. In what follows, we illustrate each and show what kind of theories and questions will guide the setting of priorities in the future. Our editorial policy is to address such priority issues by using more general approaches in the social sciences, exploring how they relate to available work in the globalization field, and then posing questions that could become the topic of individual chapters.

The complex and increasingly troubled relationship between *identities* and globalization is a case in point. Both individual identity and collective identity are involved here, both the individual subject and the cultural community (Touraine 1997). Two long-standing strands of social science theory shape our understanding of personal or individual identity. One is rooted in developmental psychology and sees identity as the result of 'deep socialization', i.e., early value-forming experiences and learning processes that make up the core personality traits and character dispositions. This psychological understanding is close to what could be called the 'hard-wired' aspect of identity as a sense of self – once formed, it is fairly stable throughout the life course, and relatively resistant to political, cultural and social changes.

The other approach is more sociological in nature and sees it as the outcome of ongoing search processes. Individuals try to forge, negotiate and reconcile their own 'worldviews' and notions of self with that of collectively defined expectations. Given the multiple roles people perform in modern, diverse societies, however, this more 'soft-wired' form of identity is not only evolving, it is also precarious and precious. It refers less to identity as 'self' but more to identity in relation to categories such as nation, religion, place, or belonging (Calhoon 1994).

Are these approaches useful in the context of globalization? What are some of the drivers shaping identity in a globalizing world, and what policy implications can be suggested? What are the social and cultural outlets of identity formation? These questions would form the basis for a chapter on the relationship between globalization and individual identity. By the same token, other chapters could address collective identity, including the cosmopolitan, as well as organizational and professional (or 'social') identities. How are such identities and the possible conflicts between them acting as forces for social change or stasis? As regards tensions and conflicts, what are the factors of escalation or resolution? The important point is that the critical relationship between cultures, globalization and identity would be examined from different theoretical perspectives and different units of analysis.

The globalization literature suggests a number of approaches that can be useful for examining the relation between globalization and culture looking for patterns and structures across different units of analysis. The work of Castells (1996, 1997) and Held et al. (1999) are cases in point. Castells (1996) argues that networks among organizations and individuals increasingly form meta-networks at the transnational level and create a system of 'decentralized concentration', where a multiplicity of interconnected tasks takes place in different sites. Since the 1970s, enabling technologies such as telecommunication and the Internet brought about the ascendance of a 'network society', whose processes occur in a new type of space – the space of flows. The space of flows, comprising a myriad of links and exchanges, has come to dominate the older space of place (including territorially defined units such as states and neighborhoods), thanks to its flexibility, and its compatibility with the new logic of the network society. The social organization of the network society is constructed by nodes and hubs in this space of flows, where most of the social action occurs. Hence, the manifold spaces of flows are at the core of understanding globalization, and are where we need to explore the role and place of culture. What is the 'culture' of these spaces, and how do they affect cultural changes, and at what level or unit of analysis?

Following Held et al. (1999: 17–27), we suggest that some of the major contours of the more organizational aspects of cultures and globalization can be described by four related characteristics:

- *Extensity* as a measure of the geographical expansion of activities, i.e., movements of objects (goods, services, resources etc.), meaning (symbols, knowledge) and people across regions and intercontinental space, as indicated by the number of 'nodes' (e.g., organizations, informal networks, artists, and participants) that constitute the overall spread of a 'network' or practice. Extensity refers to the range of cultural globalization;

- *Intensity* of the overall volume of such movements relative to the national and the local; it refers to the number and types of connections involved among the various 'nodes'. Intensity indicates how densely the elements are connected amongst each other;
- *Velocity* of the overall interactions as a measure of the frequency to which movement connections are made or used among nodes; and
- *Impact* of globalization on cultures. This is the most difficult one to conceptualize and measure, and involves processes such as homogenization, hybridization, contestation, indifference, evolution, decline or, on the positive side, liberation or emancipation, that can be described in terms of the resulting cultural infrastructures, practices and repertoires; the institutionalization of interactions; patterns of stratification, power, inclusion and exclusion.

The modes of interaction are of particular interest, and include:

- *Imposition*, which implies cultural power differences and stratification, hierarchy and unevenness in the establishment and use of institutional infrastructure across societies, regions, etc.; such power needs organizational, institutional infrastructure (media, professionals, knowledge).
- *Diffusion*, whereby elements from one 'culture' find their way into another.
- *Relativization*, whereby cultural elements take shape relative to other elements.
- *Emulation*, as the creation of a common cultural arena in which actors can selectively choose from an increasingly global arsenal.
- *Glocalization*, whereby universal ideas, patterns values are interpreted differently; refers to the way in which homogenization and heterogenization intertwine.
- *Interpenetration*, whereby the universalization of particularism and the particularization of universalism combine.
- *Resistance,* whereby local culturalist claims and identities are asserted in reaction to the perceived imposition of the global.

These interactions involve a communication and media infrastructure of cultural production, transmission and reception, although the extent to which flows and processes are institutionalized varies across time and space. For different cultural areas and issues, we would ask what kinds of interactions prevail among what units of analysis to produce different kinds of outcomes, and policy implications, in terms of:

- *Thick* cultural globalization (high extensity, high intensity, high velocity, and high impact), with the Internet, mass tourism as cases in point.
- *Diffused* globalization (high extensity, high intensity, high velocity, and low impact), e.g., global art markets.
- *Expansive* globalization (high extensity, low intensity, low velocity, and high impact), e.g., elite cultural networks.
- *Thin* globalization (high extensity, low intensity, low velocity, and low impact), e.g., international cultural organizations.

D. Models and policy positions

What are some of the initial positions and policy approaches in sociology, for example, that can be relevant for our purposes, and that can be examined empirically in a range of cultural fields and areas? Specifically, for the positions illustrated below, we would ask: what are the policies and policy implications concerning the relationship between culture and globalization for the movements of objects, meanings and people in terms of identities, patterns and structures, and the processes, communications and flows?

Held et al. (1999) identify the *Hyperglobalizers* who predict a homogenization of the world's cultures along the American model of mass culture and consumerism. They are set apart from the *Skeptics* who lament the loss of 'thick' national cultures and point to the 'thinness' and ersatz quality of globalized culture, whereas the *Transformationalists* shift attention to the intermingling of cultures and the emergence of hybrid global cultural elements and networks.

Berger (1997) suggests that globalization involves four conflicting 'cultures' that themselves are closely allied to specific institutions: the *Davos Culture* is the increasingly globalized corporate culture, lifestyle, career patterns and expectations of the international business community; the *Faculty Club* is the intellectual response to globalization that is largely on reform course, trying to 'tame' and 'humanize' the process; *McWorld* refers to the spread of consumerism and Americanization of popular culture (Barber 1995); and *religious revival* refers to the efforts of largely protestant and Islamic groups to proselytize and gain greater influence. The value systems around these cultures are on a collision course as they make very different claims on the nature of globalization, leading to rather different policy implications.

Kaldor, Anheier and Glasius (Kaldor et al. 2003) develop a different, though complementary, approach and identify political/value positions on globalization. These positions are held by actors such as NGO leaders as well as political parties, governments, business executives and individuals. They argue that there are very few out and out *supporters* of globalization (i.e., groups or individuals who favor all forms of global connectedness such as trade, money, people, law and politics); at the same time, there are very few total *rejectionists*. Rather, the dominant responses to globalization are mixed. Specifically, 'regressive globalizers' are individuals, groups and governments who favor globalization on their own terms and when it is in their particular interest. Reformers or 'redistributive globalizers' are groups, individuals, governments and multilateral institutions that, like Berger's 'Faculty Club,' favor 'civilizing' or 'humanizing' globalization.

Viewing the various positions from the vantage point of the sociology of culture, Crane (2002) has identified the following four broad models as heuristic markers:

1. *The cultural imperialism model*, which focuses upon the roles of governments and of multinational and trans-national corporations in the dissemination of different forms of global culture. It hypothesizes that this culture is disseminated from rich and powerful countries located at the core of the world cultural system to poorer and less developed countries on the periphery. The theory presupposes a relatively homogeneous mass culture that is accepted passively and uncritically by mass audiences. Cultural imperialism is viewed as purposeful and intentional because it corresponds to the political interests of powerful capitalist societies.
2. *The cultural flows or network model* sees the transmission process as a set of influences that do not necessarily originate in the same place or flow in the same direction. Receivers may also be originators. In this model, cultural globalization corresponds to a network with no clearly defined centre or periphery (see, for example, Appadurai 1996) but shifting configurations. Globalization as an aggregation of cultural flows or networks is a less coherent and unitary process than cultural imperialism and one in which cultural influences move in many different directions to bring about rather more hybridization than homogenization.
3. *The reception model* argues that audiences vary in the way they respond actively rather than passively to mass-mediated culture, and that different national, ethnic, and racial groups interpret the same materials differently. Hence the different empirical responses to cultural globalization by publics in different countries, a phenomenon one observes readily in many developing countries where 'cultural pride' is strong. This model does not view globally disseminated culture as a threat to national or local identities. Multiculturalism rather than cultural imperialism is the dominant trend.
4. Finally, *a negotiation and competition model*, based on the recognition that globalization has stimulated a range of strategies on the part of nations, global cities, and cultural organizations to cope with, counter, or facilitate the culturally globalizing forces. They include strategies for preserving and protecting cultural forms inherited from the past, strategies for rejuvenating traditional cultures, strategies for resisting cultural imposition, and strategies that aim to process and package – maybe even alter or transform–local and national cultures for global consumption. In this perspective, globalization impels these entities to try to preserve, position, or project their cultures in global space.

It is clear that these positions involve very different policy preferences in all the areas of concern.

Setting priorities

As suggested at the outset, a clear analytical framework should spell out the organizing principles and substantive foci of *Cultures and Globalization*. Thus, in the context of globalization drivers and processes, we are primarily interested in describing and analyzing different units of analysis, cultural identities, patterns, structures and flows, and the models, theories and policy options they suggest. We would do so through four lenses that each highlight specific aspects of culture: artistic,

Figure I.1 Framework for the Cultures and Globalization Series

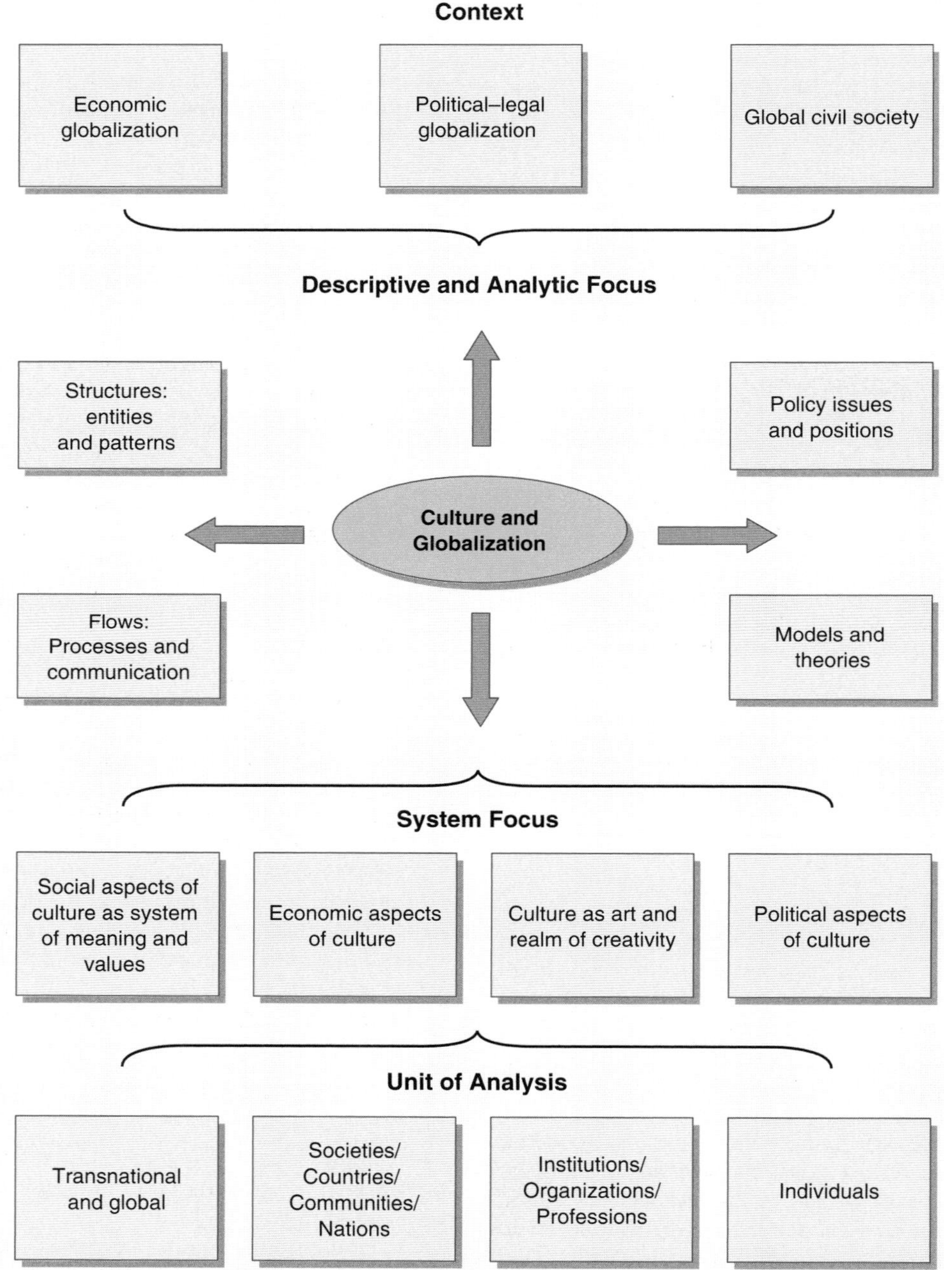
Context
Economic globalization
Political–legal globalization
Global civil society
Descriptive and Analytic Focus
Structures: entities and patterns
Policy issues and positions
Culture and Globalization
Flows: Processes and communication
Models and theories
System Focus
Social aspects of culture as system of meaning and values
Economic aspects of culture
Culture as art and realm of creativity
Political aspects of culture
Unit of Analysis
Transnational and global
Societies/ Countries/ Communities/ Nations
Institutions/ Organizations/ Professions
Individuals

social, economic, and political. This framework, presented in Figure 1, shows our intellectual terrain in the context of other forms and drivers of globalization, the various systems and units of analysis that can become relevant, and the core descriptive and analytic foci pursued. As elaborated in the chapter 'Introducing Cultural Indicator Suites', Figure 1 also offers both framework and guidance for the 'Profiles of World Cultures', the data section of the *Cultures and Globalization Series*.

We see this framework as an analytic tool for breaking down the relationship between culture and globalization, and the shifting nexus between culture and society. In terms of setting priorities and for keeping focus as well as editorial coherence, each edition examines, though not exclusively, the relationship between globalization and culture with the help of a particular emphasis. This could be a specific theme or set of related themes, a critical policy approach or some other topic. The thematic foci for the first five include, beginning with this year's theme Conflicts and Tensions; The Cultural Economy; Creativity and Arts Practice; Identities and Values; and Innovation and Regression.

REFERENCES

Anheier, H. K., Glasius, M. and Kaldor, M. (2001) *Global Civil Society 2001*. New York: Oxford University Press.

Appadurai, A. (1996) *Modernity at Large: Cultural Dimensions of Globalization*. Minneapolis: University of Minnesota Press.

– (2001) (ed.) *Globalization*. Durham, NC: Duke University Press.

Barber, B. (1995) *Jihad vs. McWorld: How Globalism and Tribalism are Reshaping the World*. New York: Times Books.

Beck, U. (2000) *What is Globalization?*. Cambridge, UK: Malden, MA: Polity Press.

Berger, P. L. (1997) 'Four Faces of Global Culture', *The National Interest* (49): 23(7).

Bourdieu, P. (1987) *Distinction: A Social Critique of the Judgment of Taste*. Cambridge, MA: Harvard University Press.

Calhoon,C. (ed.) (1994) *Social theory and the politics of Identity*. Cambridge, MA and oxford, Blackwell.

Castells, M. (1996) *The Rise of Network Society*. Oxford: Blackwell.

– (1997) *The Power of Identity*. Oxford: Blackwell.

Crane, D. (2002) 'Cultural globalization from the perspective of the sociology of culture'. Paper presented at the Symposium, Statistics in the Wake of Challenges Posed by Cultural Diversity in a Globalization Context, UNESCO Institute of Statistics, Montreal, October 21–23.

Dicken, P. (1999) 'Globalization: An Economic-Geographical Perspective', in W. Halal and K. Taylor (eds), *Twenty-First Century Economics*. New York: St Martin's Press.

– (2003) *Global Shift: Reshaping the Global Economic Map in the 21st Century*, 4th edn. Thousand Oaks, CA: Sage Publications.

Durkheim, E. (1965) [1912] *The Elementary Forms of the Religious Life*. Trans. by Joseph Ward Swain. New York: The Free Press.

Eisenstadt, S.N. (2000) 'Multiple Modernities', *Daedalus*, Vol. 129, No. 1, Winter 2000.

Featherstone, M. (1995) *Undoing Culture: Globalization, Postmodernism and Identity*. London: Sage.

Freud, S. (1961) *Civilization and its Discontents*. Trans. and ed. by James Strachey. New York: Norton.

Friedman, J. (1996) *Cultural Identity and Global Process*. London: Sage Publications.

Gaonkar, D. (ed.) (2001) *Alternative Modernities*. Durham, NC: Duke University Press.

García Canclini, N. (1995) *Hybrid Cultures: Strategies for Entering and Leaving Modernity*. Minneapolis: University of Minnesota Press.

Geertz, C. (1983) *Local Knowledge: Further Essays in Interpretive Anthropology*. New York: Basic Books, Inc.

Giddens, A. (1991) *Modernity and Self-Identity: Self and Society in the Late Modern Age*. Cambridge, UK: Polity Press.

Gilroy, P. (2004) *After Empire*. Abingdon: Routledge.

Gramsci, A. (1971) *Selections from the Prision Notebooks*. Trans. and ed. by Quintin Hoare and Geoffrey Nowell-Smith. London: Lawrence and Wishart.

Guillen, M.F. (2001) 'Is Globalization Civilizing, Destructive or Feeble? A Critique of Five Key Debates in the Social Science Literature', *Annual Review of Sociology*, pp. 235–60.

Habermas, J. (1987) *The Philosophical Discourse of Modernity*. Cambridge, MA: MIT Press.

Habermas, J. (1994) *Multiculturalism and 'The Politics of Recognition': an essay*. Princeton, NJ: Princeton University Press.

Hall, S. and Du Gay, P. (1996) *Questions of Cultural Identity*. Thousand Oaks, CA: Sage Publications.

Hannerz, U. (1992) *Cultural Complexity: Studies in the Social Organization of Meaning*. New York: Columbia University Press.

Hartman, G. (1997) *The Fateful Question of Culture*. New York: Columbia University Press.

Held, D. and McGrew, A. G. (2000) *The Global Transformations Reader: An Introduction to the Globalization Debate*. Malden, MA: Polity Press.

– (2002) *Global Transformations: Politics, Economics, and Culture*. Cambridge, MA: Polity Press (revised and updated edition).

–, Goldblatt, D., and Perraton, J. (1999) *Global Transformations: Politics, Economics, and Culture*. Cambridge, MA: Polity Press.

Ilczuk, D. and Isar, Y.R. (eds) (2006) *Metropolises of Europe: Diversity in Urban Cultural Life*. Warsaw: CIRCLE.

Innis, H.A. (1950) *Empire and Civilization*. Oxford: Oxford University Press.

Isar, Y. R. (2006) 'Cultural diversity', *Theory, Culture and Society*, Special Issue on *Problematizing Global Knowledge*, Vol. 23, Nos. 2–3 March–May 2006.

Jameson, F. and Miyoshi, M. (1998) *The Cultures of Globalization*. Durham, NC: Duke University Press.

Kaldor, M., Anheier, H. and Glasius, M. (2003) 'Global Civil Society in an Era of Regressive Globalization', in M. Kaldor, Helmut, Anheier and Marlies Glasius (eds), *Global Civil Society 2003*. Oxford: Oxford University Press.

Kroeber, A. L. and Kluckhohn, C. (1952) *Culture: A Critical Review of Concepts and Definitions*. Cambridge, MA: The Museum.

Lomborg, E. (ed.) (2004) *Global Crisis, Global Solutions*. Cambridge: Cambridge University Press.

Marx, K. (1978). *The Marx-Engels Reader*. New York: Norton.

Mercer, C. (2002). *Towards Cultural Citizenship: Tools for Cultural Policy and Development*. Stockholm: The Bank of Sweden Tercentenary Foundation and Diglunds Förlag.

Meyer, J. W., Boli, J., Thomas, G. M. and Ramirez, F. O. (1997) 'World Society and the Nation-State', *American Journal of Sociology* 103(1): 144–81.

Murray, W. (2006) *Geographies of Globalization*. London: Routledge.

Rabinow, P. and Rose, N. (eds) (2003) *The Essential Foucault*. New York: New Press.

Rao, V. and Walton, M. (2004) *Culture and Public Action*. Stanford, CA: Stanford University Press.

Robertson, R. (1992) *Globalization: Social Theory and Global Culture*. London: Sage Publications.

Sassen, S. (1998) *Globalization and Its Discontents: Essays on the New Mobility of People and Money*. New York: The New Press.

Simmel, G. (1983) *Soziologie. Untersuchungen über die Formen der Vergesellschaftung*. Berlin: Duncker & Humblot.

Stevenson, N. (2003) *Cultural Citizenship: Cosmopolitan Questions*. Maidenhead: Open University Press.

Stiglitz, J. (2003) *Globalization and Its Discontents*. New York: Norton.

Tönnies, F. (1991) *Gemeinschaft und Gesellschaft. Grundbegriffe der reinen Soziologie*. Berlin: Wissenschaftliche Buchgesellschaft.

Tomlinson, J. (1999) *Globalization and Culture*. Cambridge: Polity Press.

Touraine, A. (1997) *Pourrons nous vivre ensemble? Egaux et différents*. Paris: Fayard.

United Nations Development Program (2004) *Human Development Report 2004: Cultural Liberty in Today's Diverse World*. New York, NY: Oxford University Press.

UNESCO (1998) *World Culture Report: Culture, Creativity and Markets*. Paris: UNESCO Publishing.

UNESCO (2000) *World Culture Report: Cultural Diversity, Conflict and Pluralism*. Paris: UNESCO Publishing.

UNESCO (2001) Universal Declaration on Cultural Diversity http://unesdoc.unesco.org/images/0012/001271/127160m.pdf

Warnier, J-P. (2004) *La mondialisation de la culture*. Paris: La Découverte.

Weber, M. (1978) *Economy and Society: An Outline of Interpretive Sociology*. Berkeley and Los Angeles: University of California Press.

Wieviorka, M. and Ohana, J. (eds) *(2001) La différence culturelle: Une reformulation des débats*. Paris: Balland.

Williams, R. (1976) *Keywords: A Vocabulary of Culture and Society*. New York: Oxford University Press.

Wolton, D. (2003) *L'autre mondialisation*. Paris: Flammarion.

World Commission on Culture and Development. (1996) *Our Creative Diversity*. Paris: UNESCO Publishing.

INTRODUCTION

Yudhishthir Raj Isar and Helmut K. Anheier

Behind the concern for 'culture' that is increasingly evoked in contemporary public debate lurks the specter of conflict: the cultural dimensions of conflict on the one hand, and the conflictual dimensions of culture on the other. The duality inherent in this concern is, however, not always overtly stated. Yet, like so many other phenomena that characterize or are generated by globalization, conflict–culture relationships are inadequately analyzed and little understood. Hence they are easily politicized by ideologues of many different types and persuasions. This applies in particular to the question of cultural identities, both individual and collective, and their forms of expression, maintenance, representation, recognition, and renewal.

What exactly do we mean by 'conflict'? At one level, we mean the tensions between individual and collective values on the one hand and economic and political interests on the other. These are an integral part of the human and social condition; they have always re-asserted themselves in times of accelerated change. Nor are they all inherently negative or harmful, on the contrary. Many observers make the point that the arts, for example, flourish during times of change and tension as tools of critique and dissent. Or take the 'creative conflicts' that sociologists from Simmel (1983) to Dahrendorf (1994) have written about, or the 'creative destruction' economists such as Schumpeter (1962) and others identified. Globalization has given a new 'edge' to such conflicts, however. Harnessing them through adequate institutions and ways of conflict regulation is now the challenge (see, e.g., Berger 1998).

Yet there are also violent conflicts, including conventional inter-state wars, ethnic strife and religious riots. Such conflicts are not only hideously wasteful of social energies and acutely harmful to all their protagonists. They also endanger future generations by creating a legacy of grievances and a 'culture of memory' that, as will become clear below, are likely to sow the seeds of future conflicts as well.

Addressing a broad range of conflicts, their cultural content and their relationships to globalization processes – within and among nations as well as across the world's geo-cultural regions – is our focus for this maiden issue of the *Series*. We shall use the framework outlined in the Introductory chapter to this volume in order to break down these relationships and the shifting nexus between cultures and societies. In so doing, we shall have to examine two facets of culture-related conflict, in other words: i) the extent to which conflicts generated by globalization in other areas appropriate the cultural dimension and ii) the extent to which the cultural dimension itself may have its own inbuilt conflict dynamics and tensions that might be either amplified or suppressed by globalization processes.

Although conflictuality is constitutive of the human condition, today we live in a particularly conflict-prone global environment, as the contributors to this volume will demonstrate, even though scholars disagree about the assessment and interpretation of different types of conflicts, their intensity and impact. Culturally driven and culturally implicated conflicts have been and are unfolding throughout the world. A myriad of tensions constantly surface with respect to cultural claims and assertions of many different kinds. A new commonplace is to see culture as a 'security issue'. Yet fact-based and theoretically informed debate about the causes and consequences of such conflicts and tensions in the context of globalization has not become easier, but more difficult. One of the reasons is the increasing tendency to reify and essentialize the concept of culture, to instrumentalize 'culture' as a thing, an agency, and to ascribe causality to it, when often culture is only a pawn and the tensions are in fact generated by contests over power and resources.[1]

The duality of cultural conflict: path-dependency, worldviews and interests

What, then, can be done to 'deconstruct' this relationship? First, we suggest that even the most complex reality should not deter us from proposing explanatory models, if only to discard them after having explored their utility. Second, we think that such models, like the framework already proposed for breaking down the relationship between globalization and cultures, should be parsimonious, allow us to focus on essential features and issues, encourage further thinking, and be relevant to policy. This may be easier to advocate than to accomplish, however, and so here we can do little more than sketch what kind of model we have in mind.

Let us make a risky proposition as a starting point, although we are aware that it may well not be fully testable with the limited evidence available: in our opinion, many of today's conflicts, though not all, and rarely in their entirety, are tied to globalization processes.

Why might this be the case? In making this proposition, we have in mind a broad range of conflicts, including overtly ethnic conflicts, conflicts over resources and power, inter-state and civil wars, which are the focus of many of the chapters in this book, but also industrial, work-related conflicts, peasant revolts and student demonstrations, etc. We see globalization not primarily as the single cause of such conflicts but as a process penetrating and changing the 'causal chemistry' and 'fabric' of existing conflicts as well as emerging and re-emerging ones. Finally, in putting forward our proposition, we are invoking a broader historical perspective on globalization similar to that of many contemporary analysts when they point to the expansion of direct foreign investment and world trade since the end of the Cold War as the critical period but not the only one. Thus we see the current globalization spurt, as indeed previous ones in the nineteenth and early twentieth centuries, in the context of a long-term though uneven expansion of world rationalization *and* capitalism. While in operational terms, we fully share contemporary readings of globalization as greater connectedness of flows of finance, knowledge, goods and services, and people across time, nations, regions and inter-continental space, we treat it conceptually as part of an ongoing historical process with *cultural roots* reaching back many centuries.

In other words, rather than a process that may have started in the late twentieth century, we regard today's globalization as the latest phase of historic developments whose major impetus was the rise of capitalism in Europe and North America, but which for centuries have spurred and interacted with specific dynamics in other parts of the world in terms of economic and political development (e.g., Japan) or underdevelopment (e.g., Sub-Saharan Africa). At some level, the spread of rationality and capitalism has engendered conflict dynamics, i.e., colonialism, imperial wars, and struggles for self-determination and independence. At another level, these conflict dynamics, while often economic and political on the surface, have also been deeply cultural.

By 'cultural conflict' we mean nothing as dramatic as some 'clash of civilizations' or 'epochal fight' of ethnicities or religions. What we have in mind is more subtle and long-term: the cultural dynamics of rationalism and capitalism have long brought diverse cultural worldviews into contact with each other.[2] In many cases, such contact implied domination, but frequently it also involved some form of 'meshing' or partial inter-penetration of worldviews over time, encouraging cultural learning, cross-fertilization, imitation and innovation. Not surprisingly, the ways in which worldviews interact and relate to each other reflect power relations and changing elite interests over time. Some of these worldviews are religious, for example those of Catholicism or Sufism, while others are secular ideologies such as socialism, liberalism or Baathism, while yet others are eclectic mixtures, such as fascism or many forms of nationalism. Some are more coherent than others, and they vary in terms of openness and capacity for adaptation. Critically, these worldviews have been, and are, affected by globalization in varying ways, and vice versa, but they also have their own dynamics. The important point is that such worldviews have existed and evolved for many centuries, sometimes millennia, and typically antedate the more pronounced globalization periods of the late nineteenth and twentieth centuries. Indeed, Christianity, Islam and socialism have been transnational creeds from their very beginning, and are certainly not the products of national societies or cultures.

Thus, when exploring the relationship between globalization and conflict we have to be mindful that some types of conflicts are deeply rooted in history, and that they are not the result of current events, even though the latter may well have contributed new impetuses and triggers. Instead, some conflicts are closely linked to worldviews held by different populations, groups and individuals, and how these worldviews line up with prevailing economic, political, and cultural realities. For example, the 'culture wars' in nineteenth-century Germany were a conflict between a politically and economically weakened Catholic Church and the rising secular power of Prussia. The culture wars of late twentieth-century America, however, take place between a cosmopolitan urban-industrial elite, and a religiously minded lower-middle class in danger of losing the socioeconomic status they worked so hard to attain.

Yet, if globalization involves more frequent movements of objects, meanings and people across transnational space, then it also implies, at the very least, a greater exposure of different collectivities to each other, and hence also greater contact among worldviews. Such contacts may challenge or reinforce long-held cultural assumptions and they may also increase the frequency of 'meshing' and depths of interpenetration, including acceptance and rejection as well as patterns of innovation and diffusion. Whatever the outcome, such contacts may also generate a greater conflict potential.

Yet what specifically could be such greater conflict potential in the historic and current relationship between globalization and culture? Let us step back and remind ourselves of Weber's observations about the relationship between ideas and interests. In his comparative analysis of world religions (Weber 1988), he concluded that material and ideal interests, and not specific ideas, govern human behavior. Yet the worldviews, i.e., the sum of ideas and their assumptions, act as a 'switch' and determine the 'tracks' along which actions are then being pushed by the dynamics of interests, be they political or economic. Thus, interests are path-dependent on patterns suggested, if not largely determined, by worldviews (see Tenbruck 1999; Schluchter 2005).

The parallel argument could be made for conflicts: not specific ideas, but material and ideal interests, govern human actions leading or responding to conflict. The worldviews, again, provide both structure and context to these conflicts and help shape specific conflict dynamics. As a result of globalization processes, the relationship between worldviews and interests has become more complex; and increasingly, through greater interpenetration and more frequent 'meshing', conflicts are nested in each other, either in latent or manifest ways.

An example of such nested conflicts is provided by the current morass in Iraq, with several layers of latent inter-ethnic and inter-religious strife that were 'ignited' to become manifest conflicts after the US-led invasion produced a power vacuum in an inconclusive post-war scenario. In other words, not only are conflicts, like interests, path-dependent on worldviews, they are also path-dependent on each other, as the illusion that World War I was a 'war to end all wars' profoundly and tragically demonstrated. In sum, in an age of globalization, the duality inherent in the relationship between culture and conflict stems from the path-dependent interplay between worldviews and interests.

Taking a closer look

The preceding paragraphs implied a rather abstract notion of 'conflict'. How to make our understandings more concrete? In the most general terms, conflict is a disagreement through which parties involved perceive a threat to their needs, interests and concerns. In other words, conflict is more than a disagreement; it is that plus a perceived threat. It is also a social configuration in that it establishes a relation among conflicting parties, even if that relationship is very uneven and contested in content and form. Several aspects are worth noting.

It is the perceived threat that matters, not the actual one; and parties act according to their perception of the situation, which points to the importance of worldviews, values and belief systems as 'filters' but also to the role of information and recall (memory) of prior experience in interpreting threats. In other words, as shown above conflicts are culturally and socially embedded.

Power plays a crucial role in any conflict situation; conflict involves a confrontation among conflicting parties, each with some capability (real or imagined, specific or diffuse) to produce some effect in addressing the disagreement about needs, interests and concerns. Power is closely linked to resource availability and legitimacy, as well as to the potential of inflicting violence and the deployment of military means. Conflict is a clash of power, a pushing and pulling, a giving and taking. In this balancing process of powers confronting each other, the capabilities of the involved parties vary and may shift. In other words, conflicts are dynamic and rarely static.

Conflicts are manifest tensions that arise from perceived disagreements, as opposed to latent conflicts where parties may be largely unaware of the level of threat and power capabilities. Once conflicts are manifest, however, the conditions for communicating, mobilizing and organizing them are critical for the process and outcome. As we will suggest below, the wider availability of information technology, combined with a steep decline in communication costs, facilitates the transformation of latent into manifest conflicts.

While modern societies are conflict-prone they tend to seek ways and means of managing, i.e., institutionalizing, conflicts (panels, hearings, political parties, social movements, judiciary, etc.) rather than seeking settlement through domination alone. Such institutionalized conflicts are seen as creative conflicts that reduce the tensions that could otherwise build up along major societal cleavage structures. Such tensions could threaten the social fabric of societies, while managed conflicts contribute to social stability and 'tamed' social change.

However, over-institutionalization of conflicts can create inertia and stifle social change and innovation, whereas under-institutionalization can lead to a spreading of the conflict into other fields and generate unintended consequences. Moreover, deep-seated core conflicts (labor–capital; value conflicts; ethnic conflicts) have the tendency of amassing complicating factors around them that in the end can make some conflicts intractable.[3] Such basic insights into conflict are useful for our purposes as they allow us to probe deeper into the complex relationship between globalization, culture and conflict.

While Table I.1 applies to conflicts in general, globalization has the potential of changing the dynamics of conflict as well as the forms conflicts can take. For instance, conflicts spill across national boundaries, and create latent and manifest conflicts among parties that hitherto have not been connected in that way. Outsourcing is an obvious example, as are environmental problems or the influx of Western cultural products ('Hollywood') in Asia or the Middle East.

Global governance problems are important here. Because of globalization, the management of conflicts towards some form of institutionalization is more difficult to achieve today. Because of the limited capacity of the system of international institutions to deal effectively with global, transnational issues such as the environment, crime, epidemics, or economic exploitation, virtually all nation-states find it more challenging to address such problems with regulatory tools geared to dealing with domestic policy settings.

At the same time, globalization offers greater opportunity structures for movements of many kinds and a greater range of framing options, flowing from worldviews, for bringing grievances about divergent needs, interests and concerns forward (e.g., via global media networks). Moreover, technological developments have reduced the cost of communication, mobilizing and organizing (e.g., the Internet). Entry barriers for entering conflicts are reduced. In sum, latent and manifest conflicts exist in an environment of higher global connectivity at lower costs.

Persistent global governance problems, greater opportunities, reduced barriers and lower costs may well encourage a more frequent transformation of latent conflicts into manifest ones, and, related to this, of oppressed and dormant conflicts into open and active ones. In essence, we would expect globalization to free up existing conflicts as well as generate new ones, which have become salient in two ways:

- First, through identity politics, which generate conflicts largely but increasingly across established political boundaries, and have a tendency to instrumentalize culture for other ends; and
- Second, through what has become known as the 'clash of civilizations' discourse that exercises a certain hegemony upon academics, journalists and politicians as well as in the popular imagination.

Both types of conflicts are variations of the pattern or questions Weber identified: how current economic and political interests are aligned with prevailing worldviews, and the extent to which path-dependencies of interests play themselves out in a world characterized by increased interpenetration.

Identity politics and mobilization

The first avatar of the 'cultures and conflict' binomial is based on increasing group recourse to culture in connection with politicized and often conflict-saturated discourses of ethnicity and nationalism. A renewed politics of identity, often bloody, emerged forcefully at the end of the Cold War, whose bloc confrontations had masked a multitude of local claims and tensions over scarce resources or over the sharing of newly acquired

Table I.1 Analytic dimensions of conflict

Dynamics of conflict phases	Process of latent conflicts becoming manifest		Process of manifest conflicts becoming resolved	
	Possibility of conflict (disagreement and perceived level of threat) filtered through worldviews, and assessed relative to opportunity structures, grievance issues, framing processes, and instrumentalization options; politics of memory and path-dependencies	Conditions of communicating, mobilizing and organizing, resources available and resource dependencies	Power differentials and technical, organizational capacity for collective action; range of complicating factors, conflict forms, channels, and forums; learned conflict behavior	Conditions for conflict balancing and reaching settlement, conflict outcomes; of alignment of outcome with worldview and current as well as anticipated interests

ones. Once freed, these claims began to push collectivities of many different kinds into the narrow walls of group identity, often the 'narcissism of small differences' posited by Freud, feeding a new tide of smaller confrontations between, ethnic, religious and national communities. Religion as a marker of group identity has come particularly to the fore in recent years. In the psychoanalytical perspective (one that is regrettably not represented in this volume), Sudhir Kakar (1996: 192) has observed:

> *The involvement of religious rather than other social identities does not dampen but, on the contrary, increases the violence of the conflict. Religion brings to conflict between groups a greater emotional intensity and a deeper motivational thrust than language, region or other markers of ethnic identity.*

The collapse of the USSR and other regimes in Central and Eastern Europe revealed the resilience of apparently widespread nationalist sentiment hitherto hidden under the mantle of Soviet universalism. The cultural vocabularies of this resilience, in Europe and elsewhere, revealed the strength with which the 'bent twigs' of suppressed or wounded *Volksgeist* spring upright, to quote the image Isaiah Berlin often used, borrowed from Schiller. And the story has been repeated elsewhere across the world, as a world system centered on transnational corporate power and globally-ranging financial markets has taken hold, generating strong local reactions in worldviews, sentiments and aspirations. The values of different ways of life have risen to consciousness to become the rallying cry of diverse claims to a space in the planetary culture. Before, culture was just lived. Now it has become a self-conscious collective project (Sahlins 1994).

As populations shift and societies change, people turn to cultural distinctions embodied in their traditions to resist what is perceived as a threat to their integrity and prosperity, even their very survival in terms of transmission of identities and values. This recurrent mobilization around group identity has led to a cultural politics whose stakes include gaining control of (or access to) political and economic power. Where ethnic groups have enjoyed relatively equitable positions, tensions have arisen as soon as one or several of them has begun to feel that their relative position is slipping. Such tensions, often inevitable as economic conditions change, have led to contentions over rights to land, education, the use of language, political representation, freedom of religion, the preservation of ethnic identity, autonomy or self-determination.

The standard 'development' models have paid little attention to cultural values and differences, assuming that functional categories such as class and occupation are more important. We suggest, however, that many conflict-haunted development failures and disasters stem from an inadequate recognition of precisely these cultural complexities. In these situations, culture has been a determining factor in the nature and dynamic of conflict, as different markers such as language, race or religion have been used to distinguish the opposing actors. All too frequently, one specific group has assumed state power, and state building has rendered many other groups devoid of power or influence. Where it is perceived that the government either favors or discriminates against groups identifiable in cultural terms, this encourages the negotiation of benefits on the basis of cultural identity and leads directly to the politicization of culture. The dynamics of this process are such that when any one group starts negotiating on the basis of its cultural identity, others are encouraged to do likewise; and it has often been cumulative (Tambiah 1996).

'Civilizations' and conflict

The idea of a cultural conflict at world level has been generated by Samuel Huntington's thesis that 'the principal conflicts of global politics will occur between nations and groups of different civilizations' (Huntington 1996). Although the empirical foundation of the thesis is highly contestable, the phrase 'clash of civilizations' has become a contemporary cliché, abundantly thrown around by academics, politicians and journalists who have read neither Huntington nor his many critics. The thesis itself, reductionist and highly abstract, is a significant step backwards when compared to the Weberian understanding presented above. It treats culture with little heed for the internal dynamics and plurality of every so-called 'civilization', or for the fact that the major contest in most cultures concerns the diverging definitions and interpretation of each of them (see in particular Senghaas 2003).

Indeed, this is precisely what is happening with 'Islamic civilization', which has such a central place in Huntington's theory (Kepel 2004). This is particularly ironic post-September 11, when we realize that the thesis is identical with the reasoning of the chief protagonist of that horrific event, Osama Bin Laden himself, and this may well be the case as well of many who have since waged latter-day 'Crusades', if subsequent events in Iraq are any indication. Nonetheless, it appears necessary to present empirical evidence that either supports or rejects the thesis, and to shift the debate away from its highly ideological justification to evidence-based reasoning.

Against the background presented above, we have enlisted a group of experts from a range of social science or other analytical disciplines to explore different facets of the culture, conflict and globalization relationship. We were interested in comparative studies that explore this relationship at the global level, and across a larger number of cases. We were particularly keen to explore regional variations and realities, and also decided to focus on a number of cross-cultural tensions and cultural/political fault lines in today's world. Finally, we decided not to focus only on conflict as such, but also on its prevention, reconciliation and resolution. Although it was clear from the start that the theme of this inaugural volume encompassed culture principally in the 'ways of life' sense, we were also determined to bring culture as the arts and heritage into the equation as well. For the two dimensions of the culture concept are often closely intertwined. We wanted to be able to pinpoint current tensions within the arts and in the practices of commemoration that accompany heritage, to uncover how both are articulated with the broader meanings and, most specifically, how 'cultural capital' of various kinds can be either conflict's pawn or its remedy.

Conclusion

The results of our contributors' efforts are presented in twenty-seven chapters, organized in four sections, each with a separate introduction to help orient the reader. All in all, this is a project based on great expectations shared by those of us (including the co-editors and the authors) who believe deeply in the central importance of the 'cultural'. The theme this volume addresses, as we have unpacked it in these introductory remarks, is one that crystallizes, behind those great expectations, great anxieties and perhaps equally great illusions. The great anxieties arise from the persistent abuse of culture, both as a concept and as a reality. The great illusions are the result of overblown visions, of simplifications that are reductive, and readings that are instrumental. The illusions can be dispelled, the anxieties allayed (and the expectations justified), however, by the patient and methodical marshalling of evidence in an informed and conceptually sensitive way. It is our hope that this volume will contribute meaningfully to that task.

Notes

1 Academic anthropologists have long been familiar with the pitfalls of reification and essentialization that dog the 'culture' concept. But since culturalist discourse is now pervasive in much broader circles and has invested the public rhetoric of governments, intergovernmental organizations and civil society bodies alike, it seems important to reiterate a number of points for the benefit of a less specialized readership. Despite growing sophistication about the constructed nature of this contemporary culturalism, a number of misleading ideas persist whenever the notions of culture and 'cultural identity' are deployed, viz., that *culture is homogeneous,* which leads to the idea that *culture is a thing* that can act and have causality; that it *is uniformly distributed among members of a group;* that *an individual possesses but a single (generally 'national') culture;* that *culture is custom,* in other words tradition, something fixed and unchanging; finally, that *culture is timeless*, as when some speak of the 'Arab mind', as though a unitary cognizing element has come down to all Arabs straight from the Mecca of the Prophet Mohammed (see Avruch 1998).

2 Worldviews refers to ways of making sense of the world and accounting for realities so perceived, within prevailing circumstances. We use the term worldview rather than 'civilization' for two reasons. First, worldview, close to Weberian thinking, suggests greater plurality and fluidity than the term civilization. Second, the term civilization has become overly politicized through Huntington's clash of civilizations thesis and the ensuing debate around it.

3 These distinctions and ideas owe much to the sociology of conflict, in particular the work of Simmel,(1983), Dahrendorf (1994), Coser (1956), and others.

REFERENCES

Avruch, K. (1998) *Culture and Conflict Resolution.* Washington, DC: United States Institute of Peace Press.

Berger, P. (ed.) (1998) *The Limits of Social Cohesion: Conflict and Mediation in Pluralist Societies. A Report of the Bertelsmann Foundation to the Club of Rome.* Boulder, CO: Westview Press.

Coser, L (1956) *The Function of Social Conflict.* New York: Free Press.

Dahrendorf, R. (1994) *Der moderne soziale Konflikt: Essay zur Politik der Freiheit.* Munich: DTV.

Huntington, S. P. (1996) *The Clash of Civilizations and the Remaking of World Order.* New York: Simon & Schuster.

Kakar, S. (1996) *The Colors of Violence: Cultural Identities, Religion, and Conflict.* Chicago: University of Chicago Press.

Kepel, G. (2004) *Fitna: Guerre au coeur de l'Islam.* Paris: Editions Gallimard.

Sahlins, M. (1994) 'A Brief cultural history of culture'. Unpublished paper prepared for the World Commission on Culture and Development (UNESCO).

Schluchter, W. (2005) *Handlung, Ordnungen und Kultur: Studien zu einem Forschungsprogramm im Anschluss an Max Weber.* Tübingen: Mohr.

Schumpeter, J. (1962) *Capitalism, Socialism and Democracy.* New York: HarperPerennial.

Senghaas, D. (2003) *The Clash within Civilizations: Coming to Terms with Cultural Conflicts.* New York: Routledge.

Simmel, G. (1983) *Soziologie: Untersuchungen über die Formen der Vergesellschaftung.* Berlin: Duncker & Humblot.

Tambiah, S.J. (1996) *Leveling crowds: Ethnonationalist Conflicts and Collective Violence in South Asia.* Berkeley and Los Angeles: University of California Press.

Tenbruck, F.(1999) *Das Werk Max Webers.* Tübingen: Mohr.

Weber, M. (1988) *Gesammelte Aufsätze zur Religionssoziologie I.* Stuttgart: UTB.

INTRODUCTION

This first section presents cross-cutting approaches that address basic questions about the 'whys and hows' of tensions and conflicts linked to cultural identity and belonging as well as to forms of cultural expression. The six contributors share the conviction that cultural conflicts are not natural but constructed, not necessarily cultural in their origins but often sited at the intersection between political and economic interests and the universes of ideas, values, meanings, memories, representations. On the basis of empirical and interpretive observation or comparative data, they analyze the stances of different actors and institutions – the nation state, political elites, local communities, artists and arts institutions, or intellectuals – as stakeholders.

The 'institutional' approach in political science has long argued that cultural conflicts are induced first and foremost by economic and political inequities. In the opening chapter, Beverly Crawford analyzes a number of current conflicts in this perspective and links them directly to changes brought about by globalization. State institutions attempt to deal with inequities but frequently find that the very processes they try to counteract are rapidly undermining their capacity to do so. Instead, these processes open up opportunities for political actors to become 'cultural entrepreneurs' as it were, by politicizing culture for economic or political gain. According to Crawford, effective institutions are the key factor in enabling societies to combat such pressures. The contribution entitled 'Ethnicity and War in a World of Nation-States' is a longitudinal and cross-cultural analysis by Andreas Wimmer and Brian Min that combines the insights of political science and sociology. The authors demonstrate that the number of interstate wars has decreased, while civil wars have increased. However, they argue that the formation of the modern nation-state is an often-disregarded cause of conflict and has influenced both forms of violent conflict, and in two ways. First, nationalist movements during nation-state formation were often rooted in violence and contention. Second, the nation-states that were created then sought to include diverse ethnic or cross-national groups, and this meant increased competition within the nation-state for political and institutional power.

What happens when nation-states develop policies and mechanisms to the sorts of cultural pressures brought about by globalization? This is the question Laura Adams, Miguel Centeno and Charles Varner take up in their comparative analysis of resistance to globalization. Some governments actively institutionalize resistance: Canada's regulations against influences from the United States, Kazakhstan's regulation of Russian culture, and Malaysia's attempts to limit the influence of local Chinese and Indian immigrant populations. Resistance to globalization is a complex process that always takes place within a local context where the globalization process is represented by a concrete target of resistance. In these three countries, the state has employed three different frameworks in resisting globalization processes: anti-hegemonic, post-colonial, and diasporic. Policies are generated in response to a specific threat related to cultural globalization and are related to cultural trade, media, language, and religion. Like Crawford, these authors argue that institutions are especially responsible and powerful for both exacerbating and mitigating cultural conflict.

The three social scientific approaches are mirrored by the three chapters written from the perspective of artistic practice and heritage preservation. As an Asian performance scholar, Rustom Bharucha draws on the latent dimensions of conflict in on-the-ground cultural practice of 'subaltern' groups. He takes as a case study India's *Siddi* community, people of African origin or descent, who now live in scattered settlements in different parts of the country, and focuses on what he calls the 'intra-cultural' contexts by which local and regional differences interact with global forces and opportunities. In emphasizing the disjunctions between global theoretical discourse and grassroots activism in representing subaltern communities, he questions 'the capacity to aspire' dimension of culture posited by Arjun Appadurai, highlighting the limits of global networking and performance in favor of a more nationally grounded cultural praxis.

Dragan Klaic asks whether culture is the cause or the victim in cases of globalized conflict. He too demonstrates how what appears to be cultural conflict, is often politics, economics, or religion advancing masked behind culture, so that passions are enlivened and key stakeholders and audiences engaged. Globalization, he argues, fuels the processes of 'culturization' or 'ethnicization' – and this interpretation will be returned to several times in the volume as a whole. For example, globalization allows worldwide involvement in the memory wars of different locales because of worldwide media streams and global associations. Memory wars evoke values, authorities, and beliefs and in countries without viable, functioning institutions, these rifts can explode into violence. The intensity of these protests relies more on politics, on deeply ingrained anger and feelings of repression, than on culture per se.

Cultural heritage is 'collective memory' made tangible: Dacia Viejo Rose explores how both are attacked in present-day armed conflict: through the deliberately targeted destruction of monuments, the theft of artifacts, the replacement of important imagery and symbols, and the imposition of politically charged propaganda. She too suggests a typology, but of destruction, according to the kind of action, the type of object destroyed or damaged and the type of conflict. She assesses the ways in which globalized forces such as movements of people and international normative instruments act against or in favor of heritage conservation. Finally, she discusses international reconstruction efforts while also demystifying them: post-conflict societies need to recognize new meanings and symbols and an interpretation of heritage and history that encourage concord over the long term.

## CHAPTER 1

GLOBALIZATION AND CULTURAL CONFLICT: AN INSTITUTIONAL APPROACH

Beverly Crawford

The links between economic globalization and cultural conflict are found at the level of the state and the level of the society. Global economic forces can weaken state institutions that ensure social peace, and can cause distinct cultural groups in multi-ethnic societies to suffer disproportionate economic hardships and gains. This suffering provides a concrete justification for grievances that can be transformed into a resource for political mobilization by cultural entrepreneurs. If political institutions provide a legitimate arena for those entrepreneurs to compete and if resources are allocated fairly, cultural politics, like other kinds of political competition, can be legitimate and stable. But when demographic and economic changes – often brought on by the forces of globalization – undermine the 'rules of the game', and lead to perceptions that the balance of political power is unfair, cultural politics can escalate to cultural conflict and violence.

Introduction

What is the impact of globalization on social cohesion and political integration? Does globalization nourish social and political integration and tear down cultural barriers that divide people? Does it signal a 'vital step toward both a more stable world and better lives for the people in it' (Rothkopf, 1997)? Or does it hasten social disintegration and exacerbate social conflict? Is there really a link between globalization and 'cultural' conflict or harmony? If so, what is it?

Migratory flows, the tidal wave of global information, and the imperatives of economic liberalization and fiscal reform – the markers of globalization – have reshuffled social relations all over the world. As the flood of immigrants to the industrial West has given birth to a nascent heterogeneity in previously homogeneous societies, social pressures and plummeting income levels accompany it. In some countries, a spike in hate crimes against foreigners seems to correspond to the influx of immigrants. And people have watched in horror as Islamic radicals have committed brutal acts of violence, justified as revenge against cultural oppression or religious deviance.

Although globalization has been called an integrating force, cultural conflict has become the most rampant form of international violence as globalization has accelerated. Of the 36 violent conflicts raging around the world in 2003, the Iraq invasion was the sole international war. The remaining 35 were internal wars within the territory of 28 countries, and all but four of these were communal conflicts, inspired by ethnic, sectarian, or religious grievances (Marshall 2005). Nonetheless, the number of those conflicts has begun to decline, and many have ended. Indeed, in vast areas of the world, conflicts are being resolved peacefully, and people of different cultures live together or side by side without hostility or prolonged violent conflict.

But as some conflicts ended, new conflicts ignited. Despite the end of the wars in ex-Yugoslavia, continued violence plagues Kosovo and Bosnia. Even in the presence of foreign peacekeeping troops, violence in Kosovo took between 4,000 and 12,000 lives between 1999 and 2004. And between 1999 and 2004, Chechnya erupted in a war of secession, causing the deaths of close to 30,000 civilians. Attacks on dark-skinned people, often identified as Chechens or Dagestanis were reported in Moscow and other major Russian cities beginning in 1994, and escalated as the conflict continued (Human Rights Watch (2003)). Between 1989 and 2003, more than 65,000 people, mostly Muslim civilians were killed in Kashmir and the conflict there continues to take over 2,000 lives per year. These examples suggest significant differences in the kinds and levels of conflict and the conditions under which it breaks out. In this essay, I present a conceptual framework for understanding these differences. It relies on the role of economic forces triggered by globalization that drive both 'cultural' conflict and integration. It looks to the role and strength of political institutions as the key to conflict provocation, exacerbation, and mitigation. It focuses on those institutions that channel economic forces to create cultural winners and losers in the globalization process, and those that channel political participation and treat group 'rights' in ways that mitigate or intensify the violence that members of one culture perpetrate against those who belong to another.

Argument

Many analysts (Rothkopf 1997; Sadowski 1998; Telo 2001; Kuran, 2001; Dutceac, 2004) critique the idea that economic globalization fuels cultural conflict, arguing that cultural conflicts are found in almost every society, whether it experiences high levels of globalization or not. And in fact, these conflicts are likely to be much less lethal in societies that are receptive to globalization (Bhalla 1994; Whitehead 1995; Geddes 1994).[1] There is evidence to support this view. For example, Malaysia had much in common with Sri Lanka in terms of economy, society, and culture, including ethnic composition and inequalities between ethnic groups (Bruton 1992). Unlike Sri Lanka, however, whose economy stagnated with economic liberalization, Malaysian prosperity expanded the economic pie through its participation in the global economy, providing abundant resources to Chinese and Malay alike. Because the allocative institutions that distribute these resources in ways that are widely perceived as 'fair', rising prosperity denies extremist groups – bent on pitting these two communities against each other – the grievances that could fuel cultural conflict (Athukorala 2001).

The Indian State of Punjab between 1992 and 1998 provides a second example. There, after violence was repressed, the federal government abolished many restrictions, and market-stimulated growth benefited disgruntled Sikh farmers who were previously disadvantaged by discriminatory regulations. But this social harmony may be difficult to sustain, as the costs of participation in the global economy outweigh the benefits. By 2002, because of extreme fluctuations in global agricultural markets, Punjab experienced *both* chronic economic crisis, and the renewed escalation of social unrest.[2] The stories of Punjab and Malaysia suggest that as long as states 'win' in market competition, and when both advantaged and previously disadvantaged cultural groups benefit, economic transformation resulting from globalization can mute cultural conflicts.

While many analysts suspect that there is a link between economic globalization and the current round of cultural conflict[3] (e.g., Lapidus et. al. 1992; Woodward 1995; Kapstein 1996; Schulman 2000; Bandarage 2000; Alesina et al. 2003; Biziouras, forthcoming), few have investigated causal forces that might explain that relationship.[4] I suggest here that such causes operate at two levels, the level of *the state* and the level of *the society*. Global economic forces can weaken those state institutions that ensure social peace, and can cause distinct cultural groups in multi-ethnic societies to suffer disproportionate economic hardships and gains. I suspect that although the forces of globalization have created a common commercial culture – particularly among elites – they have also deepened cultural divides in many societies where those elites live. Few would disagree that integration in the global economy – even if the result is net aggregate growth – creates winners and losers in the domestic economy. If economic hardship – whether in a growing or declining economy – falls disproportionately on distinct cultural groups, they have a concrete justification for political grievances that can be transformed into a resource for political mobilization. Groups with grievances are ripe for recruitment efforts by those I term *'cultural entrepreneurs' – individuals or agencies that politicize culture or protest cultural discrimination for political or economic gain.* These entrepreneurs will be successful if they have resources to distribute in exchange for support. These resources will be available if a 'cultural machine' is in place – either in or out of government – to acquire and distribute those resources and if 'cultural brethren' abroad provide support targeted to extremist political entrepreneurs. States weakened by the forces of globalization have fewer means to cope with social disintegration. And violence may be the only alternative course for groups making non-negotiable resource demands.

The myth of liberalization

This argument challenges the claim that the rapid and simultaneous construction of liberal economic and democratic political institutions – a process for which 'globalization' is sometimes a code word – can mitigate cultural conflict. Free markets create wealth for all, the argument runs, erasing the need for violent struggle over resources. And democracy permits political aggregation and representation of all social interests, allowing conflicts of interest to be adjudicated in the political arena and trump identity conflicts that are more difficult to negotiate.

Despite widespread acceptance of these claims, however, I would argue that *perceived economic inequities, particularly those that arise from current policies of economic liberalization and the longer term effects of globalization can undermine liberal political practices and, combined with illiberal politics, can be an explosive trigger for cultural conflict*[5]. Where communal differences had already become politically relevant in the past, today the ethnic or religious card may be the easiest one to play in the effort to mobilize political support in the face of economic decline, in the shift from welfare to market economies, and in the move from centralized to decentralized polities. The policies of economic liberalization require the 'dismantling' of state institutions, and weakened states cannot provide equal protection for all who live within their territory.

Liberal democracies can mute cultural conflict with institutions of inclusiveness, universal representation, and electoral systems designed to encourage elite compromise. Indeed, a robust liberal democracy may be one of the strongest defenses against cultural conflict. But 'democracies' are not all liberal; many *illiberal* democracies have emerged in the last fifteen years that possess some democratic attributes, such as free elections, freedom of speech, freedom of movement, freedom of association, and freedom of religion. But they pay only lip service to the rule of law, minority and citizen rights, and independent judicial review (Zakaria 1997, 2003; Pigliucci 2004). Illiberal democracies exacerbate cultural conflict. In periods of economic uncertainty and political transition, when states that once provided entitlements are dismantled, when illiberal democracies are so constructed that they fail to protect rights, and when the introduction of markets leads to deep insecurities, the rich symbolic resources of culture offer hope in their promise of collective empowerment to populations who feel powerless.

Illiberal democracies can arise in the absence of economic liberalization and globalization. At the time of independence in Sri Lanka, for example, there were about 4.6 million Sinhalese and 1.5 million Tamils living there,[6] and Sri Lanka's 'democratically' elected majority Sinhalese government discriminated against the Tamil minority. The Citizenship Act of 1948 deprived Tamils – whose ancestors had lived in the country for more than a century – of citizenship in the independent state of Sri Lanka. In fact, Tamils were only allowed to *apply for* citizenship in 2003. From the 1950s on, the Sinhalese-controlled parliament enacted discriminatory legislation against the Tamil minority, starting with the 'Sinhala-only Act', replacing English with Sinhala as the only official language, effectively excluding Tamils from employment in the civil service if they could not speak Sinhala. The 1972 Constitution made Buddhism the state religion, threatening the Tamil practice of their Hindu faith, and Tamils were excluded from institutions of higher education by strict quotas.

I am therefore not suggesting that the forces of globalization and economic liberalization directly 'cause' cultural conflict. In Sri Lanka, as we shall see, violence broke out as the country entered the global economy, but, as a result of the creation of an illiberal democracy, tensions churned long before. In places like Malaysia (Lubeck 1998; Biziouras, forthcoming), integration into the global economy has brought growth and a distribution of income that has helped to attenuate cultural conflict. Clearly, the link between economic liberalization, illiberal politics, and cultural conflict is not a linear one. Here, I explore the role of globalization by conceptualizing both its differential impact on cultural groups in multicultural societies and its impact on the state's ability to support institutions that provide social order. I argue that the institutions of political participation and resource allocation are the crucial factors affecting social integration, and the nature and strength of these key institutions differ among societies.

Globalization: factor flows and state 'shrinking'

Two aspects of the globalization process may be significant triggers for cultural conflict: migration, and trade. While the expansion of trade and its requirement for state-shrinking impacts both the developed and underdeveloped world, immigration can ignite conflict in the industrialized West, turning homogeneous nations into heterogeneous societies with vast differences in wealth, values, and cultural practices. Combined with the state-shrinking imperatives of trade openness, conflict can increase, triggering the intervention of opposing diasporic communities. This mixture can be lethal (see contributions by Estrada, Grimson and Wong below).

For roughly half a century, from the 1930s to the 1980s, immigration rates were historically low, compared to rates from 1850 to 1920. Now the tide has turned. Net immigration rates have more than doubled in the United States and Western Europe since the 1960s. Ironically, this upward surge occurred during a period in which immigration policy in the most developed countries became increasingly restrictive.[7] Indeed, some 500,000 undocumented migrants enter the European Union each year, and over 150 million people are on the move every year – one out of every 50 people worldwide. This migration surge has broken the back of cultural homogeneity, particularly in the industrialized West, where most migrants are headed. Table 1.1 shows the dramatic surge of migration to Europe between 1992 and 2001.

Immigrants rarely arrive in their host countries today without bringing with them ties to family and community in their homeland. These bonds heighten the importance of diaspora communities in the globalization process. With decreasing costs of transportation and communication worldwide, interactions within such communities are increasing in depth. This intensity can be partially captured in the evidence of growth in cross-border remittances worldwide. For example, remittances to Latin America and the Caribbean from Latinos in the United States doubled in the last half of the 1990s (Suro 2003). Official remittances from immigrant labor to 24 countries worldwide have grown almost 4 percent per year between 1980 and 2002, and grew three times faster than the GDP of most developing countries during the same period (Adams 2003). In addition to the increase in migration over the last 50 years, there has been a marked expansion in the flow of goods worldwide. The ratio of worldwide exports to worldwide GDP rose from about 8 percent in 1960 to 20 percent in 2001. The most important contributor to this growth was a dramatic lowering of trade barriers across the globe. Average tariffs in the United States, Germany, and Japan fell by more than half. The membership of the World Trade Organization rose from 18 countries in 1948 to 146 countries in 2003. And free-trade areas, led by the European Union and NAFTA, have increased from 1 in 1958 to 16 in 2003.

Political power lies behind the growth of world commerce. Trade expanded because trading states replaced policies that protected some producers from global competition with policies that removed that protection, such as tariffs and subsidies and other non-tariff trade barriers. States open their economies to trade by also assuring that their currencies are convertible, and lifting controls on the flow of capital. Governments have also enacted 'reform' policies that they believe will make their products more competitive in the global market place. We can call these economic liberalization measures policies of 'state-shrinking,' because their goal is to remove the state from interference with the market.

Globalization and economic hardship

Political and economic forces unleashed in the globalization process can drive each other in a vicious circle that often ends in conflict. In particular, these policies of 'state-shrinking' can cause social disruption and radical dislocation of communities. In multicultural societies, the resulting hardships can be disproportionately allocated among various cultural groups, especially where there is a cultural division of labor in which different cultural groups are segmented into distinct economic sectors. Existing political cleavages based on cultural difference are then exacerbated and new ones are created. In the industrialized world, this result is perhaps nowhere more obvious than in countries with large immigrant communities.

In Europe, for example, immigrants from non-European states suffer from much lower wage rates and much higher rates of unemployment than native populations, despite the fact that nearly 88 percent come with a secondary education or higher (Adams 2003). Figure 1.1 shows that in France and Germany, immigrant unemployment is twice the national rate, and in Denmark, Finland, The Netherlands, and Sweden, it is three to four times the national average. These rates suggest persistent exclusion, disadvantage and even discrimination (The European Monitoring Centre on Racism and Xenophobia 2003).

With the exception of the 2005 youth riots in French suburbia, immigrants have rarely engaged in violent protest against these conditions. It is most

Table 1.1 Stocks of Foreign Population in selected OECD Countries
Thousands and percentages

	1992	1993	1994	1995	1996	1997	1998	1999	2000	2001
Austria	623.0	689.6	713.5	723.5	728.2	732.7	737.3	748.2	757.9	764.3
% of total population	7.9	8.6	8.9	9.0	9.0	9.1	9.1	9.2	9.3	9.4
Belgium	909.3	920.6	922.3	909.8	911.9	903.2	892.0	897.1	861.7	846.7
% of total population	9.0	9.1	9.1	9.0	9.0	8.9	8.7	8.8	8.4	8.2
Czech Republic	41.2	77.7	103.7	158.6	198.6	209.8	219.8	228.9	201.0	210.8
% of total population	0.4	0.8	1.0	1.5	1.9	2.0	2.1	2.2	1.9	2.0
Denmark	180.1	189.0	196.7	222.7	237.7	249.6	256.3	259.4	258.6	266.7
% of total population	3.5	3.6	3.8	4.2	4.7	4.7	4.8	4.9	4.8	5.0
Finland	46.3	55.6	62.0	68.6	73.8	80.6	85.1	87.7	91.1	98.6
% of total population	0.9	1.1	1.2	1.3	1.4	1.6	1.6	1.7	1.8	1.9
France	–	–	–	–	–	–	–	3 263.2	–	–
% of total population	–	–	–	–	–	–	–	5.6	–	–
Germany	6 495.8	6 878.1	6 990.5	7 173.9	7 314.0	7 365.8	7 319.5	7 343.6	7 296.8	7 318.6
% of total population	8.0	8.5	8.6	8.8	8.9	9.0	8.9	8.9	8.9	8.9
Greece	–	–	–	–	–	–	–	–	–	762.2
% of total population	–	–	–	–	–	–	–	–	–	7.0
Hungary	–	–	137.9	139.9	142.5	143.8	–	127.0	110.0	116.4
% of total population	–	–	1.3	1.4	1.4	1.4	–	1.2	1.1	1.1
Ireland	94.9	89.9	91.1	96.1	118.0	114.4	111.0	117.8	126.5	151.4
% of total population	2.7	2.7	2.7	2.7	3.2	3.1	3.0	3.2	3.3	3.9
Italy	925.2	987.4	922.7	991.4	1 095.6	1 240.7	1 250.2	1 252.0	1 388.2	1 362.6
% of total population	1.6	1.7	1.6	1.7	2.0	2.1	2.1	2.2	2.4	2.4
Japan	1 281.6	1 320.7	1 354.0	1 362.4	1 415.1	1 482.7	1 512.1	1 556.1	1 686.4	1 778.5
% of total population	1.0	1.1	1.1	1.1	1.1	1.2	1.2	1.2	1.3	1.4
Korea	55.8	66.7	84.9	110.0	148.7	176.9	147.9	169.0	210.2	229.6
% of total population	0.1	0.2	0.2	0.2	0.3	0.3	0.3	0.4	0.4	0.5
Luxembourg	122.7	127.6	132.5	138.1	142.8	147.7	152.9	159.4	164.7	166.7
% of total population	31.0	31.8	32.6	33.4	34.1	34.9	35.6	36.0	37.3	37.5
Netherlands	757.4	779.8	757.1	725.4	679.9	678.1	662.4	651.5	667.8	690.4
% of total population	5.0	5.1	5.0	4.7	4.4	4.3	4.2	4.1	4.2	4.3
Norway	154.0	162.3	164.0	160.8	157.5	158.0	165.0	178.7	184.3	185.9
% of total population	3.6	3.8	3.8	3.7	3.6	3.6	3.7	4.0	4.1	4.1
Poland	–	–	–	–	–	–	–	42.8	–	–
% of total population	–	–	–	–	–	–	–	0.1	–	–
Portugal	123.6	131.6	157.1	168.3	172.9	175.3	177.8	190.9	208.0	223.6
% of total population	1.3	1.3	1.6	1.7	1.7	1.8	1.8	1.9	2.1	2.2
Slovak Republic	–	11.0	16.9	21.9	24.1	24.8	27.4	29.5	28.3	29.4
% of total population	–	0.2	0.3	0.4	0.5	0.5	0.5	0.5	0.5	0.5
Spain	393.1	430.4	461.4	499.8	539.0	609.8	719.6	801.3	895.7	1109.1
% of total population	1.0	1.1	1.2	1.3	1.4	1.6	1.8	2.0	2.2	2.7
Sweden	499.1	507.5	537.4	531.8	526.6	522.0	499.9	487.2	477.3	476.0
% of total population	5.7	5.8	6.1	5.2	6.0	6.0	5.6	5.5	5.4	5.3
Switzerland	1 213.5	1 260.3	1 300.1	1 330.6	1 337.6	1 340.8	1 347.9	1 368.7	1 384.4	1 419.1
% of total population	17.6	18.1	18.6	18.9	18.9	19.0	19.0	19.2	19.3	19.7
United Kingdom	1 985.0	2 001.0	2 032.0	1 948.0	1 934.0	2 066.0	2 207.0	2 208.0	2 342.0	2 587.0
% of total population	3.5	3.5	3.6	3.4	3.4	3.6	3.8	3.8	4.0	4.4

Note: Data are from population registers or from registers of foreigners except for France and Greece (Census), Italy, Portugal and Spain (residence permits) Poland (estimates), Ireland and the United Kingdom (Labour Force Survey). The data refer to the population on 31 December of the years indicated unless otherwise stated.

Figure 1.1 Unemployment rate of EU and non-EU nationals in 2001 (percent of their active population 16–64)

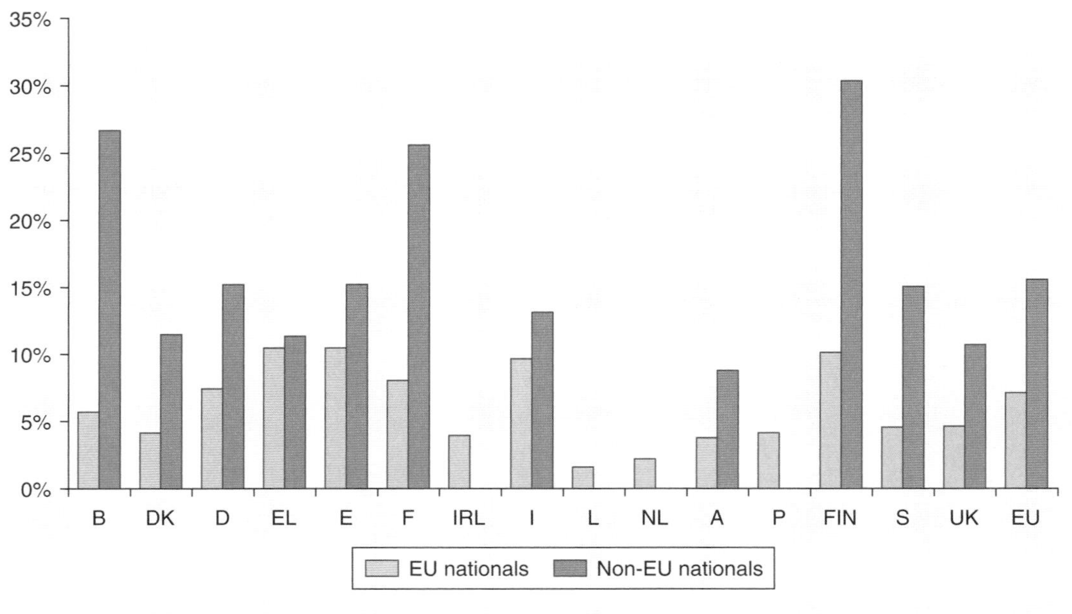

Source: LFS, Eurostat

often the native population that threatens or engages in violence against foreigners. This is because unemployed immigrants are often legally eligible for welfare and unemployment compensation. When majority native populations also suffer high unemployment rates as the shrinking state removes its social safety net, they often blame those same immigrants. As European economies stagnate, and as governments engage in 'state-shrinking' policies to revive them, we have witnessed throughout Europe a heightened awareness of hate crimes against foreigners and a growing number of those crimes in some countries. Anti-immigrant violence is fueled by political rhetoric that portrays immigrants as an economic burden.

Examples of this rhetoric abound. The European Commission against Racism and Intolerance reported in 2004 that immigrants in Austria were typically portrayed as being responsible for unemployment and increased public expenditure, as well as posing a threat to the preservation of Austrian 'identity' (McClintock 2005). In England, as industry declined in the early 1980s, and as Margaret Thatcher's policies of 'state-shrinking' took hold, many industries preferred cheap immigrant labor to an expensive native workforce. And although immigrant workers bore the brunt of economic recession, as indicated by higher than average unemployment rates, native workers were not protected from rising unemployment by the immigrant buffer (Money 1997). The immigrant communities invariably had higher levels of unemployment than the native workforce and were gradually pushed into the slums of the cities where they had worked. But slum removal projects required that slum occupants be housed in public housing. Thus unemployed immigrant slum dwellers leapfrogged over natives who had long waited for public housing. It was not long before immigrants were being blamed for taking the jobs and housing away from the white workforce.

In Germany a similar story can be told. Between 1987 and 1991 unemployment increased five-fold, while two million immigrants streamed into the country. One million were ethnic Germans from the East, about 500,000 were East Germans fleeing west, and about 600,000 were asylum seekers. And as in England, foreign workers were more likely to become unemployed and eligible for social services than natives. Extremist neo-Nazi groups targeted asylum seekers as the foreigners who undermined German social stability and committed numerous acts of violence against them.

Countries elsewhere are now experiencing similar pressures too. In recent years, Hindu immigrant labor has flooded into Punjab seeking employment in low wage jobs. Census data for 2004 showed that the Sikh population in Punjab, which had hovered around 60 percent for decades, had begun to drop, as Sikhs migrate abroad and as Hindus enter Punjab in search of jobs (Singh 2004). Tensions began to rise as letters to the editor of local newspapers blamed migrants for causing social, economic, and housing problems (*Chandigarh Tribune*, 22 January 2004.) Both churning up and capitalizing on this discontent, *Dal Khalsa*, a radical Sikh organization, began a drive against migrants from the poorer states of Bihar and Uttar Pradesh, who have settled in Punjab, saying they are a drain on the state's economy, and warning that 'if allowed to come into Punjab unchecked and unhindered, migrants would hold the key to the state's political power' (Indo-Asian News Service 2004). Publicly calling migrants a 'population bomb', a *Dal Khalsa* march against immigration portrayed banners and placards intended to alarm migrants that they were not welcome in Punjab.

Immigrants are not the only targets of violence when economies stagnate and states reduce entitlements to native populations who have come to depend on them. In Bulgaria, the introduction of markets and the restitution of land created disproportionate unemployment among the Muslims, leading to accusations of 'genocide' of the Turkish population against the Bulgarian majority. In Yugoslavia, Croatia fared better in global economic competition than the less developed republics and yet was forced to transfer resources to them, fostering deeper and deeper resentments against federal Yugoslavia that took the form of ethnic discrimination and privilege.

In 1977 Sri Lanka initiated a structural adjustment program that included trade liberalization, reduction in public expenditures, de-control of prices and interest rates, promotion of private sector development and foreign investment, and financial sector reforms. But the reforms could not halt a decline in economic growth.[8] Although the reforms transformed Sri Lanka from an agricultural to an industrial and service economy, growth rates were some of the lowest in the Asian developing world. And the Tamil population suffered disproportionately. Gunasinghe (1984) argues that trade liberalization swept away the main agricultural activities in the North, hurting the Tamil farmers. And Biziouras (forthcoming) shows that during the entire liberalization process, the state continued to give preferential treatment to the Sinhalese: the vast majority of export-oriented industrialization projects were targeted for Sinhalese-dominated regions; food subsidies were reduced across the board for Sinhalese and Tamils alike, but savings were then allocated to loss-making enterprises dominated by the Sinhalese. And, despite policies of 'state-shrinking', the state remained the most important source of employment. As noted above, strong patronage networks allocated jobs to Sinhalese, while Tamil employment options – particularly for Tamil youth – were extremely limited (Kelegama 1997; Tiruchelvam 1984). Although Tamil groups began to commit sporadic acts of violence shortly before the state-shrinking began, after the 'reforms' they had entered a civil war with the aim of carving out a separate Tamil state in Sri Lanka.

As these examples suggest, economic hardships can lead cultural groups to distrust each other and to no longer trust the state to protect all of its citizens. Hardships can make these groups available for reassignment to new political identities. The losers in economic transformation will attempt to use their political resources and position to resist changes that disadvantage them. It is often under these circumstances that we see the rise of cultural entrepreneurs as the catalysts of conflict.

The role of 'cultural entrepreneurs': political interpreters of economic hardship as cultural discrimination

Cultural entrepreneurs often emerge in the face of economic hardship to articulate grievances of distinct cultural groups, thus mobilizing support that can place them in positions of political power. These organizations, political parties, or would-be political leaders are entrepreneurial, in that they have discovered that if they politicize cultural identity, they can transform it into a reliable and efficient basis for ethnic group cohesion, and that group can then become an effective political base. Cultural entrepreneurs resemble their economic counterparts in that while the economic entrepreneur seeks to maximize wealth, the cultural entrepreneur seeks to maximize political power by mobilizing support around cultural identity (Laitin 1985; Brass 1976).

Cultural entrepreneurs increase the odds of political conflict because they heighten the role of 'identity politics' in multicultural societies. Identity politics are said to be more prone to conflict than interest-based politics. While *interests* are malleable and multiple, making compromises and logrolling possible, *cultural identity* is fixed and non-negotiable. Identity groups – distinct cultural communities – often lay exclusive claims to resources, and the more power they gain, the more ability they have to deny those resources to other cultural groups. Disputes over resources among 'identity groups' are thus particularly difficult to negotiate, raising the odds of violence.[9]

Examples abound of individuals who become cultural entrepreneurs. In Bulgaria, two stand out: Ahmed Dogan and Kamen Burov. The first led a newly organized Turkish party after Communism's collapse, calling on past grievances to mobilize collective support. It was Dogan who pointed to disproportionate unemployment among Turks, calling it 'genocide.' Burov led the Democratic Labor Party, formed to represent the Bulgarian Muslims, who called themselves Pomaks. As the Pomak mayor of the village of Zhîltusha, he purveyed the notion that Pomaks were entitled to resources on the basis of their distinct cultural identity. In England, in the 1960s, cultural entrepreneur Enoch Powell took advantage of the explosive combination of widespread economic dislocation and the presence of immigrant communities described above and stigmatized 'immigrants as strangers, as objects of justifiable fear and hatred, and as a source of future division in the nation'. He received overwhelming support for his position from the native population. In Punjab, the radical Sikh, Jarnail Singh Bhindranwale gathered a following of unemployed Sikh youth, who were denied jobs in industry, the military, and even farming. Claiming that Hindu immigrants were snapping up Sikh jobs, and condoning guerrilla tactics, he fomented violence and urged his followers to fight for a separate state for Sikhs only, where 'the Sikhs could experience the glow of their freedom'.

A cultural entrepreneur does not need to be an individual. In Germany, although individuals participated in the formation of right wing parties that fomented violence against immigrants, the cultural entrepreneurs were the parties themselves. Although Jörg Haider, the leader of Austria's extreme right wing freedom party, has been singled out as an important cultural entrepreneur – linking immigration and unemployment in almost every speech – the right wing parties themselves are currently playing that role. In Punjab, after the death of Bhindranwale, groups like *Babbar Khalsa*, the International Sikh Youth Federation, *Dal Khalsa*, and the Bhindranwale Tiger Force continued to link economic deprivation and cultural discrimination – and continued to engage in guerrilla tactics. Even after the violence was quelled in 1992, new cultural entrepreneurs began to spring up. A previously unknown group, for example, the *Saheed Khalsa Force*, claimed credit for marketplace bombings in New Delhi in 1997.

In Sri Lanka, in both the Sinhalese and Tamil populations, rival political parties as cultural entrepreneurs competed for political power, using different mobilization tactics and appealing to different sectors of the population. The Liberation Tigers of Tamil Eelam (LTTE) known as the 'Tamil Tigers', became (and continue to be) the most powerful cultural entrepreneurs among the Tamils, and have been willing to turn to violence in pursuit of their aims. They have built an organization by actively seeking out socially and economically marginalized groups, lower castes, young rural peasants, coastal fishermen, and all those without land. In particular, the Tigers have been able to recruit the young, who had been denied both education and employment and were ripe for political mobilization.

Legacies of ascriptive resource allocation

People will flock to cultural entrepreneurs and join their cause in those places where legacies of discriminatory resource allocation are still entrenched. In many regions where cultural conflict is most intense, resources have been traditionally allocated according to ethnic or religious criteria, and an ethnic division of labor persists. In Abkhazia, populated by Abkhazis and Georgians before the onset of civil war, Abkhaz farmers received more subsidies and experienced less central control than Georgian farmers; likewise, ethnic 'machines' provided a disproportionate share of jobs in the government bureaucracy for Abkhazis. Yugoslavia, under Tito, was governed by the institutions of 'ethnofederalism'. Five culturally defined groups – Serbs, Slovenes, Croats, Macedonians, and Montenegrins were territorially organized in constituent republics in which, as the titular nationality, they held the status of 'constitutive nation'. The 1971 census recognized Muslims as a separate nation, and Bosnia-Herzegovina was recognized under the national principle as a republic, consisting of three constitutive peoples: Serbs, Croats, and Muslims.[10] Investment funds from the central government were provided to distinct ethnic republics by the central state according to political and ascriptive criteria rather than economic 'rationality'. Ascriptive allocation fostered both bitterness among some groups, and perceptions of intrinsic 'rights' to further resources from the center among others. This system churned up mutual resentments and suspicions of other republics; this solidified the political relevance of ethnic identity, weakened loyalty to the central government, and reinforced the dominant logic of identity politics at the federal level.

The disintegration of federal control over resources created opportunities for regional officials – nascent cultural entrepreneurs – in ethnic republics to seize assets and gain political support. After 1973, the four-fold increase in oil prices fused with a decline in the economic growth rate to trigger expanded borrowing on international markets. Although there was a sense of well-being on the surface because consumption was financed by debt, overall economic growth ground to a halt by 1982. As the economy worsened, regional fragmentation increased; conflicts among the republics over the distribution of rapidly declining economic resources contributed to economic decline. The regionally based allocation of resources increased local power and the political strength of local ethnically motivated political entrepreneurs at the expense of the central state. Cultural entrepreneurs such as Slobodan Milosevic, Franjo Tudjman, and a host of local Serb and Croat politicians found that they could use funds distributed from the center to the republics to build a political power base at the local (republic) level. They used these funds as patronage to mobilize and gain the political loyalty of their culturally defined populations and then exploited ethnic differences and whipped up ethnic hatred.

As noted above, Sri Lanka allocated resources based on cultural criteria, using the Sinhala-only act to remove Tamils, who were more proficient in English, from employment in the state bureaucracy and the army. The act also mandated that children be educated in their birth language, effectively preventing Tamils from learning the official language and further reducing employment opportunities. Tamils also lost educational opportunities because of discriminatory policies, when the parliament replaced the merit system in higher education with preferential treatment for Sinhalese students.[11] The Tamils became increasingly radicalized by these exclusionary policies and their effects, and in 1976 declared independence for 'Tamil Eelam', the name they adopted for what they claimed as the traditional Tamil homeland in Sri Lanka. The Sinhalese majority, with their preponderance of economic resources and military might, moved to quell the Tamil Tigers, leading to the civil war of 1983.[12]

Under conditions of resource scarcity and institutional uncertainty and weakness, in societies where an entrenched tradition of cultural privilege and discrimination prevailed earlier, politicians are tempted to privilege – or promise to privilege – the members of one ethnic or religious community over others. In Yugoslavia, for example, the weaker the central government became, the more allocative authority fell into the hands of regional party elites. The deepening economic crisis and the collapse of the social welfare system made their role and their patronage networks increasingly important because their aid became indispensable in keeping both enterprises and individuals afloat; they made significant allocative decisions in the economy, as well as political and administrative appointments based on ethnic and cultural bonds created in their local communities. In Sri Lanka, Biziouras (forthcoming) shows that, 'economic decline from 1970–1977 increased the demands of the Sinhalese community on the state for employment and assistance at the expense of the Tamil minority.'

Contributions by the diaspora cultural community and other external sources of support to cultural entrepreneurs

The odds of violent ethnic conflict increase when diasporic communities funnel resources to cultural entrepreneurs in order to fight an opposing cultural group believed to be a cause of hardship and suffering. The Tamils fared surprisingly well in the civil war, despite a ban on the possession of weapons and the overwhelming power of the Sinhalese army, because of an infusion of resources from the diaspora Tamil community. Because diaspora groups abroad often see their 'brethren' under an oppressive yoke in their own land from which they must be liberated, they channel these resources to those extreme groups who argue for secession or a form of 'ethnic cleansing'. Ethnic Kosovars living abroad sent funds directly to the KLA; before the wars of Yugoslav succession, Croats abroad sent support to the HDZ, Tudjman's extremist party.

Support from the diaspora is particularly important when distinct cultural communities in their homeland are excluded from other resources. Local Abkhaz officials, for example, were cut off from their patronage networks in Moscow with the Soviet collapse. Bereft of internal resources, they looked outward to potential alliances, and received enough military support from Russia and Trans-Caucasus alliances to defeat the Georgians. In Sri Lanka, the Tamil Tigers, with financial help from Tamils overseas, evolved into a formidable military force, with technologically sophisticated arms, including weaponry such as rocket-propelled grenade launchers and night-vision glasses. By 2002, the Tamil Tigers had created a fighting force of 10,000 men who used guerrilla tactics that included everything from suicide bombings to surface-to-air missiles acquired through Tamil networks abroad.[13] Similarly, in Punjab, radical groups needed money from abroad to sustain their activities. Many Sikhs living in Britain, Canada, and the United States had been campaigning for an independent nation of Khalistan for many years. When Bhindranwale began to campaign in Punjab for a separate state, he was bolstered by foreign funds from the Diaspora Sikh community.[14] He used funds from these groups to purchase arms for a military buildup in the area surrounding the Golden Temple in Amritsar, the traditional seat of spiritual and temporal authority of the Sikhs, and scene of some of the worst violence in the conflict.

The community offering support does not necessarily have to be of the same ethnic or religious group. Support can come from those who sympathize with the cultural 'cause' or simply from those groups who perceive a common enemy. Abkhazi separatists called on former KGB members, elements of the Soviet army, and the Confederation of the Mountain Peoples of Caucasia for material support in their war of secession. These groups came to the aid of the separatists because they each had a separate grievance against Georgia or had previous ties to the separatists. Other external support can be 'grabbed' by well-positioned extremist groups, even if that support is not necessarily targeted to bolster their position. Western human rights organizations and aid agencies unwittingly abetted the agendas of ethnic and religious entrepreneurs in post-communist regions and helped to swell the ranks of their supporters. They have done this by providing or promising to provide material or symbolic support to targeted cultural groups and excluding other groups.

The strength of cultural entrepreneurs – often armed with external support – will grow as central authority weakens. Established authority can be weakened by the globalized forces of 'state-shrinking' because liberalization policies tend to reduce government resources that can be distributed in return for support. It is to the issue of state strength in the face of the imperatives of globalization that I now turn.

Globalization and state strength

All stable countries are characterized by political and social arrangements that have some form of historical legitimacy. Sometimes these arrangements or 'social contracts' are written in constitutions; sometimes they are found instead in a country's political and social institutions. In either case, such social contracts structure the terms of citizenship and inclusion in a country's political community, the rules of political participation, the political relationship between the central state and its various regions, and the distribution of material resources within a country. When political institutions make ascription – that is, cultural distinctions – a criterion for membership, participation, and resource allocation, 'identity politics' is played out in the political arena. When the institutions of central authority are strong, and perceived as legitimate, and when resource allocation is considered 'fair', political conflicts are less likely to become violent. Indeed, perceptions of fair resource allocation are a key pillar of institutional legitimacy. Strong and legitimate institutions provide broadly accepted channels of political competition within which political actors operate in 'normal' times. They allow central authorities to make credible commitments to distribute benefits and structure bargaining among various groups in ways that will be perceived as mutually advantageous. Institutional legitimacy enhances institutional capacity, reducing the threat of cultural conflict by increasing the benefits of peaceful dispute resolution and reducing the benefits of violence. Although these institutions may privilege some groups over others, they can counter the threat of backlash with offers of side payments and compensation to those who see themselves as harmed by the preferential practices.

It would be wrong to assert that perfect social harmony is the result. These institutions often foster resentment because of these practices of privilege and compensation. But where they are considered essentially legitimate, their behavioral rules are echoed in other organizations and in the society at large. The opposite is true when state institutions are considered unfair, illegitimate and oppressive. Often, privilege is granted to one group, and others are excluded from the privileged resource allocation. Resentment is likely to build but will be repressed as long as the state is strong enough to exert coercive power to maintain social order. For example, in the 1970s, both Punjabi Sikhs and Georgian peasants in Abkhazia were excluded from privileged resource allocation. Thus both sought to secede from the governing state that they perceived as oppressive. As long as that state remained strong enough to repress dissent and as long as these two groups continued to be deprived of resources for mobilization, their grievances festered, but they did not resort to violence until the institutions of the central state weakened.

There are many reasons why a central state would weaken: corruption, inefficiency, and overextension come readily to mind. In addition, however, upholding these social contracts becomes more difficult when globalization weakens the state through its imperatives for 'state-shrinking'. This is exemplified in the case of Bulgaria after Communism's collapse. There, the former Communist regime provided the Turkish minority with economic security: ethnic Turks were concentrated in the tobacco industry; the state purchased tobacco, ensuring full lifetime employment. With the fall of Communism, however, the inefficient and uncompetitive tobacco industry was privatized, and its failure in global markets left the majority of Turks unemployed and destitute. Turkish political entrepreneurs in Bulgaria began to label unemployment ethnic 'genocide' in their effort to mobilize the Turkish population against the liberalizing policies of the new regime. Similarly, as noted above, the worsening of the Sri Lankan national economy in 1970–1977 only increased the demands of the Sinhalese community on the state for employment and assistance, often at the expense of the Tamil minority.

In short, policies of state-shrinking that reduce the state's role in the economy and reduce its sovereignty over political membership – and exacerbate social cleavages along cultural lines – are important causes of broken social contracts and failed coercive policies. National economic growth and decline and the level of external debt affect the level of resources that the state can allocate, and short-term policies of economic liberalization yield up the state's distributive powers to the market. Indeed, when states make the decision to allow the market to pick economic winners and losers, they often break the social contract that once permitted them to soften some of the disadvantages suffered by particular cultural groups.

Coping with cultural conflict: the role of institutions

A perception of unjust political and economic resource distribution among distinct cultural groups lies at the heart of many of today's cultural conflicts. Therefore, political leaders in multicultural societies must take care to maintain strong, legitimate institutions in the face of globalization's state-shrinking imperatives. Institutions should be fashioned so that economic hardships and benefits are allocated in ways that integrate rather than fragment the political community. Federal systems in multi-ethnic states must create a strong center if they are to survive. They must be strong enough to protect and maintain the rule of law and civil and political rights of groups as well as individuals. And governments must be committed to those rights. An independent judiciary not captured by political forces is essential. Institutions of the presidency and parliament must be constructed so that stalemates do not repeatedly occur and in which negative majorities – able to veto decisions but unable to take positive action – do not dominate. A system of political competition that fosters compromise will buffer against perceptions of further unfair resource distribution as state budgets shrink.

Even globalization in the form of market rationality can actually be a coping mechanism that can mitigate cultural conflict: markets can reduce the influence of unjust patronage networks, including ethnic and sectarian ones. Coping with globalization in multi-ethnic societies must mean more than reducing fiscal deficits, privatization, currency stabilization, and creating economic efficiencies; coping with globalization must also mean refashioning institutions that both depoliticize and respect cultural identity. Below I tell two stories that highlight the role of institutions in coping with those effects of globalization that heighten cultural conflict.

Coping with globalization and mitigating cultural conflict I: Bulgaria

Bulgaria is strikingly similar to Yugoslavia in terms of historical legacies, social composition, and economic structure: yet Yugoslavia erupted in communal conflict with the fall of Communism, and Bulgaria did not. Below I sketch out a brief explanation for Bulgaria's relative social harmony, which suggests that political institutions played a significant role in channeling Bulgarian cultural conflict into non-violent political competition.

Pre-1989: impact of institutions on social integration in the face of international pressures

The roots of Communism's collapse can, in part, be traced to the forces of globalization and the position of communist countries in the international economy. Communist countries found themselves on the sidelines in the race for economic prosperity as their technical expertise in commercial industry began to lag far behind the industrial capitalist nations. Throughout the Cold War, technology gaps between them and the West widened and multiplied (Crawford 1993).

While both Bulgaria and Yugoslavia pursued autarky and central planning that brought economic hardship to all social groups, they were marked by differences in the structures of their political institutions. Despite the tight grip of the Communist party on both countries, Bulgaria was a centralized state while post-war Yugoslavia was constructed as a federal system. These different structures made a crucial difference in filtering the forces of globalization when they began to change economic and political calculations within each country.

In contrast to Yugoslavia, Bulgaria was a unitary state, with political power concentrated in the center (Curtis 1992). The Bulgarian Communist Party (BCP) program specified an orthodox hierarchical party structure of democratic centralism, each level responsible to the level above. The lowest-level party organizations were based in workplaces: all other levels were determined by territorial divisions, which were weaker than the workplace organizations (Bell 1986). Allocative institutions privileged party members and functionaries rather than particular ascriptive groups.

This centralization was reflected in the forced inclusion of Muslim minorities into the state. From the outset, the Communist regime sought to overcome the 'backwardness' of the Turkish population through policies of forced inclusion, for example, the destruction of autonomous local organizations and decrees of mass public de-veilings of Turkish women – not unlike the recent French ban on the *hijab* (or head scarf) – in public schools.

In 1984–85, the Bulgarian regime tightened the screws of 'inclusion'. It declared that Bulgarian Turks were not really Turkish, but rather they were Bulgarians who had been forcibly Islamicized and Turkified under Ottoman rule. It forced all Turks to change their names from Turkish to Slavo-Christian ones, and prohibited most religious rites, closing down mosques, and destroying public signs of an existing Turkish culture (Neuburger 1997: 6; Curtis 1992: 82).

The Bulgarian Muslims, or 'Pomaks', suffered much less repression. Because, historically, there had only been a weak and ultimately failed effort to construct a Pomak political identity, there was no need for the Communist regime to single them out, either for special repression or privilege (Todorova 1998). If anything, the Pomaks were coincidentally privileged because they enjoyed 'border benefits', that is, development funds that the state doled out to the border regions of the Rhodopes in which they lived. They thus attained a higher than average standard of living for the region. And, unlike the case in Yugoslavia, there were no intermediary political entrepreneurs who could control the distribution of those benefits in order to enhance their own power base.

Despite these policies, an 'ethnic' division of labor characterized the Bulgarian economy. The majority of Turks and Pomaks worked in agriculture, particularly in the tobacco industry, and in light manufacturing, sectors privileged by the regime in its industrialization drive. The sectors in which Turks and Pomaks toiled were completely tied to domestic demand and to exports to other CMEA countries. As long as those exports remained strong, as long as the domestic market was sheltered from international competition, and as long as they were granted equal welfare benefits, these minorities did not experience disproportionate economic hardships. But as Bulgaria became increasingly integrated into the global economy during the 1980s, those hardships manifested themselves.

Unlike Yugoslavia, which was integrated into the international economy throughout the Communist period, Bulgaria staved off an opening to the West until the 1980s. But as it too began to open to the world, it was hard hit by the global recession and debt crisis of the 1980s. By 1990, Bulgaria had suspended both principal and interest payments on its foreign debt. Meanwhile, in 1989, as a result of both the forced assimilationist policies and the growing economic crisis, 300,000 ethnic Turks left Bulgaria for Turkey, in what some observers called the largest post-war civilian population movement in Balkan history. The exodus resulted in an acute loss of agricultural personnel during the harvest. And the two-thirds of the Turks who eventually returned found that the authorities had given their homes to Bulgarians (Tzvetkov 1992: 40).

In short, with Communism's collapse, Bulgaria was ripe for 'cultural' conflict. A highly centralized state engaged in extremely repressive policies against its ethnic minority. Economic hardship as a result of integration into the global economy had fallen disproportionately on Bulgaria's Muslim population, creating conditions for the creation of an opposition movement, able to call on shared memories of oppression, and ready to mobilize politically.

After Communism's collapse: democratic competition in Bulgaria

After Communism's collapse, economic conditions worsened for Bulgaria's Muslims. Throughout the 1990s, the country was brought to the brink of economic disaster several times; CMEA trade all but disappeared, leaving it with a huge debt and no export markets. The unemployment rate skyrocketed.[15] And, as a UNDP report states, 'The changes [dwindling of the external markets due to the disintegration of the CMEA] ... disproportionately affected the canning and the tobacco industry, where workers of Turkish and Gypsy origin predominated'. (UNDP 1996: 6–11).[16]

While the market brought suffering to the Muslim populations, democracy brought the right to organize in the political arena. Ethnic Turks were permitted to take back their Turkish names. The BCP voted to condemn the policy of forced assimilation and restated the constitutional rights of ethnic Turks to choose their own names, practice Islam, observe their religious customs, and speak Turkish.

Bulgarian nationalists countered these moves toward political liberalization and the establishment of cultural rights. On December 31, 1989, there were demonstrations against political liberalization measures in Kurdzhali, and, in early January 1990, a series of demonstrations in Razgrad and Kurdzhali and a nationalist march on Sofia, protesting the 'Turkification' of Bulgaria. There is some evidence to suggest that BSP (Bulgarian Socialist Party) resources supported these nationalists[17] (Troxel 1993: 414; Neuburger 1997: 8).

The regime's response to this explosive situation was to both affirm the constitutional rights of minority groups and ban ethnic political parties. Nonetheless, the Movement for Rights and Freedom (MRF), led by Ahmed Dogan – described above – was formed, which, while not officially a Turkish Party, did represent the Turkish minority in Bulgaria. After its formation, nationalist opposition rapidly increased both at the level of social protest and in a complaint to the Supreme Court. On

November 22, 1990, the National Committee for the Defense of National Interests (a right-wing nationalist group whose members included many former communists who had participated in the implementation of the various Bulgarization campaigns) proclaimed the 'Bulgarian Republic of Razgrad' (a city with a large Turkish population) as a response to the 'treacherous pro-Turkish policy' of the National Assembly (Curtis 1992: 215). Indeed, in 1991, the BSP actively courted the nationalistic right wing, and its political rhetoric claimed that its UDF rival and its alliance with the MRF would reawaken Turkification that would increase the chances for secession and threaten the territorial integrity of the Bulgarian state (Perry and Ilchev 1993; Nikolaev 1993; Dainov 1993: 10; Troxel 1993: 421). Further nationalist protests followed.

The BSP also tried to outlaw the MRF. Once the 1991 Constitution was ratified by the National Assembly in the July of 1991 it presented the MRF with an obvious problem because Article 6 prohibited the creation of parties along ethnic lines. Despite the MRF leadership's comments to the contrary, it had become increasingly apparent to all observers that the MRF was the Turkish party in Bulgaria. The BSP sought to exploit this for strategic benefits and sued to prevent the registration of the MRF for the 1991 parliamentary elections.

In this period of heightened ethnic tensions, the MRF began a campaign to politicize the Turkish minority, calling on past grievances to mobilize collective support. It announced the party's plan to introduce the Turkish language in the school curriculum in Turkish-dominated cities and villages. Kamen Burov (the other Bulgarian 'cultural entrepreneur' described above) also pointed to discrimination in his bid to mobilize the Pomak minority and politicize its cultural identity.

But unlike 'ethnic' political parties in the former Yugoslavia, Burov received little political support. And Dogan and the MRF did not possess an existing regional party machine that it could use to mobilize for an alternative political authority in opposition to the central government. Indeed, both minority cultural groups lacked the organizational and material resources of the regional party elites of Yugoslavia. Further, the Bulgarian Supreme Court decided to allow the MRF to register and thus compete in elections and represent the Turks in the Parliament (Ganev 1997). This effectively legitimated the MRF in the political arena, allowing it to participate in democratic competition rather than be excluded or marginalized. By legitimizing the MRF the court left it without resources to organize opposition outside the political arena.

The absence of a federalized political structure along ethnic lines, as had been the case in Yugoslavia, meant that the MRF lacked any substantial means of resource allocation that would enable it to resist participation in the mainstream of Bulgarian politics. Unlike Tudjman and Milosevic, Dogan did not have the 'luxury' of inheriting an organized and well-funded political base. Thus he was forced to participate in the 'normal' bargaining processes of post-communist Bulgaria, structurally induced to temper his demands. Similarly, the existence of a politically independent Supreme Court served as an effective veto point that preserved the democratic politics of post-communist Bulgaria. Under these conditions, the MRF managed to become a power broker in the Bulgarian government. Despite the fact that the UDF won the parliamentary elections in 1991, it did not gain a clear majority and thus was unable to govern without the MRF – which had become the third largest party in Bulgaria. In 1993, the MRF led strikes for higher tobacco prices in order to pressure the caretaker government to increase revenues that would cushion the transition to the market, and Dogan opportunistically supported a deal – together with the UDF and BSP – to construct a gas pipeline from Russia to Greece through Bulgaria under the assumption that Russia could be paid partly through sales of Bulgarian tobacco (EIU. Bulgaria. Country Profile, 1993).

But disproportionate economic hardship persisted as the state withdrew from the economy and both agriculture and industry were privatized. By 2001, almost half of Bulgaria's Turks lived below the poverty line, and though they made up only 9 percent of the population, they accounted for one quarter of the country's poor (Ivaschenko 2004). At first there was very little pressure on the party elite from the Turkish constituency to reduce poverty rates and the declining economic prospects of the Turkish minority. But starting 1997, the party split over economic issues (EIU, 1997a; EIU 1997b). The MRF continues to behave like a normal, interest-based party in democratic competition, and cultural conflict is channeled through the political process.

Clearly institutions matter in the Bulgarian case. Healthy political competition, an independent judiciary, and the absence of ethno-federalism all worked to channel potential cultural conflict into the trenches of peaceful political competition.

Coping with globalization and mitigating cultural conflict II: Europe and its immigrants

Throughout this essay I have suggested that Europe is increasingly vulnerable to cultural conflict, as globalization has led to the growth of immigrant populations and the simultaneous shrinkage of the welfare state. Europe's uneven ability to integrate its immigrants, combined with the steep social ladder, the rise of the xenophobic right, and resistance to immigration have created a volatile mix of resentment, hatred, and rancor on the part of the native population that can translate into violence.

It is probably no exaggeration to claim that Muslim populations in Europe are growing exponentially. Conservative estimates project that, within a generation, Muslims will be the majority in major German, French, and Dutch cities. France is already home to 5 million Muslims, almost 10 percent of its total population. Twenty-three million Muslims now live in the European Union, and they are overrepresented in unemployment, crime, and poverty. At the same time, the birth rates of ethnic Europeans are imploding, exacerbating fears that Muslims will one day become a dominant majority on the continent. In the pages above we have encountered European cultural entrepreneurs whose rhetoric warned of the day when immigrants – particularly Muslim immigrants – would become a dominant majority on the European continent, stirring up fears that feed prejudice and hatred.

And as Muslim populations grow throughout Europe, they are increasingly exposed to Islamic radicalism that incites cultural conflict. Shore (forthcoming) cites studies that show that young Muslims who were born in Europe are increasingly repelled by liberal European values and drawn to extreme views. He writes that:

> *in one large-scale study of Turkish-German Muslims in their twenties and teens, almost one-third agreed that Islam must become the state religion in every country. Even though they live in Europe, 56 % declared that they should not adapt too much to Western ways but should live by Islam. Over 33 per cent insisted that if it serves the Islamic community, then they are ready to use violence against nonbelievers. Perhaps most disturbing, almost 40 per cent stated that Zionism, the European Union, and the United States threaten Islam.*

Radical clerics have become cultural entrepreneurs, whose sermons plant and nourish these views. They can be found in both local mosques and in the pages of the Internet. Indeed, radical Imams in Syria, Jordan, Afghanistan, and Saudi Arabia can transmit their messages instantly to the Muslims in Europe, exerting the pull of pan-Islamism in an effort to unite the diaspora community to oppose Western culture.

And European states themselves often fan these fundamentalist flames by enacting anti-terror legislation which many view as anti-Muslim, or by banning symbols of Islamic faith, such as headscarves in schools and the workplace. Holland, once a safe haven for refugees, will deport 26,000 asylum seekers, many of them Muslim, in an effort to stem the tide of its burgeoning Muslim underclass. Furthermore, Muslims in Western Europe are underrepresented in parliaments, have lower incomes and less schooling than indigenous Europeans and other immigrant groups. In public policy, many European countries have withdrawn financial and legal support for integration of Muslims in their schools. After 9/11 there was a significant decline in state funding of Islamic schools in Britain; there was a decline in funding for Islamic instruction in public schools in Germany, and in France the *hijab* was banned in public schools (Fetzer and Soper 2005: 143f).

Together these factors churn up the volatile mix of ingredients for violence that I have described throughout this essay: growing economic suffering as the welfare state disappears, the uneven distribution of economic hardship, the discriminatory allocation of political and economic resources, and the rise of radical cultural entrepreneurs, some of whom are fed by diaspora cultural communities.

But immigrants themselves have rarely perpetrated violence against native populations, and conflict in the form of violent hate crimes perpetrated against immigrants has not risen significantly in Europe since the early 1990s. In Table 1.2, I show the number of reported violent crimes against foreigners in five European countries. In Germany, where the data seem to be most complete and

Table 1.2 Violent crimes per 1000 foreigners[i]

	1993	1994	1995	1996	1997	1998	1999	2000	2001
Austria[ii]									0.44
France							~0.18		
Germany	0.19	0.11	0.08	0.08	0.1	0.09	0.1	0.13	0.09
Sweden					0.87	1.05	1.20	1.20	1.17
Switzerland[iii]									0.08

[i] **Data based on OECD population data and racial violence statistics from RAXEN (2003); European Monitoring Centre on Racism and Xenophobia (2003); The Stephen Roth Institute (2003).**

[ii] **Includes anti-Semitic acts.**

[iii] **Foreign population data is available up to 2001. Crime data are available from 2002. Crime statistics for 2001 are estimated based on average of 2002 and 2003. Includes anti-Semitic acts.**

most accurate, the number of these crimes has actually decreased, even as the number of immigrants has grown. Switzerland, France, and Austria are also low and comparable to Germany. The only 'outlier' is Sweden, where hate crimes have skyrocketed in proportion to the number of immigrants that have made their home there.

All of these countries have institutions that protect immigrant individual and group rights and provide some form of political integration, measured by voting rights for foreigners (Minkenberg 2005). Sweden has the strongest institutions protecting both individual and group rights – the most inclusive policies, permitting voting rights for foreigners. So why would violent hate crimes spike in Sweden and remain low in most other European countries?

Sweden may keep better track of these crimes, but probably the mechanisms used to track crimes there are not much better than those in Germany. My hunch is the following: strong integrative and allocative institutions matter, but they do not operate in a vacuum. Sweden is a country that has only recently accepted immigrants; social relations have thus shifted quickly, in comparison to other European countries, as economic growth has stagnated. The government quickly established a welcoming approach to immigration in general, and opponents of immigration had little voice. So, although integrative and allocative institutions are strong, there is a growing backlash against immigrants in the form of a large Neo-Nazi network formed outside legitimate channels of political participation. This creates the potential for the rise of informal organizations and anti-immigrant cultural entrepreneurs as 'loose cannons', active in crime rather than politics.

If my hunches are correct, the European case shows that strong liberal institutions matter, particularly those that channel conflict through a legitimate and non-violent political process. But as globalization proceeds and the European welfare state is forced to shrink and shed its social safety net, we may see more anti-immigrant violence there in years to come.

Conclusions

Vulnerability to cultural conflict does not automatically bring on cultural violence. When resources are provided or withheld from groups on the basis of their cultural identity, cultural entrepreneurs attempt to mobilize their cultural brethren to protest an unjust resource allocation or shore up resources for their own group. If political institutions provide a legitimate arena for those entrepreneurs to compete and if resources are abundant and allocated in ways that are widely considered to be fair, cultural or identity politics, like other kinds of political competition, can be legitimate and stable. It is when demographic and economic changes – often brought on by the forces of globalization – undermine the 'rules of the game', and lead to perceptions that the balance of political power is unfair, that identity politics, like other forms of political competition, can escalate to cultural conflict and violence. States whose institutions promote social integration are not immune to cultural strife. Historical, ideological, and sectarian legacies can provide incentives to politicize culture. And economic discrimination and advantages can push cultural leaders into the political arena to protest grievances or protect privilege. If governments wish to avoid cultural conflict, institutions must provide ample resources and rules to make social divisions like class, interest or ideology more relevant than culture in the political arena. And they must distribute resources in ways that promote social integration and redress past grievances.

Notes

1 Cultural conflicts in industrial and industrializing societies tend either to be argued civilly or at least limited to the political violence of marginal groups.

2 Still the second richest state in India, the gap is narrowing as other states have begun to grow more rapidly. Punjab is now trapped in a crisis, which is reflected by: stagnation in the productivities of principal crops, namely, wheat and rice; declining returns from agriculture; a declining rate of growth; and the degradation of environmental resources. A number of factors are also hindering the industrialization of the land-locked state, including a lack of mineral resources, a location disadvantage in relation to major national markets, and its proximity to a sensitive international border.

3 The 'boom' in this literature began with the appearance of Samuel Huntington's 1993 'Clash of Civilizations' article in *Foreign Affairs* which suggested that the current round of ethnic and sectarian violence is a backlash against the apparent triumph of the 'West' in the form of economic globalization and institutional transformation – the opening of new markets for goods, services, capital, and people, the construction of new democracies, and the implementation of 'state-shrinking' ideologies that have swept the globe.

4 Alesina et al. (2003) argue that trade openness leads to the secession of wealthier regions in multi-ethnic societies because they can compete successfully and no longer wish to transfer resources to their poorer compatriots whose ethnicity or religion is different. Biziouras (forthcoming) argues that medium levels of economic liberalization can permit the state to continue and increase selective patronage to various cultural groups in ways that trigger conflict between those targeted for patronage and those who are excluded.

5 Benjamin Barber makes similar connections, although his logic of explanation diverges from the logic presented here. He argues that economic globalization also globalizes politics by creating new sources of dominance, surveillance, and manipulation, thereby weakening the nation-state. The state is thus increasingly less important as a focus of political life. Global processes do not require democracy to expand. With the decline of the nation-state as the locus of political life and the increasingly undemocratic globalization of political and economic life, sub-national communities governed by fanatical hierarchies attempt to localize politics. These groups are also undemocratic, in that they demand loyalty to the group above loyalty to the individual, and rights are only real for the dominant group. The result is the decline of democracy and democratic, integrating nation-states. Barber does not explain why local politics would take a non-democratic form. (see Barber 1995).

6 It was widely believed that Sri Lanka had inherited a highly competitive pluralistic political system, which was considered an outstanding model of third world democracy (Jupp 1978; Kearny 1973; Wilson 1979).

7 Eurostat, the European Union's statistical unit, in 1994 began commissioning a series of research studies to improve understanding of the trends underlying immigration (Salt and Singleton 1995). In 2000, the United Nation's Population Division released *Replacement Migration: Is It a Solution to Declining and Ageing Populations? See also* Organisation for Economic Co-operation and Development (2004), *Trends, in International Migration 2004* (Paris: OECD) and OECD Migration database for latest available year, 2002.

8 In 1955, Sri Lanka's per capita income was greater than that of other major Asian countries, except Malaysia. South Korea and Thailand continued to lag behind Sri Lanka in terms of per capita income even by 1960 (Abeyratne, 2002). But between 1965 and 1980, Sri Lanka achieved a growth rate of only 2.8 percent of GNP per capita, less than half that of Indonesia, and little more than half that of Thailand. And between 1990 and 1995, the percent of GNP per capita growth rate in Sri Lanka was only 3.2 percent, compared to Thailand's growth rate of 6.3 percent and Indonesia's 4.8 percent (World Health Organization 2002).

9 This assumption has not been systematically tested. A good test would compare the intensity of conflict and level of violence of 'identity group' conflicts with 'interest group' conflicts, ideological conflicts, class conflicts, and interstate conflicts.

10 Susan Bridge (1977: 345–7) argues that the structure of formal political representation throughout the post-war period discouraged minority participation and representation through the single-member district in both party and government. But the single member district worked to the advantage of minorities in two defined regions where the 'nationality' was a majority of the population. After the constitutional changes of 1974, Kosovo, with a majority Albanian population, and Voivodina, with a majority Hungarian population, gained increasing autonomy throughout the post-war period and enjoyed equal participation at the federal level with the same representative status as the constituent nations. Kosovo would become a trigger for the wider conflict that ensued.

11 The percentage of Tamil students able to gain admission to university medical courses fell from 50 percent

in 1970 to 20 percent in 1975. The percentage of Tamil students entering engineering courses fell from 40.8 percent in 1970 to 24.4 percent in 1973, and 13.2 percent in 1976. The percentage of Tamil students entering science courses fell from 35 percent in 1970 to 15 percent in 1978.

12 In fact, Sri Lanka's political conflict, developed since the 1970s, has two major facets. One is the Tamil separatist movement, which is widely known to be between the majority Sinhala and the minority Tamil communities. The other is the militant movement of the Sinhala community, which erupted twice into armed struggles with the aim of changing the existing political regime. Due to the concurrent escalation of the conflict the two facets of the political cannot be separated analytically. I focus here on the Tamil–Sinhalese conflict.

13 Kopel (2004) argues that Sinhalese uncertainty and paranoia added to economic uncertainty in these acts. He writes, 'Despite their clear majority, Sinhalas fear the large numbers of foreign Tamils who, including those in India's [state of] Tamil Nadu, are said to number around 50–60 million between Southeast Asia through Middle East to the Caribbean. On the other hand Ceylon Tamils, despite being only 11.2 percent of the population, consider themselves strong in terms of the global Tamil brotherhood.'

14 Most prominent continue to be the World Sikh Organization and the International Sikh Youth Federation.

15 Unemployment increased from 1.7 percent in 1990 to over 11 percent in 1991 and 16 percent in 1993. Growth rates plummeted to –10.9 percent in 1997, and industrial output all but ceased (NSI 1996: 10–11).

16 Some figures illustrate: in the predominantly Muslim districts of Blagoevgrad and Smolyan, unemployment rates hit 90 percent; in Borino, unemployment was 96 percent; in all other Muslim districts – Girmen, Bregovo, Strumyani, Khadzhidimovo, Razlog, Yakoruda, Sandanski, Gotse Delchev, Kirkovo, Devin, Kresna, and Nedelino, the unemployment rate was over 90 percent (Todorova 1998: 493) while in Bulgaria as a whole, the registered unemployment rate fluctuated between 1.7 percent in 1990, 11.1 percent in 1991, 15.3 percent in 1992, 16.4 percent in 1993, 12.4 percent in 1994, 11.1 percent in 1995 and 12.5 percent in 1996 (ILO 1997:447).

17 The BSP is the former Communist Party, formerly named the Bulgarian Communist Party.

REFERENCES

Abeyratne, Sirimal (2002) 'Economic roots of political conflict: the case of Sri Lanka'. ASARC Working Paper, No. 2002–03. Australian National University, Australia South Asia Research Centre.

Adams, Richard H., Jr. (2003) 'International migration, remittances, and the brain drain: a study of 24 labor exporting countries'. World Bank Policy Research Working Paper 3069. Washington, DC: World Bank.

Alesina, Alberto, Devleeschauwer, Arnaud, Easterly, William, Kurlat, Sergio and Wacziarg, Romain T. (2003) 'Fractionalization', *Journal of Economic Growth,* 8(2): 155–94.

Athukorala, P. (2001) *Crisis and Recovery in Malaysia: The Role of Capital Controls.* Cheltenham: Edward Elgar.

Bandarage, Asoka. (2000) 'The Sri Lankan conflict: broadening the debate'. Talk given at the Sri Lanka Symposium, Carnegie Council on Ethics in International Affairs and Asia Society, New York. (June 13, http://www.afsc.org/pwork/1000/102k06.htm.)

Barber, Benjamin, R. (1995) *Jihad vs. McWorld: How Globalism and Tribalism Are Reshaping the World.* New York: Ballantine Books.

Bell, John, D. (1986) *The Bulgarian Communist Party from Blagoev to Zhivkov.* Stanford: Hoover Institution Press.

Bhalla, Shurjit (1994) 'Freedom and economic growth: a virtuous cycle?' Paper presented at the South Asia Seminar, Harvard University Center for International Affairs. (February)

Biziouras, Nikolaos (forthcoming) 'Economic liberalization and the propensity for ethnic conflict in multi-ethnic societies: A cross-regional analysis with illustrative case studies (Sri Lanka, Bulgaria, Ethiopia, and Malaysia)', PhD Dissertation, University of California, Berkeley.

Brass, Paul R. (1976) 'Ethnicity and Nationality Formation', *Ethnicity,* 3(3): 225–39.

Bridge, Susan (1977) 'Some Causes of Political Change in Modern Yugoslavia', in Milton J. Esman (ed.), *Ethnic Conflict in the Western World.* Ithaca: Cornell University Press. pp. 345–47.

Bruton, H.J. (1992) *The Political Economy of Poverty, Equity and Growth: Sri Lanka and Malaysia.* New York: Oxford University Press.

Chandigarh Tribune. Various Issues.

Crawford, Beverly (1993) *Economic Vulnerability in International Relations.* New York: Columbia University Press.

Curtis, Glenn. (ed.) (1992) *Bulgaria: A Country Study.* Washington: Federal Research Division.

Dainov, Evgenii (1993) 'Losing readers in Bulgaria', *The Warsaw Voice.* 8 August.

Dutceac, Anamaria (2004) 'Globalization and ethnic conflict: beyond the liberal-nationalist distinction', *The Global Review of Ethnopolitics*, 3(2): 20–39.

Economist Intelligence Unit (EIU) (1997a) *Turkey, Country Report* Quarter 2 (May 9). (1997b) *Turkey, Country Report*, Quarter 3 (July 18).

The European Monitoring Centre on Racism and Xenophobia (2003) *Migrants, Minorities and Employment: Exclusion, Discrimination and Anti-Discrimination in 15 Member States of the European Union*. (October.) http://eumc.eu.int/eumc/material/pub/comparativestudy/CS-Employment-en.pdf.)

Fetzer, S. Joel and Soper, J. Christopher (2005) *Muslims and the State in Britain, France, and Germany*. Cambridge: Cambridge University Press.

Ganev, Venelin I. (1997) 'Bulgaria's Symphony of Hope', *Journal of Democracy*, 8(4): 125–41.

Geddes, Barbara (1994) 'Challenging the Conventional Wisdom', *Journal of Democracy*, 5(4): 104–118.

Gunasinghe, N. (1984) 'Open economy and its impact on ethnic relations in Sri Lanka', *Lanka Guardian*. Issues of 7, 14 and 21 January.

Human Rights Watch (2003) 'Briefing paper on the situation of ethnic Chechens in Moscow'. (24 February. http://www.hrw.org/backgrounder/eca/russia032003.htm.)

Indo-Asian News Service. Various Issues.

International Labor Organization. Various Publications.

Ivaschenko, Oleksiy (2004) 'Poverty and inequality mapping in Bulgaria'. World Bank (http://siteresources.worldbank.org/INTPGI/Resources/342674–1092157888460/Ivaschenko.MappingBulgaria.pdf.)

Jupp, James (1978) *Sri Lanka: Third World Democracy*. London: Frank Cass and Company Limited.

Kapstein, Ethan B. (1996) 'Workers and the world economy', *Foreign Affairs*, 75(3): 16–37.

Kearney, R.W. (1973) *The Politics of Ceylon (Sri Lanka)*. London: Cornell University Press.

Kelegama, Saman (1997) 'Sri Lankan economy in the context of the north-east war, rehabilitation and reconstruction'. Paper presented at Conference on the Political, Economic and Social Reconstruction of Sri Lanka, Harvard University. (November)

Kopel, David. (2004) 'Lions vs. tigers', *National Review Online*. (3 March)

Kuran, T. (2001) 'The religious undercurrent of muslim economic grievances', Social Science Research Council. (http://www.ssrc.org/sept11/essays/kuran_text_only.htm.)

Laitin, David (1985) 'Hegemony and Religious Conflict: British Imperial Control and Political Cleavages in Yorubaland', in Peter B. Evans, Dietrich Rueschemeyer and Theda Skocpol (eds), *Bringing the State Back In*. New York: Cambridge University Press. pp. 285–316.

Lapidus, Gail W., Zaslavsky, Victor and Goldman, Philip (eds) (1992) *From Union to Commonwealth: Nationalism and Separatism in the Soviet Union*. Cambridge: Cambridge University Press.

Lubeck, P. M. (1998) 'Islamist responses to globalization: cultural conflict in Egypt, Algeria, and Malaysia', in B. Crawford and R. Lipschutz (eds.), *The Myth of 'Ethnic Conflict': Politics, Economics and 'Cultural' Violence*. Berkeley: IIS/IAS-University of California Press. pp. 293–319.

Marshall, Monty G. (2005) 'Current status of the world's major episodes of political violence'. Report to Political Instability Task Force. (3 February)

McClintock, Michael (2005) *Everyday Fears: A Survey of Violent Hate Crimes in Europe and North America*. A Human Rights First Report. (http://www.humanrightsfirst.org/discrimination/pdf/everyday-fears-080805.pdf.)

Minkenberg, Michael (2005) 'Religion, immigration and the politics of multiculturalism: a comparative analysis of western democracies'. Paper presented at the workshop 'Immigration Policy Post-9/11', University of Pittsburgh. (9–10 September)

Money, Jeannette (1997) 'No vacancy: the political geography of immigration control in advanced, market economy countries', *International Organization*, 51(4): 685–720.

Neuburger, Mary (1997) 'Bulgaro-Turkish encounters and the re-imaging of the Bulgarian nation (1878–1995)', *East European Quarterly*, 31(1): 1–21.

Nikolaev, Rada (1993) 'Bulgaria's 1992 census: results, problems and implications', *RFE/RL Research Report*, 2(6): 58–62.

Perry, Duncan M. and Ilchev, Ivan. (1993) 'Bulgarian ethnic groups: politics and perceptions', *RFE/RL Research Report*, 2(12): 35–42.

Pigliucci, Massimo. (2004) 'Liberal vs. illiberal democracy', Rationally Speaking blog, N. 49. (May)

RAXEN (2003) 'Table A.1.5. Stocks of foreign population in selected OECD countries', *Trends in International Migration and in Migration Policies*. OECD. (http://www.oecd.org/document/36/0,2340,en_2649_33931_2515108_1_1_1_1,00.html.)

Rothkop, David (1997) 'In praise of cultural imperialism?' *Foreign Policy*, 107: 38–53.

Sadowski, Y. (1998) *The Myth of Global Chaos*. Washington, DC: Brookings Institution Press.

Salt, J., and Singleton, A. (1995) 'Analysis and forecasting of international migration by major groups'. Report prepared on behalf of Eurostat. London: Migration Research Unit, University College of London.

Schulman, M. (2000) 'Urban policies in the Nordic countries', *North*, 11(2/3): 12–17.

Shore, Zachary (forthcoming) *Breeding Bin Ladens: America, Islam and the Future of Europe*. Washington, DC: Johns Hopkins University Press.

Singh, Bajinder Pal (2004) 'Blame migration, Sikh footprint smaller in Punjab', *The Indian Express*. September 9.

The Stephen Roth Institute (2003) 'Switzerland', *Antisemitism Worldwide*, The Stephen Roth Institute, Tel Aviv University. (http://www.tau.ac.il/Anti-Semitism/asw2003–4/switzerland.htm.)

Suro, Roberto (2003) 'Latino remittances swell despite US economic slump', Migration Information Source. (1 February) http://www. migrationinformation. org/Feature/ display.cfm?ID=89.)

Telo, Mario (ed.) (2001) *European Union and New Regionalism: Regional Actors and Global Governance in a Post-hegemonic Era.* Aldershot, England; Burlington, VT: Ashgate.

Tiruchelvam, Neelan (1984) *The Ideology of Popular Justice in Sri Lanka: A Socio-Legal Inquiry.* New Delhi: Vikas.

Todorova, Maria (1998) 'Identity (trans)formation among Bulgarian Muslims', in B. Crawford and R. Lipschutz (eds), *The Myth of 'Ethnic Conflict': Politics, Economics and 'Cultural' Violence.* Berkeley: IIS/IAS-University of California Press. pp. 471–510.

Troxel, Luan (1993) 'Socialist persistence in the Bulgarian elections of 1990–1991', *East European Quarterly*, 26(4): 407–421.

Tzvetkov, Plamen S. (1992) 'The politics of transition in Bulgaria: back to the future?' *Problems of Communism*, 41(3): 34–44.

United Nations Development Programme (UNDP). Various Publications.

Whitehead, Laurence (1995) 'Political democratization and economic liberalization: prospects for their entrenchment in Eastern Europe and Latin America'. Paper presented at the Southern California Workshop on Political and Economic Liberalization, University of Southern California, Los Angeles. (30 January)

Wilson, A.J. (1979) *Politics in Sri Lanka, 1947–1979.* London: Macmillan.

Woodward, S. (1995) *Balkan Tragedy.* Washington, DC: Brookings Institution.

World Health Organization. (2002) 'Health situation in the South-East Asia region, 1994–1997'. (http://w3.whosea.org/health_situt_94–97/socioeconomic.htm.)

Zakaria, Fareed (2003) *The Future of Freedom: Illiberal Democracy at Home and Abroad.* New York: W.W. Norton.

– (1997) 'The rise of illiberal democracy', *Foreign Affairs*, 76(6): 22–43.

## CHAPTER 2

DIMENSIONS OF CONFLICT IN GLOBALIZATION AND CULTURAL PRACTICE: A CRITICAL PERSPECTIVE

Rustom Bharucha

Drawing on the latent dimensions of conflict in cultural practice, this essay focuses on those intracultural contexts by which local and regional differences interact with global forces and opportunities within the larger framework of the nation-state. Working through two distinct contexts of the 'African Indian' Siddi community, one represented by caste-bound agricultural labor and the other privileged through the benefits of global performance, the essay questions the relationships of globalization to 'capability', de-syncretization and communalism. Emphasizing the disjunctions between global theoretical discourse and grassroots activism in representing subaltern communities, the essay works towards a critical reading of 'the capacity to aspire' by indicating the limits of global networking and performance in favor of a more nationally grounded cultural praxis.

In the collusion of languages between postmodernism and neo-liberal globalization theory, conflict is almost always elided under the spectral energies of 'flow'. Identities, goods, and practices are imagined to be in a perpetual state of metamorphosis, flux, and mutation, as they cross borders, circumventing the strictures of trade regulations and the protocols of nation-states. If there are obstacles encountered in this seemingly unregulated global flow, they are invariably absorbed along the way, with dichotomies and oppositions giving way to hybrid mixtures and intercultural conversations. Even when 'disjuncture' (Appadurai, 1990, 1996) is marked as a central component of such globalization discourse, it is never allowed to disrupt the momentum of cross-border exchange. If anything, it catalyzes the exchange without allowing it to break down under the pressure of irreconcilable differences.

Against this increasingly hollow utopian scenario, what makes the insertion of 'conflict' in globalization discourse so productive is precisely its interruptive capacity to break the easy equations between the flow of global capital and its impact on new modes of cultural production and reception. Conflict brings us back to earth, within the immediacies and contradictions of specific locations. It reminds us that globalization impacts on different locations in significantly different ways. Even when its commodities and services appear to be distributed at mass levels, this dissemination registers through a spectrum of inequalities and imbalances, if not exclusions of large sections of the world's population. Far from being anachronistic, therefore, conflict has the potential to be the soundest arbiter of differences, if not the most potent means of questioning the dominant hegemonies of our times.

Without conflict, there can be no action: this truism, drawn from and tested through the practice of theater and cultural activism, continues to be oddly tenacious, not just at a performative level, but in the social and political developments of the public domain as well. In the world of theater, it is well known that when conflict appears to disappear altogether, by entering the subtexts of silence or stasis, there are more unprecedented and enigmatic dimensions of conflict than what gets articulated in the agonistic confrontation of differences. These non-conflictual dimensions of conflict that seem divested of all violence and tension are best described as 'latent', to adopt the felicitous category adopted by the editors of this series. I would argue that the latent dimensions of conflict can be more intractable than those manifest dimensions of conflict where the differences are emphatically marked. Likewise, the invisible traces of conflict can be more corrosive than what meets the eye. More critically, the attempt to deny conflict, or to settle it once and for all, as in many sincere and failed experiments in conflict-resolution, can be more problematic than the embrace of conflict as an integral part of human endeavor and change.

In this essay, I will elaborate on some conflictual dimensions of globalization through a specific focus on cultural practice, particularly in the subaltern sectors. Even as 'culture', a talismanic category with multivalent associations, seems to be catalyzing new alliances across the disciplines of economics, sociology, anthropology, and development studies (Rao and Walton 2000), cultural practice continues to be a glaring absence or else a tokenistic inclusion in globalization studies. Here I will be extending the notion of 'practice' from 'artistic practice', as in theater, music, painting, and dance, towards a broader notion of 'cultural practice', whereby the knowledge of these artistic disciplines, supplemented by the critical insights derived from material culture and the politics of identity, can be translated into a new set of competencies in dealing with the real. Inevitably, the cultural practice highlighted here will cross the limits of artistic disciplines to explore new interstitial relations between the civil and the political domains of everyday life. While the interstice has been much valorized in postmodern theory as 'the cutting edge of translation and negotiation, the *in-between* space' (Bhabha 1996: 38), it can also be the site of the deepest misunderstandings and breakdowns. Conflicts are not always reconcilable, which doesn't mean that they are not necessarily productive. Indeed, the myth of reconciliation could be the greatest stimulus for the perpetuation of conflict itself.[1]

Locating the intracultural

Before presenting my evidence on subaltern cultural practice in a larger global perspective, it would be useful to situate how 'conflict' has figured in my understanding of culture at an 'intracultural' level, through the minutiae of local and regional differences within the larger borders of the nation-state. A neologism which entered my critical discourse in the 1980s (Bharucha, 1993a, 2000a, 2000b), the 'intracultural' was my strategic means of countering the 'intercultural', characterized by a voluntarist exchange of cultures of choice by individuals and non-official social groups functioning across nations. As I have argued in these early writings, the liberal individualism underlying the advocacy and acquisition of cultures of choice fails to take into account that cultures are not readily chosen by millions of people in the world, and even when they are chosen in the realms of fantasy or desire, this doesn't mean that they necessarily materialize. The access to cultures has to be negotiated and claimed through any number of mediations and regulatory regimes, beginning with the mechanisms of the nation-state, which are invariably ignored by the privileged First World votaries of the intercultural who imagine themselves to be free of national affiliations altogether.[2]

As a term which gained currency in American performance studies in the mid-1970s, interculturalism was endorsed with little theoretical rigor against the official sterilities and bureaucratic mechanisms of internationalism. Far from being annexed to the discourse of globalization as a postnational phenomenon, interculturalism was valorized as a pre-national, primordial force of human togetherness that somehow transcended the immediacies of politics, ethnicity, and national sovereignty. Countering this ahistorical perspective, I would argue that the intercultural, mediated through the legacies of trade, war, migration, and colonization, can exist only in and through the national, past the national, against the national, perhaps (in very idealized circumstances) beyond the national, but it cannot entirely displace the national. Ironically, this very attempt to displace the national in order to avoid conflict at ideological levels is also the surest means of camouflaging conflict at a latent level, which clashes with the upsurge of virulent new nationalisms all over the world.

Against the naïve endorsement of non-national readings of interculturalism, it is heartening to acknowledge the recent qualifications in globalization discourse, particularly in relation to the 'global city', which inscribes the national in increasingly candid and pragmatic ways. Far from playing into the myth of free-floating borderlessness, Saskia Sassen, for example, has emphasized that, 'The global city represents a strategic space where global processes materialize in national territories and global dynamics run through national institutional arrangements' (2001: 347). Denying the 'exogenous' force of globalization, she argues that it operates as a 'function of a cross-border network of strategic sites' from 'the inside of national corporate structures and elites' (2001: 347–8). These are technical, but precise illuminations of how globalization functions at an economic level, but their lessons have yet to be adequately translated into intercultural theory and practice. In this essay, I will explore how the global manifestations of cultural practice are inseparable from the political, social, and economic conditions in which culture is produced at local, regional, and national levels. The global cannot be adequately understood outside the intricate network of these mediations.

Unlike the intercultural, which ostensibly functions across and beyond the borders of nation-states, the multicultural has no other choice but to frame its management of cultural and ethnic diversities within the norms of state-determined citizenship. At a purely descriptive level, both the 'intra' and the 'multi' would seem to share a common ground insofar as they assume the coexistence of regional and local cultures within the larger framework of the nation-state. However, while the 'intra' prioritizes the interactivity and translation of diverse cultures through an acknowledgement of internal differences, the 'multi' upholds a notion of cohesiveness that is invariably built around loyalties to larger associations of national heritage, tradition, civilization, and patriotism (Bharucha 2000b: 81).

Against the onslaught of these official, multicultural, state-determined norms, the 'intra' is a dissident category precisely because it works against the pieties of national mantras like 'unity in diversity'. Not only does the 'intra' remind us that within diversities there are differences; diversities, at times, are the very outcome of differences relating to social and economic disparities (Sangari 1995: 3303). More critically, diversities do not necessarily constitute a plurality, which is the assumed ideal of the multicultural nation-state, based on an essentially quantitative assessment of the sheer variety of distinct cultural practices and traditions upheld by differentiated ethnic groups, which are invariably sealed within constituencies with seemingly impermeable boundaries. This kind of segregated multiculturalism where different cultures co-exist in 'mere spatiality, without interpenetrating' (Al-Azmeh, 1993, quoted by Sangari, 1995: 3309) is not to be equated with plurality, which only begins to make sense through a cognizance, interaction, and exchange of differences. Plurality, in other words, is not merely symptomatic of a seemingly harmonious coexistence of diversities, which are assumed to embody an intrinsic tolerance; rather, it is a political principle that has to be shaped and constructed through an active engagement with differences – not just cultural differences, but those emerging out of the inequalities and injustices that divide communities at social, political, and economic levels.[3]

Some of these differences can be very minute; indeed, they may be almost invisible within the imagined homogeneities of people sharing the same space, food, religion, ethnicity and language constituting a specific 'cultural diversity'. Undetected, or denied the possibility of voice in democratic forums, these differences can fester and explode unexpectedly into fierce conflicts, testifying to Freud's prescient observation that, 'the smaller the real difference between two peoples, the larger it looms in their imagination… [I]t is precisely when external markers point towards the absence of any major differences that people act as if they are deeply divided' (quoted by Bhargava 1999: 33). An intracultural analysis of cultural practice is perhaps one way of retaining some vigilance on these little differences before they ignite into seemingly inexplicable and irreconcilable manifestations of violence.

The Siddi of India

With these preliminary remarks, I will now proceed to focus on the Siddi community of African origin or descent, living in scattered settlements in different parts of India, primarily in the states of Gujarat, Karnataka, and Andhra Pradesh, who constitute an unrecognized diaspora of approximately 40,000 individuals in the Indian subcontinent.[4] Generally, when we talk about the diaspora in India, it is located 'out there' – the millions of indentured laborers from India, for instance, who were exported to South Africa, Fiji, Mauritius, and the West Indies between 1820–1914, and who are now citizens in these countries or elsewhere, are part of a recognized Indian diaspora. But the African diaspora in India has been far less recognized not least because it is too scattered, too marginal, and, above all, too impoverished, to qualify as a vote-bank, quite unlike the upwardly mobile middle-class professional Indians in the UK and the US, who are among the key players in the global economy of the subcontinent. While these privileged migrants pravasis (non–resident or diasp) have been granted the status of 'Persons of Indian' origin, with the promise of dual citizenship, the possibilities of Siddi being granted a 'Person of African' status is not in sight.

While travelers from Africa have been coming to India over the centuries through waves of migration as soldiers, merchants, sailors, mercenaries, and domestic servants (Banaji 1932; Harris 1971; Catlin-Jairazbhoy and Alpers 2004), the ones I wish to call attention to are, in all probability, the descendants of slaves who fled from Goa, or were freed from bondage, approximately 150 years ago, to seek refuge in the forest regions of the Western Ghats. It is one such community living in a forest settlement in the district of Manchikere, Karnataka, that is the focus of my attention here. How the Siddi migrated from Goa to Manchikere is a history that has yet to be written. What is of concern in this essay is their present condition, which could be described as caste-bound servitude, a condition that I will contrast with the globalization of a small section of upwardly mobile Siddi from Gujarat. How this globalization manifests itself I will leave you to read in the following pages, but not before preparing a basic context which is embedded within a network of institutions whereby the most seemingly distant global opportunities become available to local communities through regional mediations.

Neither an anthropologist nor an ethnologist, I did not seek the Siddi out in the wilds of the tropical forest; rather, they entered my theater practice through the mediation of the Ninasam Theatre Institute located in the village of Heggodu in Karnataka, which has served as the site for my intracultural research since 1987 (Bharucha 1993c: 220–39). In 1986, Ninasam, a self-sufficient grassroots cultural organization patronized by a socialist constituency of the Havyaka Brahmin community, had accepted a modest grant from the Ford Foundation in India, one of the biggest global players in the area of culture and development, with its headquarters in New York and numerous branches in Third World metropolitan cities operating with a semblance of decentralized autonomy. Tellingly, this grant from a global funding agency to a regional organization facilitated Ninasam's first cultural interaction with the Siddi community, those agricultural laborers working on the fields of the Havyaka Brahmins themselves, who have lived in near seclusion in forest settlements, as in Manchikere.[5] The specific interaction with the Siddi was facilitated by a theatrical adaptation of Chinua Achebe's classic *Things Fall Apart*, which was adapted in the form of a low-tech, song-and-dance, grassroots production. This production was historic not least because for the first time in living history, the Siddi from this locality were seen not merely as laborers and as lazy, fun-loving, alcoholic, irresponsible blacks, but as actors in their own right.

Building on this interaction within my own intracultural investigations at Ninasam, I conducted a workshop in 2000 with a group of Siddi from Manchikere on Land and Memory. Land, because they live on what the Ministry of Environment and Forests in India chooses to designate as forest land, which, in effect, makes the Siddi, among other forest-dwelling tribes, encroachers in their own habitat. I wanted to work on memory more out of curiosity than anything else because I knew that the Siddi had come from Africa. But, on working with the group from Manchikere, I learned that there was no tangible evidence of their links to Africa through musical or oral traditions, genealogy, or local history. This would seem to be quite different from the cultural memory of the Siddi community in Gujarat, which traces its origins to the Sufi saint Gori Pir, and whose instruments like the *mugarman*, or footed drum, is almost identical to the *ngoma* drum to be found in Zimbabwe today, while the *malunga*, or braced musical bow, seems to resemble the *berimbao* used in the Afro-Brazilian martial arts dance form of *capoeira* (Catlin-Jairazbhoy, 2004: 187, 189). I found no such connections in my encounter with the Hindu Siddi of Manchikere who had probably not heard of Gori Pir, and whose only musical instrument was a simple drum (*damami*).

Indeed, I was compelled to acknowledge that, to the best of my knowledge, the Siddi of Manchikere had no living memory of Africa. Nor were they particularly traumatized by the fact of their forgotten origins. In fact, I question the veracity of calling the Siddi 'African Indians', which is the designated category now being hegemonized by global scholars, when the link to Africa is not a particular concern for most of the Siddi living in India today. One is compelled to ask: Who constructs the diaspora and for whom? And what defines the diaspora? Is it its point of origin, or its actual location and struggle in a new habitat? At what point in time does the origin cease to be relevant?[6] These questions have some bearing on the larger hegemony of global categories determining local realities from which globalization discourse relating to culture and public action is not free. The only way to counter this hegemony is to present counter discourses that have emerged through specific local, regional and national histories.

Tellingly, the Siddi of Manchikere were less concerned about their diasporic cultural identity in relation to Africa than they were eager to resolve the actual confusions surrounding their political identity in relation to the official categories of the Indian state. In the last session of the workshop on Land and Memory, the Siddi created a choric poem in which they raised critical questions: 'Who are we? What are we? SC? ST? OBC?' For those readers who may be unfamiliar with the political rhetoric of the Indian state, these seemingly surreal abbreviations stand for Scheduled Caste, Scheduled Tribe, Other Backward Classes. Dehumanizing and offensive as these categories may seem to liberal sensitivities, they are among the most deeply internalized and coveted of affiliations by a vast spectrum of low-caste communities in India because they are linked to quotas and reservations for jobs, loans, housing facilities, free education, and hostel accommodation. Today, the Siddi of Manchikere can claim the status of ST, even though they have yet to learn how to deploy its benefits, just as they have yet to be adequately informed about the ongoing debates in the Indian Parliament on the forthcoming 'Scheduled Tribes (Recognition of Forest Rights) Bill', which acknowledges the 'historical injustice' that has been inflicted on forest-dwelling tribes by agencies of the State and the conservation lobby upholding vested interests in the name of environmental and wildlife protection.

It would be useful at this point to emphasize the obvious fact, but frequently exaggerated in antiglobalization discourse, that conflict arising from injustice is not a global prerogative. There are many intense conflicts that are already at work within national scenarios, which global interventions merely aggravate in blind pursuit of their own vested interests. For the Siddi it is clear that the complications around their political identity have been enhanced through the institutionalization of the Scheduled Tribe status, which has been inexplicably denied to large sections of the Siddi on bureaucratic grounds. So, within the ranks of the marginalized, the ostensibly democratic intervention of the State to provide an oppressed community with the benefits of affirmative action creates further divisions of 'minorities within minorities' through the arbitrary withholding of the ST status to all members of a particular community. Some Siddi are ST; others are not.

Likewise, despite its attempts to legislate democracy for grassroots communities through constitutional procedures, the State enhances its exclusivity through its sheer inability to disseminate information on progressive bills like the 'Scheduled Tribes (Recognition of Forest Rights) Bill' to those very communities in whose name the bill is being passed.[7] At one level, the multiple conflicts surrounding the bill are being thrashed out by opposing members of political parties, ministries, environmental activists, and proponents of the timber lobby – in other words, the educated members of civil society and the recognized citizens of the State.[8] But, in contrast, the very non-inclusion of the Siddi in the debate is what contributes to the larger challenge of realizing social justice in the absence of democratic decision-making at ground levels. What develops in the process is a mere tokenization of minority rights without a real empowerment of minorities themselves.

The politics of practice

Let me splice into the discussion here some indication of my actual cultural practice with the Siddi, which enabled me to learn about their condition. When 'practice' is theorized in the social sciences, particularly in the emergent literature around practice-based globalization theory, it is generally neutered of an experiential base. Even among those anthropologists whose articulations of practice seem to be increasing in almost direct proportion to their decline in actual fieldwork, it would seem as if the observation of other people's practices constitutes a practice in its own right. Writing and cultural action are conflated and collapsed into each other's priorities, resulting in a tautology whereby theory becomes practice, instead of being dialectically interrelated. In my experience, practice is invariably ahead of theory even as the existing grounds of practice have been prepared through embodied and internalized theoretical premises. Practice has the capacity to stretch theory into the difficulties of acknowledging the unknown, messy, and chaotic dimensions of everyday life.

What is my cultural practice in interacting with groups like the Siddi? Drawing on my experience in theater, I basically work through the exercises and techniques of improvisation that prioritize processes of mutual learning and dialogue over the shaping of fully realized 'artistic' productions. I tend to prioritize improvisations of everyday life, which, arguably, can be regarded as an improvisation in its own right – a 'necessary' and 'regulated' improvisation, as Pierre Bourdieu would have us believe (1977: 8). In a reflexive mode, theatrical improvisation has enabled me to expose the internalization of what Bourdieu would describe as the *habitus*, that tacit realm of 'embodied history, internalized as a second nature, and so forgotten as history' (1990: 56), which rests on the extraordinary paradox that, 'It is because subjects do not, strictly speaking, know what they are doing that what they do has more meaning than they know' (1977: 79). The 'logic of practice' that fuels the business of everyday life can be discerned in 'the intentionless invention of regulated improvisaton' (1990: 57), which seems to function almost implacably under the immanent laws of 'conductorless orchestration' (1990: 59).

Improvisation in theater works differently. At one level, like the *habitus*, it is an invention, generally 'made from scratch', without the help of a script, where, in actuality, almost anything can happen out of the accumulated experiences of a particular community. However, 'intentionless' as it may appear, the theatrical improvisation is driven by the need to make choices and to define certain gestures and relationships, however tenuous and processual; without these minimal provisions, it would fail to make sense. Improvisations may not have scripts, but they work within spatial, temporal, and conceptual frames which are, more often than not, orchestrated by the director, whose 'conductorlessness' is at best a strategy for a close observation of the accidental and the deviant. Basically, my practice in theater has enabled me to question the seeming normalization of the social and economic conditions stabilizing the *habitus* of groups like the Siddi of Manchikere, but it has also compelled me to push the regulatory norms of this *habitus*.

So, for example, when the Minister of Social Welfare from Karnataka visited our workshop with a perfectly gratuitous official visit, where he proceeded to enact the Theater of the State in which the Siddi were patronized and reduced to lazy natives, I had an opportunity as a director to play back the scene the day after he had left. In this improvisation, one of the Siddi became the minister, and the other Siddi proceeded to question him vigorously, thereby articulating their previously silenced rage, but also their logic in countering the bureaucratic mechanisms of the State in relation to land ownership with their own ecological verifications of what constitutes land (and land rights) in the first place. Theater can disturb the protocols of the *habitus* through the illusion of play and, in this sense, it is both a profoundly reflexive activity and an impetus for change. The challenge is to extend this impetus beyond the civil domain of theater practice into the actual confrontation of power in the political domain.

This is where I ran up against walls in Ninasam. More precisely, I was made to confront its hegemonic structure, which, for all its good intentions, was not prepared to betray either the limits of theater or its implicit endorsement and preservation of brahmanic caste norms in its propagation of a communitarian ethos. Moreover, as much as I wanted to link the Siddi of Manchikere to other Siddi groups in Karnataka itself, I was unable to find the appropriate infrastructure for such an intracultural exchange. This irony needs to be highlighted: in the age of globalization when messages and images are being beamed and transmitted across the world, in split-seconds of virtual communication, there is no infrastructure of communication between individuals belonging to a particular marginalized group living in the same region, within the boundaries of the same nation-state. Confronting this impasse in my research on the Siddi, I had no other choice but to think of other mediations that could cut across the stranglehold of local cultures within regional hegemonies. The global enters my narrative at this point.

The Siddi go global

I would like to shift the context now to Gujarat where the Siddi live in somewhat more resilient economic conditions than the Siddi of Manchikere, with more employment opportunities outside of agricultural labor, and even some dubious cultural recognition through their participation in Republic Day Parades, performances for dignitaries like Nelson Mandela, and tours organized by the Zonal Cultural Centres and other cultural departments of the Indian State.[9] Unlike in Manchikere, where the primary cultural intervention with the Siddi was mediated through theater, in Gujarat, the primary interventions in cultural activism have been fueled through ethnomusicology and applied anthropology, resulting in a global performance of Sidi Sufi-related songs and dances for the international stage.

Some unraveling of the interrelationship of different institutions becomes necessary at this point to contextualize the links between the global and the local. In 1975, the ethnomusicologist Nazir

Jairazbhoy from UCLA had recorded the songs of the Pakistani Shidi from Lyari, Pakistan, in preparation for their trip to Washington D.C. for the Smithsonian Institution's Bicentennial Festival of American Folklife held in 1976. While the role of festivals in globalizing cultural practices across the world is now well established as a source of generating capital, employment, and tourism, what is not often acknowledged is that the performances selected from the South are invariably 'traditional' or 'folk', with a strong visual and kinetic appeal as opposed to the historically grounded and less translatable specificity of the spoken word. Tellingly, Rajasthani folk musicians from the Langa and Manganiyar communities, who are socially underprivileged, could have far more global opportunities for performance than the middle-class, educated, and internationally cognizant performers of the contemporary Indian theater (Bharucha 2003: 236–288). The global does not necessarily favor the 'modern' in its propagation of performance, particularly from Third World countries.

Following the Smithsonian Festival, in 1998, a three-minute excerpt from the recordings of the Pakistani Shidi was included in a video made by Jairazbhoy and his wife, Amy Catlin, on the *Musical Instruments of Kacch and its Neighbors*. This kind of video can be regarded as a new manifestation of what Bourdieu would describe as 'educational capital' whereby the power of the printed word is, to a large extent, being substituted by an electronic representation of 'local knowledge' that is sold as an educational resource and learning aid to global academic consumers. Based on the reception to the video, Catlin realized that the 3–minute excerpt of the Shidi in the documentary proved to be a 'hook' to Americans and Indians alike, who had 'never imagined an African presence on Indian soil' (2004: 180). Capitalizing on this voyeuristic interest in 'black Indians' and building on her own American affinities to the civil rights movements in the United States, which she imagined could be extended to the Indian context by recognizing the human rights of unrecognized blacks in the subcontinent, Catlin began a long-term collaborative project with the Siddi near Rajpipla, Gujarat, on a Siddi CD Project. By 2002, she had organized the first performance tour of the 'Siddi Goma: Black Sufis of Gujarat' as part of a cross-cultural festival of the Music of the Mystics, which opened in Aberystwyth, Wales, precipitating a series of performances in the UK, the United States, and Africa. The Siddi had not just become 'mystical'; they had gone global.

Judging from one of the more recent manifestations of this performance, which I witnessed in Delhi, under the sponsorship of the American Resource Center for Ethnomusicology, it was obvious that the 'sacred' dimensions of Sufism in the Siddi performance were inextricably linked to an exotically packaged 'invention of tradition' (Bharucha 1993b: 192–210). Beginning on a solemn ritualistic note, with the white-robed performers invoking Allah and Bismillah in devotional group singing and simulations of trance, the performance built in the second half to a climactic *dammal*, or state of ecstasy, in which the performers, now costumed in peacock feathers, hurled coconuts in the air and smashed them with their skulls, with all the virtuosity of budding Ronaldinhos and Ronaldos. The most obvious question that emerged from the performance is whether the Siddi dances, songs and revelry performed within the shrine (*dargah*) of Gori Pir, the patron saint of the Siddi, can be meaningfully transported to metropolitan festival circuits outside of the contradictions of secularization. To what extent does the sacred remain 'sacred' when its elements are decontextualized from actual worship? What kind of 'sacred' gets simulated through global packaging? And can this 'sacred' effectively link the seeming transference of 'divine revelry' from shrine to stage? Or is it more accurately regarded as a robust form of interactive cultural tourism in which First World cosmopolitans in the audience are invited to dance with the natives at the end of the show?

While these questions open up large ethical issues concerning the commodification of indigenous performances with sacred elements, I am more concerned in this essay with the consequences of the social and economic development of the Siddi through global mediation. A purely material analysis would indicate that the Siddi have earned a substantial amount of money, at least by their standards, through global performance, which has also enabled them to enhance their cultural and social capital. Their self-confidence would also seem to have increased in almost direct proportion to the enlarging of their social contacts and networks in the UK and the United States. While it is not yet theoretically clear how cultural practice gets transformed into what Amartya Sen has defined as 'capabilities' (Sen 1985, 1999), the potential of individuals to convert entitlements over goods and services into active choices for a larger social well-being, what cannot be denied is that the 'terms of recognition' (Appadurai, 2004) of the foreign-returned Gujarati Siddi would seem to have increased. In contrast, one is compelled to acknowledge that the Siddi of Manchikere continue to be relatively unrecognized within the hegemonic constraints of land-owning upper-caste Hinduism.

In his normative conceptualization of 'How Does Culture Matter?' (2004), Amartya Sen has stressed that there are plenty of opportunities involved in combining cultural pursuits with economic use, though he does sound an obligatory note of caution concerning the 'commercial' use of 'religious objects or sites' (2004: 39). Without elaborating on the possible pitfalls of such commercialism, Sen emphasizes that 'economically remunerative cultural activities and objects' (2004: 39) need to be actively pursued, if necessary across national borders. This openness to the free exchange and absorption of cultures compels him to insist that any attempt to thwart the importation of 'foreign' cultural influences on grounds of contamination should be vigorously countered. Not only does 'the threat of being overwhelmed by the superior market power of an affluent West' not contradict in any way 'the importance of learning from elsewhere' (2004: 52), the 'prohibition of cultural influence from abroad', as Sen puts it in a more magisterial mode, is 'not consistent with a commitment to democracy and liberty' (2004: 54). In dealing with the 'asymmetry' of foreign influence, which is one of the most familiar charges brought against globalization, Sen concedes that the opportunities available to local cultures need to be strengthened, and some 'positive assistance' may need to be provided to them so that they can 'compete in even terms' (53–4).

Clearly, the 'how' in Amartya Sen's proposition relating to 'how culture matters' lacks the contradictory dimensions of practice. For a start, the dichotomy that he outlines between the global and the local is too narrowly confined within the registers of the foreign influence coming from outside, and the local culture receiving this influence from within the borders of a particular nation-state. The fact that the global can be produced *within* the indigenous resources of local cultures, as in the case of the Siddi Goma performance, is not acknowledged as a possibility. The issue in question, I would argue, is not contamination resulting from external 'foreignness' but the production of local exotica for global consumption. What happens to the self-image of local communities when they exoticize themselves in order to earn a living? If this local manufacture of the exotic could be acknowledged as a pragmatic means of income generation linked to cultural tourism, it would be less problematic, to my mind, than its dubious legitimization of sustaining and extending the cultural 'authenticity' of indigenous people.

Tellingly, the globe-trotting Siddi of Bharuch district, Gujarat, would seem to be building their credentials on a specifically 'sacred' ground of 'Siddi culture', while their less fortunate brothers from Ahmedabad, who also have a thriving Siddi Goma troupe but who have yet to go abroad, are more than prepared to sell their 'African' artifacts (costumes, headgear, and jewelry) as an additional means of augmenting their income.[10] For the Bharuch Siddi, this kind of commodification of Siddi artifacts is viewed disparagingly as a means of diluting the authentic premises of 'traditional Siddi culture'. 'Why should we let go of our tradition by sharing it with others?' is the thrust of their argument, which can be more meaningfully read, to my mind, as a strategic means of holding on to their monopolistic control of 'Siddi culture'. The more it gets diffused, the less exotic (and therefore, the less marketable) their performance. It is worth keeping in mind that the so-called traditional 'African' artifacts of the Siddi, notably the peacock-feather skirts, headgear, and painted faces, were first invented by a contemporary non-Siddi theater director from the National School of Drama in New Delhi, who used the Siddi as 'demonic' presences in an amateur experimental production dealing ostensibly with nuclear war (see Catlin-Jairazbhoy 2006: 8). So much for traditional 'authenticity'.

The manufacture of this factitious neo-traditional 'authenticity' would seem to increase in almost direct proportion to the decrease in the syncretic dynamics of Siddi performance. On the international stage, the Sufi-related songs and dances get schematized within a larger grid of devotional solemnity and play. More emphatically, the religious identity of all the performers is marked 'Muslim'. However, within the intimate performative context of the Siddi shrine itself, where the healing of afflicted persons from all kinds of psychophysical ailments is made possible through trance and spirit possession, we are presented with a palpable syncretism, which cannot be fixed within the boundaries of any one religious tradition or genealogy. In contrast, both at the levels of performance and reception, the globalizing of the Siddi performance would seem to exemplify a process of de-syncretization, working against the liberal myth of global cultural production, which tends to valorize the generation of new forms of cultural hybridity. This, indeed, is not always the case, as 'hybridity' is increasingly branded within dominant global tastes and fashions, exemplifying the homogenizing tendencies of the market.

While an extended ethnography of syncretic Siddi ritual practices is not possible within the limits of this essay – read the thick description and analysis provided by Helene Basu 1993, 1998, 2004 – what needs to be emphasized is that these practices reveal a mélange of many diverse ceremonial and material constituents, drawn not only from Sufi but diverse Hindu trance-related practices, which are available in hundreds of shrines scattered in the rural areas of western Rajasthan and Gujarat. Gods and goddesses have multiple identities in such shrines as they reach out to diverse constituencies of followers. Over the years, as Basu has elaborated in her numerous writings, the *dargah* (shrine) of Gori Pir in Gujarat, for instance, has drawn worshippers not only from the Siddi, but from Sunni Muslims, Bohras, low-caste Hindus, the tribal community of Bhils, and even a small number of Parsi Zoroastrians. Both in its ritual practices and in its openness to diverse religious communities, who are not expected to relinquish their own religions in celebrating Gori Pir, the Siddi shrine can be regarded as an embodiment of a charismatically charged syncretism that spills into the cross-cultural textures and dynamics of everyday life.

Significantly, this shrine was targeted by a group of former Hindu worshippers abetted by communal thugs in the wake of the Babri Masjid demolition in Ayodhya in December 1992. Like many other shrines that continue to be pillaged and desecrated in India on account of their mixed Hindu-Muslim cultural heritage, this shrine was not spared. Indeed, it continues to be communalized through the intricate politics surrounding the administration of the shrine whereby Siddi custodians have been replaced by Bohras under the apparently 'neutral', and ostensibly 'secular' supervision of the Charity Commission's Office in Gujarat (read Basu 2004: 69–81 for a detailed account of the manipulations). While it is not possible to draw any direct causality between the intensification of globalization and the equally widespread communalization of Indian society, particularly in the state of Gujarat where Muslims in Godhra were targeted by Hindu extremists in 2002 in a pogrom masterminded by the custodians of the State,[11] the point is that globalization and communalism are coterminous phenomena that feed on each other's agendas. Indeed, one of the unanswered enigmas of globalization is its proximity to the rise in xenophobia, sectarianism, and Islamophobia, so much so that it becomes almost impossible not to acknowledge the interconnectedness of these two seemingly distinct and opposing phenomena. As the world gets smaller and more seemingly intimate through the outreach of global facilities, the 'mind forg'd manacles' of narrow sectarian constituencies would seem to be widening on a global basis.

Conflicting agendas

Returning to the tensions between the Siddi groups from Bharuch and Ahmedabad, it is clear that the competition arising from the globalization of indigenous performance can create new divisions between marginalized people. The disparities, between those who have access to global resources and opportunities and those who don't, intensify, when one considers the predicament of the Siddi of Manchikere, who are still relying on agricultural labor to earn a meager living, with no hope for a significantly altered future. Given these rifts between the Siddi of Karnataka and Gujarat – and I haven't begun to inscribe the middle-class aspirations and apparent acculturation into mainstream 'Indian' society of the Siddi of Hyderabad – how does one build the 'capabilities' of the Siddi on a more equitable basis across the inequities of different constituencies and regions? Before the Siddi of Manchikere can begin to 'compete in even terms', to adapt Sen's normative recommendation, it would seem necessary that their context should be infused with new economic and social opportunities and a much wider communicative network. It is unlikely that the creation of another Siddi Goma troupe in Manchikere would facilitate this agency in a positive way. Other more contextualized and material entitlements over goods, services and education would need to be made available before the *capabilities* of the Siddi of Manchikere can precipitate concrete change.

What is clear is that this change is not likely to be facilitated by the existing agencies of the State for whom the Siddi are too marginal to matter, or by the existing caste hegemony whose paternalism is the soundest way of keeping the Siddi bound within a state of compliant servitude. Almost by default, the most potentially dynamic catalysts of change at this point in time could be NGOs and a global network of scholars, *The African Diasporas in Asia (TADIA)*, which has attempted to transform itself from a virtual network into an organization committed to the long-term social, economic and political development of the Siddi within the larger academic framework of African and diasporic studies. The transition of a network into an organization is not always a smooth process, and the complications increase with the conflicting agendas and politics of scholars and activists, and of differing orientations within the same constituencies. Clearly, the historians of TADIA are divided between prioritizing the African-American and African-Asian diasporas, with the latter being linked to the newly emerging field of the Indian Ocean World Studies. To what extent does slavery continue to be the dominant motif linking these diasporas?

Involuntarily, the Siddi are linked to these discursive formations emerging around their identities, even as these formations relating to 'diasporic consciousness' may have little to do with their specific difficulties relating to caste, religion, the politics of identity surrounding Scheduled Tribes, and the economic possibilities of gaining control over forest resources. Indeed, to what extent does the hegemonic global discourse around the 'Slave Route' program, institutionalized by UNESCO and now formally linked to TADIA's social objectives, have any concrete relevance in the Siddi context? Or is the annexation of the Siddi to the Slave Route just another means of amplifying the considerable intellectual capital that has been built around the narrative of this particular history of suffering at the expense of recognizing other histories of marginalized people in Asia, who may not be linked to the phenomenon of African slavery at all?[12]

With these questions, we enter the conflictual dimensions that are bound to emerge out of global academic discourses and local histories of struggle linked to particular cultures of activism. While, at a normative level, one would want these contexts to be closely interrelated, they are, in actuality, bound within distinct constituencies marked by specialized languages, grammars, modalities, modes of expertise, and political priorities. The translation of cultural discourse into social and political action is, indeed, a hard task. At times the discourse could project a form of action that may not in fact be relevant to the people concerned. A lot has been written, for instance, on intellectual property rights by which indigenous cultures across the globe have been appropriated and marketed by corporate agencies preoccupied with the marketing of culture through monopolistic production and distribution practices. I am in fundamental agreement with the premises of this anti-globalization critique (see, for instance, the extremely comprehensive document of the Copy South Project (2006)). However, I would also acknowledge that a protectionist attitude towards the poor cultures of the South has emerged through such discourses, which often exist in total (or relative) ignorance of the actual cultural practices of the poor, which remain largely undocumented. Against this insufficiently informed global vigilance, one needs to acknowledge that the very idea of copyright may not be a burning issue for subaltern communities, who may need to be protected from the more local and regional modes of exploitation to which their cultural practices are subjected on a habitual basis. Anti-globalization should not make one immune to local abuse.

Take the case of Methi, a legendary female Rajasthani singer from the low-caste Hudkal community, a prolific composer of contemporary folk songs, who used to receive a pittance for a one-shot recording deal with regional cassette manufacturers, who would then proceed to sell thousands of her cassettes all over Rajasthan. Methi's voice was recognized everywhere – in construction sites, *dhabas* (roadside restaurants), weddings, pilgrimage sites, *melas* (fairs). But this recognition of her singing voice, which was not necessarily linked to her name, never extended to an acknowledgement of her economic and social predicament. The much-theorized issue of authorship in relation to the alleged anonymity of 'folk' singing traditions is not the issue here. More to the point is the painful reality that this phenomenal singer was beaten to death by her own co-singer, the co-singer's husband and son, in a drunken brawl in Methi's village. There was no NGO, no women's organization, at a regional, national, or global level, not even a *panchayat* at a local level, that attempted to intervene in Methi's life, which was marked by the realities of poverty, caste, alcoholism, and illiteracy. Her life has been cut short and the world is poorer for it.

There are two questions that need to be raised at this juncture in the essay, as I shift the indeterminacies of cultural practice into the demands of social activism. First, how does one extend one's knowledge of the voice of a particular performer to what Appadurai describes as the 'cultural capacity' (2004: 66) of voice to debate, contest, inquire and participate critically in the political domain of life? At a purely visceral and pleasurable level, Methi's singing voice did have considerable 'local cultural force' (2004: 67), but it was unable to engage with social, economic and political realities, beginning with her own predicament. She had control over her metaphors and rhetoric, but she lacked any affiliation to activist organizations and public forums, which could have enabled her to extend her terms of recognition through the social transformation of her voice.

A second question that needs to be drawn from Methi's predicament concerns the possible extension of 'cultural recognition' beyond the cultural domain into the actual economic 'redistribution' of resources (Appadurai, 2004: 63). As Appadurai puts the question pithily: Can the politics of dignity and the politics of poverty be viewed in the same framework? (2004: 63). In the case of Methi, this would not seem possible. It is one thing, I would argue, to acknowledge the politics of recognition, as Appadurai does, on the lines of Charles Taylor's insistence on the 'ethical obligation to extend a sort of moral cognizance to persons who share world views deeply different from our own' (2004: 62). This could be one of the soundest and most humane interventions in the discourse of multiculturalism, but Taylor assumes a common ground of *citizenship* with conflicting ethnicities – a citizenship which cannot be readily applied to the protagonists of this narrative, including the Siddis and folk singers like Methi. For all their nominal identities as citizens of India, they inhabit the fragmented, illegal, and unstructured domain of 'political society', as Partha Chatterjee (2004), has defined it, where fundamental rights cannot be readily assumed in accordance with the laws and rules of behavior constituting civil society. Subalterns like Methi have to be recognized as citizens, and respected as individuals in their own right despite their low-caste status, before the honorary status given to their voice as singers can extend to a real cognizance of their material reality and capacity-building faculties.

Capabilities and Aspirations

This would be an appropriate point in the essay to return to the problematic of 'capability' indicated by Methi's condition and addressed earlier in the context of the Siddi of Manchikere. Within the framework of cultural practice, I would now like to push the seeming limitations of 'capability' against the 'capacity to aspire', as articulated by Arjun Appadurai (2004), in an attempt to inflect, if not circumvent, the overly economistic determinants of development. While the 'capacity to aspire', for Appadurai, 'provides an ethical horizon within which more concrete capabilities can be given meaning, substance, and sustainability', at a converse level, 'the exercise and nurture of these capabilities verifies and authorizes the capacity to aspire and moves it away from wishful thinking to thoughtful wishing' (2004: 82). Perhaps, there are too many assumptions being made in these swift equations, which could be meaningfully challenged less through the assumptions of symbiosis linking 'capability' and 'aspiration' than through their *conflictual* dynamics, which Appadurai does not address.

At the messy and complicated levels of practice, in long-term activist engagements with the poor on the realities of income generation, for instance, the capacity to aspire can only be built on a sufficiently solid and sustainable base of capabilities in terms of education, access to and control over resources, intra-community dialogue, communication with the outside world, and the acquisition of new productive skills and knowledge (Nathan, 2005: 40). Assuming the availability of this capability base, Appadurai's theoretical pitch for deepening the capacity to aspire is built on the premise that aspirations *will* by the sheer intensity of their underlying desire and volition create new capabilities. The possibility that some aspirations could work against the development of existing capabilities, or could be destructive, is never considered as a problem.

Secondly, while Appadurai correctly acknowledges the 'uneven distribution' of the capacity to aspire (2004: 68), he undermines the conflictual effects of this unevenness, which is not merely symptomatic of the stark differences between the rich and the poor, with the former in a more privileged position than the poor to 'produce justifications, narratives, metaphors, and pathways through which bundles of goods and services are actually tied to wider social scenes and contexts, and to still more abstract norms and beliefs' (2004: 68). Against this discrimination, one needs to emphasize the infinitesimal differences in the capacity to aspire to be found *within* the ranks of the poor, and more emphatically, between men and women belonging to the same families. From grassroots activist ethnography, there is much evidence to indicate that women in subaltern communities, for example, are more prepared than men to make critical adjustments in household resources and management in order to facilitate the realization of new aspirations – for example, the education of their daughters with the hope that they will be in a better position to find employment in a local industry (Nathan 2005: 37). The men, on the other hand, may continue to hold on to the comforts provided by a subsistence economy. Within these clashes of aspiration and apathy, how does the capacity to aspire negotiate differences, if not violence, at familial, communal, and inter-communal levels?

Thirdly, while Appadurai insists that 'aspirations are never simply individual' but are 'always formed in interaction and in the thick of social life' (2004: 67), he inadvertently upholds a cohesive notion of 'community' without taking into account the communal divides that are at work in precisely those slums in Mumbai which he valorizes. Here conflict is part of everyday life, consolidated through the intracultural differences of caste, religion, language, and custom, and intensified by the agencies of communalism. How does the capacity to aspire negotiate these differences outside of the assumptions of intrinsically well-managed communities functioning under the auspices of enlightened NGOs?

Furthermore, in acknowledging the media as one of the most powerful and deceptive generators of aspiration through its propagation of images (Nathan 2005: 40), the question to be asked is whether the capacity to aspire can be so neatly separated from market-driven consumerism. Through what circuits of communication are media-driven aspirations received if not through the networks of global capitalism? Here there needs to be some kind of positioning as to what kinds of aspiration are viable within specific contexts of poverty, or else, there is an implicit valorization that all inputs carry the same weight and value. What are the critical filters through which the aspirations of the market can be discriminated at ethical levels, and if necessary, countered with an alternative value-system?

Severing the possible links of aspiration to the immediacies of political struggle, it is telling how Appadurai avoids any engagement with the processes of democratization that are available *within* the national scenario of India. Instead of exploring the expedient affiliations that large sections of the poor do adopt in relation to political parties, electoral politics, the *dalit* movement, trade unionism, and the politics of reservations, Appadurai opts for global cross-border activism whereby local alliances of NGOs in cities like Mumbai can be linked to larger global organizations like the Slum/Shackdwellers International (SDI). While such alliances operate through the tactics of dialogue and negotiation, they seem to circumvent the necessity of oppositional strategies, which Appadurai almost makes into a virtue. Drawing on the dubious assumption that the proverbial 'patience' of the poor could be their 'biggest weapon' (2004: 81), he somewhat misses the point. Today, India's increasingly politicized downtrodden communities are *impatient* for a significant change in their lives. And, for the vast majority of them, this impatience is manifest not in forming links with global movements and NGOs, but in entering the political fray through a blatantly opportunistic use of the politics of caste and reservations, in addition to running for elections. The conflicts emerging through this embrace of the political battleground are harsh, but they are also potentially lucrative and empowering.

The Limits of Performance

This critique of the 'capacity to aspire' may seem overstretched in the context of my argument on globalization and cultural practice. But I make it for two reasons. First, the concept denies the dynamics of conflict in building aspiration within a national context. More critically, however, I am skeptical of the performativity of Appadurai's evidence, supplemented by its overly discursive modes of persuasion. Indeed, performances provide the primary sites of his eloquent documentation of grassroots activism in Mumbai, which is specifically linked to two subaltern cultural practices – housing exhibitions and Toilet Festivals (*sandas melas*). These are different kinds of grassroots performances from the ritualized export-oriented Siddi performance described earlier in the essay, but both of them have a global reach with somewhat different implications.

With housing exhibitions, a 'creative hijacking of an upper-class form' (2004: 77), the slum-dwellers are in a position to demonstrate their greatest expertise, which is to 'build adequate housing out of the flimsiest of materials and in the most insecure of circumstances' (2004: 77). Such demonstrations enable the slum-dwellers to realize their own unacknowledged skills as architects and engineers, which is, indeed, a sound way of building on their own existing capabilities to realize new aspirations. These aspirations, however, are acknowledged not within the intimacies of closed-doors workshops, but through performances for larger audiences – not just the peers of the slum-dwellers, but the agencies of the State, municipal authorities, heads of NGOs, and, at times, foreign funders as well. It is through these public performances that the slum-dwellers enter, as Appadurai emphasizes, 'a space of public sociality, official recognition, and technical legitimation' (2004: 78).

In a more euphoric mode, Appadurai celebrates the phenomenon of Toilet Festivals, which are a 'brilliant effort to turn [the] humiliating and privatized suffering [of shitting in public] into scenes of technical innovation, collective celebration and carnivalesque play' (2004: 79). By building real public toilets and drawing cosmopolitans like World Bank officials into dialogue, the so-called 'shitters' are in a position to transform their 'abjectivity' into 'subjectivity', while consciously voicing a script of their own in which a 'recognition from below' is enacted and celebrated (2004: 79). This script extends to the lobby of the United Nations building, where a model house as well as a model children's toilet are built, through which Kofi Annan walks 'in the heart of his own bureaucratic empire', surrounded by 'poor women from India and South Africa, singing and dancing' (2004: 80). Appadurai describes this event as a 'magical moment, full of possibilities for the Alliance, and for the Secretary-General, as they engage jointly and together with the global politics of poverty' (2004: 80). He adds that, '[N]o space is too grand – or too humble – for the spatial imagination of the poor and for the global portability of the capacity to aspire' (2004: 80).

What we have in effect here, I would argue, is the global portability of a particular kind of globalization theory, whose reference points to local cultural practices are, in actuality, far less disseminated within the municipal boundaries of cities like Mumbai than Appadurai's rhetoric would suggest. To whom are these practices directed – the official world of global decision-makers or to the people of India? While I would not necessarily dismiss housing exhibitions and Toilet Festivals as 'political charades' (2004: 78), I would definitely see them as instances of the 'Theater of Development' that play into the feel-good, palliative, non-confrontationist, civil measures of how the poor can aspire under the auspices of global patrons like the World Bank. It is ironic, indeed, that social scientists in their need to re-ignite their arguably burned-out imaginaries should be turning to performances at precisely the same point in time when the limits of performance need to be inscribed in activating agendas of social transformation.

Today, as the cultures of activism get increasingly spectacularized and consumed by the global media, it is necessary to ensure that they are not reduced to mere performances. And yet, that is the dominant trend if one considers the anti-globalization rallies and Word Social Forums, whose periodic upheavals appear to incarnate the seemingly spontaneous uprising of the multitudes against the forces of global capital, only to disappear into anonymity without any sustained political consolidation. Against the hype of global performance, the specter of Gandhi looms large, both in relation to performance and to the blatant injustices of economic globalization. When Gandhi picked a fistful of earth from the banks of the River Dandi and symbolically converted it into salt, it would be a mistake to detach the performativity of this political gesture from the larger mass political movement and critique of colonial economics that provoked this gesture at multiple levels. In itself, the gesture was almost banal, flaunting its ordinariness and almost improvised quality. However, if it had the power to capture the hearts and minds of an entire nation and beyond, it is because of its political grounding that enabled Gandhi's activism to cut across regional and sectarian constituencies, working through differences, and above all, *embracing the immediacies of conflict* without surrendering to violence.

What is needed, perhaps, in the age of globalization is not an avoidance of conflict to circumvent violence, but rather, a critical engagement with conflict that combines performance with the cunning of reason, incorporating the strategies of negotiation and opposition. Only then will it be possible to arrive at a new ethics of global cultural practice, whereby the capabilities and aspirations of the poor can be brought into sharper critical dialogue, facilitating a more viable future without surrendering the realities on the ground.

Notes

1 See, for example, my analysis of how the rhetoric of Truth and Reconciliation has not contributed to the cessation of violence and conflict in post-apartheid South Africa (Bharucha 2002: 361–88).

2 Interculturalists based in the South have fewer illsions of such postnational freedom not least because the right to travel and to cross borders is increasingly circumvented by the non-availability of visas. The surveillance of immigration and anti-terrorist agencies has also intensified since September 11, 2001.

3 The discrimination between 'diversity' and 'plurality' has been finely enunciated in the contemporary Indian discourse on secularism (Alam, 1994; Vanaik 1997) in opposition to anti-secularist valorizations of an intrinsically 'pluralist' and 'tolerant' traditional Hindu culture, as espoused by communitarian theorists like Ashis Nandy (1990).

4 I shall be adopting the spelling 'Siddi' throughout the essay to represent the groups in all the states of India, though there are regional variations – in Gujarat, the word 'Sidi' is more common; 'Sidhi' is also used in Karnataka alongside 'Siddi', and, in medieval historiography, the words *habshi* and *kaffir* have also been used to designate persons of African origin in the Indian subcontinent. Though for a long time the word Siddi was linked to the honorific and 'established Arabic religious and/or aristocratic title "Sayyid"', which often got translated as a descendant of the Prophet Mohammed, more recent etymological research indicates that the word 'Siddi' could mean 'captive' or 'prisoner of war' (see Lodhi 2004: 2, for a closer linguistic analysis).

5 While the Ford Foundation has one of the biggest endowments for the arts in the world amounting to millions of dollars, it is telling that Ninasam received around Rs.275,000 for its two-year theater and film program in which the Siddi production of *Things Fall Apart* was included as one of the activities. The Siddi themselves received Rs.9 per day during the rehearsal process of the production, which was the exact amount of their daily wages as agricultural laborers in 1986.

6 Campbell (2006) provides a succinct critique of some of the dominant tropes that have emerged around 'diaspora' by the proponents of the African-American diaspora. They include: 1. 'displacement from a homeland to two or more peripheral or foreign regions'; 2. the 'formation of a "relatively stable community in exile"'; 3. 'social rejection by, and alienation from, the locally dominant society'; 4. an 'awareness, real or imagined, of a common homeland and heritage, and of the injustice of removal from it'; 5. 'efforts to maintain links with and improve life in the homeland'; and 6. a 'desire ultimately to return permanently'. As Campbell correctly points out, the Siddi, among many other migrants in the African-Asian diaspora, do not fulfill these criteria, and their condition, accordingly, has to be historicized differently.

7 In a recent workshop that I conducted for approximately 130 Siddi from different parts of India, organized by the TADIA Society as part of the conference on *The Siddis of India and the African Diasporas in Asia* held in Goa, January 2006, I was struck by the fact that not one of the Siddi in the workshop was aware of the ongoing debates in Parliament. This contrasted sharply with their strongly articulated dissatisfaction about the role of the State in denying the ST status to some sections of the Siddi on an arbitrary basis.

8 See special section on 'Tribal Bill', *Economic and Political Weekly*, 19 November 2005, pp.4888–901, for a trenchant summary of the controversies surrounding the Bill.

9 All the factual information included in this section on the 'The Siddi Go Global' is drawn from two publications by Amy Catlin-Jairazbhoy (2004, 2006) on the modalities and consequences of international touring.

10 The oppositional contrast in the attitudes of the two groups both to tradition and to the projection of their cultural practice was emphatically articulated in the TADIA workshop in Goa, January 2006. It was clear that the Ahmedabad group resented the fact that they had not received the same global opportunities as their colleagues from Bharuch, and this compelled them to adopt a more pragmatically commercial attitude in relation to their use of tradition.

11 For a detailed report on 'Genocide: Gujarat 2002', read the special issue of *Communalism Combat*, Mumbai, March–April 2002.

12 The historian Gwyn Campbell's plea to work against the 'universalizing' agenda of UNESCO's African Slave Route program has drawn much heat from many of TADIA's members who do not see the African-Asian diaspora functioning in a fundamentally different trajectory from that of the African-American diaspora. Ironically, the 'ethical' priorities of UNESCO upheld against Campbell's ostensibly academic (and implicitly insensitive) 'objectivity' fail to take into account that the master narrative of an intrinsically 'African' slavery needs to be complicated through what Campbell has described as 'overlapping histories of reversible dependence and servitude'. This would seem to be a more accurate way of examining the multitudinous histories of the Indian Ocean World where slavery is just one reality in a larger spectrum of diasporic survivals and reinventions of identity. This important debate, drawn from e-mail exchanges following the TADIA conference in Goa in January 2006, has yet to be adequately theorized in the form of a critical discourse rather than an exchange of polemics.

REFERENCES

Alam, Javeed (1994) 'Tradition in India under interpretive stress', *Thesis Eleven*, No. 39.

Al-Azmeh, Aziz (1993) *Islam and Modernities*. London: Verso.

Appadurai, Arjun (1990) 'Disjuncture and difference in the global cultural economy', *Public Culture*, Vol. 2, No.2.

– (1996) *Modernity at Large: The Cultural Dimensions of Globalization*. Minneapolis: University of Minnesota Press.

– (2004) 'The Capacity to Aspire: Culture and the Terms of Recognition', in Vijayendra Rao and Michael Walton (eds), *Culture and Public Action*. New Delhi: Permanent Black.

Banaji, Dady Rustomji (1932) *Bombay and the Sidis*. Bombay: Macmillan.

Basu, Helene (1993) 'The Sidi and the Cult of Gori Pir in Gujarat', *Journal of Indian Anthropology*, 28: 289–300.

– (1998) 'Hierarchy and Emotion: Love, Joy and Sorrow in a Cult of Black Saints in Gujarat, India', in Pnina Werbner and Helene Basu (eds), *Embodying Charisma: Modernity, Locality and the Performance of Emotion in Sufi Cults*. London and New York: Routledge.

– (2004) 'Redefining Boundaries: Twenty Years at the Shrine of Gori Pir', in Amy Catlin-Jairazbhoy and Edward A. Alpers (eds), *Sidis and Scholars: Essays on African Indians*. New Delhi: Rainbow Publishers.

Bhabha, Homi (1996) *The Location of Culture*. London and New York: Routledge.

Bhargava, Rajeev (1999) 'Introduction', in Rajeev Bhargava, Amiya Kumar Bagchi, and R.Sudarshan (eds). *Multiculturalism, Liberalism and Democracy*. New Delhi: Oxford University Press.

Bharucha, Rustom (1993a) *Theatre and the World: Performance and the Politics of Culture*. London and New York: Routledge.

– (1993b) 'Notes on the Invention of Tradition', in Rustom Bharucha, *Theatre and the World: Performance and the Politics of Culture*. London and New York: Routledge.

– (1993c) 'Ninasam: A Cultural Alternative', in Rustom Bharucha, *Theatre and the World: Performance and the Politics of Culture*. London and New York: Routledge.

– (2000a) *The Politics of Cultural Practice: Thinking through Theatre in an Age of Globalization*. London: The Athlone Press and Hanover: Wesleyan University Press.

– (2000b) 'Thinking Through Culture: A Perspective for the Millennium', in Romila Thapar (ed.). *India: Another Millennium*? New Delhi: Viking.

– (2002) 'Between Truth and Reconciliation: Experiments in Theater and Public Culture', in Okwui Enwezor et al. (eds). *Experiments with Truth*. Germany: Hatje Kantz.

– (2003) *Rajasthan: An Oral History*. New Delhi: Penguin.

Bourdieu, Pierre (1977) *An Outline of a Theory of Practice*. Cambridge: Cambridge University Press.

– (1990) *The Logic of Practice*. Stanford: Stanford University Press.

Campbell, Gwyn (2006) 'The African-Asian diaspora: myth or reality?'. Keynote address presented at the TADIA conference on 'The Siddis of India and the African Diasporas in Asia', at International Centre, Goa, 9–20 January 2006.

Catlin-Jairazbhoy, Amy (2004) 'A Sidi CD? Globalization of Music and the Sacred', in Amy Catlin-Jairazbhoy and Edward A. Alpers, (eds), *Sidis and Scholars: Essays on African Indians*. New Delhi: Rainbow Publishers.

– (2006) 'Consequences of international touring among Sidis of Gujarat'. Paper presented at TADIA Conference on 'The Siddis of India and the African Diasporas in Asia', at International Centre, Goa, 9–20 January 2006.

– and Alpers, Edward A. (2004) *Sidis and Scholars: Essays on African Indians*. New Delhi: Rainbow Publishers.

Chatterjee, Partha (2004) *The Politics of the Governed*. New Delhi: Permanent Black.

Copy South Research Group (2006) *The Copy South Dossier: Issues in the Economics, Politics and Ideology of Copyright in the Global South*. http://www.copysouth.org

Harris, Joseph (1971) *The African Presence in Asia: Consequences of the East African Slave Trade*. Evanston: Northwestern University Press.

Lodhi, Abdul-Aziz Y. (2004) 'Sidhi, an East-African community in Gujarat: globalization in earlier days and their situation today'. Paper presented at the 18th European Conference on Modern South Asian Studies, 6–9 July Lund, Sweden.

Nandy, Ashis (1990) 'The Politics of Secularism and the Recovery of Religious Tolerance' in Veena Das. (ed.), *Mirrors of Violence*, New Delhi: Oxford University Press.

Nathan, Dev (2005) 'Capabilities and aspirations', *Economic and Political Weekly*, January 1.

Rao, Vijayendra and Walton, Michael (eds) (2000) *Culture and Public Action*. New Delhi: Permanent Black.

Sangari, Kumkum (1995) 'Politics of Diversity: Religious Communities and Multiple Patriarchies', *Economic and Political Weekly*, December 23 and 30.

Sassen, Saskia (2001) *The Global City: New York, London, Tokyo*. Princeton and Oxford: Princeton University Press.

Sen, Amartya (1985) *Commodities and Capabilities*. Amsterdam: Elsevier.

– (1999) *Development as Freedom*. New York: Knopf.

– (2004) 'How Does Culture Matter?', in Vijayendra Rao and Michael Walton (eds.), *Culture and Public Action*. New Delhi: Permanent Black.

Vanaik, Achin (1997) *Communalism Contested: Religion, Modernity and Secularization*. New Delhi: Vistaar Publications.

## CHAPTER 3

ETHNICITY AND WAR IN A WORLD OF NATION-STATES

Brian Min and Andreas Wimmer

A recent surge in fundamentalist terrorism, ethnic strife, and guerrilla insurgencies has led some to argue that the violence that characterizes the post-Cold War era reflects new imbalances in global and domestic economies, market changes in the availability of weapons, and the expansion of transnational markets for blood diamonds and oil to fund insurgencies. This chapter presents a historical perspective on rates of war around the world and evaluates some of the theories linking recent conflicts to globalization. We then present an alternative understanding of war trends, one that links war to the diffusion of the nation-state form across the globe over the past two centuries. The recent wave of wars may not be a qualitatively new phenomenon linked to unprecedented levels of globalization, but rather a new episode in a story that has evolved discontinuously over time.

Introduction

Over the last two centuries, periods of global peace and war have led observers to alternate between the hope for eternal peace and faith in institutions that would secure it and the fear that humanity will never be able break the cataclysmic cycles of violence that have characterized its history. In recent years, the end of the Cold War led to renewed optimism about a coming era of perpetual peace within a new global world order. Yet it seems that the end of the Cold War has led not to a pacific 'end of history' populated by friendly liberal democracies as Fukuyama (1992) once envisioned, but to a new global disorder replete with fundamentalist terrorism (Juergensmeyer 2000), ethnic strife (Chua 2003), guerrilla insurgencies (Fearon and Laitin 2003), an intensifying clash of civilizations (Huntington 1996), and a general increase in domestic and international political instability.

According to most observers, the violence that characterizes the post-Cold War era is more reflective of new imbalances in global and domestic economies, market changes in the availability of weapons, and the expansion of transnational markets for blood diamonds and oil to fund insurgencies, than simply a result of the shift in the global balance-of-power that the end of the Cold War has brought about. Indeed, so the argument goes, the increasing density of economic, cultural, and political connections between peoples around the world have created new political fault lines as well as new opportunities for ideologues, rebels, and terrorists to exploit these divides. In other words, these new theories of conflict suggest a strong link between globalization and the patterns of conflict observed in recent decades.

Some of these explanations share a concern for the way in which ethnic differences have been exacerbated in an era of globalization, and propose that the flames of ethnic conflict have been fanned by the breezes of rapid and unchecked economic, political, and cultural integration. This chapter presents a historical perspective on the rates of conflict and warfare around the world over the last two centuries and evaluates some of these theories linking recent conflicts to patterns of globalization. We then present an alternative understanding of war trends, one that links war to the diffusion of the nation-state form across the globe over the past two centuries. We maintain that the recent wave of wars may not be a qualitatively new phenomenon linked to unprecedented levels of globalization, but rather a new episode in a story that has evolved discontinuously over the past few centuries.

Rates of conflict around the world

Before we engage the literature on globalization and war, we evaluate some basic trends in the occurrence of war that have characterized the past two centuries. The historical record shows an enduring history of violence between and within

Figure 3.1 Number of ongoing wars around the world, 1816–2001

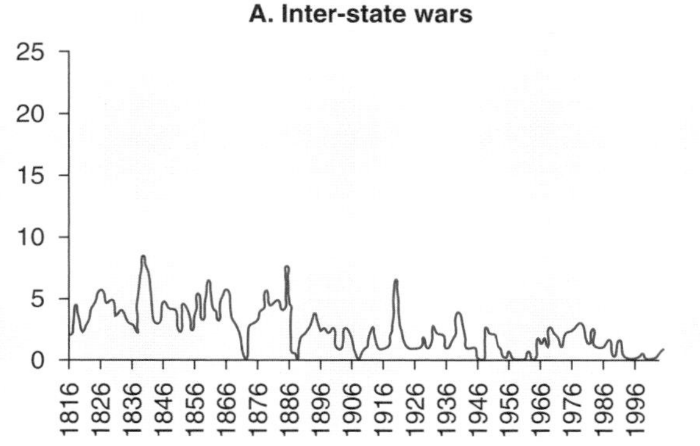

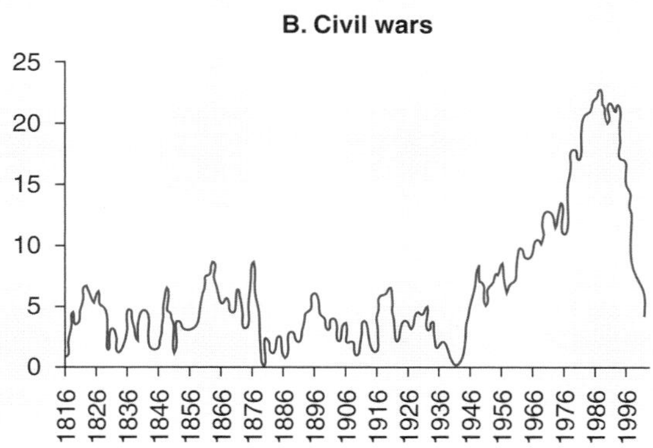

Source: Wimmer and Min, forthcoming

countries. Remarkably, there has not been a single year void of war over the last two hundred years, and perhaps for much longer than that. In every year for which we have reliable data, there has been at least one, and typically several more, violent civil or inter-state wars being fought whose death toll exceeded a thousand battle-deaths, the standard threshold for war used in most quantitative datasets. Figure 3.1 shows the number of ongoing civil and inter-state wars from 1816 to 2001.

Some observers at the end of the nineteenth century hoped that the future would bring pacific interdependence between the 'nations of the world' and peaceful human advancement. While the number of inter-state wars did decline, from 106 inter-state wars in the nineteenth century to 59 wars in the twentieth, there was no such emergence of a new peaceful order. The twentieth century would be marked by crisis over the collapse of empires and new geopolitical conflicts over the rise of fascism and communism. These would be fueled by advances in the killing efficiency of military technologies, helping to make the wars of the twentieth century significantly bloodier than those of the previous century. The number of wars, while exhibiting a secular decline, masks the real level of carnage and bloodshed associated with war since counting wars does not take the number of engaged state participants or the geographic scope of a war into account. Notably, the two World Wars count as one war each.

In the second half of the twentieth century, a slight surge in inter-state wars occurred during the 1970s and 1980s as the Cold War reached its height, followed by a near absence of inter-state war after the fall of the Berlin Wall. The only inter-state conflicts since 1989 with casualties exceeding the 1,000 battle death threshold include the first Gulf War in 1991, the Eritrean-Ethiopian conflict of the late 1990s, the Kosovo war in 1999, the long-standing skirmish in Kashmir between Pakistan and India, and the current conflict in Iraq.

Civil wars emerged in the twentieth century as an even more acute form of conflict. By some estimates, five times more people have died in civil wars (16.2 million) than in inter-state wars (3.3 million) in the post-World War II era (Fearon and Laitin 2003). It may surprise some that the average death toll of 130,000 per civil war has been roughly the same as the toll for inter-state wars since 1945.

During the nineteenth century, 115 civil wars were fought, a number that increased to 180 in the twentieth. It is not well known that the bloodiest civil war ever fought was the Taiping Rebellion in China (1850–1866) during which some 30 million lives were lost amid battle and famine. The uprising pitted Hong Xiuquan and his band of Heavenly

Brothers against the Qing court of Emperor Hsien-Feng. While the first half of the twentieth century indicated some promise of a decline in the rate of civil conflict, an extraordinary surge in the number of civil wars began in about the 1960s, peaking in the late 1980s. While the number of civil wars has dropped in the 1990s, they are still at historically high levels compared to the pre-World War II period. The timing of this surge and decline roughly mirrors the rise and fall observed for inter-state wars, leading some observers to link this pattern to the emergence and later the disappearance of Cold War rivalry between the superpowers. In 2004, there were ongoing civil wars in Darfur (Sudan), Uganda, Colombia, Chechnya (Russia), Nepal, and Kashmir (India).

What explains these fluctuations in the rates of war? How can we account for these changes in the pattern, scope, and purpose of wars? Why has the rate of inter-state wars declined while that for civil wars has risen? Among the difficulties in establishing coherent explanations of war has been a long-standing division of labor between scholars and analysts of inter-state wars and of civil wars (e.g., Levy 1998). This distinction emerged out of quantitative studies of war that began during the Cold War. Among the most important of these early studies were Quincy Wright's *A Study of War* (1942) which lists 278 wars of 'modern civilization' from 1480 to 1940, and Lewis Richardson's *Statistics of Deadly Quarrels* (1960) which lists 108 wars from 1820 to 1949. Both works introduced systematic classification of wars into different categories of intensity and purpose. Later, the groundbreaking Correlates of War (COW) project begun by J. David Singer and Melvin Small (1972; 1982) established an influential threefold typology of wars that included inter-state wars (between two or more independent state actors), intra-state wars (between an independent state actor and domestic rebels, as in civil wars), and extra-state wars (between an independent state and a non-state unit, as in colonial wars). Systematic country-level data generated by the COW project nourished an increasingly focused quantitative research tradition on wars and at the same time fostered a split between scholars of inter-state war and those interested in domestic conflicts, with each group adopting their own approaches, methods, and explanations.

In recent years, a new wave of scholarship has hastened a blurring of the traditional boundaries between the study of inter-state and of civil wars. While these war categories may have been useful during the Cold War era, some scholars have argued that the character of war has fundamentally changed in recent decades as a result of dramatic leaps in the intensity and reach of global interconnectedness. In purpose and in form, scholars like Kaldor (2001) argue, today's wars are intrinsically different from the traditional Clausewitzian state-to-state warfare that defined the 'old' wars of the era before the advent of globalization. We now discuss this first version of the globalization argument.

New wars

In today's globalized world, organized violence has taken on new forms that differ from the classic inter-state or civil wars of the past. These 'new wars' are occurring in greater frequency, particularly in Africa and Eastern Europe, and pursue a fluid set of objectives incorporating traditional violence between governments and political groups over state power, organized crime in pursuit of financial gain, and large-scale terrorizing of the civilian population. The wars are fought by armed networks of non-state and state actors, including paramilitary groups, terrorist cells, organized criminal groups, private military companies, and mercenaries. These networks tend to be formed around extreme political ideologies, often linked to nationalist and fundamentalist movements. To Kaldor and others, recent conflicts in Bosnia-Herzegovina, Somalia, Mozambique, and the Nagorno-Karabakh in the Transcaucasus typify the 'new war', which can be contrasted from wars of earlier eras in their differing goals, methods of warfare, and sources of financing.

According to these authors, the new wars are the results of two interrelated processes of globalization: the emergence of a global weapons market and the erosion of the capability of governments to uphold a monopoly on violence. The increased availability of weapons is linked to both the growing interconnectedness of states and non-state actors in the marketplace, as well as the surplus of weapons resulting from the buildup of arms during the Cold War. New networks among widely dispersed diasporas also facilitate the trade and flow of small arms and light weapons. Arguments about the weakening of the state cover more varied ground. Kaldor (2001) emphasizes the increasing role of international actors vis-à-vis the state. In the new wars, state institutions are under increased global scrutiny by non-governmental organizations like Médecins Sans Frontières, Oxfam, and the International Red Cross, international institutions like the Organization for African Unity (OAU), the North Atlantic Treaty Organization (NATO), or the United Nations (UN), and the watchful eye of the international press and media. The state monopoly on violence is eroded not only by well-armed domestic rebel groups but also by the growing role of international peacekeeping troops from the UN, foreign rebel groups, and private mercenaries and military companies like the South African-based Executive Outcomes. The privatization of violence has occasionally even been sanctioned by governments, as in the Balkan wars when political leaders encouraged the organization and activation of roving gangs (Eppler 2002).

States are also undermined by weakened government legitimacy, especially as globalization reduces the financial resources available to states to exercise power. International financial actors like the International Monetary Fund (IMF) and the World Bank (WB), through their emphasis on lean governments and tight fiscal and monetary controls, impose heavy financial pressures on states that are already weak and cash-strapped and perhaps further weakened by bad governance. Globalization thus speeds up the decline of state power and provides rebels with opportunity and motive to challenge their governments for control over land, resources, and people (Brzoska, 2004). Where states lack the resources to govern effectively, Munkler (2005) suggests that they are less able to compete with armed challengers who can fund themselves through participation in trade and smuggling or remittances from diasporas. With advances in the technology of warfare, even small and undisciplined bands of rebels can challenge and perhaps defeat better-equipped armed forces.

Other 'new war' accounts emphasize the lack of apparent political ideology or motive among insurgents. While many scholars implicitly hold that old civil wars were motivated by broad, well-defined, clearly articulated programs of social change, new civil wars tend to be motivated by concerns that often boil down to little more than simple private gain. For Kaplan (1993), civil conflicts in Africa are criminal pursuits fought by bandits, teenage hooligans, disenfranchised soldiers, and child-soldiers on drugs. Enzensberger (1994) describes the competing factions in new civil wars as 'warrior gangs'. These de-politicized entrepreneurs of violence use ethnic cleansing or even genocide as deliberate strategies to intimidate and terrorize and thus gain control over the civilian population.

Yet it remains doubtful whether the anecdotal evidence presented in the 'new war' literature is convincing. Kalyvas (2001) argues that perceived differences between post-Cold War conflicts and previous civil wars are attributable more to the lack of readily available conceptual categories and vocabulary in the post-Cold War era than to any structural change per se in the nature of war. Moreover, many new war accounts suffer from poor access to information, an over-reliance on journalistic accounts, and serious selection bias. The categorization of new wars may also reflect ethnocentric biases – a desire to characterize the conflicts of others as worse than one's own. The seeming irrationality of violence rests on a subjective judgment according to which the maimings by machete in Sierra Leone are less rational than killings by precision-guided bombs in Afghanistan. While violence appears meaningless in a large number of wars today, this may also be an appropriate judgment for previous conflicts. The levels of brutality, its seeming randomness, and its seeming lack of a rational logic, may not be as new as is claimed.

A central argument advanced by new war scholars is that the number of low-intensity guerrilla insurgencies has increased in recent years. Global time-series data reveal a less pronounced trend, however (Figure 3.2). While the absolute number of low-intensity conflicts has increased in recent decades, so also has the number of high-intensity wars. Thus in comparison, the share of low- and high-intensity conflicts has remained relatively stable in the post-World War II era. Three-quarters of all internal conflicts were of minor or

Figure 3.2 Civil conflicts by level of intensity

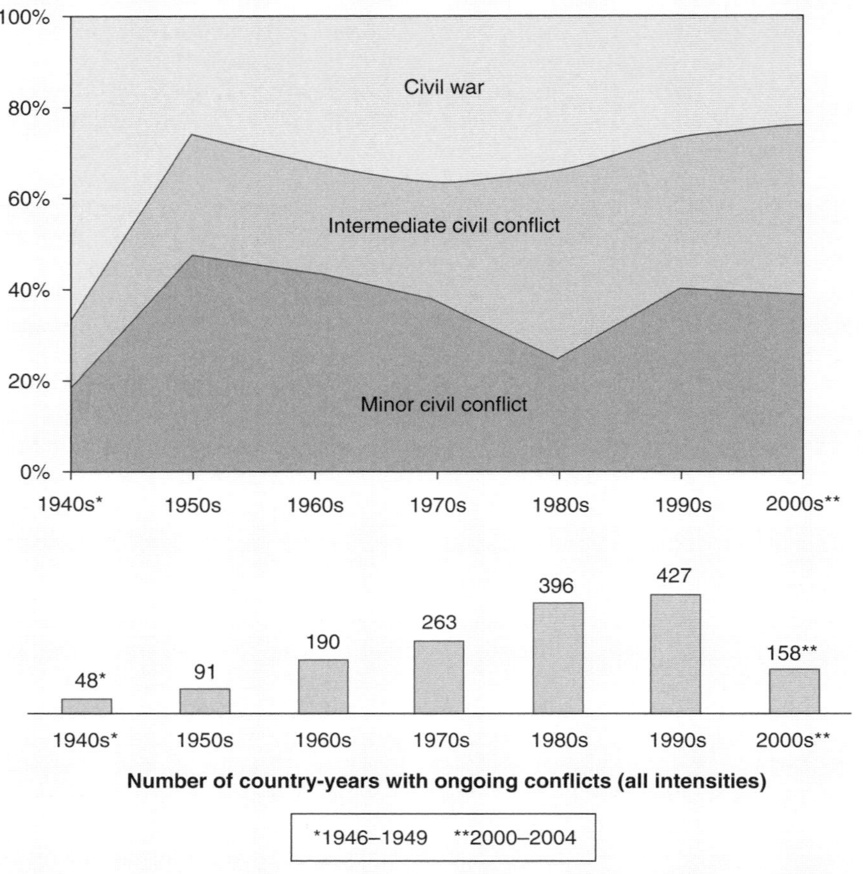

Source: Gleditsch et al. (2002)

intermediate intensity in the post-1990 era, compared with two-thirds in the prior two decades. This increase in the proportion of lower intensity conflicts should not be ignored, but neither does it seem to validate the strong claim that the nature of conflict has fundamentally changed in recent decades.

Still, the new war literature has provided important insights and many of the themes it emphasizes are now echoed in other strands of the research on war. Within the highly influential political economy literature on civil war , weak governments and access to lootable resources are among the most important predictors of civil conflict (Collier and Hoeffler 2001; Fearon and Laitin 2003; Sambanis 2004). The most common form of civil war in the post-World War II era has been stalemated guerrilla insurgencies fought in relatively confined rural areas in poor, post-colonial states (Fearon 2005), a conclusion consistent with the expectations of new war scholars. Most importantly, the new wars literature has contributed to a helpful softening of the long-standing division between research on inter-state wars and civil wars. Many recent wars, including conflicts in Congo, Sierra Leone, Liberia, Nigeria, and Rwanda, spill across borders and involve complex webs of foreign and transnational military and paramilitary troops (Rotberg and Mills 1998), defying any conventional categorization into a neatly contained domestic conflict or a state-to-state war fought by competing governments.

Ethnicity and war

What role does ethnicity play in international and domestic wars? This question has been widely debated in recent years as many influential scholars postulated that ethnic schisms are the basis of conflict in the post-Cold War era. Four variants of this argument can be discerned. Since the unifying force of ethnic identity that binds together individuals can also be the basis upon which others are excluded, the first argument suggests that ethnic or religious antagonisms may lead to friction and conflict both within countries and across them, especially once the centripetal power of authoritarian, communist states melts away in the thaw of the post-Cold War era (we call this the 'defrosting' hypothesis, as advocated by Barber (1992) and Kaplan (1993)). Secondly, many have pointed to the fact that most of the new states that have emerged after the end of Communism are extraordinary heterogeneous in ethno-religious terms and thus will experience higher levels of conflict than older, more homogeneous nation-states (the diversity argument, see, e.g., Nairn 1993). At the global level, the well known clash of civilizations hypothesis suggests that cultural and religious fault lines dividing humankind are likely to be the central source of conflict now that the struggle between capitalism and communism has largely been decided. Finally, Chua (2003) establishes a more direct link between ethnic violence and globalization: in many nations, global economic integration has enriched economically-dominant minorities while democratization has empowered poorer ethnic majorities, providing demagogues the opportunity to blame ethnic minorities for the impoverishment that open markets have brought to the less fortunate and competitive. We discuss this scapegoat hypothesis first.

In the era of globalization, Chua suggests that enterprising Chinese entrepreneurs have expanded their already significant wealth across Southeast Asia, where ethnic Chinese control all but 3 of the 70 most powerful business groups in Thailand, hold 70 percent of the market capitalization in Malaysia, and own all of the Philippines' largest and most lucrative department store, supermarket, and fast-food restaurant chains. Across these lands, anti-Chinese sentiment among the native populations has raged in recent years. In May 1998, violent rioting, looting, and fire-bombing across Indonesia targeted ethnic Chinese shop owners and their families, leaving over 2,000 dead and resulting in tens of billions of dollars of capital flight. To her eyes, globalization is fanning the flames of such ethnic conflicts around the world.

Chua supplements her story with case studies of Jews in Russia, Spaniards in Bolivia, whites in Zimbabwe, the Ibo in Nigeria, and other successful minority groups who have benefited from globalization at the perceived expense of an increasingly disgruntled ethnic majority. But hers is a selective list, selecting on the dependent variable in classic fashion by discussing only cases that support her argument. She overlooks the scholarship on trading minorities (Horowitz 1985: 113–24; Zenner 1991), which shows that rivalries between ethnic groups with uneven economic power are common throughout history but that violent episodes are rare given the prevalence of such relationships around the world. Chua squeezes as many conflicts as she can into her narrative, but some of her stories are less plausible than others. For instance, she is content with explaining Robert Mugabe's seizure of white-owned farms in Zimbabwe as a direct consequence of globalization without acknowledging the role of his Bonapartist ambitions to maintain power. She does not provide systematic empirical evidence to convincingly demonstrate that conflicts between ethnic groups on unequal economic footing are more severe or frequent today than in the past.

Let us now turn to the diversity and defrost arguments, which maintain that the new states created after the fall of Communism were so heterogeneous that conflict and war were almost inevitable once their centrifugal tendencies were no longer held in check by authoritarian governments. Many quantitative studies of the link between ethnic diversity and civil conflict have now been completed, though the results remain far from conclusive. In a widely cited study, Collier and Hoeffler (2001) found that during the 1960–99 period, the ethnic diversity of a country was a very poor predictor of civil war once differences in per capita income were taken into account. Some more recent research has generally confirmed this result (Fearon and Laitin 2003; Sambanis 2004). Others have argued that the polarization of a country (which is highest when a population is split evenly in two groups) is more important that its diversity (which is higher as the number of groups increases). Reynal-Querol (2002) finds that a country's religious polarization is an effective predictor of ethnic civil wars, although linguistic polarization seems to have no effect.

Many of these studies have relied upon estimates of ethno-linguistic diversity that are calculated on the basis of the survey of ethnic groups performed by Soviet scholars in 1960 (the so-called *Atlas Narodov Mira*). Users of this diversity measure can evaluate whether ethno-demographic constellations – the share of particular ethnic groups in a population – explain conflict. However, Cederman and Girardin (forthcoming) convincingly argue on the basis of their own cross-national research that rather than mere ethno-demographics, it is imbalances in the distribution of political power across different ethnic groups that matter, a thesis to which we will return.

The most prominent theory that relates ethno-cultural difference to new configurations of conflict is Samuel Huntington's well known thesis of a 'clash of civilizations' (Huntington 1996) replacing the old competition between communism and capitalism. The new conflicts would pit Western Christianity against Eastern Christianity, the Muslim World, Sub-Saharan Africa, Latin America, the Confucian Far East, or Hindu India. Conflicts between members of such civilizational blocks result from the re-shuffling of alliances after the end of the Cold War and from the increased levels of regional co-operation in the globalized world that has emerged since the 1970s. Despite some prominent recent cases that seem to lend support to the Huntington thesis, notably in the current Middle East conflicts, broad cross-national empirical analysis has not found strong support for the idea that conflicts have realigned along civilizational lines. Gurr (1994) finds that while communal conflicts across the Huntingtonian civilizational lines are more intense than others, their relative frequency had not increased in the first few years after the end of the Cold War. Russett, Oneal, and Cox's (2000) analysis of the Cold War years suggests that pairs of states split across civilizational boundaries are no more conflict-prone once traditional realist factors such as contiguity, alliances, relative power, and democratic interdependence are taken into account. Evaluating the 1946–1997 period, Chiozza (2002) finds no evidence linking civilizational differences to increased rates of conflict.

These arguments all predict an increase in levels of ethnic or nationalist conflict in recent years as a direct and indirect result of globalization. Figure 3.3 presents data on the proportion of civil wars that have been fought in the name of ethno-nationalist goals – either the establishment of new national states or a shift in the ethnic balance of power within existing states. The most pronounced trend visible from the graph is a steady and unprecedented rise in the share of ethno-nationalist civil wars beginning around 1930. This trend does not correspond to global trends in globalization as measured by flows of foreign capital, which only took off from the 1970s onwards; nor is it the effect of the end of the Cold War in 1989, as the defrost argument would predict. Rather, the constant rise in the share of ethno-national conflict may relate to the growing global legitimacy of nationalist claims from Wilson's 14 point program onwards. Second, when looking at both the nineteenth and twentieth centuries together, there appears to be no correlation between economic patterns of interdependence and rates of ethnic violence. The United Kingdom's celebrated repeal of its protectionist Corn Laws in 1846 helped usher in a 'Golden Age' of free trade embraced by many of Europe's great powers throughout the 1860s and 1870s. Yet this period coincides with the lowest rates of ethno-nationally-motivated civil wars witnessed during the last two centuries. Thus the recent rise in the share of such conflict could be linked to a diffusion process that is independent from economic globalization. To this diffusion process we now turn.

Figure 3.3 Ethno-nationalist civil wars as a share of all civil wars, 1825–2001

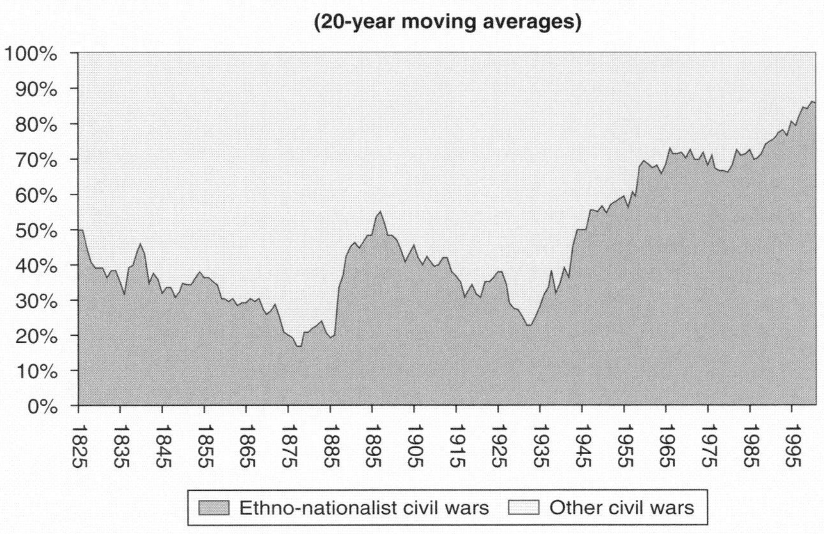

Source: Authors' coding; Wimmer and Min, forthcoming

The global diffusion of the nation-state form

Many of the accounts described above commonly assume that the wars of recent years are a new phenomenon, linked to processes of globalization that have been manifested in recent decades. But a different concept of globalization, one that emphasizes processes of diffusion of forms rather than growing interconnectedness, might recognize an even larger trend unfolding over the last two centuries – the global spread of a particularly modern form of political organization, the nation-state. Many of the wars of the modern era may be linked in timing and through actual causal mechanisms to the processes associated with the creation of nation-states. Indeed, many of the conflicts of recent decades have occurred in places where the nation-state form has only recently been introduced (e.g., the successor states of the Soviet Union), where the nation-building project is incomplete or in transition (e.g., Iraq), where attempts to build nation-states have failed or are under great duress (e.g., Congo-Kinshasa), or where nationalist movements pursue secession and seek their own nation-state (e.g., Chechnya). Seen from such a diffusionist, global point of view, the wars of recent decades are not dramatically different from the conflicts over the establishment of nation-states in earlier eras.

Today, almost all political units that make up the 'international community' are modern nation-states. Mainstream research on war assumes that such modern states are the relevant units of analysis to study, even in longitudinal studies that look across history. But only two centuries ago, the world represented a hodgepodge of imperial powers, dependent colonial territories, city states, absolutist kingdoms, and tribal societies. Today, over 95 percent of the world's surface area is governed by nation-states – polities that are based on the principle that each nation, i.e. a large group bound together by shared ancestry, culture, or language, should be housed in its own state. The pattern through which this regularity has emerged, as well as variations in the success with which nation-building projects have been pursued, can help illuminate many of today's global dynamics, including enduring and new patterns of violent conflict.

The nation-state form emerged out of developments in Europe including the Treaty of Westphalia and the emergence of national identities, particularly in France and England during the seventeenth and eighteenth centuries. This ideal spread rapidly throughout the nineteenth century, hastened by improvements in literacy, the development of civil societies, and discontent at rising taxation by warfaring absolutist states (Mann 1995). At the time, the world was dominated by empires which governed through indirect rule over a diverse and multi-ethnic populace that shared little common identity besides a vague notion of belonging to the same civilizational sphere.

Beginning in the early nineteenth century, waves of nation-state creation swept the world, sparked by the sequential crisis and dissolution of the world's major empires. The first wave followed the collapse of the Spanish empire. The second wave occurred after the First World War with the break up of the Ottoman and Habsburg empires. Another wave resulted after the Second World War when the Middle East as well as South and Southeast Asia were decolonized, followed by the final dismantling of the British and French colonial empires around 1960. The fifth occurred when the Portuguese colonial empire finally dissolved, and the sixth wave rolled over the Soviet and other communist empires during the early 1990s. As empires fell, new states were formed, established upon a new ideal that sought to house peoples of shared national ancestry within their borders. The six main waves of nation-state creation are discernible in Figure 3.4.

Throughout these different waves, nation-states emerged from nationalist movements who shared a common ideal: that each national group should govern itself, and that the government in turn should be representative of the ethno-national make-up of the population. In places where a common ethnic ancestry did not exist, new national identities were forged out of the memories of heroic struggles against the imperial enemy. Many of these nationalist movements encountered the resistance of the imperial center, for which losing territory represented a major set-back and challenge, given that territorial expansion represents a basic raison d'être of imperial polities. But the ability to repress nationalist movements diminished in parallel to the growing global acceptance of the principle of national self-determination. For example, the British Empire governed roughly a quarter of the world's population and a third of its land surface at its height near the beginning of the twentieth century. But by World War II, it was evident how threadbare and strained the power and reach of its colonial rule had become, ultimately portending the collapse of an empire over which the sun had once never set.

The spread of the nation-state represents one of the most important features of global political history of the past centuries. Never before has the world shared such an agreement about the form in which peoples and territories should be governed and about how these governments relate to one another in an international community (Meyer et al. 1997). This development is, obviously, not the result of some teleological force, but rather of the victory of powerful states which had an interest in the proliferation of international institutions. Since Woodrow Wilson declared his Fourteen Points plan in 1918, the global hegemon has become a major promoter for the spread of the nation-state form. From the League of Nations onward, the United Nations (UN), the World Trade Organization (WTO), the Organisation for Economic Co-operation and Development (OECD), are all clubs of nation-states that accept only similar entities as members – an important incentive for state-builders to organize along the principles of citizenship, democracy, and nationality that define modern statehood.

War in a world of nation-states

As the face of the globe changed from a world of empires to a world of independent, sovereign nation-states, politics also underwent fundamental changes, as did the aims and forms of war (Wimmer and Min forthcoming). In the imperial world, balance of power struggles were often aimed at securing geo-political advantages through the acquisition of new territories. But in the emerging world of nation-states, conquest for the purposes of territorial gain was less common. Acquisition of foreign lands and peoples lacked the same appeal for a nation-state established upon the principle that the state should be home to citizens of its nation alone.

The domestic relationship between governments and their citizens also changed dramatically. In

Figure 3.4 Number of nation-state creations (five-year periods), 1800 to 2000

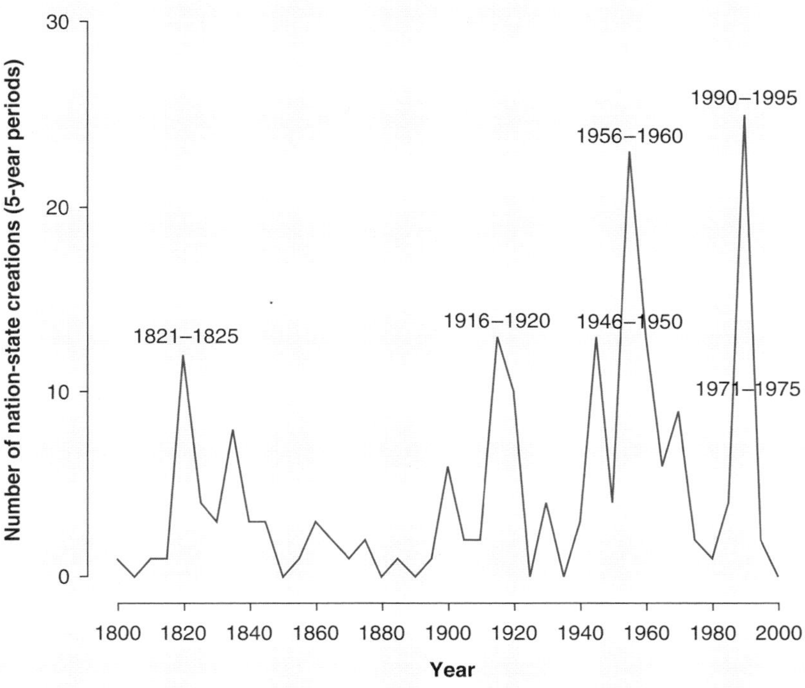

Source: Wimmer and Min, forthcoming

the new nation-states, governments were to be representative of the nationally defined people they ruled over; 'foreign rule' was thus no longer legitimate and became an indignity against which nationalist movements mobilized. Even given wide variations across democracies and autocracies, the principle of ethno-national representation is shared by all modern nation-states and sets them apart from imperial polities which ruled in the name of transcendental principles: the spread of modern civilization, the enlargement of the domains of Allah, the advancement of class-based revolution. These new patterns of political legitimacy would result in dramatic changes both in the purpose and scope of conflict in the modern era.

The emergence of the modern nation-state is linked to patterns of conflict in two important ways. First, the process of nation-state formation pursued by nationalist movements has often been contentious and mired in violence. The crisis that befell many of the world's empires opened a window of opportunity for nationalists seeking to break their stone out of the imperial mosaic of various ethnic, religious, and language groups. As mentioned before, nationalist movements were usually met by fierce resistance from imperial rulers. Moreover, competition within nationalist movements between factions with differing conceptions of the form, extent, and inclusiveness of the new state were often aggravated by competition from neighboring nationalist movements that sought claim to the same territory or peoples. In these struggles, ownership of the new state, its institutions, and its resources would be the ultimate prize, one whose value was often deemed worth the cost of war (Wimmer 2002). The recent wars in Yugoslavia are a good example of such complex processes in which various nationalist movements fight over the borders of the nation-state they envision against the receding forces of the central state. The first and second Balkan wars in Rumelia or the various Central American wars over the shape and borders of the successor states of the Spanish empire are other examples here.

Second, the new nation-states that emerged out of the ashes of fallen empires were far from perfect realizations of the nationalist ideal that 'like' should rule over ethnic 'likes'. The victories of nationalist movements were often products of compromise, political constraints, and geo-political negotiations. Many new states inherited at least some of the ethnic or linguistic or religious diversity of imperial society. However, following nationalist doctrine and institutional practice, political participation, equality before the law, and protection from arbitrary violence were reserved for members of the nation in the name of which the new state was supposed to govern (Wimmer 2002). The ruling elite, more often than not, systematically excluded ethno-national minorities from power, neglected their language or religion in the curricula of the newly founded 'national' schools, banned their language from official use, excluded their cultural heritage and history from the national sanctuary of museums and officially codified historical narratives. The legal and political status of minorities thus worsened dramatically (Noiriel 1991; Wimmer 2002) compared to what it had been in empires, when imperial rulers cared little about the ethno-national background of their subjects. The rise of the modern nation-state thus has been accompanied by increased competition over state institutions by groups frequently aligned along ethnic or national lines (Wimmer 1997), increasing the likelihood of violence and civil war in the years after nation-state creation.

Empirically, it is possible to investigate the relationship between nation-state creation and war by looking at *when* wars occur relative to moments of nation-state creation. In particular, do wars tend to occur with greater frequency either during or near periods of nation-state formation? The historical record reveals a clear pattern. Of 551 wars for which we have reliable data since 1816, 233 wars (42 percent) occurred within the 50-year period centered on the year of nation-state creation. In comparison the 50-year window preceding this formative period witnessed 71 wars (13 percent), while the 50-year window after the nation-state-formation period saw 113 wars (21 percent). The graph in Figure 3.5 reveals this time-dependency by depicting the likelihood of war in each year before and after the creation of a modern nation-state.

The basic pattern of a rising likelihood of war peaking around the time of nation-state formation remains remarkably constant across the several cohorts of nation-state formations described in Figure 3.4. Throughout history, periods of intense conflicts have been associated with the fall of an empire and the formation of new nation-states. Thus the fact that several of the most prominent recent wars have taken place in Sub-Saharan Africa and Eastern Europe is consistent with a pattern that has been observed in Western Europe, Southeast Asia, and the Far East in the decades following the collapse of empires in those regions. Seen from this point of view, the wars of the early twentieth century that accompanied the dismantling of the Ottoman empire and the subsequent conflicts between and within its successor states in the Balkans are structurally equivalent to the bloody conflicts that accompanied the end of imperial rule on the Indian subcontinent or the collapse of the Soviet empire and the wildfires of nationalist and separatist strife it ignited on its southern rim.

Recognition of this historical regularity linking nation-state formation to war should complement contemporary accounts of conflict that emphasize the role of globalization in accentuating societal divisions around the world. The weakness of states, for example, is often attributed as a root cause of domestic unrest and rebellion, and globalization is seen as an important reason why the state capacity to govern is deteriorating in many places. But state weakness may not simply be a product of globally-imposed fiscal and monetary constraints and the loss of steering capacities now controlled by supra-national institutions. Instead, the fundamental weakness of governments in many parts of the world may represent a crisis of legitimacy born out of struggling nation-building projects, especially as a result of failures to successfully offer equality before the law, protection from arbitrary violence, and political participation to all its citizens independent of their ethnic background. Members of excluded groups thus challenge the authority of the government, weakening its political support base and complicating its ability to perform even the most basic acts of collecting revenues and providing public services. In such environments, state weakness is directly linked to a particular form of nation-state formation, characterized by a weak

Figure 3.5 Nation-state creation and rates of war

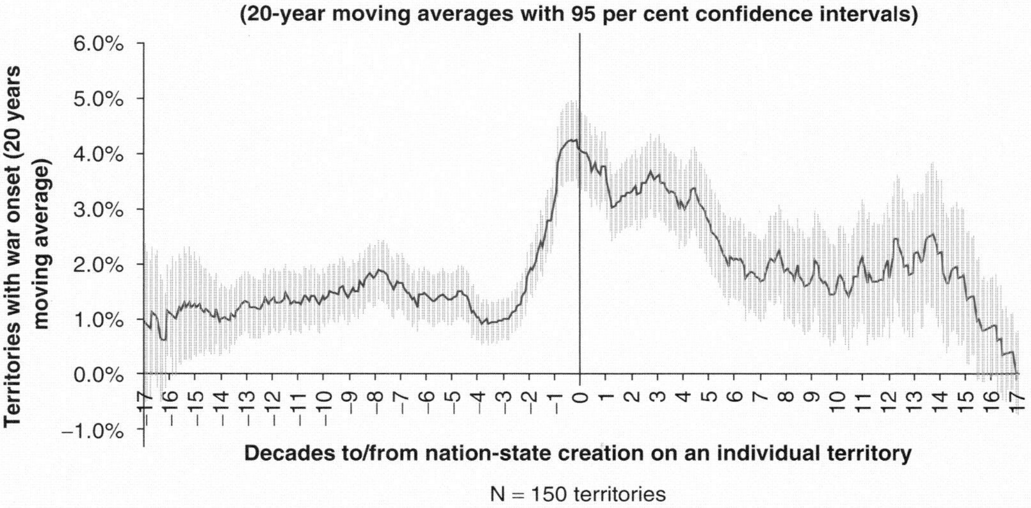

For date sources and codings see Wimmer and Min, forthcoming

civil society and strong , politically mobilized ethnic communities (for a more detailed argument see Wimmer 1997).

Ethnic conflicts thus have to be understood within this context of nation-state formation. It is not ethnodemographic heterogeneity per se, but rather the politics of exclusion and discrimination along ethnic lines which may lead to ethnic political mobilization and the spiraling up of conflicts. It is not ethnic diversity or cultural heterogeneity as such that led to conflictive relationships between Hutu and Tutsi in Rwanda, Jews and Palestinians in Israel, Sunni and Shi'a Muslims, Maronite Catholics, and the Druze and Alawite sects in Lebanon, but rather critical choices made by political elites during the transition from colonial dependency to independent nation-state, which led to the exclusion of Muslim and Christian Arabs in the late 1940s in Israel, Hutus in the early 1960s in Rwanda, etc. For reasons beyond the scope of this chapter, a more inclusive, multi-ethnic nation-building project was pursued in Switzerland from 1848 onwards, in Canada after Confederation, Cameroon after de-colonization and in independent Malaysia.

From the point of view that we are advocating here, globalization is seen as a discontinuous process of the diffusion of political and cultural forms, rather than a continuous process of growing inter-connectedness. The effects of this diffusion, to be sure, are far from uniform and homogeneous (cf. Wimmer 2001). The introduction of the nation-state form in the late eighteenth-century United States had different consequences and followed a different political logic than the transformation of Bosnia into a multi-ethnic national state some 200 years later. And yet, the shift from universalist claims of political legitimacy and trans-ethnic political inclusion to the nation-state model that rests on the particularistic logic of nationalism triggered structurally similar processes of transformation – even if these unfold along different pathways and lead to widely varying political outcomes. Many of these pathways of transformation imply a heightened risk of both inter-state and civil wars. Seen from this perspective, the waves of war that swept over the globe after the end of the Cold War may not so much be a product of intensified 'globalization,' but rather the result of yet another episode of transformation: the emergence of a new cohort of young nation-states from the ashes of the various Communist empires. While history never repeats itself, some of the causal forces at work may remain constant (cf. Collier and Mazukka forthcoming).

Conclusion

Without question, the world has been changing rapidly in recent decades. Globalization is leading to unprecedented levels of economic, political, and cultural integration between and within states. Many observers have linked globalization to the surge in violent conflicts that has accompanied the end of the Cold War. Some have maintained that globalization has weakened the capacity of existing states to uphold the monopoly of violence. Others believe that those who lose out in an increasingly competitive and unsure economic environment turn their frustration against successful minorities, thus igniting the fires of ethnic conflict. According to still others, the new states that have appeared after the end of Communism are ethnically too heterogeneous to evolve peacefully. Finally, Huntington has argued that the end of the Cold War has led to a re-alignment of global constellations of alliances along the lines of the major world religions, thus leading to intensified conflict on the borders between such civilizational areas.

Yet a longer historical perspective suggests that many of the conflicts of recent years may be comparable in purpose and cause to those of earlier periods. One of the major stories of institutional history over the last two centuries has been the demise of empires and their replacement by a system of sovereign nation-states. The processes associated with the formation of the nation-state, particularly over the national character of the state and decisions about who to include or exclude from the privileged state-owning nation, have been the source of many of the world's conflicts, and represent the basis upon which many of today's conflicts unfold.

REFERENCES

Barber, Benjamin (1992) 'Jihad vs. McWorld', *The Atlantic Monthly*, 269 (3): 53–65.

Brzoska, M. (2004) '"New wars" discourse in Germany', *Journal of Peace Research,* 41 (1):107–117.

Cederman, Lars-Erik, and Girardin, Luc (Forthcoming) in *American Political Science Review.* Beyond Fractionalization: Mapping Ethnicity onto Ethno-Nationalist Insurgencies.

Chiozza, G. (2002) 'Is there a clash of civilizations? Evidence from patterns of international conflict involvement, 1946–97', *Journal of Peace Research,* 39 (6): 711–34.

Chua, Amy. (2003) *World on Fire: How Exporting Free Market Democracy Breeds Ethnic Hatred and Global Instability*, 1st edn. New York: Doubleday.

Collier, P., and Hoeffler A. (2001) *Greed and Grievance in Civil War.* Washington: World Bank. http://www.worldbank.org/research/conflict/papers/greedandgrievance.htm

Collier, Ruth Berins and Mazzuca, Sebastián. (Forthcoming) 'Does History Repeat?' in Charles Tilly and Robert E. Goodin, *Contextual Political Analysis.* Oxford: Oxford University Press.

Enzensberger, Hans Magnus (1994) *Civil Wars: from L.A. to Bosnia.* New York: New Press: Distributed in the United States by W.W. Norton.

Eppler, Erhard (2002) *Vom Gewaltmonopol zum Gewaltmarkt? [From the Monopoly of Violence to a Market of Violence?].* Frankfurt am Main: Suhrkamp.

Fearon, J. D.(2005) 'Civil war since 1945: some facts and a theory'. Paper read at Annual meeting of the American Political Science Association, September 1–4, at Washington, DC.

– and Laitin, D. D., (2003). 'Ethnicity, insurgency, and civil war', *American Political Science Review,* 97 (1): 75–90.

Fukuyama, Francis (1992) *The End of History and the Last Man.* New York: Free Press.

Gleditsch, Nils Petter, Wallensteen, Peter, Eriksson, Mikael, Sollenberg, Margareta, and Strand, Hirard (2002) 'Armed Conflict 1946–2001: A New Data set', *Journal of Peace Research*, 39 (5): 615–37.

Gurr, T. R. (1994) 'Peoples against states – ethnopolitical conflict and the changing world-system 1994 Presidential–Address', *International Studies Quarterly,* 38 (3):347–77.

Horowitz, Donald L. (1985). *Ethnic groups in conflict.* Berkeley: University of California Press.

Huntington, Samuel P. (1996). *The Clash of Civilizations and the Remaking of World Order.* New York: Simon & Schuster.

Juergensmeyer, Mark (2000) *Terror in the Mind of God: The Global Rise of Religious Violence. Comparative Studies in Religion and Society: 13.* Berkeley: University of California Press.

Kaldor, Mary (2001) *New and Old Wars: Organized Violence in a global era; with an afterword, January 2001.* Stanford, CA: Stanford University Press.

Kalyvas, S. N. (2001) "New" and "old" civil wars a valid distinction?' *World Politics* 54 (1): 99–118.

Kaplan, Robert D. (1993) *Balkan Ghosts: A Journey Through History*, 1st edn New York: St Martin's Press.

Levy, J. S. (1998) 'The causes of war and the conditions of peace'. *Annual Review of Political Science* 1:139–165.

Mann, Michael (1995) 'A Political Theory of Nationalism and its Excesses', in Sukumar Periwal, *Notions of Nationalism*. Budapest: Central European University.

Meyer, John, Boli, John, Thomas George M. Ramirez and Francisco O. (1997) 'World society and the nation-state', in *American Journal of Sociology,* 103 (1): 144–81.

Munkler, Herfried (2005) *The New Wars*. Cambridge, UK; Malden, MA: Polity.

Nairn, Tim (1993) 'All Bosnians now?', *Dissent,* Fall: 403–10.

Noiriel, Gérard (1991) *La tyrannie du national, le droit d'asile en Europe (1973 – 1993)*. Paris: Calmann-Lévy.

Reynal-Querol, M. (2002) 'Ethnicity, political systems, and civil wars', *Journal of Conflict Resolution,* 46 (1): 29–54.

Richardson, Lewis Fry (1960). *Statistics of Deadly Quarrels*. Pittsburgh: Boxwood Press.

Rotberg, Robert I. and Mills, Greg (1998). *War and Peace in Southern Africa: Crime, Drugs, Armies, and Trade*. Washington, DC: Brookings Institution Press.

Russett, B. M., Oneal, J. R. and Cox M. (2000). 'Clash of civilizations, or realism and liberalism déjà vu? Some evidence', *Journal of Peace Research,* 37 (5): 583–608.

Sambanis, N. (2004) 'What is Civil War? Conceptual and Empirical Complexities of an Operational Definition'. *Journal of Conflict Resolution* 48 (6): 814–858.

Singer, J. David and Small, Melvin (1972) *The Wages of War, 1816–1965: A Statistical Handbook*. New York: Wiley.

Small, Melvin and Singer, J. David. (1982) *Resort to Arms: International and Civil Wars, 1816–1980*. 2nd edn. Beverly Hills, CA: Sage Publications.

Wimmer, Andreas (1997) 'Who owns the state? Understanding ethnic conflict in post-colonial societies', *Nations and Nationalism,* 3 (4): 631–65.

– (2001). 'Globalisations *avant la lettre*. A comparative view on isomorphization and heteromorphization in an interconnecting world', *Comparative Studies in Society and History* 43 (3): 435–66.

– (2002) *Nationalist Exclusion and Ethnic Conflict: Shadows of Modernity*. Cambridge, UK; New York, NY, USA: Cambridge University Press.

– and Min, Brian. (Forthcoming) 'From Empire to Nation-state: Explaining Wars in the Modern World, 1816 to 2001' Manuscript under review.

Wright, Quincy (1942) *A Study of War*. Chicago, IL: The University of Chicago Press.

Zenner, Walter P. (1991) *Minorities in the Middle: A Cross-cultural Analysis, SUNY Series in Ethnicity and Race in American Life*. Albany: State University of New York Press.

## CHAPTER 4

RESISTANCE TO CULTURAL GLOBALIZATION – A COMPARATIVE ANALYSIS

Laura Adams, Miguel Centeno and Charles Varner

Resistance to globalization is a complex process that always takes place within a local context where the globalization process is represented by a concrete target of resistance. We examine cases where the state has employed three different frameworks in resisting cultural globalization processes: anti-hegemonic, post-colonial, and diasporic. In Canada, Kazakhstan, and Malaysia respectively, policies are generated in response to a specific threat related to cultural globalization. Specifically, we examine policies related to cultural trade, media, language, and religion and explore how states employ these policies within their local framework of resistance.

From the first discussions of contemporary globalization, its documented rise has been accompanied by an almost simultaneous wave of resistance. For every Thomas Friedman extolling the beneficent inevitability of globalization, a José Bové has expressed a reluctance to be part of a single world system. Obviously, economic tensions and anxieties have played a significant role, but no issue seems to bring forth more of an emotional response than the threat (or promise) of cultural globalization.

In a few cases, this opposition simply reflects a generic and isolationist aversion to external influences. Jingoistic 'know-nothingness' may be found in practically every nation, with few historical or geographical exceptions. Much more common, however, is an explicit fear of a particular form of cultural imperialism. In this case, it is not so much that a society rejects external links in a blanket manner, but that another culture is seen as representing a specific threat; that is, the opposition does not come from a simple desire to be autarkic, but reflects a strongly felt fear of cultural subjugation by a powerful outsider. In this essay we emphasize the latter form of anti-globalization; our attention is on binary oppositions. We do not do this because the more general form of cultural conflict and resistance is unimportant. Rather we emphasize these more 'bilateral' fights because: a) they tend to be more concrete and involve policy actions, and b) even in a globalized world, conflicts tend to be between individual players.

We begin by sharing the definitions of culture and globalization discussed in the co-editors' 'Introduction'. For us, globalization involves increasing connectivity, while culture includes a broad sense of national identity. What we are calling resistance stems from the perception of a threat that increasing connectivity will lead to the dilution or even pollution of a national culture. These threats are particularly significant when power is seen as asymmetric. The asymmetries may arise out of political or military threats, demographic competitions, or simply perceptions that the external culture is just 'too attractive'. While many individuals in a variety of societies may perceive these threats, we are focusing on the manner in which resistance has been institutionalized through government policy. We believe that these deserve privileged attention as they are the first challenge to the creation of any form of global governance that would allow for conflicts to be mediated.

While focusing on three cases, we believe that they represent generalizable examples that will allow us to think about larger questions dealing with culture and conflict including notions of intractable 'civilizational' clashes, oppositions between 'modern' and 'traditional' forms of life, the coexistence of differing cultures within the same nation-state, and the balance between the defense of the freedom to choose and the defense from imperial practices. We next provide a framework with which to study and compare these resistances and then provide three examples of resistance that allow us to explore them in greater detail.

Frameworks of resistance to cultural globalization

While a great deal of attention has been devoted to broad movements criticizing a general form of globalization, specifically economic integration, we contend that a much more important area of contention includes active resistance to cultural globalization. By resistance we mean concrete steps either to establish barriers preventing 'external' influences from becoming dominant, or to provide support for 'authentic' or indigenous cultural practices. These forms of interactions do not necessarily involve a rejection of a globalized world or of greater integration, but originate in a desire to maintain at least a modicum of the 'local' within the more broadly 'global'.

We are interested in resistance rather than some sort of assimilation. Resistance is interesting because cultures are usually quite flexible at adapting new elements. Usually this indicates a politicization of culture. We are especially interested in how this resistance is transformed into policy. Obviously this means that we are ignoring many other conflicts. For example, for a form of resistance to have a policy outcome it must already include powerful actors among its allies. The fact that a 'threatened' culture can create policies meant to defend itself already implies a significant amount of influence if not national dominance. We are particularly interested in analyzing why resistance emerges, how it institutionalizes itself and the degree to which it seems to succeed in creating privileged spaces.

We start our discussion with the notion of frameworks of cultural resistance. By frameworks we mean how a particular population and its political agents see their situation: the origin and power of the threat and the best way to resist it. Our categories do not necessarily reflect the realities of cultural conflict (but by definition these may be impossible to establish), but focus rather on how threats are perceived and policies implemented to resist those perceptions. Resistance to cultural globalization is an example of a larger phenomenon of responses to cultural conflict. In this section we will examine the analytical dimensions of cultural conflicts more generally and specify what we see as those that are especially significant for the case of resistance to cultural globalization. These dimensions are not exhaustive, but account for the significant things to look for when comparing different kinds of conflict. Also, this schema (Figure 4.1) represents conflicts in an overly simple way, as consisting of two opposing forces, a protagonist and an antagonist, if you will:

- The first dimension is whether the target of the response (the antagonist) is internal or external to the protagonist society. Perceptions of the origin of the 'threat' are obviously important, not just for categorizing the perceived other, but also in defining the possible tool kit of policies available.
- The second dimension focuses on the action proposed by the response or how the protagonist determines to react to the threat. A reactive or negative response ('we must stop this') seeks to create walls around the host society in order to prevent the 'contamination'. A positive or proactive response ('we must create something new') seeks to create a privileged space for the domestic culture.
- Our third dimension is the scope of the response, ranging from a total attack on all aspects of the threat to a partial response dealing with particular aspects of the perceived threat. This is important for distinguishing between across the board rejections of a culture (usually with racialist or essentialist overtones) to more specific objections regarding one or another manifestation of its relationship to the domestic culture.
- The fourth and final dimension is the tone of the response which can range from offensive ('this is bad') to defensive ('we're just as good'). In the former, emphasis is placed on why a domestic culture needs to be protected while in the latter the emphasis is more on what it has to offer.

We can use these four dimensions to discuss specific cases of cultural conflict and isolate critical structural properties. For example, according to our schema, efforts such as the Nuremberg racial laws can be categorized as internal, reactive, total, and offensive. 'Red scares' are similar, but with more of perception of externality. Fundamentalist movements share some characteristics of these, but may differ as to scope and tone. Post-colonial movements, on the other hand, often were much more proactive and partial in their responses. 'Obscenity' regulations for cultural imports involve reactive, partial, and defensive frames.

It is also important to understand that conflicts take place on different levels of society, and that the scale of analysis chosen has implications for what you will find in terms of a response's efficacy, impact and durability. The three basic levels of analysis are states, non-state institutions, and grassroots movements.

Figure 4.1 Dimensions of cultural conflicts

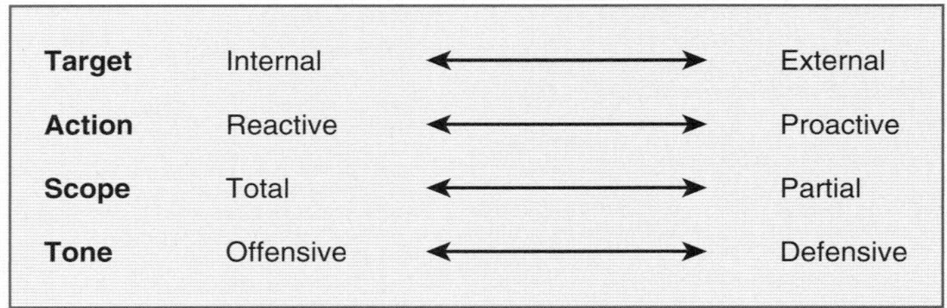

States have varying capacities, which affects the efficacy of their responses to conflict, especially when the state response does not resonate with the population or is not practical to implement. However, state responses can have a higher impact and be more durable than the responses of other societal groups. Non-state institutions are fairly efficacious at implementing specific responses which tend to be fairly durable, but the impact tends to be limited since it is only within the purview of that particular institution or organization. On the grassroots level of analysis, responses tend not to be very efficacious in attaining the desired results (without the help from organizations or the state), but, if widespread and enacted in daily life practices, can have a high impact and be very durable. For the sake of brevity, in this chapter we focus on state responses to cultural conflict and examine in more detail the efficacy, impact and durability of legislation designed to resist cultural globalization.

The defining feature of resistance to cultural globalization, as opposed to other types of cultural conflict, is located on the first dimension of response: target. By definition, the target of resistance to globalization will be located in some respect at a distance from the protagonist community. However, this distance varies, with a varying relationship to other aspects of resistance, such as the tone of resistance. In order to illuminate these differences within the category of resistance to cultural globalization, we will examine three cases at differing points along the dimension of target location, and we will examine how cultural legislation in these three cases accordingly differs in its proposed action, scope, and tone depending in part on the protagonist's physical distance from the target of its resistance.

The three cases we will examine are Canada, whose cultural legislation reflects what we term an anti-hegemonic response to its target, the United States; Kazakhstan, whose legislation is wrapped up in a post-colonial framework that targets both local Russian populations and the continuing dominance of Russian culture coming from Russia; and Malaysia, whose legislation reflects an anti-diaspora framework that targets local populations of Chinese and Indian immigrants who are seen as posing a threat to indigenous local culture.

Canada and the anti-hegemonic framework of resistance

A globalizing force can appear 'hegemonic' if its domination is so pervasive and inescapable that nations and cultures feel that some resistance is critical for survival no matter its futility. Such resistance need not be a product of a rejection of the dominant culture (although that may play a role), but a defensive measure to hold back the flood. We may expect that it would be expressed not so much as antipathetic to the culture in question, but defensive of the ability of the local culture to survive. We use the term hegemonic in this instance not to describe a 'Gramscian' reality of cultural domination, but the perception of a hegemonic project by a society.

How to control such cultural trade? Should such transactions be controlled by the same mechanisms that apply for merchandise trade with perhaps more neutral content? The US media industry

Table 4.1 Foreign Market Share (1997)

Cinema	95%
Music Sold	84%
Magazines	83%
Radio	70%
Books	70%
English Language TV	60%

Source: Heritage Canada

Table 4.2 Canada

	Broadcasting and Mass Media: Canada has established quotas requiring Canadian content on TV and radio (usually around 30%, but some ambiguity regarding times and definition of Canadian content). Subsidies of around US$50 million per year. Some preferential licensing for Canadian satellite channels. Attempts to tax "split-run" magazines.
Target	US
Action	Reactive: limit investment by US media companies (MAI).Quotas for Canadian production in TV and radio.Controlling flow of split-run magazines.
Scope	Partial—does not seek to exclude dominant culture, but protect some areas for Canadian products. Some complaints from European firms that efforts to limit US media flow adversely affect them as well. Interesting intra-Canada concerns as French language restrictions in Quebec (requiring 65% French language content) mean that English language Canadian acts get underplayed.
Tone	Defensive. Relatively little effort to foster a 'Canadian' product through subsidies, etc. (à la France). Recent (2003) reductions in Canadian federal government support for Canadian television Fund.
Efficacy/impact	Moderate efficacy: compliance of letter of law is significant, but consumer reaction limits real reach of Canadian media. (enforced at high level; low level not clear), moderate–low impact (most adults not affected).

has been active in making sure that cultural products are covered by the standard free trade agreements. GATT's 1947 agreement, however, allowed for national quotas. These battles (largely against US media if implicitly, not explicitly) continued in the Uruguay and Doha rounds and are being fought within the WTO. The extent to which a different set of rules will apply to cultural products will be a major point of discussion in the ongoing debate regarding twenty-first century globalization.

The Canadian experience will no doubt serve as a major reference point. Earlier than any other country affected by globalization's cultural flows, Canada has had to deal with the 'Mouse–Elephant' problem: what does a smaller country with its own cultural framework do to defend itself from the influence of a next door giant? These have been issues in Canada ever since the creation of the Dominion in the nineteenth century, but the willingness, ability and perceived need of the Canadian state to respond to American cultural dominance dramatically increased in the post-World War II era. Beginning in the late 1960s with Prime Minister Trudeau, Canada created a series of cultural barriers assuring some presence of Canadian arts in mass media. More recently, Canada has partnered with France in seeking 'cultural exemptions' from WTO regulations. After the ratification of NAFTA, fears of a 'cultural meltdown' (*New York Times*, July 18, 2001, p. E10) have made these regulations even more salient. What is particularly interesting in the Canadian case is the perceived similarity between the 'origin' and 'host' countries: the fear is that 'too little' difference between the United States and Canada will make the eradication of Canadian culture easy. The pressures on Canada to maintain some cultural autonomy are clear from any perusal of the penetration of foreign (overwhelmingly US) media (Table 4.1).

There is a very clear political line here with some advocating the openness and greater efficiency of a continental media market and others expressing fear that Canada will become a 'northern Puerto Rico with an EU sensibility' (*Mcleans*, November 25, 2002, p. 18.) According to our schema, the Canadian case may be analyzed as in Table 4.2.

Kazakhstan and the post-colonial framework of resistance

Post-colonial societies perceive the threat of cultural globalization as looming on two fronts. The first is global consumer culture, which threatens to replace traditional culture with imported commodities. The second is the culture of their colonizer, which threatens both from the outside, via continued domination of local markets by the colonizing country, and from the inside, via the internalized colonial mentality that relegates the local culture to a lower status (Prakash 1995: 3). However, in post-colonial societies, defenders of local culture are also learning how to make use of the networks and flows of globalized culture to defend against the culture of the colonizer (Tomlinson 1991). Globalization in some ways helps post-colonial societies manage the asymmetrical cultural relationships that are a product of colonialism.

The introduction of both globalized consumer culture and the open struggle against the culture of the colonizer come into focus if we examine a case such as Kazakhstan, which is in the process of developing its post-colonial framework during a time of intensive globalization. The Kazakhs are a Turkic people who lived as pastoral nomads until the Soviet period. The proportion of Slavs in the population grew from the late 1800s thanks to policies of the Russian and Soviet empires encouraging agricultural colonization and, under the Soviets, the assignment of technical specialists to developing regions. The proportion of Kazakhs in the population declined during the 1930s due to death and migration caused by the Soviet collectivization campaign. Just before independence, Kazakhs were less than 40 percent of the population of Kazakhstan (Gosudarstvennyi Komitet SSSR po Statistike 1992). Following a mass emigration of Europeans in the mid-1990s, the population of Kazakhstan stood at 15 million in 1999, 53 percent of whom were ethnic Kazakhs (Agentstvo Statistike 2000: 21–22).

The Kazakh response to Russian colonialism has been mild, with the exception of some uprisings in the early part of the twentieth century and a few violent protests toward the end of the Soviet period (Schatz 2005). For the most part, Kazakhs have internalized the worth of European culture and many urban Kazakhs grew up in the Soviet period speaking Russian as their first language (Dave 2004). In this context, we can explore the dimensions of cultural conflict in post-Soviet Kazakhstan as an example of a post-colonial framework of resistance to cultural globalization: the target is both internal (the colonized mentality and the remaining settler population) and external (the continuing colonial domination of culture markets); the actions proposed tend to be proactive, intended to reaffirm and bolster local culture rather than being concerned with 'pollution', (in part because the colonized mentality sees local culture as more polluting in the first place); the scope of the response varies among post-colonial societies and is related to the political conditions of decolonization; and the tone of the response tends to be defensive, in part because of continued dependence on the colonizer and, again, in part because of the colonized mentality. In Kazakhstan, the post-colonial framework of resistance will be examined in light of two pieces of legislation adopted in the decade following independence: language laws and broadcasting laws.

Kazakhstan's language laws

During the Soviet period, Kazakh language schools, publications and broadcasts existed, but took a second place to their Russian counterparts. Promoting the status of Kazakh was one of the main issues around which nationalists rallied in the late 1980s (Olcott 1995). Independent Kazakhstan's constitution specifies that Kazakh is the state

Table 4.3 Kazakhstan

	Official Language	Broadcasting and Mass Media
Target	Internal – local Russophones	External – primarily Russian media companies
Action	Proactive – teach more Kazakh	Reactive – stop domination of Russian language and content
Scope	Partial – consequences only for politicians, implementation not specified at other levels	Total, within the sphere of broadcasting – applied to state- and privately-owned outlets
Tone	Defensive	Defensive
Efficacy/impact	Moderate efficacy (enforced at high level; low level not clear), moderate–low impact (most adults not affected)	Low efficacy (low capacity to enforce), moderately high impact (widespread attempts to comply)

language, but its scope is partial because Russian has equal status to Kazakh in state institutions. This is rather different from the post-colonial reaction of some other former Soviet republics, which instituted barriers to full citizenship based on command of the local language (Laitin 2002). The 1997 language law was a proactive measure to restore Kazakh rather, though some supported it as a sanction against those who continued to use Russian.

This outcome was the result of a broader process of cultural globalization related to the spread of two kinds of cultural norms: both Soviet internationalist norms and globalized norms of governance support Kazakhstan's attempt to promote its own language and culture so long as the legislation does not infringe too much on the rights of minorities. Although the cultural opportunities for linguistic minorities are not legally restricted, those with political aspirations who refuse to learn Kazakh are restricted because the president and the heads of parliamentary bodies must have 'perfect command of the state language'. Unfortunately, the state lacks the capacity to create the kind of mass adult education campaign that would provide opportunities to learn Kazakh to all who want them, limiting the impact this law can have (Dave 2004).

Kazakhstan's broadcasting laws

In contrast, Kazakhstan's broadcasting laws are a reactive move against both Russian dominance over local media and against the saturation of local markets with global media products. Kazakhstan's 1999 law on the mass media states that 50 percent of all programming broadcast on radio and television must be in the Kazakh language. An amendment to the law also limits the rebroadcast of foreign-produced programming to 20 percent of a broadcast station's total airtime. Again, implementation is a problem as the government and independent media producers alike lack the capacity to fulfill this mandate, due to the lack of available programming and the expense involved in dubbing or producing new content. In 2003, the lower house of parliament passed a law further restricting foreign ownership of newspaper and television outlets, but President Nazarbayev vetoed the law.

Malaysia and the diasporic framework of resistance

Diasporas within national boundaries can transform amorphous fears of external influence into concrete perceptions of specific threats to national identity. We might expect such perceptions to generate reactive responses. However, the relative size and economic strength of diasporas limit the ability of the titular population to use exclusion as a means of cultural resistance. In Malaysia, large and prosperous Chinese and Indian diasporas have led ethnic Malays to pursue a more subtle form of resistance. Laws and policies promote commonality but at the same time preserve special cultural spaces for ethnic Malays (see the contribution of Diana Wong, chapter 22).

Ethnic Malays have a long history of external influence. B. W. Andaya and L. Y. Andaya suggest that Malays have developed a 'self-confident' approach to outsiders (1982: 299). However, British colonial rule created economic demands for Chinese laborers and businesspeople and Indian plantation workers (Haque 2003; Harding 1996). Concentrated in lower paying agricultural jobs, ethnic Malays' socioeconomic status declined relative to the two immigrant groups. By 1957, the average ethnic Malay earned 59 percent of the average Indian income and only 46 percent of the average Chinese income (Mah, as cited in Haque 2003). Malaysia gained independence in this context of increasing demographic and economic competition. The departing British helped orchestrate a political coalition among the three groups (Lee 2004). Ethnic Malays would retain political dominance in exchange for Chinese and Indian citizenship and economic dominance (Van der Westhuizen 2002).

Ethnic Malays have used their political majority as the primary means of resistance to Chinese and Indian cultural influences. Chinese and Indian populations remain large – 26 and 7.7 percent respectively in the 2000 census (Department of Statistics, as cited in Haque 2003) – and integral to the national economy. Although state of emergency declarations have been used several times since independence to quell or supposedly prevent race riots, sustained attempts to stifle diaspora cultures make little sense. Instead, ethnic Malays have sponsored state laws that attempt to institutionalize a Malay culture. The hope is that these laws will promote socioeconomic redistribution to ethnic Malays and prevent inter-ethnic conflict. Below, we examine specific cultural laws and their effectiveness in achieving these goals.

Religious laws

Article 160 of the Malaysian constitution defines Malays to be Muslim and Islam as the state religion (Mohd and Abas 1986). Muslims are subject to Islamic law and may not convert to another religion. The state courts have stated that jurisdiction over the conversion policy resides solely in the Islamic courts, which have handed down prison terms for convicted heretics (US Department of State 2004). Non-Muslims are, for the most part, free to practice their own religions. The US Department of State (2004) reports some limitations on publications that 'might incite racial or religious disharmony' and slow permitting processes for non-Muslim places of worship.

Religious laws have generated moderately effective resistance to alternative religions insofar as they have built Sunni Islam as a state religion that is legally protected against encroachment. Ethnic Malays may not legally recant their Muslim identities without fear of fairly severe penalties, nor may non-Muslims proselytize Muslims. Furthermore, other Islamic groups (e.g., Shia) are closely monitored and restricted (US Department of State 2004). However, fears of recent political inroads made by fundamentalist Islamic groups may have the unintended consequence of bringing non-Malays and moderate Malays together (Lee 2004).

Language laws

Article 152 of the constitution makes Malay the national language, although laws would be published in both Malay and English. The most debated laws relate to the language to be used in education. In the 1970s and 1980s, the government pursued a gradual approach to convert English schools into Malay schools (Haque 2003). This policy was somewhat reactive in its aim to remove the upward mobility advantage gained by children – mostly Chinese and Indian – who had begun to attend English-language schools (Lim Mah Hui, as cited by Van der Westhuizen, 2002). Since the language policy applied only to formerly English schools, it was partial in scope. Chinese and Tamil schools could continue to operate. The tone of the policy was defensive. English was not seen as bad; rather, proponents thought that Malay should be just as good for economic pursuits and that ethnic Malays should not be economically disadvantaged due to language.

These language policies seem to have been moderately effective. Most Chinese and Indians can speak Malay but tend to use their own languages when communicating with co-ethnics (Haque 2003). In 2002, the government reversed course and began to require that science and math courses in all primary schools be taught in English. Chinese, Tamil, and Malay activists all protested the removal of their respective mother tongues

Table 4.4 Malaysia

	Religion	Language	Speech	Media
Target	Internal – non-Muslims, including Chinese and Indians	Internal – Chinese and Indians seen to gain advantage through English education	Internal – Chinese and Indians who might challenge Malay special position	Internal and external
Action	Proactive – build a strong Sunni Islam with state support	Reactive shifting to proactive	Reactive	Proactive – promote 'national identity and global diversity'
Scope	Partial – special laws that apply only to ethnic Malays (Muslims)	Partial – applied only to English schools. Chinese- and Tamil-language schools could continue to operate (with some being outside the national education system)	Total	Total – applies to any broadcast received in Malaysia
Tone	Defensive	Defensive	Offensive	Defensive
Efficacy/impact	Moderate – Muslims have been imprisoned for 'heretical' beliefs, but non-Muslims are generally free to practice their own religions	Moderate – most Chinese and Indians can speak Malay; recently, global pressure and some domestic (including Malay) support for policy shift back to English	Moderate – speech has been quelled, although emergency declarations have been required several times	To be determined (new law and content code)

from the schools, but increasing global pressures to conduct business in English seem to have convinced some parents that a shift to English is necessary. The activists may be out of touch with the majority of their co-ethnics (Collins 2005).

Free speech and press laws

Freedoms of speech and press are limited in Malaysia, specifically with regard to topics that might challenge preferential policies for ethnic Malays. Under the Sedition Act of 1948 as amended in 1970, it is illegal to discuss issues related to 'citizenship; the national language and the languages of other communities; the special position and privileges of the Malays, the natives of Sabah and Sarawak, and the legitimate interests of other communities in Malaysia' (Lee 2004: 241).

However, the government seems to be shifting to a more proactive approach. The Communications and Multimedia Act of 1998 calls for 'the representation of Malaysian culture and national identity' (Section 213(d)). This act is total in scope, applying to all broadcasts received in Malaysia. However, the actual content code published by the media regulatory agency promotes the local within the global. Media should 'grow and nurture local information resources and cultural representations that facilitate the national identity and global diversity' (The Communications and Multimedia Content Forum of Malaysia, 2004, Section 1.1(d)).

Conclusion

Canada's policy of cultural resistance may be unique in that while forceful and strictly policed, it is not based on ethnic animosity or even totalist rejection. The logic behind the Canadian position is the need to counter the likely popularity of American cultural products by creating reserves for Canadian content. The major problem with the Canadian model is that the failure to subsidize Canadian content in a significant way (and the necessity of this given the economies of scale involved in a global market) means that the supply of 'local culture' does not match its institutionalized demand.

Kazakhstan's reactions to the globalization of culture can be seen to strike out first against the culture of the former colonizer and then against the encroachment of other foreign cultures. However, globalization also facilitates these reactions by legitimating the importance of indigenous culture, providing models for legislation, and guaranteeing acceptance for these actions if they comply with international norms.

Since independence, Malaysian laws have promoted a common national identity while privileging ethnic Malays and Malay/Muslim culture. Yet elites have also recognized increasing global integration. The recent policy reversal encouraging English use in schools provides one example of this recognition. This shift toward the global also has a local element. As English is incorporated into the national identity, the relative positions of the Chinese and Indian diasporas shift in two ways. Previously, these groups had secured socioeconomic advantage through command of English while maintaining their own cultures with informal Mandarin or Tamil. As English becomes universal in Malaysian schools, both processes are constrained.

REFERENCES

Agentstvo RK po statistike. (2000). Itogi perepisi naseleniia 1999 goda v Respublike Kazahstana. Tom 1. Almaty: Agentstvo RK po statistike.

Andaya, B. W. and Andaya, L. Y. (1982) *A history of Malaysia*. New York: St Martin's Press.

Collins, A. (2005). 'Securitization, Frankenstein's monster and Malaysian education', *The Pacific Review*, 18(4): 567–88.

Dave. B. (2004). 'Entitlement through numbers: nationality and language categories in the first post-Soviet census of Kazakhstan'. *Nations and Nationalism*, 10(4), 439–59.

The Communications and Multimedia Content Forum of Malaysia (2004) The Malaysian communications and multimedia content code (English, Version 6). Retrieved from the Web January 12, 2006. http://www.cmcf.org.my/HTML/cmcf_content_code_extension.asp.

Gosudarstvennyi Komitet SSSR po Statistike. (1992). Itogi Vsesoiuznoĭ perepisi naseleniia 1989 goda. v. 7. Minneapolis: East view publications.

Harding, A. (1996) *Law, government, and the constitution in Malaysia*. The Hague: Kluwer Law International.

Haque, M. S. (2003) 'The role of the state in managing ethnic tensions in Malaysia', *American Behavioral Scientist*, 47(3): 240–66.

Laitin, D.D. (2002). 'Culture and national identity: "The East" and European integration'. *West European Politics*, 25(2): 55–80.

Laws of Malaysia (1998) Act 588 Communications and Multimedia Act 1998. Retrieved from the Web January 12, 2006. http://www.mcmc.gov.my/the_law/legislation.asp.

Lee, H. P. (2004) 'Competing Conceptions of Rule of Law in Malaysia', in R. Peerenboom (ed.), *Asian Discourses of Rule of Law: Theories and Implementation of Rule of Law in Twelve Asian Countries, France and the U.S.* London: RoutledgeCurzon. pp. 225–49.

Mohd, T. H. and Abas, S. B. (1986) 'Traditional elements of the Malaysian constitution', in F. A. Trindade and H. P. Lee (eds), *The Constitution of Malaysia: Further Perspectives and Developments*. Singapore: Oxford University Press. pp. 1–17.

Olcott, M.B. (1995) *The Kazakhs*. Stanford, CA: Hoover Institution press.

Prakash, G. (1995) *After colonialism: Imperial histories and postcolonial displacements*. Princeton. NJ: Princeton University Press.

Schatz, E. (2005) Reconceptualizing clans: kinship networks and statehood in Kazakhstan. *Nationalities Papers*, 33 (2), 231–254.

Tomlinson, J. (1991) *Cultural imperialism: a critical introduction*. London: Pinter Publishers.

US Department of State (2004) International Religious Freedom Report. Retrieved from the Web January 5, 2006. http://www.state.gov/g/drl/rls/irf/2004/35405.htm.

Van der Westhuizen, J. (2002) *Adapting to Globalization: Malaysia, South Africa, and the Challenge of Ethnic Redistribution with Growth*. Westport, CT: Praeger.

## CHAPTER 5

CULTURAL EXPRESSION IN GLOBALIZED CONFLICT: CAUSE OR VICTIM?

Dragan Klaic

This chapter identifies the major axes of conflicts and tensions within the cultural realm, among cultural operators and policy-makers. It describes the interests and behaviors of various extended constituencies that are implicated or involved in such conflicts and describes how globalization accentuates discord. The primary tension identified is between the commercial interests of the cultural industry and non-commercial artistic creativity. Within the non-commercial culture, another growing friction exists between cultural heritage and contemporary creativity and then within the contemporary artistic field, the tension is rising between the institutionalized and non-institutionalized sectors. The antagonism between Nationalists and Neo-liberals represents another major axis of conflict. Finally, clashes between religious notions of cultural production and its secular versions are also developing.

Internal conflicts, invisible tensions

Cultural production is often a hotbed of conflict in which the distinct and often contradictory interests of artists, funders, producers and presenters become entangled. The field of cultural production is inherently fragmented and disharmonious, primarily because of the strong individuality of all artists and their need to assert their uniqueness, but also because most artistic processes favor an individual or small-group setting. Esthetic and political antagonisms are intertwined with professional jealousies within and among disciplines, directions and styles; between generations or between more-established and less-established players. There is a shared feeling of vulnerability among individuals, collectives and institutions alike because of the high dependence on private and public support and the increased pressures now exerted by the commercial cultural industry. Some of the tensions escalate into open conflicts, but most are hardly visible to outsiders. Only occasionally do they draw the attention of the media as gossip or scandal. In short, they are largely unexplored by cultural researchers.

Conflicts also occur between artists and their audiences. Many of these have little to do with globalization. But when in 2004 some four hundred young British Sikhs successfully block entrance to the Birmingham Rep for the premiere of *Behzti*, a play written by a Sikh woman, Gurpreet Kaur Bhatti and considered offensive by religious militants, globalization indeed plays a role. For migration brought some 60,000 Sikhs to the Birmingham area and continues to shape the sensitivity of the community's young radicals and their readiness to resort to violence in the defense of their 'dignity'. And it has resulted in the clash of norms and expectations and contributed directly to the anxieties attached to 'minority' status.

The conflict between French cultural workers and their employers about special unemployment benefits that led to the cancellation of the major French summer festivals in 2003 remained chiefly a French affair. The public got its money back and the foreign companies were compensated by the French Ministry of Culture for their canceled guest appearances. The economic damage caused to the tourist industry was only roughly estimated and was left uncompensated. For most observers, even the French, the conflict about *les intermittents,* or artists entitled to special unemployment benefits, is too complex to be fully grasped (see www.intermittents-unedic.com). Despite the strong criticism of globalization in France, however, the extent to which this particular labor conflict was driven by globalization passed unnoticed. A welfare scheme, originally designed for some 10–15 thousand individual artists in the performing arts, has been systematically abused by an entertainment industry that in the last 25 years has grown exponentially on the coattails of globalization, employing in France alone ten times more workers and keeping their employment flexible by giving them access when needed to the provisions of the welfare state.

This multifaceted conflict between the commercial interests of the *cultural industry* on the one hand and the interests of non-commercial *artistic creativity* on the other is the primary ongoing tension within the cultural sector. And it too is driven by globalization. The two sides are interdependent and implicated in various ways in each other's modes of operation. Each is driven, however, by distinct motivations and value systems: profit on the one hand and artistic originality on the other. The more cultural industry becomes globalized and dominant, the more contemporary creativity becomes forced into collaboration with it. Cultural industry has demonstrated great flexibility and absorptive capacity, to appropriate and integrate artistic goods, ideas, styles, and modes and turn them into mass-produced global products. While many artists like to assert their autonomy and oppose the instrumentalization of the arts, whether at the hands of the distributors of public subsidy or the market, they are in fact increasingly dependent on the cultural industry. If they do not work directly for it, they are nevertheless affected by the trends, hypes and fads that the cultural industry orchestrates and the impact these have on consumer tastes. With the cultural industry imposing a growing uniformity, it is becoming more difficult for the artists to assert their uniqueness and have it recognized as such by the public. Even when they opt for a nomadic, highly mobile mode of existence, or choose to operate on the margins of society and established cultural realms, artists can hardly escape the ubiquitous presence of the cultural industry and shelter themselves from its corrupting impacts. They can no longer seek secluded, isolated zones of comfort and peace, such as those certain artists' colonies in the south of France or the southwest of the United States were once able to offer. They cannot step out of globalization. That is probably why this opposition does not manifest itself as an open conflict (Smiers 2003).

Within the non-commercial culture, there is also a tension – again not necessarily an open conflict – between *cultural heritage* and *contemporary creativity*. The confrontation between the two may appear to be just competition for public subsidies, sponsorship and public appreciation. Behind this façade of parallel economic interests and shared vulnerability, however, lie more intricate loyalties and myth-making manipulations. The unsettling impact of globalization is visible in the explosion of the identity concerns and anxieties that the cultural heritage seeks to appease and control by stressing its capacity to provide continuity, invoke tradition and preserve collective identity. In contrast, contemporary artistic production stresses its originality, celebrates individual talent. If at all concerned with cultural heritage, artists today tend to treat it merely as a free source of creative material. The heritage sector is more institutionalized than the world of artistic creativity and operates in a clear preservationist mode. Heritage resources both material and immaterial are used to draw markers in time (periodization) and assert borderlines in cultural space, dividing cultural groups, appropriating and 'peripherizing' some cultural products. Those considered most precious are foregrounded, inserted in curricula, or endowed with canonical status. The heritage world is still very much concerned with the great narratives of national cultural history, and with efforts to safeguard the homogeneity of the national culture and its exclusive traits. In some places it is willing to sell out to the interests of the tourist industry.

Contemporary creativity on the other hand tends to be more idiosyncratic and to project itself as free of history, tradition and canons, a self-propelling agent of change, perpetuating in this manner another modernist myth. Yet because of its appeal to collective sentiments or anxieties, because of its invocations of tradition as supposedly authentic values and not truncated cultural practices, heritage preservation can expect more public support and more generous treatment at the hands of the public authorities than contemporary creativity. This status inequality increases jealousies and widens the gap between the two: their relationships oscillate between mutual indifference and charged competition. Yet they share a common uneasiness over the encroachments of the cultural industry and its tendency to exploit them both.

In the contemporary arts, there is a rising tension between the *institutionalized* and the *non-institutionalized* sectors. This is again a dispute primarily about the allocation of public subsidies, equity and access. The institutions tend to use the vocabulary of high professionalism and excellence and claim advantages of scale, while the non-institutionalized operators criticize them for their bureaucratic style and feudal hierarchies, insinuating that they are either conservative and elitist or dangerously close to mainstream commercial culture. The non-institutional forces tend to embellish their position with such notions as independence, freedom and radicalism, while they are at the same time criticized for their subsidy-dependence, fragmented and inefficient ways of operating, and supposed indifference to their potential public. Non-institutionalized forces seek access to institutions and ultimately to control them for the sake of stability, prestige and enhanced influence, but they also understand that the typology of cultural institutions that has reigned for the last two centuries has become obsolete.

Globalization reveals this anachronistic feature of cultural institutions, set up originally to define, preserve and promote national culture and identity. It is reasonable to argue that if increased market pressures and the growth of the cultural industry make individual cultural operators outside the institutions increasingly vulnerable and the prevailing institutional shelter offers a diminishing set of advantages, the solution is to conceive new types of cultural organization that can respond to the challenges of globalization, step out of the ideology of the nation-state and national culture, use the benefits of the ICT revolution for a more extensive and continuous impact and at the same time appeal to a multicultural urban public. This is a tall order for sure. In Europe, experimentation as regards rethinking the institutional profile is curbed by the steady flow of subsidies to existing clients. Elsewhere, market pressures make experimentation less likely to occur. Strangely, more attention is given to the leadership qualities in culture than to institutional typology (Dragicevic Sesic and Dragojevic 2005).

Globalization colors some other tensions in cultural production, such as the rivalries between majority and minority cultures in a given territory or tensions between the supposed center and periphery that are driven by status, empowerment and impact concerns. The fading ideology of the nation-state and the multiplication of access channels to the world market offer, for instance, new opportunities for so-called 'second tier' cities to profile themselves internationally, side-stepping the nominal primacy of the national capital and its central infrastructure. The climate of competition between domestic and imported cultural production results in various forms of protectionism (extra subsidies, tax abatements, minimal programming quotas, etc.). These measures have been extracted from national governments through aggressive lobbying that uses a battery of arguments, ranging from identity protection to the enhancement of cultural diversity. There is also a clash between the controlling prerogatives of the public authorities and their monitoring and evaluating agencies on the one hand, driven by the notions of transparency and accountability, and the autonomous strivings of cultural producers on the other.

Culture within conflict and in its aftermath

The cultural stakes *within* or in the midst of a violent local or regional conflict easily acquire global significance today and thanks to the globalizing reach of the media they deliver metaphors with a global appeal and global associations. During the 1992–95 war in Bosnia and Herzegovina, one of the protracted episodes of the armed conflicts that caused the disintegration of Yugoslavia, the city of Sarajevo was besieged by Serbian forces. The city survived for almost a thousand days with a weak, improvised military defense and high incidence of civilian deaths from artillery and sniper fire. The inhabitants were without electricity, gas and running water, with only scarce provisions barely trickling in. From June 1992 the conflict was internationalized by occasional convoys of peacekeeping UN troops bringing small quantities of humanitarian aid; a symbolic military contingent was stationed at the Sarajevo airport. Through this point of entry the late Susan Sontag arrived in 1993 to stage a production of Samuel Beckett's play *Waiting for Godot*. Her engagement with famished and freezing professional actors encouraged the explosion of an intense culture of resistance, with dozens of productions, concerts, screenings, exhibits and even festivals held during the war, mostly in underground shelters, and lit only by candles and solar batteries (Munk, 1993; Sontag, 1994).

Sontag's example prompted a steady flow to Sarajevo of artists from all over the world who helped enliven, sustain and intensify its cultural life as a form of civic resistance and at the same time demonstrated a form of global solidarity with the inhabitants. Paradoxically, although cut off from the rest of the world and exposed to brutal attacks, the city experienced as a result of the international media attention the artistic solidarity attracted, the greatest possible globalization of its cultural life in the midst of a regional conflict. This was greater than it had ever been in times of peace, with the possible exception of the Winter Olympics that Sarajevo successfully hosted in 1984. Unfortunately, the ties thus forged between Sarajevo's cultural operators and foreign artists were neglected after hostilities ended in 1995 – thus cultural and social capital has been squandered instead of being deployed for the renewal of the cultural infrastructure and cultural production.

Violent conflicts almost inevitably destroy cultural property and infrastructure and inflict great suffering on cultural operators. Brutal destruction of cultural heritage during armed conflict sometimes provokes global outrage (Dubrovnik, 1991; the Buddhist stone sculptures destroyed by the Taliban in Afghanistan in 2001; see also Dacia Viejo Rose's contribution in Chapter 6 below), but not much more – no efficient protective intervention, at least not before the end of the conflict. Eventually, some aid in reconstruction might come from the outside after the conflict de-escalates. The broad scale pillaging of the National Library, the National Museum and the National Archive in Baghdad in April 2003, at the very beginning of the US invasion, could occur because of the stunning indifference of the US forces. Afterwards, suspicions were voiced that some of the pillage was planned and even commissioned by foreign art dealers and collectors. Cultural heritage specialists and organizations across the world then stepped in to palliate the situation.

The plight of Iraqi artists, however, who were caught up in the protracted violence in the country or in extended exile from Saddam Hussein's dictatorship, attracted little attention. Efforts to reach out to them and provide support from abroad to renew, even minimally, cultural production in post-Saddam Iraq have been rare. Germany's *Theater an der Ruhr* gathered together some of the Iraq theater exiles and took them under its wing just as it did with the Roma theater company *Pralipe* whose existence in Skopje, Macedonia, became unsustainable after the breakup of Yugoslavia in 1991. Such gestures of global cultural solidarity in the midst of a protracted violent conflict remain rare, however. Systematic efforts to build up networks of global solidarity with artists affected by a conflict usually succumb to indifference, self-centeredness and compassion fatigue. Rare individuals might become well known worldwide and be idolized as embodiments of resistance or victims of repression, while thousands of anonymous, unrecognized and unaided others remain in distress and dire need.

Globalized information flows are not of much help to cultures caught up in a violent conflict. We know, we watch, we notice, we read about and hear an occasional first-hand testimony, but destruction and repression continue. For long, it was believed that the industrialized destruction of human beings during the Holocaust was possible because it was hidden from public view. Now we know better. Knowing, noticing, observing does not automatically bring relief or resistance. In violent conflicts, humanitarian interventions are usually the priority; these do not address cultural issues and neglect cultural capital. Cultural protection is less urgent, less supported and more difficult to carry out. Campaigns to defend cultures in danger simply do not take off. Or they lose steam quickly.

There is nevertheless a role for culture in post-conflict reconstruction: to inspire, engage, reconnect, help process anger, hate, trauma. To get the timing and proper sequence right is difficult, however. A festival planned in Kabul in 2004 by the Goethe Institute had to be cancelled because of security concerns. If this was a premature gesture to signal the return of cultural normalcy, some months later Ariane Mnouchkine's *Théâtre du Soleil* troupe could go to Afghanistan with the support of George Soros' Open Society Institute to apply their performance techniques to rehabilitation work with refugees and Taliban victims. In Afghanistan, like in Darfur and many other places of wretchedness that lack even the most basic provisions for normal and dignified human life, cultural intervention can hardly be imagined. Nor can it ever compensate for the lack of security, food, water and shelter. In Lebanon, where 16 years of civil war spared the economic elite from total ruin, small scale festivals appeared in the 1990s as signs of political normalization and as rich hoteliers invested in the revival of the tourist industry. In post-apartheid South Africa, festivals were organized in order to regain international contacts, build a new inter-racial public, diffuse new skills, break the previous monopoly control of whites over the cultural infrastructure and create a sense of cultural ownership for the underprivileged. And because globalization exposed South Africa's post-apartheid transition to world attention, new festivals organized there could count on a great deal of peer cooperation and funder goodwill at the international level (Engelander and Klaic 1998). In the rural north of Uganda, Roel Twijnstra brought his Rotterdam company *Het Waterhuis* to perform *The Girls of Aboke* in a large clearing, where it was watched by 20,000 people. This production on the children kidnapped and turned into soldiers by the Ugandan rebel Army of God, made originally in 1999 for the intimacy of a Dutch classroom, thus reached out to the traumatized children and their parents at the very edge of the ongoing conflict, a proof of globalized attention and solidarity finally secured.

A visual arts exhibit, set up on the 'green line', which since 1974 has cut off the Turkish controlled part of Cyprus from the rest of the island and runs straight through Nicosia, sought in 2005 to make sure that small steps that had been made towards a thaw in a long-frozen conflict did not get blocked by political bickering. Artists inserted their works between the conflicting sides and marked the territory of confrontation as a micro-topography of communication and mutual discovery. Consequently, a mobile and biennial visual arts event called *Manifesta 6* was to take place in the autumn of 2006 in the form of a four-months-long arts school. Its goal was to offset the isolation of Cypriot artists, insert some energy and status into the contemporary arts scene and break the dominance of the cultural heritage that is the chief resource of the tourist industry. Most importantly, the event sought to further defuse conflictuality on the island by internationalizing it in an artistic way, after its internationalization through the buffer presence of the UN military froze it for decades. This concurrent internationalization, driven by the spirit of cultural solidarity that inspired Susan Sontag, Blue Shield and Roel Twijnstra, is embedded in the belief that artists can retain their inherent autonomy and challenge reigning realities at the same time. Yet sometimes political or ideological forces retaliate in blatant disregard of cultural autonomy. In June 2006, the host organization of *Manifesta 6*, Nicosia for Arts, suddenly cancelled the event, fired all 3 curators and prohibited them from taking their work elsewhere under the threat of punitive damages. Even though the host organization originally accepted the idea that *Manifesta 6* would be a 'bi-communal' event, involving both Greek and Turkish Cypriots, and that it would take place on the entirety of the island, the Greek Cypriot authorities seem to have refused the very notion that durable cultural infrastructure would be created in a part of the island that is beyond their control. Efforts to mediate this conflict failed and the opposing parties now seem set for a long legal battle. Whatever its outcome, it will not resurrect *Manifesta 6* nor help any of the contemporary artists on the island.

Broader conflicts acquire a cultural mask

When the Egyptian writer Naguib Mahfouz asks via his publisher the permission of the Al-Azhar Islamic authorities to republish his novel *Children of Gabalawi*, is he seeking to avoid a cultural conflict? Or is he only becoming pious in his old age – since he even suggested that a prominent member of the Muslim Brotherhood should write a preface if the publication is authorized (Vloet 2006). Or is the Nobel laureate concerned for his own safety after being stabbed in 1994 by a fanatic who acted after an Al-Azhar *fatwa* that banned the novel after its initial publication in the daily *Al Ahram* in 1959? Mahfouz' request and his explicit acceptance of Al-Azhar's censorial prerogatives, officially sanctioned in 2004 by the Egyptian government, have caused a cultural conflict in Egypt that touches on matters of politics, morals and religious belief. Some of Mahfouz' colleagues and friends are outraged by his defense of the positive impact of censorship in general, forgetting that Mahfouz actually headed the government's film censorship department for a short while in the 1950s. He claims that he promised President Nasser 45 years ago that he would publish his novel abroad and consider an Egyptian publication only with Al-Azhar approval. He is simply a man of his word, he claims.

When the municipal council of Rotterdam formulates a citizen 'charter' of desirable behavior at the end of 2005 and insists that immigrants should speak only Dutch in public, is this an effort to reduce cultural conflict in a multicultural city or is it a gesture that only exacerbates such conflict? The Rotterdam 'Dutch Only!' initiative was quickly endorsed by the Immigration and Integration Minister Rita Verdonk, a hardliner who regularly antagonizes the very immigrant communities whose integration she is supposed to facilitate. No penalties are planned (yet!) for the violators of the

Rotterdam charter since the document is envisaged as a consensual, declarative commitment on the part of individual citizens. But even the draft prompted angry protestations and some more rational objections regarding the feasibility of such a rigid linguistic regime. Rotterdam's demography has been radically altered in the last 40 years by global migratory patterns and as a result its inhabitants are thought to speak some 170 different languages. Indeed, some newcomers hardly learn any Dutch. More than 50 percent of children attending elementary school have at least one parent born outside the Netherlands. This linguistic constellation brings with it a predictable web of cultural frictions and frequent communication blockages. The insistence on the use of Dutch in public could be seen as an expression of the anxieties that grip some of the autochthonous residents who occasionally feel estranged in their own city or shut out by the use of languages they do not understand. For many migrants and their offspring, regardless of their degree of fluency in Dutch, as well as many natives, the proposal is yet another sign of increasing discrimination and xenophobia in this country, once admired for its supposed tolerance. The resulting debate is linguistic, cultural, sociological and of course political. The primary interest of the initiative was to capture some anti-foreigner votes in the March 2006 municipal elections and therefore various, often rather outrageous and legally unsustainable initiatives to further integration and curb migration with repression and control appeared almost daily in Dutch public life. It seems that some of the Dutch have had it with globalization and now fantasize on how to shut themselves off. The 'Dutch Only!' initiative backfired on its proponents who were heavily beaten in recent elections in Rotterdam and some other cities – this was partly a result of the immigrant vote.

When Google, a company of truly global reach, bowed in January 2006 to the pressure of the Chinese government and accepted its request to keep some 'undesirable' web sites out of the reach of its search engines, one could see here a conflict between the global notion of free access to information, shared by many Google users, and the Chinese government's censorious preferences. Is the large and global Google community threatened in its cultural values and convictions by the decision of the company's senior management? This manifestation of corporate greed, prompting Google to comply with the censor in return for a strong presence in the Chinese market – as many multinationals and its competitors Yahoo and Microsoft had already done by meekly accepting the same governmental restrictions – has affected freedom of communication and free access to information. Can it be seen as a business decision with a moral shadow, a paradigm of the kind of corruption the steady appeal of the growing Chinese market seems to be forcing upon global capitalist forces? A new wall has been erected around China, a virtual wall, concludes Egbert Dommering (2006). But thanks to the globalization of technical knowhow, many cyber holes will be for sure created in this wall by hackers whose individual ingenuity will find ways to avoid Google's scrutiny. If Google users had responded to this blatant instance of corporate opportunism with a mass boycott of their favorite search engine, this would have been a consumer revolt driven by the defense of some shared cultural values. But no such boycott has taken place. Moral criticism has not led to deeds of moral and cultural solidarity.

Instead, what we saw in early 2006 was the affair of the Danish cartoons. The global confrontation between European norms of press freedom and Islamic outrage briefly made Huntington's paradigm of the clash of civilizations appear less hypothetical than is usually presumed. Sensing this heat, European politicians switched gears and resorted to polite phrases of appeasement, upholding press freedom in the most general terms but also stressing the need to respect all religious feelings. They have also identified artificial symmetries between the Danish cartoons and the anti-Semitic cartoons common in the Arab press, and have engaged in an exercise of political correctness and opportunistic whitewashing that is quite similar to the corporate behavior referred to above. Their soothing platitudes, repeated by their US peers, implicitly deny any critical function of the arts and renounce satire as a means of public debate. Those European papers that reprinted the cartoons saw themselves only too easily as valiant defenders of their sacrosanct principles – but without thinking much about how to advance the cause of the free press in countries where it does not exist at all. A Jordanian weekly that followed them by publishing the same cartoons intelligently tested the limits of its own society, but the editors – who simply wanted their

Arab readers to see for themselves how press freedom is abused in the West – were promptly arrested nevertheless.

Forty years or so ago, publishing a cartoon of a local bishop, not to mention the pope himself, would have caused enormous outrage in most Catholic countries of Europe and religious forces would have been mobilized to attack the blasphemers. But the incident would have remained an isolated one, confined to its national setting, and would have been noted elsewhere only as a minor news item. Today, because of globalization, a local incident of this sort easily attains planetary scale. And Islamic radicals are not the only opponents of the artistic freedom of expression. The threat of New York Mayor Giuliani in 1999 to strip the Brooklyn Museum of its subsidy for displaying a painting of the Virgin Mary by Chris Ofili, made with the use of elephant dung (a signature practice of the artist), resulted in a great deal of publicity for the exhibit and much global ridicule for the Mayor. A US judge subsequently ruled that no subsidy cut could be imposed as punishment. In the UK in 2005, radical Christians staged demonstrations against performances of *Jerry Springer – the Opera*, a supposedly satanic, blasphemous musical which had moved from Broadway to London's West End and on to tour throughout the country. Some venues refused to program it so as to avoid picket lines.

As I write these lines in March 2006, the editorial decisions of a Danish newspaper of no European significance are being echoed, reproduced and countered worldwide, confirming the notions of extensity, intensity and velocity of globalization presented in the introductory chapter to this volume. And yet, the fact that the mass planetary outrage erupted several months after the publication of the infamous cartoons signals discontinuities in the globalization dynamics. Or rather, does it reveal the complexity of its engineering? For the mass protests exploded only after months of limited and rather local dissatisfaction in Denmark, after the Prime Minister refused to receive the protesting ambassadors of Islamic countries and after some Arab governments withdrew their envoys. The supposed spontaneity of the mass protests is to be doubted. Globalization is not just a faceless and irresistible force but a dynamics that can be carefully orchestrated. Global Muslim rage about the Danish cartoons was stoked by a Copenhagen-based imam and his cohorts who lobbied Arab politicians and clerics for several months (Fattah 2006). A secondary factor was the political motivation of Islamic clergy and ruling elites to instigate, allow and amplify the protests. The intensity of the latter should be seen more in terms of politics than of culture: as an expression of protracted frustration, accumulated anger and a deeply internalized sense of individual and collective powerlessness among the poor, repressed and uneducated masses for whom their religion with its untouchable notions is the last bulwark of identity and the only promise of possible redemption.

In all these cases what appears to be a cultural conflict turns out to be something else: an epiphany of cowardice on the part of an aged novelist in Cairo; political demagoguery to pick up votes by acting tough towards foreigners in Rotterdam; corporate expansion drift, oiled by opportunism in Beijing. The cultural elements are incidental and superficial: artifacts, systems and values are implicit and are shaped as religious, political and business arguments. These arguments in turn engage many players and consume a great deal of polemical passion, so that the initial cultural elements drift gradually into the background. Globalization, however, has played a key role in all three situations and has expanded the dimensions of the conflict. Globalized political Islam swayed Mahfouz into submission; identity anxieties made Rotterdammers feel uneasy in their globalized city; China is a geographic priority on a globalized market of digital services. As regards the Danish cartoons, however, culture stands at the center here, not so much as a cause but as a consequence: the clash of cultural systems, the culture of a free press versus the culture of untouchable religious norms. The face-off between satire and revengeful physical violence ultimately questions the legitimacy of satire and invective as forms of artistic or journalistic discourse. Caricature as a specific cultural product seems to be in acute danger, faced with the prospect of being discarded or rather sacrificed to the imperative of inter-religious harmony and mutual respect by opportunistic politicians, publishers, advertisers and readers in Europe, North America and elsewhere. This cultural sacrifice, however, cannot be expected to disarm the wellsprings of conflict, for these are fueled by injustice, inequality and oppression.

Memory wars and outrageous blasphemies

In cultural practice, *memory wars* explode regularly over the cultural/artistic rendering, presentation, interpretation and evaluation of controversial past events and processes. At the core of the polemic is usually a cultural practice or work (a film, a book, a monument, an exhibit, a performance) whose truthfulness is hotly contested. Divergent historic interpretations are read into the single artifact and used to confirm or contest its evocative impact. The artifact is, so to speak, sucked into incompatible historic narratives. Instead of being allowed to function autonomously, it is appropriated as an icon, proof or banner of provocation for specific groups and their interests. The autonomy and the complex, multiple potential meanings of the work are reduced and denied. Moreover, the representational authority of the author(s) is contested as well: Who has the right to refer to some collective historic experience, invoke it and rephrase it and who does not? What are the qualifications and credentials required? What is the truthful way of rendering it? The discussion of true versus false, authentic versus artificial slides quickly into the discussion of proper versus improper, acceptable versus offensive, permissible versus outrageous. Those who feel offended always feel so in the name of someone or something else. They invoke values, beliefs, authorities, illustrious ancestors and current leaders who are supposed to endow them with contestatory authority, establish them as a legitimate group of complaint and outrage, as sufferers and victims. Their opponents tend to invoke principles of autonomy, freedom of expression, inquiry and debate, and present themselves as true heirs of the Enlightenment. They inevitably become slightly discomfited when somebody like the Holocaust denier David Irving, sentenced to jail in Austria, appropriates their rhetoric.

In countries with stable and functioning institutions, unambiguous legislation and an impartial judiciary that all protect freedom of expression, the offended party might go to court to seek relief and excise prohibition, corrective measures and punitive compensation. But in countries where freedom of expression is not so respected, where notions of propriety are stronger than the value of artistic autonomy, and where there is no independent judiciary, the contestation often turns wild, taking the form of a turbulent street protest, often violent. In countries where there is not even rudimentary freedom for self-organization of social groups and for the articulation of particular interests in a legal manner, disagreements easily explode into anger and anger into violence as no other channels seem to be available. Passionate protests against the Danish cartoons coincided in Teheran with the strike of urban bus drivers who were not allowed to form a union. The mass enthusiasm manifested for Iran's right to develop atomic energy without the scrutiny of the UN Atomic Energy Commission came in handy to eclipse the two other concurrent causes and rephrase and reappropriate their frustrations for the benefit of the radicals. The mass violence between dispossessed and powerless Sunni and Shiite radicals in Iraq also draws on a vague memory of a conflict between the successors of the Prophet centuries ago.

One of the longest lasting memory wars of more recent times has been waged globally by the Armenians who have accused the Turks of genocide in 1915. Armenian organizations worldwide have been successful in mobilizing international acknowledgment of their martyrdom and manifold expressions of sympathy, while the Turkish state and much of Turkish public opinion remain in staunch denial. The recent, much-publicized trial of the Turkish novelist Orhan Pamuk for an interview that supposedly offended 'Turkish identity' could be seen as an effort to consolidate the denial front, especially after an academic conference on the issue was held in Fall 2005 at Bilgi University in Istanbul. Here ultra-nationalist lawyers attempted to use the law, as they often do to counter the 'unpatriotic' behavior of some Turks or indict Kurdish human rights activists. A vaguely worded article in the recently reformed penal code gave them a peg to demonize the novelist, who in an interview to a Swiss paper had alluded to a protracted conspiracy of silence about the 1.5 million Armenians murdered in 1915 and the 30,000 Kurds killed in the 1990s. This specific memory war is culturally loaded insofar as both the Armenians in the diaspora and those in independent Armenia seem to have made the trauma of the 1915 genocide the core of their collective experience and have allowed it to color all their options for the future – a disastrous choice for a small, poor, isolated country in the neighborhood of Turkey. For the nationalist

Turks, admitting the genocide seems to be perceived as a gesture that could dismantle the entire Kemalist ideology of an authoritarian secular republic, a nation-state of Turks only, one that is exposed to the pressure of Islamic forces and to a reformist agenda, prompted by the prospect of integration in the EU.

In another bizarre twist, the conspiracy of silence asserted itself violently over resurrected memory: in 1955 the Turkish secret police organized two days of riots by nationalists in Beyogly/Pera, the part of Istanbul which had at the time a high concentration of residents of foreign origin. Stores and apartments were ransacked and plundered, people were killed, beaten up and raped and the exodus of foreigners, especially Greeks, was accelerated. Consequently, the city lost much of its cosmopolitan character. The event was practically forgotten when some negatives of the photographs made during the riot were discovered. The photographs were displayed in September 2005 by a small gallery in the same part of town and again nationalist youth rushed in and destroyed them as a trace of something that supposedly never happened (Pamuk 2005). However, this effacement of a xenophobic outburst of 50 years ago by another xenophobic intervention cannot stop Istanbul reinventing itself as a cosmopolitan city that is busy rediscovering and reviving its historic layers of intercultural experience.

Other memory wars are waiting to erupt. The first visit to Athens of Pope John Paul II in 2001 prompted violent demonstrations by Greek Orthodox priests, monks and nuns in memory of the Crusaders' ransacking of Constantinople in 1204, as if this event had occurred last year and not eight centuries ago. This was the phenomenon of collapsed time, flattened like an accordion. But one could also apply the notion of 'chosen trauma' Vamik Volkan (1997) used to interpret the Serbian Kosovo myth and all the grievances derived from it. The Crusaders' plunder of Constantinople was blamed for the city's subsequent weakening, decay and ultimate fall in 1453. Protracted conflicts such as the Israeli – Palestinian one or the Hutu – Tutsi animosity also contain the confrontation of contentious memories and an ongoing, current conflict nourished by traumatic remembrance.

The impact of globalization on those memory wars is difficult to gauge. To be sure, it leads them to transcend their local and regional dimensions, become widely known and solicit worldwide supporters and allies. It means that they are increasingly fought with the whole world as a courtroom. Armenians, for instance, have been using their massive diaspora to arrange for official gestures of support and sympathy and the erection of public monuments in memory of the 1915 genocide, while Turkish émigré communities have been slow and far less efficient in countering them. Many of those memory wars are being fought out on the Internet, including hackers' assaults on their opponents' web pages.

It would be wrong to assume that the memory wars all oppose religious and secular cultures, one, oversensitive and prone to overreact and another, rational and capable of handling irony and multiple interpretations. The Armenian–Turkish genocide controversy is chiefly a secular affair, fought out by secularists and on secular ground. Sunni–Shiite conflict occurs within Islamic eschatology. Religious belonging and concepts are used predominantly to reinforce existing oppositions, escalate confrontations and strengthen the loyalty and passion of the opposed sides.

Yet it is difficult to explain why the publication of some cartoons in European newspapers prompts more protracted, more massive and more violent protests by Muslims, particularly Arabs, than the photos from Abu Ghraib prison that showed the actual physical and psychological abuse of Iraqi prisoners (Muslims and Arabs). Is it because many Arabs know or can imagine what horrendous tortures are being practiced on prisoners in the prisons run by their own governments? Similarly, why do some outrages caused by supposed religious blasphemy fizzle out quickly and remain local affairs while others become global events? The cancellation in 2000 of the production *Aisja* by the *Onafhankelijk Toneel* in Rotterdam, just before rehearsals were to begin, was caused by a rumor that a *fatwa* would be issued against the Moroccan artists involved in the project. Even though the company had already put on a series of well-received Dutch–Moroccan co-productions, enjoyed high credibility among the Moroccans in The Netherlands and had even commissioned a translation of the adaptation of Nadia Djebbar's novel *Women of Medina* from the contemporary Moroccan to the classical Arabic in order to stress the distance of *Aisja* from the historic setting, the prospect of putting the Prophet and his family on stage provoked rumors of intimidation. But the affair remained localized and some other adaptations of the same novel were staged without incident in Germany and Italy.

Similarly, some 60,000 Sikhs living in the greater Birmingham area remained indifferent to the staging of *Behzti* in the Birmingham Rep and only 400 Sikh youngsters reacted with violence to what they perceived as an offense of their religion and its priests. The irony is that the Birmingham Rep invited the young Sikhs to the production process and to the previews, hoping to 'develop' them as a regular theater audience with such a culturally diverse repertoire. Instead, the latter turned violently against the production, blocked access to other spectators and forced the Rep to cancel the run. A bizarre incident indeed in the audience development strategies of cultural organizations, eager to enhance cultural diversity as their subsidy-givers expect them to do, never surpassed local circumstances – in contrast to the protracted campaign waged worldwide against Salman Rushdie and his *Satanic Verses*, with his Norwegian translator shot, Italian and Japanese publishers stabbed and many booksellers threatened. Stopping a theater production as a blasphemous act seems to be easier than preventing the publication of a text or image, which can be instantaneously reproduced in other press outlets and on the Internet. Similarly, the Internet and mobile telephones rapidly spread a sense of outrage and mobilize potential demonstrators.

Such conflicts now give rise to much global punditry: as the new commentators join or seek to arbitrate the controversy, they add their own points of view, often drawing false analogies and defining misleading symmetries, so that the cultural dimension of the conflict becomes even more obscure or disappears altogether as it is reduced to a clash between fundamentalist secularism and fundamentalist religiosity. Cultural wars run in parallel. Some extreme positions tend to cancel each other out: the satirical *Charlie Hebdo* (Paris) publishes the problematic cartoons while an Iranian paper calls for a competition of cartoons devoted to the Holocaust and Israel. 'Death to Europe!' chant angry demonstrators in Teheran around European embassies, kept carefully in check by the riot police. Some evenings earlier, in the Ferdosi Hall of the Teheran University, a concert by SDS, an Iranian dead metal band, was interrupted by the police when it became impossible to prevent the audience from singing along and swaying with the band – an impermissible 'Western' habit. The audience of 300 (90 percent male, dressed in dead metal style, with the women all in black) was promptly ejected and yelled angrily at the police: 'Fascists! We hate you! Death to the regime!' (Wieringa, 2006). These two invocations of death, one on the part of a religious sensibility offended by permissive foreigners, and the other on the part of the Iranian followers of a global music fad ostracized by domestic puritans, exemplify the extreme forms of cultures in conflict in the shadow of globalization. Globalization is usually seen as causing cultural uniformization. My tentative reformulation of this proposition would be that globalization tends to accelerate the formation of antagonistic group solidarities, pro or con some cultural forms, but in so doing tends to politicize those cultural forms, destroying their autonomy and their inherent multiplicity of meanings, flattening them into reductionist binary oppositions. Cultural expression is thus not the reflection nor the instigator of globalized conflicts but their well-targeted victim.

Box 5.1 The Memory and Reconciliation Virtual Library: Sarajevo–Belgrade–Frankfurt

The *Memory and Reconciliation Virtual Library (MRVL)* is a joint project of three national libraries located in Sarajevo (Bosnia and Herzegovina), Frankfurt (Germany) and Belgrade (Serbia). The initiative is based on the shared experience and shared memory of wartime destruction.

On 6 April 1941 Nazi Germany's *Luftwaffe* bombed and completely destroyed the National Library of Serbia. Thirty-two years later, on 6 April 1973, the new building of the National Library of Serbia was opened. On 6 April 1992 the three-year Serbian siege of Sarajevo began. On the night of 25–26 August 1992 Serbian shells hit the Town Hall and destroyed the National and University Library of Bosnia and Herzegovina. In a macabre way, the destruction of April 1941 was echoed by that of August 1992. How could those who experienced the trauma of the first destruction do exactly the same thing to others several decades later?

Because it was at the center of this double experience, it was the Belgrade library that initiated a project expressly designed to serve a culture of memory, reconciliation and dialogue. In the 'Founding Statement' for the project, the following statements were made by the library authorities:

> It is easier to forgive someone else than to forgive oneself. We shall never forget what we did. We cannot forgive ourselves. We repent. We sincerely hope that this confession will contribute to others forgiving us. We beg for forgiveness. We believe that true repentance can be the pledge of true reconciliation. At the same time, we cannot forget what was done to us. But our memory is of no use if it remains passive. We want that no one ever experiences the misfortune that we experienced. If we contribute to reconciliation, we contribute to that too. It is harder to forgive oneself than someone else. The Serbian partner would like to invite the other two partners to accept this statement and join.

The libraries of Sarajevo and Frankfurt took up this offer. The purposes of this triangular initiative are both concrete and symbolic. Concretely, it involves the establishment, maintenance and development of a specialized Internet portal as a multi-dimensional on-line resource, a virtual library based on the pooled technical and professional capacities of the three partners. Symbolically, it permanently regenerates the spirit of memory, reconciliation and dialogue. Its motto is the words of Danilo Kiš: 'Danger comes from the conviction gathered from one book only.' The following shared dedications connect and bind the three sides:

- to memory
- to the good
- to the happiness of our descendants and to the heritage of our ancestors
- books, reading and understanding of meaning
- to trust and mutual esteem
- to peace in the world
- to the vision of a united Europe and a united world
- to truth and dialogue.

Prepared on the basis of information supplied by Sreten Ugričić, Director National Library of Serbia

REFERENCES

Dommering, Egbert (2006) 'De Chinese muur'.www. netkwesties.nl/ editie139/column2.html

Dragicevic Sesic, Milena and Dragojevic, Sanjin (2005) *Arts Management in Turbulent Times: Adaptable Quality Management*. Amsterdam: Europ. Cultural Foundations/ Boekmanstudies.

Engelander, Rudy and Klaic, Dragan (eds) (1998) *Shifting Gears*. Reflections and reports on the contemporary performing arts (articles by L. Niclas, H. Bakker and G. Schiphorst). Amsterdam: Theater Instituut Nederland.

Fattah, Hassan M. (2006) 'At Mecca Meeting, Cartoon Outrage Crystallized' *New York Times* 9 February 2006.

Munk, Erika (1993) 'Reports from the 21st century: a Sarajevo interview', 'Notes from trip to Sarajevo', 'Only the possible: an interview with Susan Sontag', *Theater* 3: 9–36.

Pamuk, Orhan (2005) *Istanbul*. London: Faber & Faber.

Smiers, Joost (2003) *Arts Under Pressure*. London: Zed Publishers.

Sontag, Susan (1994) '*Waiting for Godot* in Sarajevo', *Performing Arts Journal*, 16: 2, 87–106.

Vloet, Corine (2006) 'Nobelprijswinnaar verradt eigen werk', *NRC*, 23 January 2006.

Volkan,Vamik (1997) *Bloodlines: From Ethnic Pride to Ethnic Terrorism*. New York: Farrar, Straus & Giroux.

Wieringa, Kees (2006) 'Het publiek prevelt "We hate you",' *NRC*, 27 January 2006.

## CHAPTER 6

CONFLICT AND THE DELIBERATE DESTRUCTION OF CULTURAL HERITAGE

Dacia Viejo Rose

Contemporary conflicts are increasingly imbued with cultural references and claims to particular cultural identities and histories. While cultural differences are not the cause for conflicts, cultural rhetoric is affecting our perceptions of the place of culture in relations between countries. As the world becomes increasingly interdependent, the need for communication and mutual understanding is greater than ever and yet culture is being used as a barrier rather than a facilitator in this process. This has a direct impact on the fate of cultural heritage which becomes a target for destruction and a hostage to fortune. This paper looks at some of the ways in which cultural heritage is targeted, destroyed and reconstructed as a result of the confluence of current trends in conflicts and globalization.

Introduction

The stories that a society tells itself about its past are often represented and transmitted through the images contained in the archaeological, architectural, historical and artistic heritage. These objects of the past are used to define the present and are today increasingly imbued with an ideological dimension. This is revealed in stark terms by the processes of destruction and reconstruction of cultural heritage. By tracing recent trends in this area, we can infer some lessons about the relationships between cultural heritage, conflict and globalization.

The cultural heritage in both its tangible and intangible manifestations – physical structures and objects as well as traditional knowledge, beliefs and forms of expression – has become central to contemporary perceptions of collective memory. An increasing number of cultural groups now articulate their struggles for rights and recognition around the ownership and representation of their cultural heritage (as Dragan Klaic has just argued). And these representations – or negations of them – have often become conflictual, yoking history and culture to the purposes and acts of war. Cultural heritage has long been a target for deliberate destruction in wartime. Today, how do the dynamics of contemporary globalization shape the ways in which this destruction is presented and perceived? How does cultural heritage come to be at the center of conflicts and, conversely, can it play a constructive role in sustainable development and peace-building?

This chapter seeks to address questions such as these. It will do so in two parts. First, I shall develop a typology of destruction and attempt to link the various motivations to the influences of globalization. The second section is dedicated to the reconstruction of cultural heritage in post-conflict scenarios. I must underline at the outset, however, that in this area robust empirical data are notoriously difficult to come by. Statistics pertaining to conflicts concentrate on casualties, expenditure and the destruction of key infrastructure; rarely do they include destruction of cultural heritage. Furthermore, the wartime destruction of cultural heritage has become such an important propaganda tool that in the case of conflicts where data have been collected (as in the former Yugoslavia) it is almost impossible to gauge their reliability. Damage is particularly difficult to assess because proper inventories of cultural heritage and its state of preservation prior to the conflict rarely exist. However, by analyzing recent trends, attitudes towards them and the discourse that has emerged, it is possible to gauge whether any change has occurred in the quality, if not quantity, of this type of destruction.

Destruction

The destruction of buildings and the theft of artifacts appear to be inseparable from violent conflict throughout recorded history. Often this destruction

Table 6.1 Tentative typology of the destruction of cultural heritage caused during conflicts

Destructive action	Object destroyed or damaged	Type of conflict[2]
• Plunder and looting • Deliberate targeting • Deliberate misuse/reuse • Neglect and selective memory • Vandalism • Collateral damage • Military reasons • Iconoclasm • Official cultural policy • Failure to safeguard	• Religious building/objects • Civilian building • Museum • Heritage site • Library or archive • Historical monument/site • Cemetery • Official building • Public art • Political memorial/site • Archaeological site • Infrastructure (bridges) • Natural heritage[3]	• Stable states with disorderly transfers of power, continuity of bureaucratic/governance • State failure due to predatory or ineffectual governance • State erosion or failure due to ethnic/regional conflict • Sate failure due to ideological conflict • State change imposed from outside as a residual form of old imperialist intervention

has even occurred within legal frameworks. There are countless stories of cities sacked – Carthage, Constantinople, Jerusalem, Rome – and moments of iconoclasm – Byzantium, the Reformation, the French Revolution, Taliban-ruled Afghanistan. Colonial conquest was also a privileged vehicle for the wide-scale destruction of cultural heritage. The conquest of the New World was accompanied by a war of images in which the Conquistadors razed entire cities, destroying Mayan temples and images of gods, replacing them with symbols of Christianity. All the colonial powers assaulted the material culture of colonized societies, pillaging, destroying and supplanting these with their own symbols (Gamboni 1997: 35).

Revolutions too have been characterized by the destruction of cultural symbols and heritage. During the French Revolution, the Legislative Assembly ordered that monuments built in pride, prejudice and tyranny be they in public places or private homes should be destroyed (Law passed on 14 August 1792, for more on this see Leith 1965). 'It was thus argued that the French Revolution would not have been so extreme in its iconoclasm had the French monarchy not resorted to art as a political instrument to the degree that it did, while the link between Communist monumental propaganda and the wholesale pulling down of statues in Central and Eastern Europe after 1989 is readily apparent' (Gamboni 1997: 27).

The increase in civilian targeting and the massive means of destruction available today have made it more difficult to ascertain when cultural heritage is a deliberate target and when it merely suffers 'collateral damage'. What is clear, though, is the increased salience of destruction as a propaganda tool, which first appeared in significant ways during World War I (for example, with the destruction of Louvain's library and the Reims cathedral) and increased during World War II (Gamboni 1997: 42–5).[1]

Because cultural heritage is self-consciously deployed as a key signifier of belonging and difference, it is very often targeted in conflicts between cultural groups. As a result, studying the destruction of cultural heritage would seem to be one way to shed light on the matrix created by the interrelation of cultures, conflict and globalization.

A tentative typology of destruction

A detailed typology of the destruction of cultural heritage in conflict situations would require parallel typologies of conflict, of cultural heritage and of forms of destruction – a mammoth task. I have attempted nonetheless to set out a tentative typology (Table 6.1) and will 'annotate' the various types of destructive action briefly.

Plunder and looting have always been a part of belligerent action; they can be motivated by a desire to collect trophies of war, to gain economic benefit, or as a symbolic gesture of taking from others what is dear to them or recovering what they have taken from you. The Roman Empire provides some early examples of art treasures and libraries being carried off by conquerors. The conquest of Volsinii in 264 BC is said to have produced booty of 2,000 statues, and when Sulla occupied Athens in 86 BC he took Aristotle's library and installed it in his home in Rome. The triumphal processions in Rome which involved the display of looted treasures were later copied by Napoleon (Treue 1960: 13).[4] Looting can supply the illegal trade in art and antiquities, it can become a *monnaie d'échange* in crime rings, running in parallel to the trafficking of weapons and drugs, or it can serve to launder money earned through activities like trafficking. It is a form of destruction that despoils a country of its cultural heritage; countries weakened by conflicts are particularly vulnerable. This is intrinsically linked to the illicit trade of artifacts discussed in the next section.

Deliberate targeting is very difficult to categorize because the intent is so difficult to pin down. Even the interpretation of eye-witnesses who lived through the destruction is influenced by everything they have heard about the event; the destruction of symbolically charged heritage is lived emotionally and mythologies around the destruction quickly emerge, encouraged by the propaganda machinery.[5]

The most evident form of *deliberate misuse* of cultural heritage, rendered illegal by the Hague Convention (Box 6.3), is its requisitioning for military purposes. The use of cultural monuments, buildings or sites to store weapons, as sniper posts, or other bellicose activities renders them legitimate targets and the 'military necessity' clause of the Hague Convention applies to them. In terms of religious heritage, the misuse can take various forms – in the citadel of Berat in Albania, for example, churches were transformed into bars and restaurants.

The *reuse* of stone masonry from a previous period has been a common destructive practice throughout history. Architectural elements from previous constructions are exploited and as new religions or values come to power new symbols and buildings are built over the old (Box 6.1). As a result, many religious sites are built on layer upon layer of other sites; this practice, extant today, can result from and/or give rise to violent conflict. For example, in 1992 a mosque dating from 1528 was pulled down in the Indian city of Ayodhya because Hindu fundamentalists claimed it had been built on the site where the deity Lord Rama was born. The demolition of the mosque caused riots across the country, in which dozens of temples and mosques were burnt and an estimated 2,000 people died (CNN, 2002).

Box 6.1 The Mosque of Cordoba

Between 780 and 785 AD Abd-al-Rahman I built the Mosque of Cordoba on what is believed to have been the remains of a Christian building. Many of the 800 columns used in this magnificent building were pillaged from Roman and Visigothic remains. After the Christian conquest of Cordoba in 1236, the Mosque was turned into a cathedral. This transformation resulted in the construction of a closed-off choir area. On seeing the results, and despite having given his permission for the modification, the Holy Roman Emperor and King of Spain Charles V declared: 'You have built here what you, or anyone else, might have built anywhere; to do so you have destroyed what was unique in the world.' (Quoted in Fletcher 1992: 3).

Selective memory and neglect. The presence of physical remains establishes the truth of a story. Finding this proof can consequently become a serious political venture of the same weight as erasing evidence of alternative stories. During Enver Hoxha's rule in Albania, for example, considerable resources and efforts were concentrated on uncovering tangible evidence that the Albanians were the direct descendants of the Illyrians. Hence archaeological work along the coast and especially in Apollonia and Butrint was given priority. In contrast, the Byzantine heritage was neglected and misused, causing it to fall into ruin as was the fate of the town of Voskopojë (Box 6.2).

Vandalism has occurred throughout history both in armed conflict and as a result of social unrest. A recent instance is documented in UNESCO's report on the *Protection and Preservation of Cultural Heritage in KOSOVO* (UNESCO 2005). Most of the destruction reported occurred in 1995 or in 2004 and a frequent description of damage reads as follows: 'In 1999 it was destroyed with dynamite and the cemetery was desecrated.'[6]

Collateral damage is a term used to explain the unintentional casualties and destruction caused by military campaigns. Built heritage, architecture, monuments, museums and their collections inevitably suffer from bombing. The considerable amount of collateral damage caused by NATO's bombing of Kosovo and Serbia in 1999 showed that even the most sophisticated 'smart' weapons can result in substantial unintended destruction.

Box 6.2 The story of Voskopojë[7]

Voskopojë was an important Byzantine metropolis and trading center, which at its peak in 1769 boasted a population of 20,000 and had 26 Orthodox churches with frescoes decorated by some of the best painters of the time; the forgotten town now has a population of 500 and only five churches in various stages of collapse. Since 2002 it has been on the World Monument's Fund World Monuments Watch list of The 100 Most Endangered Sites. While the churches of Voskopojë and the surrounding villages have undeniably suffered from destruction caused by wars – three against the Ottomans in the second half of the eighteenth century, the Balkan wars of 1912–1913 and the two World Wars – a totalitarian regime and a rough transition period, neglect is the most serious cause for their current desperate state. This becomes evident when the state of these churches is compared with that of their equivalents on the other side of the border in Ochrid, Macedonia. The churches around Ochrid, several of which have frescoes painted by the same artists that worked on the churches of Voskopojë, are in good condition, having been carefully conserved in the past decade. The damage suffered by the churches of Voskpojë represents many of the types discussed in the text, but also includes iconoclasm, official cultural policy and failure to safeguard. Iconoclastic destruction became political as a result of emperors wanting to reduce the influence of local monks and saints. Reduced funding, together with the often-disastrous state of conservation, makes this a prolonged emergency. Today, harsh weather conditions and dampness are the greatest dangers facing the cultural heritage. Many of the structures are so weakened that neglect is tantamount to destroying them.

Whilst the form of violence the destruction takes reveals some of the intention behind it, this needs to be examined in relation to the nature of the heritage destroyed and the context of the conflict. Even a brief sketch of what a typology of the destruction of cultural heritage might be raises two issues: motivation and protection.

Motivations

It is the importance that we give to cultural heritage and the identity symbols that it embodies that render it vulnerable to deliberate destruction. When cultural symbols are successfully presented as marks of group identity, anyone intending to injure that group will have the incentive to target it. This targeting can be motivated by several factors: striking an enemy by destroying what is held most dear to him; obliterating any historic trace of the Other; erasing reminders of a painful or contested past; eliminating perceived symbols of oppression to assert self-determination; 'wiping the slate clean' in moments of regime change. Often it is a combination of factors, as was the case in the destruction of the Bamiyan Buddhas, where religious iconoclasm and the urge to defy the international community came together. 'The discriminatory intent, reflected in the sheer will to eradicate any cultural manifestation foreign to the Taliban ideology, and the deliberate defiance of the United Nations and international public opinion make this destruction a very dangerous precedent' (Francioni and Lenzerini 2003). These are only some of the possible motivations for destruction. Tracing motivations is necessary in order to discover if there is a plan or method behind the destruction. Yet, as these examples indicate, motivations are not a straightforward, black and white affair. As such, one-dimensional attempts at preventing the destruction cannot be effective in the long term.

With the growth of tourism as a key economic sector, targeting cultural heritage can also be at par with targeting natural resources or infrastructure. The shelling of Croatia's Adriatic coast damaged not only cultural heritage but the tourist infrastructure so important to the region (on its way to recovery, in the year 2000 tourist spending in Croatia was estimated at $US 3,328 million, or 12.5 percent of the country's Gross National Product).

An indication of intent is the destruction that goes on away from the immediate zones of combat. That churches, mosques, monasteries, cemeteries, libraries and archives were often destroyed outside these zones throughout the former Yugoslavia reveals a targeting of symbols. The destruction of cemeteries is another telling action. In some cases this destruction illustrates an attempt to rewrite history to erase physical evidence that the other party was ever there, in order to prevent claims to return to the land, as well as claims to property. However, refugees also disinterred the remains of their dead and removed them with them out of fear that their loved-ones' tombs would be desecrated.

Difficulties in discovering intent

The destruction of symbolically infused heritage is quickly engulfed in a mythology, making it difficult to discover intent. The bombing of the town of Guernica during the Spanish Civil War, like the bombing of the *Stari Most* (Old Bridge) of Mostar cannot be disentangled from its mythology. Ask ten people about the motivations behind the destruction of the Mostar bridge and you will get ten different stories, each told with absolute conviction. Anyone who tried to follow the story of the Museum of Baghdad from early April 2003 will be aware of the conflicting stories that emerged, each one with supporting material evidence and eye-witness reports.[8]

The propagandist use of destruction also masks original intent. From the beginning of the Spanish Civil War, the Spanish Catholic Church aligned itself with the military uprising. The widespread burning of churches that took place throughout the conflict was not an attack on religion but on the Church. In other words, it had a socio-political basis (Álvarez Lopera 1982). Yet, the deliberate targeting of churches was portrayed by the nationalist side as a battle between believers and heretics using the language of a crusade.

The power of language

The language used in conflicts can shape how the struggle takes shape in people's imaginations, especially when the words chosen and metaphors invoked are powerfully symbolic. The term 'cleansing' was a recurrent theme throughout the Spanish Civil War and was used by both sides, which after taking a town claimed to proceed in cleansing it of undesired elements. The Battle of Kosovo of 1389 was one of the inflammatory memories that Milosevic drew on and it was the town of Kosovo Polje that he chose, on the 24th of April 1987, to launch his battle cry thus: 'First I want to tell you, comrades, that you should stay here. This is your country, these are your houses, your fields and gardens, your memories... You should stay here... Otherwise you would shame your ancestors and disappoint your descendants' (Quoted by Bet-El in

Müller 2002: 208). Milosevic was not alone in using historic symbols to inspire fear and hatred. Franjo Tudjman, in his electoral campaign of 1990, repeatedly evoked the Independent State of Croatia, stimulating painful memories for Bosnians and Serbs of the Ustachi regime's collaboration with the Nazis.[9]

The words used to talk about a conflict can weave a symbolic discourse around it that distorts our ability to understand it. Uneasiness about genocide and ethnic cleansing that sprouted from the sense of horror and guilt at the Holocaust, for example, coupled with the vow that the international community made to never let such a horror recur, means that alarm bells ring whenever these words are used. The power of the media to elaborate a symbolic robe around a conflict in this way can considerably shape public opinion.

Rewriting history

A certain reinterpretation of history accompanies all regime change, but authoritarian regimes have a particular predilection for establishing a clean slate on which to build their visions. Mussolini's urban renewal involved the *sventramento* or disembowelling of Rome, a project he initiated personally with a pickaxe in hand. In the late 1980s, Ceausescu pursued his vision of a uniform countryside by building modern complexes throughout rural areas of Romania and razing over 7,000 villages in the process (Gamboni 1997: 213). In the wars of the 1990s in the former Yugoslavia, religion became the principal identifier of difference; attacking religious buildings was thus a way of attacking symbols of the enemy. Secular heritage was also destroyed, a practice that continues today, as throughout the countries of the former Yugoslavia, museums and monuments dedicated to the Partisan struggle during World War II, chosen as a unifying symbol by Tito, are taken down (Klaic, 2002)[10] and replaced by new symbols.

Protection and its limitations

Behind the drive to understand the motivations behind the deliberate destruction of cultural heritage lies the issue of responsibility and protection. The first attempts to create an international body or agreement dedicated to the protection of cultural heritage against wartime destruction, date back to the aftermath of World War I and evolved rapidly after World War II, culminating in the so-called Hague Convention of 1954 (Box 6.3).

Box 6.3 Protection measures

As early as 1899, the Convention with Respect to the Laws and Customs of War on Land contained references to the protection of cultural heritage in wartime (Nafziger 2003). However, it was the important destruction of cultural heritage during World War II that spurred the elaboration of a normative instrument to address the issue. The Convention for the Protection of Cultural Property in the Event of Armed Conflict was adopted at The Hague in 1954. This was the first international agreement focusing exclusively on the protection of cultural heritage, both movable and immovable. The repeated destruction of cultural property in conflicts since the 1980s has revealed the deficiencies of the Convention. Consequently, a review was undertaken that sought to incorporate some of the lessons learnt. This effort resulted in the adoption in March 1999 of a Second Protocol to the Convention. Spurred by the destruction of cultural heritage in the former Yugoslavia and the destruction of the Bamiyan Buddhas, UNESCO adopted in 2003 a 'Declaration Concerning the Intentional Destruction of Cultural Heritage'. The Blue Shield, a non-governmental organization, was created by the International Council on Archives (ICA), the International Council of Museums (ICOM), the International Council on Monuments and Sites (ICOMOS) and the International Federation of Library Associations (IFLA), to collect and disseminate information, and coordinate action to protect cultural heritage in crisis situations spurred by natural and complex emergencies (Hladík 2001).

The idea that it is morally wrong to destroy the cultural heritage, even of an enemy, can be traced through the legal instruments developed to protect heritage and by examining the attitudes of the perpetrators. Considerable embarrassment in Britain over the bombing of Dresden could be detected in Churchill's speeches following the bombing and the treatment that 'Bomber Harris' received in its aftermath. Similar embarrassment on the part of the Allies can be found with regard to the destruction caused in Italy and France. In the context of the current boom in humanitarian action sparked by the actions of the Red Cross, voices protesting the destruction of cultural heritage were muted, fearing accusations of callousness and indifference to human suffering and more urgent needs of safety, shelter and food. However, the attitude expressed in a Council of Europe report relating to its monitoring activities in Bosnia is increasingly common: '*Our* view is that people suffering is of first priority, never mind the monuments. But that is not *their* view. They take global destruction of their monuments very seriously indeed. It is time that their attitude about what is happening to their cultural heritage should be taken seriously by us.'[11]

While the protection measures mentioned have not been demonstrably effective in preventing destruction, they have been used to allocate responsibility. Despite the difficulty in determining motivations, the International Criminal Tribunal for the former Yugoslavia at The Hague (ICTY) has attempted to pin down responsibility for the deliberate destruction of cultural heritage. On January 31, 2005, in the case of *The Prosecutor v. Pavle Strugar* concerning the shelling of the Old Town of Dubrovnik, the court found the accused Lieutenant-General guilty of 'destruction or willful damage done to institutions dedicated to religion, charity and education, the arts and sciences, historic monuments and works of art and science, a violation of the laws or customs of war under Article 3 of the Statute' (ICTY, 2005).[12] The Court arrived at this conclusion partly due to Strugar's responsibility as commander of the forces that perpetrated the shelling of the Old Town of Dubrovnik and to the fact that the Old Town as a whole figured on UNESCO's World Heritage List (ICTY, 2005).

Processes of globalization and cultural heritage

Three aspects of globalization have influenced cultural heritage: the translation of values into *international normative instruments* for the safeguarding of cultural heritage, *the increased internationalization* of markets and trade and the large-scale *movement of people* as immigrants, refugees and tourists.[13]

International organizations, UNESCO in particular, have since their inception developed *normative instruments* for the protection of culture and cultural heritage. Since the first meeting in 1978 of UNESCO's World Heritage Committee, a list of monuments and sites considered the 'heritage of mankind' has been developed. The translation of this international standard of valuation to the local level becomes difficult, however, when it is contested or disregarded (as in the former Yugoslavia or Afghanistan).

The *internationalization of markets* has facilitated the trade in art and artifacts. While this has had many positive aspects, it has also facilitated the illicit trade and made these items notoriously difficult to trace. This illicit trade has reached considerable proportions, comparable in terms of volume and monetary importance to trade in drugs and weapons.

The *movement of people* has had an impact on cultural heritage in different ways, the most obvious being perhaps cultural tourism, which each year dispatches millions of people around the world to travel and experience the cultural heritage of others (See the indicator suite on tourism in the data section). For many nations and regions, tourism has become an essential economic engine. Yet marketing or packaging cultures to attract visitors simplifies them into two-dimensional brochures, thus encouraging stereotypes and making dialogue outside of this framework difficult (Robinson 1999). In addition, anti-globalization movements have invoked cultural rights and the protection of cultural heritage and traditions as a rallying cry against a perceived homogenization. This has further accentuated the ideological exploitation of cultural difference.

Cultural heritage, conflict and globalization

Apart from the effects already discussed, the globalization process can combine two or more of its aspects to impact on cultural heritage. I shall analyze two of these possible combinations below.

International art market + Conflict + Cultural heritage = Illicit trade and Decontextualization.

In many ways, consumer culture has become the response to the Kantian search for categorical and unifying imperatives. After all, in the global village, cultural differences are if anything extolled as exotic and merchandisable products, rather than as sources of tension. Linked to the argument that the past, art and heritage are being perceived as consumer items is the monetary value ascribed to them. One destructive effect of this market value is the important volume of illicit trade. This illegality makes it difficult to accurately trace transactions and assess volume of trade.[14] Yet works of art and artifacts are pieces of history, evidence of stories about the societies that produced them; part of their value lies in their context, a wealth which is lost when objects are illicitly excavated and sold. Conflict makes a country vulnerable to illicit excavations and export of its movable heritage. This is so much the case that there are not a few instances of wartime archaeology. For example, during the First World War, British and French armies stationed in Greece sent a considerable number of artifacts home, a practice described by Ernest Gardener, a naval intelligence officer and head of the Salonica Headquarters Museum during the war.[15]

Box 6.4 Looting, illicit trade and conflict

While there are few statistical data on how political instability affects the looting and illicit trade of cultural heritage, there is enough empirical evidence to be able to affirm that there is an obvious correlation. In March 2002, in a visit to UNESCO, the then interim leader of Afghanistan, Hamid Karzai, urged the Organization to help stop the looting of archaeological material and antiquities that was going on in Afghanistan as the country did not have the resources to prevent it . An issue of the newsletter *Culture without Context* covered some of the looting going on in Afghanistan in 2001–02, emphasizing that in the wake of the Taliban regime looting was on the rise. This shows that destruction does not only occur during conflict but also in the environment of instability, lawlessness and poverty that ensues (*Culture Without Context*, Issue 10, Spring 2002: 19–20). The same issue of the newsletter contains an account of the looting of Javanese cultural heritage since the fall of the Suharto government in Indonesia in 1998. A more recent issue notes the results of a six-year survey in Pakistan and Iran indicating that 90 percent of major archaeological sites have been looted and another study on Israel and Palestine alleging that illegal digging in the Palestinian Authority territory was up 50 percent (*Culture without Context*, Issue 15, Autumn 2004: 9–10). 'Trafficking in material culture is a multimillion industry, second only to trade in narcotics,' says George Abungu, former Director-General of the National Museums of Kenya and president of the International Standing Committee on Illegal Trafficking in Material Culture (Shipepechero, 2002). He acknowledges that Kenya was a transit country for antiquities from countries in the Great Lakes region and the Horn of Africa that have been through conflicts in the past 15 years. While Ethiopia and Eritrea were at war, for example, insiders at the National Museums of Kenya observed how pieces that were highly valued on the international market made their way from Ethiopia to Nairobi through refugees from both the warring parties.

Since demand and the market are global, so too have been the means to thwart such trade. For example, on 22 May 2003, the UN Security Council passed Resolution 1483, which approved new post-war arrangements and imposed a worldwide ban on trade in or transfer of Iraqi cultural property illegally removed since 2 August 1990.

While political and social instability and conflict render countries vulnerable to the pillaging that feeds the illicit trade in artifacts, poverty is also a key motivator. Thus today, the biggest threat to cultural heritage in Southern Albania is deterioration resulting from lack of attention rather than targeted destruction. ICOMOS's *Heritage@Risk* report on Albania points to the impact of the Albanian Transition on the cultural heritage of the country, including in the city of Berat with its fortress, Byzantine churches and old city center.

Conflict + Movement of people + Culture = Exile and Decontextualization

When a conflict generates large-scale flows of refugees and when their exile becomes prolonged, the memory of this group becomes fragmented. For example, the civil war in Spain resulted in the exile of thousands of Republican supporters and others, ranging from politicians to intellectuals, artists, and moderate liberals. While many went to France and Mexico, other groups dispersed throughout the world. This dispersal resulted in the fragmentation of the memory of the defeated while the war, the reason for their circumstances and sole commonality, became a foundation myth for their new lives. Each group, depending on its composition and how it experienced exile, developed a different memory of the war, together with varying symbols and meanings. In contrast, in Spain, there was only one official history of the war that was taught, recalled and represented. The victors had the monopoly of the story that was told and they erased any evidence of an alternative through urban planning, cultural policies, rewriting textbooks and school curricula and also through censorship. In the same way as Trotsky disappeared from photographs, so cultural and historical Spanish figures disappeared from textbooks and townscapes. The destruction wrought by globalization in these cases is principally that of decontextualization, whether objects are removed from their original settings without records being made of where they were found and with what, or through the demands of the tourist and culture industry on the production of marketable goods and services. Cultural heritage, be it in the shape of statues torn from buildings or dances torn from their spiritual or cultural meaning, loses its potential to transmit knowledge when it is viewed without regard or understanding for its context. The objects and forms of expression are vehicles for the transmission of values, stories and knowledge – the loss of one means the loss of the other.

Incitation, propaganda and rhetoric

As mentioned above, motivations are notoriously difficult to identify and the best that can be done is to examine the rhetoric surrounding a conflict, the speeches made and the media's portrayal of it, as well as the propaganda. Even a thorough study of destruction cannot provide a definitive account of the motivations and intention behind the actions (for such a study see Lambourne 2001). A look at accounts of British Bomber Command's raids on Lübeck and Rostock in March 1942 indicates that the aim was to experiment large-scale area bombing, not to destroy historic centers. The fact that these raids mainly affected historic and cultural buildings was picked up by German propagandists who portrayed the destruction as proof of British barbarism. In retaliation, the *Luftwaffe* responded with a series of attacks on targets of cultural and historic interest in Exeter, Bath, Norwich, York and Canterbury, attacks that came to be known as the Baedeker raids. Five days after the raids began, Goebbels wrote in his diary that 'like the English, we must attack centers of culture' (Lambourne 2001: 142). Thus these raids helped cement the idea of cultural targeting.

As already mentioned, one of the difficulties of uncovering some sort of 'truth' to the data and motivations behind the destruction of cultural heritage is the propaganda machinery that immediately appropriates it. Propaganda aims to spark emotions, define a conflict and influence its development. The media and propaganda machinery was so crucial in the war in the former Yugoslavia that NATO targeted Serbian media centers (NATO bombing began on March 24, 1999). While propaganda uses have been made of the media to launch accusations of 'barbaric' destruction, this mediation has also contributed to building an awareness of the issue. This awareness as well as the way the destruction has been interpreted has contributed to changing attitudes.

The international community's rhetoric

Changes in attitudes towards the destruction of cultural heritage began in World War II and were further crystallized as a result of the destruction in the 1991–95 conflict in Bosnia. The damage caused to cultural heritage, whether intentional or not, is carefully monitored by the parties to the conflict, by the media and by international organizations, as manifested in the international community's rhetoric.

The state museum of East Timor, established in 1995 by the Indonesian Department of Education and Culture, was used as a field hospital in the period after the referendum on East Timor's independence in August 1999. It suffered from vandalism, insect infestation and damp; while some objects were removed for safeguarding, only a tenth of the original collection remained intact. In the wake of the wave of destruction that erupted immediately after the referendum, and which swept away any cultural heritage in its path, UNESCO's Director-General declared: 'This heritage has been targeted because of its significance for national identity, which should on the contrary cause it to be safeguarded as a symbol of community and the promise of a shared future' (UNESCOPRESS, Press Release No. 2002–28).[16]

When the Mostar Bridge and the Bamiyan Buddhas were destroyed, many international organizations protested and issued statements underlining their understanding that this heritage was targeted because of its symbolic nature. For example, the President of the World Monuments Fund issued a statement in response to news reports that Afghanistan's ruling Taliban militia had begun demolishing statues across the country. The statement began as follows:

> *The Taliban's edict to destroy all pre-Islamic statues in Afghanistan and their subsequent demolition of the great Buddhas in Bamiyan was a disturbing reminder that cultural destruction can be a potent weapon in campaigns of political oppression and tyranny. From the Ch'in emperor's burning of books in the 3rd century* BC *to Hitler's leveling of Eastern European cities, history is full of examples of cultural destruction as punishment against a victimized people. But this recent act of violence against cultural icons exhibits a troubling new twist. It represents full-fledged cultural terrorism, with the perpetrators using irreplaceable works of art as hostages. The Buddhas of Bamiyan and the statues from the Kabul museum were targeted because their destruction could draw just as much attention – and revulsion – as a far riskier act against human life. (Burnham 2002)*

Finally, the Israeli–Palestinian conflict has given rise to countless accusations of the destruction, misrepresentation and appropriation of cultural heritage on both sides. A poignant example is how Ariel Sharon's visit in September 2000 to the Temple Mount or Haram al-Sharif was seen as a provocation or pretext for the al-Aqsa Intifada (Scham 2004). Any account of destruction, such as the report of destruction of cultural heritage in Nablus provokes immediate retorts from the other side. (See Jean-François Lasnier's report in *The Art Newspaper* of June 2002 and reactions including Robert Bevan's reply in November of the same year)

Reconstruction and its discontents

> *If we are interested in arresting cycles of violence to produce less violent outcomes, it is no doubt important to ask what, politically, might be made of grief besides a cry for war. (Butler 2004)*

Concurrent with the increased reference to cultural references in the discourse surrounding conflicts is the increased involvement of the international community in both peace-building missions and the safeguarding of cultural heritage. The two trends come together in post-conflict reconstruction work. Through heritage reconstruction, an intangible fabric of meaning and memory is added to a society's capability to recover from the trauma of war. Post-conflict scenarios are often ones in which wars of meaning and history are fought. For example, Paul Preston's analysis of the post-Civil War period in Spain is that the writing of history under Franco 'was the continuation of the war by other means' (Preston 1995: 30). Clearly, violence and destruction do not end when a conflict officially does. Even when reconstruction in the former Yugoslavia had begun, with the participation of the international community, cultural heritage continued to be destroyed. A baroque Serb Orthodox diocese building was dynamited in the Croatian town of Karlovac on Christmas Day of 1993 and three mosques were blown up a few months later, despite agreement over a Muslim – Croat federation in Bosnia (Marlowe 1994). The legacy of history can be a heavy burden in the effort to move towards peace and stability and memories of the destruction of cultural heritage can prolong hatred and conflict. In instances when the destruction of cultural heritage has been heavily used for propaganda purposes in wartime rhetoric, the reconstruction process is delicate to say the least:

> *Archaeology has become a key issue in this process (reconstruction). In Pocitelj (Bosnia and Herzegovina), there is an agenda to undertake excavation to define the Christian origins of the settlement and thus prevent full reconstruction of the mosque and return of the Muslim population. The belief that the mosque was built on the site of a church was an important factor in its destruction. (Barakat et al. in Layton et al. 2001: 173)*

The interpretation of cultural heritage is fundamental to this process, but it requires the courage to address its less benign meanings. In the aftermath of war, as the symbolic landscape gets rebuilt, the visual narratives of a society's past and of the conflicts themselves, create a new sense of group belonging. It is crucial to understand how this happens if long-term peace-building is to result, for a symbolic landscape can easily be built that carries the violence of the war into the post-war period, planting signposts of discord that continue to provoke fear and hatred and work against reconciliation.

Much reconstruction today is in the hands of foreign NGOs and donors. This is not without its perverse impact; for these donors tend to advertise their participation in reconstruction projects and this branding process creates a new symbolic landscape. When, for example, a large panel thanking the Greek government stands in front of a rebuilt Orthodox church, one thanking the Vatican in front of a Catholic church or a religious NGO and one thanking Saudi Arabia in front of a mosque, each of these markers reinforces the respective divides and takes agency and ownership away from the local population. In both Bosnia and Herzegovina and Kosovo a Saudi Arabian aid agency, the Saudi Joint Relief Committee, has been building mosques that have little to do with the 400-year-old edifices of which they are supposed reconstructions. 'Reconstruction' has meant painting or plastering over the ancient frescoes that are unique to Balkan Muslim architecture but run counter to Wahhabi religious codes. Conversely, in Pristina, Kosovo, an undamaged eighteenth-century mosque (the *Kater Lula* or Four Fountains) was torn down and replaced with a new one that includes a shopping mall. In the town of Rahoves, in western Kosovo, the town's seventeenth-century mosque was torn down, bulldozed and replaced by one made of reinforced concrete.[17]

Countries or organizations that offer funding often earmark their contributions for particular purposes. For instance, a country might allocate funds towards an IGO or NGO's activities in the reconstruction of cultural heritage in Bosnia and Herzegovina, on the condition that these funds are used exclusively for the rebuilding of the Muslim heritage. To make things even more complicated, donors – guided by their own values and good intentions – might make their support rest on the condition that all of the previously warring groups participate in a joint project and work together. However, after a conflict has broken the bonds of trust between communities and fomented fear and humiliation, not everyone will be ready to collaborate in this way. Some communities will need to recuperate and rebuild their confidence before being able to take that step. As a result, projects implemented by various organizations often end up using the same people, those willing to work together, while ignoring the communities in greatest need: those who are the most vulnerable to the influences of people who wish to perpetuate an environment of fear and hatred.

While each conflict is unique, all share a common characteristic: regardless of the complexity and the layers of struggles and forms of violence that make them up, they inevitably get simplified. Often this simplification reads along 'good guys vs. bad guys' lines. NGOs can easily get caught up in this and choose sides in the reconstruction work, igniting resentment, marking differences and potentially sowing the seeds of future conflict.

Post-conflict environments can be full of contradictions, making good intentions and intuition insufficient. Far more applied research is needed in order to develop appropriate and agreed reconstruction and peace-building methodologies. So, while Walter Benjamin defended the idea that pseudo-healing, or the patching up of deep wounds, prevents us from addressing the deeper trauma that needs to be faced in order for lasting recovery to take place, Archbishop Desmond Tutu argues for repentance and forgiveness as fundamental to healing. What is clear from the cases of Spain, South Africa and the former Yugoslavia, is that healing takes time. The time such healing has to take is not often reflected in the timescales of projects developed by organizations constrained to gain support from funders before a new cause pulls the interest of the latter in a completely different direction. When it is a matter of rebuilding elements of a symbolically charged heritage, the need for time might be even greater.

Box 6.5 Rebuilding religious symbols in Sarajevo

The international community mobilized itself to reconstruct the iconic buildings of the major religions of Sarajevo: the main Orthodox Church, the Catholic Church, the Mosque and the Synagogue. Yet beneath this tolerant inter-religious façade lies a reality that fits less with the rhetoric as new symbols of contention continued to be erected. Notable is the case of the mosque that has been built since the end of hostilities. It is perhaps the biggest that the city, once known as the city of the hundred mosques, has ever known. Built largely in concrete, with powerful loudspeakers to announce the call to prayer, it has been placed strategically, center stage to the amphitheatre of the Serbian neighborhood created by the geography of the river valley. This is echoed throughout the region with the construction of a Catholic church with an enormous bell tower in Mostar, or the construction of an equally large Orthodox and impossible to ignore church in Banja Luka. Rebuilding the symbolic religious buildings in Sarajevo's old town was a necessary and valuable action but without a parallel effort to engage with interpretations of destruction and reconstruction, it failed to fully utilize its mediating potential.

Lessons and policy implications

When foreign governments, NGOs and international organizations make reconstruction plans, the need to act efficiently in terms of limited time and resources can come to supersede long-term foresight.[18] Consultations with local communities are time-consuming and risk not delivering consensus over reconstruction plans. As a result, they often get sidestepped in the name of efficiency with the result that actions can appear patronizing, leaving local communities passive bystanders.

To illustrate the case, let us imagine a situation in which the UK or France had been devastated by war and international organizations and NGOs made up mainly of Croatian, Serbian, and Bosnian experts were called in to organize the reconstruction of Notre Dame, the Pont Neuf, St Paul's or Big Ben, with local populations being consulted only after key decisions had been made. Would it even matter that the experts involved were perfectly able to reproduce and rebuild these sites? Would these sites, rebuilt by foreigners, still 'belong' to the French or UK populations? What new meaning and symbolism would these places retain? Such questions must be addressed whenever foreign intervention is involved in the rebuilding of cultural heritage, no matter how well intentioned it may be.

For reconstruction projects to have long-tem peace-building effects on communities they need to embrace the complexity of post-conflict environments. Consultations can reflect conflicting interests and risk delaying projects if they are held early on in the planning stages. Yet, in environments characterized by volatile politics in which leaders change often, it is necessary to be able to assess the attitudes of the beneficiary communities. Otherwise, intervention can adopt a paternalistic role with echoes of colonialism and sap autonomy from the very groups it seeks to help. A consultative methodology that is carefully timed and continued throughout a project cycle can become a key tool in developing civil society by giving it a say in decision-making.[19]

Interpretation in the public sphere

Developing an interpretation that can be negotiated and offer a diverse reading of a site makes it possible to make the heritage a tool for integration, cultivating a pride of place. This requires an open dialogue that allows multiple perspectives to emerge. As interviews in Voskopojë revealed, there are different stories to explain the downfall of the city, the damage suffered by the churches and the fate of Voskopojë's inhabitants. This diversity of narratives is part of the wealth of the site. Integrating it into the physical restoration can encourage the local populations to take ownership of the space by giving their stories public recognition rather than favoring one account to the detriment of another.

In 1999, an international conference was held on combating stereotypes and prejudice in history textbooks in South-East Europe (*Disarming History.* Visby, Sweden). A similar dialogue with regard to the post-war interpretation of cultural heritage would be an equally valuable endeavor.[20]

Conclusion

> *In 1453, Mehmed the Conqueror called the task of reviving Constantinople after its conquest the 'mightiest war' compared with which the business of taking it had been merely one of the 'lesser wars'. (Mazower 2004: 31)*

Because the motives, forms and intensities involved in the destruction of cultural heritage are so diverse, 'quick and easy' reconstructions inevitably fail to protect the wealth and depth of meanings and symbols that make cultural heritage so important to societies. But we still have not learned enough about these meanings and symbols. We need international comparisons of conflicts and reliable statistics on destruction. We need also to be able to compare these findings with other data such as the percentage of teachers and intellectuals killed, for instance, in order to establish whether there are direct correlations between these various forms of violence as an indication of the motivations and intentionality behind the targeting of cultural heritage (in for example Sri Lanka, South Africa, Nicaragua, El Salvador, Uganda, East Timor, Lebanon, Cambodia or Haiti).

In post-conflict trauma work, the interrelation between the appropriations that the nation makes of memory and individual rejection or acceptance of these memories is part of the process of creating new meanings. It is through this negotiation that a public space can be created for people to express grief and come to terms with the psychological and emotional impact of loss (Hamber and Wilson, 1999).

Reluctance in traumatized post-conflict societies to confront responsibilities and reinterpret the loyalties and identities born of the conflict can entrench division, if left unaddressed (Boswell and Evans 1999). The decisions made on what cultural heritage is rebuilt and how it is interpreted affect the development of meaning and symbols in societies, and their relations to others. Therefore, forging a narrative of the past that does not carry the seeds of conflict into the future is essential. This can only be done with the involvement of the society that will create or/and legitimize the new meanings and symbols. If war in its destruction of cultural heritage can also destroy communal memory, then those responsible for rebuilding after war have some power to determine the messages, meanings and history that is constructed.[21]

War is not fought over cultural differences. However, the rhetoric that is built up around war is shot through with talk of values, historical references and – especially today – of cultural allegiances and commonalities on the one hand and irreconcilable differences on the other. This rhetoric has a powerful grip on our understanding of conflict and can mould our ways of thinking. Hence the overriding need to disarm in terms of cultural and historical weaponry so that historical hatreds and unbridgeable cultural differences are seen for what they are: constructions designed to manipulate emotions and inspire fear and hatred, not define truths, and that all too often mask the inequality, poverty and quest for political and economic power that are the root causes of conflict. The post-conflict reconstruction of cultural heritage can offer us a space in which we can begin to disarm the minds of men.

Notes

1 Nicola Lambourne (2001) provides an important blow-by-blow account of the destruction to historic monuments during World War II. Her systematic and thorough study shows how cultural heritage was rarely a deliberate target but every occasion was taken to portray it as such, making it of far greater interest to the propaganda machinery than to the military.

2 Kreimer, Eriksson, Muscat, Arnold, and Scott (1998). The World Bank's Experience with Post-Conflict Reconstruction. Washington: World Bank Publishing. The paper identifies five categories of conflicts with examples; I have developed their categorization a bit further to account for recent conflicts in Afghanistan and Iraq. In the paper, the authors argue that each category of socio-political emergency requires a different post-conflict reconstruction approach.

3 German forests were another type of cultural target identified by the British Air Ministry in World War II; the Hartz mountains and the Black Forest were particularly singled out as important material and psychological targets (Lambourne 2001: 143).

4 Wilhelm Treue's now classic book on the topic, *Art Plunder: The Fate of Works of Art in War, Revolution and Peace*, provides a thorough history of wartime looting in Europe from Antiquity through World War II. Amongst other accounts, Treue also relates the looting of Constantinople by the Crusaders and the sack of Rome.

5 The damage that conflict can cause does not only come in the shape of bombs. Conflicts inevitably cause the weakening of state structures and shifts in funding so that there is no money for salaries, maintenance, security, or training. Sanctions aggravate this situation, limiting resources for essential preventive care and inventorying activities. They also make looting archaeological sites a lucrative business. International isolation also makes emergency measures and rescue difficult.

6 This particular instance refers to the Church of St Nicholas, in Kijevë/Kijevo and Malishevë/Malisevo, the report also says that: 'The destruction is ongoing, as well as the use of the site as a dumping ground.'

7 This and further references to Voskopojë derive from the participation of the author in a restoration project run by two French organizations, the NGO *Patrimoine Sans Frontières* and the *Institut National du Patrimoine.*

8 Whether the museum was used by Iraqi military as a defensive position or not; whether some of the looting was the work of insiders with keys or not.

9 In 1941 an Ustashi Minister made a speech saying that 'there are not methods that the Ustashi will not use to make this land truly Croatian, and cleanse it of the Serbs'. Part of a quotation in Marcus Tanner (1992) *Croatia: A Nation Forged in War.* New Haven: Yale University Press.

10 Dragan Klaic (2002) "Lieu de mémoire: Partisan Hospital Franje". *Transeuropéennes* (Paris), 22, Spring/Summer 2002, 270–4.'The irony is that in the last decade hundreds of the partisan monuments, especially in Bosnia and in some parts of Croatia, were systematically destroyed by fanatic warriors who wanted to assert their own nationalist and anti-communist truth by erasing the partisan-written version of history – by dynamite or artillery. With this explosive handwriting the history of World War II was rewritten. ...' Some of the substitute monuments can be quite surprising, for instance the statue of Bruce Lee unveiled in Mostar in November 2005.

11 Comment by Roger Shipman, cited in Council of Europe document 6904, *Third Information Report on War Damage to the Cultural Heritage in Croatia and Bosnia-Herzegovina*, September 1993. Quoted by Lambourne, 2001, pp. 5–6. More recently, the US military was criticized for its failure to protect the National Museum of Baghdad during its invasion of Iraq in the name of democracy in April of 2003.

12 CT/P.I.S./932e Judgement in the case *The Prosecutor v. Pavle Strugar.* The Hague, 31 January 2005. Available on internet at *www.un.org/icty/pressrelease/2005/p932–e.htm*

13 These are not the only dynamics that affect cultural heritage. Further research needs to be done on: a) how differences or similarities between warring factions can influence the degree of destruction; b) how new weapons technology influences the ability to choose targets and the level of destruction; c) how the time factor, the capacity of immediate destruction, affects protective measures.

14 For a complete discussion of illicit trade, see : Neil Brodie, Jenny Doole, and Peter Watson (2000) *Stealing History: The Illicit Trade in Cultural Material.* Cambridge: The McDonald Institute for Archaeological Research.

15 C. Picard, 'Les recherches archéologiques de l'Armée Française en Macedoine, 1915–1919', *Annual of the British School at Athens*, 23 (1918–1919), 1–9. Cited by Mazower, 2004.

16 UNESCO's Director-General was referring to the massive destruction that followed the referendum on East Timor's independence in August 1999.

17 See an appeal signed by Ivo Banac, Shlomo Fischer, Rusmir Mahmutcehajic, Michael Sells and Adam B. Seligman published in *Bosnia Report.* New Series No: 32–4, December–July 2003. London: Bosnian Institute. Also, an article by Peter Ford. 'Mosques face new danger', first appeared in the *Christian Science Monitor* 25 July 2001 and reproduced by the *Bosnia Report.* No: 23/24/25, June–October 2001. London: Bosnian Institute.

18 Skotte, Hans 'NGOS Rebuild in Bosnia without Planning', on the Reuters Foundation's Alert Net at *www.alertnet.org/thefacts/reliefresources/600083.htm*, seen 3 July 2003.

19 Channeling reconstruction money through local officials can be faster but it also risks deepening divides. Local officials will be inclined to distribute aid to 'their sides' and preferred beneficiaries, as happened in many cases throughout Bosnia (Demichelis, 1998).

20 For a discussion of training policies in countries emerging from armed conflict see Martha Walsh (1997) *Post-conflict Bosnia and Herzegovina: Integrating women's special situation and gender perspectives in skills training and employment promotion programmes.* Geneva: International Labour Organization.

21 Ivo Maroevic (1998) 'Museums and the Development of Local Communities After the War', in *Towards a Museology of Reconciliation* at *www.maltwood. uvic.ca/tmr/maroevic.* See also Zlatko Isakovic (2000) *Identity and Security in Former Yugoslavia.* Aldershot: Ashgate Publishing, and Hakan Wiberg and Christian P. Scherrer (eds) (1999) *Ethnicity and Intra-State Conflict.* Aldershot: Ashgate, for descriptions of the stereotypes that different groups in the Balkans have of each other and the negative myths that reinforce them.

REFERENCES

Álvarez Lopera, José (1982) *La politica de bienes culturales del gobierno republicano durante la Guerra Civil Española*. Madrid: Dirección General de Bellas Artes, Archivos y Bibliotecas.

Barakat, Sultan, Wilson, Craig, Sankovic Simcic, Vjekoslava and Kokakovic, Marija (2001) 'Challenges and Dilemmas facing the Reconstruction of War-damaged Cultural Heritage: The Case Study of Pocitelj, Bosnia-Herzegovina', in Robert Layton et al. (eds.), *Destruction and Conservation of Cultural Property*. London: Routledge.

Boswell, David and Evans, Jessica (eds) (1999) *Representing the Nation: A Reader: Histories, Heritage and Museums*. New York and London: Routledge in association with the Open University.

Boylan, Patrick (1993) *Review of the Convention for the Protection of Cultural Property in the Event of Armed Conflict, The Hague Convention of 1954*. Paris: UNESCO publishing.

Burnham, Bonnie (2002) 'Countering cultural terrorism: a response to the destruction in Afghanistan'. World Monuments Fund accessed on 12/7/05 at: www.wmf.org/html/programs/Afghanistan.html

Butler, Judith (2004) *Precarious Life: The Powers of Mourning and Violence*. New York: Routledge.

CNN (2002) 'Ayodhya: India's religious flashpoint'. December 6.http://edition.cnn.com/2002/WORLD/asiapcf/south/12/06/ayodhya.background/

Demichelis, Julia (1998) *NGOs and Peacebuilding in Bosnia's Ethnically Divided Cities*. United States Institute of Peace, Special Report 32. www.usip.org/pubs/specialreports/early/BosniaNGO.html

Fletcher, Richard (1992) *Moorish Spain*. Berkeley: University of California Press.

Francioni, Francesco and Lenzerini, Federico (2003) 'The destruction of the Buddhas of Bamiyan and international law', *European Journal of International Law*, Vol. 14, No. 4, pp. 619–51.

Gamboni, Dario (1997) *The Destruction of Art: Iconoclasm and Vandalism since the French Revolution*. London: Reaktion Books.

Hladík, Jan (2001) 'Protection of cultural heritage during hostilities', *Museum International*, UNESCO, Paris, No. 211, Vol. 53, No. 3.

Hamber, Brandon and Wilson, Richard (1999) 'Symbolic closure through memory, reparation and revenge in post-conflict societies'. Centre for the Study of Violence and Reconciliation (CSVR), (www.wits.ac.za/csvr). Paper presented at the Traumatic Stress in South Africa Conference, Johannesburg South Africa, January.

International Criminal Tribunal for the former Yugoslavia. CT/P.I.S./932e Judgement in the case *The Prosecutor v. Pavle Strugar*. The Hague, 31 January 2005. Available on internet at *www.un.org/icty/pressrelease/2005/p932–e.htm*

Klaic, Dragan (2002) 'Lieu du mémoire: Partisan Hospital Franje', *Transeuropéennes* (Paris), 22, Spring/Summer 2002: 270–74.

Kreimer, Alcira, Eriksson, John, Muscat, Robert, Arnold, Margaret, and Scott, Colin (1998) *The World Bank's Experience with Post-Conflict Reconstruction*. Washington: World Bank Publishing.

Lambourne, Nicola (2001) *War Damage in Western Europe: The Destruction of Historic Monuments During the Second World War*. Edinburgh: Edinburgh University Press.

Lasnier, Jean-François (2002) 'Palestinian heritage under attack', *Art Newspaper*. June.

Layton, Robert, Stone, Peter G. and Thomas, Julian (eds) (2001) *Destruction and Conservation of Cultural Property*. London: Routledge.

Leith, James A. (1965) *The Idea of Propaganda in France – 1750–1799*. Toronto: University of Toronto Press.

Marlowe, Lara (1994) 'Destroying souls', *Time*, 8 August, No. 32, p. 43.

Mazower, Mark (2004) *Salonica: City of Ghosts, Christians, Muslims, Jews 1430–1950*. London: Harper Perennial.

McDonald Institute for Archaeological Research *Culture without Context,* Issue 15, Autumn 2004: 9–10.

Müller, Jan-Werner (ed.) (2002) *Memory and Power in Post-War Europe: Studies in the Presence of the Past*. Cambridge: Cambridge University Press.

Nafziger, James A.R. (2003) 'Protection of cultural heritage in time of war and its aftermath', *International Foundation for Art Research Journal*, Iraq Double Issue: Vol. 6, Nos. 1 & 2, www.ifar.org/heritage.htm

Preston, Paul (1995) *The Politics of Revenge: Fascism and the Military in 20th Century Spain*. London: Routledge.

Robinson, Mike (1999) 'Is cultural tourism on the right track?', *UNESCO Courier. August*. At http:// www.unesco.org/courier/1999_08/uk/dossier/txt11.htm

Scham, Sandra. (2004) 'High places: symbolism and monumentality on Mount Moriah, Jerusalem', *Antiquity*, Vol. 78, No. 301. September.

Shipepechero, Pedro 'Loss of artefacts may diminish role of museums', *African Church Information Service*. Posted to the web October 8, 2002. http://www.museum-security.org/O2/html#3

Tanner, Marcus (1992) *Croatia: A Nation Forged in War*. New Haven: Yale University Press.

Treue, Wilhelm (1960) *Art Plunder: The Fate of Works of Art in War, Revolution and Peace*. London: Methuen & Co. Ltd.

UNESCO (2005) *Protection and Preservation of Cultural Heritage in KOSOVO*: Consolidated Summary of an International Donors Conference organized by UNESCO in cooperation with the United Nations Interim Administration Mission in Kosovo (UNMIK), Council of Europe and European Commission. Paris,13 May 2005.

UNESCOPRESS, Press Release No.2002–28.

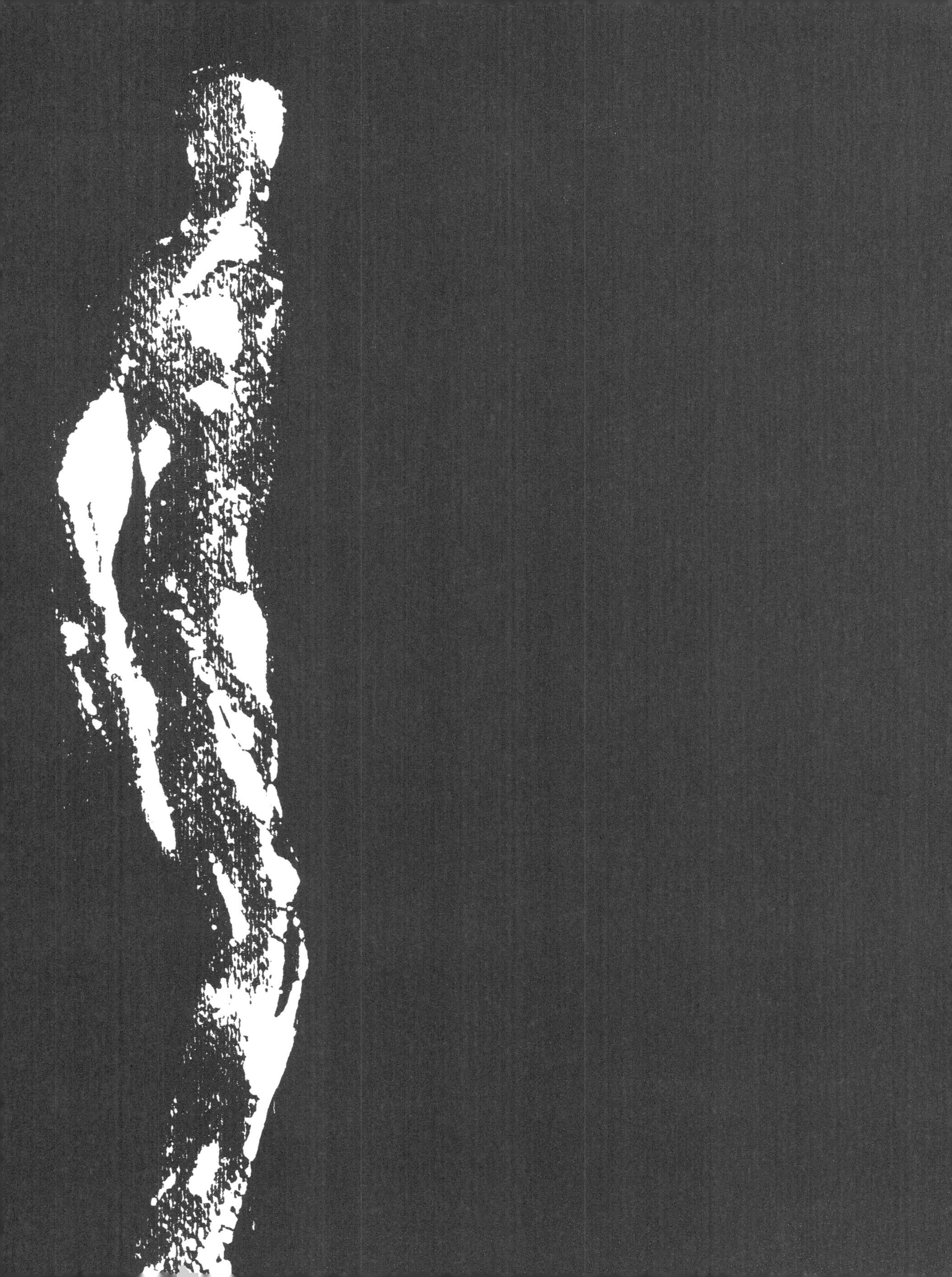

INTRODUCTION

Globalization has broken, or is challenging, the nexus between culture, polity and society virtually everywhere. Yet it is an uneven process, affecting different countries, regions and territories in unequal ways. David Held has used the terms extensity and intensity to describe this modulated presence of globalization across the globe, and Peter L. Berger coined the phrase 'many globalizations' to emphasize that both the process and its underlying drivers, are far from uniform. In this section, we bring together different refractions of this core theme.

Four analysts explore the conflict dimensions of cultures as they interact with the drivers of globalization in different regions – Francis Nyamnjoh looks at Africa, Ahmad Moussalli at the Arab world, Janadas Devan at Southeast Asia and Aníbal Ford at Latin America. Ronnie Lipschutz and Yuanxiang Yan deal with large nation-states of quasi-civilizational scope: the United States of America as the world's 'superpower' and its cultural hegemon in the view of many, and China, the emerging economic and political center of the twenty-first century. Anthony Giddens examines the European situation, in particular the 'European Social Model (ESM)' as a set of consensual socio-cultural values, and shows how globalization threatens both the social and the cultural in this now fragile consensus.

Each analyst is aware of the pitfalls of generalization and of the over-simplification to which it can lead. Common to all of these chapters, however, are the shared paradoxes and aspirations of a globalizing world. On the one hand, simultaneous cultural flows and closures; essentialist articulations of culture and belonging; the re-actualization of boundaries or the erection of new ones; the hardening of attitudes towards different categories of cultural others. On the other hand, the yearning for new fusions of horizons with regard to cultural difference; for the fluid, dynamic nature of 'identity' to be recognized both in principle and in practice; and for cultural conviviality as the seemingly natural outcome of a world of flexible, increasing mobility.

CHAPTER 7

CULTURES, CONFLICT AND GLOBALIZATION: AFRICA

Francis B. Nyamnjoh

Globalization and cultural conflict cannot be understood separately from the hierarchies that continue to inform social relations. African encounters, especially with Western colonialism and consumerism, have engineered a complex set of cultural conflicts: between indigenous African cultures and Western cultures; between advocates of cultural autonomy and those who have subscribed in varying degrees to Western cultures; and among different cultural associations, movements or groupings defending, contesting or appropriating inherited hierarchies from colonial classifications of African humanity and creativity. Cultural differences should be tolerated beyond tokenism, in order for the dynamic nature of culture to be accommodated in principle and practice and for cultural conviviality and interpenetration to be recognized as the natural outcomes of a world of flexible mobility.

Introduction

Neither globalization nor cultural conflict is a new phenomenon in Africa, even if the recent revolution in information and communication technologies has greatly intensified both. I shall argue that neither can be understood divorced from the hierarchies of race, ethnicity, geography, class, gender and citizenship that continue to inform social relations, although science and rhetoric both wave the flags of equality of humanity and opportunity. I shall demonstrate how encounters with Western colonialism and consumerism have negatively affected African humanity and creativity, and engineered a complex set of cultural conflicts. These conflicts are of various kinds: between indigenous African cultures and 'Western' cultures; between advocates of cultural autonomy and those who have subscribed in varying degrees to Western cultures; and among different cultural associations, movements or groupings that defend, contest or appropriate hierarchies inherited from colonial classifications. I shall conclude with a call for cultural differences to be tolerated beyond tokenism, for the dynamic nature of culture to be accommodated in principle and practice, and for cultural conviviality and interpenetration to be recognized as the natural outcomes of a world of flexible mobility.

Globalizing Africa, Africanizing globalization

Intensified globalization, in Africa as elsewhere, is marked by accelerated flows and, paradoxically, accelerated closures. The rhetoric of free flows and dissolving boundaries is countered by the intensifying reality of borders, divisions and violent strategies of exclusion. As the possibility of free and unregulated movement provokes a ready response by disadvantaged labour in search of greener pastures, the neo-liberal doctrine of globalization becomes more shadow than substance for most – with the exception of global capital, which is altogether unfettered in comparison to global labour. This glorification of multinational capital is having untold consequences, especially in marginal sites of accumulation such as Africa where devalued labour is far in excess of cautious capital. The accelerated flows of capital, goods, electronic information and migration induced by globalization have only exacerbated the insecurities and anxieties of locals and foreigners, citizens and subjects, insiders and outsiders, bringing about an even greater obsession with essentialist articulations of culture and belonging.

One stark result is the building or re-actualization of boundaries and differences through xenophobia and related intolerances. The response in many places is for states to tighten immigration regulations, and for local attitudes to harden towards foreigners, strangers and outsiders as cultural others. When unskilled migrants are reluctantly accepted, they are expected to fill the menial jobs which even the most destitute nationals reject. And should they succeed despite the odds in making ends meet from the margins, their success is likely to be at the root of xenophobia by excluded locals who feel more entitled.

In situations such as that of post-apartheid South Africa, where the majority of nationals are yet to graduate into meaningful citizenship, the competition with migrants for the lowest level jobs is keen, and so is the potential for cultural conflict. Claims of belonging are aggressive; feelings of hostility to migrants and their cultural values are excessive. The tendency is for migrants not only to be treated as labour zombies but also as hailing from inferior cultures (Nyamnjoh 2005a, 2006). In general, when 'cheap' outsider workers are readily available from foreign countries or from poorer regions and segments of the same country, 'the dirty, dangerous and difficult jobs' become stigmatized, racialized and ethnicized, as they are associated with outsiders as inferior cultural, racial or ethnic others to such a degree that those who consider themselves insiders are reluctant to undertake them (Geschiere and Nyamnjoh 2000; Shipler 2004; Nyamnjoh 2005a, 2006). As they are elsewhere, such accelerated closures are creating manifold problems in Africa, where flexible mobility has been part and parcel of life and livelihood since precolonial times (de Bruijn et al. 2001; MacGaffey 1995; Appiah 1992; Owolabi 2003).

For various reasons of race, ethnicity, geopolitics and socioeconomic interests, African cultures are among the most subjected and marginalized in the globalization process, even if relatively less so at the dawn of the twenty-first century than in the past (van Binsbergen and van Dijk 2004; Nyamnjoh, 2004a, 2004b; Oguibe 2004). Although global capitalism has facilitated harmonization and interconnection between 'seemingly disparate and incompatible zones of accumulation and production' (Surin 1995: 1191–6), its logic of 'winner-takes-all', of 'one-size-fits-all', of 'undomesticated agency', and of 'Barbie democracy' (Nyamnjoh 2005b: 25–80) plus its practice of putting 'profit over people' (Chomsky 1999) have largely informed how, by whom and for what purposes advances in information and communications technologies (ICT) are appropriated. Its obsession with binaries compels its converts either to choose its one-best-way logic, or to be at conflict with their own selves by living a lie, appearing to be less than what they actually are through constantly trying to suppress identities that make of them melting-pots of cultural influences. Technology has indeed created the possibility and even the likelihood of a global culture (Berger and Huntington 2002), although the extent to which such a culture is built on a global consensus and on a common sense of humanity and creativity remains to be established. The fax machine, satellite, television, Internet and cell phone are simultaneously sweeping away and reinforcing cultural boundaries. True, the global culture industries are shaping the perceptions and dreams of ordinary citizens and subjects regardless of their geographies or cultures of daily articulation, but who and whose culture have access to recognition and representation depend not only on economic factors, but also on the hierarchies of race, ethnicity, class, gender and geography that temper the dominant rhetoric of unregulated flows (Nyamnjoh 2006; Oguibe 2004).

Privileged in this flow of values, norms and cultures are Western ideals of consumer capitalism. The celebration of an aggressive, determined and globally mass-mediated consumerism as the ultimate unifier, the supreme indicator of sophistication, the symbol of civilization, or the very mark of existence for individuals, communities and peoples, has, in a context of structural hierarchies had the effect of taking the globe hostage to a very narrow idea of culture, creativity and humanity. In the interest of predictability, calculability and profitability, the tendency is to standardize, streamline, routinize and transnationalize cultural production in ways insensitive to creative diversity and ultimately to the humanity of those at the margins of power and privilege (Ritzer 1996; Thomas and Nain 2004; Oguibe 2004).

It is hardly surprising, as UNESCO notes, that more than half the world's population are presently in danger of cultural and economic exclusion. Of the world's approximately 6000 languages only 4 per cent are used by 96 per cent of the world population, 50 per cent are in danger of extinction, while 90 per cent are not represented on the Internet. Some 5 countries dominate world trade in the cultural industries. In the field of cinema, for instance, 88 countries out of 185 have never had their own film production[1] (see also Rourke 2004; Oguibe 2004). Even when popular alternatives with relevant cultural content such as the Nigerian home video entertainment industry (Nollywood) are initiated, technological and distribution difficulties make it impossible for such initiatives to compete with, let alone challenge, the dominance of the Western culture industries.

The reality of unequal access for the world's cultures, combined with the aggressive targeting of budding, young and often innocent consumers poses a real threat to the marginalized cultures of Africa in the global arena. Poor African countries seduced by mass advertising by the global machines of desire are flooded with first- and second-hand cultural goods, to which their citizens and subjects succumb to varying degrees. Sentiments of cultural insecurity and of being besieged are on the increase among Africans, including even among those who would ordinarily subscribe to cultural dynamism and interpenetration. Thus, instead of broadening cultural possibilities in a significant way, globalization has, in its 'culture game' tended to homogenize, standardize, streamline and routinize the consumer palates of non-Western others, ensuring that emphasis is on passive internalization and regurgitation of Western menus, not on global buffets, critical digestion and engagement. In this way, 'the global culture game' succeeds not in annihilating or in bringing about conviviality, but rather in making of difference an 'obsession' and 'an essence that neither reality nor the imagination seems able to dislodge' (Oguibe 2004: xiv).

Even when token attention is paid to other cultures in its streamlined menus, the emphasis on commercialization has been known to have a disturbing impact on people, as what once were elements of their ways of life with great symbolic and spiritual value become mere commodities for consumer tourism and entertainment. At the same time, people are increasingly bombarded with new images, new music, new clothes and new values, even when the new is in reality second-hand and second-rate. The familiar and old are to be discarded or undermined not consistently or the world over, but only in those regions and cultures purged, a priori, of the privilege and power to define themselves into relevance, recognition, representation, competitiveness and visibility. The role of local cultures as spontaneous and integral parts of ordinary lives is eroded and their impact as a means of constructing societal values, reproducing group identity and building social cohesion, diminishes. The end result of global integration without obvious benefits for all and sundry is achieved at the risk of local uncertainties, insecurities and overt conflicts.

Regions or states insist on cultural recognition through national media at their own peril, at the risk of losing audiences to cheap, affordable packages delivered by satellite by the global conglomerates. In Africa, fear of losing viewers or the inability to provide local content, has pushed many a local television station in various countries to fill their transmissions with cost-effective Western content: superficial and often irrelevant news broadcasts, quiz shows, sports, sex and violence, all of which are sensational advertisements luring Africans to join the global consumer bandwagon. The desires awoken by the global consumer bandwagon push thousands to move to already overcrowded sprawling commercial capital cities. There, they risk their lives attempting to emigrate to the West and other purported centres of accumulation. The majority of these new immigrants end up devalued, zombified and in abject poverty, often unable to contain the rising expectations of remittances by family and friends (Nyamnjoh 2005a).

The cumulative effect in Africa is a crisis of cultural confidence, combined with increased economic uncertainty and the inability of African states to defend the best interests of Africans. This creates real problems for social solidarity, whether it is at the level of states, communities or families, as, faced with the ever widening circles of exclusion, the natural response is to diminish or tighten the circles of inclusion or belonging.[2] The globalization of consumerism thus appears to wage war upon all other cultures, eclipsing, subordinating or confining them to particular localities, while inviting its converts within those cultures to bid farewell, in the name of freedom, to their traditions and practices whatever their achievements and relevance. The appearance of Christian fundamentalism in the very heartlands of the globalizing forces of the world, suggests that even here, there is a sense that values, beliefs and faith are being sacrificed to global necessity, and there has been an effort even by the most spectacular beneficiaries of economic globalization to salvage what they see as some of their most precious truths. The stigmatizing of the bearers of resistance as extremists, terrorists or those who hate freedom is too simple a formulation for these complex and painful processes. To be unable to acknowledge the profound and complex social and religious disruptions that come as inseparable spectral companions of economic globalization has been the most grievous failure of the rich and powerful. That this strikes at the roots of human search for meaning ought to have been clear, particularly to those who invest so much in intelligence and security – abstractions which have become as insubstantial as the terror against which these are supposed to be deployed.[3] (See also Clinton 2001; Mamdani 2004.)

Yet, because real life is larger than media representations, because global consumerism is like a bazaar to which many are called but few rewarded, and because not everyone is attracted (to the same degree) by the consumer bandwagon, mass mediated cultural exclusion is not always synonymous with cultural death. Opinion is mixed even among social scientists on the cultural opportunities and encumbrances of globalization (Berger and Huntington 2002; Appadurai 2001; van Binsbergen and van Dijk 2004; Smith 1990; Hall 1992). The global character and ramifications of consumer capitalism notwithstanding, people's responses to it are far from homogeneous, simple, or predictable. Various factors inform how different peoples and regions relate to the globalization of uncertainties and insecurities: the commonalities and particularities of regional and local histories, politics, cultural and material realities, as well as the social configurations developed among individuals, groups and communities. The aggressive spread of the streamlined consumerist culture often under the control of Western multinationals brings new challenges to local cultures and communities. In the case of Africa, the situation is worsened by the fact that states are increasingly unable to handle their own cross-border flow of ideas, images and resources that affect cultural development.

Cultural encounters, marginalization and the violence of cultural conversion

Given the paucity of positive and mass cultural production by Africans and on Africa at the global market place and the low level of ICT domestication in Africa, non-Africans and Africans alike are forced to draw on an overwhelmingly negative catalogue of cultural representations of the continent by others. Film, art and publications by Africans, or that capture the richness and dignity of African humanity and creativity, are hard to come by, and often, even well-meaning people interested in Africa are fed by caricatures, stereotypes and prejudices that date back to the colonial period and beyond. Thus even Africans, in the face of compounding uncertainties and their own insecurities, draw on these same negative images as they seek to outgrow one another. Elite Africans have tended to articulate their acculturation in ways that conflict with the mainstream though often devalued cultures of ordinary Africans in urban ghettos and rural villages. Tensions have emerged between Africans who have adopted and adapted to cultural values and interests perceived as foreign, and their families and communities seen as largely faithful to their age-old cultural traditions. Themes of 'creative conflicts' or 'creative destruction' abound in popular culture, ranging from music to art through fiction, that demonstrate not only the tensions embedded in cultural encounters, but also the psychological and emotional violence of conversion that Africans have suffered thanks to cultural marginalization through slavery, colonialism, education, and the globalization of consumer capitalism.

Although Africans have always had cultures, encounters with others have not always acknowledged African creativity nor credited their cultures with much worth preserving. Unlike Asia (the Orient) which the West, upon initial contact, credited with some degree of civilization and therefore opted for cultural interpenetration, Africa (the Dark Continent) was considered virgin ground in matters cultural, with little to boast of but savagery and babyishness. Thus instead of cultural interpenetration, the West went for wholesale cultural conversion (Bryceson 2000), and if it has succeeded more with the post-colonial elite, this by no means implies only they were targeted (Walker 1911; Comaroff and Comaroff, 1997; Magubane 2004; Landau and Kaspin 2002). Subjected to white racism and its unilinear logic of the pursuit of a universal civilization through a eurocentric index of modernization and globalization (Winant 2004), Africans and their cultures have been depicted and related to as inferior, as belonging to the margins of humanity and creativity, and as deserving to be despised and outgrown. Modernity or development, since contact with Europe, has traditionally been conceived, presented and pursued as something induced from without, a process that favours imitation over originality and appropriation. Such a concept of modernity to Africans has entailed self-denial, self-abandonment, or self-humiliation, and the adoration of most things Western – packaged and presented as the norm in a variety of ways, both crude and subtle. Supposedly universalistic and achievement-oriented, Western cultures are expected to penetrate the backward-looking cultures with their values through a unilinear process of inter-cultural communication (Oguibe 2004). Everything new is considered to be progress, as long as it is the uncritical reproduction of the 'McDonaldized' and 'CocaCola-ized' versions of society perfected in the West and spearheaded by the United States of America (Ritzer 1996; Warnier 1999). Such expectations of westernization have only accelerated with the globalization of consumerism and of poverty (Nyamnjoh, 2005a and 2005c).

Globalization to Africans thus entails the celebration of Western achievements, prejudices and stereotypes. Salvation, comfort or self-betterment is seen as something possible only with Westernization, as African civilizations and cultures are perceived as constrictive and conservative – crushing opponents of progress that must be countered with the assistance of the media and culture industries as 'magic multipliers' of knowledge, information and propaganda. Globalization has thus intensified a long-standing tradition of inviting Africans to devalue themselves, their institutions and their cultures by cultivating an uncritical empathy for Western economic, cultural and political values which are glorified beyond impeachment by the hegemonic structures that underpin them. They are presented as having little chance of progress as Africans or blacks, and invited to intensify their assumed craving to become like the whites in Europe and North America. The rhetoric of tolerance to cultural difference notwithstanding, the entire paradigm is in reality impatient with alternative systems of thought and practice, and seeks cultural homogeneity by imposing the Western consumer outlook and approach as the one best way of achieving betterment (Warnier 1999). Modernity as hegemonic 'modes of social life and organisation' of European origin (Giddens 1990) thus poses as a giant compressor determined to crush every other civilization and culture in order to reduce them to the model of the industrialized West.

Instead of recognizing and accommodating the fact that 'people are fiercely proud of their heritage, language, customs, religion and traditional ways of life' (Halloran 1993: 4), Western ambitions of dominance have set about suppressing African pride, creativity and self-esteem through physical conquest, coercion and persuasion, as Vernon February's study of the 'coloured' stereotype in apartheid literature in South Africa demonstrates (February 1981). There was and there still very much is, even by social scientists, 'the unconditional condemnation of African culture[s]' and 'the unconditional affirmation of the colonisers' world view' (Nnoli 1980: 2).

This not only dispossesses Africans of their own cultures, it infantilizes and debases them by forcing them to learn afresh, under the guidance of condescending and overbearing Western overlords, new ways of seeing, doing and being. Undermining, marginalizing and distorting African cultures minimizes the empowerment that Africans and their communities are able to draw from these cultures to fight domination. This, as Franz Fanon has argued, creates and sustains the myth of the inferior native and a justification for domination. The harbingers of Western cultural values, by alienating the Africans from their traditions through 'cultural estrangement', reinforce in Africans a self-hatred and a profound sense of inferiority that compels them 'to lighten their darkness' for white gratification (Fanon 1967: 169). Thus skin lightening creams and culture-bleaching products are made available to Africans as if to suggest that 'black cannot be the ideal of beauty' (Hamelink 1983: 2), or that black cultural achievements could not be pacesetters. Whiteness has come to symbolize power, authority, status, and above all, the good life even for the most fragile or the most mediocre of whites (Nyamnjoh and Page 2002). It is hardly surprising that the tendency for Africans subjected to such pressure has been to join the global consumer bandwagon, and only when denied access to promised consumer goodies do they turn round to seek cultural revalorization as a way of coping with the uncertainties and insecurities that come with globalization as a process of flows and closures.

Globalized uncertainties and the quest for security through autochthony

Through its policy of inventing indigenes/natives, colonialism created or reinforced hierarchies among the native populations of its African colonies, whereby Africans who came closest to Europeans either through physical attributes or culturally through educational achievements and mimicry, were placed at the top of the hierarchy of the subjected. This arbitrary racist and administrative system of categorization was internalized and reproduced at independence by the post-colonial states, to give rise to a lethal cocktail of competing identities. Privileging divide and rule, the system thrived on freezing individuals into citizens and subjects, depending on whether their lives were governed by the civic regime of laws or by culture and tradition, hardly providing for the reality of those straddling both regimes in their daily lives. Even in the world of total subjection to the registers of culture and ethnic tradition, the craving to divide and rule was such that there was all to gain in polarizing or freezing identities, by ensuring that invented ethnic (cultural) citizens and ethnic (cultural) strangers put asunder by colonial racism and administration shall never meet and work in harmony (Mamdani 1996, 2001; Nnoli 1998; Gourevitch 1998; Akinyele 2000). In the case of Rwanda, which was later to turn genocidal in 1994, the colonial and post-colonial authorities refused to recognize the age-old cultural conviviality of the Hutus and Tutsis that they were so determined to keep asunder. They would not acknowledge, until it was too late, the sociology of the Hutus and Tutsis who had come to speak the same language, follow the same religion, intermarry, and live intermingled, without territorial distinctions, on the same hills, sharing the same social and political culture in small chiefdoms (Maquet 1961; Gourevitch 1998: 47–74).

The result has been for people to increasingly embrace the Western obsession with boundaries, binaries, hierarchies and belonging in very essentialist terms. This is an obsession that brings with it the questioning of previous assumptions about nationality, citizenship, solidarity and interconnectedness. This is as true of how nationals and citizens perceive and behave towards one another as insiders, as it is of how they behave towards immigrants, migrants, and/or foreigners as outsiders. The crisis of citizenship and subjection flamed by mutually exclusionary discourses and claims of entitlement and injury by the Hutu–Tutsi divide in Rwanda that resulted in the genocidal extravaganza of 1994 (Gourevitch 1998; Mamdani 2001; Melvern 2000), along with the current conflict in Côte d'Ivoire fuelled by competing and exclusionary claims of *Ivoireté* [Ivorianness] (Fanon 1967: 125; Akindès, 2004; Vidal, 2003; Zongo 2003; ICG, 2004) are sufficiently indicative of how increasingly difficult it is to be sanguine about belonging in Africa under liberal democracy and global consumer capitalism (Geschiere and Nyamnjoh 2000; Bayart et al. 2001; Englund and Nyamnjoh 2004; Nyamnjoh, 2005b). Inspired by the global culture game of obsession with difference (Oguibe 2004), Africans desperate for recognition and representation at local and global levels, are using various cultural platforms to stake competing and conflicting claims.

In Nigeria the oil rich Niger Delta minority ethnic groups who have seen themselves victimized 'by the politicization and ethnicization of the resource allocation process by the Nigerian state and its elites', have resorted to autochthony to lay claim to priority and privileged access to oil revenue and resources, as sons and daughters of the Delta soil. And when Shell and the Nigerian state have not heeded their demands, these minorities have resorted to various strategies, including violence and the use of cultural associations to seek entitlements and to attract attention and sympathy (Anugwom 2005). Indeed, not only ethnic minorities are contesting the idea of 'one Nigeria' under which independence was obtained. It has been noted that many of Nigeria's constituent units are regrouping under regional and ethnic cultural umbrellas, often in violent contestations that threaten the state (Alubo 2004; Aluko 2003; Owolabi 2003).

Feeding on images of surging global tensions between Islam and Christianity, relations between Christian and Muslim communities in Nigeria have often been conflictual, sometimes resulting in violent clashes, especially in cases of territorial encroachment, perceived trivialization, or attitudes of disrespect vis-à-vis their respective religious values (Harnischfeger 2004). The media not only reflect such tensions and conflicts, their coverage has tended to be biased in favour of this or that religious community, depending on whether ownership of the media and the journalists involved are Christian or Muslim. Such politics of belonging and polarization in the media are well evidenced in and around the debate on the introduction of Sharia law in the predominantly Muslim northern states of Nigeria (Adebanwi 2005). After the September 11th terrorist attacks against the United States, violence between Christians and Muslims spread to the city of Kano. Over 200 people were killed in Kaduna, in response to a journalist's comments in a Nigerian newspaper *This Day* regarding the Prophet Mohammad and the likelihood that he would have taken one of the contestants of the Miss World beauty pageant due to take place in Nigeria during Ramadan for a wife. The February 2006 worldwide violent protests by Muslims over Danish newspaper cartoons of the Prophet Mohammed played into the hands of the Muslim–Christian divide in Nigeria, resulting in the deaths of Christians in the north and Muslims in the south. However, the conflict also lies in competition for jobs, patronage, control of government, and Muslim fears that they are being overtaken by faster birth rates in the Christian south (Henneman 2003).

In Sudan, where an intractable war has raged for decades between 'the Arabs and Arabised largely Muslim Northern Sudanese' on the one hand, and 'non-Arabised black largely Christian Southern Sudanese' on the other, at stake are bitter feelings of debasement, exclusion and exploitation on racial and cultural grounds amongst the latter (Akinyele 2000). Currently in the global spotlight is the Darfur region where the Sudanese government has been accused of encouraging widespread rape and genocide. The conflict is endemic, 'including inter-communal violence, the depredations of Chadian militias using the region as a springboard for their ambitions in their own country, banditry, and counter-insurgency by the Sudanese armed forces and their proxy militias', a situation worsened by the proliferation of small arms (De Waal 2005: 127).

In the Horn of Africa, Assefa argues, elites find ethnic prejudices and stereotypes fertile ground in which they can easily cultivate support for their political and economic aspirations. Expressing their objectives in ethnic or nationality terms (such as 'advancing the interest of our own people' or 'protecting ourselves from another ethnic group') ennobles the pursuits and gives them more legitimacy. As we have seen in many instances in the continent, the major beneficiaries of such aspirations might be the elites, but the whole ethnic group becomes associated with these aims since they are pursued in the name of the entire group. Once this cycle starts and conflict begins to be waged in the group's name, fear and further animosity pervade the whole group, since all members become perceived as the enemy by those against whom the conflict is being waged. Thus, a conflict started by the elites ends up, in a self-fulfilling prophecy, engulfing the entire ethnic group.[4]

Even countries like Botswana, where ethnic citizenship and belonging had almost disappeared in favour of a single political and legal citizenship and of nation-building, there has, in recent years, been a resurgence of cultural identity politics. Tensions over belonging have mounted, as various groups seek equity, better representation and more access to cultural representation, natural resources and opportunities (Werbner and Gaitskell 2002; Werbner 2004; Nyamnjoh 2006: 82–112). In such situations and in the light of inherited colonial hierarchies compounded by globalization, while every national can assert their legal citizenship, some see themselves or are seen by others to be less authentic claimants. The growing importance of cultural identity politics and more exclusionary ideas of citizenship are matched by the urge to detect difference and to distinguish between 'locals', 'nationals', 'citizens', 'autochthons' or 'insiders' on the one hand, and 'foreigners', 'immigrants', 'strangers' or 'outsiders' on the other, with the focus on opportunities, economic entitlements, cultural recognition and political representation (Nyamnjoh and Rowlands 1998; Nnoli 1998; Geschiere and Gugler 1998; Geschiere and Nyamnjoh 2000; Werbner 2004; Harnischfeger 2004; ICG 2004; Nyamnjoh, 2005b).

Customary African values (for example, the widely shared philosophy of life, and conceptions of agency and responsibility that assert interdependence over autonomy) and policies of inclusion are under pressure from the politics of entitlements in an era of sharp downturns and accelerated flows of opportunity-seeking capital and migrants. Voices have been raised claiming autochthony over certain lands, especially those deemed to promise greater opportunity, and Africans almost everywhere are foraging in colonial archives for maps either to legitimate or contest claims of belonging. The creation of elite cultural and development associations that often tend to serve more overtly political than cultural ends and targeting the state and international NGOs for resources, recognition and representation, is the order of the day throughout the continent (Nyamnjoh and Rowlands 1998; Werbner 2004). Ethnic communities have bought into world heritage projects, building memorials, museums and websites, and organizing festivals to showcase their claims for cultural authenticity as a way of earning financial, political and symbolic capital through re-imagined traditions. Autochthony or the ever growing obsession with purity and belonging to ever diminishing circles seems to be the reality everywhere. National and regional boundaries are deployed strategically to reinforce stratified access to resources by race and ethnicity as in the case of the 1989 conflict between Senegal and Mauritania. With regard to the Casamance conflict in Senegal, Sonko argues that upon independence the Senegalese government implemented a system of territorial division and administration that did not take into account the local cosmogony and the territorial and social systems like ethnic, religious and regional affiliations and political expressions. By imposing regional administrators from other parts of Senegal in the name of nation-building, the feeling of the people in Casamance is that of being under foreign occupation. Scarcity of social and economic resources reinforces this feeling, in particular due to the 'prebendal, tribalistic and embezzlement practices of some civil servant'. Autochthony remains meaningful in the Casamance conflict and the local leadership invoke it to legitimize their claims. 'The antagonism between the indigenous populations and fellow Senegalese seen as foreigners, occur in a context of scarcity of the social and economic resources' (Sonko 2004: 30-1).

Outsiders are increasingly unwelcome, and even those who are welcome are not socially accepted, as various cultural indicators (e.g., the ability to speak the local language) are used to ensure that their outsider status is never lost. This is especially the case in countries where the economies are still attractive to local and foreign devalued labour, as is the case in industrialized (e.g., South Africa), mineral rich and relatively better governed (e.g., Botswana), or oil rich (e.g., Gabon, Equatorial Guinea, Nigeria) countries. Taking the example of South Africa and Botswana, immigrants from other black African countries (e.g., Zimbabwe, Nigeria, Congo) where economies have suffered greater downturns, are referred to derogatorily as *Makwerekwere*, depicting not only their inability to articulate the local languages, but also the savagery of their own languages and cultures of origin (Nyamnjoh 2006). In Gabon and Equatorial Guinea, clashes with and expulsion of foreigners are not uncommon, as citizens and indigenes seek to confine opportunities to the tested sons and daughters of the soil. In mineral-rich Democratic Republic of Congo, post-Mobutu political chaos has combined with cultural politics to reverse achievements in national citizenship with wars flamed by ethnic belonging. In all countries, even the citizenship of one another is increasingly subjected to scrutiny, using ever-tighter culturally determined criteria of belonging.

Thus in Cameroon, although foreigners (especially the dynamic Nigerian trading community from the Igbo ethnic area) are accused of 'arrogance and ostentation' (Nkene 2003), the cultural tensions and conflicts are often between Cameroonians themselves, whose claims of belonging are articulated around land and entitlements as 'authentic sons and daughters of the ethnic soil'. Anglophone and Francophone Cameroonians are always warring (verbally) over their inherited English and French colonial values, and so are the various groups within and between the two colonial divisions, which adds an interesting dimension to identity politics and mobilization in Cameroon. Anglophones and Francophones from the Bamenda and Bamileke grassfields are the most migratory group in the country, with a nose for opportunities that is unequalled, and are thus derogatorily referred to as 'come-no-go', together with a catalogue of other negativities meant to portray them as culturally inferior. Political clashes since the reintroduction of multiparty politics in the 1990s have been largely between cultural others, and migrants from this region of Cameroon, who are seen as a threat to diminishing opportunities. ((Nyamnjoh and Rowlands 1998; Geschiere and Nyamnjoh 2000; Konings and Nyamnjoh 2003; Nyamnjoh 2005b).

Scholarly, political, popular doctrines and ideologies of cultural valorization

Doctrines and ideologies asserting the importance of African creativity, symbolic representations and worldviews have proliferated since independence. Among the most well known have been: *authenticité* of Mobutu (Zaire), *négritude* of Senghor (Senegal), *Consciencism* of Nkrumah (Ghana), *Ujamaa* of Nyerere (Tanzania), *Harambee* of Kenyatta (Kenya), *African Renaissance*, and *Ubuntu* of Mbeki (South Africa). These are parallel to similar movements by Africans in the diaspora, who are keen to reassert perceived lost cultural roots as a result of forced and voluntary migration. In certain scholarly and artistic circles, the belief in an essential African culture and identity has become very popular, the aim being, at least in rhetoric, to distance Africans from the corrupting influence of white supremacy and its morally degenerate consumer culture. Afrocentricity is the name of this perception of what it means to be culturally African. Together with religious fundamentalism inspired by Islam and local variants of Christianity such as healing charismatic churches (Devisch 1996; Mamdani 2004), this Afrocentricity has sometimes resulted in violent clashes with icons of Western cultures.

A case in point is the clashes in Northern Nigeria against the hosting of the Miss World/Miss Universe beauty contest, which resulted in deaths and the movement of the event from Abuja to London. Clashes over religion are commonplace in Nigeria, especially between the largely Muslim Hausa and Fulbe communities of the North, and the mainly Christian Igbo traders who hail from the South East. In South Africa where until 1994 black cultures were either deprived of meaningful existence or caricatured for instrumental purposes in the service of apartheid, conscious efforts at re-traditionalization are now under way. Traditional chieftaincy, initiation and circumcision rites, occultism and traditional beliefs are being revived among black ethnic groups and cultural communities, resulting in tensions between advocates of such cultural revivalism on the one hand, and those who associate these practices with slowing down modernization, development, democracy and struggles to contain the HIV/AIDS pandemic in South Africa. Naming and renaming of cities and public places, the enactment of monuments to celebrate African cultural figures, are contentious issues in post-apartheid South Africa. Cultural revivalism through claims of autochthony are increasingly deployed by elites either to seek political power in a context of multipartyism or to secure or maintain access to land and resources otherwise endangered by universal civic citizenship.

Conclusion

The way forward from the above scenarios is in recognizing and providing for the fact that culture and belonging are processes subject to renegotiation. For one thing, political, cultural, historical, and, above all, economic realities, determine what form and meaning the articulation of belonging assumes in any given context. The possession of rights is something individuals and communities may be entitled to, but who actually enjoys rights does not merely depend on what individuals and groups may wish.

Addressing the cultural uncertainties and anxieties that have intensified with globalization is hardly to be accomplished through a narrow and abstract definition of belonging. The answer is not simply to shift from a state-based to a more individual-based universal conception of citizenship, as some have suggested, since this fails to provide for the rights of collectivities, however construed. The answer to the impermanence of present-day achievements, lies in incorporating 'outsiders' without stifling difference, and in the building of new partnerships across those differences. The answer, in other words, is in a cosmopolitan life informed by allegiances to cultural meanings drawn from different sources in the rich repertoire of multiple, kaleidoscopic encounters.

Some have argued in favour of a cosmopolitanism informed by relationships that stress 'a deterritorialized mode of belonging', that makes it possible to feel at home away from home (Englund 2004). As noted above, African communities are historically renowned for their flexibility of mobility and belonging, a reality only enhanced by the arbitrary nature of colonial boundaries on the one hand and a mainstream philosophy of life, agency, meaning and responsibility that privileges people over profit. The tendency especially in Africa has been for scholars to de-emphasise small-scale 'ethnic' in favour of large-scale 'civic' citizenship, whose juridico-political basis is uncritically assumed to be more inclusive than the cultural basis of ethnic citizenship (Mamdani 1996, 2001). The mistake has been to focus analysis almost exclusively upon institutional and constitutional arrangements, thereby downplaying the hierarchies and relationships of inclusion and exclusion informed by race, ethnicity, class, gender and geography that determine belonging in real terms (An-Na'im 2002; Englund and Nyamnjoh 2004; Harnischfeger 2004; Alubo 2004). There has been too much focus on 'rights talk' and its 'emancipatory rhetoric', and too little attention accorded the contexts, meanings and practices that make belonging possible for some but an aspiration relentlessly deferred for most. The concept of cultural citizenship has actually won itself more disciples recently, not least from among scholars, who are no longer simply keen on juridico-political citizenship but also on claiming belonging over and beyond the essentialist identities the state has to offer.

What should therefore be celebrated about globalization in Africa and elsewhere is its potential to offer a type of unity in diversity, where the fact of belonging to the same consumer club does not guarantee cultural synchronization (Lapham 1992). As Halloran puts it (quoting a cynic) in reference to warring Serbs, Croats, Slovenes, Bosnians and Macedonians of the former Yugoslavia, all watching the same television for years has done for them is that they 'may march to fight each other wearing the same T-shirts whistling the same pop tune and with a can of coke and a Mars bar in their packs'. They have little else in common 'other than a tribally based hate and a need to "cleanse"' (Halloran 1993: 2). We may as well come to terms with the fact that despite the increasing synchronization of consumer tastes and habits at a global level, the cultural heterogeneity of the modern world seems to get deeper instead. Difference should be seen as 'something that relates disparate realms of experience rather than separates them' (Erlmann 1994: 166). Globalization should thus be able to harmonize seemingly disparate and incompatible zones of accumulation and production, without necessarily posing identification with a global culture as a pre-condition.

The challenge is clearly to hearken to the reality of Africans and their communities at work in laboratories that experiment with different configurations, as they seek broader, more flexible regimes of belonging. Here meaningful cultural, political, economic recognition and representation could be negotiated for individuals and groups to counter the ever diminishing circles of inclusion. Just as cultural, economic and social citizenship are as valid as juridico-political citizenship, collective, group or community citizenship is as valid as individual citizenship, to be claimed at every level, from the most small-scale local to the most mega-scale global level. The emphasis should be on the freedom of individuals and communities to negotiate inclusion, opt out and opt in with flexibility of belonging in consonance with their realities as straddlers of a kaleidoscope of identity margins.

Obviously, such flexible belonging is incompatible with the prevalent illusion that the nation-state is the only political unit permitted to confer citizenship in the modern world. Nor is it compatible with a regime of rights and entitlements that is narrowly focused on yet another chimera – 'the autonomous individual'. Everywhere the price of perpetuating these illusions has been the proliferation of ultra-nationalism, chauvinism, racism, tribalism and xenophobia that have consciously denied the fragmented, multinational and heterogeneous cultural realities of most so-called 'nation-states'. Almost everywhere, this narrow model has cherished hierarchies based on race, ethnicity, class, gender and geography, that have tended to impose on perceived inferior others decisions made by those who see themselves as more authentic or more deserving of citizenship. Belonging that hails from such a celebration of insensitivities is not a model for a future of increased mobility, or for the satisfaction of its individual and collective victims.

Notes

1 http://portal.unesco.org/culture/en/ev.php-URL_ID=11605&URL_DO=DO_TOPIC&URL_SECTION=201.html

2 'The drawbacks of cultural globalization' by Wole Akande *Yellow Times* November 10, 2002. http://globalpolicy.igc.org/globaliz/cultural/2002/1110cult.htm

3 Jeremy Seabrook 'Localizing cultures', in the *Korean Herald* January 13, 2004. (http://globalpolicy.igc.org/globaliz/cultural/2004/0113jeremyseabrook.htm)

4 Hizkias Assefa 'Ethnic conflict in the Horn of Africa: myth and reality'. http://www.unu.edu/unupress/unupbooks/uu12ee/uu12ee06.htm#2.%20ethnic%20conflict%20in%20the%20horn%20of%20africa:%20myth%20and%20reality

REFERENCES

Adebanwi, W. (2005) 'Media, narratives and identity politics: the Shari'a debate and secularism in Nigeria'. Paper presented at the 2005 CODESRIA Governance Institute, Dakar, Senegal.

Akindès, F. (2004), *Les Racines de la crise militaro-politique en Côte d'Ivoire.* Dakar: CODESRIA.

Akinyele, R.T. (2000) 'Power-sharing and conflict management in Africa: Nigeria, Sudan and Rwanda', *Africa Development*, Vol. 25 (3&4): 209–33.

Alubo, O., (2004) 'Citizenship and nation making in Nigeria: new challenges and contestations', *Identity, Culture and Politics*, Vol. 5 (1&2): 135–61.

Aluko, M.A.O. (2003) 'Postcolonial manipulations of ethnic diversity in Nigeria', *Identity, Culture and Politics*, Vol. 4 (1): 73–84.

An-Na'im, A.A. (ed.) (2002) *Cultural Transformation and Human Rights in Africa*, London: Zed Books.

Anugwom, E.E. (2005) 'Oil minorities and the politics of resource control in Nigeria', *Africa Development*, Vol. 30 (4): 87–120.

Appadurai, A. (2001) *Globalization.* Durham, NC: Duke University Press.

Appiah, K.A. (1992) *In My Father's House: Africa in the Philosophy of Culture.* New York: Oxford University Press.

Bayart, J.-F., Geschiere, P. and Nyamnjoh, F. (2001) 'Autochtonie, democratie et citoyenneté en Afrique', *Critique Internationale*, No. 10: 177–94.

Berger, P.L. and Huntington, S.P. (eds) (2002) *Many Globalizations: Cultural Diversity in the Contemporary World.* Oxford: Oxford University Press.

Bryceson, D.F. (2000) 'Review article: Of criminals and clients: African culture and afro-pessimism in a globalized world', *Journal of Canadian African Studies*, Vol. 34 (7): 417–42.

Chomsky, N. (1999) *Profit Over People: Neoliberalism and Global Order*, New York: Seven Stories

Clinton, B. Press. (2001) *The Struggle for the Soul of the 21st Century*, http:// bbc.co.uk/arts/news_comment/dimbleby/print_clinton. shtml.

Comaroff, J. and Comaroff, J. (1997) *Of Revelation and Revolution: The Dialectics of Modernity on a South African Frontier* (Vol. 2). Chicago: University of Chicago Press.

De Bruijn, M.E., van Dijk, R.A., Foeken, D.W.J. (eds) (2001) *Mobile Africa: Changing Patterns of Movement in Africa and Beyond.* Brill: Leiden.

Devisch, R. (1996) '"Pillaging Jesus": healing churches and the villagisation of Kinshasa', *Africa*, Vol. 66 (4): 555–85.

De Waal, A. (2005) 'Briefing: Darfur, Sudan: Prospects for Peace', *African Affairs*, Vol. 104 (414): 127–35.

Englund, H. (2004) 'Cosmopolitanism and the devil in Malawi', *Ethnos*, Vol. 69 (3): 293–316.

– and Nyamnjoh, F.B. (eds) (2004) *Rights and the Politics of Recognition in Africa*. London: Zed Books.

Erlmann, V. (1994) 'Africa civilised, Africa uncivilised: local culture, world system and South African music', *Journal of Southern African Studies*. pp. 165–79.

Fanon, F. (1967) *The Wretched of the Earth.* Harmondsworth: Penguin Books.

February, V.A. (1981) *Mind Your Colour: The 'Coloured' Stereotype in South African Literature.* London: Kegan Paul International.

Geschiere, P. and Gugler, J. (eds) (1998) *The Politics of Primary Patriotism*, *Africa,* Vol. 68 (3).

— and Nyamnjoh. F.B. (2000) 'Capitalism and autochthony: the seesaw of mobility and belonging', *Public Culture*, Vol. 12 (2): 423–52.

Giddens, A. (1990) *The Consequences of Modernity*, Cambridge: Polity Press.

Gourevitch, P. (1998) *We Wish To Inform You That Tomorrow We Will Be Killed With Our Families.* New York: Farrar, Straus and Giroux.

Hall, S. (1992) 'The Question of Cultural Identity', in S. Hall, D. Held and A. McGrew (eds), *Modernity and its Futures*, Cambridge: Polity Press.

Halloran, J.D. (1993) '*The European image: unity in diversity – myth or reality*'. A presentation at the IAMCR Conference, Dublin, June.

Hamelink, C.J. (1983) *Cultural Autonomy in Global Communications: Planning National Information Policy.* Longman: London.

Harnischfeger, J. (2004), 'Sharia and Control over Territory: Conflicts between 'Settlers' and 'Indigenes' in Nigeria', *African Affairs*, Vol. 103 (412): 431–452.

Henneman, K. (2003), 'Responding to Religious Communal Conflict in Northern Nigeria'. http:www.maxwell.syr.edu/parc/Henneman%20communal%Confilict%20Paper.pdf

ICG (2004), *Côte d'Ivoire: No Peace in Sight*, Africa Report No. 82, 12 July, Dakar/Brussels: International Crisis Group (ICG).

Konings, P. and Nyamnjoh, F.B. (2003) *Negotiating an Anglophone Identity: A Study of the Politics of Recognition and Representation in Cameroon.* Brill: Leiden.

Landau, P.S. and Kaspin, D.D. (eds) (2002) *Images and Empires: Visuality in Colonial and Postcolonial Africa.* Berkeley: University of California Press.

Lapham, L.H. (1992), 'Who and what is American?', *Harper's Magazine,* January, pp. 43–49.

MacGaffey, W. (1995) 'Kongo Identity, 1483–1993', in V.Y. Mudimbe (ed.), *The South Atlantic Quarterly. Nations, Identities, Cultures* (special issue). Duke University Press: Durham, NC. pp. 1025–37.

Magubane, Z. (2004) *Bringing the Empire Home: Race, Class, and Gender in Britain and Colonial South Africa.* Chicago: The University of Chicago Press.

Mamdani, M. (1996) *Citizen and Subject: Contemporary Africa and the Legacy of Late Colonialism.* Cape Town: David Philip.

– (2001) *When Victims Become Killers: Colonialism, Nativism, and the Genocide in Rwanda.* Fountain Publishers: Kampala.

– (2004), *Good Muslim, Bad Muslim: America, the Cold War, and the Roots of Terror.* New York: Pantheon Books.

Maquet, J.J. (1961) *The Premise of Inequality in Ruanda.* London: Oxford University Press.

Melvern, L.R. (2000) *A People Betrayed: The Role of the West in Rwanda's Genocide.* London: ZED Books.

Nkene, B.-J. (2003) 'Les immigrés nigérians à Douala: Problèmes et stratégies d'insertation sociale des étrangers en milieu urban', *Africa Development*, Vol. 28 (3&4): 142–67.

Nnoli, O. (1980) *Ethnic Politics in Nigeria.* Fourth Dimension Publishers: Enugu.

— (ed.) (1998) *Ethnic Conflicts in Africa.* Dakar: CODESRIA.

Nyamnjoh, F.B. (2004a) *'Globalization and Popular Disenchantment in Africa',* in J.M. Mbaku and S.C. Saxena, (eds), *Africa at the Crossroads: Between Regionalism and Globalization.* Westport, Connecticut: Praeger. pp. 49–91.

– (2004b) 'From publish or perish to publish and perish: What "Africa's 100 Best Books" tell us about publishing Africa', *Journal of Asian and African Studies*, Vol. 39 (5): 331–55.

– (2005a) 'Images of Nyongo amongst Bamenda Grassfielders in Whiteman Kontri', *Citizenship Studies*, Vol.9 (3): 241–69.

– (2005b) *Africa's Media, Democracy and the Politics of Belonging.* London: Zed Books.

– (2005c) 'Fishing in Troubled Waters: Disquettes and Thiefs in Dakar', *Africa*, Vol. 75, (3): 295–324.

– (2006) *Insiders and Outsiders: Citizenship and Xenophobia in Contemporary Southern Africa.* London: CODESRIA/Zed Books.

– and Page, B. (2002) 'Whiteman Kontri and the enduring allure of modernity among Cameroonian youths', *African Affairs*, Vol. 101 (405): 607–34.

– and Rowlands, M. (1998) 'Elite associations and the politics of belonging in Cameroon', *Africa,* 68 (3): 320–37.

Oguibe, L. (2004) *The Culture Game.* Minneapolis: University of Minnesota Press.

Owolabi, K.A. (2003) 'Fictional tribes and tribal fictions: ethnicity, ethnocentrism and the problem of the "Other" in Africa', *Identity, Culture and Politics*, Vol. 4 (1): 85–108.

Ritzer, G. (1996) *The McDonaldization of Society.* Pine Forge Press: London.

Rourke, J.T. (ed.) (2004) *'Is Globalization Likely to Create a Better World?' Taking Sides: Clashing Views on Controversial Issues in World Politics*, 7th edn. Guilford, Connecticut: McGraw-Hill/Dushkin.

Shipler, D.K. (2004) *The Working Poor: Invisible in America.* New York: Vintage Books.

Smith, A.D. (1990) 'Towards a Global Culture?', in M. Featherstone (ed.), *Global Culture: Nationalism, Globalization, and Modernity.* London: Sage.

Sonko, B. (2004) 'The Casamance conflict: a forgotten civil war', *CODESRIA Bulletin*, Nos. 3&4.

Surin, K. (1995) 'On producing the concept of a global culture' in: V.Y. Mudimbe (ed.) *The South Atlantic Quarterly. 'Nations, Identities, Cultures'* (special issue), Vol. 94 (4): 1179–99.

Thomas, P.N. and Nain, Z. (eds) (2004) *Who Owns the Media? Global Trends and Local Resistances.* Southbound/WACC/ZED Books: London.

Van Binsbergen, W. and van Dijk, R. (ed.) (2004) *Situating Globality: African Agency in the Appropriation of Global Culture.* Leiden: Brill.

Vidal, C. (2003) 'La Brutalisation du Champ Politique Ivoirien, 1990–2003. *African Sociological Review*, Vol. 7 (2): 45–57.

Walker, F.D. (1911) *The Call of the Dark Continent: A Study in Missionary Progress, Opportunity and Urgency.* London: The Wesleyan Methodist Missionary Society.

Warnier, J.-P. (1999) *La Mondialisation de la Culture.* Paris: Editions La Découverte.

Werbner, R. (2004) *Reasonable Radicals and Citizenship in Botswana: The Public Anthropology of Kalanga Elites.* Bloomington: Indiana University Press.

– and Gaitskell, D. (Guest-eds), (2002), 'Minorities and citizenship in Botswana', *Journal of Southern African Studies*, Vol. 28 (4).

Winant, H. (2004), *The New Politics of Race: Globalism, Difference, Justice.* Minneapolis: University of Minnesota Press.

Zongo, M. (2003), 'La Diaspora Burkinabé en Côte d'Ivoire: trajectoire historique, recomposition des dynamiques migratoires et rapport avec le pays d'origine', *African Sociological Review*, Vol. 7 (2): 58–72.

CHAPTER 8

REGIONAL REALITIES IN THE ARAB WORLD

Ahmad S. Moussalli

There are three different attitudes toward globalization among the Arab in intelligentsia. There are those who reject it as the highest stage of imperialism and a cultural invasion threatening to undermine distinctive cultural personality and destroy heritage, authenticity, beliefs and national identity. The second group of Arab thinkers, secularist by inclination, welcomes globalization. A third group seeks an appropriate form of globalization that is compatible with the national and cultural interests of the people. All three groups agree that globalization is equivalent to Americanization, and they view it as a tool for disseminating American culture as a model for the whole world. Islamists express the greatest suspicion of this development and instead seek to promote an Islamic universalism that is superior to any cultural paradigm imposed by the Christian West. Radical Islamists view globalization as a new call for the elimination of the boundaries between the domain of Islam and the domain of unbelief.

Introduction

Current conditions in the Arab region hold out little hope either for the increased well-being of ordinary people or for the greater positive participation of Arab cultures in globalization. Whilst the latter is seen by a number of thinkers as a phenomenon that promises economic development and good governance (Yahyawi 1999), many individuals, groups, and states outside the Western world equate it with the control exercised by the economy and culture of the West; the political domination of the strong – the Western world – over the weak – the rest of the world and their cultures (1999: 175–81). The Arab world is a part of 'the rest' (1999: 188–204). In the 'clash' scenario, Arab and Islamic cultures are portrayed as the primary opponents of Western 'civilization'.

While there is no consensual Arab view on globalization and its effects, three key trends in thinking will be elaborated below. However, even those individuals and groups who reject globalization, including Arab Islamists, have adopted certain globalized Western doctrines such as democracy, pluralism and human rights. Nonetheless, ethical and moral problems other than the perception of globalization as Americanization have put globalization on an insecure track in the Arab world. The whole issue of globalization is complicated by the fact that the Arab peoples do not enjoy its benefits but suffer from instability, conflict and repression. As regards the political background, while there is no such thing as an 'overarching Arab-Islamic political culture' (Nonneman 2001), there is an implicit consensus on the following points:

- The results of the many political changes of the 1990s have not been promising.
- The discourses of democracy and pluralism have become widespread.
- Political culture is viewed as important, yet not-dominant.

I shall argue that the Arab world oscillates between globalization, which is associated with Americanization, and Islamization, which is associated with Islamic authenticity. Both have had tremendous positive and negative impacts on the Arab cultures. The two processes, as well as concomitant doctrines like the limited role of government and liberalization, advanced technologies, free trade, and liberal democracy on the one hand, or the Islamic state, morality, modernity, and the essential role of religion, on the other, constitute the fundamental underpinnings of both radical and moderate Arab Islamist and secular discourses. Today, all Arab intellectual, cultural and political currents have to grapple with the need to re-conceptualize traditional Western and Islamic views on morality, modernity, the role and ability of the nation-state to control or coerce, and to liberalize or socialize the economy and society. Globalization and Islamization, separately and together, have led to new perceptions, both negative and positive, about: i) the ability of Arab and Islamic culture to be sustained as a moral and political system and ii) the ability of globalization to affect the intellectual, moral, political, economic, and cultural systems of the Arab world. Together these have led to the emergence of radical Islamists who reject non-Islamist ideologies, philosophies, and technologies. Their aim is to prevent the penetration of globalization into Islamic societies and to limit Western dominance in the international order and organizations.

Globalization, religion, and development

It is clear, then, that the Arabs neither completely reject nor accept globalization. Instead, they view it differently in its diverse domains of realization. The technological domain of globalization is almost entirely accepted and uncritically embraced, as seen in the complicated progress of privatization. The neo-liberal ideology implicit within globalization brings with it new identities, values, and norms that theoretically challenge dominant institutions and sources of power (Stone 2002).

The Arabs are deeply concerned, however, about maintaining their cultural identity and independence in the face of the West's superiority – and the globalization it has spread. The Arab intelligentsia appears to have three different attitudes in this regard. First, there are those who reject globalization as cultural domination that undermines their distinctive cultural personality and threatens to destroy their heritage, authenticity, beliefs and identity. A second group of Arab thinkers, secularist by inclination, welcomes globalization. A third calls for a form of globalization that is compatible with the national and cultural interests of each 'people'. The Islamists, however, are deeply suspicious of globalization, and instead seek to promote an Islamic universalism that is considered superior to any cultural paradigm imposed by the Christian West. Radical Islamists in the Arab world view globalization as a new call for the elimination of the boundaries between the domain of Islam and the domain of unbelief, as a process that seeks to join infidels and Muslims under the banner of secularism and worldliness (Najjar 2005).

However, all Arabs agree that globalization is equivalent to Americanization. They view it as an American design to disseminate American culture as a model for the whole world. The debilitating impacts of globalization on Arab cultures have been explored by various scholars.[1] In the present context, I would agree with the image of retribalization conjured up by Benjamin Barber:

> *a threatened balkanization of nation-states in which culture is pitted against culture, people against people, tribe against tribe, a Jihad in the name of a hundred narrowly conceived faiths against every kind of interdependence, every kind of artificial social cooperation and mutuality: against technology, against pop culture and against integrated markets; against modernity itself as well as the future in which modernity issues.(1995: 4)*

This is opposed by Barber to a future painted in 'shimmering pastels, a busy portrait of onrushing economic, technological, and ecological forces' that seek integration and uniformity and that enchant 'peoples everywhere with fast music, fast computers, and fast food... pressing nations into one homogeneous global theme park, one McWorld tied together... (1995: 4).

Indeed Jihad (Islamization) and McWorld (globalization) both operate with equal strength in opposite directions: Jihad is motivated by 'parochial hatreds', McWorld by:

> *universalizing markets, the one re-recreating ancient subnational and ethnic borders from within, the other making national borders porous from without. Yet Jihad and McWorld have this in common: they both make war on the sovereign nation-state and thus undermine the nation-state's democratic institutions. Each eschews civil society and belittles democratic citizenship, neither seeks alternative democratic institutions. McWorld has no choice but to service Jihad, for neither can Jihad do without McWorld. For where would be culture without the commercial producers who market it and the information and communication systems that make it known! (1995: 6, 155)*

For instance, Arab Islamists use both the latest technologies as well as certain doctrines spread by globalization. Thus the Internet has been adopted zealously to allow Muslims to participate in the hoped-for community of the *umma* (see also Chapter 16 by Bassam Tibi) to recreate a virtual community which unites them and acts as a global launching pad for Islamic ideas. More importantly, the Internet provides religious sources that do away with the monopoly of knowledge claimed by religious authorities. The fragmentation of traditional sources of authority is hence a major issue with regard to the nexus of Islam and globalization (Featherstone 2002).[2]

The Arabs definitely need the positive effects of globalization for they are on a downward trajectory when it comes to development, The *Arab Human Development Report* (UNDP 2002) warns that the Arab world has fallen off the globe due to a poverty of capabilities and a poverty of opportunities, despite its wealth of natural resources. The population of the Arab world will increase from 280 million to 410–459 million by 2020. 'By then it will have become too late to prevent angry southerners from marching north, with the Arabs spearheading a Muslim world. The GDP of all the Arab states combined is less than that of Spain alone. There is also a freedom shortage, and on a global level, the Arab world has the lowest level of freedom' (APS Diplomat, 2002).

Scholars such as Clement Henry (2003) argue that the Arab world is indeed going through a new clash of globalizations that frames the processes of development and modernization in much of what used to be called the Third World. The pressure on them to bring about extensive political and economic reforms combines the imperialistic impulses of the Bush Administration and the dictates of multilateral proponents of globalization, such as the World Bank, International Monetary Fund, and the United Nations. (Henry 2003) Political and military instability are the principal impediments to development. While the free market is important for development, good governance, associated with constitutional democracy, it is vital to making markets work for sustainable human development. Whilst the more radical Islamist opposition parties oppose any such reform-oriented forces, the experiences with European imperialism, as well as the interventions earlier against Nasser and more recently Saddam Hussein, do affect how people and regimes in the area perceive globalization – as a new form of imperialism.

Globalization, reform, and politics

However, in reality and within each country, ever harsher repression makes it ever more difficult to reconcile the reformers who might adopt globalization and their opponents who might reject change and prefer a return to 'cultural authenticity', Islamic universalism or Arab nationalism. Still, many moderate political Islamists do not oppose market-oriented reforms and a more accountable state, as advocated by the World Bank. But the dialectics of globalization do not favor any inclusive synthesis in the tense regional climate, given international intervention in Iraq and possibly elsewhere (Henry 2003: 60–5). This is why some argue that the concepts of core and periphery, and not any culture of values, provide the basis for outlining the general geographic border of the Middle East and, therefore, the successive stages of development in the region (Ismael and Ismael 1999). In other words, it is not only internal dynamics that will encourage globalization but also the main player on the world scene who will have a tremendous impact on how the Arabs will absorb globalization.

After World War II, pan-Arabism dominated Middle Eastern politics as a consequence of colonialism: Arab societies were fragmented politically, socially and economically and their weak and unrepresentative governments were dependent on external powers. The state of Israel was created. An ever increasing population of Palestinian refugees and the establishment of a Palestinian state became the core crisis of the area. The dominant patterns of cooperation and conflict evolved in the post-war period from the efforts made by these peripheral national governments to deal with these problems as they threatened the sovereignty, legitimacy, and capability of the states themselves (Ismael and Ismael 1999).

Elsewhere in this volume Bassam Tibi downplays the impact of colonialism and imperialism on the Arabs, and finds that there is real civilizational discord that must be addressed. The Islamic threat can no longer be pursued free of context. Discord can be related to clashing worldviews and it can assume a military shape. September 11 was an assault on the values and concept of order of the West (Rubenstein 2005). Nonetheless, the appeal of Islamist ideology must be situated historically in the changing relations of global capital (and the concomitant shift from nationalist abstractions to religious ones). Invoking the clash of civilizations argument is also a way of evading responsibility for the blowback that the US imperial projects have generated (Wedeen 2003). We can see that the rise of Islamism in the 1970s was part of capitalism's war against communism. It was believed then that religious thought, especially Islamic, can constitute a palisade against the expansion of communism and socialism to protect capitalism and the Western powers.

However, while they certainly served indirectly to contain the spread of communism and socialism, it was part of the Islamists' worldview to present Islam as providing an alternative vision of Western modernity, an alternative 'Islamic modernity', underscoring its authenticity and cultural distance from the hegemonic Western discourse. This worldview stands in radical contrast to the liberal-modernist worldview, which is ready to modify an apparently unified framework empowered by the *Qur'an*, the *Hadith* (sayings of the Prophet), and the *Sunna* (the conduct of the Prophet). Thus, Arab Muslims negotiate competing claims of piety and material survival within a world defined by the technological and material progress called modernization (Pasha 2003).

However, twenty-first century global modernity foregrounds the issue of who, or what, directs and delimits the identity of individuals, nations, and cultures. The attempt to criticize the totalizing master narrative of Western modernity is part of the larger search for cultural authenticity in the non-Western world. Many people contend that Western modernity resembles a Faustian bargain in which variegated traditional familial, tribal, ethnic, religious and national identities must be sacrificed for the tediously monotonous materialism of the present age. Authenticity is tantamount to taking charge of one's existence and traditions in a manner that is genuine, trustworthy, and sincere (Boroujerdi 1997).

The resurgent influence of religion in politics and cultural identification around the world ranks as one of the most remarkable developments of the late twentieth century. It challenges long-held assumptions about the secular nature of modernization and modernity (Hefner 1998). Consequently, the common emphasis on epistemology derives from the fact that in the post-colonial world arguments for Islamic authenticity and specificity are shaped and framed by the complex dimensions of Western domination. Although globalization renders the boundaries between peoples and practices permeable, it does not do so by erasing radical inequalities between the center and the periphery, but often by maintaining and advocating them. Since globalization involves the dissemination of modern Western forms of life around the globe, it can be regarded in some ways as the newest expression of Western hegemony. One crucial dimension of this power is how Western experiences of modernity and its processes have been successfully universalized to define modernity for the West and the non-West alike. 'To be more specific, how much their attempt to delineate a distinctively Islamic approach to knowledge is at once framed by and parasitic on the very Western paradigms they contest illustrates the challenge of identifying an authentically Islamic perspective in a world defined by pervasive Western influence and power (Euben 2002).'

Globalization, fundamentalism, and identity

In the cultural arena, fundamentalism is an attempt to impose certain limits on modernization, and more particularly on post-modernism. It attempts to reverse the historical onrush towards hyper-secular consumerism and pluralism by providing, paradoxically, a traditional defense of modernity. The history of Islam revolves in part around these problems of local and global authority, giving rise to periodic social movements of Islamization in which the ascetic and literary codes were imposed upon localist forms (Turner 1991). In particular, two sets of issues impact the stability of the region and globalization in the Arab world. First, religion and history and, therefore, religious claims and symbolism question the legitimacy and policies of both Arab governments and Israel, in turn negatively affecting Arab–Israeli relations, internal Arab and Israeli policies, inter-Arab attitudes and, consequently, long-term world interests and globalization. Identity questions based upon religion and history will thus be fundamental issues that will affect ideological and cultural trends for the next few decades. As much as religious questions over land and identity have galvanized and divided public opinion in Israel, Islamic fundamentalism has opened up questions of legitimacy and the nature of the state in the Arab world.

Moreover, while the destabilizing effects of globalization started long before September 11, it is difficult to interpret this event and others like it unless we understand the structural conditions of insecurity arising from globalization. People reaffirm their identity when it is threatened. Nationalism and religion provide stable discourses and beliefs because of their ability to give a sense of security, stability and simple answers. As Kinnvall observes:

> *Globalization as increased movements of goods, services, technology, borders, ideas, and people has real social and economic consequences: increasing rootlessness and loss of ability as people experience the effects of capitalist development, media overflows, unemployment, forced migration and other forces. Old patterns of behavior have become undermined as traditional power relations have become democratized. (Kinnvall 2004: 742)*

There are two basic consequences of such processes: 1) old ways are eliminated, 2) the structures that identified the community and bound it together are also being destroyed (Kinnvall 2004). As Kinnvall argues, globalization, including the spread of Western values and practices, has accelerated such processes. In response to these developments, religious Islamist leaders talk about moral or ethical decline by pointing to modern society's immorality, loss of ethical values, corruption, and so on, and concluding that the only antidote to the current decay is a return to traditional values and religious norms (2004).

Identity is mainly contested where cultures clash and where actors struggle for authenticity and independence from cultural imperialism and seek to defend their national, ethnic, cultural, or religious identities in their own socio-political space. The tension between cultures and human agency is played out in the confrontation between global processes and localized identities. In the political and sociocultural arena, major actors try to globalize what is local in order to cope with the economic and technical push toward globalization (Khan 1998). Islamization is an example of this globalization.

Global images of Islam such as the green threat or the Islamic bomb or Islamic terrorism have presented it as an anachronistic doctrine that cannot live in harmony with the modern world. Religiously motivated Muslims are viewed as being irrational. They are now being forced to re-assess their values and beliefs from an outside-in perspective. Their view of themselves is becoming more and more defensive. Arab Muslims are attempting to reinterpret Islamic values in the Enlightenment lexicology, using terms such as Islam and human rights, Islam and pluralism, Islam and women's rights, that all indicate the acceptance of many dominant values of the West. Identity is represented by using Islamic symbols and discourses, or Islamic authenticity and Islamization, that have evolved over time (1998).[3]

Furthermore, fundamentalism has the unintended and unanticipated consequence of exposing traditional values to public inspection, with the result that their coherence and authenticity become a critical issue. But values and institutional systems do gradually change, as regards shared identity that is connected to a certain system of values, symbols, attitudes, and structures. This allows people to understand themselves and their place in history and context. This is why the perceived challenge of modernity has led to so many reaffirmations of traditional values and identities. 'Traditional values include relations between men and women, rulers and subjects, and believers and unbelievers. Furthermore, cultural flexibility and materialist pragmatism are not considered virtues' (Kasper 2005). The unintended de-traditionalization of values and practices is particularly evident in the Islamic debate about the status of women in Muslim society (Turner 2001).

On the other hand, according to Mazrui, globalization has had consequences on values and on comparative moral standards. Across the world the two organizing concepts of comparative ethics and norms are cultural relativism and historical relativism. He argues that the cultural distance between the West and Islam has narrowed. Thus, sex before marriage is widely practiced with parental consent. Even within the same country moral judgments across different cultures are also illustrated when American Muslims, for instance, try to decide how to judge President Clinton over the Monica Lewinsky affair. According to their values as Americans the adultery is not the most serious offense. It is the lying about it, especially under oath. But according to their values as Muslims, surely adultery is a much more serious offense than lying. Also, a woman may choose in the West to become a mistress of a married man but she is not allowed to marry the same man and have equal rights as a second wife. In Islam, having a second wife is legitimate and having a mistress is a crime (Mazrui 1999). This is why some writers argue that Huntington's thesis is correct: culture does matter. However, Huntington is mistaken in assuming that the core clash between the West and Islam is over political values. At this historical juncture, societies throughout the world see democracy as the best form of government.

But there is a really dangerous fault line between Islam and the West, which Huntington did not identify: this relates to gender equality and sexuality, in regard to which Muslim societies have remained the most traditional in the world. This sexual 'clash of civilizations' raises far deeper issues, such as the acceptance by Islam of modernity and its ability to survive in the modern world, than the treatment of women in Muslim countries (Inglehart and Norris 2003). For the West has also imposed on the Middle East its own brand of liberal feminism. To challenge these power structures, Arab feminists and Middle East scholars and activists still negotiate the contested terrains of women's relationships to nationalist and Islamic movements as well as the hybrid identities of Arab and Muslim women. No doubt, at the center of regional conflict and the nationalism/feminism debate stands the Palestinian struggle for self-determination and national sovereignty. Thus, viewing Islamist forces as the main source of gender discrimination is reductionist. Still, the debates about Islam as an alternative to Western liberal humanism are occurring at a time when the 'Islamic threat' has become the new enemy of the post-cold war era (Saliba 2000).

The expansion of women's organizations in the Arab world is linked to global feminism. 'This feminism is predicated upon the notion that notwithstanding cultural, class, and ideological differences among the women of the world, there is a commonality in the forms of women's disadvantages and in the forms of women's organizations worldwide. The internationalization of discourses of equality, empowerment, autonomy, democratization, participation, and human rights has been captured and indeed extended by women's organizations around the world' (Moghadam 1997). Women's groups and organizations are quite active in Egypt and in North Africa, while women's activists in Algeria, Morocco, and Tunisia network with each other. Among the Palestinians, there is a group of staunch feminists who have criticized the conservatism of the Palestinian Authority, but their efforts have been weakened by the opposition of the Islamist Hamas.

Many commentators fail to understand that the globalization of modernity stems from false expectations. Global modernity does not create global citizens, and the failure of everything local does not weaken the search for locally rooted legitimacies and systems of meaning in social life. This search does not contradict the commitment to a common global modernity. The Arab world today, and the Islamic world in general, are attuned to the concerns and issues to which modernity in general and globalization in particular give rise. Arabo-Islamic discourse and social movements today, in their emphasis on creativity and activism and the universal dimensions of ethics and social relations, and in their opposition to the post-colonial state, highlight the same fundamental trajectories of all post-national affiliations (Bamyeh 2002).

Political representation and social justice

The second set of issues that are important to the Arab world relates to newly globalized tendencies that call for proper political representation, equitable economic distribution, and open relations with the world, including the West. This means that Arab cultures have to deal with multi-layered levels of instability and change. Their future, whether they move towards moderation or radicalism, largely depends on the future of democracy in the Arab world and the Arab world's relations with the West. Arab governments are capable of destroying the military infrastructure of rising Islamic movements, but they cannot liquidate their bases or dismiss the grievances which sustain them. All of this does affect how Arab cultures deal with globalization. A common perception throughout the region is that increased globalization is a threat to political, economic and cultural independence. This threat includes imposing cultural homogeneity based on Western secular market-based values, using notions of human rights to push agendas driven by the West, including gender equality, sexual freedom, as well as destroying local industry.[4]

For instance, Saudi Arabia has long regarded change, especially rapid change, as being equivalent to instability. The regime remained relatively static for most of the twentieth century. It was ill-prepared for the implications of globalization, which was one of the main consequences of the collapse of communism. By the late 1990s, it became clear that fundamental change would become inevitable. Some measures were introduced, especially in the economic sphere. Saudi Arabia joined the World Trade Organization in 2005 ('Saudi Arabia' 2002). Saudi Arabia has been trying to reap the benefits of the economic and technical aspects of globalization while avoiding its political and cultural aspects.

The United Arab Emirates began opening up to free trade much earlier, encouraging the free movement of labor and forming joint business ventures long before it became necessary in the post-communist era. Dubai is leading the way, with the other Emirates following its lead. The UAE does not see globalization and liberalization as challenges to overcome but as opportunities from which to benefit ('The UAE' 2002). As a result, the Emirates can claim to be the most globalized country in the Middle East. By contrast, most other governments of the Arab world are largely unprepared for the economic and political impact of globalization.

Another example is Tunisia, where globalization is interpreted mainly in the economic and social perspectives. On the political front, only reforms that will not challenge the predominance of the ruling Constitutional Democratic Rally led by President Ben Ali are tolerated. Tunisia's stability rests on what is essentially an authoritarian state, with very clear limits on pluralism, freedom of speech and judicial independence. The limits of political liberalization were highlighted by the constitutional referendum in 2002, which removed the three-term limit to the presidency and also raised the age of eligibility to presidential nomination from 70 to 75 years. Nonetheless, Tunisia has become one of the most rapidly growing economies in the Arab World, steadily becoming more integrated with the EU through commercial, social and intellectual linkages as well as cooperation on security issues ('Tunisia' 2002).

Yemen was admitted to the World Trade Organization, a pillar of globalization, as an observer. Yet key aspects of Yemen's relationship with globalization, namely economic and political reform, have taken place by default. The economy was on the verge of collapse through much of the early 1990s until the multilateral agencies stepped in to provide advice with various structural reform processes. In 1995, after the end of the civil war, the President embarked on a comprehensive plan of reforms backed by the IMF and World Bank. However, given the geo-political situation after September 11, the President may calculate that such an approach would not create much of a backlash in the West ('Yemen' 2002).

Socioeconomic and geo-political globalization are affecting the way the Palestinian cause is perceived by major powers and public opinion worldwide. Because of the global war on terror, the Arab–Israeli conflict is seen through the lens of suicide bombings and retaliations ('Palestine' 2002).

For the last two centuries, the Muslim people as well as the Arab world have been quite receptive to the economic and political model of the modern world. Many have been eager to transform and redesign the socioeconomic and political structures of their societies on the model of the capitalist West (Hossein-Zadeh 2005). Most governments, however, have viewed globalization as a threat rather than an opportunity. Their focus is on the negative effects brought on by the inability to compete economically or to measure up politically within the international community. Complicating matters is the geo-political environment in the region ('The Challenge of Globalization' 2002).

Clash of civilizations between Islam and the West

Whatever 'clash of civilizations' might exist, it clearly involves reciprocal interaction. The colossal social and economic changes that have taken place in the modern capitalist West have impacted mightily on the Arab world in particular and on the modern Muslim world and thought in general. As Abu-Rabi observes, 'the fate of the Muslim world is highly intertwined with the triumphant Western capitalism.'(1998: 18) And he asks, 'What does globalization mean in the context of a postmodern, post-Soviet, post-cold war world, and in the context of aggressive/hegemonic Western capitalism?'

He argues that the Muslims have inherited a world of contradiction. Cultural and political decolonization after independence saw the forces of neo-colonialism forging economic and political relationships that would give the center the upper hand when dealing with the international and economic affairs of its former dependencies, the periphery. Hence many Arab thinkers believe that globalization is the latest stage of neo-colonialism, or the victory of Americanization (Abu-Rabi 1998: 26).

Thus, while globalization deeply affects the Arab world, anti-globalization forces are making headlines with their sometimes violent actions at meetings of international organizations in Seattle, Genoa, Gothenburg, etc. Yet all of this moved into the background after September 11. Anti-globalization leaders in Brussels as well opposed the US military campaign in Afghanistan, arguing that a military response alone was not enough to deal with terrorism. Other anti-globalization efforts were less constructive. In Pakistan, crowds organized by radical Islamic groups smashed and looted Kentucky Fried Chicken and McDonald's outlets, while burning American flags (Le Feber 2002). In the Arab world, there were attempts to blow up McDonald's stores and many calls to boycott American products were issued.

Furthermore, the Arabo-Muslim world is now negatively associated with attitudes that are not conducive to growth. On the basis of an analysis of the World Values Survey data, it is asserted that among adherents to the world's major religions, Muslims are the most anti-market; for Muslims around the world reside in poor countries. Islam is also associated with special practices such as the prohibition of *Riba* (interest) or the command to pay *Zakat* (alms giving), which could serve as the causal link between theological belief and economic performance. Yet attempts to rigorously assess the impact of these unique practices suggest that they have little, if any, impact on the accumulation and allocation of capital. Less dramatic than terrorist attacks are public attitudes toward foreigners and globalization. The 2003 Pew Global Attitudes survey revealed a significant level of discomfort with globalization in the Middle East. To the extent that adherence to Islam is a significant component of personal and communal identity, Islamic teachings will be one measure through which these developments are viewed. This apprehension is reinforced when Islam itself is seen as being part of the contested issue (Moland and Pack 2004).

Isolationism is no option, whether for globalists or Islamists, the 'Christian West' or the 'Islamic East'. Cultures, Arab or otherwise, can no longer be conceptualized as self-contained entities. Equally important, in the Arab world the state's dominant role vis-à-vis society is eroding under the hammer blows of, again, globalization and Islamization. On the one hand, because globalization is by its very essence de-centralized and elusive, it severely constrains traditional state domination of the government, economy, and culture. On the other hand, Islamization, as a global phenomenon, cannot ignore the new culture of liberalism and limited government that is emerging in the Arab world. In fact, it has begun absorbing this new culture into its discourses but with major cultural, political, and social dislocations.

The attitudes towards globalization and the West of Arabo-Islamic movements are contingent on two variables: opportunity structures and normative frameworks. The more such movements benefit from international opportunity structures shaped by globalization, the more they become pro-globalization. Thus, the more the normative framework of an Islamic movement is tolerant and open to cross-cultural interactions, the more it favors globalization (Kuru 2005).

Much of the contemporary return to Islam is driven by the perception of Muslims as a community with a mission. In encounters between the West and Islam, the struggle is over who will provide the primary definition of world order. Is it the West or Islam? This question suggests a competition between cultural traditions with distinct notions of peace, order, and justice (Rubenstein 2005).

Conclusion

At this historical juncture, the Arab and Western worlds should both make concerted efforts to dispel the perception of clashes of civilizations and wars of religions; they need to focus on more dialogue, justice, development, and freedom. Radical Islamic fundamentalism is an extreme expression of dissatisfaction with the unjust and materialist modern globalized world and it is a dangerous embodiment of religious extremism. Even more explosive issues are time bombs ready to explode. Muslim minorities in the West and religious minorities in the Arab world should not be treated as enemies; for such actions may deepen the rise of radicalism and terrorism, committed by individuals, groups, or states. Many dissatisfied and marginalized individuals and groups may resort to terrorism to bring about what they ironically believe to be justice and freedom.

Thus, the prospects of future ideological and political co-existence between globalization and Islamization through a re-conceptualization of the role of the state under a limited government, an open economic system, and a new international moralism are not very promising. In the contemporary Arab world are to be found both radical Islamic movements that call for an authoritarian state power and a controlled economy and moderate movements that call for a limited state power and a liberal economy. Both globalization and Islamization, therefore, have been and will have a great influence on state structures and political ideologies and culture. The interplay between globalization and culture should be seen in light of the repercussions of reform and development in the Arab world and the need to resolve the outstanding and major obstacles represented by the repression of Arab regimes, the radicalization of Islamic movements, the continuation of the Arab–Israeli conflict, the occupation of Iraq and the failure to build a democratic state there.

Thus, it should be made clear that while the Western world does indeed want to control the Islamic world and use its raw material and markets, it does not aim at converting Muslims. While the Islamic perspective focuses more on the religious dimension of the conflict, it is ready to share its resources with the West. The two perspectives have been misunderstood. Both sides must develop deeper channels of communication: the Western, to communicate the idea that the West does not want to undermine or abolish the Islamic faith and Arab culture; the Islamic and Arab, to communicate the idea that they do not stand against Western interests. Creating such channels of communication is the duty of both Arabs and Westerners, especially the Americans. Their futures are locked together, not only in Iraq but all over the Arab world and beyond. A new Western policy towards the Islamic and Arab world and its most explosive issues, including Palestine, Iraq, and democracy, should be developed, just as new Islamic and Arab orientations towards the West and its concerns, especially Islamic radicalism, are equally indispensable.

Notes

1 For Arab scholars' interest in globalization, see Ghazi Qusaybi, *Al-'Awlama wa al-Hawiya al-Wataniyya* (Riyadh: Maktabat al-'Ubaykan, 2002), 'Abd al-Basit 'Abd al-Mu'ti, ed., *Al-'Awlama* (Cairo: Dar al-Kitab al-Jadid al-Mutahida, 2000), Salih Abu 'Usba' and others, eds. *Al-'Awlama wa al-Hawiyya* (Amman: Manshurat Jami'at Philidaphia, 1999), *Al-'Awlama wa al-Hawiyya*, Conference Proceedings, Ribat, 1997, Al-'Awlama wa al-Thaqafa wa al-Muqawama, *Shu'un al-Awsat*, Vol. 120, Fall 2005. The whole issue of the journal is focused on globalization. See also other citations in this article's footnotes.

2 See also 'Reimagining the Ummah', by Peter Mandaville in *Islam Encountering Globalization*, p. 70.

3 On different local responses to globalization, see Christopher Merrett, 'Understanding local response to globalization: the production of geographical scale and political identity', *National Identities*, Vol. 3, No. 1, 2001.

4 On the difficulties facing globalization in the Arab world, see Robert Looney, 'Why has globalization eluded the Middle East?', *Strategic Insights*, Vol. III, Issue 12 (December 2004). See also Enid Hill, 'First World, Third World, Globalizing World: Where is the Middle East?', *Arab Studies Quarterly*, Vol. 21, Issue 3, 1999.

REFERENCES

'Abd al-Basit,' (2000) Abd al-Mu'ti, ed., *Al-'Awlama* (Cairo: Dar al-Kitab al-Jadid al-Mutahida.

Abu-Rabi, Ibrahim, (1998) 'Globalization: a contemporary Islamic response,' *The American Journal of Islamic Social Science*, 15:3, pp.18–20 and 26–8.

Al-'Awlama wa al-Hawiyya, Conference Proceedings, Ribat, 1997, Al-'Awlama wa al-Thaqafa wa al-Muqawama, *Shu'un al-Awsat*, Vol. 120, Fall 2005.

APS Diplomat Fate of Arabian Peninsula (2002 September 2), Vol. 43.

Bamyeh, Mohammad (2002) 'Dialectics of Islam and global modernity', *Social Analysis*, Summer, Vol. 46, Issue 2.

Barber, Benjamin (1995) *Jihad vs. McWorld*. New York: Times Books.

Boroujerdi, Mehrzad (February 1997) 'Iranian Islam and the Faustian bargain of Western modernity', *Journal of Peace Research*, Vol. 34, No. 1, pp. 1–5.

'The Challenge of Globalization', (2002, September) *APS Diplomat Fate of the Arabian Peninsula*, Vol. 43, Issue 3.

Euben, Roxanne, (2002) 'Contingent borders, syncretic perspectives: globalization, political theory, and Islamizing knowledge', *International Studies Review*, Spring 2002, pp. 23–48.

Featherstone, Mike (2002) 'An Introduction', in Ali Mohammadi (ed.), *Islam Encountering Globalization*. London: Routledge Curzon, pp. 7–8.

Hefner, Robert (1998) 'Multiple modernities: Christianity, Islam, and Hinduism in a globalizing age,' *Annual Reviews of Anthropology*, p. 85.

Henry, Clement (2003) 'A clash of civilizations: obstacles to development in the Middle East', *Harvard International Review*, Spring 2003, Vol. 25, Issue 1, pp. 60–5.

Hossein-Zadeh, Ismael (2005) 'The Muslim World and the West: the roots of conflict,' *Arab Studies Quarterly*, Summer, Vol. 27, Issue 3.

Inglehart, R. and Norris, P. (2003) 'The True Clash of Civilizations', found at http://www.globalpolicy,org/globalize/cultural/2003/0304clash.htm.

Ismael, Jacqueline and Ismael, Tariq (1999, June 1) 'The globalization of the Arab world in Middle East politics: regional dynamics in historical perspective', *Arab Studies Quarterly*, Vol. 21, Issue 3.

Kasper, Wolfgang (2005, May) 'Can Islam meet the challenges of modernity', *Quadrant*, Vol. 49, Issue 5.

Khan, M.A. Muqtedar (1998) 'Constructing Identity in "Global" Politics', *The American Journal of Islamic Social Science*, Vol. 15, No. 3, pp. 81–5.

Kinnvall, Catarina (2004) 'Globalization and religious nationalism: self, identity, and the search for ontological security', *Political Psychology*, Vol. 25, No. 5, pp. 741–3.

Kuru, Ahmet (2005) 'Globalization and diversification of Islamic movements: three Turkish cases', *Political Science Quarterly*, Vol. 120, No. 2, pp. 253–4.

Le Feber, Walter (2002)'The post September 11 debate over empire, globalization, and fragmentation', *Political Science Quarterly*, Vol. 117, No. 1, pp. 9–10.

Mazrui, Ali (1999) 'Globalization and cross-cultural values: the politics of identity and judgment', *Arab Studies Quarterly*, Summer, Vol. 21, Issue 21.

Moghadam, Valentine (1997) 'Globalization and feminism: the rise of women's organizations in the Middle East and North Africa', *Canadian Women's Studies*, Spring, Vol. 17, Issue 2.

Moland, Marcus and Pack, Howard (2004, June) 'Islam, globalization, and economic performance in the Middle East', *International Economics: Policy Briefs*, Number PB04-4 pp. 2–4.

Najjar, Fawi (2005) 'Arabs, Islam and globalization', *Middle East Policy*, Vol. xii, No. 3, Fall 2005, pp. 91–2.

Nonneman, Gerd (2001) 'Rentiers and autocrats, monarchs and democrats, state and society: the Middle East between globalization and hum "Agency"', *International Affairs*, Vol. 77, No. I, pp. 143–5.

'Palestine: the challenge of globalization', (2002, January 6) *APS Diplomat Fate of the Arabian Peninsula*, Vol. 43, Issue 1.

Pasha, Mustapha Kamal (2003) 'Fractured worlds: Islam, identity, and international relations' *Global Society*, Vol. 17, No. 2, pp. 115–118.

Qusaybi, Ghazi (2002) *Al-'Awlama wa al-Hawiya al-Wataniyya*. Riyadh: Maktabat al-'Ubaykan.

Rubenstein, Richard (2005, February) 'Religion and the Clash of Civilizations', *World and I*, Vol. 20, Issue 2.

Saliba, Theresa (2000) 'Arab Feminism at the Millennium', *Signs*, Vol. 25, No. 4, Summer, pp. 1087–92.

Salih Abu 'Usba' and others (eds) (1999) *Al-'Awlama wa al-Hawiyya*. Amman: Manshurat Jami'at Philidaphia.

'Saudi Arabia: the challenge of globalization', (2002, March), *APS Diplomat Fate of the Arabian Peninsula*, Vol. 43, Issue 4.

Stone, Leonard (2002) 'The Islamic crescent, culture and globalization', *Innovation*, Vol. 15, No. 2, p. 128.

'Tunisia: the challenge of globalization', (2002, June 3), *APS Diplomat Fate of the Arabian Peninsula*, Vol. 43, Issue 6.

Turner, Bryan (1991) 'Politics of Culture in Islamic Globalism', in R. Robertson and W.R. Garrett (eds), *Religion and Global Order. Religion and the Political Order*. pp. 90–1. New York: Paragon House.

– (2001) 'Cosmopolitan virtue: on religion in a global age', *European Journal of Social Theory*, Vol. 4, No. 2, p. 402.

'The UAE: the challenge of globalization', (2002, July 22), *APS Diplomat Fate of the Arabian Peninsula*, Vol. 43, Issue 1.

United Nations Development Program (UNDP) (2002) *Arab Human Development Report 2002: Creating Opportunuites for Future Generations*. New York: UNDP.

Wedeen, Lisa (2003) 'Beyond the Crusades: Why Huntington, and Bin Laden, are wrong', *Middle East Policy*, Vol. X, No. 2, Summer 2003, p. 56.

Yahyawi ,Yahia (1999) *Al-'Awlama Ayat 'Awlama*. Beirut: Ifrikiyya al-Sharq.

'Yemen: the challenge of globalization', (2002, August), *APS Diplomat Fate of the Arabian Peninsula*, Vol. 43, Issue 2.

CHAPTER 9

GLOBALIZATION AND ASIAN VALUES

Janadas Devan

Culture has emerged as a question of enormous moment, precisely because the production of cultural difference remains the only means of asserting identity and recovering value in the current stage of globalization. The concept of 'Asian values' is one such means of recovery that provides Asian states with ideological machinery for the assimilation of indigenous cultures to the demands of modernity, as well as an alternative intellectual and cultural genealogy for Asian modernity that would allow Asian societies to claim an independent basis for their capitalism.

A thesis

The project-description for the *Cultures and Globalization Series* made this observation: 'The values of different ways of life,' its authors noted, 'have risen to consciousness to become the rallying cry of diverse claims to a space in the planetary culture. Before culture was just lived. Now it has become a self-conscious collective project.'

This chapter will ask why this should be so. Using Singapore as a particular case study – and ranging further afield to consider East Asia in general – I will ask why, at this particular moment in history, when globalization has become a fact of enormous moment, cultures should insist on their uniqueness, and why the theory and practice of culture should become 'a self-conscious project'. I will argue that that very coincidence – the assertion of cultural uniqueness coinciding with the material fact of globalization – is itself the explanation. Capitalism, hitherto, had been understood to be continuous with a particular, namely Western, culture. That continuity has been broken by globalization. The very fact that capital is transnational renders capital in excess not only of nation but also of culture. The threefold link between the rationality of the Enlightenment, cultural identity and the interests of capital has become a twofold link between rationality and capital, with a purely instrumental notion of culture mediating. The fact that 'Asian values', for example, can now signify competitive economic advantage – culture on par, as it were, with a well-trained workforce, an efficient infrastructure and favourable tax structures – as much as it does an assertion of unique identity, is evidence that transnational capital is also potentially transcultural. Which means to say, the structures, habits and belief systems transnational capital requires for its functioning are to a remarkable extent quite independent of any particular cultural formation or nation-state.

It is in this context that culture has emerged as a question of enormous moment. The production of cultural differences, including all the potential uglinesses as well as affirmations that such differences involve, is a means of recovering value, including national sovereignty, in a context where the universal as such has become the province of transnational capital. Culture, in other words, has become 'a self-conscious collectivist project' because it is the only arena left for the assertion of identity and value. There is a double movement involved in that assertion: (1) a negative refusal of transnational capital as the sole arbiter of value; and (2) a positive affirmation of particular cultures as repositories of value, identity and authority.

I have chosen Singapore, in particular, as the focus of my analysis for a number of reasons. First, it is the society I know best, since I am a Singaporean. Second, its relative smallness, both in terms of its geographical size as well as population, renders it easier to study than larger Asian countries like China, India and Indonesia. Third, Singapore's ideologues have been unusually influential in the global marketplace of ideas, in part because of their eloquence, and in part because of their access to the international media through the English language. And finally, Singapore, because of its exceptional economic success, has often been cited as a cultural and political 'model' by a number of other, much larger Asian countries, including China.[1]

Local and global

The double movement described above can be observed in every Asian society – including, and most especially, in the ones that are most 'globalized'. In a sense, the double movement is rooted in their status as rapidly globalizing economies, a function of their attempt to come to grips with the contradictions of that globalization. Even the most globalized of economies must wrestle with these contradictions.

On the one hand, *socially meaningful life can only exist locally, in a particular time and place, or it cannot exist at all.* Nobody can have an immediate knowledge of society in the mass. Someone living in Tokyo or New Delhi, say, has no direct contact with something called Japanese or Indian society. What that person has is a direct knowledge of his or her own family, circle of friends, colleagues in the workplace, and so on. This is not to deny that something called Japanese or Indian society – or Chinese or American society, for that matter – has any reality. Far from it. Societies, nations, obviously act. Through the agency of the state, they go to war, make laws, administer justice, provide social safety nets, determine the socioeconomic life of countless people.

But there are different levels of immediacy governing our existence as social beings. We tend to forget this when we read, say, a newspaper. By virtue of its ability to place events from different locations (Fallujah, Somalia, Washington, Jakarta) on the uniform surface of a page, newspapers (like the rest of the media) foster the impression that these geographically separated events can exist in a common mental space.[2] That space does indeed exist, but the immediacy of its reality is in inverse proportion to its distance from the directly experienced facts of daily life, in particular local communities.

On the other hand, the *global economy is a fact completely at variance with the requirements of socially meaningful life.* The global economy doubtless exists, but it has no location. It is a vast transactional system involving people who are far more unlikely to meet each other than are people who live in the same country, and are far less likely to understand each other when they do meet. If the first stage of industrialization involved the reduction of all value to exchange value, the latest stage of capitalism involves the reduction of all communities to the status of symbols circulating in a space without location. The global economy, in other words, is everywhere and nowhere.

The problem here is how do we connect the first mode of social existence – here and now, in particular communities, in particular spaces – with that other, equally real mode, the global, which in essence has no location?

The solution obviously cannot involve shutting off the local from the global. That would be the route to economic suicide. But neither can the solution involve suppressing the local in favour of the global, for there is no society that answers to a global 'we'. The ability to say 'we' – in the absence of which there can be no meaningful social life – is only possible in local communities, rooted in particular spaces and histories.

The 'worlding' of the world, or globalization, will inevitably elicit a counterforce – a defensive insistence that the local does not coincide with the global.

'Asian values'

The assertion by many Asian leaders and intellectuals that something called 'Asian values' exists – and that these values govern the trajectory of Asian societies, economically and politically – is one example of how globalized Asian societies have dealt with the contradictions inherent in globalization. It illustrates, at once, why the category of culture can acquire such self-conscious valency in precisely those societies that deliberately assume the modalities of globalization; and how it enables them to negotiate the conflicting demands of the local and the global. In psychoanalytic terms, one might describe 'Asian values' as an apotropaic or defensive gesture – which is not to say it does not also encompass positive, even challenging and sometimes aggressive, claims.

Consider Singapore: why would a country that now has a higher per capita income than the UK, where English is spoken extensively, a country that actually feels more westernized than say Taiwan or South Korea, why would such a country insist on the Asian-ness of its modernity? And why would others, as various as China and Malaysia, want to advance similar claims?

A good place to begin would be Huntington's *Clash of Civilizations*, the work most responsible in recent times for foregrounding, in particularly stark terms, the role of culture in geo-politics. Singapore figures largely in the book, both as a figure of praise and doubt.[3] Huntington, for instance, praises Singapore's system of 'Shared Values'.

'Shared Values', of course, refers to the state-endorsed ideology that declares the basic values of Singaporeans to be: (1) Nation before ethnic community and society above self; (2) Family as the basic unit of society; (3) Community support for the individual; (4) Consensus instead of contention; and (5) Racial and Religious Harmony. As Huntington notes, these Shared Values were meant to emphasize that Singapore was in crucial respects an Asian society. As the government document announcing the Shared Values of Singaporeans explained: 'Singaporeans are not Americans or Anglo-Saxons, though we may speak English and wear Western dress. If over the long term Singaporeans became indistinguishable from Americans, British or Australians, or worse became a poor imitation of them, we will lose our edge over these Western societies,' an edge 'which enables us to hold our own internationally.'[4]

Singapore, that is, has to remain Asian in part for competitive economic advantage. The logic is startling though impeccable: Singapore fears becoming like America, not solely because it fears losing its Asian soul, but primarily because becoming like America will weaken its ability to compete successfully in the global market, become a full-blown developed economy, and thereby become like America. Singapore, in other words, has to remain Asian in order to become Western. The same logic is operative in many other Asian countries, which insist their economic modernization would be imperilled if it were to be equated with cultural westernization.

Obviously baffled by this logic, Huntington, despite his admiration for Singapore, is driven to cite the island-state as an example of why a clash of civilizations – between the Sinic and the Western in this instance – is inevitable. Singapore's founding prime minister Lee figures so prominently in the book, not only because Huntington admires him, but also because Mr Lee, more articulately than any other Asian political figure, has denied the universality of something called Western values, and insisted forcefully that a different system of values informs the logic of Asian modernity.[5]

Singapore, then, is a strange case – at once evidence of a threat to Western universalism as well as reassuringly familiar. The peculiar position Singapore occupies in the imaginary of someone like Huntington – 'Goodness gracious,' you can almost hear him say, 'this lot want to become more like us in order to remain more like themselves' – this curious but understandable reaction makes Singapore a good test case for asking: What precisely is at stake in asserting the priority of cultural identities or civilizational affinities over, say, economic or political ones? What is being obfuscated or denied in asserting that a clash of civilizations is inevitable?

At bottom, the similarity between Singapore's position and Huntington's – between Asian cultural conservatives, in general, and American cultural conservatives – is a re-formulation of political choices as cultural choices, and the fashioning of those cultural choices in ways that best support the local manifestations of what is, for better or worse, a single global economic system. Indeed, 'Asian values' is a construct that achieves the same ideological effects as Huntington's own insistence on the Judeo-Christian tradition as the informing genius of Western civilization.[6] The effects of both ideological constructs are so similar that it is difficult to tell whether we are witnessing a Westernization of Oriental values or an Orientalization of Western values, or what either of these categories – Western or Oriental – might mean in the context of globalization. In both instances we find an attempt to legitimize strikingly similar political and economic agendas by locating their source in what is offered as the essential identity of a culture or civilization. The question is this: Given the remarkable similarities of political agendas, why then is there an insistence on cultural difference, differences so insistent, according to Huntington, that they may well result in clashes? Why must the same be distinguished as threateningly different?

Significantly, the ideological and economic challenge posed by East Asia in general to the hegemony of the West, has been represented, in both the West and Asia, for not entirely incompatible reasons, as a conflict within capitalism. Both parties seem to agree that global capitalism is now riven by a cultural division *between*, and not a political division *within*, each of its contrasting manifestations across the Pacific Ocean. Thus, for Asian ideologues, the division that matters is between a communitarian East and an individualist West. Thus, for figures such as Huntington the division that matters is between an Eastern 'authoritarian capitalism' and a Western 'liberal capitalism'.

The protagonists in this particular transoceanic cultural war, we ought to note, have only recently discovered their suspicions of each other, after having cooperated closely in the Cold War. The distinction between 'authoritarian' and 'liberal' capitalism is less an argument over the spoils of victory than an argument as to what that victory means.

Consider, for instance, the great play that has been made in organs like the *Wall Street Journal* of the fact that the economies of a good many East Asian countries are dominated by their governments. This, coupled with the political controls at the disposal of various Asian regimes, is supposed to render East Asian capitalist miracles demotic versions of true capitalism. Leaving aside for a moment why capitalist systems dominated by big government-linked enterprises should be any worse (or better) than capitalist systems dominated by big private conglomerates, the distinction is too pat for more immediate reasons.

First, contrary to what is commonly believed, the active participation of governments in market economies is not exactly an East Asian invention. Bismarck's Germany got there first before Meiji Japan. Indeed, if there is any one particular ideological inspiration for the form of capitalism that countries like Singapore practise, it comes from the West: namely, that model of the mixed economy that Fabians of Britain's Labour Party successfully exported to many former British colonies. (Singapore's ruling party even produced a manifesto in the 1970s that christened the system of managed capitalism it had instituted, 'Socialism that Works' – in contrast to the versions in Western Europe that didn't.)

Second, though the extent of public sector participation in Singapore's economy might well shock free-market orthodoxies in the US, what has powered Singapore's transformation is not indigenous but foreign capital – to be exact, multinational capital, much of it from the US. If so-called authoritarian capitalism is dramatically different from liberal capitalism, admirers of the latter ought to explain why so many Fortune 500 companies have found the miracle economies of East Asia such salubrious destinations. To dismiss the relationship as purely exploitative – greedy Western corporations exploiting cheap labour; or ruthless Eastern despotisms taking advantage of Western gullibility – is to miss the mutualities involved altogether.

This is the discomfiting truth that liberal, Western critics of East Asian regimes have considerable difficulty recognizing. It is easy enough to dismiss as irrational a system that you find objectionable; but if the objectionable system possesses all the features of a rationality of which you approve, then you are faced with the disagreeable task of extricating yourself from a judgment that is not also a self-condemnation.

Singapore, for example, is an economic powerhouse precisely because its political, social and legal institutions have been shaped in ways to ensure its assimilation into a global economic system that emanates from the West. Contract law, for instance, the mother's milk of international commerce, functions in Singapore in the same way it does in the US or the UK or the European Union. Entities like Hewlett-Packard and Microsoft know that; the Singapore government knows they know; and all the cutting things that liberal capitalists have said about authoritarian capitalists have not prevented any of them from operating in Singapore.

It is within this context, I believe – the convergence of global economic interests – that a construct like 'Asian values' should be understood. Western liberalism reads 'Asian values' as merely a challenge to liberalism's ideological sway. In many respects, 'Asian values' does constitute such a challenge; various East Asian governments have indeed invoked it to represent civil liberties as Western importations, or to limit the growth of democracy beyond the exercise of a free vote at periodic intervals. But to read 'Asian values' as merely an ideological challenge to the West would be to underestimate its power and scope, its continuation of a logic that remains thoroughly (and paradoxically) Western.

To begin with, the very discovery of 'Asian values' was driven by the need to manage, not to resist, increasingly successful industrial states. The invocation of 'Asian values' functions, that is, not merely to contain the growth of rights beyond those already granted to achieve modernity, but also as a means of shaping indigenous cultures into fit instruments of modernity. This is why the concept has proven attractive to political and intellectual elites in countries as various as Singapore (a first-world economy), China (an emerging economy), and Malaysia (a Muslim-majority country).[7]

In Singapore, 'Asian values' was largely a substitute term for the Confucianism that was believed to underpin the worldview of its Chinese majority. Rediscovered in East Asia after its presence was detected by Western academics like Ezra Vogel to explain the startling growth of East Asia, Confucianism was offered by East Asian intellectuals as their answer to the Protestant work ethic.[8] In the space of a decade, a philosophy that 50 years ago had been an object of almost universal derision among Chinese intellectuals as the cause of China's backwardness, was transformed into a system of 'communitarian' beliefs and values – at once the factor explaining the genesis of Asian capitalism as well as ensuring its continued growth.[9]

Linked to rationality, providing the justification even for radical rearrangements of traditional social structures,[10] this half-rediscovered, half-invented tradition affords the state a means of assimilating its population to a structure of values whose chief beneficiaries are the distinctly modern protocols of capitalism, even as the state stages that modernity as a continuation of an unchanging past. By yoking in this fashion the past to the present, the local to the global, 'Asian values' provide Asian elites with the means of accomplishing two purposes: first, founding an efficient ideological machinery for completing a process that has been going on for more than a century – the assimilation of indigenous cultures to the demands of modernity; and second, providing an alternative intellectual and cultural genealogy for Asian modernity that would allow Asian societies to claim an independent basis for their capitalism.

These purposes encompass the double movement referred to above: a negative rejection of transnational capital as the sole repository of value; and a positive affirmation of an independent cultural formation. And in accomplishing both purposes, the invention of 'Asian values' also enables these societies to negotiate the conflicting demands of the local and the global.

On the one hand, 'Asian values' constitutes an ideological machinery that is continuous with the Orientalism of the nineteenth-century metropolitan powers, and re-figures it in such a manner as to be fully consonant with the requirements of modern market economies. Successful East Asian economies, indeed, are arguably modern fulfilments of the Orientalist project – conceived and executed, this time, by Orientals themselves. Few other Asian countries have created as efficient a mechanism for selecting and defining an 'Asian' (or indigenous) identity that is so fully consonant with the requirements of the modern market economy, even as they set aside what they deem decadent or dangerous, harmful or useless in the West. The re-ethnicization of identity that this involves is not quite the re-discovery of essential cultural identities, as much as it is an ideologically-driven but globally-informed reformulation of those very same identities so as to meet particular political and economic exigencies.

On the other hand, by representing possibilities *within* modernity as a choice *between* Eastern and Western cultural identities, the invocation of 'Asian values' also allows for the assertion of a specifically local – or 'rooted', 'national', 'cultural', and sometimes 'racial' or 'racialized' – 'we'.

Ironically, Western ideologues like Huntington, who fail to note that the source of such contradictory possibilities is Asian modernity itself, and choose instead to regard the contradictions as evidence of a flawed modernity diametrically different from their own, confirm (negatively) the very terms of the debate that Asian ideologues seek (positively). Ironically, both sides in this debate find common cause in representing differences *within* as differences *between*, for neither can make culture 'a self-conscious collective project' otherwise. Ironically, both find themselves embarking on similarly structured cultural projects just when the socioeconomic differences between their societies are vanishing, and their patterns of production and consumption, as well as their systems of governance and economic regulation, are converging.

Conclusion: multiculturalism?

This re-discovery of cultural identities in Asia may have a geo-political impact, and may well shape the emerging tussle for influence between the US and China in East Asia. It is difficult, however, to predict what precisely that impact would be, or how precisely cultural politics will influence geopolitics. Affiliations and alliances in Asia may not be as clear-cut as civilizational theorists like Huntington would have them, and a number of other factors, besides the cultural, may influence the behaviour of nation-states. Singapore, for example, though the prime originator of the concept 'Asian values', is also one the United States' most reliable partners in East Asia. Singapore leaders openly state their preference for a continued US presence in the region, for they, like many in the Association of Southeast Asian Nations (or ASEAN), do not wish to see the region dominated by China. An ideological interest in sustaining an alternative intellectual and cultural genealogy for Asian modernity is not likely to trump every other geo-political calculation.

It would be foolish, nevertheless, to assume that the machine-like logic of globalization would be so over-powering that it would be bound to erase cultural differences. 'The world is flat,' neo-liberals like Mr Tom Friedman of the *New York Times* have announced, suggesting that the reality of economic globalization will force not only economic barriers to wither, but also cultural ones.[11] But the world has been flat before – most recently, prior to World War I – only to see that flat world explode in an orgy of violence.

It would be premature, too, to assume that multiculturalism is the obvious solution to cultural separatism. As a social value, there can be no doubt about the virtues of multiculturalism: try to be a little kinder to each other, try to be a little more understanding of cultural differences. Such values are always valid, now perhaps more than ever.

But multiculturalism as an ideology is more than just a message of tolerance or even acceptance. It is also, fundamentally, an assertion of the priority of culture as a category of understanding. If cultural identity exists today as a category of exclusive value primarily because of globalization – as a form of self-defence, almost – the question naturally arises: Can assertions of the priority of cultural categories, like multiculturalism, be a sufficient solution to a problem whose structure it shares? Can the category of culture, in other words, even if it comes dressed up as inherently multiple and relative, function usefully in an arena where culture as such – a 'self-conscious collectivist project' – has become a problem? Can the fox be asked to look after the chicken-coop?

Fundamentally, the doubt about multiculturalism concerns the validity of substituting identity politics for the project of modernity. What becomes of the 'We' in 'We, the people' in the absence of a radical secularism whose protocols of rationality are not coincident with any particular culture or race?

Notes

1 And not only by other Asian countries. Western scholars too have referred to the 'Singapore model' or the 'Singapore School'. See Huntington, 1996; and B. Friedman, 2005.
2 I owe this concept to Anderson, 1991: 187–206.
3 Huntington's book mentions Mr Lee Kuan Yew, Singapore's founding Prime Minister, and now Minister Mentor, more often than it does almost any other contemporary political figure. Mr Lee gets ten entries in the book's index. By contrast, former Taiwanese President Lee Teng Hui appears four times, former Indonesian President Suharto three, and former Malaysian Prime Minister Tun Dr Mahathir Mohammad four. Other Singaporean figures, like diplomats Tommy Koh and Kishore Mahbubani (the author of *Can Asians Think*?), also make appearances in the book – Mr Mahbubani three times, as many occasions as the next name in the index, Mao Zedong, the Great Helmsman himself.
4 See Huntington, 1996: 318–20. See also Government of Singapore, 1991: 2–10.
5 Mr Lee, unlike others in the so-called 'Singapore school', has referred usually to 'Confucian values', rather than 'Asian values'. In many respects, 'Asian values' functions in Singapore as a substitute for 'Confucian values', given Singapore's multiracial make-up.
6 Huntington, for instance, bemoans the 'moral decline, cultural suicide and political disunity' of the West in terms remarkably similar to those which many Asian ideologues adopt in criticising Western culture. It is worth noting here that Huntington's thesis of a global clash of civilizations is not unrelated to his fears about cultural developments within the US. 'The futures of the United States and of the West,' he says in one typical passage 'depend upon Americans reaffirming their commitment to Western civilization. Domestically this means rejecting the divisive siren calls of multiculturalism. Internationally it means rejecting the elusive and illusory calls to identify

the United States with Asia.' As his most recent book (2004), makes plain, Huntington's paradigm of a global clash of civilizations is in fact motivated and accentuated by a vision of the US riven by similar conflicts within its borders. His willingness to jettison the universalist claims of Western culture is not unrelated to the recognition that those universalist claims, which must of necessity be inclusive, can be at odds with the desired racial composition of the US. An unwillingness to work a 'multicivilizational' US must result too in an unwillingness to work a 'multicivilizational' US foreign policy; thus, Huntington's recommendation for the US to reassert the primacy of the Western alliance – against, among other things, 'the elusive and illusory calls to identify the US with Asia'. Given these policy recommendations – domestically, a uni-cultural US, and internationally, a US – European military and economic combine – it is fair to ask: Is the US foreign policy Huntington urges the logical corollary of a world divided into nine self-enclosed civilizations impossibly at odds with one another; or does the world have to appear so treacherously impossible for the sake of the policy? Must the West place itself in purdah because it has to or because it wants to?

7 It is significant that Malaysia, a Muslim-majority state, has found 'Asian values' to be a usable concept. That it can be found attractive in countries as different as Malaysia and Singapore is evidence at once of its power and scope as well as of its lack of cultural, ethnic or national specificity. Malaysia's Prime Minister Abdullah Ahmad Badawi has even assimilated 'Asian values' into a vision of a progressive, tolerant and modern Islam, what he has called *Islam Hadhari,* or Islamic Governance.

8 It is worth noting that what is now taken to be a truism – namely, that the economic success of East Asian societies can be traced to the presence in them of certain cultural traits attributable to Confucianism – would have struck numerous scholars, no more than a few decades ago, as an absurdity. Max Weber, at the turn of the century, thought that Confucianism lacked the dynamism of Protestantism (Weber 1968). Development sociologists in mid-century held that a certain number of culturally-specific social and psychological qualities had to obtain in societies before economic modernization was possible. If one had taken a look at some of these qualities in the 1960s – radical individualism, for one; the personal achievement motive, for another; both foreign if not anathema to traditional Confucianism – one might well have concluded East Asian societies had no business succeeding. But succeed, they did.

9 See Chua, 1995. Chua, borrowing from Gramsci, describes Confucianism as the ground of the 'ideological hegemony' of the state. For a description of the views of early 20th century Chinese intellectuals of Confucianism, see Spence, 1981.

10 For example, in the promotion of Mandarin, in preference to the various dialects traditionally spoken by Chinese Singaporeans. This policy has been justified on both pragmatic grounds – increasingly English-educated Chinese Singaporeans are more likely to remain sufficiently proficient in Chinese if they speak one, not half a dozen, dialects; as well as on cultural grounds – the widespread use of Mandarin will facilitate the transmission of traditional values. Singapore's 'Speak Mandarin Campaign' has been remarkably successful, especially among the young, though many older Chinese Singaporeans continue to speak Hokkien, Cantonese and Teochew.

11 See T. Friedman, 2005. For a brilliant critique of Friedman's arguments, see Gray, 2005. 'There is no systematic connection between globalization and the free market,' Gray points out. 'It is no more essentially friendly to liberal capitalism than to central planning or East Asian dirigisme… Neither does it augur an end to nationalism or great-power rivalries.'

REFERENCES

Anderson, Benedict (1991) *Imagined Communities: Reflections on the Origin and Spread of Nationalism.* London and New York: Verso.

Chua, Beng-Huat (1995) *Communitarian Ideology and Democracy in Singapore.* London and New York: Routledge.

Friedman, Benjamin M. (2005) *The Moral Consequences of Economic Growth.* New York: Alfred A. Knopf.

Friedman, Thomas L. (2005) *The World Is Flat: A Brief History of the Twenty-First Century.* New York: Farrar, Straus and Giroux.

Government of Singapore (1991) *Shared Values.* Singapore: Command Paper No. 1.

Gray, John (2005) 'The world is round,' *New York Review of Books,* 52 (13).

Huntington, Samuel P. (1996) *The Clash of Civilizations and the Remaking of World Order*. New York: Simon and Schuster.

– (2004) *Who Are We? The Challenges to America's National Identity*. New York: Simon and Schuster.

Spence, Jonathan D. (1981) *The Gate of Heavenly Peace: The Chinese and their Revolution*, 1895–1980. New York: Viking Press.

Weber, Max (1968) *The Religion of China: Confucianism and Taoism*. New York: Simon and Schuster.

## CHAPTER 10

GLOBALIZATION AND THE EUROPEAN SOCIAL MODEL

Anthony Giddens

Underlying the European Social Model (or ESM) is a general set of values: sharing risk widely across society; containing the inequalities that might threaten social solidarity; protecting the most vulnerable through active social intervention; cultivating consultation rather than confrontation in industry; and providing a rich framework of social and economic citizenship rights for the population as a whole. Globalization, therefore, threatens not only the 'social' in the ESM but also the cultural values the model embodies. In contrast to the recent past, when the cultural, social and the economic were more aligned, the present sees the rise of conflicting pressures and trends that might threaten the very survival of the ESM. With the cultural–social consensus breaking up, if not already broken, what will be the future of the ESM in the face of these challenges?

Europe's welfare system is often regarded as the jewel in the crown – perhaps the main feature that gives the European societies their special quality. In May 2003 two of Europe's most distinguished intellectuals, Jürgen Habermas and Jacques Derrida (2005), wrote a public letter about the future of European identity in the wake of the Iraq war. The welfare state's 'guarantees of social security', 'Europeans' trust in the civilizing power of the state' and its capacity to correct 'market failures' brooked large. Most other observers sympathetic to the European Union project today would agree. The 'European social model (ESM)' is, or has become, a fundamental part of what Europe stands for.

The ESM, it has been said, is not only European, not wholly social and not a model (Diamantopolou 2003). If it means having effective welfare institutions, and limiting inequality, then some other industrial countries are more European than some states in Europe. For instance, Australia and Canada surpass Portugal and Greece, not to mention most of the new EU member states after enlargement. The ESM is not purely social, since, however it be defined, it depends fundamentally upon economic prosperity and redistribution. It is not a single model, since there are big divergences between European countries in terms of their welfare systems, levels of inequality and so forth.

Hence there are many different definitions of the ESM around, although they all home in on the welfare state. Daniel Vaughan-Whitehead (2003), for example, lists no less than 15 components of the ESM. We should probably conclude that the ESM is not a unitary concept, but a mixture of values, accomplishments and aspirations, varying in form and degree of realization among European states. My list would be:

- A developed and interventionist state, as measured in terms of level of GDP taken up by taxation.
- A robust welfare system, that provides effective social protection, to some considerable degree for all citizens, but especially for those most in need.
- The limitation, or containment, of economic and other forms of inequality.
- A key role in sustaining these institutions is played by the 'social partners', the unions and other agencies promoting workers' rights. Each trait has to go along with
- Expanding overall economic prosperity and job creation.

The ESM is not only a social model; underlying the ESM is a general set of values: sharing risk widely across society; containing the inequalities that might threaten social solidarity; protecting the most vulnerable through active social intervention; cultivating consultation rather than confrontation in industry; and providing a rich framework of social and economic citizenship rights for the population as a whole. Globalization, therefore, threatens not only the social in the EMS but also the cultural values the model embodies. In contrast to the recent past, when, roughly speaking, the cultural, social and the economic were more aligned, the present sees the rise of conflicting pressures and trends that might threaten the very survival of the

EMS. With the cultural–social consensus breaking up, if not already broken, what will be the future of the EMS in the face of these challenges?

The past and the future

It is agreed by supporters and opponents alike, that the ESM is currently under great strain, or even failing. We should begin, however, by putting this situation into context. Some speak of the 1960s and 1970s as a 'Golden Age' of the welfare state, when there was good economic growth, low unemployment, social protection for all – and when citizens were able to feel much more secure than today. From this perspective, the ESM has been 'attacked' by external forces, particularly those associated with liberalization, and progressively weakened or partly dismantled.

The reality is more complex. For countries such as Spain, Portugal, Greece and later entrants to the European Union, there was no 'Golden Age' at all, since welfare provisions were weak and inadequate. Even in those nations with advanced welfare systems, everything was far from golden in the 'Golden Age'. The era was dominated by mass production and bureaucratic hierarchies, where management styles were often autocratic and many workers were in assembly-line jobs. At that period few women were able to work if they wanted to. Only a tiny proportion of young people entered further or higher education. The range of health services offered was far below those available now. Older people were put out to pasture by a rigid retirement age. The state generally treated its clients as passive subjects rather than as active citizens. Some of the changes in welfare systems over the past thirty years have been aimed at correcting these deficiencies and hence have been both progressive and necessary.

The world, of course, has shifted massively since the 'Golden Age'. The ESM, and the EU itself, were in some large part products of a bi-polar world. The 'mixed economy' and the Keynesian welfare state served to differentiate Western Europe from American market liberalism on the one hand and state-centred Soviet Communism on the other. The fall of the Berlin Wall – Europe's 11:9 (Friedman 2005) – more or less completely changed the nature of the EU, giving rise to identity problems that still remain unresolved – and indeed were reflected in the refusal of the proposed EU constitution by the people of France and The Netherlands.

The demise of Keynesianism in the West, and the collapse of Soviet Communism, were brought about by much the same trends – intensifying globalization, the rise of a worldwide information order, the shrinking of manufacture (and its transfer to less developed countries), coupled to the rise of new forms of individualism and consumer power. These are not changes that came and went; their impact continues today.

Fundamental although the trends mentioned above are, it is essential to recognize that the problems of the ESM today don't just stem from changes happening in the global environment. Some of the core difficulties are internal, or at most only loosely connected with wider transformations in the wider world. They include primarily demographic changes, especially the ageing population, the associated issue of pensions, and the sharp decline in birthrates; changes in family structure, with many more one-parent families than before, and more women and children living in poverty; and high levels of unemployment coming in some part from unreformed labour markets.

A few commentators tend to underplay the difficulties Europe faces, especially when the EU15 is compared with the US.[1] Europeans, they say, have made a life-style choice. They have traded in a certain level of possible growth for more leisure than most Americans enjoy. Productivity in some EU countries rivals that of the US. Precisely because of Europe's stronger welfare systems there are fewer working poor in the EU states than in the US.

But these ideas are not convincing, as recent work has demonstrated (Sapir et al. 2003). Average growth in the EU15 has declined in relative terms year on year since the 1980s. GDP per head has not got beyond 70 per cent of the US level over that period. Not only has the US had higher growth, it has also had greater macroeconomic stability over that time. About a third of the contrast in per capita GDP with the US comes from lower average productivity of labour, a third from shorter working hours and one third from a lower employment rate. However, none of these come purely from choice, and all affect the sustainability of the ESM. Twenty million people are unemployed in the EU. There are 93 million economically inactive people in the EU, a far higher rate than in the US. The employment rate of older workers (over 55) is 40 per cent in the EU, compared to 60 per cent in the US and 62 per cent in Japan.

Some of these differences certainly do come from a 'preference for leisure' in Europe, and a better balance between home and work than is found in the US. But there are very many in Europe, including many young people – and over 55s – who want to work but can't. This comment also applies to immigrants. The US has done a much better job of integrating immigrants into its labour market than have the EU countries. The jobless rate of non-nationals in the EU15 in 2002 was more than twice the rate for nationals. In the US the two rates are almost the same. Enlargement has brought with it a series of issues that are very remote from a 'preference for leisure'. It has increased the EU population by 20 per cent, but GDP by only 5 per cent. Problems of inequality and cohesion are heightened, both across the EU as a whole and within the member states.

There is therefore good reason to support the conclusion that over recent years 'the sustainability of the "European Model" has become more and more questionable' (2003: 97). Achieving higher average levels of economic growth and of job creation must be placed at the forefront, since the current combination of low growth and higher public expenditure cannot continue.

Policy controversies

There is intense debate among policy specialists about how far in European welfare systems there is 'path-dependency', inhibiting mutual learning. Following the work of Gosta Esping-Andersen (1989) it is widely accepted that there are three or four main types of 'welfare capitalism' in Europe. These are the Nordic type, based upon high taxation and extensive job opportunities provided within the welfare state itself; the Central European type (Germany, France), based mainly on payroll contributions; and the Anglo-Saxon type, which supposedly is a more 'residual' form of welfare system, having a lower taxation base and using more targeted policies. The fourth type, alongside the three Esping-Andersen originally recognized, is the Mediterranean one (Italy, Spain, Portugal, Greece), which also has a fairly low tax base and depends heavily upon provision from the family.[2]

Esping-Andersen has made much of the 'service economy trilemma' – originally formulated by Torben Iversen and Anne Wren (1998) – that limits the degree to which policies can be applied across these different types. The idea is that it is impossible, in a modern service economy, simultaneously to have balanced budgets, low levels of income inequality and high levels of employment. Two of these goals can be successfully pursued by governments at any one time, but not all three. The different types of system are distinguished partly because they have chosen varying combinations.

In the Nordic countries, for instance, the welfare state acts as employer, providing an expanding number of public-sector service jobs. Taxation has to be very high and puts a continual strain on borrowing levels. The Anglo-Saxon countries, such as the UK and Australia, have generated large numbers of private-sector jobs, and have maintained fiscal discipline, but are marked by high levels of poverty. In the Central European type, such as Germany or France, by contrast, there is a commitment to limiting inequality and (at least until recently) to budgetary constraint. However these countries are dogged by low levels of job growth.

But how far in fact does path-dependency operate? Is the 'trilemma' real? Hemerijk and his colleagues have argued persuasively that the empirical evidence for all of this is 'surprisingly shaky' (2002). The recent history of Scandinavia suggests that it is in fact possible to have sound public finances, low inequality and high levels of employment. Per contra, it also seems possible to have only one. Germany, for example, now has high levels of unemployment and a burgeoning public debt. Moreover, the various 'types' are not very clear-cut. The Nordic states differ quite widely from one another, for example. It is not obvious that Germany and France belong to a single type. The UK is supposed to be a 'residual' welfare state, but its net taxation levels are now about the same as Germany's. In the shape of the NHS, it has the most 'socialized' system of medicine in Europe (Barysch 2005). Hemerijk has concluded that the welfare states that have adapted best to changing conditions have created 'hybrid models', borrowed in some part from elsewhere. It is a case I find convincing, and I shall suggest below that a great deal of mutual learning is possible.

Lisbon and after

Unlike other major achievements of the European Union, such as the Single Market, the Single Currency and enlargement, the ESM has been only minimally shaped by the EU itself. The welfare state was built by nations, not by international collaboration. Some of the member countries with the most established welfare institutions signed up to the EU only relatively late on. Given the grip that member states have on social policy, most real change will have to come from within nations.

We don't lack for reports suggesting what should be done to get the underperforming parts of Europe back on their feet again, and generally to make the EU states more competitive. They stretch back well before the proclamation of the Lisbon Agenda in 2000. There is a good deal of unanimity on policies to be followed. Andre Sapir's six points would be agreed upon by many: (1) Make the Single Market more dynamic. (2) Boost investment in knowledge. (3) Improve EU macroeconomic policy. (4) Reform policies for convergence and restructuring. (5) Achieve more efficiency in regulation. (6) Reform the EU budget, cutting back on agricultural spending and deploying the resources elsewhere (Sapir et al. 2003).

The Single Market has certainly benefited Europe. It is estimated EU GDP in 2002 was 1.8 per cent higher than it would have been without the progress that has been made. However the Lisbon Agenda has proved much harder to implement, and the ambition of making Europe the most competitive knowledge-based economy in the world by 2010 has come to seem remote indeed. The EU countries are supposed to reach an average employment ratio of 70 per cent by that date, but at the moment the target looks unrealizable. There are still states where the level of employment is below 60 per cent of the available labour force, including Belgium (59.6 per cent), Greece (57.8 per cent), Italy (56 per cent), Hungary (57 per cent) and Poland (51.2 per cent).[3]

There are clear tensions between the Single Market and the ESM, as many authors have noted – and which recently have centred upon the Services Directive that seeks to deregulate and increase competition within services across Europe. As Fritz Scharpf has pointed out, the Directive could even impact directly upon the 'best practice' sector of Europe, Scandinavia. Electoral support for the Nordic welfare state depends in a vital way upon the provision of universal public services of high quality. However, suppose European competition law is 'opened up' to liberalize those 'markets'? Some services could come to be provided, say, from Latvia, meeting only local criteria of costing and effectiveness. There could be a drift towards an American-style system, as services become differentially priced and diverted to those who could most afford them (Scharpf 2002).

The Services Directive is the focus of some of the most bitter controversies about the future direction of Europe. For those in favour, it is an absolutely essential part of the drive to cope with the EU's problems of unemployment and underemployment. For those opposed to, or worried about it, the Services Directive could have largely harmful consequences. The Commission insists that core public services will be protected, but for critics the guarantees offered are inadequate. To those same critics, the Directive also signals the triumph of a market-based Europe over social Europe. For it is all about deregulation and competition. What has happened to the core European values of equity and solidarity? Won't the Directive simply produce greater inequality and economic insecurity?

Debate about the ESM has a special significance in this context. For it could be argued that although the Lisbon Agenda, Sapir report, Kok report and other similar contributions all talk about the ESM, social exclusion and so forth, they have little to say about them in a direct way. They lack a systematic discussion of how the innovations they propose can be reconciled with *social justice*. One could even say that this missing dimension is part of the reason why their prescriptions have been so hard to realize.[4]

Lessons to be learned

With these difficulties in mind, let us set out what the experience of the past few years in Europe shows us about combining competitiveness and social justice. We should be cautious about success stories of today – they may turn out to be the failures of tomorrow. But they supply our best guesses for the moment. As given here, the points are schematic – each could be developed in far more detail. And the devil, one should remember, is always in the detail.

One

It is right to put growth and jobs at the forefront. A high level of employment, above a decent minimum wage, is desirable for more than one reason. The greater the proportion of people in jobs, the more money is available – other things being equal – to spend on social investment and social protection. Having a job is also the best route out of poverty. The Lisbon aim of getting an average of 70 per cent or more of the workforce into jobs is not in principle unrealistic. But all depends on the will to reform in those countries where the employment ratio is well below this figure.

Many factors, of course, go into creating more net jobs. However it cannot be accidental that all the countries that have employment ratios of over 70 per cent in Europe have active labour-market policies. Such policies provide training for workers who are unemployed or threatened by unemployment and also try actively to match up workers with job vacancies. They were first of all introduced in Sweden many years ago, but since have spread quite widely. They are not all of a piece. The most effective combine social partnership and universal access to benefits that provide for retraining and resettlement – 'flexicurity'.

The Danish example is widely quoted, even if some have expressed doubts about how far it could be instituted elsewhere.[5] However, many in societies with high unemployment levels are now expressing interest in such policies, including political leaders. Agenda 2010 in Germany is a prime example, although of course it has proved politically extremely difficult to implement. Some reforms have been introduced in France and it is said that in that country there is 'a vogue for the "Danish model"', (Barbier 2005).

Two

Those on the right side of the political spectrum argue that only low-tax economies can prosper in a world of intensifying competition. Yet the evidence to the contrary seems unequivocal. There is no direct relationship between taxation as a proportion of GDP and either economic growth or job creation. There probably is an upper limit, as is indicated by the case of Sweden, which has for some while had the highest tax rate among the industrial countries, but saw its level of income per head slip markedly in relative terms. But more important than the size of the state is how effective the state institutions are and the nature of economic and social policies pursued.

Three

Flexibility in labour markets is an essential part of the policy framework of the successful states. It does not mean American-style hire and fire. In an era of accelerating technological change, however, 'employability' – being willing and able to move on – becomes of prime importance. 'Moving on' often has to happen within the same job because of the importance of technological change. It has been estimated that in the EU15 economies 80 per cent of the technology in use over the period 1995–2005 is less than ten years old. However, 80 per cent of the workforce was trained more than ten years ago.

Flexibility has a bad name, especially among some on the left. For them it means sacrificing the needs of the workforce to the demands of capitalistic competition. But the nature of labour-market regulation is at least as important as its extent. Many labour rights can and should remain. They include rights of representation and consultation, the regulation of working conditions, laws against discrimination and so forth. Ireland has enjoyed its phenomenal growth while implementing all relevant EU labour legislation of this sort (Wickham 2004).

Many employees in fact want flexible working, and part-time work, in order to accommodate family demands. Flexibility also meshes to a considerable degree with wider trends in everyday life in modern societies. Most citizens are accustomed to a much wider range of life-style choices than a generation ago, including, if it is feasible for them, when, where and what work to do.

Four

The much-touted knowledge economy is not just an empty term, an invention of the Lisbon Agenda that lost its relevance when the dot.com bubble collapsed – although it should be more accurately called a knowledge and service economy. Only 17 per cent of the labour force on average in the EU15 countries now work in manufacturing and that proportion is still falling. To put it the other way around, over 80 per cent of people now must get their living from knowledge-based or service jobs.

Full employment is possible in the knowledge economy – it has been attained in some of the better-performing European economies mentioned above.[6] But there is a price to be paid. More than two-thirds of the jobs created in the knowledge economy are skilled. They are so-called 'lovely jobs' – and they are becoming more plentiful. Over the period 1995–2004, the proportion of jobs in the EU15 needing advanced qualifications went up from 20 per cent to 24 per cent.

Low-skilled jobs – 'lousy jobs' – fell from 34 per cent to 25 per cent. But a lot of people must still work in such jobs – serving in shops, supermarkets, petrol stations or coffee shops. The minimum wage cannot be set so high as to exclude the lousy jobs, or we also lose the lovely jobs that come with them. We have to try to ensure that it is set at the right level so that there are no working poor; and to make sure that as far as possible people don't get stuck in those jobs.

Five

Investment in education, the expansion of universities, the diffusion of ICT are crucial parts of the modernization of the ESM. Finland is an interesting example of a society in the vanguard of ICT and also with a strong welfare system. As Manuel Castells has pointed out, the country shows that the thesis that a high-tech economy must be modelled after Silicon Valley – in a deregulated environment – is mistaken (Castells and Himanen 2002). Finland has a greater degree of IT penetration than the US. Its growth rate in 1996–2000 was 5.1 per cent. It also ranks near the top of all industrial countries in terms of measures of social justice and has a high tax base. Finland, Castells concludes, offers hope for others. Only three generations ago, Finland was a very poor, heavily rural society.

Six

It is often said that 'our societies are becoming more unequal', but in many respects this is not the case. The position of women, gays and the disabled, for instance, has improved almost everywhere over the past 30 years. Income inequality has grown in most industrial countries over that period, but there are signs this process is now levelling off. Some societies have managed to stay remarkably egalitarian, with the Nordic countries once more being in the lead. We can and must sustain values of equality and inclusiveness. We do not all have to become Scandinavians in order to do so, at least if this means having highly elevated tax rates. The superiority of the Nordic countries in terms of their low levels of inequality does not come primarily from redistribution through taxes and transfers (Sapir 2005). The main explanation is their superior investment in human capital. The distribution of poverty risk directly matches levels of education if we use the four-fold typology of welfare states. The Nordic and Continental welfare states have the largest proportion of the population aged 25–64 with at least upper secondary education (75 per cent and 67 per cent respectively). The Anglo-Saxon and Mediterranean types have the smallest (60 per cent and 39 per cent). We have to invest heavily in early years education since so many capabilities are laid down then. Investment in early education and child care is a key element in reducing levels of child poverty.

Seven

Ecological issues must be brought much more to the forefront than in the past. The best way to do so is through the theme of ecological modernization, originally pioneered by the German Greens in the 1980s. The idea was developed in conscious opposition to the 'limits to growth' arguments coming from an earlier generation of ecological thinking. Ecological modernization means seeking wherever possible to find environmental innovations that are compatible with economic growth. These can involve green technologies and the use of market-based and tax-based incentives for consumers, companies and other agencies to become more environment-friendly in their actions.

However, ecological policy can never be only technological or economic – it also has to be political. Like other types of reform, ecological modernization impinges on the interests of many different groups, including nations. The difficulties involved in producing an international consensus on the Kyoto protocol provide an obvious case in point.

Eight

Immigration has become one of the hottest of hot topics across Europe, far too complex to discuss in any detail here. As societies become multicultural, do they inevitably lose an overall sense of social solidarity? Will the majority be prepared to support policies aimed at helping those who are newcomers and culturally different? Comparative studies seem to suggest a tentative 'yes' to this question, so long as certain conditions are in place (Rossi 2003). These include ensuring that immigrants cover all skill levels – that they are not predominantly unskilled; that access to full welfare benefits is deferred; and that concrete steps are taken to ensure that immigrants accept overall norms of the host culture.

The term 'immigrant', of course, covers a multitude of differences. There are immigrants from 150 different countries living in the UK, for example. Great variations can exist among those coming from the same country, depending upon differences in socioeconomic background, ethnicity, culture and other factors. Some migrants or minorities fare much better than others. Thus in the UK first or second generation immigrants from Pakistan or Bangladesh on average earn far less than the indigenous population. Indians, by contrast, earn more on average than native-born whites.

Nine

The ageing population should be seen as an opportunity, not just as another 'problem'. We know what has to happen – the difficulties in most countries depend upon mustering the political will to make the changes. We have to invest more in children. We have to persuade younger people to save more. The main cause of the ageing society is not that people on average are living longer – although they are – it is the low birth rate. The state has to provide people with incentives to have more children, and make sure the right type of welfare measures are in place. No matter what innovations are made to help or force people to save, there is only one main way to solve the issue of unaffordable pensions commitments. We have to persuade or motivate older people to stay in work longer. Such a goal is surely not just a negative one. We have to contest ageism both inside and outside the workplace. If it means people over 55, or over 65, 'old age' is no longer the incapacitating factor it once was.

Ten

Continuing reform of the state itself, and of public services, is just as important to the future of the ESM as any of the factors noted above. Where needed, decentralization and diversification are the order of the day. Plainly there has to be a balance between these and integration. The relations of national states within the EU, with power moving both upwards and downwards, are a core example, but nevertheless only one example, of the inevitability of multi-layered governance today. Of course, the issue of the privatization of state services, or putting them more in the hands of not-for-profit agencies, continues to be a matter of widespread controversy. Public services should become just as responsive (in some ways, more responsive) to the needs of those they serve as commercial organizations are.

Some have suggested Keynesian solutions both to reform of the ESM and to job generation in Europe. François Hollande (2005) has proposed a strengthening of economic government in Europe, including persuading the European Central Bank to add job creation to its concern for managing the stability of prices. Business taxes should be standardized across Europe and programmes of 'great works', in transport, communications and energy, should be launched on a European level, financed through borrowing. But why should an approach that has failed everywhere at a national level suddenly work at a transnational one? Some kinds of new infrastructural projects for Europe may very well be worth considering, particularly in the area of ICT, but not solely or even primarily as a means of creating jobs.

Although there are those who insist otherwise, the future of the ESM does not come down to a choice between a Keynesian Europe and a 'deregulated, Anglo-Saxon' Europe. Some have suggested that there was in fact a 'plan B' for Europe in the event of the rejection of the constitution. It was the 'British plan of liberalisation and deregulation' favoured by Tony Blair (Moscovići 2005). But this assertion makes no sense in either political or analytical terms. Blair signed up to the Constitutional Treaty, as did all other European political leaders.

Much more importantly, the future of the ESM does not lie in 'becoming more Anglo-Saxon' – certainly not if this means in some sense taking the UK as a model for the rest of Europe. Other countries can learn from what has been achieved in Britain – after all, the UK has a high rate of employment, is the only EU15 country to have actively increased its investment in public services over the past few years, and has significantly reduced its poverty rate. However, the standard of public services in the UK still lags well behind Continental best practice and levels of economic inequality remain high in spite of progress made.

A template for reform

Previous thinking has been rather dazzled by the 'three/four worlds of welfare capitalism', but while real differences do exist, the EU and its member states should be pushing for convergence here as in other areas. Most of the core difficulties facing the ESM are not specific to any country; they are structural. In a globalizing era, solutions can often, or even normally, in principle be generalized.

A future ESM, to repeat, would not be the British model. It would not be the French model. It would not be the Swedish or Danish one either. What I sketch in below is something of an ideal type – a list of traits that might be adopted in varying ways by specific reforming countries. A template for a revised ESM (RESM) might be guided by the following overall characteristics:[7]

- A move from negative to *positive welfare*. When William Beveridge developed his plan for the post-war welfare state, he thought – as did almost all others – of the welfare state as a corrective device. The point of his innovations was to attack the 'five evils' of ignorance, squalor, want, idleness and disease. We should not forget about any of these, but today we should seek much more to make them positives. In other words, we should be promoting education and learning, prosperity, life choice, active social and economic participation, and healthy life-styles.
- Such goals presume *incentives* as well as benefits, and *obligations* as well as rights, since the active compliance of citizens is required. The connection of welfare with citizenship is not, as T.H. Marshall (1950) suggested in his classic formulation, brought about only by the expansion of rights, but by a mixture of rights and obligations. Passive unemployment benefits were defined almost wholly as rights – and proved to be dysfunctional largely for this reason. The introduction of active labour market policies makes it clear that the able-bodied unemployed have an obligation to look for work if they receive state support, and there are sanctions to help ensure their compliance.
- The traditional welfare system sought to *transfer risk* from the individual to the state or community. Security was defined as the absence, or reduction of risk. But risk in fact has many positive aspects to it. People often need to take risks to improve their lives. Moreover, in a fast-moving environment it is important for individuals to be able to adjust to, and if possible actively prosper from, change. This statement is as true of the labour-force as it is of entrepreneurs; it is as valid for those affected by divorce or other social transitions as it is for the economic world. The creative use of risk, however, does not imply the absence of security – far from it. Knowing that there is help when things go wrong may often be a condition of entertaining the risk in the first place. I take it this is part of the logic of 'flexicurity' in active labour market policy.
- An RESM has to be, at least in many spheres, *contributory*. Services designed to be free at the point of use may be designed with nobility of purpose, but are prone to essential difficulties. Since they have few mechanisms to contain demand, they become over-crowded and over-used. Two-tier systems tend to develop, in which the affluent simply opt out. Contributions, even if relatively small, can help not only with this issue, but can also promote responsible attitudes to the use of services. The contributory principle – contributions from direct users – is therefore likely to play an increasing role in public services, from pensions and health through to higher education.
- An RESM must be *de-bureaucratized*. The pre-existing welfare state was based almost everywhere upon treating citizens as passive subjects. Collectivism was acceptable in a way it isn't, and shouldn't be, today. De-bureaucratizing means standing up against producer interests, promoting decentralization and local empowerment (for interesting examples, see the changes introduced into health provision and education in Sweden and Denmark in the early 1990s). These endeavours should be sharply distinguished from privatization, which is one among other means of potentially pursuing these goals.
- An RESM would differ quite radically from the 'American model' (Aiginger 2002: 114):

- Costs may be trimmed, and new contributions introduced, but the welfare system continues to offer wide protection on a range of fronts, in terms of social, economic and health risks. Levels of taxation are high in international terms.
- The scope for active government and the state remains large, although more geared to investment in human capital than in the past. The RESM may aptly be regarded as involving a 'social investment state'.
- Welfare policy is more egalitarian than in the US.
- Solidarity is promoted by ensuring that welfare systems remain attractive to more affluent groups.
- The 'social partners' play a key role in determining wage levels and other conditions of work.
- Environmental goals are central to the agenda.

Such a 'best guess' RESM provides a very real way forward for Europe, including for new member states. Of course the practical/political barriers to reform in some countries remain formidable. Even where generalizable, best practice as we can discern it at the moment leaves question marks and difficulties. For instance, how can those countries where inequalities are marked, and where child poverty is common – such as Greece, Ireland, Portugal and the UK – reduce them in a radical way? The immigration that Europe, in fact, needs to better its economic performance might be blocked by the rise of right-wing populism and by the sentiments of the wider public. Even countries that have come closest to embodying an RESM, such as Denmark or The Netherlands, have fallen prey to such influences. In addition, the wider global environment is shifting rapidly because of the increasing prominence of China, India and other developing countries in world markets.

Fears connected with migration and external competition played a big role among 'no' voters in France and The Netherlands in the constitutional referenda and it is to this issue I turn now.

Citizens' anxieties, fair and unfair competition

Referenda are notoriously unreliable as a means of assessing opinions. They almost always flood over well beyond the question or questions actually asked. Moreover the referendum on the proposed constitution was a highly unusual one. It is very uncommon for a referendum to be held on such a lengthy and complex document as the Constitutional Treaty. It isn't surprising that after the 'no's' in France and The Netherlands everyone had a field day reading into the results whatever their prejudices dictated.

Polls offer a more reliable source of assessment. We know that the issues that most worried voters in France and The Netherlands weren't in fact primarily constitutional. Seventy-five per cent of all French voters in the referendum and, extraordinarily, fully 66 per cent of 'no' voters, still believed a constitution for Europe was necessary. The main worries were social and economic. In France, in particular, there were widespread fears about social security and the other welfare provisions that make up the ESM.

The now celebrated Polish plumber played a major role in the referendum – in his absence, of course. Anxieties about unfair tax competition from the new member states, and about 'social dumping', are felt not only at the level of the lay public, but also by political leaders too. They underlie the calls for the harmonization of business taxes, as well as worries about the Services Directive.

One of the main dividing-lines that has opened up across Europe is between those able to take advantage of the opportunities offered by the knowledge society and the open cosmopolitan world linked to it; and those denied those opportunities and uncomfortable with, or openly hostile to, such a world. Feelings of the latter sort, in turn are closely bound up with worries about immigration and the swamping of national identity in a globalizing world. They explain why The Netherlands, which by and large has been an economic success story over the recent period, should have voted 'no' in the referendum.

It is crucial, however, to separate well-founded anxieties from false ones, bracketing off for a moment the immense political problems, and populist pressures, involved. How far are living standards in the richer EU countries really threatened by 'social dumping' from the poorer ones? Could a 'race to the bottom' within the EU be initiated as a result? A relatively new, but related question has come to the fore recently, although it has not as yet received as much attention in Europe as in the US – the outsourcing of service jobs to poorer countries, where workers are paid much lower wages than in the West.

Fears about a potential race to the bottom with enlargement seem to be misplaced. They have been expressed before, in two different contexts. One was in relation to intensifying global competition generally; the other was in the context of earlier EU expansion, which took in the Mediterranean countries. The anxieties expressed by many that economic globalization would force cut-backs in European welfare states have proved to be almost wholly unfounded. Taxation revenue as a proportion of GDP has remained stable in virtually all the industrial countries, although with a few exceptions, such as the UK, it is no longer climbing. Some of the most important difficulties facing the ESM, as mentioned earlier, are in any case internal rather than external.

Studies of the economic impact of Portugal, Spain and Greece after their accession show positive rather than negative effects on the more affluent EU countries. There were no cut-backs to welfare programmes within the three states. On the contrary, the welfare systems developed over the past twenty years have been marked by strong expansionary trends (Guillen and Matsaganis 2000). Many at the time of their accession thought the rich states would get even wealthier, while the new entrants would get relatively poorer. The scenario proved false, even if large differences remain. The EU has acted as a 'convergence machine' (Tsoukalis 2005).

Of course it could be argued that in the current round of enlargement, the incoming states are poorer in relative terms, and have adopted more aggressive tax policies than the earlier periods. Yet the gap is not nearly as great as that between the developed countries and poorer countries on a world level.

Harmonizing of business taxes is extremely unlikely to be achieved, even if it were desirable. Is there a case for, and more possibility of achieving, greater harmonization of labour standards at European level? The most that could be accomplished is probably a set of minimum prescriptions that could be accepted by all countries. Dialogue between social partners at a European level might create some sort of consensus. However, it should be noted that unions tend to represent the interests of workers in jobs rather than the unemployed, while employers' federations usually speak more for larger corporations and less for small business (Bean et al. 1998).

Concluding thought

The question is always asked: Can Europe afford its social model and the culture it embodies? But perhaps we should turn it the other way around: Can Europe afford *not* to have its social model? The levels of inequality that exist in the US could cause that country immense problems in the years that lie ahead. The US, for example, may have the best universities in the world, but it also has the highest illiteracy rate among the industrialized countries. According to the Programme for International Assessment, 15-year-olds in the US rank no higher than 24th out of 29 nations compared; and only 24th also in tests of problem-solving skills. At a time when the knowledge economy is itself becoming globalized, a reformed European social model might mean that Europe may be better placed than the US.

Notes

1 See, for example, Jeremy Rifkin: *The European Dream*. New York: Tarcher Penguin, 2004.

2 Maurizio Ferrera seems to have been the first to identify the fourth type, in his *Le Trappole del Welfare*. Bologna: Il Mulino, 1998.

3 Figures are for 1993.

4 The Lisbon Strategy has recently been supplemented by a new five-year Social Agenda. See European Commission: *Communication on the Social Agenda,* Brussels, 9 February 2005.

5 Denmark radically revamped its social security policy in the early 1990s. Workers can be dismissed at short notice. Severance pay is not high. Unemployment benefits, however, are good and paid over four years, with lower-paid workers receiving up to 90 per cent of their working wage. Retraining is obligatory after a certain time. It is provided in a highly decentralized way, with extensive involvement from the unions and civil society agencies. The unemployed are obliged to take up offers of employment or retraining made by local departments of employment.

6 However, there are problems with the rising numbers of people claiming disability or sickness benefits. In Sweden in 2004, for example, 6 per cent of people of working age were on sick leave or registered as disabled.

7 A different formulation appears in Karl Aiginger: 'The new European model of the reformed welfare state', European Forum Working Paper, Stanford University, 2002. I have learned a great deal from Aiginger's perceptive writings on the future of European welfare.

REFERENCES

Aiginger, Karl (2002) 'The new European model of the reformed welfare state'. European Forum Working Paper, Stanford University.

Barbier, Jean-Claude (2005) 'Apprendre vraiment du Danemark?', *Connaissance de l'emploi*, No. 18. July.

Barysch, Katinka (2005) 'Liberal versus social Europe', Centre for European Reform Bulletin. August/September.

Bean, Charles et al. (1998) *Social Europe: One for All?* London: Centre for Economic Policy Research.

Castells, Manuel and Himanen, Pekka (2002) *The Information Society and the Welfare State*. Oxford: Oxford University Press.

Diamantopolou, Anna (2003) 'The European social model – myth or reality?' Speech at Labour Party Conference, Bournemouth, 29 September.

Esping-Andersen, Gosta (1989) *The Three Worlds of Welfare Capitalism*. Cambridge: Polity Press.

European Commission: *Communication on the Social Agenda* 9 (February 2005), Brussels.

Ferrera, Maurizio (1998) *Le Trappole del Welfare*. Bologna: Il Mulino.

Friedman, Thomas (2005) *The World is Flat*. New York: Allen Lane.

Guillen, Ana M. and Matsaganis, Manos (2000) 'Testing the "social dumping" hypothesis in Southern Europe', *Journal of European Social Policy*, Vol. 10.

Habermas, Jürgen and Derrida, Jacques (2005), 'February 15, or, what binds Europeans together', in Daniel Levy et al.*, Old Europe, New Europe, Core Europe*. London: Verso.

Hemerijk, Anton (2002) 'The Self-transformation of the European Social Model(s)', in Gosta Esping-Andersen, *Why We Need a New Welfare State*. Oxford: Oxford University Press.

Hollande, François (2005) 'L'Europe dans la tourmente', *Revue Socialiste*, Vol. 30.

Iversen, Torben and Wren, Anne (1998) 'Equality, employment and budgetary restraint: the trilemma of the service economy', *World Politics*, Vol. 50.

Marshall, T.H. (1950) *Citizenship and Social Class*. Cambridge: Cambridge University Press.

Moscovići, Pierre (2005) 'L'Europe dans la tourmente', *Revue Socialiste*, Vol. 30.

Rifkin, Jeremy (2004) *The European Dream*. New York: Tarcher Penguin.

Rossi, Nicola (2003) 'Managed diversity', in Anthony Giddens, *The Progressive Manifesto*. Cambridge: Polity Press and Policy Network.

Sapir, Andre (2005, 9 September) 'Globalisation and the reform of European social models', background document for ECOFIN meeting, Manchester. Available at www.bruegel.org

– et al. (2003) *An Agenda for a Growing Europe*. Brussels: European Commission, July.

Scharpf, Fritz (2002) 'The European social model: coping with the challenges of diversity'. Koln: Max-Planck-Institute Working Paper.

Tsoukalis, Loukas (2005) *What Kind of Europe?* Oxford: Oxford University Press.

Vaughan-Whitehead, Daniel (2003) *EU Enlargement versus Social Europe?* London: Elgar.

Wickham , James (2004) *The End of the European Social Model Before it Began*? Dublin: Irish Congress of Trade Unions.

## CHAPTER 11

LATIN AMERICA: DIVERSITY, INVENTION AND CRISIS IN CULTURAL PRODUCTION

Aníbal Ford[1]

Latin America is strongly marked by differences among the regions that compose it, differences in the formation of its societies, historical patterns, and in levels of development. Sophisticated forms of Western culture exist alongside pockets and areas of instability and marginal cultural production. These areas, however, display many different forms of creativity. Despite the recent trend of concentration and convergence of symbolic industries, which results in a loss of cultural autonomy, there is a space that allows Latin American people to communicate their socio-cultural problems and to generate innovative and creative expressions that are based around their own unique identities. The following report strives to give an account of cultural diversity in the face of conflicts that arise in the new globalized scene.

Introduction

In the pages that follow, I shall explore the globalization-related tensions in contemporary cultural production in Latin America. At the outset, I stress that any reflection on the current situation across this continent requires constant diachronic revision not only of the way that the countries which make it up were constituted, but also of the way in which the very concept of 'Latin America' emerged. For the latter is a grouping of countries that share many problems but whose economies are highly diverse, whose societies are constituted in highly different ways, and whose institutions and cultural formations, levels and strategies and conceptions of development, and relationships with modernity and the rest of the world vary very greatly.

The term Latin America refers to those countries on the American continent to the south of the Río Grande, i.e. the US–Mexican border. But the term itself, which emerged during the nineteenth century in the midst of complex political discussions and projects, raises several issues. First, the fact that from the outset it has encompassed concepts of unity or solidarity – often utopian – between the national entities, along with the autonomous and often chaotic development of each of those nation-states. Second, the term has been intended to signify a clear demarcation from Anglo-Saxon North America, especially the US, and its frequent military interventions in the southern countries. Finally, in spite of the fact that all the countries of Latin America accept the term, the term itself embodies discrimination because it prioritizes Latinness, ignoring the original pre-Hispanic indigenous and Black populations that resulted from the massive slave trade,[2] not to mention the fact that the population also contains immigrants[3] from non-Latino ethnic groups. This explains the use by many of the broader term 'Latin America and the Caribbean'.

When asserting the unity of Latin America it is indispensable to simultaneously underline its diversity, complexity and richness – if only to counter the reductionism practiced by the West, which, through its domination, administration, commercialization and even marketing, has both simplified and impoverished this complex reality. Indeed many in Latin America echo the classic refutation of this discourse provided by Edward Said's *Orientalism* (2004), a position that must be taken into account in view of the huge changes taking place in international communication systems.[4] But this does not mean that there are no common characteristics and projects, as well as shared problems and failures. As the Mexican writer and essayist Carlos Monsiváis says in *Aires de familia*:

> *The question, 'Is there such a thing as the unity of Iberoamerica?' seems a little irrelevant. Yes, of course there is. And, if we don't want to take into account the great formative processes of language and the historical similarities, we can just look at a couple of elements: the look of the cities (leaving aside the natural beauty and architectural achievements) homogenized by the*

> *pressures of profitability; the weight of foreign debt; the huge concentration of profits; the incessant assimilations of Americanization; the effects of the neo-liberal economy; the regulating role of functional illiteracy; the predictable results of changing fashions in architecture and sculpture; the zones of ecological devastation and the levels of contamination caused by savage capitalism; the rise in unemployment and underemployment; the failure of public education and, yes, private education, which is nevertheless compensated by the success of its graduates. On the other hand, there are more or less simultaneous cultural processes: the development of civil society (with human rights first on the agenda); a genuine internationalization of culture, and a gradual liquidation of the sense of 'the peripheral' in arts and letters. (Monsiváis 2000: 113)*

At the same time, Eduardo Galeano, author of *Las venas abiertas de América Latina* (1971) and of *Memorias del fuego* (1982; 1984; 1986) states: 'The passion of Latin American diversity can be found in everything I have written, and it is difficult, or impossible, to break it up into parts.'[5] And, when necessary, he criticizes Latin American failures with an ironic twist:

> *They say we missed our date with History, and it´s true we´re usually late to appointments. Neither have we been able to take power, and the fact is we do sometimes lose our way or take a wrong turn, and later we make a long speech about it. We Latin Americans have a nasty reputation for being charlatans, vagabonds, troublemakers, hotheads, and revelers, and it´s not for nothing. We´ve been taught by the law of the market that price equals value, and we know we don´t rate for much. What´s worse, our good nose for business leads us to pay for everything we sell and buy every mirror that distorts our faces. We´ve spent five hundred years learning how to hate ourselves and one another and work heart and soul for our own ruin. That´s what we´re up to. But we still haven´t managed to correct our habit of wandering about daydreaming and bumping into things or our inexplicable tendency to rise from the ashes.*[6]

These critical reflections by two important students of Latin America continue to ring true, along with hypotheses that foresee a more equitable reality for this region, in view of current transformations, both here and in the wider world. And it is in this sense that a range of development possibilities is being explored. Thus Alcira Argumedo (2004) states that in order for each of the nations of the region to survive on the world stage, Latin America must construct 'an autonomous and federative continental integration,'[7] as many have proposed in the past. But as a continent of utopias, of 'crazy' projects, of high levels of intellectual speculation and invention, of as many attempts to imitate the central countries and orthodox belief in modernity as of quests for autonomy and for their own knowledge systems, Latin America continues to be a region of exaggerated contrasts, full of festivals and fighters, as Galeano says. Difficult to tame.

Differences and Asynchronicities

As regards the diversities to which I referred at the outset, Rossana Reguillo (2005:17) points out key areas such as the following: 'the specificity of conquest and colonization; the greater or lesser presence of the Catholic Church, which through its evangelizing efforts put a profound stamp on the culture that emerged; the way in which the local elites understood access to modernity; the construction of nation-states; the precariousness of political forms and organization, subject to significant transformations.' In spite of many displacements and interruptions throughout Latin America's history – fundamentally due to the repression of military dictatorships, necessitated by the neo-liberal projects that they attempted to impose – an understanding of Latin America requires a *long-range* perspective, one that some current research projects tend to ignore or minimize.

It is important to bear in mind, for example, the persistence of old cultures in the complex and rich Andean region, which maintain many of their original patterns at the same time as they survive in the megacities of the twenty-first century. In other words, the triumph of Evo Morales, the first indigenous president of Bolivia, is not fortuitous. Also, in another cultural arena, the phenomenon of a continent marked – from Ushuaia to the Rio Grande – by the tropical music of Afro-Brazilian, or specifically Afro-Caribbean origin. This also has its impact on other, more socially critical expressions, such as the *narcorrido* in Mexico, the *cumbia villera* in Argentina, or the different varieties of the *ballenato* in Colombia. The fact is that in Latin America there is this coexistence of cultures with differing socio-cultural and historical matrices – and we can say this without falling either into evolutionism or categorizations such as 'traditional' or 'pre-industrial' cultures versus 'modern' cultures. Also, it may be the one area in the world where the differences between the rich and the poor are the greatest, and where large zones of extreme precariousness, of alternative or marginal cultural production, coexist – not without conflict – with the most sophisticated forms of 'Western' culture.[8]

This, taken together with the flood of Latin Americans now emigrating elsewhere, especially to the United States, has given rise to the idea, not so much of a Latin American culture, but rather of a 'Latin American socio-cultural space' (Garretón 1999: 3), 'which is characterized by a territorial and non-territorial arena. In other words, there is a communicational or virtual arena, composed of spaces and circuits in which ethnic and historical roots are recognized, and intercultural communities are identified, which goes beyond the territory identified as Latin America' (García Canclini 2004a: 133). In short, when we speak of Latin America, a zone of immigration of the greatest possible cultural variety, we are also speaking of multiple ethnic, national and gender identities, contained within this space.[9]

In terms of the relation between socio-cultural space and geographic space, we must keep in mind the importance of Latin American migration to the US, because it affects cultural production, much of it centered in Miami, which then spreads into Latin America.[10] The role of Miami is fundamental, therefore, in analyzing the relation of forces which act on the Latin American socio-cultural stage. (Mato 2000; Mazziotti 1999)[11]

The fact is that all this is analyzed both academically and by essayists as well as through other, more free and less clearly defined systems of writing and analysis. It is indeed characteristic of Latin America that while it has not conceded totally to modernity, it has not cultivated an orthodox and positivist vision of the various discourses either. For this reason, research does not confine itself to academic fields. On the other hand, the role of the 'literati' who have been writers, news reporters and politicians all in one, has been a fundamental feature of Latin American culture from its very beginning, its struggles, its modernizing utopias. Perhaps Martí is the paradigmatic figure of this current which has persisted until very recently (see also Hugo Achugar in Chapter 14).[12]

In the Latin American perspective, we must therefore deal with the culture-communication-information grouping with reference both to the practices of construction of meaning – from public opinion to the social imaginary and the arts – and the complex infrastructures which correspond to this grouping.[13] Also relevant are the strong economic growth and the emergence of the industries of the symbolic as significant contributors to GNP, in the central countries as well as in Latin America. The discussion of these problems, which began in the middle of the nineteenth century, intensified during the twentieth. In that period, concern with communication or with meaning – which at bottom are one and the same thing – was always related to societies which, with the advance of industrialization and modernity, were becoming ever more opaque and complex. It is in the ensuing decades that different systems of mediation of representation multiply, arising out of increased cultural exchange, from the complexities of cities in modernity, to the development of the first mass-communication media and the first techno-electronic advances in the reproduction of sounds and images. And these systems, which continue to grow – making a great leap after the Second World War – also have impacted Latin America, especially in the urbanization and modernization of the rural sectors and of other primary activities.

These changes have provoked a significant growth of traditional or new communications media due, in part, to the influx of cheap equipment from East Asia. Material poverty, which has increased due to the great crises caused by neo-liberalism, has not impeded the advance of communication. There is no poor zone which does not have its parabolic antenna (Muniz Sodré 1992; Ford 1999), no small town which does not have a public Internet site in its central plaza, however low the quality of its equipment may be. This brings together cultures based on wealth and consumption, with cultures based on poverty and lack of basic necessities, generating a number of questions about the socio-cultural future. These questions are different from those that were posed by the technological changes of the 1970s (Muraro 1987). The new technologies are being used by social movements, the popular classes and the third sector. Research in this area is still in its infancy, taking up simplified visions of the digital gap, and other systems, such as teaching, in which even the popular sectors often enter school with a certain level of digital culture, superior in many cases to that of teachers who are formally trained.[14] This is one of a number of changes that affect daily life; also there is the close relation of the new technologies to the 'society of vigilance', the workplace, and in a more macro sense, the development of finance capital. But it also affects our systems of research and documentation to the extent that it alters the systems of classification, hierarchies and selection, which are influenced by the categories of knowledge of the 'central' countries (Ford and Chicco 2002).

On the Latin American Structural Context

> *Statistics on cultural investment, production and consumption give basic data, which we must correlate to other information and experiences to determine the meaning of the cultural resources of a society. The meaning of cultural development is not just a question of the number of books, records or movies produced and purchased; it is necessary to draw a correspondence of these figures to the educative level, creativity, the uses and disuses of cultural capitals, life expectancy and socio-cultural conflicts. Therefore, the cultural field must be correlated to other spaces which contain educational indicators, forms of social organization and participation which have their own logic, superposed in part by the cultural area, but also related to other social processes or forces. (García Canclini 2005)*[15]

In other words, cultural analysis must be based on a contextual framework that takes into account the particularities of the region: from the structural to the super-structural. These features, on the level of content production, definitely influence the forms of use and access of the new technologies – which have considerably increased the symbolic mass in terms of socially conscious output – as well as in their appropriation and the meanings attached to them.[16]

It is estimated that 200 of Latin America's 500 million inhabitants live below the poverty line.[17] Sixty-nine percent of the rural population[18] has no access to drinking water; one of every five lacks sanitary services; and less than a third have social insurance.[19] During the decade of the 1990s, Latin American foreign debt grew from 400 billion to more than 700 billion dollars. Four percent of the GNP and almost 50 percent of the income from export of goods and services, is devoted to the amortization of this debt.[20] The index of inequality of the region (calculated between the richest 10 percent of the population and the poorest 10 percent) is indicative of the inequality in income distribution in Latin America. For example, in Brazil the index of inequality is 68 percent; in Colombia, 57.8; in Mexico, 45; and in Argentina, 39.1 percent. These statistics also permit the comparison of Latin America's situation to the central countries; for example, using the same index, France is 9.1 percent; Japan, 6.2; and the US is 15.9.[21]

While the structural differences are considerable, if we compare Latin America with the central countries in terms of consumption of traditional media and new technologies, the gap is smaller. For example, in the case of mobile telephone subscribers, Latin America has 239 for every 1000 inhabitants, while Europe has 287. [22] This indicates a higher level of intercommunication among the poorer sectors, who are the principal users of cellular telephones.

Material scarcity, however, is not entirely correlated to the lack of access to new technologies: Brazil has the lowest index of income distribution[23]; however, it is also the country with the highest number of television sets per capita in Latin America; it has 369.4 sets per 1000 inhabitants, a higher index than Latin American countries with higher per capita GNP, as in the case of Mexico with 282 sets, or Argentina with 235.8. Meanwhile the United States has 937.5; France, 631; and the United Kingdom, 950.5.[24] In the last decade, as these gaps have grown, and economic, political and social crises have intensified, many more Latin Americans have been connected to the Internet. For example, in Brazil access increased from 50,000 inhabitants in 1991, to 143 million in 2003; in Argentina, from 1000 to 4.1 million; in Mexico, from 5000 to 12.3 million.[25]

Globalization and the Transformations of Cultural Production

The Brazilian researcher Renato Ortiz began his book *Mundialización y cultura* by stating the premise of 'the existence of global processes which transcend groups, social classes and nations'

(1994: 17). And on this basis he analyzed how changes that have taken place during this period: the phenomenon called globalization is not harmonious, regular, and systematic; it affects not only systems of social organization and daily life, but even the conceptual tools and concepts of the social sciences. For example, the crisis of the concepts of state, nation, class and the need to consider the world system as a specific phenomenon; the levels of deterritorialization of culture; the radicalization of modernity, and the need to work diachronically as well as synchronically; accelerations or decentralizations of productivity; the rupture of binaries such as global/local, centralization/decentralization; homogeneity/heterogeneity, etc.[26]

Understanding the current situation, then, requires examination not only of the 'indicators of cultural development, but also the indicators of underdevelopment and counter-development' (García Canclini 2004b: 288), along with empirical data that demonstrate the loss of local control of the Latin American cultural patrimony and the ways in which the traditional relations infrastructure and superstructure have been transformed, together with systems of mediation and representation (Ford 2005 and 2005a).

Beginning in the 1990s, the ecology of Latin American media was framed by increasing international competition of capital, agreements, purchases and fusions of info-communication enterprises. 'The high level of oligopolistic concentration of telecommunications and audiovisual is one of the elements that explains the convergence that leads toward unification of two worlds in communication, which thanks to informatics can converge on at least three levels: technological, and that of actors and services.' (Mastrini and Becerra n.d.) In this way, the large multimedia groups in the region took shape, for example *Televisa* in Mexico, *Cisneros* in Venezuela, *Globo* in Brazil and *Clarín* in Argentina. But it should also be recalled, as Jesús Martín-Barbero states:

> *In Latin America what happens in and through the media cannot be understood outside the cultural discontinuities which mediate the significance of the mass- media discourse and the meaning of its social uses. This is so because what is produced by the communication processes and practices, does not respond only to mercantile logic, and technological inventions, but rather to profound changes in the everyday culture of the majority, and the accelerated de-territorialization of cultural demarcations such as: modern/traditional, noble/vulgar, cult/popular/mass. (Martín-Barbero 2002: 178)*

In other words, not all transformations can be reduced to economic processes, while many transformations are taking place, the consequences of which we still are not aware:

> *The experiences of indigenous movements lining up with ecologist movements and with cyberspace (Internet) show that new … dynamics are occurring in Latin America which, far from signifying a loss of identity, can empower it, especially when it involves groups which have been clearly suppressed in the nation-building process, as has been the case of ethnic groups, youth and women. Because of globalization, intellectuals and artists in the provinces perceive opportunities which traditional capital city centralism never gave them. So there are indications of a trans-national cultural information, with signs of cultural multiculturalism and pluralism. (Subercaseaux 2002)*

In summary, then, in dealing with the issues of globalization and conflict in the cultural sphere we must take into account not questions of contents, but also the relationships between contents and structural dimensions, systems of production, distribution and consumption of culture as a whole, with information and communication in the sense of equipment and technologies – film, television, Internet and other forms of digital communication – as well as with new modalities of formation of public opinion and the social imaginary (Ford 2005).

The processes of globalization have diminished regional cultural production significantly. National industries have ceased to play a principal role in the generation of cultural products. With the establishment of multinational corporations in the region and the massive imports of symbolic products, Latin America's previously expanding cultural industry has clearly suffered setbacks in the international market. Nevertheless, as regards internal consumption the process is the reverse. 'The development and consolidation of the cultural industry in Brazil, Mexico and Venezuela took place mainly in the decade of the seventies. This phenomenon altered the previous panorama in which the importation of U.S. products was the rule and was linked to the strengthening of the internal audiovisual market and the increasing consumption of nationally-produced dramatic fare (mainly *telenovelas*).' (Ortiz 2003: 57) For example, Mexico and Brazil produce between 15 and 20 *telenovelas* per year. This genre, in turn, saw strong growth in the area of exports (Mazziotti, 2004).[27] In this framework of concentration and convergence of media, of loss of cultural autonomy, as in the case of publishing, generally due to purchase by Spanish conglomerates, Latin American production ranges from examination of critical socio-cultural problems, to avant-garde productions.

Historically, Latin American film has known many ups and downs. Unlike the large, profitable production and distribution enterprises of the US, film here has depended mainly on state aid to develop, and for that reason it has been affected by political fluctuations, and the lack of subsidies and measures aimed at regulating the industry. The symbolic industries are not an important part of the gross national product as in many 'central' countries and 'the conditions of production and the extreme improvisation, have imposed in Latin America a "poor-man's cinema" where scarcity is a sign of sincerity and spontaneity' (Monsiváis 2000: 64). However, in recent decades film has received a significant push forwards.[28] Not only in Brazil, Argentina and Mexico – with its long tradition of cinematographic production – but also in Peru, Bolivia and Cuba, 'the new Latin American film' has become an important phenomenon. According to some writers (Daicich 2004), it is based on personal projects, of writer-directors who use film as a means to communicate their ideas, their emotions, and their particular aesthetic, and attempt to reflect the identity of their country. We can also observe the clear stamp of critical exploration of identity and socio-cultural issues. Some examples: *La virgen de los Sicarios* by Barbet Schoeder (2000), *Estación Central* (1998), *Diarios de Motocicleta* (2004) by Walter Salles, *Amores perros* by Alejandro González Iñarritu (2004), *Ciudad de Dios* by Fernando Meirelles (2002), *Nueve reinas* by Fabián Bielinsky (2000), *Luna de Avellaneda* by Juan José Campanella (2004), etc. Another type of film involves the exploration and development of memory of the horrors of the military processes – for example: *Garage Olimpo* by Marco Bechis (1999). As Monsiváis (2000: 76) observes, 'since 1990, the thriller has become an indispensable genre for those talented filmmakers convinced of the incestuous links between politics and crime.'

However, the big international conglomerates (Disney and Sony, for example) still have the greatest share of cinematographic production. In many cases alliances have been created with Latin American enterprises to distribute films in the region (e.g. *Estación Central* in Brazil and *El hijo de la novia* in Argentina) and in some instances to participate in production, such as 'Motorcycle Diaries' (*Diarios de motocicleta*). But this growth in production is not accompanied by a comparable increase in film distribution, either to other Latin American countries or outside Latin America. In fact it could be said that a serious cultural issue – which applies equally to television, film and academic publishing – is poor distribution. The massively attended book fairs at Buenos Aires, Guadalajara or Bogotá are neither systematic nor organic.

On the other hand, the massive presence of US productions in mass communication media in Latin America can also be seen in cable television programming. For example, in Argentine cable TV, 67 percent of the programming is of US origin, and on the other hand there is very little exchange of cultural products among the countries of the continent.[29] As regards public television, which involves much more local production, the situation is different. In their attempt to expand the Latin American television market, US networks have developed alliances and exchanges with Latin American networks, especially with the four which together make up 90 percent of television, film and video exportation: Televisa, Rede Globo, Venevisión and Radio Caracas TV[30] (Mastrini and Becerra n.d.; Sánchez Ruiz 2005). The sale of television formats has been another variant of international exchange of cultural products. This modality developed abroad, at first with entertainment programs (local versions of *Big Brother* or *Survivor*) which were imported. The sale of formats involves acquisition of the libretto, the production book, participation in casting, etc. – questions intimately linked with the development of the product itself. This phenomenon has also transferred itself to fiction. An important case, although of low quality, is the Argentine *costumbrista* novel, *Los Roldán*, sold in Mexico as *Los Sánchez* and in Colombia as *Los Reyes*. Perhaps in the process there may be significant possibilities for development and export in Latin America, as is also the case with the development of software.

In the book-publishing industry, while the 1940s and 1960s were periods of glory in terms of national development and in the integration of the societies of this region, during the last decade of the twentieth century the majority of Latin American book publishers were acquired by foreign, primarily Spanish, companies. This caused a loss of autonomy, both in terms of selection of national products and in the complex and strategic field of translations. The policy toward translations in Spain is not the same as former practice in Mexico or Argentina, countries with other socio-cultural necessities. On the other hand, the structure of the Latin American market makes book distribution rather difficult, both within each country and across the continent. This seriously hampers cultural exchange, and the relation between reading and education, including the exchange of scientific works in the fields of humanities and the social sciences.

Since the 1990s, six transnational enterprises have appropriated 96 percent of the world music market (EMI, Warner, BMG, Sony, Universal Polygram and Phillips) and have purchased smaller music and book-publishing houses of many countries in Latin America, Africa and Asia; regions which function as zones of exploration and innovation, because the marginal areas are often very creative in the music arena. (Yúdice 2002; Ochoa 2002; García Canclini 2004b)

As we have pointed out already, a large percentage of entertainment and information is produced outside the region, and this often results in wooden stereotypes, and images characterized on the one hand by social violence, constant internal conflict, and unstable democracies, and on the other hand, an aspect more linked to exoticism. Aníbal Ford (2001) and Rossana Reguillo (2002) analyze the stigmatizing features which accompany the vision that the central countries have of Latin America – ideas linked to violence, the inability to politically and socially realize the values of modern democracy – and the fact that new types of representations have been developed, drawn up by the cultural industries, which reinforce the negative image of the 'visibility of difference' or the idea of 'contamination' by the dangers implied by the 'other' in the respective countries. Also there is the vision of Latin America in terms of magical realism, or the pre-logical mentality.

In other words, cultural differences arise in terms of the quality of information and the differences of informational and cultural flows – these have deteriorated as far as 'developing' countries are concerned – whose different patrimonies, cultural, physical, institutional, labor, social, legal, etc., are often displaced. This situation generates an informational gap in the poor countries which poses obstacles to what Herbert Schiller (1996:18) calls 'socially necessary information.'

As regards literature, Latin America had a strong international presence in the 1970s which it subsequently lost. (Monsiváis 2000; Franco 1983). Crises and dictatorships weakened cultural production, but they also modified it, promoting the development of alternative cultures, social movements, an increased presence of the Third Sector – which in many cases was problematic – and different forms through which the democracies of the continent reestablished themselves.

Today, we are in a transition stage: while the worldwide presence of Latin culture is very limited, internal artistic and cultural production is beginning to be strengthened. For example, in digital-artistic forms and in popular or folk genres, which are often related; in the recuperation of autonomous, often pre-Columbian, artistic expression, and fusions with music of other cultures, in which the Brazilian *bossa nova* has achieved a very high level; in classical music, together with reworking of popular genres of other countries, which involves major creative development of the borrowed genre, as has happened with formats derived from rock music and in crafts, etc.

Latin America oscillates between powerful expressions of its socio-cultural problems, of its social life on the one hand, and on the other works of avant-garde experimentation now displayed in museums and in experiences such as the Memorial de San Pablo, the Malba de Buenos Aires and many others, as well as in graphics and electronic art.[31] In terms of literature, which has seen a drop-off in 1970s-type experimentalism, advances can be observed in investigative reporting, and 'best-sellerism', often involving everyday stories from the different countries of the continent.[32] There is also a great deal of academic production.[33] At the same time, there is the growth, not only of institutes and centers dedicated to the study of Latin America, for example, the *Fundación para un Nuevo Periodismo Iberoamericano* (Foundation for a new Iberoamerican Journalism) created by Gabriel García Márquez, but also research or career centers.

According to the *Federación Latinoamericana de Facultades de Ciencas de la Comunicación Social* (Latino-American Federation of Faculties of Social Communication), there are 1000 universities dedicated to communications in Latin America today. This indicates the strong presence on the continent of fields and activities in regards to culture, communication and information, in the midst of great conflicts within these fields and in the social context in which they are developing. In recent years they have had to deal with everything from dictatorships, to strong commercial pressures from outside. These pressures are not holding them back, and this is being perceived on the micro and independent level with countless experiences of cultural research and development which bear the potential for significant advances, in the midst of great contrasts, on this conflictual and paradoxical continent.

Notes

1 With Anabella Messina and Mariana Rivas as research assistants.
2 A detailed history of the term can be found in the first part of Ángel Núñez (2001)
3 Compare with Note 9.
4 We have analyzed the differences in the quality of information about the countries of the third world in: Aníbal Ford (1999).
5 Personal correspondence with Eduardo Galeano in e-mails, December 31, 2005.
6 Ibid.
7 These ideas are updated in Argumedo, Alcira, '*La crisis de la Cultura Occidental dominante*' (to be published in Dina Picotti [compiler] *De los estudios culturales a los sujetos históricos*. Instituto de Pensamiento Latinoamericano. Buenos Aires, Third of February National University.
8 These zones attract the attention of the multinationals, for example, because of the high level of creativity in their music.
9 In the region there are more than 400 indigenous towns, with 50 million inhabitants. Five countries together represent almost 90% of the regional indigenous population: Peru (27%), Mexico (26%), Guatemala (15%), Bolivia (12%), Ecuador (8%). For its part, the Black, Afrolatin and Afrocaribbean population totals almost 150 million, located principally in Brazil (51%), Colombia (21%), the Caribbean subregion (16%), and Venezuela (12%). At the beginning of the millennium the indigenous, Afrolatin and Afrocaribbean population has the worst economic and social indicators and scarce cultural influence and access to public decision-making power. *CEPAL report, Twenty-ninth session*. (2002) Brazil, Brasilia, May 10 to 16.
10 According to the International Organization for Migration, it is estimated that in 2002 there were 20 million Latin Americans and Caribbeans living outside their countries of birth. Seven of 10 reside legally or illegally in the United States. The remaining 30% live in countries of Latin America and the Caribbean, and the rest of the world, such as Canada, Italy, Spain, Holland and the United Kingdom. In *Report of the International Organization for Migration* (2000), United Nations.
11 At the beginning of the 1990s, 300,000 professionals and technicians from Latin America and the Caribbean – around 3 percent of those available in the region – were living outside of their countries of birth. Over two-thirds of them were in the United States, where it is estimated that 12 percent of those with higher qualifications in science and engineering are foreign-born. Report of the Economic Commission for Latin America, Twenty-ninth session, Brasilia, May 2002.
12 See Núñez, Angel (2001); Ramos, Julio (1989). In terms of the relation between literature and politics, the chapter in Piglia, Ricardo (2005) dedicated to Ernesto 'Che' Guevara is important.
13 We should mention that the discussion of these terms is ongoing, as is the variety of proposed definitions. First put forward in 1952 by Kroeber, Alfred and Kluckholm, Clyde (1952), the discussion continues to the present day. See García Canclini, Néstor (2004a). Also, this variety of definitions has strong ideological foundations, as Antonio Gramsci perceived in the 1930s.
14 Giezzi Lasso, *Los usos de Internet como herramienta informativa en la comunidad indígena guambiana, de Colombia*. Master's thesis in progress, University of San Andrés, Buenos Aires; and Villanueva Mansilla, Eduardo (in publication), *Comunicación interpersonal en la era digital*. Bogotá: Editorial Norma.
15 Another type of comparison can be found in Chapter 3 of Ford, Aníbal, and Contreras, Silvana, 'Memorias abandonadas o las brechas comunicacionales' in: Ford, Aníbal (1999) *La marca de la bestia. Identificación, desigualdades e infoentretenimiento en la sociedad contemporánea*. Buenos Aires: Editorial Norma. We consider these comparisons to be fundamental because they have changed the relationship between material goods and symbolic values.
16 A study carried out by the University of California, Berkeley, states that the amount of information contained in book, film, magnetic and optical formats grew in 2002 to five hexabytes of new information, which is the equivalent of 37,000 new libraries the size of the US Library of Congress. See 'How Much Information 2003' at http://www.sims/berkeley/edu/research/projects/how-much-info-2003/execsum.htm#summary
17 The poverty threshold is calculated as that part of the population living on less than $US 2 per day. World Bank, *World Development Indicators* 2001.
18 According to the Report on Human Rights 2005 of the United Nations Development Program, the rural

population in Latin America is 23.3% of the total, and there are countries such as Guatemala or Nicaragua where the percentage of rural population reaches 46.3% and 57.3%, respectively.

19 According to the World Bank's *World Development Indicators*, 2001.

20 World Bank. *World Development Indicators*, 2001.

21 United Nations Development Program, *Human Development Report, 2005.*

22 United Nations Development Program, *Human Development Report, 2005.*

23 United Nations Development Program, *Report on Human Development. International cooperation at a crossroads. Aiding Development, Commerce and Security in an Unequal World*, 2005.

24 *Global Civil Society 2005/6*. Sage Publications, London, 2005.

25 *Millennium Development Goal Indicators Database*, United Nations, 2003.

26 *Cfr. Hopenhayn, Martín, 'Educación y cultura en Iberoamérica: situación cruces y perspectivas, en Iberoamérica 2002, Santillana, OEI, México, 2002.*

27 In the last ten years, Brazil exported 190 productions.

28 The most successful program of communicational integration, Ibermedia, through which the Iberoamerican Summits promote audiovisual coproduction in the region, reached 59 films coproduced by Spain and Latin American countries in the 15 years previous to this program. In the period 1998–2004, this number grew to 158. In García Canclini, Néstor, (2005).

29 Data extracted from a programming guide of Cablevisión de Argentina television distributor.

30 Televisa does the most business with Latin America, with close to 50% of the total operations: 'Their net foreign sales rose, from 9.9% in 1993 to 17.5% in 1997. 75.3% of the value of its exports and 97% of its imports in 1997 originated in the United States.' (Mastrini and Becerra n.d.)

31 From that period two literary figures remain, representing very different positions: Gabriel García Márquez and Mario Vargas Llosa.

32 Among others, Isabel Allende, Ángeles Mastretta, Marcela Serrano and Laura Esquivel.

33 In the field of letters a series of anthologies or compilations have emerged which confronts the problems of Latin America, for example: Josefina Ludmer (comp) (1994) *Las culturas de fin de siglo de América Latina.* Rosario: Beatriz Viterbo Editora. Also authors who have dealt a great deal with these themes, such as Jorge Lafforgue (2005), who directed important collections on Latin America in the Centro Editor de América Latina, where significant efforts were made to develop Latin American collections in the 1970s. This publisher's books were destroyed by fire, by order of the military government. In Ford, Aníbal (2005), *La pira. La quema de los libros del Centro Editor en Junio de 1978.* Buenos Aires, Lezama, May, No. 13. Also important are Latin American productions such as those of Carlos Altamirano (director), *Términos críticos de sociología de la cultura.* Buenos Aires: Editorial Paidós, 2002, and the collection from Norma, *Enciclopedia de sociocultura y comunicación*, compuesta por libros realizados por autores latinoamericanos (2000).

REFERENCES

Argumedo, Alcira (2004) *Los silencios y las voces en América Latina. Notas sobre el pensamiento nacional y popular.* Buenos Aires: Ediciones del Pensamiento Nacional. Ediciones Colihue.

Daicich, Osvaldo (2004) *Apuntes sobre el nuevo cine latinoamericano. Entrevistas a realizadores latinoamericanos.* La Habana: Fundación del Nuevo Cine Latinoamericano. Escuela Internacional de Cine y Televisión.

Ford, Aníbal (1999) *La marca de la Bestia. Identificación, desigualdades e infoentretenimiento en la sociedad contemporánea.* Buenos Aires: Editorial Norma.

– (2001) 'La construcción discursiva de los problemas globales. El interculturalismo: residuos, commodities y pseudofusiones', *Iberoamericana*, University of Pittsburgh, Vol. XVII, No. 197, October-December

– and Chicco, Ivana (2002) 'Una navegación incierta: Mercosur en Internet'. Working paper prepared for the MOST seminar (UNESCO) on 'Mercosur: Spaces of Interaction, Spaces of Integration'.

– (2005) *Resto del Mundo. Nuevas mediaciones de las agendas críticas internacionales.* Buenos Aires: Grupo Editorial Norma.

– (2005a) 'Del infodesing a los registros con rayos X. La estetización del control social' in Espinosa Vera, Pablo (comp.) *Semiótica de los mass media. Discurso de la comunicación visual.* Monterrey: Universidad Autonónoma de Nuevo León.

Franco, Jean (1983) *La cultura moderna en América Latina.* México D.F: Colección Enlace, Editorial Grijalvo.

Galeano, Eduardo (1971) *Las venas abiertas de América Latina.* México D.F.: Siglo XXI.

– (1982) *Memorias del Fuego. Los Nacimientos*. México D. F.: Siglo XXI.
– (1984) *Memorias del Fuego. Las caras y las máscaras*. Buenos Aires: Catálogos.
– (1986) *Memorias del Fuego. El siglo del viento*, Buenos Aires: Catálogos.
García Canclini, Néstor (2004a) *Diferentes, desiguales y desconectados. Mapas de la Interculturalidad*. Barcelona. Gedisa Editorial.
– (2004b) 'Preguntas sobre el nacionalpopulismo recargado' en *La cultura en las crisis Latinoamericanas*, Buenos Aires.:Colección Grupos de Trabajo CLACSO.
– (2005) 'Cultura y comercio: desafíos de la globalización para el espacio audiovisual latinoamericano'. Inaugural speech at confence on 'Latin American Visual Space', organized by UNESCO and the Universidad de Guadalajara, Guadalajara, June 14. http://www.comminit.com/la/pensamientoestrategico/pensamiento2005/pensamiento-82.html
Garretón, Manuel Antonio (ed.) (1999) *América Latina: un espacio cultural en un mundo globalizado*. Bogotá, Colombia: Convenio Andrés Bello.
Kroeber, Alfred and Kluckholm, Clyde (1952) *Culture: A Critical Review of Concepts and Definitions*. New York: Peabody Museum.
Lafforgue, Jorge (2005) *Cartografía Personal. Escritos y escritores de América Latina,* Buenos Aires: Taurus.
Martín-Barbero, Jesús (2002) *Oficio de Cartógrafo. Travesías latinoamericanas de la comunicación en la cultura*. Santiago de Chile: Fondo de Cultura Económica.
Mastrini, Guillermo and Becerra, Martín (n.d.) *Estructura y concentración de las Industrias Culturales y las Telecomunicaciones en América Latina*. mimeo.
Mato, Daniel (2000) '*Miami en la transnacionalización de la industria de la telenovela: sobre la territorialidad de los procesos de globalización*'. Speech at Congress of the Latin American Studies Association (LASA) Miami, March 16–18.
Mazziotti, Nora (1999) 'El show de cristina y la construcción de lo latino' en: Guillermo Sunkel (comp.) *El consumo cultural en América Latina*, Bogotá: Convenio Andrés Bello.
– (2004) 'La fuerza de la emoción. La telenovela: negocio audiencias, historias' in Maria Immacolada Vasallo de Lopez (org.): *Telenovela. Internacionalizacao e interculturalidade.* San Pablo: Loyola.
Monsiváis, Carlos (2000) *Aires de Familia. Cultura y sociedad en América Latina.* Barcelona: Anagrama, Colección Argumentos.
Muniz Sodré (1992) *O social irradiado: violência urbana, neogrotesco e mídia*. Rio de Janeiro: Cortez Editora.
Muraro, Heriberto (1987) *Invasión Cultural Economía y Comunicación.* Buenos Aires: Editorial Legasa.
Núñez, Ángel (2001) *El canto del quetzal. Reflexiones sobre la Literatura Latinoamericana.* Prologue by Antonio Cándido. Buenos Aires: Editorial Corregidor.
Ochoa, Ana María (2002) *Músicas locales en tiempos de globalización*, Buenos Aires: Grupo Norma Editores.
Ortiz, Renato (1994) *Mundialización y cultura.* Preface by Aníbal Ford, Editorial Alianza, Buenos Aires.
– (2003) 'Revisitando la noción de imperialismo cultural' in *Comunicación, Cultura y Globalización*, Bogotá: Centro Editorial Javeriano, Colección Biblioteca del Profesional, Línea Comunicación, medios y Cultura.
Piglia, Ricardo (2005) *El último lector.* Buenos Aires. Editorial Planeta.
Ramos, Julio (1989) *Desencuentros de la modernidad en América Latina. Literatura y política en el siglo XIX.* México D.F.: Fondo de Cultura Económica.
Reguillo, Rossana (2000) *Emergencia de culturas juveniles*, Buenos Aires: Grupo Editorial Norma.
– (2002) 'Pensar el mundo en y desde América Latina. Desarrollo intercultural y políticas de representación'.Speech at the 23rd Conference and General Assembly of the AIECS/AMCR/AIERI. Barcelona, July 21–26.
– (2005) *Horizontes fragmentados. Comunicación, cultura, pospolítica. El (des)orden global y sus figuras.* México D.F.: Instituto Tecnológico y de Estudios Superiores de Occidente (ITESO).
Said, Edward (2004) *Orientalismo.* Barcelona: De Bolsillo.
Sánchez Ruiz, Enrique (2005) *Medios de comunicación y democracia.* Buenos Aires: Grupo Editorial Norma.
Schiller, Herbert (1996) *Information Inequality.* New York and London: Routledge.
Subercaseaux, Bernardo (2002) *Procesos complejos, preguntas múltiples* en http://www.mav.cl/foro_cult/suberca02.htm.
Yúdice, George (2002) *El recurso de la cultura. Usos de la cultura en la era global.* Barcelona: Editorial Gedisa.

CHAPTER 12

MANAGING CULTURAL CONFLICTS: STATE POWER AND ALTERNATIVE GLOBALIZATION IN CHINA

Yunxiang Yan

Cultural flows in China since the late 1980s have integrated the country into the global economy and international community. Consequently, a new consensus of defending and promoting the national identity emerged in the mid-1990s and expressed itself in four trends of thought and social action: nationalism and anti-Americanism, cultural conservatism, critique of cultural globalization, and finally the discourse on the Beijing Consensus. Together these trends reveal an emerging model that emphasizes the centrality of the state in forming a Chinese alternative of globalization and in managing cultural conflicts. Potential fault lines of cultural conflicts are identified in this chapter and possible ways of managing cultural conflicts are discussed.

In November 2004, the American company Nike aired an advertisement called 'Chamber of Fear' on a number of Chinese television stations. In this commercial the NBA superstar LeBron James defeated an old Chinese martial arts master (a cartoon figure), a Chinese lady, and two dragons all of whom tried to stop the basketball player during his journey running up a five-story building. The central message of the ad is, of course, the power of the new Nike sports shoes, but the story line provoked strong criticism from Chinese audiences who felt that Chinese culture and national pride were being insulted. Angry citizens called the television stations, wrote to newspapers, and bombarded Internet chat rooms. The State Bureau of Radio, Film, and Television responded quickly, issuing an order on December 3 prohibiting the broadcast of the ad on all Chinese television stations (Qiu 2004). Under mounting pressure from both public opinion and the government, Nike thereafter issued a public apology and withdrew its commercial (BBC 2004).

Similar cultural conflicts occur frequently in today's world due to the increasing speed of globalization and cultural flows. A recent and now celebrated example is the Muslim protest over the publication of some controversial cartoons of Muhammad in the Western media. The twelve cartoons, including one that showed Muhammad wearing a turban in the shape of a bomb, were first published by the Danish newspaper *Jyllands-Posten* in late 2005 and then reprinted by other West European media in early 2006. The mass anger quickly developed into a global and often violent anti-Western protest movement by Muslims in European and Asian cities (Fleishman 2006a; Watson and Ali 2006).

What makes the Chinese case noteworthy, however, is that the strong governmental power of the Chinese state intervened and resolved the conflict arbitrarily. By contrast, in the case of the Danish cartoons the Western governments could do little to prevent the escalation of the protests from angry reactions to violent attacks, which were fueled by the continuing publication of the cartoons by the Western media in a gesture to protect freedom of speech. Unlike the Chinese state that has long been determined to keep both the cultural flows and conflicts under its control (Yan 2002), the leaders of the European countries seem to have been caught in confusion and unprepared to face the explosive nature of such cultural conflicts (Fleishman 2006b).

These two cases reveal an interesting clue that may help us better understand the relationships among cultures, conflict, and globalization: the role of the powerful state in dealing with cultural conflicts. In the following, I will first briefly review the cultural flows in China, arguing that globalization is in full swing in Chinese society where the state has to carefully balance out the pros and cons of opening up to the outside world. Second, I will examine several trends that may well be indicative of the cultural conflicts caused by the ongoing process of globalization. In my opinion, these trends also reveal an emerging Chinese model of globalization that features the centrality of the state in managing cultural conflicts in particular and in forming a Chinese alternative to globalization in general. I will conclude the chapter with some remarks on potential fault lines in cultural conflicts and possible ways to reduce the development of such conflicts.

Cultural flows and managed globalization in China

Since China adopted the opening-up policy and market-oriented reforms in the late 1970s, it has seen robust economic development, with an average annual GDP growth of more than 9 percent. During this period, the flow of capital, images, information, and people in and out of China – the defining features of globalization – has been accelerated in both scope and quantity. For example, China's two-way trade with the world increased from $236.6 billion in 1994 to $1,154.8 billion in 2004. In 2004, Chinese exports totaled $593 billion and Chinese imports totaled $561 billion. In the same year, China also drew $60.3 billion in foreign direct investment (FDI). In terms of US – China trade, US exports to China increased from $9.3 billion in 1994 to $34.7 billion in 2004, and US imports from China increased from $41.4 billion in 1994 to $210.5 billion in 2004, making the United States China's second largest trading partner (USCBC 2005). According to the latest official data, total FDI in January 2006 went up 11 percent compared to January 2005, a clear sign of continuing strong interest among foreign companies to invest in China (Dai 2006). The cross-border flow of people is equally impressive as the total number of people who legally entered or left China increased by an annual rate of 10 percent from 1999 to 2004. In 2002, for example, while 1.63 million Chinese citizens traveled abroad, 1.34 million foreigners visited China (Yu 2005).

For ordinary people in China, a clear presence of economic globalization is seen in the influx of foreign goods, which started from Japanese electronics and quickly expanded to encompass almost all aspects of everyday consumption (Zhao 1994). It was reported that imported fax machines and videotape recorders took 98 percent of the market share in China, and foreign cellular phones took 80 percent by the mid-1990s. At the same time, popular Chinese brand names were either defeated or bought out by foreign companies: Coca Cola and Pepsi bought seven of the eight leading Chinese soft drinks brands, and more than 70 percent of the beer breweries were bought out by foreign capital. Although it caused a new round of national debate about the fate of the domestic film industry, the Chinese government finally decided to allow Kodak to purchase six Chinese film makers in 1998, leaving only the Lekai brand on the market. Competition between domestic and imported products was so severe that it was proclaimed 'a war without gun smoke' (Wang and Lin 1996). This war of domestic and foreign brands continues in the twenty-first century, with more foreign brands taking up the Chinese urban market and now turning to the vast rural areas (see Dolven 2003).

Along with the flow of capital, technology, and people into China, there has also been an influx of various cultural products, ranging from fashion, sports, pop songs, movies, and TV programs, to books, cultural values, and social movements. It is the transnational movements of these cultural products that constitute the process of cultural globalization. Peter Berger (1997) describes the emergence of a global culture that contains four distinctive faces or domains: the transnational business elite culture, the global popular culture, the worldwide intellectual culture, and the new social movements that transcend national borders. Another collaborative investigation led by Berger on cultural globalization in ten countries, however, reveals more diversities of cultural globalization, including the 'alternative globalizations; that is, cultural movements with a global outreach originating outside the Western world' (Berger 2002: 12). As a member of Berger's international research team, I conducted research on the Chinese case of cultural globalization in 1998 and 1999 and discovered that by the late 1990s, the strong presence of global (mostly American but also East Asian) cultures was obvious in all four aspects of social life in China, although the local influences varied across different social groups, genders, and social domains. My follow-up research in 2005 reconfirms the findings in the late 1990s, but also reveals some noteworthy new developments, which will be discussed in the next section.

Among the Chinese business elite, although some individuals indeed live very Westernized lifestyles, are familiar with Western culture, and behave in work similarly to their counterparts in New York or London, a distinctive 'Davos culture' has yet to be formed. More importantly, because of the remaining influence of public ownership over important economic sectors and the strong presence of state power in economic life, when there is conflict between company interests and national interests or cultural traditions, Chinese business elites do not act as part of a transnational capitalist class (Sklair 1991). Rather, many prefer to be labeled as an indigenous 'Confucian merchant' (*rushang*) type of business elite. In the second domain of academic culture, the Chinese intellectuals found that the best way to achieve success is to be Western in one way or another. By resorting to various Western thoughts and research paradigms, Chinese intellectuals could achieve more scholarly freedom and space without directly challenging the Communist Party and the state (hereafter, the party-state); even the advocates of anti-globalization and anti-Western hegemony have to rely on the imports of dependency theory and post-colonialism (Gao 2004). Many also rely on foreign foundations for funding, which, as some Chinese scholars have pointed out, also help to sustain the dominance of Western academic culture in China (Yan 2002: 21–7).

Popular culture is no doubt an area where the global influence is dominant. Sit-com TV series from both the West and neighboring countries like Japan and Korea, Hollywood blockbusters, pop music from Hong Kong and Taiwan, Japanese cartoons, and NBA and World Cup soccer matches are among the hot ticket items of cultural consumption sought by a majority of ordinary Chinese consumers, so much so that when Michael Jordan retired in early 1999, many sports fans were devastated, and stories about Jordan covered the Chinese printed media for weeks. American fast foods (McDonald's and KFC in particular) and Hollywood blockbuster movies, the two icons of American popular culture, have dominated the Chinese market since the late 1990s (Yan 2002: 28–9).

Social movements – religious movements in particular – are kept under the careful watch of the party-state because they have the potential of developing into opposition forces. Nevertheless, the 1990s also witnessed the rapid development of various kinds of social movements. The estimated number of Christians reached 40 million, and secular movements such as consumer rights, environmental protection, and feminism also took shape during this period, mainly due to the intellectual and financial support of global organizations (Yan 2002: 30–3). According to official statistics, by 2004 more than 100 million Chinese were religious believers, and there were more than 300,000 clergy of various religions. NGOs and NPOs also mushroomed, reaching a total number of 289,000 (State Council 2005). There are, however, various official regulations for associations, and many of these NGOs have government sponsorship in one way or another, thus earning them the nickname of 'GONGO'.

The influx of foreign cultural elements also resulted in important social changes manifested in the everyday life of ordinary people, such as the rising demands for romantic love and sexual freedom, the escalating divorce rate and the emergence of single-parent families, the triumph of consumerism and the fetish for commodities, the fever for MBA degrees and to learn English, and the competition to be 'cool' among urban youths (He 2000).

Another result of the decades-long importation of foreign cultural products is the so-called 'cultural trade deficit', a popular topic discussed in the Chinese media in 2005. It is interesting to note that although China has had a favorable economic trade balance, which has become a major issue in Sino – US relations, the flow of cultural products constitutes a very different story. China has imported many more cultural products and has exported very few. Recent statistics show that in the book trade, China imported seven times more books than the number of books it exported; in copyright trade, the ratio between imports and exports is 10.3 to 1. The largest gap or deficit, however, is found in the publication of translated books. In recent years China has authorized publication of more than 12,000 foreign books in Chinese translation, but only 81 Chinese books have secured foreign publishing rights (Jin and Zhang 2005; see also Buckley 2005). China's weak position in the cultural flow at the global scale was first mentioned by Zhao Qizheng, the chief spokesperson of the State Council, during a high-level roundtable conference in May 2005 (Di and Chen 2005). Zhao's warning was soon coined by the media as China's 'cultural trade deficit' and it triggered a wave of public discussion. In response to the cultural trade deficit, a set of new policies was promulgated by the central government to promote cultural exports and regulate cultural imports (Buckley 2005).

On the basis of my research in the late 1990s, I concluded that the Chinese party-state had strategically positioned itself as the ultimate manager of the globalization process by promoting China's integration into the global economy and international community on one hand and carefully controlling this process on its own terms on the other. As far as the four aspects of cultural globalization are concerned, the party-state has thus far taken different strategies to maintain control and at the same time to facilitate growth. The business elite culture seems to be the least worrisome for CCP leaders, and the official media have actually been crucial in promoting a Western-style management system and corporate culture. Popular culture is another area that the state has seemingly decided to leave alone, presumably because it can be used to lessen the social tensions of the post-1989 era and to create an image of prosperity and happiness. In contrast, the state has always closely watched and tightly controlled areas of intellectual development and social movement, because the former pose a direct challenge to the Communist ideology and the latter may lead to collective action on a large scale, a source of great fear to the party-state (Yan 2002).

The party-state's management role applies to the transnational companies in China as well. Because the state still controls many important resources and, more importantly, access to the Chinese cultural market, foreign companies and cultural agencies have to be careful not to challenge the state's authority and must make necessary concessions, otherwise they will be denied opportunities to conduct business in China. For example, the Internet is arguably the most important and efficient domain for the flow of images, ideas, and information in the age of globalization. Thus, many in the West have argued that the Internet will be the most powerful weapon to bring down various boundaries and barriers and to transform authoritarian regimes into democracies (see for example Friedman 2005). Transnational companies did take a large share of the vast Internet market in China, reaching more than 100 million users by 2005. But they hardly had any impact on the way the party-state controls freedom of speech over the Internet. Instead, the party-state has successfully changed the way these companies conduct their businesses in China. For example, Yahoo! has been criticized repeatedly for providing the Chinese government with key information from its server that led to the arrest of a Chinese dissident (Ni 2005). Microsoft, Google, and Cisco all participate in the government-imposed censorship on the Internet in China (Gutmann 2004: 127-72), a common practice that has led the US Congressional Human Rights Caucus to hold a hearing and conduct an independent investigation (Zeller 2006). The active role played by the party-state defines a fundamental feature of the Chinese model of globalization, or 'managed globalization' as I prefer to call it (Yan 2002). Such a model can also be seen in the domain of cultural conflicts as shown in the new trends in tensions and tension management discussed below.

Emerging tensions and conflicts since the 1990s

The above-mentioned discussion on China's cultural trade deficit and the government's efforts to control the cultural market in 2005 signify an increasingly strong and clear consensus on the necessity to defend and promote Chinese national identity and Chinese culture. This recently developed consensus, which is shared among political and cultural elites and supported by the populace, expresses itself in four new trends of thought and social action: nationalism and anti-Americanism, critiques of cultural globalization, cultural conservatism, and, finally, the new Beijing Consensus. Some of these trends emerged in the late 1990s but gained momentum in recent years, while others represent the latest Chinese responses to globalization. What makes these trends remarkably different from the social-cultural trends in the 1980s and 1990s is a shared critical undertone toward American hegemony, the core values of Western culture, and the Hellenistic or Western-dominated model of globalization.

The rise of nationalism and anti-Americanism

The rise of nationalism in China since the 1990s has taken three different forms: official, intellectual, and popular. In order to regain its political legitimacy after 1989 and to maintain political stability in the dynamic 1990s which witnessed the collapse of the former Soviet Union and East European bloc, the Chinese party-state promoted a special form of nationalism – patriotism – as the new official ideology. As Zheng notes, patriotism is interpreted as a devotion to and love of the socialist state, which is in turn regarded as the only force that can lead the Chinese people to the wonderland of modernity. Specifically, this official patriotism calls for the

Chinese people's loyalty to the state and commitment to political stability, a consensus to constrain the 'narrow nationalism' of ethnic groups, and realization of the goal of national unification (Zheng 1999: 90–5).

The development of nationalism among Chinese intellectuals followed a more dramatic path because most intellectuals regarded Westernization as the only way for China to modernize itself. The strong pro-West tendency among intellectuals, later criticized as worship of the West, culminated in a six-part TV documentary 'River Elegy' that was aired in 1988–1989. This TV series discredited traditional Chinese culture and called for an unconditional embrace of Western culture (see Chen and Jin, 1997, especially pp. 215-38). In the 1990s, some scholars tried to rediscover useful resources in Chinese tradition, thus returning to Confucianism, while others continued to explore Western liberal thought, but with a new focus on property rights and individual freedom. The most active scholars, however, were the Neo-leftist intellectuals who used deconstruction theory, post-colonialism, and other post-modernist theories to critique the previous pro-Western illusions, the invasion of global capitalism, and the decline of Chinese national identity (Gao 2004).

The most radical nationalist scholars are from the so-called 'fourth generation' who grew up under the relatively open environment of economic reform and material prosperity, such as the authors of the 1996 book *Zhongguo keyi shuo bu* (China Can Say No). In this national bestseller, the authors (Song et al. 1996) cite American efforts to block China's Olympic bid, opposition to China's entry to GATT/WTO, the Taiwan strait issue, support for Tibetan independence, among other examples, to show that the United States is an hegemonic power making every effort to prevent China from becoming wealthy and powerful (see also Li et al. 1996). The intellectual promotion of nationalism and anti-Americanism reached a new high when militant nationalists like Wang Xiaodong began to warn of the danger of China's extinction and to advocate a martial spirit and self-sacrifice for the nation (see Fang, Wang, and Song, 1999).

It should be noted that until the late 1990s the majority of Chinese intellectuals showed tremendous self-restraint when they faced the dilemma of how to deal with Western hegemony on the one hand and how to fight for freedom and democracy in China on the other. Among other concerns, they were primarily worried that the party-state might manipulate nationalistic emotions among the younger generations and utilize political nationalism as a means to maintain the authoritarian regime. They thus made efforts to prevent the surge of narrow-minded nationalism (see Xiao 1997; Le 2004). This has changed since the late 1990s. An increasingly large number of intellectuals have abandoned their previous conviction that China should adopt the American way of modernization and many of them have begun to criticize the United States and the West for trying to block China's development. Through lectures, publications, and media presentations, these intellectuals have had a great influence on college students, and, through the latter, on Chinese youth in general. One of the most noteworthy events in the media was the publication of a series of essays in a widely read newspaper that criticized American arrogance, unilateralism, and the insidious nature of American values including human rights, democracy, and freedom of the press (*Beijing qingnian bao* 1999; for a detailed analysis of these essays, see Rosen 2003: 111–112). Such a shift to reassess American culture was also fed by the international discourse on the 'China threat'. Chinese audiences, especially popular audiences reflected in the mass media, reacted strongly to the 'China threat' theory, viewing it as clear evidence that the foreign powers were conspiring to block China's rise as a modern and powerful nation (Yee and Zhu 2002).

The mass media played a key role in spreading the intellectual discourse of nationalism to the public, and a series of conflicts in Sino–US and Sino–Japanese relations during the 1990s fueled the growth of a third form of nationalism – popular nationalism among the ordinary people, especially the Chinese youth. NATO's accidental bombing of the Chinese embassy in Belgrade in 1999 and the collision of an American spy plane with a Chinese fighter jet off China's southern coast in 2001 played particularly important roles in provoking popular nationalism, on both occasions resulting in student protests in major cities (Gries 2004). A number of surveys have shown that negative views toward the United States and American culture began to grow among Chinese youth in the mid-1990s (Yang 1997) and have continued to develop since then. A 1999 survey of 1,600 high school students, for example, found that 70 percent of the respondents gave a negative rating to the United States (Rosen 2003: 108). The most noteworthy development, however, is not the impression that the US government is the world police; instead, it is the reassessment of a set of values such as democracy, freedom of speech, and human rights that motivated the previous generation of college youth to stage demonstrations and to launch a hunger strike in Tiananmen Square. Popular nationalism also elicits many emotional responses, such as sympathy toward the terrorists and the celebratory reaction to the terrorist attacks on American targets (see e.g., Gong 2003; Kristof 2002).

The emotional and radical form of popular nationalism, however, does not always fit with the official line of nationalism. As Zheng (1999) and Rosen (2003) point out, while the party-state is promoting patriotism as a strategy to maintain political stability, which includes stable Sino–US and Sino–Japan relations, popular nationalism has often been critical of Chinese foreign policy for being too soft. Thus, nationalism is a double-edged sword to the Chinese state, and this is why the government has been carefully controlling popular nationalism and attempting to channel it to best serve the interests of the state.

A good example in this connection can be found in several nationalist demonstrations that took place since the late 1990s. College students in Beijing, Shanghai, and several other major cities took to the streets in 1999 after the NATO bombing of the Chinese embassy in Belgrade, in 2001 after the mid-air collision of an American spy plane and a Chinese fighter jet (for a detailed account, see Gries 2004), and, most recently, after Japanese government leaders insisted on visiting the Yakasune Shrine in 2005. The intriguing point is not the radical reactions of the Chinese students but the organizational work behind these demonstrations. In all major cities, students were loaded onto buses and unloaded in the designated areas; yet, once the government sensed the danger of losing control over the demonstrations it called for their cessation and transported the student demonstrators back to their campuses. Almost without exception, the leaders of these demonstrations were student cadres who were loyal to the party-state.

Confucianism strikes back: the rise of cultural conservatism

As indicated above, some intellectuals turned to study and to promoting the Chinese classics – mainly Confucian texts – after the government crackdown on the 1989 Tiananmen Square movement. This renewed interest in tradition developed into a new trend of cultural conservatism during the 1990s, claiming that it could rediscover new spiritual and ideological resources in Confucianism for China to respond to globalization. By 2005, the cultural conservatism had moved onto the center stage of public opinion in two ways: a popular movement to study the classics and an elite movement to construct China's soft power.

Dissatisfied with contemporary Chinese education that transmits primarily modern knowledge of the sciences and social sciences from the West, some Chinese scholars launched a movement to 'study the classics' among kindergarten and primary school students in the late 1990s, whereby they returned to features of ancient Chinese pedagogy, requiring students to memorize and recite the classic Confucian texts. This started as a small experiment in home schooling, but quickly became a nation-wide movement, reportedly enrolling more than 3 million children or teenagers in various kinds of reading classes by late 2004. Capitalizing on the publicity of this movement, a group of leading advocates of Confucianism held a summit to announce the formal entry of cultural conservatism onto the central stage of Chinese intellectual life. Jiang Qin, the founder of the movement, openly stated that his purpose was to restore Confucianism to the center of state ideology and political power, thus creating for China a new religion (see Zeng 2006). Other leaders praised Confucianism as a much superior cultural treasure and contrasted Confucianism with the hypocritical democratic values of the West. From this point onward, the movement to study the classics became a carefully designed political movement of the conservative intellectuals (Cheng 2005; Liu 2004).

The scholarly craze for the study Confucianism reached a new high in 2005 when the People's University established a new school of classical studies and the university president Ji Baocheng published a series of articles urging reconciliation with the traditional culture (Ji 2005; Zeng 2006). It is interesting that although the liberal intellectuals opposed the Neo-leftist scholars when they debated China's strategy in dealing with globalization and realization of the goal of modernization (Gao 2004), many of them converged to support the revitalization of Confucianism. What brought them together was a quest for indigenous resources to reconstruct the Chinese spirit or the soft power of China. In this connection, Gan Yang stands out as the most noteworthy figure because he played a key role in introducing Western thoughts and values into China during the 1980s and then became a leader of the Neo-leftist circles in the 1990s, calling for a more critical reassessment of Western culture and values. Gan (2003) then began to argue that China's long history is its greatest resource for modernization, calling for a return to traditional culture, the tradition of Maoist socialism, and the new tradition of Deng's economic reforms. Among the three traditions, socialism is the most important for China to build up its soft power (Gan 2006).

The core of cultural conservatism, therefore, is to promote the superiority of traditional Chinese culture so as to resist Western values and build up China's cultural strengths. The increasing popularity of cultural conservatism should also be understood as a reconfirmation of Chinese national identity, which over the last two decades has become more and more relevant to China's overall national power. Interestingly, the Chinese government has shown some ambivalence toward this increasingly radical push for a return to tradition by turning a deaf ear to the political appeals of cultural conservatism on one hand and supporting some traditional cultural activities on the other. For example, the year 2004 featured government-sponsored ceremonies on a grand scale to commemorate the founding leaders of Chinese civilization, such as the mystical Yellow Emperor and Confucius (Liu 2004; Wu 2004). Given the history of the Chinese Communist Party as the most radical opponent of tradition, it is clear that the party-state now cautiously hopes to maintain a balance between its own Western Marxist roots and the current needs to cultivate new cultural resources from within Chinese cultural tradition.

Changing attitudes toward globalization

Until the late 1990s, the Chinese discourse on globalization focused on economic globalization, presenting it as a continuation of modernization. This differed from most Western discussions that treated globalization as a post-industrial and post-modern phenomenon. Most intellectuals and policy-makers regarded globalization as a historical trend that was both inevitable and unavoidable, with a strong flavor of historical teleology. The entire modern history of China, as Yang and Wang argue (1998), can be seen as a series of attempts to meet the challenges of the outside world and to regain China's status in the global community of nation-states. The period from 1840 to 1949 was the first stage when the Chinese state became a vassal of the Western powers during the process of globalization. The second stage (1949–1978) was marked by the Chinese Communist Party's efforts to resist the West-dominated globalization by taking the socialist road that was modeled after the Soviet Union. Although the resistance to globalization secured China's political independence, it also caused China to fall farther behind in terms of its economy and culture. It is only during the current third stage that China has participated positively in all aspects of the globalization process, for which, the reform efforts of the party-state should be credited (Yang and Wang 1998). Along with the continuing economic growth, this enthusiasm for globalization has also developed into a more confident expression to restore China's glory on the global stage. This is best illustrated in the three leading slogans regarding China and the world during the past twenty years.

In 1987 an article caught the attention of public opinion by warning that unless China were to speed up its reform process, the country would likely again be left behind in the new era of the post-industrial economy (see Lu 1989). Should this occur, China would eventually lose its membership in the emerging global village (coined in Chinese as '*qiuji*', or 'global membership'). Underlying this discussion of China's global membership was an urgent push for a more radical reform, more openness in Chinese society, and a strong identification of modernization with Westernization, as mentioned above.

In the late 1990s, the leading slogan '*Zhongguo zouxiang shijie, shijie zouxiang Zhongguo*' (China to the World, and the World to China) caught the national imagination. There is a two-fold hidden message in this slogan. At one level, it depicts a two-way process in which China is reaching out to the world, while the world is similarly entering China. At a deeper level, the slogan emphasizes that the out-reaching approach toward foreign cultures is on China's terms when China takes the proactive step to march to the world. This strategy is known as '*jiegui*' or '*yu guoji jiegui*' in policy implementation and practice (see Zhao 2003). Literally, the term '*jiegui*' means the re-connection of tracks in railroad operations, and it is used here to encourage all sectors in China to get back on the international track of development and modernization. A good example in this connection is the state-sponsored campaign to learn English. Not only must all school students learn English and pass numerous exams, all academics, researchers, and civil servants also must now take an English exam in order to keep their jobs or to be promoted. In preparation for the 2008 Olympics, the Beijing municipal government even established a new bureau called the 'Division of English Learning for All Beijing People'. The rationale behind this campaign is that fluency in English will help put China onto the international track of development, namely, *jiegui*.

From the changes in these three slogans, we can see that the Chinese state and intellectuals are taking a proactive approach to welcome and embrace economic globalization, and, more importantly, they regard globalization as a golden opportunity for China to realize its ultimate goals of modernization. The Chinese reactions toward the cultural aspects of globalization, however, were diversified in the 1990s and in recent years have become more critical.

As indicated above, an anti-globalization voice began to be heard among a group of Chinese scholars who simply copied the dependency theory and post-colonialism from Western academic circles and criticized globalization at a rather abstract level, which, as can be expected, hardly reached the public (Gao 2004; Yan 2002). What has changed since the late 1990s, however, is that there are new voices that connect the critique of cultural globalization with Chinese reality.

The first of these voices is the nationalist discourse, particularly the more radical and militant version, such as that of Song Qiang and Wang Xiaodong. The 1996 book *Yaomohua Zhongguo de beihou* (Li et al.) effectively destroyed the credit of the Western media among Chinese audiences (Rosen 2003) and has had a profound influence on how Chinese journalists report on foreign affairs, paving the way for a nationalist attack on the negative results of cultural globalization. Another critical voice came from a Marxist perspective, claiming that globalization was nothing new, but rather a continuation of capitalist expansionism. As a result, people on the receiving end of the globalization will suffer from more exploitation, including cultural exploitation (Fang, Wang, and Song 1999; Zhu 2003: 148-205). A further danger of cultural globalization is China's loss of cultural sovereignty to the uncontrolled influx of foreign cultures (Jin 2004: 87–159). In light of Bourdieu's theory, He Qing argues that cultural globalization is actually a conspiracy or trap set by the neo-imperialist United States to undermine the national consciousness of developing countries and thus he calls for a further strengthening of state power in China as a strategy to fight against such a conspiracy (He 2003: 21–93). The advocates of cultural conservatism constitute another main critique of cultural globalization but their focus is on the superiority of Chinese culture over foreign cultures, as mentioned above (see e.g. Gan 2003; Ji 2005). Finally, the rise of anti-globalization voices in China also relates to Chinese intellectuals' awareness of a global anti-globalization movement and their efforts to participate in this movement (see Pang 2002).

Despite these anti-globalization voices and the media sensation of cultural colonialism, there has been no organized anti-globalization movement in China. Here the Chinese state again plays a key role. Although the state has always been suspicious of the influx of cultural products and thus controls the cultural market tightly, it also makes every effort to prevent the outbreak of any anti-globalization social movement for fear of the associated challenges to its own monopoly over political power. Thus, the party-state prefers to use government policies and regulations to manage the flow of cultural products, as in the above-mentioned case of the 'cultural trade deficit', and by and large ignores the appeals for more anti-globalization actions from the more radical, nationalist, or conservative intellectuals. For the same reason, the party-state has also been quite firm in cracking down on social protests by peasants or migrant laborers against real estate developers and private companies, many of which are closely related to global capital or transnational companies in China. In this connection, the Chinese state actually helps global capital maintain a stable and profitable environment for investment. It is not inconceivable, without the state control, the anti-globalization discourse among the cultural elite might have reached the lower strata of the society and become a new ideology of social resistance, helping the angry and deprived villagers and workers to organize themselves for collective actions, which could have in turn led to a full-blown anti-globalization movement, such as that has occurred elsewhere in the world.

From Asian values to the Beijing consensus

In March 1993, representatives of most Asian countries met to prepare a document that would reflect the Asian stance on human rights at the World Conference on Human Rights to be held later in the year. This document, known as the 'Bangkok Declaration of Human Rights', surprised many Western observers with its bold opposition to a universal notion of human rights which does not accord with Asian values. Unlike the Western notion of human rights that focuses on the primacy of the individual, argues the Bangkok Declaration, the Asian notion of human rights also takes into consideration the community, the society, and the country; moreover, the Asian notion of human rights emphasizes the basic rights of survival, instead of political rights. Although the declaration has strong political implications, it also indicates the increasing importance of culture and intellectual heritages in East – West exchanges and/or conflicts. The Chinese leaders were pleased to see such a rising awareness of Asian-ness among Asian countries and successfully adopted the discourse of Asian values, particularly the Asian notion of human rights, to defend their own policies of political control.

Many intellectuals and journalists in the West tend to dismiss Asian values as merely a cloak for the authoritarian leaders of Asian states, from Lee Kuan Yew to Hu Jintao, to hang on to a monopoly of power or to resist universal ideas of democracy, freedom, and human rights (see Steinglass 2005; Zakaria 1998). The 1997 Asian financial crisis further discredited the validity of Asian values, leading many to question the actual existence of Asian values. For example, Francis Fukuyama, a leading advocate of globalization, commented in 1998 that 'This crisis has certainly taken the wind out of the sails of the Asian-values argument that authoritarian states have an advantage in promoting economic progress' (quoted in Lohr 1998). The Western critique or denial marks a sharp contrast to the serious efforts by Asian leaders and intellectuals to rediscover and promote Asian values, clear evidence of conflicts in basic values. Janadas Devan's chapter in this volume offers an insightful perspective to understand the rising awareness and discourse on Asian values. According to Devan, it is the irresistible trend of globalization that forces non-Western countries around the globe to find or invent their own ways to assert the uniqueness of their own cultures and identity. Taking Singapore as an example, Devan argues that despite the fact that the Singaporeans have lived a Westernized lifestyle, the Singapore state would no longer have its edge and advantages in global competition if it were to lose its Asian identity and become culturally Westernized. The 'shared values', the Asian values officially endorsed by the Singaporean government, asserts Devan, actually function as an effective cultural and psychological mechanism to deal with globalization and to defend Asian modernity.

Indeed, although Asian values have been interpreted differently in different Asian countries, they all serve a common purpose, that is, to underscore the cultural identity of a particular Asian society so that it can resist the homogenizing power of Western modernity and the ongoing process of globalization. In this connection, the recent notion of a Beijing Consensus may have even a wider influence among non-Western countries.

In May 2004, the European think-tank Foreign Policy Centre published Joshua Cooper Ramo's long article 'Beijing Consensus,' in which the author declares the discovery of a new, alternative model of development, modernity, and globalization:

> *To the degree China's development is changing China it is important; but what is far more important is that China's new ideas are having a gigantic effect outside of China. China is marking a path for other nations around the world who are trying to figure out not simply how to develop their countries, but also how to fit into the international order in a way that allows them to be truly independent, to protect their way of life and political choices in a world with a single massively powerful centre of gravity. (Ramo 2004: 3–4)*

This Chinese model of development, or the Beijing Consensus as referred to by Ramo, consists of three theorems. The first repositions the value of innovations, the second stresses chaos management and prioritizes sustainability and equality, and the third contains a theory of self-determination, 'one that stresses using leverage to move big, hegemonic powers that may be tempted to tread on your toes' (Ramo 2004: 12). By calling it a 'Beijing Consensus', Ramo unmistakably describes the Chinese model as an alternative to the well-known 'Washington Consensus', a set of Neo-liberal ideas of Western economics that can be considered responsible for the accelerated process of economic globalization since the 1990s.

As many commentators have pointed out, the model that Ramo tries to describe is filled with inner contradictions. For instance, the first theorem idealizes the power of innovations and thus does not differ from the 'Silicon Valley model of development' (Dirlik 2006). The emphasis on sustainability and equality, Ramo's second theorem, derives mostly from the speeches of the current Chinese leaders who want to correct some serious consequences of the single-minded pursuit of economic growth over the past two decades, such as the devastating pollution and the rapid increase in inequality. What makes the Chinese model really unique, and thus attractive to other developing countries, however, is the third feature that Ramo generalized in his Beijing Consensus, that is, China's ability to insist on self-determination and independence. As Dirlik notes: 'I think it is here that the so-called Beijing Consensus offers a genuine alternative to the Washington Consensus; not in the economy or social policy, but in reshaping the global political environment that is the context for economic development' (2006: 5). In other words, with its tight grip on both political power and important market sectors, the Chinese state has been able to promote integration with the global economy while resisting various pressures to make political concessions, showing the possibility of managing the process of globalization (Yan 2002).

While the Washington Consensus features unilateralism and the universality of certain Western core values including the limitation of state power, the Beijing Consensus offers an alternative that relies on multilateralism, refuses to accept the hegemony of Western core values, and insists on a strong state in economic development and globalization. There is, therefore, a conflict of core values behind the stand-off between these two development models, leading some observers to speculate that a clash of soft powers between China and the United States may emerge (see Chow 2006).

Such speculation is not entirely ungrounded. In a sense, the Beijing Consensus is a repackaged model of the Asian values that emphasize self-determination and state suzerainty. With its remarkable achievements in economic growth and increasing military power, China stands out as a much more attractive model than other East Asian tigers and thus has had much wider and deeper influences on some African and Latin American countries by offering an alternative (Kurlantzick 2005; Thompson 2005). The Beijing Consensus, or the Chinese model, has changed global diplomacy, and, in the eyes of American right-wing thinkers, constitutes a real threat to American superiority and the Western model of development (Kurlantzick 2005). This in turn reinforces the China threat theory (Yee and Storey 2002) and increases the possibility of future conflicts.

Conclusions

Remarking on China's effort to enter the world, the late paramount leader Deng Xiaoping also commented: 'When you open the window, flies and mosquitoes come in.' The flies and mosquitoes that Deng was referring to is the inevitable influx of foreign – mainly Western – thoughts and cultural values that accompany the foreign investment, technology, and management skills, and which could pose serious challenges to the Communist regime by 'peaceful evolution'. Therefore, by nature this is an inherent tension.

Despite the fear of peaceful evolution and the repeated attempts to fence off foreign influences, the Chinese party-state has maintained the open-door policy and has integrated China much further into the international community during the last twenty-five years or so. Consequently, social life and cultural values in the society have changed to a great degree, including the rise of individuality, the popularity of romantic love and no-fault divorce, the pursuit of individual freedom and privacy, consumerism and a consumer movement, environmentalism, and the mushrooming of NGOs. When these foreign cultural ideas, values, and behavioral patterns first entered Chinese society, almost all of them were regarded as political 'flies and mosquitoes' by the party-state and 'unhealthy and strange' by conservative citizens; they naturally caused tensions and conflicts with existing Chinese ideas, values, and behavioral patterns. Yet, as time went by, the initial tensions and conflicts turned out to be inspirations and catalysts for positive social changes, leading to more constructive and creative results, that is, an increasingly open and globalizing Chinese society.

Other cultural importations, such as the values of democracy and human rights, or the idea of a shrinking state, have had different encounters in China, causing much stronger and critical responses from both the elite and the populace. Why the difference? A close reading of the several trends in the tensions and conflicts since the 1990s reveals that, almost without exception, the tensions developed into cultural conflicts whenever state sovereignty, national self-determination, the dignity of the core values, and the popular psyche regarding perceived national status and face were being seriously challenged by the influx of foreign cultures, especially by the imposed influx. These might also be identified as the potential fault lines or mine fields in cultural globalization, which could be triggered by ethno-centralism, unilateralism, or simply the lack of cultural sensitivity in cultural exchange and flows.

To illustrate the crucial importance of avoiding ethno-centrism and unilateralism, let us return to the two cases mentioned at the beginning of this chapter. When commenting on a series of foreign advertisements that were considered insulting or offensive by the Chinese, a high-level executive in a Western advertising giant simply attributed the perceived insults to the lack of mutuality among Chinese customers who could not stand for the creativity and rebelliousness that were so common in the commercials in the West (see Ni 2005). This sharply contrasts with the reflection of a Chinese marketing specialist after the insulting Nike commercial, who said that one cannot challenge or ridicule anything in a given culture, 'some things are sacred and have to be respected' (personal interview). In a similar vein, the Western media focused on freedom of the press and thus continued to challenge Muslim culture by publishing the controversial cartoons after the angry and often violent protests had spread to many cities in the world. This led UN Secretary-General Kofi Annan to call the continuing publication of the cartoons 'insensitive' and to state that freedom of speech entails 'exercising responsibility and judgment' (see Farley 2006).

What made the final ending of these two cases so different depended to a great extent on whether there was an intervening power and how that power worked. In the Chinese case, as I have reiterated throughout this chapter, a strong party-state played a key role in managing cultural conflicts, intervening with administrative orders or government policies, and often ending conflicts arbitrarily. For the same reason, there has not been any organized anti-globalization movement in China, even though the social causes for such a movement have become at least equally as strong as anywhere else in the world. This is what I call managed globalization, a distinctive Chinese model of globalization (Yan 2002).

Managed globalization, however, may prove itself to be a double-edged sword, because it seeks to control, instead of facilitating, global cultural flows and thus will reduce mutual understanding and dialogue across cultural and national boundaries. As a result, while it can solve some existing cultural conflicts, it also likely will create more misunderstandings, tensions, and conflicts due to the low availability of information flows and cultural exchanges. For example, the same Nike advertisement 'Chamber of Fear' was aired in Hong Kong, among other Chinese societies, but did not cause any negative reactions from Hong Kong residents. Is this because the Hong Kong residents were less sensitive, or because they were more open-minded in a much more open society where the flow of information was much less controlled?

It is important, therefore, to promote more cross-cultural dialogues, to construct freer environments for cultural flows and mutual understanding, to avoid ethno-centrism, to cultivate cultural sensitivity, and, more importantly, to shift more responsibilities and power for managing cultural conflicts to civil society and NGOs so as to balance state power. Moreover, it is also important to recognize the complexity and diversity of the globalization processes, or, as the title of the book by Berger and Huntington (2002) bluntly states, to recognize the 'many globalizations' going on in today's world. In this connection, the Chinese alternative may provide a lot of food for thought.

REFERENCES

BBC (2004) 'China tightens up TV ad. rules', BBC News, December 12.

Beijing qingnian bao [Beijing Youth Daily] (1999) 'Reassessing human rights', May 15; 'Reassessing freedom of the press,' May 16; 'Reassessing national strength', May 17; 'Reassessing globalization', May 18; 'Reassessing American blockbuster movies', May 19; 'Reassessing Western civilization,' May 20; 'China taking another look at the US,' May 20.

Berger, Peter (1997) 'Four faces of global culture', *National Interest* 49: 23–9.

– (2002) 'Instruction: The Cultural Dynamics of Globalization', in Peter Berger and Samuel Huntington (eds), *Many Globalizations: Cultural Diversity in the Contemporary World*. Oxford: Oxford University Press.

– and Huntington, Samuel (eds) (2002) *Many Globalizations: Cultural Diversity in the Contemporary World*. New York: Oxford University Press.

Buckley, Chris (2005) 'Beijing to clamp down on foreign media', *International Herald Tribune*, August 4.

Chen, Fong-ching and Jin, Guantao (1997) *From Youthful Manuscripts to River Elegy: The Chinese Popular Cultural Movement and Political Transformation 1979–1989*. Hong Kong: The Chinese University Press.

Cheng, Qing (2005) 'Dujing yundong yu zhengzhi baoshou zhuyi' [The movement of reading the classics and political conservatism], *Tianya* [Frontiers], No. 1.

Chow, Eric Teo Chu (2006) 'U.S. – China ideological rivalry heats up', *Japan Times,* January 6.

Dai, Yan (2006) 'FDI continues to rise, Up 11% in January', *China Daily*, February 21.

Di, Jianrong and Chen, Chunyan (2005) 'Wenhua maoyi nicha buliyu shijie liaojie Zhongguo' [Cultural trade deficit hinders the world's understanding of China], *Jiefang ribao* [Liberation Daily], May 17.

Dirlik, Arif (2006) 'Beijing Consensus: Beijing 'Gongshi'. Who recognizes whom and to what end?', Globalization and Autonomy Online Compendium, at www.globalautonomy.ca. Position paper posted on January 17.

Dolven, Ben (2003) 'Into China's new frontier: foreign brands, successful in cities, head for tough rural markets', *Wall Street Journal*, February 20.

Fang, Ning, Wang, Xiaodong, and Song, Qiang (1999) *Quanqiuhua yinyingxia de Zhongguo zhi lu* [China's Road under the Shadow of Globalization]. Beijing: Zhongguo shehui kexue chubanshe.

Farley, Maggie (2006) 'Freedom of speech carries responsibility, Annan says', *Los Angeles Times*, February 10, A11.

Fleishman, Jeffrey (2006a) 'Protesters burn Danish Embassy in Syria over cartoons of Prophet', *Los Angeles Times*, February 5, A3.

– (2006b) 'Rage over cartoons perplexes Denmark', *Los Angeles Times*, February 9, A1.

Friedman, Thomas L. (2005) *The World Is Flat: A Brief History of the Twenty-First Century*. New York: Farrar, Straus and Giroux.

Gan, Yang (2003) 'Cong minzu-guojia zouxiang wenming-guojia' [From nation-state to civilization-state], *Ershiyi shiji jingji baodao* [The 21st Century Economic Times], December 30.

– (2006) 'Shehuizhuyi chuantong: Zhongguo zuijiben de ruanshili' [Socialist tradition: the most basic soft power of China], *Ershiyi shiji jingji baodao* [The 21st Century Economic Times], January 14.

Gao, Mobo (2004) 'The Rise of Neo-nationalism and the New Left: A Postcolonial and Postmodern Perspective', in Leong H. Liew and Shaoguang Wang (eds). *Nationalism, Democracy and National Integration in China*. London: RoutledgeCurzon. pp. 44–62.

Gong, Haoqun (2003) 'Gonggong lingyu de shuangchong yaoqiu: Pingxi 9.11 shijian yu Zhongguo de meijie shijian' [The double-demand of the public sphere: an analysis of the 9.11 incident and the media event in China], *Wenhua yanjiu* [Cultural Studies], No. 4: 120-8.

Gries, Peter Hays (2004) *China's New Nationalism: Pride, Politics, and Diplomacy*. Berkeley: University of California Press.

Gutmann, Ethan (2004) *Losing the New China: A Story of American Commerce, Desire and Betrayal*. San Francisco: Encounter Books.

He, Qing (2003) *Quanqiuhua yu guojia yishi de shuaiwei* [Globalization and the Decline of National Consciousness]. Beijing: Renmin daxue chubanshe.

He,Wei (2000) *Ku* [Be Cool]. Jilin: Jilin sheying chubanshe.

Ji, Baocheng (2005) 'Yu chuantong hejie' [To reconcile with tradition], *Nanfang zhoumo* [The Southern Weekend], May 26.

Jin, Minqing (2004) *Wenhua quanqiuhua yu Zhongguo dazhong wenhua* [Cultural Globalization and Popular Culture in China]. Beijing: Renmin chubanshe.

Jin, Yuanpu and Zhang, Jiangang (2005) 'Miandui wenhua maoyi nicha, Zhongguo gaidang hewai?' [Facing the cultural trade deficit: what should China do?), *Banyuetan* [Fortnightly Chats], July 28.

Kristof, Nicholas D. (2002) 'The chip on China's shoulder', *New York Times*, January 18, A23.

Kurlantzick, Joshua (2005) 'Cultural revolution: how China is changing global diplomacy', *The New Republic*, June 27.

Le, Shan (ed.) (2004) *Jianliu: Dui xiaai minzuzhuyi de pipan yu fansi* [The Under Currents: Critique and Reflections on Narrow Nationalism]. Shanghai: Huadong shifan daxue chubanshe.

Li, Xiguang et al. (1996) *Yaomohua Zhongguo de beihou* [Behind the Scene of Demonizing China]. Beijing: Zhongguo shehui kexue wenxian chubanshe.

Liu, Ruonan (2004) 'Dalu ruxue fuxing yundong' [The Movement to Revitalize Confucianism in Mainland China]. *Fenghuang zhoukan* [Phoenix Weekly], at www.lys123.home.sunbo.net/show_hdr.php?xname=5HFUG01&dname=67BPL01&xpos=8.

Lohr, Steve (1998) 'Asian values may change in wake of economic crisis', *New York Times*, February 7.

Lu, Yi (ed.) (1989) *Qiuji: Yige shijixing de xuanze* [Global Membership: A Choice of the Century]. Shanghai: Baijia chubanshe.

Ni, Ching-Ching (2005) 'Yahoo accused of aiding China in arrest', *Los Angeles Times*, September 5, A3.

Pang, Zhongying (ed.) (2002) *Quanqiuhua, fanquanqiuhua yu Zhongguo* [Globalization, Anti-globalization, and China]. Shanghai: Shanghai renmin chubanshe.

Qiu, Hongjie (2004) 'Guangdian zongju: Ge dianshitai dingbo Nike ad "kongju doushi"' [The state administration of radio, film and television stopped the broadcast of the Nike ad "Chamber of Fear"], New China News Agency, December 8.

Ramo, Joshua Cooper (2004) *The Beijing Consensus: Notes on the New Physics of Chinese Power*. London: Foreign Policy Centre.

Rosen, Stanley (2003) 'Chinese Media and Youth: Attitudes toward Nationalism and Internationalism', in Chin-Chuan Lee (ed.), *Chinese Media, Global Context*, London: RoutledgeCurzon. pp. 97–118.

Sklair, Leslie (1991) *Sociology of the Global System*. Baltimore: Johns Hopkins University Press.

Song, Qiang et al. (1996) *Zhongguo keyi shuo bu* [China Can Say No]. Beijing: Zhonghua gongshang lianhe chubanshe.

State Council (of the People's Republic of China) (2005) 'Zhongguo de minzhuzhengzhi jianshe' [The construction of democratic polity in China]. See http://news.xinhuanet.com/ziliao/2005-10/26/content_3685106.htm

Steinglass, Matt (2005) 'Whose Asian values?' *The Boston Globe*, November 20.

Thompson, Drew (2005) 'China's soft power in Africa: from the "Beijing Consensus" to health diplomacy', *China Brief* (Jamestown Foundation) 5, No. 21 (October 13).

USCBC (The US – China Business Council) (2005) 'US-China trade statistics and China's world trade statistics'. See http://www.uschina.org/statistics/tradetable.html

Wang, Yuxian and Lin, Yang (1996) 'Guohuo yu yanghuo: Meiyou xiaoyan de zhanzheng' [National products vs. foreign products: a war with the smoke of gunpowder], *Shidian* [Perspectives], No. 6: 16–18.

Watson, Paul and Ali, Zulfiqar (2006) 'Three Afghans killed in protest of cartoons', *Los Angeles Times*, February 8, A6.

Wu, Zhaomin (2004) 'Honghong leilei ji shenme?' [What are the grand ceremonies for?], *Zawenbao* [Essay Weekly], November 12.

Xiao, Pang (ed.) (1997) *Zhongguo ruhe miandui xifang* [How China Should Face the West]. Hong Kong: Mirror Books Ltd.

Yan, Yunxiang (2002) 'Managed Globalization: State Power and Cultural Transition in Contemporary China', in Peter Berger and Samuel Huntington (eds), *Many Globalizations: Cultural Diversity in the Contemporary World*. New York: Oxford University Press. pp. 19–47.

Yang, Dongping (1997) 'Qiguai de minjian yizheng' [The Strange Civil Debate of Politics], in Xiao Pang, (ed.), *Zhongguo ruhe miandui xifang* [How China Should Face the West]. Hong Kong: Mirror Books Ltd. pp. 206–17.

Yang, Xudong and Wang, Lie (1998) 'Guanyu quanqiuhua yu Zhongguo yanjiu de duihua' [A Dialogue Regarding Globalization and China Studies], in Hu Yuanzi, and Xue, Xiaoyuan (eds), *Quanqiuhua yu Zhongguo* [Globalization and China]. Beijing: Zhongyang bianyi chubanshe. pp. 1–21.

Yee, Herbert and Storey, Ian (eds) (2002) *The China Threat: Perceptions, Myths and Reality*. London: Routledge Curzon.

– and Zhu, Feng (2002) 'Chinese Perspectives of the China Threat: Myth or Reality?', in Herbert Yee and Ian Storey (eds), *The China Threat: Perceptions, Myths and Reality*. London: RoutledgeCurzon. pp. 21–42.

Yu, Keping (2005) 'Rehuati yu lingsikao: Guanyu Beijing gongshi yu Zhongguo fazhan moshi de duihua' [Hot Topic and Calm Thinking: A Dialogue about the Beijing Consensus and the Chinese Model of Development], in Huang Ping and Cui Zhiyuan (eds), *Zhongguo yu quanqiuhua: Huashengdun gongshi haishi Beijing gongshi?* [China and Globalization: The Washington Consensus, or the Beijing Consensus?]. Beijing: Shehui kexue wenxian chubanshe. p. 209.

Zakaria, Fareed (1998) 'Will Asia Turn Against the West?' *New York Times*, July 10.

Zeller Jr., Tom (2006) 'Microsoft amends its policy for shutting down blogs', *New York Times*, February 1.

Zeng, Jun (2006) 'Sixiang yu xueshu zai dangdai wenhua zhong heliu: 2005 nian renwen xueshu redian saomiao' [The convergence of thoughts and scholarship in contemporary culture: scanning the hot topics of cultural studies in 2005], *Xueshujie* [Academic Circles], No. 1.

Zhao, Bo (1994) 'Xingxing sese yang xiaofei' [Varieties of consumption of foreign goods]. *Shichang jiage* [Market Price], No. 3: 9.

Zhao, Yuezhi (2003) '"Entering the World': Neo-liberal Globalization, the Dream for a Strong Nation, and Chinese Press Discourses on the WTO"', in Chin-Chuan Lee (ed.), *Chinese Media, Global Context*. London: Routledge Curzon. pp. 32–56.

Zheng, Yongnian (1999) *Discovering Chinese Nationalism in China: Modernization, Identity, and International Relations*. Cambridge: Cambridge University Press.

Zhu, Xiaomei (2003) *Dazhong wenhua yanjiu* [A Study of Popular Culture]. Beijing: Qinghua daxue chubanshe.

## CHAPTER 13

CAPITALISM, CONFLICT AND CHURN: HOW THE AMERICAN CULTURE WAR WENT GLOBAL

Ronnie D. Lipschutz

Cultural conflicts emerge when the hegemony of a dominant elite is challenged by social changes related to transformations in capitalism and by the social turmoil that follows. In the United States such periods of disruption and conflict are associated with what are generally called 'industrial revolutions', periods during which capitalism eats away at the foundations of social structures and hierarchies through, in Joseph Schumpeter's terms, 'creative destruction' and 'churn'. Churn weakens the ideologies and relations that naturalize and justify particular institutionalized forms of domination, social organization and hegemony, and when these begin to erode, the legitimacy of a social order is challenged.

Introduction

Every society has its myths, its Golden Ages, its foundational principles and beliefs, its naturalized social hierarchy (Morgan 2005). And all societies undergo periods of stress, change and instability, leading their members to yearn for the 'good old days'. A central element of Golden Age mythology is that everyone was happier and better off, things and people 'were in order', and following the rules offered its just rewards – even if such was rarely the case. Cultural conservatives such as Huntington believe the American Golden Age was the 1950s, when the country was prosperous and at peace, Ike was in the White House, fathers were at work, mothers were in the kitchen, and everyone who counted was White and Protestant. For African-Americans, radicals and homosexuals, among others, that particular decade was hardly a golden one. And one need only recall the case of the Irish during the first half of the nineteenth century to recognize that 'Americans of all races, ethnicities, and religions' have not always been embraced by the country's dominant Anglo-Protestant culture. For other groups, such rejection still remains true today. Why, then, make patently absurd claims such as Huntington's?

For more than 35 years, even before Ronald Reagan became President, a *kulturkampf* for social and political hegemony[1] has been raging across the United States. This culture war pits elites and their followers who see themselves as the guardians of 'traditional' norms, values and hierarchies – social and cultural conservatives, nostalgic Cold Warriors and pre-millennialist Christians (Herman 2000) – against a cabal of putative liberals, secular humanists, multiculturalists, and others (Hunter 1991; Himmelfarb 1999; McConkey 2001; Horowitz 2003; but see also Wolfe 1998; Fiorina 2005; and Abramowitz and Saunders 2005).[2] Thus, in 1991, a cultural critic (Gray 1991:13) at *Time* magazine wrote:

> *[T]he customs, beliefs and principles that have unified the U.S....for more than two centuries are being challenged with a ferocity not seen since the Civil War... Put bluntly: Do Americans still have faith in the vision of their country as a cradle of individual rights and liberties, or must they relinquish the teaching of some of these freedoms to further the goals of the ethnic and social groups to which they belong?*

And, in his speech to the 1992 Republican Convention, Pat Buchanan warned:

> *My friends, this election is about much more than who gets what. It is about who we are. It is about what we believe. It is about what we stand for as Americans. There is a religious war going on in our country for the soul of America. It is a cultural war, as critical to the kind of nation we will one day be as was the Cold War itself. And in that struggle for the soul of America, Clinton and Clinton are on the other side, and George [H.W.] Bush is on our side. And so, we have to come home, and stand beside him. (1992)*

Thus were the lines drawn, the forces committed and the battles fought.

While some thought the culture wars would come to an end after September 11, 2001, this was not to be. The invasion of Iraq in 2003, with its strong religious overtones (Northcott 2004), the re-election of George W. Bush in 2004 and his declining popularity, vacancies on the nation's Supreme Court in 2005, and the specter of a 'war against Christmas' in 2005 evoked ever more fierce attacks from the Right (Frum and Perle 2003, Coulter 2003, 2004; Hannity 2004). But more than this, the attacks on New York and Washington, as well as the shooting wars that followed, seemed to suggest that the American culture wars might be spreading beyond the United States, to other parts of the world. It began to appear as though cultural conflict was also engaging the Catholic Church in Europe and America (Wills 2005) as well as Islam (Pew 2003).

What I argue in this chapter is that there is nothing new about such cultural conflicts. They are, in large part, artifacts of modernity and globalization, of the tendency, as Marx and Engels put it in *The Communist Manifesto* (1848/1964: 63) and *The German Ideology* (1932/1970), that 'all that is solid melts into air.' Cultural conflicts emerge when the hegemony of a dominant elite is challenged by social changes related to changes in capitalism and the social turmoil that follows. Indeed, as we shall see, in the United States such periods of disruption are associated with what are generally called 'industrial revolutions', and they tend to revolve around conflicts within elites, over changing belief and status systems and practices.[3] In the United States, these structures have, historically, been rooted in religion – even though social and political elites themselves are not always particularly devout.

I begin with a general discussion of the relationship between culture, conflict, and globalization. I argue, from an historical materialist perspective, that capitalism eats away at the foundations of social structures and hierarchies through the 'creative destruction' and 'churn' that it generates, in the present case linked to globalization (Schumpeter 1942; see also Cox and Alm 1992; Boo 2004a, 2004b). Churn weakens the ideologies and relations that naturalize and justify particular institutionalized forms of domination, social organization and hegemony. When these begin to erode, the legitimacy of a social order comes under challenge. One result is cultural conflict, of the sort we see in America today. In the second part of the chapter, I give a brief historical account of this phenomenon in the United States, beginning with challenges to Puritanism in the 1730s and ending with the current religious revival and cultural conflict that began during the 1970s. This cycle is important because, since the early eighteenth century, there have been interesting, if mostly unremarked, cultural-religious conflicts correlated with phases of global capitalist expansion and social change. In this section, I also extend my analysis from the territory of the United States to the ROW (Rest of the World). I argue that the great, world-girdling struggle(s) of the early twenty-first century, between 'freedom' and 'terror', might be better seen as the latest episode in recurrent patterns of cultural conflict within the American social system, now extended beyond the country's borders. Finally, I conclude with some theoretical speculations on the arguments presented in this chapter.

Culture, conflict and globalization

How are culture, conflict, and globalization linked?[4] I start from the premise that all human societies are constituted by and organized through social relations based on specified rule sets embodied in culture, religion and law, among other things.[5] These rule sets explain not only how one should act to succeed and be socially-acceptable but also what constitutes 'right order' and 'virtuous behavior' (these, nonetheless, may be quite unfair, unjust, and even violent). These rule sets, or 'creeds' in Huntington's (2004) terms, are generally learned from birth, communicated to children (and adults) at home, in schools and churches, through public rituals, and by the media (Tétreault and Lipschutz 2005: ch. 2). They are acknowledged as 'truths' by members of a society, even if some individuals and groups flatly reject them as a basis for normal social relations. In most cases, the social relations normalized by these rule sets stand in an explicit or implicit hierarchy, placing individuals and groups in dominant–subordinate roles on the basis of kinship, descent, contract, wealth, power, office, style, or other attributes read off of appearance, dress, speech, attitude, texts, gender, race, ethnicity, history and material accoutrements (e.g., cars, swords, cellphones, MP3 players).

In so-called traditional societies, hierarchies tend to be relatively fixed and, in the absence of demographic catastrophes such as the Black Plague, the potential for social mobility is limited or non-existent (Diamond 2006). Generally speaking, one's place is determined by and at birth, and that's pretty much that. In modern societies, rule sets, practices, and hierarchies are legitimized through what Antonio Gramsci (1971) called 'hegemony'. Hegemony is necessary to a modicum of stability under capitalism, and it rests on society's broad consent to and acceptance of the social order, even if, from an 'objective' economic perspective, that order is clearly disadvantageous to large segments of society. Hegemony is to be differentiated from the notion of 'false consciousness', in that it fosters inter-class solidarity on the basis of social and cultural characteristics, such as religious belief, morality, and identity. People may be fully aware of economic cleavages, but these may matter less than social and cultural differences (Frank 2004; Rupert 1995; Fonte 2001; see also below).

Under conditions of capitalist growth and expansion, as Marx and Engels (1848/1964, 1932/1970) pointed out, the fixity of rules and social relations cannot be taken as given. Without going into the specific details of capitalist transformation and social change (see, e.g., Berman 1982; Lipschutz 1998a, 2000), I only note that the possibility of upward social mobility is one of the most attractive elements of American capitalist and political discourse. A critical element of American social relations is the deeply held and almost religious notion that the only obstacles to individual 'success' are one's own shortcomings, which may be organic, inherited, or learned (Herrnstein and Murray 1994). The conviction that anyone can succeed if s/he works hard enough and obeys the rules is often articulated in terms of 'entrepreneurship' and 'opportunities' to be seized. American children are taught that, in the United States, 'anyone can be President' (no one would think to say such a thing in France). In this sense, therefore, life is very much like business: an accounting of profit and loss.

But almost certainly, this belief is incorrect (Jacoby and Glauberman 1995). Even the United States, a society with arguably the highest degree of upward (and downward) mobility in the world, is nevertheless characterized by relatively stratified social and racial relations as well as class structures (Scott and Leonhardt 2005; Brown and Wellman 2005).[6] Moreover, as is widely recognized but rarely admitted, the capacity to 'seize' an opportunity, to accumulate wealth, and to move upward in the social hierarchy, is not merely a matter of either individual merit or Fortuna (e.g., Isbister 2001: ch. 5; Sen 1999). Success breeds success. Those who already have wealth are well-poised to acquire more, and rarely operate in isolation from others similarly well-off (Herbert 2005). They are well embedded in webs of social relations with people who are wealthy and well placed economically and politically, whose families and background are of a particular sort, and who know the ropes (which is why going to Harvard is so often a stepping stone to riches and public office; see Douthat 2005). Those lacking such advantages are rarely offered entry into that upper-class world (Wilkerson 2005). Social hierarchies are closely linked to societal divisions of labor which, in turn, are historically related to group, rather than individual, status, attributes and practices (e.g., Tilly and Tilly 1994; Brown and Wellman 2005). At the very least, those lower in the economic hierarchy must work all the harder to build the necessary networks. Efforts to remedy disadvantage have been half-hearted, at best (Katznelson 2005). As practiced in the United States, affirmative action, widely criticized as providing unfair advantages to excluded groups, in fact seeks to promote *individuals*, and not groups, on the basis of some indicator of merit and behavior (see, e.g., Fullinwider 2005; Brown and Wellman 2005). As a racial group, for example, most African-Americans remain at the bottom of the American social hierarchy and division of labor (Daniels 2005), while those who have risen to political and economic prominence constitute a relatively small middle class. Still, the very essence of social stability requires that the possession of power and wealth by some be recognized as legitimate by those who lack these attributes (and who can hope that they may, someday, be as well-off). Moreover, that established hierarchy must constantly be naturalized through invocation of belief in the possibility of 'self-improvement'.[7]

Globalization exposes such social relations to relentless attack by the acidic powers of capitalism, as commodification, accumulation, and cultural change expose the fluidity and hollowness of what appeared to be stable social relations, and downsize or eliminate people's niches in the societal division of labor.[8] This has happened to blue- and white-collar workers in the United States, as the country's industrial base has become less competitive and corporations have moved to outsourcing and offshoring both manufacturing and services (see, e.g., Cox and Alm 1992; Gereffi and Korzeniewicz 1994; Boo 2004a, 2004b). For reasons having to do with historical racial and ethnic exclusions in certain parts of the United States, as well as pure demographics (Royster 2003), the vast majority of blue-collar and middle-management workers are white Protestants.[9] The industrial and corporate reorganizations of the past 30 years have had a significant effect on them, even though minorities tend to be 'first fired' and have experienced greater impacts as a result of organizational change (Rimer 1996). Whatever the numbers say, the 'natural order of things' has been upset and 'all that is solid melts into air.'

I should note that although there is a class character to the impacts and consequences of churn, political and social alliances tend to be based on cultural relations rather than strictly economic factors (which is why the international proletariat has never 'lost its chains'). This explains the paradox noted by Thomas Frank (2004) in *What's the Matter with Kansas?,* a book that asks why those whose economic interests are so severely affected by Bush Administration policies have nonetheless overwhelmingly been supporters of the Republican Party. Frank invokes religious solidarity (rather than false consciousness) to account for this phenomenon and, as we shall see below, this is an important element, although not the only one. Still, in the United States, when culture and economic interests cross swords, so to speak, it is often the former that best explains the odd political coalitions sometimes observed.

There is a second aspect to globalization's churn. Depending on political and economic conditions at a given time, the disadvantaged may find it possible to acquire some economic resources through exploitation of the very niches in the division of labor to which they have been relegated as a result of the social hierarchy (Chua 2002). Improvement in the economic well-being of members of such groups then spills over into the cultural realm, as the market caters to changing tastes, growing incomes and accumulated savings.[10] Because these new cultural products often differ from what was previously on offer – Gay Days at Disneyworld, billboards in Spanish – they acquire a high degree of visibility and attention and make disadvantaged groups seem more prominent and influential than their numbers. The rise in the social and economic status of American gays and lesbians between 1980 and today, as well as growing numbers of migrants from Mexico into the United States, illustrate this point. As a formerly subordinated and closeted group, now with growing income, wealth, and social power, gays and lesbians represent an attractive market for businesses who cater to their needs and desires, as well as a source of capital for office-seekers and other entrepreneurs (von Hoffman 2004). While migrant incomes remain low, they nonetheless constitute a growing market demographic across the United States, too (Lowry, Ulanov and Wenrich 2003).

Practices and behaviors that, at one time, were forbidden, such as same-sex marriage, become more widely accepted, as new forms and patterns of livelihood and economic organization undermine the material bases of the better-off (Fiorina 2005: ch. 4, 5; Lipschutz 1998a). Those who paint themselves as guardians of 'traditional values' warn of the imminent collapse of the social order if people are not disciplined (e.g., Sheldon 2004; Kurtz 2003). Unwilling to criticize the market, these elites search for non-economic sources of the disorder and disrespect that are symptoms of the coming calamities. Foreigners, communists, gays, adolescents and progressives are, among others, easy targets, for these are the people most likely to violate or stray from real or imagined social and cultural verities (Lipschutz 1998b). The division of society into those who are 'good' and those who are not follows rather easily (Coulter 2003, 2004; Hannity 2004; Frum and Perle 2003).

Even minor cultural changes may come to be interpreted as a challenge to the hegemonic power and privileges of elites and become the basis for political mobilization of those who are linked to elites through religious beliefs and practices (Lipschutz 1998a, 1998b). Such mobilized groups may seek to restrict or roll back those changes, through rhetorical references to cultural 'naturalness' (Carlson and Mero 2005), laws that impose limits on work opportunities and property ownership, or invocation of 'natural' law. In some extreme cases, as in the case of Nazi Germany and Rwanda, mobilization may be followed by wholesale genocide. Note, moreover, that even if most members of these groups remain relatively poor and powerless, as in the case of African Americans and Latinos, the upward mobility of the few may come to be seen as a synecdoche of a threat from the subordinate group as a whole (as, apparently, does Huntington).

Finally, it is not necessary that such changes be accepted as problematic or threatening by even a majority of a given society. Polling data in the United States suggest that most of the American public is only marginally aware of the culture war, much less engaged in it. Most of those involved appear to be those who Fiorina and his associates (2005) call 'activists and partisans,' that is, those who are either fairly conservative or liberal (see also Abramowitz and Saunders 2005). While Fiorina et al. see this division more as a product of electoral competition between Republicans and Democrats seeking to capture voters from the 'center', there is, as I have argued above, a more fundamental matter at stake: hegemony. This is, after all, not only about what society takes as 'common sense,' but also about how and what policies and programs are legitimated and funded and how and what children, students and adults are taught and told is the 'truth'. Hegemony even shapes the cultural products delivered by the mass media, which resists at the peril of loss of market share and unfriendly takeovers. Such forms of socialization, in turn, support and legitimate the social order that enables elites to maintain their material and ideological hegemony and assures them that they are the 'natural' leaders of society. Clearly, hegemony is a focus of constant political and social struggle, for which it is worth fighting (Halperin, 2004).

Religion, culture and conflict in the United States

What, then, is the specific role of religious belief in this culture war? Religion, as suggested above and as various writers point out (Frank 2004; Peterson 2001; Swidler 2003), is central to naturalizing social arrangements and distinctions and maintaining their legitimacy and 'rightness'. This is not so much because religions specify or command particular social relations and hierarchies – although, as in the case of feudalism or the nuclear family, they often do. Rather, religion provides an external, authoritative framework of 'truths' and linked practices that validates the existing social order and promises eventual rewards to those who obey the rules and accept their place in that order (Weber 1958). Furthermore, it is in the interest of elites that such truths come to be internalized and accepted as natural and, most of all, *static* and not open to challenge or change. But here arises another contradiction: religion is cultural in a very foundational way and, as with other aspects of culture, it is hardly static or unchanging (Swidler 2003). Indeed, both culture and religion are extremely labile, syncretic and adaptive, and their beliefs, texts and practices can be 'read' in ways that support or attack all manner of social changes (see, e.g., Miller 1954: esp. ch. 14; Miller 1953: ch. 11, 19). One need look only so far as, for example, Vatican II and the subsequent backlash against it in the Catholic Church (Wills 2005), or contemporary debates within Islam (Moghissi 2005), to see such fluidity in action.

Mass religious reactions to churn and change seem especially evident in the United States.[11] It is not only that Protestantism was so central to the country's founding, and that cultural change seems repeatedly to issue challenges to Anglo-Protestant hegemony. It is also that the conventions of religious belief and practice come into question whenever capitalism experiences an 'industrial revolution' and the accompanying 'churn'. Notably, perhaps, these also tend to be periods of higher rates of capital accumulation, job opportunities, and destabilization of social hierarchies. Indeed, beginning in the early eighteenth century, religious upheavals have broken out every 50 to 75 years among Protestant communities in North America (Table 13.1).[12] These 'Great Awakenings' are characterized by mass mobilizations of believers, eruptions of religious movements of 'purification', and onrushing waves of xenophobia and social conflict. As McLoughlin (1980: 2) puts it, these Great Awakenings develop during 'periods of cultural distortion and grave personal stress, when we lose faith in the legitimacy of our norms, the viability of our institutions, and the authority of our leaders in church and state'.[13] And even though the absolute numbers involved in such movements do not constitute national majorities (see, for example, www.adherents.com n.d.), they do tend to draw heavily on religious and cultural elites and to attract widespread attention in the media and public discourse.

The most recent Great Awakening began in reaction to the protest movements of the 1960s, followed by the emergence of the what was then

Table 13.1 Great Awakenings and their salient features

Great Awakening	Approximate Dates	Character	Nature of economic change
First	1730–1780(?)	Purification movement against Puritanism and individual success, leading to the rise of Congregationalism	Integration of North American colonies into British imperial system
Second	1830–1855	Reaction against Congregationalism and mainline denominations; rise of millennialist and literalist Protestant sects; abolitionism	Penetration of first industrial revolution into US economy; integration through rails and roads
Third	1880–1930	Prairie populism and evangelism; Social Gospel; rise of fundamentalist churches	Corporate monopoly, depressions and currency crisis, farm modernization
Fourth	1975–present	Growth in evangelical, premillennial churches, and their expansion into the Third World; reaction against social liberalism	Post-Fordism, aka, the Information Revolution, outsourcing, downsizing, etc.

Source: McLoughlin, 1980; author's research

called the 'New Right' around 1975 (Bennett 1988; Lienesch 1993; Harding 2000). Since that time, this has grown into a political-social-religious coalition encompassing neo-conservatives, Christian premillennial dispensationalists,[14] ardent supporters of Israel, both Christian and Jewish, and others, generally associated with the Republican Party (Boyer 2005). 'Family values' is the general code for the social content of this revival and, while not easily defined, it includes, among other things, respect for duly constituted authority, fidelity to the patriarchal nuclear family, strictly defined gender roles within the household and without, patriotism, and allegiance to religious strictures (Buss and Herman 2003; Kline 2004).[15] These beliefs and practices are predicated on a vision of social stability rooted in the prosperity and white Protestant hegemony of the 1950s, when racial, religious, and ethnic minorities, in particular, had not yet begun to challenge the 'natural' order of things (Weyrich 2005; Carlson and Mero, 2005).

Whether that hegemony is really threatened is debatable. In particular, by 2005, with a few localized exceptions, the traditionalist coalition had won resounding political victories across much of the United States, taking control of all three branches of the US government, exercising enormous influence over the tone and content of the public media, and re-instating the authoritative role of religion in American public life. The opposition, as it were, appeared to be on the run. Polling data, however, suggest that victory is far from certain (Fiorina 2005), and the decline in President Bush's fortunes are, perhaps, indicative of a gradual sea-change even in conservative sentiments (Hadar 2005). Nevertheless, it is unlikely that the culture war will soon be over, although, as we shall see, there are to be fundamental contradictions in the relationship between culture and market, which may well, ultimately, lead to the decline of traditionalist forces.

In North America, the first three Great Awakenings were largely domestic affairs (albeit mirrored in Britain and Europe in reaction to both the Napoleonic Wars and the first industrial revolution; see Halperin 1993). For the most part, however, the effects of American revivalism on the Rest of the World (ROW) were limited (Merk 1963).[16] In recent years, however, borders have been crossed. To a growing degree, the Fourth Great Awakening has gone abroad and engulfed the ROW through the intentional extension and expansion of neo-liberal capitalism and US 'culture' (Northcott 2004; Lipschutz 2006) and, more recently, in pursuit of democratization in the Middle East via the invasion of Iraq. As President George W. Bush proclaimed in his January 2003 State of the Union address, 'America is a nation with a mission, and that mission comes from our most basic beliefs,' and, he continued, speaking of the Middle East, 'I believe that God has planted in every human heart the desire to live in freedom.' Indeed, there is a teleological quality to the American faith in markets and democracy (Lipschutz 2006) not far removed from evangelical notions about salvation through good works and belief in Christ (Weber 1958; see also Northcott 2004).

The Bush Administration's foreign policies can be seen, in part, as a response to the globalized, socially disruptive character of American capitalist expansion during the 1980s and 1990s. Parallel to the domestic struggle for hegemony, these policies represent efforts on the part of the dominant world power to buttress social stability in the international system (Bush et al. 2002) while maintaining domestic order.[17] Social change within and across societies has led to formation of an odd transnational movement among the American Christian Right (now joined in the traditionalist coalition to the Bush Administration), the conservative elements in the Catholic Church (supported by Pope John Paul II and, now, Pope Benedict XVI), and even the governments of certain Muslim countries (invoking the eternal verities of Sharia law; see Buss and Herman 2003). But neo-liberal globalization and capitalist churn have also given rise to the global justice movement (Notes from Nowhere 2003)[18] as well as the transnational Salafist *jihadi* movement (the latter concerned about issues of representation, problems of political corruption, and the unjust exercise of power; see Lubeck and Lipschutz forthcoming). This is not to suggest an alliance between the global justice movement and the *jihadis;* only to point out that, at the margin, they may share some objectives. Space precludes an extensive discussion of the globalization of American culture war, or how it might play out over the coming years and decades. Suffice it to say that it is a thoroughly *modern* phenomenon, although those social forces in confrontation hold somewhat different views of what constitutes a proper social order and how that order is to be achieved (Lipschutz 2006).

Concluding thoughts about capitalism, culture and conflict

Patterns of religious revivalism and cultural conflict that appear throughout American history and practice may, of course, simply be correlations, artifacts of coincidences among disconnected struggles, structures, and effects. I think not. There is a set of specific contradictions inherent in the structure and organization of an American-style democratic capitalist society that renders it subject to periodic culture wars. These contradictions arise between the legitimating functions of the democratic state and the constant erosion of rules and norms due to the churn of capitalism.[19] In more authoritarian societies, police power and economic control can stabilize the social order (although, as we observe repeatedly, even such states are not immune to churn and challenge; see, e.g., Woodruff 2001). Rule may lack legitimacy but, in the absence of *intra*-class struggle, elites generally manage to maintain themselves for some period of time. Capitalist *democracies*, by contrast, must limit the use of police power in order to sustain the legitimacy of their social choice mechanisms as well as their status and hierarchy relations, and to manage active opposition to domestic distributions of power and authority.[20]

Given that socially dominant groups tend to hold political power, even in capitalist democracies (Chua 2003), it is fairly straightforward to avoid or head off *political* and *social* policies that could lead to radical redistributions of power and wealth and threaten hegemony (Polanyi 2001; Halperin 2004). Social democracy, in particular, relies on both political mechanisms and redistribution to maintain social hierarchies and 'traditional' culture. Libertarian democracies such as that of the United States, eschew such regulatory practices, with considerable potential and real costs to longer-term social stability. High rates of economic growth, as well as the disappearance of those forms of regulation that underpinned the welfare state and fostered some limited degree of resource redistribution, do not reduce but, rather, exacerbate the gap between the better-off and the worse-off (Frank 2005). Under such conditions, it becomes increasingly difficult to construct the social and political coalitions necessary to acquisition or maintenance of power. Moreover, as seems to have happened to the Democrats' New Deal coalition, they can dissolve if based purely on economic interests. In the United States, economic mobility is at least partly divorced from hierarchy and status, and can pose a challenge to hegemony's 'natural order' of things and people, thereby generating various forms of paradoxical resentment. Such anger and confusion can be mobilized and used to build cultural solidarity against an opponent, to reinforce hegemony and, parenthetically, to organize winning political coalitions (Lipschutz 1998b). Nonetheless, continued conservative prosecution of the 'culture war' may prove difficult. For one thing, the white Protestant population in the United States is declining as a percentage of the whole (Huntington 2004; Smith and Kim 2004), and a fair fraction of that demographic – perhaps as much as half [21] – remains both liberal and even secular (Fiorina 2005).

Another key problem for the traditionalist coalition is, as I have argued throughout this chapter, globalization. Cultural and religious conservatism is a form of behavioral regulation, just like any other, and it is also subject to the dynamism of lightly regulated global capitalism. Religious solidarity around cultural values probably cannot indefinitely survive growing material gaps between rich and poor. Globalization will continue to exacerbate that gap unless and until the Republican coalition governing in Washington decides to institute an extreme protectionist regime and a draconian immigration and travel policy (disputes over what to do about China or how to handle illegal immigration offer examples of internal conflicts that could destroy the coalition). But a 'Fortress America' would generate such a ferocious depression and decline in living standards as to permanently wreck the Right (much as happened during the Great Depression).

Moreover, even culture wars can produce unexpected outcomes. The Third Great Awakening pitted farmers and urban labor against Eastern bankers and business, in a context of deepening poverty and growing corporate power and corruption. Christians were active not only in the rising Populist movement but also in working for social reform (Gorrell 1988). Progressivism, based on technical expertise and a notion of the 'common good', emerged in reaction to both Populism *and* the corporate excesses of the time, and succeeded in dampening social and cultural conflict. The same could well happen again. Between the dying-off of the aging traditionalist vanguard and broad acceptance of new mores, practices, and values by younger adults (Fiorina 2005), in another 10 or 20 years, the culture wars may fade away. But the social peace that follows is unlikely to last very long. Given capitalism and churn, it never does.

Notes

1 I define 'hegemony' here in Gramsican terms: the elite ideological and cultural beliefs to which members of society 'consent' and which generate normalization and what Gramsci called 'common sense'. (see, e.g., Gramsci 1971; Rupert 1995)

2 It should be noted that not everyone finds that there is such a culture war under way, or that it has become more intense (see, e.g., McConkey 2001; Fiorina 2005).

3 Campbell (2004) has made a similar argument, claiming that 'globalization undermines moral consensus' through relativization, that is, 'calling into question such things as the definitions, boundaries, categories and conclusions through which they have understood the world and established their identity.' But he does not link this process to material or economic change.

4 Here I rely on the definitions of these concepts offered by the editors of this volume.

5 I do not want to fall into functionalism here; these are not rule sets that have somehow been consciously and deliberately devised to govern the operation of society, but neither are they 'spontaneous,' as suggested by Friedrich Hayek (1945).

6 Although the potential for mobility among income quintiles is considerable – more than half of each quintile moved up or down between 1968 and 1991, almost 47% of the lowest and 42% of the highest quintiles did not move up or down (McMurrer and Sawhill 1996: Table 2).

7 This is one reason why the Bush Administration's response to the destruction of New Orleans has been attacked so vociferously. Not only was it a dereliction of duty, it also exposed to the light of day the extent to which social hierarchy is so fundamental to American society, yet so naturalized as to be invisible to most. The notion of 'self-improvement' is also a very Lockean one, which should come as no surprise (see *New York Times* Class Project 2005, especially questions 26–30).

8 The British have a marvelous word for this: to be made 'redundant' (see MacErlean and Bachelor 2005).

9 Although precise data are difficult to come by, there are about 125 million self-identified 'born-again' or 'evangelical' Protestants in the United States (44% of the total population), out of 151 million Protestants (Adherents.com. n.d). Thus, simple demographics would suggest they have been the most affected. There is also strong evidence that, on the one hand, conservative Protestants tend to be the highest percentage of the Christian population in the American South, which remains the poorest part of the country with high unemployment rates, even as, on the other hand, the counties in which conservative Protestants live tend to be the more prosperous ones (ARDA 2005). Other data also seem to suggest that conservative Protestants are fairly well off in terms of education and income (see, e.g., IFAS 1998).

10 This does not mean that these groups become fabulously wealthy; only that they are able to accumulate and make a cultural mark on society at large (Severson 2004; Quinone 2005).

11 Religion has been central to political and nationalist mobilization for centuries (Marx 2003), although it does not seem quite so central to the contemporary politics of industrialized states other than the United States (Buss and Herman 2003).

12 The English Civil War and Puritan Commonwealth of the 17th century can be seen as manifestations of an earlier 'Great Awakening' setting the Puritan movement against backsliding Anglicans and Catholics.

13 Not all scholars agree that such Great Awakenings actually occurred (Lambert 1999; Finke and Stark 1992).

14 Premillennial dispensationalists believe that the Second Coming may happen at any time, indicated by 'the Rapture'. One of the critical signs of Jesus's return and the 'End Times' is the re-establishment of Israel (Herman 2000; Buss and Herman 2003: 10–13).

15 It is no small irony, then, that a number of leaders of this coalition (e.g., Newt Gingrich and Tom DeLay) have been caught out in either infidelity or corruption.

16 I ignore here the French and Indian War, the American Revolution, the War of 1812, the War with Mexico, the Civil War, the Spanish–American War, World War One, and various incursions, all of which might be correlated with the first three Great Awakenings (Lipschutz 2006).

17 War and external threats have long been known as means of fostering domestic social cohesion (see, e.g., Waltz 1959: ch. 4).

18 I should note that the Third Great Awakening, during the latter part of the 19th century, saw the emergence not only of conservative Christianity but also the Social Gospel (Gorrell 1988).

19 Space precludes a more detailed discussion of the tension between the capitalist state's regulatory and accumulation functions; some of these points are discussed in Lipschutz 2005.

20 Capitalist police states may not be so encumbered by this problem, so long as the bourgeosie is fully on board, as suggested by the relative economic success of Pinochet's Chile, on the one hand, and the apparent decline of middle-class support for the Saudi monarchy, on the other.

21 Data from 2001 suggest that, while 76% (211.5 million) of the American population identifies as 'white', only 53% (151 million) claim to be Protestant and 44% (125.3 million) are 'born-again' or 'evangelical'. Of the latter, only 22 million are 'theologically' evangelical (Adherents.com, n.d.).

REFERENCES

Abramowitz, Alan and Saunders, Kyle (2005) 'Why can't we all just get along? The reality of a polarized America', *The Forum* 3 (2): article 1, at: http://www.bepress.com/forum (16 Dec. 2005).

Adherents.com (n.d.) 'Composite U.S. demographics', at: http://www.adherents.com/adh_dem.html (16 Dec. 2005).

American Religion Data Archive (ARDA) (2005) 'Religious congregations and membership maps and reports', at: http://www.thearda.com/RCMS/2000/RCMS_report2000.asp (17 Dec. 2005).

Bennett, David H. (1988) *The Party Of Fear: From Nativist Movements to the New Right in American History*. Chapel Hill, NC: University of North Carolina Press.

Berman, Marshall (1982) *All that is Solid Melts Into Air.* New York: Simon and Schuster.

Boo, Katherine (2004a) 'The churn: creative destruction in a border town', *The New Yorker*, March 29, at: http://

www.newyorker.com/fact/content/?040329fa_fact (22 Sept. 2005).

– (2004b) 'The best job in town: the Americanization of Chennai', *The New Yorker*, July 5, pp. 54–69.

Boyer, Peter J. (2005) 'The big tent', *The New Yorker*, August 22, pp. 42–55.

Brown, Michael K. and Wellman, David (2005) 'Embedding the color line: The accumulation of racial advantage and the disaccumulation of opportunity in post-civil rights America', *Du Bois Review* 2 (Fall).

Buchanan, Patrick (1992) Speech to the 1992 Republican National Convention, at: http://en.wikisource.org/wiki/Patrick_Buchanan's_Speech_to_1992_GOP_Convention (21 Sept. 2005).

Bush, George W. (2003) 'State of the Union,' at: http://www.whitehouse.gov/news/releases/2003/01/20030128-19.html# (23 Sept. 2004).

–, et al. 2002. *The National Security Strategy of the United States* (Washington, DC: The White House, September), at: http://www.whitehouse.gov/nsc/nss.pdf (29 Sept. 2002).

Buss, Doris and Herman, Didi (2003) *Globalizing Family Values — The Christian Right in International Politics.* Minneapolis: University of Minnesota Press.

Campbell, George Van Pelt (2004) 'Everything you know is wrong: how globalization undermines moral consensus'. Paper presented at the annual meeting of the Association for the Sociology of Religion, San Francisco, 14 August, at: http://hirr.hartsem.edu/sociology/sociology_online_articles_campbell.html (28 Oct. 2005).

Carlson, Allan C. and Mero, Paul T. (2005) 'The natural family: a manifesto', The Howard Center for Family, Religion and Society, at: http://www.familymanifesto.net (23 Sept. 2005).

Chua, Amy (2003) *World on Fire: How Exporting Free Market Democracy Breeds Ethnic Hatred and Global Instability.* New York: Doubleday.

Coulter, Ann (2003) *Treason – Liberal Treachery from the Cold War to the War on Terrorism.* New York: Crown Forum.

– (2004) *How to Talk to a Liberal (If You Must): The World According to Ann Coulter.* New York: Crown Forum.

Cox, W. Michael and Alm, Richard (1992) 'The churn – the paradox of progress', Federal Reserve Bank of Dallas, Reprint from *1992 Annual Report*, at: http://www.dallasfed.org/fed/annual/1999p/ar92.pdf (6 Dec. 2005).

Daniels, Lee A. (ed.) (2005) *The State of Black America, 2005.* New York: National Urban League.

Diamond, Jared (2006) *Guns, Germs, and Steel: The Fates of Human Societies*, new edn. New York: Norton.

Douthat, Ross Gregory (2005) *Privilege: Harvard and the Education of the Ruling Class.* New York: Hyperion.

Fiorina, Morris P. with Abrams, Samuel J. and Pope, Jeremy C. (2005) *Culture War? The Myth of a Polarized America.* New York: Pearson Longman.

Fogel, Robert W. (2000) *The Fourth Great Awakening and the Future of Egalitarianism.* Chicago: University of Chicago Press.

Fonte, John (2001) 'Why there is a culture war – Gramsci and Tocqueville in America', *Policy Review* 104, at: http://www.policyreview.org/dec00/Fonte.html (8 Feb. 2006).

Finke, Roger and Stark, Rodney (1992) *The Churching of America, 1776–1990: Winners and Losers in Our Religious Economy.* New Brunswick, NJ: Rutgers University Press.

Frank, Robert H. (2005) 'The income gap grows', *The Philadelphia Inquirer*, Nov. 17, at: http://www.philly.com/mld/philly/13263286.htm (6 Jan. 2006).

Frank, Thomas (2004) *What's the Matter with Kansas? How Conservatives Won the Heart of America.* New York: Metropolitan Books.

Frum, David and Perle, Richard (2003) *An End to Evil – How to Win the War on Terror.* New York: Random House.

Fullinwider, Robert (2005) 'Affirmative action', in Edward N. Zalta (ed.), *The Stanford Encyclopedia of Philosophy*, Spring 2005 Edition, at: http://plato.stanford.edu/archives/spr2005/entries/affirmative-action (20 Dec. 2005).

Gereffi, Gary and Korzeniewicz, Miguel (eds) (1994) *Commodity Chains and Global Capitalism.* Westport, CT: Greenwood Press.

Gorrell, Donald K. (1988) *The Age of Social Responsibility: The Social Gospel in the Progressive Era, 1900–1920.* Macon, GA: Mercer University Press.

Gramsci, Antonio (1971) *Selections from the Prison Notebooks*. Trans. by Quintin Hoare and Geoffrey Nowell-Smith (eds). London: Smith, Lawrence and Wishart.

Gray, Paul (1991) 'Whose America?' *Time*, July 8, pp. 13–17.

Hadar, Leon (2005) 'Innocents abroad – Karen Hughes' mission impossible', *The American Conservative*, Dec. 19, at: http://www.amconmag.com/2005/2005_12_19/print/articleprint2.html (14 Dec. 2005).

Halperin, Sandra (1993) 'Religious Revivalism in Nineteenth Century Europe and the Contemporary Middle East: A Comparison', Paper presented at the Annual Meeting of the American Political Science Association, Washington, DC, 2–5 Sept.

– (2004) *War and Social Change in Modern Europe: The Great Transformation Revisited.* Cambridge: Cambridge University Press.

Hannity, Sean (2004) *Deliver Us from Evil – Defeating Terrorism, Despotism, and Liberalism.* New York: ReganBooks.

Harding, Susan Friend (2000) *The Book of Jerry Falwell: Fundamentalist Language and Politics*. Princeton, NJ: Princeton University Press.

Hayek, Friedrich A. (1945) 'The use of knowledge in society', *American Economic Review*, 35: 519–30.

Herbert, Bob (2005) 'The mobility myth', *New York Times*, June 6, at: http://www.nytimes.com/2005/06/06/opinion/06herbert.html?ex=1135227600&en=a16a00d882f98da9&ei=5070 (20 Dec. 2005)

Herman, Didi (2000) 'The New Roman Empire: European envisionings and American premillennialists', *Journal of American Studies*, 34 (1): 23–40.

Herrnstein, Richard J. and Murray, Charles (1994) *The Bell Curve: Intelligence and Class Structure in American Life.* New York: Free Press.

Himmelfarb, Gertrude (1999) *One Nation, Two Cultures.* New York: Knopf.

Horowitz, David A. (2003) *America's Political Class under Fire: The Twentieth Century's Great Culture War.* New York: Routledge.

Hunter, James Davison (1991) *Culture Wars: The Struggle to Define America.* New York: Basic.

Huntington, Samuel (2004) *Who are We? The Challenges to America's National Identity.* New York: Simon and Schuster.

Institute for First Amendment Studies (IFAS) (1998) 'Survey of Christian Right activists', cited at 'Christian fundamentalism exposed', www.sullivan-county/news/ (28 Oct. 2005).

Isbister, John (2001) *Capitalism and Justice – Envisioning Social and Economic Fairness.* Bloomfield, CT: Kumarian Press.

Jacoby, Russell and Glauberman, Naomi (eds) (1995) *The Bell Curve Debate: History, Documents, Opinions.* New York: Times Books.

Katznelson, Ira (2005) *When Affirmative Action was White: An Untold History of Racial Inequality in Twentieth-Century America.* New York: W.W. Norton.

Kline, Scott (2004) 'The Culture war gone global: "family values" and the shape of U.S. foreign policy', *International Relations,* 18 (4): 453–66.

Kurtz, Stanley (2003) 'Beyond gay marriage – the road to polyamory', *The Weekly Standard* 8 (45), August 4, at: http://www.weeklystandard.com/Content/Public/Articles/000/000/002/938xpsxy.asp (23 Sept. 2005).

Lambert, Frank (1999) *Inventing the "Great Awakening".* Princeton, NJ: Princeton University Press.

Lienesch, Michael (1993) *Redeeming America: Piety and Politics in the New Christian Right.* Chapel Hill, NC: University of North Carolina Press.

Limbaugh, David (2003) *Persecution: How Liberals are Waging War Against Christianity.* Washington, DC: Regnery.

Lipschutz, Ronnie D. (1998a) 'From "Culture Wars" to Shooting Wars: Cultural Conflict in the United States', in Beverly Crawford and Ronnie D. Lipschutz (eds), *The Myth of 'Ethnic Conflict': Politics, Economics and 'Cultural Violence'.* Berkeley, CA: International and Area Studies Press, University of California. pp. 394–433.

– (1998b) 'Seeking a State of One's Own: An Analytical Framework for Assessing Ethnic and Sectarian Conflicts', in Beverly Crawford and Ronnie D. Lipschutz (eds), *The Myth of 'Ethnic Conflict': Politics, Economics and 'Cultural Violence'.* Berkeley, CA: International and Area Studies Press, University of California. pp. 44–78.

– (2000) *After Authority – War, Peace and Global Politics in the 21st Century.* Albany, NY: State University of New York Press.

– (2002) 'The clash of governmentalities: the fall of the UN republic and America's reach for imperium', *Contemporary Security Policy,* 23 (2): 214–31.

– with Rowe, James (2005) *Globalization, Governmentality and Global Politics – Regulation for the Rest of Us?* London: Routledge.

– (2006) 'The empire of faith: American religion, imperial absolutism and global struggle', at: http://people.ucsc.edu/~rlipsch/Empire.doc

Lowry, James, Ulanov, Alex and Wenrich, Thomas (2003) 'Advancing to the next level of Latino marketing: strike first, strike twice,' Boston Consulting Group, Feb. 15 at: http://www.bcg.com/publications/publication_view.jsp?pubID=791&language=English (20 Dec. 2005).

Lubeck, Paul and Lipschutz, Ronnie D. (Forthcoming) 'The clash of global discourses: explaining the relationship between neo-liberalism and Islamism', Center for Global, International, and Regional Studies, University of California, Santa Cruz.

MacErlean, Neasa and Bachelor, Lisa (2005) 'Lost your job? Here's how to get back on the road to work', *The Observer,* April 24, at: http://money.guardian.co.uk/work/howto/story/0,1456,1469825,00.html (6 Jan. 2006).

Marx, Anthony (2003) *Faith in Nation: Exclusionary Origins of Nationalism.* Oxford: Oxford University Press.

Marx, Karl and Engels, Friedrich (1848/1964) *The Communist Manifesto.* New York: Pocket Books.

– (1932/1970) *The German Ideology,* C.J. Arthur (ed.). New York: International Publishers.

Merk, Frederick (1963) *Manifest Destiny and Mission in American History.* New York: Knopf.

McConkey, Dale (2001) 'Whither Hunter's culture war? Shifts in Evangelical Morality, 1988–1998', *Sociology of Religion,* 62 (2): 149–74.

McLoughlin, William (1980) *Revivals, Awakenings and Reform.* Chicago: University of Chicago Press.

McMurrer, Daniel P. and Sawhill, Isabelle V. (1996) 'Economic mobility in the United States', Urban Institute, Oct. 1, at: http://www.urban.org/publications/406722.html#tab1a (19 Dec. 2005).

Miller, Perry (1953) *The New England Mind: From Colony to Province.* Cambridge, MA: Harvard University Press.

– (1954) *The New England Mind: The Seventeenth Century,* 2nd edn. Cambridge, MA: Harvard University Press. (1st edn, 1939.)

Moghissi, Haideh (ed.) (2005) *Women and Islam: Critical Concepts in Sociology.* London: Routledge.

Morgan, Edmund S. (2005) 'The other founders', *New York Review of Books,* 52 (14): 41–3.

Northcott, Michael (2004) *An Angel Directs the Storm – Apocalyptic Religion and American Empire.* London: I.B. Tauris.

Notes from Nowhere (ed.) (2003) *We Are Everywhere – The Irresistible Rise of Global Anticapitalism.* London: Verso.

Peterson, Anna (2001) *Being Human – Ethics, Environment, and Our Place in the World.* Berkeley: University of California Press.

Pew Research Center (2003) 'Religion and politics: contention and consensus', July 24, at: http://pewforum.org/publications/surveys/religion-politics.pdf (19 Dec. 2005).

Polanyi, Karl (2001) *The Great Transformation,* 2nd edn. Boston: Beacon. (1st edn 1944.)

Quinone, Sam (2005) 'From sweet success to bitter tears', *The Standard*, Jan. 21, at: http://www.thestandard.com.hk/stdn/std/Focus/GA21Dh01.html\ (6 Jan. 2006).

Rimer, Sarah (1996) 'A hometown feels less like home', *The New York Times*, March 6, at: http://www.nytimes.com/specials/downsize/06down1.html (22 Sept. 2005).

Royster, Deirdre A. (2003) *Race and the Invisible Hand: How White Networks Exclude Black Men from Blue-Collar Jobs.* Berkeley: University of California Press.

Rupert, Mark (1995) *Producing Hegemony: The Politics of Mass Production and American Global Power.* Cambridge: Cambridge University Press.

Schumpeter, Joseph (1942) *Capitalism, Socialism and Democracy.* New York: Harper.

Scott, Janny and Leonhardt, David (2005) 'Class in America: shadowy lines that still divide', *New York Times*, May 15, at: http://www.nytimes.com/2005/05/15/national/class/OVERVIEW-FINAL.html?ex=1135227600&en=bf8e0a8c461091e8&ei=5070 (16 May 2005).

Sen, Amartya (1999) *Development as Freedom.* New York: Anchor.

Severson, Kim (2004) 'The hole truth – can America build a better doughnut? Does it need to?', *San Francisco Chronicle*, March 17, at: http://www.sfgate.com/cgi-bin/article.cgi?f=/chronicle/archive/2004/03/17/FDGDM5J57Q1.DTL (6 Jan. 2006).

Sheldon, Louis (2004) 'Constitutional attorney sees polygamy as next stage of sexual revolution', Traditional Values Coalition Press Release, Oct. 5, at: http://traditionalvalues.org/modules.php?sid=1935 (22 Sept. 2005).

Smith, Tom W. and Kim, Seokho (2004) 'The vanishing protestant majority', NORC/University of Chicago, July, GSS Social Change Report No. 49., at: http://www.norc.uchicago.edu/issues/PROTSGO8.pdf (20 Dec. 2005).

Swidler, Ann (2003) *Talk of Love – How Culture Matters.* Chicago: University of Chicago Press.

Tétreault, Mary Ann and Lipschutz, Ronnie D. (2005) *Global Politics as if People Mattered.* Lanham, MD: Rowman and Littlefield.

Tilly, Chris and Tilly, Charles (1994) 'Capitalist Work and Labor Markets', in Neil J. Smelser and Richard Swedberg (eds), *The Handbook of Economic Sociology.* Princeton, NJ: Princeton University Press. pp. 283–312.

Von Hoffman, Constantine (2004) 'Out and about', *CMO Magazine*, November, at: http://www.cmomagazine.com (20 Dec. 2005).

Weber, Max (1958) *The Protestant Ethic and the Spirit of Capitalism.* Trans. by Talcott Parsons. New York: Scribner's.

Waltz, Kenneth N. (1959) *Man, the State and War – A Theoretical Analysis.* New York: Columbia University Press.

Weyrich, Paul M. (2005) 'Traditional family values', *The American Daily*, May 4, at: http://www.americandaily.com/article/7675 (23 Sept. 2005).

Wilkerson, Isabel (2005) 'A success story that's hard to duplicate', *New York Times*, June 12, at: http://www.nytimes.com/2005/06/12/national/class/12angelaside-final.html?ex=1135227600&en=22b685aacbca029c&ei=5070 (20 Dec. 2005).

Wills, Garry (2005) 'Fringe government', *New York Review of Books,* 52 (15):46–50.

Wolfe, Alan (1998) *One Nation, After All: What Middle-Class Americans Really think about: God, Country, Family, Racism, Welfare, Immigration, Homosexuality, World, the Right, the Left and Each Other.* New York: Viking.

Woodruff, David M. (2001) 'Power and prosperity: outgrowing communist and capitalist dictatorships', *East European Constitutional Review* 10 (1), at: http://www.people.fas.harvard/~dmwoodr/materials/olson_review.htm (17 Aug. 2005).

INTRODUCTION

'Conflict' in the context of culture and globalization often takes the form of tensions and fault lines that crystallize or bring to the fore issues, patterns and processes that in other circumstances may have been far less visible or clear-cut. This section explores a range of such cases, many of which have been alluded to already, directly or indirectly, in the preceding chapters.

The 'clash of civilizations', that seemingly ubiquitous, almost unavoidable trope, is a popular, perhaps even populist fault line, posited by Samuel Huntington to anticipate the impending conflict scenarios of a post-Cold War world. Even many who do not support this apocalyptic hypothesis, have unconsciously allowed this vision some discursive purchase. Recent world events, in particular 9/11 and the invasion of Iraq in 2003, have singularly reinforced this propensity, giving credence to the spectre of fault lines that cause unbridgeable antagonisms between massive blocks of peoples.

But the reality is infinitely more complex and differentiated, as the chapters in this section will demonstrate. Basing his analysis on Latin American realities and perceptions, Hugo Achugar looks at how contemporary globalization inflects the North–South divide inherited from centuries of Western empire; symbolic production remains asymmetrically distributed across the world, but the imbalance is articulated in new ways. Georges Corm for his part identifies the traumatic geopolitical and historical roots of the divide between the Arab world and the West. These must take precedence over the culturalist explanations now in vogue, he argues, for only when these traumas are recognized can the antinomies be bridged. But there are great divides *within* 'civilizations' as well and Bassam Tibi, whose analysis departs from Corm's in many respects, explores the intense quarrels of doctrine and sentiment that are prevalent among the Muslim peoples and how, despite the many values, symbols, traditions, memories and fears of threatened identity they may all share, they simply cannot be seen as a single, unified monolith. Similarly with 'Western civilization': mutual perceptions of the cultural commonality between Europe and the United States have oscillated over the last four centuries. On the basis of data from the World Values Survey/European Values Survey, Chris Welzel and Franziska Deutsch contextualize today's value divergences, identifying the moral rigidity and the vigour with which Americans defend individualism (along with their self-righteousness and their belief in the morality of retaliation) as the main tension-generating feature. On the same issue, Nathan Gardels identifies divergent 'cultures of belief' or mindsets in four key domains: security, the social model, immigration and technological advance. The power of religion is another area of divergence – indeed the very notion of 'culture' is often a coded reference to contemporary reassertions of religious values, particularly of the fundamentalist variety, and especially in Islam. Religion matters. Inglehart and Norris also use World Values Survey data to explain why the world as a whole now has more people with traditional religious views than ever before and argue that while secularization has reduced subjective religiosity in these countries a broader type of spiritual concern has become increasingly widespread.

For others, the tensions arise elsewhere, at the national or local level, as the unprecedented mixings of peoples brought about by globalization, and reinforced by economic and social insecurities, generate confrontations between cultural identities and their representations, between different levels of belonging. Because the massive movement of peoples is at the same time a key driver and concomitant of globalization, this section closes with three analyses of the impacts of migratory flows. What changing, different and complex interactions are occurring *within* nations between the cultural and other socioeconomic dimensions as a result of these flows? Leo Estrada looks at how migration-caused cultural tensions in the United States have been altered by immigration from Latin America and Asia; how, as a consequence of 9/11, new fears regarding Muslim or Arab or Middle Eastern immigrants are now articulated within a newly defined 'national security' context. The present immigration scenario in Argentina, on the other hand, emblematic of patterns found throughout the Global South, leads to readings of social conflict as cultural conflict. As Alejandro Grimson points out, immigration from Bolivia, Paraguay and Peru, linked to the changes introduced by neo-liberalism, has brought a new ethnic politics to the fore, generating new ideas and definitions of nationality, class and citizenship. Finally, in Malaysia, massive inflows of global capital have also generated massive inflows of foreign workers from the region; initially, their assimilation and political incorporation were informal and unproblematic, but now, with the introduction of formal labour recruitment, competition over scarce urban resources such as jobs and housing is causing friction; here too, immigrants now labelled 'illegal' are increasingly perceived as a subversive threat to national security.

CHAPTER 14

TENSIONS BETWEEN NORTH AND SOUTH

Hugo Achugar

The symbolic situation of the 'North' versus the 'South' represents the asymmetrical economic, commercial, political, and cultural flows of globalization. North–South tensions relate specifically to the unequal distribution of symbolic artistic, scientific, and theoretical production, and of cultural labor. Current cultural globalization implicitly favors the 'universalization' of rules and paradigms of what should be understood as 'valid' systems of symbolic production. It is precisely this wide field of representations and symbolic production that generates unevenness between the North and the South (as geo-symbolic, rather than geographical places). In essence, cultural globalization stifles local production of culture, language, and memory, and gaps in access fuel North–South tensions and conflicts.

> *The four cardinal points are three: North and South.*
>
> *Vicente Huidobro (1919–1931), Altazor*

There are many North–South tensions contained within the processes of globalization; in this chapter I shall focus on the representational aspects. When globalization is represented and analyzed, space and time are always centrally important; they become even more pertinent when globalization is conceptualized beyond the frame of 'First World thinking', in an historical perspective defined from the 'periphery' or a Southern location.

Globalization old and new

It has been said that current globalization is but a new phase of an old process. According to some scholars, 'if the sixteenth century Iberian expansion was better known, we could not speak of globalization as an unprecedented and recent situation' (Gruzinski 2000). In this perspective, notions such as the 'planetary melting pot' in cultural or ethnic terms do not constitute novelties as such. Nevertheless, even if globalization today – both economic and cultural – is qualitatively different from prior stages or phases of global processes, this difference lies only in the technological and informational transformations experienced in the last two decades of the twentieth century. This is the reason why, we can argue, along with Braudel (1967), that there are *longue durée* trends which existed in the past and laid the ground for contemporary globalization. These long-term trends were in operation even before the Iberian expansion. We must not forget the earlier Arab expansion into Europe which began well before the tenth century.[1] But even if we decide to concentrate on Western Europe as a site where contemporary globalization has its most ancient origins, many of the effects of globalization could reasonably be seen as mere technological adjustments to earlier, existing cultural phenomena. Some of these cultural phenomena have played a role since the dawn of imperial expansionism and have generated various forms of 'cultural tensions' – racism for instance. But there have also been other aspects, such as contempt for languages, arts, theories and thoughts considered not to be 'rational', 'Western' or 'scientific' that were then translated into forms of 'Orientalism', 'New Worldism' and other visions of 'exotic' cultural and ideological productions (Said, 1994; Gruzinski 2000). These 'cultural tensions' arose not necessarily from a 'clash of civilizations' or as a result of 'religious differences', but out of economic, territorial and power interests that were a fundamental feature of various imperial expansionisms.

By this I do not mean to suggest that the global process initiated by Western Europe around the sixteenth century remained the same in perpetuity. In fact, each process has had distinct features as well as a different pace. Throughout the nineteenth century and especially during its last decades, most parts of the world underwent – along with the growing expansion of world markets and the rapid development of the means of transport and information – a sort of 'culture shock' qualified or understood by many as 'modernization'. This 'culture shock' was very marked among artistic communities in Western Europe, the US and Latin America. It is well known that artistic and cultural endeavors such as the mid-nineteenth century British Arts and Crafts movement, or French *Art Nouveau*, German *Jugendstil* and Spanish-American *Modernismo* at the turn of the twentieth century were part of the 'spiritual reaction' against the positivistic philosophy of the industrial revolution, mass production and market values in the West and its peripheries. This resistance to the market and 'materialistic' society did not imply, however, a condemnation of globalization itself; actually, in many countries these and other artistic movements were features of 'cosmopolitanism' – the word of the day for a sort of social or cultural 'globalization' (see Timothy Brennan among many others) that was quasi-synonymous with modernity.

It is precisely during this nineteenth-century phase of globalization that communications grew to be a quasi-global reality; major news agencies started at the time and if we can not speak yet of 'global journalism' it is possible by the end of the century to find 'world sections' in many newspapers.[2] It was also during this epoch that notions such as *Weltliteratur* (World Literature) appeared. On January 31, 1827, Goethe coined, in his conversations with Eckerman, his idea of the notion when he said: 'Nowadays, national literature does not mean a great deal; the moment has arrived of World Literature, and we all should contribute to advance the coming of this epoch'. In a similar vein, a few years later, Marx and Engels claimed in the *Communist Manifesto*: 'The intellectual creations of individual nations become common property. National one-sidedness and narrow-mindedness become more and more impossible, and from the numerous national and local literatures, there arises a world literature' (from the authorised English translation of the text of 1848, http://www.anu.edu/polsci/marx/classics/manifesto.html). This assessment appeared in a context that described the ways the world market works and in which, according to Marx and Engels, 'the bourgeoisie has given a cosmopolitan character to production and consumption in every country.' Clearly, many people in the nineteenth century, at least among the elite or intelligentsia, were conscious that the world they were living in was, if not a global system, a world system. It was not just Europeans who felt this way: the writings of Latin American intellectuals like José Martí, José Enrique Rodó, Rubén Darío and North Americans like Henry James and others testify to a similar global awareness.

What I have been arguing is, on the one hand, that there have been several predecessors to current globalization and on the other that globalization is a process that can and should be described in historical terms or 'historicized'. In this regard, there are different 'periods' in this historical process known as 'globalization'. There is also another relevant issue: the fact that 'globalization' is a constructed notion, a representation of the ways we think of the world or our societies.

It is possible to identify different features that characterize globalization in terms of 'World culture'. According to the Brazilian writer Renato Ortiz, globalization should be differentiated from *mundializaçao* ('worldization'): the former refers to financial and economic aspects while the latter should be reserved for social and cultural features. The discussion around 'cultural globalization' is nevertheless tied according to some analysts to 'global markets' and to the 'World system'.

In Franco Moretti's words, for instance, the 'World system' is one that at the same time is:

> ... one and unequal: with *a heart and a periphery (and a semi-periphery) that are united in a relation of growing inequality. One and unequal ... but a system that is different from the one on which Goethe and Marx pinned their hopes, since it is profoundly unequal. (2000: 1)*

Moretti's remark – made in the context of the notion of 'world literature', supposedly in the realm of 'global academia' – emerges from his belief that we are thinking 'against the background of the unprecedented possibility that the entire world may be subject to a single center of power – and a center which has long exerted an equally unprecedented symbolic hegemony' (Moretti 2003). US-based Moretti, Mexico-based García Canclini and others identify current cultural globalization with this 'unprecedented symbolic hegemony' of the entire world.

This transnational shared characterization of globalization as the pre-eminence of a 'single cultural model' is not a universally shared view. The French literary critic Pascale Casanova has argued that this idea has served as a neutralizer term that purports to conceptualize the totality as the generalization of the same model applicable everywhere (Casanova 2001). It is true that Casanova is dealing with literature and, as she prefers to name it, with the *République mondiale des Lettres* ('World Republic of Letters'), but she supports the idea of 'internationalization' instead of *mondialisation* because she believes that 'competition' is what characterizes the world republic of letters and not submission to a sole hegemonic model.

What is a stake here is more than just the characterization of globalization; it is even the notion itself which is being questioned. Should cultural globalization be understood as the hegemony of a single model – a 'pop culture' or a 'US model'? Should we equate cultural globalization to the two faces of the same coin, where the main tension is the local versus the global? To what extent is cultural globalization the same object of knowledge when considered from different locations and different cultural traditions? To what extent can the lived experiences of cultural phenomena be independent of their location?

Moretti's view of the 'one and unequal' cited above, does not reinforce a paradox but rather underscores the idea that globalization does not mean universal homogeneity. In this sense, inequality becomes one of the main features of globalization. This inequality is based on the existence of different locations regarding the global process: core and periphery. Recognizing these different sites works against the grain of 'Internet-views' of globalization that support the idea that locations – local or national – have become obsolete.

In this sense, there are many conflictive representations of cultural globalization. There are those who consider globalization to be a process leading to the erasure of the local; there are those who consider that globalization implies tensions between local and global but do not believe that symbolic hegemony implies the obsolescence of local traditions. There are others who see the 'glocal' or 'hybridization' as the outcomes of cultural globalization and 'fusion' – be it ideological or 'cultural' – as its trademark.

Regardless of differences in the lived experiences and notions of globalization, the specificity of today's cultural globalization or globalizations remains. Thus, if we agree that globalization/s is/are historical process/es, then the question is what makes the current version different from previous ones? And also, is the necessary previous phase of globalization the nineteenth century one? One could argue that globalization can be periodized in different ways. In this sense, it could be said that World War 1, World War 2 or the 1929 Stock Exchange Crash are revealing moments or symptoms of the tensions unleashed by global processes. On the cultural side, one could argue that the 'discovery' of African art by Modigliani, Picasso and the cosmopolitan avant-garde were also revealing moments of these global processes, at least within a World War 1 perspective. The same could be argued for international or 'global' ideologies such as Bolshevism and Fascism and one could consider the expansion of these ideologies as symptoms of globalization. In fact, many cultural and ideological tensions within current globalization can be traced to most if not all of the symptoms listed above. Even more, 'cultural industries' or 'mass culture' have their origins in these different periods, as film, radio, sound recordings, posters and other mass-culture products began to generate transnational 'world' audiences in ways that prefigured the 'global' of today. But even if we can trace many aspects of globalization – especially in cultural terms – to previous stages or phases, the question of the extent to which the contemporary version is different from previous forms remains open.

According to some scholars, cultural globalization today means the 'Americanization of the world' (García Canclini 1999) in the sense of US hegemony; others support the idea that if 'Americanization' is valid for Latin-America or some regions of Western Europe this is not the case for the whole planet; thus you could also speak of 'Japanization', 'Russification', etc. (Appadurai 1996). In most of these views, the cultural dimension of globalization is equated with the growing impact or hegemony of 'Pop Culture', especially through films, music or audio-visual production originated in the US.

In a certain sense, all discussions about globalization or 'world culture' arise from the same ambivalent place or 'structure of feeling': fear or celebration. Fear of symbolic hegemony, fear of annihilation of local and national cultures, fear of a 'one thought world', and fear in sum of the extinction of 'cultural diversity'. Celebration on the other hand of the disappearance of localisms and other forms of 'fundamentalism', celebration of the universalization of 'enlightened' values, celebration of a democratic and universal public sphere that will extinguish different claims to regionalism or localism by local or national elites as mere anachronisms.

There is also another 'place' or symbolic location in discussions about globalization; one that some analysts despise as 'The Delocalized Realm of Thinking'. Globalization has been understood as economic, demographic and informational flows (Appadurai 1996); in general, this idea is accompanied by distinctively geographical directions that show that these flows have a North–South or South–North drive depending on whether they are economic, demographic, informational or cultural in nature. Northern representations of these flows generally fail to account for the patterns of circulation within Southern regions. In other words, there are flows that are not necessarily from North to South but from 'northern south' regions to 'southern south' ones; sometimes even within the space of a nation or within Southern regions.[3] In this regard, Northern media and academia, because of their hegemonic role in global scenarios often tend to 'universalize' or make global their own colonial and post-colonial history and their national or local experience/everyday life (I have referred to this elsewhere as 'Commonwealth academic theories'). In this regard, Judith Butler's remarks regarding 'universality' are germane:

> *The question of universality arises maybe in a more critical way in those left discourses that have noted the use of the doctrine of universality at the service of colonialism and imperialism. The fear, of course, is that what has been named as universal is the provincial propriety of dominant culture, and that 'universability' is not dissociable from imperial expansion. (Butler et al. 2000: 41)*

And she asks more questions, as follows: 'What, then, is a right? What ought universality to be? How do we understand what it is to be a "human"?' As Butler herself explains it 'it is not then to answer these questions, but to permit them an opening, to provoke a political discourse that sustains the questions and shows how unknowing any democracy must be about its future.' Finally, she states: '…universality is not speakable outside of a cultural language, but its articulation does not imply that an adequate language is available. It means only that when we speak its name, we do not escape our language, although we can – and must – push the limits'. It is precisely this unspeakable outside of a cultural language that is relevant to the different scenarios out of which cultural globalization/s is thought and even more relevant to the tensions between universalism and globalization.

North–South tensions: what are they?

Conflicts or tensions between North and South have a long history that can be traced back to imperialism, but also in more recent times, to commercial negotiations in global forums. In this regard, though the North–South divide is clearly geographical, it seems to me that the geographical sites are more than just physical locations, especially if cultural or symbolic production is taken into account.

The North–South binary is also an ideological and cultural one.[4] First, because not all countries and regions thought to belong to either zone are necessarily located in those geographical locations all the time. Geographically speaking, Australia, for instance, belongs to the South, though culturally it is considered to be part of the North. To a certain extent these cases – especially, but not only Australia – appear to be 'ectopic North' societies. On the other hand, Albania or Haiti, while geographically located in the North are without doubt culturally Southern, so to speak 'ectopic South' societies.

Economic or commercial factors, though central or fundamental, are not the only ones to create this divide. Political and cultural issues are also relevant to North–South tensions . Language is one of them. Language itself and 'cultural language' (Butler) have become a battleground in which symbolic hegemony is debated. The unbalanced flow of translations (see data section), not only in literature but in scientific, technological and scholarly publications, shows that Southern production/writing is almost nonexistent in the North. Conversely, Northern production overwhelms the South. This imbalance is due to the economic, technological and scientific gaps between North and South. Such gaps do not exist with regard to artistic or cultural production, however, and this leads to another tension that arises around the very definition of artistic production. Consider the existing 'World Histories' of art, music or literature. Most of these manuals – even sophisticated scholarly publications – deal entirely with the history of European and US artistic production. Southern accounts, on the other hand, are either reproductions of Northern views or attempts to rewrite world history by inserting the periphery in world analysis.

Is this enough to assess the existence of North–South tensions? The answer to this question, as always, varies depending on who has the chance to do so. There are many scenarios, many symbolical locations from which this question can be posed.

One such location, as much symbolical as it is geographical and political, is Latin-America. José Martí's *Nuestra América* ('Our America') is a canonical, foundational text for Latin-Americans. In his poetic prose Martí warns Latin-Americans to be aware of two different dangers: first, the danger coming from within, at least from those Latin-Americans who try to rule ignoring their own realities, and second, a danger rooted that comes 'from the difference of origins, methods and interests between the two continental elements and the fact that an enterprising and pushy country that knows her but little and disdains her will soon want to establish close relations with her.' Martí fears this coming conqueror because of this ignorance and disdain. *Nuestra América* was published in 1891. In the eyes of Latin-American intellectuals, Martí foresaw what was to come in the twentieth century. At least this is the way the text has been read by the Latin-American elite through the years.[5] A similar text could have been written by an intellectual from another 'weak' country or region neighboring a powerful one; after all peripheries share common ground in worldwide power struggle.

Could such a text have been written regardless of the North–South divide? Maybe… Yet I for one strongly believe that there is a specificity to North–South tensions, at least seen from Latin-America or from powerless regions.[6] Are East–West tensions, for instance, different from North–South tensions? And if so, how different? Although I believe they are, I shall also argue that the answer depends on what we understand by East–West tensions. In different historical moments East–West tensions were supposedly ideological/political ones – capitalism versus socialism – while at other times they were religious or cultural, even racial. They were not tied mainly or necessarily to economics, although there were differences that could imply economic dimensions such as those related to the 'cultural infrastructure' or 'cultural capital': the amount and characteristics of technical and cultural apparatuses and traditions that entailed differences both in use value and in exchange value.

A second scenario is staged not just by Latin-America but the bulk of countries which are members of the Cairns Group, the G-20, IBSA or similar groupings of nation-states.[7] Or even better, by so-called 'South-South' groups that bring together countries from various regions whose positions, as Gary M. Mersham points out when discussing South African–Australian relations, 'feed into the broader South–South versus the North discourse'.[8] Here East–West tensions are erased not only culturally and geographically but mainly economically. Yet this 'South–South' scenario is very heterogeneous. This heterogeneity is different from Latin-American heterogeneity (Cornejo Polar 1994) and is mainly based on economic and productive factors. At the same time, while the economy is the fundamental cement of transnational alliances it does not override cultural differences linked to their traditions, languages and ethnicities.

In this sense, the South itself is heterogeneous. How to speak, then, of 'North–South' tensions? The tensions I am referring to here are not only – though fundamentally – the ones you can find between the 'I' or the 'eye' of the center and the 'Other' or the 'object of the ethnocentric gaze', but also the ones revealed by the extremely unequal distribution of symbolic production, in other words artistic, scientific and theoretical production. For a precise and uneven distribution of cultural labor pervades: the South is viewed by the North as the locus of 'exoticism' – from 'magical realism', to 'primitive' or 'pre -modern' cultural artifacts – as well as the site of 'alternative' or 'non-scientific' knowledge and of 'local' as opposed to 'universal' culture. Although this dichotomy may be supported by some concrete realities – most scientific activity is indeed produced in the North – it is also true that this hegemony of scientific and technological activity implies a 'brain drain' from the South towards the North (Pellegrino 2001).

It is not just the absence of acknowledgement, but a recognition that is performed by the way you 'identify' an exotic 'Other'; an identification that promotes, as Jesús Martín Barbero has observed, a strong demand for meaning. Today, identities are galvanized in their struggles by something that is inseparable from demands for acknowledgement and meaning. Neither one nor the other is to be thought of in mere economic or political terms, since both refer to the core of culture as a realm of shared *belonging*. For the Northern gaze, the South is where exotic or magical realities are produced. This entails a sort of 'invisibility' – in Hannah Arendt's sense of a lack of 'citizenship' (Lefort, 1988) – and it also implies the belief that all production that does not 'belong' to the North is just 'mimicry', not real work nor valid thought.[9]

On representations

It is precisely in the wide field of representations and symbolic production that one can observe the conflictive unevenness between North and South. Or, in other words, the tensions that can be discovered when we look at what 'North' and 'South' actually mean in different 'geo-symbolic places', in the sense illustrated by Chilean poet Vicente Huidobro's apparently incoherent line: 'The four cardinal points are three: North and South.' Written in the aftermath of World War I, this idea was shared by other Latin-American artists familiar with both Western European and North American cultural life. In 1935, Joaquín Torres García's map (Illustration 14.1) expressed a similar view.[10] His powerful and eloquent motto 'Our North is the South' was used as a title for one of the lectures he gave against Northern cultural hegemony upon his return to South America after several decades in Europe and a brief sojourn in New York.

Although Torres García's map predates [11] the world of today it can be understood as a sign of current North–South cultural tensions.[12] In his writings and paintings, the 'North' is a play on words between two different meanings: in a purely geographical sense as well as in an orientation sense. The reversal of orientation proposed by Torres García expresses his idea of putting Europe aside as a model or paradigm while refocusing Latin-American symbolic production towards itself; his motto 'Our North is the South' expresses this 'cultural turn' – this moving away from Europe or the North is a form of symbolic revolution or artistic resistance.

Current cultural globalization threatens attempts to preserve local production and liberate the South from the hegemony on cultural production exerted by Northern centers. It implicitly favors 'universalization' of rules and paradigms that determine 'valid' kinds of symbolic production. Thus, languages, memories and narratives are challenged and sometimes despised. In this regard, it is no accident that 'memory' and 'cultural patrimony' have become such salient issues of international cultural politics in recent years, especially at the level of UNESCO.

Cultural consumption could be a fruitful way of conceptualizing these conflicts, for it is not only a matter of economic exchange but also of content. Cultural products convey views and values based on ideological assumptions that are rooted in different histories and societies – in both North or South – hence global flows – and their 'glocal' aspects – reinforce pre-existing tensions at the same time as they generate new ones. Here globalization needs to be analyzed also in terms of memory versus the present. This framing would explain the emergence of new tensions in different parts of the world between on the one hand the preservation of memory, the protection of cultural patrimonies and the like, and on the other the enunciation of so-called 'universal' histories, arts and values. It also could be argued that these new tensions dominate the content or 'message' of symbolic production in many parts of the world.

Today's globalization is not really global. In Heloisa Buarque de Holanda's words (2002), there is 'a Southern side to cyberspace and academia'. This Southern side has been understood primarily as the 'locus of absence' for economic reasons: the figures on Internet and Broadband in the South speak for themselves as regard the disparity.[13] The promised 'global explosion of knowledge' through computer science and technology was indeed portrayed by former World Bank President James D. Wolfensohn (quoted by Carreón Granados 2001.) as a means to *widen* the gap between rich and poor nations: 'the promise of the era of new information – knowledge for all – can remain the most distant star in the universe'. But this gap is also related to educational and linguistic factors: 'computer illiteracy' both technical and linguistic also explains this 'Southern side of cyberspace'. A dark, despised or dispossessed side that feeds its anger on this growing gap. It is also true that there is another side within the South – that of the 'happy few' in Stendhal's terms – who celebrate and profit from globalization. And these two opposing sides reinforce social tensions that are sometimes understood as mirroring North–South tensions. The Social Forum in Sao Paulo or Caracas as well as recent violent protests in many Southern countries, including those whose protagonists hailed from the South but were living in Europe – especially during the urban riots in France of late 2005 – show the significant fault line within globalization along the North–South axis.

Illustration 14.1 Our North and South

Joaquín Torres García, 1943 (artist)

The gap in access to new global technology is not the only element fueling North–South tensions. Neither is it the lack of acknowledgement nor the predetermined place that the North accords the South in terms of expression and representation. The predetermined place of the South implies a sort of Orientalist vision that because of the hegemony of Northern media representational power leaves no alternative to the South but that of so-called mimicry, hybridization, fusion, or local and regional 'fundamentalism'.

None of these options, all of which are present in contemporary art and academia, are foreign to the ongoing tensions between North and South; at least from a Southern point of view. It is also true, as García Canclini (1995) has said, that there is a growing though partial dialogue among artists and scholars from both sides of the fault line.[14] Some of these dialogues are considered or analyzed as an opportunity to celebrate postmodern times. On the other hand, there are those (for example, Monsonyi) who consider these postmodern dialogues as an expression of neo-liberalism and thus something to be fiercely resisted; others, like Daniel Mato, argue in favor of 'globalization from below' as a way to resist cultural hegemony by the Northern version of globalization. Martín Hopenhayn has analyzed these different views of globalization in Latin-America as part of the ongoing struggle over cultural and social transformations in the region. He stresses the 'gaps between material and symbolic integration in the new phase of Latin-American modernization; the field of cultural industries as central to the dispute over cultural integration and hegemony; the symbolic asymmetries of cultural globalization and the problems of cultural integration/subordination supposed by them.' (Hopenhayn 2001:77, my translation).

Finally, given that the Northern countries represent less than 20 percent of world population while the rest of the world is overrun by Western cultural products[15] we can understand the challenges that globalization poses to Southern countries today, in particular for those whose 'native languages' are far from hegemonic. And by 'native language' I do not refer only to English, French or any other of the widely spoken tongues, but also to language in a wider sense, as a set of tools to produce and understand life and society. It is precisely these 'languages' or sets of tools which allow representation in the twin senses of being a way to portray oneself or one's society or culture and a way to speak for oneself or one's society/culture.

There is extensive official concern in international fora such as UNESCO with the challenge of redressing unbalanced cultural flows. There are also efforts by regional fora in the South, such as the Ibero-American Summit, to counter some of these asymmetries. These efforts will not erase or solve the current cultural tensions: they are in fact their most visible symptoms.

Notes

1 Even if you do not take the Arab expansion into account, recent claims by Chinese scholars date the first world map to the beginning of the fifteenth century – well ahead of Europe's so-called 'voyages of discovery'.

2 See for instance the ways in which *The New York Times* or *El Mercurio* (Chile), *La Nación* (Argentina) reported 'world news' at the end of the nineteenth century.

3 Northern scholars analyzing migrations tend to 'forget' or not see the sorts of South–South phenomena discussed by Leo Estrada and Alejandro Grimson further on in this volume.

4 At a certain level, North–South divisions can be found within 'North' and 'South', in other words not only within regions or continents but also within countries: compare for instance what 'North' means culturally or economically in Brazil, South Africa, Italy or the US. The connotations are quite different.

5 This a long tradition running from José Martí to Eduardo Galeano, Commandante Marcos and most of today's Latin-American intelligentsia.

6 The question of language is also relevant in these tensions, particularly because of the hegemony of Northern languages and, more to the point, the hegemony of English, not only in communication but also in the social sciences and other fields. (See a forthcoming volume by Renato Ortiz on this topic).

7 IBSA stands for India, Brazil and South Africa. The G-20 grouping currently includes Argentina, Bolivia, Brazil, Chile, China, Cuba, Egypt, India, Indonesia, Mexico, Nigeria, Pakistan, Paraguay, Philippines, South Africa, Thailand, Tanzania, Venezuela and Zimbabwe. The Cairns Group is made up of Argentina, Australia, Bolivia, Brazil, Canada, Chile, Colombia, Costa Rica, Guatemala, Indonesia, Malaysia, New Zealand, Paraguay, Philippines, South Africa, Thailand and Uruguay (the inclusion of Canada may differentiate it from the other two groups).

8 Mersham also points out that the Non-Aligned Movement, together with UNCTAD (United Nations Conference on Trade and Development) and the G-77 (The Group of 77 is the largest Third World coalition in the United Nations) are seen by states as bulwarks against the creeping disempowerment and disenfranchisement of the South. Since the world is no longer polarized between East and West, the cleavage between rich and poor is now more pronounced than ever. The Non-Aligned Movement 'is therefore one of the primary arteries capable of infusing fresh blood into South–South cooperation' (Le Pere 1997: 5, in Mersham, 2005).

9 In this sense 'mimicry' – as Homi Bhabha has described it, though I do not completely agree with him – is emblematic of the division of labor between North and South: the role of the South is not to produce meaning but to imitate; at least according to some scholars speaking from the North.

10 Though they are close there is a difference between Huidobro and Torres García. In 1932 Huidobro expressed in his manifest 'Total': 'Enough with your wars … The North against the South, the South against the North' (Huidobro *Obra selecta*, 337; my translation).

11 There are different versions of Torres García's map. The first one is from 1935, while the one shown here is from 1943. In his essay, 'The School of the South' of February 1935 Torres García argues the following: 'A great School of Art should rise up here in our country. I say it without any hesitation: *here in our country*. And I have my reasons for affirming it. I have said School of the South; because in reality, *our north is the South*. There should be no north, for us, except in opposition to our South. Therefore right now we're turning the map upside down, and thus now we have a just idea of our position, and not one that the whole World wants us to have. The tip of America, from now on, extending itself, persistently points to the South, our north. Likewise our compass: it unpardonably always slants towards the South, towards our North Pole. When the ships leave from here, they continue downwards instead of upward. Because the north is now underneath. And the east, facing our new south, is on our left. This rectification was necessary; in this way now we know where we are' (italics by Torres García 1944: 213).

12 Various scholars (García Canclini, Yúdice, among many others) have proposed explicitly or implicitly the idea of several waves of globalization; some of them have even proposed that the first was initiated by the voyage of Christoper Columbus in 1492.

13 Topics discussed at the UN's 'International Summit on Information' held in Tunisia in November 2005 included the informatics gap as well as the debate on who should 'govern' the Internet.

14 See El diálogo norte-sur en los estudios culturales., Néstor García Canclini and also Daniel Mato.

15 Though it must be recognized that the reception of these products is influenced by local conditions and is never mechanical or passive.

REFERENCES

Appadurai, Arjun (1996) *Modernity at Large: Cultural Dimensions of Globalization*. Minneapolis: University of Minnesota Press.

Bhabha, Homi K. (1994) *The Location of Culture*. London and New York: Routledge.

Braudel, Fernand (1967) *Civilisation matérielle et capitalisme. XVe-XVIIIe siècle*. Paris: A. Colin.

Brennan, Timothy (2003) 'The Empire's new clothes', *Critical Inquiry*, Vol. 29, 2.

Buarque de Holanda, Heloisa (2002) 'La academia al sur del cyberspace', in Hugo Achugar and Sonia D'Alessandro (eds), *Saberes locales/saberes globales*. Montevideo: Trilce.

Butler, Judith, Laclau, Ernesto and Zizek, Slavoj (2000) *Contingency, Hegemony, Universality: Contemporary Dialogues on the Left*. London, New York: Verso.

Carreón Granados, Juan José (2001) 'América Latina e Internet: avances recientes' in (http://www.comminit.com/la/pensamientoestrategico/lasth/lasld-740.html)

Casanova, Pascale (2001) *La República mundial de las Letras*. Barcelona: Editorial Anagrama.

Cornejo Polar, Antonio (1994) *Escribir en el aire. Ensayo sobre la heterogeneidad socio cultural en las literaturas andinas*. Lima: Editorial Horizonte.

García Canclini, Néstor (1995) 'El diálogo norte-sur en los estudios culturales' in *Consumidores y ciudadanos: conflictos multiculturales de la globalización*. México: Grijalbo.

– (1999) *La globalización imaginada*. Buenos Aires: Paidós.

Goethe, J.W. (1984) *Conversations with Eckerman (1823–1832)*. Trans. by John Oxenford. San Francisco: North Point Press.

Gruzinski, S. (2000) *El pensamiento mestizo*. Barcelona: Paidos Ibérica.

Hopenhayn, Martín (junio de 2001) '¿Integrarse o subordinarse? Nuevos cruces entre política y cultura' in *Estudios latinoamericanos sobre cultura y transformaciones sociales en tiempos de globalización*. Daniel Mato (comp.) Buenos Aires: FLACSO.

Huidobro, Vicente (1989) 'Total' en *Obra selecta*. Caracas: B. Ayacucho. pp. 336–7.

Lefort, C. (1988) 'Hannah Arendt and the Questions of the Political' in *Democracy and Political Theory* (trans. by David Macey). Minneapolis: University of Minnesota Press. pp. 50–1.

Martí, José (1977). 'Nuestra América' en *Nuestra América de José Martí*. Prólogo de Juan Marinello, Cronología de Cintio Vitier. Edición y notas de Hugo Achugar. Caracas: Biblioteca Ayacucho.

Martín Barbero, Jesús (2002) 'La globalización en clave cultural: una mirada latinoamericanna' in *2002 Bogues. Globalisme et pluralismo. Colloque International*. Montreal, April 22–7.

Marx, Karl (1848) *The Communist Manifesto*: annotated text; prefaces by Marx and Engels; edited by Frederic L. Bender, New York: W.W. Norton, 1988.

Mato, Daniel 'Des-fetichizar la 'globalización': basta de reduccionismos, apologías y demonizaciones, mostrar la complejidad y las prácticas de los actores' in http://www.globalcult.org.ve/pub/Clacso2/mato.pdf (accessed 9/25/05).

Mersham, Gary (2005) 'Australia and South Africa: neighbours or strangers in the South' http://www.arts.uwa.edu.au/Mots Pluriels/MP1300gm.html (accessed 9/25/2005).

Monsonyi, Esteban (1982) *Identidad nacional y culturas popularesl*. Caracas: Editorial La Enseñanza nueva.

Moretti, Franco (2000) 'Conjectures on world literature', *New Left Review*, 1, January–February, 54–68.

– (2003) 'More conjectures', *New Left Review*, 20, March–April, 77–81.

Ortiz, Renato (1997) *Mundialización y Cultura*. Buenos Aires: Alianza.

Pellegrino, Adela (2001) 'Trends in Latin American skilled migration: brain drain or brain exchange?', *International Migration*, 39 (5), 111–32.

Said, Edward (1994) *Orientalism*. New York: Vintage Books.

Torres García, Joaquín (1944) *Universalismo constructivo: Contribución a la unificación del arte y la cultura de América*. Buenos Aires: Editorial Poseidón.

Wallerstein, Immanuel (1974) *The Modern World System: Capitalist Agriculture and the Origins of the European World Economy in the Sixteenth Century*. New York: Academic Press.

World Bank (http://siteresources.worldbank.org/INTGEP2005/Resources/overviewspan.pdf) (accessed 9/27/ 2005).

THE WEST VERSUS THE ARAB WORLD: DECONSTRUCTING THE DIVIDE

Georges Corm

The main geo-political and historical roots of the sense of divide existing between the Arab world and the West do not originate in any kind of clash of religious and cultural differences of an essential nature, but come rather from the different historical traumas suffered by Europe and the Arab world, both in their own specific history and in their thorny historical relations. Any attempt to reduce tensions should first recognize these different traumas. Too often in the media and the academic world different religious arguments are advocated to analyze purely political issues. It is only by recognizing the complex historical plight suffered by both groups that hostility and tensions can be diffused and reduced. This requires restraint in the media and the academic world, so that the political changes needed on both sides of the divide to reduce tensions and clashes can be encouraged.

Introduction: globalization and the resurrection of mega-identities

The nineteenth century and the first half of the twentieth were dominated by the nation-state system and the secular nationalisms associated with it. But the Cold War recreated the forgotten sense of belonging to what could be called a mega-identity structure, as the Soviet bloc and the Western democracies confronted each other, with their respective institutions[1] and ideologies[2] in a hostile face-off. Such a confrontation between groups of diverse societies and nations had not been seen since the end of the Middle Ages, when Christendom and Islam constituted two different and opposed worlds. Its modern reincarnation was the East/West confrontation.

As the Soviet bloc crumbled in 1989, a major power vacuum emerged in the international system. However, contrary to optimistic expectations, the generalization of the democratic system based on the rule of law and the respect for individual human rights did not take place.[3] Rather, what emerged was a new divide between the 'Muslim' World (centered on the Arab countries) and the 'Judeo-Christian' World. This divide has become central in international relations. It has been constructed on various old and new cultural and historical backgrounds belonging to the respective new mega-identities.[4] Globalized communications augment the perception of threat on both sides of the divide, as epitomized by Samuel Huntingon's 'clash of civilizations' thesis based on religious identity.[5] Recently, President George Bush has lent credibility to the Huntingtonian vision by describing what he sees as an all-out war in which the United States is pitted against Islamic militants supposedly attempting to establish a radical Muslim empire from Indonesia to Spain, with the aim of destroying 'civilization'.[6]

This chapter will attempt to deconstruct the mutual feelings of hostility between the Arab World, Europe's next-door neighbor, and the Western world, whose self-definitions allude increasingly to Judeo-Christian values. It is to be hoped that uncovering the roots of hostility and fear may contribute to easing the tensions now being fueled by most official political discourse.

Israel in the perspective of radically different historical traumas

All too often, Western decision-makers presume that Arab public opinion has the same feelings and emotions concerning key issues in international affairs as Westerners do. In so doing, they forget that the Arabs (as well as people in other non-Western nations, whether Muslim or non-Muslim), have not experienced the same historical traumas and have been only indirectly exposed to European history. These traumas should be clearly identified because they continue to influence considerably the 'Western' view on the conduct of world affairs, particularly in the Middle East.

The terrible Wars of Religion between Catholics and Protestants were one of the first European traumas of modern times, followed later by the explosion of secular nationalisms and the conflicts that devastated Europe, culminating in the two

World Wars.[7] Narrow nationalism and anti-Semitism grew together in European culture.[8] The Zionist Movement, launched at the end of the nineteenth century, was a reaction to this monstrous alliance.[9] And when the horrors of the Nazi incarnation of European anti-Semitism were fully revealed at the end of World War II, it was understandable at that Europeans were convinced that the Jews should be given a State of their own in Palestine as a compensation for the tragic fate of the European Jewish communities.[10]

The Arabs and other non-Western peoples who were not exposed to the same trauma could not develop the same kind of political culture and sentiment. There is no way the Arabs could ever feel the same emotions about the Israeli endeavor as a European or an American does. Of course individuals may develop considerable sympathy for the suffering of the Jews during World War II. But the Arabs and other non-Western nations cannot collectively respond in any comparable way to this very specific European trauma.

Long-standing European historical traumas vis-à-vis the Arab East

Europeans have accumulated a succession of historical traumas in their relations with their Arab and Muslim neighbors. Chief among them has been the fear of Muslim invasion and domination, as occurred first when the Arabs conquered Spain, Sicily and Southern Italy and later when the Ottoman Turks conquered the Balkans and Hungary and twice set siege to Vienna, the capital of the Habsburg Empire. These old traumas were refreshed and aggravated when, under the pressure of guerrilla movements and armed resistance, Europe was forced to relinquish its colonial possessions in the Arab and Muslim world. And in relation to the Christian-Jewish trauma mentioned above, is there not a clear link between implicit or explicit Western support for the expansionist settlement policies of the State of Israel in what remains of Palestinian land and memories of the Crusades that failed to secure the permanent settlement of European Christians in the Arab East?[11] And isn't nostalgia for lost French or British colonial possessions involved as well?

As regards the invasion of Iraq by the United States, Britain and the symbolic battalions of a few other Western countries, one could also argue that the old historical background is still an active, albeit unconscious factor in shaping Western policies in the Arab East. This is not to deny the existence of other geo-political factors that motivated President Bush (the control of oil, the security of Israel, the encirclement of China, etc.), but might help to understand why this invasion took place in spite of massive popular opposition and the condemnation of the Pope. Controlling the Arab East and controlling Islam are dreams anchored in the unconscious that has shaped the Western mega-identity. And reverse traumas are to be found in the Arab East.

Arab historical traumas

The Arabs for their part have entirely different historical traumas. For centuries, they lived in a state of peace within various non-Arab empires (first the Mamluks and then the Ottomans). While they lost their political power at the beginning of the tenth century, they were not exposed to either invasion or war after the end of the Crusades and the Mongol invasions. Although tensions certainly existed among various different Muslim creeds, the Arab lands remained at peace except for minor internecine wars between feudal lords. Relations between Kurds, Berbers and Arabs were multisecular and did not pose specific problems. Relations between Muslims and non-Muslims, namely Christians and Jews of Arab or Berber or Spanish origin were not characterized by violence, except very sporadically and locally. There was no displacement of population, no genocide, no systematic persecution as was the case in Europe since the beginning of the Wars of Religion.

The Arab trauma was in fact created by European colonial policies (the invasion of Algeria beginning in 1830; the invasion of Egypt in 1882; the troubles between the Maronites and the Druze in Mount Lebanon between 1840 and 1861 because of the confrontation between the British and the French empires).[12] Arabs witnessed the crumbling of their protector, the Ottoman Empire, in the face of the greed of the colonial powers, their rivalries over how to divide up the Arab lands among themselves and influence the different religious and ethnic communities. The trauma was amplified by the creation of Israel in 1948. Arab decision-makers and public opinion could not understand why Palestinians should be evicted from their ancestral land to compensate for

Jewish suffering in Europe, in which they had played no part. In their view, such compensation, if it were to consist of territory that would become exclusively Jewish, should take place in Europe and not in Palestine, where the holy sites of the three monotheistic religions are located and where the local Jewish communities had always lived at peace with their Muslim and Christian neighbors.

In relation to Palestine, as the Arabs had absorbed so many different types of migrants in their history, public opinion could have accepted individual Jewish migration. The historical reference for the Arabs was not an homogeneous nationalist State of the German or the French type; rather it was a pluralistic society organized along the lines of the Ottoman *millet* system, under which different religious or ethnic groups coexisted; each religious community was autonomous in managing its own civil affairs (education, marriage, inheritance, religious endowments or *wakfs*). Lebanon was cited as an example of the modernization of the *millet* system and served as a basis for the functioning of a parliamentary system along the liberal European model of consociative democracy.[13]

Hence the idea of a State exclusively based on one religion in Palestine appeared totally irrational and inconsistent with Arab social and cultural historical experience in religious and ethnic pluralism. Displacing the Palestinian people to realize the Jewish National Home in Palestine appeared unfair, unjust and politically unacceptable.

The recent invasion of Iraq by the United States and its allies has not only revived the trauma of the occupation of Arab land by the European colonial powers; it has also revived other, older historical traumas such as the Crusader invasions of the Arab East or the expulsion of the Arabs from Spain (*Al Andalus*) and Southern Europe. This dramatic and painful event has reinforced the feeling that the divide between the Arab East and the West is in fact permanent. It has caused Westerners to be seen as essentially hostile to the Arabs, interested above all in dominating them. Moreover, the Arabs feel that the West wants full control of Arab oil in its own strategic interest.

Why the West assumes that Arabs are anti-semitic

The Arab attitude vis-à-vis Israel is not well understood by many in the West who, influenced by their own traumatic experience of anti-Semitism, tend to believe that the Arab so-called rejection of Israel is the result of a deeply rooted local anti-Semitism and that it should be repressed and suppressed by all means available, including wars such as those waged by the State of Israel in 1948, 1956, 1967 or 1982, with the invasion of Lebanon, or by the re-occupation of large tracts of the West Bank and Gaza in 2001, or the invasion of Iraq by the United States. Moreover, Western governments tend to pressurize Arab officials, intellectuals and civil society organizations to fight this 'local' variant of anti-Semitism. In spite of the fact that Israel still occupies Arab and Palestinian territories in violation of UN resolutions, Western decision-makers persist in pressuring Arab governments to establish diplomatic and economic relations with it. What is more, these officials, whether American or European, are imprisoned in an implicit or unconscious prejudice: guided by their own history, through which so many forced displacements of populations took place, they do not understand why the Palestinians should stick so hard to their land and why they insist on the right of return.[14] After all, in Europe, the displacement of populations had long been a solution to many intractable problems. This was the case during the Wars of Religion, from which emerged the famous Westphalian principle *cujus regio, ejus religio*, as well as during various nationalist wars of territorial expansion in the nineteenth century, culminating in the two World Wars. The design of new national borders after 1945 provoked the displacement of millions of Europeans. As for North and South America, the large-scale displacement and shrinking of native populations was at the heart of the modern history of both. This we believe is the reason why the Israelis as well as parts of Western public opinion cannot understand why the Palestinians do not simply migrate and settle in neighboring Arab countries, so as to enable the Middle East to live in peace at last.

Why some Arabs see Western support for Israel as a continuation of the Crusades

On the other hand, many Arabs and Palestinians are puzzled by the moral pressure brought to bear on them by the West. It is as if the latter wants them to regard Israel as a normal and peaceful country simply addressing its problems of security and terrorism, as if the occupation of Palestinian land did not exist. Against this, what the Arabs see is prolonged occupation and the suffering of Arab populations in the West Bank, Gaza and the Golan Heights, as well as the continuous expansion of settlements in the occupied territories, in addition to three Israeli invasions of Lebanese territory (one of which lasted for 22 years). They cannot understand what logic can justify depriving them of their ancestral land where they have lived since Biblical times or depriving Palestinians who have been refugees for the last 40 years of any right of return, while any citizen from any country in the world can migrate to the same territory, provided he can prove his Jewish origin.

Naturally, Arab public opinion tends to rationalize the Western bias vis-à-vis Israel in the light of the last two historical traumas – the Crusades and colonialism. For the vast majority, who have no detailed understanding of the history of Europe and its traumas, the emergence of Israel and the support it receives can be explained only as a new colonial and religious Crusade. This perception is reinforced by the fact that the Western powers do not implement the universal values contained in international law fairly in the region.

Credibility and double standards in the Middle East

This existence of double standards is the second issue on which Arab and Western public opinion can only diverge and which must be seriously debated. Unfortunately, however, most Western decision-makers do not grasp the destabilizing impact of the misuse of international law and the United Nations in the management of the Middle Eastern conflicts. These double standards are apparent in the following areas:

On Palestine and Israel

- The large number of US vetos on draft resolutions presented to the UN Security Council that condemned Israel for violent and disproportionate acts of reprisal against Lebanon (invasion in 1978 and 1982) or against the Palestinians in the occupied territories.
- The non-implementation of Security Council resolutions asking Israel to withdraw from occupied territories (the opposite was true when Iraq occupied Kuwait).
- No international sanctions have ever been adopted against Israel (except when the European Union barred products from Israeli settlements in the occupied territories) , while so many sanctions have been applied against other countries (Rhodesia, South Africa, Argentina, Libya, Sudan, Iraq, China and Russia during the Cold War).
- While the international community has provided military protection to suffering populations as in the case of Namibia, East Timor, Bosnia or Kosovo, nothing of the sort has been envisaged for the Palestinians, despite their suffering over the last 75 years.
- Contrary to what happened in other places (Chechnya, East Timor, Bosnia, Sri-Lanka,[15] South Africa, etc.), resistance to occupation doesn't appear to be recognized as legitimate either on the part of Palestinians, or on the part of the Lebanese in resistance to the Israeli occupation of large parts of South Lebanon between 1978 and 2000. In both cases, the occupied population has in fact been asked not to resist.
- In 1947–1950 the United Nations produced the best possible compromise on the Palestinian issue between universal values and principles embodied in modern secular international law on the one hand, and the need in the Western view to create *ex-nihilo* a state for Jews on the other hand. This compromise included, *inter alia*, the right of return or compensation for Palestinians evicted from their ancestral land and the need to make Jerusalem an open international city, since its many holy places belong to the three monotheistic faiths. This international legislation appears to have been forgotten in the West. In sharp contrast, UN resolutions on Iraq were promptly implemented and backed by military force, including the economic embargo that created so much civilian suffering.
- The policies of the UN Atomic Energy Agency are firmly implemented with regard to Arab countries and Iran but not as regards Israel; policies concerning weapons of mass destruction are only applied to Arab countries (and, as is well known, it turned out that Iraq in fact had none).
- When Security Council resolution 1559 recently ordered Syrian troops to withdraw from

Lebanon, international pressure was put on the two governments to implement it forthwith. Although most of the Lebanese are rightly satisfied to see their country free of the Syrian military presence, how can we forget that Security Council resolution (425) of 1978 asking Israel to withdraw its army from the south of Lebanon was implemented only 22 years later and that only as a result of the armed resistance of Lebanese to Israel? The same could be said of the 1982 resolution demanding all foreign forces to leave Lebanon after the invasion of Lebanon by Israel. More recently, under the pretext of resolution 1559, the whole of Lebanon has again been targeted by Israel, together with a maritime and air blockade, in reprisal for the kidnapping of two Israeli soldiers by Hezbollah. This has led to massive destruction of Lebanese civilian infrastructure and tragic loss of innocent lives. This is a repetition of its major aggression of 1982 under the pretext of eradicating Palestinian terrorists operating from southern Lebanon.

Arab public opinion perforce concludes that for most Western decision-makers international law does not have to be enforced on the State of Israel, but only on the Arab States, as if they implicitly believe either that Israel is always right in its military actions, or that the specificity of this State and its historical origins justify the waiving of internationally-agreed principles and values, including those embodied in the Geneva Convention and in numerous UN provisions for the settlement of the Arab/Israeli conflict. The recent ruling of the International Court of Justice that the separation wall being built by Israel on Palestinian land is totally illegal[16] has already been forgotten by Western decision-makers and, unfortunately, by all Arab governments as well. The construction of the wall continues unabated.

On Iraq

- In response to the Iraqi invasion of Kuwait, a military force under a UN resolution went to war, whereas no other military invasion anywhere in the world during the last decades has been dealt with this way.
- The economic embargo of Iraq, again under UN auspices, was one of the cruelest acts of the international community. It savagely punished the Iraqi population, mainly children, while reinforcing the grip of the dictator. In spite of the fact that Kuwait had been liberated from the Iraqi army a few months after its occupation, this cruel embargo was maintained until the US-led invasion of Iraq.
- North Korea, although it has acknowledged that it is developing nuclear weapons, has never received the same harsh treatment as Iraq, either politically or militarily.
- There have been, and still are, many terrible dictators in the world, but never – with the exception of the tiny island of Grenada invaded by the United States in 1983 – has a major Western power invaded a country to liberate its population from oppression or to search for weapons of mass destruction (whose existence was in any case questionable, as we now know).
- No link has been proven to exist between the Iraqi regime and Al Qaeda terrorist group. True, there was an alliance between this group and the Taliban regime in Afghanistan, but nothing of the sort regarding Iraq.
- As in Palestine, the right to resist a foreign occupation is denied by the United States and all its Middle Eastern policy sympathizers.

To convince the Arabs that Western decision-makers are fair in their management of the international system and earnest in preaching democratic values to the Middle Eastern countries, there should be a fair and just implementation of international law and of UN decisions and body of laws on all concerned countries.

The practice of such double standards destroys the credibility of the democratic values that are so badly needed in the Middle East. If there is to be a stable regional order in the Middle East, the core principles and values embodied in international law must be implemented consistently with regard to every country. But many Western decision-makers do not even appear to be aware of the double standards they practice in this part of the world. This is one of the biggest threats to the future of international peace, for it leads Arab public opinion to consider that the 'West' merely manipulates general principles of law and justice against the legitimate interests of the people of the region. A minority Arab radical fraction is thus reinforced in its belief that Muslims should reject all modern political principles originating in the philosophy of the European Enlightenment. This same fraction preaches the most rigid of the many interpretations of the Koran dating back to the time when the world was effectively divided between Christendom and Islam.

Muslim double standards

By exactly the same token, the reluctance of many governments in the Islamic world to recognize the importance of key ethical and political standards promotes the growing sentiment in the West of a civilizational 'clash' with the Arab and Muslim world. Respect for minorities, gender equality, freedom of expression, freedom of creed and to change religion, judicial guarantees against arbitrary arrest and imprisonment, are key values that originated in the Enlightenment but have all become universal, accepted by people throughout the world. Unfortunately, the human rights record of the Arab world in the last 50 years has been very negative and political liberalization has been slow and superficial.

To make things worse, secular Arab nationalism has been embodied by political parties of the Nasserist and Baathist type with a very poor record in terms of human rights. Arab nationalism has failed to secure order, stability and freedom in the Arab region, while various kinds of fundamental Islam that have tried to replace it have also failed. The so-called 'Islamic revival' has produced various forms of cultural alienation from the modern world, as well as the creation of an international entity based on religion (the Organization of the Islamic Conference) which comprises countries with large Muslim populations. The OIC has adopted an Islamic Declaration of Human Rights which is not really compatible with the Universal Declaration.[17]

In fact, this 'revival' encouraged as a tool to fight the extension of various forms of Marxist ideology, takes a closed view of the world, creating an artificial feeling of deep division between Muslims and non-Muslims. Many components of this revival have degenerated into violent political movements opposing both Western culture and local political systems. This violence, exported first to Europe and then to the United States in 2001, is largely responsible for aggravating the divide between the Arab World and the West.

Moreover, a few regimes (Saudi Arabia, Sudan, Pakistan – a non-Arab country – and the late Taliban regime in Afghanistan – also non-Arab) implement Islamic law according to the strictest and most rigid criteria:[18] gender inequality, physical punishment, forced separation of the sexes in all aspects of public life, refusal to acknowledge liberal and modernized interpretations of the Koran. This contributes to creating a very negative image of Islam in public opinion worldwide, thus increasing the divide, although many other Arab regimes do not implement Islamic *Sharia* in this brutal way.

How to bridge the divide?

The need to go back to a coherent secular view of the world

The simplistic traditional view established by European philosophy and sociology is that democracy and individualism originate exclusively in Judeo-Christian monotheism. It is however rather simplistic to differentiate Islam from the two other monotheistic faiths and consider it alien to the values produced by the latter. Islam too is a monotheistic faith originating in the same Biblical roots that are fully acknowledged and honored in the Koran. Western secularism and recognition of individual rights originate in the cruel and extended religious wars between the Church of Rome and the various protestant creeds that contested its autocratic and monopolistic rule, as well as in the English, American and French revolutions. In the Islamic world, there was no Church to impose its control on political matters; rulers were always laymen free of the tutelage of a religious establishment.[19] Secularism as it emerged in European history has no historical meaning in a non-European context, whether Muslim or Buddhist or Hindu. However, the most hotly debated issue in the Arab and Islamic worlds is the extent to which the text of the Koran and its well-established interpretations can evolve and adapt to new economic and social conditions. This issue was actually debated in the first centuries of Islam before being abandoned. It has been reopened during the last 150 years concomitantly with institutional and political modernization, but Muslim conservative movements reject any evolution of this kind.[20] They focus largely in fact on non-political issues such as the restriction of women's rights, polygamy, adultery, etc. On the political front, their views are geared to promoting Jihad against the infidels, i.e., any Muslim or non-Muslim who does not adhere to their rigorist approach to Islam. The various Israeli occupations as well as the invasions of Afghanistan and Iraq lend credibility to their call for Jihad against the 'new Crusaders'. Unfortunately, as secular Arab nationalism has failed, the Jihadist call to fight the occupation of Arab land by Western infidels is the only current expression of nationalist anger.

The key issue here is the way, in a certain historical context, political decision-makers can misuse religion to encourage conflicts and wars, while the same religion can inspire the highest moral values in a setting that encourages peace and development. Suffice it to recall that 50 years ago secularism was a universal value, even in the developing countries. The Non-Aligned Movement in its heyday of the 1960s and 1970s never made any allusion to moral or religious values in explaining the differences between the developed and the developing worlds.

It is also to be remembered that secularism is a basic principle of modern democracy and political life. It should be so in international life as well. International law cannot be subverted by religious or ethical considerations; it should remain secular, based on humanitarian principles that have developed since the sixteenth century. Unfortunately, since religion was heavily mobilized against the Soviet Union and socialist or Marxist segments of public opinion during the last phase of the Cold War, secularism appears to be on the retreat everywhere.[21] Discussions are now heavily focused on religious revivals in different parts of the world. So-called conflicting Islamic or Judeo-Christian values are in the foreground for most people and top the political agendas internationally.

For a moratorium on discussing Islam in the West

The pervasiveness of this discussion is an enormous obstacle to clear thinking about the real political issues at stake. In our view, what is really needed today for positive dialogue to take place on the historical and legal issues underpinning them is self-restraint, or a kind of self-imposed and voluntary moratorium on discussion of the religious issues. In reality, current dialogue all too often solidifies existing sentiments and positions and thus deepens the artificial sense of a clash of religious values. What is urgently needed is a common attempt to grasp real objective issues within the secular framework of Enlightenment values and principles – all of which had a major impact in the Middle East after the French Revolution, leading Arab, Iranian and Turkish clerics and intellectuals to adopt most of them in the nineteenth century.[22] The diffusion of these principles to broader segments of the population was hindered by the colonialist excesses of the French and the British, which contradicted the principles they preached. Conservative elements in our Arab societies were thus reinforced in their opposition to adopting and adapting these values locally.[23]

Conditions are similar today. The Western powers preach democracy, reform and the rule of law, but their behavior in the region directly or indirectly contradicts these basic principles. Secularists and democrats in the region are thus looked upon with suspicion by conservative or Muslim radical fundamentalists; in addition, they are not considered sufficiently representative by Western decision-makers or the media who always prefer to dialogue with or speak to conservative religious personalities or tribal chiefs. Moreover, some of the latter have abandoned any critical view of US policies in the region and are vocal critics of secular Arab nationalism, which is considered to be old-fashioned and to have inspired autocratic regimes. This attitude denies them a solid popular base in their own countries: the more they are admired and promoted in the Western media, the more they are looked upon with suspicion by their own people.

A code of conduct for media and academic research

The presentation of the confrontation between the West and the Arab world by the media – and by academic researchers popular with the media – needs to be changed. Stereotyping and cliché-mongering should be more closely monitored. This is valid for both the Arab media and the Western media. A good example of media misuse is the way the issue of the Islamic veil in France has been dealt with on both sides of the divide. On the Western side, whether French or not, the issue is dealt with in a highly politicized way; secularists and multiculturalists have entered into furious battles between themselves and have used young Muslim girls or Muslim intellectuals to approve or disapprove of the very restricted measure taken by the French government to ban the wearing of any religious sign in the public school system. The American press attacked the French government as if it was taking revenge for the French disapproval of the war in Iraq. The Arab media were no better. They confused their audiences by not explaining that the veil ban was restricted to government schools, letting ordinary Arabs believe that the veil was banned everywhere. This contributed to the general atmosphere of hostility. Western and Arab media did not care to report to the public the very lively and democratic debate that took place within and around the work of a special Commission appointed by the French Government to explore the issue in consultation with various interested parties (students, parents, teachers, and religious institutions). The media mishandling was as big in the West as it was in the Arab East and incited many demonstrations and rallies against the French decision in the streets of Paris and many Arab capitals, including Baghdad. The same mishandling is apparent with regard to the nuclear issue. For years, media talked about the 'Islamic' bomb when reporting on Pakistan's efforts.[24] Would anybody have ever termed the Western nuclear arsenal 'Christian' or called the Israel nuclear capability 'Jewish'?

Self-restraint should be promoted in the media so that religion is not implicitly or explicitly mixed up with political issues.[25] If certain violent radical and anarchist groups in Arab countries pretend to act on the basis of Islam does this necessarily imply that Islam as a religion is the culprit? Did anybody in the Western media accuse the Christian faith or the Marxist view of history as responsible for the violent anarchists or leftist movements or for the violence of the IRA or the Basque ETA movement in Spain?[26]

And academic research should not focus exclusively on radical anarchist movements advocating Islam or on the rigid and dogmatic expressions of the Islamic creed advocated by fundamentalist movements. Instead, it should try to give a full view of the intellectual life in the Arab East. More translations of books written in Arabic by eminent Muslim reformists or by Arab secular nationalists of both yesterday and today should be made available to Western readers.

After all, the world is now confronted with a resurgence of fundamentalism in religious faith. This phenomenon is not a monopoly of Muslim societies. Islamic fundamentalism is paid much greater attention because of the violent acts committed by anarchist groups advocating Islam, but people forget that many more acts of terrorism are perpetrated *within* the Arab world or in countries such as Indonesia and Pakistan than in the West. Furthermore, the Arab East itself is devastated by conflicts and wars and its huge oil reserves are a magnet for the interference of the major powers.

The Arab media and academic researchers also need to heed the lesson of self-restraint. They should cease to treat the 'West' as a single unified bloc that wants to dominate the Muslim East at any price. More focus should be placed on intellectual trends in the West that have strongly condemned colonialism and more recently the invasion of Iraq and that support the legitimate rights of the Palestinians. Western secularism needs also to be discussed more objectively. It is high time that the history of secularism is properly explained in the Arab and Muslim world. The recent wave of Muslim fundamentalism has propagated the idea that secularism is equal to atheism and thus antagonistic to Islam, and that the West wants to impose it on Muslim believers so as to dilute the strength of Islam. This simplistic view should be confronted, and secularism should be explained as having been the solution to endless religious wars in European history and the means to promote democracy and individual rights without suppressing religion and religious liberty. Properly understood and adapted to the historical background and specific problems of Arab societies, secularism could ease many internal tensions within them, where different kinds of Islam must coexist (Syria, Iraq, Lebanon, Saudi Arabia, Kuwait, Bahrain, Yemen) or where Christians and Muslims must live together (Egypt, Sudan, Lebanon, Syria and Iraq). Secularism might also become an appropriate solution in the future for a bi-national State or federated State in Palestine/Israel where Jews, Christians and Muslims could live peacefully side by side.

An additional key issue to be addressed in the Arab media is the growing view that the Jews are conspiring collectively against the Arabs, in association with the West. This view, as already mentioned, results from the wholesale import of the Western anti-Semitic tradition and writings into the Arab world. It is also attributable to Western writings about the pervasive influence of the so-called Jewish lobby in the United States. In this sense, there is also a Western responsibility for the view that the Arabs are now developing. In the 1950s and 1960s Arab secular nationalism used to make a distinction between the Zionist creed advocating the conquest by force of the Holy Land and the Jewish religion. Today this distinction has disappeared. This is not only due to fact that this brand of Arab nationalism has been totally marginalized by the ascending trend of political Islam, but also to the fact that Zionism in the West is now considered to be an essential element of the Jewish faith, despite the fact that it is contested within Judaism itself. [27] The only way to counter this expanding view both in the West and the Arab East is to stop analyzing tensions and conflicts as being the mere expression of religious mentalities and psychologies. In the case of Israel, no doubt there exist powerful American sympathies based on the religious feeling that America was the 'promised' land three centuries ago and that Israel is the archetypal one today, legitimately re-conquered by its ancient founders.[28]

But more important is the non-religious and exclusively political belief that because Israel supports US imperial policy in the Arab East it should not be made to implement UN resolutions and hand back land conquered in 1967. The fact that most Arab governments have now become so supportive of American policy in the region allows the US Government to pursue its almost blind support to Israel regardless of the cost to its real national interest in the region.[29] The Jewish lobby in the US is certainly powerful, but its influence stems not from 'Jewish' power as such, but rather from an American context that is extremely favorable to its views.[30] As a result, very few people both in the West and in the Arab and Muslim world resist the view that US policy in the Middle East is exclusively dictated by the Jewish lobby.[31]

There will be no way to reduce the divide between the West and the Arab East without media restraint in coverage of Middle Eastern and Arab affairs and without a much needed diversification of academic research to analyze the complexities of Arab societies and report the lively debate taking place in the intellectual and political circles of these societies. There should also be more awareness that the American geo-political agenda should not be become the agenda for dialogue between the two parties. Rather, such an agenda should discuss the real issues that we have attempted to identify here as a basis for reducing tensions. Only by so doing may we attain a better understanding of what really divides East and West and set aside inadequate anthropological and religious conceptualizations that are of little help for conflict-resolution in our time.

Notes

1 The Warsaw Pact and COMECON on the one hand and NATO and the OECD on the other.

2 See the very interesting book by Frances Stonor Saunders, *The Cultural Cold War: The CIA and the World of Arts and Letters* , New Press, New York, 1999.

3 See Francis Fukuyama, *The End of History and the Last Man,* Free Press, New York, 1992.

4 For the colonial cultural heritage that has shaped discourse on Islamic societies see Edward Said, *Orientalism,* Vintage Books, New York, 1978 and *Culture and Imperialism*, Knopf/Random House, New York, 1993; for an historical enquiry into the roots of this new divide, see Georges Corm, *Orient-Occident. La fracture imaginaire,* La Découverte, Paris, 2003 (paperback edition 2005).

5 Samuel P. Huntington, *The Clash of Civilizations and the Remaking of World Order*, Simon & Schuster, New York, 1996.

6 See the text of the President's speech in October 2005 at the National Endowment for Democracy (www.whitehouse.gov/news/releases/2005/10/print/20051006-3.html)

7 The best description of the trauma created in European culture by the long wars between Catholics and Protestants is in Arnold Toynbee, *An Historian's Approach to Religion,* Oxford University Press, 1956; see also the famous book written in 1852 by Edgar Quinet, *Le christianisme et la Révolution française,* Fayard, Paris, 1984.

8 See the classical study of Hanna Arendt, *The Origins of Totalitarianism,* Harcourt, New York, 1951.

9 See Zeev Sternhell, *The Founding Myths of Israel: Nationalism, Socialism, and the Making of the Jewish State*, Princeton University Press, 1999 and Alain Dieckhoff, *The Invention of a Nation: Zionist Thought and the Making of Modern Israel,* Columbia University Press, 2002.

10 See Raul Hilberg, *The Destruction of European Jews,* Homes & Meier, New York, 1985 and *The Politics of Memory: Experiences of a Holocaust Researcher,* Ivan R. Dee, Chicago, 1996.

11 One French writer did not hesitate to make the comparison between the Crusades and the emergence of the State of Israel, stating that this time everything was done to secure an eternal Western presence in the Arab East through the State of Israel. According to this writer, while the Crusades failed, the West should not allow the Israeli experience to fail. See Jean-Claude Guillebaud, *Sur la route des Croisades*, Arlea, Paris, 1993. This book is a reprint of a long reportage by the author that had appeared in a series of articles published by the French daily *Le Monde.*

12 See the classic book on the emergence of modern Arab nationalism by George Antonius, *The Arab Awakening,* Capricorn Books, London, 1938.

13 See Albert Hourani, *Arabic Thought in the Liberal Age. 1798–1939*, Oxford University Press, London, 1967 and Georges Corm, *Histoire du pluralisme religieux dans le bassin méditerranéen,* Geuthner, Paris, 1998 and *L'Europe et l'Orient. De la balkanisation à la libanisation: histoire d'une modernité inaccomplie,* La Découverte, Paris, 1989 (pocket book 2004).

14 We have these types of misunderstanding at length in the latest reprints of our history of the contemporary Middle East, *Le Proche-Orient éclaté: 1956–2005*, Gallimard, Folio/Histoire, 2006.

15 It is to be noted that it is in Sri Lanka that the first suicide bombers emerged in 1987 as a new form of guerrilla warfare employed by the Tamil Tiger armed revolt, many years before the Palestinian resistance. The Tamil rebels say 240 of their members have carried out suicide attacks over the years (see Frances Harrison report to the BBC on July 5 2005 available on BBC website: www.news.bbc.co.uk/1/hi/world/south_asia/2098657). It is also to be noted that Chechen resistance to Russia includes also very bloody suicide bomb attacks against civilians. However, in both cases Western public opinion is not as moved or revolted against these attacks as is the case for Palestinians or Iraqis.

16 'Legal Consequences of the Construction of a Wall in the Occupied Palestinian Territory Advisory Opinion', International Court of Justice, General List No. 131, 9 July 2004.

17 This Declaration states that 'Islam is the natural religion of human beings' and that nothing should allow 'changing of religion' (article 10); see the text in www.oic-oci.org/index.asp. It also states the equality of all in dignity and responsibility, but refrains from stating equality in 'rights'. There are other official Declarations on Islamic rights as the one adopted by the Islamic Council of Europe (www.aidh.org/Biblio/) in 1981 and the Decca Declaration adopted in 1983.

18 It is to be noted in this respect that Iran is not an Arab country.

19 It is to be noted here that the recent Iranian experience of *Wilayet Fakih* introduced by Imam Khomeini whereby Muslim clerics would control and scrutinize the acts of secular political power is quite new even in the Shia brand of Islam. It is also contested by many eminent Shia religious scholars.

20 There are very lively discussions in the Arab world about flexibility in interpreting the sacred text. Brilliant Arab scholars have continued to write extensively on this delicate issue, producing books that have a big impact, e.g. Mohammed Shahrour in Syria or Nasser Hamed Abou Zeid of Egypt who was forced into exile due his teaching and writings at Cairo University. Western media and academic work on Islam ignore almost totally the work of these scholars and concentrate exclusively on Islamic radical movements and their propaganda pamphlets. See the (unpublished) text of the lecture given at the Library of Congress in Washington on April 7, 2004 by Ziad Hafez, *The New Arab Thinkers in Islam.* A prior condensed French version of this talk was published in France under the title 'Les nouveaux penseurs de l'Islam' *in Manière de Voir,* July/August 2002, special issue on Islam published by *Le Monde Diplomatique*, Paris (e-mail of Dr Hafez: Zhafez@aol.com to ask for the full text).

21 However, for a precise and well informed worldwide view of the state of secularism, see Pippa Norris and Ronald Inglehart, *Sacred and Secular: Religion and Politics Worldwide*, Cambridge University Press, 2004. See also their contribution on religion in this volume.

22 See Albert Hourani, *Arabic Thought in the Liberal Age,* op. cit.

23 On this point, see Georges Corm, *La question religieuse au XXIè siècle. Géopolitique et crise de la postmodernité,* La Découverte, Paris, 2006.

24 Steve Weissman and Herbert Krosney, *The Islamic Bomb: The Nuclear Threat to Israel and the Middle East,* Times Books, New York, 1981 and D.K. Palit, *Pakistan's Islamic bomb*, Vikas, New Delhi, 1979.

25 See Edward Said, *Covering Islam: How the Media and the Experts Determine How We See the Rest of the World,* Pantheon, New York, 1981.

26 In this respect, see the very interesting article on the nature of the various jihadist movements by Mary Evans under the title: "For jihadist, read anarchist", *The Economist,* August 18, 2005.

27 On anti-Zionist trends in Judaism see the very detailed and documented book by Yakov Rabkin, *Au nom de la Torah. Une histoire de l'opposition juive au sionisme,* Les presses de l'Université Laval, Québec, Canada, 2004.

28 See on this point, Elise Marienstrasse, *Nous le peuple: les origines du nationalisme américain,* Gallimard, Paris, 1988 as well as Richard E. Wentz, *American Religious Traditions. The Shaping of Religion in the United States,* Fortress Press, Minneapolis, 2003 (chapter 2 titled 'Myths, Legends, and the Promised Land') and Anatol Lieven, *America Right or Wrong,* Harper Collins, New York, 2004 (chapter 6 titled 'American Nationalism, Israel and the Middle East').

29 See Georges Corm, 'Avoiding the obvious: Arab perspectives on US hegemony in the Middle East', *Middle East Report*, No. 208, Fall 1998.

30 See J.J. Goldberg, *Jewish Power. Inside the American Jewish Establishment,* Addison Wesley Publishing Co., New York, 1996.

31 See Stephen Zunes, 'Israel not to blame for Iraq mess', *The Asia Times,* January 11, 2006 and his article 'The influence of the Christian Right on U.S. Middle East Policy', Foreign Policy in Focus – *FPIF Policy Report*, June 2004. The author underlines different complex factors in the fabric of US policy in the Middle East and the fact that there are as many liberal Jews in the Democratic Party and in the academic world in the US as there are in the Administration and the neo-conservative group around President Bush.

REFERENCES

Antonius, George (1938) *The Arab Awakening.* London: Capricorn Books.

Arendt, Hanna (1951) *The Origins of Totalitarianism.* New York: Harcourt.

Corm, Georges (1998) *Histoire du pluralisme religieux dans le bassin méditerranéen.* Paris: Geuthner.

– (1998a) 'Avoiding the obvious: Arab perspectives on US hegemony in the Middle East', *Middle East Report,* No. 208.

– (2004) *L'Europe et l'Orient: De la balkanisation à la libanisation; histoire d'une modernité inaccomplie.* Paris: La Découverte.

– (2005) *Orient-Occident: La fracture imaginaire.* Paris: La Découverte

– (2006) *Le Proche-Orient éclaté: 1956–2005.* Paris: Gallimard, Folio/Histoire.

– (2006a) *La question religieuse au XXIè siècle. Géopolitique et crise de la postmodernité.* Paris: La Découverte.

Dieckhoff, Alain (2002) *The Invention of a Nation: Zionist Thought and the Making of Modern Israel. New York:* Columbia University Press.

Evans, Mary (2005) 'For jihadist, read anarchist', *The Economist,* August 18.

Fukuyama, Francis (1992) *The End of History and the Last Man.* New York: Free Press.

Goldberg, J.J. (1996) *Jewish Power: Inside the American Jewish Establishment.* New York: Addison Wesley Publishing Co.

Guillebaud, Jean-Claude (1993) *Sur la route des Croisades.* Paris: Arlea.

Hafez, Ziad (2002) 'Les nouveaux penseurs de l'Islam', *Manière de Voir, Le Monde Diplomatique,* July–August. Paris.

Hilberg, Raul (1985) *The Destruction of European Jews.* New York: Homes & Meier.

– (1996) *The Politics of Memory: Experiences of a Holocaust Researcher.* Chicago: Ivan R. Dee.

Hourani, Albert (1967) *Arabic Thought in the Liberal Age: 1798–1939.* London: Oxford University Press.

Huntington, Samuel P. (1996) *The Clash of Civilizations and the Remaking of World Order.* New York: Simon & Schuster.

International Court of Justice (2004) 'Legal Consequences of the Construction of a Wall in the Occupied Palestinian Territory Advisory Opinion', General List No. 131, 9 July 2004.

Lieven, Anatol (2004) *America Right or Wrong.* New York: Harper Collins.

Marienstrasse, Elise (1988) *Nous le peuple: les origines du nationalisme américain.* Paris: Gallimard.

Norris, Pippa and Inglehart, Ronald (2004) *Sacred and Secular: Religion and Politics Worldwide.* Cambridge: Cambridge University Press.

Palit, D.K. (1979) *Pakistan's Islamic Bomb.* New Delhi: Vikas.

President George Bush's speech in October 2005 at the National Endowment for Democracy (www.whitehouse.gov/news/releases/2005/10/print/20051006-3.html).

Quinet, Edgar (1984) *Le christianisme et la Révolution française.* Paris: Fayard.

Rabkin, Yakov (2004) *Au nom de la Torah. Une histoire de l'opposition juive au sionisme.* Québec: Les presses de l'Université Laval.

Saïd, Edward (1978) *Orientalism.* New York: Vintage Books.

– (1981) *Covering Islam: How the Media and the Experts Determine How We See the Rest of the World.* New York: Pantheon.

– (1993) *Culture and Imperialism.* New York: Knopf/Random House.

Saunders, Frances Stonor (1999) *The Cultural Cold War: The CIA and the World of Arts and Letters.* New York: New Press.

Sternhell, Zeev (1999) *The Founding Myths of Israel: Nationalism, Socialism, and the Making of the Jewish State.* Princeton, NJ: Princeton University Press.

Toynbee, Arnold (1956) *An Historian's Approach to Religion.* Oxford: Oxford University Press.

Weissman, Steve and Krosney, Herbert, (1981) *The Islamic Bomb: The Nuclear Threat to Israel and the Middle East.* New York: Times Books.

Wentz, Richard E. (2003) *American Religious Traditions: The Shaping of Religion in the United States.* Minneapolis: Fortress Press.

Zunes, Stephen 'Israel not to blame for Iraq mess', *The Asia Times,* January 11, 2006 and 'The influence of the Christian Right on U.S. Middle East policy', in *Foreign Policy in Focus – FPIF Policy Report*, June 2004.

## CHAPTER 16

ISLAM: BETWEEN RELIGIOUS-CULTURAL PRACTICE AND IDENTITY POLITICS

Bassam Tibi

The late 20th and early 21st centuries are characterized by the rise of the Islamic civilization to the forefront of world affairs. A belief within Islam of a cross-cultural umma, or a collective civilizational community, has taken hold in response to the perceived cultural threat of modernity and the forces of structural globalization. This has politicized culture and religion; this politicization in turn has given rise to a conflict-saturated discourse of Islamic civilization that causes tensions amongst Muslims themselves and between Muslims and non-Muslim others. Within contemporary Islam, new forms of 'imagined community', identity politics, invention of tradition, selective revival of cultural heritage, and construction of collective memories, all serve to reinforce the line drawn between the self and others. A global democratic peace is needed that accepts cultural and religious pluralism. Only a rethinking of Islamic doctrines and precepts may result in a civil Islam compatible with democratic peace.

Introduction

When discussing the dynamics of the cultures–conflict–globalization triad across the culturally diverse world of 'Islam' it is essential to distinguish between 'culture' and 'civilization' rather than use the two notions interchangeably. While there is no scholarly consensus – the terminology is *un*settled – the working definition of culture I use in regard to contemporary trends in the Islamic world is the local social production of meaning (Geertz 1973). In contrast, I see 'civilization' as a grouping of cultures linked to one another by a 'family resemblance' in terms of values and worldviews (Tibi 2001, updated 2005). This understanding applies to Islam as both a social reality and a belief system, shared cross-culturally from Asia through Africa stretching to Europe (which is now home to 20 million Muslim immigrants). While we speak here, in the plural, of many diverse cultures, the collective recourse to Islam and the belief in its imagined cross-cultural *umma* as a civilizational community have become politicized. This politicization has given rise to a cross-cultural, conflict-saturated discourse of Islamic civilization as a collective reference shared by all Islamic local cultures.

This has led to an Islamic identity politics based on the perception of a cultural threat. In this context, the revival of collective memories of Islamic glory is not just nostalgia (Kelsay 1993: 25) but represents a divergent vision of the world as well as a certain defensiveness (on defensive culture see Tibi 1988: 1–8). This identity politics also involves tensions arising from subdivisions in Islamic identity (e.g. Sunna vs. Shi'a in Iraq, see Jabar, 2003 and Anderson and Stansfield, 2004) as well as from the Arabo-centric interpretation of Islam that plays down the place of non-Arab cultures in Islamic civilization.

The idea of the West (Gress 1998) is related to the cultural claim of universal Westernization (Laue 1987) that historically infringed on and superseded *Dar al-Islam* through colonial conquest. In the early nineteenth century, Muslims were willing to accommodate to a world dominated by Europe (Abu-Lughod 1963). Islam was separated from politics. In contrast, the contemporary Muslim and Arab revival (Kramer 1996) returns the sacred to politics and not only targets Western hegemony, but also contests so-called 'cultural globalization'. Cultural Islamization aims to purify through de-Westernization. Indeed, long before the theories of Samuel Huntington, Islamist thinkers and Imams conceptualized Islam as a united *umma* (the community of Islam) and viewed it as a civilization (Qutb 1983). The fourteenth-century philosopher Ibn Khaldun, the very last great thinker that the Islamic civilization produced before it began to decline, was the first thinker to establish a 'science of civilization' (*Ilm al-Umran*) (Mahdi 1957).

Islam's predicament with modernity

The First World War contributed to the breakdown of the Ottoman Empire and the Sunni Caliphate, which was the last Islamic order in world history (Lord Kinross 1977), and in the aftermath, the world of Islam began to be mapped into the international Westphalian system of nation-states (Tilly 1985). Yet national flags and symbols have only concealed the tensions between the uniting modern nation-state and fragmenting ethnic, tribal and sectarian communities. The new nation-states that grew from the dissolution of the universal Islamic order made efforts to impose a superordinate national identity on their peoples (Oomen 1997), but have barely succeeded in this pursuit, because beyond formal sovereignty they lack the key substantive features of the modern state. The current sectarian and ethnic strife in Iraq (Anderson and Stansfield 2004) following the breakdown of the nominal Iraqi nation-state held together by the repression of Saddam Hussein's 'Republic of Fear' (al-Kahlil 1989) is an illustrative case in point.

In Islamic countries as elsewhere, structural globalization results in cultural fragmentation that contributes to the construction of ethnic-cultural and religion-based loyalties, which in turn shape collective identity politics. Local-cultural ethnic and universal Islamic-civilizational revived collective memories are combined, exacerbating the tensions arising from the perception of a cultural threat. In this context, a distinction is often made between political and social conflicts and their cultural perceptions and/or articulations. Terms such as 'culturalization' or 'religionization' imply that culture and religion are means for the articulation of conflicts. At issue is a real interplay of culture, religion society, economy and politics. In contrast, the popularized Marxist understanding that all conflicts must have social and economic roots overlooks the fact that culture is neither determined nor determinative, but is a part of the interplay. For instance, neither the 'Arab dream palace' (Ajami 1999), nor Moroccan authoritarianism (Hammudi 1997) nor Arab neo-patriarchy (Sharabi 1988) are economic issues; they are intrinsically related to culture. This is by no means an essentializing culturalism, however.

We must be wary of both economic reductionism and the opposite trap of culturalism. In Islam, culture is related to a distinct and intrinsic process of production of meaning and is therefore always in flux, ever changing. Therefore there exists no immutable culture based on Islamic rulings and all cultural production is now embedded in a global environment shaped by modernity. Yet Muslims themselves who have politicized Islam present their religious faith in an essentialized manner as a cultural ideology leading to conflicts on two levels: within Islam, and with non-Muslims. Essentialization is thus not only a flaw of Orientalism, but also of an Islamist 'Orientalism in reverse' (al-Azm 1992: 17–86).

Both economico-political reductionism and essentializing culturalism contribute to a misinterpretation of cultural conflicts in Islam. These are not merely a reflection of a 'clash of interests' (Gerges 1999), nor do they flow from an Islamic essence. Socioeconomic, political and cultural factors interact; and they are all embedded in globalizing structures (Tibi in G. Atiyeh). None of the cultural or structural factors can be properly understood in their own terms alone, nor can the former be reduced to the latter. Islam's predicament with modernity generates identity politics; it is both instrinsic to culture and structurally embedded.

The 'identity politics' generated by the politicization of religion, the religionization of politics and the culturalization of conflict are becoming a major source of tensions, creating fault lines based on new collective memories and 'wars' between them. These 'cultural' attitudes are not simply reflections of economic structures but stem from a threat perception that is intrinsically Islamic in nature. Muslims involved in conflicts determine their identity in the faith that they are acting *fi sabil Allah*/in the path of God, i.e. as 'true believers' and not as parties to a mere economic 'clash of interests'. These cultural-religious beliefs and the revival-related memories are part of the time and space of globalization, but they are not fully determined by it.

The return of the sacred in cultural garb: Islamist ideology and the contestation of globalization

Islam may be conceptualized as the identity pattern of a cross-cultural civilization. Despite the fact that the Arab world and the broader Islamic Middle East (including non-Arab Iran and Turkey) constitute only one segment of the more than 1.6 billion people (and 57 states of OIC) of the Islamic *umma*, this region is considered to be the cultural core of Islamic civilization (Tibi 1998: chapter 2). Undergirding this reality is the birth of Islam in Arabia, the Arab descent of its messenger, the Prophet Mohammed, and the revelation of the Koran in Arabic. These facts explain the Arab configuration of the entire civilization (most non-Arab Muslims have Arab names and pray and use cultural rituals in Arabic). This Arab cultural centrality was questioned when the Republic of Turkey was established and the caliphate was abolished (Berkes 1998), leading to processes of secularization and modernization. Today's repoliticization, however, which has given rise to the cultural ideology of Islamism, was launched in the Arab heartland, thus returning to this region its centrality and challenging the secular model in Turkey itself (Howe 2000).

What we see today is the call for an Islamic state (Tibi 1998a: chapter 8). The process began only a few years after the abolition of the Caliphate when the Muslim Brotherhood was established in Egypt in 1928 (see Mitchell 1969). This was followed by the call for an Islamic world order to be accomplished by an 'Islamic World Revolution' (Qutb 1992: 172–3) and can be traced back to the first variety of political Islam established in the Arab world which later spilled over to the entire world of Islam, from Southeast Asia (Indonesia) to West Africa (Nigeria and Senegal). At present, immigration is bringing this process into the core of the West itself and is broadening the scope of Islamic identity politics (Al Sayyad and Castells 2002; Katzenstein and Byrnes 2006).

What is at stake here is the return of the sacred in the shape of a cultural resurgence. Its articulations are essentially defensive (Tibi 1988: 1–14) but become offensive as well through the call for an Islamic state and Islamic world order based upon Islamic universalism. It is true that a contestation of the present world order is the driving motive. However, this contestation is based on cultural-religious foundations; its anti-secularism is much more than anti-globalization (Philpot 2002: 66–95). It is a claim to global power that combines religion, culture and politics. I conceptualize this phenomenon as the simultaneity of structural globalization and cultural fragmentation (Tibi 2001: updated 2005: chapters 4 and 11); the 'religionization' of politics, the 'politicization' of religion, while the cultural articulation of conflict expresses a cultural fragmentation. By fragmentation I mean five areas of discord over norms, rules and values accompanying the processes of structural globalization, viz. 1) identity politics; 2) imagined community; 3) invention of tradition; 4) selective revival of cultural heritage and 5) the construction of collective memories. In all these five areas, as addressed by the cultural ideology of political Islam, the cultural self is defined in opposition to the Other, creating tensions and fault lines.

First, the construction of Islamic *identity politics* needs to be seen in the context of the perception of the Muslim self as a collective *umma* viewed as a civilizational entity. Only those who lack the capability of reading Islamic sources, primarily Arab ones – and these include Huntington himself – could argue that the idea of a 'clash of civilizations' is the invention of a Harvard professor. For it can be found in the early writings of political Islam since the 1930s, for example, the idea of Islam as a civilization of universal power as articulated in the writings of Sayyid Qutb (1983) (on his views see Euben 1999: chapter 3). In a way Huntington is unwittingly in line with political Islam's polarization between Islam and the West, but not the inventor of this tradition. Also, those who refer to the creation of Israel and to the Arab–Israeli conflict as the major motivation overlook the fact that the anti-Western and anti-Jewish sentiments of political Islam predate the birth of Israel in 1948 and the American engagement in the Middle East following the Suez war of 1956, not to speak of the Iraq War in 2003. The context is not contemporary politics, but rather the challenge of cultural modernity and Islamic responses to it. The Western–Islamic rivalry is historically rooted, and its current shape is essentially constructed, while reviving collective memories in a context of a return – definitely not the end – of history.

Relating the numerous local Islamic cultures to one another by shared values and a common worldview results in the self-perception of an *imagined community* (Anderson 1991). When I work in Senegal and Indonesia, as an Arab Muslim I am always treated not as a foreigner, but rather welcomed as a member of the Islamic *umma* living as a brother in *Dar al-Islam*. In contrast, I am viewed as an alien in Germany, that is, in the European country where I am a citizen and have lived for more than 40 years. The underlying reason is cultural: most Muslims and Germans are in this regard culturally pre-modern and have no sense of the identity of the citizenship based on cultural modernity. In general, Muslims are treated in Europe as aliens, which undermines an integration and thus leads to cultural attitudes of hostility on both sides. This is a sign of a fragmentation despite the intensification of globalization. Under these conditions the imagined *umma* community in civilizational terms anchors its legitimacy on an *invention of tradition* (Hobsbawm and Ranger 1986). This process is taking place and can be observed in the spreading new understanding of two Islamic cultural concepts: *shari'a* and *jihad*. The shari'atization and jihadization of Islam become sources of conflict by contesting Westernization and seeking to bring about de-Westernization. In the search for authenticity of the self a selective *revival of Islamic heritage* is also being undertaken. However, the real authenticity of tradition is not in line with the revived and constructed *collective memories*. The war of memories centers on two competing models of globalization: the Islamic and the Western (Tibi 1999) and not on the real heritage of Islam (Rosenthal 1994). The rationalists of Medieval Islam were eager to learn from others (e.g. the Hellenization of Islam, see Watt 1962: chapters 2 and 3); they did not construct exclusiveness as some Muslims do today.

The five issue areas related to the return of the sacred do not indicate an end of history (Fukuyama 1992, in contrast Tibi 1995a: 28), but rather a 'return of history' in cultural and conflict-inducing terms. The cultural identity politics of the Islamists as based on their belief in an imagined exclusive *umma* community contributes to dissociating Muslims from the rest of humanity. In the European Islamic diaspora this is consequential, because it culturally separates Muslim immigrants as an 'enclave' (Kelsay 1993: 118) from the polity they live in. This perception of the self as an Islamic civilization in contrast to the others in 'us against them' terms is the seed-bed for cultural fault lines.

Politically, a cultural power for Islam is claimed and it is attached to four concepts promoting tension and conflict.

The first is the neo-Islamist concept of *Nizam* (system) and of *Hakimiyyat Allah* (rule of God). In both, one encounters a political-cultural redefinition and a reinvention of Islam. In this context, the concept of *Nizam Islami* (Islamic order for the state and the world, not to be confused with the traditional caliphate) and *Hakimiyyat Allah* (God's rule) are set in contrast to the popular sovereignty of the secular nation-state. Those who describe political Islam as a scenario for establishing a 'new caliphate' are not well informed and lack knowledge of the literature produced by the Islamists themselves. There are some (e.g. *Hizb al-Tahrir*) who talk about re-establishing the Caliphate, but this view does not reflect the mainstream (Tibi 1998a, updated 2002, chapter 8 on the Islamic state).

Second is the concept of Islamic constitutional law based on the reinvention of Islamic *shari'a* as divine Islamic state law. The term shari'a occurs only once in the Koran (sura *al-Jathiya* 45/18). In the eighth century, Muslim scribes developed shari'a into a legal system of civil law (*Mu'amalat*), but without any codification (Schacht 1979; Coulson 1964). There is a systematic explanation for this: Shari'a is, in contrast to legislative law, interpretive in character and therefore cannot be codified. Dogmatization or rigidization of the shari'a is not to be confused with codification. In political Islam today it is understood as the constitutional matrix of an Islamic order within Islam as well as for the world at large. The tensions ignited by this call for *tatbiq al-shari'a*/implementation (Tibi, 1998a, updated 2002, chapters 7 and 8) are nicely illustrated by the case of Iraq where the constitution elaborated by the Islamic parties includes provisions that no legislation can contradict 'Islamic rulings' (a clandestine term for shari'a). The faltering democratization of Iraq shows how the fault lines related to ethnic and sectarian tensions are established constitutionally in the name of freedom. It is argued that there is a 'clash of shari'a and democracy' (the title of my article in the *International Herald Tribune*, September 17/18, 2005, 6). In other parts of Islamic civilization the shari'atization of Islam ignites conflicts between Muslims and non-Muslims.

Third is the rebirth of *jihad* resulting in the concept of jihadism (Tibi 2005). The Islamic revivalist al-Afghani first called for jihad in an anti-colonial spirit as a response to imperialism (Keddie 1983). However, jihad was subsequently linked to the creation of political Islam by the Muslim Brotherhood in Egypt. With Hasan al-Banna, jihad becomes an ideology of jihadism. It is therefore a falsification of history to draw a line between al-Afghani and al-Banna, as is done in an apologetic manner by Tariq Ramadan, the latter's controversial grandson.

The fourth concept is the 'Islamization of Knowledge' (The International Institute of Islamic Thought 1989, and Tibi 1995). The vision of human beings as not only entitled to universal human rights but as being also related to other humans as equals despite all cultural diversity is implicitly questioned by this concept. At its height, Islamic civilization was capable of producing great scientific accomplishments because distinguished medieval Muslim rationalists such as Farabi, Ibn Sina and Ibn Rushd, embraced the Hellenist legacy and shared the concept of common human reason-based knowledge. Science in Islam (Turner 1995) was closely linked to an open mind that allowed this cultural borrowing (Davidson 1992). This open-minded Islam is no longer shared by Islamists who advocate an 'Islamization of knowledge' based on the Islamist politico-cultural program of de-Westernization (Tibi 1995). In so doing, they not only hold back Islamic civilization, but also generate tensions between Muslims and others. As much as there can be no Western or Islamic physics there can be no rational religion-based knowledge in contrast to human reason.

The major fault lines

The problem of Islam and cultural modernity under conditions of globalization is related to the claim of both to universality. Earlier, secular Muslims and modernizers were willing to accommodate the two together (Hourani 1962). In contrast, today's political-cultural Islamists speak with contempt of Muslims who are 'infected' by the virus of modernity and secularity. This disparagement is articulated by the global al-Jazira TV-Mufti Yusuf al-Qaradawi (chapter 8 in Schaebler and Leif 2004). The modernizing project is decried by representatives of political Islam as 'inner colonization' and 'Orientalism from within', as for instance by Islamists in Turkey who contest Kemalism. All Islamists draw a false historical line from the First Crusade in 1096 to the colonial incursion of Europe beginning in the eighteenth century (Napoleon in Egypt, 1798). They stretch this line to the present (US troops in Iraq). Islamists see in this line a 'Western globalization' viewed as a conspiracy carried out by the 'new Crusaders'. Even the Jews are included in this conspiracy-driven view of history, yet the Jews of Jerusalem stood with the Muslims in defending the city against the invading Crusaders (Runciman, German translation, 1995: 274) and in retaliation the latter burned the Jews alive in their synagogue. The present return of history is reduced to nostalgia about Islamic *futuhat* (expansion) aimed at mapping the entire globe into *Dar al-Islam*, the Islamic version of globalization that was undermined by the Crusaders and the Jews, then by colonialism, and now by globalization. The revival of the Islamic project is opposed to the so-called 'Jewish-Christian conspiracy' in the service of Western globalization (Kassab 1991).

The return of history and the nostalgia revolve around the following question: which model of globalization will be victorious and shape the future world order? (Kelsay 1993: 117). Westernization is viewed as *ghazu*/conquest and is contested by the call for jihad aimed at an all-encompassing de-Westernization of the world; the *umma* must mobilize against the West and defeat the conspiracy targeting Muslims worldwide. While accusing the West of Islamophobia Islamists in themselves develop an acute 'Westphobia.' A Muslim writer qualifies this sentiment as cultural schizophrenia (Shayegan 1992).

There are three levels in which this polarization appears to be making the 'clash of civilizations' a self-fulfilling prophecy: at the *global level*, with tensions between the world of Islam and the rest, primarily the West (Scruton 2002: chapters 3 and 4); *within Islam*, with the jihad of political Islam against secular Islamic elites suspected to be infected by the virus of Westernization (e.g., Kemalists in Turkey, the Francophones in Algeria and other Muslim secularists); and *in the diaspora* in Europe: Islamists agitate against integration in the name of preserving Islamic identity (Tibi 2002). Here, Islam has become ethnicized and hence a source of conflict. A superimposed Islamic ethnic identity is constructed to supersede real local Islamic identities (Turks in Germany, Maghrebis in France) and create a diasporic unity of Islam in Europe viewed as an extension of *Dar al-Islam*. This provokes tensions between immigrants and settled populations in Europe as much as the European right-wing extremists do.

Wars of collective memories and of ideas over world order are being waged on all three levels and becoming violent in the process. In this context, tragedies such as Bosnia, Palestine and Iraq become material for agitation. History is degraded to serve as a source for propaganda materials that support allegations of a Judeo-Christian genocide targeting Muslims as a race (whereas the *umma* is a multiracial community based exclusively on shared faith). It is intriguing to see how this phenomenon assumes the surface form of anti-globalism, a spirit which then unites the forces of political Islam. It is most disturbing to see this Islamist ideology of an extreme political right embraced by a European left that knows little or nothing about its new bedfellow. It is sad to see that seriously flawed Western policies (e.g., Bosnia, Palestine, Iraq) and silence over crimes (Chechnya, Kashmir) help strengthen Islamists in the war of ideas and of collective memories, enabling them to feel morally superior to the West. In these wars without armies a line is drawn from Jerusalem to Cairo and Baghdad, stretching to the Islamic periphery in Asia and to the diaspora in Europe, demarcating the battlefield in a cosmic fight between believers and *kafirun*/unbelievers.

Jihad and jihadism

Among the tension-igniting concepts of political Islam listed earlier the one that generates the most fault lines is jihad. As already mentioned, the concept has been reinterpreted to become an instrument of identity politics. The new meaning is quite different from the classical jihad concept in Islam (Tibi, 1996, 128–46). A sense of victimhood is cultivated to underpin the conceptualization of jihad as a measure of self-protection to counter real, perceived or constructed assaults by the Other (the West) considered to be the enemy of the cross-cultural *umma* community. This vision of jihad also bridges diverse Muslim communities to join forces against the perceived hostilities of the Western enemy.

One needs to explain the cultural tradition of jihad and how it has turned into jihadism. Jihadists are non-state actors waging an irregular war legitimated culturally by the idea of purifying the *umma*. The target of *kafirun*/unbelievers includes all non-Muslims as well as Muslim deviators. Qutb (executed in Cairo 1966) made the message crystal clear in a quasi-Marxist phrasing: Jihad is a 'permanent Islamic world revolution' (Qutb 1992, reprint: 172) aiming to de-center the West in order to replace its order by the *Hakimiyyat Allah*/God's rule, first within Islam and then globally. In their practice of cultural purification, early pre-al-Qaida Islamists always honored Qutb's distinction between two steps, the local and the global. The jihadist strategy aims first to topple secular regimes at home, and after accomplishing this, to move to global jihad. The change through al-Qaida is not that it is fighting somebody else's war (i.e., fighting against the US instead of toppling Muslim leaders), as some pundits suggest, but rather that it conflates the two steps in the jihadist strategy. The conflation results not just from intellectual short-sightedness; it is also related to the novelty of Islamic migration **that blurs** the cultural boundary between Europe and *Dar al-Islam*. The emerging Muslim diaspora in the West is a phenomenon that was of course unknown to Qutb. It is a new reality that undermines civilizational boundaries (e.g., Algeria in France, Silverstein 2004), yet is embedded in a context of globalization (Weiner 1995: chapters 5 and 6)

The jihadist mindset is a major source of tension and conflict within Islamic civilization and is also heavily muddying the waters of Muslim–Western cultural relations. In explaining traditional jihad some speak of non-violence and argue that it is to be understood purely as self-exertion. This reading is belied by the Koran in that its text allows Muslims to resort to *qital*/physical fighting for the benefit of Islam, but this is clearly not terrorism. In Islamic history the fighting of jihad wars as *qital* was subjected to strict rules as listed in the Koran. In contrast, terrorism is by definition a war without rules (Tibi 1996, and 2005). In the new Islamist interpretation of jihad an 'ism' is added to the term, utterly changing its meaning, while keeping the Islamic claims bound to it. Unlike restricted traditional jihad, the new *jihadiyya* is an expression of unrestricted irregular war, in other words a variant of modern terrorism. What matters here is the cultural-religious justification of violence by the jihadists who view themselves as true believers acting in the 'Mind of God' (Juergensmeyer 2000); other Muslims are disparaged as deviators. In many mosques, including those of the Islamic diaspora in Europe, the mindset of jihadism in which young Muslims are taught and socialized is fraught with tension and conflict, clearly as a 'revolt against the West' (Bull 1984). As a public choice it enjoys tremendous popularity in the ongoing war of ideas. In order to combat jihadism, Muslim cultural alternatives are needed, such as a cultural education in democracy (Tibi 2004, 2005a), an enlightened Islamic rationalism (al-Jabri 1999) and above all overcoming cultural predicament with modernity to facilitate an embracing of cultural pluralism (Tibi 2006).

The mindset of jihadism that promotes cultural fault lines can be combated by a strategy for 'Preventing the Clash of Civilizations' (Herzog 1999).

It is a war between global jihad and democratic peace as paradigms to shape our century (Tibi 2005). At issue are different cultural concepts. Among them is the concept of law underpinning competing political orders. In this war of ideas creating culturally legitimated tensions, jihad is pursued for *Hakimiyyat Allah*/God's rule, an order based on shari'a. For this reason, we need to ask why the call for the implementation of the latter contributes to tensions and conflicts.

Shari'a and the cultural shari'atization of Islam

The shari'a is advanced as a claim for a divine order on all levels. The mindset of shari'a is adversial to both pluralism and democratic peace. There is a cultural concept of shari'a in Islam (Schacht 1979; Coulson 1964). However, the shari'atization of Islam, as an invention, creates an obstacle to democracy in the world of Islam. The related tensions can be stated globally and locally. Within nation-states shari'a contributes to all kinds of divides, especially in multi-ethnic and multi-religious societies. In spring 2005 a variety of civil-society-based religious communities of all major segments of multi-ethnic Malaysia launched an initiative of an inter-religious dialogue among these communities for establishing a consensus over values and rules for ensuring an international peaceful coexistence. Only the Muslim community rejected the bid. Its justification for this behavior was that Muslims base their conduct on the shari'a and non-Muslims have no right to co-determine Muslim conduct. Non-Muslims are expected to subject themselves as protected minorities to a Muslim majority on the grounds of shari'a (Ye'or 2002). When Muslims are a minority they often insist on the application of shari'a – by claiming the cultural right, as in India, to the application of Muslim personal law.

Among the cultural inventions of tradition is the contemporary understanding of shari'a as 'constitutional law'. This issue was discussed at the 3rd International Congress for Comparative Constitutional Law held in Tokyo in September 2005, where it was argued that international terrorism is menacing international society. In this context it was asked whether religion as a faith and a cultural view of the world could deliver peace instead of tensions among rival religious communities (cf. my earlier discussion on the return of the sacred in political form). The connection between religion and law is cultural, for one encounters different cultural understandings of the rule of law. The Islamization of law through the introduction of the shari'a does not bridge, but creates tensions and fault lines. For instance the new Iraqi constitution stipulates that Islam is 'a fundamental source of legislation'; it further states that 'no law' can be legislated that 'contradicts the ruling of Islam'. Because of American pressure the term shari'a is not used, but the implementation of shari'a is clearly meant. The rivalry between Sunnis and Shi'as in Iraq is not about this understanding of law as shari'a being *lex divina*/sacred law of Islam, but only about whether shari'a should be 'the only' or just 'a' source of law. Add to this the Sunni–Shi'a discord on what shari'a actually is. One is reminded of the cultural tradition that views Islam as not only a religion, and hence includes shari'a as an essential part of 'Islamic culture' (Schacht reprint, 1979; Tibi 2001: chapter 7). Traditionally, Islamic law, never codified, was mostly restricted to civil law, in contrast to the present call for the political order of a constructed Islamic state. In this context it is alleged throughout the world of Islam that shari'a is tantamount to constitutional law. The question then, if shari'a really offers grounds for constitutional law, is to ask how Muslims could take part in a global order of 'democratic peace' (Russett 1993) if this is their only understanding of the rule of law, which also claims to be universal.

Indeed shari'a as it is proposed is not consonant with democracy and peace in a pluralist society. Aceh in Indonesia provides another demonstration of the shari'atization of culture, a process launched under the peace accord reached with the central government. At issue are two different understandings of democracy and rule of law. First, the Western secular versus the Islamic shari'a-based understanding of constitutional law. Due to the historical fact that there exists no law-book entitled shari'a, because Islamic law is based on the interpretation of the Koran and – as already stated – has never been codified, there exists among Muslims no common understanding of what shari'a is. It follows that the call for shari'a also creates rifts within the Muslim community itself. In addition it alienates Muslims from the rest of humanity. The call for shari'a is a source of tension and could even lead to war as was the case of Sudan (Petterson

2003). Non-Muslim Sudanese do not accept being subjected to shari'a and therefore have been rebelling for decades against this imposition.

Intercultural peace requires that Muslims view non-Muslims as equal to them: neither as protected minorities/*dhimmi* (Ye'or 2002) nor as *kafirun*/unbelievers. The diversity of cultures needs to be related to establishing and accepting commonalities, one of which is to insist on a common concept of law shared by all cultures. A reform of Islamic shari'a law may allow an embedding of Islamic civilization into a democratic peace based on the recognition of commonalities in constitutional law (An-Na'im 1990). Without 'rethinking Islam' (Arkoun 1994), above all the shari'a, there can be no Islamic contribution to a cultural foundation of the rule of law in transforming the world of Islam towards democracy. It follows that some secularization is required (Tibi 2000).

Conclusion: towards a civil Islam

Globalization has exacerbated Islam's predicament with modernity. While there is no single, monolithic Islam, there is to be sure one Islamic civilization in terms of a worldview shared by the thousands of Islam-linked local cultures in the world. Yet even these are permanently in flux and characterized by inner diversity. Islamic identity politics have homogenized this plurality. The collective Islamic memories now being constructed revolve around the history of jihad and crusade, forcing Islamic identity into a sense of victimhood. The West is blamed for ending the Islamic *futuhat*-expansion that took place from the seventh to the seventeenth centuries, in the interest of its own globalization, thus contributing to the present misery of the *umma*. World peace requires different options. I have proposed a cross-cultural morality as a bridge (Tibi in Herzog 1999: 107–26) and would argue that cultural modernity (Habermas 1987) provides a rational worldview that can be shared between Muslims and non-Muslims alike. Is this only wishful thinking? What can be done? What is feasible?

It was the historical intrusion of Europe into the lands of Islam in the late eighteenth century that first compelled Muslims to ask themselves: 'How could this happen to us when the Koran **says** we are *Khair umma*/the foremost community?' This question was reiterated in the early twentieth century by the revivalist Shakib Arslan in the title of his book 'Why Muslims are backward while others have progressed?' (Arslan reprint, 1965). Today, the choice is between failed 'adaptation' (secular nationalism as the legitimacy of the nation-state) and the unfolding Islamic revival (Kramer 1996). But political Islam is incapable of realizing its vision: it pronounces order, but delivers disorder (Tibi 1998a, updated 2002). What policies, then, can be recommended to policy-makers under these conditions?

I maintain that the seeds for the disenchantment (*Entzauberung)* described by Max Weber once existed in Islamic civilization. In Hellenized medieval Islam an Islamic rationalism emerged, but it was suppressed by the Muslim Fiqh-orthodoxy (Makdisi 1981; Tibi 2001 and updated, Chapter 8). The Moroccan philosopher Mohammed al-Jabri is among those Muslims now pleading for a revival of Islamic medieval rationalism (Averroism), for in his view 'the survival of a philosophical tradition to contribute to our time can only be Averrist'(al-Jabri 1999). It can be argued that the decline of science and technology in Islamic civilization (Turner 1995) led to an Islamic decay and then to the rise of Europe and its expansion replacing Islamic with European globalization. Yet the current cultural revival of Islam focuses on the historical competition between both civilizations in terms of a 'blame game', contributing permanently to cultural tensions leading to political conflicts. The conflict over the Danish cartoons is a case in point.

Are the tensions between Islam and the West really the 'culturalization' of a structural conflict (with regional varieties) or is culture itself the ground of conflict? The answer is that an interplay is at work. This interplay is partly determined by the structural constraints underlying the current defensive-cultural Muslim attitudes; at the same time constructed cultural views are part and parcel of triggering the conflict itself (e.g., jihad and shari'a). Rejecting both reductionism and culturalism, as I argued earlier, efforts should be made to counter the politics of Islamization of the Islamic diaspora in Europe by enlightenment and educational policies. The Islamic revival in the world of Islam itself is a more complicated issue, as the complex case of Turkey demonstrates (Howe 2000;). Political Islam and its cultural concepts could not be successful in establishing cultural divides if they were not supported in the interplay between cultural, social and economic factors. The marginalization of Muslims in Europe (Tibi 2002) and the failure of Kemalism as a 'Revolution from above' have supported the appeal of Islamic and Islamist culturally divisive concepts, but they are not the primary cause of these concepts and the related worldviews.

For all these reasons particular efforts are needed in education and conflict-resolution. An acceptance of pluralism needs to be developed within Muslim civilization, but this requires that Muslims themselves engage in cultural-religious reforms. The contribution of the West would be better understanding of Islam combined with justice and more democracy in international relations.

To be sure, this mutuality does not yet exist. Hence I conclude by stressing that for an adequate understanding of the world of Islam, its diverse peoples and its different countries, 'culture matters' (Harrison and Kagan 2006) as much as the economy, power politics and other pivotal issue areas. Despite their great diversity the people of the world of Islam base their identity politics on shared values and worldview. This civilizational identity and its collective memories (Hodgson 1977 are tangible social facts; they are not essentializations.

REFERENCES

Abu-Lughod, Ibrahim (1963). *The Arab Rediscovery of Europe*. Princeton, NJ: Princeton University Press.

Ajami, Fouad (1999) *The Dream Palace of the Arabs*. New York: Random House.

Al Sayyad, Nezar and Castells, Manuel (eds) (2002) *Muslim Europe or Euro-Islam: Politics, Culture and Citizenship in the Age of Globalization*. Berkeley and Lanham: Lexington. This book includes Tibi chapter 2 on Euro-Islam, 31–52.

Anderson, Benedict (1991) *Imagined Communities*, revised edn. London: Verso.

Anderson, Liam and Stansfield, Gareth (2004) *The Future of Iraq*. New York: Palgrave.

An-Na'im, Abdullahi (1990) *Toward an Islamic Reformation*. Syracuse, NY: Syracuse University Press.

Arkoun, Mohammed (1994) *Rethinking Islam*. Boulder, CO: Westview.

Atiyeh, George and Oweiss, Ibrahim (eds) (1998) *Arab Civilization: Challenges and Responses*: Studies in Honor of Constantine K. Zurayk. Albany, NY: SUNY Press.

Arslan, Shakib (1965, reprint) *Limatha ta'akharra al-Muslimun wa taqaddama ghairauhum* (Why Muslims are backward while others have progressed).

al-Azm, Sadik Jalal (1992) *Dhihniyyat al-Tahri* [The Mentality of Taboos]. London: Riad.

Berkes, Niyazi (1998) *The Development of Secularism in Turkey*. New York: Routledge.

Bull, Hedley (1984) 'The Revolt Against the West', in Hedley Bull and Adam Watson (eds), *The Expansion of International Society*. Oxford: Clarendon Press.

Coulson, N.J. (1964) *A History of Islamic Law*. Edinburgh: Edinburgh University Press.

Davidson, Herbert (1992) *Alfarabi, Avicenna and Averroës on Intellect*. New York: Oxford University Press.

Euben, Roxanne L. (1999) *Enemy in the Mirror: Islamic Fundamentalism and the Limits of Modern Rationalism*. Princeton, NJ: Princeton University Press.

Fukuyama, Francis (1992) *The End of History*. New York: Avon Books.

Geertz, Clifford (1973). *The Interpretation of Culture*. New York: Basic Books.

Gerges, Fawaz (1999) *America and Political Islam: Clash of Cultures or Clash of Interests*? Cambridge: Cambridge University Press.

Gress, David (1998) *From Plato to Nato: The Idea of the West and its Opponents*. New York: Free Press.

Habermas, Juergen (1987) *The Philosophical Discourse of Modernity*. Cambridge, MA: MIT Press.

Hammudi, Abdellah (1997) *Master and Disciple: The Cultural Foundations of Moroccan Authoritarianism*. Chicago: University of Chicago Press.

Harrison, Lawrence and Kagan, Jerome (eds) (2006) *Developing Cultures*, Vol. I Essays of the Culture Matters Project. London: Routledge. This volume includes a chapter on Islam by B. Tibi. Vol. II, Case Studies.

Herzog, Roman, and others (1999) *Preventing the Clash of Civilizations,* New York: St Martin's Press, herein a chapter by B. Tibi, 107–126.

Hobsbawm, Eric and Ranger, Terence (eds) (1996) (reprint) *The Invention of Tradition*. Cambridge: Cambridge University Press.

Hodgson, Marshall (1977) *The Venture of Islam: Conscience and History in a World Civilization*. Chicago: University of Chicago Press.

Hourani, Albert (1962) *Arab Thought in the Liberal Age*. London: Oxford University Press.

Huntington, Samuel P. (1996) *The Clash of Civilizations and the Remaking of World Order*. New York: Simon & Schuster.

Howe, Marvine (2000) *Turkey Today: A Nation Divided Over Islam's Revival*. Boulder, CO: Westview Press.

Jabar, Faleh (2003) *The Shi'ite Movement in Iraq*. London: Saqi.

al-Jabri, Mohammed Abed (1999) *Arab Islamic Philosophy*. Austin/Texas: University of Texas.

Juergensmeyer, Mark (2000), *Violence in the Mind of God*, Berkeley: University of California Press.

Kassab, Mohammed Yacine (1991) *L'Islam face au nouvel ordre mondial*. Algiers: Edition Salama.

Katzenstein, Peter and Byrnes, Tim (2006) *Religion in an Expanding Europe*. Cambridge, UK: Cambridge University Press.

Keddie, Nikki (1983) *An Islamic Response to Imperialism*. Berkeley: University of California Press.

Kelsay, John (1993) *Islam and War*. Louisville, KY: John Knox Press.

al-Khalil, Samir (1989) *Republic of Fear – The Politics of Modern Iraq*. Berkeley: University of California Press.

Kinross, Lord (1977) *The Ottoman Centuries*. New York: Morrow Quill.

Kramer, Martin (1996) *Arab Awakening and Islamic Revival. The Politics of Ideas in the Muslim Middle East*. New Brunswick, NJ: Transaction Publishers.

Laue, Theodore von der (1987) *The World Revolution of Westernization*. New York: Oxford University Press.

Mahdi, Muhsin (1957) *Ibn Khaldun's Philosophy of History: A Study in the Philosophic Foundation of the Science of Culture*. London: George Allen and Unwin.

Makdisi, George (1981) *The Rise of Colleges*. Edinburgh: Edinburgh University Press.

Mitchell, Richard (1969) *The Society of the Muslim Brothers*. London: Oxford University Press.

Oomen, T.K. (ed.) (1997) *Citizenship and National Identity: From Colonialism to Globalism*. Sage: London and New Dehli, herein chapter 7 by B. Tibi, 199–226.

Petterson, Dan (2003) (updated) *Inside Sudan*. Boulder, CO: Westview.

Philpot, Daniel (2002) 'The challenge of September 11 to secularism in international relations', *World Politics*, Vol. 55, issue 1 (October), 66–95.

Qutb, Sayyid (1983) (reprint) *al-Islam wa mushkilat al-hadarah* [Islam and the problem of civilization]. Cairo: Dar al-Shuruq, 9th legal printing.

– (1992) (reprint) *al-Salam al-Alami wa al-Islam* [World Peace and Islam], Cairo: Dar al-Shuruq, 10th legal printing.

Rosenthal, Franz (1994) (reprint) *The Classical Heritage in Islam*. New York: Routledge.

Runciman, Steven (1995) *A History of the Crusades* [German translation: Geschichte der Kreuzzüge]. Munich: C.H. Beck-Verlag.

Russett, Bruce (1993) *Grasping Democratic Peace*. New Haven: Yale University Press.

Schacht, Joseph (1979) (reprint) *An Introduction to Islamic Law*. Oxford. Clarendon Press.

Schaebler, Birgit and Sternberg, Leif (2004) *Globalization and the Muslim World: Culture, Religion and Modernity*. Syracuse, NY: Syracuse University Press.

Scruton, Roger (2002) *The West and the Rest: Globalization and the Terrorist Threat*. Wilmington, Delaware: ISI Books.

Sharabi, Hisham (1988) *Neopatriarchy: A Theory of Distorted Change in Arab Society*. Oxford: Oxford University Press.

Shayegan, Darjush (1992) *Cultural Schizophrenia: Islamic Societies Confronting the West*. Syracuse, NY: Syracuse University Press.

Silverstein, Paul A. (2004) *Algeria in France*. Bloomington: Indiana University Press.

Tibi, Bassam (1988) *The Crisis of Modern Islam*. Salt Lake City: University of Utah Press.

– (1990) 'The Simultaneity of the Unsimultaneous: Old Tribes and Imposed Nation-States', in Philip Khoury and Joseph Kostiner (eds), *Tribes and States in the Middle East*. Berkeley: The University of California Press. pp. 127–152.

– (1995) 'Culture and knowledge. The politics of Islamization of knowledge as a post-modern project? The fundamentalist claim to de-westernization', *Theory, Culture, Society*, Vol. 12, issue 1 (February), 1–24.

– (1995a) *Krieg der Zivilisationen*. Hamburg: Hoffmann & Campe.

– (1996) 'War and Peace in Islam', in Terry Nardin (ed.), *The Ethics of War and Peace*. Princeton, NJ: Princeton University Press.

– (1998) *Conflict and War in the Middle East: From Interstate War to New Security*, 2nd enlarged edn. New York: St Martin's Press.

– (1998a) (updated 2002) *The Challenge of Fundamentalism: Political Islam and the New World Disorder*. Berkeley: The University of California Press.

– (1999), *Kreuzzug und Djihad. Der Islam und die christliche Welt*. München: Bertelsmann.

– (2000) 'Secularization and De-Secularization in Modern Islam' in *Religion-Staat-Gesellschaft*, 1, 1: 95–117.

– (2001) (updated and expanded 2005), *Islam Between Culture and Politics*. New York: Palgrave.

– (2002) *Islamische Zuwanderung. Die gescheiterte Integration*. München: Deutsche Verlagsanstalt.

– (2004) 'Education and democratization in an age of Islamism', in Alan Olson (ed.), *Educating for Democracy*. Lanham, MD: Rowman & Littlefield Publishers. pp. 203–219.

– (2005) 'From Islamist jihadism to democratic peace? Islam at the crossroads in post-bipolar international politics', *Ankara Papers*, 16, London and Ankara: Frank Cass/Taylor & Francis.

– (2005a) Islam, Freedom and Democracy in the Arab World, in: Michael Emerson, ed., *Democratisation in the Neighbourhood*, Brussels: Centre for European Policy Studies/CEPS, pp. 93–116.

(2006) 'The Pertinence of Islam's Predicament with Democratic Pluralism for the Democratization of Asia' in *Religion-Staat-Gesellschaft*, 7, 1: 83–117.

The International Institute of Islamic Thought (1989) *Toward Islamization of Disciplines*. Herndon, VA: International Institute of Islamic Throught.

Tilly, Charles (ed.) (1985) *The Formation of the Nation State*. Princeton, NJ: Princeton University Press.

Turner, Howard (1995) *Science in Medieval Islam*. Austin: Texas University Press.

Watt, William Montgomery (1962) *Islamic Philosophy and Theology*. Edinburgh: Edinburgh University Press.

Weiner, Myron (1995) *The Global Migration Crisis*. San Francisco: Harper & Row.

Ye'or, Bat (2002) *Islam and Dhimmitude*. Cranbury, NJ: American University Press.

CHAPTER 17

EUROPE VERSUS AMERICA: A GROWING CLASH WITHIN THE WEST?

Nathan Gardels

There has been much talk since 9/11 about how the 'clash of civilizations' posited by Huntington is really a clash within Islam. But is there a clash within the West as well? This essay looks at that growing clash between America and Europe. Though contrasting cultures of belief and disbelief might mark the most dramatic difference between America and Europe today, there are other dimensions of the divide as well. Essentially, this clash within the West arises from two different cultural systems that are coming to grips with geo-political shifts, globalization and technological revolution in divergent ways. A largely aging, post-nationalist, secular, social and satisfied Europe proposes to cope with the future far differently than a youthful, largely nationalist, religious, individualist and aspirational America. The outcome could well leave Europe in elegant retirement as America joins Asia in shaping the 21st century.

In December 2004, just after the US presidential election, a group of editors, scholars and political leaders gathered under the auspices of *Aspen Institute Italia* in Rome to discuss the impact on American–European relations. Gianni Riotta from the Italian daily *Corriere della Sera* best captured the concern around the table. While there had been much talk in recent years about the clash between moderates and fundamentalists *within* Islam, he said, now perhaps it was time to talk about the clash *within* the West. Riotta was referring to the growing rift between American and European worldviews revealed by the emergence of the 'faith gap' in which a religious majority mobilized to re-elect George Bush as president even as the European Union was pointedly rejecting its Christian heritage in the preamble to its constitution. While the churches are empty and the mosques are full in Europe – something ever truer even in Catholic Italy – the mega-churches of what Ayatollah Khomeini called the Great Satan are overflowing every Sunday.

Though contrasting cultures of belief and disbelief might mark the most dramatic difference between America and Europe today, there are other dimensions of departure as well. Essentially, this clash within the West arises from how two different cultural systems are coming to grips with geo-political shifts, globalization and technological revolution in divergent ways. A largely aging, post-nationalist, secular, social and satisfied Europe proposes to cope with the future far differently than a youthful, largely nationalist, religious, individualist and aspirational America.

To be sure, within this distinction there are still further internal cleavages. Which America? The red or blue states? Which Europe? Old or new? Even so, in general terms one can identify four core areas that are the likely terrain of trans-Atlantic tension in the times to come. These areas are: the hard versus soft approach to security; the European versus the American social model; the related issues of immigration, integration and hybrid culture and, finally, attitudes toward religion and technology, particularly, biotechnology and the environment.

These zones of divergence are by no means the whole story. Deep economic links remain the bedrock under emerging differences. As Chris Patten, the former External Affairs Commissioner of the EU, has pointed out, Europe has accounted over the past decade for half the total global earnings of US companies (Patten and Lamy 2003). And, of course, Europe and America are both mature market democracies with widely shared norms and practices.

Hard versus soft security

One need only look at the career path of the former German chancellor Gerhard Schroeder to trace the dramatic arc of transformation of the European security situation in the past three decades. He started his career in the 1970s leading the Jugos (young socialists) in their opposition to the American-based euromissiles against Moscow and has ended up in political retirement on the board of the europipeline bringing energy supplies from Russia to Germany.

This surely signifies that, historically speaking, the Atlantic Alliance is past its prime. NATO is obviously no longer needed either to contain Russia or constrain Germany, which has been absorbed within the European Union. Whatever the democratic shortcomings in today's Russia, they are not for export. Indeed, as a kind of institutional atonement for the past century when two great criminal ideologies – fascism and communism – foisted hot and cold war on the world, Europe has begun the revolutionary postmodern process of integrating sovereignties. In terms of the history of governance, Donald Rumsfeld had it exactly backwards: American nationalism is what's old, Europe's post-nationalism is what's new.

Consequently, the central threat to world peace – and to American interests – no longer comes from Europe, but elsewhere: from terrorists seeking Hiroshima scale weapons to global pandemics like the avian flu, to climate change and to the rise of China and India. Simply put, trans-Atlantic ties are no longer the central relationship of the world order.

American–European relations in the security dimension have gone through three distinct phases since the collapse of the Soviet Union. First, were the immediate post-Cold War years, including the Balkan wars as the former Yugoslavia broke up; then came the period from 9–11 through the US invasion and occupation of Iraq; and now the period marked by Iran's pursuit of nuclear weapons and the accelerated rise of China as a major world power followed by India.

In the immediate years following the end of the Cold War, geo-political habits and addictions died hard. Jean-Francois Revel was right to say that in those times American unilateralism was primarily the result of the power failure of Europeans to act, particularly in Bosnia and Kosovo, no less in the Middle East (Revel 2003). This American unilateralism by default, however, became the Bush Administration's unilateralism by choice as it sidestepped the United Nations and multilateral institutions of every kind when it invaded Iraq in the name of the new post-9/11 policy of preemption.

Paradoxically, the manifest failure of the go-it-alone hard power approach in Iraq boosted the legitimacy of the European claim that the multilateral soft approach to resolving conflicts through international rule of law, diplomacy and political negotiation was the better course in coping with the new challenges of the twenty-first century. Rightly believing its peace and prosperity was no longer a function of the American security umbrella, as it was in the Cold War, Europe found a new self-confidence in the US debacle in Iraq it had warned against. As illustrated in its economic-benefits 'carrot' approach to keeping Iran from going nuclear, Europe asserted itself, taking the lead on a key global security issue.

Yet, if Iraq has shown the limits of hard power, the now-evident failure of negotiations by the Europeans with Iran has shown the limits of soft power absent the real threat of force. The Iranian hardliners who seek nuclear weapons and openly call for wiping Israel off the map know hollow power when they see it. The problem now is that by squandering its hard power on Iraq, the US has, in effect, disarmed itself militarily in the face of a real threat from Iran. At the same time, the collapse of a negotiated settlement over the Iranian nuclear program has just as effectively disarmed Europe diplomatically absent any credible force structure of its own. Interestingly, the diplomatic front on Iran has shifted from the US-British lead on the Security Council to Russia and China.

While the Europeans are right that most conflicts in this globalized, information age are best dealt with politically and economically, including the roots of extremism, some are not: Al Qaeda, Iran, North Korea and possibly China vis-à-vis Taiwan are cases in point.

Iran will thus be the test. The outcome in the years ahead will show whether soft power can work in preventing a hard threat or whether Europe must retreat again behind the American shield. Or, will Europe at last develop credible military capacity of its own to back up its carrots with sticks? There is plenty of grist for tension as the new balance between hard and soft power becomes established, no less because China, which adheres to its own *realpolitik*, is the new player at the global table.

European social model versus American-led globalization

One of the greatest divergences between Europe and America today involves their differing responses to globalization. Clearly, the same forces that hastened the collapse of communism – technological change and the free movement of capital, skills and information across borders – are swinging their wrecking ball at the welfare state.

What the late Christopher Lasch pointed out about America is doubly true of Europe: the middle class was created by the nation-state (Lasch 1991). With the nation-state on the wane, the idea of relatively egalitarian societies dominated at their core by a secure middle class is at risk. With the nation-state no longer in control of the primary levers of economic life, such as Keynesian fiscal policies in which demand creates *national* employment, it is difficult to capture the wealth required to sustain expensive systems of social protection.

America has responded to the opportunities of globalization by simply accepting growing inequality coupled with social mobility. As the late economist Milton Friedman argued in a recent conversation, 'the issue is not how much inequality there is, but how much opportunity there is for the individual to get out of the bottom classes and into the top. If there is enough movement upward people will accept the efficiency of the markets. If you have opportunity, there is a great deal of tolerance for inequality' (Friedman, M. 2006). It is significant that China has also embraced this raw aspirational market model.

By contrast, if there is one fundamental pillar of all the variations across nations of the European Social Model it is an aversion to inequality in the name of 'social solidarity' (at least among non-immigrants).

This contrast between the American individual and the social European even extends to environmental sensibilities. I recall a discussion some years ago with the Green foreign minister of Germany, Joschka Fischer, about how America's individualistic culture can lead to retail sanity, but wholesale madness. This molecular self-interest is most evident in California, the greenest state in America, where smoking has long been banned for health reasons, but global warming SUVs abound. In Germany, Fischer noted, Green Party members smoke like chimneys, but wouldn't be caught dead driving a large vehicle (Fischer 2001).

Deregulated markets, flexible labor rules and immigration all undermine the idea of solidarity. The European model is not so much anti-aspirational as non-aspirational, characterized by complacency and a sense of entitlement. And that seems to be the problem as the continent's political leaders try to push Europeans into joining their demographically diminishing fortunes together against the American and Asian onslaught on their way of life.

That Europe feels besieged by the forces of globalization pushing its member states closer together was evident in the rejection of the EU Constitutional Treaty in 2005. Facing the commitments of a constitution many believed would wed their fates to Polish plumbers and Turkish honor killings, the French and Dutch ran away from the future their paternal elites had charted out for them. Instead of saying 'I do,' they said 'No.'

Perhaps this embarrassing rejection announced proper anxiety over a step too far more than it meant a step backward. After all, Europeans will still be friends, not enemies. They aren't about to go to war, least of all the French and pacifistic Germans. They will share the same currency, cross-border cell phones and budget airlines as before. As a common public opinion, they will continue to oppose US unilateralism and worry about Asians taking their jobs.

Certainly the no voters were right to doubt whether greater centralization in Brussels was the best way to go in an era of networked and distributed power. What value would another layer of bureaucracy have added when the trend of history is, in any case, toward devolution?

Like people everywhere, ordinary Europeans are incremental creatures with human scale horizons. They want to get used to each step forward before moving on, pushing the inexorable shock into the future as far as possible.

At the time of the vote, there had been just too much change too quickly for one generation what with all the fallen walls, reunifications, expansions, extinguished currencies, ethnic cleansings and murdered filmmakers. Where once there was Cold War, understandably now there are cold feet.

The larger issue looming over it all, however, was the sense of systemic blackmail globalization brings.

In a *New York Times* column last June, Tom Friedman scolded the Parisians from his perch among the sacred cows and software engineers in Bangalore: If you don't shed your long lunches and welfare state you are finito, he told them. You should give up your 35 hour week to work 35 hours a day like the Indians, he preached (Friedman, T. 2005).

Whoa! To be sure, Europe needs remodeling. Productivity and the slow food movement need to be reconciled. If you want the good life, you have to pay for it. But demolition is a reckless idea. Is it really necessary to discard the fruits of over a century of labor struggles in order to out-sweat the wretched of the earth, albeit now aspiring, or stand up to the sole superpower?

It seems all the French and Dutch voters wanted to do was retain some grasp over their destiny – relative sovereignty – and instill a more incremental pace of change. Is it such a crime to not want to surrender a good way of life entirely to anonymous forces, invisible hands or distant bureaucracies?

If Europe learned anything from the disasters of the twentieth century, it is that the middle way is the best course. This is the message of Anthony Giddens and the Third Wave crowd around British Prime Minister Tony Blair who talk about 'flexisecurity' – the need for both flexible labor markets AND social protection. Indeed, the Nordic countries have put this idea into practice. As Goran Persson, the Swedish premier, has said, 'It is precisely social protection that enables the personal security to take economic risks in a freer labor market' (Campbell 2005).

Just as Europeans chose social democracy over communism or cowboy capitalism the approach of the Swedes and others suggests a way in our time of globalization to both savor the local goat cheese AND pay for retirement without reverting to the primitive accumulation of a Wal-Mart world order. What's so wrong with that?

Immigration and hybrid culture

In the 1940s, the Swedish social scientist Gunnar Myrdal anticipated the American civil rights movement in his seminal book, *An American Dilemma*, which decried racial segregation as contrary to America's democratic aspirations (Myrdal 1944). In those days, leading black American artists and writers, like James Baldwin, moved to France to escape discrimination. Though a black underclass excluded from social mobility persists in America's urban centers, integration has been largely successful over the past several decades in creating a large black middle class.

By 2005, it was the *banlieue* ringing Paris instead of the American inner city that burned with rebellion over the racism and exclusion Europeans so righteously condemned at the height of America's post-war influence. Only the situation is worse because it involves immigrants and their children with roots in another civilization – Islam.

America's underclass problem concerns integrating the descendants from the broken culture of its only involuntary immigrants – slaves. But America has been largely successful in creating a hybrid culture out of voluntary immigrants not only from Europe, but from Arabia to Asia. This has led European observers to marvel at how America is a kind of geocultural therapy for history's wounded masses. When they come to America immigrants leave their troubles behind. The soil, so to speak, is taken out of the soul and becomes real estate.

Ryszard Kapuscinski sees America as the cultural realization of '*La Raza Cosmica*' – the universal mixed race – envisioned by Jose Vacsoncelos, Mexico's education minister at the time of the Revolution (Kapuscinski 1997). For Kapuscinski, America is a 'collage of cultures'. Bernard-Henri Lévy is also quite right to note how well assimilated the Arab-American community around Dearborn, Michigan is compared to St Denis in France, where Arab-French youth rioted. 'What is good about America,' he says, 'is that in order to be a citizen you are not asked to resign from your former identity. You have to erase from your mind the ancestors you had.' 'America,' he concludes admiringly, is a 'factory' of citizens (Lévy 2006).

As with so many other aspects of American life, the integration of everyone as a '*citoyen*', which France only theoretically imagines, has been more or less realized in practice in the US. As Jean Baudrillard often chides his fellow French intellectuals who look down upon America, 'What did you expect the practical implementation of French ideas to look like?' (Baudrillard 1989).

To be sure, the presence of scores of millions of Mexicans in the US today represents a new order of immigration not so easily absorbed. Mexican immigration is different than all past immigration to the US because Mexicans come from a contiguous culture and they are mostly illegal. Far from having left their homeland behind, Saturday soccer matches in Los Angeles pit teams of immigrants from different Mexican states against each other; on holidays the border is jammed with people going home to visit. Mexicans haven't left their identity behind at all; they still live with it, but within the US economy.

While immigration to Europe has led to a widespread sense of 'identity crisis', Mexican immigration to the US has meant an identity crisis for Mexico. Is Mexico's destiny linked more to North America than Latin America? Mexican political elites and intellectuals, especially of the left, look South; its impoverished majority looks North. 'Los Angeles,' the Mexican social critic Carlos Monsivais says, 'is the heart of the Mexican dream' (Monsivais 1991).

Because of their Catholic, if Counter-Reformation, roots, there are no essential civilizational issues between the loose hybridity of the American mainstream and Mexicans. The main problem is class. Since the immigrants are predominantly peasants, successful integration depends on the social mobility of successive generations through education and opportunity. Everything depends on this, and here there is cause for worry about our consumer democracy's capacity to keep up the requisite social infrastructure.

The European situation could not be more different. Growing immigration to fill the labor demands of an aging, depopulating continent could well lead to a set of localized clashes of civilizations within Europe. In 2000, for example, net migration to the EU was 816,000, more than twice the population growth of 343,000 – what India adds to its population in a week (Chamie 2001). Though policies to end early retirement can help, that trend will certainly grow.

The problem is the incapacity of the European immigration models so far to absorb its mainly Muslim immigrant groups from Turkey and North Africa whose traditional culture clashes with Europe's secular and liberal lifestyle. This has given rise to the 'postmodern populism' of people like the late journalist Oriana Fallaci or the late Pim Fortuyn who, unlike Jean-Marie Le Pen or Jorg Haider, opposed immigrant influence not on racist grounds, but on the ground that 'liberal norms' like women's rights or homosexuality are not respected by the new arrivals. Indeed, it is the most culturally liberal states in all of Europe – The Netherlands and Denmark – that are the key points of conflict with Islamic immigrants. Holland is where the film-maker Theo Van Gogh had his throat slit on an Amsterdam street; Denmark is where the popular daily newspaper *Jyllands-Posten* first published satirical cartoons of the Prophet Mohammed that caused an uproar among Muslims globally and boycotts of Danish products in the Arab world.

Both the most liberal multicultural model – The Netherlands – AND the most integrationist model (at least theoretically) of France – have failed to cope with this issue.

Salman Rushdie unfavorably compares the European situation not only to the US, but also to India. 'In Europe', he says, 'integration has been held up as a bad word by multiculturalists, but I don't see any conflict. We don't want to create countries of little apartheids. No enlightenment will come from multicultural appeasement' (Rushdie 2006). Similarly, the Somali-born Dutch legislator, Ayaan Hirsi Ali, argues for assimilation as the necessary path – for Muslim immigrants and Europeans. 'What Africans, Asians and Muslims must go through in Europe, the Europeans have experienced in their past, during many transitions from underdevelopment to development, from religion to secularization, from a rural environment to a city culture. Multiculturalism freezes the status quo instead of allowing further development' (Hirsi Ali 2006).

This is Europe's deepest dilemma, not least because it is tied up with how demographic demise undercuts Europe's ability to maintain the social model at the root of its identity.

Religion and technology

Despite the pharmaceutical triumphs of the Swiss companies like Novartis or the Nordic success of Nokia, Alvin Toffler, the American futurist, has long regarded Europe as hopelessly 'technophobic'. My personal experience year in and year out at the Davos World Economic Forum confirms Toffler's suspicion: American technologists like Bill Gates of Microsoft, John Chambers of Cisco Systems or Eric Schmidt of Google inevitably dominate the conclave.

Undeniably, there remains a robust romantic strain among Europeans that runs from Heidegger in his mountain hut railing against American technology and consumerism in the 1950s to Jose Bové trashing McDonald's and free trade as a terminal threat to Europe's way of life. Whether one has sympathy with this romantic strain or not is beside the point. America's utilitarian pragmatism, coupled with the open embrace of technological advance, has created a growing productivity gap with Europe. GDP per head – the broadest measure of productivity – in the 15 longest-established members of the EU was only 73 percent of US levels in 2005. The R & D budget of Europe is nearly half that of the US as a percentage of GDP (Wolf 2006).

The integration of technology into the daily life of Americans has been enabled not only by work rule flexibility but by consumer enthusiasm. This is even truer of key Asian countries. Broadband penetration into Korean homes is approaching near totality. As Mayor Myung Bak Lee told me as he handed me his digital business card recently, Seoul has 100 percent broadband penetration (Lee 2006). One almost never sees a Japanese teen separated from his or her DoCoMo. The Shanghai middle class is notoriously gadget crazy. Bill Gates predicts China will become a 'broadband power' sooner rather than later (Gates 2006).

There is also a gap between Europe on the one hand, and Asia and America on the other when it comes to biotechnology. In China, genetically modified crops are readily accepted as a necessary means of making arid farmlands more productive, far less of a threat than poultry with the flu. The fear of contamination which has made so many Europeans fond of the ecological principle of 'precaution' has even less resonance in most of Asia than in America.

Surely, the world is dividing between those willingly 'committed to our mutuation', as Teilhard de Chardin once put it, and those more resistant (Teilhard de Chardin 1959). The rapid clip of change means the tentative space between willing and resistant will grow into a chasm overnight. 'Relative decline' is the term historians use to describe the fate of those in the slow lane.

Particularly with biotechnology, this gap illuminates yet another paradoxical difference between America and Europe. Europe is secular, but suspicious of technology overrunning human dignity. America is a kind of religio-secular hybrid, as the theologian Martin Marty has put it (Marty 2005), with the religious aspect ever more pronounced in areas having to do with the blurring boundaries of the person, or what President Bush likes to call 'the culture of life' – abortion, assisted suicide, stem-cell research – albeit not capital punishment.

Increasingly, pragmatic Americans speeding toward the future are looking to traditional religion for moral and ethical guidance as they commit to their mutation in the new age of biology. This is not surprising: new advances in science seem to have resurrected the religious imagination by raising anew all the questions of origins and destiny.

Leon Kass, the chairman of President Bush's Council on Bioethics, for example, has returned to a study of the Biblical book of Genesis for answers about bioethics in the 21st century. In his book, *The Beginning of Wisdom: Reading Genesis*, he sees genetic engineering as our contemporary equivalent to the limitless hubris of the Tower of Babel, which God struck down (Kass 2003). What is paradoxical is that the great European voice of secular reason, Jürgen Habermas, has arrived at a similar conclusion. In a conversation with Cardinal Ratzinger before he became Pope, Habermas asked whether 'modern democracies of necessity must draw from moral – especially religious – sources that they cannot themselves produce'. He concludes that liberal democracies must leave a wide open space for religious expression and religious forms of life, particularly when confronting issues at the frontiers of science. 'A liberal political culture can even expect that secularized citizens will participate in the efforts required to translate relevant contributions from religious language into a publicly accessible one' (Habermas 2004).

In a new book, *A Time of Transitions*, Habermas is even clearer, saying that the West's Judeo-Christian heritage is the ultimate foundation of liberty, conscience, human rights and democracy – the benchmarks of Western civilization. 'To this day we have no other options. We continue to nourish ourselves from this source. Everything else is postmodern chatter.' Habermas goes on to contest 'unbridled subjectivity' which he sees as clashing with 'what is really absolute; that is ... the unconditional right of every creature to be respected in its bodiliness and recognized in its otherness as an "image of God"' (Habermas 2006).

All this suggests that not only might Europeans be losing out with their romantic hesitations over technological advance, but that they must also keep an open ear to that most religious of democracies, America, to answer their doubts and concerns about where secular society is headed.

Chris Patten recently published a memoir-reflection entitled *Cousins and Strangers: America, Britain and Europe in a New Century* (2006). My sense is that we are becoming more strangers and less cousins. When I worked for the California governor thirty years ago, we prematurely touted the Pacific Century. In 2006, that idea is no longer premature. The centers of gravity of population, technology and trade are shifting back to the East after centuries of European domination. America, with its heavy-hitter economy but weightless culture, as Jean Baudrillard has put it, will go with the flow. Europe, for better and worse, will remain behind, perhaps mired in a crisis of 'civilizational morale' as the Catholic writer George Weigel has put it. Hopefully, it will be an elegant retirement.

Box 17.1 The French suburbs and the violence of exclusion

Jean-Joseph Boillot

The following reflections are based on the working hypotheses and preliminary findings of a socio-economic audit launched recently by the author on behalf of the Académie (the French term for the different regional branches of the ministry of education) of the eastern Paris suburb of Créteil. This area has been the heartland of recurring violent incidents in recent years; it also has a school dropout rate of over 50 percent. The audit is designed to lead to a new educational strategy for the integration of the young people concerned.

The extent and violence of the autumn 2005 riots in the French suburbs astonished the entire world and called to mind those of America's inner cities in the 1960s. The ethnic origins of many of the rioters and the use of terms such as ghetto, discrimination, racism or minorities in the media coverage of these events were another striking parallel. The difference, however, was that these rioters were not only 'blacks' but also young people from North Africa – known as '*Beurs*' in today's urban slang (or '*Robeux*' as they call themselves in *Verlan*, the French equivalent to English 'backslang') – as well as underprivileged indigenous French youths. In other words, they were the 'Black-Blanc-Beur' (Black-White-Beur), so called after the composition of the French soccer team that won the World Cup in 1998, itself emblematic of the real heterogeneity of the country's urban population. In the background to the violence also hovered the great debate on 'France and its Muslims', the title of a recently released report by the International Crisis Group.[1] The undeniable resurgence of Islam piety among some 'second generation' immigrants in France is sometimes represented as a transposition of the Israeli–Palestinian conflict. Indeed Salafist doctrine does appear to have inspired some of the most highly educated among them, as revealed by Zacarias Moussaoui during his recent trial concerning his responsibility as regards the September 11 attacks.

The turmoil caused by the 'war of the veil', in other words the Islamic headscarf issue, after the adoption of the 2004 law prohibiting the sartorial display of visible religious symbols in schools, had already reinforced the impression that the French model of integration was in crisis and needed to be adapted to the realities of a 'multicultural' society. The appeal of the 'multiculturalist' solution, however, was diminished by the way in which similar urban violence led the Blair government in the United Kingdom to toughen its legislation on immigration laws and freedom of speech, in particular after the London bombings of 2005. In short, both these ideal models of integration would seem to be in an impasse. Yet the search for 'culturalist' explanations of and solutions to the violence in Europe's suburbs continues.

The audit now under way takes a different tack. Rather than foreground cultural, ethnic or religious approaches to the urban violence affecting almost one million pupils and students in the eastern suburbs, our hypothesis is that the economic and social impacts of accelerated globalization in the 1980s have created a vicious circle in which 'cultural' explanations serve as surrogates for the blockages of French society in the face of the challenges of globalization. These blockages affect all levels of the society. There is a parallel between the urban violence and the rejection of the European Constitutional Treaty in 2005 which was based *inter alia* on a deep wave of anti-capitalist sentiment among young indigenous French who are much better off. Ironically, it is the latter who recently took to the streets in the Spring of 2006 to protest the so-called 'CPE' contract, a liberal new labor law designed to promote employment for workers under 26, only to find themselves attacked during the mass demonstrations by 'gangs from the suburbs'.

Our initial results show that using the prisms of culture, ethnicity or religion leads nowhere and even generates a vicious circle as demonstrated by the reassertion of economic nationalism in Europe, particularly in France. In the face of the destructive features of economic change, of which globalization is only one vector, French society is increasingly divided into two distinct groups: not the traditional *ex ante* winners and losers, but rather insiders and outsiders. The insiders deploy offensive and defensive strategies which effectively exclude the outsiders from the competitive process itself. Urban space is fractured along the lines of the center-periphery model of the new economic geography à la Paul Krugman and others. The center reinforces itself, capturing all resources, in particular, mobilizing economic and social capital, by setting up protectionist barriers including the symbolic, for example through the increasingly stringent scholastic selection, while employment declines. The topography of an area such as Paris and its region (12 million inhabitants, 30 per cent of the French GDP) is in this respect very revealing: a Western crescent concentrates modern industries, the new tertiary sector services, the elites *Grandes Ecoles*, the centers of R&D and innovation, while the Eastern crescent is increasingly segregated with the multiplication of urban, education and cultural ghettos. Half of its young people leave school without any diploma or professional education and their real unemployment rate is as high as 50 percent in the industrial wastelands with no future.

Vis-à-vis the strategy of avoidance deployed by the insiders and the growing discourse of victimization of the outsiders, who live increasingly assisted lives, the intellectual elites tend to turn to culture, religion or race in order to explain the emergence of a caste society or a Greek democracy (the Citizens and the others). France contaminated by 'communitarianism', as the star soccer player Lilian Thuram put it recently, is in fact an implicit response of the French elites allied with the white upper middle class as the French economy declines. However they don't see or don't want to see that this decline is due precisely to the large-scale waste of human resources since half of the young people in the region around Paris are the offspring of immigrants. Nor do they seem to grasp the negative impacts, such as the recent riots that the exclusion of these young people has led to, affecting the attractivity of Paris for millions of tourists. The country's economic growth has averaged barely 1.5 percent since 1980, in other words a level of quasi-stagnation per capita. And globalization's winners are reacting like the CAC 40 companies (with the stock exchange rising 30 percent in 2005) as they move more and more of their business out of France. The best qualified engineers are also leaving France when, even according to official sources, the number of people living in poverty is increasing as a result of the unemployment rate of 10 percent of the active population. Unemployment exceeds 25 percent in the suburbs of the large cities and can attain as much as 50 percent among young people and reach 80 percent in the most affected areas.

Like any crisis, the revolt of the suburbs could hold ways out of the blockages of French society. For instance, a recent report of the Economic Analysis Council shows how liberalization in some sectors such as the hotels and restaurant industry alone could create up to 3.4 million jobs, particularly for less qualified young people, typically those from the suburbs. Similarly, the initiative taken in 2000 by the director of the prestigious *Institut de Sciences Politiques* to recruit some of the best students from the suburbs through affirmative action mechanisms was not only a great media success but also had positive outcomes. Nearly 200 young people have gained entry to 'Sciences Po' as a result, whereas the proportion of young people from the lowest income brackets entering the elite educational establishments fell from 29 percent at the beginning of the 1950s to approximately 5 percent today.

But a race is now on between the demons of elitism, racism and negative discrimination which make globalization, particularly migration, the source of all evil and thus see the solution only in repression and the modernization of the police. In the same way, the middle path of 'multiculturalism' is likely to prove illusory, for recent research shows that the deprived young people of the suburbs are essentially 'multi-colored' (Black-White-Beur). Thus the mechanisms that apply to them are those of the 'underclass' well described by American sociology of immigration. Rather than borrowing from their so-called 'cultures of origin' which they have in fact never known, they produce their own culture, a sub-culture of adversity which rejects dominant standards and values. Suffice it to observe the boom in artistic expression – Rap yesterday and Slam today – and among the hundreds of young people who congregate at the *Café culturel* in Saint-Denis and share poetry in the French language not seen since that of François Villon (1431 – ?). This 'ethnic' assertion is that of a composite culture which becomes violent only against the violence of exclusion to which it is subjected.

---

[1] ***La France face à ses musulmans: Émeutes, jihadisme et dépolitisation,*** Rapport Europe No. 172, 9 mars 2006, International Crisis Group (http://www.crisisgroup.org/home/ index.cfm?id=4019&1=2)

REFERENCES

Baudrillard, Jean (1989) 'After Utopia', interview with Nathan Gardels, *New Perspectives Quarterly,* 6 (2): 52–4.

Campbell, Gordon (2005) 'Lessons from Sweden', *New Zealand Listener,* (197) 3383, March 12–18.

Chamie, Joseph (2001) 'The new population order', *New Perspectives Quarterly,* 18 (2): 25–8.

Fischer, Joschka (2001) Unpublished interview with Nathan Gardels in Davos, Switzerland, January 28.

Friedman, Milton (2006) 'Free Trade and The End of History', interview with Nathan Gardels, *New Perspectives Quarterly,* 23 (1): 37–43.

Friedman, Thomas (2005) *New York Times*, June 3.

Gates, Bill (2006) Unpublished interview with Thomas Friedman at the World Economic Forum in Davos, Switzerland, January 27.

Hirsi Ali, Ayaan (2006) 'Islamic Reformation will come from Europe', interview with Andrea Seibel, *New Perspectives Quarterly,* 23 (1): 20–4.

Habermas, Jürgen (2004) Excerpts from 'A post-secularist consensus: the Habermas–Ratzinger exchange': Catholic Academy in Bavaria, January 19, 2004. Cited at www.heythrop.ac.uk.

– (2006) *A Time of Transitions.* Oxford: Polity Press. Cited in TNR on-line Daily Journal of Politics by Reihan Salam (May 3, 2005) www.tnr.com.

Kapuscinski, Ryszard (1997) 'One World, Two Civilizations', in Nathan Gardels (ed.), *The Changing Global Order: World Leaders Reflect.* Oxford: Blackwell. pp. 3–8.

Kass, Leon (2003) 'Biotech and the new Babel', interview with Nathan Gardels, *New Perspectives Quarterly,* 20 (4), 2003: 5–19.

Lasch, Christopher (1991) 'Why liberalism lacks virtue', interview with Nathan Gardels, *New Perspectives Quarterly,* 8 (2): 30–5.

Lee, Myung Bak (2006) Unpublished interview with Nathan Gardels at the World Economic Forum in Davos, Switzerland, January 26.

Lévy, Bernard-Henri (2006) *Weekend Interview* by Tunku Varadarajan, *Wall Street Journal,* January 21.

Marty, Martin (2005) 'Righteous empire: the faith gap in American politics', interview with Nathan Gardels, *New Perspectives Quarterly,* 22 (1): 24–8.

Monsivais, Carlos (1991) 'Los Angeles: heart of the Mexican dream', interview with Nathan Gardels, *New Perspectives Quarterly,* 8 (1): 51–2.

Myrdal, Gunnar (1944) *An American Dilemma: The Negro Problem and Modern Democracy*. New York: Harper's.

Patten, Chris (2006) *Cousins and Strangers: America, Britain and Europe in a New Century.* New York: Henry Holt.

– and Lamy, Pascal (2003) 'Transatlantic appeal: put away the megaphones', Global Viewpoint, *Los Angeles Times* Syndicate, April 7.

Revel, Jean-Francois (2003) 'Contradictions of the anti-American obsession', *New Perspectives Quarterly*, 20 (2): 11–27.

Rushdie, Salman (2006) 'Inside the mind of jihadists', interview with Nathan Gardels, *New Perspectives Quarterly,* 23 (1): 7–12.

Teilhard de Chardin, Pierre (1959) *The Phenomenon of Man.* New York: Harper & Row.

Weigel, George in conversation with Walter Russell Mead at the Council on Foreign Relations, February 22, 2006. Unpublished.

Wolf, Martin (2006) *Financial Times*, January 25, p. 13.

CHAPTER 18

VALUE PATTERNS IN EUROPE AND THE UNITED STATES: IS THERE A TRANSATLANTIC RIFT?

Christian Welzel and Franziska Deutsch

We examine empirical evidence for a widespread stereotypical assumption: the alleged cultural rift between Europe and the US. With respect to individualistic values emphasizing human self-expression, we find little division between Western Europe and North America. Rather, they are mostly unified as the individualistic, liberal and democratic West against the 'rest' of the world. By contrast, we observe a massive transatlantic separation regarding community norms. Despite internal divisions, the US is on average considerably more religious, rigid, and absolute in its moral values than any society of continental Western Europe. Moral value rigidity is not a reflection of 'American Exceptionalism' but rather an attribute characterizing all Anglophone societies.

Introduction

'It is time to stop pretending that Europeans and Americans share a common view of the world … Americans are from Mars and Europeans are from Venus.' Robert Kagan's (2003) famous first lines in *Of Paradise and Power* are typical of recent debates on transatlantic relations. Following Kagan and many other voices, it does indeed seem as if the rift between the US and Europe has never been wider. The anecdotal evidence at least is overwhelming. Consider, for instance, Donald Rumsfeld's branding of Germany and France as 'Old Europe' in reaction to their critical stance on the US war in Iraq. Further evidence of an Atlantic rift has been provided by reports saying that Americans are boycotting French products to express their anger at the French position in the Iraq question. On the other side of the Atlantic, hundreds of thousands of people all over Europe demonstrated against the Iraq war and the Bush administration in spring 2003. Moreover, European governments have been estranged by the US's blunt refusal of the Kyoto Protocol and the International Criminal Court (ICC).[1] Europeans tend to see a stunning discrepancy between the missionary vigor by which Americans portray themselves as the guardians of universal human rights and the deficiencies in the realization of this ideal – these deficiencies being obvious from the treatment of Muslim prisoners in Abu Ghraib and Guantánamo, and the practice of the death penalty in many US states. These grievances are reflected in a serious decline in positive opinion towards the US in all European publics, accompanied by a new wave of latent anti-Americanism (Berman 2004).

It has by now become a widespread belief that these US–European differences do not reflect rationally manageable conflicts of interests between different governments but instead indicate a deeply rooted cultural rift that is not easily bridged. There seems to be an increasing belief that American and European publics (and politicians) do not understand each other. Not coincidentally, one finds a growing number of articles on the cultural differences in religious values between Europe and the US and speculations on the related potential for international conflicts (see for example Ian Buruma's essay in *The Guardian*, 7 January 2006).

The focus on differences between the US and Europe is not new. Ever since Alexis de Tocqueville's classic *Democracy in America* in 1835/40, social scientists have continuously emphasized significant differences when comparing the US to other modern societies. There is a tradition of treating the US as an exceptional and deviant case in many ways (see among others Lipset 1963, 1990, 1996; Lind 1996; Madsen 1998; Lockhart 2003). As Lipset argues, the country is an outlier in various perspectives:

> *With respect to crime, it has the highest rates; with respect to incarceration, it has the most people locked up in jail; with respect to litigiousness, it has the most lawyers per capita of any country in the world, with high tort and malpractice rates. It also has close to the lowest percentage of the eligible electorate voting, but the highest rate of participation in voluntary organizations. The country remains the wealthiest in real income terms, the most productive as reflected in worker output, the highest in proportions of people who graduate from or enroll in higher education (post-grade 12) and in postgraduate work (post-grade 16). It is the leader in upward mobility into professional and other high status and elite occupations, close to the top in terms of commitment to work rather than to leisure, but the least egalitarian among developed nations with respect to income distribution, at the bottom as a provider of welfare benefits, the lowest in savings, and the least taxed. (1996: 26)*

In light of this notion of American Exceptionalism, the question arises of whether the stereotype of a cultural rift between Europe and the US can be empirically validated. If such a cultural rift exists, US Americans and Europeans must differ in basic value orientations and the value differences between them must be greater than the value differences within Europe and the US. This is the empirical question that this chapter addresses: is there only a 'rift rhetoric' or is there a real and widening cultural rift between Europe and the US?

European–American value differences are an all the more pressing issue in light of the increasingly widespread belief in the existence of irresistible homogenization processes summarized under the term globalization. It is often said that advancing global integration is not only an economic but also a cultural process (Castells 1996). With a rapidly growing flow of knowledge via Internet, telephone and satellites, ideas and worldviews that have once been specific to particular cultures become ever more intermingled with one another, ending up in just one global cultural mix. If cultural change were to follow this 'global village' metaphor, we would expect a convergence of formerly distinct American and European values. Others, however, have claimed that exposure to different worldviews and values can lead to a more deliberate emphasis on one's own cultural identity, strengthening rather than weakening cultural differences. The increasing awareness of seemingly fundamental differences between Europe and America could be a process of this kind, in which case a divergence of European and American values should be observable. In order to be more certain about which of these two opposing possibilities, cultural convergence or cultural divergence, comes closer to the truth, we cannot rely on an impressionistic reading of news media. We have to look at representative empirical data.

For this purpose we will use survey data from the World Values Survey/European Values Survey 1981–2000, looking at the relative size as well as the dynamic of the value differences between the US and core Western European societies.[2] As Baker (2005) and Inglehart and Welzel (2005) have shown, one can map the most fundamental value differences on two major dimensions of cross-cultural variation. The first dimension ranges from traditional values reflecting a morally rigid mentality at one extreme end to secular-rational values reflecting a morally permissive mentality at the other extreme end. The second dimension ranges from survival values reflecting a collectivist orientation at one extreme end to self-expression values reflecting an individualistic orientation at the other extreme end. A society's prevailing beliefs can be located and the change of these beliefs can be traced on a map involving these two dimensions.

First we locate the average American and European *value positions* on the two-dimensional cultural map, looking whether the value differences are greater between the two continents or within them. For that matter we subdivide the US and Europe into various cultural regions. The stereotype of an American–European rift would be justified only to the extent that the value distances between Europe and the US are larger than the differences between their regions.

In a next step we look at *value changes.* Have American and European values been converging or diverging over the past 20 years, or is there no trend at all? Over the past years in the US there has been considerable debate about an American crisis of values (Bellah et al. 1996(1985); Himmelfarb 1996; Bennett 1999, 2001; Putnam 2000), more precisely the perception of a crisis (Baker 2005). Findings of numerous studies ('social regression', the 'loss of a moral compass', the 'collapse of community' or changes in 'fundamental values about right and wrong, good and evil, noble and base') indicate that US society is losing some of its distinct 'American' characteristics. Conversely, Europe (and not just Europe) has been facing a wave of Americanization, affecting various aspects of society, such as politics, economic relations, everyday language or consumerism. Both trends suggest that the respective societies have been converging in their value patterns. Contrary to this expectation, the cultural rift stereotype suggests a divergence of values between the US and Europe. Which of the two is true is a question for empirical investigation and cannot be decided on the grounds of impressionistic guesses.

Value patterns

Value orientations tell us what people want out of life (Inglehart and Welzel 2005). To be sure, no society is homogeneous in its value orientations, simply because different people aspire to different things in their lives. Societies differ, however, distinctively in the *frequency* with which one can find certain value orientations among people. In this sense, certain value orientations are more typical of some societies than they are of others. Western societies have been said to be individualistic in their value orientations, not because every member of Western societies is individualistic but because one can find individualistic values in higher frequency in Western societies than in other societies (Triandis 1995). Thus, one can use the relative frequency of particular value orientations to describe the cultural location of an entire society, disregarding the fact that the values of relevant minorities will differ from a society's prevailing value orientation.

As has been demonstrated by Baker (2005) and Inglehart and Welzel (2005), a society's prevailing value orientation can be located on the two major value dimensions mentioned above. If, on the traditional versus secular-rational dimension, a society is closer located to the secular-rational pole, moral obligations to such traditionally sacrosanct institutions as the family, religion, and fatherland are less rigid and looser than in societies that are more closely located to the traditional value pole. As Inglehart and Welzel have shown, societies tend to change their prevailing value orientation from more traditional (rigid) values to more secular-rational (permissive) values when the rise of industrial technology increases human control over basic life risks and thus nurtures a basic sense of existential security, making traditional moral obligations superfluous.

If, on the survival versus self-expression dimension, a society is closer to the self-expression pole, survival-driven collective constraints on individual freedom diminish and more room is left to individual self-expression. Societies tend to change their prevailing value orientations from survival (collectivist) values to (individualistic) self-expression values when the rise of a postindustrial 'creative economy' (Florida 2002) de-standardizes economic activities, social role models, and life courses and, by doing this, nurtures a fundamental sense of individual autonomy, making collective restrictions of self-actualization superfluous.

As Inglehart and Welzel have demonstrated, differences on these two value dimensions are highly indicative of various major aspects of a society's well-being and florescence. For instance, low fertility rates, high life expectancies, high literacy rates, high levels of income equality and large-scale welfare states are reflected in less moral rigidity (less traditional values) and more moral permissiveness (more secular-rational values). On the other hand, high levels of tertiary education, high income levels, vibrant civil societies, as well as transparent, accountable and democratic governance, are all reflected in less collectivist orientations (less survival values) and more individualist orientations (more self-expression values). Because these connections are very close, mapping societies on the two value dimensions does not only give us a good idea of their closeness in major values but also of their closeness in basic living conditions. Based on survey data from the World Values Surveys, Figure 18.1 presents such a map, using cultural clusters as presented earlier by Huntington (1993, 1996) and more recently by Inglehart and Welzel (2005).

Comparing the US to some core Western European societies, the results are ambivalent. In terms of moral rigidity (traditional values), Americans seem to be far apart from most of Europe, being as traditional and rigid in their morality as the most conservative Catholic societies, such as Ireland, Poland, or Portugal. In terms of individualism (self-expression values), the US and core Western European societies such as France, Germany, or Sweden are on roughly the same level of individualism. Individualism indeed is the common cultural heritage that the West (especially the Protestant West) obtained from its early entrance

Figure 18.1 Global cultural map

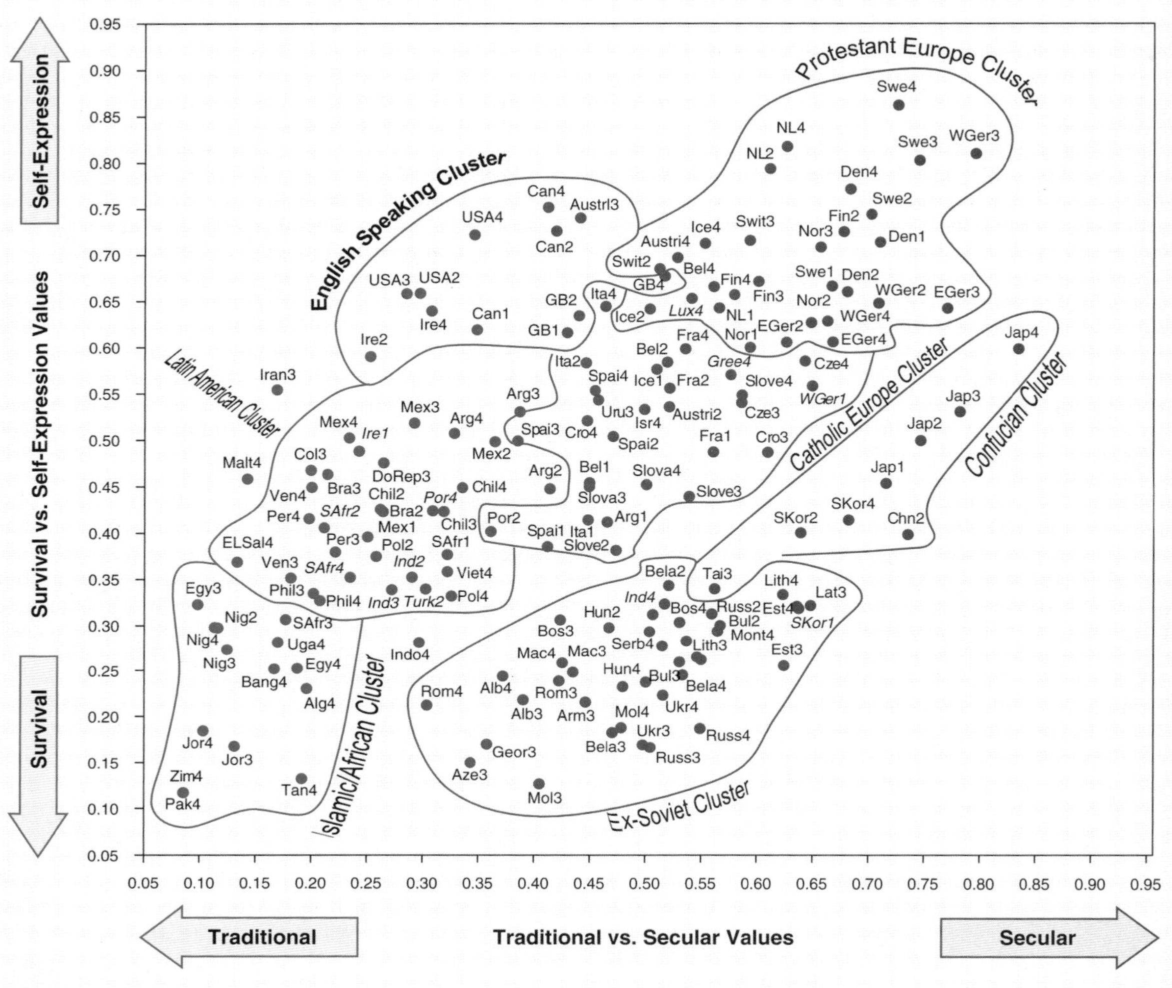

Source: World Values Survey 1981–2001. The numbers next to the country abbreviations indicate when the society participated in the four waves of the world values survey: 1 = 1981; 2 = 1990–91; 3 = 1995–98; 4 = 1999–2001.

into full-fledged capitalism. In this point at least, the (Protestant) West has still a distinct cultural feature that sets it clearly apart from other world regions. Hence, there is no Atlantic rift in individualism. Let us look at this ambivalence in more detail.

Interestingly, as much as Protestant societies are unified in their common emphasis on individual self-expression, they are divided in their emphasis on traditionally rigid values. This division indeed follows a division between continental Europe and North America or between the English-speaking and non-English speaking world, with the US taking one of the most extremely traditional positions (besides Ireland). Moral rigidity is based on the conviction that God is important for one's life and an emphasis on obedience and religious faith as values that children should be taught at home. In general, faith in God, fatherland and family are closely related to each other, indicating a worldview in which moral obligations to these holy institutions are rigid and have to be followed. While the overall picture suggests a pronounced support for such values in the US, a great deal of variation can be found among European countries. Protestant European societies are less rigid (less traditional) and more permissive (more secular-rational) in their moral orientations than Catholic and English-speaking European societies. In fact, English-speaking societies show about the same level of moral rigidity as that which has been observed in Latin America.

The overall impression of Figure 18.1 seems to support Lipset's American Exceptionalism, even though it would be more precise to generalize the US's Exceptionalism to the world of Anglophone European settled countries, in which case we might state Anglophone Exceptionalism (so the US is somewhat less unique than many like to see it). In any case, Anglophone societies differ from other individualistic societies in the postindustrial world in that they are considerably more traditional in their emphasis on rigid moral values.

Figure 18.2 allows us to take a closer look at the value changes that occurred over the past 20 years. To provide a more comprehensive picture, the US, Sweden (Protestant Europe) and Spain (Catholic Europe) were supplemented by societies from other cultural zones.

In 2000, both the US and European societies show a slightly less traditional (rigid) value pattern than in 1980, with the US indicating the greatest change towards more moral permissiveness. Thus, even though the US shows an exceptionally rigid morality it is at the same time the country that has moved the most towards more secularity, rationality, and moral permissiveness. This seems counterintuitive in light of the resurgence of evangelical vigor and creationism that the US has experienced in recent years. But it is not. There is a resurgence of fundamentalism and dogmatism in the US precisely because the society has moved towards more moral permissiveness, especially in domains that touch traditional family values, such as divorce, abortion, and homosexuality. This change has alerted the conservatives and has mobilized them so that they became more active and visible (but not more numerous) than before (cf. the discussion by Ronnie Lipschutz in this volume).

At the same time, all Western societies show a further move towards more emphasis on self-expression values (individualism), the widest move occurring in Protestant Sweden. Interestingly, the variation over time is limited by cultural boundaries as shown in Figure 18.1. Despite considerable cultural changes, cross-national value differences remain largely unaltered. Sweden, Spain and the US all became considerably more secular (morally permissive) from 1980 to 2000. But even in 2000 most Swedes are more permissive and secular than most Spaniards who, in turn, are more permissive and secular than most Americans – as it was in 1980. Likewise, all three societies became more individualistic from 1980 to 2000. But the differences in 2000 are the same as in 1980: self-expression values are still most pronounced in Sweden, somewhat less in the US, and least in Spain. Overall, the picture suggests that Western societies have undergone similar cultural changes, insofar as they share a great deal of common experience in the context of post-industrialization and globalization. Still, despite the similarities of these changes, cultural traditions show a sustained impact in that they preserve the relative distances between societies. Value differences are as large as ever, irrespective of the supposed homogenizing forces of globalization.

Our findings indicate significant differences between core societies in Western Europe. Catholic European societies are generally less individualistic and morally more traditional than Protestant European societies. English-speaking Europe, for its part, is as individualistic as most of the

Figure 18.2 Value changes in selected societies

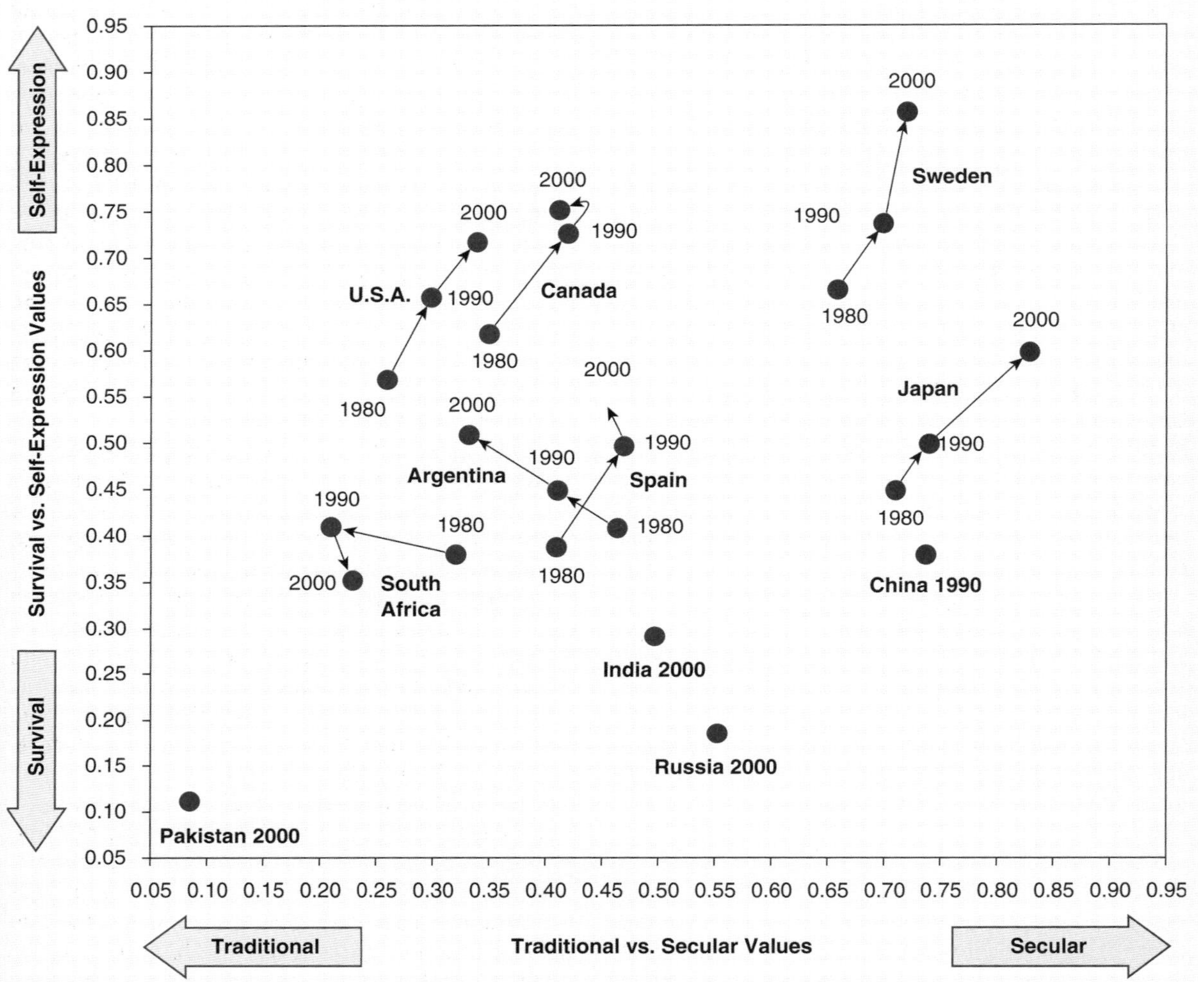

Protestant societies on the European continent but even more traditional than most of the Catholic societies on the continent. With this combination, English-speaking Europe takes a special position, located somewhere between the US and the non-English Europe. In addition to Europe's categorization, we apply a comparable regional classification to the US. The regionally highly unequal results of the 2004 Presidential election (the Pacific states and the vast majority of the North East and the Great Lakes voted for the Democratic candidate, the Southern and Western States voted in favor of the Republican George W. Bush) suggest that the US population is not homogeneous in its value orientations but is itself divided into sub-national cultural zones (most of which are larger than most European nation-states). To see how large inner-American value differences are in comparison to the differences between America and Europe, we have grouped the different US states into regional divisions, largely following the classification by the US Census Bureau.[3]

Using this classification, Figure 18.3 maps the absoluteness of people's belief system, plotting the importance of religion in people's lives against the question of whether people think that there are always and in each situation clear guidelines for what should be considered good or evil. To allow conclusions about the changes occurring over time in both dimensions, the figure documents the results for 1990 and 2000 in different regions in the US and Europe.[4]

On the one hand, the results of Figure 18.3 support our previous findings: The US clearly shows a more traditional (rigid) value pattern than the European societies. For a majority of the US population God is very important in their lives. Similarly, significantly more Americans than Europeans consider the distinction between good and evil to be an absolute one, implying strict moral standards that are always applicable. The figure suggests that US society is more strongly driven by absolute rules than are European societies.

On the other hand, mean differences obscure considerable differences within the US. For example, the Southern states are by far the most morally rigid part of the US (also the part where support for the death penalty is most pronounced), followed by the Western region and the Great Lakes. By contrast, the Progressive US (Pacific Coast and North East) is morally more permissive, almost at the same level as the English-speaking part of Europe. In a way, the latter provides a 'transatlantic bridge' between the most permissive parts of the US and the morally most rigid parts of Europe.

Figure 18.4 directs attention to a central component of self-expression values, tolerance of human diversity. Let's have a look how strongly the various parts of the US and Western Europe 'resist' the rise of tolerance values. On the x-axis, we document intolerance towards foreigners (immigrants or foreign workers, people of a different race). On the y-axis, the rejection of new or alternative lifestyles (divorce, homosexuality) is displayed.

In all societies, intolerance towards foreigners seems to be a minority phenomenon, nowhere getting support from more than 20 percent of the population. Overall, the rejection of immigrants or people of a different 'race' is slightly more pronounced in Western Europe than in the US, in particular in 2000. With the exception of English-speaking Europe and the Great Lakes region in the US, none of the societies shows an increase in rejection of foreigners. This result is surprising in light of the prevailing frame in public debate, which discusses migration largely as a threat to domestic job owners. It is supported, however, by the results of another question (not documented here), asking people whether they think that employers should give priority to nationals instead of immigrants, in case jobs are scarce. With the exception of English-speaking Europe and the Western region of the US, a decline in assenting to this statement can be observed between 1990 and 2000.

Looking at people's judgments about divorce or homosexuality and their tolerance of other people's decisions to live their lives as they want, more variation can be observed. Yet, again the picture does not show a simple rift between the US and Western Europe. Protestant Europe shows the most liberal attitudes towards diversity but the Progressive US is closer to Catholic Europe than to the rest of the US. Vice versa, English-speaking Europe can be located among the other US regions. As expected, the Southern part of the United States is characterized by the highest level of intolerance towards alternative lifestyles, with more than 50 percent of the population rejecting divorce or homosexuality. However, all societies, including the US South, show an enormous increase in tolerance between 1990 and 2000, indicating changing values towards more individual autonomy, lifestyle pluralism and freedom

Figure 18.3 Absolute beliefs, in %

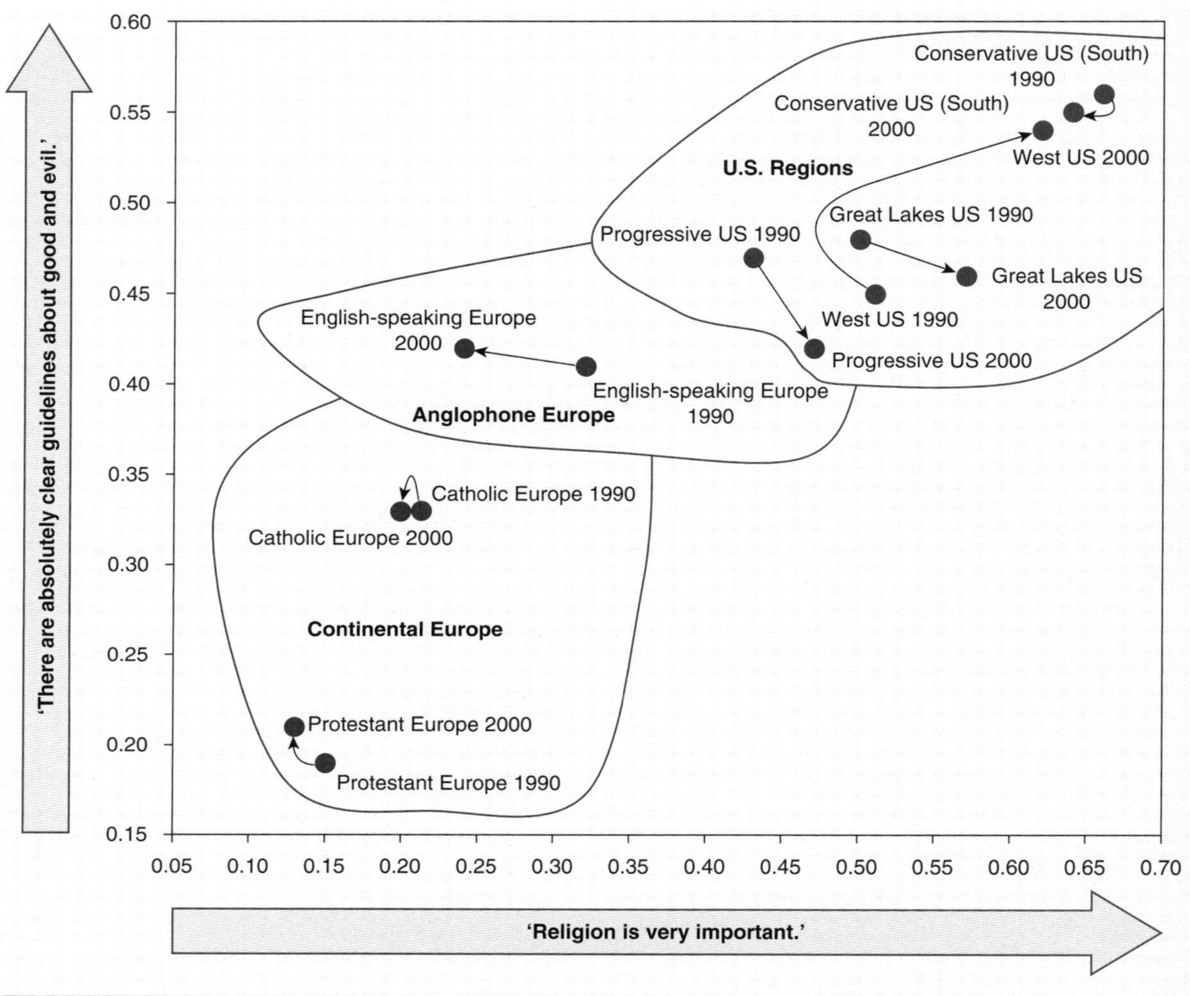

Religion is very important:

'How important is religion in your life?' (1 = very important to 4 = not at all important). Answers 'very important' are depicted in percent.

There are absolutely clear guidelines about good and evil:

'There are absolutely clear guidelines about what is good and evil. These always apply to everyone, whatever the circumstances.' Answers agreeing with the statement are depicted in percent.

Figure 18.4 Intolerance towards 'The Other', in %

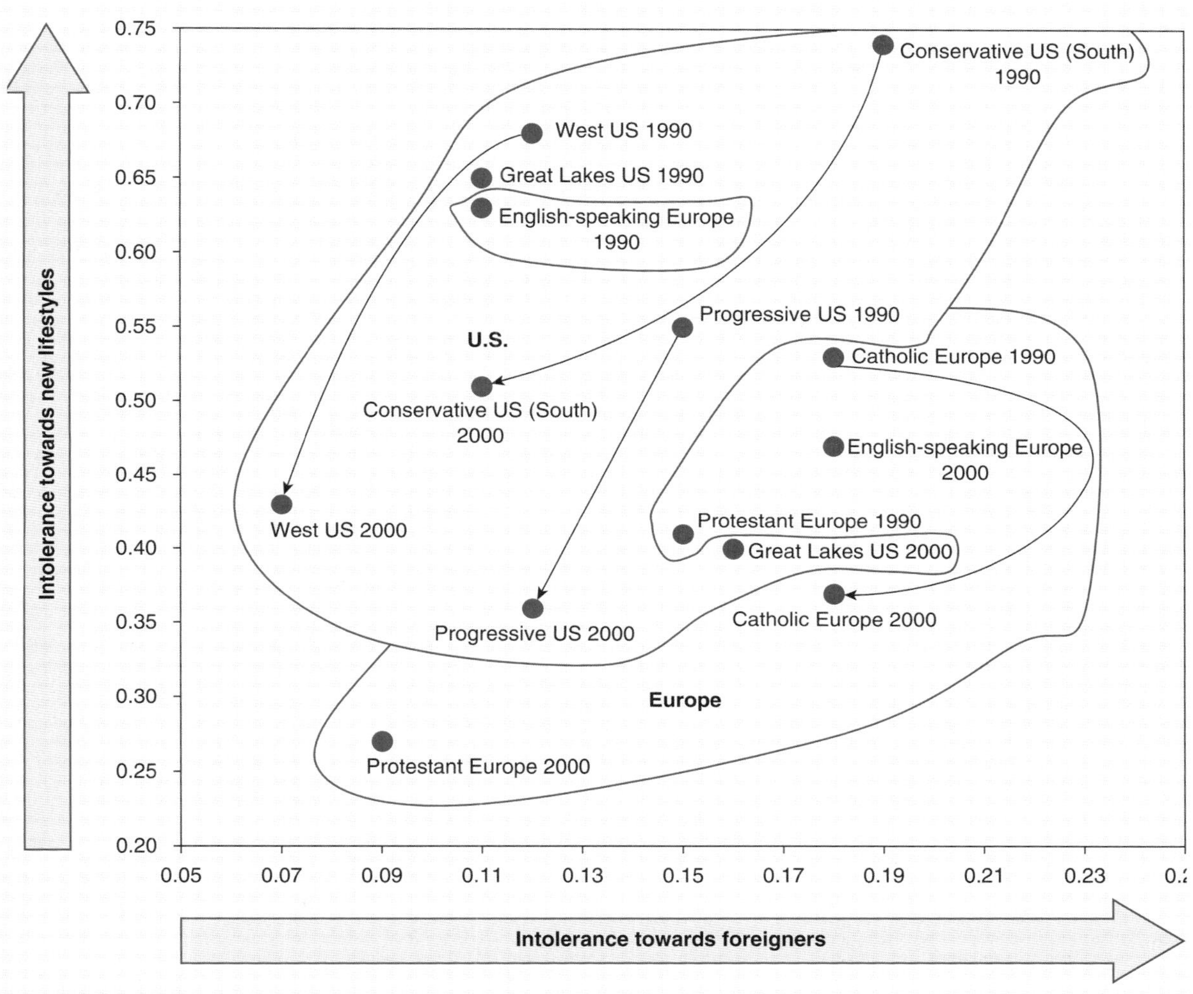

Intolerance towards foreigners:

'On this list are various groups of people. Could you please sort out any that you would not like to have as neighbors? Answers mentioning any of 'people of a diferent race' or immigrants/foreign workers' are depicted in percent.

Intolerance towards new lifestyles:
'Please tell me whether you think that divorce can always be justified, never be justified, or something in between. ... Please tell me whether you think that homosexuality can always be justified, never be justified, or something in between (1 = never justifiable, 10 = always justifiable)'. Answers 1 to 3 on any of the scales are depicted in percent.

of choice. In any event, in terms of tolerance values there is no simple rift between the US and Western Europe. The major rift is rather within the US, dividing its progressive coastal regions from the conservative South.

Conclusion

Is there an Atlantic rift dividing North American and Western European values into two sharply separated zones? The answer to this question varies, depending on what type of values one is looking at. With respect to individualistic values that place emphasis on human self-expression, there is little division, if any, between North America and Western Europe. In this respect, Europe and America are pretty much unified as the individualistic West against the 'rest' of the world. As is known from the analyses of Inglehart and Welzel (2005), individualistic values are most closely associated with such institutional features as transparent, accountable, and responsive government. These are the core characteristics of liberal democracy and there is little difference in these characteristics between Western Europe and North America. There is no Atlantic rift in matters of democracy.

Yet there is an important internal differentiation within the Western world when it comes to the role of rigid traditional moral codes. On the whole, the US is considerably more religious, rigid, and absolute in its prevailing values than any society of continental Western Europe. But one should be cautious in considering this as an indication of American Exceptionalism or as an indication of an American–European chasm. For one, the morally fundamentalist stance is not a specificity of the US alone. This characteristic is shared by Ireland, Canada, Australia, New Zealand, and Great Britain to a somewhat lesser extent. Thus, a tendency to moral rigidity is not an exceptionally US American phenomenon; it is a general characteristic that is shared (though to different degrees) by all economically advanced Anglophone societies. It is an Anglophone phenomenon. But what unifies these societies and makes them so distinct in questions of moral strictness? Usually, value orientations become less traditional, sacred, rigid, and absolute and more permissive, secular, and rational when the risk sharing mechanisms of the welfare state nurture a sense of existential security, making traditional obligations superfluous. Compared to the Christian Democratic and Social Democratic versions of an extended welfare state, all Anglophone societies entertain a small-scale 'liberal' welfare state. This feature is coupled with higher rates of social mobility but also with more unequal incomes, higher risks of job loss and of poverty and thus less existential security. In such a situation, strict moral guidelines and rigid obligations to such institutions as religion, the family, and the nation appear as a safeguard in an economically insecure world. Thus, as little as the Anglophone and the non-Anglophone parts of the West differ in matters of democracy, as much do they differ in matters of the welfare state. This is reflected in the stronger presence of religious and strict worldviews in the Anglophone world. Societies in the Anglophone world tend to have an anti-state orientation but not an anti-nation orientation. Quite the contrary, they are rather patriotic.

The differences between the US and Western Europe in questions of moral strictness are considerable. This is very likely to become manifest in international politics. When it comes to democratic values and universal human rights, North America and Western Europe stand for the same set of human-centric values, which reflects their common individualistic heritage. But they differ tremendously in the moral vigor with which they advocate these values. Western Europeans are constantly annoyed about the missionary zeal by which US Americans advocate their case. This tendency to absoluteness makes much of American society receptive to the morality of retaliation. Combined with a considerable amount of self-righteousness, the 'eye for an eye, a tooth for a tooth' logic of retaliation easily justifies the freedom to wear guns, the death penalty as well as unilateral US action in international politics. This is a potential source of conflicts between the EU and the US.

How much of this potential becomes virulent largely depends on who is in power in the US. By now the potential definitely is virulent. When US President George W. Bush claimed God to be an ally of the US after September 11, when he discriminated between 'good' and 'evil', 'us' and 'them' (Katzenstein 2003: 756), characterized some countries as the 'axis of evil' or stated 'Either you are with us, or you are with the terrorists',[5] he pretty much hit a nerve with the American public. As our analyses have shown, Americans are more inclined to think along dimensions of 'good' and 'evil' than Europeans.

Still, we should not forget that on the issues that divide the US from the European Union, the US itself is a divided society. There are two different Americas if we compare the value orientations of the coastal regions with those of the South and the lower Midwest. Hence, the extent to which the cultural differences between Europe and America become effective in international politics depends on which America is in power. With a slightly different electoral system, Al Gore would have followed Bill Clinton in office. In that case, the American–European divide would probably not be much of an issue today.

As is currently the case, a conservative Republican administration poses a greater challenge to the European Union (and to the international system in general). But it also means a greater chance to market the European model of international politics, emphasizing cooperative multilateralism rather than self-righteous unilateralism, rational dialogue rather than missionary declarations, mutual responsibility rather than national egoism, and a stronger emphasis on foreign aid in relation to national defense.

Notes

1 In 2002, the US Congress passed the 'American Servicemembers' Protection Act' (ASPA) which gives the US President extensive authorities to protect US servicemembers from ICC hearings and convictions. The ASPA was criticized for containing, although hypothetically, an option for military intervention. The law became also known as the 'Hague Invasion Act'.

2 We are perfectly aware of the fact that there is no authoritative definition of core Western European societies. Hence, our proposal does not claim to be authoritative. It is simply a definition based on convention.

3 Four regions: (1) Progressive US: New England, Middle Atlantic, Pacific, California; (2) Great Lakes: East North Central; (3) West: West South Central, Mountain States; (4) Conservative US (South): East South Central, West South Central, South Atlantic. For the United States Bureau of the Census, see: http://www.census.gov.

4 Three regions: (1) Protestant Europe: Denmark, Finland, Iceland, The Netherlands, Sweden, West Germany; (2) Catholic Europe: Belgium, France, Italy, Spain; (3) English-speaking Europe: Ireland, Great Britain, Northern Ireland.

5 George W. Bush in his 'Address to a Joint Session of Congress and the American People', 20 September 2001. He underlined his position by taking up this statement at further occasions.

REFERENCES

Baker, Wayne (2005) *America's Crisis of Values: Reality and Perception.* Princeton and Oxford: Princeton University Press.

Bellah, Robert N. et al. (1996/1985) *Habits of the Heart: Individualism and Commitment in American Life*, updated edn with a new introduction. Berkeley: University of California Press.

Bennett, William J. (1999) *The Death of Outrage: Bill Clinton and the Assault on American Idols.* New York: Free Press.

– (2001) *The Broken Hearth: Reversing the Moral Collapse of the American Family.* New York: Random House.

Berman, Russell A. (2004) *Anti-Americanism in Europe: A Cultural Problem.* Stanford, CA: Hoover Institution Press.

Buruma, Ian (2006) 'Cross purposes. Conflicting views about religion threaten to divide Europe from the US', *The Guardian*, 7 January.

Castells, Manuel (1996) The Information Age: Economy, Society, and Culture. Volume 1. *The Rise of the Network Society.* Oxford and Malden, MA: Blackwell Publishers.

Florida, Richard (2002) *The Rise of the Creative Class.* New York: Basic Books.

Himmelfarb, Gertrude (1996) *The De-Moralization of Society: From Victorian Virtues to Modern Values.* New York: Vintage Books.

Huntington, Samuel P. (1993) 'The Clash of Civilizations', *Foreign Affairs*, 72 (3): 22–49.

– (1996) *The Clash of Civilizations and the Remaking of World Order.* New York: Simon & Schuster.

Inglehart, Ronald and Welzel, Christian (2005) *Modernization, Cultural Change, and Democracy: The Human Development Sequence*. Cambridge: Cambridge University Press.

Kagan, Robert (2003) *Of Paradise and Power: America and Europe in the New World Order.* New York: Alfred A. Knopf.

Katzenstein, Peter J. (2003) 'Same war – different view: Germany, Japan, and counterterrorism', *International Organization*, 57: 731–60.

Lind, Michael (1996) 'The American creed: does it matter? Should it change?', *Foreign Affairs,* 75 (2): 135–9.

Lipset, Seymour Martin (1963) *The First New Nation: The United States in Historical and Comparative Perspective*. New York: Basic Books.

– (1990) *Continental Divide. The Values and Institutions of the United States and Canada*. New York and London: Routledge.

– (1996) *American Exceptionalism. A Double-Edged Sword.* New York and London: W.W. Norton & Company.

Lockhart, Charles (2003) *The Roots of American Exceptionalism: History, Institutions and Culture*. New York: Palgrave Macmillan.

Madsen, Deborah L. (1998) *American Exceptionalism.* Edinburgh: Edinburgh University Press.

Putnam, Robert D. (2000) *Bowling Alone: The Collapse and Revival of American Community.* New York: Simon & Schuster.

Tocqueville, Alexis de (2000 [1835/40]) *Democracy in America.* Trans., ed., and with an introduction by Harvey C. Mansfield and Delba Winthrop. Chicago: University of Chicago Press.

Triandis, Harry C. (1995) *Individualism and Collectivism.* Boulder, CO: Westview Press.

## CHAPTER 19

WHY DIDN'T RELIGION DISAPPEAR? RE-EXAMINING THE SECULARIZATION THESIS[1]

Ronald Inglehart and Pippa Norris

The publics of virtually all advanced industrial societies have been moving toward more secular orientations since the 19th century. Nevertheless, the world as a whole now has more people with traditional religious views than ever before – and they constitute a growing proportion of the world's population. These two seemingly contradictory claims are actually closely related, because secularization is linked with steeply declining human fertility rates, so that virtually all rich, secularized countries are now below the population-replacement level. Another reason that religion has not disappeared is that since about 1990, subjective religiosity seems to have stopped declining in advanced industrial societies and a broader type of spiritual concern has become increasingly widespread.

Major social analysts of the nineteenth century, from Marx and Weber to Durkheim and Freud, predicted that religion would cease to be significant with the emergence of industrial society. In recent years, however, this thesis has experienced a sustained challenge. Critics claim it is time to bury the secularization thesis.

It would be premature to do so. The critique relies too heavily on selected anomalies and focuses too heavily on the United States (a striking deviant case) rather than comparing systematic evidence across the full range of societies. This study draws on a massive base of new evidence generated by the four waves of the World Values Survey/European Values Survey, which has carried out representative national surveys in eighty societies, covering all of the world's major faiths and including 85 percent of the world's population.

It is obvious that religion has not disappeared from the world, nor does it seem likely to do so. Nevertheless, the concept of secularization captures an important part of what is going on. This chapter presents a revised version of secularization theory that emphasizes the extent to which people have a sense of existential security – that is, the feeling that survival can be taken for granted. The feeling that survival is uncertain has shaped the lives of most people throughout most of history, and the need for a sense of reassurance in a highly uncertain world, has been a key factor underlying the mass appeal of religion. As this need diminishes, a systematic erosion of religious practices, values and beliefs tends to occur. The need for a sense of assurance in face of existential insecurity is not the only motivation underlying religion. Throughout history, philosophers and theologians have turned to religion in seeking answers to the meaning of life. But for the vast majority of the population, the prime appeal of religion was that it helped them cope with existential insecurity.

During the twentieth century in nearly all post-industrial nations church attendance has declined markedly. The United States remains exceptional, showing much higher rates of church attendance, and higher emphasis on religion, than is found in almost any other advanced industrial society (though ranking far below most pre-industrial societies).

But despite clear evidence of secularization in rich nations, the world as a whole has not become less religious. Two things are true:

1. The publics of virtually all advanced industrial societies have been moving toward more secular orientations during the past fifty years. Nevertheless,
2. The world as a whole now has more people with traditional religious views than ever before – and they constitute a growing proportion of the world's population.

Though these two propositions may initially seem contradictory; they are not, as we will demonstrate.

Theories of secularization

The idea that the rise of a rational worldview has undermined the foundations of faith in the supernatural, the mysterious, and the magical predated

Weber, but was strongly influenced by his work. Leading sociologists advanced the rationalist argument farther during the 1960s and 1970s, arguing that the rise of science and technology rendered the central claims of the Church implausible in modern societies, blowing away the vestiges of superstitious dogma.

Weber viewed the mysterious as something to be conquered by human reason. The dazzling achievements of medicine, engineering, and mathematics – and the material products generated by the rise of modern capitalism, technology, and manufacturing industry during the nineteenth century – reinforced the idea of mankind's control of nature. The division of church and state, and the rise of secular-rational bureaucratic states and representative governments, displaced the rule of spiritual leaders, ecclesiastical institutions, and hereditary rulers claiming authority from God. According to Weber, industrialization brought the fragmentation of the life-world, the decline of community, the rise of bureaucracy, and technological consciousness – all of which made religion less arresting and less plausible than it had been in premodern societies. But if a rational worldview generates widespread skepticism about the existence of God, then those societies which express most confidence in science might be expected to prove least religious; in fact, as data from the World Values Survey demonstrates, exactly the opposite is true: today, the advanced industrial societies in which secularization is most advanced, show the *lowest* levels of confidence in science and technology – far lower than those found in low-income societies. Moreover, the Weberian interpretation emphasizes cognitive factors that tend to be irreversible and universal: the spread of scientific knowledge does not disappear in times of crisis or economic downturn. If it were the dominant cause of secularization, we would not expect to find fluctuations in religiosity linked with varying levels of security – but we do.

A related explanation for secularization was offered by Durkheim's theory of functional differentiation in industrialized societies. By the 1950s this perspective had become the predominant sociological view. Functionalists argue that religion is not simply a system of beliefs and ideas; it is also a system of rituals and ceremonies that help sustain social cohesion and stability. But in industrialized societies specialized professionals and organizations, dedicated to healthcare, education, social control, politics, and welfare, replaced most of the tasks once carried out by religious organizations. Stripped of their core social purposes, religious institutions play greatly diminished roles. If this thesis is correct, one would expect that religion should have declined most in affluent societies that have developed extensive welfare states, such as in Sweden, The Netherlands and France – and indeed much of the evidence is consistent with this account.

Yet in recent decades growing numbers of critics have expressed reservations about the core claims of the functionalist interpretation, pointing to a resurgence of religiosity evident in the success of Islamic movements and parties, the popularity of Evangelicalism in Latin America, ethno-religious bloodshed in Nigeria. Traditional secularization theory is now widely challenged and the supply-side school of rational choice theorists, that emerged in the early 1990s, has become the most popular alternative. This school assumes that the public's demand for religion is constant, and focuses on how conditions of religious freedom, and the work of competing religious institutions, actively generate its 'supply'. The earlier view was that pluralism *eroded* religious faith, destroying the unquestioned power of a single pervasive theological faith, sowing the seeds of skepticism and doubt. Drawing on the analogy of firms struggling for customers in the economic market, supply-side theory assumes the opposite. Its core proposition is that vigorous competition between religious denominations has a *positive* effect on religious involvement. The more churches, denominations, creeds and sects compete in a local community, the harder rival leaders need to strive to maintain their congregations. This school argues that the continued vitality of religious beliefs and practices in the United States reflects strong competition among many religious institutions. By contrast, where a single religious organization predominates through government regulation and subsidies, it encourages a complacent clergy, just as state-owned industries and corporate monopolies generate inefficiency and lack of innovation in the economic market. Thus, the state-subsidized churches of Northern Europe have produced an unmotivated clergy and an indifferent public.

Nevertheless, after more than a decade of debate, the supply-side claim that religious pluralism fosters religious participation remains in dispute. It has difficulty accounting for the relative vigor of church attendance in Southern European countries where the Roman Catholic Church has a near-monopoly. Moreover, evidence from the World Values Survey demonstrates that religious belief is far more intense in Islamic societies than in the highly pluralistic United States. The publics of almost all low-income countries – Islamic or non-Islamic, and religiously monolithic or pluralistic – place more emphasis on religion than does the American public. The dominant factor seems to be economic development, rather than market competition. Regardless of how one measures it, religion tends to be much more important in agrarian societies than in industrial or post-industrial societies, as Figure 19.1 demonstrates.

The thesis of secularization based on existential security

We propose an alternative interpretation, linked with the fact that rich and poor nations around the globe differ sharply in their levels of development and socioeconomic inequality, and thus in their levels of existential security – the feeling that one can take survival for granted. Economic development has significant consequences for religiosity; sharply rising levels of economic resources, interacting with the emergence of the welfare state, reduce the need for religion. Virtually all of the world's major religious cultures provide reassurance that, even though the individual alone can't understand or predict what lies ahead, a higher power will ensure that things work out. This belief reduces stress, enabling people to shut out anxiety and focus on coping with their immediate problems. Without such a belief system, extreme stress tends to produce withdrawal reactions. Individuals under stress need rigid, predictable rules. They need to be sure of what is going to happen because their margin for error is slender. Conversely, people raised under conditions of relative security have less need for the absolute and rigidly predictable rules that religions provide.

But, while rising levels of existential security lead to secularization, the latter has a dramatic negative impact on fertility rates. Thus, rich societies are becoming more secular but they are becoming a diminishing part of the world's population. By contrast poor nations remain deeply religious – and display far higher fertility rates and growing populations. One of the most central injunctions of virtually all traditional religions is to strengthen the family, to encourage people to have children, to encourage women to stay home and raise children, and to forbid abortion, divorce, or anything that interferes with high rates of reproduction. As a result of these two interacting trends, rich nations are becoming more secular, but the world as a whole is becoming more religious.

Conclusions

Evidence from 80 societies indicates that due to rising levels of human security, the publics of virtually all advanced industrial societies have been moving toward more secular orientations. 'Modernization' (the process of industrialization, urbanization, and rising levels of education and the transition from agrarian to industrial and post-industrial society) greatly weakens the influence of religious institutions making religion subjectively less important in people's lives.

Within most advanced industrial societies, attendance at religious services has fallen over the past several decades; and religious authorities have largely lost their authority to dictate to the public on such matters as birth control, divorce, abortion, sexual orientation and the necessity of marriage before childbirth. Secularization is not taking place only in Western Europe, as some critics have claimed; it is occurring in most advanced industrial societies including Australia, New Zealand, Japan, and Canada. Even in America, there has been a lesser but perceptible trend toward secularization; the trend has been partly masked by massive immigration of people with relatively traditional worldviews (and high fertility rates) from Hispanic countries – and by relatively high levels of economic inequality; but when one controls for these factors, even the United States shows a significant movement toward secularization.

Nevertheless, it would be a major mistake to assume that religion will eventually disappear throughout the world. The world as a whole now has more people with traditional religious views than ever before – and they constitute a growing proportion of the world's population. Rich societies are secularizing but they contain a dwindling share of the world's population; while poor societies are not secularizing and they contain a rising share of

Figure 19.1 Religiosity by type of society

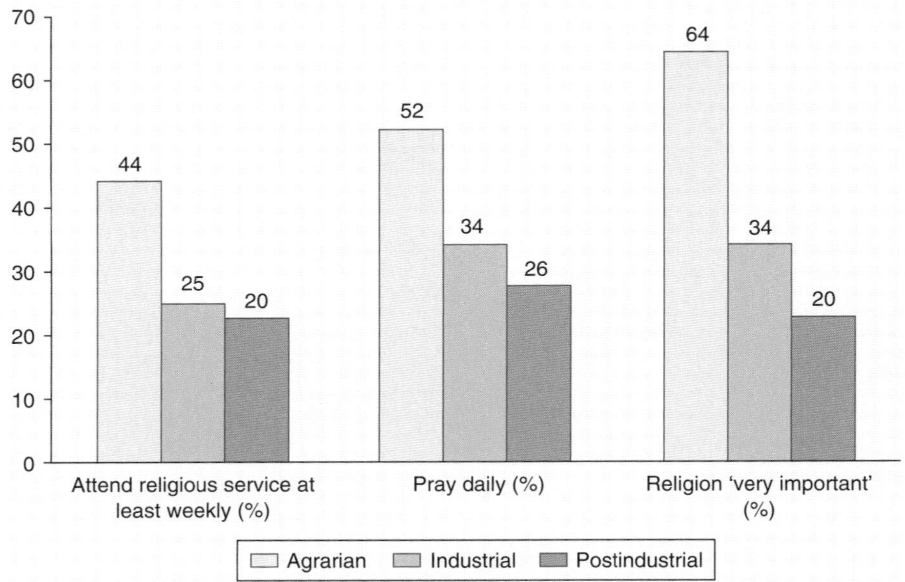

Figure 19.2 Percentage who 'often' think about the meaning and purpose of life

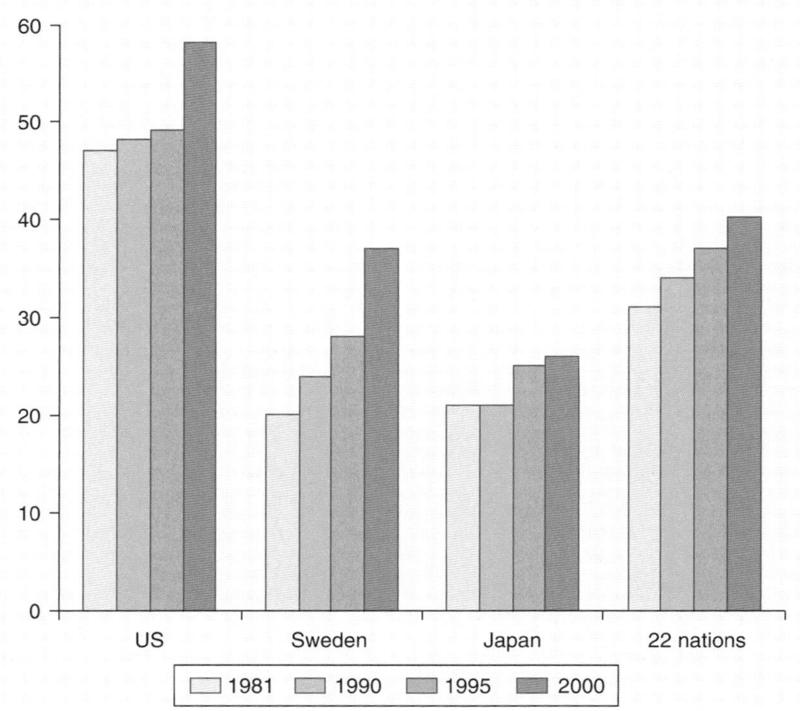

the world's population. Thus, modernization does indeed bring a de-emphasis on religion within virtually any country that experiences it, but the percentage of the world's population for whom religion is important is rising.

There is one more twist in this complicated story. Although the established religions are losing the allegiance of the public throughout advanced industrial society, evidence from the Values Surveys indicates that from 1981 to 2001, a growing percentage of the public in virtually all of these countries spent time thinking about the meaning and purpose of life. Figure 19.2 shows this pattern in the relatively religious United States, in two of the most secularized industrial societies – Sweden and Japan – and in 22 advanced industrial societies as a whole. Organized religion is losing its grip on the public, but spiritual concerns, broadly defined, are taking on growing importance.

Note

1. This paper appeared in September 2004 in WZB-Mitteilungen Heft 105, and is available online at: http://www.wz-berlin.de/publikation/pdf/wm105/s7-10.pdf

MIGRATION, SECURITY AND CULTURE IN THE USA

Leo F. Estrada

The question of migration in the United States of America is now increasingly dominated by security issues that are raised with regard to Arab immigrants or Muslims in general, whereas during the last decades of the twentieth century labor issues were central and pertained to people from Latin America and Asia. As a consequence of 9/11, however, the focus is on those immigrants who are now associated with potential danger and the threat of violence. These concerns have added sentiments of fear, unfrairness and racism to previously articulated issues of employment and cultural identity. As the US Government has aligned its immigration and national security policies a new migration-security nexus has emerged in this country.

Introduction

Migration-caused tensions in North America have so far revolved around labor and cultural issues and have concerned immigrants from Latin America and Asia. As a consequence of 9/11, however, new tensions have arisen regarding Muslim or Arab or Middle Eastern immigrants. These issues are located within a new national security context, in which the US Government has aligned immigration and national security policies. Foreign agencies, social service agencies, citizen patrols, and even employers have become new actors in this scenario. It has been a time of reliance on emerging and untested principles of human security. The emerging new tensions have added sentiments of fear, unfairness and racism to existing concerns about employment and cultural identity. The unintended yet hazardous long-term consequences of these emerging policies will fall more heavily on some immigrant groups as well as on immigrant host countries' security provision capacities.

It is necessary, therefore, to broaden our understanding of the new migration pressures in the perspective of the security dimension. It will be argued that global migration-caused tensions are highly diverse and complex phenomena and that they require a new conceptualization of international migration.

The dynamics of global migration

Although large-scale movements of people have a long history, the extent, intensity and velocity of human migration and its impact on host and home societies and states have reached an unprecedented scale today. With more than an estimated 200 million people living as immigrants outside the countries of their birth, international migration has become one of the primary drivers of global change.[1] The increasing scale and scope of international migration is a symbol of globalization in the twenty-first century as much as global trade and investment were at the end of the nineteenth. And its impact has the potential to prompt violent local backlashes when its causes, conditions and implications are not understood and addressed.

There are many global examples of movements or intended movements of people. The wave of Sub-Saharan and North African immigrants accosting the Italian island of Lampedusa, migrants attempting hazardous crossings of the Eurotunnel, the indefinite detention of refugees in Nauru island by Australia, Haitians who drown crossing the turbulent sea to Puerto Rico, or the casualties among migrants crossing the perilous US/Mexico Sonora desert, all exemplify the intensifying pressure that new trends of global migration place on growing numbers of migrants as well as their home and host countries.

Demographic aspects

The scope and scale of current migration trends make it difficult to establish an accurate picture of the phenomenon and the new pressures it causes. In North America, for example, international migration is the major determinant of population growth. For the most part, fertility and mortality rates have been constant in the United States and Canada over the past decade. What determines the amount and rate of growth today and into the future in North America is immigration from Mexico, Central America, and Asia where a majority of North American migration originates.

Migration flows alter the size and composition of the population of the host country as well as regions in the country of origin. Internal population growth has slowed and in some cases gone into decline in most Western countries. The populations of Western countries are undergoing significant ageing as life expectancy increases and birth-rates fall. For these nations, immigration adds population but also brings younger workers into the workforce, entrepreneurs who rejuvenate inner-city business districts and children to sustain public school enrollments. The difference in age structure between the older and more mature host populations and the newcomer and younger immigrants also creates tensions when their respective interests and priorities clash.

In this context, the current trend of immigration contributes positively to population growth, alleviating some of the population ageing problems in OECD countries.[2] According to OECD estimates, immigration has been the most important factor in population growth in Austria, Germany, Italy, Luxembourg, Sweden and Switzerland. It contributes to population growth as much as indigenous population growth in the United States, Canada, Australia, Greece, Norway and The Netherlands. The exceptions seem to be France, the UK, Belgium, Portugal and Spain where immigration plays a marginal role in population growth. The diversity of cases makes it a perilous exercise to try to establish a general map of future population growth and demographic change due to immigration. Thus, to gauge the current conditions and long-term consequences of global movements of people we need to analyze the phenomenon beyond its demographic elements.

The globalization of migration trends

Generally speaking, immigration is viewed negatively in host countries. Conventional wisdom on the impacts of immigration is based on a Neo-Malthusian rationale and the xenophobic arguments of negative pressure on both welfare state and cultural traditions.

A single typology of migration motives cannot be drawn from the diversity of cases. Migration dynamics include: chain migration (the first immigrant brings other members of the family over successive years), network migration (migration that relies on a social network that extends beyond the family), serial migration (non-continuous migration extending over decades), individual migration (a single decision), family migration (a collective decision), transnational migration (different family members go to different counties), recruited migration (resulting from direct employer recruitment), etc. Each process leads to differences in immigrant composition and expectations as regards the country of destination and the amount of time spent there. Migration is generally an individual decision with collective implications that number in the millions. However, international migration is not distributed evenly and interesting regional differences in migration persist. Generally, international migration flows move from south to north (from Mexico, Central and South America) and from west to east (from Asia, Southeast Asia). But international migration can suddenly arise anywhere as the outcome of a natural disaster, a political upheaval, or a family dislocation.

The traditional approaches to explaining migration decisions are rooted in neo-classical economic rational actor models that argue in favor of a strong labor market component. Cornelius and Rosenblum maintain that when the returns on labor are sufficiently high in foreign markets, such that the expected increase in wages exceeds the cost of migration, rational individuals choose to emigrate.[3] The case of the United States illustrates this clearly: every year more than 1 million immigrants legally enter the United States. The need for skilled and semi-skilled labor[4] justifies such sizeable migration. Undocumented immigrants enter to provide a workforce for blue collar and occasional workforce needs. The proposed Bush Administration immigration reform proposal highlights a 'guest worker' program that acknowledges the need for foreign labor and underlines, as Tirman suggests, that the 'American economy needs immigration.'[5] Others oppose a 'guest worker' program until all able-bodied US citizens are employed or unless it is limited to programs for specific skills.

This trend is not exclusive to the United States, or to the current period. Three main countries of immigration in the postwar period, the United States, Germany and France, already shared an acute need for foreign labor at that time. The United States has received 25 million immigrants in the last fifty years.[6] Immigration to Europe's industrialized nations has totaled over 75 million. There are no indications that these migratory flows will abate and if migration to industrial countries follows a similar trend, the contemporary pattern of migration will supersede its predecessors in terms of intensity and extent.

Global immigration impact

Explanations for global migration are often forced into an economic discourse surrounding employment that circumvents the complexity of the migration question. This is not surprising, since increasing insecurity of employment or the lack of it has for many years now focused public opinion attention on immigrants 'taking jobs'. Yet no event identified and exposed the impact of international movement of people as 9/11. What was most decisive in galvanizing the migration question was the fact that the nineteen attackers in the four planes that participated in the attacks were all foreigners on temporary visas in the United States. September 11 *shifted the global movement of people into the realm of security*. Furthermore, it reinforced perceptions of danger and contributed to new tensions associated with migration even in multicultural and traditionally migrant-welcoming countries such as Canada and the United States. Suddenly, new homeland security directives linked immigration and security. Given these legal and administrative changes, it is crucial to establish a general view of current global migration trends under its new security rubric.

The migration-security nexus is fivefold. First, migration may be caused by threats to human security (civil unrest, political repression, human rights violations, ethno-religious conflict, gender/sexual persecution). Secondly, the movement of people can itself be securitized and suggested as a threat to national security if it is massive and uncontrolled. Third, migration can result in other security threats such as ethnic violence and xenophobia if migrant integration is not a priority. Fourth, high rates of migration can alter the demographic structure of a nation. The final nexus of security and migration that cannot be underestimated is its cultural dimension.

Global cultural production

Global migration brings world culture to a new context that often clashes with local culture. For example, the extensive increase in the use of other languages in a purely English-speaking nation creates highly emotional resistance and fears despite the evidence of the benefits of a multilingual society. This response is best understood as a form of ethnocentrism that is concerned less with language than with preferred images that clash with non-English cultural production in the media, music, art and other cultural forms. The irony is that the United States, the nation that exports its films, music and other cultural products the most is resistant to immigrant-based cultural production.

Immigrants and their communities contribute to what Michael Mann calls 'transcendent cultural power' in which the movement of people and texts helps establish a pattern of shared cultural belief over an extensive area, and creates patterns of reciprocal interaction in which cultural ideas in one place influence those in another.[7] The impact of global migration on global cultural production is difficult to calibrate. However, it is reasonable to believe that migrant communities contribute a great deal to spreading phenomena as different as homogenization, contestation, and hybridization, doing so in relation to shifting contexts, conditions and national allegiances. The growing religious orthodoxy among young members of immigrant communities regardless of their faith needs to be viewed in this context. The Muslim community in the United States. as Tirman argues, shows 'changes in identity and spirituality demands of members, interacting with like-minded individuals in the global community'. The quest for religious orthodoxy with its social implications is thus another example of the entanglement of cultural practices in migrants' transnational identities. The idea that immigrants leave their culture behind when they move is belied by the growth of 'home town associations' among Hispanic and Asian migrants. These home town associations form permanent linkages with their towns and villages in their homeland and allow for continuous communication and the development of cross-national projects.

Migration as a factor of tension and conflict

The increase of global migration has led to increasing anti-immigrant sentiment and ethnic tension. The growing weight of extremist anti-immigration political parties has translated into open expressions of xenophobic sentiments in industrial countries. The case of the Front National totaling 18% of the votes in the 2002 Presidential election in France or the Austrian Freedom Party garnering 27% of the votes in the 1999 general election illustrate such sentiments. In the United States, the Republican Party has proposed repressive immigration laws including the building of a 1,200 mile wall between the United States and Mexico and, along the lines of certain European initiatives they also seek to deny citizenship to children born in the United States to foreign parents. The rejection of the European Constitutional Treaty in 2005 by French and Dutch voters was viewed by many as motivated by the enlargement of the European Union and the possible admission of Muslim Turkey. These anti-immigrant sentiments trumpeting economics (challenges to indigenous jobs), costs and benefits ('they take more than they give'), and cultural collision (the 'balkanization' of the nation) are increasingly contributing to ostracizing foreign migrants in most of the host countries. In the United States, Arizona voters have limited the access of immigrants to public services and in California, voters voted against bilingual education at school. The examples are too numerous to list but the emerging debate on immigration reform legislation in the United States and Canada will surely exhibit the ugly side of anti-immigrant sentiments. For centuries, the linguistic and religious identity demands of immigrants have been viewed as threats to the host country's cultural and political identity. Ethnicity and national identity have been a contested terrain in the United States since its inception. Furthermore, immigrant integration models have been dismissed by the general public; that is, few believe that immigrant distinctions will disappear over time. The debate on American identity has fuelled subsequent debates on citizenship rights and multicultural models of the Republic. Though the roots of these debates are different from those in other migrant host countries, there are similarities in the responses.

In the United States, since all the 9/11 attackers were Muslim Arabs tens of thousands of legal aliens of Muslim descent or hailing from those countries were questioned, finger-printed and profiled by the immigration authorities.[8] The Patriot Act further expanded Federal powers to prosecute aliens deemed to threaten national security and imposed special registration procedures which distinguished this group from others. The focus on Muslim and/or Middle Eastern migrants has thus affected the broader Muslim/Middle Eastern community.[9] Consequently, as Tirman suggests, after decades of gradually improving negative perceptions, the social place of the Muslim migrant in America has deteriorated. Middle Eastern people or Arabs are perceived today as a potential danger to the national security. Given the immense number of immigrants from Mexico and Latin America, one can only imagine what the situation would be had the attackers been from that region. Nonetheless, the current situation has developed into a deeper sense of blame, or open retribution; accepted anger and the explicit targeting of groups.[10]

This sentiment of marginalization, as Kymlicka and Straehle (1999) suggest, derives from the fact that immigrants feel unprotected when the nation-state fails to accept and provide institutional elements for the existence of a truly multicultural state. The lack of commitment by the nation-state signals a refusal to initiate a total acceptance of different social practices, conventions and rules. The evolution of the American identity question in the United States has established political and institutional barriers in recent years and underlines this need for a more comprehensive definition of citizenship within a national society that, culturally, is increasingly diverse.

The migration-security nexus

The new migration-security nexus is often described as the step-child of globalization. The September 11 attackers took advantage of the networks surrounding diasporas to recruit conspirators. The attackers also engaged in international communication and financial remittances to the homeland. Consequently, the immigrant phenomenon is now associated with potential violence. The United States is in the process of trying to distinguish between two types of global migration: the large-scale traditional global migration based on seeking greater opportunity and those few who migrate with the intention of committing violence. What will be the place of global migrants in American society? What kind of migration policy can address security concerns without clustering whole communities into relative isolation? What kind of migration policy is possible in the context of the increasing anti-immigrant sentiment?

Conclusion

Our point of departure was the security context in which global migration movements have entered a new phase and as a result of which new and increasing tensions are developing. In the United States, in particular, these tensions could affect recently arrived immigrants or those communities perceived as sensitive to national security and influence their interest in and ability to stay in contact with their homeland ethnic and religious politics. Both of these processes reverberate through the communities concerned and challenge their participation in the society at large. Cultural diversity can only be recognized and flourish if opportunities for reciprocal recognition are granted to migrant communities, opening up the twenty-first century metropolis to the richness of its diversities. Tuan (1996) argues therefore that a new approach to immigration and citizenship should consider two alternatives: how much of the world to keep out so as to allow personal and local virtues to grow that can then be offered to the world, and how much of that world to let in so as to prevent sterility or the development of traits that are pathological or merely eccentric. The answer to Tuan's questions lies in the capacity of the host culture to offer immigrants a new model of pluralist citizenship that respects their human security and rights at the same time as it guarantees security at large.

Notes

1 United Nations, International Migration, ST/ESA/SER.A/219. New York, Population Division, Department of Economic and Social Affairs, UN Secretariat, 2002.
2 OECD, 1993a.
3 Cornelius, W. and Rosenblum, M. 'Immigration and politics', The Center for Immigration Studies, University of California, San Diego.
4 Skilled labor for information technology and semi-skilled for agriculture and garment industries.
5 Tirman, J., 'The migration-security nexus', GSC Quarterly.
6 US Department of Commerce, Statistical Abstract, various years.
7 Mann, M. *The Sources of Social Power, Vol.1: A History of Power from the Beginning to AD 1760*. Cambridge: Cambridge University Press.
8 Tirman, J. 'The migration-Security nexus', GSC quarterly, Vol.13.
9 Now numbering around three to six million immigrants.
10 Exposed by opinion surveys showing the American public supports more control on Muslim immigration and civil liberties.

REFERENCES

Cornelius, Wayne and Rosenblum, M. (2004), 'Immigration and politics', *Annual Review of Political Science*, Vol. 8, June.

International Organization for Migration (IOM) (2006) *World Migration Report 2005*. Geneva: IOM.

Kymlicka, Will and Straehle, C. (1999) 'Cosmopolitanism, nation-states, and minority nationalism: a critical review of recent literature', *European Journal of Philosophy*, Vol. 7, No. 1.

Lahav, Gallya (2003) 'Migration and security: the role of non-state actors and civil liberal democracies. Paper prepared for the Second Coordination Meeting on International Migration, Department of Economic and Social Affairs, Population Division, United Nations, New York 15–16 October.

Mann, Michael (1986) *The Sources of Social Power, Vol.1: A History of Power from the Beginning to AD 1760.* Cambridge: Cambridge University Press.

Tirman, John (2004) 'The migration-security nexus', *Global Security and Cooperation Quarterly*, Social Science Research Council, Vol.13, Summer/Fall.

Tuan, Yi-fu (1996) 'Space and Place: Humanistic Perspective', in John Agnew, et al. (eds), *Human Geography: An Essential Anthology*. Oxford: Blackwell.

Système d'Observation Permanente sur les Migrations (2005) (SOPEMI) *Trends in International Migration.* Organization for Economic Cooperation and Development (OECD), Paris.

United Nations (2002) *International Migration Report, 2002, Department of Economic and Social Affairs, Population Division, (* ST/ESA/SER.A/220). New York.

## CHAPTER 21

MIGRATION: THE EXPERIENCE OF ARGENTINA

Alejandro Grimson

The contemporary flows of migration into Argentina are quite different from the transatlantic migrations of the late nineteenth and early twentieth centuries, for today's immigrants are from the border countries of Bolivia, Paraguay and Peru. While the Argentine government has read this as a sign of Argentina's entry into the 'First World', globalization and the changes introduced by neo-liberalism have led the ensuing social conflicts to be seen and represented as cultural conflicts. Ethnic identities and politics have thus become new players on the political scene. These trends are now at the heart of new debates and definitions of nationality, class and citizenship.

During the 1990s the Argentine government and media regularly announced the entry of a new wave of immigrants, comparable to the transatlantic migration of the late nineteenth and early twentieth centuries. This time around, however, the immigrants were from the border countries of Bolivia, Paraguay and Peru. The Argentine government took this to mean that Argentina had entered the First World: Germany had Turkish immigrants; the United States had Mexicans, and Argentina, Bolivians, Peruvians, and Paraguayans.

This idea of joining the First World was the way that Argentina inserted itself into the increasingly globalized world from 1990 and was directly related to the country's traditional self-image as a European enclave in Latin America. People proudly affirmed, in accordance with the racist ideology of the era, that Argentina was a country with no African-born or indigenous population. Yet globalization and the changes introduced by neo-liberalism produced a new scenario in which social conflict began to be seen as cultural conflict. Ethnic identities and ethnic politics became relevant as State and subaltern politics. Bolivians and migrants from other neighboring countries came to the center of new ideas and definitions of nationality, class and citizenship.

But overshadowing the celebration was an official xenophobia that blamed the newcomers for the country's growing social and economic ills. According to government and media accounts, the torrent of immigrants from bordering countries was causing an explosion in unemployment and crime. But demographic data showed that there was no jump in immigration rates. The proportion of the population made up of immigrants from neighboring countries increased but a fraction of a percent during the 1990s. Between 1991 and 2001 their representation within the total population increased only from 2.6 per cent to 2.8 per cent.

Neo-liberal globalization has made borders flexible and porous in order to facilitate the movement of capital, while exerting a restrictive effect on the population. States and their political frontiers have been transformed, not erased. The objective of the new policies is not primarily one of controlling territory; it is to control circulation. The key is no longer space but flow. MERCOSUR has tried to activate 'integration from above', while at the same time generating new frontiers between populations and citizens down below.

The public authorities have an alternative. They can either foment policies that hinder migration, criminalize undocumented immigrants and encourage xenophobia, all of which only make immigrants more vulnerable to exploitation and social exclusion. Or they can truly embrace the spirit of solidarity expressed in the declarations of regional summits by rejecting the narrow, nationalistic policies that currently marginalize immigrants. The Argentinean case shows how migration, in the contemporary phase of globalization, is constitutive of the ways in which a social conflict scenario is actually defined. The ethnicization of migrant groups is the way in which the culturalization of social and political conflict is now taking place.

Migration and diversity in the Argentinean imaginary

Clearly, the fiction of exploding immigration rates has been motivated, at least in part, by the need to

Table 21.1 Percentage in the population of immigrants from neighboring countries and Peru in Argentina (1869–2001)

Year	per cent
1869	2.4
1893	2.9
1914	2.6
1947	2
1960	2.3
1970	2.3
1980	2.7
1991	2.6
2001	2.8

Source: INDEC, Censos Nacionales de Población, 1869–2001

find a scapegoat for the country's economic and social crisis. But the nature of ethnic visibility in Argentina has also been changing. In the past, 'diversity' had been rendered invisible, but by the 1990s difference was increasingly highlighted, or 'hyper-visibilized'. This tendency toward ethnicization has been driven, in part, by the organizing efforts of migrants seeking legal status and their attempts to counter negative stereotyping through the celebration of their 'culture'. Their heightened visibility provoked alarmist, racist and xenophobic responses across society, even at the level of public pronouncements and policy. In 1995 Foreign Minister Guido Di Tella, warning of an influx of 'horrible people', predicted that 'in 2020, 20 percent of Argentines will be Bolivian or Paraguayan.'

Specific renditions of Argentina's national imaginary around race and ethnicity have accompanied the country's social and economic transformations ever since the 1930s. In the 1940s and 1950s, however, ethnic and racial differences were subsumed within the political polarization with regard to the populist government in power. With the consolidation of neo-liberalism in the 1990s, traditional political identifiers became diluted; social segregation and fragmentation increased; and ethnicity emerged as a meaningful social category. The crisis of the neo-liberal model (Grimson and Kessler 2005), however, seems to have reversed this process of increasing ethnic visibility.

Argentina's national narrative, like Brazil's, tells of the country forging its population in a racial 'melting pot'. In the Brazilian imaginary, the 'races' that mixed were whites, indigenous peoples and Afro-descendants (DaMatta 1997; Segato 1998), whereas in Argentina's, the 'races' were entirely European: the only things Argentines descended from were the boats arriving from Europe![1] But of course Argentina has never been culturally, ethnically or racially homogeneous. In fact, the country has a proportionately larger indigenous population than Brazil.[2] But the portion of the population that would be considered *mestizo* in other Latin American contexts has been subjected to a unique process of 'de-ethnicization' here. Ethnic differences have been removed from public view and political language. And state pressures have made assimilation the only route for ethnically marked persons to attain the full rights of citizenship. Government antidotes against diversity have included the white dustcoat worn over regular clothes by public school children, the prohibition of indigenous languages, universal conscription and restrictions against giving infants names considered too exotic. By shedding ethnic markings, each generation has been promised closer proximity to equal status within strictly defined 'Argentine' cultural parameters.

By the 1940s, ethnic identities in Argentina had lost all relevance in the national political scene. The myth of homogeneity prevailed and, importantly, the dominant understanding of Argentine social and political reality revolved around the dichotomy of Perónism and anti-Perónism (Segato 1998;

Neiburg 1997). Social divisions and political identities, that is, were subsumed within the split between those who supported and those who opposed the policies associated with the figure of Juan Domingo Perón, who ruled from 1946 to 1955, and again in 1973–1974. The degree of cultural and ethnic homogenization, while concealing differences, did not eliminate racism. Racism in Argentina was simply expressed differently than in other contexts; 'blackness' was constructed around characteristics other than the conventional African phenotype. One example is the term *cabecita negra.* When the import-substitution economic model stimulated migration from rural to urban areas in the early 1930s, this stigmatizing formula was used by the upper and middle classes to refer to the migratory masses. As was pointed out above, in Argentina *negro* is not related to phenotypical features associated with Africa. In everyday speech, *negro* or *cabecita negra* was used to refer to someone who was poor (thus preserving the myth that Argentina was a country without blacks).

This form of racism played a role in political discourse for several decades. 'Blacks' – meaning the poor, workers, provincials of indigenous ancestry – were equated politically with Perónism, because of its populist appeal to lower classes (Ratier 1971; Guber and Visacovsky 1998). For the upper and middle classes, Perónists were 'blacks'. In this context, immigrants from neighboring countries, particularly Bolivians and Paraguayans, who, since the nineteenth century, had accounted for less than 3 percent of the population were not considered 'foreigners.' Rather, they were simply counted as part of the undifferentiated mass of *cabecitas negras*. Any distinction based on national origin or ethnicity was dissolved within this overarching class identity, though this identity in turn was racially marked with 'darkness'.

Neo-liberalism and xenophobia

This conceptualization changed in the 1990s. As neo-liberalism transformed the country's social and economic landscape, ethnic visibility in Argentina was also transformed. Official discourse blamed immigrants for the country's growing social and economic problems, and the national and local governments responded with similarly anti-immigrant initiatives and policies. For example, Eduardo Duhalde, when Governor of the province of Buenos Aires, launched a 'Labor Plan' in June 1995 that sought to not only pave roads, but also to crack down on undocumented workers in 'defense of Argentine jobs'. Meanwhile, Secretary of Migration Hugo Franco announced that immigrants were responsible for 60 percent of the misdemeanors committed in Buenos Aires – even though statistics showed only 10 percent of such offences were attributable to immigrants. 'Crime in the capital has been taken over by foreigners,' proclaimed Franco, while President Carlos Menem asserted that Argentina would close its doors 'to those who come to commit crimes against our country.'

The Construction Workers' Union (UOCRA) added its voice to the xenophobic campaign, claiming that government, business or labor were not responsible for unemployment, on-the-job accidents and low wages didn't belong to the government, but rather that they were caused by *bolitas* and *paraguas* – derogatory names for Bolivians and Paraguayans respectively – who stole jobs from Argentine workers. The Union then demanded from the government stricter control over illegal immigration and more severe penalties for undocumented border immigrants. After a number of fatal on-the-job accidents, on August 5, 1998, the UOCRA held a demonstration attended by more than 10,000 construction workers, protesting against unsafe working conditions that were costing the lives of an average of 85 workers each month. Since unsafe working conditions do not discriminate against any nationality, Bolivian workers attended the demonstration too. But they were obliged to march in a separate column along with Peruvians and Paraguayans, who were also discriminated against by their fellow workers. From the mainstream column, chants like 'We are Argentines and Perónists' and 'We are Argentines and not *bolitas* (Bolivians)' could be heard. A worker stated to a reporter that 'They (foreigners) are to blame for us earning less and less.' Bolivians have in fact been construction workers in the big cities since the 1950s, but before the 1990s ethnicity was not relevant as an identity in labor unions.

Congress considered legislation for harsher penalties against illegal immigrants, sanctions against companies that employed them, increasing resources for deportation purposes and a mandate allowing the executive to establish new criteria and time frames by which to regulate the admission of foreigners. These public pronouncements and acts met with significant public approval. A poll in 1996 found that 81 per cent of Argentines agreed that foreign labor should be strictly limited, 91 per cent felt that Argentines were hurt by immigration and half of those polled supported the expulsion of 'illegal immigrants' (see Oteiza, Novick and Aruj 1997).

The sudden increase in the visibility of these immigrants was not due to any major change in their demographic significance. Instead, it was Argentina's socioeconomic reality that had changed. The consolidation of the neo-liberal model brought with it not only heightened expectations about Argentina's future, but also contradictions that required rationalization. Ethnicity had a new role to play in the re-imagining of Argentina under neo-liberalism. Various anthropological studies from the 1990s confirm this. Many Argentines began using the term 'Bolivian' to refer to not only those born in Bolivia, but also those born in Argentina of Bolivian parents. The gradual loss of ethnic markers across generations, as had been the case before, was stopped in the 1990s, marking a new conceptualization of the relationship between ethnicity and national belonging (Briones 1998; Escolar 2000; Caggiano 2005).

However, one can also add to this growing visibility the revealing trend that in many contexts 'Bolivian' had become a generic label encompassing both 'poor' and 'black'. Members and fans of the soccer team River Plate, for example, refer to the fan-base of their principal rival, Boca Juniors – the most popular team in the country and traditionally associated with the lower and working classes – as *la boliviana*. If Bolivians were once absorbed into the category of 'the poor', then during the 1990s the poor were often transformed into 'Bolivians', The socially excluded became 'foreigners'. The elite-driven national myth insisted that the neo-liberal model had made Argentina an affluent First World country, meaning that the mass of poor people appearing everywhere could not possibly be Argentines. The national imaginary sought to de-nationalize the negative social consequences of neo-liberalism. Arguably, 'Bolivian' — rather than Brazilian, Chilean, Paraguayan or Uruguayan — was used to de-nationalize exclusion because from the perspective of the dominant classes in the capital city, Bolivians occupied the lowest rung in the Argentine ethnic hierarchy. For those who perceive the country as a European enclave, nothing is as evocative of extreme difference as the indigenous 'otherness' of a person from the Andean *altiplano* (highlands). In this sense, equating the domestic poor with Bolivians is indicative of just how significant the social and symbolic rifts had become among different sectors of Argentine society.

Another social change that affected the role of ethnicity in national thinking took place in the realm of work. Traditionally, immigrants from neighboring countries tended to occupy specific occupational niches, usually in jobs considered unpalatable to native-born Argentines. These included seasonal farm work in the border regions as well as unskilled manual labor and domestic service in Buenos Aires. Historically, then, these immigrants filled gaps in the Argentine labor market. They complemented the existing labor force instead of competing with it. This changed in the 1990s, but not because of immigration. Rather, it was the boom in unemployment that altered the landscape of work for Argentines. New processes of social exclusion led those who previously would not accept the working conditions tolerated by immigrants to become suddenly willing to work under more precarious conditions. It was not immigrants who began to compete with Argentines for their jobs but the latter who began to compete for jobs traditionally held by immigrants. Immigration did not change; it was Argentina that changed – dramatically.

Ethnicization: the Bolivian example

Increased governmental and societal insistence on Argentine nationality as the basis for civil and political rights coincided with the social mobilization of the immigrant groups. Confronted by a hostile environment, exclusion and the impossibility of articulating broader social identities in the xenophobic context of the 1990s, immigrants began to organize around their ethnic-national identities. This was evidenced, for example, by the upsurge in immigrant-based fairs, celebrations, radio stations, soccer leagues, and rights organizations. Immigrant rights organizations not only fought for equal rights in terms of access to work, health and education, but also for cultural rights. Likewise, it was during this period that Argentina's native-born indigenous and Afro-descendent communities began making similar claims.

Bolivian immigrants respond in different ways to the exclusion and discrimination that they suffer

(Grimson 1999). Although fear and resignation prevail among incoming groups, many who have been in the country for some time create organizations and coordinate events that strengthen social ties and stimulate collective action. Markets and fairs have flourished in cities with a substantial Bolivian presence. Traditional Bolivian foods can be bought there and they also provide a meeting point for immigrants who replicate some of the large market-places in Bolivia. Some restaurants and discotheques are also identified with Bolivian culture. Celebrations such as the patron saint's day of Urkupiña, Copacabana and Socavón which covers several cities from Juyuy in the north to Buenos Aires, give way to new traditions like the designation of the Virgin of Guadalupe as the 'Patron of Bolivian Immigrants in Argentina'. They facilitate the necessary unification and integration process. The markets and fairs are part of a debate over the meaning of Bolivian identity – viewed negatively by Argentine society but reaffirmed with pride by Bolivians. The celebrations take place in visible places such as certain popular neighborhoods or even in downtown Buenos Aires. According to the immigrants, 'being Bolivian' is felt more strongly outside of their home country. Many who had never participated in traditional dances do so in Argentina because of 'nostalgia'. Those who dance see it as a way to 'do something for Bolivia'. At the same time, these encounters strengthen the social networks of immigrants, facilitating mutual collaboration in order to tackle various work, housing and documentation issues.

Additionally, Bolivian radio stations have emerged. Radio programs create and rely on the feelings of nostalgia and melancholy. The 'music of the nation' and the constant references to 'national traditions', provide imaginary roots on foreign soil. The media circulates certain objects identified with being Bolivian, such as folkloric music, stories of the Incas, and phrases in Quechua and Aymara, thus providing the public space for immigrants' social and cultural debates. Bolivian social organizations have flourished as well, including civil associations that defend neighborhood rights and social groups such as the Bolivian Textile Workers. In 1995, the Federation of Bolivian Civil Associations (FACBOL) was created to unite legally constituted civil associations. Its objectives are to improve the living conditions of immigrants, especially those who are facing greater difficulties, by promoting health centers in neighborhoods with a high Bolivian population and solving documentation problems. This and other immigrant federations have strongly rejected the new General Migration and Immigration Law promoted by the government. In 1999, during the government's xenophobic campaign, the Latin American Confederation was created to unite several federations of diverse immigrant groups in Argentina.

The combination of social exclusionary practices and the new urban-focused destinations create the need for the construction of 'Bolivian spaces' that can transcend local barriers. In this way, although Bolivian presence in Argentina goes back to the nineteenth century, the construction of a Bolivian identity as a reference of the strengthening of social ties and the demands for civil rights has increased steadily in the last three decades. In this way, Bolivian identifications, while they run a certain risk of ghettoization, have expanded to counter discrimination and exclusion. These migrants find in *Bolivianidad* a way to extend their solidarity networks to help them find homes, work and ways to legalize. Bolivian radio stations circulate news of work opportunities, and news also circulates by word of mouth in immigrant soccer leagues and during feast day celebrations. Bolivian nationalism has thus become a political resource in confronting a society that discriminates against Bolivian immigrants. At the same time, of course, it isolates Bolivians from Peruvians, Paraguayans and Argentines from the provinces, who live similar situations of exclusion and exploitation.

The appearance of ethnic categories had the potential for transforming historically established social relations and conflict in Argentina. Yet it also created cultural chauvinism that reinforced existing processes of discrimination and segregation. Indeed, amid the growing organizing of immigrant groups, the State reacted with more discriminatory policies – such as tighter migratory controls – and rhetoric. This fed into the already prevailing climate of xenophobia, and robbed immigrant groups of the strategy used in the past of invisibility through assimilation. In the context of severe social crisis and widespread exclusion, nationality became a political justification for affording differential rights, thus exacerbating the growing rift between social groups.

Social crisis and cultural changes: Argentina in Latin America

When Argentina was supposedly entering the First World, these immigrants were marked for their difference and 'foreignness'. They came to be interpreted as members of underprivileged nations who aspired to partake of Argentina's success, and they were blamed for any of the blemishes in Argentina's neo-liberal promised land. But in 2001 and 2002 Argentina's reigning economic, political and cultural model fell into definitive crisis, as did the congruent national narrative (Grimson and Kessler 2005). The crisis generated a new national narrative with a fresh, shared understanding of what was happening to the country and where it was going. In this new story, the place of immigrants from neighboring countries was also destined to change.

During the most acute moments of the crisis, newspapers announced an exodus of immigrants to their home countries. The scale of return was probably exaggerated, but since these announcements were accompanied by ongoing increases in unemployment, it became less and less believable that these immigrants had been the cause of Argentina's employment problems. The sheer dimension of the socioeconomic crisis belied the notion that they had been to blame. In 2002, Eduardo Duhalde, who as governor of Buenos Aires had scapegoated immigrants in 'defense of Argentine jobs', became Argentina's interim President. During his nearly 18 months in office, he did not make a single reference to illegal immigration or its supposed negative impacts. No doubt he realized that in 2002 few would believe the argument that unemployment was caused by immigration from neighboring countries. The structural causes were, by then, laid utterly bare. With this exposure came a general change in the way Argentines perceived immigrants. An opinion poll in 2002 found significantly fewer respondents supporting restrictions on immigration, as well as the idea that there was a relationship between immigration and insecurity, as compared with respondents in a 1999 poll.[3] At the same time, immigrants changed their way of intervening in public space, ceasing to make their own, group-specific claims. Their most basic demands, for food and work, had acquired new-found political weight. How could one advocate for a minority when the viability of the entire country was in doubt?

Ethnic-specific claims thus subsided during 2002. Minority groups participated in actions geared toward broader social ends. Indigenous protests linked up with marches of unemployed workers, or *piqueteros*, in Buenos Aires; Bolivian and Paraguayan immigrants joined the *piquetero* movement and in some cases became key players in factory takeovers and efforts to demand employment programs. No longer were unionized workers protesting against immigrants from neighboring countries, accusing them of 'stealing our jobs', as in the 1990s. In 2002, the unemployed organized themselves into groups that incorporated the residents of poor neighborhoods, regardless of nationality. As in the past, members of these immigrant groups became ethnically unmarked as they were re-absorbed into Argentine society as neighbors, as fellow workers or as yet more victims of the crisis. Of course this should not be taken to mean that everyday discrimination against border immigrants in Argentina has come to an end. What it does mean is that ethnic stigmatizing became – temporarily at least – much less relevant than it had been in the 1990s. While the reappearance of an ethnicizing dynamic in the future cannot be ruled out, we want to stress that during the worst moments of the crisis, between 2001 and 2002, a change occurred in the Argentine social imaginary that has affected the way migrants are seen and referred to. If in the 1990s they confirmed Argentines' view of their country as a European enclave, after 2001 the official discourse shifted to the desire 'to be a normal country'. Above and beyond the polysemic nature of the formula, there is no doubt that pretensions to power and first-world status have been definitively laid to rest. By the same token, for economic and political reasons, Argentina finds itself farther from the United States and closer to its neighbors, no longer taking its superiority for granted.

There is a new perception of globalization as well. As Argentina seeks to redefine its place in Latin America, the country may once again be forced to grapple with questions of immigration and ethnicity. As it does so, it must question regional integration projects that only seek to facilitate the free movement of capital without allowing for the free movement of people within a regional labor market. To reduce social inequality, a precondition

Table 21.2 Argentine and migrant population of Buenos Aires City: 1869 and 1914

	1869			1914		
	Argentines	Non-Argentines	Per cent of non-Argentines	Argentines	Non-Argentines	Per cent of non-Argentines
Totals	94,963	92,163	49,1	798,553	778,044	49.3
Men 20–45 years old	11,359	47,570	79,6	139,365	341,395	71

Source: Rofman and Romero, 1973

to the construction of a genuine democracy, it will be necessary to conceive of citizenship in regional, rather than national, terms. Paradoxically, the processes of globalization that stimulate cross-border migration have not resulted in the formation of a transnational or global sense of citizenship. Rather, these processes have pushed thousands of people into a 'Fourth World' in which they have no citizenship privileges at all. In this context, the nations that make up the Southern Common Market (MERCOSUR), are at a crossroads. They will need to develop a vision of regionalization aimed not only at economic development, but that seeks to achieve comprehensive human development as well. If public policy and intergovernmental accords do not emphasize the granting of full social and cultural rights to all citizens of the region, then regional economic development will lack the necessary social underpinnings to make it viable in the long run.

Notes

1 This narrative is directly related with the historical experience, in the sense of the percent of migrant population.

2 Indigenous people in Brazil were estimated to number between 236,000 and 300,000 during the 1990s, representing 0.2 percent of the national population (Ramos 1998: 3–4). In Argentina, estimates ranged between 250,000 and 450,000, representing between 0.7 and 1.2 percent of the national total (Vázquez 2000: 133-4). Nonetheless, while the indigenous are excluded from the national imaginary in Argentina, in Brazil they constitute 'a powerful symbol of nationality' (Ramos 1998: 4).

3 In 1999, 77 percent of those polled agreed that the admission of immigrants, and their right to remain, ought to be restricted. Only 51 percent felt this way in 2002. In 1999, only 18 percent opposed increased restrictions on immigration; 42 percent did so in 2002. In 1999, 45 percent thought tighter immigration laws would resolve the country's crime problems while 46 percent thought otherwise. In 2002, the numbers were 77 percent and 18 percent, respectively (Casaravilla 2003).

REFERENCES

Briones, Claudia (1998) '(Meta) cultura del estado-nación y estado de la (meta) cultura', Brasilia, *Série Antropologia*, no. 244, Departamento de Antropologia/UnB.

Caggiano, Sergio (2005) *Lo que no entra en el crisol.* Buenos Aires: Prometeo.

Casaravilla, Diego (2003) 'Crisis social, discurso y xenophobia', in *Buenos Aires. Ciudad con migrants.* Buenos Aires: Direccion General de la Mujer, Gobierno de la Ciudad de Buenos Aires.

DaMatta, Roberto (1997) *Relativizando.* Río de Janeiro: Rocco.

Escolar, Diego (2000) 'Identidades emergentes en la frontera argentino-chilena', en Grimson, A. (comp.): *Fronteras, naciones e identidades*, Buenos Aires, CICCUS-La Crujía.

Grimson, Alejandro (1999) *Relatos de la diferencia y la igualdad. Los bolivianos en Buenos Aires.* Buenos Aires: Eudeba-Felafacs.

– and Kessler, Gabriel (2005) *Argentina and the Southern Cone: Neo-liberalism and National Imagination.* New York, Routledge.

Guber, Rosana and Visacovsky, Sergio (1998) 'De las "antropologías nacionales" a la nacionalidad en la antropología. Un caso argentino', Brasilia, *Série Antropologia*, 235, Departamento de Antropologia/UnB.

INDEC (Instituto Nacional de Estadísticas y Censos) (1996) *La población no nativa de la Argentina, 1869–1991.* Buenos Aires: INDEC.

Neiburg, Federico (1997) *Os intelectuais e a invenção do peronismo.* Buenos Aires: San Pablo: Universidade de São Paulo.

Oteiza, Enrique, Novick, Susana and Aruj, Roberto (1997) *Inmigración y discriminación. Políticas y discursos.* Buenos Aires: Universitaria.

Ramos, Alcida (1998) *Indigenism:, Ethnic Politics in Brazil. Madison,* Wisconsin: The University of Wisconsin Press.

Ratier, Hugo (1971) *El Cabecita Negra.* Buenos Aires. CEAL.

Rofman, Alejandro and Romero, Luis A. (1973) *Sistema socioeconómico y estructura social en la Argentina.* Buenos Aires: Amorrortu.

Segato, Rita (1998) 'Alteridades históricas/Identidades políticas: una crítica a las certezas del pluralismo global', *Anuário Antropológico/97*, Rio de Janeiro y Brasília, Tempo Brasileiro.

Vázquez, Héctor (2000) Procesos identitarios y esclusión sociocultural. La cuestión indígena en la Argentina. Buenos Aires: Biblos.

## CHAPTER 22

MIGRATION, CONFLICT AND ILLEGITIMACY: A MALAYSIAN CASE STUDY

Diana Wong

Massive inflows of global capital into the Malaysian economy in the past three decades have generated huge inflows of foreign workers which have been of a distinctly regional provenance. The first two decades of labor migration, characterized by informal, undocumented chain migration from the neighboring state of Indonesia, saw the easy assimilation and political incorporation of the migrants. After 1990, such migration, which continued unabated, was labeled 'illegal' in light of the state's attempt to put in place a formal system of labor recruitment. The early accommodation of the migrants has given way to friction arising from localized competitition over scarce urban resources such as jobs and housing. There has also been a generalized antipathy toward the 'illegal' migrant because of his subversive threat to national security, much of it due to the flawed conceptualization and implementation of state policy.

Introduction

In 2002, the Malaysian flag was burned outside the Malaysian embassy in Jakarta by Indonesian demonstrators angered by changes to the foreign labor policy that had been recently announced by the Malaysian government, which were seen as directed against migrant workers from Indonesia. Leading Indonesian politicians called for 'action' to be taken against the 'smaller country'. At the height of the bilateral tensions generated by this migration issue, the Malaysian government issued a call for its citizens to refrain from traveling to Indonesia.

Clearly, migration flows – and policy changes – have the potential for generating conflict (see the Introduction, page, for its definition, adopted here, as a disagreement involving a perceived threat), not merely within, but also between nation-states. What needs further exploration, however, is the role played by *culture*, and by *globalization*, in migration-generated conflict.

The present standard account of globalization, migration and cultural conflict stems from the West European experience of long-distance guest-worker, asylum and illegal migration of the past four decades. Global migration is here seen as the funnel through which cultural diversity is introduced into a previously homogeneous society, resulting in the formation of new ethnic minorities with different cultural values in conflict with those of the established majority. The actual instances of conflicts which have arisen, especially those with a threateningly violent character, such as the recent controversy over the publication of cartoons deemed to be blasphemous in a Danish newspaper, have tended to reinforce this interpretative template.

This case study examines the contemporary Malaysian experience of globalization, high levels of foreign labor recruitment, and conflict. Malaysia is itself a post-colonial state and multi-ethnic society with a history of migration. Indian and Chinese immigrants came largely during the colonial period, and acquired citizenship with the granting of independence. The indigenous Malays comprise a number of ethnic sub-groups, many of whom are descendants from migrants from present-day Indonesia. Violent internal ethnic conflict in 1969 preceded the new migration which this chapter discusses.

The migration landscape in Malaysia

In July 2004, the Malaysian Home Minister announced plans for yet another major deportation exercise (the last one had just been completed in 2002 and had led to the above-mentioned demonstrations in Indonesia) of 'more than a million illegal immigrants'. In addition to this figure, there were some 1.3 million legally documented migrant contract workers in July 2004. UNHCR figures for 2003 show 78,682 persons of concern, of whom 7,424 were refugees and 9,205 were asylum seekers. Those without official refugee or asylum seeker status tend to be treated by the government as 'illegal immigrants' (Amnesty International 2004).

The migration landscape in Malaysia is thus overwhelmingly one of *labor* migrants, both legal and illegal. Assuming a total labor migrant population of 1.3 million legal plus 1.2 million undocumented (figures vary from 700,000 to 1.5 million) in 2004, foreign labor would have constituted some 25 percent of the total labor force of 9.8 million, and some 10.4 per cent of the total population of 24 million. How did a stock of such magnitude come about? Where do they come from? Why the high percentage of undocumented migrants? What have been the societal and the policy responses to this influx?

Global capital, economic growth and labor market scarcity

Two waves of labor migrant flows account for the present stock of foreign workers in Malaysia (The following account is taken largely from Kanapathy 2001). The first began in the early 1970s and lasted till the mid-1980s' recession. Between 1970 and 1980, the manufacturing sector recorded an annual average growth rate of 11 percent, due in large part to the influx of foreign capital into export-oriented manufacturing. The first wave of foreign workers came in to fill the gaps in the agricultural sector left behind by workers departing for the manufacturing and urban sectors of the economy. By 1984, there were an estimated 500,000 undocumented migrants in the country.

In the second half of the 1980s, the forced revaluation of the Japanese yen, in conjunction with a sweeping liberalization of the economy, led to a renewed resurgence of foreign investment in the country. Sustained economic growth of 8 percent per annum since 1988 (till 1997) came with an annual job creation rate of 4.6 percent. As the labor force expanded only by 3.1 percent during this period, the shortfall had to be met by the importation of foreign labor. It should be noted however that the vast majority of the new jobs created were for low-end, unskilled or semi-skilled labor. As the domestic labor force upgraded its educational qualifications as a result of state development policy, these jobs could increasingly be filled only through foreign workers. In 2004, 67 percent of legal migrant workers had an educational attainment of six years or less. It is likely that the percentage would be much higher for undocumented workers.

Whereas they had been absorbed primarily into the agricultural sector during the first wave, migrant workers were now spread throughout all sectors, including manufacturing, where their presence has been steadily increasing. In 1990, 47.9 per cent of legally documented foreign workers were employed in the agricultural sector, compared to 9.8 per cent in manufacturing. In July 2004, 30.5 percent were employed in the manufacturing sector, as against 24.7 per cent in agriculture, 25 percent in services, and 19.8 per cent in construction. There are no comparable statistics for undocumented workers, but it is likely that they are also to be found in all these sectors, but in the employ of local capital (Kassim 1997).

Clearly, without globalization, migration flows of such magnitude would not have occurred. What however, was the nature of the migration?

Formal and informal recruitment of foreign labor from the region

Foreign capital was largely of American, European and regional (East Asian) provenance, the last assuming greater prominence during the second wave of growth. Foreign labor, however, has been drawn entirely from the region. The first wave of migrant flow occurred virtually outside of state intervention and supervision and involved, apart from some Thais and Filipinos, the spontaneous and locally organized movement of people from the neighboring islands of Sumatra and Java to the west coast of Malaysia.

It should be recalled that together with the peninsula of Malaya and thousands of other islands which today form the post-colonial nation-states of Indonesia, Malaysia and the Philippines, the whole area had for centuries constituted a maritime Malay-Muslim world characterised by high levels of trade and mobility. The iconic pre-colonial kingdom of Malacca, which fell to Portuguese invaders in the fifteenth century, was founded by a prince from present-day Sumatra. The sixteenth and seventeenth centuries saw the establishment of new royal houses in the south of the peninsula by migrants from Sumatra and Sulawesi (Celebes). In the nineteenth and early twentieth centuries, under British colonial rule, large numbers of Javanese and other Indonesian migrants settled in the country. Their descendants today form part of the indigenous Malay population of the country.

One of the first pieces of legislation passed by the new nation-state when it gained independence in 1957 was an Immigration Act (1959), which regulated the movement of non-citizens into its territory. While it ended long distance immigration from India and China, migration from the neighboring islands of the Archipelago, such as Sumatra and Java, was allowed to continue. It was an acknowledgment that the movement across the Straits occurred between related peoples, albeit of different nationalities. Not until the outbreak of military hostilities between the two new nation-states of Malaysia and Indonesia in the mid-1960s did this steady flow of people movement across the Straits come to a complete halt.

The spontaneous and undocumented resumption of migration across the Straits in the early 1970s in response to the labor shortages faced by an increasingly dynamic economy in Malaysia was thus facilitated by existing social ties and networks which proved extremely effective in the organisation of the migration to the Malaysian labor market. No effort was made by the Malaysian state to prevent the inflow of Indonesian migrants who gained access to work immediately upon entry into the country, and in countless instances, also acquired Malaysian permanent residential status within months of their arrival. Chain migration rapidly ensued and family formation and settlement was common. By 1985, an estimated 500,000 Indonesian migrants were in the country, all undocumented, except for those who had acquired residential status, as there was no administrative machinery in place for the official recruitment of foreign workers.

This was to change in the late 1980s. As economic growth resumed after the mid-1980s recession, and economic planners braced for another round of high labor demand, it was decided to establish a formal recruitment system based on temporary contracts, and drawing on regional labor. The status of existing migrants was to be regularized through an amnesty. All future entry had to be channeled through the formal system to be set in place. The formal system, now largely in place, is based solely on *off-shore recruitment*. Under this work permit system, foreign workers are recruited abroad, from designated countries, and are issued with calling visas for entry into the country; once in the country, the calling visas are converted into work permits, or in the official terminology, visit passes (temporary employment). As is evident in the terminology itself, the system is designed for temporary employment. The passes are employer and location-specific. The worker is not allowed to bring in his family. He/she has to leave the country upon cancellation or expiry of the visit pass.

The establishment of the formal system of labor recruitment was accompanied by a relentlessly shrill and harsh attempt to 'weed out' what had now become illegal migration. Apart from the numerous amnesties (more than five have been conducted so far), highly publicised detention and expulsion exercises have been part of the decade-long endeavor to manage migration. Two enforcement exercises known as *Ops Nyah* I (literally, *Get Rid Operations*) and *Ops Nyah* II, the first directed at the prevention of illegal landings, the second at the detection of existing migrants at their work places or homes, are still ongoing. Detention centers have been set up for holding detainees until their expatriation, with conditions at the camps subject to charges of severe over-crowding, degrading treatment and official abuse. Every now and then, as in 2002, large-scale expulsion exercises have been held, accompanied by threats of flogging (as provided for under the law) and other 'stern' action.

The conversion from an informal system of labor recruitment to a formal one which would meet efficiently the demands of the labor market has been an exceedingly difficult, and not entirely successful, policy endeavor. The effectiveness of the formal system can be seen in the fact that in 2004, there were 1.3 million workers registered in the country, compared to 31,420 in 1989. However, at the same time, there were still an estimated 700,000–1.5 million illegal migrants in the country. The intractability of their presence is due in no small measure to the regional character of the migration, which lowers the transportation and transaction costs of illegal migration for the migrant, and makes control over entry exceedingly difficult for the state. Many of those expelled are known to return again when border controls are loosened. Obviously though, their survival within the national borders would not be possible without a certain degree of unofficial tolerance (and corruption) by the local and police authorities, as well as acceptance by local society.

Mapping the conflicts

Concern over the influx of 'foreigners' was first voiced by a non-Malay opposition party in the mid-1970s, who feared that a deliberate policy of demographic readjustment was being unofficially pursued. Not until the recession of 1985, however, did the growing migrant presence attract much media, or policy, attention. By then, Indonesian migrants were not just confined to remote plantations, but had established a presence in the capital city, at construction sites, as well as in petty trading. Their success in these two sectors, and especially in petty trading, pitted them in direct competition with local Malay rural-urban migrants in the city, for whom the informal sector of petty trading was also a key means of survival. Furthermore, having done well for themselves, they were seeking accommodation in the city, which meant renting a room or a house in a Malay Reservation area, or buying or renting in a Malay-dominated squatter area. With the migrant tendency to congregate together, visibly Indonesian settlements had sprung up in these areas by the mid-1980s.

Local resentment and hostility toward the Indonesian migrants, felt primarily by the local working class poor and concentrated in the metropolitan region around the capital city, known as the Klang Valley, thus arose largely over competition for the same urban jobs, livelihoods, and space. It was indeed to a large extent competition between two different sets of migrants – as the local working class poor was drawn largely from fresh rural migrants from the countryside. This resentment was channeled through the media, and the political parties, and found expression in the new term '*Indon*', with its derogatory undertone, to designate new migrants from Indonesia. The 1985 recession was sharp but brief however, and local resentment, although visible, remained fairly muted.

The economic growth which resumed in the late 1980s and accelerated in the early 1990s led to an acute labor shortage, resulting not merely in a massive expansion of the numbers of foreign workers, but in their distribution across more and more sectors of the economy, including manufacturing and services. Under the new formal system of recruitment set in place by government policy, labor was now being sourced not just from Indonesia, but also from South Asia, in particular Bangladesh. This second wave was thus more diverse, more numerous and more visible. Subject as it was to the new contract labor recruitment regulations in place since 1990, this second wave was also characterized by the presence of more single young men and women, as well as by what were now known officially as illegal migrants.

Even as the old sources of friction – competition over jobs and housing, especially in the informal urban market – continued to rankle, new complaints arose and became particularly vocal in the mid-1990s. One key issue revolved over women and sexuality. The existence of a large male migrant population led to the development of a sex industry catering to them, as well as to local males. Most of the sex workers were themselves migrants in the country under irregular circumstances. Other women migrants not engaged in the sex trade were nevertheless associated with the taint of sexual promiscuity and charges of female bigamy were made in the press. Relationships also developed between foreign male migrants and local women, often working in the same factory. It was in fact over women that the most serious instances of group violence between locals and migrants have occurred. In 1996, a series of such clashes broke out between local youth and Bangladeshi workers in various towns in the country and was widely reported in the press.

The increasingly hostile press coverage in the mid-1990s also associated migrants with criminality, infectious diseases, illegal clearing of state land, undue access to scarce hospital and educational resources, and above all, of illegality – of wanton subversion of the state's boundaries and hence of posing a threat to national security. Up until 1989, an Indonesian migrant could enter the country without any documents and count on getting Permanent Resident status within a short while of his arrival. From 1990 onwards, he was an illegal migrant, enemy of the state, against whom the full force of the state control and punitive apparatus was to be brought to bear. The press coverage of this epic battle between the state and the illegal migrant – police raids, illegal landings, Ops Nyah 1, Ops Nyah 2, amnesties, detentions, expulsions – dominated by far all other issues related to migration in the last decade. In these reports, the terms 'migrants' or 'workers' were hardly used. Instead, these were 'illegals', the derogatory new term for those who had previously been, and still were, called 'Indons' – and the others who had joined them.

It is telling that the two other episodes of violent conflict between migrants and locals (group fights involving different migrant groups are often reported) were actually directed against representatives of the state. In 1998, some illegal Indonesian migrants being held at a detention centre in Semenyih rioted at the camp, leading to damage to property as well as deaths. In 2002, some 500 legal Indonesian factory workers attacked police officers at the factory premises, during a drug inspection exercise. These acts of violence against the state, given massive publicity in the local media, reaffirm in the public mind the figure of the migrant as an illegal, violent-prone threat to national security.

Conclusion

If indeed globalization, taken to mean the increased velocity of global flows – of finance, trade, ideas, people etc. – is linked to cultural conflict, then flows of people, or migration, are arguably more likely than the flow of material goods, or of consumer cultural goods (see Yan in this volume), or indeed of any other type of flow, to generate such conflict. For migrants, it could be argued, are the embodiment and bearers of distinctive cultural ideas and values, whose existence at a safe distance would be of no immediate import, but whose proximity could lead to conflict.

The Malaysian case study suggests that long-distance migration flows in response to the mobility of global capital may be more of an exception rather than the rule. Domestic labor market scarcity is more easily met by recruitment of regional sources of labor, be it through formal or informal channels. Little evidence was found of cultural conflict per se; the conflicts which did arise were centered in the big towns, and in particular around the capital city. They were essentially localized instances of social conflict arising out of competition over urban employment, housing, livelihoods and women between the local working poor, themselves migrants from the countryside, and the foreign migrants.

In the context of increasing state intervention and 'management' of the issue however, a politicization and nationalization of the conflict occurred. Migrant violence, to some extent in response to increasing state violence in the form of raids, harassment etc., has been directed at the state apparatus and has generated even stronger images of the threatening character of migration in the public mind. Cultural explanations – 'Indonesians are violent people' – although not explicitly stated in the public domain, begin to circulate in everyday discourses.

Policy on migration has to be cognizant of the possible impact of its own doing, especially of the impact of flawed implementation. As the forces of globalization create the conditions of possibility for more frequent clashes or conflicts over divergent core values, it is imperative that the necessary dialogue over these conflicts not be skewed or hindered by culturally-loaded political constructions. Notwithstanding the differences in the pattern and dynamics of migration and conflict between Western Europe and Malaysia alluded to earlier, there has been a notable policy – and discourse – convergence on the figure and position of the 'illegal migrant'. Although not a cultural category – indeed, it is above all a policy-generated category – the term has become a powerful cultural signifier for the illegitimacy of migration *as such*. Through the medium of these discourses, a shared global imaginary of migration is being culturally constituted, in which local conflicts over migration become invested with global meaning, and vice versa.

If *cultural* globalization, following Robertson (1992) entails the self-reflexive awareness of the Other, global migration flows have contributed to a global imaginary in which the quintessential Other is the '*Illegal migrant*'. In this conflation of categories, migration as such becomes invested with the aura of the illegitimate, the anomic and ultimately, the conflictual. In a world in which migrant flows will continue to remain essential, this convergent construction of the 'global' migrant as illegal and anomic constitutes in itself an additional potent source of conflict, even where, in everyday life, the migrant speaks the same language, shares the same religion and partakes essentially of the same culture.

REFERENCES

Amnesty International (2004) 'Malaysia. Human rights at risk in mass deportation of undocumented migrants' at http://web.amnesty.org/library/index/ENGASA280082004, accessed 9 Feb. 2006.

Kanapathy, Vijayakumari (2001) 'International migration and labor market adjustments in Malaysia: the role of foreign labor management policies', *Asian and Pacific Migration Journal*, Vol. 10 (3-4): 429–61.

Kassim, Azizah (1997) 'International migration and alien labour employment in Southeast Asia: an insight from the Malaysian Experience'. Paper presented at the conference on India, Southeast Asia and the United States. New Opportunities for Understanding and Cooperation, 31 January – 1 February, Institute of Southeast Asian Studies, Singapore.

Robertson, Roland (1992) *Globalization: Social Theory and Global Culture.* London: Sage.

INTRODUCTION

For most cultural activists, the words 'culture and conflict' would probably mean the ways in which artistic creativity and 'cultural heritage' provide tools to prevent or resolve emerging socioeconomic tensions as well as violent conflicts and heal their consequences. For others, the binomial could refer to the ways in which inherited meanings and practices – often performative – can be used to transmit or inculcate 'modern' or reconciliatory values, particularly in so-called 'traditional' societies, when cultural differences have become conflictual. Both perceptions are typical of the contemporary urge to *use* 'culture', not only as a value or an end in itself, but also as a contributor to social 'goods' – which could include economic growth, social cohesion, citizenship, or social cohesion in addition to post-conflict reconciliation. This instrumentalization of culture now produces discourses that range from patently cynical political rhetoric, i.e., populist identity politics and racial stereotyping, to genuine socio-political engagement on the part of artists and community groups who define themselves as socially – hence 'culturally' – committed.

The contributions to this section focus on the latter, and show how different facets of culture can become a critical tool and enabling element for overcoming conflict rather than cause or concomitant factor. Barbara Nelson, Kathryn Carver and Linda Kaboolian open with an international overview of 'concord' organizations in divided societies that create mediating institutions to humanize the 'Other'. James Thompson assesses various forms of theatre- and performance-based responses to conflict in one such divided society: Sri Lanka. Ananda Breed explores the potentials and shortcomings of *Gacaca*, a traditional form of community mediation that is now being used in post-genocide Rwanda. Silvia Ramos highlights the ways in which cooperation between the police and the youth-led Afro Reggae Cultural Group is building peace in the context of extreme urban violence in Brazil. Finally, Clemencia Rodriguez and Amparo Cadavid show how, in rural Colombia, citizens' radio stations act as mediators in intra-community conflicts, in conflicts among political opponents, among communities and local authorities, and between communities and armed groups.

## CHAPTER 23

CREATING CONCORD ORGANIZATIONS: INSTITUTIONAL DESIGN FOR BRIDGING ANTAGONISTIC CULTURES

Barbara J. Nelson, Kathryn A. Carver and Linda Kaboolian[1]

Communal violence within countries and regions has been on the rise since the end of the Cold War. By contrast, there has been another less visible trend wherein some societies with deep communal divisions have moved toward greater democratic accommodation, toleration, and a sense of a shared future. Mediating institutions are necessary for the adoption of democratic communal problem solving. We examine one of the mediating institutions and processes that activate the structural advantages of liberal polities: concord organizations, which bring together people with fundamentally opposing views or identities for the purpose of promoting civil society while recognizing group differences. We draw attention to the cultural content of communal violence and explain the 'how and why' of concord organizations.

Introduction

Communal violence within countries and regions has been on the rise since the end of the Cold War.[2] To give two of many possible examples, 60,000 people have died from fighting or its consequences in Ethiopia and Eritrea and 30,000 have died in Chechnya. Against the drum beat of violence and death, there has also been another, less visible, trend. Some societies with deep communal divisions have moved toward greater democratic accommodation, toleration, and a sense of a shared future. South Africa, Northern Ireland, Israel and Palestine in the Oslo period, some troubled cities in India and the United States, and more recently the Greek and Turkish enclaves on Cyprus are all examples of 'societies' moving toward less violent and more accommodating communal relations. To use the terms popularized by Lipschutz and Crawford, most of these societies are moving from the question of 'Who Dominates?' (that is, illiberal states with contested participation) to the question of 'Who Belongs?' (that is, liberal states still struggling with constitutive issues).[3]

One problem with the categorization of communal conflict proposed by Lipschutz and Crawford is that it rests on large structural arrangements. They say little about how societies move toward less violent, more effective inter-communal relations. Certainly, the formal establishment of democratic rule of law, competitive parties, and honest administration creates the preconditions for liberal regimes, which in turn create frameworks for equitable communal inclusion. Likewise, communal strife is diminished by policies that expand economic growth and respond to those who cannot succeed by market means. But liberal and (re)distributive regimes do not *automatically* convert conflict over domination into conflict over belonging. Democratic theory and practice tell us that *mediating institutions* are necessary for the adoption of democratic communal problem solving. For instance, Varshney found that it takes successful cross-community organizations, including the Hindu – Muslim alliance in the old-style Congress party, to activate the advantages embedded in somewhat favorable structural relations. He noted that Indian cities with more cross-community organizations of all kinds had lower levels of communal violence. Importantly, he also found that in Indian cities cross-community contacts by themselves, such as going to the wedding of a friend from another community, are not predictive of lower levels of communal violence.[4]

This chapter examines one of the processes that activate the structural advantages of liberal polities, specifically, the creation of cross-community, or 'concord', organizations in divided societies. Concord organizations bring together people with fundamentally opposing views or identities for the purpose of promoting civil society while recognizing group differences. Concord organizations engage in dialogue, witness activities, education and training, conflict management and mediation, community service, or economic development. The Concord Project researched over 100 cross-community organizations in Northern Ireland, South Africa, the United States, and Israeli and Palestinian groups working in the United States.

This chapter has four objectives. The first is to enlarge and reframe structural arguments about the nature of communal violence with attention to cultural content. We assert that the cultural meanings given to communal conflicts are as important as the power relations they represent. In everyday life, the content of conflicts must be addressed by mediating institutions like concord organizations as part of the way to make the promise of liberal inclusion real. The second objective is to locate the impetus toward cross-community activities in larger global forces, especially the growth of formal democracy. We suggest that the spread of democracy promotes the preconditions for developing concord organizations, although weak democratic institutions put a brake on that growth. The third objective is to present 'a logic of collective investment' which explains in theory and practice why and how concord organizations are formed. Creators of concord organizations are investors rather than consumers. They are sensitive to interest rates, unlike the purchasers of public goods posited by Mancur Olson, who are only sensitive to price. Social investors, especially if they are brought together from antagonistic communities, need conditions and rules that will make their investments safe and worth while. Our research provides ten design principles and necessary practices that safeguard and amplify the investment made in cross-community institutions and their work.

The fourth objective is to provide specific recommendations to policy-makers, international investment institutions and foundations, and business and civic leaders about how to increase bridging social capital through the work of concord organizations.[5]

Beyond structural categories of communal conflict

Lipschutz and Crawford argue that ethnic and sectarian conflicts are fundamentally conflicts about power:

> *What we have come to call 'ethnic and sectarian conflict' is neither ethnic nor sectarian, per se. Rather it is about struggles over the levers of power and wealth within societies and countries in which ethnicity and religion provide the cultural and historical resources for mobilizing support for particular elites. These countries are almost always caught in the throes of economic and political transformations, brought on by external factors and forces.*[6]

We disagree with the exclusive quality of this statement. We do agree with the importance of seeing communal strife as representing struggles over material and political resources. Similarly we agree with their additional argument that liberal regimes must make groups belong economically as well as politically. They must create distributive and redistributive policies that 'bring in' those who, for whatever reason, do not benefit from the market.[7] But we disagree that ethnic and sectarian strife has little or no meaningful content beyond the symbolic.

The absence of attention to the cultural meaning of conflict is problematic. On the ground, people belonging to an ethnic, religious, linguistic, or racial group understand their experience not only in terms of their access to constitutive and economic structures of power. They also understand their experience in terms of the *content* of their history, their beliefs, and their hopes from their standpoint.[8] These beliefs and histories are often non-divisible. As one commentator in Northern Ireland said, 'The Pope cannot be the Vicar of Christ on even days, but not on odd days.'[9] This non-divisible difference in religious belief is a part of the alloy of communal conflict in Northern Ireland. It is just as real as the English imposition of the Plantation system or the recent stunning bank robbery by the IRA. So too, the search for political and economic power has human consequences. The dead and dispossessed in all Northern Irish communities are a source of grief, and that grief has more than political meaning.

Successful societies with deep communal divisions require more than new or improved political and economic structures. They require mediating institutions that humanize 'the Other' in everyday contexts and create opportunities for people with different histories and beliefs to act together to solve problems in ways that benefit all participating communities. Activities in mediating institutions are closer and more meaningful than participation in state decision-making and more personal and reliable than interactions in the market. Concord organizations, which build bridging social capital in societies with a surfeit of bonding social capital, are one form of mediating organization that augments structural changes. Concord organizations provide mechanisms that promote useful joint futures rather than the separate futures of vertically integrated and antagonistic communal groups.

Across the globe, thousands of concord organizations provide durable, thoughtful settings for people from antagonistic communities to act together to solve their joint problems. Concord organizations are mostly found in civil society, among non-profit institutions and non-governmental organizations (NGOs), operating independently of state control and market forces. In Northern Ireland, Corrymeela sponsors dialogue programs and education that bring together Protestant/unionists with Catholic/nationalists. In the United States, the National Conference for Community and Justice (formerly the National Conference of Christians and Jews) undertakes hundreds of training and education projects to improve cross-community leadership skills. In South Africa, IDASA emphasizes community strength within racial, tribal, and linguistic groups in order to create equal bargaining strength to build a more equitable economy. A small group of Muslims and Jews located in greater Washington, D.C. met in private for two years after 9/11 working on the hard task of mutual understanding, emerging to act together in the Hurricane Katrina relief effort.[10]

Occasionally, decentralized and somewhat autonomous public institutions are also constituted as concord organizations. In Northern Ireland, the nearly 50 tax-supported 'integrated' schools that educate Catholic and Protestant children together are examples of public concord organizations. In South Africa, the government-supported National Centre for Human Rights Education and Training (NACHRET) Division of the South African Human Rights Commission teaches skills that help cross the chasms of color and community.

Globalization, democracy, and concord organizations

It is easier to give examples of concord organizations than to estimate their numbers. The United States has an estimated 1.6 million non-profit organizations. Figures from other, especially poorer, countries are less available and accurate.[11] Thus it is no surprise that there are no reliable numbers of cross-community organizations, and even more difficult, single-community organizations that routinely engage in cross-community work.[12]

The conditions that promote the creation and longevity of concord organizations are well known, however. Our research shows very clearly that cross-community work and the creation of bridging social capital are more likely to develop and thrive where three conditions are met. First, a society needs reasonably effective democratic institutions. Second, it needs a commitment to the reduction of violence by state actors and those in civil society. And third, it must develop strong concord organizations and activities.[13] In real life, these conditions are met in different ways and to different degrees, but the trends are absolutely clear. The more a society has of these resources, the more it will be able to engage in successful cross-community work and to create enduring bridging social capital.

The many forms of globalization have had a mixed effect on the rise of concord organizations, their success, and their recognition. The democratic revolution of the past two decades, which brought the number of partial or full democracies from 90 to 143, helps to meet one of the crucial preconditions of successful cross-community work.[14] The World Values Survey shows that support for democratic principles is almost universal as national economies develop and societies evolve from survival values toward self-expression values.[15] Nor is it surprising that countries that score high in democratic ratings also report the highest levels of citizens' subjective well-being and satisfaction with life.[16] But many new democracies have weak or corrupt institutions, do not espouse or achieve lower levels of state and civil violence, and have leaders and publics with limited tolerance for minorities.[17] Thus the global democratic revolution both increases and restricts the development of concord organizations.

Similarly, elite mobilization of ethnic differences in intra-state or regional conflicts can intensify and reconfigure communal identity in ways that make concord work much more difficult. In the Balkans, central Africa, and the Caucasus, bloody and vicious violence has been unleashed in part by elites who use reconfigured communal identity as a resource for increased political and economic power. These conflicts create intense suffering and amplify hatreds in ways that make the creation of concord organizations extraordinarily difficult. Indeed, one of the objectives of elites in these clashes is to 'demonize the Other' (often not hard to do once the war is underway), and therefore to reduce the legitimacy of contact and cooperation.

To the extent that the other preconditions for successful cross-community work are achieved – working democratic institutions and a commitment to reduction in violence – concord organizations can emerge once the fighting has stopped, even in areas emerging from horrific ethnic conflicts. The numbers of concord activities will, however, be low immediately after the cessation of the violence. The few joint ventures for economic development among Tutsi and Hutu widows in Rwanda and Burundi are examples of such activities.[18] The Straw Mat Project of the Kimbimba Peace Committee was one such initiative. In 1998 a mat-making project was begun as a way to bring Hutu and Tutsi women together so they could have informal dialogues. The weekly time spent together working allowed trust to develop and friendships to grow. The mats themselves then became an income generating program as the mats were sold to aid groups for distribution to people in the displaced persons' camp or those whose homes and villages had been looted. The mats themselves are important to the infrastructure of Burundi villages and perform many critical day-to-day functions.[19] This initial project has germinated several other income initiatives that the women are seeking additional funding to pursue.

As the discussion (found in the next section) of institutional design principles for concord organizations shows, communities emerging from internecine warfare have a great and often unidentified need to undertake what is often called 'single-community' or 'single-identity work.' By this we mean that communities like Tutsis and Hutus (or Northern Irish Protestants and Catholics) must undertake the difficult work of learning to identify themselves not solely in terms of their relationships of power or oppression with other groups, but in terms of their own self-rooted aspirations.[20] Cross-community work is always very difficult, uncomfortable, often misunderstood, dangerous, and not always successful. This difficulty is not always obvious to those who live in stable, relatively well-to-do democracies. The time line to develop concord organizations is longer when the wounds are fresh, when everyday survival is uncertain, when sponsoring organizations like outside NGOs are unavailable, or when community leaders are not present or willing to engage with members from other communities.

The logic of collective investment

Given the difficulty of establishing concord organizations and their importance in linking disparate communities, it is important to ask: How are concord organizations established? What makes them succeed or fail? In many ways, concord organizations should not form. A person joins a union, a congregation, or a professional association because of unity of interests, that is, similarities that are important and differences that do not matter. Even people *with* unity of interests often 'free ride', waiting for others to establish the union or congregation, before they join. Concord organizations face the 'no takers' problem, where people separated by antagonistic views rarely want to form a joint organization.

The first task of concord organizations, then, is to find an overarching value that supersedes the differences that divide people who might create the group. This value, which can be transcendental or material, does not replace the differences that divide potential members. Sharing generalized bridging beliefs, such as the belief that all people are the children of God or disgust for violence can bring together otherwise divided communities. Likewise, members of concord organizations can be brought together by such concrete objectives as wanting their children to be able to walk to school safely or to save money by sharing sanctuaries for religious programs. Thus concord organizations are always balancing the values that bind members and those that separate them. This makes them more difficult to form and less likely to succeed than ordinary organizations.

Our research showed that people who create concord organizations think of themselves as social investors, rather than individual spenders. Thinking theoretically, people who create concord organizations are more attentive to interest rates than costs. People concerned about costs, as Olson noted, will often free ride, wanting to participate in the benefits of an organization at the lowest price, that is, without doing the work to establish it. [21] In contrast, social investors seek an adequate net pro-social interest rate. They recognize the danger, the pleasures, the obstacles, the immediate costs, the opportunity costs, and the benefits of individual action for collective ends – even if they could not perfectly calculate each component. In particular, social investors are attentive to the opportunity costs of the status quo, that is, of not acting, which they consider to have a high and enduring price. People who create concord organizations are motivated by the logic of collective investment, rather than by a race to the bottom competing on ever-lower prices.

Thinking practically, people who establish concord organizations consider them to be 'social banks' where cross-communities ideals, skills, and programs are held. Because concord organizations are social banks, they need rules in practice for protecting their assets. As Ostrom has shown, the structure of institutions and their rules are crucial to creating social capital.[22] Specifically, Ostrom wrote that 'the rate of contribution to a public good [like a concord organization] is affected by various contextual factors including the framing of the situation and the rules for assigning participants, increasing competition among them, allowing communications, authorizing sanctioning mechanisms, or allocating benefits.' In this vein, we determined ten rules for creating successful concord organizations, regardless of where they form or what tasks they undertake. These rules include four design principles and employ six necessary practices in order to keep the values that bind members in ascendance over the values that divide them. Strong concord organizations use all these principles and practices as an integrated whole.

Design principle: promote overarching values

Successful concord organizations find and continually enhance overarching shared values. In fact, this is the first task of concord organizations. The founders of such organizations, through a series of small, transformational encounters, often discover these shared values by getting to know individuals from other communities. They learn that they share generalized overarching beliefs that bridge their differences.

More than 90 percent of children in Northern Ireland go to sectarian schools. The creation of the first integrated (Catholic and Protestant) school in Northern Ireland is a good example of finding an overarching value – educating children together for a better life together. The founders of Lagan College, as it was ultimately called, were drawn in part from a group of Catholic families who sent their children to Protestant schools because the Protestant schools were closer to home or perceived as better for their children. But there were significant problems, not the least of which was that Catholic children were often 'passing' in these Protestant schools and they were required to take a Protestant-oriented religious curriculum. Catholic parents first identified themselves by, very bravely, allowing Mass cards to peek out of pockets or purses or bags so that other Catholic parents could identify them. One or two Catholics had, unusually, Protestant friends who had worked outside of Northern Ireland and were conversant with religiously integrated education and who were willing to discuss integrated education in Northern Ireland. Bit by bit they explored and reinforced their belief that educating their children together was immensely valuable. They did so even in the face of significant religious and political conflicts. And they did so at a time when there were tens of thousands of British troops in Northern Ireland and no direct rule.

Design principle: balance bridging and bonding values

Concord organizations have two enduring sets of values, bridging and bonding, and these values are always in contest within the members of organizations. Therefore, successful concord organizations deal with issues that divide their members as well as issues that bind them. Said another way, concord organizations do not avoid conflicts; they contextualize them together. They help people to hold several competing views of the same problem simultaneously and to keep the shared view in the ascendancy in their organizational work.

The late John Wallach, the founder of Seeds of Peace, which runs a summer camp in the United States for children from divided communities including the Middle East, Afghanistan, and the Balkans, described the demands of this balancing act. The three-week program recognizes the stages its campers go through. In the first week, the youngsters are either unwarrantedly idealistic or completely certain their side is right. In the second week, they begin to see that there might be other views and why people might hold them. In the third week, Wallach reported that the campers 'realize that they have to deal with the hatred and still need to accept each other anyway.[23] The Seeds of Peace International Camp would fail if it had a jolly 'we are all one under the skin' approach. In this way, the camp recognizes that it cannot succeed in its mission if it does not acknowledge what divides campers as well as what unites them.

Design principle: establish rules of engagement

The most successful concord organizations do not rush to action without attention to rule making in organizational life. They begin with well-stated democratic decision-making mechanisms, with specific attention to leadership transition and to basic mechanisms of solving future conflicts.

In Ann Arbor, Michigan, a small American college town, Genesis, the shared religious space of St Clare Episcopal Church and Temple Beth Emeth, has successfully undertaken a capital campaign for and the building of an extension for educational and community activities. This expansion was made possible by open and transparent decision-making rules embodied in a joint council established in the by-laws when the congregations decided to share space and by the deliberative and consultative processes the two congregations and the joint council undertook. In contrast, another group of congregations sharing buildings has increasingly functioned like a religious condominium with multiple tenants, in part because the original founders thought that their good intentions alone would be sufficient to deal with any conflicts in the future.

Design principle: recognize and reward investment

Successful concord organizations foster an organizational culture of social investment. People involved in concord organizations see themselves first and foremost as investors, not consumers, and they recognize and reward investment. They understand the long historical time frames of their conflicts and are realistic about the kinds of efforts necessary to bring about change. They see the organizations they form as 'banks' that hold and reinforce the often fragile visions for a better, shared future. They cultivate a hard-headed hopefulness.

Some of the investments concord organizations make are monetary. The grants given by The Abraham Fund or the Community Foundation for Northern Ireland are concrete examples of financial investment in interethnic community organizations. But most investments are more intangible – skills, relationships, new worldviews, and cross-community activities to solve shared problems. The Conflict Mediation and Transformation Practice mediated a violent conflict between ethnic gangs running competing taxi services in Cape Town. These taxis are crucial for economic well-being in poor neighborhoods with very limited public transportation and few cars. The conflict also had the potential to create a widening spiral of economic destabilization. The conflict disrupted a critical mode of transportation. The clashes also created real fear of traveling into and out of certain neighborhoods which further limits people's access to employment and the flow of goods and trade.

Many concord organizations demonstrate their commitment to investment by running programs for young people. In the United States, the high school training programs of Facing History and Ourselves and Leadership Development in Intergroup Relations are just two of many examples. The investment approach is also illustrated by the many concord organizations that act as incubators for new initiatives, spinning them off rather than growing themselves.

Necessary practice: prevent proselytizing

Successful concord organizations develop techniques where members can hold their views, but do not seek to impose them on others. Strong norms against proselytizing are important both organizationally and personally. Organizationally, strong norms against proselytizing keep the values that bridge viewpoints in the ascendancy, thus preventing organizations from drowning in the whirlpool of contested views. An individual's commitment not to proselytize demonstrates a profound and concrete recognition of the legitimacy of the people who hold views fundamentally different from, and often in opposition to, one's own. It means participants must restrain themselves from engaging in 'memory wars' or attempting to gain the upper hand through a strategy of asserting a 'hierarchy of oppression': your group may have a grievance but my group has been more greatly wronged. This practice also requires a focus on the current or immediate conflict rather than starting with the historical debates over 'where the graves of one's grandparents are located'. Neither party is allowed to harken back to injustices they have experienced to the exclusion of recognizing injustices that have been experienced by others. The self-restraint involved in not proselytizing becomes a basis for a larger social practice of restraint, listening, and efforts at mutual problem solving.

Most participants in concord organizations say that not proselytizing is one of the hardest values to internalize. Six abortion activists – three leaders in favor of legal abortion and three opposed – engaged in a five-year mediated dialogue that began after a murderous attack on abortion clinic personnel in Boston. When describing the procedures of their dialogue they said, 'We also made a commitment that some of us still find agonizingly difficult: to shift our focus away from arguing for our cause. This agreement was designed to prevent rancorous debates.'[24]

Necessary practice: acknowledge and receive legitimacy

Successful concord organizations provide mechanisms of legitimization, recognition, and respect on a personal level. Social techniques for legitimization are well known. They include such devices as using the language of the 'other' when referencing them, refraining from using words that incite those from other communities, paying attention to the balance of viewpoints presented, developing vehicles for the expression of community viewpoints within the context of concord activities, and having an organizational culture that allows people to change their minds.

Legitimization is not easy or unproblematic. It does not mean personal acceptance of the position or values of the other group. Rather, legitimization involves having one's own narrative of the conflict heard and hearing the narratives of others. The intended purpose is not to argue for the superiority of one's own narrative or to win the 'oppression Olympics' but instead to learn the sources of deeply held values and the effects of the conflict on one's self and others. For example, in American abortion dialogues participants came to call their positions by the phrases each group used for itself – 'pro-choice' and 'pro-life'. This practice was successful in part because the preferred names did not include antagonistic references to the positions of the other side. In Northern Ireland, Catholic and Protestant released prisoners discussed with each other the effects that their violent actions and subsequent internment had on their families and communities, recognizing the costs they shared. On the West Bank, The Parents' Circle – Families Forum brings Jewish and Palestinian families together to discuss their shared experience of losing a loved one to violence. Schools and community programs try to teach legitimization skills. The South African Human Rights Commission's Training Centre has fielded a national program that tries to develop intercultural competencies in school children, and The Center for the Study of Violence and Reconciliation, an NGO working in Johannesburg, has made similar efforts for youth not in school.

Necessary practice: avoid 'gotcha'

'Gotcha' is the practice of highlighting to others their failures to see a group the way the group sees itself. 'Gotcha' is American slang for, 'I got you,' meaning I caught you doing something you should not be doing. An example of 'gotcha' might be someone purposefully derailing an otherwise successful conversation to complain that the speaker had used, say, 'Hispanic' rather than 'Latina/o'. (Both are respectful names used in the United States for Americans from Spanish speaking countries in South and Central America. In many communities, 'Latina/o' is considered more authentic and attentive to cultural preferences.) The purpose of the interrupter was not to engage in a discussion on respectful names, but to show that the speaker was thoughtless and not to be trusted and that the interrupter was the guardian of true understanding.[25]

Successful concord organizations avoid 'gotcha' because it undermines the inquiring, learning culture of concord work. In practice, avoiding 'gotcha' means that people in concord groups are committed to engaging with those in opposing camps even when they cause some pain or frustration. It means being able to see oneself making the kinds of mistakes others have made about one's own group. Such norms create a virtuous circle of both attentiveness to others and flexibility and generosity in the process of learning. Avoiding 'gotcha' is a way of avoiding political correctness, which tends to emphasize monitoring behavior for failures.

Necessary practice: learn to 'not understand' and to 'not be accepted'

Successful concord organizations promote awareness that complete understanding of and acceptance by the 'Other' is neither likely nor necessary. Understandings of reality are products of lived experience and are not transferable in their entirety to those without the experience. Nor is it likely that a totally satisfactory joint definition of reality will emerge from cross-community work. Instead, the multiple narratives of lived experiences will reside simultaneously and, in the best circumstances, with respect and acceptance.

The Oakwood Integrated Primary School in Northern Ireland held a meeting for parents where the Protestant/unionist and Catholic/nationalist symbols used during the violent struggle were placed in the middle of the room. These included balaclavas, paramilitary badges, and posters. Most people had never touched or seen up close these potent symbols, even those from their own community. In a mediated discussion, parents talked about what the symbols meant to them and to Northern Ireland. This process increased awareness of their common experience of violence, upheaval, and loss. But in the end, empathy and information do not equate with the experience of being Catholic in British-ruled Northern Ireland or Protestant in IRA-besieged Northern Ireland.

Necessary practice: support single-community work

Successful concord organizations help individuals and communities develop strong, positive, single-community (that is, within home community) identities.[26] Concord organizations do this in two ways: by including single-community opportunities as part of their programming and by strengthening the capacities of single-community organizations to do cross-community work. These activities both advance concord organizations and protect their participants. Cross-community work needs talented people, many of whom are drawn to these activities from outward-looking, single-community organizations. Equally important is the fact that most people who work in concord organizations are deeply connected to, and are nurtured by, single-community groups. It is jarring and disheartening to return to a single-community organization that is hostile to cross-community engagement.

Genesis, the shared governance structure of the facility housing Temple Beth Emeth and St Clare Episcopal Church made a profound commitment to the needs of one of its congregations. Over the life of the relationship one congregation grew while the other contracted. Genesis decided that in order to meet the developing needs of one community, a new sanctuary and a school facility would be built, requiring considerable indebtedness for both congregations. Genesis, the concord organization, recognized the need to keep its individual congregations strong by building a new sanctuary, a decision that allowed it to continue its cross-community work. The commitments of two South African organizations to individual communities are different but no less vital. U Managing Conflict (UMAC), a conflict mediation organization working mostly in Cape Town, and IDASA, which works nationwide, are successful multi-ethnic organizations that work as needed with single, often geographically defined, tribal or linguistic communities. They work to develop the problem solving skills necessary to respond to disagreements both within and outside these single-community groups. Paul Graham, the executive director of IDASA, notes that their single-community work is done very much with bridging in mind.

Necessary practice: develop leaders

Successful concord organizations develop leaders, in their own organizations and in single-community groups, who can maintain legitimacy 'at home' while encouraging engagement with 'the other'. Concord organizations often challenge conventional definitions of leadership in divided societies and demand complex thinking about the value of joint activity. They ultimately depend on leaders who have enough political resources to withstand suspicions of disloyalty. Leaders with a tenuous hold on their own positions of authority or who fail to deliver value to their single-community members are seldom able to withstand attacks for participation in concord organizations or cross-community work. Strong leaders are those who can successfully engage in concord organizations, who know how simultaneously to understand and to satisfy some of the basic needs of their followers, and who encourage followers' learning and critical thinking.

At least one concord organization, NCCJ (the National Conference for Community and Justice) has made the training of leaders for cross-community work in the United States one of its main missions. As its president Sanford Cloud, Jr. noted, NCCJ's task is 'transforming communities to be more whole and just by empowering leaders to engage in institutional change'. Across the ocean, the Belfast Interface Project enhances leadership in a different way. It supports the development of effective mobile phone networks across the city. Through these networks local community activists can respond quickly to reports of tension and violence at interfaces. Relevant information can be passed within, and where possible, between communities as well as to appropriate agencies, reducing rumors and miscommunication. The mobile phone networks help local activists reduce the number of incidents at interfaces and lessen the likelihood that those that do occur will escalate.

Recommendations: supporting concord organizations

Concord organizations are culturally attentive mediating institutions that activate the implicit promise of liberal structural arrangements to improve participation and economic fairness. When designed and implemented with care, concord organizations can create the bridging social capital that increases communal understanding, promotes joint projects, and reduces bloodshed. Concord Organizations are more likely to emerge and succeed when democratic institutions work and when major actors in state and civil society disavow violence.

Concord organizations are often a node in a virtuous circle of improved communal relations. The public goods created by concord organizations are unimaginable to most people caught up in intractable, culturally-rooted, conflicts. A vision that sees an alternative and better future for all communities is a precious and fragile asset. Creating this asset requires, in the first instance, the identification of mutually desirable overarching values. Once established and nurtured, these values can be expressed in dialogue, and more durably in joint endeavors, by designing institutions that balance the overarching shared value and exclusive communal values, in ways that the overarching value dominates in these organizations.

Governments acting with large scale formal mediating institutions – like businesses, foundations, and banks – can promote cross-community work in civil society and the creation of concord organizations. Public policies that support the civic sector, especially laws that encourage the creation of independent and transparent non-profits and NGOs free of government interference make creating bridging social capital easier. A joint future with former adversaries requires a physical, cultural, and social place to find solutions. This social space needs a public-regarding ethos that emerges from the citizenry not the state, and is separate from the profit demands of the market. These are the qualities of the non-profit or civic sector.[27]

The large institutions that benefit from reduced communal violence need to invest in the community based organizations that promote cross-community asset creation. Think for a moment of the growth in the Gross Value Added (GVA) of Northern Ireland since the Good Friday Agreement, which was signed in 1998. In 1990, Northern Irish GVA per person was £6,438. By 2003, the GVA per person was £12,971. During the same period the official unemployment rate declined from 8.7 percent to 4.2 percent.[28] Not all of the economic growth came from the (imperfect) stability arising from the Good Friday Agreement. Northern Ireland's economy improved with growing European integration, declined in the worldwide slump after the events of September 11, 2001, and rebounded somewhat as a new and different equilibrium has been established. Nonetheless, few places in the industrialized world have almost doubled their GDP or GVA per person and halved their unemployment rate in just over a decade. Northern Ireland benefited from an extensive public investment strategy by the European Union and the governments of the Republic of Ireland and the United Kingdom as part of the peace process. Private investment has been important as well. In 2000 the Private Finance Initiative/Public Private Partnerships (PFI/PPS) exceeded £300 million.[29] Previously, private companies were unwilling to sink funds into communities with no future except continuing sectarian violence.

At the same time, the EU, the governments of the Republic of Ireland and the United Kingdom, plus foundations supported a remarkable growth in non-profit cross-community organizations. At the beginning of this rapid investment, Northern Ireland benefited from having cross-community organizations like Corrymeela that had started before 'The

Troubles' and had endured, with difficulty, throughout them. These organizations had developed practices and relationships that served as a place to begin creating additional institutional resources.

The World Bank, the International Monetary Fund, the regional economic development banks, large foundations, international and domestic businesses, international development NGOs, and governments can all learn from the Northern Irish experience. Investments in bridging social capital pay off, and the pay off is highest when support for concord work begins when conflict is simmering rather than raging; continues over time including, if possible, when conflict is rampant; promotes dialogue leading to joint projects; and teaches cross-community leadership skills. The ability to undertake successful concord work is in very short supply in societies, like Northern Ireland, where people work, live, and worship in separate spheres.

One of the most important lessons for governments, businesses, banks, and foundations to learn is that cross-community work requires face-to-face, trusting encounters. As a result individual concord organizations can only grow to the point where they can successfully maintain this personal learning environment. This means that funding entities can not simply 'scale-up' an existing organization. Another important limitation is the focus on a core mission and values. As concord groups gain the trust of the participants it is not uncommon for new needs to be identified in a community. It is important that the group be intentional in its choice of projects and the breadth of work it embraces. The cross-community organization has to be vigilant about 'mission-creep' so that the group does not evolve out of its effective role or abandon its core mission as new and separate immediate challenges arise. But organizational growth and social coverage can come in other forms. For instance, groups can grow using a federation model, in which the principles and practices of a group are replicated in separate settings with participants in each location. Additionally, concord organizations can address new challenges and needs by incubating targeted projects that can then spin off as new separate organizations.

Generating more and enduring bridging social capital can save money over time, in small ways at first, and then in more dramatic ways. In the Apartheid period, a small city in South Africa would have needed from three to six high schools, at least one for each group (whites, coloreds, and blacks) or perhaps two for each community, if boys and girls were educated separately. This was a great public investment burden, which in the Apartheid era was lowered by gross underinvestment in schools for colored and black children.[30] Similarly, the historical development of schools in Northern Ireland resulted in a four-part system of (now) tax-supported schools: separate boys' and girls' schools for Protestants and Catholics. The integrated school movement in Northern Ireland created religion *and gender* inclusive schools. Only five percent of the students attend integrated schools, but they are among the most academically and socially successful in Northern Ireland, and certainly a source of the next generation of cross-community leaders. Implementing *the choice* of integrated schools in Northern Ireland probably increased costs (more schools needed to be built[31]), but the principle of educating children together is one that would reduce costs, or increase investments per pupil.

Extrapolating from these examples, it is easy to argue, theoretically, that a large village in a divided society with no high school is better off building one school available to all children than building several high schools each available to only one group, or one high school available only to the dominant group. Practically, this approach only works if the groundwork in terms of successful cross-community relations exists or can be developed, which in turn, often requires addressing larger cultural forces that change only slowly. Nonetheless, against enormous odds and using very different political and civic levers, both South Africa and Northern Ireland did invent ways, in principle, to reduce educational costs through building bridging social capital. They have certainly invented mechanisms that use some schools to span – with imperfect but real success – antagonistic communities.

When governments, business, banking, and formal civic organizations support cross-community work, they help the concord organizations change the cultural time frame in divided societies. Concord organizations create places to imagine a different future, to learn, to make mistakes and try again, to humanize the 'Other', and to contribute together to reaching mutually determined goals. Creating concord organizations is extraordinarily hard work. Good intentions usually fail because they do not embody cultural recognition of the depth of difference between communities. Concord organizations can create enduring bridging social capital, the most scarce resource in divided societies. It takes hard-headed optimism, aided by the thoughtful design of cross-community organizations, supported by formal institutions that benefit from a peaceful joint future. The ideas and the practices exist to do so.

Notes

1 Barbara J. Nelson, Dean of the UCLA School of Public Affairs, can be reached at Nelson@spa.ucla.edu; Linda Kaboolian, a faculty member of the Kennedy School of Government at Harvard, can be reached at Linda_Kaboolian@Harvard.edu; and Kathryn A. Carver, a health and human rights lawyer who is the Executive Director of The Concord Project, can be reached at KAC@spa.ucla.edu. For more information about creating a concord organization, see: Nelson, Barbara J., Kaboolian, Linda and Carver, Kathryn A. (2003) *The Concord Handbook.* Los Angeles: UCLA. The *Handbook* is available at the website of The Concord Project at http://concord.sppsr.ucla.edu.

2 Human Security Centre of the University of British Columbia, Canada, (2005) *Human Security Report 2005: War and Peace in the 21st Century.* New York, London: Oxford University Press. p. 23.

3 Lipschutz, Ronnie and Crawford, Beverly (1996) 'Economic Globalization and the "New" Ethnic Strife: What is to Be Done?' Berkeley: University of California: Institute on Global Conflict and Cooperation.

4 Varshney, Ashutosh (2002) *Ethnic Conflict and Civic Life: Hindus and Muslims in India.* New Haven: Yale University Press.

5 Social Capital – the personal, relational, and organizational resources available to improve community life and solve social problems – comes in two forms: bonding and bridging. Bridging social capital spans social differences. Bonding social capital connects people of similar identities and values. Nelson, Barbara J., Kaboolian, Linda and Carver, Kathryn A. (2003) *The Concord Handbook.* Los Angeles: UCLA. p. 9.

6 Lipschutz, Ronnie and Crawford, Beverly (1996) 'Economic Globalization and the "New" Ethnic Strife: What is to Be Done?' Berkeley: University of California: Institute on Global Conflict and Cooperation. p. 6.

7 Lipschutz, Ronnie and Crawford, Beverly (1996) 'Economic Globalization and the "New" Ethnic Strife: What is to Be Done?' Berkeley: University of California: Institute on Global Conflict and Cooperation. p.15.

8 Harding, Sandra (1998) *Is Science Multicultural? Postcolonialisms, Feminisms, and Epistemologies.* Bloomington and Indianapolis: Indiana University Press.

9 See Nelson, Barbara J. Kaboolian, Linda and Carver, Kathryn A. (2004). 'Bridging Social Capital and An Investment Theory of Collective Action: Evidence from The Concord Project'. Chicago: The American Political Science Association; and Nelson, Barbara J., Kaboolian, Linda and Carver, Kathryn A. (2005) 'A Theory of Collective Investment: Creating Cross-Community Organizations In Divided Societies'. Washington, DC: Association of Public Policy Administration and Management.

10 Duin, Julia (2005) 'Jews, Muslims Pledge Peace, Stand Against "Hate" Crimes', Washington, DC: *The Washington Times,* Sunday, September 18th, 2005, p. A2.

11 Data from the Foundation Center indicate that there are approximately 1.6 million NGOs in the United States. See, Anheier, Helmut (2005) *Non-profit Organizations: Theory, Management, Policy.* London and New York: Routledge. p. 65.

12 Even nomenclature works against routinely gathering information on the numbers of concord organizations and cross-community work. The Northern Irish use the term 'cross-community' to describe concord work, while those in Palestine and Israel often use terms including 'peace' and in the United States the activity is, imperfectly, categorized as 'anti-racist' or 'multicultural'. Interestingly, South Africans engaged in concord work tend not to label their activities, or to lump them under 'building democracy' and emphasize that South Africa strives to be, as its constitution says, a 'non-racial' democracy. A senior person in the National Centre for Human Rights and Training in South Africa said to us in an interview that he was happy to have a name for what he was doing. He likened it to the old joke about learning that you were speaking prose. Indeed, the reason we coined the term 'concord organizations' was to find a phrase that captured the concept behind the many local names and that could be used internationally without being overly connected to one specific regional experience.

13 Nelson, Barbara J., Kaboolian, Linda and Carver, Kathryn A. (2003) *The Concord Handbook.* Los Angeles: UCLA. p. 3.

14 The trend toward democratization can be seen by comparing data from 1975 and 2005 from Freedom House that ranks nation-states and selected territories as Free, Partially Free and Not Free. The change in the political landscape is reflected in the number of states ranked Free or Partially Free. In 2005 there were 40 more states measured than were included in 1975 because of the break-up of the USSR and Yugoslavia and in 2005 there were ten states that had ceased to exist since 1975 due to reunification (e.g. North and South Vietnam, East and West Germany, etc.) or the previously mentioned dissolutions. Freedom House does not measure the activity solely of governments but rather conducts an annual survey of freedom as experienced by individuals. In 2005 the survey included 192 countries and 14 selected territories. The rankings of Free, Partially Free, and Not Free are determined by

evaluating analytical reports and numerical ratings measuring 10 political rights and 15 civil liberties. Also, states with participatory electoral governments are assigned an electoral democracy designation based upon factors such as competitive multiparty system, universal adult suffrage, regularly contested elections etc. The general trend has been overwhelmingly toward increased freedom within each country and in general worldwide. However, not all national cases are consistently positive. Russia moved from Free to Not Free in 2005 for the first time since the break-up of the Soviet Union. See, the Freedom House rankings and methodology at www.freedomhouse.org. Accessed January 16, 2006.

15 See The Inglehart Values Map and description in the World Values Survey. The World Values Surveys were designed to provide a comprehensive measurement of all major areas of human concern from religion to politics to economic and social life. To date there have been four waves of surveys conducted internationally. The fifth wave of the World Values Survey went into the field in the July of 2005 and will continue until late 2006. www.worldvaluessurvey.org, accessed January 24, 2006. Similar information on support for democracy is available from the Pew Global Attitudes Project (2003) *Views of a Changing World June 2003.* Washington, DC: Pew Research Center For The People & The Press. The report shows support for a democratic political process exceeding 80 percent of respondents in the countries surveyed.

16 World Values Survey, Figure 5 Subjective well-being and democratic institutions plotting Freedom House ratings of societies as Free, Partially Free and Not Free against the mean of percent happy and satisfied with life as a whole. www.worldvaluessurvey.org, accessed January 24, 2006. Citing Inglehart, Ronald and Klingeman, Hans-Dieter 'Genes, Culture, and Happiness', MIT.

17 Inglehart, Ronald and Norris, Pippa (2003), 'The True Clash of Civilizations', *Foreign Policy* March/April: 67–74.

18 Ningabira, Aloyse and Dance, Rosalie 'Making Peace in Kibimba: Healing and Peacemaking in Burundi', www.aglionline.org/PDF/Making%20Peace%20in%20Kibimba1.pdf, describes joint economic ventures of Tutsi and Hutu widows in Burundi. pp. 6–8. Accessed January 24, 2006.

19 Mats are used for everything from a place to sit or sleep, to a place to sort or store food and most importantly a place to care for an ill person and to wrap their body after death. www.aglionline.org/PDF/Making%20Peace%20in%20Kibimba1.pdf p. 7. Accessed January 24, 2006.

20 For information on single-community work – also called single-identity work – see the Community Relations Council (2003), 'Training Support: Single Identity Work' http://www.community-relations.org.uk/progs/train/siw.htm citing work in Belfast, NI.

21 Olson, Mancur (1965) *The Logic of Collective Action: Public Goods and The Theory of Groups.* Cambridge: Harvard University Press. p. 2.

22 Ostrom, Elinor (2000) 'Collective Action and the Evolution of Social Norms', *The Journal of Economic Perspectives,* 18 (3): 137–58. (Quote p. 14). See also, Ostrom, Elinor (1990) *Governing the Commons: The Evolution of Institutions for Collective Action.* Cambridge and New York: Cambridge University Press, and Ostrom, Elinor (1992) *Crafting Institutions for Self-Governing Irrigation Systems.* San Francisco: Institute for Contemporary Studies.

23 Ellenson, Ruth Andrew (May 23, 2002.) 'My Friend, My Enemy', *The Los Angeles Times.*

24 Fowler, A., Gamble, N. N., Hogan, F. X., Kogut, M., McComish, M., and Thorp, B. (January 28, 2001) 'Talking with the Enemy', *Boston Globe.*

25 Nelson, Barbara J. (1999) 'Diversity and Public Problem Solving: Ideas and Practice in Policy Education', *Journal of Policy Analysis and Management,* 18: 134–55.

26 The Northern Irish have coined two terms, cross-community work and single-community (often single-identity) work to distinguish between those skills needed when working across communities and others needed when working to develop greater capacities for cross-cultural engagement within communities. Single-community work refers to efforts within a community to develop community identities, skills, and organizational capacities that permit successful cross-community work.

27 See, Anheier, Helmut (2005) *Non-profit Organizations: Theory, Management, Policy.* London and New York: Routledge, and website of the International Network on Strategic Philanthropy (INSP), www.insp.efc.be.

28 *Northern Ireland Economic Bulletin, 2005* (2005) Belfast, NI: Department of Enterprise, Trade and Investment. June: 14–15. In the United Kingdom, Gross Domestic Product is measured in three ways: by output, by income, and by expenditure. Since the mid-1990s GDP statistics for regions in the United Kingdom have rarely been produced. Instead, regional GVA numbers are used. According to the National Statistics Office 'gross value added (GVA) measures the contribution to the economy of each individual producer, industry, or sector in the United Kingdom …The link between GVA and GDP can be defined as GVA (at current basic prices, available by industry only), plus taxes on products (available at whole economy level only) less subsidies on products (available at whole economy level only) equals GDP (at current market prices: available at whole economy level only).' The definitions are available at http://www.statistics.gov.uk/CCI/nugget.asp?ID. Accessed February 6, 2006.

29 Northern Ireland Expenditure Plans and Priorities 1999–2000 to 2001–2002, Table 11.10, http://www.nics.gov.uk/expenditure/. Accessed January 29, 2006.

30 In the apartheid period, one of the ways the government reduced the cost of providing multiple separate schools was to fail to build schools for 'colored' or 'black' children. Post-apartheid public schooling in South Africa is quite complex. Many white parents removed their children from public schools, and spatial

housing segregation creates many single-group schools. Nonetheless, the argument shows that educating children together, if there is a strong commitment to creating bridging social capital, can save money, and therefore provide greater educational coverage or meet other social needs.

31 The government of Northern Ireland shifted many of the costs of integrated schools to parents and teachers who wanted to establish them, requiring them to find and buy buildings and removing teachers from the public pension programs if the integrated schools failed to establish themselves and thrive in three years.

CHAPTER 24

PERFORMANCE, GLOBALIZATION AND CONFLICT PROMOTION/RESOLUTION: EXPERIENCES FROM SRI LANKA

James Thompson

This chapter examines performance projects as they relate to globalization and conflict resolution in Sri Lanka. It explores the history of the conflict and relates how competing nationalisms have used cultural programmes to maintain or undermine certain configurations of the Sri Lankan state. Although the conflict left many areas of the island isolated, the 2002 ceasefire has increased the impact of globalization. Three theatre projects are explored to illustrate how cultural events have been used as part of conflict resolution programmes. One is a traditional performance project in the eastern war-affected area, one a cross-community arts organization and one an activist theatre group from the north of the island. Cultural work has a complex relationship to the forces of globalization and local national movements.

Introduction

This analysis of theatre or performance initiatives in Sri Lanka accepts the definitions of culture and globalization offered in the Introduction to this volume, while seeking to extend the perspective that culture is constitutive of both collective and individual identity. Cultural action is *performative* in that it seeks to create a certain form of identity as much as it represents or constitutes it. Cultural performance in this context becomes as much aspirational as representational – seeking to bring about as much as announce certain inter-group or inter-communal relations. The performance projects discussed here are concerned with developing change in the conflict and are not only constitutive or the products of it.

History of a conflict

Sri Lanka has experienced nearly 20 years of highly destructive civil unrest and violence.[1] The country's previous history is one of conquest, colonial rule and the influence of competing global powers that have sought to exploit the wealth of its natural resources and its strategic position in the Indian Ocean between the Arabian Sea and the Bay of Bengal. Portuguese, Dutch and finally British rule can be broadly divided into equal 150-year blocks ending with independence from Britain in 1948. More recently, the country's post-independence non-alignment policies have been revoked as Sri Lanka positions itself within a global economy, heavily reliant on the garment industries, tourism and the labour of large numbers of emigrants in the Middle East[2].

Sri Lanka is a country of approximately 20 million people, divided between Sinhalese, Tamils, Muslims (also called Moors), Malays and Vedas. The Sinhalese are the largest national group (74 per cent) while the Tamils are the largest minority group, representing 18 per cent of the population. All the world's major religions are represented on the island, but Buddhism is the dominant religion and is linked particularly with the identity of the Sinhalese. The Tamils are predominantly Hindu, but the influence of Portuguese missionaries led to a substantial Tamil Catholic community, particularly in the coastal areas. In 1956 controversial legislation introduced Sinhala as the 'only' language of government partly as a response to the post-colonial dominance of English. This, however, started a process of marginalization and discrimination against the Tamil minority, which developed into armed militancy from the late 1970s after the Tamil United Liberation Front (TULF) was banned from parliament after the 1977 election. After an attack on the Sri Lankan Army (SLA) in Jaffna in 1983, an anti-Tamil pogrom swept the capital, Colombo, killing and displacing many thousands of Tamil civilians. This led to the flight of many Tamils overseas (Canada, the UK and France were the major destinations) and proved a major stimulus to an underlying 'armed struggle'. Many now mark 1983 as the start of the civil conflict that has continued to this day. Since then 70,000 people have lost their lives and many more have been displaced both within the country and internationally. Although at the beginning of the conflict the Government of Sri Lanka (GOSL) was fighting a number of armed

Figure 24.1 Map of Sri Lanka

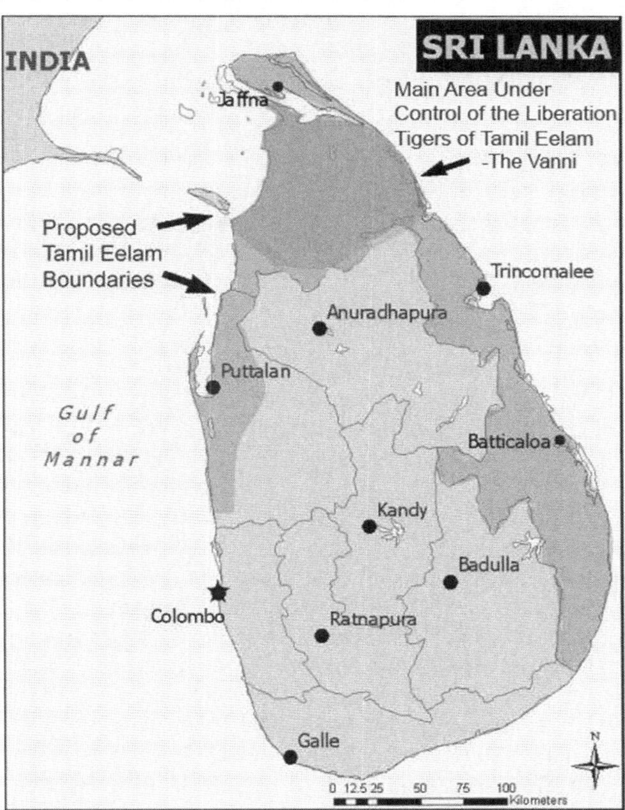

Tamil militant groups, since the late 1980s the war has been dominated by the Liberation Tigers of Tamil Eelam (LTTE). The GOSL and the LTTE have now been locked in a 20-year battle, characterized as a struggle between those that want to maintain a unitary state and those proposing an island divided between a Sinhala Lanka and a Tamil Eelam (see Figure 24.1). Recent political negotiations have suggested a compromise might be found in a form of regional autonomy between the Tamil dominated north and East and the Sinhala dominated south, but a final settlement is far from close.

In its early years very little international attention was paid to the Sri Lankan conflict. Although the Tamil militants were deliberately trained and sponsored by the Indian government in the 1980s as a means of gaining a strategic foothold in the affairs of a neighbour, this project backfired after the Indian Peace Keeping Force, sent to Sri Lanka at the end of the 1980s to implement a peace deal, became embroiled in a guerrilla war with the LTTE. The bitterness of this conflict led eventually to the assassination of the Indian Premier Rajiv Gandhi by a Tiger suicide bomber and the end of Indian patronage of Tamil militant groups. Since September 11th, however, international stakes in the Sri Lankan situation have increased. The global 'war on terror' is perhaps the key motivator for the current ceasefire as the Tamil diaspora, the traditional supporters and financers of the LTTE, are pressured to reconsider their support in light of new concerns about terrorism. The LTTE is a banned terrorist organisation in both the USA and the UK and its 'pioneering' use of the suicide bomber (purportedly potentially 'made available' to other groups in the world[3]) increased the demands for it to be drawn into the current ceasefire agreement.

The negotiations promised by the ceasefire however were suspended in 2003 after the previous President, Chandrika Bandaranaike Kumaratunga, retook control of the government and the current situation was further complicated by a split in the LTTE when the eastern commander, Vinayagamoorthy Muralitharan, led a revolt against perceived discrimination against his fighters by the Northern command of the LTTE. Although his group was rapidly defeated by the LTTE, these divisions have led to a series of assassinations and murders particularly in the east of the country. The stand-off between the government and the LTTE was made more volatile by the 26th December 2004 tsunami. Arguments about the distribution of international aid were partially resolved in July 2005 with the signing of the Post-Tsunami Operational Management Structure (P-TOMS) that permitted the coordinated distribution of aid between the GOSL and the LTTE. This, however, angered sections of the Sinhala community who saw this as official recognition of a 'terrorist' group and a further concession that threatened the integrity of the state. The anti-P-TOMS stance was one of a number of grievances taken up by the Sinhala hardliner Mahinda Rajapakse during the Presidential election of November 2005. His subsequent victory and his call for the re-negotiation of the ceasefire agreement have led to ominous responses from the LTTE.

The strategic position of Sri Lanka, its untapped potential as a major port for sea traffic, its economic reliance on tourism, tea, garments and foreign labour, and the international interest in rebuilding the country after the tsunami, create a context in which the demands of a 'national liberation struggle' confront the pressures of globalization. It is within this context that the cultural programmes that are the focus of this chapter will be discussed.

Culture[4] and conflict in Sri Lanka

Both the Sinhala and Tamil communities have strong traditional performance practices as well as lively theatre traditions. It would be inaccurate and a simplification to divide these between 'modern' or urban forms and rural and 'folk' traditions. Although there are clearly distinct practices, for the purposes of this analysis the connections between them rather than their separation will be emphasized. The political struggles in the post-independence period are an important site from which to understand current performance practices. The ways in which theatre practitioners have drawn on different stories or forms to assert 'national identities' are also important markers in an investigation of the cultural practices that have appeared in response to the current conflict. Any claim for *culture as a tool for conflict prevention or resolution* can only be understood by examining a context in which cultural practices have also been instrumental in maintaining or encouraging a conflictual situation. In addition, the arguments about 'modern' or 'traditional' forms have been made more acute in light of a ceasefire that certain practitioners see as opening up their communities to what are considered to be the threats of non-local cultural forms. As the social isolation forced by the war has started to erode, the impact of globalization has become a priority concern. This is touched upon in more detail later.

An example of the link between national identity and cultural expression can be found in the 1956 play *Maname* by the Sinhala artist and director Ediriweera Sarachchandra. This piece is now often viewed as the first example of a modern Sinhalese play and it played to hugely enthusiastic audiences at the time and has done so in subsequent revivals. It is no coincidence that it premiered in the year of the 'Sinhala Only' Act at a moment of widespread assertion of Sinhala identity and the Sinhala people's increasing dominance within the national polity. Although the effects of this policy were discriminatory against the Tamil community, it cannot be forgotten that this was also a response to the colonial legacy of the pre-eminence of the English language in all spheres of government. Although Sarachchandra's association with questions of Sinhala identity were taken further in his version of *Sinhabahu* (a retelling of the myth of origins of the Sinhala people) a brief inspection of *Maname* reveals an important part of the history of cultural practice in the island.

Maname was constructed from a diverse set of sources which included Roman Catholic *koooththu*, British proscenium arch theatre, Sinhala folk storylines, and inspiration from the Sinhala artist Gunasinghe Gurunnanse who was an expert in what in Sinhala is called the *Demala beraya* (Tamil drum). Roman Catholic *kooththu* has its origins in the coastal Tamil communities near Mannar in the northwestern part of Sri Lanka. *Kooththu* as a dance-drama form associated with ritual performances of the Mahabharata and Ramayana had been transformed through interactions with the Catholic Church in this predominantly Christian area of the island. So although *Maname* became a totem for Sinhala cultural renaissance, this cursory glance at the performance practices that were assembled in its creation, indicates a more heterogeneous vision of cultural practice. While the rich and culturally complex origins of this performance are now more frequently acknowledged, during the years of hostilities pride in your national heritage found no space for admitting that the 'enemy' had always been integral to the construction of that cultural practice. *Maname* was in those early years thus cleansed to be the quintessential example of 'modern *Sinhala* theatre', denying its association with and borrowing of a number of Tamil (and other international) cultural practices. This point is emphasized by the academic Neluka Silva when she writes:

> *In scenarios of ethnic conflict, historically mixed and hybrid communities and identities are often reinvented in terms of ethnic purity, as conflicting groups lay exclusive claims to previously multicultural territories, memories, histories and heritage.*[5]

Following Silva, Sri Lanka is more helpfully understood as a 'hybrid' island where generations of interactions between communities have left complex and interrelated performance practices. This is not only between communities on the island but between Sri Lanka and external cultural practices. Catholicism, Indian dance, and the European stage have influenced performance forms. These global trends continue to this day with the influence of Hindi film, American dance and even International NGO-sponsored participatory theatre programmes.[6] This is not to deny that certain cultural forms have strong connections to particular communities in specific geographical areas of the island, but to assert that emphasizing the interactions seeks to counter the myths of single origins and culturally homogeneous practices. Similarly, acknowledging hybridity is not to deny the problematic inequalities of power between cultural forms and also that some practices have restricted the space for the development of others. The Catholic adaptation of *kooththu* was for example as much a process of erasure as synthesis. However, heterogeneity is emphasised here in order to insist on the complexity of the relationship between the processes of globalization and local cultural practices and avoid the simplistic binary of the pure local and the contaminating global. Cultural activities in Sri Lanka have for generations been influenced by global movements of people, ideas and practices and therefore examining globalization's impact on culture today needs to acknowledge past interactions between the local and the non-local.

The process of assertive identity-formation after independence sought to carve out clear nationalist positions that in turn tended to give singular identifications to practices that in fact had multiple forms dancing or beating through them. *Maname* had elements of a Tamil dance and Tamil drumming within its structure. The war that emerged from this assertiveness further entrenched these divisions, encouraging discourses that resulted in an ethnic cleansing of forms. One dance was now Sinhala only and another Tamil only. The war was both sustained by these developments as well as being a generator of them. Culture was constitutive in that its shape was partly determined by the conflict and it was *performative* in that its execution helped to maintain the divisions. Years of conflict, with the subsequent demands for assertions of difference, have now prevented further interactions between communities entrenching the idea that cultural practices are homogeneous, and stultifying the process of engagement between communities that had been taking place for generations. The process of forced isolation caused by travel restrictions and ongoing violence has maintained these divisions and cultural practices are now very often exclusionary emblems of community identity rather than potential vehicles for inter-community understanding. These problems and difficulties are of course crucial for understanding those cultural practices that have developed within the war-affected communities and for a discussion of their potential role in conflict transformation. In addition, they explain why many artists and activists viewed the ceasefire and the subsequent opening of areas to the influence of external (and global) cultural forms, paradoxically, as threatening.

Controversies and questions in the cultural response

There are many examples of arts projects in Sri Lanka that have sought to respond to or have developed in spite of the conflict. In terms of theatre and performance these have included NGO-sponsored participatory theatre, street theatre, agit-prop political dramas, drama-therapeutic initiatives, ritual practices and large-scale spectacles. The three examples of practice discussed below have been chosen for their different approaches and for their locations in zones particularly affected by the war. They illustrate the diversity of possible relations between culture, conflict and globalization and the difficult questions that arise in all cases of theatre and performance in sites of conflict.

The role of kooththu

Kooththu is a dance-drama form that has been weakened by restrictions imposed by the conflict and has more recently been used to revitalize a sense of community in chronically conflict-affected regions. Historically, *kooththu* has been strong in the east of the country because it was an isolated area where the influence of colonial rule was minimized. It is thus positioned as a form that although weakened by the war is used as a symbol of the strength of the local as opposed to external or 'global' knowledge. Sivagnanam Jeyasankar and the Third Eye Local Knowledge and Activists Group in the eastern town of Batticaloa have worked with up to four different village *kooththu* groups in rural areas. The main group in the village of Seelamunai has had such a group for over one hundred years, but the practice has struggled to maintain itself with the curfews and restrictions on movement imposed by the war. *Kooththu* is an all-night performance of sections of Hindu epics sung and danced in the open-air *kaleri* (circular raised sand stages) to large village audiences. The Third Eye Group engages with what it calls a process of 'reformulation', where it supports a local group in reinvigorating its skills base while at the same time promoting an engagement with the issues inherent in the performed texts. In Seelamunai this has included a rewriting of the scripts so that they better represent low caste communities and permit the participation of women. In a region that has suffered violence, displacement, disappearances and since 2004 has been the site of the dispute between two factions of the LTTE, the space for debate and creative expression that the reformulation process permits is crucial. The performance does not foreground the issue to be discussed. Instead, through Third Eye's engagement with the community and through the performance of adapted scripts of traditional stories, discussions about caste and gender are instigated. In an area where space for open dialogue is much contested and outspoken comments on public issues are dangerous, the performance provides an *aesthetic* space through which concerns, questions and issues can be explored safely. Batticaloa has a civil society much weakened by the war and the recent LTTE divisions. The space of *kooththu* is perhaps a rare place of free debate done through the content and structure of the epics.

To connect this to a number of the concerns raised earlier, Third Eye is working with a cultural form that is strongly associated only with the Tamil community. However, they recognize that the form, rather than a site to construct singular impressions of Tamil national identity, is one through which to debate the multiple divisions that affect this community. By staying with *kooththu,* the participants ensure that they are safely associated with a Tamil form in an area of strongly (and violently) asserted nationalist politics. However, they offer an impressive model of practice because they manage to carve out a space for debate within this restricted arena.

In addition the 'reformulation' process is situated explicitly as a response to the pressures of globalization that are viewed with suspicion in the region, both post-ceasefire and post-tsunami. The influence of branded soft drinks, Indian film, plans for new tourist complexes, the practices of the plethora of International NGOs and so forth, are set against acts that validate 'local knowledge'. This is a new form of the division discussed in Georges Corm's chapter between 'modernity' on the one side and 'authenticity' on the other. It would be wrong to represent this as an argument of a unified Batticaloa community with those coming from without, as it is as much a debate about how to protect local knowledge, practices and cultural forms within this community. There is an argument even within the *kooththu* groups about whether any use of the 'European' proscenium arch as opposed to the more traditional circular *kaleri* should be permitted. Third Eye suggest their work in reformulating *kooththu* within the villages provides a bulwark against the influence of other cultural forms, but questions remain as to whether the global and local are in fact as oppositional as these formulations suggest. As stated earlier, few cultural practices in Sri Lanka have not somehow been the product of interactions between traditions. *Kooththu* at some point in its history travelled from the *terukkuttu* practices in Southern India.[7] The geographical and conflict-related isolation of Batticaloa is on the one hand the cause of a weaker *kooththu* practice but is also claimed as the reason for its very existence. The struggle to resolve this paradox revolves around allowing an emerging openness to increase the strength of the form through revitalized opportunities for training, practice and performance without the real or imagined threats of new external cultural practices weakening its appeal. The threats, challenges and opportunities from a post-conflict opening of the region to the global economy are exactly the arena of Third Eye's work.

Cross-community arts projects

The Centre for Performing Arts (CPA) was founded in the Northern town of Jaffna in 1965 by Professor Rev. Fr. N. M. Saveri, originally under the Tamil name *Thirumarai Kalamandram*. It has subsequently opened 20 centres across the country and many branches amongst exiled Sri Lankan communities internationally. CPA centres exist in all communities where they aim to involve young people in inter-cultural activities that promote peace and mutual understanding. This is done through a number of related activities. They teach traditional arts (for example 'Tamil' *kooththu* dances and 'Sinhala' Kandian dances) and then tour these to their different centres, thus sharing the art forms with different language and religious communities. They encourage the creation of contemporary performances by young people, often on the theme of the conflict and perform these to large audiences both within and beyond the communities where they originated. Finally they organize inter-community camps where young people from different communities work together on performance and arts projects. These activities have been conducted by CPA both during the conflict and they have continued since the ceasefire.

CPA thus seeks to work with and against the divisions in performance practice fostered by the war. They support and enhance the knowledge of traditional performance forms within Tamil, Sinhala and Muslim communities, but seek then to share the resulting performances with people from different areas. This engagement includes teaching Tamil young people dances usually associated with the Sinhala community and vice versa. The historical interaction of cultural practices is therefore deliberately developed by CPA. However, in bringing young people together in cross-cultural programmes they are also seeking to resist the divisions in cultural forms by encouraging joint practice, whereby performances are created drawing on the skills of all participants.

Cross-community work of this type is very difficult to organize during periods of actual war. When movement is difficult and dangerous and inter-community suspicion is extremely high, it takes great tenacity to persevere with such initiatives. The wartime work of CPA raises important questions about arts and conflict resolution. It is important to consider whether inter-community work through the arts merely raises false expectations because acts of war continue to recreate distrust. Does any progress made become undone by the next atrocity or can this work provide a possible bridge to future peace? This is not a judgement on the work of CPA, but their practice raises the question of when cross-community projects should start. The arts do provide a vehicle through which a dialogue based on creative activity rather than words can be initiated, but the dangers of creating these moments when the guns are still firing needs to be carefully considered.

CPA, since the ceasefire, has brought people together in multiple acts of creation and it is through the making of joyful, entertaining or challenging performances that some of the past mistrusts can be dissipated. As argued above, art forms in Sri Lanka are often experienced as emblems of certain communities' identities and ideologies. By offering contexts where these can be read as offers of exchange or examples of mutual respect, rather than as signs of exclusion and chauvinism, they could become a means of traversing conflict-sustaining divisions.

The Pongu Thamil phenomena

One of the leading community theatre groups in Sri Lanka, the Theatre Action Group (TAG), has been pioneering participatory community theatre projects for 20 years. It formed in the University of

Jaffna in 1985 and the group originally concentrated its theatre productions across the Jaffna peninsula in the north of the island. They have engaged in a diverse range of theatre activities: from political stage plays, to street theatre, to educational and health campaigns in refugee camps to children's theatre for schools. These activities have been developed to respond to the different war-imposed challenges faced by the Tamil people in this area.

TAG's work has always had a particular focus on stimulating emotional response in audiences and participants.[8] It is concerned that the war has repressed people's feelings and believes that events using song, dance, music and bold imagery can stimulate recovery. Across the different contexts in which it works, it seeks to release people's distress through energetic displays of drumming, singing and dance. Since the ceasefire, part of this format has been developed and it now helps coordinate large-scale spectacles that aim to provide a focus for Tamil grief. These events are called *Pongu Thamil* [9] and started as small celebrations but are now more akin to mass rallies. They take place particularly in areas of GOSL control, where, TAG would argue, the pain inflicted on the community has been greatest and outward displays of emotion have been most repressed.

These events are controversial within Sri Lanka. Some people suggest they are propaganda and recruiting exercises for the Tamil Tigers; others argue that they are spontaneous outpourings of Tamil emotion.[10] In addition, they are controversial within the arts communities, some believing that they are purely political and others arguing that they are *theatrical* events.[11] What are the questions for arts and conflict resolution that these events, and the debates surrounding them, raise? Their controversial nature is an important challenge to all arts projects. The capacity of a theatre company and the event it creates to be variously interpreted indicates that arts projects at the service of conflict prevention (in this case nominally a release of grief) do not have stable meanings. Because of the nature of conflict, activities that may seem well intentioned to one community can be viewed as chauvinism or support for war by another. Creators of arts projects cannot assume they control impact or the interpretation of that impact when working in a situation saturated by competing discourses, histories and myths. They need to pay attention both to the activity and the subsequent explanations of it in local and national arenas, so that aspiration for conflict resolution does not get transformed through the different readings into something else.

An additional question the work of TAG raises is the relationship between the arts and the relief of emotional harm. There is a long tradition within both western and eastern performance practices of such a link: from rituals in many Sinhala and Tamil traditions[12] to the *catharsis* in Aristotelian tragedy.[13] The therapeutic or curative possibilities of arts processes are complex, but perhaps the important point to note here is that many of these processes only make sense within a wider system of knowledge and practice. So Sinhala exorcism rituals are tied into a complex system of belief about devil possession and health, and Aristotelian catharsis sought to contribute to the rule of law within the Greek city-state. Arts-based healing rituals, therefore, cannot be interpreted in isolation but must be understood as part of a wider belief system. If that belief system is not clear or explicit, the grief displayed or emotion released will, as in the problem of interpretation discussed above, become easily attached to any system of belief that organizers, participants or observers choose. And that may not be one that an organizer of the event intends or one that seeks to reconcile and resolve conflicts.

As the funding of theatre or arts-based projects in Sri Lanka is increasingly tied into the agenda of powerful NGOs, this awareness of local systems of knowledge becomes more crucial. In addition, this has become even more acute in the post-tsunami period since 2004, at a time when funding for 'cultural' and 'psychosocial' initiatives has grown exponentially. The belief that there is a global threat to local cultural practice will be more justifiable if knowledge and practice brought to the country are not properly understood as culturally particular with little immediate currency beyond the place of their inception. So Post Traumatic Stress Disorder (PTSD) counselling, for example, becomes an imposition if there is an assumption that its development in the particularities of western contexts gives it automatic translation to a Sri Lankan one.[14]

Conclusion

This chapter has examined three examples of Sri Lankan theatre practice from the context of a war and recent ceasefire (but not yet 'post-war') period. The reformulation of traditional *kooththu* that seeks to create spaces for debate in a restricted civil society; the hope for cross-community arts practices in a geography divided by conflict and performance processes that elicit strong emotional release within a terrain where forces compete to define and own that grief. All of these both seek to be arts responses to conflict and have difficult relations to processes of reconciliation and globalization. The potential they create for safe places, dialogue and relief are enormous, but each in their own way also struggles with the demands placed by the context.

It is important to note that these are only three examples drawn from many. Artists, theatre companies and social organizations from all communities have been prompted to contribute to resolving conflict in their country. However, it should also be noted that at different times theatre and performance have been vehicles for entrenching divisions and stoking hostilities. The arts of course have no essential quality and therefore all projects where the arts are suggested as a mechanism or approach need to interrogate the form, content and processes involved.

This has become more acutely necessary since the tsunami in December 2004. Appalling physical and human destruction has once again galvanized the local and international arts communities to respond, but good intentions must always be questioned, to ensure that theatre or arts-based projects do not contribute to existing divisions, misconceptions and inequalities. A vital part of this questioning is to examine the relationship between the forms of practice proposed and the existing anxieties about threatened local practices and dominating international ones. The myths of pure 'ethnically cleansed' cultural forms have been maintained by the conflict and have been subsequently manipulated to foster conflict. Allowing new interactions to be conceptualized or experienced as the domination of the local by the global will maintain the cultural isolationism that can so easily be fanned to continue the war.

To conclude, I shall offer 6 points for action and consideration. It is hoped that these will be useful to organizations or policy-makers proposing to develop theatre and arts-based initiatives in sites of armed conflict:

1. It is important to consider the cultural forms used in projects. All cultural forms have 'telling links'[15] that mean they enact connections to ideologies and identity formations that might not be obvious to a person from outside the community. Does a particular dance form in fact have association with one language, religious or minority community? Does one practice in fact demonstrate the imposition of cultural forms from past rulers, or is the subtle change in existing practices due to a mutually enriching process of intercommunity engagement?
2. All art practices have complex genealogies and exist as changing processes more than static forms. They are rarely 'pure' and are often the product of interactions between different people and communities. In supporting theatre and the arts it is important to consider whether in doing so a dynamic process will be stultified. Does *protection* of cultural practices become a form of *preservation* that in fact maintains certain configurations of power more than the health of the arts practice? For example, does the funding of a particular performance troupe maintain the restrictions for women on access to the arts in a certain community? Or does the lack of protection mean that inequalities of global cultural exchange will ensure that international/non-local practices will be given free reign to dominate?
3. For cross-cultural or intercommunity work through the arts to be effective, the timing of projects in terms of their relation to the wider conflict is crucial. The sustainability of the benefits of these types of projects is threatened if the war is continuing and therefore must be considered fully before they are undertaken.
4. Projects that offer the potential to share cultural practices can break down barriers created by long-term conflict. However, the equality of exchange cannot be taken for granted. In sites of complex conflict different cultural practices will have different associations with formations of power. Sharing can shift to domination too easily if these different dynamics are not fully taken into account.
5. Cultural events are not singular in their meaning or in the interpretations that will be given of them. So when sponsoring or supporting cultural events the widest possible interpretations of the event need to be considered. Steps of a dance or beats of a drum can have embedded in them markers of different wars, sustaining ideologies that might counter the good intentions of reconciliation. Therefore the reception of cultural projects and the multiple acts of interpretation

need to be taken into account and planned as much as the events themselves.

6. The division between global and local in terms of cultural practice often naturalizes the global systems of practice and exoticizes the local. So for example psychological approaches to war trauma have become the norm, but Sri Lankan ritual practices are exceptional. For policy-makers to create culturally sensitive practices they must understand the power that has allowed certain practices to become *generic* and others to be categorized as *particular*. Rather than adapting a 'generic' approach to a local one – adding 'local colour' to the 'accepted' practice – projects must start from the systems of knowledge and cultural practices that exist already.

Notes

1 Sporadic violence including assassinations, small bombs and shootings have continued since the ceasefire however.

2 Sri Lanka was 20th in the league of top 20 countries receiving remittances from abroad in 2001. This constituted 7 per cent of GDP.

3 Rohan Gunaratna (1998) argues:

> In many ways, the technology generated by the LTTE has been a model for many other groups. There has been technology transfer or technology emulation. Today, suicide bomb technology is used by the Hamas, Algerian FIS, Kurdish PKK and the Punjabi Sikh insurgents. The LTTE body suit is more advanced than the body suits used by any of the other groups. The Western agencies watch a possible transfer of suicide technology from the LTTE particularly to the Middle Eastern groups, where the suicide bomb technology is still very rudimentary compared to their South Asian counterparts.(http://www.ict.org.il/articles/articledet.cfm?articleid=57 Accessed 28/1/05)

4 This chapter concentrates on theatre and performance practices as examples of cultural expression.

5 Silva, Neluka (ed.) (2002) *The Hybrid Island: Culture Crossings and the Invention of Identity in Sri Lanka*. Colombo: Social Scientists Association. p. i.

6 It needs to be acknowledged that this author's personal connection to Sri Lanka started when he was a consultant with UNICEF running 'applied theatre' programmes for young people affected by the conflict.

7 See Frasca, Richard Armando (1990) *The Theater of the Mahabharata: Terukkuttu Performances in South India*. Honolulu: University of Hawaii Press.

8 See Sithamparanathan, K. (2003) 'Intervention and methods of the theatre action group', *Intervention: The International Journal of Mental Health, Psychosocial Work and Counselling in Areas of Armed Conflict*. Vol. 1, No. 1, p. 44–7.

9 Linked to the Tamil *pongul* harvest festival when milk is boiled in an earthenware pot until it overflows.

10 See University Teachers for Human Rights (Jaffna)/ UTHR(J) (2002) *'Towards a totalitarian peace: the human rights dilemma'*. Special Report No. 13.

11 See Thompson, James (2006) 'Performance of pain, performance of beauty', *Research in Drama Education*. Vol. 11, No. 1. pp. 47–57.

12 See Kapferer, Bruce (1991) *A Celebration of Demons: Exorcism and Aesthetics of Healing in Sri Lanka*. Oxford: Berg Smithsonian Institution Press; and McGilvray, Dennis (1998) *Symbolic Heat: Gender, Health and Worship among the Tamils of South India and Sri Lanka*. Ahmedabad: Mapin Publishing.

13 Sithamparanathan (2003) uses the term 'catharsis' to explain TAG's work. For example, 'The movements during this dancing often become quite intense, suggesting that an emotional catharsis takes place' (ibid. p. 46).

14 For a detailed explanation of this position see Edmondson, Laura (2005) 'Marketing trauma and the theatre of war in Northern Uganda', *Theatre Journal*, 57: 451–74.

15 See Thompson, James (2005) *Digging Up Stories: Applied Theatre, Performance and War*. Manchester: Manchester University Press. p. 37.

REFERENCES

Edmondson, Laura (2005) 'Marketing trauma and the theatre of war in Northern Uganda', *Theatre Journal,* 57: 451–74.

Frasca, Richard Armando (1990) *The Theater of the Mahabharata: Terukkuttu Performances in South India.* Honolulu: University of Hawaii Press.

Gunaratna, Rohan (1998) *International and Regional Implications of the Sri Lankan Tamil Insurgency.* http://www.ict.org.il/articles/articledet.cfm?articleid=57 (accessed 28/1/05).

Kapferer, Bruce (1991) *A Celebration of Demons: Exorcism and Aesthetics of Healing in Sri Lanka.* Oxford: Berg Smithsonian Institution Press.

McGilvray, Dennis (1998) *Symbolic Heat: Gender, Health and Worship among the Tamils of South India and Sri Lanka.* Ahmedabad: Mapin Publishing.

Silva, Neluka (ed.) (2002) *The Hybrid Island: Culture Crossings and the Invention of Identity in Sri Lanka.* Colombo: Social Scientists Association.

Sithamparanathan, K. (2003) 'Intervention and methods of the theatre action group', *Intervention: The International Journal of Mental Health, Psychosocial Work and Counselling in Areas of Armed Conflict.* Vol. 1, No. 1, p. 44–7.

Thompson, James (2005) *Digging Up Stories: Applied Theatre, Performance and War.* Manchester: Manchester University Press.

– (2006) 'Performance of pain, performance of beauty', *Research in Drama Education,* Vol. 11, No. 1, pp. 47–57.

University Teachers for Human Rights (Jaffna)/UTHR(J) (2002) *Towards a Totalitarian Peace: The Human Rights Dilemma.* Special Report No. 13.

CHAPTER 25

PERFORMING *GACACA* IN RWANDA: LOCAL CULTURE FOR JUSTICE AND RECONCILIATION

Ananda Breed

This essay examines the Gacaca, a traditional form of community mediation being used post-genocide in Rwanda, in relation to culture, globalization, and conflict. The Rwandan government deliberately sought out a time-honored local form of justice in reaction to the larger global forces impacting Rwanda, prior to and following the genocide. Although the traditional Gacaca provides a potential device for reconciliation, the integration of modern systems of justice into the re-invented version may limit its effectiveness. Two case studies illustrate the performance of Gacaca from a local to an international level, displaying the complexities of the internal socio-political and international forces impacting the Gacaca courts.

Introduction

The *Gacaca* is a response drawn from Rwandan culture to repair the social and judicial fabric of the nation in the wake of tragedy.[1] Rwanda's 1994 genocide left the country in a state of devastation: over 1 million Tutsis and moderate Hutus had been killed, 400,000 women widowed, and over 500,000 children orphaned in the course of the 100 day long genocide, with the perpetrators most often coming from the same village as the victims.[2] The re-invented Gacaca has been established to deliver justice to the thousands of perpetrators who have been imprisoned since 1994, while serving as a restorative device for reconciliation in the larger community.

The word Gacaca means a grassy place in Kinyarwanda, a Bantu language that is the official language of Rwanda. The term actually refers to a pre-colonial form of justice in which opposed families sat on the grass as the community mediated the conflict. The National Service of Gacaca Courts defines Gacaca as, 'an institution inspired by Rwandan culture, charged with managing and resolving family conflicts. Rwandan people used to sit together on the grass '*aGacaca*' to settle disputes with open minds and to reconcile the protagonists without taking sides in the matter. As the saying goes in Kinyarwanda '*Ukiza abavandimwe arararama'*, literally, 'to settle brotherly disputes, you must put aside your family ties'.[3]

This essay examines the Gacaca in relation to culture, globalization, and conflict. I argue that the Rwandan government deliberately sought out a time-honored local form of justice in reaction to the larger global forces impacting Rwanda before and after the genocide. Although the traditional Gacaca provides a potential device for reconciliation, the integration of modern systems of justice into the re-invented version may limit its effectiveness. I will close with two case studies to illustrate the performance of Gacaca from a local to an international level, displaying the complexities of the internal socio-political and international forces impacting upon the Gacaca courts.

Genocide and globalization

The socio-political environment in Rwanda prior to the genocide was characterized by escalating tensions related to extreme poverty, harmful international funding incentives, lavish military support by the French government, and the manipulation of the masses through the local media.[4] The IMF and World Bank promoted cash crop initiatives that focused heavily on producing coffee for export, in a country where the vast majority of the population depends on agriculture for its subsistence. When the coffee market crashed in 1989, prices fell by 50 percent. The impact was devastating, as 60 percent of the Rwandan trade economy depended on the coffee industry. According to Johan Pottier, 'The collapse sentenced many poor to unprecedented levels of despair, making them vulnerable to manipulation by politicians in search of extreme solutions to their country's (and their own) growing insecurity.'[5] Escalating pressures on the Rwandan population created fertile ground for the government to seek out a scapegoat. In 1990, the Tutsi-led Rwandan Patriotic Front (RPF) staged an invasion from neighboring Uganda. From then on, the RPF, and Tutsis generally, provided a convenient target for the Hutu-dominated Habyarimana regime to deflect blame for Rwanda's deteriorating economic situation. At the same time, the international community pressured the Habyarimana government through the Arusha Peace Accords to adopt multi-party democracy in place of the established single-party system. Peter Uvin has remarked on the impact of development aid leading up to the genocide in the following terms: 'donors adopted what can only be called a policy of voluntary blindness to the politics of prejudice, injustice and human rights violations in Rwanda'[6]. Meanwhile, the French government aided the stockpiling of weapons and military training to assist the Hutu-led government to combat the Tutsi threat. After President Habyarimana's plane was shot down on 6 April 1994 the country rapidly descended into genocide.[7]

History of *Gacaca*

The justice system of Rwanda was shattered following the genocide. There remained only five judges and 50 lawyers countrywide.[8] Although the international community established the International Criminal Tribunal for Rwanda (ICTR) in Arusha, Tanzania to try individuals responsible for organizing the genocide, only 21 cases had been passed down by the end of 2004 at the price tag of two billion US dollars.[9] At the same time, in Rwanda, there was an enormous backlog of cases and desperately overcrowded jails. As the Rwandan government struggled to re-establish its justice system, it was estimated that it would take over 150 years to try the over 120,000 prisoners accused of participating in the genocide.[10] The eventual solution to speed up the trial of cases, and to gain more control over the justice process in Rwanda, was the Gacaca courts. The pilot phase began in 2002 with trials in a select 751 pilot courts, while the national launch of over 1,500 Gacaca courts on a sector level began on 10 March 2005.[11]

Gacaca versus Truth and Reconciliation Commission

The Gacaca emerged in a decade of mounting international justice systems including the Truth and Reconciliation Commissions and the International Criminal Tribunals. The government of Rwanda had originally requested the UN to establish the International Criminal Tribunal in Arusha, although subsequently was the only country to reject it.[12] In reaction against increasing international justice interventions, Gacaca was re-imagined as a pre-colonial form of justice from a pre-colonial unified past. Rwanda's mythic past as a unified nation began being performed through the Gacaca courts.

Gacaca billboards throughout the country advertise the slogan, 'Tell what we have seen, admit what has been done, and move forward to healing.' Gacaca intends to script the history of the genocide through testimonies, but unlike the TRC, opposes impunity for justice, claiming the genocide was in part made possible from a legacy of impunity since the beginning of Tutsi massacres in 1959. The difference between Rwanda's model of justice that does not allow impunity and the South African Truth and Reconciliation Commission's use of amnesty is due in part to the political forces in power within each country. According to Kimberly Lanegran, 'In Rwanda, where the Hutu forces were defeated, the government stresses retributive justice via prosecutions. In contrast, with South Africa simmering in violence, ANC leaders explicitly determined that they needed to use amnesty in order to convince authorities to negotiate the country's transition to democracy.'[13] Justice systems controlled by international agencies like the TRC and ICTR, did not allow the government of Rwanda to implicate the role of the international community in the crimes of the genocide. 'The government of Rwanda wanted the ICTR to examine crimes from 1 October 1990 through the genocide, but the Security Council refused. Therefore the ICTR has no power to examine allegations that the United Nations or its member states were negligent or complicit in the planning leading up to the genocide.'[14] I will show in due course, through the Gacaca case study of Guy Theunis, how Gacaca may be potentially used to incriminate the international community.

Case studies

The following two case studies illustrate the complex interplay of justice and reconciliation in post-genocide Rwanda. The trial of Emmanuel in Gahini provides an example of how culture is used on a local level through traditional dance and Gacaca, potentially serving as a tool for reconciliation between the perpetrators, the survivors, and the community at large. By contrast, the second case study, the hearing of Belgian priest Father Guy Theunis, illustrates the role of the international community through the symbolic representation of the colonization by Belgium, the ambiguous impact of francophone nations during the genocide, the globalized marketplace of war, the role of the media in terms of international impact, the role of churches in the genocide, and the intervention by international forces in the internal justice system of the current Gacaca courts.

Gahini

The Gacaca court in Gahini Province began with a dance performance by the association *Abiyunze* (Kinyarwanda for 'united').[15] The blending of reconciliation and justice took place in the same location, underneath a giant Umunyinya (*acacia sieberiana*) tree in the middle of an open dirt expanse. One person carried the sign *Ishyirahamwe Abiyunze Ry Igahini Dushyigikiye Ubumwe N'Ubwiyunge* (meaning the association of those who are united). The company was made up of 30 perpetrators, 40 survivors and 60 community members. Drumming started the performance, and two lead dancers stepped into the centre of the gathering. Their arms stretched into the air like bird's wings, arms weaving over and under one another's. Footwork patterns (right foot, left foot, left foot, right foot) kicked up dust as they circled one another.[16] The male dancer was a perpetrator and the female dancer a survivor; he had killed the woman's uncle during the genocide. After several dances and songs, the drumming and singing faded into the more serious tone of the Gacaca justice court. A single bench and table were placed in front of the seated audience. Ceremoniously, nine judges walked in a single-file line across the dirt expanse to the desk, wearing sashes of the Rwandan flag across their chests. The sashes had the label *Inyangamugayo* (persons of integrity, elected by the local population) written across the blue, green and yellow national colors.

The crowd stands for a moment of silence. The dance space suddenly becomes a commemoration space for the atrocities of the genocide. The president of the Gacaca recites several articles including Organic Law Article 34 that states that the cases to be tried in the Gacaca courts are solely related to genocide, an ethnic group being hunted down for extermination.[17] Crimes committed by the RPF are not tried in the Gacaca courts, but in the ordinary courts. This issue has controversial implications concerning the Gacaca as a reconciliatory form, since only one discourse or narrative is being staged. Briefly, the fact that RPF crimes are not being considered within Gacaca predetermines who is a victim and who is a perpetrator. The division of victim and perpetrator in the Gacaca, then, will continue to be divided along a primarily ethnic line. Emmanuel, an accused *génocidaire* (perpetrator of genocide), turns to face the audience of over 600 persons. He testifies to the crimes committed, including the murder of David Twamugabo. According to the scripted narrative of testimony requested, the perpetrator gives a full account of how he murdered seven individuals with the tools of grenades, arrows, and machetes. The audience gives Emmanuel their full attention during his confession, often making soft clicks in their mouth.

Emmanuel begins telling the story of David Twamugabo, introducing it by recalling that the *interahamwe* (youth militia)[18] was reluctant to go to the house of David, a giant man who was feared. When they first arrived, David stepped out of his house into the open air. Several members of the group attacked him, but were fought off. The group continued to attack him, throwing a grenade. The grenade did not explode. David picked up the grenade and warned them to leave or he would throw the grenade back at them, and he re-entered his home. The *interahamwe* continued their attack from a distance, shooting arrows. Eventually, David was struck. The perpetrator recited the names of accomplices who first hit David with a hammer over his head, then struck his legs with a machete, and finally sliced his throat with the machete.

At this point in the confession, the perpetrator is openly weeping. The resident trauma counselor makes her way through the audience to offer him tissues. The audience simultaneously dries their eyes with shirtsleeves or collars. Following the Gacaca, the grief counselor states that because the community participates in the Gacaca and local association activities, people become comfortable around one another. The Gacaca provides a space for the possibility of reconciliation.

Kigali

The trial of Father Guy Theunis represents the performativity of Gacaca enacted from the local to the international level. The Belgian Priest was arrested on charges of inciting genocide through the media and was brought before a court in central Kigali, the first European to appear before the Gacaca. Theunis had worked as the editor of a journal, *Dialogue,* which published translations of articles from Kinyarwanda into French for an international audience. The trial was held on 11 September 2005, and attracted over 1,000 observers and press agents, making the hearing a high-profile event. The appearance of the Belgian priest before the Gacaca called into question the roles of a number of international actors in the Rwandan genocide of 1994, including the role of Belgium in Rwanda from the time of colonization onwards. As Theunis was a priest the affair suggested that the churches played a role during the genocide, and as he was also a news writer, the case raised questions about the role of the media, such as *Radio Mille Collines,* in the enactment of the genocide. Over 20 Rwandans testified against Theunis. The sole person to speak in his defense was Alison des Forges, an internationally-known American specialist on Rwanda from Human Rights Watch, who highlighted the role he had played as a human rights advocate and questioned whether it was possible to incite genocide if the publication in question was addressed to an international, rather than Rwandan, audience.[19]

The staging of the Guy Theunis trial illuminates critical issues regarding international involvement in Rwandan politics, before, during and after the genocide, in other words the role of the international community in the local justice system and during the genocide. While on a local level, those who picked up the machete to kill are being held accountable, there were powerful international and political forces at play that allowed the machete to be used. The responsibility of war becomes a larger issue than the local enactment of genocide.

Conclusion and recommendations

The traditional form of Gacaca may allow for positive community redress, but the reinvented tradition formulated by the government can inhibit the natural progression of mediation at a local level because of stipulations made upon what can or can't be testified as a crime and the devices through which nationhood is being performed. There are potential negative impacts of Gacaca. Instead of offering answers to the dilemmas that Gacaca raises, I pose some questions to be considered and close with possible recommendations.

Questions

- *Retribution versus Justice*. The Gacaca is in its embryonic stage, thus it is yet to be determined if it becomes an instrument for survivors to enact revenge or forgiveness. There is potential for both. The Chief of Mission for Penal Reform International, a Gacaca monitoring agency, stated his concern for the future of Rwanda considering the number of citizens that will be accused and prosecuted through Gacaca.[20] If the estimated number of suspects, close to one million, come under trial and potentially serve twenty-five years in prison and/or community service, what are the social and economic ramifications for the nation? How will this effect lasting peace?
- *Witness, Jury, and Judge*. There is no defense council in Gacaca; instead, the local community stands as witness, jury, and judge. An evaluation of Gacaca administered by the National Unity and Reconciliation Commission stated that some of the problems with Gacaca included

corruption of judges, tampering with case materials, and misinterpretation of the Gacaca laws.[21] With little to no training in judicial procedure, will the local community be able to administer a fair trial? Is the state-mandated participation in Gacaca too much to ask of a nation in the aftermath of genocide?

- *Remembering or Forgetting.* Testimonies evoke memory. There is a correlation between trauma, memory, and testimony. If memory is fragmented or erased because of trauma, it will be difficult for an individual to give his or her testimony. Several community members in Gahengeri stated that they had never told their story because they felt they would become re-traumatized, thus could not give their testimonies in the Gacaca proceedings.[22] Thus, the success of a Gacaca court is inextricably linked to the process of 'telling'. Although 'telling' may create healing on an individual and community level, when analyzed through the construct of the government narrative being shaped through Gacaca, the 'telling' goes from being a personal to a political act. Is forgetting or remembering a personal choice towards one's own healing, or does it become a state controlled device to be manipulated towards a collective memory, shaped by the Gacaca proceedings, to serve the government's formation of a new nation?

Gacaca can be a powerful cultural tool for justice and reconciliation, but the two objectives may require different structures or mechanisms for their effectiveness. Gacaca is a process that occurs weekly from village to village. How the local community responds to its own problems will eventually be the deciding factor of its success or failure. In a Gacaca court held in Butare, a young boy accused a released perpetrator of genocide ideology.[23] A survivor stepped forward in defense of the perpetrator, stating that the perpetrator had spent 12 years in prison and that it was the duty of the community to invite him back respectfully. Moments like this illustrate the potential of reconciliation through Gacaca, although justice, in this case, depended on the personal advocacy of the community for the rights of the perpetrator to be protected during the judicial process. The aim for both justice and reconciliation to be addressed within the single system of Gacaca may be too great a task for the re-imagined traditional justice system to arbitrate genocide.

Recommendations

- Provisions must be made for either collecting information about RPF crimes through Gacaca courts in the information-gathering phase or informing the public about how the RPF war crimes are being tried. For reconciliation to be possible, multiple narratives must be honored and personal expression enhanced.
- Governments that fund and mobilize war crimes need to be held accountable. Likewise, international funding and interventions are political acts that may aid reconciliation, but might also cause further conflict. While Rwanda is currently considered a post-conflict zone, it could easily turn into a pre-conflict zone once again.

Notes

1 Pronounced (Ga Cha Cha).

2 Norwegian Helsinki Committee for Human Rights (2002) 'Prosecuting genocide in Rwanda: the Gacaca System and the International Criminal Tribunal for Rwanda'. *International Helsinki Federation for Human Rights.* http://www.nhc.no.rapporter/landrapporter/rwandrap

3 Republic of Rwanda National Service of Gacaca Courts (2005), Report on Activities of Gacaca Courts in the pilot Phase. Unpublished document.

4 There has been rigorous analysis regarding the role of international aid by Uvin (1995, 2003) and Oomen (2005).

5 Pottier, Johan (2002) *Re-Imagining Rwanda: Conflict, Survival and Disinformation in the Late Twentieth Century*. Cambridge: Cambridge University Press. p. 21.

6 Uvin, Peter (2001) 'Difficult choices in the new post-conflict agenda: the international community in Rwanda after the genocide.' *Third World Quarterly*, Vol 22: 177.

7 For further references regarding the genocide, see Berkeley (2001), Mamdani (2002), and Prunier (1995).

8 Daly, Erin (2002) 'Between punitive and reconstructive justice: the Gacaca Courts in Rwanda', *NYU. International Law and Policy*, 34: 355–96 (p. 368).

9 Oomen, Barbara (2005) 'Donor-driven justice and its discontents: the case of Rwanda', *Development and Change*, 36: 887–910 (p. 896).

10 Stockman, Farah (2000) 'The People's Court: crime and punishment in Rwanda', *Transition,* 9: 20–41 (p. 22).

11 The traditional Gacaca dealt with lesser crimes such as cattle, property, and family disputes. The contemporary Gacaca addresses the crimes conducted in the genocide that affected groups of people, hunted down due to their ethnicity, as stated in the Gacaca Courts Organic Law Article 51 (Organic Law Number 16/2004 of 19th June 2004). On rare occasions of homicide in traditional courts, the affected family seeking retaliation would act out their vengeance upon the trunk of a banana tree with a machete. The courts are separated into three categories with the gravest offenses in category 1 for rape and genocide leadership, to category 3 involving looting and property damage. The cell level courts administer trials for category 3 and make case files through data gathering courts. The sector level courts try category 2 crimes of genocide according to the case files and the witnesses in public. Category 1 crimes are judged at the high court, not the Gacaca courts. Information was obtained through official reports from the National Service of Gacaca Courts and interviews conducted by the author with the Executive Secretary Domitilla Mukantaganzwa.

12 Lanegran, Kimberly (2005) 'Truth commissions, human rights trials, and the politics of memory', *Comparative Studies of South Asia, Africa and the Middle East*. 1 (25) Duke University Press., Vol. 25, No. 1: 111–121.

13 Lanegran, Kimberly (2005). p. 116

14 Lanegran, Kimberly (2005). p. 114.

15 The Gacaca trial of Emmanuel was held on 4 August 2005. The full name of the perpetrator is not released for the Gacaca in Gahini, while Guy Theunis is named in the Kigali Gacaca, due to the publicity of the Guy Theunis trial. The trial was attended by the author.

16 The current government of Rwanda claims that there is only one culture, with the same dances and language. However, several government officials have differentiated between dances as being regional and loosely connected to divisions between Tutsi, Hutu, and Twa. In this way, dances of reconciliation may actually have stronger political affiliations.

17 Official Organic Law No. 16/2004 of 19/6/2004, Article 34.

18 Mahmood Mamdani states that the interahamwe was formed as a youth organization in 1990 and was eventually trained to execute the genocide as death squads largely responsible for the mass killings of 1994 (Mamdani 2002).

19 Trial of Priest Guy Theunis held on 11 September 2005 was observed by videotape at the National Service of Gacaca Courts on 20 September 2005.

20 Interview with Jean Charles Paras, Penal Reform International. Interview by Author. Kigali, Rwanda: 17 August 2005.

21 Interview with Theophile Rudangarwa, National Unity and Reconciliation Commission. Interview by Author. Kigali, Rwanda: 13 November 2005.

22 Interviews conducted with several residents of Gahengeri (names are omitted for interviewees' privacy). Interview by Author. Gahengeri, Rwanda: 19 July 2005.

23 The Gacaca in Butare was observed by the Author on 14 September 2005.

REFERENCES

Berkeley, B. (2001) *The Graves are Not Yet Full: Race, Tribe and Power in the Heart of Africa.* New York: Basic Books.

Daly, Erin (2002) 'Between punitive and reconstructive justice: the Gacaca Courts in Rwanda', *NYU. International Law and Policy*, 34: 355–96 (p. 368).

Lanegran, Kimberly (2005) 'Truth commissions, human rights trials, and the politics of memory', *Comparative Studies of South Asia, Africa and the Middle East.* 1 (25) Duke University Press., Vol. 25, No. 1: 111–121.

Mamdani, M. (2002) *When Victims Become Killers: Colonialism, Nativism, and the Genocide in Rwanda.* Princeton, NJ: Princeton University Press.

Oomen, Barbara (2005) 'Donor-driven justice and its discontents: the case of Rwanda', *Development and Change*, 36 (5): 887–910.

Pottier, Johan (2002) *Re-Imagining Rwanda: Conflict, Survival and Disinformation in the Late Twentieth Century.* Cambridge: Cambridge University Press.

Prunier, G. (1995) *The Rwanda Crisis: History of a Genocide.* London: Hurst & Co.

Stockman, Farah (2000) 'The People's Court: crime and punishment in Rwanda', *Transition,* Vol. 9, No. 4, Issue 84: 20–41 (p. 22).

Uvin, P. (1995) *Aiding Violence: The Development Enterprise in Rwanda.* West Hartford, CT: Kumarian Press.

– (2001) 'Difficult choices in the new post-conflict agenda: the international community in Rwanda after the genocide.' *Third World Quarterly,* Vol 22: 177–189.

Uvin, P. (2003) 'The Gacaca Tribunals in Rwanda', in D. Bloomfield, T. Barnes and L. Huyse (eds), *Reconciliation after Violent Conflict: A Handbook.* Stockholm: International Institute for Democracy and Electoral Assistance. pp. 116–29.

CHAPTER 26

FROM VIOLENCE TO DISCOURSE: CONFLICT AND CITIZENS' RADIO STATIONS IN COLOMBIA

Clemencia Rodríguez and Amparo Cadavid[1]

The Colombian internal armed conflict is considered one of the worst in the world. Colombia's 'multiple violences' emerge from power struggles engendered by unequal access to material resources. More than half a century of continuous social and political violence has had a tremendous impact on Colombians' collective imaginaries and everyday cultural practices. The mixture of patron–client relationships; an absent, corrupt, or negligent state; and the presence of armed groups, have normalized a cultural fabric that privileges individual agency, perceives difference as something to be annihilated, and favors violent forms of conflict resolution. A network of 15 citizens' radio stations operating in a Colombian region known as Magdalena Medio are succeeding in changing the cultural fabric and moving conflict from the realm of violence to the realm of dialogue and discourse. We analyze how citizens' radio stations play significant roles as mediators in conflicts between communities, political opponents, communities and local authorities, and communities and armed groups.

Introduction

The armed conflict in Colombia is considered one of the worst in the world. Some estimates speak of 35,000 violent deaths, over a thousand kidnappings, and 800 citizens missing every year; all these with a staggering impunity rate of over 90 percent (García and Uprimny 1999: 40). In 1990, the homicide rate per 100,000 in Colombia was 80, four times as much as in the rest of Latin America (Romero, 2003: 27). Sixty percent of all murders committed against trade unionists worldwide take place in Colombia, and the same is true for journalists (40 have been assassinated in the last five years; thirty Colombian journalists now live in exile) (González Uribe 2003). In the last 40 years, armed conflict has claimed the lives of 200,000 Colombians and has forced two million others to flee their homes in terror (Berrigan, Hartung, and Heffel 2005).

Unlike elsewhere, (cf. cases from Rwanda, Sri Lanka, Africa in this volume), social violence in Colombia is not related to cultural, ethnic, or religious differences. Although Colombia endures a 'multiplicity of violences' (Sánchez 2001) that includes leftist guerrillas, right-wing paramilitaries, drug trafficking networks, and common delinquency, all these forms emerge from power struggles engendered by unequal access to material resources. However, more than half a century of continuous social and political violence has had a tremendous impact on Colombians' collective imaginaries and everyday cultural practices. The mixture of patron–client relationships; an absent, corrupt, or negligent state; and the presence of armed groups and their militaristic approaches, have normalized a cultural fabric that privileges individual agency, perceives difference as something to be overpowered and annihilated, and favors violent forms of conflict resolution.

In this chapter we document how a network of 15 citizens' radio stations operating in a Colombian region known as *Magdalena Medio* [Middle Magdalena or MM] are succeeding in changing the cultural fabric and moving conflict from the realm of violence to the realm of dialogue and discourse. These Colombian citizens' media are moving conflict from the fatal social place of action to the manageable social place of culture.

Conflict, culture, and resource distribution in Colombia

Although the causes of the Colombian conflict are diverse and complex, most of them originate in structural problems associated historically with the difficulties inherent in the creation of a nation capable of giving breathing space to all its inhabitants. The main roots of armed conflict have always been and continue to be the struggle for access to economic and political power; enormous levels of inequity in the distribution of resources and a particularly critical situation of unequal land distribution (see Legrand 1986; Zamosc 1986, 1997); a state that cannot or is not willing to protect civil rights (Sánchez 2001; Romero 1998; Romero 2003); and a traditional bi-partisan system that leaves no room for new voices, new identities, new social movements, new 'structures of feeling', and thus new politics of the nation (Mueke cited in Ginsburg 2002).

Colombia presents some of the world's worst levels of inequity of resources and access to economic opportunity; a 2004 report from the Center for International Policy found that:

> *On paper, Colombia is not among the world's poorest countries. Its per capita income of US$1,820 per year is well above the developing-country average of US$1,170 . . . [however] Colombia is now the third most unequal country in Latin America, the world's most unequal region. The wealthiest 10 per cent of Colombians earned 80.27 times more than the poorest 10 per cent in 2003. Landholding statistics reveal a starker inequality: a Colombian government study released in March 2004 found that 0.4 per cent of landholders – 15,273 holdings – account for 61.2 percent of registered agricultural land. 97 percent – 3.5 million landholders – share only 24.2 percent.(Calligaro and Isacson 2004)*

A political elite entrenched in two traditional parties has maintained an iron grip on access to political power and participation in policy-making (Berquist 2001, 204; Uprimny 2001: 42). Thus, social and political violence and its resolution through armed mobilization is the result of decades-long struggles for participation in the process of nation-building. It is access to economic and political power that frames, produces, and feeds armed conflict in Colombia.

The persecution of peasant organizations mobilized during the first half of the twentieth century around land tenure issues was the origin in 1966 of what today is the largest leftist guerrilla organization – the *Fuerzas Armadas Revolucionarias de Colombia* [FARC – or Revolutionary Armed Forces of Colombia] (González, Bolívar and Vázquez 2003: 53). Today FARC has approximately 17,000 combatants organized in fronts that operate throughout the national territory. A second guerrilla organization, the *Ejército de Liberación Nacional* [ELN or National Liberation Army] has approximately 7,000 combatants. One of the main areas of influence of the ELN is the *Magdalena Medio*.

The Colombian internecine conflict has worsened since the late 1980s, mainly as a result of the country's articulations with the global drug economy. Their widespread repercussions worldwide are well known; and their impact on Colombian economic, social, political, and cultural life has been enormous. During the 1980s Colombia became one of the main locations of world drug production and trade. Between 1979 and 1992, drug money entering Colombia increased from US$2.5 billion to US$3.7 billion (Kalmanovitch 1995) and by 2001 Colombia received between 2 and 4 billion dollars a year from drug earnings (Reina 2001: 77). The accumulation of power and money in the hands of the Medellín and Cali drug cartels originated a new type of social and political violence. In order to defend and strengthen their business, drug traffickers eliminated any social force that attempted to oppose them; corrupted thousands of judges, policemen, government officials, and even senators; murdered political candidates that supported a law of extradition; and, finally, imposed a climate of terror among the general population – in only three weeks, more than 40 bombs exploded in Bogotá alone in 1989. According to economist Salomón Kalmanovitch, drug trafficking is responsible for 85 percent of all crimes committed in the country (Kalmanovitch, 1995).

In 1981 the Medellín drug cartel founded MAS, that was to become the first of many right-wing paramilitary organizations in the country. MAS – which stands for *Muerte a Secuestradores* [Death to Kidnappers] – was charged with persecuting and executing anyone who participated in or supported guerrilla organizations – thus turning all progressive social movements and leaders into military targets. Today, right-wing paramilitary groups spread throughout the national territory are organized under the *Autodefensas Unidas de Colombia* [AUC or Colombian United Self-defense Forces] – a national association of approximately 10,000 right-wing sectarian combatants.

Immense profit margins resulting from drug trade feed into all illegal armies. Both leftist guerrilla organizations and right-wing paramilitary militias fund their operations thanks to drug monies. Although not necessarily controlling drug production and marketing processes, guerrillas and paramilitaries tax marijuana, coca leaf, and poppy plantations as well as processing labs.[2] Thanks to ransom monies, illegal taxes, and particularly drug money, both guerrilla and paramilitary organizations amass significant amounts of capital that subsidize weapons, uniforms, and salaries for combatants.[3] Finally, the Colombian army also benefits from the drug problem as the United States government has approved large packages of aid to fight 'the war on drugs'. Known as Plan Colombia, (more recently re-labeled as the Andean Initiative) this aid package consists of $2 billion dollars, 80 percent of which is spent in training for the Colombian army and police (see http://www.state.gov/p/wha/rt/plncol/).

Wealth, poverty, war, and globalization: *Magdalena Medio* and its paradoxes

Local scholars have labeled Colombia *un país de regiones* [a country of regions], meaning that the nature of Colombian historical processes of colonization, economic development, and formation of cultural identities are better understood when examined region by region and not through a national lens (see Aldana et al. 1998; García 1996; González, 1994; González et al. 1998; Guzmán and Luna 1994; Jimeno 1994; Reyes 1999; Uribe 1992).

As we center our analysis on the region of the *Magdalena Medio* we focus on a very specific and unique case of social and political violence as it has evolved in this region. The MM has a critical strategic location for the country's economy, its development, its viability to integrate into globalization and overall, for the future of Colombia as nation.

The MM lies in the center of the country, covering the middle course of the Magdalena river, which crosses the country from south to north and forms a long valley between the east and central Andean ranges that likewise cross the country south to north. It covers 30,000 square kilometers which approximately 800,000 Colombians call home; the region comprises territories in four different departments (Antioquia, Bolívar, Santander, and Cesar).[4] It is well connected to national and international markets, which explains why the 27 municipalities[5] that form the MM make the highest tax contributions to their respective departmental budgets. Six of these municipalities are well known as oil producers (for a case in point, ECOPETROL, the Colombian government oil exploitation and processing corporation located in MM made $552.5 million dollars in profit in 2003 (ECOPETROL 2003). Five of the MM municipalities stand over the country's richest gold deposits; some are important agricultural and livestock centers thanks to a long agro-industrial tradition that includes oil palm, cotton, sorghum, plantain, fruit trees, and meat products. Crucial communication and trade infrastructures necessary for the development of the nation go through the core of this region, including the Magdalena river (the most navigable course in the country); the main interstate highway and railroad (connecting the capital city to the Atlantic coast on the north); the main fiber optic lines; the main oil production facility[6]; and the main gas and oil pipelines.

Paradoxically, these same municipalities are the poorest and more marginalized in each of the four departments. The region itself has lagged behind in terms of economic development and 'progress' that these same infrastructures have brought to other regions. The region also has some of the highest violence rates in the country; in 2002 the rate for homicides per 100,000 inhabitants was 250 (Katz García n.d). Widespread forms of violence in both rural and urban areas in the region include guerrilla and paramilitary activity, drug trafficking, oil mafias, and common delinquency.

The region maintains several different and complex articulations and connections to global spheres. First, MM generates 75 percent[7] of all Colombia's oil,[8] which is significant since the nation is the fifth largest producer in South America (The World Factbook)[9]. Second, the region is one of the main growers of oil palm in a country that is 'the world's fourth biggest exporter of palm oil and other oil palm products after Malaysia, Indonesia and Nigeria' (Fog 2005). Third, illegal drug production and trafficking connect the MM to global drug trade and international mafia networks. And fourth, it is traversed by two of the main routes for an illegal arms trade of 45 thousand weapons (News VOA Com 2004) that enter Colombia every year, coming from the United States, Central America, Mexico, Israel, Brazil, Venezuela, and Spain (one from Ocaña and the second one from Cúcuta) and end up in Barrancabermeja, the main urban center of the region (Cragin and Hoffman 2003).[10]

Despite all this, up to the end of the twentieth century the region remained uncharted territory.

Historians (Aprile-Gniset 1997; Archila 1986; Murillo 1994; Vargas 1992) usually agree in considering it as a sort of 'inner frontier', ironic as this might sound. In fact, the *Magdalena Medio* has had the bearings of a landlocked island geographically placed in the heart of the country.

The first economic studies ever focusing on the MM showed that its contribution to the GDP should be enough for its inhabitants to have the living standards of a European country like Spain (SEAP-CINEP 1996). However, its people live in communities that resemble those of the poorest African nations. This paradox has originated the moniker of 'a perverse economy' to refer to the economic model prevalent in the region which, since the nineteenth century, has extracted natural resources with very little ending up in the pockets of the local communities. In the past the products exploited for international markets were quina, rubber, and wood; today it is oil, coca, palm oil, sorghum, and cotton.

Development and peace-building in *Magdalena Medio*

Toward the end of the twentieth century Colombia seemed on the verge of collapsing under pressure from armed conflict and social and political violence. These dynamics seemed to want to spill over into other regions within the national territory, and into neighboring nations as well; evidence of arms trade and guerrilla and paramilitary activity were clear in border areas in Venezuela and Ecuador. Drug production, processing and marketing were being exported to Central America, México, Bolivia, and Peru.

In this context, the *Programa de Desarrollo y Paz del Magdalena Medio* [PDPMM or Peace and Development Program for Middle-Magdalena], was born in 1995, as an attempt to decrease levels of violence and increase the quality of life of local communities. The PDPMM was developed by several institutions, including ECOPETROL, the Diocese of Barrancabermeja, and CINEP a well-known Colombian NGO, which, concerned with the growth of armed conflict, decided to join forces in a comprehensive development project for the entire region. The PDPMM is an experiment in regional development, trying to implement a model that tackles all needs and hopes of local communities simultaneously; the PDPMM includes 300 initiatives that activate local economies; strengthen civic participation and consensus-building in local and regional decision-making processes; rebuild transportation, energy, health and educational infrastructures; encourage local cultures; and nurture pluralism, diversity, and tolerance.

The PDPMM partnership has had the financial support of ECOPETROL, the United Nations Development Program, Caritas, the governments of Japan and Sweden, and the World Bank. In 2002, in an attempt to counter the militaristic angle of Plan Colombia, the European Union decided to invest in the PDPMM as a Peace Laboratory.[11]

AREDMAG: a network of citizens' radio stations in *Magdalena Medio*

Toward the early 1990s media activists had begun developing citizens' radio initiatives throughout the country. In 1995 the PDPMM found five community radio stations run by citizens' groups and collectives in *Magdalena Medio*. These stations had emerged as an attempt of local collectives to strengthen their capacity to participate in local governance, monitor public institutions, and express local concerns (see Atton 2001; Downing et al. 2001; Rodríguez 2001 for scholarship on citizens' media). Common participants in these citizens' media ventures were PTAs, teachers' collectives, cultural groups, religious organizations and churches, community leaders, and local authorities.

As part of its communication and culture component, the PDPMM decided to support the citizens' radio stations of *Magdalena Medio*. From 1995 to 2000 five more radio stations were helped until they, too, secured a broadcasting license and all the necessary technical infrastructure. Today, ten citizens' radio stations and five communication collectives[12] in 15 municipalities throughout the region are organized as the Network of Community Radio Stations of *Magdalena Medio* – AREDMAG (*Asociación Red de Emisoras Comunitarias del Magdalena Medio*).

In 2004 a research team was consolidated to design and implement an evaluation study focusing on the impact of AREDMAG's radio stations on the social fabric of the MM. The team – comprising three communication academics[13] and AREDMAG's board of directors – worked collectively on the design of a participatory, qualitative evaluation methodology. Every aspect of the methodology – sampling, data collection techniques, and questionnaires – emerged from collective discussions and decisions between the academic team and AREDMAG's leadership.

The following pages are based on verbal and visual data collected as part of this study in August 2004. Working with a sample of 60 participants from all AREDMAG's 15 citizens' radio initiatives, we collected a total of 160 individual narratives and 18 group discussions about the role(s) of citizens' radio in processes of social change. The evaluation study of AREDMAG sheds light on how these radio stations are having an impact on the social and cultural fabric of their communities. Our entire evaluation study tackles the following questions: Are AREDMAG's stations generating stronger public spheres? Are these stations increasing participation in community decision-making processes? Are they improving transparency of local governments? Are they enhancing conditions of governance? Are they strengthening local cultures and values? Are they nurturing processes of peacebuilding, mediation and/or non-violent conflict resolution? What follows is the answer to the last of these questions.

We found that the role of AREDMAG's radio stations in local processes of peace-building can not be reduced to a formula. In each context, the radio stations have found their own unique ways to cultivate a culture of peace, to mediate in specific conflicts, or to keep legal and illegal armed groups (guerrilla organizations, paramilitary groups, drug traffickers, and the state's army) at a distance, therefore protecting civilians. What follows is a description of the most salient ways in which they are playing important roles as peace-builders.

Citizens' radio as mediator in inter-communal conflict

The radio stations of AREDMAG serve as peace-builders in the region as they mediate among groups within the same community when everyday life conflicts emerge and can easily escalate into aggression and violence. In all communities conflict is a necessary element of everyday life. However, in communities such as those of *Magdalena Medio*, where for generations the violent resolution of quotidian conflicts has been legitimized and normalized, simple conflicts can easily end in bloodshed. Issues such as the use of public space, conflicts around land tenure, or a community celebration can easily turn into violent episodes. In the testimony cited below, we can see how the local radio station was used as a tool to mediate and help solve a conflict among local parties:

> *[Woman – Puerto Wilches] I am going to talk about a situation that happened in our municipality that had to do with the use of a public space. There was a time when the main park in our town resembled more a Persian market than a park; little by little it filled with street vendors and their booths; the park was nothing more than clothes hanging, trinkets everywhere ... a hullabaloo. So that when people arrived by boat to Puerto Wilches, they really could not see that we had a park, all they could see was multicolored ropes from which dozens of clothes for sale hung.*
>
> *That's when the conflict began, because we [the station] began a campaign to recover the park as a public space; so we began talking to the municipal authorities and also to negotiate among the two parties; because one party was the people who used the park to make a living selling stuff, and they have the right to work, and there was the other party, the people of the community who wanted to re-claim the park as a public space. So we looked at all that, and started promoting a dialogue among all the parties involved and today I can say with pride that we have a proper park in Puerto Wilches. The park has been re-appropriated by the community and here [See Illustration 26.1.] is what the park used to look like and here is what you will find today, totally different, re-built ... this was a very significant moment for us at the station because we triggered the whole thing, we worked very close to the vendors, trying to raise their awareness of the need for public spaces, and then we began working with the municipal authorities trying to find a solution to the problem. The solution was that the vendors were able to remodel their own commercial center where they were all transferred; the municipal government gave them a facility and together they re-conditioned it and now all of us from Puerto Wilches can say that we have a public space for our leisure and enjoyment.*

Illustration 26.1 Re-claiming a park in Puerto Wilches

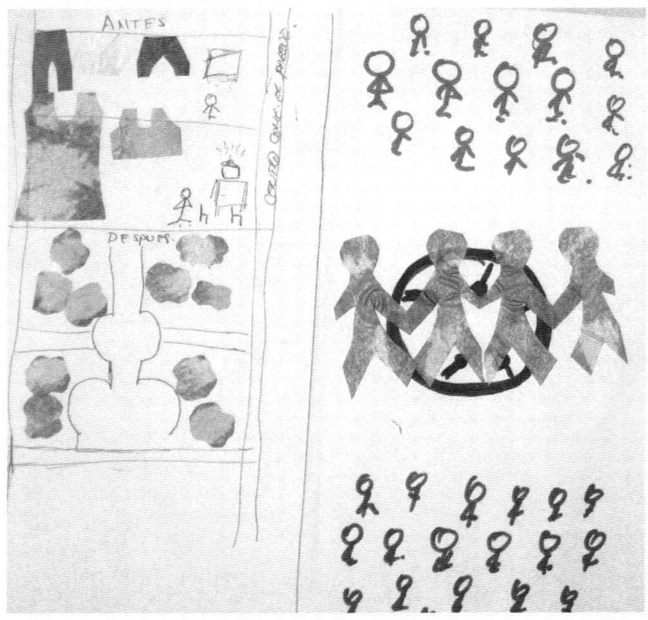

This testimony shows two different ways in which this communication space impacts this local community's social fabric. First, the radio station has transformed everyday life in Puerto Wilches as the park has been re-appropriated and is now used as a public space where people meet, interact, and monitor who comes and goes from the nearby river port. Thanks to the station, the park was recovered from market interests and made available to public ones – strengthening the local commons and thus the public sphere. Second, participating in this citizens' communication initiative is transforming this radio producer into a visionary with clear ideas about the importance of public spaces in building relationships based on interaction, solidarity, and familiarity among members of the community. For this woman, it is clear that the protection of public spaces and their impact on a peaceful social fabric is an important element of her utopia for Puerto Wilches. With visions of utopia such as this one, community leaders like her counteract the idea that 'building a future by force' is the only good option.

By making access to a public sphere accessible to this woman, the radio station invigorates her visions for a future, making them a real alternative to the aggressive proposals to solve everyday conflict put forward by armed groups (paramilitaries, guerrillas, drug mafias). The radio station operates here as a loudspeaker of peaceful utopias. Looking at the communication aspect of this case we can see that the radio station opened a communication space within the community that was used by the different parties in conflict to engage in dialogue. Clearly, the station had enough legitimacy within the community to be accepted as a mediator; leaders of both camps agreed to come to the studio to dialogue with their opponent; members of the community called in to offer their opinions. It is important here to stress the role of the technology in itself. It is not the same to engage in dialogue with one's opponent in a private space as doing so into a microphone that will bring one's version of things to the entire community. When what I say can be heard by the entire community, my identity and social image are at stake. Anything I say will be used by my community to construct their image of me; in this sense, I have to be much more careful about what I say. This technology-mediated communication

Illustration 26.2 Mitigating aggression among political candidates

space makes subjects engage in a process of self-reflection about the social image they want to cultivate, thus keeping impulsive hot tempers in check.

Finally, it is clear that the station was not able to come up with a definitive solution to the conflict; local authorities had to be brought in. In this sense, the station is putting pressure on public authorities to assume their responsibility to protect and defend citizens' rights (such as public spaces). However, if local authorities do not follow through with the commitments assumed on the radio, the station could ultimately lose its legitimacy in the community.

Citizens' radio as mediator in conflicts among local political figures

A common theme that emerged in our study revolves around instances in which the radio stations play a role diffusing conflict among opposing political parties or political figures. During the first half of the twentieth century, Colombia was marked by intense and violent conflict among the two traditional political parties (the Liberals and the Conservatives). As a result, the idea of solving political dissent by violently eliminating one's opponent has been 'normalized' in the Colombian imaginary. Here, citizens' radio stations are playing a significant role by re-directing the resolution of political violence from the realm of violence and aggression to the realm of discourse:

> *[Man – Gamarra, describing Illustration 26.2.] What I have drawn here is three political personalities – three candidates in the forthcoming election for mayor in our municipality – and, every time they talked to each other, or met in a public space, they began insulting each other; I drew little red bombs under them, because the situation was becoming a time bomb in our community. Seeing this, the youth collective at the radio station decided to organize what became known as the First Forum for Democracy in Gamarra; we wanted to seek ways to enhance peaceful coexistence in the municipality, that is one of our objectives. The three candidates agreed to come to the station and the Forum began at nine in the morning; it was supposed to end at ten, but the conversation was so exciting that the Forum kept going until twelve thirty; and the three candidates, who had insulted each other just ten minutes before the Forum started, left the station arm in arm — here [in my drawing] you can see them draped by the yellow, green and white of the Gamarra flag. How did we accomplish this? Well, as the dialogue began, we realized that the three had gone to high school together; so*

> *they each began remembering all their escapades, when they skipped school together to go to the river, or to play pool . . . this changed the mood of the conversation, they felt at ease with each other, they began looking at each other as human beings, and not just as rivals in a political race . . . we managed to lower the volume of the violent tone among the three candidates and to cultivate a more fraternal relationship. A woman and a school teacher is the director of this program; she works with the radio production youth collective and the way she conducted the interview was key to our success.*

In this case, what is to be stressed is the mediating role played by the woman who directed the program. Originally, the producers of the Forum had planned to start with 30 minutes in which the collective would ask questions about the candidates' youth, their lives when they were in school etc.; the remainder of the program was to focus on more 'serious' subjects such as their political agendas; more mature interviewers were supposed to take over from the youth collective at this point. However, during the first part of the interview the director realized that it is precisely the young interviewers who can enable the candidates to find common ground around their teenage past. It was key that at that moment, midway through the program, she made the decision to change the production plan and to allow the young interviewers to conduct the program for the entire three and a half hours duration of the Forum.

This type of ad hoc knowledge – or communication competence – seems to have played a key role in this situation. We need to emphasize two elements: first, that the director was able to detect the emerging bonds of identification and solidarity among the opponents; and second, that she valued these as the building blocks of conflict resolution and peace-building. She envisions peace as the product of quotidian gestures and interactions among the members of a collectivity; she understands the nature of these gestures and interactions, including non-verbal expressions, and, as she begins detecting them among the three political candidates, she takes the necessary decisions to nurture them. The radio station is simply allowing this community leader to use her competences and wisdom to intervene in the public sphere; her wisdom and competences are now part of the social and cultural capital with which the community of Gamarra will shape its future.

Citizens' radio as mediator in conflict among the community and local authorities

A long tradition of patron–client relationships plus a precarious Colombian state has legitimized the notion that local authorities do not have to respond to community grievances. As citizens witness the neglect of local government authorities, they lose faith in the rule of law and commonly decide to take the law into their own hands. In this type of scenario, the citizens' radio stations are playing an important role as they put pressure on the authorities to address community grievances and to be accountable to local citizens. In the following narrative we observe precisely this aspect of peace-building and conflict resolution:

> *[Man – Simití] The day of love and friendship[14] a major riot erupted … a major scuffle between the local police and the community. The fight began for nothing really, just because some kids were being rowdy and the police tried to get them to quiet down, and the people saw this and didn't like it, so they attacked the police … the police retreated but then they came back with reinforcements and that's when things got really bad … four people ended up with wounds, bullet wounds … there was gas … in all of the 457 years since this town was founded we have never been gassed. People were terrified … so the radio station began mediating; we formed a community security council and the first meeting was held on the air at the station and thankfully that defused the conflict between the police and the community; although not everyone was satisfied with the outcome, in general the community acknowledged that the police are the legitimate authority and we cannot just attack them, and also the police recognized that they had over-reacted … unfortunately the day of love ended prematurely in Simití … it wasn't even midnight!*

Here, the community confronts the local police on what is perceived as an abuse of power. The radio station opens a communication space in which the local authorities and community members can explore non-violent ways to restore the rule of law and the legitimacy of state institutions. Also, the station pressures the police to engage in dialogue with the community about their questionable actions, thus activating processes of transparency and good governance. Our evaluation of AREDMAG elicited numerous qualitative testimonies about how citizens' radio stations are mediating between the community and local state authorities around issues such as public services (water, electricity, garbage collection), community security (police and army presence), and municipal expenditure (budgets and spending priorities), among others.

Usually, citizens' media are marginalized because they are perceived as 'tools of dissidence' used to erode governmental authority; for example Downing et al. (2001) have labeled them 'radical media'. However, here we can see how citizens' media in *Magdalena Medio* are in fact strengthening the rule of law and the state – understood not as a repressive state, but as a set of public institutions responsible for overseeing the rights and responsibilities of citizens.

Citizens' radio stations as mediators in conflict with armed groups

Without doubt the most dramatic and significant aspect emerging from our evaluation study is the role that citizens' radio stations play in processes of mediation and conflict resolution between the community and illegal armed groups. For decades the *Magdalena Medio* has seen a strong presence of armed groups and guerilla organizations. The ELN was born in 1965 in San Vicente de Chucurí. During the late 1990s right-wing paramilitary groups broke into the region with the intention of 'cleansing' it from guerrillas and thus causing some of the highest levels of bloodshed in the history of Colombia. In the following narratives we begin to understand the complex role(s) that citizens' media can take in contexts of armed conflict. The first testimony says:

> *[Man – Santa Rosa del Sur] Five years ago I had a horrible experience, when our station director, José Botella, was kidnapped by the ELN; they took him to the Serranía de San Lucas, 15 hours away from downtown Santa Rosa. No one knew what had happened until a farmer who witnessed the kidnapping came to the station and told us. At the station we discussed what to do, because to say something on the air could make the station a military target of the guerrillas. But we decided to broadcast a press release where we demanded that the captors respect his life and well-being as a civilian. As soon as we aired this, messages, letters, official press releases from hundreds of local grassroots organizations and citizens began pouring into the station, all with similar demands and words of support for José. In all we got more than 1000 letters and more than 2000 signatures in a document that was sent to the President and also to the ELN. As messages continued to pour in, we shifted to a kind of sad musical selection as an expression of protest. The ELN responded with a challenge to the community: if we wanted José back, if it was true that the community loved him so much, the community had to go get him. Immediately the station began communicating this new demand and in six hours we had 480 people willing to travel the several hours to the place known as Micoahumado, way high in the mountains … we gathered in more than 40 cars, trucks, there were women, children, men, all carrying white flags. We left almost at midnight and got there by seven in the morning. First we got to a guerrilla checkpoint on the road, close to where José had been kidnapped; the guerrilleros began shooting in the air saying we could not go through; but then they called their superiors and told them that the road was totally covered with people and cars and they were only six guys. Finally they were given orders to let us go through; they warned us that the rest of the way was mined, but we insisted and kept on our way toward the guerrilla camp … it looked like a snake of cars and trucks going up the mountain! Until we got to the camp, it's like a small town … we got to the central plaza and asked to speak with the comandante. They told us he wasn't there and we had to wait, so in no time we set up tents and began lighting fires … we had brought pots and pans, potatoes, yucca, we bought a steer and we proceeded to feed everybody 'cause we were not going to leave until we reached a resolution. The next morning the so-called comandante showed up and we told him we needed José back, and not just his family but the entire community, as they could see; he didn't know what to do, so he called his superior and they told him to just make us wait, that we would surely give up and leave; when they realized we were not leaving and that we had formed a negotiating commission, they freed José Botello*

Illustration 26.3 Rescuing José Botello from the ELN

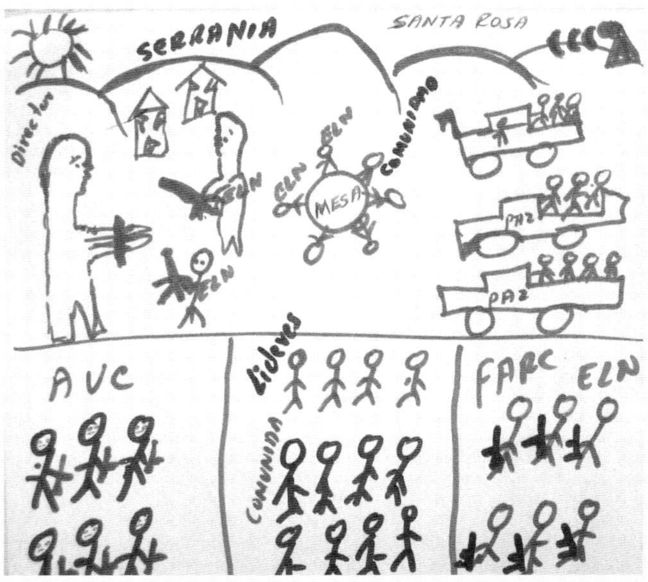

> *... from beginning to end it was seven days of horror and seven days of hope ... when we came back to Santa Rosa with José we had two days of festivities, everybody in the central plaza, celebrating, which the station also transmitted live, from the streets, thanks to our mobile unit.*

The second narrative in this section comes from San Vicente de Chucurí, where right-wing paramilitary groups attempt to intimidate young men and women by imposing strict codes about fashion, hair styles, piercing, and everyday-life practices and behaviors; for example, paramilitaries commonly forbid long hair for young men, low-cut jeans for young women, and piercing in general. Blacklists with the names of young people who defy these codes are then posted on visible public places and if the questionable behavior continues, these marked youth can end up dead or disappeared:

> *[Man – San Vicente de Chucurí] Our communities are cornered by the terror imposed by armed groups. There was a moment in San Vicente where the blacklists began multiplying, especially targeting those youth that wanted to be themselves. So one day I'm listening to the station and I hear this short message that addressed the lists issue; all you heard was someone taking attendance and a second voice responding:*
>
> *– 'So and so'*
> *–'Present!'*
> *– 'So and so'*
> *– 'Present!'*
> *–'So and so'*
> *And then, complete silence ...*
> *'He is not here. He is on a different list!'*
>
> *The message was so strong! What I am expressing in my drawing is how the community is cornered and in the middle of all this the station is trying to open a communication space to play, to sing, to love, and also to scream, because we are all terrified but at the same time we are listening to these different proposals coming from the station. The station is playing an important role, especially for young people, who are the ones more affected by the war, and at the same time, they are the ones with different life options, alternative proposals, including their musics ... they are using the station to put forward their voice and their proposals in the middle of the generalized terror and death.*

Illustration 26.4 A radio station trying to offset the terror of war

As explained earlier, our evaluation methodology elicited qualitative data of two kinds: verbal and visual. Respondents were asked to accompany their narrative with drawings or collages that would express what they were trying to convey. The central theme of illustrations 26.3 and 26.4 is the permanent state of siege imposed on civilians by armed groups. The first shows different armed groups – the ELN and FARC guerrillas on one side and the paramilitary (AUC) on the other. The community is depicted literally in between these three armed groups. The drawing about San Vicente de Chucurí shows the community surrounded by gigantic weapons which represent the strong presence and impact of armed groups in this municipality; these visual testimonies aptly express the intense levels of fear and feeling 'cornered' experienced by civilians confronted with the annihilating power of armed force. Ironically, even though the role of the station as an important voice in the community is stressed in both cases, it is depicted as almost a miniature entity. The visual narratives seem to be saying that although the station tries to maintain a communication space autonomous of the armed groups, it, too, feels intimidated and terrorized by these groups. The stations emerge as communication spaces for peace, but spaces that exist in permanent tension with the presence of armed groups.

These two testimonies express two very different ways in which the stations are contributing to peaceful conflict resolution with illegal armed groups in *Magdalena Medio*. In the first narrative the station mediates between the ELN and the community when a community leader was kidnapped; here the station decides to make the kidnapping a public event, and not just a private tragedy that affects the family and friends of the victim; the entire community is addressed by the station as victimized by the ELN and the community responds as a unified and very strong front. Assured by the resolute response from the community, the station decides to go one step further and engages the guerrilla group in a process of negotiation. Clearly the station benefits from a high level of legitimacy among the local community; it is because the community feels one with the station and feels that the station is truly at its service, that the station can trigger such a strong response (see issues of sustainability of community media as explained by Gumucio Dagron 2003).

In this case, thanks to the station, the community was able to galvanize forces and to act collectively and peacefully to confront the guerrilla group. Here again the station has opened a communication space that can be used by the community on an ad hoc basis; peaceful conflict resolution emerges from communication and interaction, but not in the form of pre-designed messages or communication strategies, and more as communication competences that the community has learned to use in moments of crisis.

The role of the station in the second narrative is of an entirely different nature. In a case of bravery (which could easily be suicidal), these young radio producers in San Vicente de Chucurí produce a high impact and well-designed message protesting the blacklists of paramilitary groups in their municipality; they protest the demonization of difference and the pressure to conform imposed on local youth. Here the station allows these young radio producers to open a communication space where difference is not only accepted but also celebrated, where being young means to be different, to explore, to play with and tease out not-yet legitimized social and cultural codes.

Conclusion

The narratives of citizens' radio producers of *Magdalena Medio* are clear evidence of how citizens' media open communication arenas in which conflict management has been shifted from the realm of aggression and violence to the realm of discourse. We have seen how different types of conflict, from conflict among community groups, conflict among the community and local authorities, conflict emerging from political differences, and conflict with armed groups have found non-violent resolution thanks to the role played by the stations.

We cannot stress enough that these are not communication discourses *about* mediation and conflict resolution; rather, they are communication spaces to be used to mediate and interact. The stations are not sending messages to the community *about* how to solve conflict in non-violent ways. Instead, the stations themselves are mediating conflicts; their communication competence is not being used to design messages about peaceful coexistence, but instead the stations are constructing peaceful coexistence through communication. This is important because most communication-for-peace initiatives conform to what has been called an 'epidemiology approach' to communication for social change that 'conceives situations of social and political violence as a result of a "disease" that affects a specific community at a certain point in time. For example, negative ethnic stereotypes are seen as having "infected" a community, and this infection degenerates into ethnic violence. From this perspective, the goal of media initiatives is to intervene in a conflict situation with pre-designed messages that address the negative factor and propose specific changes decided by "experts." Communication and media are used to persuade individuals to adopt specific behaviors or attitudes, for example to dismantle negative ethnic stereotypes' (Rodríguez 2004). Appreciated by donors because they are designed according to clear formulas, easily evaluated with pre- and post-surveys, and replicable, epidemiology initiatives receive major funding and wide support.

Instead, citizens' radio stations in *Magdalena Medio* seem more in tune with a 'social fabric approach' which understands 'social and political violence as very complex phenomena that emerge at the intersection of various factors ranging from unequal distribution of resources, weak state presence, corrupt government officials, impunity, and strong presence of illegal economies. All these, working in conjunction, erode the social fabric and normalize a culture of strong individuality, disbelief on the rule of law, fear and isolation, exclusion of difference, and lack of solidarity among individuals. In these contexts, "social fabric" communication for peace initiatives emerge as attempts to "re-knit" the social fabric. Here, the goal is to open communication spaces where individuals can – collectively – construct links among each other based on mutual respect, solidarity, and collective enjoyment of public spaces' (Rodríguez 2004). Instead of dissecting social reality and transmitting pre-designed messages that address violent behavior as a fragment of that reality, AREDMAG's radio stations open communication spaces to be used by their communities; thanks to these new communication spaces, *Magdalena Medio* citizens are learning to develop innumerable communication competences that they can use throughout their daily lives as they search for alternative, non-violent ways to solve conflict.

Notes

1 Many thanks to Orley Durán, Melba Quijano, Julio Oyos, Manfry Gómez Ditta, Omaira Arrieta and all the other people from the citizens' radio stations in Magdalena Medio who believed in us, and trusted us with their stories and their lives. It is thanks to their faith in the power of communication, their courage, and especially their love for Colombia that this text is possible.

2 Coca paste, cocaine, and heroin labs are taxed by guerrillas and paramilitaries – whoever controls the area – by grams produced; this practice is known as '*gramaje*'.

3 A large number of guerrilla and paramilitary combatants join these groups as a way out of multi-generational cycles of poverty (see González 2002). Thus it is common to see combatants switching from a guerrilla group to a paramilitary militia and vice versa (González, Bolívar and Vázquez 2003: 210–12); more than ideological affinities, young Colombians are joining these illegal armies as an economic option.

4 Departments are the geographic units in which the national territory is divided; departments are the Colombian equivalent to states in the United States.

5 The municipalities of the Magdalena Medio are: Cimitarra, Landázuri, El Peñón, Puerto Parra, Puerto Berrío, Bolívar, Puerto Nare, Barrancabermeja, San Vicente, Bajo Ríonegro, Sabana de Torres, Betulia, El Carmen, Puerto Wilches, Yondó, Bajo Simacota, San Alberto, Aguachica, San Martín, Gamarra, La Gloria, San Pablo, Morales, Cantagallo, Santa Rosa del Sur, Simití, Río Viejo, Regidor.

6 Located in Barrancabermeja (department of Santander) and processing 541,000 barrels of oil daily.

7 Available at http://www.thirdworldtraveler.com/South_America/Quagmire_Colombia.html

8 According to *Oil and Gas Journal* (O&GJ), Colombia had 1.54 billion barrels of proven crude oil reserves in 2005. The country exports about half of its oil production, with the bulk of those exports (142,000 bl/d) going to the United States in 2004 (see Energy Information Administration available at www.eia.doe.gov/emeu/cabs/Colombia/Background.html and NationMaster.com). The major energy operators in Colombia are Empresa Colombiana de Petróleos (Ecopetrol – Colombia), BP (UK), Occidental (USA); Empresa Colombiana de Gas (Ecogás – Colombia), ChevronTexaco (USA); Carbones del Cerrejon consortium (multinational), Drummond (USA), and Glencore (multinational).

9 Available at http://www.cia.gov/cia/publications/factbook/rankorder/2173rank.html.

10 From 2000 to 2004 Colombia received US$515 million in weapons, making the country the 34th recipient of weapons in the world (Wezeman and Bromley 2005: 450). From 1994 to 2003 the United States sold $656,472,000 in arms to Colombia (see Table 2. US Weapons Sales to 25 Active Conflict Nations, available at http://www.worldpolicy.org/projects/arms/reports/WatWTable2.html). Colombia holds the 17th place in terms of countries in the developing world that receive arms from the United States (see Berrigan, Hartung, and Heffel 2005, Table 1. Human Rights Records of Top 25 US Arms Recipients in the Developing World, available at http://www.worldpolicy.org/projects/arms/reports/WatWTable1.html). Between 2001 and 2006 military aid to Colombia from the United States increased by 429 percent (see Table 3 ibid. for increases in U.S. Military Aid between 2001 and 2006 under the FMF Program). A report by the Rand Corporation on black-market and grey-market sources of small weapons in Colombia found that 36 percent of small weapons come from Central America; other sources of small weapons coming into Colombia include Mexico, Israel, Brazil, Venezuela, and Spain (Cragin and Hoffman 2003).

11 The Peace Labs and Development and Peace Projects models have multiplied in the country and in 2005 seventeen DPPs covered approximately 50 percent of the national territory and the worst conflict-ridden regions. All PDPs work in coordination under a coordinating body called REDPRODEPAZ.

12 These five communication collectives are in the process of securing a broadcasting license.

13 Clemencia Rodríguez (University of Oklahoma – USA), Amparo Cadavid (Universidad Javeriana – Bogotá, Colombia), and Jair Vega (Universidad del Norte, Barranquilla, Colombia). The board of directors of AREDMAG consists of six members; Orley Durán, Julio César Hoyos, and Manfry Gómez Ditta have been the three AREDMAG board members more involved with the evaluation study.

14 National holiday equivalent to Saint Valentine's Day in other countries.

REFERENCES

Aldana, Walter et al. (1998) *Conflictos regionales. Atlántico y Pacífico*. Bogotá: FESCOL and IEPRI.

Aprile-Gniset, Jacques (1997) *Génesis de Barrancabermeja*. Bucaramanga: Instituto Universitario de la Paz.

Archila, Mauricio (1986) *Aquí Nadie es Forastero*. Bogotá: CINEP.

Atton, Chris (2002) *Alternative Media*. London: Sage.

Berquist, Charles (2001) 'Waging War and Negotiating Peace. The Contemporary Crisis in Historical Perspective', in Charles Berquist, Ricardo Peñaranda and Gonzalo Sánchez (eds), *Violence in Colombia, 1990–2000: Waging War and Negotiating Peace*. Wilmington: Scholarly Resources, pp. 195–212.

Berrigan, Frida, Hartung, William D. and Heffel, Leslie (2005) 'Promoting freedom or fueling conflict? U.S. military aid and arms transfers since September 11'. A World Policy Institute Special Report. Available at http:// www.worldpolicy.org/projects/arms/reports/wawjune2005.html#6.

Calligaro, Kate and Isacson, Adam (2004) 'Do wealthy Colombians pay their taxes?', Center for International Policy. Report available on line at http://www.ciponline.org/colombia/040804cip.htm.

Cragin, Kim and Hoffman, Bruce (2003) 'Arms trafficking and Colombia'. Report prepared for the RAND National Defense Research Institute, available at http://www.rand.org/pubs/monograph_reports/MR1468/MR1468.pdf.

Downing, John et al. (2001) *Radical Media: Rebellious Communication and Social Movements*. Thousand Oaks, CA: Sage.

ECOPETROL (2003) 'Annual Report'. Available at www.ecopetrol.gov.co.

Fog, Lisbeth (2005) 'Oil palm research takes off in Colombia'. *SciDev.Net*, 21 January. Available at http://www.scidev.net/News/index.cfm?fuseaction=readNews&itemid=1866&language=1.

García, Clara Inés (1996) *Urabá: Región, actores y conflicto, 1960–1990*. Bogotá: CEREC.

García, Mario and Uprimny, Rodrigo (1999) 'El Nudo Gordiano de la Justicia y la Guerra en Colombia,' in Alvaro Camacho and Francisco Leal (eds), *Armar la Paz es Desarmar la Guerra*. Bogota: CEREC, IEPRI, and FESCOL. pp. 33–72.

Ginsburg, Fay (2002) 'Screen Memories: Resignifying the Traditional in Indigenous Media,' in F. Ginsburg, L. Abu-Lughod and B. Larkin (eds), *Media Worlds: Anthropology on New Terrain*. Berkeley: University of California Press. pp. 195–212.

González, Fernán, E. (1994) 'Poblamiento y conflicto social en la historia colombiana', in Renán Silva, (ed.), *Territorios, regiones, sociedades*. Bogotá: Universidad del Valle and CEREC. pp. 13–33.

– Bolívar, Ingrid J. and Vázquez, Teófilo (2003) *Violencia política en Colombia. De la nación fragmentada a la construcción del estado*. Bogotá: CINEP.

González, José Jairo et al. (1998) *Conflictos regionales. Amazonía y Orinoquia*. Bogotá: IEPRI and FESCOL.

González Uribe, Guillermo (2002) *Los niños de la guerra*. Bogotá: Editorial Planeta.

– (2003) 'Cultura y Guerra. Colombia y Estados Unidos', *Revista Número,* No. 37.

Gumucio Dagron, Alfonso (2003) Arte de Equilibristas: la Sostenibilidad de los Medios de comunicación Comunitarios'. Paper presented at the OURMedia III Conference, Barranquilla, Colombia.

Guzmán, Alvaro and Luna, Mario (1994) 'Violencia, conflicto y región. Perspectivas de análisis sobre el Valle del Cauca y el Cauca', in Renán Silva (ed.), *Territorios, regiones, sociedades*. Bogotá: Universidad del Valle and CEREC. pp. 180–207.

Jimeno, Myriam (1994) 'Región, nación y diversidad cultural en Colombia', in Renán Silva (ed.), *Territorios, regiones, sociedades*. Bogotá: Universidad del Valle and CEREC. pp. 65–78.

Kalmanovitch, Salomón (1995) 'Análisis macroeconómico del narcotráfico en la economía colombiana', in Ricardo Vargas (ed.), *Drogas, poder y región en Colombia*. Bogotá: CINEP. pp. 11–58.

Katz García, Mauricio (n.d.) *A Regional Peace Experience: The Magdalena Medio Peace and Development Programme*. Available at http://www.c-r.org/accord/col/accord14/regionalpeaceinit.shtml.

Legrand, Catherine (1986) *Frontier Expansion and Peasant Protest in Colombia, 1850–1936*. Albuquerque: University of New Mexico Press.

Murillo, Amparo (1994) *Un Mundo que se Mueve Como el Rio. Historia Regional del Magdalena Medio*. Bogotá: ICAHN.

News Voa Com (2004, March 8) Examinan Tráfico de Armas en Colombia. Available at www.voanews.com/spanish/Archive/a-2004-03-08-2-1.cfm.

PDPMM. Web portal of the Programa de Desarrollo y Paz del Magdalena Medio. Avialbale at http://www.pdpmm.org.co/index.htm.

Reina, Mauricio (2001) 'Drug trafficking and the national economy', in Charles Berquist, Ricardo Peñaranda and Gonzalo Sánchez (eds), *Violence in Colombia, 1990–2000: Waging War and Negotiating Peace*. Wilmington: Scholarly Resources. pp. 75–94.

Reyes, Alejandro (1999) 'La cuestión agraria en la guerra y la paz' in Camacho, Alvaro and Leal, Francisco (eds), *Armar la paz es desarmar la guerra,* Bogotá, IEPRI, 205–226.

Rodríguez, Clemencia (2004, December 6) 'Communication for peace: contrasting approaches', *The Drum Beat*, issue 278. Available at http://www.comminit.com/drum_beat. html.)

– (2001) *Fissures in the Mediascape: An International Study of Citizens' Media*. Cresskill, NJ: Hampton Press.

Romero, Mauricio (1998) 'Identidades políticas y conflicto armado en Colombia. El caso del departamento de Cordoba', in Aldana, W. et al. (eds), *Conflictos regionales – Atlántico y Pacífico*. Bogotá: FESCOL – IEPRI. pp. 59–91.

– (2003) *Paramilitares y autodefensas*. Bogotá: IEPRI and Editorial Planeta.

Silva, Renán (1994) *Territorios, regiones, sociedades*. Bogotá: Universidad del Valle and CEREC.

Sánchez, Gonzalo (2001) 'Introduction. Problems of Violence, Prospects for Peace', in Charles Berquist, Ricardo Peñaranda and Gonzalo Sánchez (eds), *Violence in Colombia, 1990–2000: Waging War and Negotiating Peace*. Wilmington: Scholarly Resources. pp. 1–38.

SEAP-CINEP (1996) *Programa de Desarrollo y Paz del Magdalena Medio: Investigación diagnóstica*. Bogotá: SEAP-CINEP.

Uprimny, Rodrigo. (2001) 'Violence, Power and Collective Action. A Comparison Between Bolivia and Colombia', in Charles Berquist, Ricardo Peñaranda and Gonzalo Sánchez (eds), *Violence in Colombia, 1990–2000: Waging War and Negotiating Peace*. Wilmington: Scholarly Resources. pp. 39–52.

Uribe, Maria Victoria (1992) *Limpiar la tierra: Guerra y poder entre los esmeralderos*. Bogotá: CINEP.

Vargas, Alejandro (1992) *Colonización y conflicto armado*. Bogotá: CINEP.

Wezeman, Siemon T. and Bromley, Mark (2005) International Arms Transfer. Stockholm International Peace Research Institute (SIPRI) Yearbook. Available at http://www.sipri.org/contents/armstrad/atpubs.html#lat.

Zamosc, Leon (1986) *The Agrarian Question and the Peasant Movement in Colombia: 1967–1981*. London: Cambridge University Press.

– (1997) 'Transformaciones agrarias y luchas campesinas en Colombia: Un balance retrospectivo', in Leon Zamosc, Estela Martinez and Manuel Chiriboga (eds) *Estructuras agrarias y movimientos campesinos en America Latina (1950–1990)*. Madrid: Centro De Publicaciones, Ministerio De Agricultura, Serie Estudios #127. pp. 76–132.

## CHAPTER 27

THE PEDAGOGY OF DRUMS: CULTURE MEDIATING CONFLICT IN THE SLUMS OF BRAZIL

Silvia Ramos

Poor black young people in the slums and peripheries of Brazil's cities are either protagonists or victims of the violence that claims at lease 50,000 victims each year. Often, the poverty that is the root cause of this violence is compounded by police violence and corruption. In the 1990s, a number of artistic and cultural initiatives to combat these scourges began to be led by young people from the conflict zones. The 'Youth and Peace Project', initiated by the Afro Reggae Cultural Group in Rio de Janeiro together with the police, is a case in point: an example of how 'new mediators' can address the issues of endemic urban violence and work towards a 'culture of peace.'

Brazil has one of the world's highest rates of violent death. Young people are at the heart of the problem – especially the poor black youth who dwell in slums and urban outskirts – either as victims or as causers of violence. The responses of both the state and civil society in Brazil to the problem of criminality and violence have been slow and unsatisfactory. Nonetheless, in the 1990s, several cities witnessed artistic and cultural initiatives led by the young people of the city peripheries themselves. Although heterogeneous and not articulated with one another, these experiences have proven to be the most important and successful endeavors to create 'cultures of peace' in opposition to the dynamics of urban conflicts.

This chapter will present a panorama of urban violence in Brazil and will identify the emergence of groups that in many aspects can be seen as 'new mediators' in the political and cultural scenario. In particular, I shall describe the case of the Afro Reggae Cultural Group in Rio de Janeiro. Together with the Center for Studies on Public Security and Citizenship, the group has been involved since 2004 in a unique pilot experience inside military-police barracks.

The Age, Color and Geography of Violent Death

In 2003, 51,534 Brazilians were murdered, at a rate of 28.8 homicides per 100,000 inhabitants. In some states like Rio de Janeiro and Pernambuco, the rates are even higher: 50 per 100,000. In the 15 to 24 age bracket, in certain urban areas we come across rates of over 200 homicides per 100,000 inhabitants: this is the case of Rio de Janeiro, Recife and Vitória (Ramos 2005). Recent studies have revealed the existence of a dramatic concentration of violent deaths among the black segment of the population. The differences among the young are very significant: the homicide rate for white men in the 20 to 24 age bracket is 184.4 per 100,000 inhabitants; for black men the rate reaches 218.5 (Cano, Borges and Ribeiro 2004). Furthermore, there is a geography of death in the cities. It is in the slums and outskirts of urban centers, areas lacking in social services, that the highest indices of lethal violence are registered.

Some authors argue that at the base of the growth in the indices of criminality and violence in Latin America lies the phenomenon of 'new poverty' that results from the re-structuring and reduction of the state following the privatization of essential services and the unequal globalization of trade and commerce leading to closure of industry, loss of jobs and growth of unemployment (Leeds, forthcoming). At the local level, the accelerated growth of violent deaths in slums and poor neighborhoods can be explained by a combination of factors: the advent of cocaine in urban centers and the big cities in the interior of the country in the 1980s, and the extraordinary profitability of drug trafficking; fighting between rival factions for control of the points where drugs are distributed and sold; the intensive use of guns; the spread of police corruption and violence. The absence of government powers in these areas – principally an efficient and honest police force – favors the establishment and spread of territorial control by armed groups of drug dealers. The drug trade in these territories exerts a strong power of seduction over children and adolescents. With scant alternatives of employment and poor future prospects, many young people envisage an attractive way out, albeit often a lethal one, in the quick profit and glamorous life-style ensured by the power and ostensive presence of arms. These practices feed a 'culture' in which there is a predominance of despotism, *machismo*, homophobia and misogyny. This set of values, discourses and practices – which contaminates a good portion of the young people in these areas, even those not directly linked to the armed groups – has been given the name 'narcoculture' by some young leaders (Júnior 2003).

The Brazilian police and security policies

The socioeconomic profile of the main victims of violence, and their limited capacity to exert political pressure, may help to explain the late awakening of Brazilian governments and civil society to the theme of public security and the need to modernize, control and democratize the police. Only in the 1990s did systematic efforts to draw up public security policies begin to be registered, based on a contemporary perspective identified by a combination of efficiency and human rights.

As a result of the absence of investments and rational public policies, some police forces in the country became violent and inefficient. Organized crime corrupted broad segments of the police corps, in some cases reaching from the bases all the way to the heads of police (Lemgruber, Musumeci and Cano 2003). In some states, police violence has become a deep problem that bears a direct effect on the poor population of the slums and city outskirts, which finds itself cornered between the violence of the armed groups of drug dealers and the violence and corruption of the police. In the state of Rio de Janeiro, the police are responsible for more than 10 percent of criminal homicides, with occurrences totaling 983 deaths in confrontation in 2004 and 1098 in 2005.

Young people in the slums and city outskirts: Afro Reggae and the new mediators

In the context of civil answers to violence, one sees an important recent process of mobilizing young people from the slums and periphery neighborhoods. These are projects, programs or local initiatives based on cultural and artistic actions that are often developed and coordinated by the young people themselves. Examples of such initiatives are the Olodum group and the Axé project in Salvador, Afro Reggae, *Nós do Morro* and the *Cia. Étnica de Dança* in Rio de Janeiro, and hundreds of groups mobilized around hip-hop culture in the outlying neighborhoods of São Paulo, the *vilas* of Porto Alegre, the *aglomerados* of Belo Horizonte and in the poor districts of Brasília and São Luís.

These groups 'dispute' the young people with the drug trade, exercising another type of seduction and using equally strong strategies of attraction. They are committed to a culture of peace in harmony with contemporary interests and spirit: in addition to culture and art, they place value on the Internet, information technology, fashionable clothes and shoes, traveling and regional and international interchange. In general, the projects are characterized by four innovative aspects in the repertoire of the 'human rights' entities and the traditional NGOs: 1) interest in the market and 'lucrative ends' combined with a commitment to the community; 2) affirmation of local territorial identity (the slum) combined with identification with signs of globalization; 3) emphasis on subjectivity, individual trajectories, success and fame, these being associated with the world of culture and art; and 4) denunciation of racism by means of aesthetic and verbal racial affirmation.

The Afro Reggae Cultural Group is a non-governmental organization founded in 1993 and based in the Vigário Geral slum in the city of Rio de Janeiro. The Group was set up in the same year as the Vigário Geral massacre, when 21 residents were killed by policemen in an illegal operation. According to the group, its objective is to 'promote social inclusion and justice by using art, Afro-Brazilian culture and education as tools to build bridges that span the gaps and serve as supports to sustain and exercise citizenship' (www.afroreggae.org.br). The Afro Reggae Cultural Group is a typical 'new mediator'. The Afro Reggae band, which enjoys considerable visibility in the media, breaks down stereotypes and establishes bridges, providing a sort of 'translation' of the perspective of young slum dwellers, either for the government or for researchers, the media or international agencies. Afro Reggae, as well as other groups of this type, produces a first-person discourse on behalf of the young excluded slum population. Aware of the traps that exist in the naive ideology of 'art for the sake of the social' (Yúdice 2004; Ochoa 2003), these groups make an enormous effort to train and qualify artists and musicians in a highly competitive market.

The youth and police project

The story of the Vigário Geral massacre, the production of clips with images of police violence, and different episodes involving young people from Afro Reggae (some of them victims of police bullets), all of this composed not only a vast repertoire of hatred and resentment that forged an 'anti-police culture' in the group, but also made the group the most emblematic in the country to develop projects concerned with drawing closer to the police. In late 2002, to everyone's surprise, José Júnior, coordinator of the Afro Reggae Cultural Group, visited the Center for Studies on Public Security and Citizenship (CESeC) of the Candido Mendes University and said that he would like to consider a project *together with* the police. A project of 'cultural invasions' of police barracks was presented to the Ford Foundation, which gave its immediate approval. The negotiations with the Military Police of Rio de Janeiro were frustrated, so developing the project in the very state where the Afro Reggae was born proved impossible. In 2004, the Military Police of Minas Gerais invited Afro Reggae and the CESeC to fashion the project in Belo Horizonte.

At first the project was undertaken as a four-stage pilot project directed towards setting up a dialogue between the young people's culture and the police culture by reducing the distance between these two groups through music and art. Afro Reggae was responsible for workshops in percussion, theater, graffiti, dancing and shows for the policemen. The surprising results of the first four weeks showed the force and enormous potential of this method of symbolically bringing the police and society closer together. In 2005, the Military Police of Minas Gerais decided that the results were so positive that the experience was continued. This time around, policemen who had been trained by Afro Reggae taught young people in the slums in workshops in percussion, *graffiti*, street dancing and theater. In 2006, due to the great impact of the project in the national media, the police of Rio de Janeiro gave in and asked Afro Reggae and the CESeC for a pilot project in the city's police barracks.

Among the most important aspects of the experience, in contrast with the traditional forms of sensitizing police forces in human rights (courses, meetings and talks), the following key elements deserve special mention:

- The experience involves not only reason but also hearts, minds and, especially, bodies. The traditionally 'defensive' position of police culture makes it difficult to attempt to teach the police about human rights in classrooms and debates based on critical argumentation.
- The instructors are young people who dress like, talk like, and have the 'attitudes' of the young slum dweller. With the intense contact inside the barracks, the young people change their stereotypes with regard to the police and at the same time challenge them in relation to rhythm, sound and plasticity. The essential point lies in the exchange that is made mainly in the aesthetic sphere, in the body and in the experience of creating a new 'attitude' on the part of the police.
- Sound and image are essential to the project. The idea is to alter the image that society and young people have of the police and the image that the police have of the young blacks who live in the slums. Police 'is image': the uniform, the gun, the military aesthetic, the characteristic vehicle. In turn, Afro Reggae 'is image': the new image of the slum and the artists from the slums. As a result of this 'pedagogy of drums', policemen and young people – who were constructed as opposing groups – become protagonists of a new scenario that produces sounds and images to which society reacts in surprise.

Of course, there are enormous barriers to be overcome as regards the police on the national level. But initiatives where young people, using the first person, through music and art, come into direct contact with policemen are powerful instruments to create a more modern and democratic police force. The most important thing in this experience is the role played by the young people from the slums themselves, who are involved in the tragedy of violence as principal victims and principal protagonists. In this case they are 'new mediators' who use a pioneer experience to show that it is possible to offer creative answers to the problem of violence in Brazil.

REFERENCES

Cano, Ignacio (1997) *Letalidade da ação policial no Rio de Janeiro.* Rio de Janeiro: ISER.

– Borges, Doriam and Ribeiro, Eduardo (2004) *Cor e vitimização por homicídios no Brasil.* Texto para o capítulo sobre raça e violência do Relatório de Desenvolvimento Humano Brasileiro 2005. Rio de Janeiro: LAV-UERJ e CESeC/UCAM.

Júnior, José (2003) *Da favela para o mundo: a história do Grupo Cultural Afro Reggae.* Rio de Janeiro: Aeroplano.

Leeds, Elizabeth. (forthcoming) 'Rio de Janeiro', in Kees Koonings and Dirk Kruijt (eds), *Fractured Cities: Social Exclusion, Urban Violence and Contested Spaces in Latin America.* London: Verso.

Lemgruber, Julita, Musumeci, Leonarda and Cano, Ignacio (2003) *Quem vigia os vigias?* Rio de Janeiro: Record.

Ochoa, Ana María (2003) *Entre los deseos y los derechos: un ensaio crítico sobre políticas culturales.* Bogotá: Instituto Colombiano de Antropología e Historia.

Ramos, Silvia (2005), *Criminalidade, segurança pública e respostas brasileiras à violência.* 3ª Conferência Nacional de Ciência e Tecnologia. Brasília: MCT.

Yúdice, George (2004) *A conveniência da cultura: usos da cultura na era global.* Belo Horizonte: Editora UFMG.

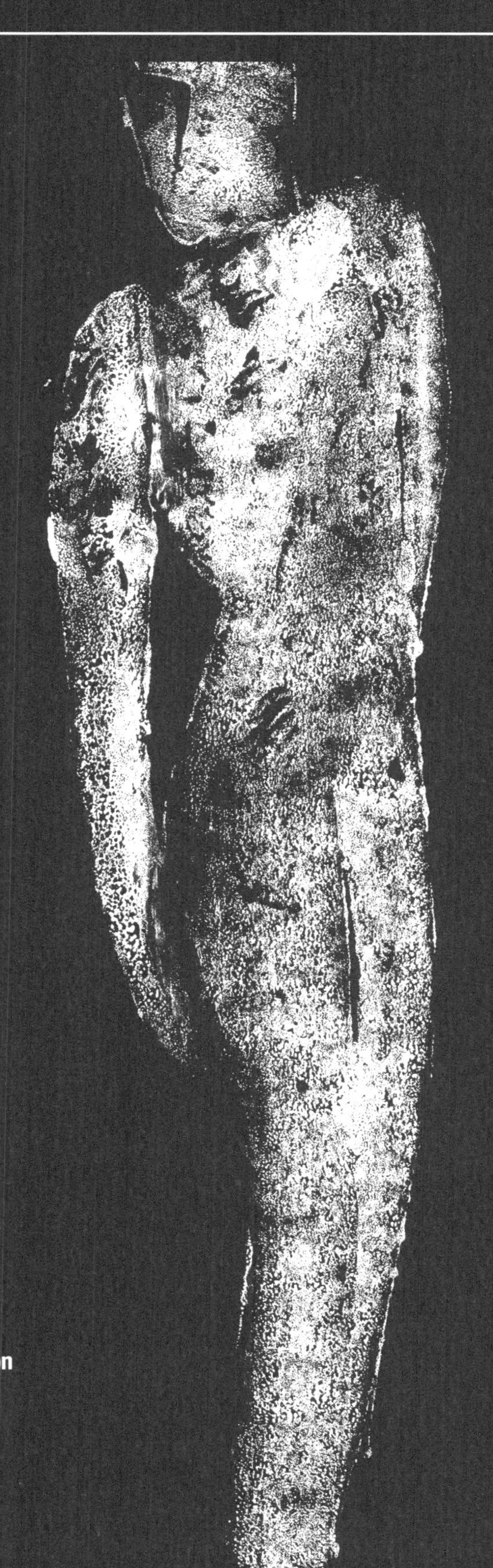

Idea and Conceptuzlization
Helmut Anheier
Design and Production
Willem Henri Lucas

INTRODUCING 'CULTURAL INDICATOR' SUITES

Helmut K. Anheier

Any indicator system requires a conceptual framework to guide its purpose, the selection of indicators and the kind of information needed. Using the framework presented in the Introduction to this volume, the present chapter proposes the development of an integrated sequence of indicators and their presentation around the notion of 'indicator suites'. These suites display information on selected facets of the relationships between cultures and globalization. In developing this integrated indicator system, we address questions like: How can we identify the most important indicators across a range of audiences, users and purposes, and why? What are the priorities in terms of data coverage, data collection, information needs as well as methodological developments in the field? How can we collect, analyze and present data in effective, efficient and user-friendly ways?

Objectives and characteristics

The purpose of the indicator system is to offer an empirical portrait of certain key dimensions of the relationships between cultures and globalization. By implication, the system would neither try to achieve a comprehensive accounting of culture as such, nor seek to report on all aspects of cultural developments and policies that might be relevant for national as well as international purposes.[1] Generally speaking, cultural indicators that refer primarily to national frameworks or that have no major theoretical or policy relevance for the culture – globalization nexus would be beyond the scope of what we are trying to measure, and will therefore receive little attention. For example, data on theater and film production by country are less important than their transnational content, share and distribution; even though obtaining the latter data assumes the availability of the former. In other words, the proposed system does not aim to become a generic indicator system for the elaboration of cultural statistics (nor does it seek to replace any existing systems). Rather, what we have in mind is a specialized system focused on a substantive core: the relationship between globalization and culture.

At the same time, the approach here is informed by work on cultural indicators research[2] that addresses either basic methodological and data issues (Bonet 2004; Duxbury 2003; European Commission 2000; Fukuda-Parr 2001; Glade 2003; Goldstone 1998; Matarasso 2001; Schuster 2002) or questions of policy relevance (Kleberg 2003; Wiesand 2002; Wyszomirski 1998). Against this background as well as the overall conceptual framework presented in the Introduction, the indicator system should aim for the following characteristics (Deutsch 1963; Anheier 2004):[3]

- *Parsimony*, i.e., the aim to 'achieve most with least':
- *Significance*, i.e., focus on the truly critical aspects of a phenomenon and its relationships;
- *Combinatorial richness*, i.e., the range of hypotheses that can be tested with the system and related to this, *Organizing power*, i.e., the ability to bring in and integrate new aspects;
- *Theoretical fruitfulness*, i.e., the extent to which the system allows theory development; and
- *Policy relevance*, i.e., the extent to which the system is useful and of interest to policy-makers.

Challenges

The relationships between globalization and culture are too abstract and multifaceted for direct observation, and need to be broken down into dimensions and sub-dimensions. In other words, we need to make the relationships 'operational' and prepare them for measurement purposes. In doing so, we face a number of critical challenges. It is important to address these issues at the onset. They are the following: the unit of analysis, the aggregation problem, indicator selection, data coverage, and normative aspects. For each challenge, we propose a solution or at least a general approach on how to address it for the purposes of the *Series*.

What is the appropriate unit of analysis? Even though we have become accustomed to think of countries or nation-states as the basic unit of analysis in international statistics and for purposes of comparative research, there are severe shortcomings to their use for studying phenomena related to globalization. For one, the implied reification of countries as actors *sui generis* in a transnational cultural space can be very misleading. For example, the United States does not 'act'; its institutions, organizations, communities and citizens do. These lower level units of analysis – and not aggregate units such as country – enact and create culture, and make up much of the relationship between globalization and culture. It is US corporations like Microsoft or the Disney Corporation, organizations like Greenpeace or Amnesty International, missionary societies, immigrant groups, art museums, artists, activists, CEOs or academics that are frequently the relevant actors. Of course, the nation-state as represented by government and governmental policies plays an important role, as do the EU, the WTO or the World Bank, but the nation-state cannot be the single focus of our attention as the primary unit of analysis.

For measurement purposes, it seems best to focus on identifiable elements that 'carry' the essential characteristics that are of interest to us. In addition, we need to put these units in the context of related phenomena such as economic globalization, global civil society, and the international rule of law.

How can the aggregation problem be solved? The excessive use of the nation-state as the unit of analysis in international statistics creates what methodologists call the aggregation problem and with it a potential for ecological fallacies. Most international data on culture are nation-based, which implies at least potentially a mismatch between the unit of observation (for example, organizations) and the *de facto* unit of analysis (country). For example, statistics indicate that the great majority of films shown in countries like the UK or Germany are from the United States (i.e., Hollywood, and hence part of the United States cultural output), yet they neglect the fact that the corporations financing, producing and distributing the movies are multinational corporations that are 'resident' in several countries and with shareholders and stakeholders in perhaps even more. If the globalization of culture is qualitatively different from national and international units of analysis, then it cannot simply be the additive score of nation-based observations

The problem behind the misattribution of data to units is primarily one of prevailing practices whereby data are aggregated and reported at national levels, and cannot be disaggregated and reconstituted at the supra-national level. This is the consequence of Scholte's (1999) and Beck's (2001) 'methodological nationalism' that plagues the social sciences. In some cases, however, the country cannot be avoided as the unit of analysis, and in others it may well be the appropriate unit, for example with respect to international legal issues or trade barriers.

Generally, the approach taken in the *Series* is to avoid taking the country as the primary reporting unit whenever data on more appropriate units are available. For example, rather than reporting only on how many book titles a country publishes per year, we would also focus on the share of the global book market held by various multinational publishing corporations; or what titles or genres are the most diffused transnationally. In the case of movies or music titles, we would look for studios, labels and corporations and report share of global output and penetration.

Clearly, given the still-limited development and availability of cultural indicators that are comparable cross-nationally, we would not be able to follow a uniform strategy, and the general approach is to develop more specific indicator-data suites around appropriate units of analysis. By indicator-data suite, we mean the range of data needed to describe the characteristics of a selected indicator. For example, for measuring the globalization of book publishing, we would use the total market share of transnational publishing houses as one indicator. The characteristics of interest would be book titles, sales, etc.; and indicators to be reported (and which can be calculated once we have the data available) would be concentration and diffusion measures. In this case, we would use organizations as the unit of analysis; in others it could be products and artifacts (e.g., books); and in others people, as in the globally most widely printed/sold/read authors in particular genres.

What actual indicators and measures are best suited for portraying the central dimensions of the relationship between cultures and globalization? Obviously, these measures range from cultural to economic, political, and social indicators, and may even involve more qualitative assessments of issues such as human rights, conflicts, and global governance. To answer the question, we need to examine available approaches and indicators, and select those that are closest to the intended meaning of the concepts involved, i.e., the conceptual framework (see below). Whenever possible, we will be guided by theoretical approaches around specific topics or issues. For example, a number of theories have been proposed to understand individual identity, and we can mine such theories when selecting indicators, and refer back to them.

What is the data coverage and availability? Much of the data needed to report on the relationship between cultures and globalization may not be readily available or not exist at all. Moreover, parts of the data may be qualitative and even involve value judgements of one kind or another. As in the case of indicators, we need to explore a broad range of potential data sources. In some cases, however, appropriate data can be found, although with limited country coverage and other aspects that reduce comparability. Thus, for each indicator-data suite selected, we conducted a detailed analysis of data coverage, quality and periodicity. We will update this search on an annual basis in the hopes that over time, data coverage will become more comprehensive and data quality improved.

Is culture essentially a normative concept? Even if culture is often seen and treated as a value-free concept in academic discourse, or as largely neutral for creative expression among art circles, it carries profound normative implications for others that range from fears about a 'clash of civilizations' (Huntington 1996), to expectations of a more humane, inclusive world and the possibility of an ethical consensus (Küng 1998). Not surprisingly, the aspirations and the norms these positions imply are contested, and the indicator system proposed here would do well to accommodate data on the normative interpretations and implications of the relationships between cultures and globalization without favoring one over the other.

How can we achieve policy relevance? Social science data tend to be somewhat removed from the information requirements of policy-makers. At best, they need 'translation' into policy terms, and at worst, they are frequently out of date (even when only 2–3 years old) and incomplete. In response, and in the medium to long term, we propose a system of scenario planning around cultural issues. This will involve an information-gathering process that relies on a global network of experts who serve as 'listening posts' and report on ongoing developments in the field of culture and globalization, as part of a systematic and coordinated survey.

Different approaches

These challenges, and we could add others as well, are formidable, to be sure, and some may question the utility and feasibility of an indicator and data system on cultures and globalization altogether. Fortunately, however, a variety of approaches have been proposed that are useful for our purposes and from which we can learn and draw critical lessons.

First, the UNDP approach in the *Human Development Report* (2000) was to select indicators and data around the Human Development Index based on a specific definition of development. Development was defined as extending choices to permit the kind of life that people wish to lead. This definition was broken down into components or dimensions of ability to make choices: leading a long and healthy life; being knowledgeable; enjoying a decent standard of living; enjoying personal security; participating in the life of the community; enjoying the respect of others. In a next step, indicators were selected such as life expectancy, literacy rates, per capita income, etc. Finally, under the umbrella of Monitoring Human Development, the indicators were integrated in a sequence of tables organized around a conceptual framework of what human development means:

Enlarging people's choices:

- Human Development Index

To lead a long and healthy life:

- Statistics on demographic trends
- Statistics on commitment to health: resources, access and services
- Statistics on water, sanitation and nutritional status

- Statistics on leading global health crises and risks
- Statistics on survival: progress and setbacks

To acquire knowledge:
- Statistics on commitment to education: public spending
- Statistics on literacy and enrollment
- Statistics on technology: diffusion and creation

To have access to the resources needed for a decent standard of living:
- Statistics on economic performance
- Statistics on inequality in income/ consumption
- Statistics on structure of trade
- Statistics on rich country responsibilities: aid, debt relief and trade
- Statistics on flows of aid, private capital and debt
- Statistics on priorities in public spending
- Statistics on unemployment

While preserving it for future generations:
- Statistics on energy and the environment

Protecting personal security:
- Statistics on refugees and armaments
- Statistics on victims of crime

And achieving equality of men and women:
- Statistics on gender-related development index

Second, in *Our Creative Diversity* (1996), the World Commission on Culture and Development linked culture and development by stating that development is 'the opportunity to choose a full and satisfying, valuable and valued way of living together, the flourishing of human existence in all its forms and as a whole'. It also set a standard for evaluating progress around the following key tenets:

- Cultural freedom of both the community and the individual
- Respect for pluralism
- Recognition that culture is dynamic but evolving
- Ethos of universal human rights

UNESCO subsequently translated these tenets into six areas (UNESCO/UNRISD, 1997; UNESCO, 1998):

- Global ethics: observance of human rights and the rule of law
- Cultural vitality: media, literacy, preservation, etc.
- Cultural diversity: access, participation, equity
- Participation in creative activity: participation of groups in creative activities
- Access to culture: do groups have access to creativity of others?
- Cultural conviviality: concern with diversity and respect of others

In contrast to UNDP's Human Development approach, the above six areas are clearly less 'clean' conceptually and some overlap exists among them. Not surprisingly, therefore, the actual tables presented in UNESCO's *World Culture Report* 1998 and 2000 do not appear to follow the operationalization of the six areas. Instead, the Report lists six rather different topics:

Statistics on Cultural Activities:
- Newspapers and books
- Libraries and cultural papers
- Radio and television
- Cinema and film
- Recorded music

Statistics on Cultural Practices and Heritage:
- Leading languages
- Leading religions
- National festivals
- Folk and religious festivals
- Most visited cultural site
- Most visited natural site
- World heritage sites

Statistics on *Ratifications:*
- Cultural and labor conventions
- Human rights conventions

Statistics on Cultural Trade and Communication Trends:
- Trends in cultural trade
- Distribution of cultural trade by type

- Tourism flows
- Communication

Statistics on Translations:

- Translations of books
- Translators
- Most frequently translated language

Statistics on *Cultural Context:*

- Education
- Tertiary education abroad
- Human capital
- Demographic and health
- Economic
- Social security
- Environment and biodiversity

The result was that the link between culture and development as postulated by the World Commission was not in fact fully explored because the conceptual framework and the empirical level of indicators and data did not match. Moreover, the distinctions between activities, practices, trade and communication and translations remained unclear and made the selection and grouping of indicators appear somewhat arbitrary.

Third, a different path has been taken by authors such as Mercer (2002: 60–1), who have proposed more systematic indicator sets:

- Cultural Vitality, Diversity and Conviviality
  i.e., Statistics measuring the health and sustainability of the cultural economy, and the ways in which the circulation and diversity of cultural resources and experiences can contribute to quality of life
- Cultural Access, Participation and Consumption
  i.e., Statistics measuring opportunities for and constraints to active cultural engagement
- Culture, Lifestyle and Identity
  i.e., Statistics evaluating the extent to which cultural resources and capital are used to constitute specific lifestyles and identities
- Culture, Ethics, Governance and Conduct
  i.e., Statistics evaluating the extent to which cultural resources and capital can contribute to and shape forms of behavior by both individuals and collectivities.

These indicator sets have then been related to the economic concept of the value production chain, as follows:

- *Creation*: the conditions and capacity for creation and innovation of values in both material and immaterial forms
- *Production and reproduction*: the transformation of values into tangible and intangible forms
- *Promotion and knowledge*: activities and capacities to gain wider use and acceptance for the produced and disseminated value and product
- *Dissemination and circulation*: the mechanisms, processes and institutions that put values and products into public and private domains
- *Consumption and use*: the processes and capacities for the use and consumption of values and products.

Finally, they were put in a matrix form to reveal distinct indicator sets presented in Table 1.

While there is much to be commended about this approach, it has two major weaknesses for our purposes: first, the comprehensive nature of the indicator matrix leaves the wider questions of 'why' and 'for what purpose' unanswered. In this sense, the indicator matrix is more like a statistical framework that can be put to different uses rather than an indicator and data system that flows from a conceptual framework serving a specified purpose. Second, most of the data needed for the indicators suggested by Mercer (2002: 156–63) are simply not available for most countries, requiring therefore a major data collection effort that is well beyond the capacities of the *Cultures and Globalization Series*.

There are, of course, important ways in which the framework proposed here differs from what Mercer, UNDP and UNESCO have achieved. First, it is not about culture as such but about the relationships between cultures and globalization; second, it is much less about countries or nation-states as the primary and near-exclusive units of analysis. The parsimony of the UNDP approach is to be commended, as is the comprehensiveness of Mercer's indicator matrix. Our search, therefore, is for a compromise between parsimony and comprehensiveness, despite the paucity of available, comparable and high-quality data.

Table 1 Indicator sets and value stages

Value stages/ Indicator sets	Creation	Production	Promotion and Knowledge	Dissemination and Circulation	Use and Consumption
Vitality, diversity, conviviality	*Indicator set*	*Indicator set*	*Indicator set*	*Indicator set*	*Indicator set*
Cultural access, participation consumption	*Indicator set*	*Indicator set*	*Indicator set*	*Indicator set*	*Indicator set*
Lifestyle and identity	*Indicator set*	*Indicator set*	*Indicator set*	*Indicator set*	*Indicator set*
Ethics, governance, conduct	*Indicator set*	*Indicator set*	*Indicator set*	*Indicator set*	*Indicator set*

Assumptions

Like the approach underlying UNDP's Human Development Index (UNDP 2000), measuring the relationship between globalization and culture must rest on the premise of parsimony and emphasize a select number of indicators that can be operationalized, are measurable, and have a reasonable degree of data availability. This approach implies that highly complex and demanding models may at present be of little use, as many indicators cannot be observed and as data are often not readily available; moreover, complex models can be difficult to communicate to diverse audiences. Specifically, we proceed from six assumptions or premises:

Assumption 1 Rather than trying to fill in data on a wide range of cultural aspects for as many countries as possible (as UNESCO tried to do), or for as many indicator matrices for as many countries as possible (as Mercer's approach would lead us to pursue), we suggest that such tasks would be futile due to the seriousness of the data problems involved and the extraordinary amount of time and resources it would take to solve them. Instead, we proceed from the assumption that only a different approach could offer a realistic way forward – an approach along the lines of the indicator suites proposed below.

Assumption 2 Any measurement of the relationship between cultures and globalization will be simpler and less perfect than the richness, variety, and complexity of what it tries to measure. As analytic and operational concepts, globalization and culture as well as the relationship between them must necessarily abstract from historical and current variations in their development, and disregard significant cultural, political, and social differences. The information presented in the indicator and data system aims to provide the essential characteristics of the relationship and its context.

Assumption 3 The relationship between cultures and globalization is a multifaceted, emerging as well as changing phenomenon that is different in different parts of the world, hence the indicator and data system must take account of this essential characteristic. In particular, some indicators may be less 'global' in their meaning and relevance than others. Put differently, not all indicators will be globalization pure; some will address international and transnational phenomena that can be limited to regions of the world that are not necessarily contiguous geographically, such as diaspora communities or transnational professions.

Assumption 4 As the essence of the relationship between cultures and globalization may vary with theoretical approach, disciplinary outlook, or policy-related interests, the indicator and data systems should be based on an open conceptual framework that emphasizes various aspects and takes account of different dimensions and orientations. For example, economists might emphasize intellectual property rights and cultural flows as critical factors, whereas sociologists would point to cultural value patterns and changes as focal areas of interest, and political scientists might focus on aspects of global governance and transnational interest groups.

Assumption 5 The operationalization and measurement of the relationship between cultures and globalization has a strategic-development dimension. We view the current profile of the relationship as an evolving system that can be perfected over time. Feedback received from the social science and policy communities will help improve the data situation over time so that future editions of the *Series* can build on each other. In other words, the proposed system is an evolving one that makes use of available information to the greatest extent possible.

Assumption 6 We no longer assume that 'country' is the preferred unit of analysis. Other units, be they organizations, communities, networks, products, artifacts or events are important as well and may indeed emerge as units more appropriate to the task. For example: leading producers of cultural products by corporation rather than country; copyright and patent holders by firm rather than country; globally relevant books, movies, TV series, stage productions, papers, websites, museums, paintings, sites, events, etc; cities with high concentrations of cultural productions, etc.

Focus and framework

For our purpose, 'culture' in the broad sense refers to the social construction, articulation and reception of meaning. It involves value systems, forms of creation, enactment, presentation and preservation as well as symbols, artifacts and objects. This definition includes 'culture' in the narrow sense as the creation, presentation, preservation, and appreciation of work of art. Figure 1 puts the focus of the indicator and data system on the relationship between globalization and culture.

This relationship exists in a context that is both analytical and factual: it is analytical because cultural globalization does not exist in isolation from other globalization processes; a book or movie is a cultural, economic and legal entity at the same time. What the analytic focus on culture does is emphasize some aspects of globalization over others it treats as contextual. The context is factual in the sense that other globalization processes are taking place, which may differ in strengths, scope, and implications. What the factual focus achieves is to bring in empirical facts from these other globalization processes as they relate to culture. For example, international trade laws may not be written with a focus on cultural matters, but the former certainly influence the latter.

Specifically, we have three contextual patterns and processes in mind: first, economic globalization in terms of trade and the rise of integrated, transnational productions and distribution systems dominated by large transnational corporations and financial markets; second, a transnational, and increasingly global, civil society has emerged more fully since the end of the Cold War, facilitated by the rise of international novgovernmental organizations, activitist networks, and civil value patterns; and third, the 'thickening' of the international rule of law has continued as well, although unevenly and with persistent enforcement problems and nationalist interpretations of global governance.

We have already suggested that we can think of culture in many ways: as a system of artistic endeavors and realm of creativity; as a social system of meaning and values; as an economic system of production, distribution and consumption; and as a political system of positions of power and influence (Figure 1). Each 'lens' or systemic view is equality valid and likely brings up different questions, leading to different insights and implications.

The relationship between cultures and globalization is not only multifaceted from a systemic perspective. Each systemic view brings different units of analysis and flows into consideration. These can be transnational and domestic, individuals, organizations, or professions as well as institutional patterns, communities, and societies, including nation-states (Figure 1). These units and flows are often connected, leading to consequences. For example, the rise of the Internet brought wide access to online news, which in turn has changed the business model of the newspaper industry, the role of journalism with the increased popularity of blogs etc.

Figure 1 **Framework for *The Cultures and Globalization Series***

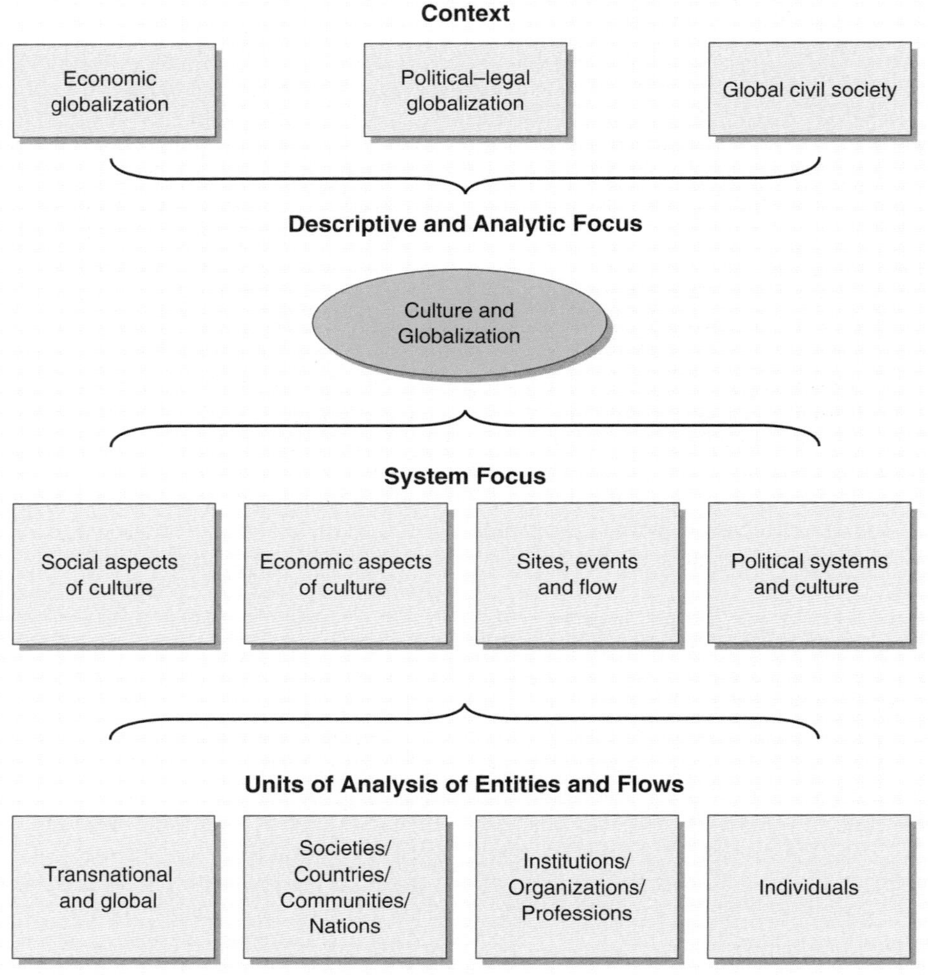

Table 2 presents the implementation of the framework. It shows the context of globalization, and the four systemic views (social aspects of culture; economic aspects of culture; culture as a system of sites, events and flows; and culture as a political system). Each 'lens' is broken down into major components and sub-components that make up individual indicator suites. For example, the social aspects of culture are broken down into values and institutions, knowledge, and practices and heritage. In turn, values are further refined in terms of identities (individual and collective), economic, social, political values, religious values and institutions, and gender. The result is an integrated, thematic hierarchy of indicators on the relationship between culture and globalization, and contextualized in relation to other globalization processes and patterns.

How to develop and present indicator suites

The notion of indicator suites is informed by Tufte's (1997; 2001) groundbreaking approach to the visual display of quantitative information, and the use of graphics in suggesting interpretations. In a departure

Table 2 Indicator Suite Matrix

The Context of Culture	Economic Globalization	Global Civil Society	Political & Legal Globalization
	• Trade flows, TNCs	• Extensity and intensity	International organizations rule of law and treaties
Social Aspects of Culture	Values and Institutions • Identities • Economics • Social • Political • Religious • Gender • Religious institutions	Knowledge • Creation • Dissemination • Storage • Innovation and Protection	Heritage and Practices • Heritage Preservation & Destruction • Environment • Participation • Sports
Economic Aspects of Culture	Economy • Industries • Global arts market • Cultural consumption & expenditures • Trade in goods and services	Professions • Artistic and cultural industries professions	Corporations and Organizations • Transnational cultural corporations • Cultural INGOs and foundations
Sites, Events and Flow	Global sites and events • Global cities • Symbolic sites and significant cities • Global events	Communication and media • Languages • Print media • Books • Music • Movies • TV & radio • TV & online news • Internet • Blogs • Telephones	Movements and communities • Transportation-Airports • Tourism • Migration • Refugees & asylum seekers • Transnational communities • Transnational social/cultural movements
Political System and Culture	Regulatory frameworks • International regulatory frameworks and agencies • International standards	Policy • Cultural diplomacy organizations	Conflict and cooperation • Current conflicts and tensions • Terrorism • Conflict resolution and UN peacekeeping • Human rights • Arms • Transnational crime – Corruption • Transnational crime – Piracy

from conventional approaches to indicators, we would neither seek to list data for indicators by country, nor strive to have a uniform layout for indicators in tabular fashion; rather we would use indicator suites and show indicator characteristics by units of analysis that seem appropriate for the purpose at hand, even if the presentation will be different across indicator suites.

The basic idea behind the notion of indicator suites is that indicators of different units of analysis, and even with incomplete data, can still be brought together in a thematic (and not in primarily statistical) way, and generate insights about relevant aspects of the relationships between cultures and globalization. What combines, and perhaps even unites, indicators to a suite is not some statistical rationale but a conceptual, qualitative one. For example, indicators or cultural tourism in terms of demand and spending, or destinations and travel patterns across the world, involve different units of analysis and time-frames, and may well vary in data coverage and quality. Hence from a statistical perspective, it would be difficult to combine these multiple indicators into one or even two.

Yet conceptually, this limitation can be a virtue: using separate indicators that capture different characteristics of phenomena such as cultural tourism or global arts markets may nonetheless allow for a qualitatively fuller presentation, description, and interpretation. Knowledge of the complexity of cultural phenomena and the paucity of comparable data leads us to search for, and embrace, diversity in measurements, (i.e., indicators), and aim for cohesion in presentation and suggested interpretations, (i.e., indicator suites).

In methodological terms, therefore, we are using (mostly) quantitative information in a (mostly) qualitative way. Indicator suites are a compromise in the sense that they take the patchy and incomplete state of quantitative cultural indicators as given, at least for the medium term, and refuse to accept the interpretative limitation this state imposes on analysis. In other words, indicator suites make do with what is empirically available, and suggest a 'story line' that is presented to diverse audiences.

The development of indicator suites is an iterative, almost hermeneutic process, as shown in Figure 2. It begins with the identification of a theme or topic, for example, communication and media. Bringing in previous indicator work on this topic, this is broken down into various dimensions such as print media, books, blogs, news and online news, music, movies, TV, radio, phones, and Internet. In each case, the questions become: What do we want to know about this topic in the context of cultural globalization, and why? And, what are some of the key policy implications and issues the data could suggest or illuminate?

For example, for the dimensions TV and Online news, it was important to learn how the viewer number and patterns of major global news outlets differ amongst each other, and what this suggests for information policy. These outlets collect, prepare and disseminate news for millions of viewers; if we include via wire services, this adds many more listeners and readers. Therefore these outlets have a major impact on global awareness and information availability as well as access. This required a look at online news consumption and audience profiles for each of the major outlets.

As the last example suggests, once we have conceptual and policy-related justification for a particular topic, an initial operationalization (news consumption, audience profile, etc.) leads to a search for possible indicators and data, with a continued process of data evaluation, incorporating data sets, and preparing them for analysis (see Figure 2). The intermediary product is an initial indicator suite that is then assessed in terms of parsimony, significance, combinatorial richness, organizing power, theoretical fruitfulness, and policy relevance. For example, the indicator suite on 'books' includes four major dimensions or subtopics:

- Annual number of books published by language and region
- The largest book markets by volume and market value
- The market share, subsidiaries and holdings of major publishers in different regions
- The number of book publishers by country.

We arrived at the relatively small number of indicators in a iterative fashion by examining alternative indicators, measures and data suggested in previous work on the subject or presented by agencies such as UNESCO's Institute of Statistics. Taken together, this parsimonious set of indicators pointed to what seems significant in the context of culture and globalization: the rise of large publishing corporations in the context of changing technologies and business models. It allowed us to relate changes in the book industry to the Internet

Figure 2 Developing Indicator Suites

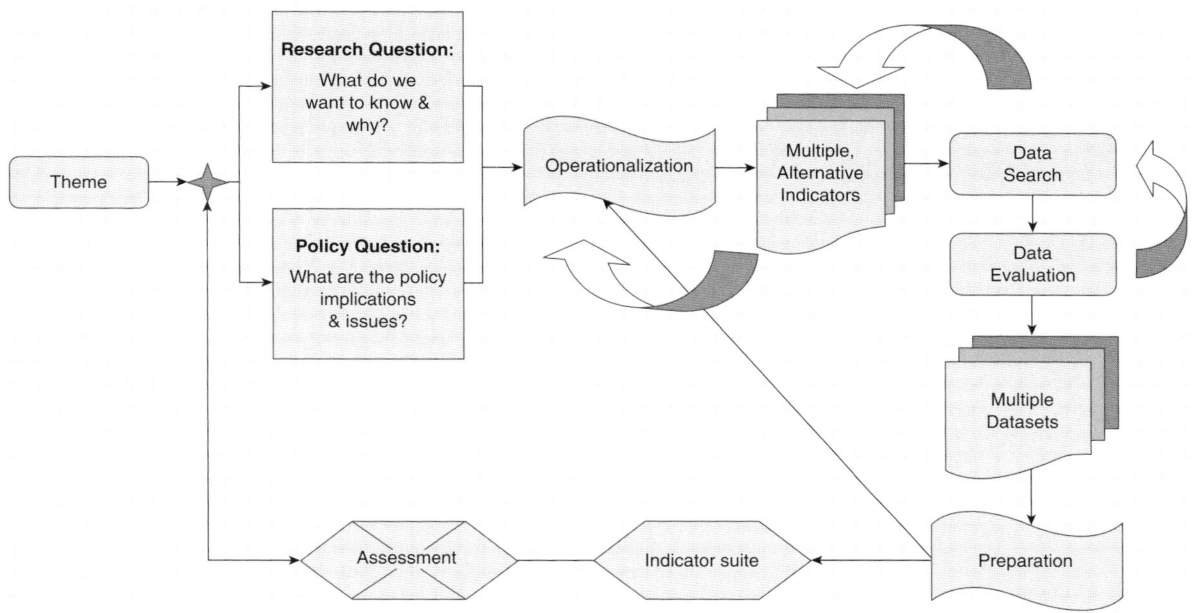

suite, the print media suite as well as others. In other words, it helped gain organizing power and combinational richness for interpretative purposes.

The data for the indicator suite on the Internet is different, of course, and offers indicators on broadband subscribers, growth in Internet usage across world regions, and the distribution of public wireless access points, among others. The suite on global arts markets includes data on major auction houses, art dealers and galleries, leading artists, etc. The indicator suites combine structural and flow measures, and make use of maps, charts and figures rather than long and complex tabular presentations. The various elements of such indicatory suites are graphically presented on double page spreads, with digests pointing to major findings, showing connections, suggesting interpretations, and providing further references and source material.

Of course, given the pioneering nature of this exercise, meeting the standards of parsimony, significance, combinatorial richness, organizing power, theoretical fruitfulness, and policy relevance is our medium- to long-term goal, and can barely be achieved in a first attempt such as the one presented here. We are aware of some of the major gaps in the indicator system. Among the most serious omissions are: indicator suites on human sexuality, food, fashion, design, architecture, performing arts and theater companies etc. Only lack of resources and time has prevented us from covering these topics in this edition of the *Series* and we are set to expand coverage in future volumes. Moreover, for those topics covered that year, it is important to keep in mind that the assessment and development of indicator suites is an open-ended process. It typically involves two, three and often more 'cycles' of interaction between topic identification and justification, indicator review and selection, data collection and analysis, and suite construction.

In terms of data gathering, we did not collect original data, and relied on secondary data exclusively. Virtually all of the data collected for the indicator suites presented here come from the great wealth and variety of online data sources available on the Internet. Of course, we are well aware that while much information is increasingly available online, much other useful information is not. The Internet, perhaps less so than more conventional data repositories, is biased in the information available and retrievable. Like others who have worked in the field of cultural indicators, we were frequently frustrated by the lack of data outside the developed world. We hope to improve the coverage of non-Western sources and data in future volumes.

Conclusion

An integrated display of indicator suites together with narrative description and analysis is meant to provide an overview of the main dimensions and contours of culture in both the broad and the narrow senses of the word. The list of indicator suites and indicators, including their operationalization and justification, is not fixed and will certainly develop and improve over time, and in consultation with international and national statistical offices as well as experts in the field. We hope to garner encouragement and constructive criticism as our work continues and as we seek to perfect what is presently little more than an initial attempt to come to terms with one of the most vexing of data problems in the social sciences.

Each volume of this *Series* includes only a portion of the full range of the indicators and data used in constructing indicator suites, with additional material available to readers on a dedicated website, Finally, as each volume takes a particular thematic focus (e.g., cultural conflicts; the cultural economy, the arts and creativity etc.), we will place a special focus on indicator suites that highlight the dimensions and trends of particular relevance to that year's topic. In this volume, the focus on cultural conflicts offers information on the frequency and patterns of different conflicts, including terrorism, and the cleavage structures and 'fault lines' involved.

Notes

1 In recent years, a number of international conferences have produced useful material on cultural indicators, mostly in the context of international statistics. See, for example: International Symposium on Culture Statistics, Montreal, October 2002, http://www.colloque2002symposium.gouv.qc.ca/h4v_page_accueil_fr.htm); *Taking the Measure of Culture*,Princeton University, New Jersey, June 7–8, 2002, http://www.princeton.edu/culturalpolicy/moc.html; *International Symposium on Culture Statistics*, Montreal, October 2002 http://www.colloque2002symposium.gouv.qc.ca/h4v_page_accueil_an.htm; UNESCO/CONACULTA *International Seminar on Cultural Indicators*, Centro Nacional de las Artes, Mexico, DF, Mexico, 7–9 May 2003, http://sic.conaculta.gob.mx/seminario/menu.html, or the *Experts meeting on cultural indicators,* Interarts, Barcelona, 20–21 November 2003.

2 IFACCA (2005) offers a useful and comprehensive overview of the state of the art in the field of cultural indicators.

3 See Pignataro (2003), Brown and Corbett (1997), and Adams et al. (2004) on similar sets of criteria that are more geared towards indicator assessments.

REFERENCES

Adams, T., Ahonen, P., and Fisher, R. (2004) *An International Evaluation of the Finnish System of Arts Councils.* Finland: Ministry of Education. http://www.minedu.fi/julkaisut/kulttuuri/2004/opm3/AnInternational.pdf.

Anheier, H.K. (2004) *Civil Society: Measurement and Policy Dialogue.* London: Earthscan.

Beck, U. (2001) 'The postnational society and its enemies'. Public Lecture: London School of Economics and Political Science, 24 February.

Bonet, L. (2004) 'Reflexiones a Propósito de Indicadores y Estadísticas Culturales', *Gestión Cultural*, No. 7(abril). http://www.gestioncultural.org/boletin/pdf/Indicadores/LBonet-Indicadores.pdf.

Brown, B., and Corbett, T. (1997) *Social Indicators and Public Policy in the Age of Devolution,* Institute for Research on Poverty, Special Report No. 71. http//www.ssc.wisc.edu/irp/ sr/sr71.pdf

Deutsch, K.W. (1963) *The Nerves of Government.* New York: The Free Press.

Duxbury, N. (2003) *Cultural Indicators and Benchmarks in Community Indicator Projects: Performance Measures for Cultural Investment?* Canada: Strategic Research and

Analysis, Department of Canadian Heritage. http://www.culturescope.ca/ev_en.php?ID=3707_201&ID2=DO_TOPIC.

European Commission (2000) *Cultural Statistics in the EU: Final Report of the LEG*. Eurostat Working Paper, European Commission. http://www.utexas.edu/cofa/ unesco/documents/FINALREP.DOC.

Fukuda-Parr, S. (2001) *In Search of Indicators of Culture and Development: Review of Progress and Proposals for Next Steps*. Second Global Forum on Human Development, Brazil, 9-10 October 2000. Text available on-line at: http://hdr.undp.org/docs/events/global_forum/2000/fukudaparr2.pdf.

Glade, W. (2003) 'Conceptualization and measurement problems in developing cross-national cultural indicators: a methodological odyssey'. A paper prepared for UNESCO/CONACULTA International Seminar on Cultural Indicators, Centro Nacional de las Artes, Mexico, DF, Mexico, 7–9 May. http://www.utexas.edu/cofa/unesco/documents/Glade%20paper.pdf or http://sic.conaculta.gob.mx/seminario/menu.html

Goldstone, L. (1998) 'Measuring Culture: Prospects and Limits', in UNESCO, *World Culture Report: Culture, Creativity and Markets*. Paris: UNESCO.

Huntington, S.P. (1996) *The Clash of Civilizations and the Remarking of World Order*. New York: Simon & Schuster.

International Federation of Arts Councils and Culture Agencies (IFACCA) (2005) *Statistical Indicators for Arts Policy*. Sydney: IFACCA. http://www.ifacca.org/ifacca2/en/organisation/page09_BrowseDart.asp.

Kleberg, C.-J. (2003) 'International co-operation for cultural policy motivated research: setbacks and promises', *Culturelink*, No. 40, Vol. 14: 99–132.

Küng, H. (1998) *A Global Ethic for Global Politics and Economics*. Oxford: Oxford University Press.

Matarasso, F. (2001) *Cultural Indicators: A Preliminary Review of Issues Raised by Current Approaches*. Comedia. http://www.comedia.org.uk/downloads/ACEIND-1.DOC.

Mercer, C. (2002) *Towards Cultural Citizenship: Tools for Cultural Policy and Development*. Stockholm: Bank of Sweden Tercentenary Foundation: Hedemora.

Pignataro, G. (2003) 'Performance Indicators', in R. Towse (ed.), *A Handbook of Cultural Economics*. Cheltenham: Edward Elgar. http://ep.eur.nl/retrieve/1379/TOWSE+EBOOK_pages0378-0384.pdf.

Scholte, J.-A. (1999) 'Globalization: Prospects for Paradigm Shift', in M. Shaw (ed.), *Politics and Globalization*. London: Routledge.

Schuster, J. (2002) *'Informing cultural policy – data, statistics, and meaning*. Paper presented at International Symposium on Culture Statistics, Montreal, October 21–23. http://www.colloque2002symposium.gouv.qc.ca/PDF/Schuster_paper_Symposium.pdf

Tufte, E. (1997) *Visual Explanations: Images and Quantities, Evidence and Narrative*. Cheshire, CT: Graphics Press.

– (2001) *The Visual Display of Quantitative Information*. Cheshire, CT: Graphics Press.

UNESCO/UNRISD (1997) 'Towards a World Report on Culture and Development: Constructing Cultural Statistics and Indicators, Report of the Workshop on Cultural Indicators of Development'. *UNRISD/UNESCO Occasional paper series on culture and development, Number 1*, Paris.

UNESCO (1998) *World Culture Report: Culture, Creativity and Markets*. Paris: UNESCO Publishing.

UNESCO (2000) *World Culture Report: Cultural Diversity, Conflict and Pluralism*. Paris: UNESCO Publishing.

United Nations Development Programme (2000) *Human Development Report 2000: Human Development and Human Rights*. New York: Oxford University Press.

Wiesand, A. (2002) 'Comparative cultural policy research in Europe: a change of paradigm', *Canadian Journal of Communication*, Vol. 27: 369–78. http://www.cjc-online.ca/title.php3?page=24&journal_id=43.

World Commission on Culture and Development (1996) *Our Creative Diversity: Report of the World Commission on Culture and Development*. Paris: UNESCO Publishing.

Wyszomirski, M. (1998) 'The arts and performance review, policy assessment, and program evaluation: focusing on the ends of the policy cycle', *Journal of Arts Management, Law and Society*, Vol. 28 (3): 191–99.

ECONOMIC GLOBALIZATION

TRADE FLOWS + TNCs

1a. OUTLOOK ON THE GLOBAL ECONOMY:

TRADE, AID, FOREIGN DIRECT INVESTMENT

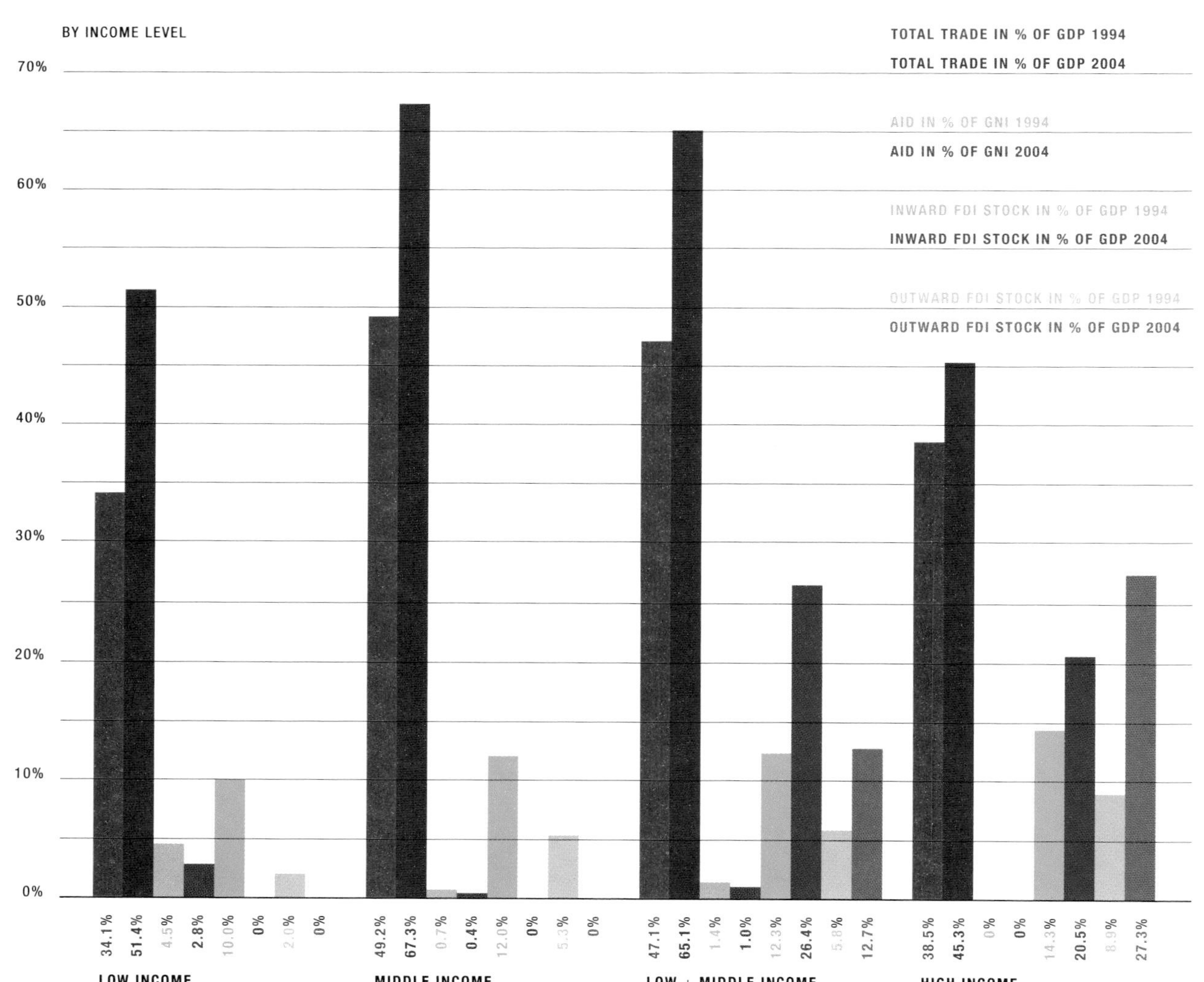

- **outlook on the global economy -** trade blocs: **trade in $us millions** 2003 + trade blocs: % **of world export** 2003
- 2003 top ten non-financial tnc's worldwide: **ranked by total foreign assets** + 2003 top ten non-financial tnc's worldwide: **ranked by transnationality index -** top twenty global companies: **rankings by forbes** (as of april 2006) **& fortune** (as of july 2005)

1b. OUTLOOK ON THE GLOBAL ECONOMY:

REMITTANCES BY INCOME LEVEL + **REGIONS** IN CURRENT $US MILLIONS + % OF CHANGE

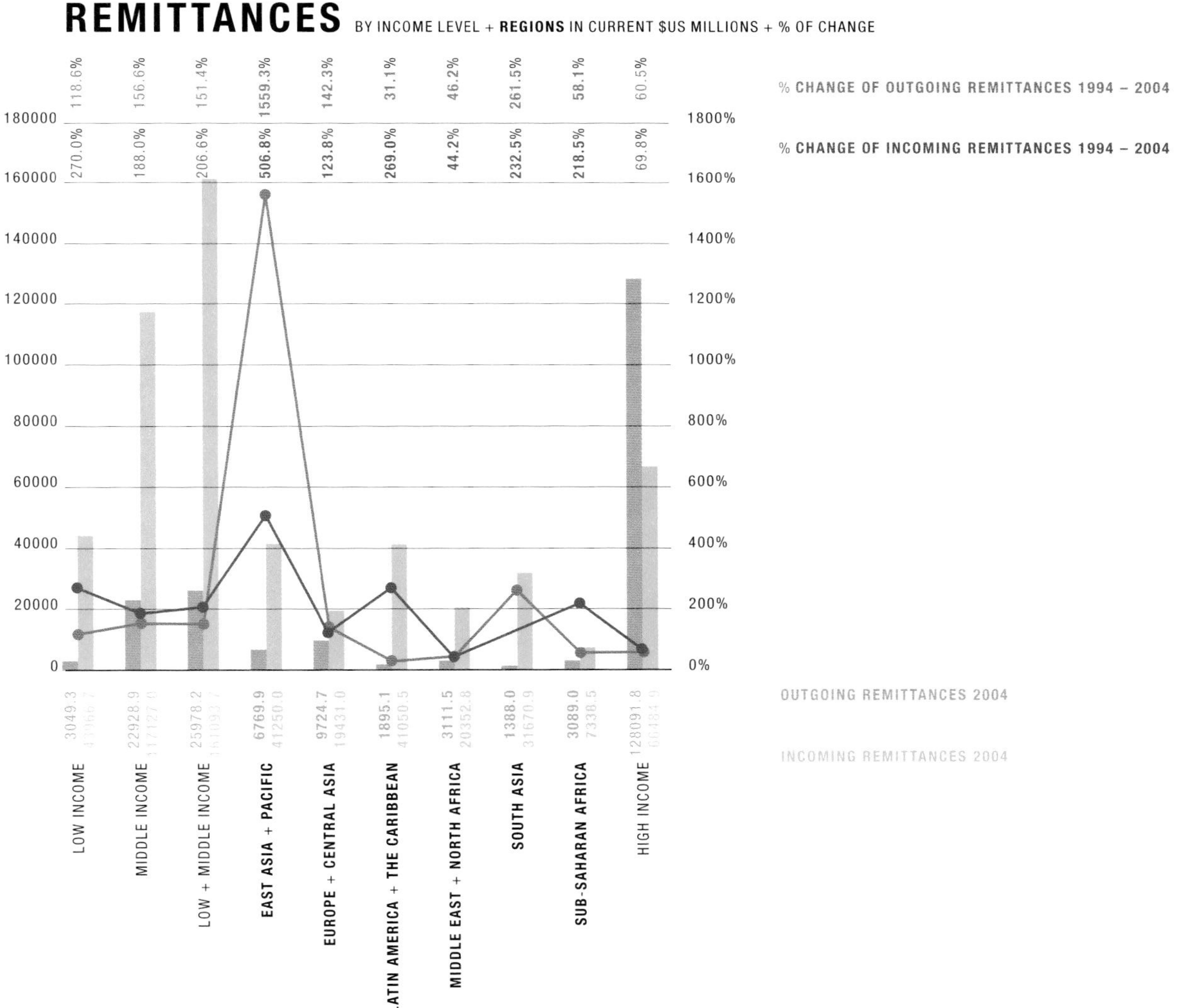

2a. REGIONAL TRADE BLOCS: % OF WORLD EXPORTS 2003

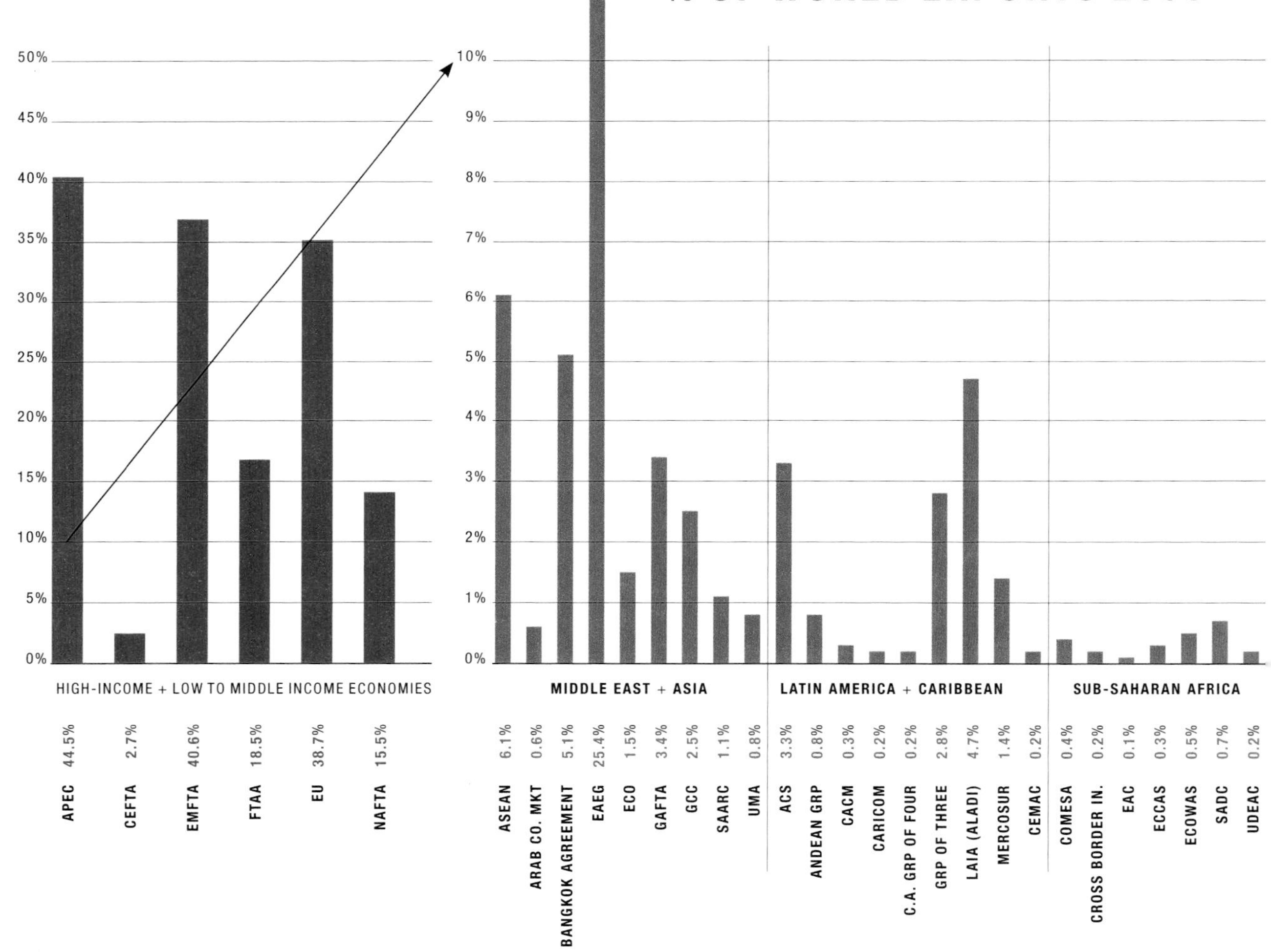

50%
45%
40%
35%
30%
25%
20%
15%
10%
5%
0%
HIGH-INCOME + LOW TO MIDDLE INCOME ECONOMIES
APEC 44.5%
CEFTA 2.7%
EMFTA 40.6%
FTAA 18.5%
EU 38.7%
NAFTA 15.5%
10%
9%
8%
7%
6%
5%
4%
3%
2%
1%
0%
MIDDLE EAST + ASIA
ASEAN 6.1%
ARAB CO. MKT 0.6%
BANGKOK AGREEMENT 5.1%
EAEG 25.4%
ECO 1.5%
GAFTA 3.4%
GCC 2.5%
SAARC 1.1%
UMA 0.8%
LATIN AMERICA + CARIBBEAN
ACS 3.3%
ANDEAN GRP 0.8%
CACM 0.3%
CARICOM 0.2%
C.A. GRP OF FOUR 0.2%
GRP OF THREE 2.8%
LAIA (ALADI) 4.7%
MERCOSUR 1.4%
CEMAC 0.2%
SUB-SAHARAN AFRICA
COMESA 0.4%
CROSS BORDER IN. 0.2%
EAC 0.1%
ECCAS 0.3%
ECOWAS 0.5%
SADC 0.7%
UDEAC 0.2%

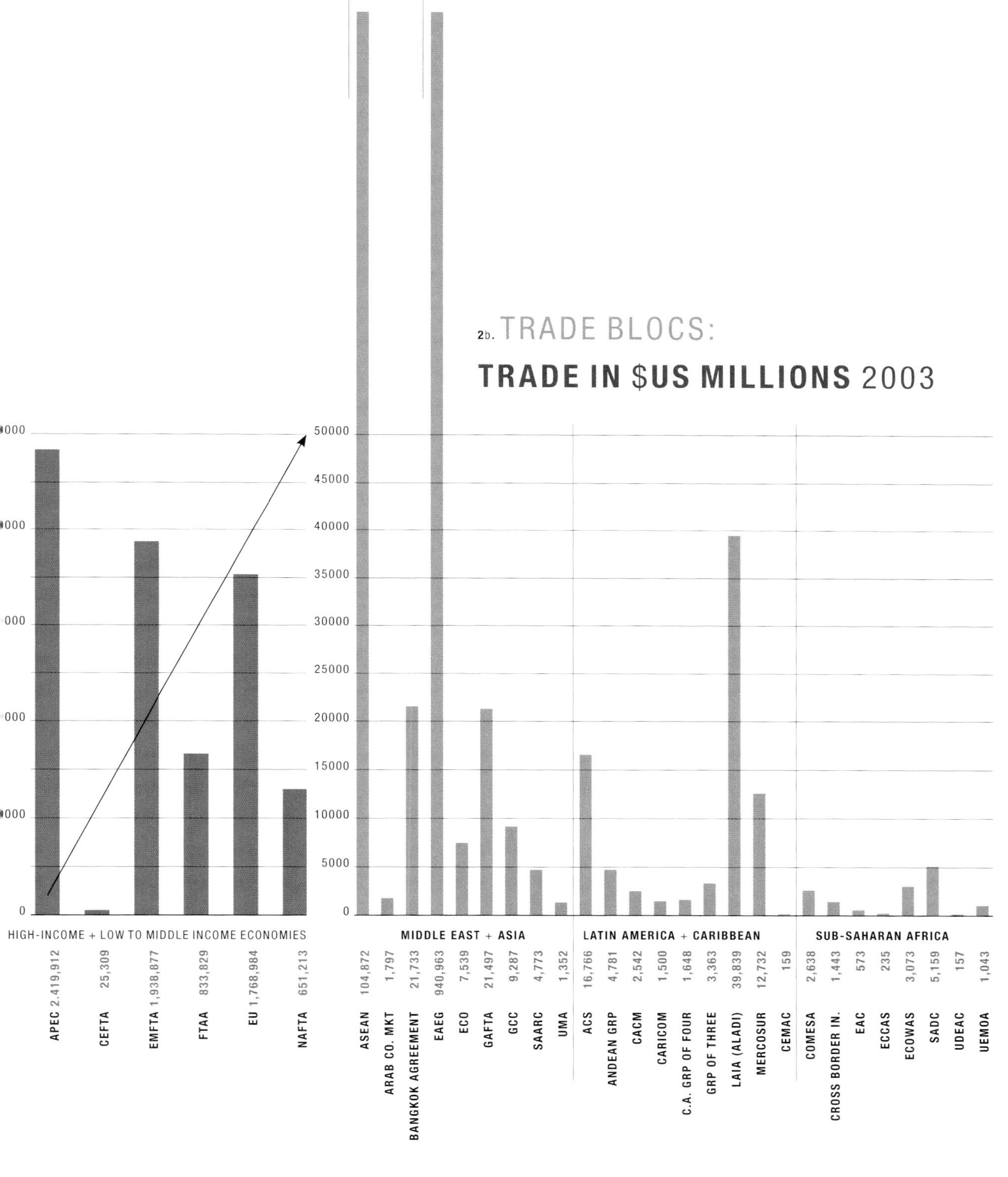
2b. TRADE BLOCS:
TRADE IN $US MILLIONS 2003
50000
45000
40000
35000
30000
25000
20000
15000
10000
5000
0
0
HIGH-INCOME + LOW TO MIDDLE INCOME ECONOMIES
MIDDLE EAST + ASIA
LATIN AMERICA + CARIBBEAN
SUB-SAHARAN AFRICA
APEC 2.419,912
CEFTA 25,309
EMFTA 1,938,877
FTAA 833,829
EU 1,768,984
NAFTA 651,213
ASEAN 104,872
ARAB CO. MKT 1,797
BANGKOK AGREEMENT 21,733
EAEG 940,963
ECO 7,539
GAFTA 21,497
GCC 9,287
SAARC 4,773
UMA 1,352
ACS 16,766
ANDEAN GRP 4,781
CACM 2,542
CARICOM 1,500
C.A. GRP OF FOUR 1,648
GRP OF THREE 3,363
LAIA (ALADI) 39,839
MERCOSUR 12,732
CEMAC 159
COMESA 2,638
CROSS BORDER IN. 1,443
EAC 573
ECCAS 235
ECOWAS 3,073
SADC 5,159
UDEAC 157
UEMOA 1,043

3a. TOP 10 NON-FINANCIAL TNCs WORLDWIDE 2003:

RANKED BY TOTAL FOREIGN ASSETS

BY $US MILLIONS + % **OF TOTAL**

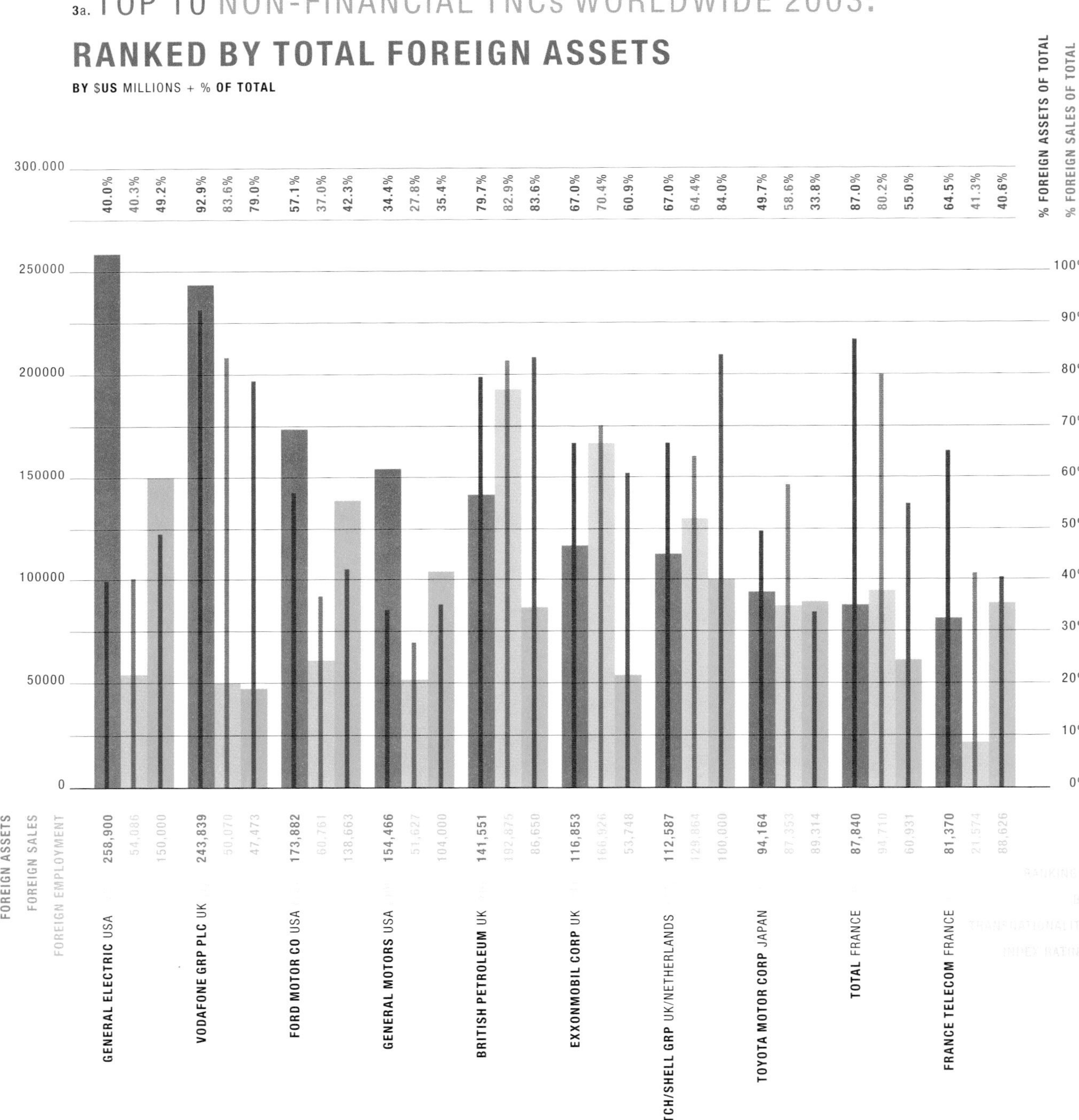

3b. TOP 10 NON-FINANCIAL TNCs WORLDWIDE 2003:

RANKED BY TRANSNATIONALITY INDEX RATING

BY $US MILLIONS + % **OF TOTAL**

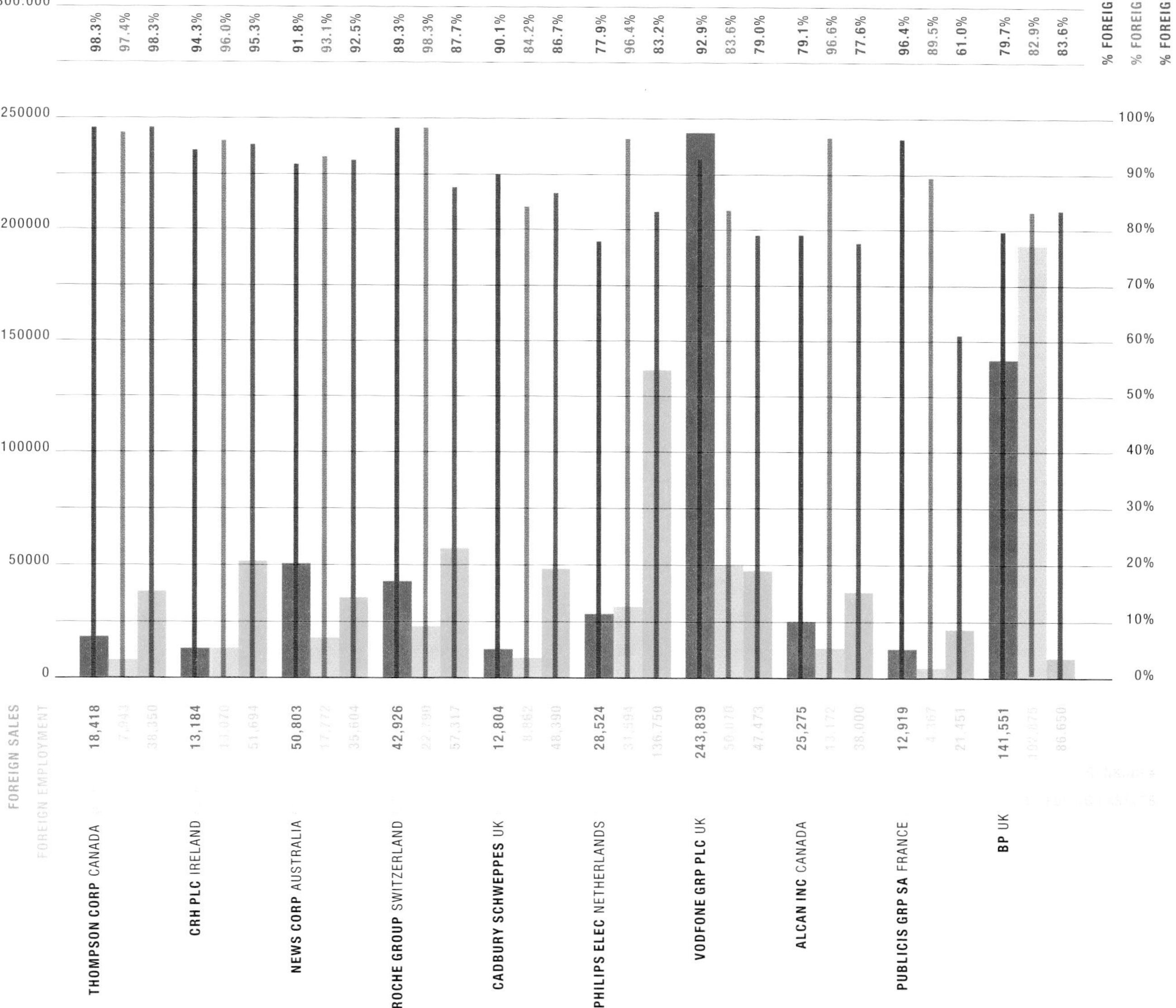

4. TOP 20 **CROSS-BORDER MERGERS + ACQUISITIONS** 2004: WITH VALUES OVER $1 **US** BILLION

RANK	VALUE	ACQUIRED COMPANY	INDUSTRY OF ACQUIRED COMPANY	ACQUIRING COMPANY	INDUSTRY OF ACQUIRED COMPAN
01	15.8	**ABBEY NATIONAL PLC** UNITED KINDOM	BANKING	**SANTANDER CENTRAL HISPANO SA** SPAIN	BANKING
02	11.1	**JOHN HANCOCK FINANCIAL** UNITED STATES	LIFE INSURANCE	**MANULIFE FINANCIAL CORP** CANADA	LIFE INSURANCE
03	10.5	**CHARTER ONE FINANCIAL** UNITED STATES	SAVINGS INSTITUTIONS, FEDERALLY CHARTERED	**CITIZENS FINL GRP** UNITED STATES	NATIONAL COMMERCIAL BANKS
04	9.6	**AMERSHAM PLC** UNITED KINGDOM	BIOLOGICAL PRODUCTS	**GENERAL ELECTRIC** UNITED STATES	POWER, DISTRIBUTION + SP. TRANSFORMERS
05	7.8	**JOHN LABATT INC** CANADA	MALT BEVERAGES	**AMBEV** BRAZIL	MALT BEVERAGES
06	4.5	**GAGFAH-HOUSING** GERMANY	DWELLING, OPERATORS, EXCEPT APARTMENTS	**FORTRESS DEUTSCHLAND GMBH**** GERMANY	INVESTORS, NEC
07	4	**BRACO SA** BRAZIL	MALT BEVERAGES	**INTERBREW SA** BELGIUM	MALT BEVERAGES
08	3.9	**EDISON MISSION ENERGY COMPANY** AUSTRALIA	COGENERATION, ALT. ENERGY SOURCES	**INVESTOR GROUP** UNITED KINGDOM	INVESTORS, NEC
09	3.9	**GRUPO FINANCIERO BBVA BANCOMER** MEXICO	BANKING	**BBVA** SPAIN	BANKING
10	3.7	**TXU AUSTRALIA LTD** AUSTRALIA	ELECTRIC SERVICES	**SINGAPORE POWER PTE LTD** UNITED STATES	INVESTORS, NEC
11	3.4	**SICOR INC** UNITED STATES	PHARMACEUTICAL PREPARATIONS	**TEVA PHARMA INDS LTD** ISRAEL	PHARMACEUTICAL PREPARATIONS
12	3.4	**MESSER GRIESHEIM-IND GAS OPS** GERMANY	INDUSTRIAL GASES	**AIR LIQUIDE SA** FRANCE	INDUSTRIAL GASES
13	3.1	**CANARY WHARF GROUP PLC** UNITED KINGDOM	LAND SUBDIVIDERS + DEVELOPERS EXCL. CEMETERIES	**SONGBIRD ACQUISITION LTD** UNITED STATES	INVESTORS, NEC
14	2.9	**DIAL CORPS** UNITED STATES	SOAP, DETERGENTS	**HENKEL KGAA** GERMANY	PERFUMES, COSMETICS ETC.
15	2.8	**MOORE WALLACE INC** CANADA	MANIFOLD BUSINESS FORMS	**RR DONNELLEY & SONS CO** UNITED STATES	COMMERCIAL PRINTING, LITHOGRAPHIC
16	2.7	**CELLTECH GROUP PLC** UNITED KINGDOM	COMMERCIAL PHYSICAL + BIOLOGICAL RESEARCH	**UCB SA** BELGIUM	MEDICINAL CHEMICALS + BOTANICAL PRODUC
17	2.7	**DYNAMIT NOBEL AG** GERMANY	EXPLOSIVES	**ROCKWOOD SPECIALITIES GRP** UNITED STATES	CHEMICALS + CHEMICAL PREPARATIONS
18	2.6	**HIDROCANTABRICO** SPAIN	ELECTRIC SERVICES	**EDP** PORTUGAL	ELECTRIC SERVICES
19	2.6	**VNU WORLD DIRECTORIES** NETHERLANDS	MISC. PUBLISHING	**INVESTOR GROUP** UNITED KINGDOM	INVESTORS, NEC
20	2.4	**JC PENNY-ECKERD STORES** UNITED STATES	DRUG STORES + PROPRIETARY	**JEAN COUTU GROUP** CANADA	DRUG STORES + PROPRIETARY

* PARENT COMPANY OF CHARTER ONE FINANCIAL IS IN SCOTLAND

** PARENT COMPANY OF FORTRESS IS BASED IN NEW YORK, USA

GLOBAL CIVIL SOCIETY

EXTENSITY + INTENSITY

EXTENSITY + INTENSITY

- ngo's + un consultative status - top 10: **ngo secretariat countries** + top 10: **ngo secretariat cities -**

location of ngo meetings by region + top 10: **ngo meeting locations** by country **- parallel summits** by type +

parallel summits by location + **parallel summits** by relation to official summit **- growth of ingo's since 1900**

- wto ministerial conference attendance

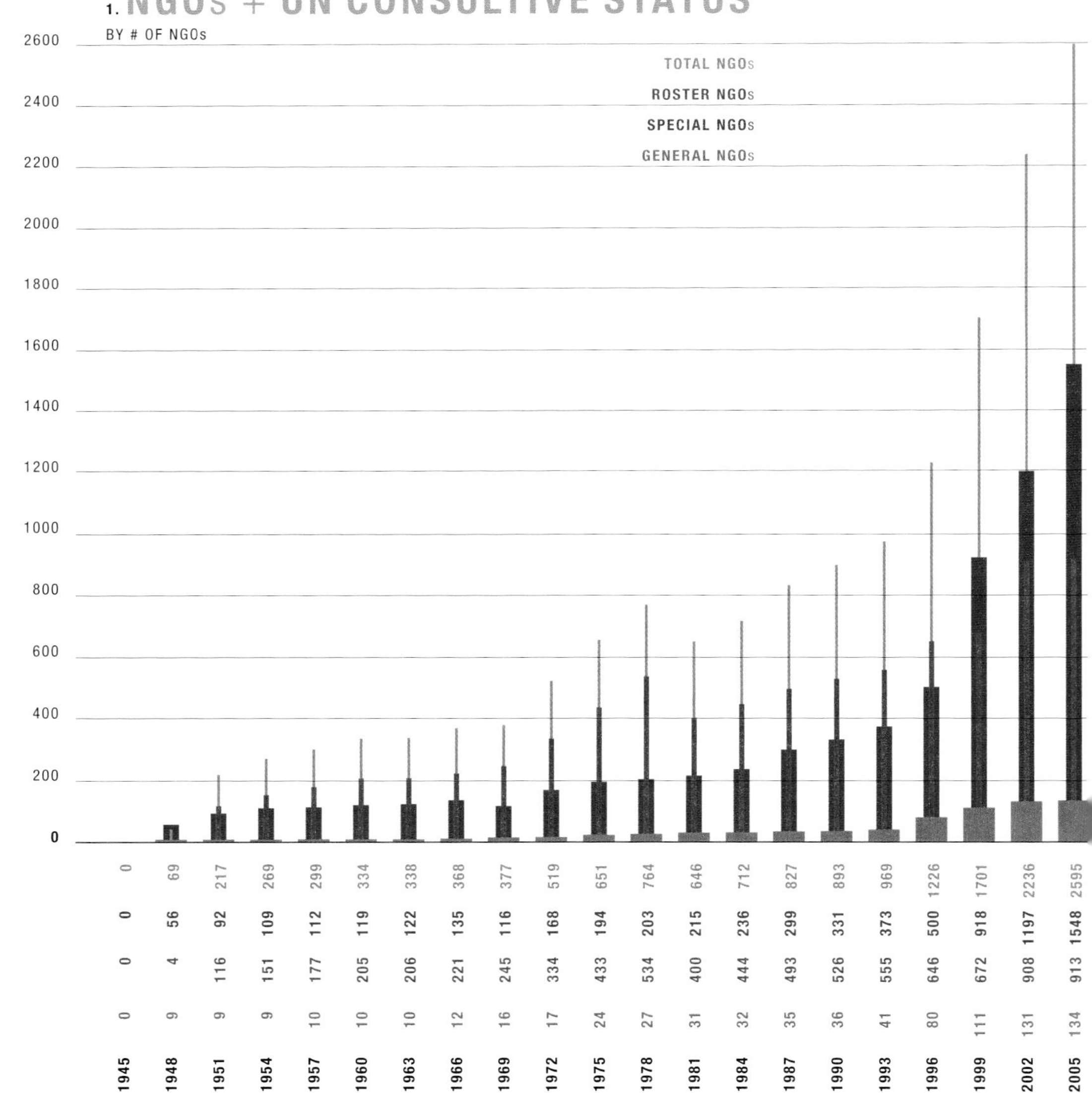

1945	1948	1951	1954	1957	1960	1963	1966	1969	1972	1975	1978	1981	1984	1987	1990	1993	1996	1999	2002	2005
0	69	217	269	299	334	338	368	377	519	651	764	646	712	827	893	969	1226	1701	2236	2595
0	56	92	109	112	119	122	135	116	168	194	203	215	236	299	331	373	500	918	1197	1548
0	4	116	151	177	205	206	221	245	334	433	534	400	444	493	526	555	646	672	908	913
0	9	9	9	10	10	10	12	16	17	24	27	31	32	35	36	41	80	111	131	134

2. TOP 10: NGO SECRETARIATS

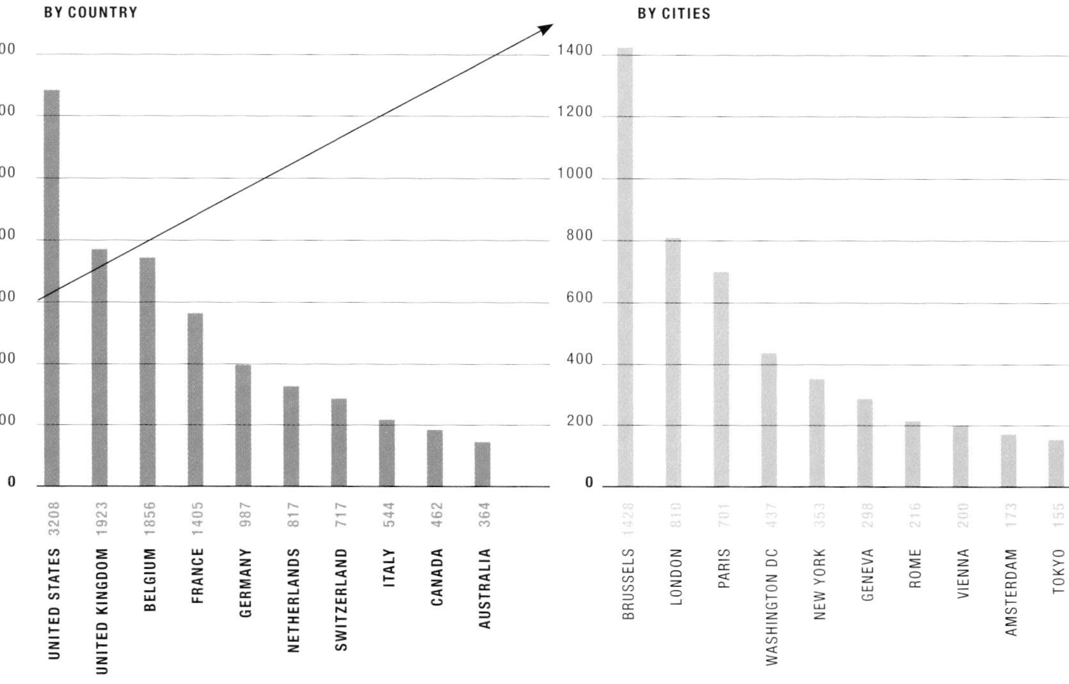

3. LOCATION OF NGO MEETINGS

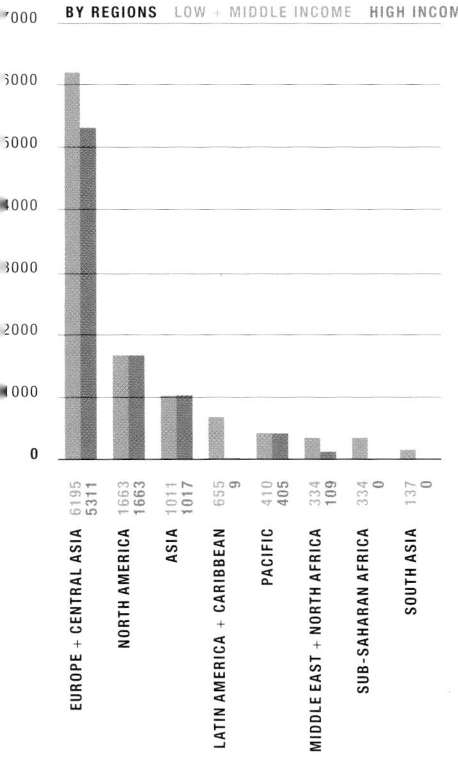

TOP 10: NGO MEETING LOCATIONS

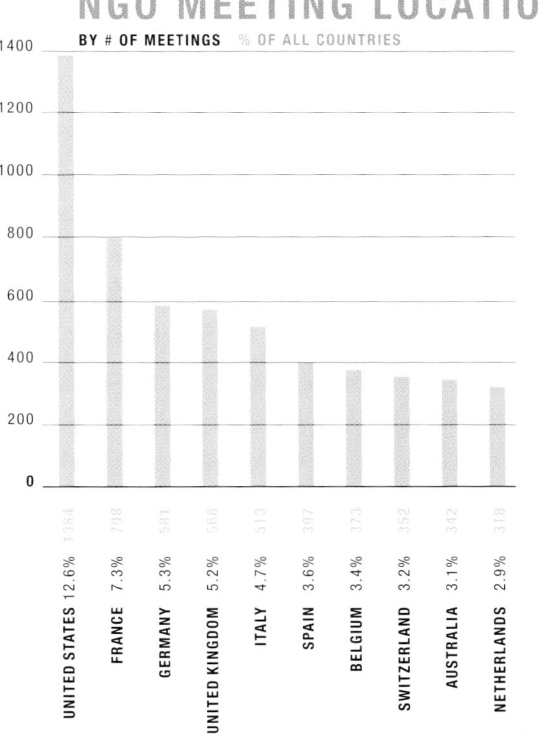

4a. PARALLEL SUMMITS: **BY TYPE OF CONFERENCE**

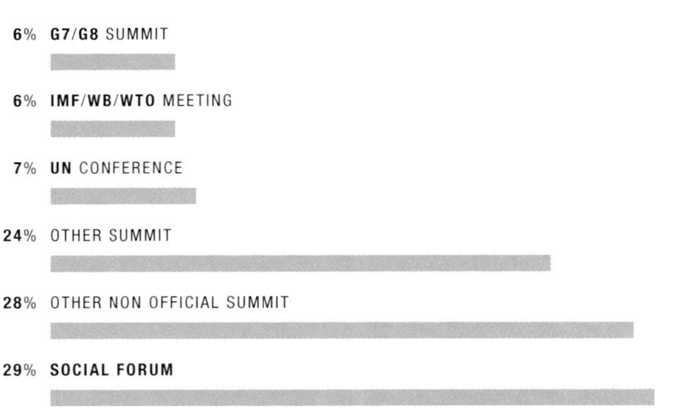

4b. PARALLEL SUMMITS: **BY LOCATION OF CONFERENCE**

4c. PARALLEL SUMMITS: **BY RELATION TO OFFICIAL SUMMIT**

5. WTO **MINISTERIAL CONFERENCE ATTENDANC**

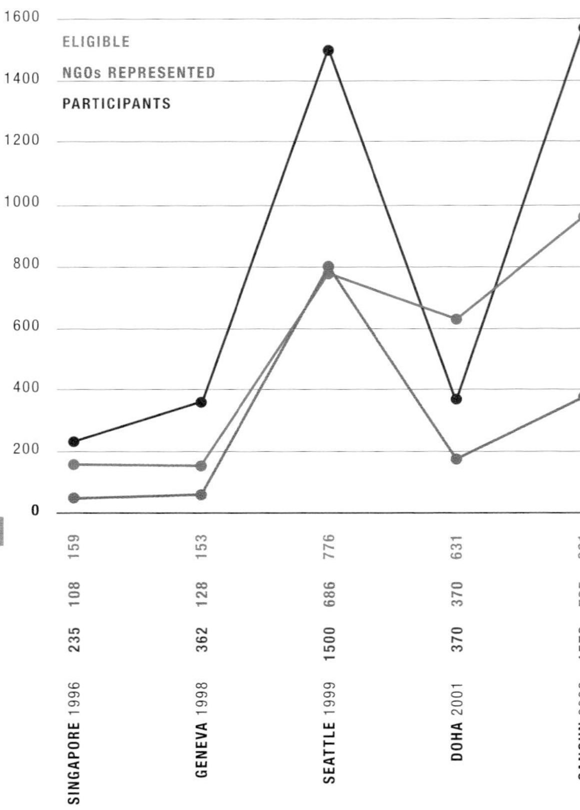

POLITICAL + LEGAL GLOBALIZATION

INTERNATIONAL ORGANIZATIONS

RULE OF LAW + TREATIES

INTERNATIONAL ORGANIZATIONS

1. RECORD OF TREATIES SIGNED OR RATIFIED BY TOP AND BOTTOM PERFORMERS

COUNTRIES THAT HAVE SIGNED ALL 22 MAJOR HUMAN RIGHTS, HUMANITARIAN + ENVIRONMENTAL TREATIES	COUNTRIES THAT HAVE RATIFIED MORE THAN 5 TREATIES SINCE 2000	COUNTRIES THAT HAVE SIGNED 5 OR FEWER TREATIES SINCE 2000	COUNTRIES THAT HAVE RATIFIED ZERO TREATIES SINCE 2000
AUSTRIA	AFGHANISTAN	BHUTAN	EL SALVADOR
BELGIUM	AZERBAIJAN	BRUNEI	IRAQ
BULGARIA	CAPE VERDE	IRAQ	SINGAPORE
CANADA	DJIBOUTI	MYANMAR	UNITED STATES
COLUMBIA	EQUATORIAL GUINEA	SINGAPORE	UZBEKISTAN
COSTA RICA	ERITREA	SOMALIA	
CYPRUS	GHANA	TONGA	
DENMARK	INDONESIA + EAST TIMOR	UNITED STATES	
ECUADOR	LIBERIA		
ESTONIA	LITHUANIA		
GERMANY	SERBIA & MONTENEGRO		
GREECE	ST. VINCENT + THE GRENADINES		
HUNGARY	SUDAN		
ICELAND	SWAZILAND		
IRELAND	YUGOSLAVIA		
ITALY			
LITHUANIA			
LUXEMBOURG			
MACEDONIA			
NETHERLANDS			
NORWAY			
PANAMA			
PARAGUAY			
ROMANIA			
SLOVAKIA			
SLOVENIA			
SPAIN			
SWEDEN			
URUGUAY			

2. HOW MANY COUNTRIES HAVE SIGNED HOW MANY TREATIES?

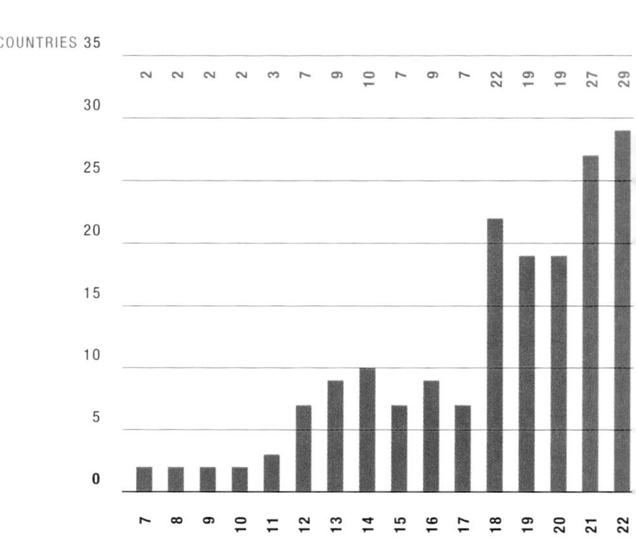

RULE OF LAW + TREATIES

- **record of treaties signed and ratified** by top and bottom performers - treaties signed: **how many countries have signed how many treaties**? - **how many countries have ratified how many treaties since 2000**? - # of **countries signing and ratifying specific treaties** by region - wef: **can the world economic forum solve our global governance problems**? - wef: **key players in global governance issues** by % of experts rating them as effective - wbi: **average percentile rank on world bank governance indicators** 2004 - un budget: **size of the united nations budget** in us $ millions - international court: **states involved in three or more contentious cases in the international criminal court** - interpol: % **increase in communications between interpol and each region** between 2002 and 2004 - interpol: **total expenditure of interpol** 2000–2005 in thousands of euros

3. HOW MANY COUNTRIES HAVE RATIFIED HOW MANY TREATIES SINCE 2000?

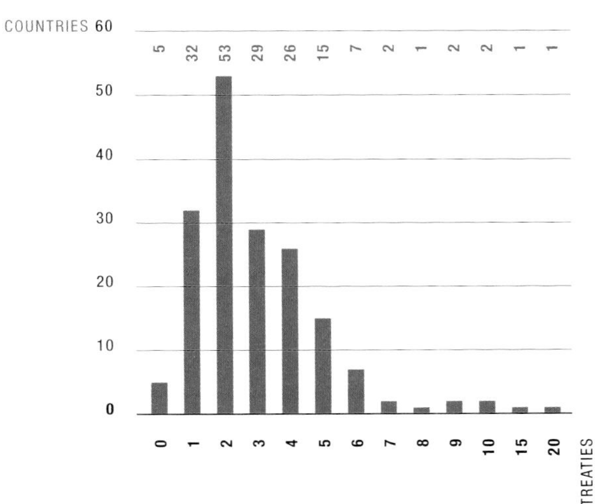

5. CAN THE WORLD ECONOM

26% UNLIKELY

14% VERY UNLIKELY

4. # OF COUNTRIES SIGNING AND RATIFYING SPECIFIC TREATIES

	HUMAN RIGHTS											HUMANITARIAN LAW						ENVIRONMENTAL LAW			
	ICESCR	ICCPR	ICCPR-OP1	ICCPR-OP2	CERD	CEDAW	CAT	Gen	ILO 87	CSR	ICC	CWC	BWC	LMC	Geneva	Prot 1	Prot 2	BC	CBD	UNFCCC	KP
EAST ASIA + PACIFIC																					
TOTAL COUNTRIES SIGNING	**13**	**11**	**5**	**3**	**16**	**21**	**9**	**16**	**9**	**12**	**8**	**21**	**21**	**13**	**23**	**16**	**15**	**16**	**22**	**22**	**17**
RATIFIED SINCE 2000	2	1	0	1	1	2	1		2	1	7	7	0	4	0	3	3	3	1	0	15
EUROPE + CENTRAL ASIA																					
TOTAL COUNTRIES SIGNING	**48**	**48**	**42**	**34**	**48**	**48**	**48**	**46**	**47**	**47**	**35**	**48**	**42**	**38**	**48**	**46**	**46**	**47**	**48**	**48**	**39**
RATIFIED SINCE 2000	4	4	3	7	4	1	3	3	4	5	34	5	1	12	2	4	3	5	4	5	36
LATIN AMERICA + CARIBBEAN																					
TOTAL COUNTRIES SIGNING	**24**	**26**	**21**	**0**	**29**	**29**	**21**	**25**	**27**	**24**	**19**	**26**	**26**	**28**	**29**	**28**	**27**	**27**	**29**	**29**	**28**
RATIFIED SINCE 2000	0	0	3	0	3	0	2	3	2	2	18	7	0	8	0	1	1	3	0	0	19
MIDDLE EAST + NORTH AFRICA																					
TOTAL COUNTRIES SIGNING	**15**	**15**	**4**	**2**	**19**	**18**	**16**	**16**	**10**	**9**	**3**	**18**	**15**	**7**	**20**	**16**	**16**	**19**	**19**	**19**	**17**
RATIFIED SINCE 2000	1	1	1	1	1	5	4	1	1	0	3	4	2	2	0	0	2	3	5	0	17
NORTH AMERICA																					
TOTAL COUNTRIES SIGNING	**1**	**2**	**1**	**1**	**2**	**1**	**2**	**2**	**1**	**1**	**1**	**2**	**2**	**1**	**2**	**1**	**1**	**1**	**1**	**2**	**1**
RATIFIED SINCE 2000	0	0	0	1	0	0	0	0	0	0	1	0	0	0	0	0	0	0	0	0	1
SOUTH ASIA																					
TOTAL COUNTRIES SIGNING	**5**	**5**	**2**	**1**	**7**	**8**	**5**	**7**	**4**	**1**	**1**	**8**	**7**	**4**	**8**	**2**	**2**	**7**	**8**	**8**	**7**
RATIFIED SINCE 2000	0	1	0	0	0	1	0	0	0	1	1	2	0	4	0	0	0	1	1	0	6
SUB-SAHARAN AFRICA																					
TOTAL COUNTRIES SIGNING	**41**	**43**	**28**	**5**	**43**	**43**	**35**	**23**	**42**	**41**	**26**	**39**	**27**	**45**	**46**	**44**	**42**	**39**	**45**	**41**	**33**
RATIFIED SINCE 2000	5	6	5	3	5	2	12	3	9	1	24	13	2	26	1	1	2	16	1	3	33
LOW INCOME ECONOMIES																					
TOTAL COUNTRIES SIGNING	**56**	**56**	**34**	**6**	**59**	**62**	**44**	**42**	**53**	**51**	**27**	**56**	**42**	**51**	**65**	**54**	**50**	**52**	**64**	**60**	**51**
RATIFIED SINCE 2000	3	4	4	0	3	4	6	1	8	1	24	9	1	24	1	0	2	10	3	5	30
MIDDLE INCOME ECONOMIES																					
TOTAL COUNTRIES SIGNING	**65**	**67**	**48**	**26**	**74**	**76**	**63**	**63**	**62**	**58**	**43**	**75**	**67**	**61**	**78**	**69**	**69**	**72**	**77**	**77**	**65**
RATIFIED SINCE 2000	5	4	6	7	5	1	6	2	6	5	38	12	1	18	1	4	4	10	5	3	43
HIGH INCOME ECONOMIES																					
TOTAL COUNTRIES SIGNING	**26**	**27**	**21**	**21**	**31**	**30**	**29**	**30**	**25**	**26**	**23**	**31**	**31**	**24**	**33**	**30**	**30**	**32**	**31**	**32**	**26**
RATIFIED SINCE 2000	0	0	0	0	1	1	2	1	1	0	22	1	0	1	0	2	1	1	2	0	20

FORUM SOLVE OUR GLOBAL GOVERNANCE PROBLEMS?

35% NEUTRAL

24% LIKELY

2% VERY LIKELY

SCR - INTERNATIONAL COVENANT ON **ECONOMIC, SOCIAL AND CULTURAL RIGHT** AS OF JUNE 9, 2004

PR - INTERNATIONAL COVENANT ON **CIVIL AND POLITICAL RIGHTS** AS OF JUNE 9, 2004

PR-OP1 - OPTIONAL PROTOCOL TO THE INTERNATIONAL COVENANT ON **CIVIL AND POLITICAL RIGHTS** AS OF JUNE 9, 2004

PR-OP2 - SECOND OPTIONAL PROTOCOL TO THE INTERNATIONAL COVENANT ON **CIVIL AND POLITICAL RIGHTS** AS OF JUNE 9, 2004

D - INTERNATIONAL COVENANT ON THE ELIMINATION OF ALL FORMS OF **RACIAL DISCRIMINATION** AS OF JUNE 9, 2004

AW - CONVENTION ON THE ELIMINATION OF ALL FORMS OF **DISCRIMINATION AGAINST WOMEN** AS OF JUNE 9, 2004

- CONVENTION AGAINST **TORTURE AND OTHER CRUEL, INHUMAN OR DEGRADING TREATMENT OR PUNISHMENT** AS OF JUNE 9, 2004

- CONVENTION ON THE **PREVENTION AND PUNISHMENT OF THE CRIME OF GENOCIDE** AS OF OCTOBER 9, 2001

O 87 - **FREEDOM OF ASSOCIATION** AND **PROTECTION OF THE RIGHT TO ORGANIZE** CONVENTION ACCESSED MAY 18, 2005

- CONVENTION RELATING TO **THE STATUS OF REFUGEES** ACCESSED MAY 18, 2005

- ROME STATUTE ON **THE INTERNATIONAL CRIMINAL COURT** AS OF MAY 12, 2005

C - **CHEMICAL WEAPONS** CONVENTION AS OF MAY 21, 2005

C - **BIOLOGICAL WEAPONS** CONVENTION ACCESSED MAY 18, 2005

- CONVENTION ON THE PROHIBITION OF THE **USE, STOCKPILING, PRODUCTION AND TRANSFER OF ANTI-PERSONNEL MINES AND ON THEIR DESTRUCTION** ACCESSED MAY 18, 2005

eva - **GENEVA** CONVENTIONS AS OF MARCH 29, 2005

t1 - FIRST ADDITIONAL PROTOCOL TO THE **GENEVA CONVENTIONS** AS OF MARCH 29, 2005

t2 - SECOND ADDITIONAL PROTOCOL TO THE **GENEVA CONVENTIONS** AS OF MARCH 29, 2005

- BASEL CONVENTION ON THE CONTROL OF **TRANSBOUNDARY MOVEMENTS OF HAZARDOUS WASTES AND THEIR DISPOSAL** AS OF APRIL 8, 2005

- CONVENTION ON **BIOLOGICAL DIVERSITY** ACCESSED MAY 18, 2005

CCC - UNITED NATIONS FRAMEWORK CONVENTION ON **CLIMATE CHANGE** AS OF MAY 21, 2005

- **BIOLOGICAL WEAPONS** CONVENTION ACCESSED MAY 18, 2005

- KYOTO PROTOCOL TO UNITED NATIONS FRAMEWORK CONVENTION ON **CLIMATE CHANGE** AS OF APRIL 29, 2005

OL - VIENNA CONVENTION FOR **THE PROTECTION OF THE OZONE LAYER** AS OF MARCH 29, 2005

6. KEY PLAYERS IN GLOBAL GOVERNANCE ISSUES

BY % OF EXPERTS RATING THEM AS EFFECTIVE

47% **EUROPEAN UNION**

26% **NATIONAL GOVERNMENTS OF DEVELOPED COUNTRIES**

24% **UNITED NATIONS**

24% **INTERNATIONAL INSTITUTIONS** E.G., WORLD BANK, IMF, WTO

18% **WORLD SOCIAL FORUM**

13% **WORLD ECONOMIC FORUM**

12% **CLINTON GLOBAL INITIATIVE**

7% **NATIONAL GOVERNMENTS OF DEVELOPING COUNTRIES**

7. AVERAGE PERCENTILE RANK ON WORLD BANK GOVERNANCE INDICATORS 2004

COUNTRIES BELOW THE 10TH PERCENTILE	COUNTRIES BETWEEN THE 47TH + 52ND PERCENTILE	COUNTRIES ABOVE THE 90TH PERCENTILE
SOMALIA	TURKEY	UNITED KINGDOM
IRAQ	MADAGASCAR	LIECHTENSTEIN
MYANMAR	VANUATU	IRELAND
CONGO, DEM. REP.	MARSHALL ISLANDS	AUSTRIA
AFGHANISTAN	EL SALVADOR	CANADA
HAITI	GHANA	AUSTRALIA
TURKMENISTAN	JAMAICA	NETHERLANDS
SUDAN	LESOTHO	SWEDEN
CENTRAL AFRICAN REPUBLIC	TUNESIA	NORWAY
ZIMBABWE	MALDIVES	DENMARK
LIBERIA	ROMANIA	SWITZERLAND
UZBEKISTAN	MONGOLIA	NEW ZEALAND
KOREA, DEM. REP.	THAILAND	LUXEMBOURG
BURUNDI	SURINAME	FINLAND
COTE D'IVOIRE	BRAZIL	ICELAND

8. SIZE OF THE UNITED NATIONS BUDGET

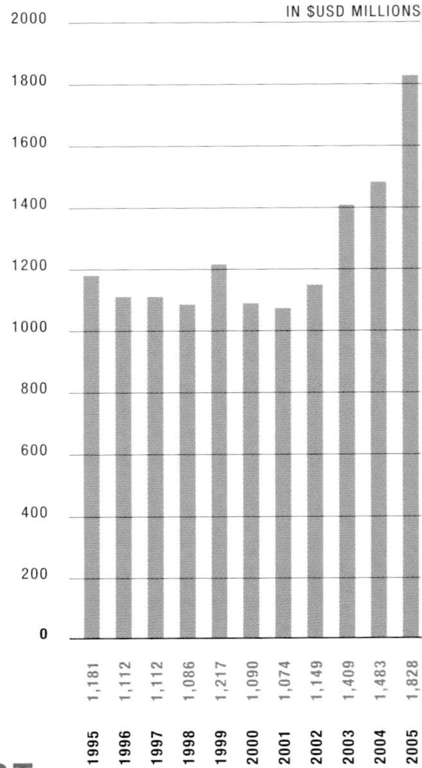

10. STATES INVOLVED IN THREE OR MORE CONTENTIOUS CASES IN THE INTERNATIONAL CRIMINAL COURT

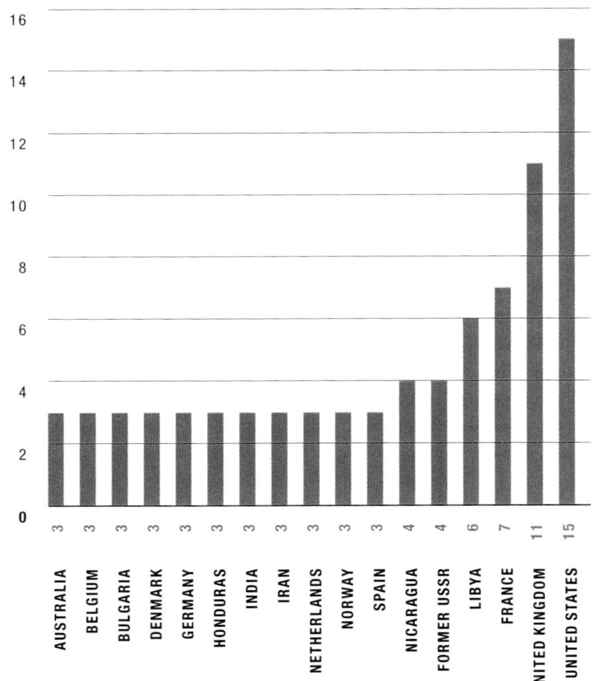

9. UNITED NATIONS REGULAR BUDGET EXPENDITURES IN CURRENT VERSUS REAL TERMS 1971 – 2003

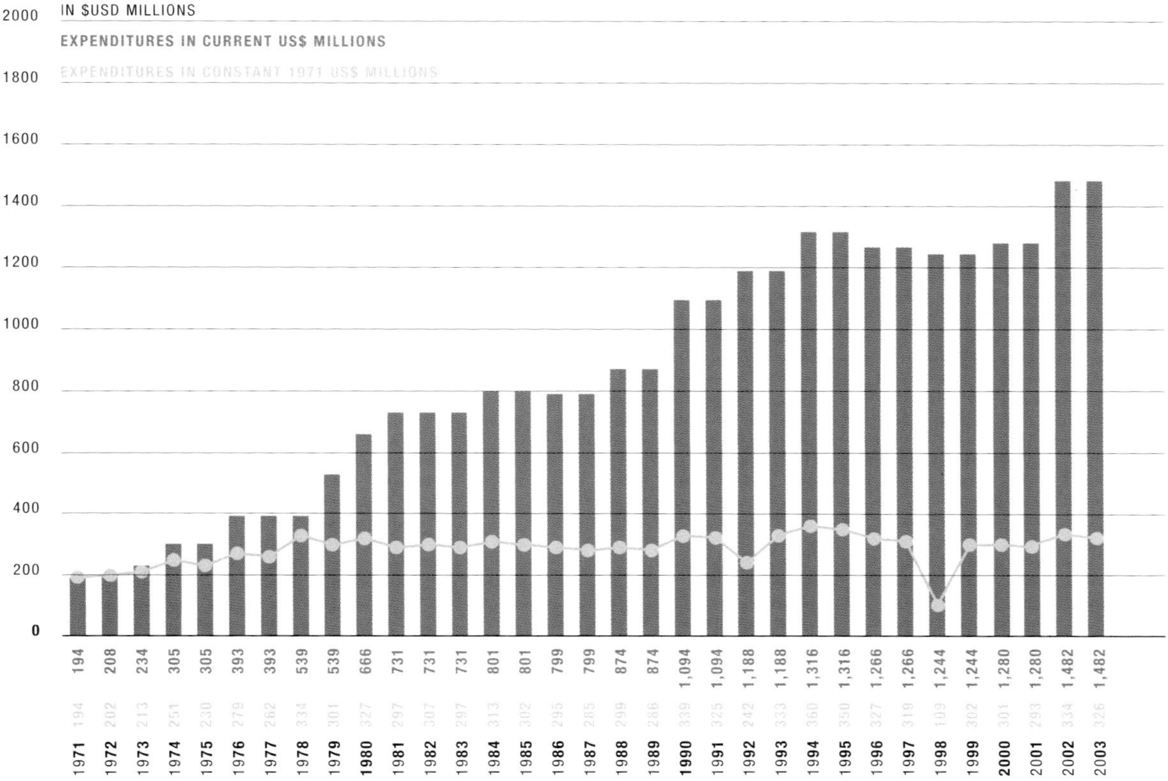

IN $USD MILLIONS

EXPENDITURES IN CURRENT US$ MILLIONS

EXPENDITURES IN CONSTANT 1971 US$ MILLIONS

Year	Expenditures in current US$ millions	Expenditures in constant 1971 US$ millions
1971	194	194
1972	208	202
1973	234	213
1974	305	251
1975	305	230
1976	393	279
1977	393	262
1978	539	334
1979	539	301
1980	666	327
1981	731	297
1982	731	307
1983	731	297
1984	801	313
1985	801	302
1986	799	295
1987	799	285
1988	874	299
1989	874	286
1990	1,094	339
1991	1,094	325
1992	1,188	242
1993	1,188	333
1994	1,316	360
1995	1,316	350
1996	1,266	327
1997	1,266	319
1998	1,244	109
1999	1,244	302
2000	1,280	301
2001	1,280	293
2002	1,482	334
2003	1,482	326

11. % INCREASE IN COMMUNICATIONS BETWEEN INTERPOL + REGIONS

BETWEEN 2002 AND 2004

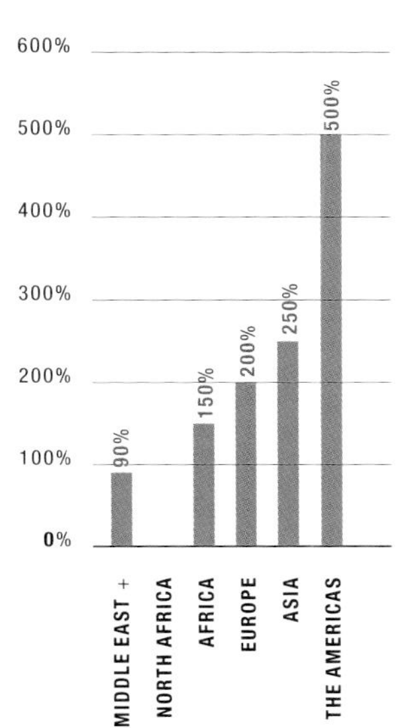

12. TOTAL EXPENDITURE OF INTERPOL 2000 – 2005

IN THOUSANDS OF EUROS

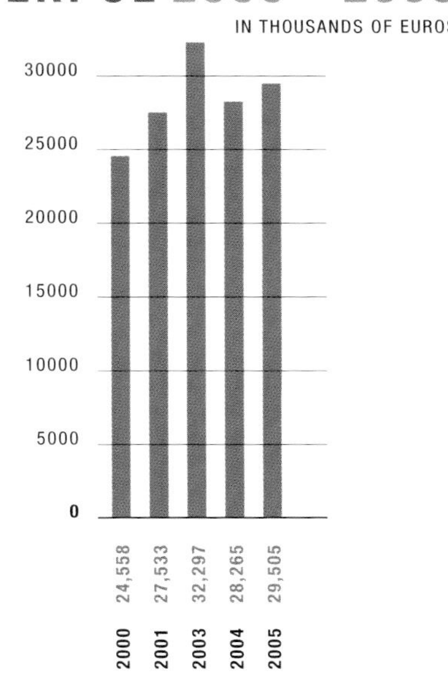

GLOBALIZATION

Contemporary globalization, as previous 'globalizing periods' in the 19th and early 20th century, is part of a long-term, though uneven, expansion of world rationalization and capitalism. While experts generally see globalization as greater connectedness of flows of finance, knowledge, goods and services, and people across time, nations, regions and intercontinental space, it is also part of an ongoing historical process with deep cultural roots reaching back many centuries. What sets the current globalization spurt apart from previous ones is the sheer scale and scope of transnational connectedness. The indicator suites on economic globalization, global civil society, and political and legal globalization show that:

- Economic globalization in terms of trade has increased significantly in the last decade; however, this growth is unevenly spread, with the world economy becoming increasingly concentrated
- The scale and role of transnational corporations (TNCs) is now more pronounced; the economic weight of some of the largest TNCs surpasses that of most national economies; and the degree of transnationality of these TNCs continues to increase
- A transnational, and increasingly global, civil society has progressively emerged since the end of the Cold War, facilitated by the rise of international nongovernmental organizations (INGOs), activist networks and civil value patterns
- The 'thickening' of the international rule of law has continued as well, although unevenly, and with persistent enforcement problems and nationalist interpretations of global governance

WHAT IS GLOBALIZATION?

Globalization is greater connectedness across universal time and space. It involves flows of investments, knowledge, cultural goods, and people across regions and intercontinental zones. These flows are facilitated by an institutional and organizational infrastructure and are patterned in terms of intensity, extensity and velocity, and show characteristic modes of interactions such as diffusion, interpenetration or domination. The notion of 'cultural globalization' involves all three movements: flows of investments and knowledge; flows of cultural goods; and flows of people. Cultures or aspects of cultures are globalized to the extent to which they involve the movement of specified objects, systems of meaning and people across national and regional borders and continents.

Cultural products and values are part of a larger process that involves economic globalization (defined as the functional integration of economic production and distribution processes across multiple national borders); the emergence of a global civil society (defined as the socio-sphere of ideas, values, institutions, organizations, networks, and individuals located primarily outside the institutional complexes of family, state, and market and operating beyond the confines of national societies, polities, and economies); and international law and the emergence of an international legal system (e.g., the International Court of Justice or the European Court of Justice).

Today's globalization as the latest phase of historic developments whose major impetus originated in the West (i.e., the rise of capitalism in Europe and the Americas), but which for centuries has spurred, and interacted with specific dynamics in other parts of the world in terms of economic and political development (e.g., Japan) or underdevelopment (e.g., Sub-Saharan Africa). At some level, the spread of rationality and capitalism engendered conflict dynamics, (i.e., colonialism, imperial wars, and struggles for self-determination and independence.) At another level, these conflict dynamics, while often economic and political at the surface are also deeply cultural.

WHAT ARE THE ISSUES?

Globalization has changed not only the economy of most countries, but the social fabric of many societies. New political positions have emerged that try to relate globalization to existing ideologies. Among them: supporters are largely in the spirit of traditional liberalism; regressives represent an outgrowth of conservative neo-liberalism; reformers constitute a reformed social democratic movement; and rejectionists favor a return to seemingly simpler world. Table 1 offers a rough outline of these positions:

TABLE 1: **POSITIONS ON GLOBALIZATION**

GLOBALIZATION OF	SUPPORTERS	REGRESSIVES	REFORMERS	REJECTIONISTS
CULTURE	**FOR:** cultures should interact freely and competition of ideas, values and practices are welcome.	**AGAINST:** national culture and identity should be cohesive and protected; core values need to be defended	**MIXED:** welcome multiple identities and cultures but conflicts need to be managed through adequate policies	**AGAINST:** favor protection of cultures and traditions
ECONOMY	**FOR:** As part of economic liberalism	**MIXED:** If beneficial to own country or group and leading stakeholders	**MIXED:** If leading to greater social equity	**AGAINST:** Greater protection of national economies needed
TECHNOLOGY	**FOR:** As part of open competition for technological innovation, e.g. gene and plant technologists	**MIXED:** For in economic terms and for military and security purposes, against for social or environmental purposes	**MIXED:** If beneficial to broader groups and the marginalized	**AGAINST:** Technology threatens local communities and traditional ways of life
LAW	**FOR:** With emphasis on international commercial law and human rights legislation	**AGAINST:** For if facilitating private investment and trade but generally against. Emphasis on strengthening national laws on property rights and domestic democracy	**FOR:** Building global rule of law not solely dependent on sovereign states. Pronounced role for International Criminal Court	**AGAINST:** Undermines national sovereignty and democracy.
PEOPLE	**FOR:** Open border policy	**MIXED:** For immigration for economic needs but against people of other cultures	**FOR:** Open policy	**AGAINST:** Closed border policy

Source: Based on Kaldor et al, 2003.

IDENTITY is an individual's or group's sense of self, and is important in that it is vital to the shaping of human behavior. In the context of globalization, a critical issue is the impact of an increasingly globalizing world on identity formation and stability. Are some identities being eroded and even pushed aside, while others evolve or dominate? For example, Huntington (2004) suggests that the erosion of America's Anglo-Protestant cultural identity is in part due to the problems of assimilation of primarily Hispanic immigrants. By contrast, Sen (2006) argues strongly against merging identities with some form of higher purpose as it suggests some "illusion of destiny" that could become dangerous and lead to violence.

APPROACHES TO IDENTITY

Two long-standing strands of social science theory shape today's understanding of individual identity:

- One is rooted in developmental psychology and sees identity as the result of 'deep socialization,' i.e., early value-forming experiences and learning processes that make up the core personality traits and character dispositions. This psychological understanding is close to what could be called the 'hard-wired' aspect of identity as a sense of self-once formed, it is fairly stable throughout the life course, and relatively persistent to political, cultural and social changes.
- The other understanding of identity is more sociological and cultural in nature, and sees it as the outcome of on-going search processes. Individuals try to forge, negotiate and reconcile their own 'worldviews' and notions of self with that of society. Given the multiple roles people perform in modern, diverse societies, this more 'soft-wired' form of identity is not only evolving; it is also precarious and precious. It refers less to identity as 'self,' but more to identity in relation to categories such as nationhood, religion, place, or belonging.

Subject to a barrage of media, advertising and other images, people learn to confront such dissonances by creating imagined worlds that offer "a series of elements (characters, plots, and textual forms) out of which scripts can be formed of imagined lives, their own as well as those of others living in other places" (Appadurai, 1990: 299). Similarly, Beck (2000: 54) suggests that "more people in more parts of the world dream of and consider a greater range of possible lives than they have ever done before," thereby dissociating their identity from territorial and value-based communities.

WHAT DO WE NOW ABOUT IDENTITY?

Among the surprising findings about changes in identities is first and foremost the stability of responses to identity-related questions over time; at the regional level and for income groups. This is in contrast to the more fluid picture suggested by analysts such as Beck or Appadurai, whose survey results point to the absence rather than the presence of rapid change in individual identities. As Table 1 shows, 63% of the population in Western Europe expressed local identities in 1980, 61% in 1990, and 63% in 2000. Likewise, the relative shares for national and supranational identities have remained stable over the last 30 years. For the Middle East (here: Turkey), Latin America and the Caribbean, and North America, the same stability prevails for the last twenty years, as it does for the group of high-income and middle-income countries.

The findings suggest that the 'deep-wiring' of identities has not yet been affected by globalization to an extent significant enough to register in population surveys, in particular in those regions and countries that are at the center of globalizing economic and political forces. At the same time, there are indications that shifts in identities are taking place, yet they seem to do so at different rates and directions, and by no means in any dramatic way. As Table 1 indicates, South Asia (India) saw an increase in national identity and a decrease of local identity, as did Sub-Saharan Africa (Nigeria, South Africa), but with a decline in supranational identity. What is more, both lower-middle income and low-income countries see an increase in national identity. Taken together, the findings suggest the absence rather than presence of a general shift in identity as a result of globalization. Where shifts have taken place they are more likely the result of national political developments (South Africa) or continued nation-building (Nigeria, India).

Within Europe, we see the emergence of a dual identity whereby over half of the respondents state 'national and European' or 'European and national' as opposed to national identities only. What is more, the dual identity is more pronounced among the younger cohorts (60%) than Europeans 55 and older (48%); among the well-educated (70%) than less well educated (45%); and higher among the self-employed, managers and professionals than among the unemployed and retirees.

Grouping countries by level of economic development, and analyzing response categories on identity and national pride by both attitudinal and macro characteristics, yields one dominant distinction: a significant difference between high-income countries on the one hand, and low and low-middle income countries on the other:

- High income countries are characterized by populations with stronger local and supranational identities, non-materialistic orientations, a regard for religion as important, and generally satisfied with life. These are countries with comparatively lower income inequality, aging and well-educated populations, and greater gender equality.
- Low and low-middle income countries have populations with stronger national identities that express great national pride, are more materialistic, regard religion as less important, and are less satisfied with their quality of life. These are countries with greater income and gender inequality, and young, less well-educated populations.

By contrast, upper-middle income countries share many of the characteristics of high-income countries but do so in a less clear-cut way.

ISSUES

Four major conclusions emerge in relation to identity: 1) National identities seem stronger in weaker economies and more peripheral countries, as seems to be the case with national pride. By contrast, local and supranational identities seem more pronounced in stronger, more developed countries; 2) In shaping and sustaining identities, the relationship between life satisfaction, religious and other value orientations is critical; 3) Globalization has not yet become a major force in changing deep-wired notions of identity, but has the potential of affecting soft-wired aspects by serving as a likely target for displaced dissatisfaction in countries/regions with lower per-capita income; and 4) There seems to be no general 'identity-based' backlash against globalization; what backlashes there are appear closely tied to persistent political and economic failures, with the Middle East and Central Asia as cases in point.

TABLE 1: **GEOGRAPHIC IDENTITIES, 1981-1999/2000**

REGION	1981 LOCAL	1981 NATIONAL	1981 SUPRA-NATIONAL	1990 LOCAL	1990 NATIONAL	1990 SUPRA-NATIONAL	1999 LOCAL	1999 NATIONAL	1999 SUPRA-NATIONAL
SUB-SAHARAN AFRICA				53%	32%	16%	52%	38%	11%
MIDDLE EAST & NORTH AFRICA				45%	46%	9%	42%	45%	12%
SOUTH ASIA				52%	39%	9%	2%	53%	5%
EAST ASIA & PACIFIC				51%	46%	4%	58%	37%	5%
LATIN AMERICA & CARIBBEAN				44%	42%	14%	45%	39%	16%
NORTH AMERICA	67%	7%	27%	49%	36%	16%	47%	35%	18%
WESTERN EUROPE	63%	28%	9%	61%	28%	10%	63%	28%	09%

WORLD BANK INCOME GROUPS	1981 LOCAL	1981 NATIONAL	1981 SUPRA-NATIONAL	1990 LOCAL	1990 NATIONAL	1990 SUPRA-NATIONAL	1999 LOCAL	1999 NATIONAL	1999 SUPRA-NATIONAL
HIGH-INCOME	64%	25%	11%	59%	31%	10%	62%	28%	9%
UPPER-MIDDLE-INCOME				56%	33%	11%	57%	33%	10%
LOWER-MIDDLE-INCOME				53%	39%	08%	41%	48%	11%
LOW-INCOME				51%	35%	15%	50%	42%	8%

Data: European Values Survey (EVS), 1981, 1990, 1999; WVS, 1990/1, 2000.

VALUES

IDENTITY VALUES

ECONOMIC VALUES

SOCIAL VALUES

POLITICAL VALUES

RELIGIOUS VALUES

GENDER

RELIGIOUS INSTITUTIONS

IDENTITY VALUES

- geographical groups - nationality + pride - nationality / religion / locality / race / continent

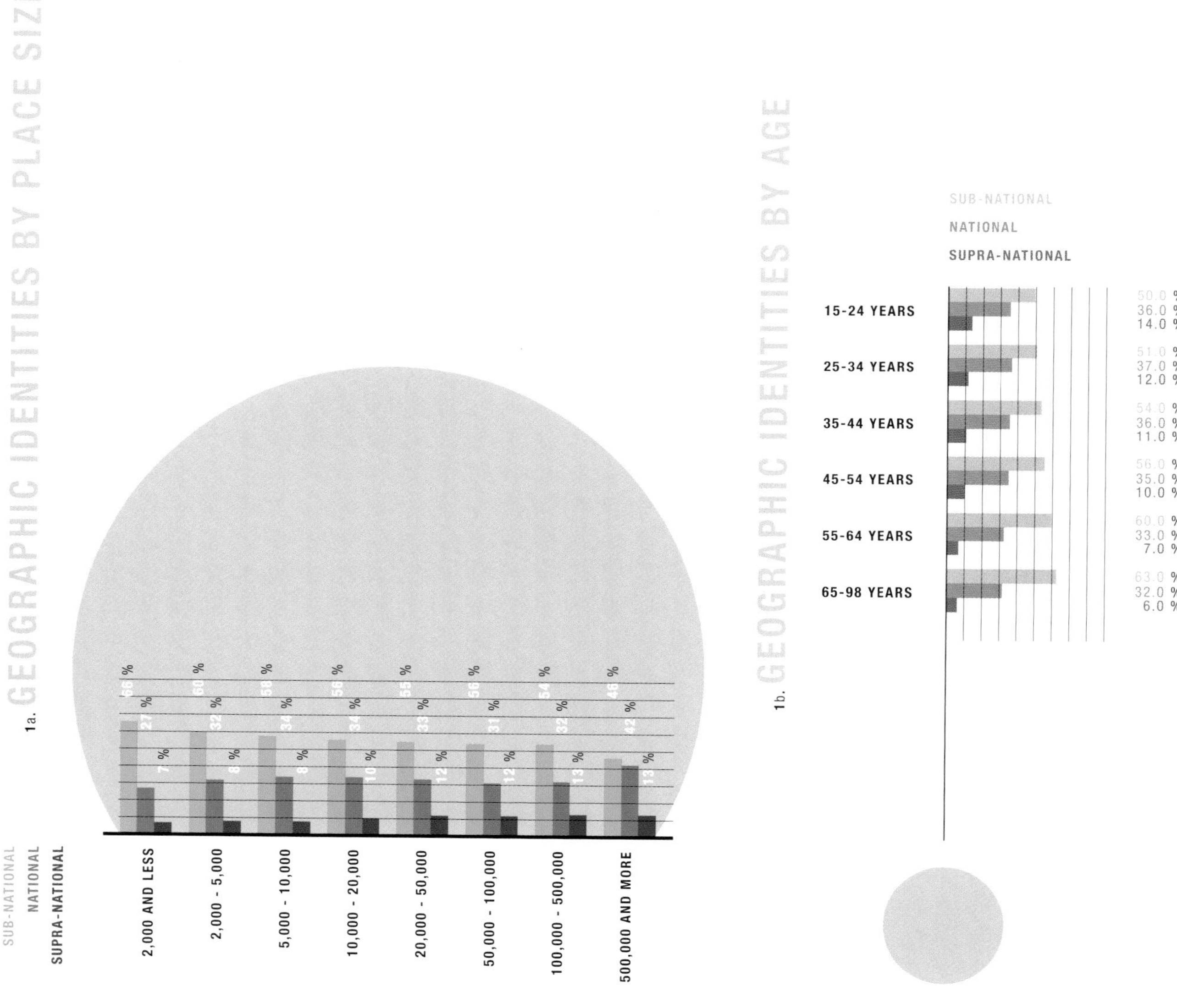

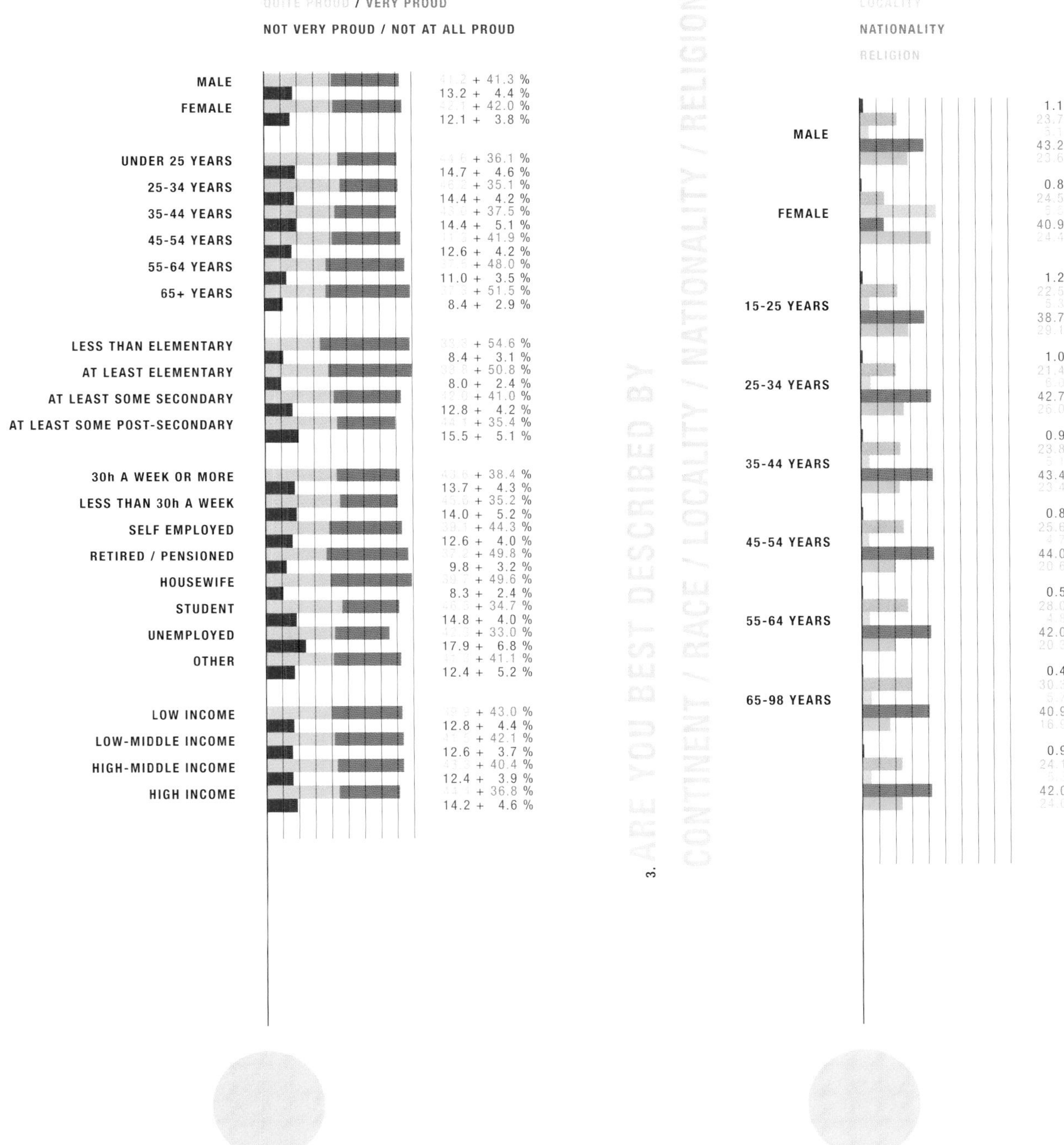
QUITE PROUD / VERY PROUD
NOT VERY PROUD / NOT AT ALL PROUD
MALE
FEMALE
UNDER 25 YEARS
25-34 YEARS
35-44 YEARS
45-54 YEARS
55-64 YEARS
65+ YEARS
LESS THAN ELEMENTARY
AT LEAST ELEMENTARY
AT LEAST SOME SECONDARY
AT LEAST SOME POST-SECONDARY
30h A WEEK OR MORE
LESS THAN 30h A WEEK
SELF EMPLOYED
RETIRED / PENSIONED
HOUSEWIFE
STUDENT
UNEMPLOYED
OTHER
LOW INCOME
LOW-MIDDLE INCOME
HIGH-MIDDLE INCOME
HIGH INCOME
41.2 + 41.3 %
13.2 + 4.4 %
42.1 + 42.0 %
12.1 + 3.8 %
44.6 + 36.1 %
14.7 + 4.6 %
46.2 + 35.1 %
14.4 + 4.2 %
+ 37.5 %
14.4 + 5.1 %
+ 41.9 %
12.6 + 4.2 %
+ 48.0 %
11.0 + 3.5 %
+ 51.5 %
8.4 + 2.9 %
+ 54.6 %
8.4 + 3.1 %
+ 50.8 %
8.0 + 2.4 %
+ 41.0 %
12.8 + 4.2 %
+ 35.4 %
15.5 + 5.1 %
43.6 + 38.4 %
13.7 + 4.3 %
45.6 + 35.2 %
14.0 + 5.2 %
+ 44.3 %
12.6 + 4.0 %
37.2 + 49.8 %
9.8 + 3.2 %
39.7 + 49.6 %
8.3 + 2.4 %
+ 34.7 %
14.8 + 4.0 %
+ 33.0 %
17.9 + 6.8 %
+ 41.1 %
12.4 + 5.2 %
+ 43.0 %
12.8 + 4.4 %
+ 42.1 %
12.6 + 3.7 %
+ 40.4 %
12.4 + 3.9 %
+ 36.8 %
14.2 + 4.6 %
3. ARE YOU BEST DESCRIBED BY
CONTINENT / RACE / LOCALITY / NATIONALITY / RELIGION?
CONTINENT
ETHNICITY / RACE
LOCALITY
NATIONALITY
RELIGION
MALE
FEMALE
15-25 YEARS
25-34 YEARS
35-44 YEARS
45-54 YEARS
55-64 YEARS
65-98 YEARS
1.1 %
23.7 %
%
43.2 %
23.6 %
0.8 %
24.5 %
%
40.9 %
24.4 %
1.2 %
22.5 %
%
38.7 %
29.1 %
1.0 %
21.4 %
%
42.7 %
26.0 %
0.9 %
23.8 %
%
43.4 %
23.4 %
0.8 %
25.6 %
4.7 %
44.0 %
20.6 %
0.5 %
28.0 %
%
42.0 %
20.3 %
0.4 %
30.3 %
5.7 %
40.9 %
16.9 %
0.9 %
24.1 %
%
42.0 %
24.0 %

ECONOMIC VALUES

- post materialist + **materialist values - competition - work attitude - government** versus **private sector**

- work versus **leisure - welfare state - income - governmental ownership**

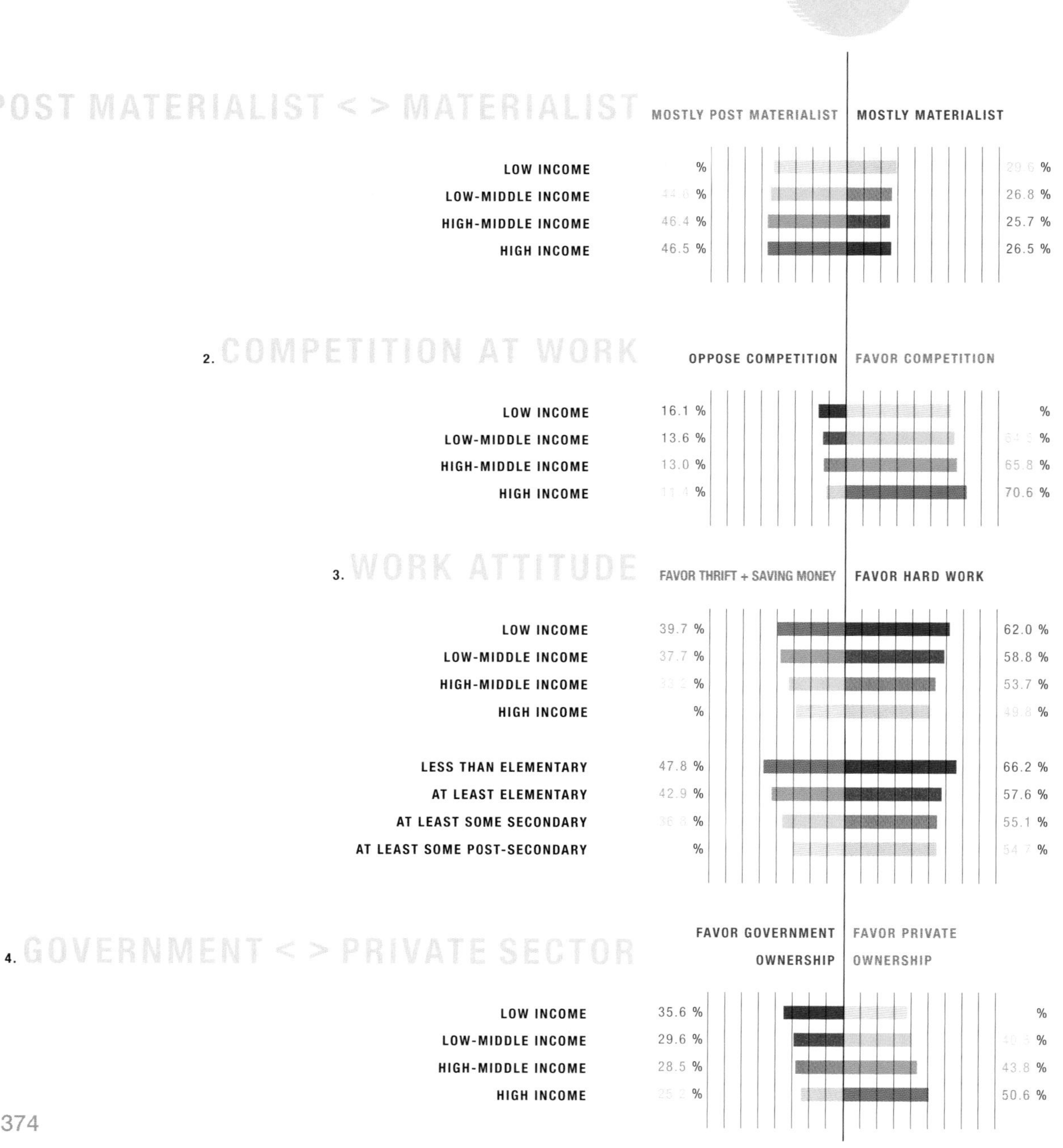

5. ATTITUDE: WORK + LEISURE

6. WELFARE < > TAXES

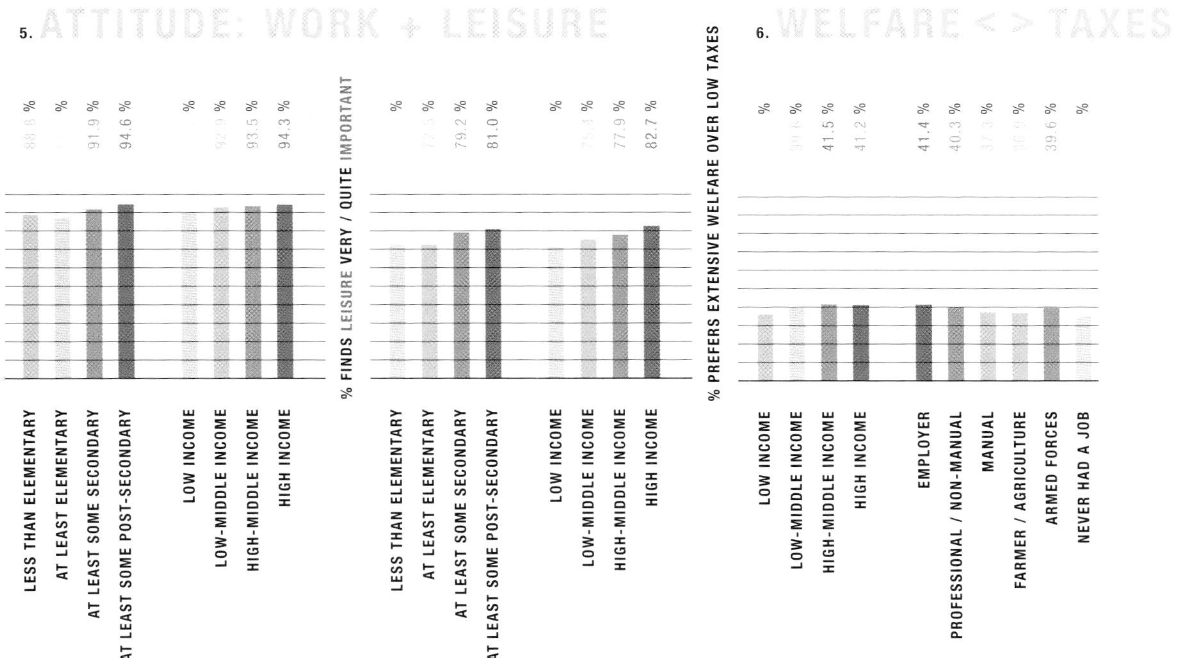

7. INCOME EQUALITY

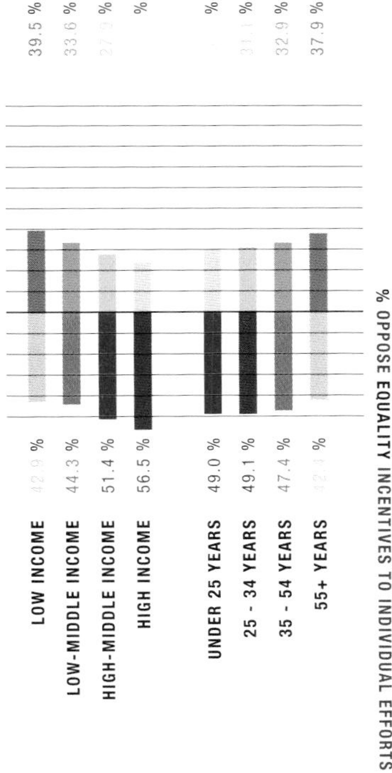

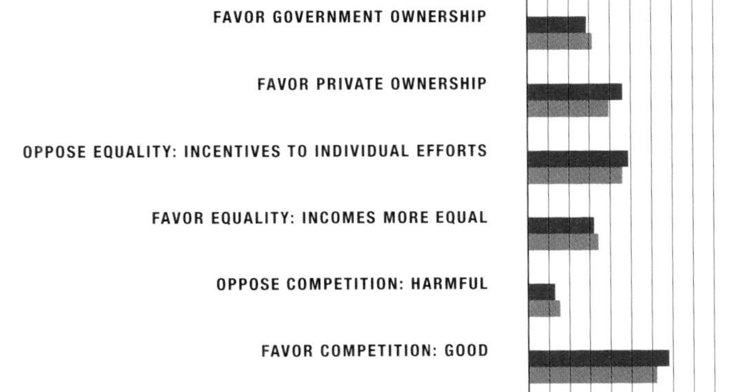

SOCIAL VALUES

- most people can be trusted - tolerance is an important value - importance of family, leisure and work

- level of prejudice based on feelings about neighbours

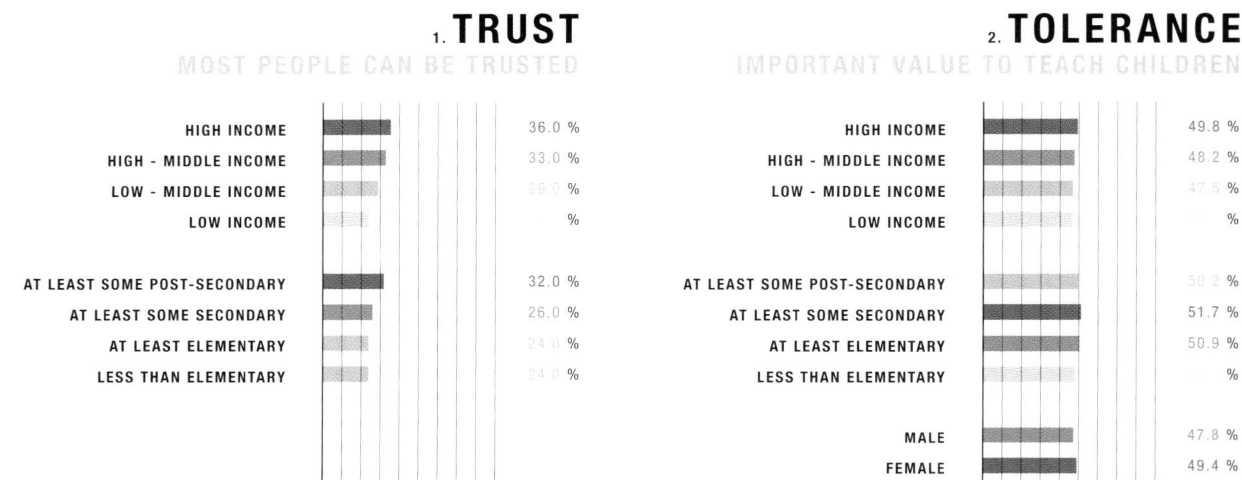

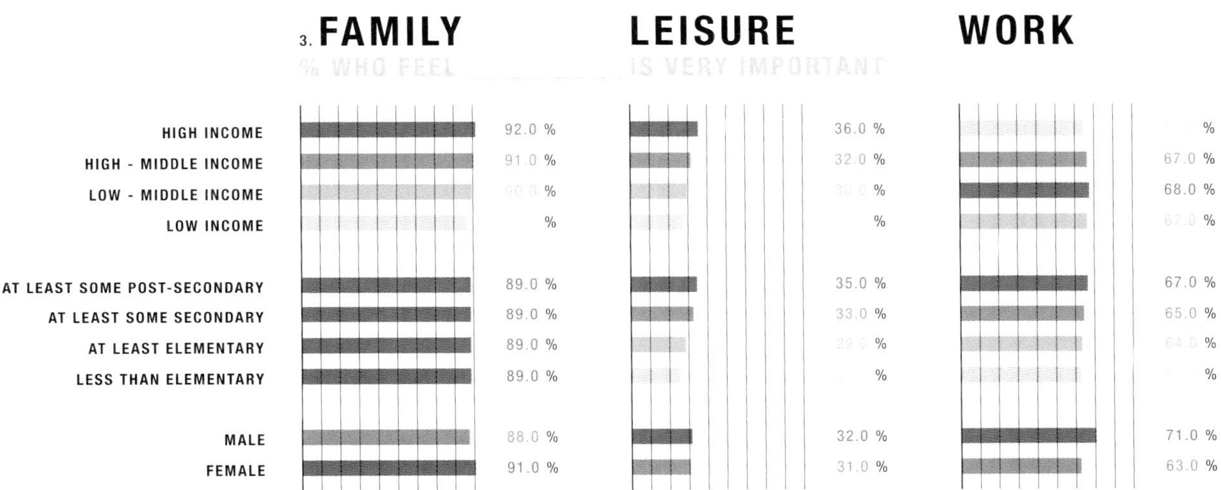

4. LEVEL OF PREJUDICE

BASED ON FEELINGS ABOUT NEIGHBOURS

HIGH INCOME	3.7 %
HIGH - MIDDLE INCOME	3.5 %
LOW - MIDDLE INCOME	3.2 %
LOW INCOME	3.0 %
AT LEAST SOME POST-SECONDARY	3.2 %
AT LEAST SOME SECONDARY	3.4 %
AT LEAST ELEMENTARY	3.7 %
LESS THAN ELEMENTARY	4.5 %
UNDER 25 YEARS	3.2 %
25 - 34 YEARS	3.3 %
35 - 44 YEARS	3.4 %
45 - 54 YEARS	3.4 %
55 - 64 YEARS	3.6 %
65+ YEARS	3.7 %

POLITICAL VALUES

- level of interest in politics + political activism - political attitudes [+ attitudes towards democracy]

1. POLITICAL ATTITUDES + EDUCATION AND CLAS

	% CHURCH STATE SEPARTISTS	% PREFER DEMOCRACY	% GOVERNMENT MORE RESPONSIBILITY
LESS THAN ELEMENTARY	27.7 %	47.3 %	51.6 %
AT LEAST ELEMENTARY	31.3 %	47.6 %	45.9 %
AT LEAST SOME SECONDARY	36.2 %	49.5 %	32.8 %
AT LEAST SOME POST-SECONDARY	36.8 %	57.3 %	36.6 %
LOW INCOME	27.4 %	45.0 %	40.9 %
LOW-MIDDLE INCOME	31.6 %	50.2 %	41.7 %
HIGH-MIDDLE INCOME	32.7 %	54.6 %	37.8 %
HIGH INCOME	37.2 %	60.8 %	34.7 %

	% PREFER DEMOCRACY
UNDER 25 YEARS	49.3 %
25 - 34 YEARS	52.7 %
35 - 44 YEARS	52.3 %
45 - 54 YEARS	53.2 %
55 - 64 YEARS	51.8 %
56+ YEARS	50.7 %

	% PREFER DEMOCRACY
MALE	52.8 %
FEMALE	50.9 %

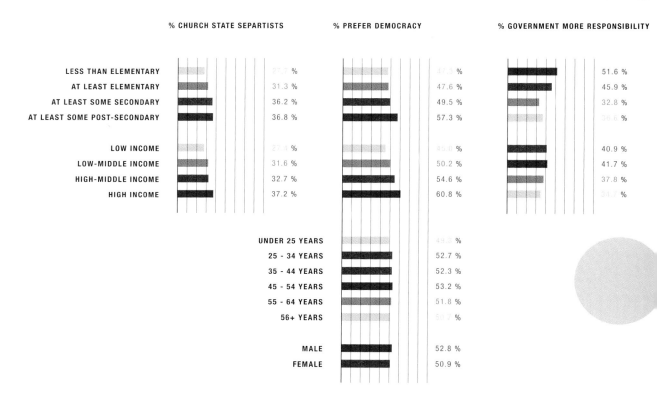

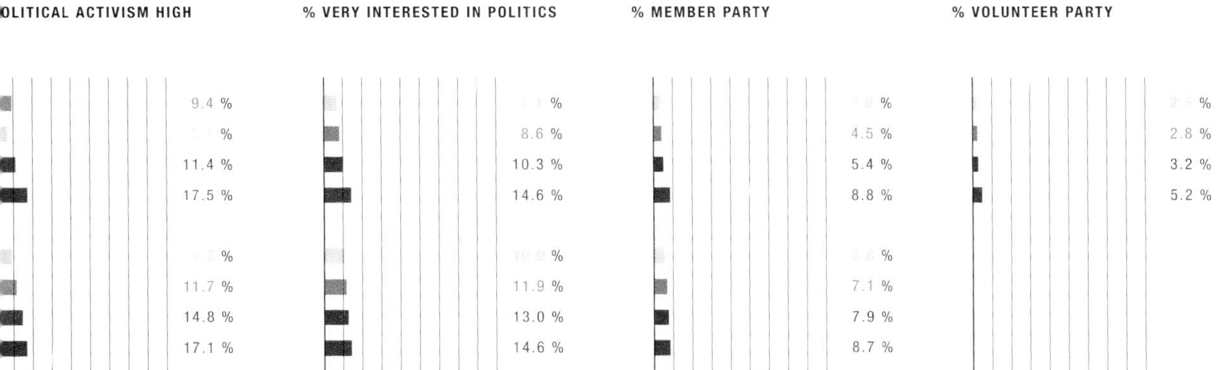

2. INTEREST IN POLITICS • POLITICAL ACTIVISM • AND AGE

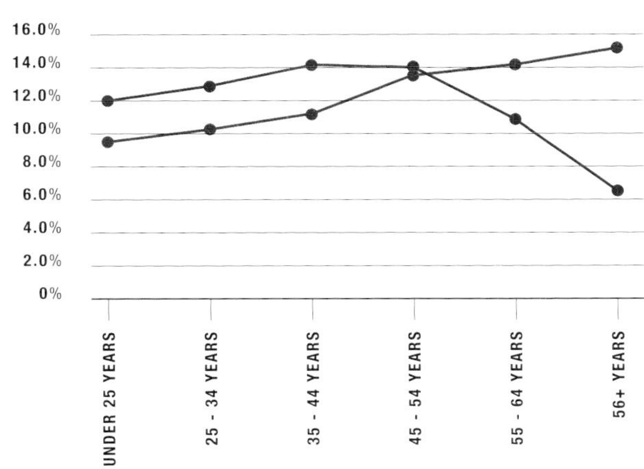

RELIGIOUS VALUES

- religious freedom rates - religious + ethnic hatred - religion + politics

- is religion important? - should children have religious faith?

- do you believe in god?

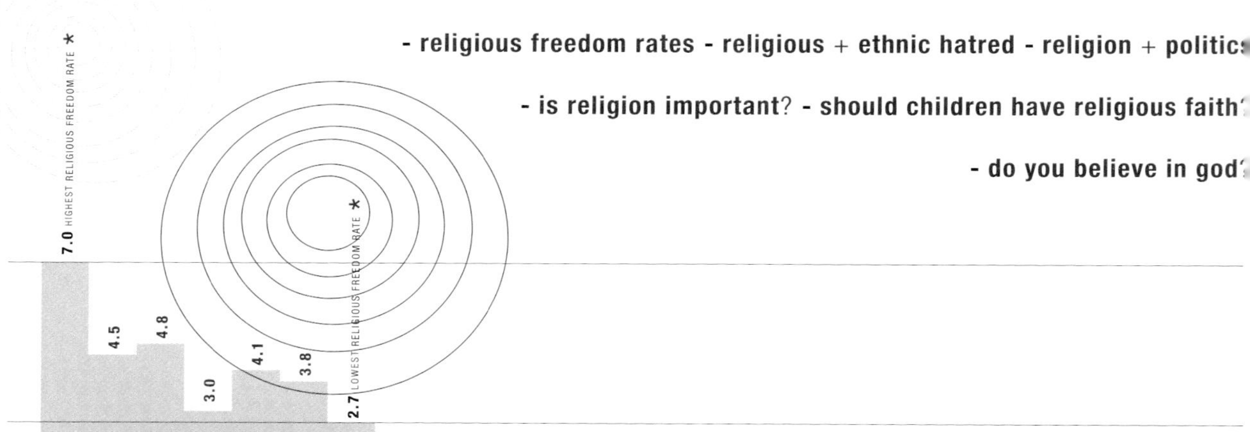

1. RELIGIOUS FREEDOM RATES:

NORTH AMERICA	7.0
LATIN AMERICA + THE CARIBBEAN	4.5
EUROPE + CENTRAL ASIA	4.8
MIDDLE EAST + NORTH AFRICA	3.0
SUB-SAHARAN AFRICA	4.1
EAST ASIA + PACIFIC	3.8
SOUTH ASIA	2.7

WORLD AVERAGE 4.2

3. SHOULD POLITICIANS BELIEVE IN GOD?

	GENDER:		AGE GROUPS:						EDUCATION ON		
	MALE	FEMALE	UNDER 25 YEARS	25-34 YEARS	35-44 YEARS	45-54 YEARS	55-64 YEARS	65+ YEARS	LESS THAN ELEMENTARY	AT LEAST ELEMENTARY	AT LEAST SOME SECONDARY
STRONGLY AGREE / AGREE	36.5 %	37.9 %	39.9 %	40.4 %	37.2 %	34.2 %	34.6 %	34 %	37.3 %	37.4 %	31 %
NEITHER AGREE NOR DISAGREE	14.7 %	16.9 %	15.0 %	14.9 %	15.7 %	15.3 %	16.6 %	19.2 %	18.9 %	16.8 %	
STRONGLY DISAGREE / DISAGREE	48.8 %	45.2 %	45.1 %	44.7 %	47.1 %	50.5 %	48.8 %	46.7 %	46.8 %	45.9 %	51.2 %

2. RELIGIOUS + ETHNIC HATRED

OTE: FIGURES ARE
NWEIGHTED AVERAGES
F COUNTRY RESULTS

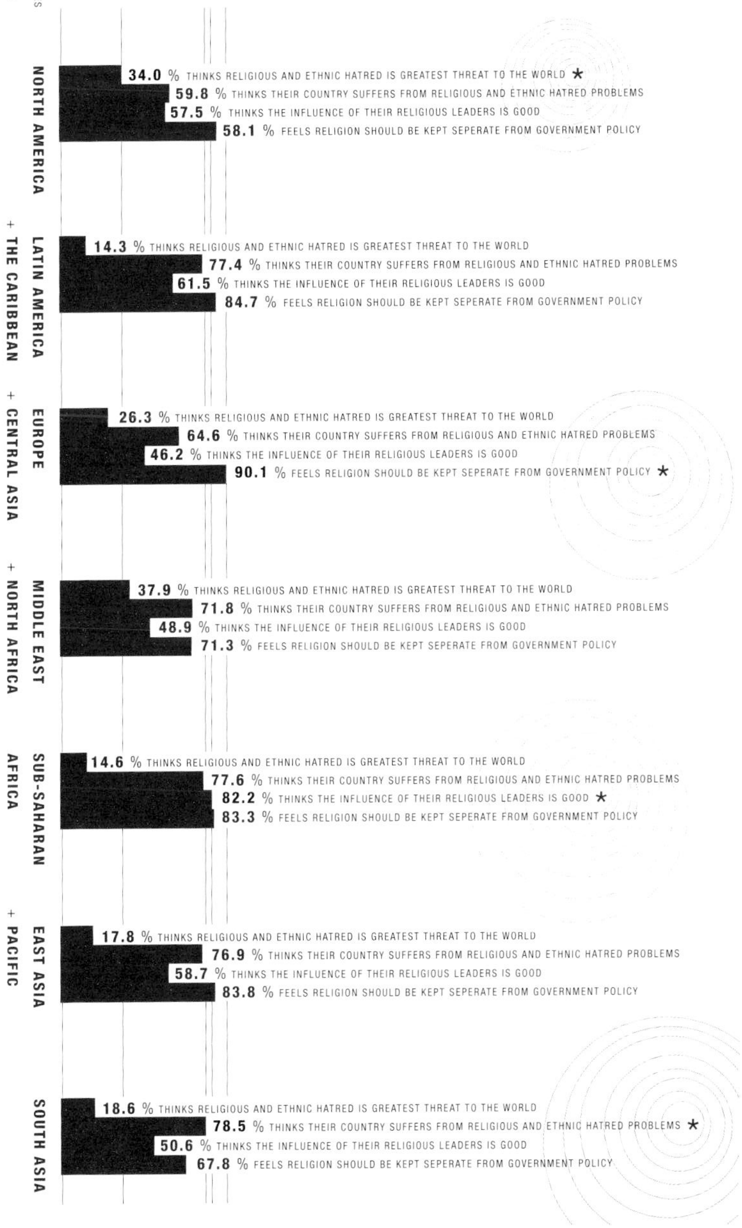

NORTH AMERICA
34.0 % THINKS RELIGIOUS AND ETHNIC HATRED IS GREATEST THREAT TO THE WORLD *
59.8 % THINKS THEIR COUNTRY SUFFERS FROM RELIGIOUS AND ETHNIC HATRED PROBLEMS
57.5 % THINKS THE INFLUENCE OF THEIR RELIGIOUS LEADERS IS GOOD
58.1 % FEELS RELIGION SHOULD BE KEPT SEPERATE FROM GOVERNMENT POLICY
LATIN AMERICA + THE CARIBBEAN
14.3 % THINKS RELIGIOUS AND ETHNIC HATRED IS GREATEST THREAT TO THE WORLD
77.4 % THINKS THEIR COUNTRY SUFFERS FROM RELIGIOUS AND ETHNIC HATRED PROBLEMS
61.5 % THINKS THE INFLUENCE OF THEIR RELIGIOUS LEADERS IS GOOD
84.7 % FEELS RELIGION SHOULD BE KEPT SEPERATE FROM GOVERNMENT POLICY
EUROPE + CENTRAL ASIA
26.3 % THINKS RELIGIOUS AND ETHNIC HATRED IS GREATEST THREAT TO THE WORLD
64.6 % THINKS THEIR COUNTRY SUFFERS FROM RELIGIOUS AND ETHNIC HATRED PROBLEMS
46.2 % THINKS THE INFLUENCE OF THEIR RELIGIOUS LEADERS IS GOOD
90.1 % FEELS RELIGION SHOULD BE KEPT SEPERATE FROM GOVERNMENT POLICY *
MIDDLE EAST + NORTH AFRICA
37.9 % THINKS RELIGIOUS AND ETHNIC HATRED IS GREATEST THREAT TO THE WORLD
71.8 % THINKS THEIR COUNTRY SUFFERS FROM RELIGIOUS AND ETHNIC HATRED PROBLEMS
48.9 % THINKS THE INFLUENCE OF THEIR RELIGIOUS LEADERS IS GOOD
71.3 % FEELS RELIGION SHOULD BE KEPT SEPERATE FROM GOVERNMENT POLICY
SUB-SAHARAN AFRICA
14.6 % THINKS RELIGIOUS AND ETHNIC HATRED IS GREATEST THREAT TO THE WORLD
77.6 % THINKS THEIR COUNTRY SUFFERS FROM RELIGIOUS AND ETHNIC HATRED PROBLEMS
82.2 % THINKS THE INFLUENCE OF THEIR RELIGIOUS LEADERS IS GOOD *
83.3 % FEELS RELIGION SHOULD BE KEPT SEPERATE FROM GOVERNMENT POLICY
EAST ASIA + PACIFIC
17.8 % THINKS RELIGIOUS AND ETHNIC HATRED IS GREATEST THREAT TO THE WORLD
76.9 % THINKS THEIR COUNTRY SUFFERS FROM RELIGIOUS AND ETHNIC HATRED PROBLEMS
58.7 % THINKS THE INFLUENCE OF THEIR RELIGIOUS LEADERS IS GOOD
83.8 % FEELS RELIGION SHOULD BE KEPT SEPERATE FROM GOVERNMENT POLICY
SOUTH ASIA
18.6 % THINKS RELIGIOUS AND ETHNIC HATRED IS GREATEST THREAT TO THE WORLD
78.5 % THINKS THEIR COUNTRY SUFFERS FROM RELIGIOUS AND ETHNIC HATRED PROBLEMS *
50.6 % THINKS THE INFLUENCE OF THEIR RELIGIOUS LEADERS IS GOOD
67.8 % FEELS RELIGION SHOULD BE KEPT SEPERATE FROM GOVERNMENT POLICY

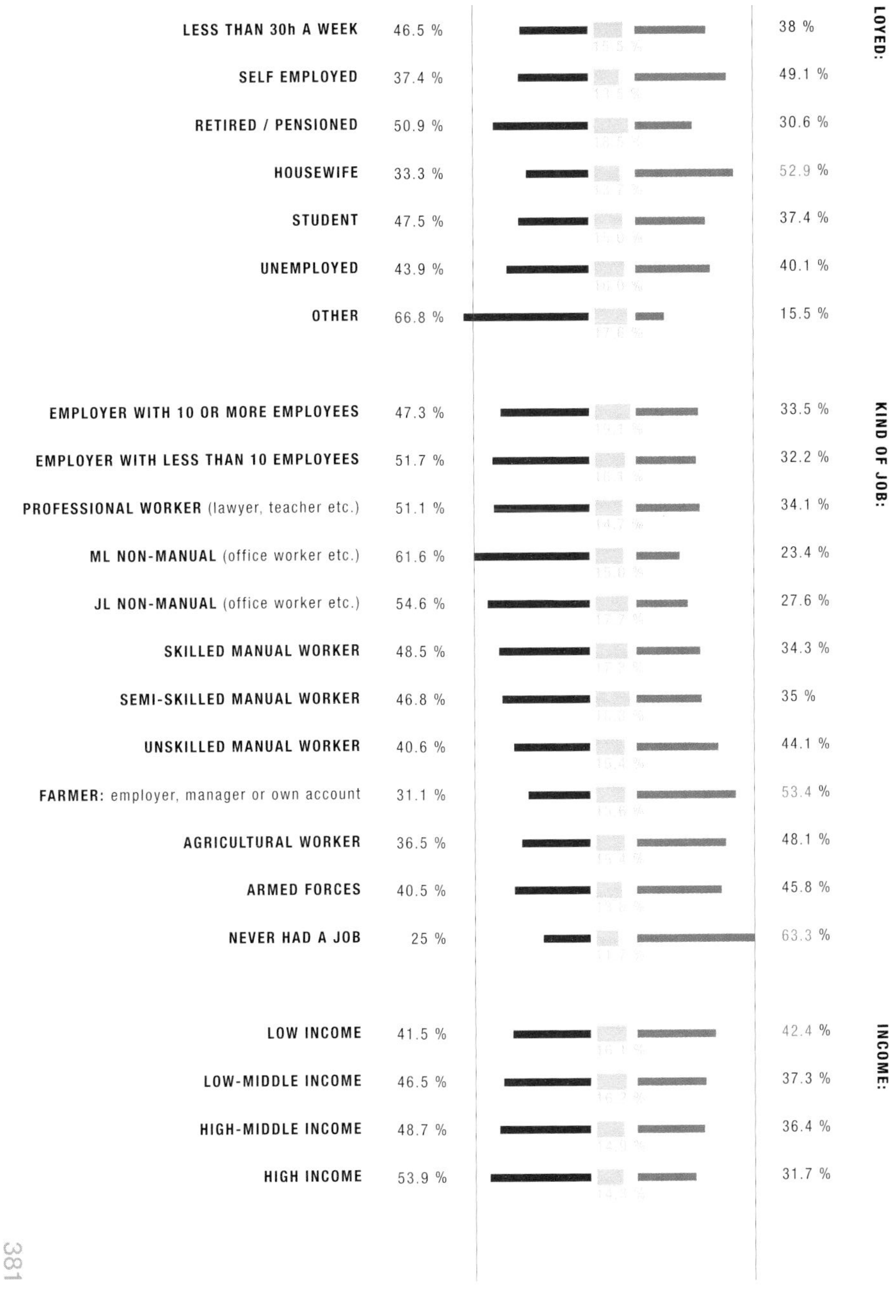

LOYED:
LESS THAN 30h A WEEK 46.5 % 38 %
SELF EMPLOYED 37.4 % 49.1 %
RETIRED / PENSIONED 50.9 % 30.6 %
HOUSEWIFE 33.3 % 52.9 %
STUDENT 47.5 % 37.4 %
UNEMPLOYED 43.9 % 40.1 %
OTHER 66.8 % 15.5 %
KIND OF JOB:
EMPLOYER WITH 10 OR MORE EMPLOYEES 47.3 % 33.5 %
EMPLOYER WITH LESS THAN 10 EMPLOYEES 51.7 % 32.2 %
PROFESSIONAL WORKER (lawyer, teacher etc.) 51.1 % 34.1 %
ML NON-MANUAL (office worker etc.) 61.6 % 23.4 %
JL NON-MANUAL (office worker etc.) 54.6 % 27.6 %
SKILLED MANUAL WORKER 48.5 % 34.3 %
SEMI-SKILLED MANUAL WORKER 46.8 % 35 %
UNSKILLED MANUAL WORKER 40.6 % 44.1 %
FARMER: employer, manager or own account 31.1 % 53.4 %
AGRICULTURAL WORKER 36.5 % 48.1 %
ARMED FORCES 40.5 % 45.8 %
NEVER HAD A JOB 25 % 63.3 %
INCOME:
LOW INCOME 41.5 % 42.4 %
LOW-MIDDLE INCOME 46.5 % 37.3 %
HIGH-MIDDLE INCOME 48.7 % 36.4 %
HIGH INCOME 53.9 % 31.7 %

	GENDER:		AGE GROUPS:						EDUCATION ON		
	MALE	FEMALE	UNDER 25 YEARS	25-34 YEARS	35-44 YEARS	45-54 YEARS	55-64 YEARS	65+ YEARS	LESS THAN ELEMENTARY	AT LEAST ELEMENTARY	AT LEAST SOME SECONDARY
4. IS RELIGION IMPORTANT? YES	65.4 %	72.3 %	69.6 %	68.7 %	66.7 %	66.1 %	69.1 %	72.4 %	73.3 %	70.3 %	62.4 %
4. IS RELIGION IMPORTANT? NO	35.5 %	27.7 %	30.1 %	31.3 %	33.3 %	33.9 %	30.9 %	27.6 %	26.7 %	29.7 %	37.6 %
5. SHOULD CHILDREN HAVE RELIGIOUS FAITH? MENTIONED / YES	67.4 %	66.5 %	73.4 %	72 %	67.2 %	63.4 %	61.7 %	57 %	73.6 %	61.7 %	58 %
5. SHOULD CHILDREN HAVE RELIGIOUS FAITH? NOT MENTIONED / NO	32.6 %	33.5 %	26.6 %	28 %	32.8 %	36.6 %	38.3 %	43 %	26.4 %	38.3 %	42 %
6. DO YOU BELIEVE IN GOD? YES	83.3 %	89 %	87.2 %	87.4 %	85.7 %	84.6 %	85.9 %	86.6 %	92.5 %	88.6 %	83.8 %
6. DO YOU BELIEVE IN GOD? NO	16.7 %	11 %	12.8 %	12.6 %	14.3 %	15.4 %	14.1 %	13.4 %	7.5 %	11.4 %	16.2 %

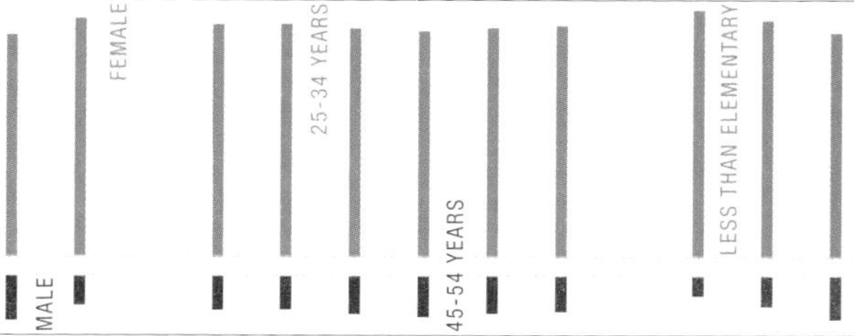

…OYED:

LESS THAN 30h A WEEK	13 %	87.0 %	31 %	69 %	31.9 %	68.1 %
SELF EMPLOYED	8.4 %	91.6 %	17.4 %	82.6 %	22.3 %	77.7 %
RETIRED / PENSIONED	15.6 %	84.4 %	49.4 %	50.6 %	32.3 %	67.7 %
HOUSEWIFE	4.7 %	95.3 %	17.9 %	82.1 %	15.3 %	84.7 %
STUDENT	12.7 %	87.3 %	27.4 %	72.6 %	30.4 %	69.6 %
UNEMPLOYED	13 %	87 %	26.1 %	73.9 %	28.6 %	71.4 %
OTHER	25.2 %	74.8 %	78.7 %	21.3 %	47.7 %	52.3 %

KIND OF JOB:

EMPLOYER, 10 OR MORE EMPLOYEES	19.5 %	80.5 %	33.5 %	66 %	39.9 %	60.1 %
EMPLOYER, LESS THAN 10 EMPLOYEES	14.8 %	85.2 %	32.1 %	65.5 %	36.5 %	63.5 %
PROFESSIONAL WORKER	16.3 %	83.7 %	35.3 %	74.5 %	34.6 %	65.4 %
ML NON-MANUAL	22.4 %	77.6 %	55.4 %	82.6 %	44.5 %	55.5 %
JL NON-MANUAL	17 %	83 %	36.9 %	68.6 %	38.5 %	61.5 %
SKILLED MANUAL WORKER	16.7 %	83.3 %	36.8 %	72 %	36.7 %	63.3 %
SEMI-SKILLED MANUAL WORKER	15.1 %	84.9 %	41.3 %	77.1 %	35 %	65 %
UNSKILLED MANUAL WORKER	9.3 %	90.7 %	27.6 %	73.3 %	25 %	75.1 %
FARMER	7.6 %	92.4 %	13.5 %	68.4 %	17.2 %	82.8 %
AGRICULTURAL WORKER	13.9 %	86.1 %	18.5 %	65.9 %	33.1 %	66.9 %
ARMED FORCES	15.1 %	84.9 %	21.4 %	68.6 %	27.5 %	72.5 %
NEVER HAD A JOB	3.2 %	96.8 %	2.7 %	66 %	10.7 %	89.3 %

INCOME:

LOW INCOME	11.6 %	88.4 %	30.4 %	69.6 %	26.8 %	73.2 %
LOW-MIDDLE INCOME	13.6 %	86.4 %	29.4 %	70.6 %	31.1 %	68.9 %
HIGH-MIDDLE INCOME	14.4 %	85.6 %	32.9 %	67.1 %	33.1 %	66.9 %
HIGH INCOME	17.4 %	82.6 %	38.1 %	61.9 %	38.3 %	61.7 %

GENDER VALUES

- life expectancy at birth - combined gross enrollment for schools - estimated earned income - literacy rat

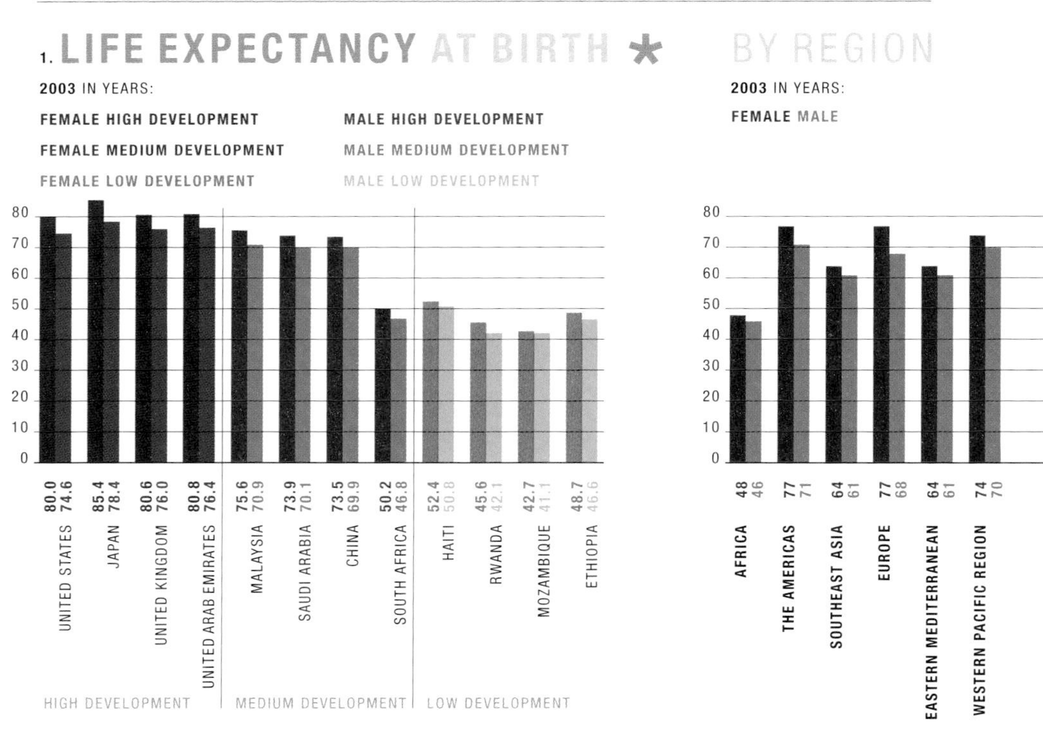

1. LIFE EXPECTANCY AT BIRTH *
2003 IN YEARS:
FEMALE HIGH DEVELOPMENT
MALE HIGH DEVELOPMENT
FEMALE MEDIUM DEVELOPMENT
MALE MEDIUM DEVELOPMENT
FEMALE LOW DEVELOPMENT
MALE LOW DEVELOPMENT
80
70
60
50
40
30
20
10
0
80.0 74.6 UNITED STATES
85.4 78.4 JAPAN
80.6 76.0 UNITED KINGDOM
80.8 76.4 UNITED ARAB EMIRATES
75.6 70.9 MALAYSIA
73.9 70.1 SAUDI ARABIA
73.5 69.9 CHINA
50.2 46.8 SOUTH AFRICA
52.4 50.8 HAITI
45.6 42.1 RWANDA
42.7 41.1 MOZAMBIQUE
48.7 46.6 ETHIOPIA
HIGH DEVELOPMENT
MEDIUM DEVELOPMENT
LOW DEVELOPMENT
BY REGION
2003 IN YEARS:
FEMALE MALE
48 46 AFRICA
77 71 THE AMERICAS
64 61 SOUTHEAST ASIA
77 68 EUROPE
64 61 EASTERN MEDITERRANEAN
74 70 WESTERN PACIFIC REGION

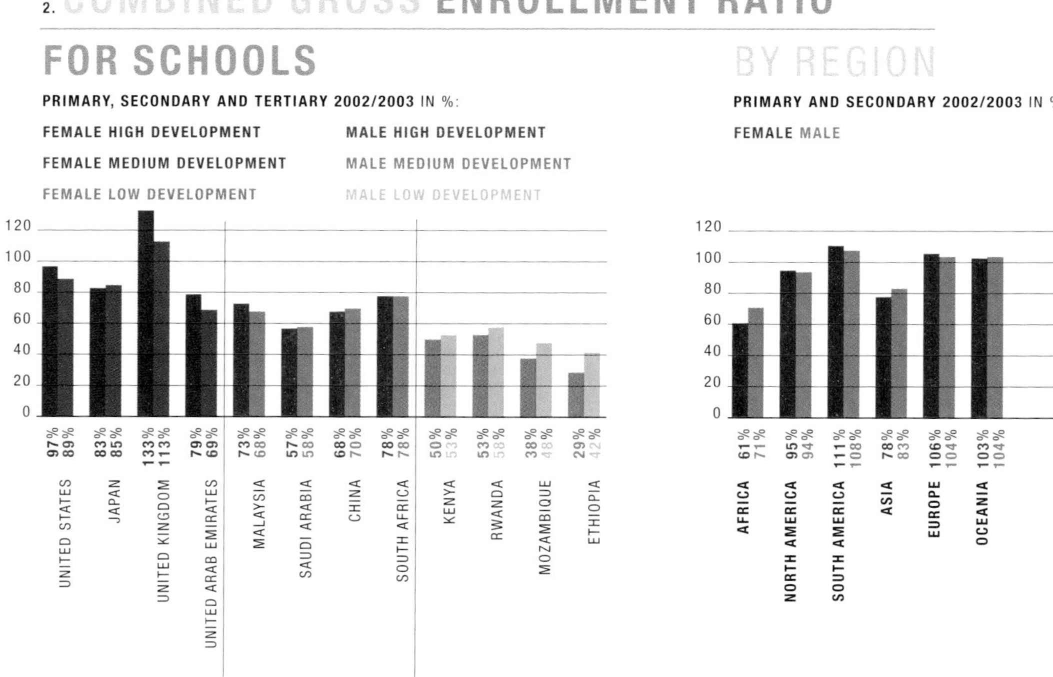

2. COMBINED GROSS ENROLLMENT RATIO
FOR SCHOOLS
PRIMARY, SECONDARY AND TERTIARY 2002/2003 IN %:
FEMALE HIGH DEVELOPMENT
MALE HIGH DEVELOPMENT
FEMALE MEDIUM DEVELOPMENT
MALE MEDIUM DEVELOPMENT
FEMALE LOW DEVELOPMENT
MALE LOW DEVELOPMENT
120
100
80
60
40
20
0
97% 89% UNITED STATES
83% 85% JAPAN
133% 113% UNITED KINGDOM
79% 69% UNITED ARAB EMIRATES
73% 68% MALAYSIA
57% 58% SAUDI ARABIA
68% 70% CHINA
78% 78% SOUTH AFRICA
50% 53% KENYA
53% 58% RWANDA
38% 48% MOZAMBIQUE
29% 42% ETHIOPIA
HIGH DEVELOPMENT
MEDIUM DEVELOPMENT
LOW DEVELOPMENT
BY REGION
PRIMARY AND SECONDARY 2002/2003 IN %
FEMALE MALE
61% 71% AFRICA
95% 94% NORTH AMERICA
111% 108% SOUTH AMERICA
78% 83% ASIA
106% 104% EUROPE
103% 104% OCEANIA

3. ESTIMATED EARNED INCOME

2003 PPP US$:

FEMALE HIGH DEVELOPMENT
FEMALE MEDIUM DEVELOPMENT
FEMALE LOW DEVELOPMENT
MALE HIGH DEVELOPMENT
MALE MEDIUM DEVELOPMENT
MALE LOW DEVELOPMENT

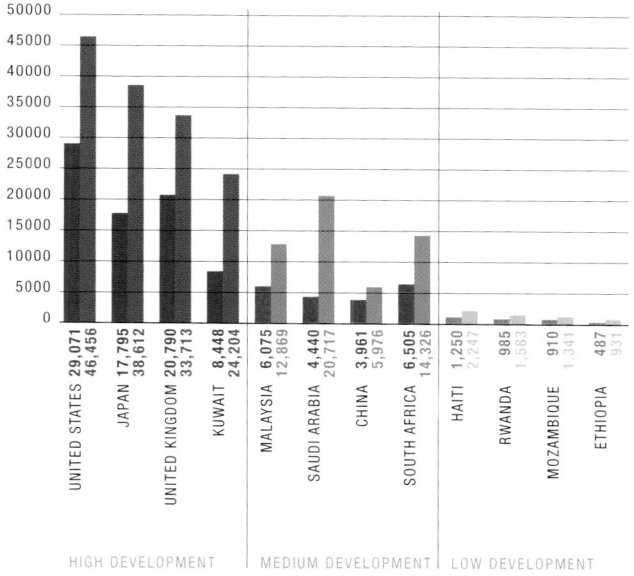

	Country	Female	Male
HIGH DEVELOPMENT	UNITED STATES	29,071	46,456
	JAPAN	17,795	38,612
	UNITED KINGDOM	20,790	33,713
	KUWAIT	8,448	24,204
MEDIUM DEVELOPMENT	MALAYSIA	6,075	12,869
	SAUDI ARABIA	4,440	20,717
	CHINA	3,961	5,976
	SOUTH AFRICA	6,505	14,326
LOW DEVELOPMENT	HAITI	1,250	2,247
	RWANDA	985	1,583
	MOZAMBIQUE	910	1,341
	ETHIOPIA	487	931

BY REGION

2003 PPP US$:

FEMALE MALE

Region	Female	Male
AFRICA	1,892	4,046
NORTH AMERICA	26,470	42,014
LATIN AMERICA	4,277	9,692
ASIA	4,897	9,420
EUROPE + CENTRAL ASIA	13,281	23,689
OCEANIA	9,928	15,069
MIDDLE EAST	5,020	15,397

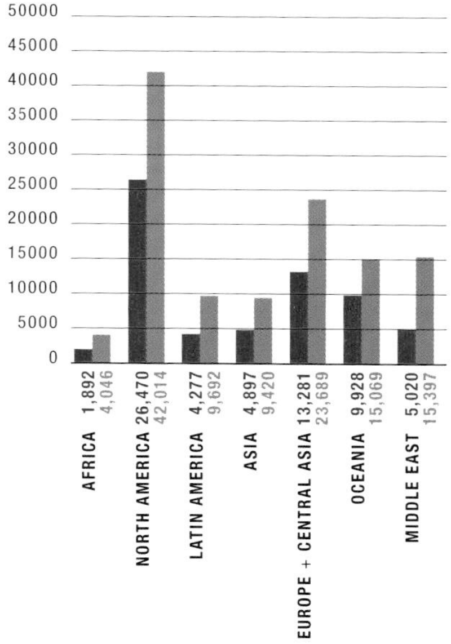

ADULT LITERACY RATE

000 – 2004, % AGES 15 AND ABOVE:

EMALE MALE FEMALE MALE

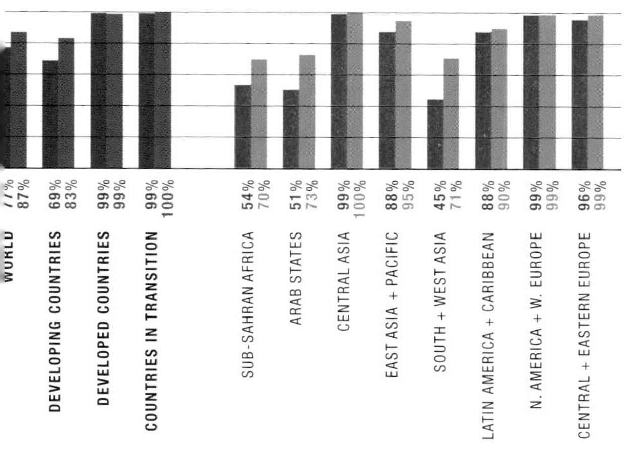

	Female	Male
WORLD	77%	87%
DEVELOPING COUNTRIES	69%	83%
DEVELOPED COUNTRIES	99%	99%
COUNTRIES IN TRANSITION	99%	100%
SUB-SAHRAN AFRICA	54%	70%
ARAB STATES	51%	73%
CENTRAL ASIA	99%	100%
EAST ASIA + PACIFIC	88%	95%
SOUTH + WEST ASIA	45%	71%
LATIN AMERICA + CARIBBEAN	88%	90%
N. AMERICA + W. EUROPE	99%	99%
CENTRAL + EASTERN EUROPE	96%	99%

YOUTH LITERACY RATE

2000 – 2004, % AGES 15 – 24:

FEMALE MALE FEMALE MALE

	Female	Male
WORLD	84%	91%
DEVELOPING COUNTRIES	81%	89%
DEVELOPED COUNTRIES	100%	100%
COUNTRIES IN TRANSITION	99%	99%
SUB-SAHRAN AFRICA	72%	81%
ARAB STATES	72%	84%
CENTRAL ASIA	98%	98%
EAST ASIA + PACIFIC	97%	98%
SOUTH + WEST ASIA	63%	82%
LATIN AMERICA + CARIBBEAN	96%	95%
N. AMERICA + W. EUROPE	100%	100%
CENTRAL + EASTERN EUROPE	98%	99%

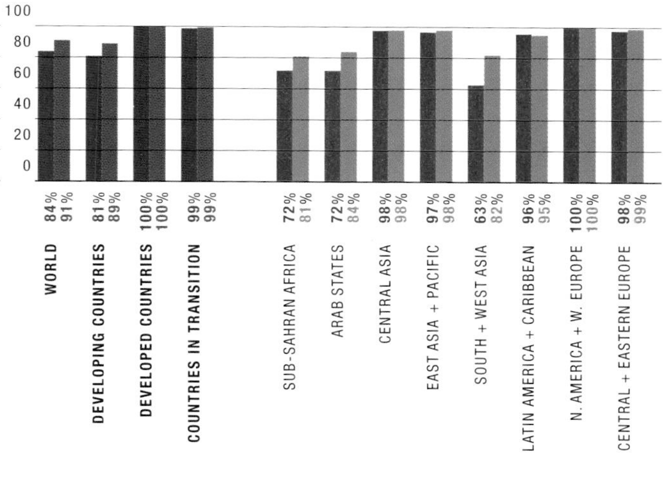

- **women should be permitted to work outside the home - seperation of the sexes** in the workplace

- **women have the right to decide if they wear a veil - women + professions** by regions

5. WOMEN SHOULD BE PERMITTED TO WORK OUTSIDE THE HOME

% OF PEOPLE AGREEING, 2002:

AVERAGE % BY REGION

% BY SELECTED COUNTRIES

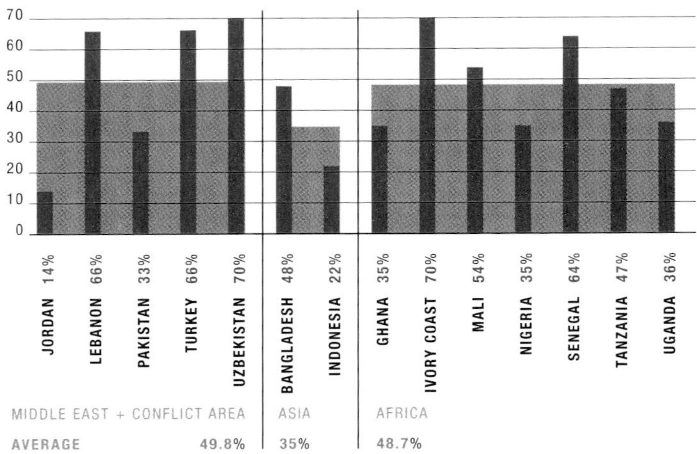

7. WOMEN SHOULD WORK SEPERATELY FROM MEN AT WORKPLACE

% OF PEOPLE AGREEING, 2002:

AVERAGE % BY REGION

% BY SELECTED COUNTRIES

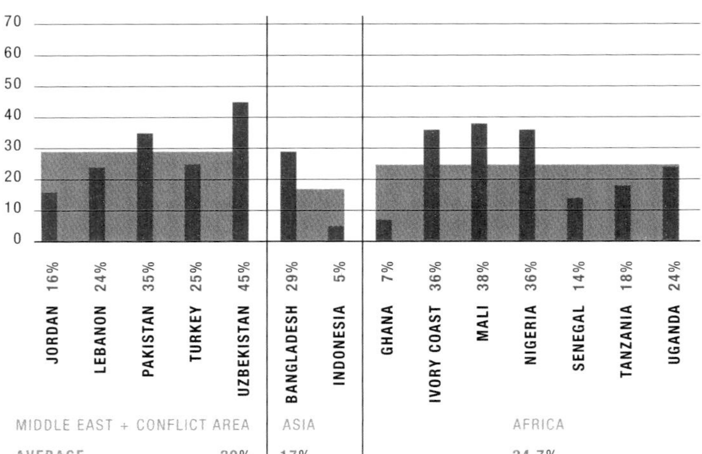

6. WOMEN SHOULD HAVE THE RIGHT TO DECIDE IF THEY WEAR A VEIL

% **OF PEOPLE AGREEING, 2002**:

AVERAGE % BY REGION

% **BY SELECTED COUNTRIES**

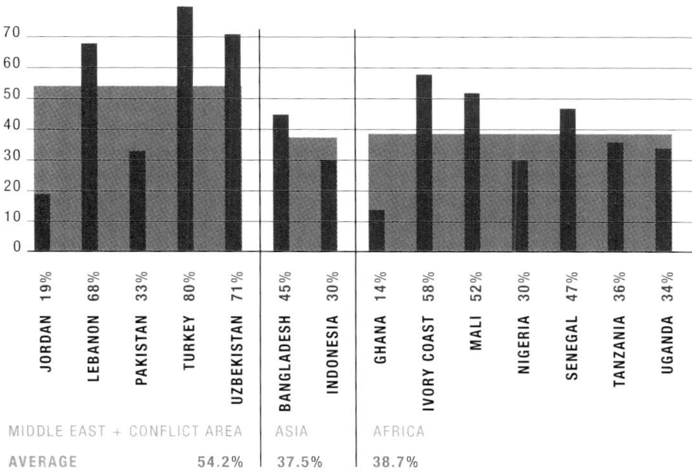

8. FEMALE PROFESSIONAL + TECHNICAL WORKERS

% **OF TOTAL** BY REGIONS

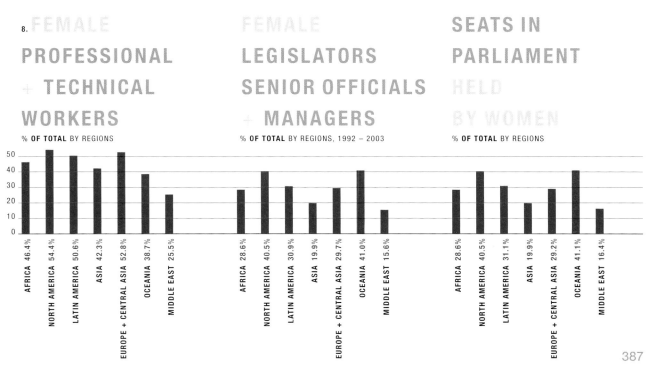

AFRICA	46.4%
NORTH AMERICA	54.4%
LATIN AMERICA	50.6%
ASIA	42.3%
EUROPE + CENTRAL ASIA	52.8%
OCEANIA	38.7%
MIDDLE EAST	25.5%

FEMALE LEGISLATORS SENIOR OFFICIALS + MANAGERS

% **OF TOTAL** BY REGIONS, 1992 – 2003

AFRICA	28.6%
NORTH AMERICA	40.5%
LATIN AMERICA	30.9%
ASIA	19.9%
EUROPE + CENTRAL ASIA	29.7%
OCEANIA	41.0%
MIDDLE EAST	15.6%

SEATS IN PARLIAMENT HELD BY WOMEN

% **OF TOTAL** BY REGIONS

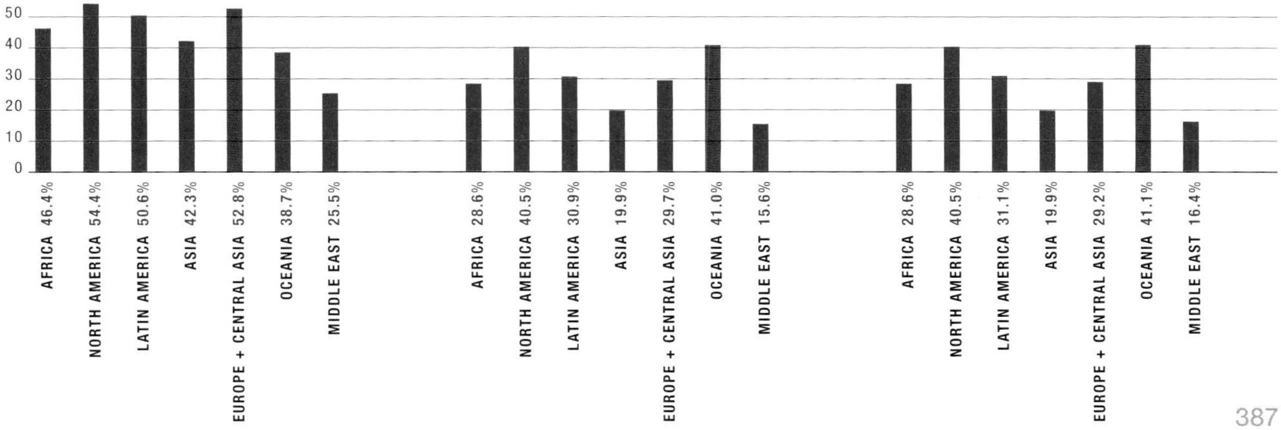

AFRICA	28.6%
NORTH AMERICA	40.5%
LATIN AMERICA	31.1%
ASIA	19.9%
EUROPE + CENTRAL ASIA	29.2%
OCEANIA	41.1%
MIDDLE EAST	16.4%

RELIGIOUS INSTITUTIONS

- world religion adherents - catholic hierarchy - dioceses / bishops / cathedrals
- parishes / priests - % roman catholic world population

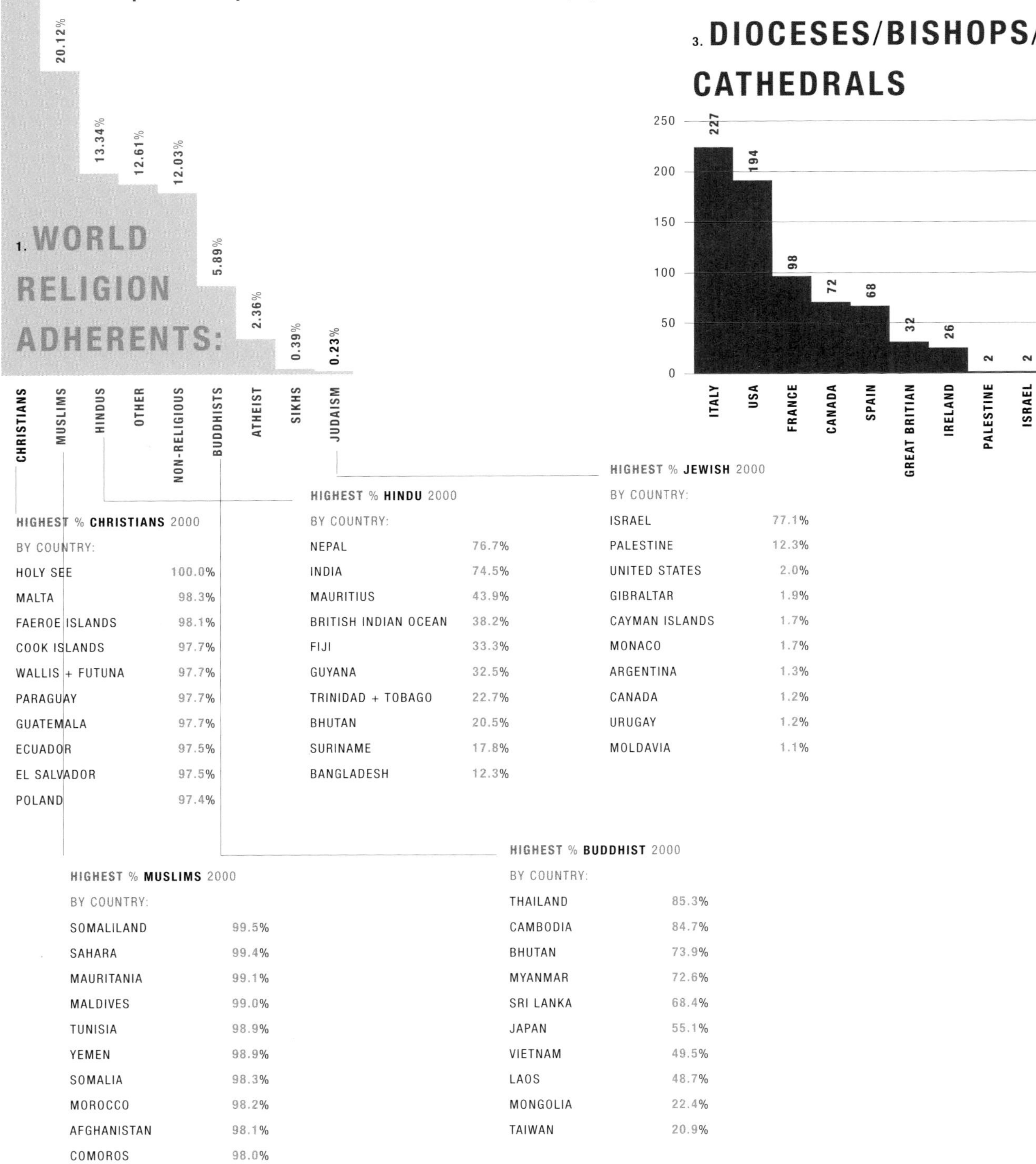

HIGHEST % CHRISTIANS 2000

BY COUNTRY:

HOLY SEE	100.0%
MALTA	98.3%
FAEROE ISLANDS	98.1%
COOK ISLANDS	97.7%
WALLIS + FUTUNA	97.7%
PARAGUAY	97.7%
GUATEMALA	97.7%
ECUADOR	97.5%
EL SALVADOR	97.5%
POLAND	97.4%

HIGHEST % HINDU 2000

BY COUNTRY:

NEPAL	76.7%
INDIA	74.5%
MAURITIUS	43.9%
BRITISH INDIAN OCEAN	38.2%
FIJI	33.3%
GUYANA	32.5%
TRINIDAD + TOBAGO	22.7%
BHUTAN	20.5%
SURINAME	17.8%
BANGLADESH	12.3%

HIGHEST % JEWISH 2000

BY COUNTRY:

ISRAEL	77.1%
PALESTINE	12.3%
UNITED STATES	2.0%
GIBRALTAR	1.9%
CAYMAN ISLANDS	1.7%
MONACO	1.7%
ARGENTINA	1.3%
CANADA	1.2%
URUGAY	1.2%
MOLDAVIA	1.1%

HIGHEST % MUSLIMS 2000

BY COUNTRY:

SOMALILAND	99.5%
SAHARA	99.4%
MAURITANIA	99.1%
MALDIVES	99.0%
TUNISIA	98.9%
YEMEN	98.9%
SOMALIA	98.3%
MOROCCO	98.2%
AFGHANISTAN	98.1%
COMOROS	98.0%

HIGHEST % BUDDHIST 2000

BY COUNTRY:

THAILAND	85.3%
CAMBODIA	84.7%
BHUTAN	73.9%
MYANMAR	72.6%
SRI LANKA	68.4%
JAPAN	55.1%
VIETNAM	49.5%
LAOS	48.7%
MONGOLIA	22.4%
TAIWAN	20.9%

2. CATHOLIC HIERARCHY

POPE 1 HEAD

THE LEADER OF THE ROMAN CATHOLIC CHURCH, ELECTED BY THE CARDINALS FOR LIFE.

CARDINALS **192**

THE CARDINALS ARE THE ELECTED "GOVERNMENT" OF THE ROMAN CATHOLIC CHURCH. THEY ELECT THE POPE FROM AMONG THEIR NUMBER.

ARCHBISHOPS **533**

RULE OVER A LARGE AREA CALLED AN ARCHDIOCESE RESPONSIBLE FOR MAKING SURE THAT THE BISHOPS FOLLOW THE CHURCH "RULES".

BISHOPS **2,496** DIOCESES, CATHEDRALS

THE BISHOP IS RESPONSIBLE FOR A DIOCESE. THE DIOCESE IS THE MAIN ADMINISTRATIVE UNIT OF THE CHURCH. THE BISHOP SUPERVISES ALL THE ACTIVITIES OF HIS CHURCH, VISITS ALL RELIGIOUS INSTITUTIONS AT REGULAR INTERVALS AND IS RESPONSIBLE FOR TEACHING THE CHRISTIAN FAITH IN HIS DIOCESE. BISHOPS ALSO HAVE A RESPONSIBILITY TO ARRANGE WORKS OF CHARITY IN THEIR AREAS AND TO SPEAK UP FOR THE POOR. EACH DIOCESE IS DIVIDED INTO A NUMBER OF PARISHES.

PRIESTS **219,583** PARISHES

CATHOLICS **1 BILLION** MEMBERS

4. PARISHES/PRIESTS

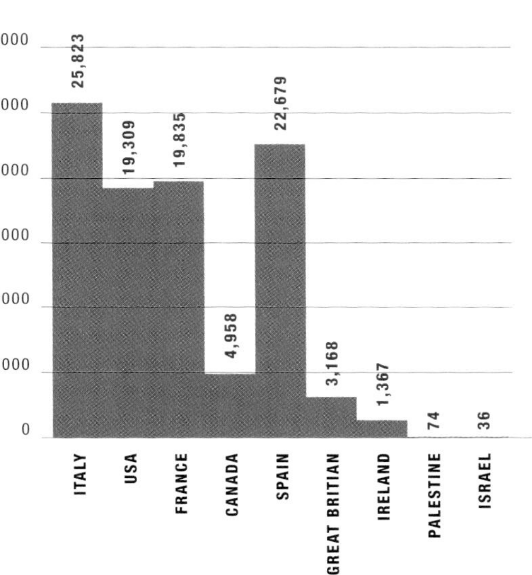

.% ROMAN CATHOLIC POPULATION

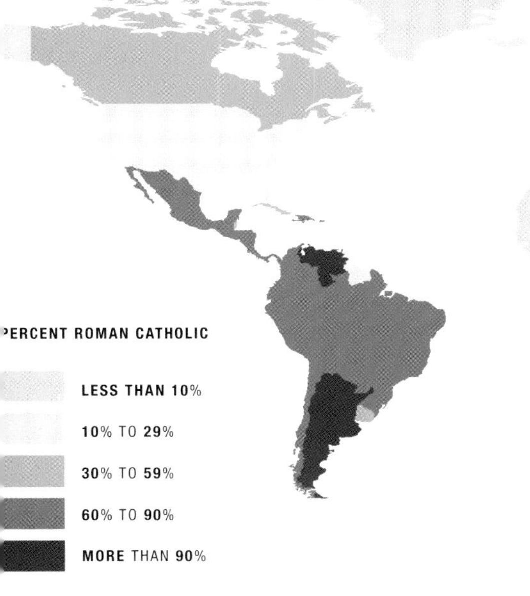

- adherents by % of population **- nominal christian world representation - christian ministry workers - christians** by income **- christian martyrs - christian resources** in 2000 **- maps**

6. ADHERENTS BY % OF POPULATION

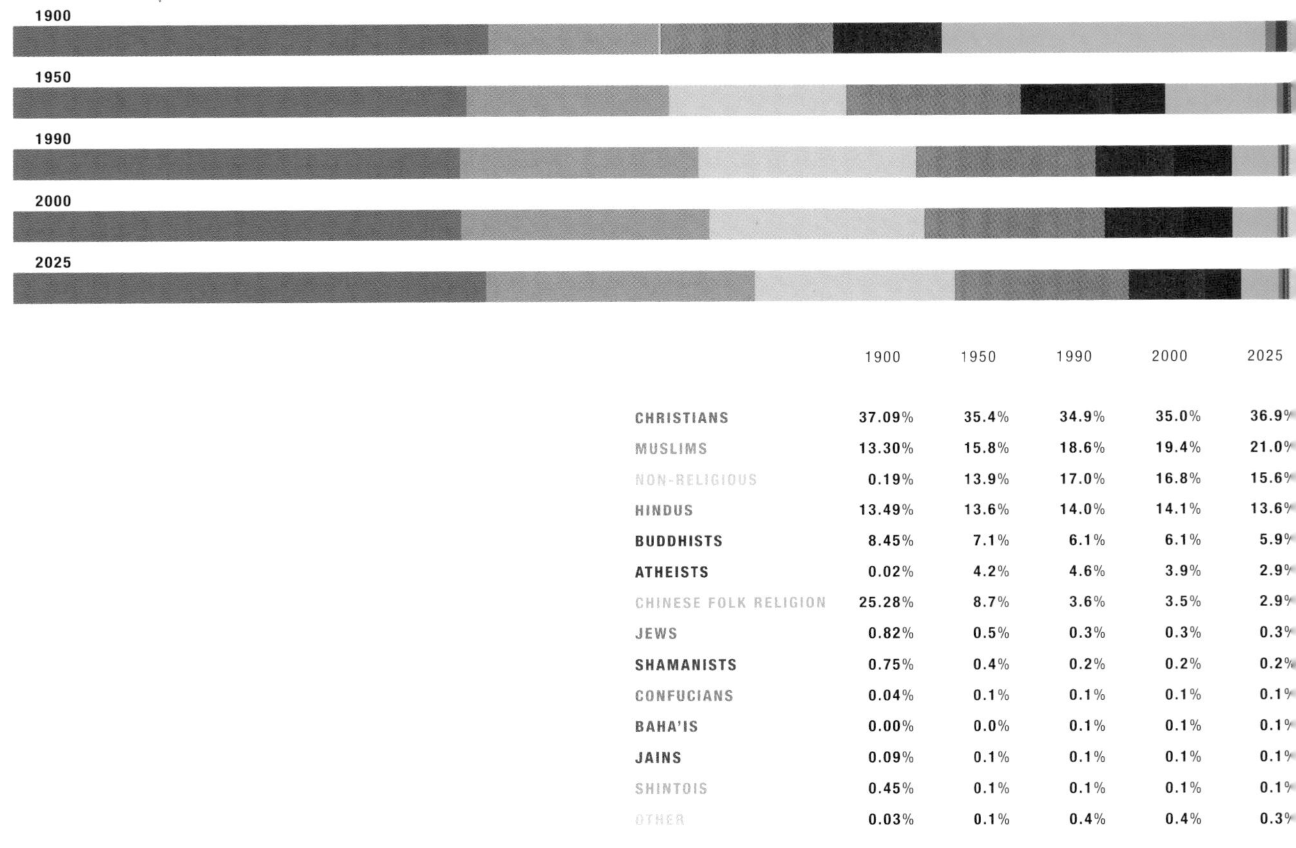

	1900	1950	1990	2000	2025
CHRISTIANS	37.09%	35.4%	34.9%	35.0%	36.9%
MUSLIMS	13.30%	15.8%	18.6%	19.4%	21.0%
NON-RELIGIOUS	0.19%	13.9%	17.0%	16.8%	15.6%
HINDUS	13.49%	13.6%	14.0%	14.1%	13.6%
BUDDHISTS	8.45%	7.1%	6.1%	6.1%	5.9%
ATHEISTS	0.02%	4.2%	4.6%	3.9%	2.9%
CHINESE FOLK RELIGION	25.28%	8.7%	3.6%	3.5%	2.9%
JEWS	0.82%	0.5%	0.3%	0.3%	0.3%
SHAMANISTS	0.75%	0.4%	0.2%	0.2%	0.2%
CONFUCIANS	0.04%	0.1%	0.1%	0.1%	0.1%
BAHA'IS	0.00%	0.0%	0.1%	0.1%	0.1%
JAINS	0.09%	0.1%	0.1%	0.1%	0.1%
SHINTOIS	0.45%	0.1%	0.1%	0.1%	0.1%
OTHER	0.03%	0.1%	0.4%	0.4%	0.3%

ADAPTED FROM SOURCE USING ADJUSTED (CORRECTED) TOTALS

7. NOMINAL CHRISTIAN WORLD REPRESENTATION INCL. NON-PRACTISING CHURCH MEMBERS

CHRISTIANS WORLDWIDE

ACTIVE CHRISTIANS 32% NOMINAL CHRISTIANS 68%

NOMINAL CHRISTIANS WORLDWIDE

CHRISTIAN WORLD 83% EVANGELIZED NON CHRISTIAN WORLD 17% UNEVANGELIZED WORLD 0.2%

8. CHRISTIAN MINISTRY WORKERS

5000000
4000000
3000000
2000000
1000000
0

YEAR 200 400 600 800 1000 1200 1400 1600 1800 2000 2200

YEAR	PASTORAL	DOMESTIC MISSIONARIES	FOREIGN MISSIONARIES
33	**200**	**200**	**0**
200	**63,000**	**12,600**	**1,400**
400	**89,000**	**17,900**	**1,800**
600	**188,000**	**37,900**	**3,700**
800	**115,000**	**23,200**	**2,400**
1000	**88,000**	**17,900**	**1,800**
1200	**280,000**	**55,800**	**3,800**
1400	**410,000**	**82,100**	**2,400**
1600	**868,000**	**173,700**	**14,400**
1700	**1,416,000**	**283,200**	**18,900**
1800	**1,748,000**	**349,500**	**29,200**
1900	**1,736,000**	**434,000**	**62,000**
1995	3,499,400	1,019,000	392,600
2000	**3,969,000**	**1,135,000**	**420.000**
2025	5,000,000	1,500,000	550,000

9. **CHRISTIANS** BY INCOME

JUST COPING 10% **NEEDY** 29% **DESTITUTE** 13% **AFFLUENT** 11% **WELL OFF** 37%

10. CHRISTIAN MARTYRS

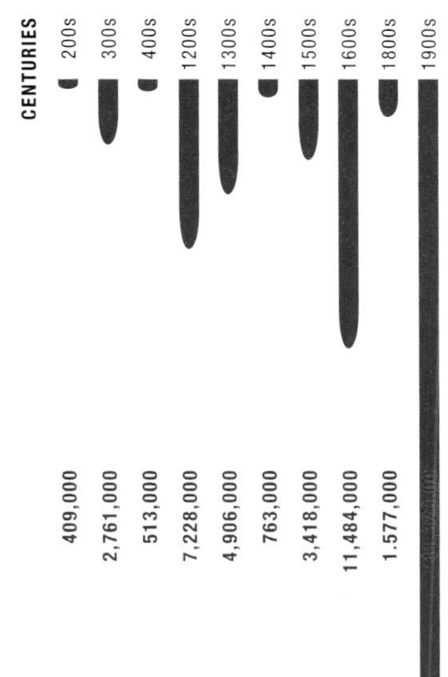

11. **CHRISTIAN RESOURCES** 2000

BIBLES DISTRIBUTED A YEAR	53,700,000
WORSHIP CENTERS (LOCAL CHURCHES)	3,450,000
MAJOR CHRISTIAN RELATED **INSTITUTIONS**	105,000
DISTINCT **DENOMINATIONS**	33,800
CHRISTIAN BOOK TITLES A YEAR	26,100
MONASTARIES, CONVENTS, ABBEYS, PRIORIES	8,000
MAJOR **COUNCILS OF CHURCHES**	6,500
HOME MISSION BOARDS	5,800
SEMINARIES/THEOLOGICAL COLLEGES	4,800
FOREIGN MISSION BOARDS	4,000
CHRISTIAN RADIO/TV STATIONS	4,000
CHRISTIAN BROADCASTING AGENCIES	1,050
CHURCH-RELATED RESEARCH CENTERS	300

12. WHAT ARE THE PREDOMINANT RELIGIONS?

PREDOMINANT RELIGION BY COUNTRY

- ANIMISM
- BUDDHISM
- CHRISTIANITY
- HINDUISM
- ISLAM
- NON-RELIGIOUS
- OTHER

13. PERCENT + GROWTH RATE OF EVANGELICALS

PERCENT EVANGELICAL

- **LESS** THEN **0.5%**
- **0.5%** TO **5%**
- **5%** TO **10%**
- **10%** TO **20%**
- **MORE** THAN **20%**

EVANGELICAL GROWTH RATE

- **FAST**
- **MODERATE**
- **SLOW**
- **NEGATIVE**
- **NONE**

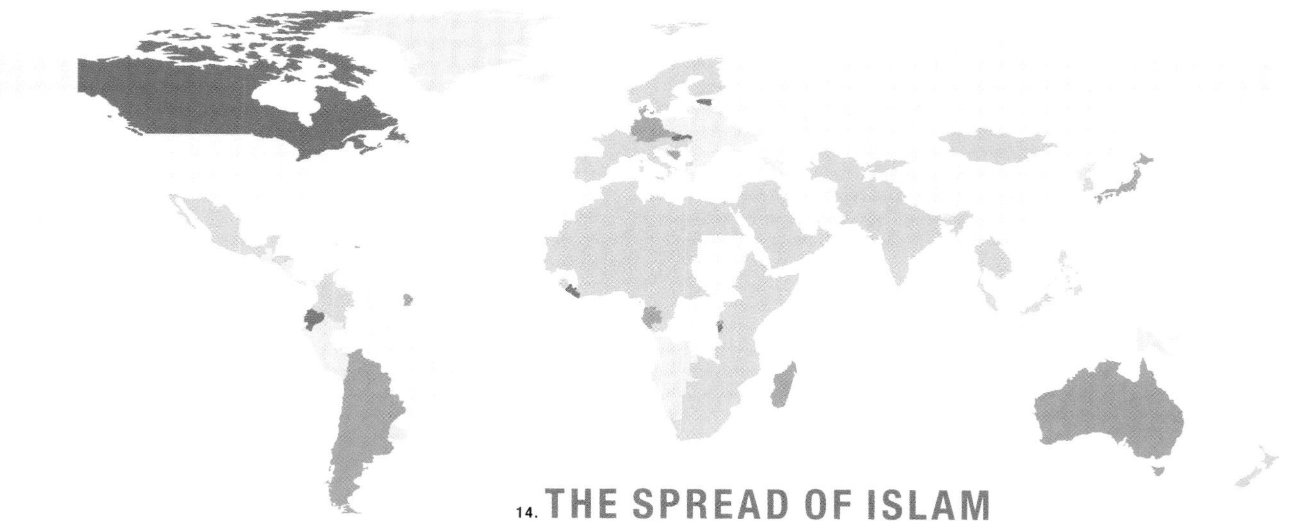

14. THE SPREAD OF ISLAM

PREDOMINANT RELIGION BY COUNTRY

- **10** TO **21**% VERY FAST
- **5** TO **10**% FAST
- **2** TO **5**% MEDIUM
- **0** TO **2**% SLOW
- **-9** TO **0**% NEGATIVE

15. WHAT PERCENT ARE EVANGELICAL CHRISTIANS?

PERCENT EVANGELICAL

- **0** TO **0.5**
- **0.5** TO **3**
- **3** TO **10**
- **10** TO **20**
- **20** TO **46.3**

ATTITUDES TOWARDS GLOBALIZATION Research on globalization has largely concentrated on transnational economic and financial activity, and the policy implications they have for national labor markets, corporate strategies, welfare states and tax regimes (Guillen, 2001). In recent years, several competing theories have been presented that focus on the interplay between different facets of globalization, in particular cultural and political reactions to economic globalization.

First, world-society researchers argue that a world-culture of institutions such as citizenship, human rights, science and technology, socioeconomic development, education, religion, and managements emerged that penetrates virtually all human endeavors (Meyer et al 1997). This global social organization of rationalized modernity has its logic and purposes built into almost all nation states, resulting in a world that shows increasing structural similarities of form among countries. At the same time, countries differ in the fit between these institutions, their needs and capacities, and therefore produce different social and economic outcomes (Meyer et al 1997). Hence we could expect public attitudes on globalization to be more positive in countries that have managed to achieve a balance between formal institutions and outcomes for the economic and social well-being of the population (see chapter 1 by Crawford).

Second, Garrett (1999) offers a dissenting perspective and argues that many governments have pursued policies aimed at buffering their citizens from the vagaries of global markets. In the presence of free capital mobility, they accept higher interest rates to keep capital at home, and shield vulnerable industries as well as population groups. In a study of over one hundred countries during the 1985-1995 period, Garrett (1999) finds no convergence in government expenditure patterns as a result of globalization, and no systematic shift away from financing the 'globalization buffer.' Hence we should find more positive public attitudes to globalization in countries that managed to shield citizens from potentially negative impacts of volatile world markets.

According to the Competitive Rankings from the World Economic Forum, the group of countries with positive attitudinal profiles has both highly competitive countries (US, UK, and Canada) as well as low competitive countries (Mexico, India). What is more, the same applies to the group of countries with more negative or cautious attitudinal patterns, with highly competitive countries such as France and Japan, and low competitive countries like Argentina or Turkey. What do results suggest about Garrett (1999) who implies that one should find more positive public attitudes to globalization in countries that managed to shield citizens from potentially negative impacts of volatile world markets? The results are inconclusive, as social welfare, education and health expenditures do not differ systematically between the two groups above.

Irrespective of these relationships, it seems that attitudes towards globalization are less directed by short-term self-interest alone, but are part of complex value dispositions. In some countries such as Canada, the US, and even India, such dispositions seem to favor the kind of openness and pro-market attitudes that seems compatible with globalization; in other countries, they seem to create more cautious agendas. Only in very few countries such as Indonesia and Pakistan, could anti-globalization feelings combine with religious fervor to bring about potentially dangerous values and attitudes.

TABLE 1. **ATTITUDES FAVORING AMERICANIZATION**

REGION:	**FAVOR AMERICAN IDEAS**	**FAVOR AMERICAN DEMOCRACY**	**FAVOR AMERICAN BUSINESS**	**FAVOR AMERICAN CULTURAL PRODUCTS**	**COMBINED SCORE**
SUB-SAHARAN AFRICA	43%	67%	62%	64%	59%
MIDDLE EAST + NORTH AFRICA	14%	37%	43%	43%	33%
SOUTH ASIA	13%	25%	28%	16%	21%
CENTRAL ASIA	33%	65%	76%	51%	56%
EAST ASIA + PACIFIC	38%	62%	51%	59%	52%
EAST + CENTRAL EUROPE	31%	50%	49%	58%	47%
WESTERN EUROPE	30%	44%	33%	68%	44%
LATIN AMERICA + THE CARIBBEAN	32%	45%	48%	61%	46%
NORTH AMERICA	58%	60%	49%	63%	57%
INCOME GROUP:					
HIGH-INCOME	40%	52%	41%	65%	49%
UPPER-MIDDLE-INCOME	30%	51%	50%	62%	48%
LOWER-MIDDLE-INCOME	30%	44%	47%	54%	44%
LOW-INCOME	34%	58%	55%	51%	50%
GRAND TOTAL:	33%	52%	49%	57%	48%

Source: Pew Charitable Trust - 2002 Global Attitudes Survey:

Q.67 Which of the following phrases comes closer to your view? It's good that American ideas and customs are spreading here, OR it's bad that American ideas and customs are spreading here.

Q.68 And which of these comes closer to your view? I like American ideas about democracy, OR I dislike American ideas about democracy.

Q.69 Which comes closer to describing your view? I like American ways of doing business, OR I dislike American ways of doing business.

Q.70 Which is closer to describing your view-I like American music, movies and television, OR I dislike American music, movies and television.

VALUES One of the most consistent findings of social research into values and attitudes is the stability of people's value patterns or 'worldviews' over time as opposed to the greater volatility of their attitudes. For example, basic values grounded in religion, and convictions about god, liberty or justice, or notions about family, tolerance, or human rights are more stable than political attitudes or opinions about public institutions or economic performance. At the same time, values and attitudes are clearly related: within the boundaries described by value patterns, people's attitudes and public opinions are more changeable and can, at times, be quite fickle, even inconsistent.

Shifts in basic value patterns are relatively rare, and if they happen, they are full of consequences and implications-from social and economic behavior and politics to the institutions of society at large. Typically, values change more between than within generations, and research attributes major inter-generational changes to differences in value formation during primary and secondary socialization (parents' economic well-being; changes in educational system etc, role of socializing agents such as religious institutions), and the impact of major events (wars, recessions, political upheavals) that, as collective experiences, shape individual value dispositions.

Over the last quarter century, and continuing into the first part of the 21st, major changes have occurred around three value-related fields: religion, role of government vs. individual responsibilities, and cosmopolitan values.

WHAT DO WE KNOW ABOUT VALUE PATTERNS?

For the developed countries of the OECD, there is general agreement that a value shift took place between 1970 and the late 1980s. Researchers have used several different labels (e.g., materialism vs. postmaterialism) to describe this value shift and the precise extent and sustainability of the changes involved continue to be debated among experts in the field. While there are many sociological correlates to this value shift and its causation, it is associated with / involves (Inglehart et al, 1998; Inglehart, 2000; van Deth and Scraborough, 1995):

- Decline in reliance on family, change in the role of women, greater emphasis on individual responsibility
- Decline in emphasis on material security, less security seeking
- Decline in allegiance to traditional institutions (church, unions etc); with other forms of organizing and participation becoming more frequent
- New search for meaning of life, and greater diversity of life styles
- Rise of cosmopolitan values (more tolerance, less nationalism, appreciation of cultural diversity)
- Preference for democratic forms of governance, and for more participatory organizations

Importantly, however, this shift did not involve many other parts of the world. In particular, developing countries are left out, and the position of Central and Eastern Europe remains somewhat unsettled. In drawing 'world value maps' to show major value clusters and fault lines, researchers like Inglehart (2000:14-15) use two major dimensions, derived from careful analysis of the World Value Survey:

- Traditional authority vs. secular-rational authority (e.g., obedience to traditional authority, adherence to family and communal obligations, etc. vs. secular view that authority is legitimated by rational-legal norms, emphasis on individual achievement)
- Survival vs. well-being values (e.g., shift from scarcity norms with emphasis on hard work and self-denial to quality of life, emancipatory values and self-expression)

The value map in the suite shows that the 43 countries fall into relatively distinct value clusters, with the poorer countries in the lower right hand corner of the map, and the richer developed countries towards the upper right hand corner. To a large extent, these value patterns reflect religious influence of the past, but current and future changes are taking place against this background: the secularization trend affects traditionally Catholic countries as it does traditional Protestant countries (with the US a major exception). The upper left-hand corner of Map 1 shows the most secularized of today's world: Central and Eastern Europe, and the Confucian countries of Asia. They are undergoing neither secularization trends (as they are basically highly secular societies already), nor a revival of religiosity. Together, this suggests that in the future an increasing secularized Western Europe, a more affluent Central and Eastern Europe and North Asia (China, Japan, and South Korea) should move closer to each other on Map 1.

WHAT ARE FUTURE TRENDS?

Value researchers expect that the following trends are likely to take place over the next 15-20 years in relation to value patterns and changes:

- A drifting apart between regions of the world that are experiencing a revitalization of religion-often combined with economic underdevelopment-and those parts that are secular or secularizing.
- A continued value shift in OECD countries toward 'post-material' values - a shift that is not taking place in most other countries, with the exception of globalized professional middle class segments in urban areas of the South.
- Cosmopolitan values have become more pronounced and widespread in recent decades, and are supported by a thickening of the international rule of law.
- Distinct value patterns and political positions are emerging around globalization; to some extent these positions are fed by domestic concerns and value patterns, but also by a strengthened cosmopolitanism and an expanding global civil society.

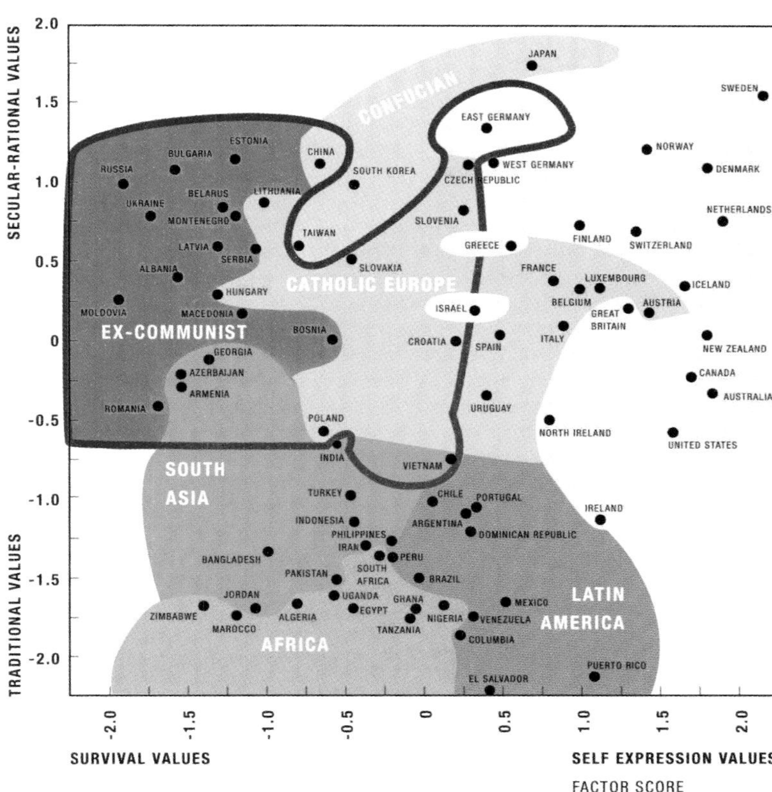

RELIGION is fundamental to the human condition and a near universal component of cultural systems. It articulates the worldviews of many societies and communities, and is central to the shaping of ideas and the production of cultural landscapes. Throughout history, humans have actively defined and maintained sacred practices and spaces. Different religions are products of their socially constituted contexts and generate different cultural patterns, including symbols, language, stories, organizations, practices, and resources. The indicator suite is largely based on the World Values Survey (1994-1999, 1999-2004) and highlights some of the following:

- Belief in a 'god' is spread equally across all high, middle and low income countries
- Men of all ages are more likely to say they are religious versus women of any age group
- Expression of religious freedom remains a privilege in most western countries and the United States, whereas South Asia experiences the lowest rate of 2.7%
- Level of education and income greatly determine views on the role of religion in politics

WHAT IS RELIGION

Defining religion has generated much controversy among theologians and social scientists, and consensus has yet to be reached. Despite the inherent difficulties in defining religion, there are certain elements of different religions that lend themselves to a cohesive generalized description. Religion loosely refers to any system of belief and/or worship, involving a philosophy of life, beliefs about deities and a code of ethics.

WHAT DO WE KNOW ABOUT RELIGION?

There are 19 major world religions, which are subdivided into 270 religious groups (Barrett, 2001). World adherents can be categorized as follows:

RELIGION (DATE FOUNDED)	SACRED TEXT	PLACE OF WORSHIP	%WORLD	GROWTH[1]
CHRISTIANITY (30AD)	The Bible	Church	**33.03**%	Dropping
ISLAM (622 AD)	The Qur'an & Hadith	Mosque	**20.12**%	Growing
HINDUISM (1500 BC)	Bhagavad-Gita, Upanishads, & Rig Veda	Temple	**13.34**%	Stable
OTHER: TRIBAL, SHAMANISM, MORMON (1830)	e.g., Book of Mormon	Various	**12.61**%	
NON-RELIGIOUS			**12.03**%	Dropping
BUDDHISM (523 BC)	The Tripitaka & Sutras	Temple	**5.89**%	Stable
ATHEISM			**2.36**%	
SIKHISM (1500 AD)	Guru Granth Sahib	Gurdwaras	**0.39**%	
JUDAISM (1900 BC)	Torah, Tanach, & Talmud	Synagogue	**0.23**%	

[1] Growth rate as % of the world population
Source: religioustolerance.org

Approximately three quarters of humanity belong to the four largest organized world religions: Christianity, Islam, Hinduism, and Buddhism. Islam is the only growing religion in the world, relative to overall population growth. Barrett (2001) suggests that Islam will maintain a stable growth rate from 2004 to 2025, whereas all other major world religions will continue to decline.

Religious adherence varies widely across cultural and geographical lines. According to the Pew Research Center, 59% of Americans say that religion is very important in their lives, as opposed to 11% of French, 21% of Germans, and 33% of Britons. Europe, particularly Western Europe, is experiencing continued secularization, with the exception of a growing Islamic population. Chadwick (1990) attributes the eroding influence of the Church to the rise of technology, increasing materialism, urbanization, the media, and the philosophies of evolutionary science and Marxism (see chapter by Inglehart and Norris).

Despite the increasing presence of the US as a "Christian" force in the world, fewer Americans identify themselves as Christians now than in previous generations. In 1947, 89% of Americans identified themselves as Christians as opposed to 82% in 2001. Furthermore, the rate of Americans identifying as non-religious between 1990 and 2000 grew 110%. Likewise, growth rates of other religions grew 170% for Buddhism, 237% for Hinduism, and 109% for Islam (Pew Forum, 2002).

In Latin America, while Roman Catholicism remains the dominant religion, the continent is undergoing a period of intense religious transformation, gravitating towards an increasing pluralization of faith. With the traditional Roman Catholic Church fading as a monolithic religious power, Catholicism in Latin America has restructured itself through the expansion of "renewal," or an increasingly Pentecostal and charismatic type of Catholicism, bringing more Protestant elements into its religious sphere (Smith & Prokopy, 1999).

Africa is currently experiencing a revival across faith lines. Christianity is growing faster in sub-Saharan Africa than anywhere else in the world, increasing at a rate of 3.5% a year. The growth of Christianity is attributed to two major waves: the rise of indigenous churches during the colonial years of the 1950s and 60s, and a more recent proliferation of evangelical and faith-healing churches (Robinson, 2000). Meanwhile, Islam's expansion in Africa is facilitated by a deluge of funding into Muslim communities by donors from Saudi Arabia and Kuwait, amounting in the billions of dollars. Traditional African religions are also experiencing a renaissance (Bunting, 2005).

WHAT ARE THE ISSUES?

As the various chapters in this volume dealing with religion have shown, the issues surrounding this phenomenon, be they theological, political, economic or social, are too numerous to be listed here and too complex for treating even a selection adequately. Three key issues are: the continued secularization of the developed world, and the proliferation of proselytizing religions, in particular Christian missions in Latin America, Russia, Asia and Africa; the growth of Islam in its role in democratic society; and the events of September 11, 2001 and their aftermath, which have brought the issue of religion, particularly Islam, to the forefront of contemporary discussion in the West, and fuelled popular discourse about a clash of civilizations. However, the conflict is less between Islam and Christianity as it is between Islam and Western secularism, as illustrated by the Danish cartoon crisis of 2005/2006.

KNOWLEDGE

CREATION

DISSEMINATION

STORAGE

INNOVATION + PROTECTION

CREATION

- top countries by # of **think tanks + staff size - world think tank matrix** - top **think tanks** by revenue - top **think tanks by staff size** + % **of staff researchers - average enrollment ratio** % of total population **in higher education** by region 2001 - **average tertiary enrollment** by region + gender, 2001 - # of **female students enrolled in tertiary education** by top 10 countries - **distribution of fields of study** by region

1. TOP **COUNTRIES** BY # OF **THINK TANKS** + **STAFF SIZE**

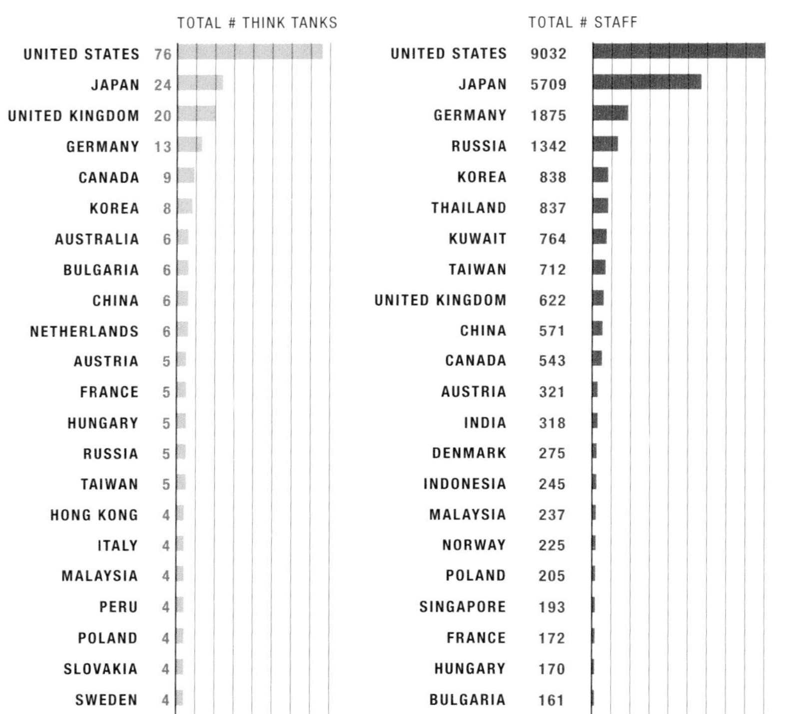

3. TOP **THINK TANKS** BY **REVENUE**

CONVERTED TO $US BY YEAR REPORTED

UNITED STATES	BROOKINGS INSTITUTION	49.80
	ASPEN INSTITUTE	58.00
	RAND CORPORATION	251.00
UNITED KINGDOM	INSTITUTE OF DEVELOPMENT STUDIES	21.20
	INTERNATIONAL INSTITUTE OF STRATEGIC STUDIES	13.90
	OVERSEAS DEVELOPMENT INSTITUTE	16.80
GERMANY	DIW BERLIN, GERMAN INSTITUTE FOR ECON RESEARCH	7.70
	IFO INSTITUTE FOR ECONOMIC RESEARCH	18.10
	KIEL INSTITUTE FOR WORLD ECONOMICS	27.60
JAPAN	INSTITUTE FOR DEVELOPING ECONOMIES JETRO	51.00
	MITSUBISHI RESEARCH INSTITUTE INC.	242.50
	MIZUHO INFORMATION & RESEARCH INSTITUTE,INC.	15.80

CONVERSIONS:

2004 1GBP = 1.93 USD
2000 1DEM = 0.48 USD
2003 1 EURO = 1.26 USD
2004 1 EURO = 1.36 USD
2004 1JPY = 0.0097 USD
2005 1 JPY = 0.0085 USD

2005 REVENUES REPORTED: BROOKINGS, ASPEN

2004 REVENUES REPORTED: RAND, INSTITUTE FOR DEVEL. STUDIES, INT'L INSTIT. FOR STRATEGIE STUDIES, ODI, JETRO, MIZUHO

2000 REVENUES REPORTED: DIW

2003 REVENUES REPORTED: KIEL INSTITUTE

- top **500 universities in the world** by region - top **100 universities in the world** by region - **countries** with the most top **100 universities** - # of **nobel prize winners** by top 5 universities in the world since 1904 - # of **international students** by top 5 universities, 2004-5 - **total expenses** + **revenue** in million $USD by top 5 universities, 2004-5 - top **20 countries with the most funding for technology** + **science** - **gross domestic expenditure on r+d** as % of GDP for 2001

2. THINK TANK COMPARISON CHART

*DOES NOT INCLUDE BOOKS PUBLISHED BY COMMERCIAL PRESSES

NAME:	LOCATION:	YEAR:	AGE:	TOTAL REVENUE:	# STAFF:	# RESEARCHERS:	ESTIMATED # PUBLICATIONS*:
BROOKINGS INSTITUTION	USA	**1916**	90 yrs	**49.8** million US$ 2005	**277**	117	**5,014**
ASPEN INSTITUTE	USA	**1950**	56	**58.2** million US$ 2005	**142**	31	**240**
CATO INSTITUTE	USA	**1977**	29	**14.0** million US$ 2005	**130**	35	**451**
COUNCIL ON FOREIGN RELATIONS	USA	**1921**	85	**32.0** million US$ 2005	**215**	70	**321**
HERITAGE FOUNDATION	USA	**1973**	33	**37.4** million US$ 2004	**195**	61	**226**
RAND CORPORATION	USA	**1948**	58	**251.0** million US$ 2005	**1,600**	730	**4,509**
INSTITUTE FOR EMPLOYMENT STUDIES	UK	**1968**	38 yrs	**5.2** million GB£ 2004	**60**	43	**318**
INSTITUTE OF DEVELOPMENT STUDIES	UK	**1966**	40	**11.0** million GB£ 2004	**200**	80	**939**
INTERNATIONAL INSTITUTE OF STRATEGIC STUDIES	UK	**1958**	48	**7.2** million GB£ 2004	**40**	23	**152**
OVERSEAS DEVELOPMENT INSTITUTE	UK	**1960**	46	**8.7** million GB£ 2004	**118**	71	**439**
DIW BERLIN, GERMAN INSTITUTE FOR ECON RESEARCH	GERMANY	**1925**	81 yrs	**16.0** million US$ 2000	**184**		
IFO INSTITUTE FOR ECONOMIC RESEARCH	GERMANY	**1949**	57	**13.3** million Euro 2004	**165**	64	
KIEL INSTITUTE FOR WORLD ECONOMICS	GERMANY	**1914**	92	**22.0** million Euro 2003	**270**	65	
INSTITUTE FOR DEVELOPING ECONOMIES							
JAPAN EXTERNAL TRADE ORGANIZATION	JAPAN	**1960**	46 yrs	**5,265** million ¥ 2004	**232**	147	**24**
UJF INSTITUTE LTD.	JAPAN	**1985**	21	**2,060** million ¥ 2005	**700**		**129**
MITSUBISHI RESEARCH INSTITUTE, INC.	JAPAN	**1970**	36	**25,000** million ¥ 2004	**767**	614	**70**
MIZUHO INFORMATION & RESEARCH INSTITUTE,INC.	JAPAN	**2004**	2	**1,627** million ¥ 2004	**4,500**	347	

4. TOP THINK TANKS BY STAFF SIZE + % OF STAFF RESEARCHERS*

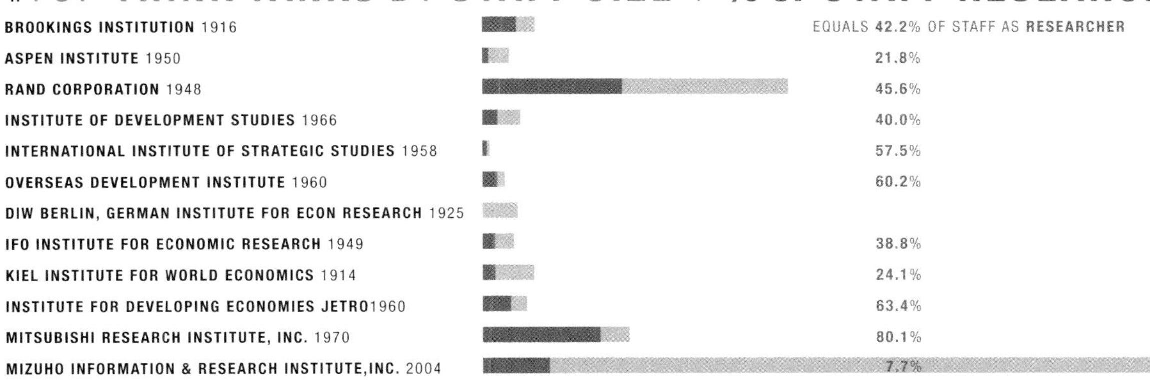

* FOR #'s SEE CHART ABOVE

5. AVERAGE ENROLLMENT RATIO

IN HIGHER EDUCATION BY REGION

% OF TOTAL POPULATION, 2001

ARAB STATES	21.6%
CENTRAL + EASTERN EUROPE	41.5%
CENTRAL ASIA	28.7%
EAST ASIA + PACIFIC	27.7%
LATIN AMERICA + THE CARIBBEAN	27.3%
NORTH AMERICA + WESTERN EUROPE	55.3%
SOUTH + WEST ASIA	10.9%
SUB-SAHARAN AFRICA	3.6%

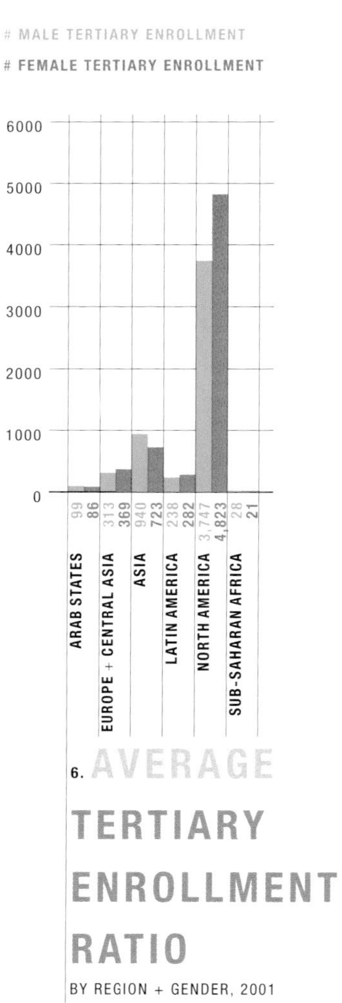

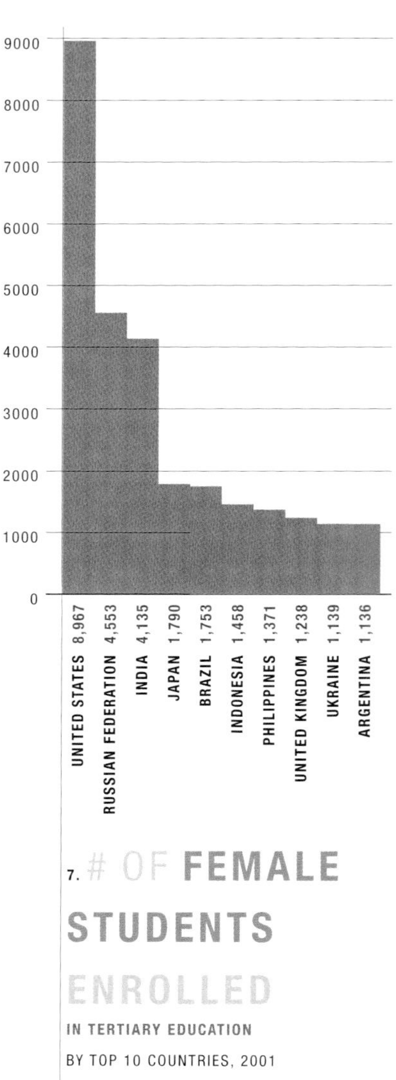

9. TOP 500 UNIVERSITIES IN THE WORLD BY REGION

AMERICAS 40% | EUROPE 40% | ASIA/PACIFIC 19% | AFRICAS 1%

10. TOP 100 UNIVERSITIES IN THE WORLD BY REGION

AMERICAS 57% | EUROPE 35% | ASIA/PACIFIC 8%

11. # OF INTERNATIONAL STUDENTS BY TOP UNIVERSITIES 2005 – 6

49% UNIVERSITY OF CALIFORNIA (10)	16% HARVARD	14% STANFORD	12% MIT	9% TOKYO
10,834	3,619	3,046	2,792	2,103

8. DISTRIBUTION OF FIELD OF STUDY

BY REGION, ★ SHOWS MOST STUDIES OF SPECIFIC FIELD

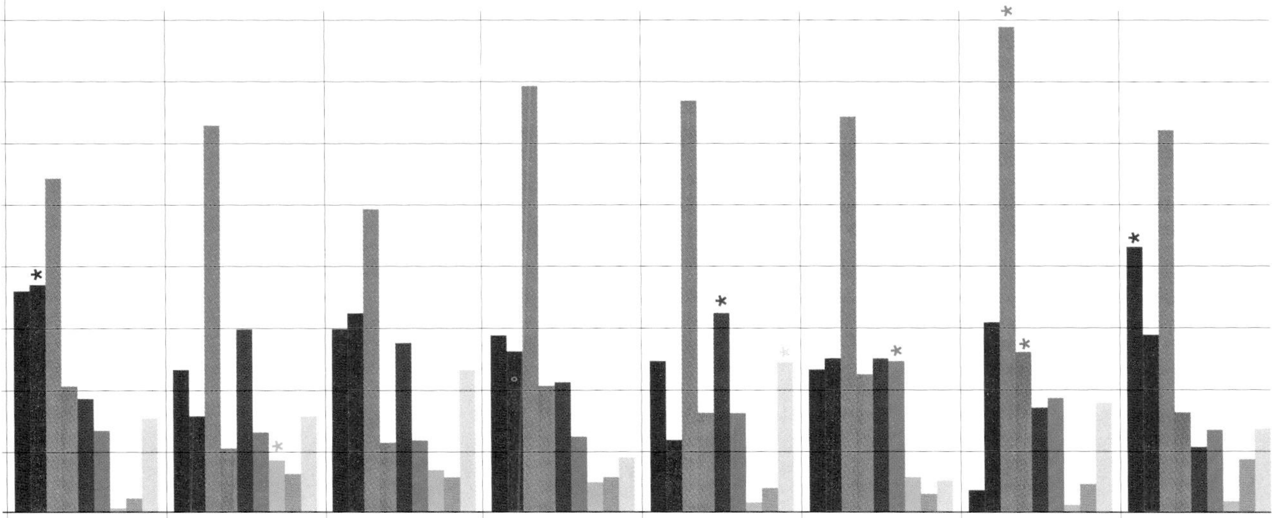

	ARAB STATES	CENTRAL + EASTERN EUROPE	CENTRAL ASIA	EAST ASIA + THE PACIFIC	LATIN AMERICA + THE CARIBBEAN	NORTH AMERICA + WESTERN EUROPE	SOUTH + WEST ASIA	SUB-SAHARAN AFRICA
EDUCATION	18.1	12.5	15.0	14.5	12.4	11.7	1.9	21.6
HUMANITIES AND THE ARTS	18.6	8.5	16.3	13.2	6.0	12.6	15.5	14.5
SOCIAL SCIENCE, BUSINESS, LAW	27.2	33.6	24.7	34.7	33.5	32.2	39.5	31.1
SCIENCE	10.4	5.7	5.8	10.4	8.2	11.3	13.1	8.2
ENGINEERING, MANUFACTURING, CONSTRUCTION	9.4	16.0	13.9	10.7	16.3	12.6	8.6	5.4
HEALTH & WELFARE	6.8	7.1	6.0	6.3	8.2	12.4	9.4	6.8
SERVICES	0.4	4.7	3.6	2.6	0.9	3.0	0.7	1.0
AGRICULTURE	1.2	3.5	3.0	3.0	2.1	1.6	2.4	4.4
OTHER/UNKNOWN	7.8	8.5	11.7	4.6	12.3	2.7	9.0	6.9

13. # OF NOBEL PRIZE WINNERS

BY TOP 5 UNIVERSITIES IN THE WORLD SINCE 1904

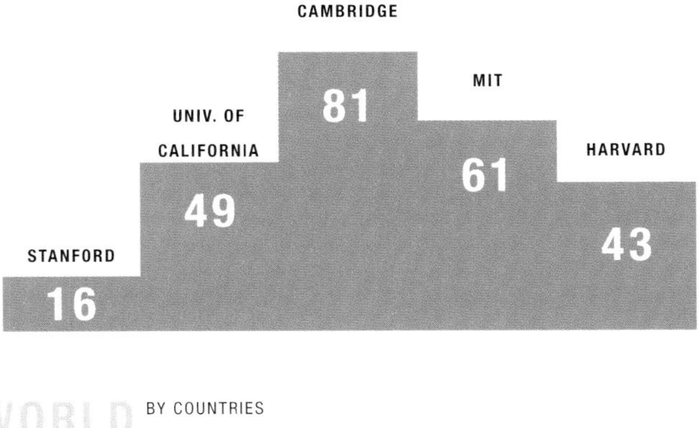

STANFORD
16
UNIV. OF CALIFORNIA
49
CAMBRIDGE
81
MIT
61
HARVARD
43

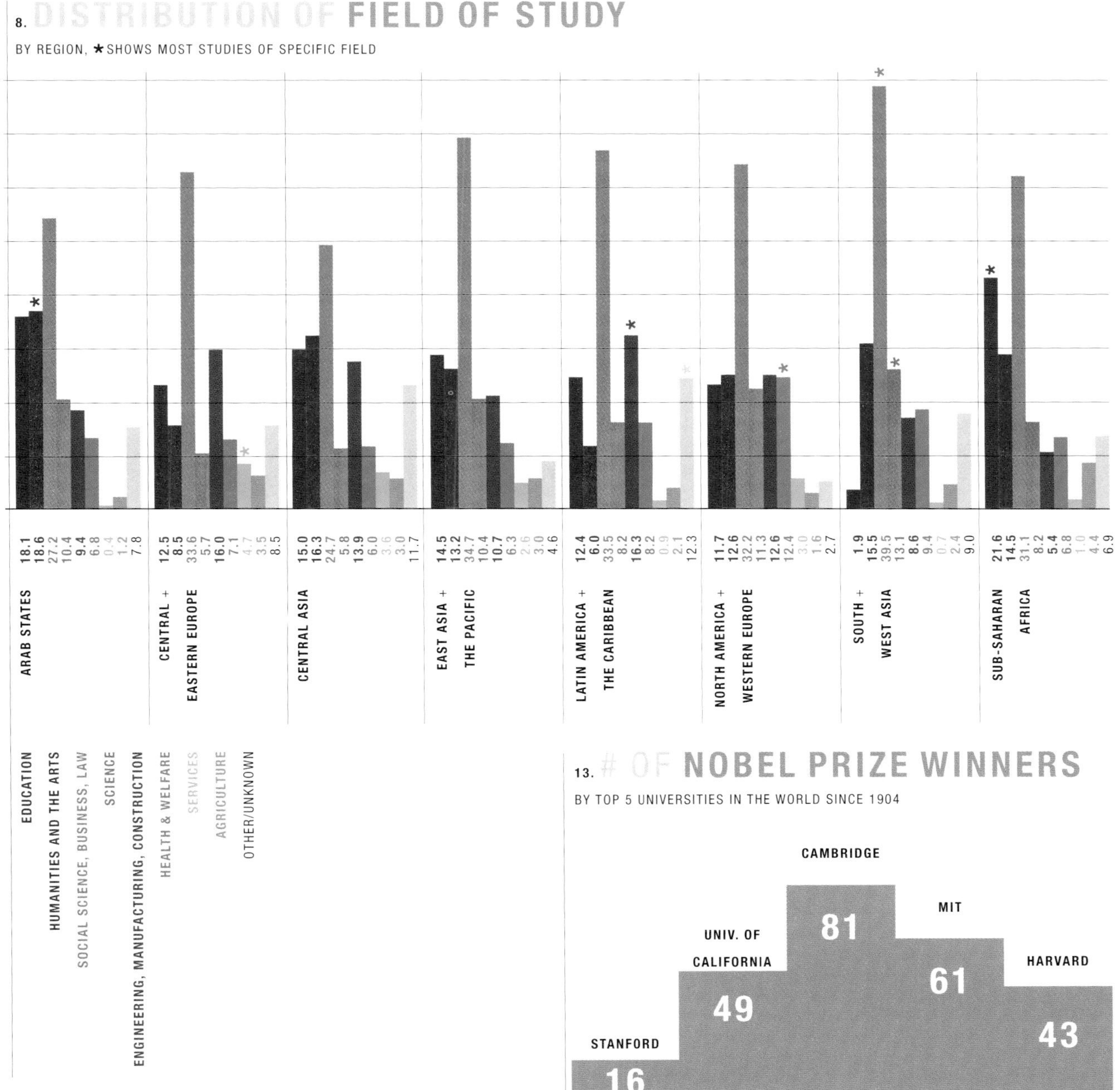

12. TOP 100 UNIVERSITIES IN THE WORLD

BY COUNTRIES

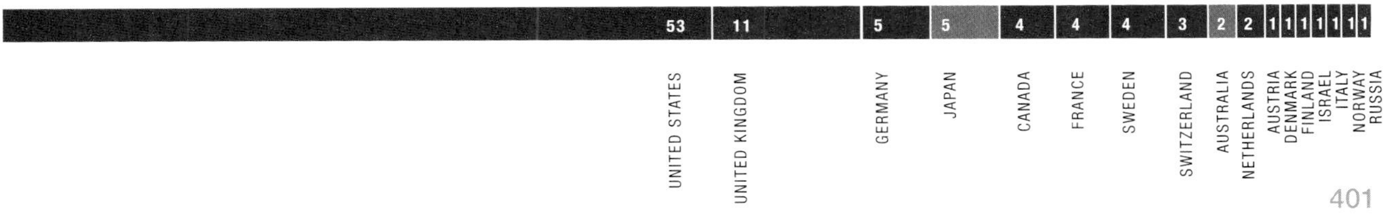

53 UNITED STATES
11 UNITED KINGDOM
5 GERMANY
5 JAPAN
4 CANADA
4 FRANCE
4 SWEDEN
3 SWITZERLAND
2 AUSTRALIA
2 NETHERLANDS
1 AUSTRIA
1 DENMARK
1 FINLAND
1 ISRAEL
1 ITALY
1 NORWAY
1 RUSSIA

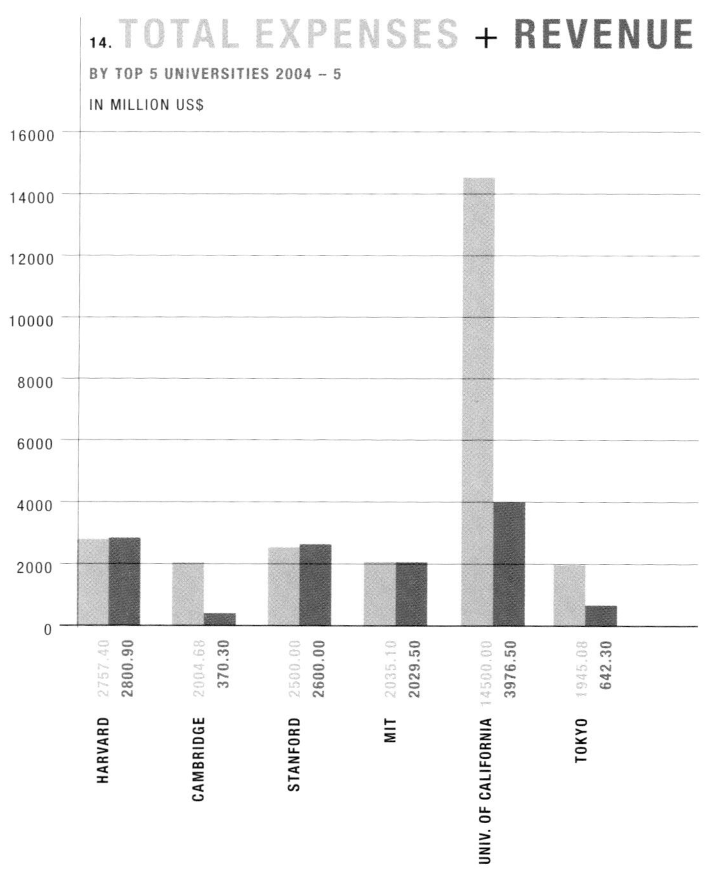
14. TOTAL EXPENSES + REVENUE
BY TOP 5 UNIVERSITIES 2004 – 5
IN MILLION US$
16000
14000
12000
10000
8000
6000
4000
2000
0
2757.40
2800.90
2004.68
370.30
2500.00
2600.00
2035.10
2029.50
14500.00
3976.50
1945.08
642.30
HARVARD
CAMBRIDGE
STANFORD
MIT
UNIV. OF CALIFORNIA
TOKYO

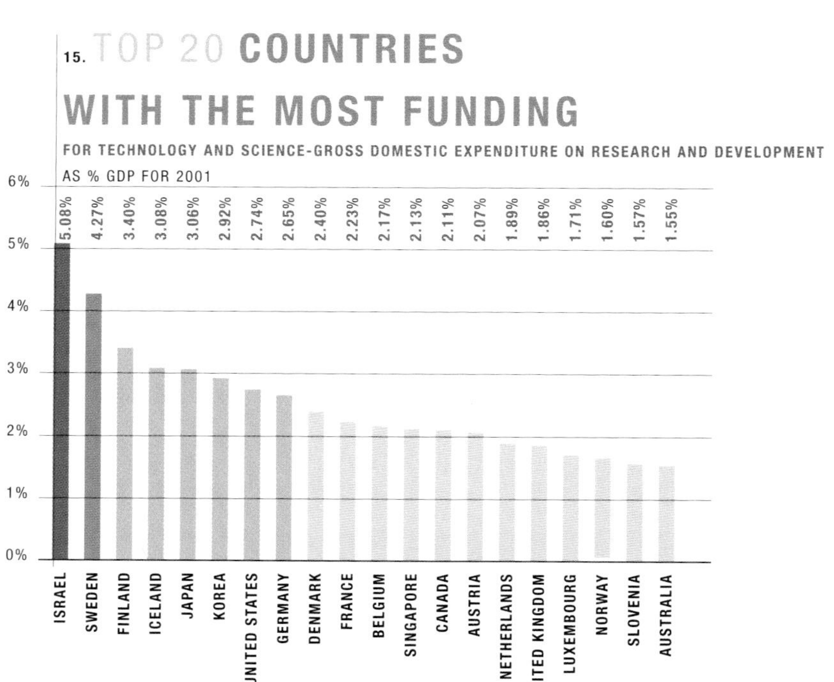
15. TOP 20 COUNTRIES
WITH THE MOST FUNDING
FOR TECHNOLOGY AND SCIENCE-GROSS DOMESTIC EXPENDITURE ON RESEARCH AND DEVELOPMENT
AS % GDP FOR 2001
6%
5%
4%
3%
2%
1%
0%
5.08%
4.27%
3.40%
3.08%
3.06%
2.92%
2.74%
2.65%
2.40%
2.23%
2.17%
2.13%
2.11%
2.07%
1.89%
1.86%
1.71%
1.60%
1.57%
1.55%
ISRAEL
SWEDEN
FINLAND
ICELAND
JAPAN
KOREA
UNITED STATES
GERMANY
DENMARK
FRANCE
BELGIUM
SINGAPORE
CANADA
AUSTRIA
NETHERLANDS
UNITED KINGDOM
LUXEMBOURG
NORWAY
SLOVENIA
AUSTRALIA

DISSEMINATION - estimated # of **academic/scholarly journal publications** by select country - estimated # of **academic/scholarly journal publishers** per select country - ten largest **academic/scholarly journal publishers** by # of journals published:UK - ten largest **academic/scholarly journal publishers** by # of journals published:USA - largest **academic/scholarly journal publishers:** # of e-published journals (as of march 06) - top 5 **academic/scholarly journal publishers** by # of journal publications

1. ESTIMATED # ACADEMIC/SCHOLARLY JOURNAL PUBLICATIONS

BY SELECT COUNTRY AS OF FEBRUARY 2006

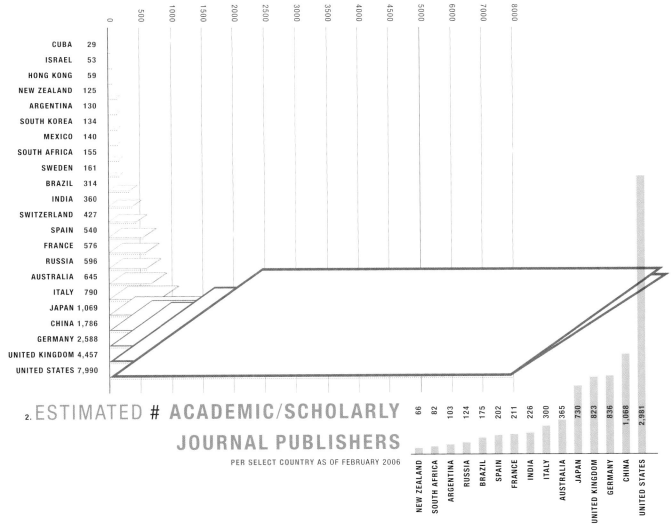

CUBA	29
ISRAEL	53
HONG KONG	59
NEW ZEALAND	125
ARGENTINA	130
SOUTH KOREA	134
MEXICO	140
SOUTH AFRICA	155
SWEDEN	161
BRAZIL	314
INDIA	360
SWITZERLAND	427
SPAIN	540
FRANCE	576
RUSSIA	596
AUSTRALIA	645
ITALY	790
JAPAN	1,069
CHINA	1,786
GERMANY	2,588
UNITED KINGDOM	4,457
UNITED STATES	7,990

2. ESTIMATED # ACADEMIC/SCHOLARLY JOURNAL PUBLISHERS

PER SELECT COUNTRY AS OF FEBRUARY 2006

NEW ZEALAND	66
SOUTH AFRICA	82
ARGENTINA	103
RUSSIA	124
BRAZIL	175
SPAIN	202
FRANCE	211
INDIA	226
ITALY	300
AUSTRALIA	365
JAPAN	730
UNITED KINGDOM	823
GERMANY	836
CHINA	1,068
UNITED STATES	2,981

3. 10 LARGEST ACADEMIC/SCHOLARLY JOURNAL PUBLISHERS UK + US

BY # OF JOURNALS PUBLISHED

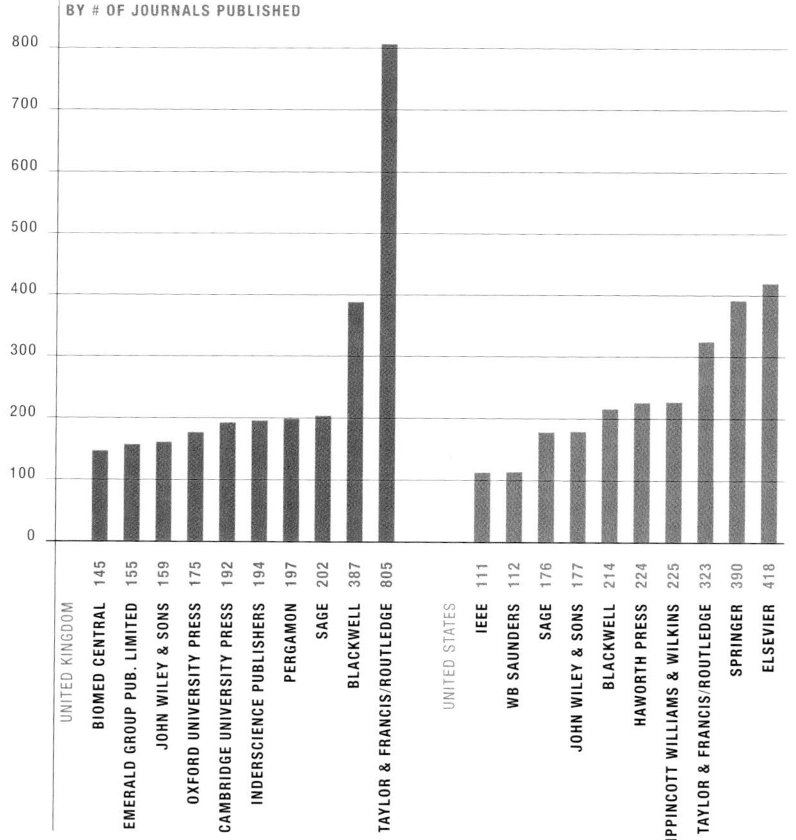

4. TOP 5 ACADEMIC/SCHOLARLY JOURNAL PUBLISHERS

BY # OF JOURNAL PUBLICATIONS # OF E-PUBLISHED JOURNALS AS OF MARCH 2006

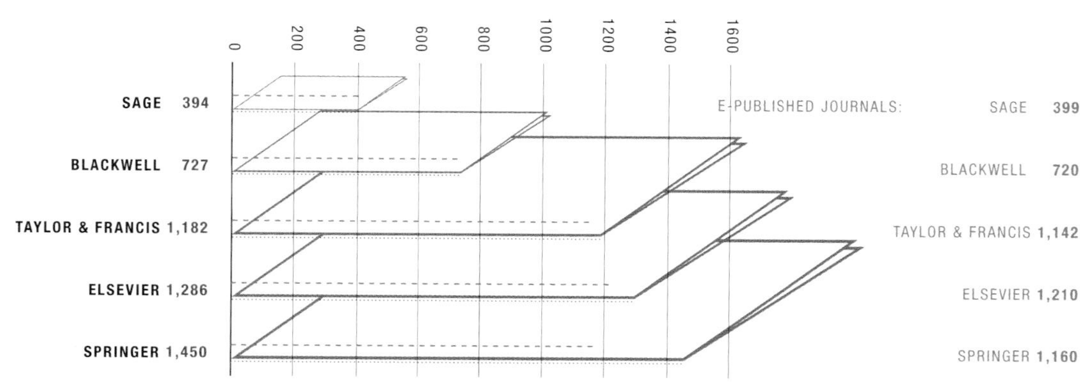

5. TOP ACADEMIC/SCHOLARLY JOURNAL PUBLISHERS MATRIX

NOTE: FIGURES ARE ESTIMATIONS

PUBLISHER (UMBRELLA COMPANY):	TAYLOR & FRANCIS	SPRINGER	ELSEVIER	BLACKWELL	SAGE
ORIGIN:	UNITED KINGDOM	GERMANY	UK/NETHERLANDS	UNITED KINGDOM	UNITED KINGDOM
DIVISION OF:	INFORMA PLC (UK)	SPRINGER SCIENCE AND BUSINESS MEDIA	REED ELSEVIER		
ESTIMATED REVENUE '05:	**983.79** MILLION GBP 2005	**783** MILLION EUROS 2005 TOTAL FOR COMPANY	**1,363** MILLION GBP 2004	**191** MILLION GBP 2004 TOTAL FOR COMPANY	**N/A**
# TITLES:	**1,182**	**1,450**	**1,286**	**727**	**394**
# IMPRINTS:	**6**	**70**	**5**	**0**	**7**
# COUNTRY OFFICES:	**7**	**19**	**25**	**8**	**3**
# OF E-PUBLISHED JOURNALS:	**1,142**	**1,160**	**1,210**	**720**	**399**
SPECIALITY SUBJECTS:	HUMANITIES AND SOCIAL SCIENCES, B2B, STM	B2B & STM	STM	HUMANITIES AND SOCIAL SCIENCES, B2B, STM	HUMANITIES AND SOCIAL SCIENCES,
EXAMPLE IMPRINTS OR FRANCHISES:	ROUTLEDGE, CARFAX, SPOON PRESS, GARLAND SCIENCE, PSYCHOLOGY PRESS, SCANDINAVIAN UNIVERSITY PRESS	BIRKHAUSER, VOGEL, BAU-VERLAG, BSMO, FORUM, PRINCETON ARCHITECTURAL PRESS, KEY CIRRICULUM PRESS	SAUNDERS, MOSBY, CHURCHILL LIVINGSTONE, BUTTERWORTH-HEINEMANN, HANLEY & BELFUS		PAUL CHAPMAN, CORWIN PRESS, PINE FORGE PRESS, RESPONSE BOOKS, VISTAAR BOOKS, SAGE SCIENCE PRESS, SCOLARI
MAIN MARKETS:	EUROPE, USA, UK, AUSTRALIA, INDIA, SINGAPORE	EUROPE, GERMANY, UK, INDIA, RUSSIA, SPAIN, TAIWAN, USA	EUROPE, USA	UK, USA, AUSTRALIA, EUROPE, JAPAN	UK, USA, INDIA,

STORAGE - ranking top 20 **countries with largest national libraries** - top 10 **larg**
national libraries - top universities worldwide: **total library collection size** - top ranked universities worldwi
total estimated # of library e-journals & e-databases - top ranked universities worldwide: **total estima**
institutions in whole library system - **encyclopaedia britannica:** revenues 1999 – 2001 - **encyclopae**
britannica online versus **wikipedia** - **encyclopaedia britannica:** # **publications by language** - # **of inter**
searches per day in millions - **share of all visits to search engines** by US web users july 2005 - **billions of text**

1a. RANKING TOP 20 COUNTRIES WITH LARGEST NATIONAL LIBRARIES

BY # OF VOLUMES

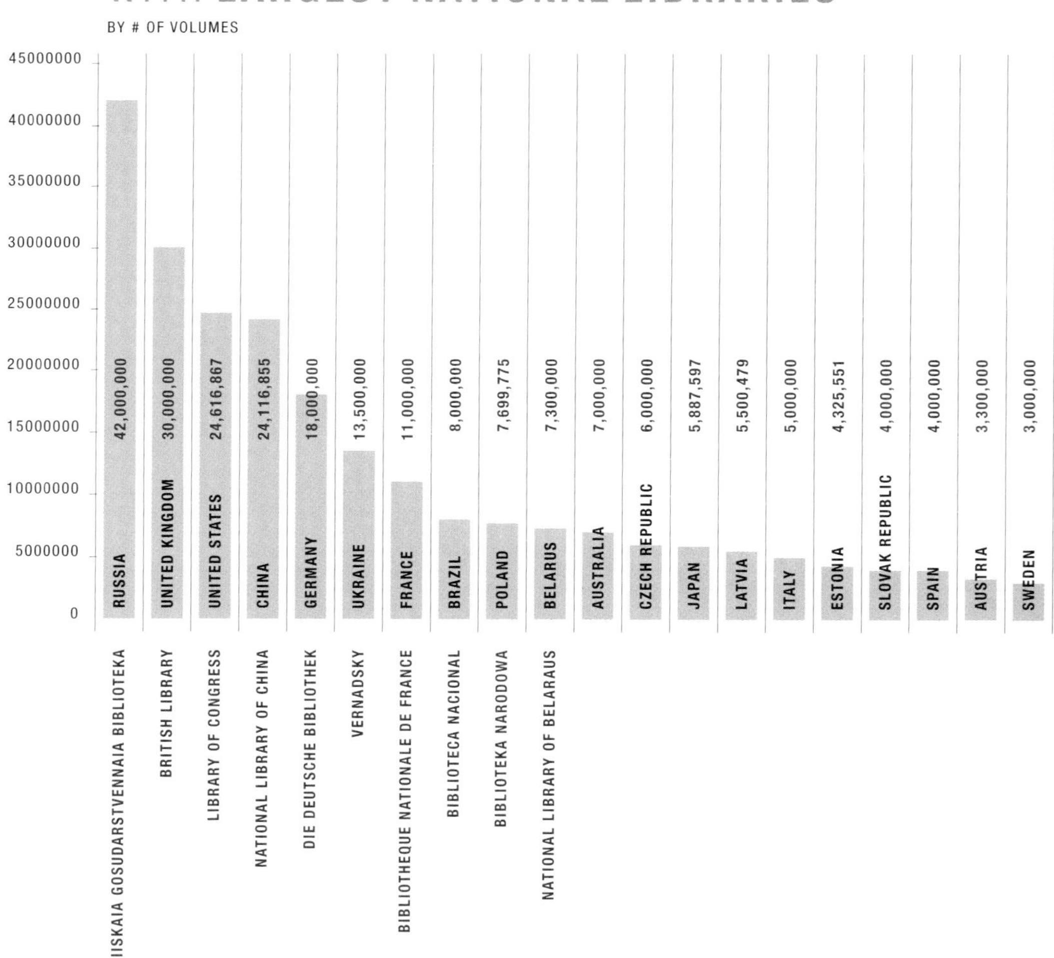

1b. TOP 10 LARGEST NATIONAL LIBRARIES

documents indexed by search engine 1996 – 2003 - **relevance of results** by search engine december 2005 - wikipedia: # **of articles and registered users** by language march 2006 - wikipedia: **total visits** per day 2002 – 2004 - wikipedia: **new articles created** per day 2001 – 2005 - comparison **literature and art archives** by region 2005 - comparison **museum archives** by region - comparison **architecture archives** by region - comparison **religious communities archives** by region - notable museums comparison: # of **visitors** in millions - notable museums comparison: # of **languages served** - **notable museums comparison matrix**

TOP RANKED UNIVERSITIES WORLDWIDE:

2. TOTAL ESTIMATED **LIBRARY COLLECTION** SIZE

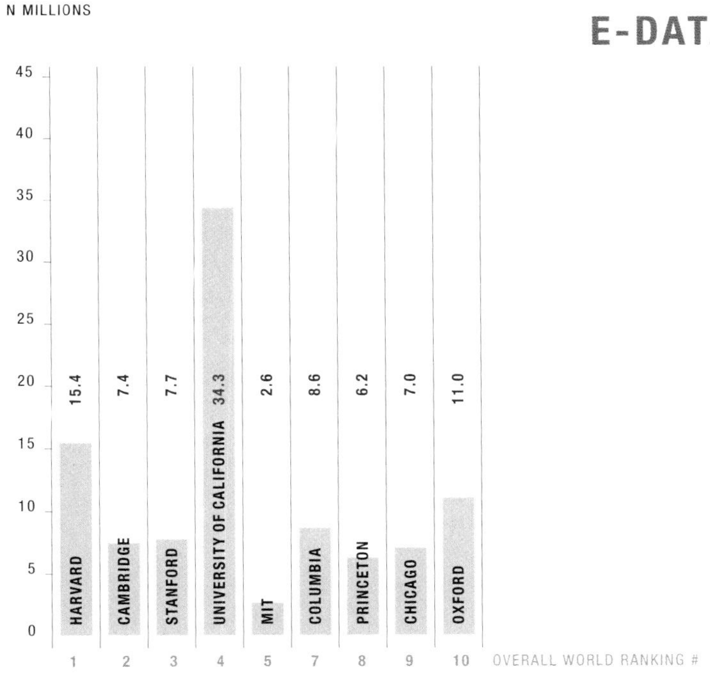

IN MILLIONS

OVERALL WORLD RANKING #	University	Collection size
1	HARVARD	15.4
2	CAMBRIDGE	7.4
3	STANFORD	7.7
4	UNIVERSITY OF CALIFORNIA	34.3
5	MIT	2.6
7	COLUMBIA	8.6
8	PRINCETON	6.2
9	CHICAGO	7.0
10	OXFORD	11.0

3. TOTAL ESTIMATED # OF LIBRARY **E-JOURNALS** + E-DATABASES

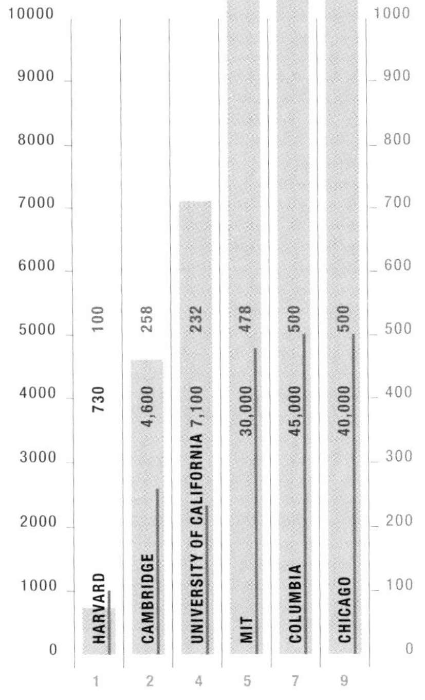

OVERALL WORLD RANKING #	University	E-journals	E-databases
1	HARVARD	730	100
2	CAMBRIDGE	4,600	258
4	UNIVERSITY OF CALIFORNIA	7,100	232
5	MIT	30,000	478
7	COLUMBIA	45,000	500
9	CHICAGO	40,000	500

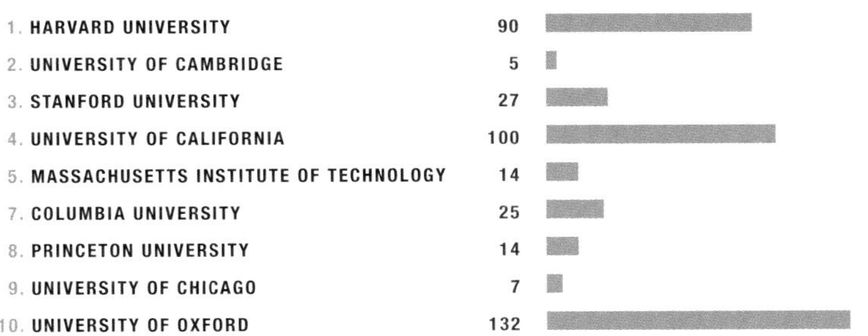

#	University	Institutions
1.	HARVARD UNIVERSITY	90
2.	UNIVERSITY OF CAMBRIDGE	5
3.	STANFORD UNIVERSITY	27
4.	UNIVERSITY OF CALIFORNIA	100
5.	MASSACHUSETTS INSTITUTE OF TECHNOLOGY	14
7.	COLUMBIA UNIVERSITY	25
8.	PRINCETON UNIVERSITY	14
9.	UNIVERSITY OF CHICAGO	7
10.	UNIVERSITY OF OXFORD	132

7. # OF INTERNET SEARCHES PER DAY + % SHARE OF ALL VISITS TO SEARCH ENGINES BY US WEB USERS

JULY 2005

6. RELEVANCE OF RESULTS BY SEARCH ENGINES

DECEMBER 2005

PROPORTION OF RESULTS

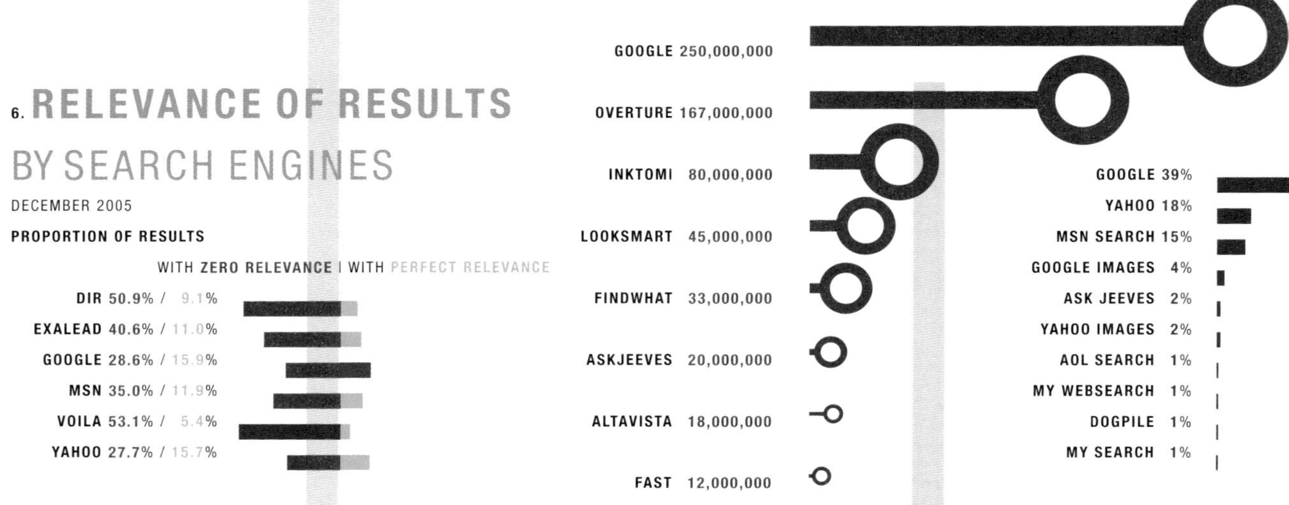

5. ENCYCLOPAEDIA BRITANNICA:

REVENUES 1999 – 2001

IN $USD MILLIONS

PUBLICATIONS BY LANGUAGE

ONLINE

ARTICLES 2004 # KEYWORDS IN THOUSANDS ● # OF LANGUAG

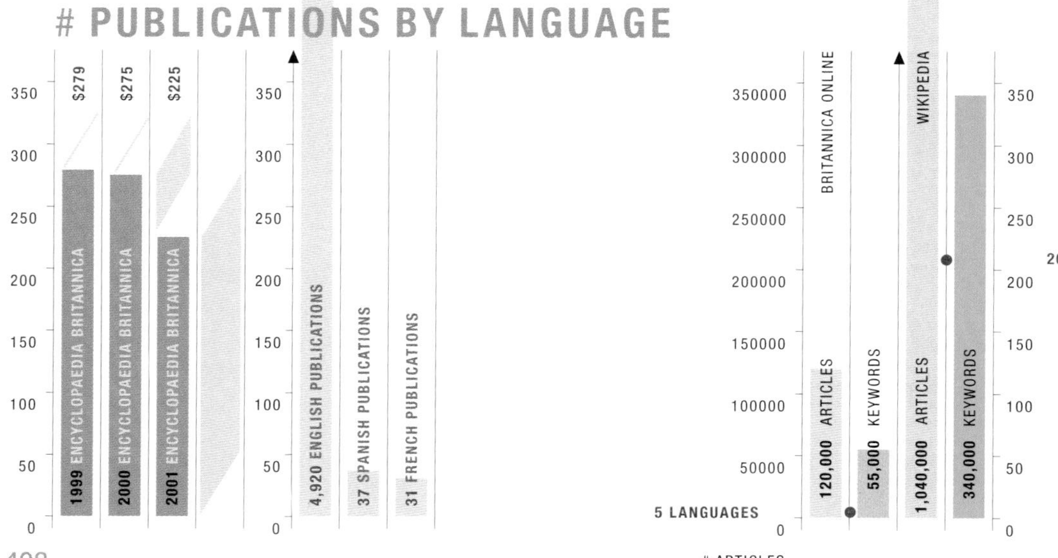

8. BILLIONS OF TEXTUAL DOCUMENTS INDEXED BY SEARCH ENGINE

1996 – 2003

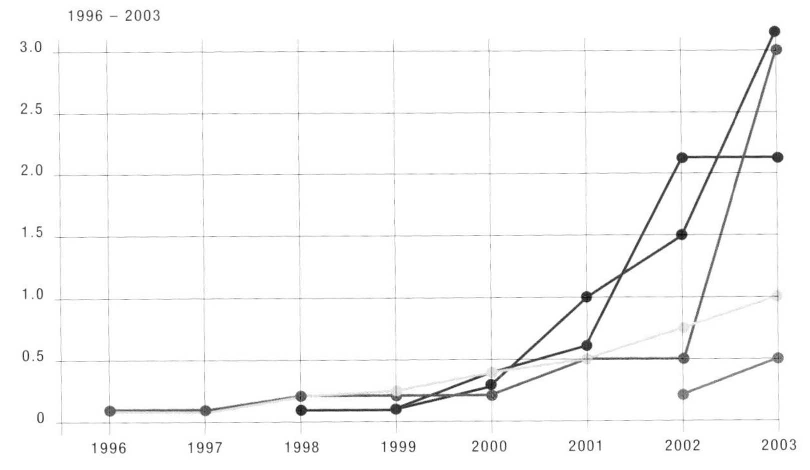

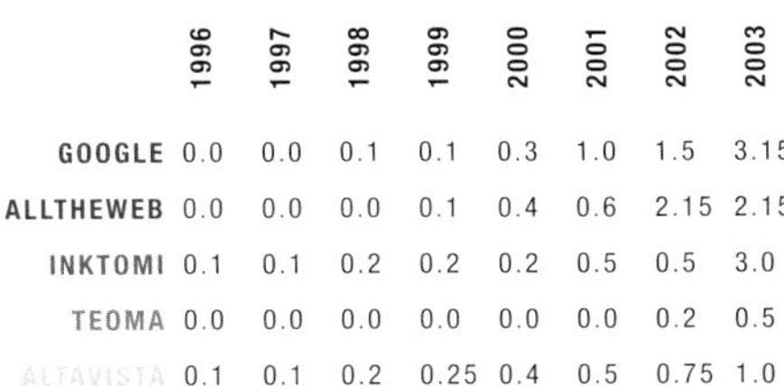

	1996	1997	1998	1999	2000	2001	2002	2003
GOOGLE	0.0	0.0	0.1	0.1	0.3	1.0	1.5	3.15
ALLTHEWEB	0.0	0.0	0.0	0.1	0.4	0.6	2.15	2.15
INKTOMI	0.1	0.1	0.2	0.2	0.2	0.5	0.5	3.0
TEOMA	0.0	0.0	0.0	0.0	0.0	0.0	0.2	0.5
ALTAVISTA	0.1	0.1	0.2	0.25	0.4	0.5	0.75	1.0

9. WIKIPEDIA: NEW ARTICLES CREATED PER DAY

2001 – 2005

10. WIKIPEDIA: # OF ARTICLES + REGISTERED USERS

BY LANGUAGE, MARCH 2006

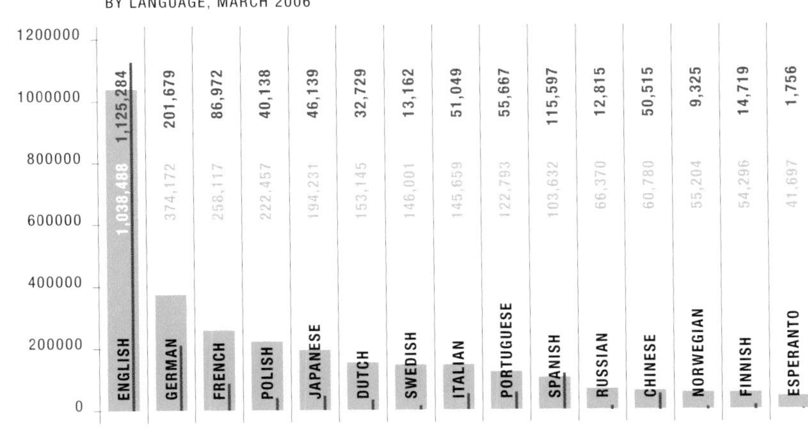

11. WIKIPEDIA: TOTAL VISITS PER DAY

2002 – 2004

OCTOBER 02 44,000

APRIL 03 97,000

OCTOBER 03 282,000

APRIL 04 593,000

OCTOBER 04 917,000

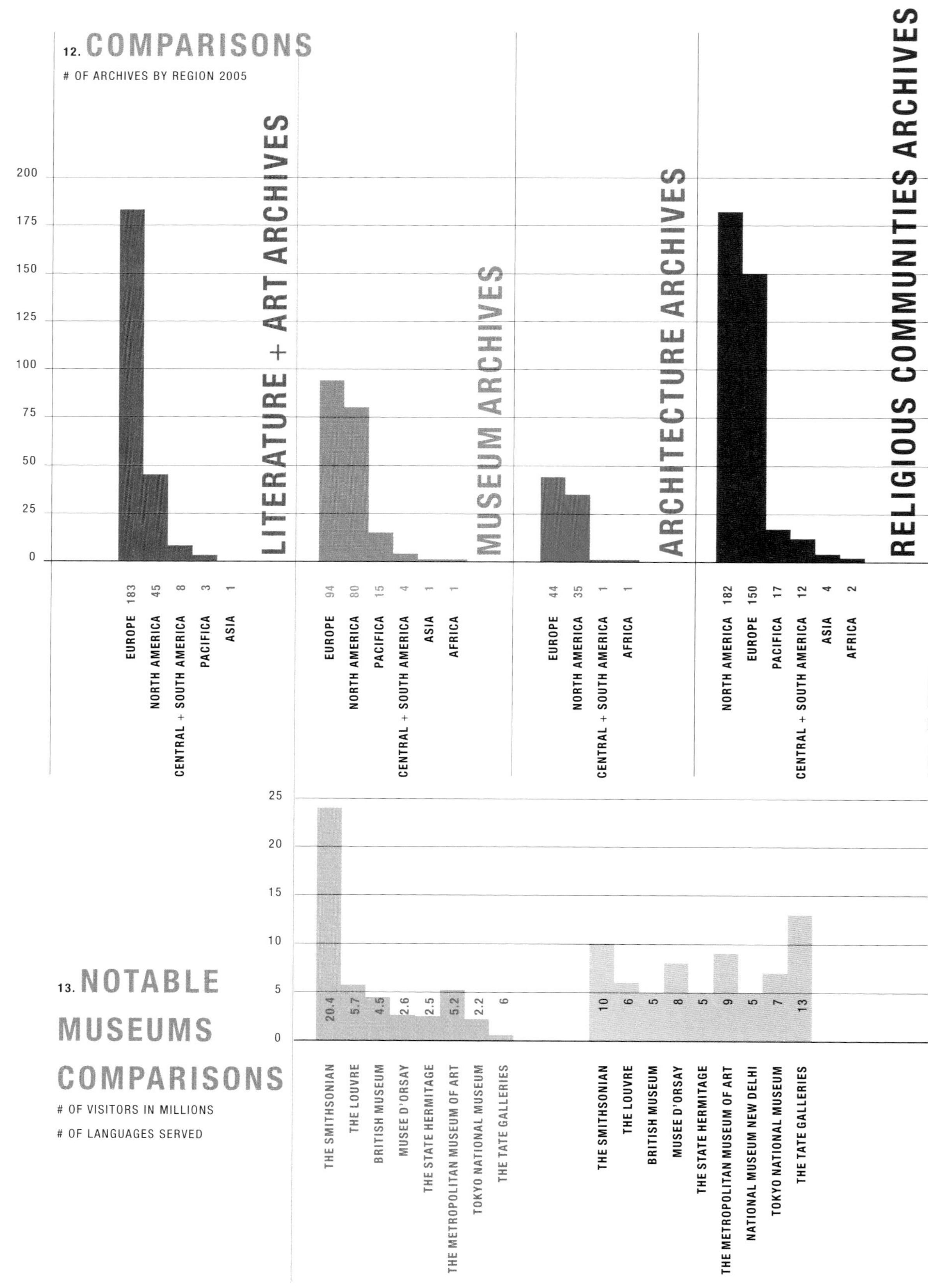
12. COMPARISONS
OF ARCHIVES BY REGION 2005
200
175
150
125
100
75
50
25
0
LITERATURE + ART ARCHIVES
EUROPE 183
NORTH AMERICA 45
CENTRAL + SOUTH AMERICA 8
PACIFICA 3
ASIA 1
MUSEUM ARCHIVES
EUROPE 94
NORTH AMERICA 80
PACIFICA 15
CENTRAL + SOUTH AMERICA 4
ASIA 1
AFRICA 1
ARCHITECTURE ARCHIVES
EUROPE 44
NORTH AMERICA 35
CENTRAL + SOUTH AMERICA 1
AFRICA 1
RELIGIOUS COMMUNITIES ARCHIVES
NORTH AMERICA 182
EUROPE 150
PACIFICA 17
CENTRAL + SOUTH AMERICA 12
ASIA 4
AFRICA 2
13. NOTABLE MUSEUMS COMPARISONS
OF VISITORS IN MILLIONS
OF LANGUAGES SERVED
25
20
15
10
5
0
THE SMITHSONIAN 20.4
THE LOUVRE 5.7
BRITISH MUSEUM 4.5
MUSEE D'ORSAY 2.6
THE STATE HERMITAGE 2.5
THE METROPOLITAN MUSEUM OF ART 5.2
TOKYO NATIONAL MUSEUM 2.2
THE TATE GALLERIES 6
THE SMITHSONIAN 10
THE LOUVRE 6
BRITISH MUSEUM 5
MUSEE D'ORSAY 8
THE STATE HERMITAGE 5
THE METROPOLITAN MUSEUM OF ART 9
NATIONAL MUSEUM NEW DELHI 5
TOKYO NATIONAL MUSEUM 7
THE TATE GALLERIES 13

4. NOTABLE MUSEUMS COMPARISON MATRIX

	LOCATION	TYPE	# OF VISITORS (MILLIONS)	VISITORS STAT YEAR	FOREIGN VISITORS	# OF LANGUAGES SERVED	COLLECTION SIZE (# OF PIECES)	# OF GLOBAL TRAVELING EXHIBITS OR LOANS	OWNERSHIP
THE SMITHSONIAN	WASHINGTON DC	ART, HISTORY, NATURAL HISTORY, SCIENCE, CULTURE	**20.4**	2004		10	**143.7** MILLION	3.9 MILLION (2004)	NATIONAL
THE LOUVRE	PARIS	ART	**5.7**	2003	**3,600,000**	6	**35,000**	± 54	NATIONAL
BRITISH MUSEUM	LONDON	ART, HISTORY, NATURAL HISTORY, CULTURE	**4.5**	2005		5	**6.5** MILLION	8	NATIONAL
MUSEE D'ORSAY	PARIS	ART	**2.6**	2004		8	**4,000**	2	NATIONAL
THE STATE HERMITAGE	ST. PETERSBURG	ART, HISTORY, CULTURE	**2.5**	2004	**400,000 – 500,000**	5	**3** MILLION	20	NATIONAL
THE METROPOLITAN MUSEUM OF ART	NEW YORK CITY	ART, HISTORY, CULTURE	**5.2**	2005		9	**2** MILLION +	20 (INTERNATIONAL LOANS, 2004)	PRIVATE/ NON-PROFIT
NATIONAL MUSEUM NEW DELHI	NEW DELHI	ART, HISTORY, CULTURE		2004		5	**2,000**	0	NATIONAL
TOKYO NATIONAL MUSEUM	TOKYO	ART, HISTORY, CULTURE	**2.2**	2004		7	**119,474**	4	NATIONAL
THE TATE GALLERIES	LONDON, LIVERPOOL, ST. IVES	ART	**6.0**	2004	± **2.400.000**	13	**65,000**	5	NATIONAL

INNOVATION + PROTECTION

- top 20 **countries with most patents filed** 2004 - **patents filed per country** 2000 + 2005 - **patents filed per country table** - top 50 **companies by # international patent applications** 2005 **& global fortune 500 rank** - top 50 **companies** 2005 # **of wipo application patents approved by type of patent** within top 15 subclasses

1. TOP 20 **COUNTRIES** WITH **MOST PATENTS FILED**

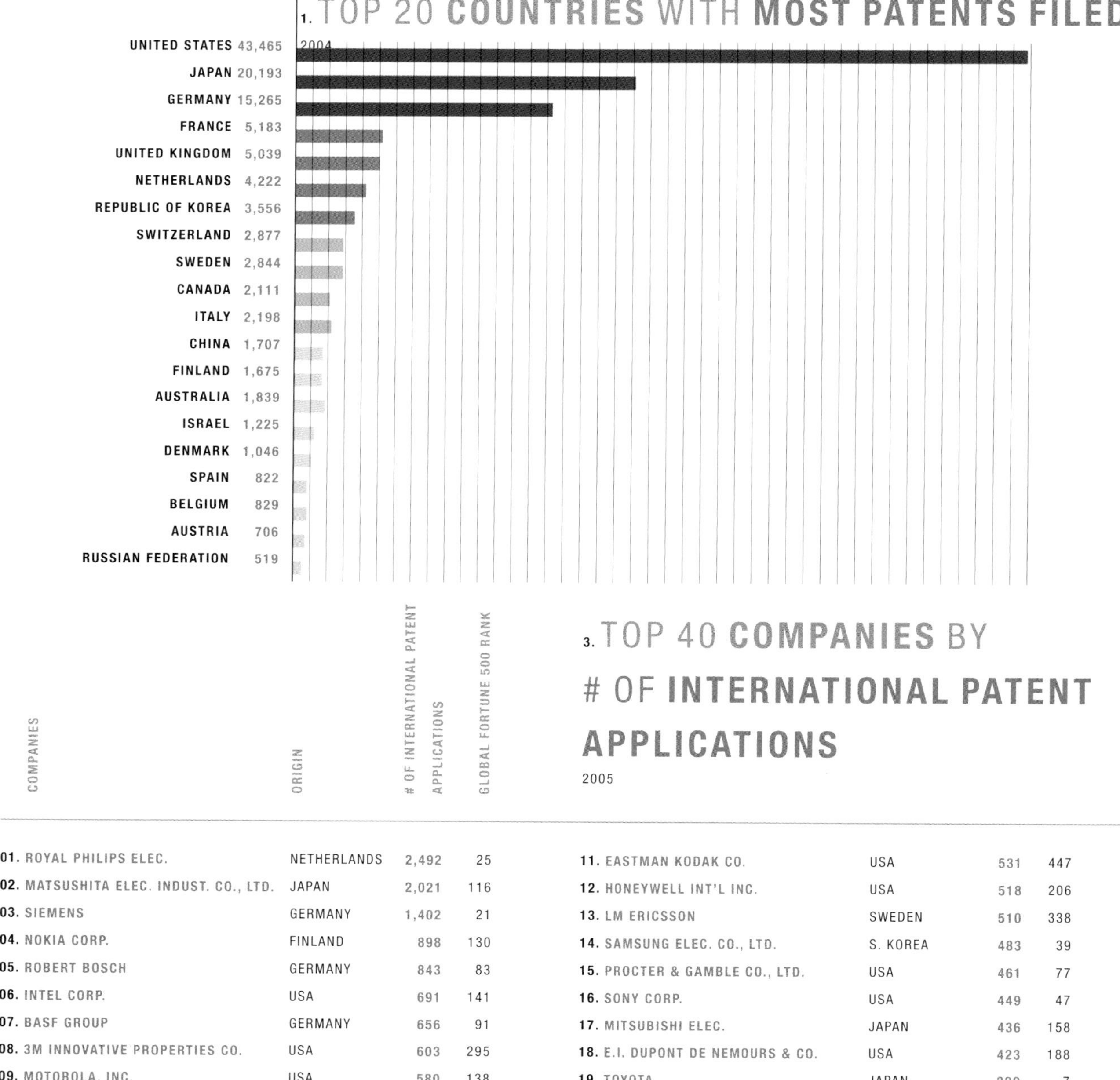

3. TOP 40 **COMPANIES** BY # OF **INTERNATIONAL PATENT APPLICATIONS**

2005

COMPANIES	ORIGIN	# OF INTERNATIONAL PATENT APPLICATIONS	GLOBAL FORTUNE 500 RANK
01. ROYAL PHILIPS ELEC.	NETHERLANDS	2,492	25
02. MATSUSHITA ELEC. INDUST. CO., LTD.	JAPAN	2,021	116
03. SIEMENS	GERMANY	1,402	21
04. NOKIA CORP.	FINLAND	898	130
05. ROBERT BOSCH	GERMANY	843	83
06. INTEL CORP.	USA	691	141
07. BASF GROUP	GERMANY	656	91
08. 3M INNOVATIVE PROPERTIES CO.	USA	603	295
09. MOTOROLA, INC.	USA	580	138
10. DAIMLER CHRYSLER	GERMANY	567	6
11. EASTMAN KODAK CO.	USA	531	447
12. HONEYWELL INT'L INC.	USA	518	206
13. LM ERICSSON	SWEDEN	510	338
14. SAMSUNG ELEC. CO., LTD.	S. KOREA	483	39
15. PROCTER & GAMBLE CO., LTD.	USA	461	77
16. SONY CORP.	USA	449	47
17. MITSUBISHI ELEC.	JAPAN	436	158
18. E.I. DUPONT DE NEMOURS & CO.	USA	423	188
19. TOYOTA	JAPAN	399	7
20. THOMSON LIC. S.A.	FRANCE	390	-

- **resident patent application per capita** 2002 - **resident patent granted per capita** 2002 - **# wto patents filed oy technical field** 2004 - top 3 **countries in subclasses:** % of total for subclasses 2004 - **sum of all national applications filed - country comparisons:** % share of world total in # of patent applications - **innovation perfor-mance** per group of indicators - **innovation performance** per capita gdp - **typology of innovation demand** 2005

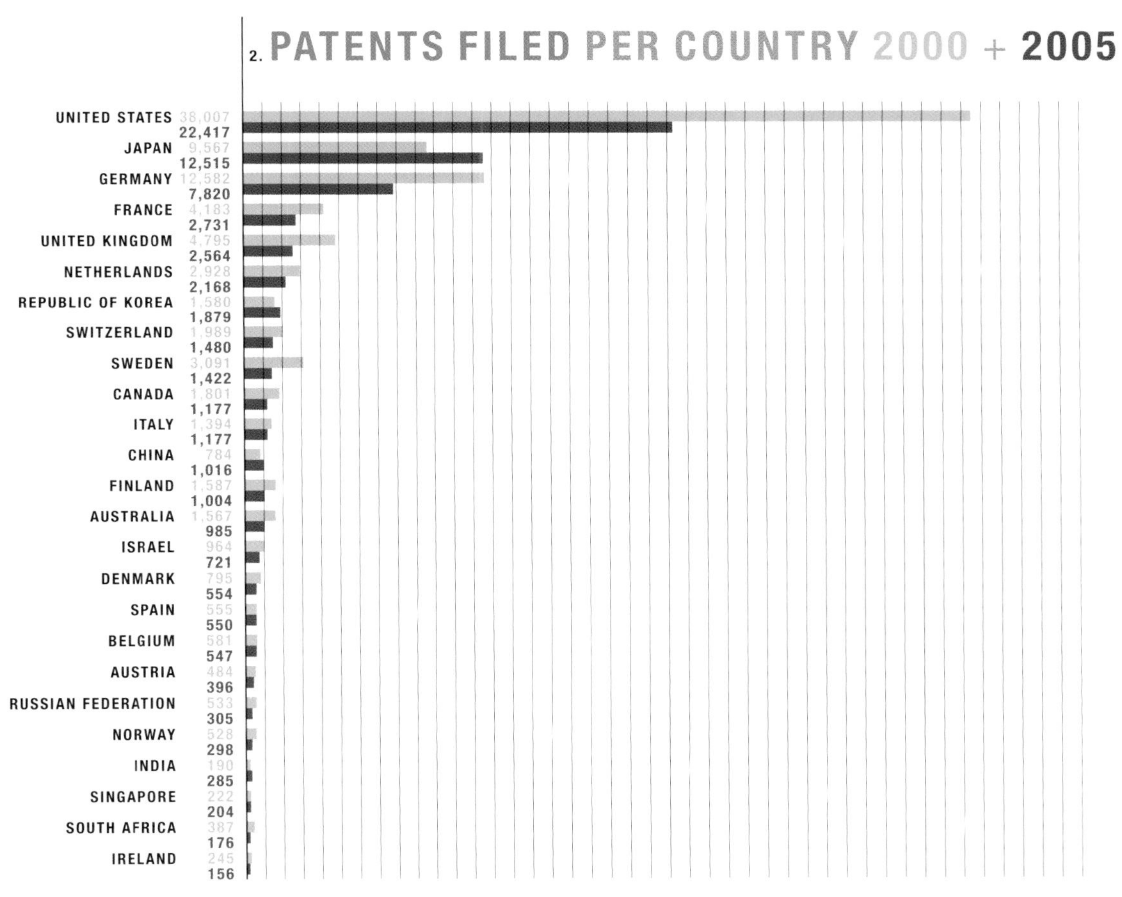

21. QUALCOMM INCORP.	USA	379	-
22. INT'L BUS. MACHINES CORP.	USA	374	20
23. FUJITSU LTD.	JAPAN	358	99
24. HEWLETT-PACKARD	USA	358	28
25. NEC CORP.	USA	353	96
26. INFINEON TECH.	GERMANY	345	-
27. THE REGENTS OF THE UNIV. OF CALIFORNIA	USA	343	-
28. KIMBERLY-CLARK WORLD., INC.	USA	336	394
29. LG ELECTRONICS INC.	S. KOREA	332	115
30. GENERAL ELECTRIC CO.	USA	321	9
31. PHILIPS INTELL. PROPERTY & STDS	GERMANY	319	-
32. BAYER	GERMANY	310	124
33. JAPAN SCI. & TECH. AGENCY	JAPAN	304	-
34. OLYMPUS CORP.	JAPAN	295	-
35. CANON	JAPAN	269	154
36. SHARP	JAPAN	269	225
37. HUAWEI TECH. CO., LTD.	CHINA	249	-
38. MEDTRONIC, INC.	USA	245	-
39. PIONEER CORP.	JAPAN	240	-
40. NOVARTIS AG	SWITZERLAND	227	186

4. TOP 5 **COMPANIES** 2005 # OF **WIPO APPLICATION PATENTS APPROVED** BY TYPE OF PATENT

TOP 15 SUBCLASSES:

G06F - **ELECTRIC DIGITAL DATA PROCESSING**
A61K - **PREPARATIONS FOR MEDICAL, DENTAL, OR TOILET PURPOSES**
C12N - **MICRO-ORGANISMS OR ENZYMES; COMPOSITIONS THEREOF**
C07D - **HETEROCYCLIC COMPOUNDS**
G01N - **INVESTIGATING OR ANALYZING MATERIALS BY DETERMINING THEIR CHEMICAL OR PHYSICAL PROPERTIES**
H04L - **TRANSMISSIONS OF DIGITAL INFORMATION (TELECOMMUNICATIONS)**
H01L - **SEMICONDUCTOR DEVICES; ELECTRIC SOLID STATE DEVICES NOT OTHERWISE PROVIDED FOR**
A61B - **DIAGNOSIS; SURGERY; IDENTIFICATION**
H04N - **PICTORIAL COMMUNICATIONS (TELEVISION)**
C07C - **ACYCLIC OR CARBOCYCLIC COMPOUNDS**
H04B - **TRANSMISSIONS OF DIGITAL INFORMATION (TELECOMMUNICATIONS)**
H04Q - **SELECTING**
A61F - **FILTERS IMPLANTABLE INTO BLOODVESSELS; PROSTHESES; ORTHOPAEDIC, NURSING OR CONTRACEPTIVE DEVICES**
B65D - **CONTAINERS FOR STORAGE OR TRANSPORT OF ARTICLES OR MATERIALS**
A61M - **DEVICES FOR INTRODUCING MEDIA INTO OR ONTO THE BODY**

ROYAL PHILIPS ELECTRONICS
NETHERLANDS

G06F	336
A61K	6
C12N	–
C07D	–
G01N	35
H04L	231
H01L	169
A61B	112
H04N	298
C07C	–
H04B	92
H04Q	45
A61F	2
B65D	6
A61M	2

MATSUSHITA ELEC. INDUST. CO., LTD.
JAPAN

G06F	307
A61K	1
C12N	6
C07D	–
G01N	35
H04L	234
H01L	138
A61B	39
H04N	276
C07C	1
H04B	162
H04Q	82
A61F	–
B65D	4
A61M	1

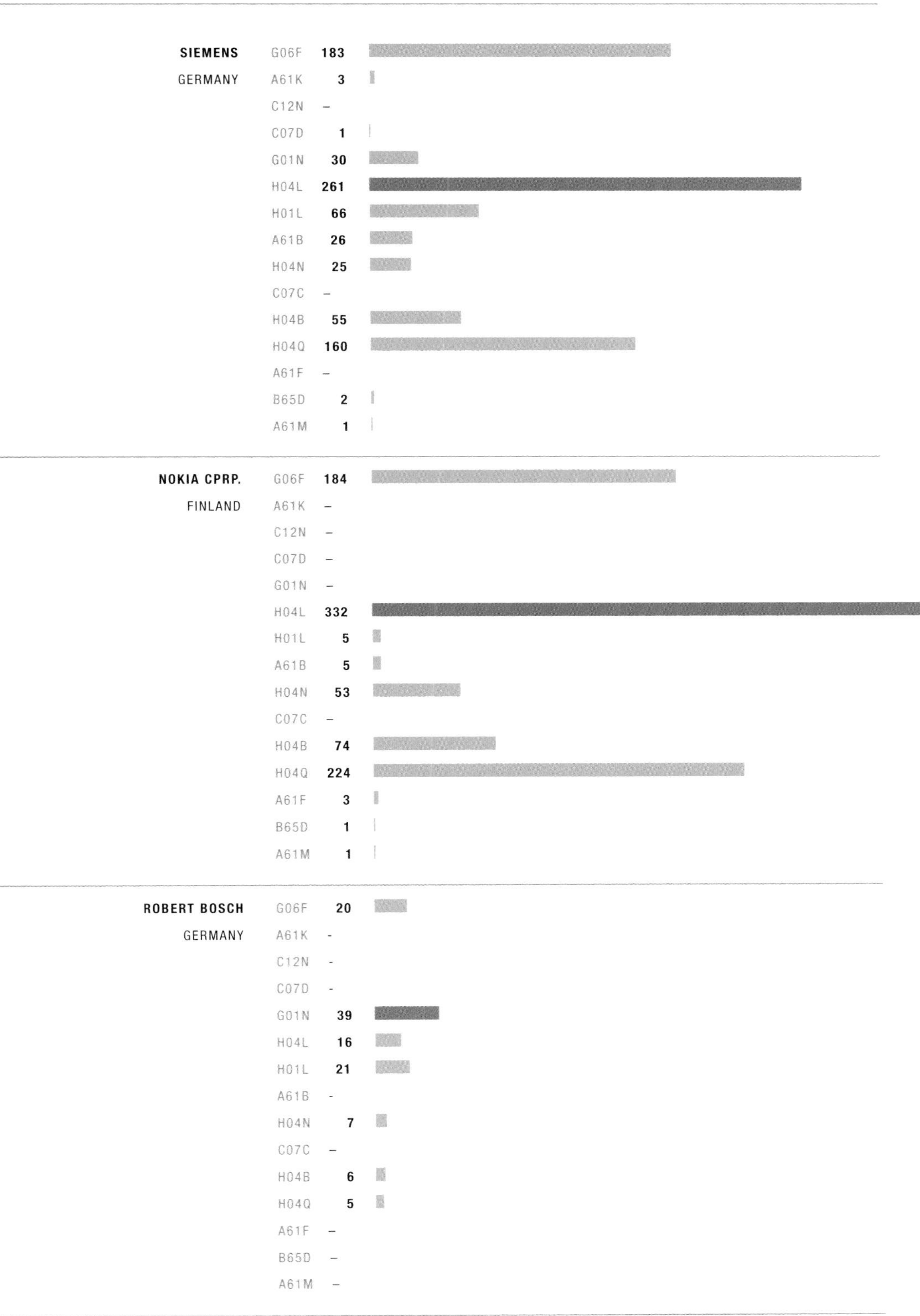
SIEMENS
GERMANY
G06F 183
A61K 3
C12N –
C07D 1
G01N 30
H04L 261
H01L 66
A61B 26
H04N 25
C07C –
H04B 55
H04Q 160
A61F –
B65D 2
A61M 1
NOKIA CPRP.
FINLAND
G06F 184
A61K –
C12N –
C07D –
G01N –
H04L 332
H01L 5
A61B 5
H04N 53
C07C –
H04B 74
H04Q 224
A61F 3
B65D 1
A61M 1
ROBERT BOSCH
GERMANY
G06F 20
A61K -
C12N -
C07D -
G01N 39
H04L 16
H01L 21
A61B -
H04N 7
C07C –
H04B 6
H04Q 5
A61F –
B65D –
A61M –

5. # WTO PATENTS FILED BY TECHNICAL FIELD 2004

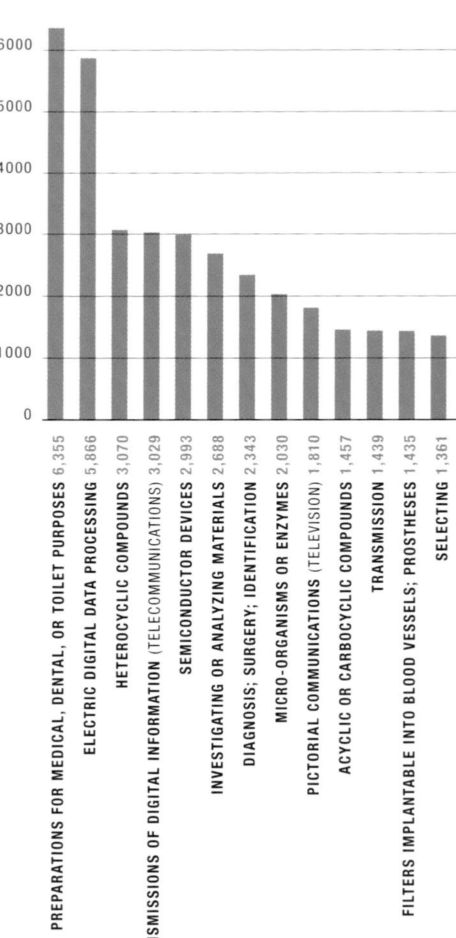

6. RESIDENT PATENT APPLICATIONS

PER CAPITA 2002

7. RESIDENT PATENTS GRANTE

PER CAPITA 2002

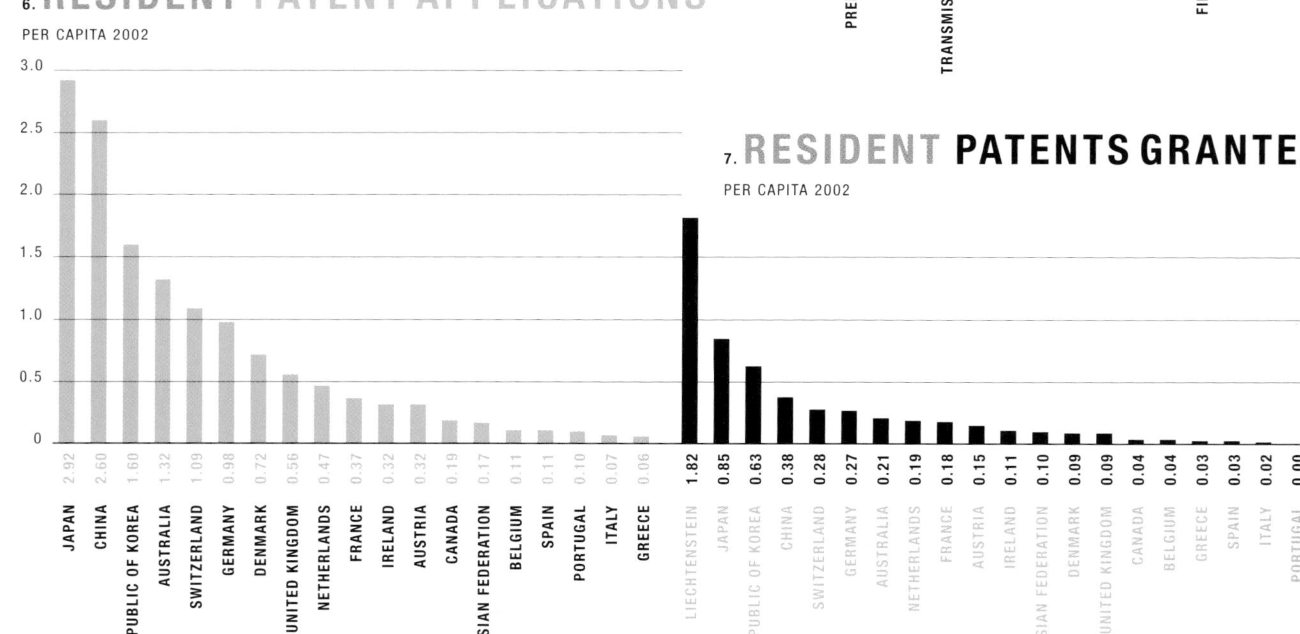

8. TOP 3 COUNTRIES IN SUBCLASSES:

% OF TOTAL FOR SUBCLASS 2004

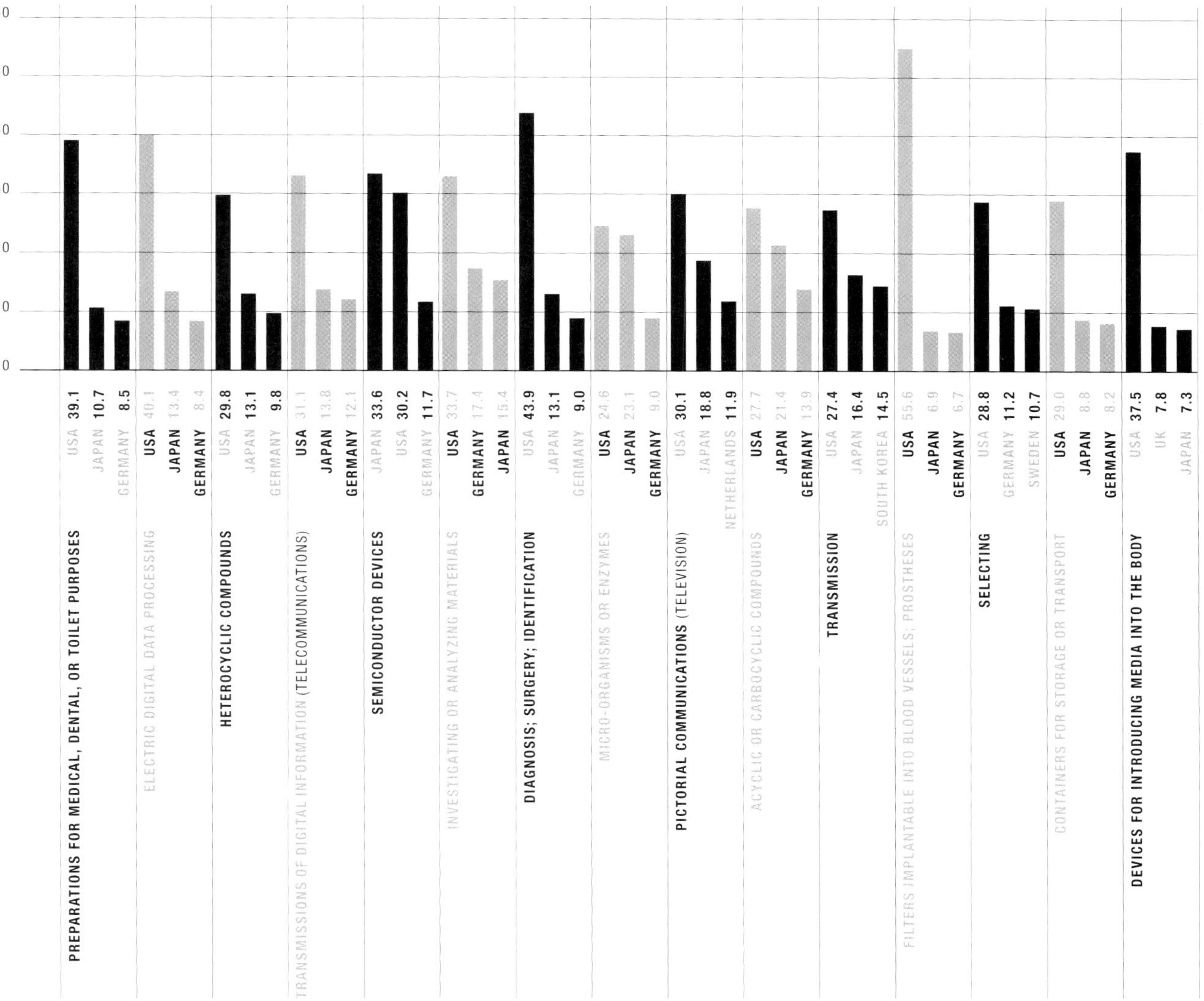

PREPARATIONS FOR MEDICAL, DENTAL, OR TOILET PURPOSES	USA	39.1	JAPAN	10.7	GERMANY	8.5
ELECTRIC DIGITAL DATA PROCESSING	USA	40.1	JAPAN	13.4	GERMANY	8.4
HETEROCYCLIC COMPOUNDS	USA	29.8	JAPAN	13.1	GERMANY	9.8
TRANSMISSIONS OF DIGITAL INFORMATION (TELECOMMUNICATIONS)	USA	31.1	JAPAN	13.8	GERMANY	12.1
SEMICONDUCTOR DEVICES	JAPAN	33.6	USA	30.2	GERMANY	11.7
INVESTIGATING OR ANALYZING MATERIALS	USA	33.7	GERMANY	17.4	JAPAN	15.4
DIAGNOSIS; SURGERY; IDENTIFICATION	USA	43.9	JAPAN	13.1	GERMANY	9.0
MICRO-ORGANISMS OR ENZYMES	USA	24.6	JAPAN	23.1	GERMANY	9.0
PICTORIAL COMMUNICATIONS (TELEVISION)	USA	30.1	JAPAN	18.8	NETHERLANDS	11.9
ACYCLIC OR CARBOCYCLIC COMPOUNDS	USA	27.7	JAPAN	21.4	GERMANY	13.9
TRANSMISSION	USA	27.4	JAPAN	16.4	SOUTH KOREA	14.5
FILTERS IMPLANTABLE INTO BLOOD VESSELS; PROSTHESES	USA	55.6	JAPAN	6.9	GERMANY	6.7
SELECTING	USA	28.8	GERMANY	11.2	SWEDEN	10.7
CONTAINERS FOR STORAGE OR TRANSPORT	USA	29.0	JAPAN	8.8	GERMANY	8.2
DEVICES FOR INTRODUCING MEDIA INTO THE BODY	USA	37.5	UK	7.8	JAPAN	7.3

9. SUM OF ALL NATIONAL APPLICATIONS FILED

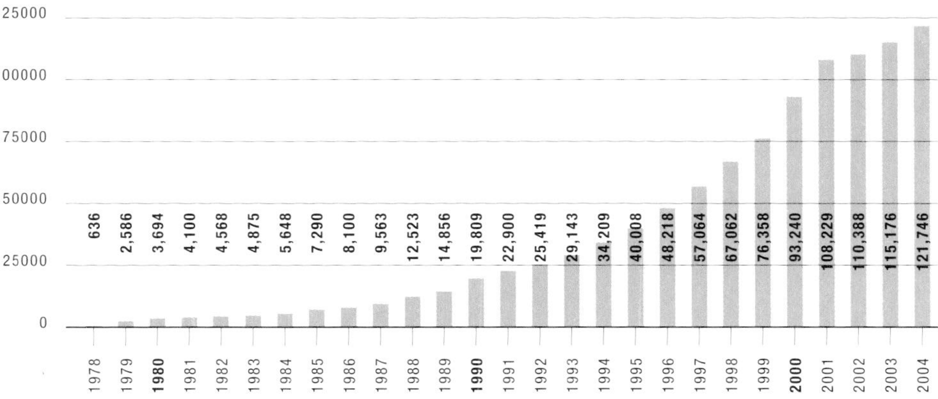

10. 2005 SUMMARY INNOVATION INDEX

SWEDEN	0.72
SWITZERLAND	0.71
FINLAND	0.68
JAPAN	0.65
DENMARK	0.60
UNITED STATES	0.60
GERMANY	0.58
AUSTRIA	0.51
BELGIUM	0.50
NETHERLANDS	0.48
UNITED KINGDOM	0.48
EU15	0.46
FRANCE	0.46
ICELAND	0.45
LUXEMBOURG	0.44
EU25	0.42
IRELAND	0.42
NORWAY	0.40
ITALY	0.36
ESTONIA	0.32
SLOVENIA	0.32
HUNGARY	0.31
SPAIN	0.30
CYPRUS	0.28
PORTUGAL	0.28
LITHUANIA	0.27
CZECH REPUBLIC	0.26
BULGARIA	0.24
POLAND	0.23
SLOVAKIA	0.21
GREECE	0.21
LATVIA	0.20
MALTA	0.20
ROMANIA	0.16
TURKEY	0.06

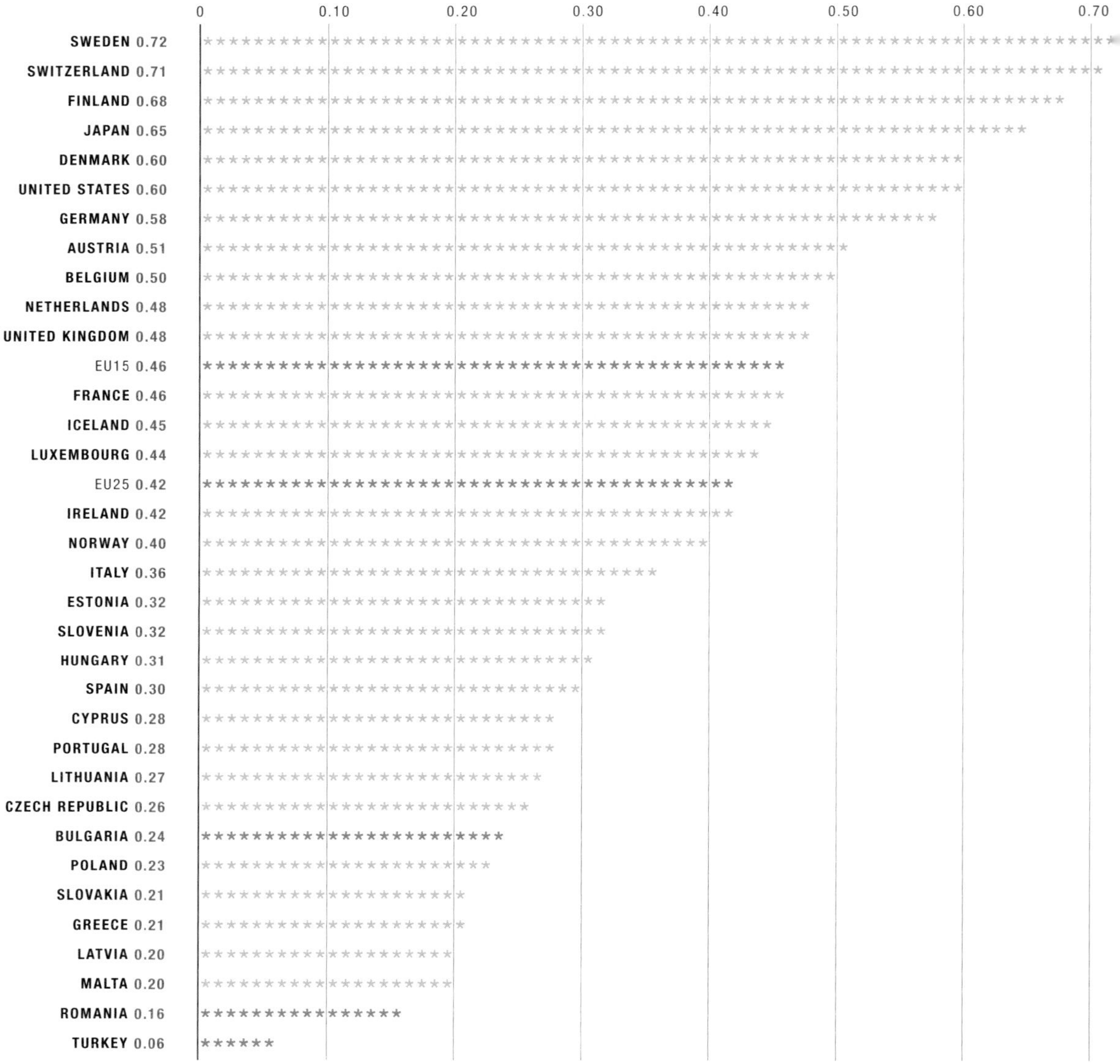

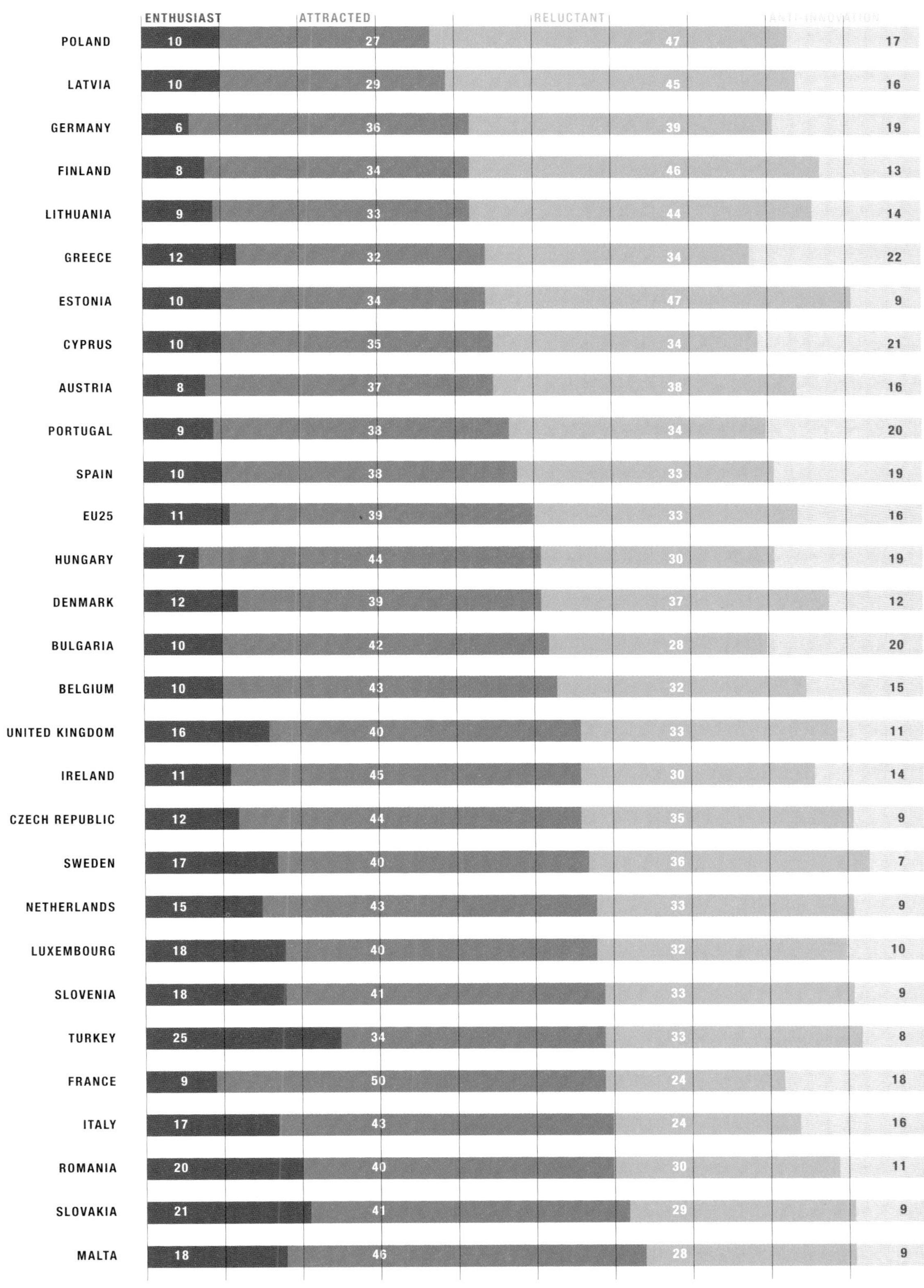
11. TYPOLOGY OF INNOVATION DEMAND
ENTHUSIAST
ATTRACTED
RELUCTANT
ANTI-INNOVATION
POLAND 10 27 47 17
LATVIA 10 29 45 16
GERMANY 6 36 39 19
FINLAND 8 34 46 13
LITHUANIA 9 33 44 14
GREECE 12 32 34 22
ESTONIA 10 34 47 9
CYPRUS 10 35 34 21
AUSTRIA 8 37 38 16
PORTUGAL 9 38 34 20
SPAIN 10 38 33 19
EU25 11 39 33 16
HUNGARY 7 44 30 19
DENMARK 12 39 37 12
BULGARIA 10 42 28 20
BELGIUM 10 43 32 15
UNITED KINGDOM 16 40 33 11
IRELAND 11 45 30 14
CZECH REPUBLIC 12 44 35 9
SWEDEN 17 40 36 7
NETHERLANDS 15 43 33 9
LUXEMBOURG 18 40 32 10
SLOVENIA 18 41 33 9
TURKEY 25 34 33 8
FRANCE 9 50 24 18
ITALY 17 43 24 16
ROMANIA 20 40 30 11
SLOVAKIA 21 41 29 9
MALTA 18 46 28 9

KNOWLEDGE The term 'knowledge' refers to the state of knowing or learning, and its acquisition and organization. Knowledge can be implicit or explicit, informal or formal, personal or institutional, scientific or traditional, and acquired or learned. While each of these are separate in content and are going through different global permutations and ownership debates, they are all part of what could be called a 'knowledge cycle' of creation, recognition, dissemination, storage and protection.

These acts involve value judgments for determining what becomes considered knowledge and worthy of incorporation into explicit (formal recorded and institutional) knowledge systems and canons. Indigenous knowledge[1] has long been overlooked as folklore or "backward", but recently, in light of large multi-national companies patenting traditional knowledge of plants and medicines for commercial purposes, there has been a rush to formalize traditional knowledge. This has proven difficult because of the culture disconnect between 'westernized' perceptions of what is classified as knowledge, and the concept that information can be stored and codified devoid of context versus a more traditional holistic concept of knowledge as culture and without separation between person, community and fact. Further adding to the debate is the construct of intellectual property (IP), which refers to creations of the human mind and their protection by law, (WIPO). Knowledge then, is intricately intertwined with patent law and protection, and defined by its ability to be codified and patented on a global scale by interested parties and local actors.

WHAT DO WE KNOW ABOUT KNOWLEDGE?

Within the field of knowledge creation is a growing concentration of actors in the production, dissemination, innovation and storage of intellectual property and historical information. The Internet, with online library and archival collections, periodical databases, hyperlinked encyclopedias, and web-based patent applications and information, further facilitates this concentration. This trend is especially apparent in scholarly academic publishing (print and online) through the acquisition and mergers of smaller or independent journal publishers, including university presses, with conglomerate publishing houses. Of the top five ranking scholarly publishers worldwide, four are based in the UK (Taylor and Francis, Elsevier, Blackwell and Sage) (Ulrich's Periodicals Directory). In 2005, the world's largest academic publisher, Springer (based in Heidelberg, Germany), printed 1,450 titles and owned 70 scholarly imprints, more than any other publishing house worldwide.

As advanced technology and communication systems spread throughout the globe, the prevalence of e-journals and online resources crowd out traditional print references. Although Encyclopaedia Britannica, a major repository of knowledge, has developed an online service to attract a larger audience, the volume and languages available for online articles is disrupted by Wikipedia (see Indicator Suite).

The decreasing number of actors in the cycle of knowledge creation is also evident in patent applications and approvals. Innovations and patents are dominated by the US, Japan and Germany (Table 1). Japan is in the top three countries in every patent subclass except for Selecting, and the US is number one in all three subcategories except Semiconductors. Four of the top ten companies worldwide with the highest number of patent applications are from Germany, and three are from the US (WIPO, 2005). Furthermore, Asian countries outpaced all countries in total growth of patents in 2005 (44% increase for China, 34% in South Korea, and 24% in Japan.)

WHAT ARE THE ISSUES?

The decreasing diversity in knowledge creation cycle highlights the tensions existing between innovation and the rights and protection of traditional knowledge. A growing urgency to protect traditional and cultural knowledge or practices is further complicated by the legal standards surrounding IP and debates on whether culture can be copyrighted at all (Brown, 1998). Today, a large majority of indigenous knowledge remains unprotected by existing IP laws and only a handful of countries are working towards identifying indigenous knowledge and traditional cultural expressions to ensure integration into IP legal definitions, or sui generis (items that stand alone and cannot be categorized due to their unique and/or cultural character). Such treaties and laws governing the protection of traditional knowledge combine two basic legal concepts: the regulation of access and the granting of exclusive rights (WIPO).

India, China and Brazil have led recent movements to create sui generis laws. The Indian government has created a Traditional Knowledge Library to collect, patent and store traditional knowledge on yoga and ayurvedic medicine. For example, the government intends to patent each yoga asana (position) and ayurvedic practice in the attempt to protect their cultural heritage from increasingly western and commercial versions (Bellman, 2005). In China and Brazil, in addition to India and many other developing nations, there is a movement towards protecting biodiversity and medicinal plants and drugs. China, in response to biopiracy, and also linked to TRIPs (Agreement on Trade-Related Aspects of Intellectual Property Rights negotiated by the WTO in 1994 at the end of the Uruguay Rounds), passed patent laws on traditional medicine usage, pharmaceutical products and methods in 1993, and updated them in 2000. This has prompted a huge flood of international patent applications for traditional Chinese medicine that has been endorsed by the government to protect Chinese culture and knowledge, and also enter into international trade agreements and respect of international patents as regulated by TRIPs (Yongfeng, 2006).

TABLE 1: **TOP PATENT COUNTRIES, 2005**

	ESTIMATE # OF PATENTS	% OF WORLD PATENT APPLICATIONS	% GROWTH
USA	45,111	33.60%	3.80%
JAPAN	25,145	18.80%	24.30%
GERMANY	15,870	11.80%	4.00%
FRANCE	5,522	4.10%	6.60%
UK	5,115	3.80%	1.50%
SOUTH KOREA	4,747	3.50%	33.60%
NETHERLANDS	4,435	3.30%	4.70%
SWITZERLAND	3,096	2.30%	7.50%
SWEDEN	2,784	2.10%	-2.10%
CHINA	2,452	1.80%	43.70%
CANADA	2,315	1.70%	9.80%
ITALY	2,309	1.70%	5.10%
AUSTRALIA	2,022	1.50%	10.10%
FINLAND	1,866	1.40%	11.60%
ALL OTHERS	5,835	4.40%	2.70%

Source: WIPO, Patents and PCT Statistics (2005)

TABLE 2: **COUNTRIES WITH LAWS PROTECTING TRADITIONAL KNOWLEDGE**

COUNTRY/REGION	YEAR	CONTENT
AFRICAN UNION	2000	Rights of local communities, Farmers and Breeders, Regulation of Access to Biological Resources
BRAZIL	2001	Regulating Access to Genetic Heritage, Protection of and Access to Associated Traditional Knowledge
CHINA	2000	Regulation on the Protection of Traditional Medicine
COSTA RICA	1998	Protection of Biodiversity
INDIA	2002	Biological Diversity Act
PERU	2002	Protection for Collective Knowledge of Indigenous Peoples Derived from Biological Resources
PHILIPPINES	1997	Indigenous Peoples Rights Act
PORTUGAL	2002	Regime of Registration, Conservation, Legal Custody and Transfer of Plant Endogenous Material
THAILAND	1999	Protection and Promotion of Traditional Thai Medicinal Intelligence
UNITED STATES	1990	Indian Arts and Crafts Act, and other relevant measures

Source: WIPO, Intergovernmental Committee on Intellectual Property and Genetic Resources, Traditional Knowledge and Folklore (2004)

[1] Also known as "traditional knowledge," refers to knowledge systems that were developed and maintained within a community in a local context. According to the World Intellectual Property Organization, this can include a wide array of topics, including but not limited to, food and agriculture; biological diversity and environment; innovation and regulation in biotechnology; economic, social and cultural development; cultural policy; and human rights.

HERITAGE + PRACTICES

HERITAGE PRESERVATION + DESTRUCTION

ENVIRONMENT

CULTURAL PARTICIPATION

SPORTS

HERITAGE PRESERVATION

- unesco properties figures: **breakdown of unesco world heritage properties** - unesco properties figures: # of **unesco world heritage properties** by region + type - unesco properties figures: # of **unesco world heritage properties added since 1994** by region + type - unesco heritage cities: # of **cities** per region **listed as unesco world heritage properties** - unesco intangible: # of **unesco proclaimed masterpieces of the oral and intangible heritage of humanity** - unesco intangible: # of **intangible masterpieces identified** by type - heritage destruction: **cultural heritage sites heavily damaged or destroyed in bosnia-herzegovina** - unesco heritage in danger: **world heritage in danger** list

1. BREAKDOWN OF **UNESCO WORLD HERITAGE PROPERTIES**

MIXED 24 - 3% NATURAL 160 - 20% **CULTURAL 628** - 77%

2. # OF **UNESCO WORLD HERITAGE PROPERTIES**

BY REGION AND TYPE: **CULTURAL** NATURAL

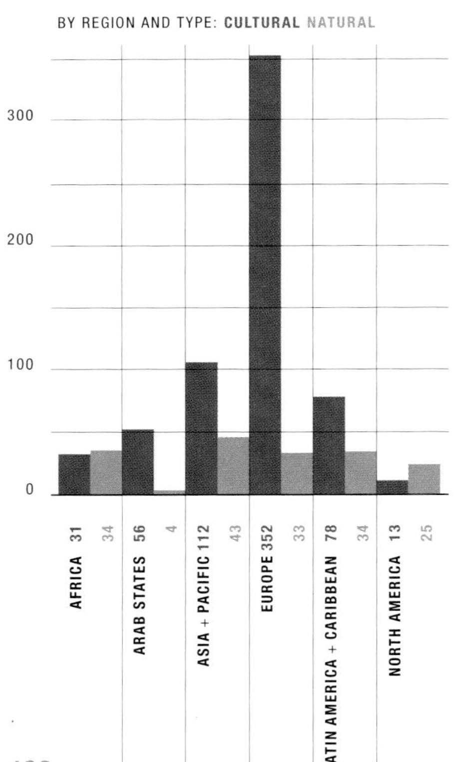

3. % **GROWTH IN WORLD HERITAGE PROPERTIES**

ADDED SINCE 1994 **CULTURAL** NATURAL

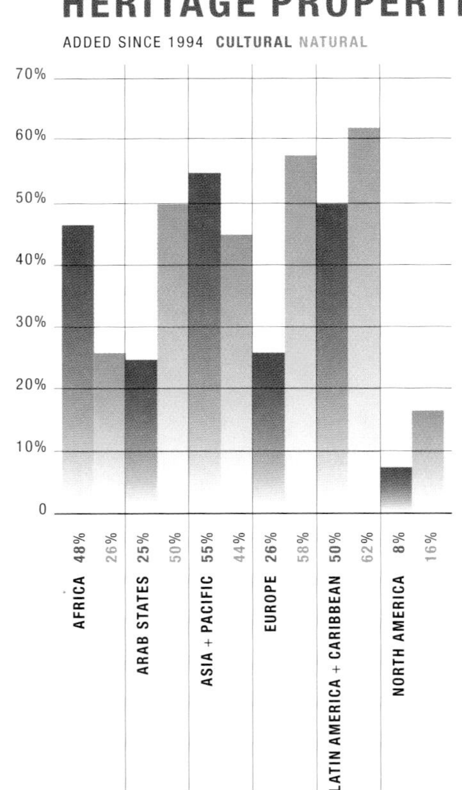

4. # OF **CITIES** PER REGION **LISTED** AS UNESCO WORLD HERITAGE PROPERTIES

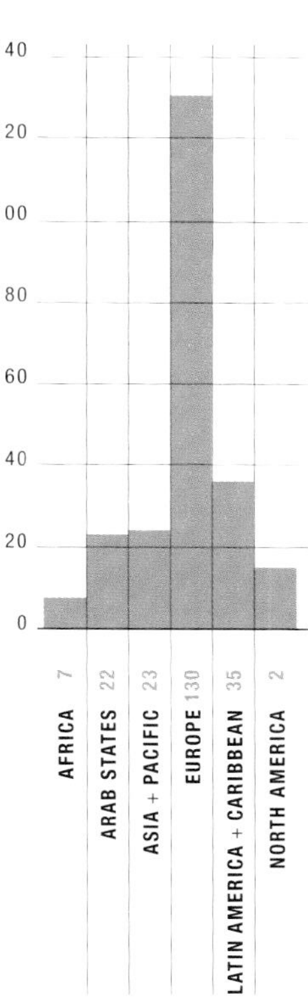

5. # OF **UNESCO PROCLAIMED MASTERPIECES** OF THE ORAL AND INTANGIBLE HERITAGE OF HUMANITY

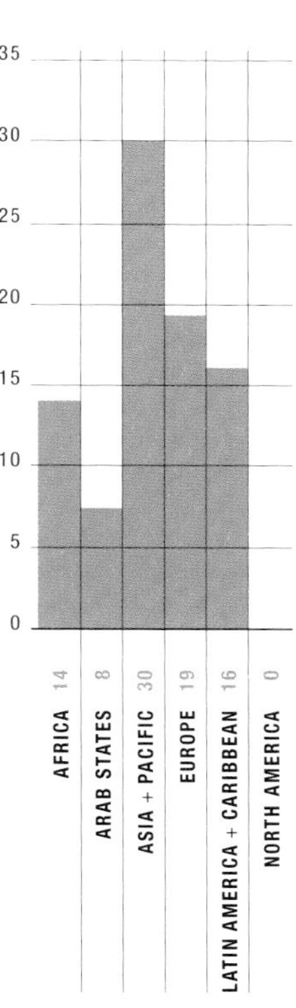

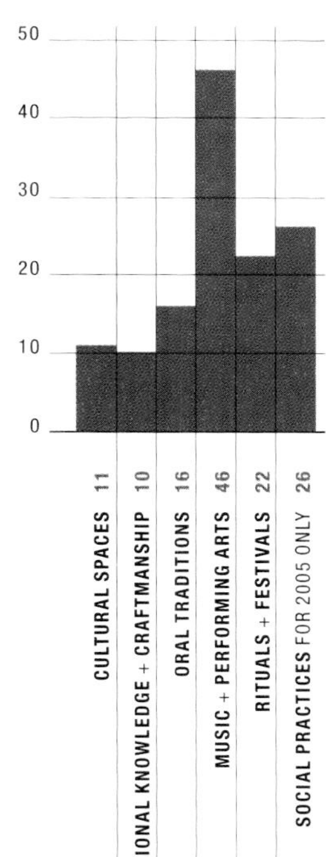

6. # OF **INTANGIBLE MASTERPIECES IDENTIFIED**

BY TYPE

CATEGORIES ARE NOT EXCLUSIVE

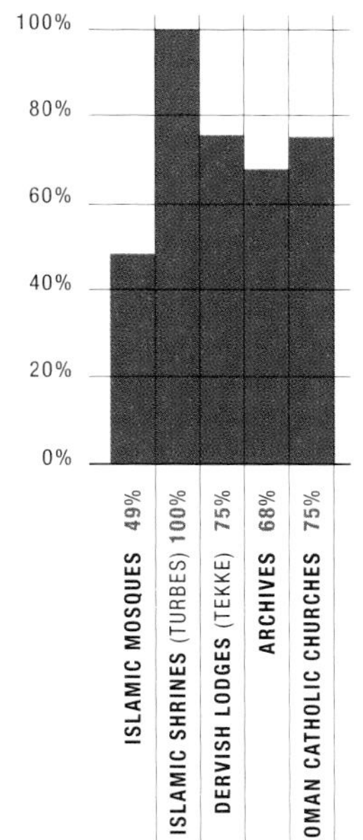

7. CULTURAL HERITAGE SITES **HEAVILY DAMAGED** OR **DESTROYED** IN BOSNIA-HERZEGOVINA

1992-1996

8. WORLD HERITAGE **IN DANGER** LIST

IN ACCORDANCE WITH ARTICLE 11(4) OF THE CONVENTION

COUNTRY	HERITAGE SITE	DATE LISTED AS **IN DANGER**
AFGHANISTAN	**CULTURAL LANDSCAPE + ARCHAEOLOGICAL REMAINS OF THE BAMIYAN VALLEY**	2003
	MINARET + ARCHAEOLOGICAL REMAINS OF JAM	2002
ALGERIA	**TIPASA**	2002
AZERBAIJAN	**WALLED CITY OF BAKU WITH THE SHIRVANSHAH'S PALACE + MAIDEN TOWER**	2003
BENIN	**ROYAL PALACES OF ABOMEY**	1985
CENTRAL AFRICAN REPUBLIC	**MANOVO-GOUNDA ST FLORIS NATIONAL PARK**	1997
CHILE	**HUMBERSTONE + SANTA LAURA SALTPETER WORKS**	2005
CÔTE D'IVOIRE	**COMOÉ NATIONAL PARK**	2003
	MOUNT NIMBA STRICT NATURE RESERVE *	1992
DEMOCRATIC REPUBLIC OF THE CONGO	**GARAMBA NATIONAL PARK**	1996
	KAHUZI-BIEGA NATIONAL PARK	1997
	OKAPI WILDLIFE RESERVE	1997
	SALONGA NATIONAL PARK	1999
	VIRUNGA NATIONAL PARK	1994
EGYPT	**ABU MENA**	2001
ETHIOPIA	**SIMIEN NATIONAL PARK**	1996
GERMANY	**COLOGNE CATHEDRAL**	2004
GUINEA	**MOUNT NIMBA STRICT NATURE RESERVE** *	1992
HONDURAS	**RIO PLÁTANO BIOSPHERE RESERVE**	1996
INDIA	**GROUP OF MONUMENTS AT HAMPI**	1999
	MANAS WILDLIFE SANCTUARY	1992
IRAN	**BAM + IT'S CULTURAL LANDSCAPE**	2004
IRAQ	**ASHUR** (QAL'AT SHERGAT)	2003
JERUSALEM (site proposed by Jordan)	**OLD CITY OF JERUSALEM + IT'S WALLS**	1982
NEPAL	**KATHMANDU VALLEY**	2003
NIGER	**AIR + TÉNÉRÉ NATURAL RESERVES**	1992
PAKISTAN	**FORT + SHALAMAR GARDENS IN LAHORE**	2000
PERU	**CHAN CHAN ARCHAEOLOGICAL ZONE**	1986
PHILIPPINES	**RICE TERRACES OF THE PHILIPPINE CORDILLERAS**	2001
SENEGAL	**DJOUDJ NATIONAL BIRD SANCTUARY**	2000
TUNESIA	**ICHKEUL NATIONAL PARK**	1996
UNITED REPUBLIC OF TANZANIA	**RUINS OF KILWA KISIWANI + RUINS OF SONGO MNARA**	2004
UNITES STATES OF AMERICA	**EVERGLADES NATIONAL PARK**	1993
VENEZUELA	**CORO + IT'S PORT**	2005
YEMEN	**HISTORIC TOWN OF ZABID**	2002

* transboundary property

removed in 2005:

BUTRINT, Albania

SANGAY NATIONAL PARK, Ecuador

TIMBUKTU, Mali

ENVIRONMENT

- **world co2 emissions from fuel combustion** 1990 - **world co2 emissions from fuel combustion** 2003 - environmental sustainability index: **regional average esi scores** - top 15 countries in **environmental sustainability** - **lowest performing countries in environmental sustainability** - world values survey: **attitudes toward the environment—protecting** versus **economic growth** - types of **international conflicts due to water** 1950 – 1999

1. WORLD CO2 EMISSIONS FROM FUEL COMBUSTION 1990

ERNATIONAL RS 0.6 - 3%

KYOTO PARTIES 8.3 - 40%

NON-KYOTO PARTIES 11.8 - 57%

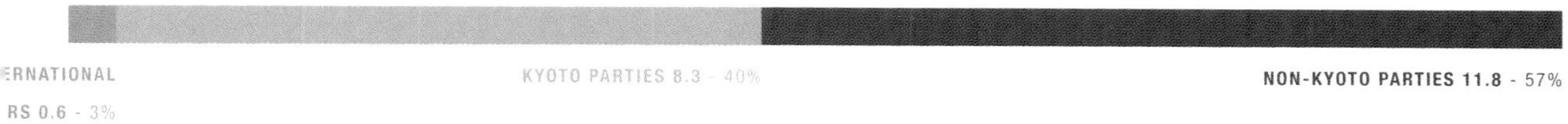

2. WORLD CO2 EMISSIONS FROM FUEL COMBUSTION 2003

ERNATIONAL RS 0.8 - 3%

KYOTO PARTIES 7.8 - 31%

NON-KYOTO PARTIES 16.5 - 66%

3. TOP 15 COUNTRIES IN ENVIRONMENTAL SUSTAINABILITY

BASED ON ESI SCORE, 2005

FINLAND	75.1
NORWAY	73.4
URUGUAY	71.8
SWEDEN	71.7
ICELAND	70.8
CANADA	64.4
SWITZERLAND	63.7
GUYANA	62.9
ARGENTINA	62.7
AUSTRIA	62.7
BRAZIL	62.2
GABON	61.7
AUSTRALIA	61
NEW ZEALAND	60.9
LATVIA	60.4

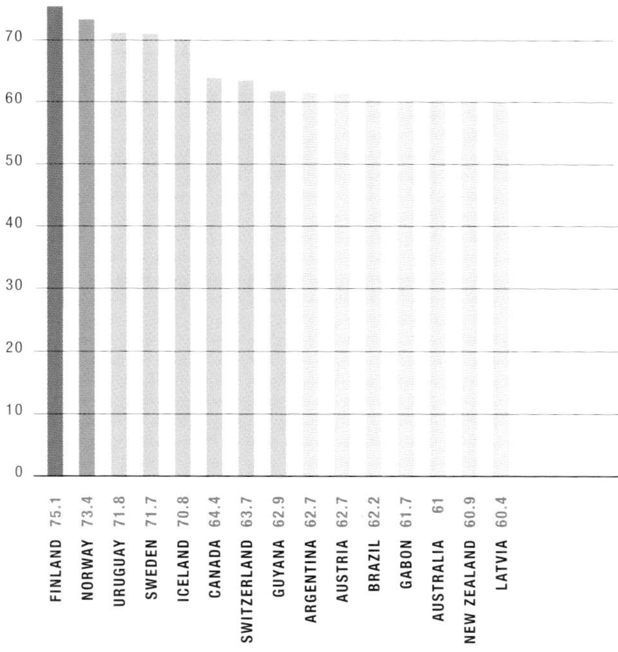

4. 15 WORSE PERFORMING COUNTRIES IN ENVIRONMENTAL SUSTAINABILITY

BASED ON ESI SCORE, 2005

PAKISTAN	39.9
IRAN	39.8
CHINA	38.6
TAJIKISTAN	38.6
ETHIOPIA	37.9
SAUDI ARABIA	37.8
YEMEN	37.3
KUWAIT	36.6
TRINIDAD + TOBAGO	36.3
SUDAN	35.9
HAITI	34.8
UZBEKISTAN	34.4
IRAQ	33.6
TURKMENISTAN	33.1
TAIWAN	32.7
NORTH KOREA	29.2

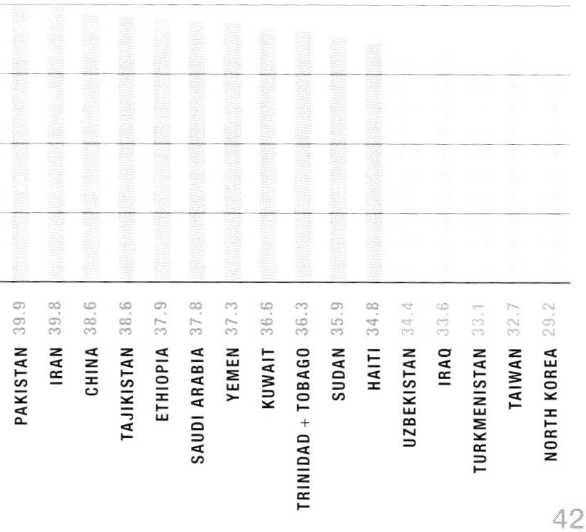

5. 2005 **ENVIRONMENT SUSTAINABILITY** INDEX

REGIONAL AVERAGE ESI RANK

LOWER SCORES (29.2 – 40.0) ARE THOSE WITH SERIOUS ENVIRONMENTAL STRESSES

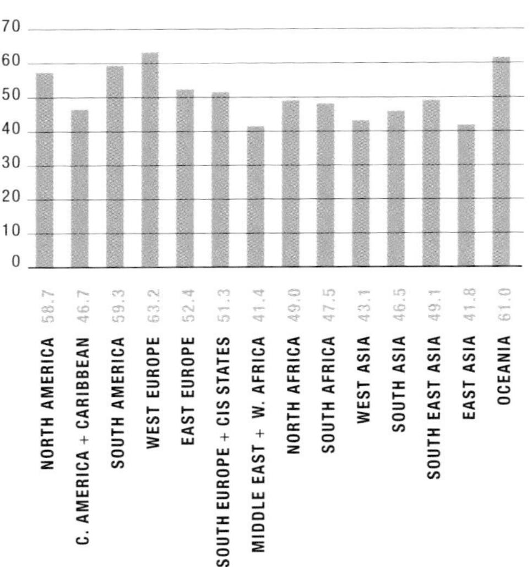

6. ATTITUDES TOWARDS ENVIRONMENT: **PROTECTING ENVIRONMENT** VERSUS **ECONOMIC GROWTH**

% OF TOTAL FOR SUBCLASSES 2004

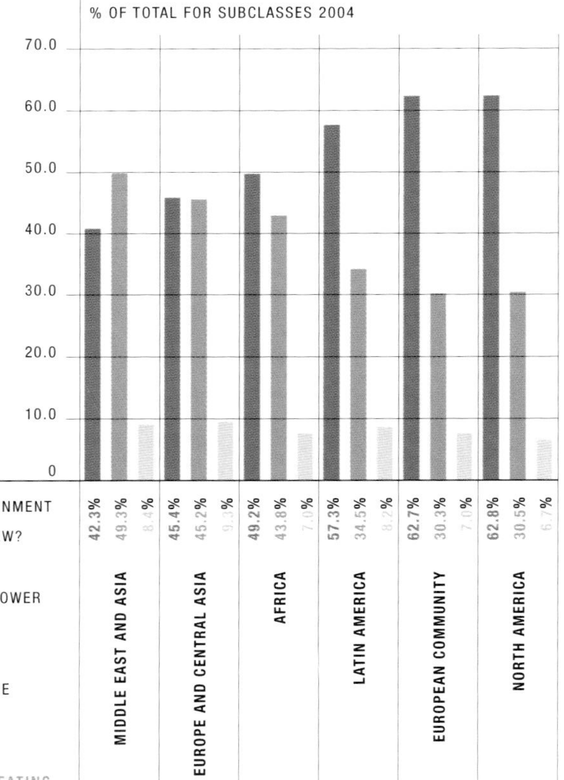

HERE ARE TWO STATEMENTS PEOPLE SOMETIMES MAKE WHEN DISCUSSING THE INVIRONMENT AND ECONOMIC GROWTH. WHICH OF THEM COMES CLOSER TO YOUR OWN POINT OF VIEW?

A. PROTECTING THE ENVIRONMENT SHOULD BE GIVEN PRIORITY, EVEN IF IT CAUSES SLOWER ECONOMIC GROWTH AND SOME LOSS OF JOBS.

B. ECONOMIC GROWTH AND CREATING JOBS SHOULD BE THE TOP PRIORITY, EVEN IF THE ENVIRONMENT SUFFERS TO SOME EXTENT.

POSSIBLE ANSWERS 1. **PROTECTING ENVIRONMENT** / 2. **ECONOMY GROWTH AND CREATING JOBS** / 3. **OTHER ANSWER**

7. TYPES OF **INTERNATIONAL WATER** CONFLICTS

1950-1999

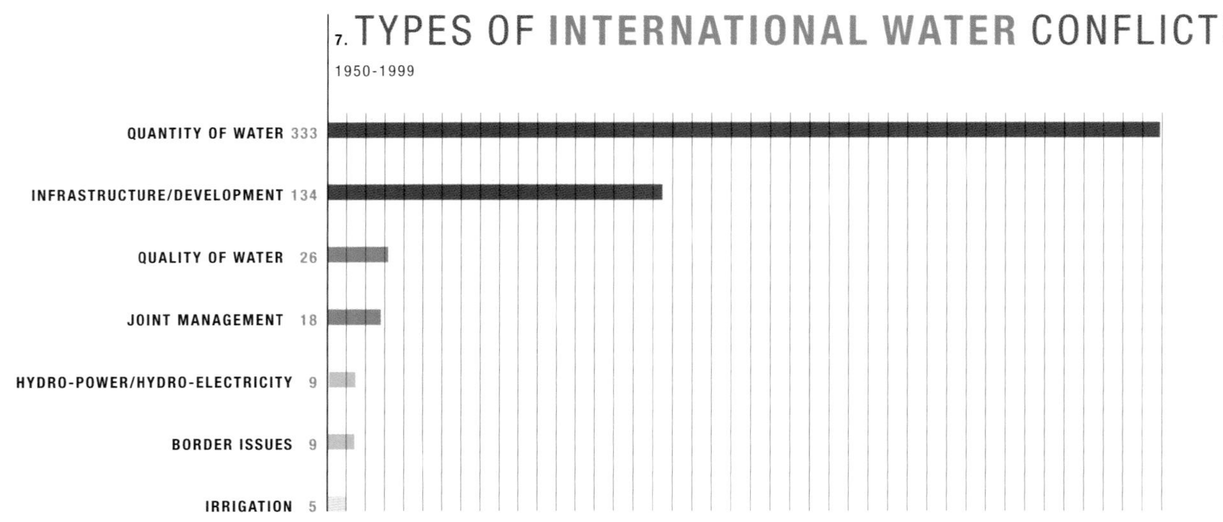

CULTURAL PARTICIPATION

- world values survey: **cultural participation** by region - world values survey: **time spent with people at a sportsclub, cultural, service or voluntary organization** by region - **european cultural activities** - **practicing artistic activities in the eu** - % of **us adults participating in the arts** at least once in a 12-month period - # of **us adults performing arts** at least once in a 12-month period - % of **us adults participating in other leisure activities** - minutes per day **spent on entertainment + cultural participation** - time spent **watching tv + videos** - proportion of **people who spent any time on entertainment + culture** % per day - % of **people who spent any time watching tv + videos** - average time spent **watching tv / videos of those who spent any time on tv / videos**

1. DO YOU PARTICIPATE IN EDUCATIONAL, ARTS, MUSIC, OR CULTURAL ORGANIZATIONS OR ACTIVITIES?

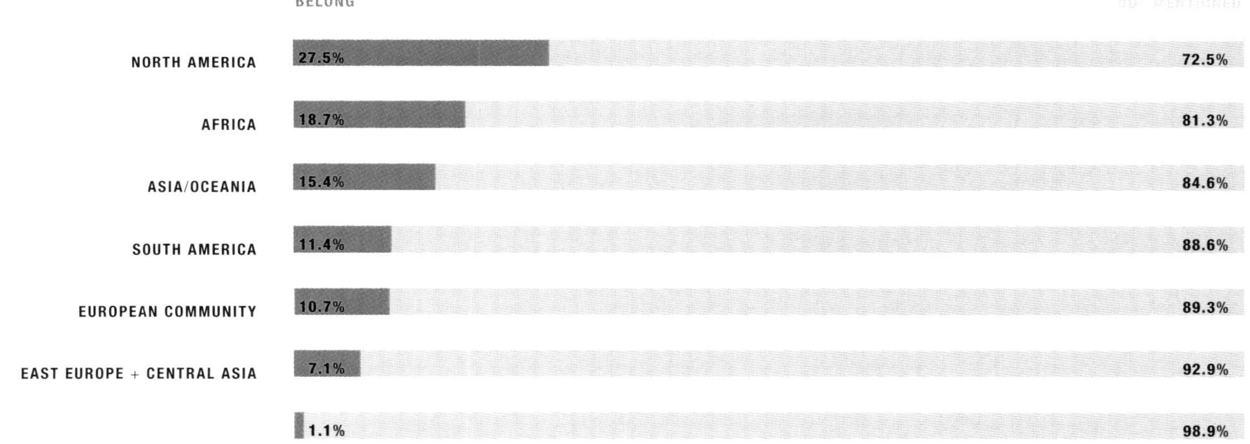

2. EUROPEAN CULTURAL ACTIVITIES

3. HOW MUCH TIME SPENT WITH PEOPLE AT A SPORTS CLUB, CULTURAL, SERVICE, OR VOLUNTARY ORGANIZATION

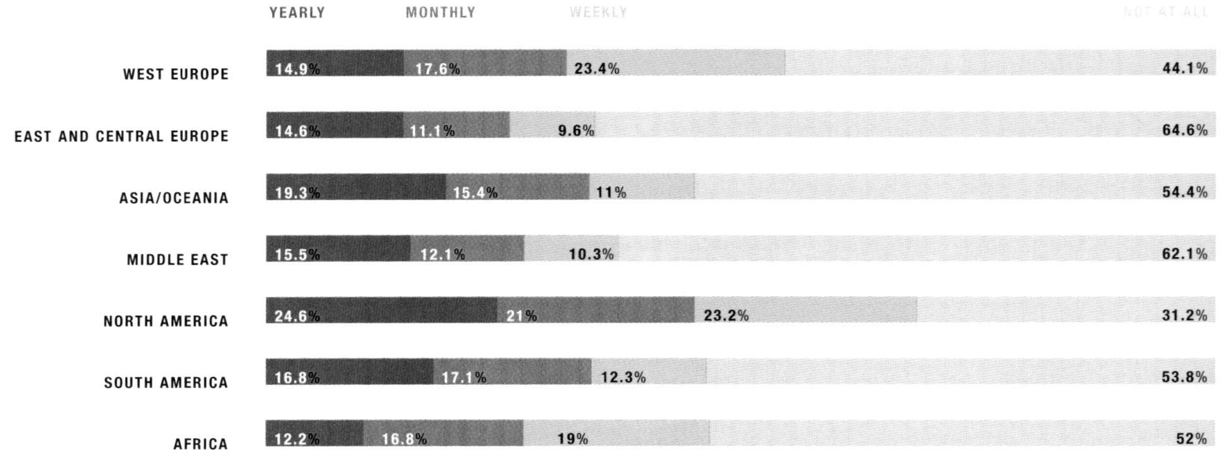

4. EUROPEAN ARTISTIC ACTIVITIES

AS A % OF THE EU POPULATION

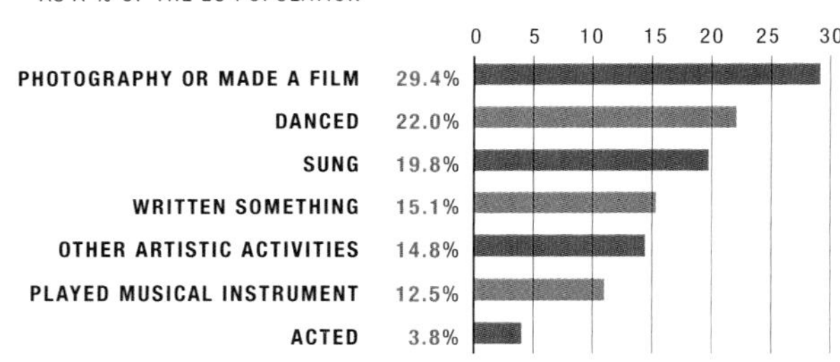

5. AMERICAN PARTICIPATION IN THE PERFORMING ARTS

MILLIONS OF U.S. ADULTS

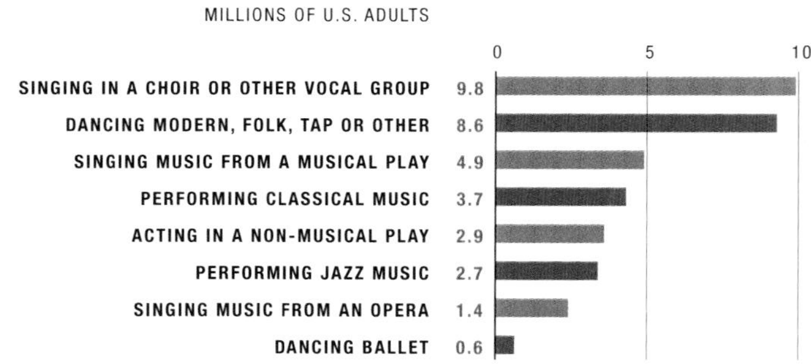

U.S. ADULTS PARTICIPATING IN THE ARTS

AT LEAST ONCE IN A 12-MONTH PERIOD IN % + MILLIONS

	% OF **ADULTS** **ATTENDING / VISITING / READING**			MILLIONS OF **ADULTS** **ATTENDING / VISITING / READING**		
	1982	1992	2002	1982	1992	2002
PERFORMING ARTS						
MUSIC:						
JAZZ *	9.6%	10.6%	10.8%	15.7	19.7	22.2
CLASSICAL MUSIC *	13.0%	12.5%	11.6%	21.3	23.2	23.8
OPERA *	3.0%	3.3%	3.2%	4.5	6.1	6.6
PLAYS:						
MUSICAL PLAYS *	18.6%	17.4%	17.1%	30.5	32.3	35.1
NON-MUSICAL PLAYS *	11.9%	13.5%	12.3%	19.5	25.1	25.2
DANCE:						
BALLET *	4.2%	4.7%	3.9%	6.9	8.7	8.0
OTHER DANCE *	N A	7.1%	6.3%	N.A.	13.2	12.1
VISUAL ARTS						
ART MUSEUMS / GALLERIES *	22.1%	26.7%	26.5%	36.2	49.6	54.3
ART / CRAFT FAIRS AND FESTIVALS	39.0%	40.7%	33.4%	63.9	75.6	68.4
HISTORIC SITES						
PARKS / HISTORIC BUILDINGS / NEIGHBORHOODS	37.0%	34.5%	31.6%	60.6	64.1	64.7
LITERATURE						
PLAYS / POETRY / NOVELS / SHORT STORIES	56.9%	54.0%	46.7%	93.3	100.3	95.3
ANY BENCHMARK ACTIVITY	39.0%	41.0%	39.4%	66.5	76.2	81.2

* denotes 'benchmark' art activity

7. U.S. ADULTS PARTICIPATING IN OTHER LEISURE

	% OF **ADULTS** **ATTENDING / VISITING / READING**		
TYPE OF ACTIVITY	1982	1992	2002
MOVIES	63.0%	59.0%	60.0%
EXERCISE	51.0%	60.0%	55.1%
GARDENING	60.0%	55.0%	47.3%
HOME IMPROVEMENTS	60.0%	48.0%	42.4%
AMUSEMENT PARKS	49.0%	50.0%	41.7%
BENCHMARK ARTS EVENTS	39.0%	41.0%	39.0%
SPORTING EVENTS	48.0%	37.0%	35.0%
OUTDOOR ACTIVITIES	36.0%	34.0%	30.9%
ACTIVE SPORTS	39.0%	39.0%	30.4%
VOLUNTEER / CHARITY	28.0%	33.0%	29.0%
TV HOURS PER DAY	3.0%	3.0%	2.9%

8. TIME SPENT **WATCHING TELEVISION** & **VIDEOS**

AVERAGE | FEMALE | MALE

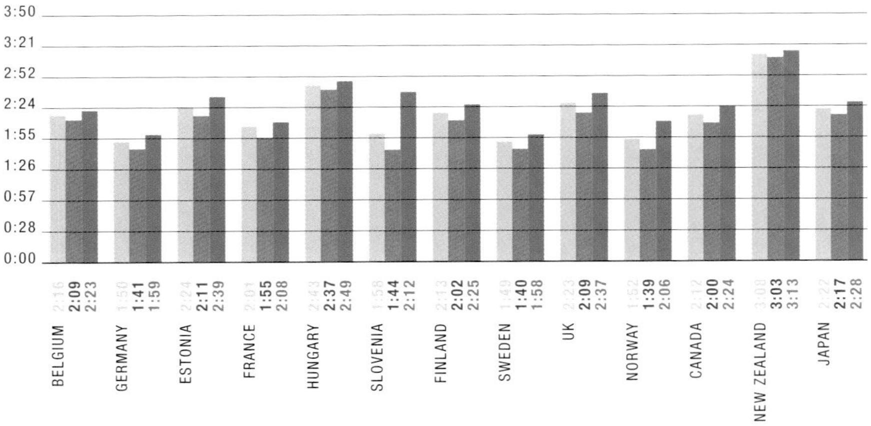

3:50
3:21
2:52
2:24
1:55
1:26
0:57
0:28
0:00
2:16 2:09 2:23
BELGIUM
1:50 1:41 1:59
GERMANY
2:24 2:11 2:39
ESTONIA
2:01 1:55 2:08
FRANCE
2:43 2:37 2:49
HUNGARY
1:58 1:44 2:12
SLOVENIA
2:13 2:02 2:25
FINLAND
1:49 1:40 1:58
SWEDEN
2:23 2:09 2:37
UK
1:52 1:39 2:06
NORWAY
2:12 2:00 2:24
CANADA
3:08 3:03 3:13
NEW ZEALAND
2:22 2:17 2:28
JAPAN

11. PROPORTION OF PEOPLE WHO SPENT ANY TIME WATCHING TELEVISION + VIDEOS

% OF DAY

AVERAGE | FEMALE | MALE

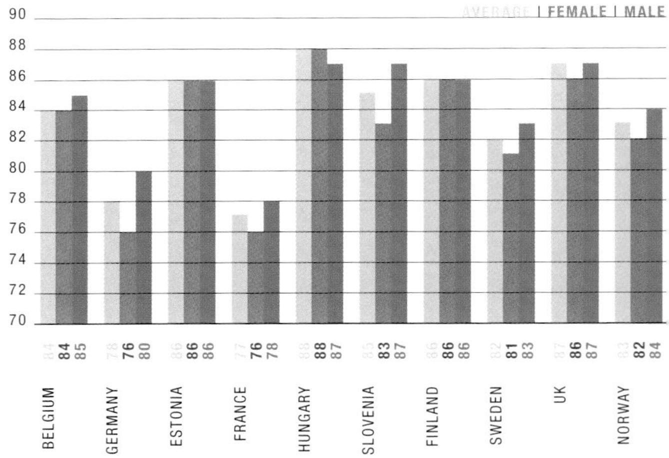

90
88
86
84
82
80
78
76
74
72
70
84 84 85
BELGIUM
78 76 80
GERMANY
86 86 86
ESTONIA
77 76 78
FRANCE
88 88 87
HUNGARY
85 83 87
SLOVENIA
86 86 86
FINLAND
82 81 83
SWEDEN
87 86 87
UK
83 82 84
NORWAY

10. AVERAGE TIME SPENT **WATCHING TV/VIDEOS OF THOSE WHO SPENT ANY TIME ON TV/VIDEOS**

AVERAGE | FEMALE | MALE

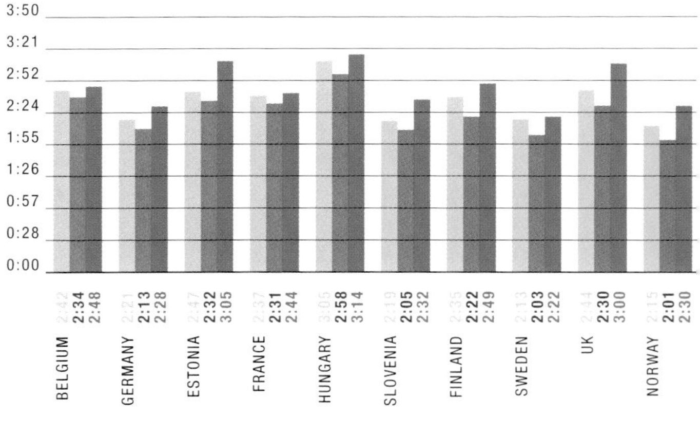

3:50
3:21
2:52
2:24
1:55
1:26
0:57
0:28
0:00
2:42 2:34 2:48
BELGIUM
2:21 2:13 2:28
GERMANY
2:47 2:32 3:05
ESTONIA
2:37 2:31 2:44
FRANCE
3:05 2:58 3:14
HUNGARY
2:19 2:05 2:32
SLOVENIA
2:35 2:22 2:49
FINLAND
2:13 2:03 2:22
SWEDEN
2:44 2:30 3:00
UK
2:15 2:01 2:30
NORWAY

9. MINUTES PER DAY **SPENT ON ENTERTAINMENT & CULTURAL PARTICIPATION**

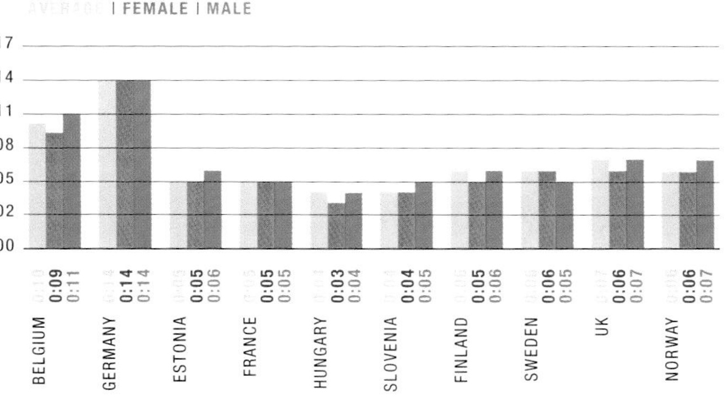

12. PROPORTION OF **PEOPLE WHO SPENT ANY TIME ON ENTERTAINMENT & CULTURAL**

% PER DAY

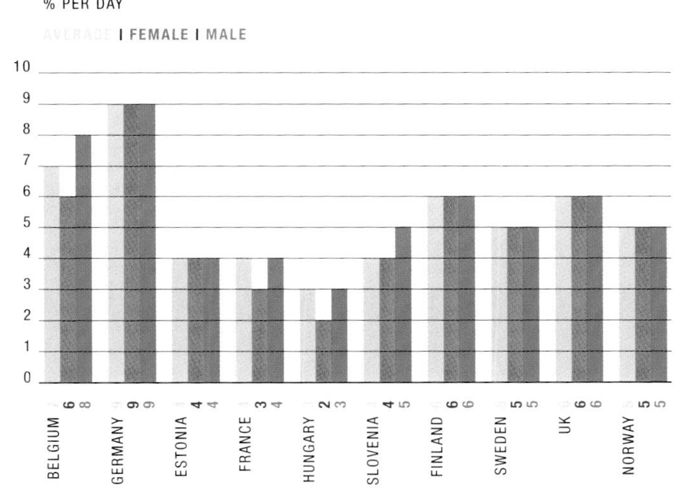

SPORTS

- world's most valuable football teams 2006 **- fifa revenue - fifa income tv rights - overview of fifa world cup - host countries** 1930 – 2010 **- fifa use of funds by fifa country associations - ioc revenue generation** by program area - olympic games: **revenue from broadcast partnerships** - olympics: **revenue from top program** - olympics: **revenue from ticketing** - olympics: **revenue from licensing - other popular international sports competitions**

1. WORLD'S MOST VALUABLE **FOOTBALL TEAMS** 2006

IN $USD MILLIONS

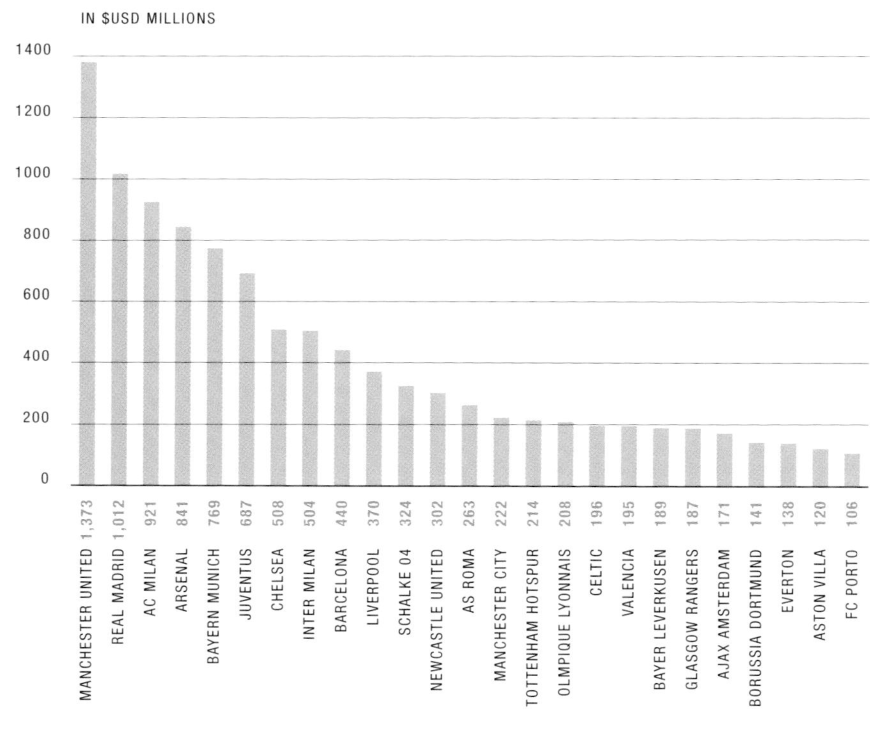

3. **FIFA** TV RIGHTS **REVENUE**

IN 1987, FIFA GRANTED THE TV RIGHTS FOR THE THREE FIFA WORLD CUP COMPETITIONS TO FOLLOW (1990-98) TO THE INTERNATIONAL CONSORTIUM OF PUBLIC SERVICE BROADCASTERS. TEN YEARS LATER, THE RIGHTS FOR THE 2002 AND 2006 FIFA WORLD CUPS WERE GRANTED TO THE KIRCHSPORT GROUP.

1990	**95** MILLION (Swiss Francs)
1994	**110** MILLION
1998	**135** MILLION
2002	**1.3** BILLION
2006	**1.5** BILLION

2. BREAKDOWN OF **FIFA REVENUE** 2005 IN CHF MILLIONS

OTHER 36 - 4%

BRAND LICENSING **21**
QUALITY CONCEPT **6**
FINES **4**
OTHER E.G. RENTAL INCOME, SALE OF FILM **5**

FINANCIAL INCOME 86 - 10%

FOREIGN EXCHANGE EFFECTS **70**
INTEREST **14**
INVESTMENTS **2**

EVENT-RELATED REVENUE 752 - 86%

TV BROADCASTING RIGHTS:
- 2006 FIFA WORLDCUP **423**
- ADDITIONAL FIFA EVENTS **12**

MARKETING RIGHTS **193**
HOSPITALITY RIGHTS **65**
LICENSING RIGHTS **14**
OTHER **45**

6. **IOC: REVENUE** GENERATION BY PROGRAM AREA

IN $US MILLIONS 2001 2004

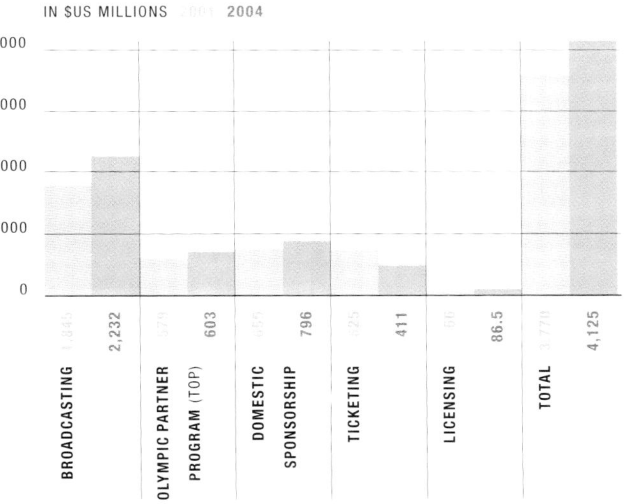

4. OVERVIEW OF **FIFA WORLD CUP HOST COUNTRIES** 1930 – 2010

1930 URUGUAY
1934 ITALY
1938 FRANCE
1950 BRAZIL
1954 SWITZERLAND
1958 SWEDEN
1962 CHILE
1966 ENGLAND
1970 MEXICO
1974 GERMANY
1978 ARGENTINA
1982 SPAIN
1986 MEXICO
1990 ITALY
1994 UNITED STATES
1998 FRANCE
2002 KOREA/JAPAN
2006 GERMANY
2010 SOUTH AFRICA

5. **FIFA** USE OF FUNDS

BY COUNTRY ASSOCIATIONS, 2001 – 2005

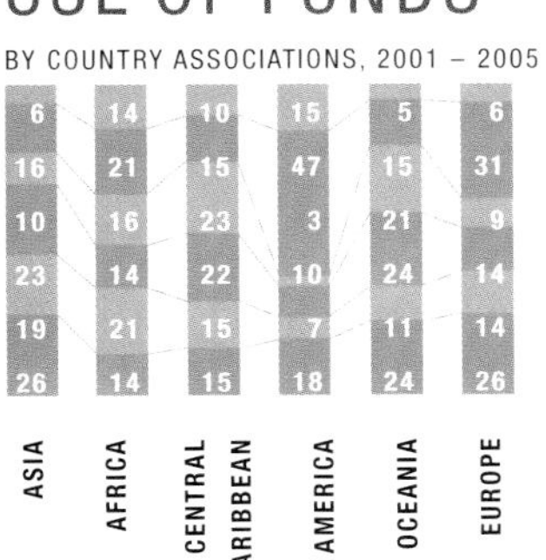

VARIOUS
INFRASTRUCTURE
PLANNING + ADMINISTRATION
TECHNICAL DEVELOPMENT
MEN'S COMPETITION
YOUTH FOOTBALL

7. **OLYMPIC GAMES:** REVENUE FROM BROADCAST PARTNERSHIP

IN $USD MILLIONS

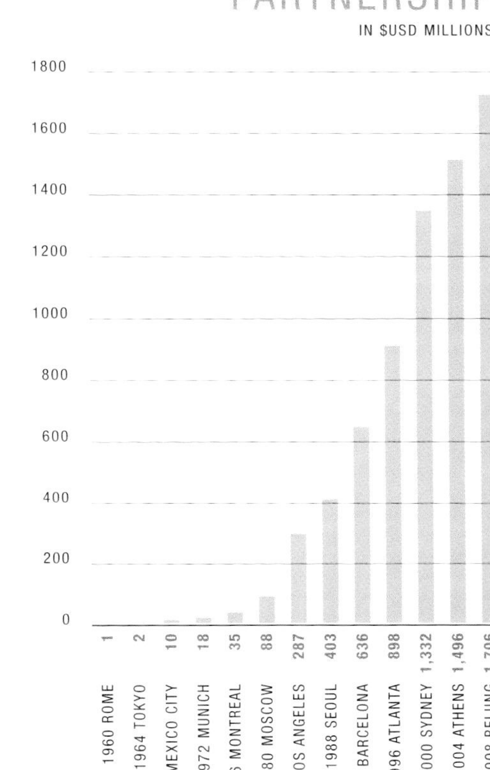

8. OLYMPICS: **REVENUE FROM TOP** OLYMPIC PARTNER **PROGRAM**

$US MILLIONS | # OF NOCS | # OF PARTNERS

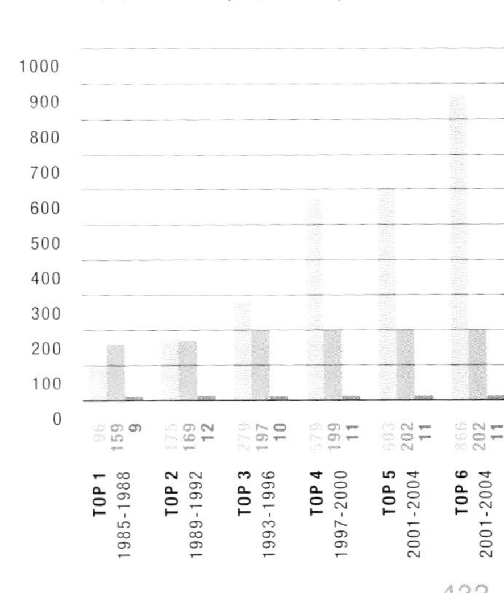

9. OLYMPICS: REVENUES FROM LICENSING

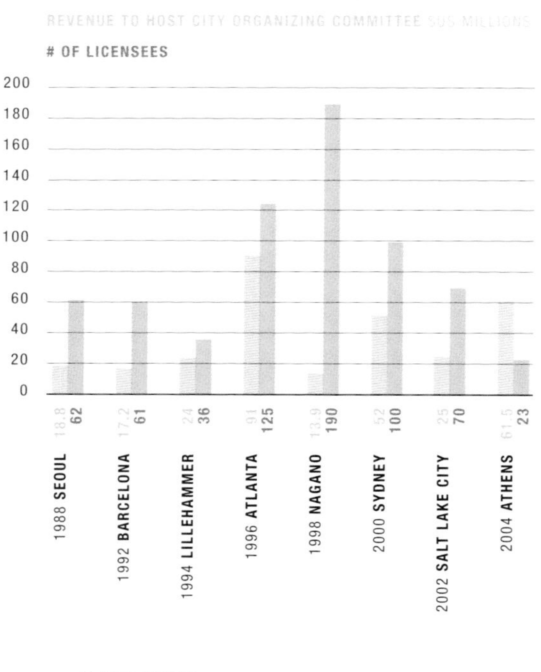

10. OLYMPICS: REVENUE FROM TICKETING

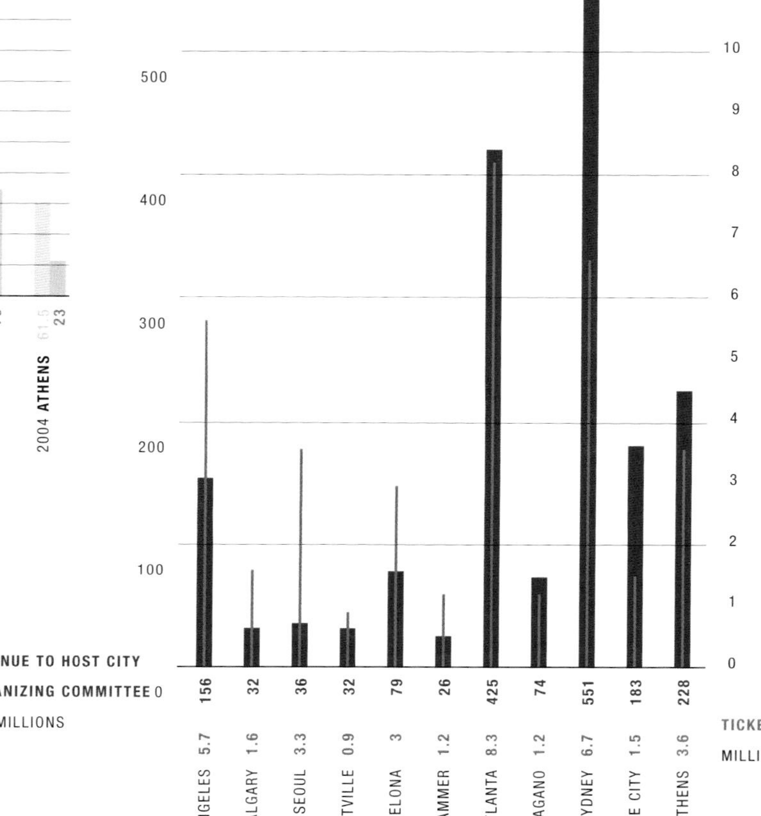

11. OTHER POPULAR INTERNATIONAL SPORTS COMPETITIONS

ESTIMATED AVERAGE ATTENDANCE

MILLIONS

16
14
12
10
8
6
4
2
0

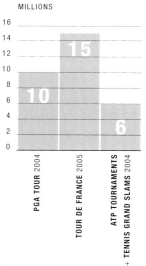

10 — PGA TOUR 2004

15 — TOUR DE FRANCE 2005

6 — ATP TOURNAMENTS + TENNIS GRAND SLAMS 2004

HERITAGE PRESERVATION AND DESTRUCTION Globalization poses new challenges for world heritage. Conflicts, lack of resources and awareness, and sometimes neglect and incompetence result in the destruction of various heritages and environments. The indicator suite on Heritage shows that:

- UNESCO world heritage sites presently number 812, with 77% being cultural, 20% natural, and 24.3% mixed
- Of identified UNESCO world heritage sites, 121 are considered intangible and divided along the categories of Music and Performing Arts (accounting for 38%), Social Practices (21.5%), Rituals and Festivals (18%), Oral Traditions (13%), Cultural Spaces (9%), and Traditional Knowledge and Craftsmanship (8%)
- Europe dominates the allocation of cultural properties (55%) and cities listed as UNESCO World Heritage Properties (59.4%)
- Threatened world heritage sites tend to be located in politically tumultuous areas of the world

WHAT IS HERITAGE?

Heritage refers to cultural legacies or traditions that are passed from one generation to the next. Physical heritage are tangible in nature, and include buildings, monuments, artifacts, and other manufactured cultural products, while natural heritage is comprised of components of the natural environment such as flora and fauna. Intangible heritage come in the form of customs, practices, belief systems, artistic expression, and languages. As heritage testifies to the socioeconomic, political, ethnic, religious, and philosophical values of a particular people, it often becomes targeted for destruction in times of war or political upheaval. Heritage preservation is the theory and practice of maintaining physical, natural, and intangible components of heritage. The process of preservation is inherently subjective, as the presiding generation determines which items are of value for future generations.

WHAT DO WE KNOW ABOUT HERITAGE IN TERMS OF PRESERVATION AND DESTRUCTION?

UNESCO's World Heritage Committee, whose purpose is to secure world cultural and natural heritage sites, determines which are important to the common heritage of humankind and in designation, allows the sites access to financial support from the World Heritage Fund.*

Of the 219 cities listed as UNESCO World Heritage Properties, 130 are located in Europe, which is more than the combined number of Latin America and the Caribbean (35), Asia Pacific (23) the Arab States (22), Africa (3), and North America (2). Europe also has the largest number of UNESCO heritage properties (352), more than Asia Pacific (112), Latin American and the Caribbean (78), the Arab States (56), Africa (31), and North America (13) combined.

On the other hand, Asia Pacific leads the world with largest number of natural heritage sites (43), while Africa (34), Latin America and the Caribbean (34), and Europe (33) have similar numbers, North America has 25, and the Arab States have 4. Asia Pacific also dominates as the region with the largest number of intangible heritage pieces (30), followed by Europe (19), Latin America and the Caribbean (16), Africa (14), and the Arab States (8). North America has no intangible heritage pieces despite the rich traditions of numerous American Indian tribes.

In 1994, the World Heritage Committee launched the Global Strategy for a Balanced Representative and Credible World Heritage List to better represent the world's less-developed areas, particularly non-European parts. As a result, Latin America and the Caribbean, Asia Pacific, and Africa have seen significant percent growth rates for cultural heritage sites, while the Arab States have seen a growing number of natural heritage sites.

In 2005 UNESCO identified 35 world heritage sites in danger. With the exception of Cologne Cathedral in Germany and the Everglades National Park in the United States, listed heritage sites tend to be located in developing countries and/or politically unstable areas of the world. On the other hand, the 2006 World Monuments Watch 100 Most Endangered Sites list compiled by the World Monuments Fund (WMF) includes more developed areas, particularly the United States, and is more architecturally oriented, featuring more buildings and villages compared to the UNESCO list, which frequently lists national parks and nature reserves.

WHAT ARE THE ISSUES?

The end of the cold war and the fall of the Soviet Union triggered a chain of events around the world, which in some instances burdened the preservation of world heritage. The war that took place in Bosnia-Herzegovina between 1992 and 1995 had devastating impacts on cultural heritage sites of the area. As a result of the conflict, all Islamic shrines listed as cultural heritage sites by UNESCO suffered heavy losses, while three-quarters of Dervish Lodges and Roman Catholic churches, 68% of archives, and almost half of Islamic mosques were severely damaged. In 2001, the Taliban destroyed the colossal 1,500 year old Buddhas of Bamiyan in central Afghanistan with dynamite and tank barrages, and more recently in Iraq, 8,000 year old artifacts have stood unprotected in the midst of war. While damage to world heritage sites is sometimes accidental, these acts are often deliberate attempts of destruction to eradicate cultural heritage and collective memory (Financial Times, 2006). As destruction itself is also a part of history, the decision to rebuild is politically charged, sometimes cleansing history of its scars and delivering an incomplete narrative.

* The World Heritage program of UNESCO, generally only deals with tangible heritage, whereas, separate programs exist for tangible and intangible heritage.
(accessed 6/1/06)

ENVIRONMENT The world's cultures exist in varied physical environments. Culture and the environment are intertwined in complex and changing ways. Globalization is challenging this relationship, putting serious pressures on resources, and bringing into question long-term sustainability as well as the adequacy of existing governance structures and regulatory frameworks. The indictor suite on the environment shows that:

• In Asia and the Middle East, 49.3% of the population believes that economic growth and creating jobs should be given priority over the environment; whereas in Latin America, Europe and North America, over 50% believe that protecting the environment should be given priority, even if it causes slower economic growth
• Of the top 15 countries on the 2005 Environmental Sustainability Index Report, four are Scandinavian
• Of the lowest 15 countries on the 2005 Environmental Sustainability Index Report, five are in the Middle East
• Between 1990 and 2003, total emissions for countries that ratified the Kyoto Protocol declined by 6%, while emissions for non-Kyoto parties grew by 39% from 11.8 gigatons to 16.5 gigatons

WHAT IS MEANT BY "ENVIRONMENT"?

The environment is the sum of circumstances, objects, and conditions impacting the form, behavior, and development of an organism. The natural environment encompasses air, water, land, natural resources, flora, fauna, and humans. In recent centuries, human activity has carried significant impacts of environmental degradation, with nature's resources being consumed faster than can be replenished. Sustainability refers to the concept of designing human activity as to actualize the greatest potential in the present while preserving the natural environment for future generations and their needs.

BASIC FACTS ON THE ENVIRONMENT

As rapid political and economic changes result in clashes over control and access to valuable natural resources, water is particularly vulnerable given its role as a human necessity and importance in agriculture, manufacturing, and energy production. According to the Transboundary Freshwater Dispute Database, between 1950 and 1999, 534 international conflicts occurred over water (2005). 62% of these conflicts were over the quantity of water, while a quarter related to infrastructure and development, 5% to the quality of water, 3% to joint management, 1.7% to hydro-power/ hydro-electricity and border issues respectively, and less than 1% due to issues in irrigation.

The Environmental Sustainability Index (ESI) is compiled by the Yale University Center for Environmental Law and Policy, Columbia University's Center for International Earth Science Information Network (CIESIN), and the World Economic Forum to gauge the sustainability of nation's environmental practices. The top five scoring countries on the 2005 Environmental Sustainability Index Report were Finland, Norway, Uruguay, Sweden, and Iceland, while the bottom five scoring nations were North Korea, Taiwan, Turkmenistan, Iraq, and Uzbekistan. The US ranked 45 out of 146, while Canada placed 6th, Japan 30th, the UK 65th, and China 133rd. With some exceptions, such as the United States, a country's environmental sustainability index score positively correlated with its degree of democratization: the more democratic countries are, the higher their environmental sustainability index.

The Kyoto Protocol, negotiated in 1997 under the United Nations Framework Convention on Climate Change (UNFCCC), seeks to reduce global climates (Table 1) via carbon dioxide and other greenhouse gas reduction. Following ratification by Russia in November of 2004, the protocol became legally binding in February of 2005. Although India and China ratified the protocol, the present agreement does not impose any regulations on their greenhouse gas emissions. Out of the 163 countries that ratified the protocol (as of April 2006), the United States and Australia rejected ratification for reasons related to potential economic impacts; furthermore, US President Bush still questions the existence of a Greenhouse Effect. The United States, Australia, China, India, Japan, and South Korea agreed to respectively curb greenhouse gas emission as signatories of the Asia Pacific Partnership on Clean Development in July of 2005; however, the document has no enforcement mechanisms.

WHAT ARE THE ISSUES?

Globalization enhances access to and production of goods and services, stimulating economic development around the world; yet, the process of producing and distributing goods and services carries environmental consequences. Clearing land for agriculture and burning fossil fuels releases carbon dioxide and other greenhouse gases which results in global warming. The effects include a thinning ozone layer, frequency of extreme weather events, and the spread of disease.

The US (representing 23% of global emissions in 2003) and China (representing 15%) contributed the largest shares to the world's total emissions, accounting for over half the growth of emissions between 1990 and 2003, and are not subject to the emissions control mechanisms of the Kyoto Protocol compared to most nations of their economic capability (International Energy Agency, 2005). Countries often fail to implement environmentally sustainable measures, prioritizing economic growth and employment rates. However, the majority of people in Europe (62.7%), North America (62.8%), and Latin America (57.3%) believe that "protecting the environment should be given priority, even if it causes slower economic growth and some loss of jobs" (World Values Survey, 1999-2004).

Among Kyoto Protocol parties, Russia, Japan, Germany, Canada, and the United Kingdom accounted for 54% of the group's total emissions between 1990 and 2003; thus, the overall decline in emissions among Kyoto parties can be attributed to diminishing emissions among Economies in Transition (EIT) such as Croatia and Slovenia. As member nations update their action plans and industrialized countries attempt to meet set goals, Kyoto parties will increasingly rely on flexibility mechanisms such as emissions trading (International Energy Agency, 2005). However, emissions are likely to increase in EIT countries as they develop their economies, decreasing the supply of emission credits so that all Kyoto parties will need to implement sustainable energy policies and practices to curb total emissions in the long run.

US preponderance in harmful emissions is partly attributable to its dependence on automobiles and consumption of oil. In the last decade, the growing popularity of the Sports-Utility Vehicle raised American gas consumption and pollution rates. Since 2004, oil prices have skyrocketed in the US and other countries due to high demand, rising crude oil prices and the destruction of oil platforms and refineries by hurricanes. Still, prices are low compared to Europe, where governments impose higher gas taxes to regulate use of a limited resource and protect the environment. A major problem in the US, China and India-the three largest and fastest growing energy consuming markets in the world-is the absence of a coordinated regulatory framework for pubic policy and market incentives to operate synergistically and reconcile short-term needs with long-term sustainability.

TABLE 1: **THE GREENHOUSE EFFECT-GLOBAL SURFACE TEMPERATURES**
reported in Celsius

YEAR	5-YEAR ANNUAL MEAN TEMPERATURE	YEAR	5-YEAR ANNUAL MEAN TEMPERATURE
1905	13.77	**1980**	14.05
1910	13.71	**1990**	14.25
1920	13.75	**1995**	14.25
1940	14.04	**2000**	14.37
1960	14.01	**2005**	14.52

Source: Carbon Dioxide Information Analysis Center, Goddard Institute for Space Studies (2006)

CULTURAL PARTICIPATION Knowledge about cultural participation has in a way suffered from contested definitions and a poor information base, in particular from a cross-national perspective. Some analysts link cultural participation to cultural citizenship, defined as "the maintenance and development of cultural lineage via education, custom, language, religion, and the acknowledgment of difference in and by the mainstream" (Lewis and Miller, 2003:1). Thus, cultural participation can be seen as the enactment of cultural citizenship.

However, much contemporary scholarship on cultural participation is based on the formation and cultivation of what Pierre Bourdieu and Jean-Claude Passeron called "cultural capital" (1977). Bourdieu (1984) theorized that cultural capital was the result of a specific socialization process whereby dominant social classes establish cultural benchmarks in terms of cultural knowledge and expertise, amplified through unequal access to educational institutions. The nurturing of cultural capital in the children of elite families (i.e., the appreciation and consumption of high-art or elite-culture by younger generations) was a way to ensure to reproduction of high social status. Education and the arts, therefore, were crucial to this process and served as signifiers of achievement and cultural attainment. In this light, the evolution of cultural capital is linked to issues of acculturation and participation in activities that influence or shape a so-called "cultured" individual within society. The suite, therefore, shows primarily cultural participation in terms of preferences, but also as active participation based on decisions on how to spend one's time.

A GLIMPSE INTO CULTURAL PARTICIPATION WORLDWIDE

Statistics on cultural participation are gathered disproportionately within countries, making comparisons across regions and countries difficult. Differing definitions of what constitutes a "cultural" activity further complicate data collection and studies. However, recently comparative studies are beginning to emerge, particularly in Europe.

Currently, Canada archives and collects the most comprehensive data on cultural participation of any country, also perhaps as part of its ongoing attempt to shield against the influence of American popular culture. In fact, 87% of Canadians feel that participation and promotion of Canadian artistic and cultural expression is essential "to remain distinct as a country" (Environics Research Group Ltd., 2000). Indeed, understanding cultural participation is in attempt to generate cultural development policies that strengthen national or collective identities against the infiltration of 'outside' cultures (DiMaggio and Mukhtar, 2004).

The European Union population study (European Commission, 2004) identified going to the cinema, library or museum, and attending sporting events as the top cultural activities participated in by those surveyed. Similarly, in the United States, 60% of the population also goes to the movies, followed by exercise (55.1%) and gardening (47.3%) (NEA, 2002). Clearly here, the United States definition of cultural activities includes leisure or recreation, whereas the European definition is based more on traditional notion of cultural participation.

THE ISSUES: CULTURAL PARTICIPATION & GLOBALIZATION

Historically, early concepts of what constitutes culture, and therefore cultural activities, have privileged western cultures over all others and painted indigenous or traditional cultures as 'backward', even 'uncivil.' The institutionalization of these concepts has indeed permeated theories related to globalization and development; as well as come into play within policies addressing the global economy. The valuation of 'Western' as dominant has privileged cultural activities in association with western culture (fine arts, Hollywood blockbuster movies, popular media, literature, and cultural institutions) over other forms of non-western art and cultural activities. This has facilitated the commodification of Western culture through mass media and entertainment as popular culture, which, in turn, has influenced citizen participation in culture.

Recently scholars have noted that globalization has not necessarily benefited dominant cultures disproportionately. They point to the growing diversity available to individuals within many societies as a result of globalization. This diversity informs and changes people's tastes, preferences and activities. Globalization of cultural activities has changed participation to include more transnational, and potentially perhaps even increasingly cosmopolitan, tastes. Whereas in Bourdieu's world, one "elite" culture was privileged among many, today the privileged person is the one that is informed and can participate in many cultures (DiMaggio and Mukhtar, 2004).

SPORTS AND RECREATION

Sport is a culturally and politically complex phenomenon, and one that is becoming increasingly lucrative from a business perspective, as the lines between sports and entertainment are blurring. Like many other cultural phenomena, sports are affected by globalization in practice (e.g. the rise of soccer as the pre-eminent global sport), organizations (e.g., the rise of 'super-clubs' such as Manchester United and global spectacles like the Olympics), and structure (e.g., more dominant sports such as soccer crowding out less popular, niche sports in terms of media attention).

Culturally, sport is a vehicle for expressing ideals of health and beauty through exercise, and, in an international context, even peace and human understanding, with the Olympic movement as the clearest expression. At times, however, sports have been instrumentalized for political reasons, with the perverted 1936 Olympics, the 1978 Soccer World Cup in Argentina, and the partially boycotted 1980 and 1984 Olympics as the perhaps most obvious examples.

WHAT ARE SPORTS?

Sports are organized game playing, regulated by rules, permitted equipment, and objectives. While some sports are cooperative and have no clear winners or losers, most involve competition, typically between two opposing teams, or individuals, playing against each other with varying mechanisms for keeping score, and determining a winner. Historically, sports has a complex heritage: linked to the celebration of youth and healthy exercise on the one hand, its competitive elements have been used to represent a country, region, city or a distinct group of people playing for the glory of winning-linking sport to various forms of cultural identity.

THE SCALE AND RISE OF GLOBAL SPORTS

Globally, the Olympics and the Soccer World Cup are the most notable world sporting events, both well attended and followed by global audiences. The globalization of football is linked to the spread of the early British Empire and later to the migration of British people to commonwealth states. Between 1850 and 1930, the British successfully introduced competitive football to the United States, Canada, Mexico, South America, South Africa, Brazil, China, Singapore, Sudan, Russia, Austria, Hungary, Greece, Italy and Portugal (Goldblatt, 2004). Although the British are largely responsible for the global spread of the game of football, its origins lie in China (10,000 BC), further highlighting the evolution and globalization of the sport (Goldblatt, 2004).

Today, the globalization of sports is highly dependent on revenues and broadcasting. In 2005, FIFA, the International Football Association, received roughly $750 million in revenue from events, including broadcasting rights for the 2006 Soccer World Cup and the qualifying matches. The revenue generated from broadcast partnerships for the Olympic Games has grown significantly: in 1996, the Atlanta Games generated $898 million, whereas in Athens in 2004 the sum was almost $1.5 billion, and projected revenue for the 2008 games in Beijing is roughly $1.7 billion.

By looking at attendance rates for international sports leagues, we can see that the league and sport with the highest average attendance per game is the National Football League (NFL-American football). However, comparing attendance per capita, we see that the NFL only draws 26 per 100,000 US citizens, whereas Australian football draws a higher proportion of their population to their games. While soccer is very popular in Europe, it is not proportionally as popular as football in the US and Rugby in Australia, New Zealand and Ireland/Scotland.

LEAGUE	AVERAGE ATTENDANCE	# OF PEOPLE IN ATTENDANCE PER 100,000 POPULATION	TYPE OF SPORT
NPB (JPN)	23,552	18	Baseball
Major League Baseball (USA/CAN)	30,970	9	Baseball
NBA (USA/CAN)	17,558	5	Basketball
Australian Football League (AUS)	35,703	176	Football
NFL (USA)	67,593	23	Football
NFL Europe (GER/NET)	18,965	3	Football
SM-liiga (FIN)	4,609	88	Hockey
Nationalliga A (SWI)	5,495	73	Hockey
Elitserien (SWE)	6,240	69	Hockey
Czech Extraliga (CZE)	5,018	49	Hockey
NHL (UCA/CAN)	16,955	5	Hockey
Russian Hockey Super League (RUS)	3,900	3	Hockey
NPC Division 1(N.ZEA)	13,356	328	Rugby
National Rugby League (AUS)	17,336	86	Rugby
Celtic League(IRE/SCO)	4,457	48	Rugby
Guinness Premiership (ENG)	9,718	16	Rugby
Eredivisie (NET)	16,789	102	Soccer
La Liga (SPA)	28,401	70	Soccer
FA Premier League (ENG)	33,893	56	Soccer
Bundesliga 1 (GER)	37,806	46	Soccer
Serie A (ITA)	25,805	44	Soccer
Ligue 1 (FRA)	21,392	35	Soccer
Football League Championship (ENG)	17,425	29	Soccer
Turkish Premier Super League (TUR)	16,799	24	Soccer
J. League 1 (JPN)	18,765	15	Soccer
Campeonato Brasileiro (BRA)	13,630	7	Soccer
Major League Soccer (USA)	15,108	5	Soccer

WHAT ARE THE ISSUES?

Some sports, soccer in particular, have loyal communities of fans. In such cases, sport is important for identity formation and maintenance, and has, at times become part of identity politics. This may range from local hooliganism to international instances, as was the case for so-called Soccer War between Honduras and Nicaragua. In such instances, sport serves as a cultural conduit focusing events that allow underlying conflicts between and among warring parties to crystallize.

The globalization of some sports such as soccer has brought about a mismatch between input markets and revenue markets. While players in major soccer clubs are increasingly internationally recruited, and now represents around half of the players in major European leagues, the major revenue source through ticket sales remains local, and grounded in deep-seated loyalties. As broadcasting revenue is increasing relative to ticket sales, soccer clubs are turning into commercial franchises, void of their original cultural roots in particular cities or regions, and the support of local fans. In other words, the globalization sports will make some sports such as soccer more lucrative from a commercial perspective, and but less cultural in terms of identity.

ECONOMY

GLOBAL ARTS MARKET

CULTURAL CONSUMPTION + EXPENDITURES

CULTURAL INDUSTRIES

TRADE IN CULTURAL GOODS + SERVICES

GLOBAL ARTS MARKET - **art basel:** cities with the largest # of **art gallery exhibitors** + art basel partners - **galleries** per country represented **at art cologne** - **galleries** per country **at the armory show** - **sotheby's: net auction sales** by year - **international art auction**

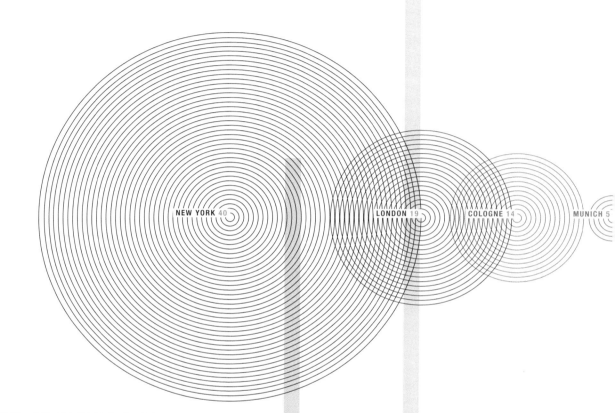

NEW YORK 40

LONDON 19

COLOGNE 14

MUNICH 5

2. THE ARMORY SHOW 2005:

3. ART COLOGNE 2005:

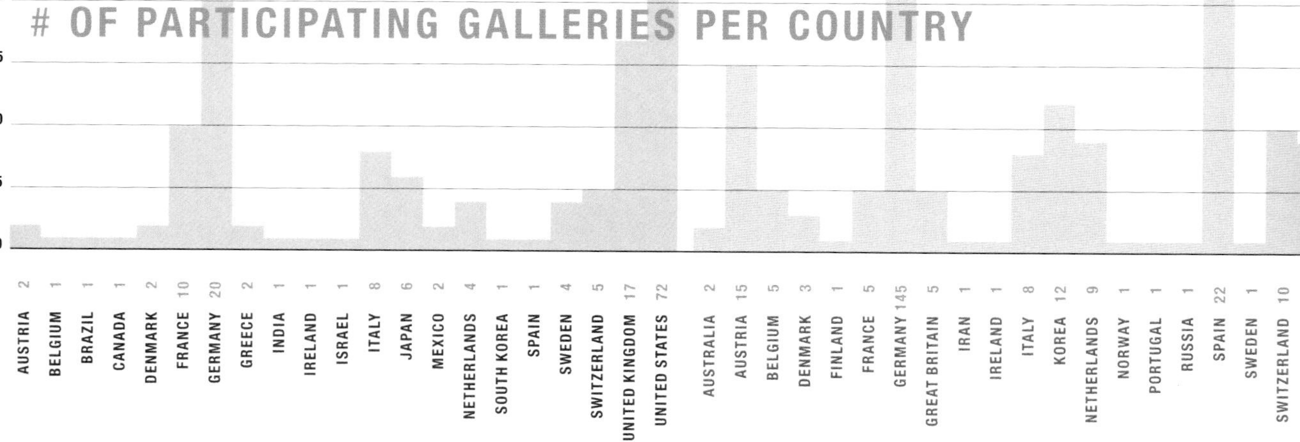

market turnover by country 2003–04 - **international art market** by period art - **us art auction market - uk art auction market - contemporary art auction sales - index of 20th c. modern artists - index of old masters** works on paper - **index of old master** paintings

1. ART BASEL, JUNE 2006:

CITIES WITH LARGEST # OF ART GALLERY EXHIBITORS

ART GALLERIES BY CITY

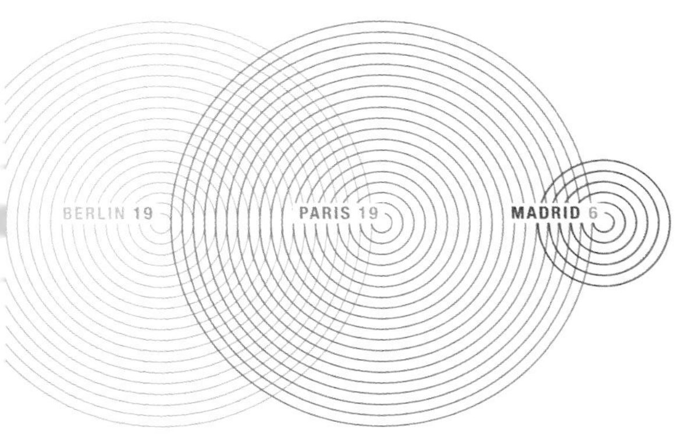

ART BASEL PARTNERS (JUNE 2006)
MAIN SPONSOR
UBS
ASSOCIATE SPONSOR
BVLGARI
HOST SPONSORS
BALOISE INSURANCE
NETJETS EUROPE
BMW GROUP
OFFICIAL NEWSPAPERS AND LIFESTYLE MAGAZINES
BASLER ZEITUNG
NEUE ZÜRCHER ZEITUNG
LE TEMPS
FRANKURTER ALLGEMEINE ZEITUNG
LE MONDE
INTERNATIONAL HERALD TRIBUNE
CORRIERE DELLA SERA
BOLERO
NEO2
ANOTHER MAGAZINE
BON MAGAZINE
OFFICIAL CARRIER
SWISS INTERNATIONAL AIRLINES

SUPPLIERS
MOËT & CHANDON
VITRA
UNIPLAN
SALATHÉ
SEMPEX
MEMBER OF TOP EVENTS OF SWITZERLAND
TOP EVENTS OF SWITZERLAND
ART CITY BASEL/MUSEUMS
ARCHITEKTURMUSEUM BASEL
FONDATION BEYELER
KUNSTHALLE BASEL
LISTE 06
JEAN TINGUELY
KUNSTMUSEUM BASEL
MUSEUM FÜR GEGENWARTSKUNST
KUNSTHAUS BASELLAND
SCHAULAGER
VITRA DESIGN MUSEUM
TOURISM INFORMATION
BASEL TOURISM
CITY MARKETING BASEL
SWITZERLAND TOURISM

ART BASEL - MIAMI BEACH PARTNERS (DECEMBER 2006)
MAIN SPONSOR
UBS
ASSOCIATE SPONSORS
BVLGARI
NETJETS EUROPE
BMW GROUP
HOST SPONSORS
MORGANS HOTEL GROUP
W SOUTH BEACH
AXA ART INSURANCE CORPORATION
OFFICIAL HOTELS
SHORE CLUB
DELANO
OFFICIAL NEWSPAPER
THE MIAMI HERALD
OFFICIAL ART RADIO
WPS1.ORG
OFFICIAL CARRIER
SWISS INTERNATIONAL AIRLINES
LOUNGE HOSTS
BLOOMBERG
DAVIDOFF
EPIC RESIDENCES & HOTEL
ST. REGIS
FOUR SEASONS RESIDENCES MIAMI

PROVIDERS
ART NEXUS
10 CANE RUM
PERRIER-JOUËT
CROBAR
TROPICULTURE
VCA
MUSEUMS
BASS MUSEUM OF ART
BOCA RATON MUSEUM OF ART
THE FROST ART MUSEUM, FLORIDA INTERNATIONAL UNIVERSITY
LOWE ART MUSEUM
THE MARGULIES COLLECTION AT THE WAREHOUSE
MIAMI ART CENTRAL
MIAMI ART MUSEUM
THE MOORE SPACE
MUSEUM OF ART FORT LAUDERDALE
MUSEUM OF CONTEMPORARY ART
NORTON MUSEUM OF ART, PALM BEACH
RUBELL FAMILY COLLECTION
UNIVERSITY GALLERIES/FLORIDA ATLANTIC UNIVERSITY
THE WOLFSONIAN, FLORIDA INTERNATIONAL UNIVERSITY

4. SOTHEBY'S: NET AUCTION SALES BY YEAR

SALES IN THOUSANDS $US

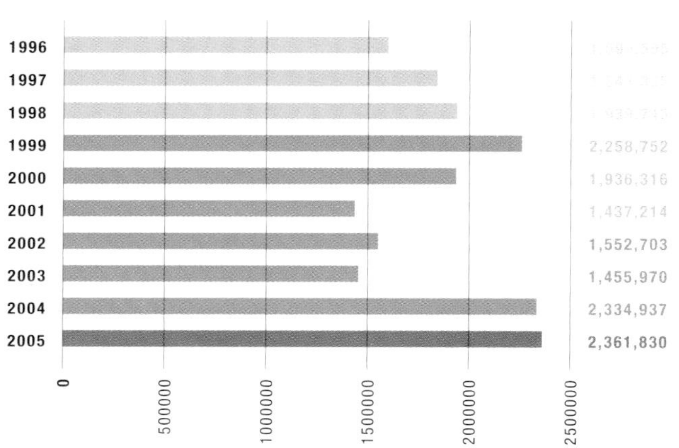

5. CONTEMPORARY ART AUCTION SALES

TURNOVER LOTS SOLD IN $USD MILLION

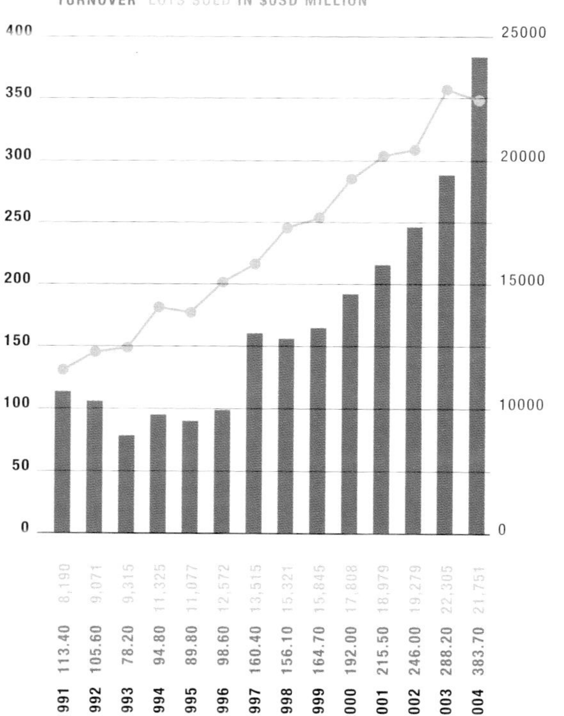

6. INTERNATIONAL ART AUCTION MARKET BY TURNOVER

2003/2004 AUCTION SEASON £1.9 **BILLION** – **$**3.3 **BILLION**

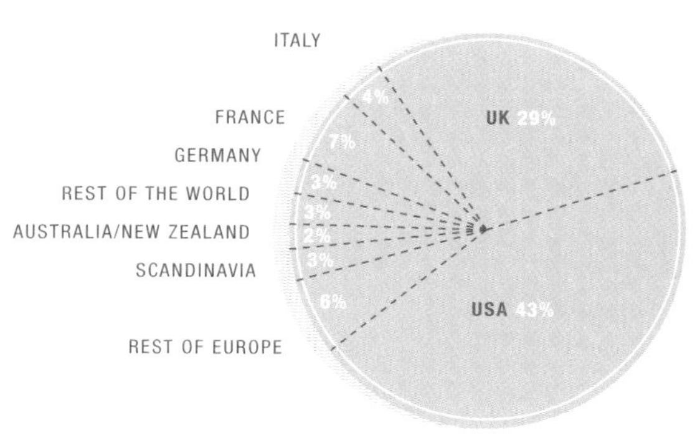

7. INTERNATIONAL ART AUCTION MARKET BY PERIOD OF ART

TURNOVER (IN MILLION £) 17 TO 18TH C. 19TH C. 20TH C.

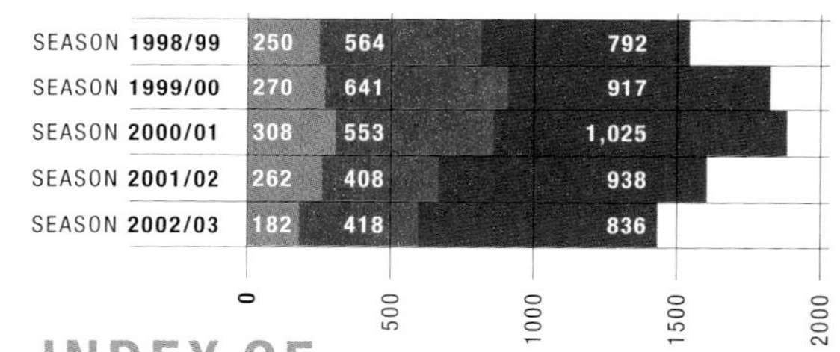

8. INDEX OF 20TH C. MODERN ARTISTS

BASE AVERAGE 1975 – 1979 US$3,040

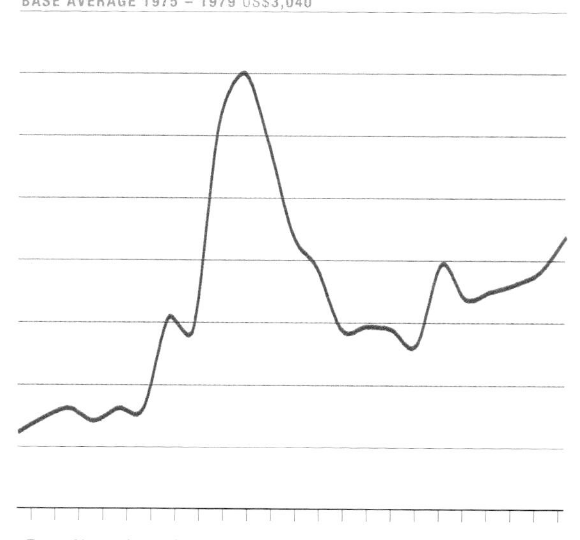

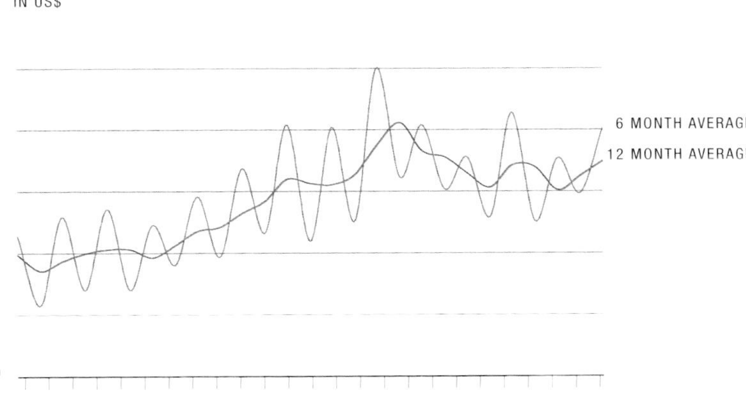
9. USA ART AUCTION MARKET 6/12
IN US$
6 MONTH AVERAGE
12 MONTH AVERAGE
JAN.-92
JUL.-92
JAN.-93
JUL.-93
JAN.-94
JUL.-94
JAN.-95
JUL.-95
JAN.-96
JUL.-97
JAN.-98
JUL.-98
JAN.-99
JUL.-99
JAN.-00
JUL.-00
JAN.-01
JUL.-01
JAN.-02
JUL.-02
JAN.-03
JUL.-03
JAN.-04
JUL.-04
JAN.-05

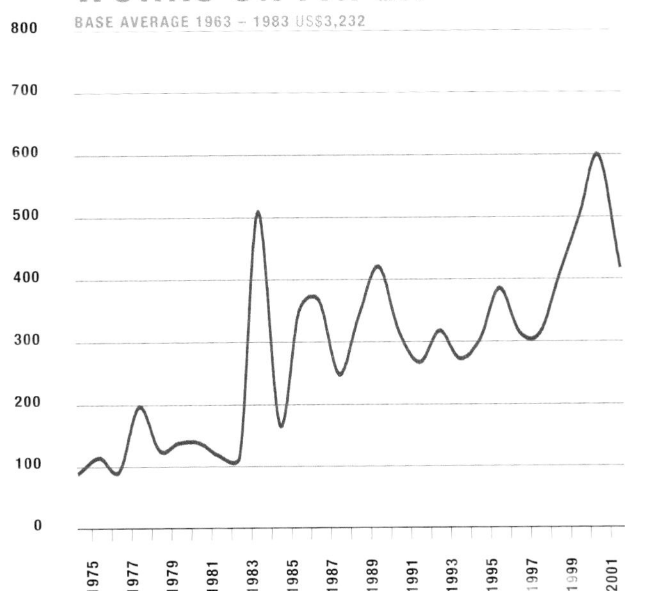
11. INDEX OF OLD MASTERS WORKS ON PAPER
BASE AVERAGE 1963 – 1983 US$3,232
800
700
600
500
400
300
200
100
0
1975
1977
1979
1981
1983
1985
1987
1989
1991
1993
1995
1997
1999
2001

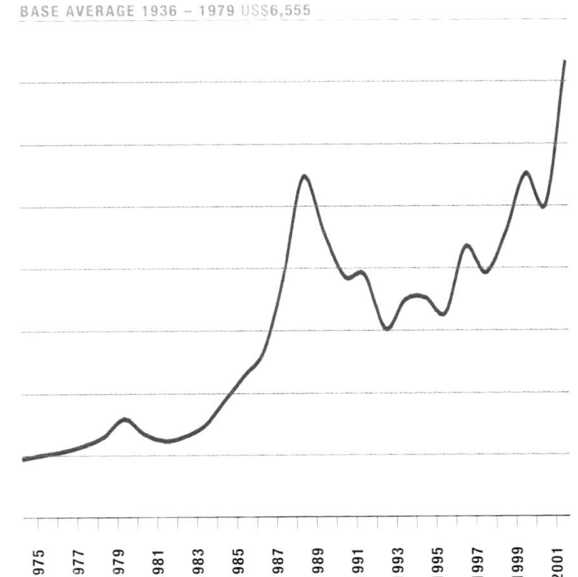
12. INDEX OF OLD MASTERS PAINTINGS
BASE AVERAGE 1936 – 1979 US$6,555
800
700
600
500
400
300
200
100
0
1975
1977
1979
1981
1983
1985
1987
1989
1991
1993
1995
1997
1999
2001

CULTURAL CONSUMPTION

- government versus **household consumption expenditures** % of total consumption by country & years of comparison: **recreation & culture** + **education - consumption expenditure of households and government in the us -** international spending on the arts: **total government spending - consumer spending on culture** by category, canada 2003 **- consumer spending on culture compared to other items**, canada 2003 **- spending on key cultural items**, canada 1997–2003

1a. GOVERNMENT VERSUS HOUSEHOLD EXPENDITURE: RECREATION + CULTURE

UN NATIONAL ACCOUNT STATISTICS - % OF TOTAL CONSUMPTION BY COUNTRY + YEARS OF COMPARISON

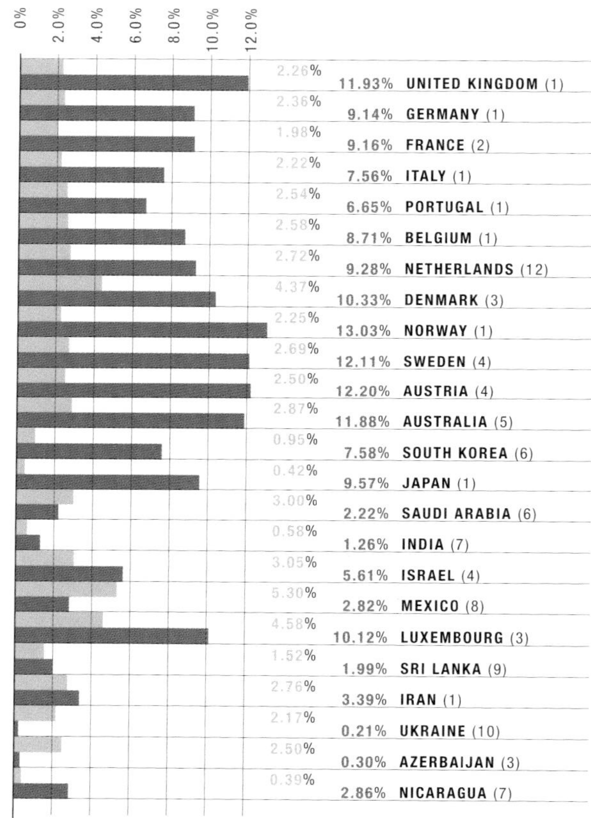

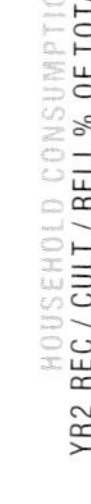

GOVERNMENT CONSUMPTION EXPENDITURE
YR2 REC / CULT / RELI % OF TOTAL CONSUMPTION

DATES OF COMPARISON:

(1) 1992 + 2002	(4) 1995 + 2002	(7) 1994 + 2000	(10) 1996 + 2000
(2) 1995 + 2001	(5) 1998 + 2002	(8) 1993 + 2001	(11) 1994 + 2002
(3) 1993 + 2003	(6) 1992 + 2001	(9) 1992 + 2000	(12) 1995 + 2003

1b. GOVERNMENT VERSUS HOUSEHOLD EXPENDITURE: EDUCATION

UN NATIONAL ACCOUNT STATISTICS - % OF TOTAL CONSUMPTION

BY COUNTRY + YEARS OF COMPARISON

0% 2.0% 4.0% 6.0% 8.0% 10.0% 12.0% 14.0% 16.0% 18.0% 20.0% 22.0% 24.0% 26.0% 28.0% 30.0% 32.0% 34.0% 36.0%

HOUSEHOLD CONSUMPTION EXPENDITURE YR2 EDU % OF TOTAL CONSUMPTION	GOVERNMENT CONSUMPTION EXPENDITURE YR2 EDU % OF TOTAL CONSUMPTION	
1.27%	17.66%	UNITED KINGDOM (1)
0.70%	18.13%	GERMANY (1)
0.64%	20.50%	FRANCE (2)
0.94%	24.69%	ITALY (1)
1.51%	29.64%	PORTUGAL (1)
0.57%	27.69%	BELGIUM (1)
7.49%	32.66%	NETHERLANDS (12)
0.77%	23.12%	DENMARK (3)
0.58%	22.21%	NORWAY (1)
0.13%	23.77%	SWEDEN (4)
0.73%	27.26%	AUSTRIA (4)
2.38%	20.17%	AUSTRALIA (5)
5.83%	26.11%	SOUTH KOREA (6)
2.25%	19.41%	JAPAN (1)
0%	26.45%	SAUDI ARABIA (6)
2.35%	16.99%	INDIA (7)
3.30%	23.66%	ISRAEL (4)
3.85%	36.90%	MEXICO (8)
0.39%	24.03%	LUXEMBOURG (3)
1.49%	13.25%	SRI LANKA (9)
0%	5.60%	IRAN (1)
1.33%	27.26%	UKRAINE (10)
3.30%	29.10%	AZERBAIJAN (3)
1.40%	15.44%	NICARAGUA (7)
8.24%	27.40%	BOTSWANA (11)

1c. U.S. GOVERNMENT VERSUS HOUSEHOLD EXPENDITURE: RECREATION / CULTURE + EDUCATION 2004

% OF TOTAL CONSUMPTION

Household	Government	
9.02%	1.57%	UNITED STATES
2.57%	27.46%	UNITED STATES

AS REPORTED BY THE US GOVERNMENT, WHICH HAS A DIFFERENT SYSTEM FOR MEASURING NATIONAL ACCOUNTS (COMPARED TO THE UN)

2. INTERNATIONAL SPENDING ON THE ARTS 1995 – 1997

TOTAL GOVERNMENT SPENDING IN $USD MILLIONS PER CAPITA IN $USD

% OF GDP
7000
6000
5000
4000
3000
2000
1000
0
0.70%
0.60%
0.50%
0.40%
0.30%
0.20%
0.10%
0%
AUSTRALIA 0.14%
CANADA 0.21%
FINLAND 0.47%
FRANCE 0.26%
GERMANY 0.36%
IRELAND 0.07%
NETHERLANDS 0.21%
NEW ZEALAND 0.60%
SWEDEN 0.29%
UNITED KINGDOM 0.14%
UNITED STATES 0.02%
438 25 AUSTRALIA
1,272 46 CANADA
460 91 FINLAND
3,275 57 FRANCE
6,886 85 GERMANY
33 9 IRELAND
714 46 NETHERLANDS
598 15 NEW ZEALAND
496 57 SWEDEN
1,518 26 UNITED KINGDOM
1,530 6 UNITED STATES

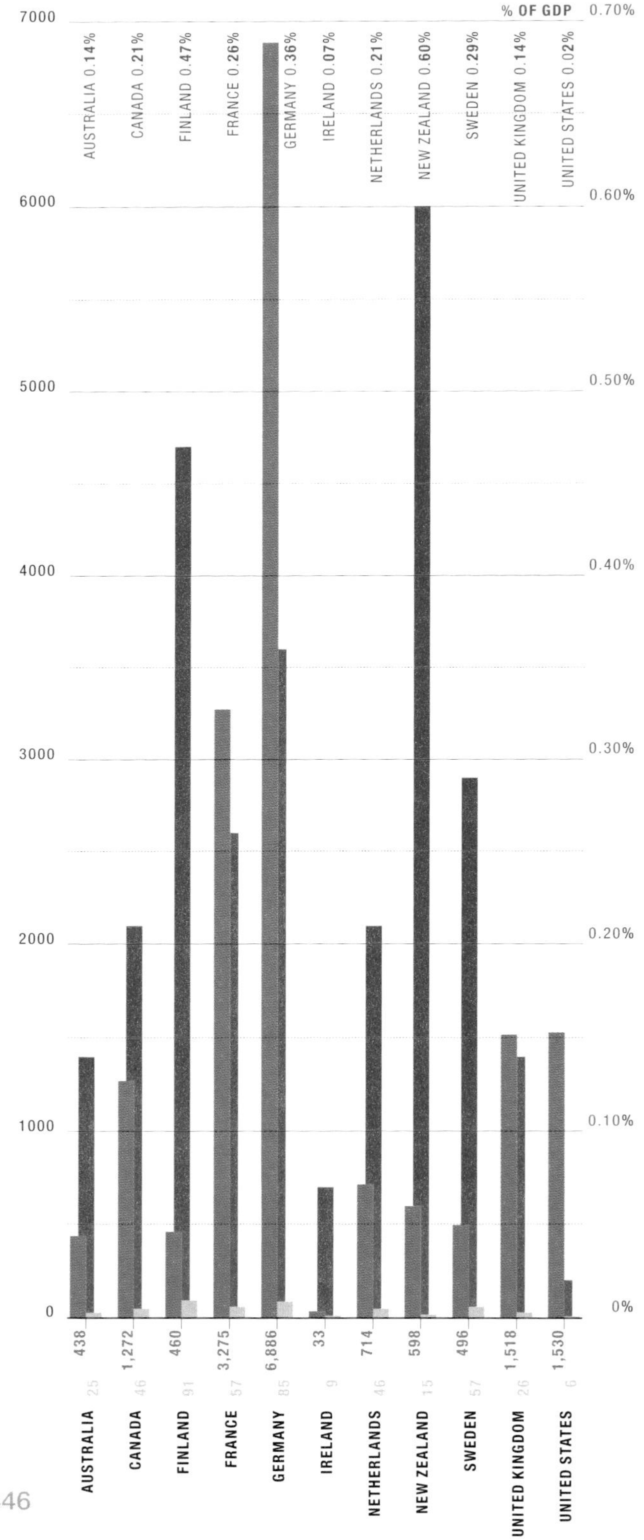

3. CANADA 2003 CONSUMER SPENDING ON CULTURE

COMPARED TO OTHER ITEMS

IN $ BILLIONS

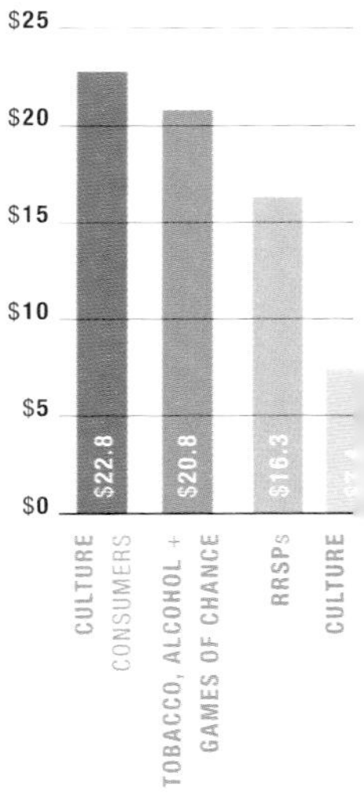

$25
$20
$15
$10
$5
$0
$22.8
$20.8
$16.3
CULTURE CONSUMERS
TOBACCO, ALCOHOL + GAMES OF CHANCE
RRSPs
CULTURE

4. CANADA 2003 CONSUMER SPENDING ON CULTURE

IN $ BILLION BY CATEGORY

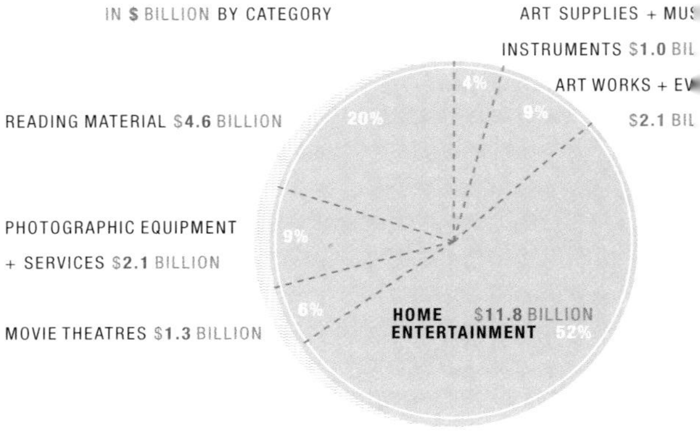

ART SUPPLIES + MUS
INSTRUMENTS $1.0 BIL
ART WORKS + EV
$2.1 BIL
READING MATERIAL $4.6 BILLION
PHOTOGRAPHIC EQUIPMENT
+ SERVICES $2.1 BILLION
MOVIE THEATRES $1.3 BILLION
HOME ENTERTAINMENT $11.8 BILLION 52%
20%
4%
9%
9%
6%

5. CANADA 97/03 SPENDING ON KEY CULTURAL ITEMS

$1.4
$1.2
$1.0
$0.8
$0.6
$0.4
$0.2
$0.0
MOVIE THEATRES
BOOKS
PERFORMING ARTS (LIFE)
WORKS OF ART, CARVINGS
AND VASES
SPORTS EVENTS (LIFE)
ADMISSIONS TO MUSEUMS
& HERITAGE
1997
1998
1999
2000
2001
2002
2003

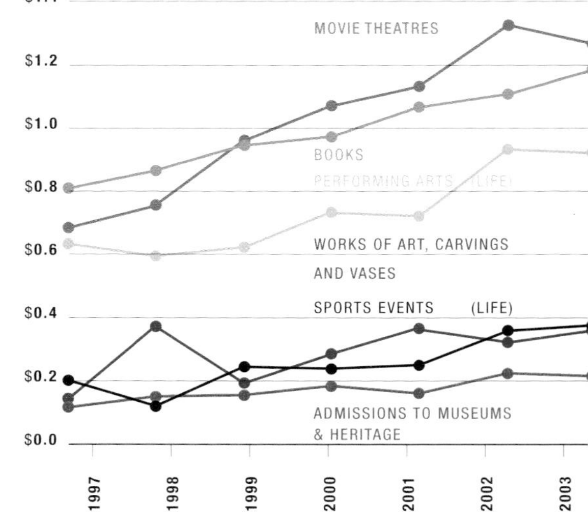

CULTURAL INDUSTRIES

largest producers of cultural goods for 2002 - cultural/creative industries as a % of GDP - cultural industries as % of total country employment - world cultural industries markets ($USD millions) 2000 - cultural employment as % of total employment in EU 2002 - fortune & forbes rankings for major tnc's in cultural industries fields 2005

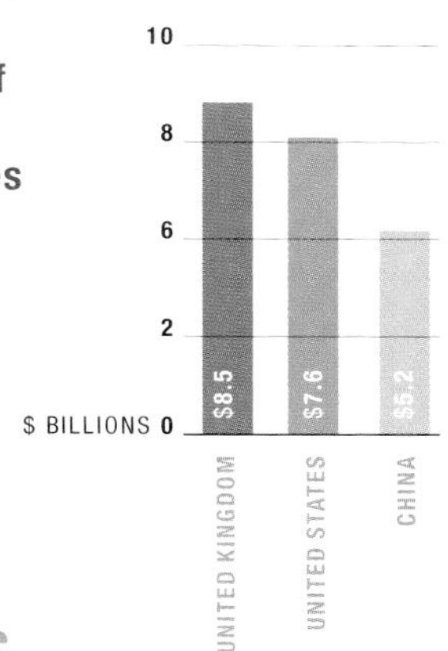

1. LARGEST PRODUCERS OF CULTURAL GOODS 2002

IN $ BILLION BY COUNTRY

2. CULTURAL/ CREATIVE INDUSTRIES

AS % OF GDP

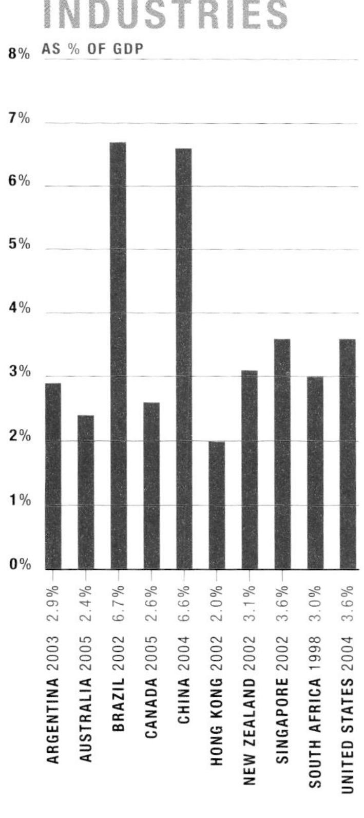

3. CULTURAL INDUSTRIES

% OF TOTAL COUNTRY EMPLOYMENT

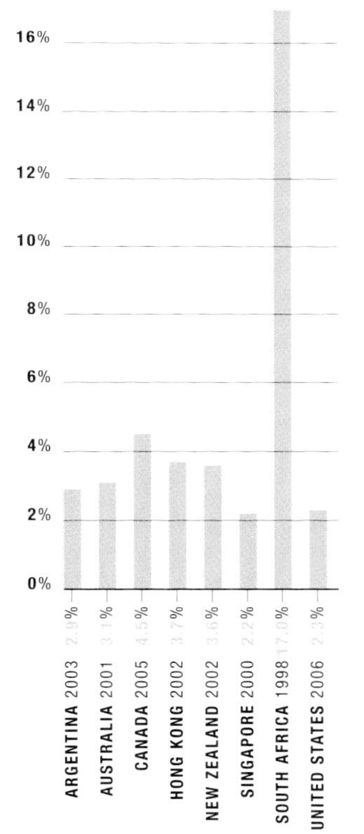

4. CULTURAL EMPLOYMENT

AS % OF TOTAL EMPLOYMENT EUROPEAN UNION 2002

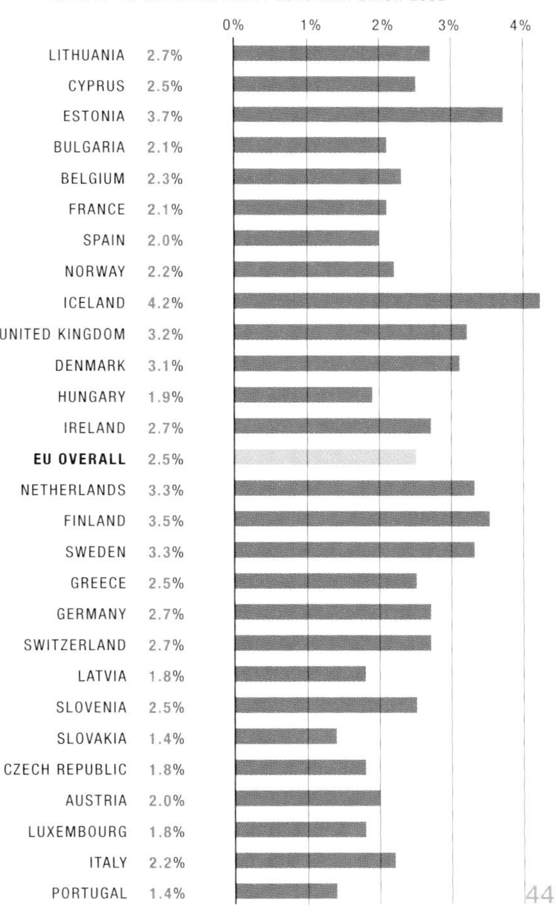

5. FORTUNE AND FORBES RANKING
FOR MAJOR TNC's IN CULTURAL FIELDS 2005

COMPANY:	COUNTRY:	FORTUNE GLOBAL 500 OVERALL & INDUSTRY RANK:	FORBES GLOBAL 2000 OVERALL & INDUSTRY RANK:	REVENUE IN MILLIONS:	PROFITS IN MILLIONS:
COMPUTER SERVICES AND SOFTWARE					
MICROSOFT	UNITED STATES	127 (1)	47 (1)	36,835	8,168
ELECTRONIC DATA SYSTEMS	UNITED STATES	274 (2)	608 (8)	21,033	158
COMPUTER SCIENCES	UNITED STATES	378 (3)	450 (6)	15,849	810
ACCENTURE	UNITED STATES	455 (4)	378 (5)	13,674	691
MEDIA/ENTERTAINMENT & PUBLISHING/PRINTING*					
TIME WARNER	UNITED STATES	100 (1)	51 (1)	42,869	3,364
WALT DISNEY	UNITED STATES	159 (2)	99 (2)	30,752	2,345
VIACOM	UNITED STATES	196 (3)	448 (12)	27,055	-17,462
VIVENDI UNIVERSAL**	FRANCE	199 (4)	454 (13)	26,651	938
BERTELSMANN	GERMANY	271 (5)	NOT RANKED	21,164	1,284
COMCAST**	UNITED STATES	290 (6)	131 (4)	20,307	970
NEWS CORP.	UNITED STATES	282 (7)	125 (3)	20,802	1,533
LAGARDÈRE GROUPE	FRANCE	345 (8)	414 (10)	17,384	475
DAI NIPPON PRINTING	JAPAN	467 (9)	420 (11)	13,259	558
TOPPAN PRINTING	JAPAN	471 (10)	623 (16)	13,153	378
TELECOMMUNICATIONS					
NIPPON TELEGRAPH & TELEPHONE	JAPAN	18 (1)	23 (2)	100,545	6,608
DEUTSCHE TELEKOM	GERMANY	37 (2)	60 (5)	71,989	5,764
VERIZON COMMUNICATIONS	UNITED STATES	38 (3)	18 (1)	71,563	7,831
VODAFONE	UNITED KINGDOM	53 (4)	377 (23)	62,971	-13,910
FRANCE TÉLÉCOM	FRANCE	63 (5)	36 (3)	58,652	3,463
SBC COMMUNICATIONS	UNITED STATES	102 (6)	40 (4)	41,098	5,887
TELECOM ITALIA	ITALY	111 (7)	85 (7)	39,228	971
TELEFÓNICA	SPAIN	114 (8)	80 (6)	38,188	3,579
BT	UNITED KINGDOM	140 (9)	112 (9)	34,673	3,360
AT&T	UNITED STATES	162 (10)	556 (32)	30,537	-6,469
SPRINT	UNITED STATES	192 (11)	489 (29)	27,428	-1,012
KDDI	JAPAN	194 (12)	205 (16)	27,170	1,866
CHINA MOBILE COMMUNICATIONS	CHINA	224 (13)	128 (10)	23,958	4,078
BELLSOUTH	UNITED STATES	244 (14)	105 (8)	22,729	4,758
MCI	UNITED STATES	247 (15)	734 (36)	22,615	-4,002
CHINA TELECOMMUNICATIONS	CHINA	262 (16)	167 (11)	21,562	2,422
TELSTRA	AUSTRALIA	401 (17)	180 (12)	15,193	2,939
KT	SOUTH KOREA	414 (18)	347 (20)	14,901	1,119
BCE	CANADA	416 (19)	206 (17)	14,842	1,224
ROYAL KPN	NETHERLANDS	418 (20)	187 (13)	14,828	1,879
QWEST COMMUNICATIONS	UNITED STATES	451 (21)	773 (38)	13,809	-1,794
NEXTEL COMMUNICATIONS	UNITED STATES	463 (22)	1,196 (53)	13,368	3,000

NOTE: TABLE INCLUDES ALL CORPORATIONS FOUND ON THE FORTUNE LIST. REPORTED REVENUE AND PROFITS ARE FROM FORTUNE, WHICH RANKS ON REVENUE ALONE. FORBES USES A COMPOSITE RANKING FROM FOUR METRICS: SALES, PROFITS, ASSETS, & MARKET VALUE

*MEDIA/ENTERTAINMENT AND PUBLISHING/PRINTING PRESENTED SEPARATELY IN FORTUNE, NOT IN FORBES. FORTUNE INDUSTRY RANKINGS WERE COLLAPSED IN THIS CATEGORY.

**VIVENDI AND COMCAST WERE LISTED AS MEDIA COMPANIES IN FORBES, AND TELECOMMUNICATIONS IN FORTUNE.

TRADE IN CULTURAL GOODS + SERVICES

- % **of export of cultural goods 2002** (by regions) - **total export value of core cultural goods 1994–2002** (by world economies) - **comparison of imports & exports of core cultural goods 2002** (by regions) - **top 10 exporters/importers** (comparison of both values) - **flow chart of 5 countries** (export/import) - **trade partners of the** usa**'s export/imports of core cultural goods 2003** - **trade partners of** china**'s export/imports of core cultural goods 2003** - **trade partners of** south africa**'s export/imports of core cultural goods 2003** - **trade partners of** brazil**'s export/imports of core cultural goods 2003** - **trade partners of** egypt**'s export/imports of core cultural goods 2003** - **top 30 most valuable brands** (as reported in the financial times, april 2006) - **top 3 brands per sector** (as reported in the financial times, april 2006)

1. TOTAL EXPORT VALUE OF CULTURAL PRODUCTS

IN $US MILLIONS 1994 – 2002

	1994	1995	1996	1997	1998	1999	2000	2001	2002
HIGH-INCOME ECONOMIES	33,136.9	38,256.7	39,437.6	41,113.3	41,779.6	45,288.4	44,944.0	40,651.2	44,920.9
UPPER-MIDDLE-INCOME ECONOMIES	1,734.4	2,171.3	2,616.4	2,983.7	3,195.9	3,546.3	4,253.0	4,577.2	6,411.1
LOWER-MIDDLE-INCOME ECONOMIES	1,207.2	1,510.8	1,693.6	1,719.6	1,746.5	1,700.9	1,538.2	1,999.3	3,005.4
LOW-INCOME ECONOMIES	143.9	210.9	225.6	292.1	309.5	349.0	462.1	274.5	329.0

2. % OF EXPORT OF CULTURAL GOODS 2002

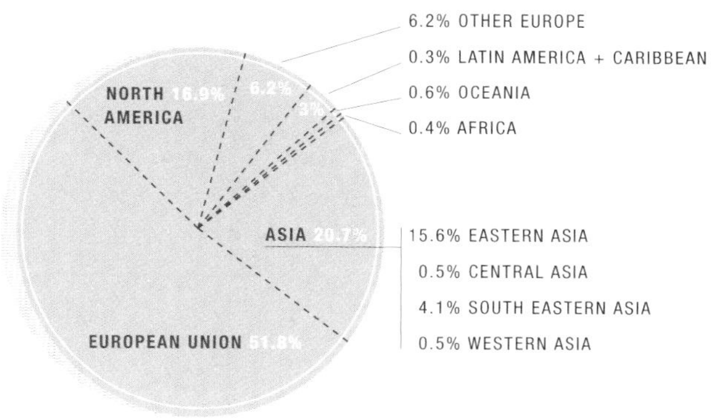

GLOBAL VALUE OF CORE CULTURAL GOODS IN BILLION US$ **2002**

18.2 BILLION US$ **RECORDED MEDIA**

15.4 BILLION US$ **PRINTED MEDIA** — 8.5 AUDIOVISUAL MEDIA; 4.5 NEWSPAPERS + PERIODICALS; 2.4 OTHER PRINTED MATTER

11.3 BILLION US$ **VISUAL ARTS**

02.2 BILLION US$ **HERITAGE GOODS**

MAIN DESTINATIONS OF BRAZILIAN EXPORTS OF CORE CULTURAL GOODS 2003

28.9% PORTUGAL
25.9% UNITED STATES
11.9% JAPAN
5.9% REST OF AVAILABLE COUNTRIES
3.3% SPAIN
1.1% FRANCE
1.1% SOUTH AFRICA
1.1% ANGOLA
1.1% ITALY
0.8% GERMANY
0.8% UNITED KINGDOM
17.2% LATIN AMERICA:
4.4% COLOMBIA
4.3% CHILE
4.0% ARGENTINA
3.8% MEXICO
0.7% PERU

3. COMPARISON OF EXPORT

OF CORE CULTURAL GOODS BY REGION

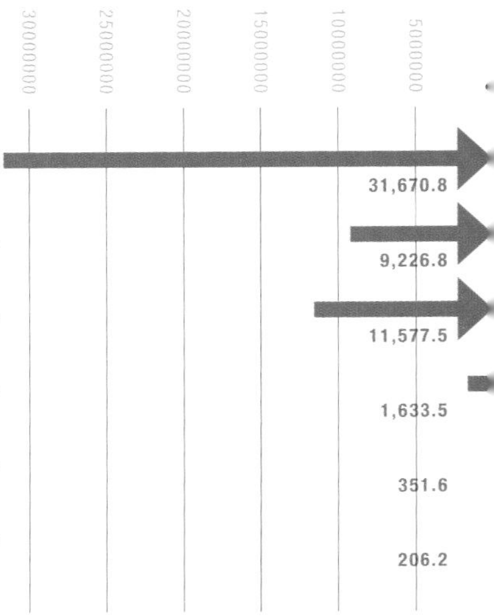

30000000 25000000 20000000 15000000 10000000 5000000

FROM **EUROPE** 31,670.8
FROM **NORTH AMERICA** 9,226.8
FROM **ASIA** 11,577.5
FROM **LATIN AMERICA** 1,633.5
FROM **OCEANIA** 351.6
FROM **AFRICA** 206.2

MAIN DESTINATIONS OF SOUTH AFRICAN EXPORTS OF CORE CULTURAL GOODS 2003

39.9% AFRICA:
10.4% ZAMBIA
4.5% MOZAMBIQUE
4.5% ZIMBABWE
3.9% TANZANIA
3.7% MALAWI
2.9% ANGOLA
2.6% NIGERIA
2.6% MAURITIUS
2.5% CONGO
2.3% KENYA
19.9% UNITED STATES
16.2% UNITED KINGDOM
3.2% GERMANY
2.2% AUSTRALIA
1.3% NETHERLANDS
17.3% REST OF AVAILABLE COUNTRIES

MAIN DESTINATIONS OF AMERICAN EXPORTS OF CORE CULTURAL GOODS 2003

40.2% CANADA
12.0% UNITED KINGDOM
5.6% SWITZERLAND
5.2% JAPAN
3.6% MEXICO
3.3% GERMANY
2.7% FRANCE
2.5% REPUBLIC OF KOREA
2.4% AUSTRALIA
2.2% NETHERLANDS
1.4% CHINA
18.7% REST OF AVAILABLE COUNTRIES

4. TOP EXPORTERS /

OF CORE CULTURAL GOODS BY SELECT COUNTRIES

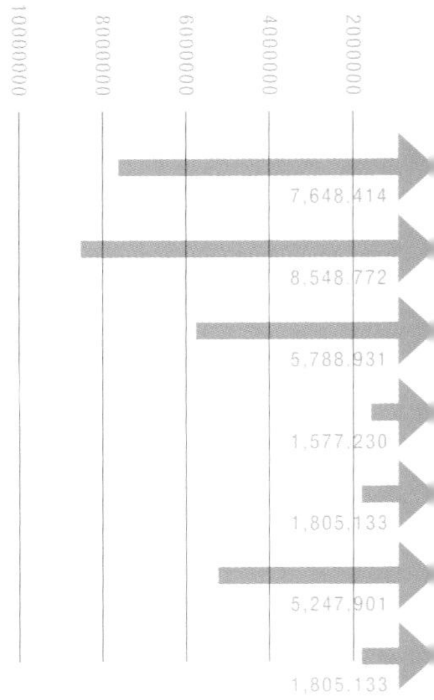

10000000 8000000 6000000 4000000 2000000

FROM UNITED STATES 7,648,414
FROM UNITED KINGDOM 8,548,772
FROM GERMANY 5,788,931
FROM CANADA 1,577,230
FROM FRANCE 1,805,133
FROM CHINA 5,247,901
FROM JAPAN 1,805,133

MAIN DESTINATIONS OF CHINESE EXPORTS OF CORE CULTURAL GOODS 2003

34.7% UNITED STATES
17.9% HONG KONG, CHINA
14.5% NETHERLANDS
6.6% JAPAN
6.5% UNITED KINGDOM
2.4% CANADA
2.3% GERMANY
2.0% AUSTRALIA
1.2% ITALY
11.9% REST OF AVAILABLE COUNTRIES

IMPORTS 2002

OF CORE CULTURAL GOODS BY REGION

5000000 10000000 15000000 20000000 25000000 30000000 35000000 40000000

30,620.7 TO **EUROPE**

19,173.9 TO **NORTH AMERICA**

9,363.2 TO **ASIA**

2,291.6 TO **LATIN AMERICA**

1,560.9 TO **OCEANIA**

658.1 TO **AFRICA**

MAIN ORIGINS OF SOUTH AFRICAN IMPORTS OF CORE CULTURAL GOODS 2003

27.2% UNITED KINGDOM
21.3% UNITED STATES
10.7% IRELAND
6.3% GERMANY
5.9% AREAS, NES
5.2% CHINA
2.6% NETHERLANDS
2.1% FRANCE
1.8% AUSTRALIA
1.6% JAPAN
15.3% REST OF AVAILABLE COUNTRIES

MAIN ORIGINS OF BRAZILIAN IMPORTS OF CORE CULTURAL GOODS 2003

28.8% UNITED STATES
16.3% UNITED KINGDOM
8.2% SPAIN
6.6% REST OF AVAILABLE COUNTRIES
5.2% CHINA
4.0% FRANCE
4.0% GERMANY
3.6% JAPAN
2.9% PORTUGAL
2.9% HONG KONG, CHINA
2.4% ITALY
1.0% SWEDEN
14.2% LATIN AMERICA:
5.2% ARGENTINA
3.3% PERU
3.2% URUGUAY
2.5% CHILE

TOP IMPORTERS 2002

OF CORE CULTURAL GOODS BY SELECT COUNTRIES

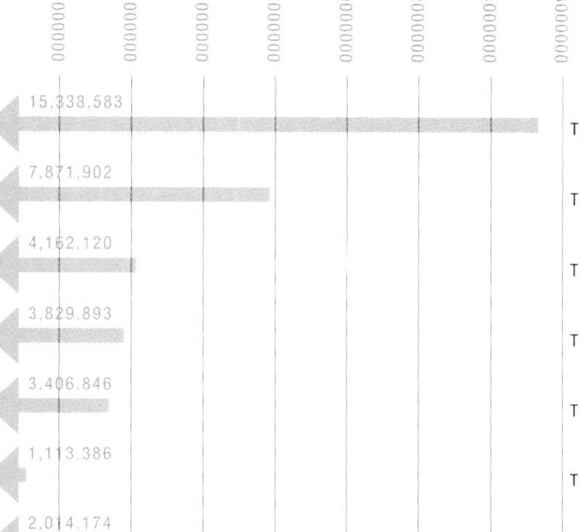

TO UNITED STATES

TO UNITED KINGDOM

TO GERMANY

TO CANADA

TO FRANCE

TO CHINA

TO JAPAN

MAIN ORIGINS OF AMERICAN IMPORTS OF CORE CULTURAL GOODS 2003

30.8% CHINA
11.0% UNITED KINGDOM
10.8% FRANCE
10.5% CANADA
4.2% GERMANY
4.0% ITALY
3.6% JAPAN
3.3% HONG KONG, CHINA
3.0% MEXICO
2.1% SWITZERLAND
1.8% SPAIN
15.0% REST OF AVAILABLE COUNTRIES

MAIN ORIGINS OF CHINESE IMPORTS OF CORE CULTURAL GOODS 2003

22.2% UNITED STATES
14.7% GERMANY
12.5% HONG KONG, CHINA
10.2% SINGAPORE
7.1% FINLAND
6.4% JAPAN
5.7% OTHER ASIA, NES
4.7% IRELAND
3.2% FREE ZONES
2.6% UNITED KINGDOM
10.7% REST OF AVAILABLE COUNTRIES

5. THE FINANCIAL TIMES: **30 MOST VALUABLE GLOBAL BRANDS**

VALUE IN $US MILLIONS, AS OF APRIL 2006

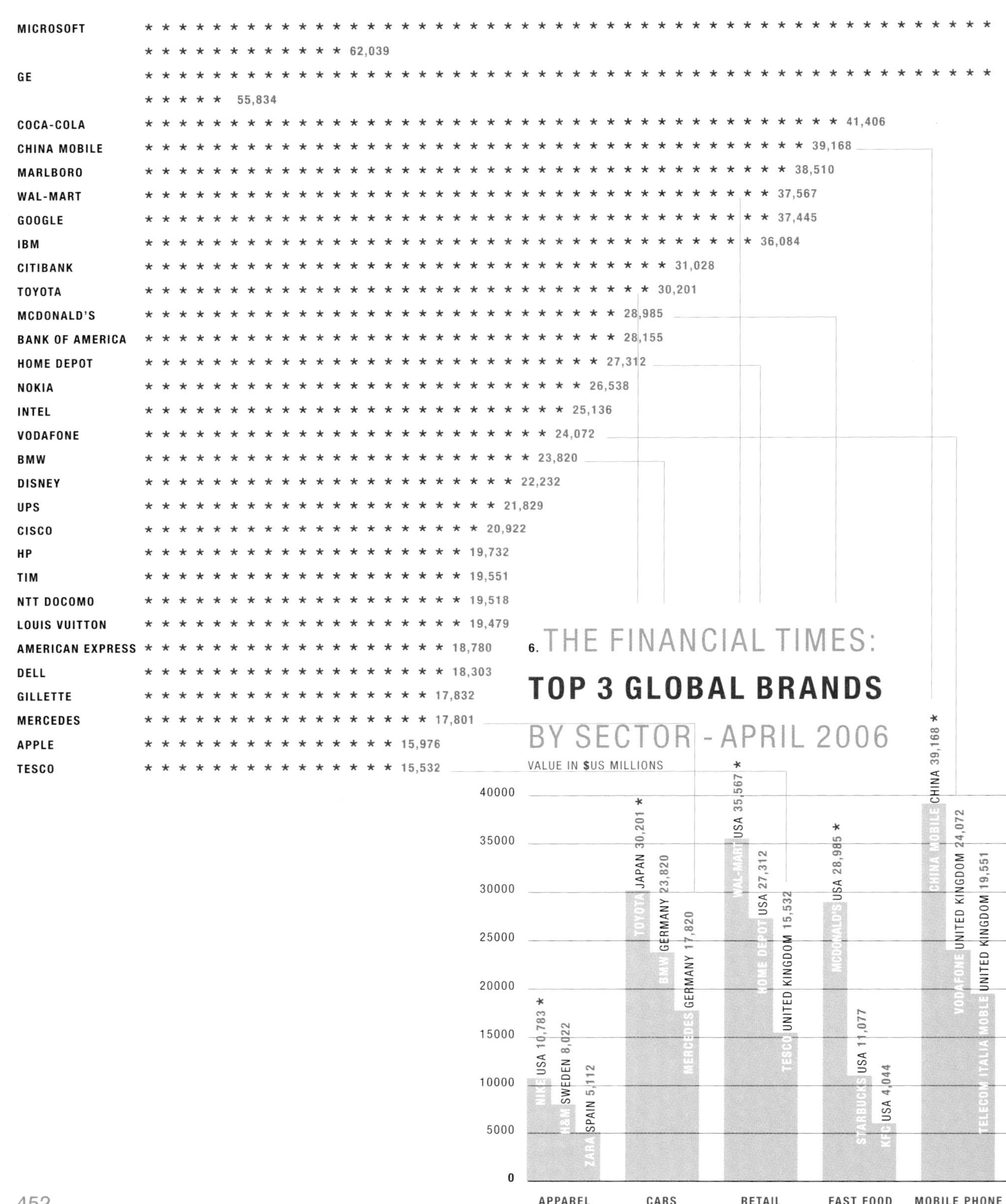

MICROSOFT 62,039
GE 55,834
COCA-COLA 41,406
CHINA MOBILE 39,168
MARLBORO 38,510
WAL-MART 37,567
GOOGLE 37,445
IBM 36,084
CITIBANK 31,028
TOYOTA 30,201
MCDONALD'S 28,985
BANK OF AMERICA 28,155
HOME DEPOT 27,312
NOKIA 26,538
INTEL 25,136
VODAFONE 24,072
BMW 23,820
DISNEY 22,232
UPS 21,829
CISCO 20,922
HP 19,732
TIM 19,551
NTT DOCOMO 19,518
LOUIS VUITTON 19,479
AMERICAN EXPRESS 18,780
DELL 18,303
GILLETTE 17,832
MERCEDES 17,801
APPLE 15,976
TESCO 15,532
6. THE FINANCIAL TIMES:
TOP 3 GLOBAL BRANDS
BY SECTOR - APRIL 2006
VALUE IN $US MILLIONS
40000
35000
30000
25000
20000
15000
10000
5000
0
NIKE USA 10,783 *
H&M SWEDEN 8,022
ZARA SPAIN 5,112
TOYOTA JAPAN 30,201 *
BMW GERMANY 23,820
MERCEDES GERMANY 17,820
WAL-MART USA 35,567 *
HOME DEPOT USA 27,312
TESCO UNITED KINGDOM 15,532
MCDONALD'S USA 28,985 *
STARBUCKS USA 11,077
KFC USA 4,044
CHINA MOBILE CHINA 39,168 *
VODAFONE UNITED KINGDOM 24,072
TELECOM ITALIA MOBILE UNITED KINGDOM 19,551
APPAREL
CARS
RETAIL
FAST FOOD
MOBILE PHONE

CULTURE AND THE ECONOMY The cultural economy includes activities for the creation, production, distribution, and consumption of cultural goods and services, such as fine arts, printing and publishing, multimedia, audio-visual, phonographic and cinematographic productions, and crafts and design. According to UNESCO's Division of Arts and Cultural Enterprise, the cultural economy comprises industries that "combine the creation, production and commercialization of contents which are intangible and cultural in nature. These contents are typically protected by copyright and they can take the form of goods or services" (UNESCO, 2006).

Like other parts of the economy, the cultural economy is undergoing a process of globalization driven by economic opportunities and technological innovations that brings up complex policy issues in terms of fair trade, cultural diversity, access to information and knowledge as well as cultural sovereignty. At the same time, comparative statistics and indicator systems of cultural activities are underdeveloped, and suffer from major classification and measurement problems.

The General Agreement on Trade in Services (GATS) covers services ranging from architecture to voice-mail telecommunications and space transport. Services are now the largest and most dynamic component of the economy in both developed and developing countries. Important in their own right, they also serve as crucial inputs into the production of most goods. Since January 2000, they have become the subject of multilateral trade negotiations with numerous amendments and special clauses with regards to specific cultural industries (especially music and movies).

The World Intellectual Property Organization (WIPO) is an international organization dedicated to promoting the use and protection of works of the human spirit. These works — intellectual property — are expanding the bounds of science and technology and enriching the world of the arts. Through its work, WIPO plays an important role in enhancing the quality and enjoyment of life, as well as creating real wealth for nations. (WIPO, 2006). WIPO is one of the 16 specialized UN agencies, with 183 nations as member states. It administers 23 international treaties dealing with different aspects of intellectual property protection. Among these are:
• Berne Convention for the Protection of Literary and Artistic Works
• Treaty on the International Registration of Audiovisual Works (Film Register Treaty)
• Paris Convention for the Protection of Industrial Property
• Rome Convention for the Protection of Performers, Producers of Phonograms and Broadcasting Organizations
• Singapore Treaty on the Law of Trademarks (not yet in force)

LONG-STANDING DEBATE

The notion of 'Kulturindustrie' (cultural industries), the critical precursor to modern terms such as cultural economy or creative industries, has its origin in the critique of modern mass culture by members of the Frankfurt School of Sociology, in particular the works of Theodor Adorno and Max Horkheimer. They disparaged what they identified as the commodification of culture perpetuated by the homogenizing and 'downgrading quality' of the capitalist system (Adorno and Horkheimer, 1947). Culture as artistic creation and appreciation became increasingly replaced by culture as products manufactured and offered for mass consumption. In this process, according to Adorno and Horkheimer, art becomes increasingly void of its deeply humane capacity to anticipate, and contribute to, a better world, and instead emerges as a conformist, legitimizing tool of capitalism.

The Adorno-Horkheimer thesis has certainly not remained unchallenged, and has been charged as elitist by some, and as biased against non-Western cultures by others. Yet debates about how culture and market are to relate to each other continue unabated, and it is particularly the process of economic globalization that has brought the question of the cultural economy to the forefront. At the center of the debate is whether or not "culture" or cultural industries should be treated as any other industry in a globalizing economy. The question is driven by fears of cultural homogenization by economically dominant cultures.

WHAT DO WE KNOW ABOUT CULTURAL ECONOMIES?

From the indicator suite we can see the range and growth of national and transnational economic activities within the cultural economy. These are very diverse, and involve, at one end, economic activities that are highly knowledge and labor-intensive with an emphasis on creativity and innovation; and, at the other, they involve mass production and distribution to vast audiences. Overall, the cultural economy is highly concentrated in geographic terms, as globally, cultural goods and services are being exported from Europe, the US, China and Japan, but being consumed by almost all other countries. Specifically:

• Global trade in cultural goods and services is dominated by the industrial North and China. Europe accounts for more than half of the world exports of cultural goods and services, and a little under half of the world imports. The UK and Germany are responsible for roughly a third of this trade, in both exports and imports.
• Asian exports are dominated by China, followed by Japan, and together they are only responsible for a third of cultural imports to Asia.
• The largest three global producers of cultural goods are the US, the European Union and China; with 6.6% of China's GDP dedicated to cultural or creative industries, second only to Canada.
• The global arts market is dominated by European artists, and traded mostly in Europe and the United States: 72% of international art auctions, measured by yearly turnover, are located in the US and the EU; only 5% of the total number of international art auctions take place outside of the US and Europe.
• New York, London, Paris and Berlin are the international centers of fine art trade.
• Sotheby's and Christies are the world's preeminent fine art auctioneers. Christie's conducts international auctions in over 80 categories-from fine art and furniture to clocks and vintage cars. Founded in 1776, Christie's now has salerooms in New York, Los Angeles, London, Amsterdam, Geneva, Madrid, Tel Aviv, Milan, Paris, Rome, Zurich, Hong Kong and Dubai. In addition, Christie's has offices in many countries. For example, in Europe it is represented in 17 countries, with six offices in Germany alone.
• Cultural industries have expanded over the course of the last five years, with the highest growth rates taking place in industrial countries (Americans for the Arts, 2005). However, there are notable exceptions in parts of the developing world, Brazil and China in particular, where growth rates surpass those of the US and Europe.
• A major factor in this case is the growth of the home entertainment industry. The global trade in cultural entertainment and media explains China's prominence as an exporter, and Europe and the US as importers.

However, lack of data and differences in the classification of goods and services make it difficult to compare economic statistics on cultural economy. This refers also to data on government and household expenditures on culture, recreation and education. As Table 1 shows, only 24 of the 185 countries in the United Nations System of National Accounts report expenditures in the field of culture, mostly from developed countries. From what limited data exist, there is a clear division between developed and developing countries. Unfortunately, the dearth of comparable and more comprehensive data continues to handicap the debate surrounding cultural industries, trade and globalization. The efforts of the Canadian government to collect data on cultural participation and cultural industries are a rare exception, as are Australia, New Zealand and a few EU member states.

WHAT ARE THE ISSUES?

A basic line of disagreement among experts is the treatment of cultural goods and services in national and international policies. Most argue that culture is different from let's say machinery or insurance, and should therefore be treated as a category of its own. While some argue that culture and cultural industries should remain "hands-off" with regard to economic policy, the majority maintain that it is the role of a sovereign state to safeguard national cultures and to encourage their development. An example of this debate arises in trade negotiations, whereby the US seeks to exclude all forms of national protection of cultural goods, services and industries to which other countries, especially Europeans and Canadians, object (Raboy, et.al, 1994; Hesmondhalgh and Pratt, 2005).

As cultural goods and services become commodified, there is also growing debate about who is gaining and who is losing out. Many developing countries are unable to take part in the international trade of culture, and are becoming more marginalized and isolated: Africa, Latin America and Oceania combined only account for roughly 4% of global cultural exports. Conversely, as we have seen, the industrialized countries dominate cultural trade and consumption, which is creating fears of cultural hegemony that might dominate and even erode non-Western cultures.

A counter-movement against the dominance of the West in the commodification of culture is under way in countries like India, China, Brazil and South Africa. They are at the forefront of creating a system of cultural heritage protection and promotion campaigns that seek to reconcile preserving indigenous culture and knowledge with capitalizing on economic values and revenue generation. In India, this includes the patenting of traditional Indian knowledge in fields such as botany; in Brazil, cultural industries are seen as having the ability to generate revenue by utilizing a wealth of cultural knowledge and practice that has previously not been commodified nor seen as products suitable for international marketing and trading.

TABLE 1: **REPORTING ON CULTURAL CONSUMPTION EXPENDITURE IN THE FIELD OF CULTURE IN THE UN SYSTEM OF NATIONAL ACCOUNTS** (SNA), 2003, BY NUMBER

COUNTRIES ...	
Covered in the SNA	**185**
Reporting government consumption expenditure on culture, recreation and education	**79**
Reporting household consumption expenditure on culture, recreation and education	**68**
Reporting both government and household consumption expenditure on culture, recreation and education	**50**
Reporting both government and household consumption expenditure on culture, recreation and education in comparable detail	**24**

Source: United Nations, 2003

PROFESSIONS

CULTURAL PROFESSIONS

CULTURAL PROFESSIONS

- eu cultural professions: % **change in employment in selected occupations**, european union 1995–1999 - ilo charts: % **of total employment in selected professions** by selected countries 2005 - **employment statistics for cultural workers versus all workers**, european union 2002 - us employment: **annual % of total employment in select professions**, united states 2005 - uk cultural occupations: **key statistics on cultural occupations in the united kingdom** - eu cultural employment & education: % **of university graduates in general employment versus cultural employment**, european union 2002 - % **of students graduating from tertiary education** by field of study and region 2002–2003 - % **of female graduates in tertiary education** by field of study and region 2002–2003

1. % CHANGE IN EMPLOYMENT IN SELECTED OCCUPATIONS EU1995 – 1999

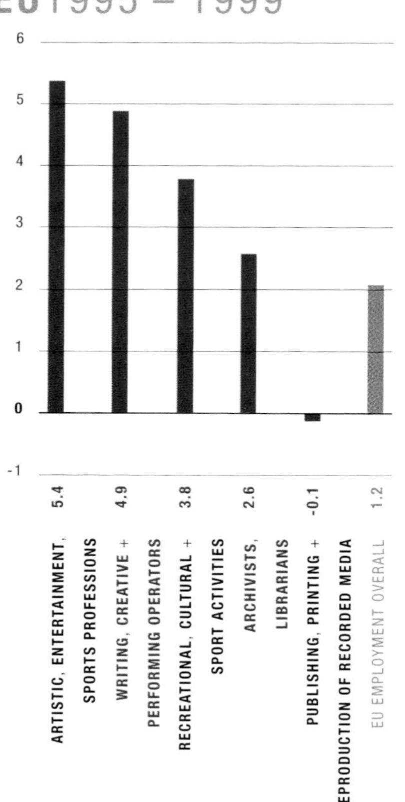

2. % OF TOTAL EMPLOYMENT IN SELECTED PROFESSIONS

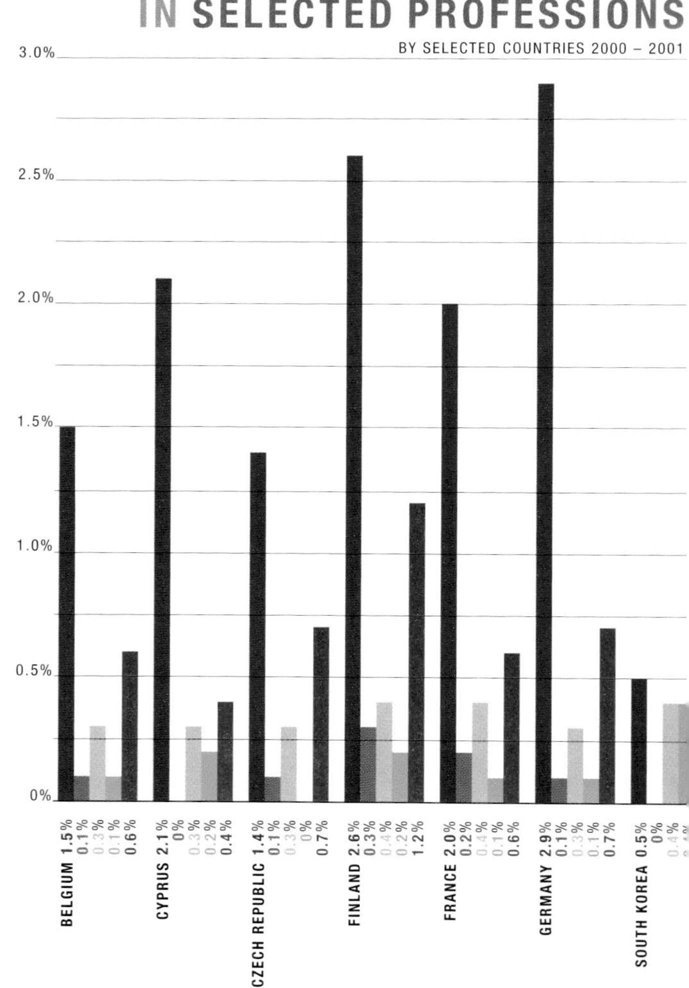

3. EMPLOYMENT STATISTICS FOR ALL WORKERS VERSUS CULTURAL WORKERS EU 2002

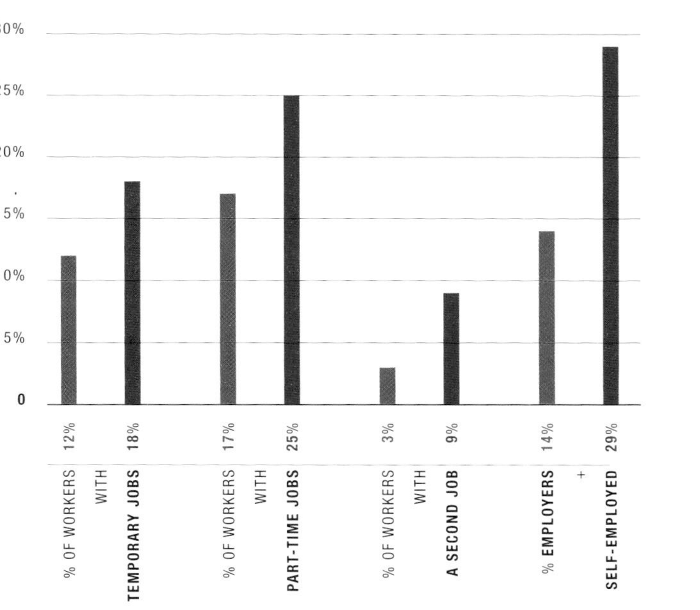

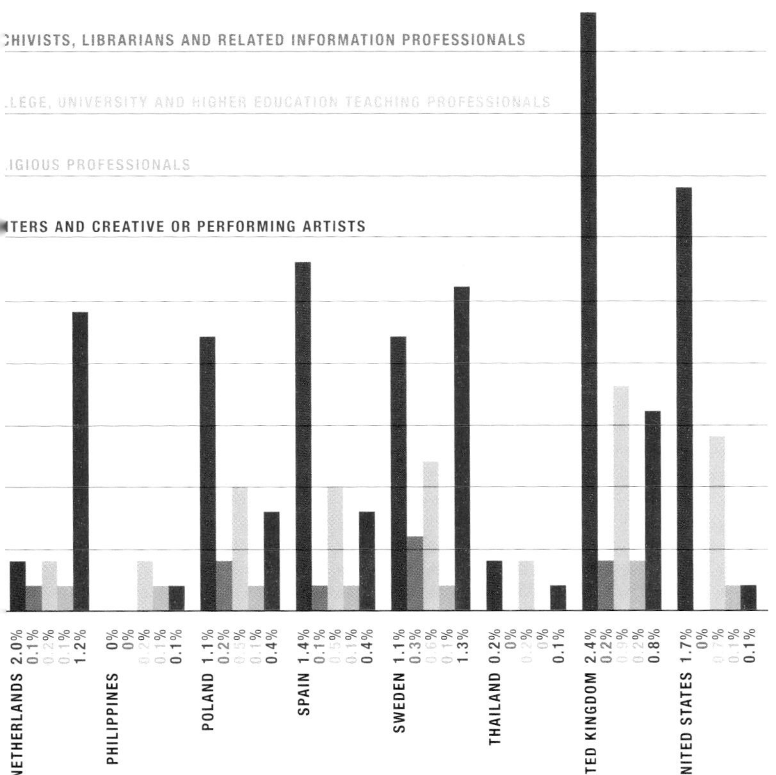

4. ANNUAL % GROWTH IN EMPLOYMENT IN SELECTED PROFESSIONS US 2005

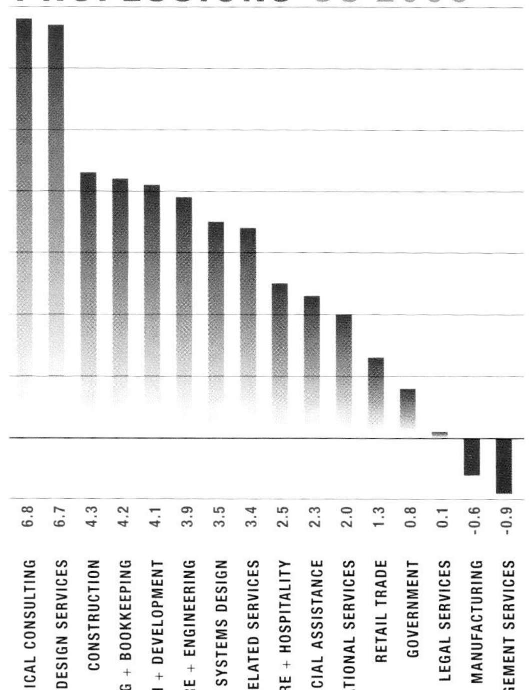

5. KEY STATISTICS ON CULTURAL OCCUPATIONS IN THE UK

	CULTURAL WORKERS	OTHERS
% SELF-EMPLOYED	39%	12%
AVERAGE LENGTH OF TIME CONTINUOUSLY EMPLOYED	7.3 YEARS	7.7 YEARS
% WHO SAY THEY WOULD WORK LONG HOURS	6%	8%
AVERAGE GROSS WEEKLY PAY	£ 368	£ 290
% EXPERIENCING AT LEAST ONE SPELL OF UNEMPLOYMENT	1.7%	1.8%
% WITH A HIGHER UNIVERSITY DEGREE	10%	4%

6. % OF UNIVERSITY GRADUATES IN GENERAL EMPLOYMENT VERSUS CULTURAL EMPLOYMENT EU 2002

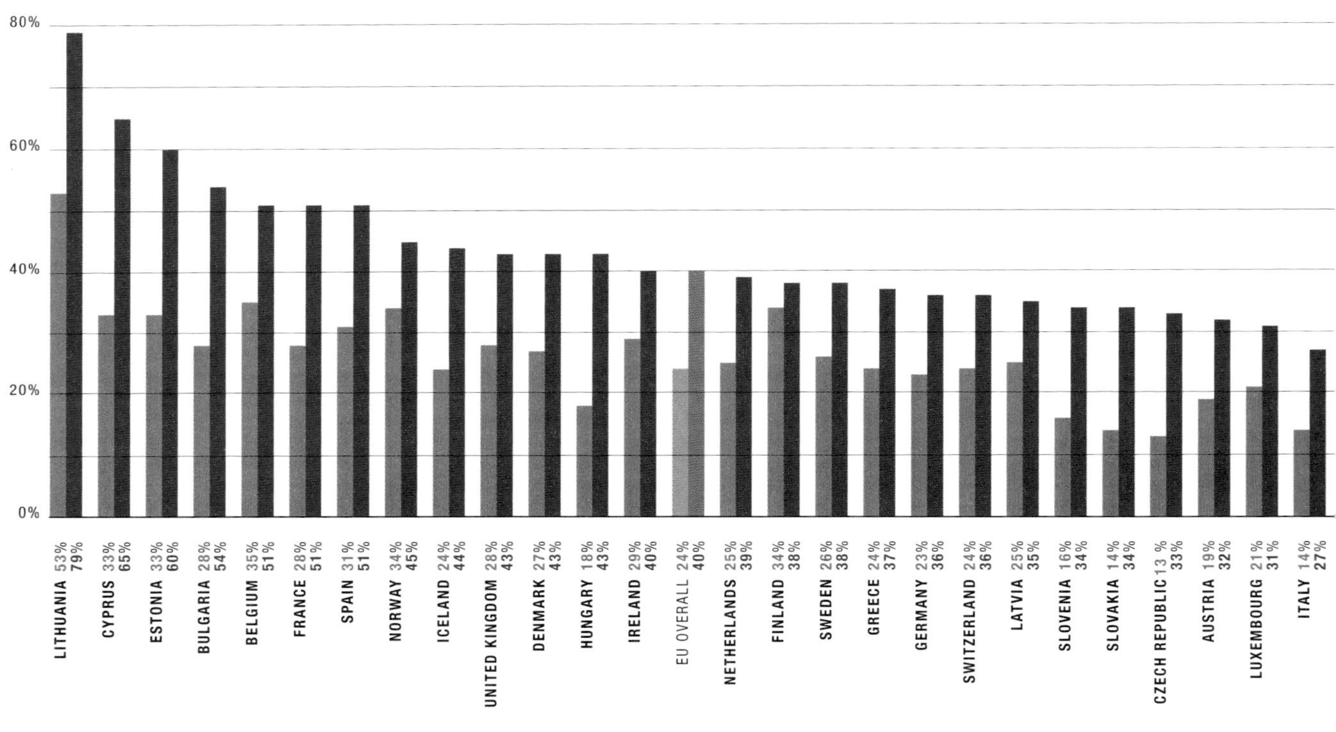

7. % STUDENTS GRADUATING FROM TERTIARY EDUCATION BY FIELD OF STUDY AND REGION 2002 – 03

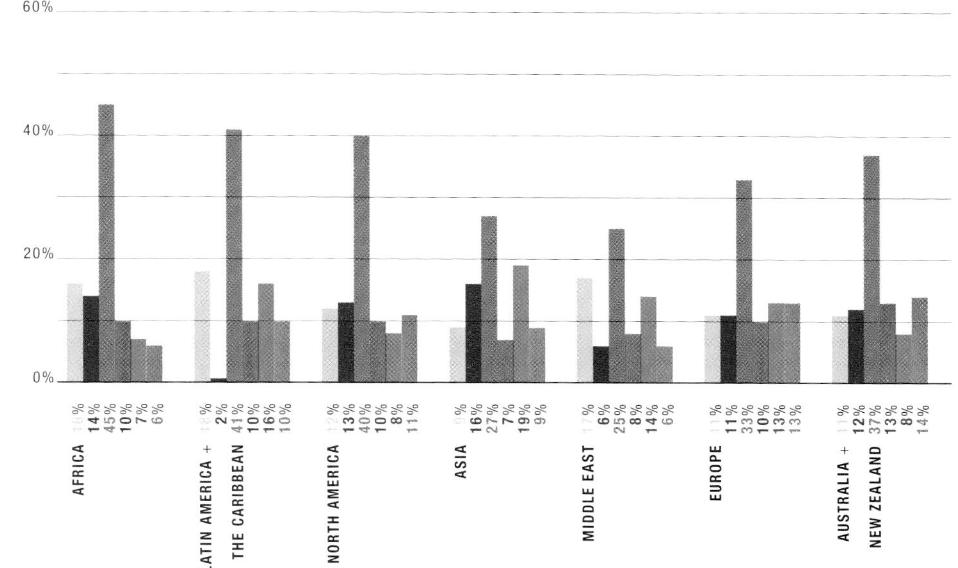

EDUCATION

ARTS + HUMANITIES

SOCIAL SCIENCES,

BUSINESS + LAW

SCIENCE

ENGINEERING, MANUFACTURING

+ CONSTRUCTION

HEALTH + WELFARE

OVERALL

8. % FEMALE GRADUATES IN TERTIARY EDUCATION BY FIELD OF STUDY AND REGION 2002 – 03

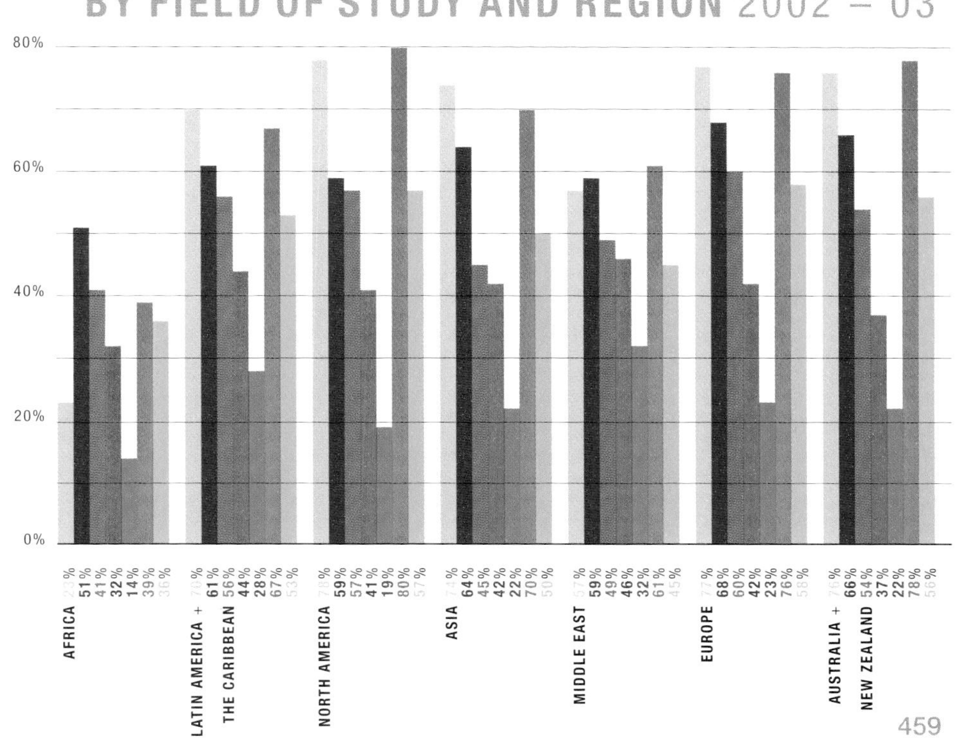

CULTURAL PROFESSIONS The growth of the cultural industries and increasing commodification of cultural products has spawned a simultaneous growth in employment in cultural occupations. This growth is changing both the types of jobs available and the nature of the work itself. Growth in cultural occupations is not evenly distributed around the world, however, as it is growing most quickly in the more developed economies, particularly in Europe. Employment in cultural professions generally requires higher education, specialized skills, and considerable risk-taking as cultural employment often takes place on a temporary or part-time basis, or within the context of self-employment. The indicator suite shows that:

• In the EU, from 1995-1999, employment in the cultural professions grew faster than overall growth in employment. Particularly, in the entertainment and sports professions, as well as writing and creative or performing arts. Growth did not occur in publishing, printing, and reproduction of recorded media, which may be due to the rapid consolidation of those industries (e.g. see suite on Books).
• The growth of cultural professions in the EU is reflected in greater percentages of university graduates in cultural employment then general employment in 2002, for all countries with available data. This trend is especially noticeable in economies in transition such as Estonia, Hungary, Slovenia, Slovakia, and the Czech Republic
• In EU countries, a higher percentage of the European population is employed in cultural professions particularly in architecture and engineering.
• In the US, employment in cultural professions is also on the rise. Fields such as specialized design services, architecture, and advertising are growing quickly, while fields such as retail and law are growing at a slower rate, and manufacturing is declining
• Conversely, cultural workers in Europe are more likely to hold temporarily or part-time jobs, to have a second job, and be self-employed than other workers overall. This suggests that cultural employment is more transitory and insecure than employment in other fields.
• Looking at the percentage of students graduating from university in select fields of study across the globe, we find that in every region the highest percentage of students graduated in social sciences, business and law. Females are highly represented in tertiary education, and particularly in fields of study likely leading to cultural employment. In every region, females make up more than half of all graduates in arts and humanities, except for Africa, as well as in education and science.

WHAT ARE CULTURAL PROFESSIONS?

There is no single definition of what occupations the term cultural professions includes. The term may include such diverse occupations as those engaged in the creative and performing arts (e.g., musicians, writers, performers, or artists), architects, designers, educators, journalists, and clergy. Strictly defined, it may only include those working in the fields of creative and artistic production, and heritage collection and preservation (such as by Statistics Canada). In common usage, however, it typically includes both those meeting the strict criteria as well as those in "knowledge" industries, such as publishing, technology, and education. Many, but not all, cultural professions are professions in the traditional sense. The term "professions" has typically been reserved for those occupations that require specialized knowledge and skills, provide significant autonomy to the worker, and benefit society as a whole and not just single individuals or corporations. Many cultural professions contain some elements of that definition but not all, and thus may be termed "occupations" by some.

WHAT DO WE KNOW ABOUT CULTURAL PROFESSIONS?

Recent work by Florida (2003; 2005) and others has proclaimed that there is an emerging "creative class" that is uniquely self-directed and high-achieving, a boon to any economy that can claim it. According to Florida (2003), who views cultural employment broadly, there are 32 million Americans in cultural employment, more than 30% of the US workforce. This may be particularly true in Europe, where cultural employment grew by 37% in France between 1982 and 1990 and 34 percent in the United Kingdom over the same period (European Commission, 2001). Although this workforce is growing, according to Florida, in the United States, this emerging creative class is increasingly threatened by current US immigration laws and the globalization of cities (2005). What has emerged in this "creative age" is rising competition for creative individuals and creative talent on a global scale (Florida, 2005).

The growth in cultural professions can be attributed to several different phenomena, including the increasing commercialization of cultural products, the digital revolution, and increased participation in higher education (European Commission, 2001). There has also been significant investment by some governments in growing this sector of their economy. France is the most prominent example; another is Denmark where the Ministry of Culture seeks to strengthen the design industry by supporting education, collaboration and professional standards in the field.

WHAT ARE THE ISSUES?

Unsurprisingly, globalization is helping to spark the growth of the cultural professions, as cultural workers are highly mobile and are able to cross borders and boundaries with their most important resource, personal knowledge, intact. The growth of digital media also promotes the spread of ideas and allows people to produce and transmit cultural products quickly and widely. Unfortunately, like many aspects of the economy that are being globalized, the global distribution of cultural professionals is uneven. Most professional cultural work is being done in more developed countries, particularly Europe.

The growth of cultural professions means that many people are experiencing new patterns of labor, more self-employment and more "flexible" work arrangements. Part of the larger post-Fordian shift, cultural employment tends to be more self-directed and project-based, taking great advantage of information and communication technologies (Milohnic, 2005). As an example of this, cultural workers in the UK are more likely to be self-employed, less likely to want to work longer hours, are more highly educated and are higher paid than other workers (Davies and Lindley, 2003). This has also led to what has been termed the "de-gendering" of the cultural professions, which includes high numbers of women in its ranks (Gottschall and Betzelt, 2001). The table below shows the growth of select cultural professions in Germany over the 1990s, with the trend toward greater participation of women, higher percentages of self-employment, and more cultural employees with university degrees.

EMPLOYMENT TRENDS IN CULTURAL PROFESSIONS (GERMANY)

	# OF WORKERS		% FEMALE		% SELF-EMPLOYED		% WITH UNIVERSITY DEGREES	
	1993	**1999**	**1993**	**1999**	**1993**	**1999**	**1993**	**1999**
JOURNALISTS (ISCO 2451)*	76,000	121,000	**38.1%**	**41.9%**	32.2%	33.8%	**45.5%**	**49.1%**
COMMERCIAL DESIGNERS (ISCO 3471)*	60,000	79,000	**43.4%**	**44.2%**	42.7%	47.7%	**33.0%**	**45.3%**
EDITORIAL WORKERS (incl. in ISCO 2451)*	no data		estimated > **90%**		estimated > **60%**		no reliable data, mostly academic	

Source: Official statistical data of Sample Census (Mikrozensus), own calculations; absolute figures rounded.
* ISCO = International Standard Classification of Occupations, 1988 (ILO)
Note: Taken from Gottschall, Karin, and Betzelt, Sigrid. 2001. "Self-Employment in Cultural Professions: Between De-Gendered Work and Re-Gendered Work and Life-Arrangements?" Paper presented at the Gender Conference on "Changing Work and Life Patterns in Western Industrial Countries", WZB Berlin, Sept. 20-21, 2001. Accessed May 25, 2006 at: www.zes.uni-bremen.de/~kgs/WZB9-01.doc.

CORPORATIONS + ORGANIZATIONS

TRANSNATIONAL CULTURAL CORPORATIONS

- DISNEY

OTHER **MAJOR MEDIA CORPORATIONS**

CULTURAL INGOs + FOUNDATIONS

TRANSNATIONAL CULTURAL CORPORATIONS - DISNEY

1a. DISNEY COMPANY STRUCTURE

7.587 MILLION US$

13,207 MILLION US$

DISNEY STUDIO ENTERTAINMENT

THEATRICAL FILM BANNERS

- WALT DISNEY PICTURES
- WALT DISNEY FEATURE ANIMATION
- DISNEYTOON STUDIOS - TOUCHSTONE PICTURES
- HOLLYWOOD PICTURES
- MIRAMAX FILMS
- BUENA VISTA INTERNATIONAL

PRODUCTION STUDIOS

- BUENA VISTA HOME ENTERTAINMENT
- BUENA VISTA HOME ENTERTAINMENT INTERNATIONAL
- BUENA VISTA THEATRICAL PRODUCTIONS
- BUENA VISTA MUSIC GROUP
- WALT DISNEY RECORDS
- BUENA VISTA RECORDS
- HOLLYWOOD RECORDS
- LYRIC STREET RECORDS

DISNEY MEDIA NETWORKS

DISNEY MEDIA NETWORKS

- THE ABC TELEVISION NETWORK:
  ABC ENTERTAINMENT
  ABC DAYTIME
  ABC NEWS
  ABC SPORTS
  ABC KIDS
- TOUCHSTONE TELEVISION
- ABC OWNED TELEVISION STATION
- ABC RADIO
- RADIO DISNEY
- ESPN RADIO
- ABC NEWS RADIO

CABLE NETWORKS

- ESPN
- DISNEY CHANNEL
- ABC FAMILY
- TOON DISNEY
- SOAPnet.
- WALT DISNEY TELEVISION ANIMATION
- FOX KIDS INTERNATIONAL
- LIFETIME ENTERTAINMENT SERVICES
- A&E TELEVISION NETWORKS
- E! NETWORKS
- BUENA VISTA TELEVISION
- BUENA VISTA TELEVISION INTERNATIONAL
- HYPERION BOOK
- WALT DISNEY INTERNET GROUP

3. DISNEY WILDLIFE CONSERVATION FUND 2005

GRANTS DOLLARS

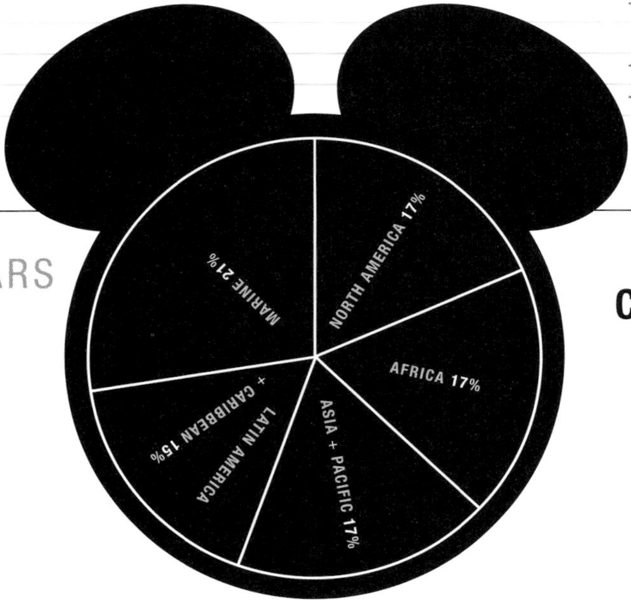

MARINE 21%
NORTH AMERICA 17%
AFRICA 17%
ASIA + PACIFIC 17%
LATIN AMERICA + CARIBBEAN 15%

- company **structure** + **annual revenue** 2005

- **audiences** - **corporate philantropy**

1b. DISNEY **ANNUAL REVENUE** 2005

IN US$ MILLIONS, EXCEPT PER SHARE AMOUNT

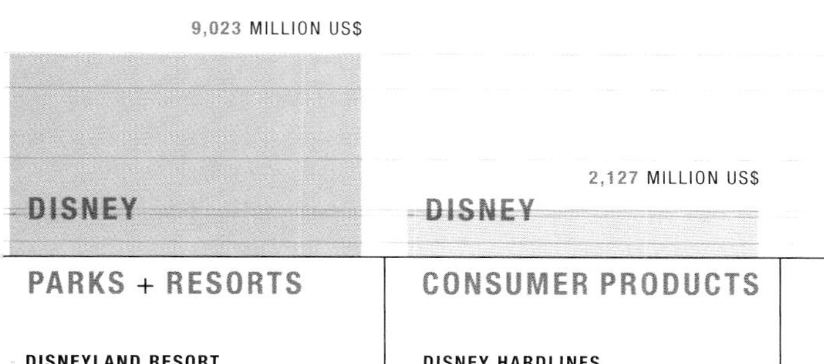

22,124 MILLION US$

3,171 MILLION US$

1,331 MILLION US$

435 MILLION US$

NORTH AMERICA

EUROPE

ASIA + PACIFIC

LATIN AMERICA + OTHER

PARKS + RESORTS

- DISNEYLAND RESORT
- WALT DISNEY WORLD RESORT
- TOKYO DISNEY RESORT
- DISNEYLAND RESORT PARIS
- HONG KONG DISNEYLAND
- DISNEY CRUISE LINE
- DISNEY VACATION CLUB
- ESPN ZONE
- WALT DISNEY IMAGINEERING

CONSUMER PRODUCTS

- DISNEY HARDLINES
- DISNEY SOFTLINES
- DISNEY TOYS
- DISNEY PUBLISHING
- HYPERION BOOKS FOR CHILDREN
- DISNEY PRESS
- DISNEY EDITIONS
- DISNEY ADVENTURES
- BUENA VISTA GAMES
- THE BABY EINSTEIN COMPANY
- DISNEY STORES WORLDWIDE
- DISNEY DIRECT MARKETING
- DISNEYSTORE.COM
- DISNEY CATALOG

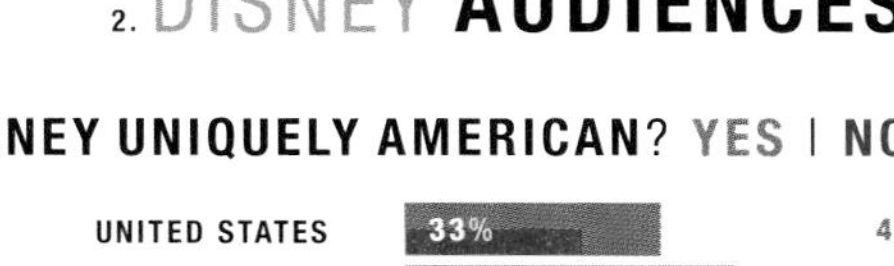

2. DISNEY **AUDIENCES**

IS DISNEY UNIQUELY AMERICAN? YES | NO

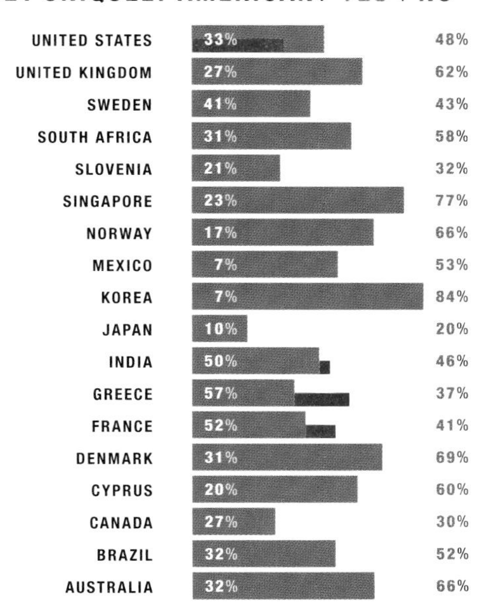

GRANTS

MARINE AREAS ASSOCIATED WITH REGIONS

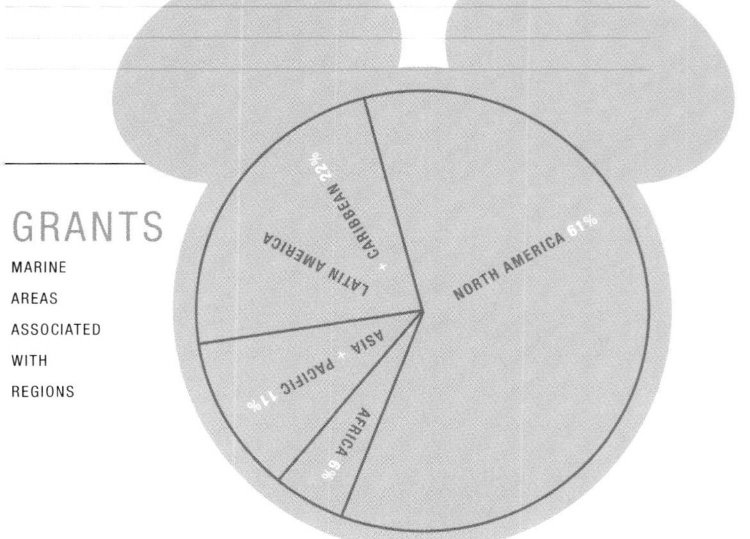

TRANSNATIONAL CULTURAL CORPORATIONS - top global media companies - news corporation

structure - top media corporations 2005

1. GLOBAL MEDIA

WORLD'S LARGEST
MEDIA COMPANIES

TIME WARNER INC.
THE WALT DISNEY CORPORATION
THE NEWS CORPORATION LTD.
SONY CORPORATION
GENERAL ELECTRIC CO.
VIACOM, INC.
BERTELSMANN AG

WORLD'S LARGEST
RECORD COMPANIES

GENERAL ELECTRIC
SONY MUSIC GROUP
WARNER MUSIC GROUP
EMI GROUP PLC
BMG (BERTELSMANN)

WORLD'S LARGEST
PUBLISHERS

BERTELSMANN AG
PEARSON PLC
TIME WARNER
WALT DISNEY CORPORATION
THE NEWS CORPORATION LTD.
VIACOM, INC.

WORLD'S MOST DOMINANT
FILM COMPANIES + THEIR PARENTS

WARNER BROTHERS
WALT DISNEY PICTURES INCLUDING **MIRAMAX**
PARAMOUNT PICTURES
COLUMBIA PICTURES / SONY PICTURES
UNIVERSAL PICTURES
TWENTIETH CENTURY FOX

2. NEWS CORPORATION: HOW IT'S RUN

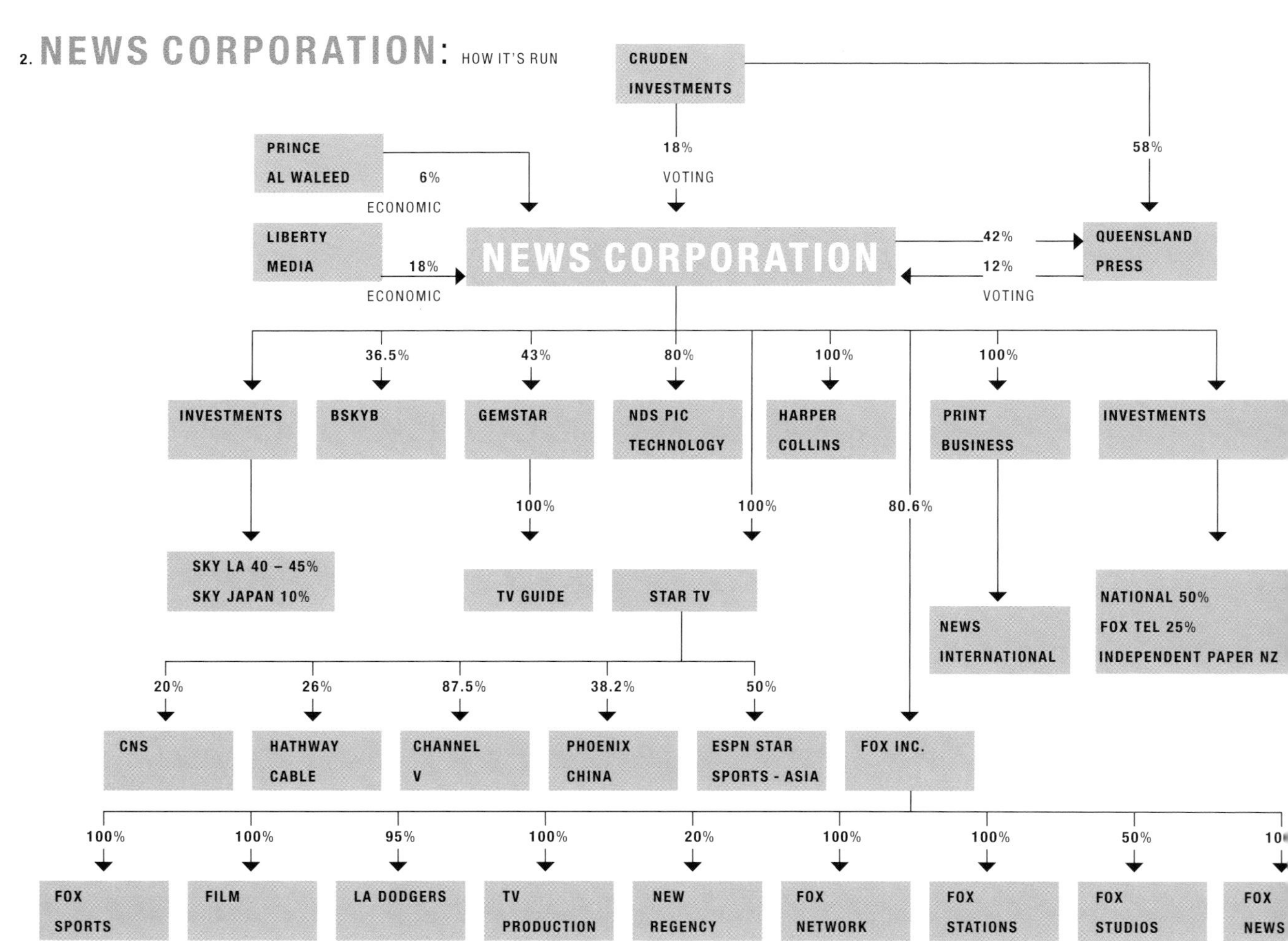

3. TOP MEDIA CORPORATIONS 2005

PARENT COMPANY	**TIME WARNER**		
HEADQUARTERS	NEW YORK CITY, NY		
REVENUE	**43.6** BILLION IN 2005		
TELEVISION	WB: **50**% HBO: **75**% CINEMAX: **75**% COMEDY CENTRAL: **37.5**% COURT TV: **37.5**% E! AND STYLE: **7.5**%	TBS: **75**% TNT: **75**% CARTOON NETWORK: **75**% TURNER CLASSIC MOVIES: **75**% CNN: **75**% HEADLINE NEWS: **75**%	CNNfn: **75**% CNN/SPORTS ILLUSTRATED: **75**% TVKO: **75**% WHOLLY AND PARTIALLY OWNED CHANNELS IN EUROPE, ASIA + SOUTH AMERICA
CABLE	SECOND LARGEST PROVIDER WITH **12.8** CUSTOMERS IN WHOLLY AND PARTIALLY OWNED SYSTEMS		
PRODUCTION	WARNER BROTHERS WARNER BROTHERS ANIMATION TELEPICTURES	CASTLE ROCK LIBRARY OF **6,500** MOVIES **32,000** TV SHOWS	**13,500** CARTOONS TIVO: **18**% DIGITAL VIDEO RECORDING
MOVIES	WARNER BROTHERS: **75**% NEW LINE FEATURES: **75**% FINE LINE FEATURES: **75**%	LIBRARY OF MGM, RKO, AND PRE-1950 WARNER BROS. FILMS WARNER HOME VIDEO: **75**%	UNITED CINEMAS INTERNATIONAL: **50**% WF CINEMA HOLDINGS: **50**%
MUSIC	OVER **40** LABELS INCLUDING: WARNER BROS. ATLANTIC ELEKTRA LONDON-SIRE	RHINO RECORDS MANUFACTURERS + DISTRIBUTES THE COMPANY'S CDs, TAPES AND DVDs, MAJORITY INTEREST IN ALTERNATIVE DISTRIBUTION ALLIANCE	QUINCY JONES ENTERTAINMENT CO.: **37.5**% COLUMBIA HOUSE: **50**% MUSIC PUBLISHER WARNER / CHAPPELL
MAGAZINES	OVER **74** TITLES INCLUDING: **> 75**% TIME LIFE PEOPLE FORTUNE ALL YOU BUSINESS 2.0 SPORTS ILLUSTRATED INSIDE STUFF	MONEY ENTERTAINMENT WEEKLY THE TICKET IN STYLE SOUTHERN LIVING PROGRESSIVE FARMER SOUTHERN ACCENTS COOKING LIGHT	THE PARENT GROUP THIS OLD HOUSE SUNSET SUNSET GARDEN GUIDE REAL SIMPLE ASIA WEEK (ASIAN NEWS WEEKLY) POPULAR SCIENCE IPC
INTERNET	AMERICA ONLINE COMPUSERVE NETSCAPE ICQ AOL INSTANT MESSENGER MUSICNET: **20**%	DIGITALCITY LEGEND: **49**% MOVIEFONE MAPQUEST SPINNER.COM WINAMP	SHOUTCAST AMAZON: **2**% DR. KOOP: **10**% ROADRUNNER CABLE MODEMS
NEWSPAPER	–		
BOOKS	WARNER BROS. LITTLE, BROWN AND COMPANY	WARNER FAITH TIME WARNER AUDIO BOOKS	TIME INC.
RADIO	–		
SPORTS	ATLANTA BRAVES ATLANTA HAWKS	ATLANTA THRASHERS GOODWILL GAMES	PHILLIPS ARENA
THEME PARKS	WARNER BROS. MOVIE WORLD THEME PARK + HOTELS (WITH AT&T)		
OTHER	TIME WARNER TELECOM: **37**% WARNER BROS, STUDIO STORES: **75**%	LICENSE RIGHTS TO DC COMICS HANNA-BARBARA CHARACTERS: **75**%	

TOP MEDIA CORPORATIONS 2005

PARENT COMPANY	GENERAL ELECTRIC		
HEADQUARTERS			
REVENUE	**149.7** BILLION IN 2005		
TELEVISION	NBC: **80%** CNBC: **50%** MSNBC: **50%** A&E: **25%** HISTORY: **25%**	BIOGRAPHY: **25%** SNAP TV: **80%** AMC BRAVO	WE INDEPENDENT FILM CHANNEL MUCH MUSIC INTERNATIONAL CHANNELS PAXTON: **32%**
CABLE	–		
PRODUCTION	NBC PRODUCTIONS RADIO CITY TELEVISION BRAVO ORIGINAL PROGRAMMING	IFC PRODUCTIONS NEXT WAVE FILMS SATELLITE DBS PROVIDER	TIVO
MOVIES	UNIVERSAL PICTURES		
MUSIC	–		
MAGAZINES	–		
INTERNET	NBC.COM: **47%** SNAP: **47%**	CNBC.COM: **10%** SALON.COM: **10%**	AUTOBYTEL.COM: **10%** POLO.COM: **50%**
NEWSPAPER	–		
BOOKS	–		
RADIO	–		
SPORTS	NEW YORK KNICKS NEW YORK RANGERS	NEW YORK LIBERTY NEW ENGLAND SEAWOLVES	HARTFORD WOLFPACK MADISON SQUARE GARDEN
THEME PARKS	–		
OTHER	–		

TOP MEDIA CORPORATIONS 2005

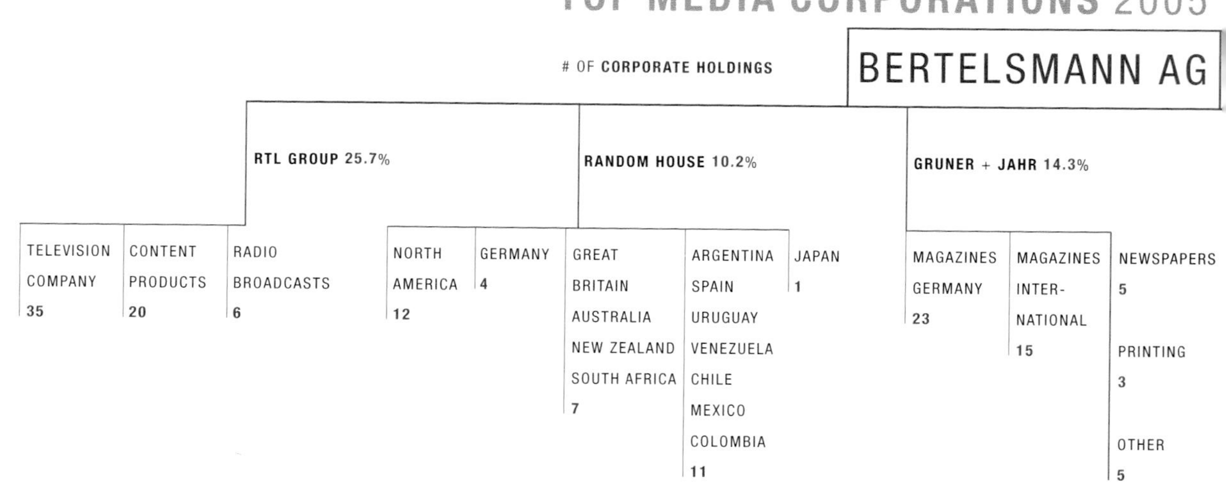

TOP MEDIA CORPORATIONS 2005

PARENT COMPANY	**SONY**		
HEADQUARTERS			
REVENUE	**53.8** BILLION IN 2005		
TELEVISION	TELEMUNDO: **34**% SOAP CITY: **50**%	GAMESHOW NETWORK: **50**% MUSIC CHOICE	25 INTERNATIONAL CHANNELS 8 TV STATIONS
CABLE	–		
PRODUCTION	_		
MOVIES	COLUMBIA PICTURES SCREEN GEMS SONY PICTURES CLASSICS	REVOLUTION STUDIOS DISTRIBUTION ARMS WHOLLY AND PARTIALLY OWNED WITH NEWS CORP.	AOL-TV AND DISNEY LOEWS THEATER: **40**%
MUSIC	**15**% OF ALL MUSIC SALES INCLUDING COLUMBIA, EPIC, AMERICA , AND SONY	RED DISTRIBUTION:**50**% COLUMBIA HOUSE: **50**%	PRESSPLAY PLANNED MUSIC SITE WHITEFIELD RECORDING STUDIO
MAGAZINES	_		
INTERNET	SO-NET, JAPANESE ISP		
NEWSPAPER	_		
BOOKS	–		
RADIO	–		
SPORTS	_		
THEME PARKS	–		
OTHER	MANUFACTURER OF BROADCAST AND ELECTRONICS EQUIPMENT PLAYSTATION AND OTHER ELECTRONIC GAMES AND EQUIPMENT	INSURANCE AND CREDIT FINANCING RETAIL STORE IN CHICAGO	

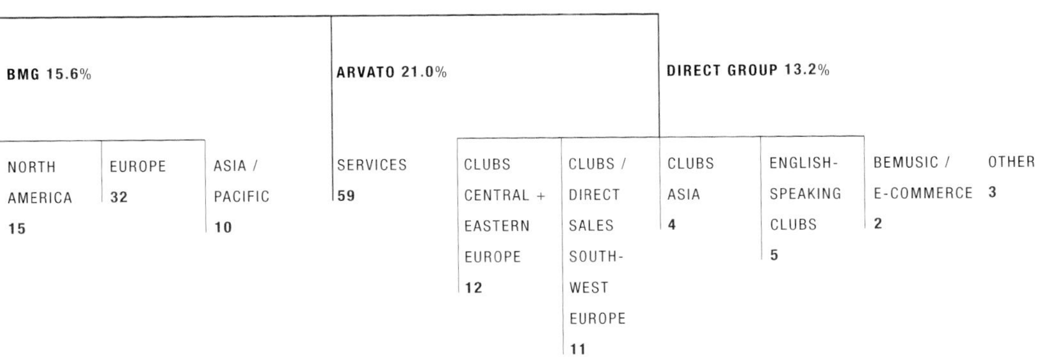

TOP MEDIA CORPORATIONS 2005

PARENT COMPANY	**VIVENDI**		
HEADQUARTERS			
REVENUE	**37.2** BILLION IN 2005		
TELEVISION	USA NETWORK: **93%** SCI-FI CHANNEL: **93%** HOME SHOPPING NETWORK: **12%** SUNDANCE CHANNEL	CANAL+: **49%** CANALSATELLITE 30 INTERNATIONAL CHANNELS	MULTITHEMATIQUE CHANNELS INTERNATIONAL CABLE SUBSCRIPTIONS ECHOSTAR: **10%**
CABLE	–		
PRODUCTION	UNIVERSAL STUDIOS: **49%** CANAL+: **49%**		
MOVIES	UNIVERSAL STUDIOS: **93%** STUDIOCANAL: **93%** POLYGRAM FILMS: **93%** GRAMERCY PICTURES: **93%**	INTERSCOPE COMMUNICATIONS AND PROPAGANDA: **93%** CANAL+: **49%** WORLD'S 2ND LARGEST FILM LIBRARY	POLYGRAM HOME VIDEO: **93%** UNITED CINEMAS INTERNATIONAL: **49%** MULTIPLEX BV: **49%** CINEMA INTERNATIONAL CORPORATION: **49%**
MUSIC	US MUSIC SALES: **27%** FROM LABELS:	INTERSCOPE GEFFEN A&M ISLAND DEF JAM	MCA MERCURY MOTOWN
MAGAZINES	L'EXPRESS L'EXPANSION	INFORMATION TECHNOLOGY MEDICAL JOURNALS	
INTERNET	VIVAZZI: **50%** INTERNET PORTALS IN EUROPE	GET MUSIC: **50%** iWON.COM: **42%**	
NEWSPAPER	FREE NEWSPAPERS IN FRANCE		
BOOKS	LEADING FRENCH FICTION PUBLISHER HOUGHTON MIFFLIN PUBLISHERS	MEDICAL AND REFERENCE BOOKS AND CDs	
RADIO	–		
SPORTS	–		
THEME PARKS	UNIVERSAL STUDIOS HOLLYWOOD UNIVERSAL CITYWALK UNIVERSAL STUDIOS ORLANDO	HOTELS AND WATER PARK: **25%** UNIVERSAL STUDIOS JAPAN: **24%** UNIVERSAL STUDIOS PORT AVENTURA: **37%**	SEGA GAMEWORKS: **12%** 12 US ENTERTAINMENT CENTERS
OTHER	BOTTLED WATER CEGETEL FRENCH PHONE SERVICE: **44%** INTERNATIONAL CELL PHONE SERVICES TICKETMASTER: **12%** 151 RECYCLING FACILITIES 119 LANDFILL SITES 83 INCINERATION PLANTS	COMMERCIAL AND INDUSTRIAL CLEANING 26 EUROPEAN RAILROADS 186 EUROPEAN AND AUSTRALIAN BUSLINES 65,000 HEATING SYSTEMS ELECTRICAL AND MECHANICAL EQUIPMENT MAINTENANCE AND SECRETARIAL SERVICES SPENCER GIFTS	DAPY GLOW STORES UNIVERSAL STUDIOS STORES SPIRIT HALLOWEEN (SUPERSTORES) 220 INTERNATIONAL ADVERTISING AGENCIES

INGOs + FOUNDATIONS

- **growth** of art + culture ngo's - **ngo's** by regional field of activity - **arts** + **culture ngo's** - **international foundations** + **main activity** - # of **foundations** - **countries** with most foundations **giving to arts** + **culture** - top **foundations in international giving** - top **non-us recepients us foundations grants** - map **international cultural foundations**

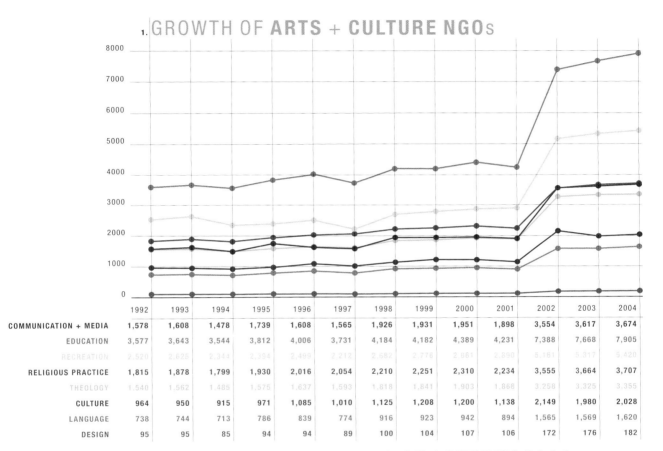

1. GROWTH OF ARTS + CULTURE NGOs

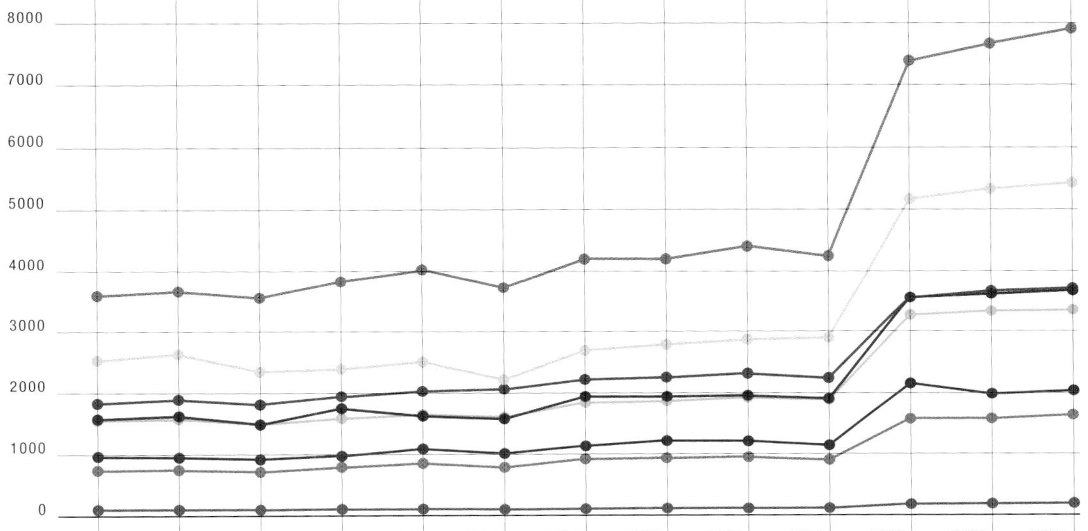

	1992	1993	1994	1995	1996	1997	1998	1999	2000	2001	2002	2003	2004
COMMUNICATION + MEDIA	1,578	1,608	1,478	1,739	1,608	1,565	1,926	1,931	1,951	1,898	3,554	3,617	3,674
EDUCATION	3,577	3,643	3,544	3,812	4,006	3,731	4,184	4,182	4,389	4,231	7,388	7,668	7,905
RECREATION	2,520	2,625	2,344	2,394	2,499	2,212	2,682	2,776	2,861	2,890	5,161	5,317	5,420
RELIGIOUS PRACTICE	1,815	1,878	1,799	1,930	2,016	2,054	2,210	2,251	2,310	2,234	3,555	3,664	3,707
THEOLOGY	1,540	1,562	1,485	1,575	1,637	1,593	1,818	1,841	1,903	1,868	3,258	3,325	3,355
CULTURE	964	950	915	971	1,085	1,010	1,125	1,208	1,200	1,138	2,149	1,980	2,028
LANGUAGE	738	744	713	786	839	774	916	923	942	894	1,565	1,569	1,620
DESIGN	95	95	85	94	94	89	100	104	107	106	172	176	182

2. NGOs BY REGIONAL FIELD OF ACTIVITY 2004

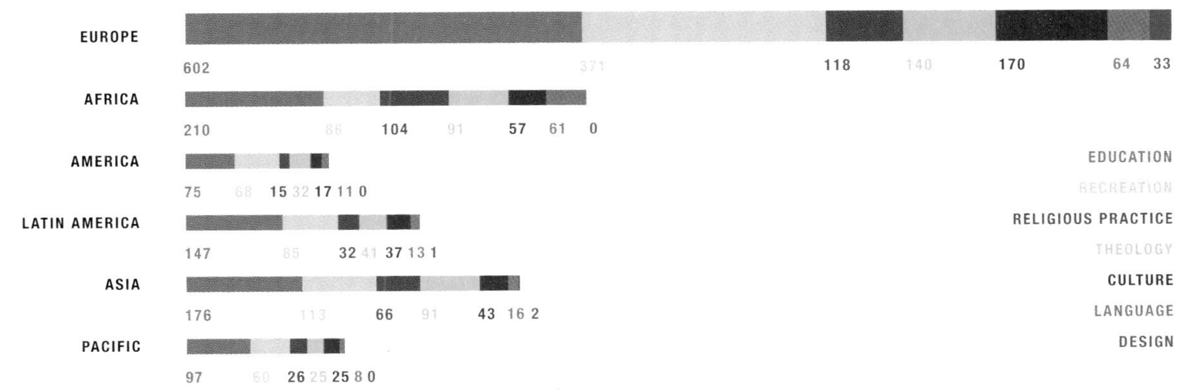

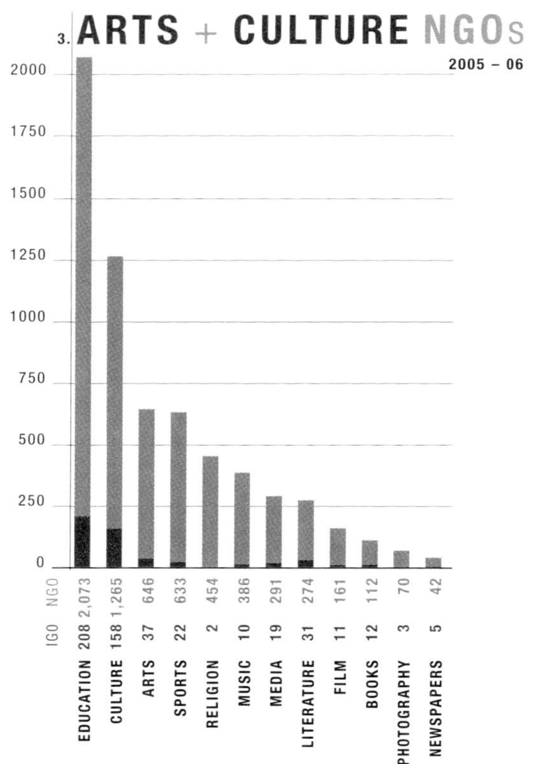
3. ARTS + CULTURE NGOs
2005 – 06
2000
1750
1500
1250
1000
750
500
250
0
IGO NGO
EDUCATION 208 2,073
CULTURE 158 1,265
ARTS 37 646
SPORTS 22 633
RELIGION 2 454
MUSIC 10 386
MEDIA 19 291
LITERATURE 31 274
FILM 11 161
BOOKS 12 112
PHOTOGRAPHY 3 70
NEWSPAPERS 5 42

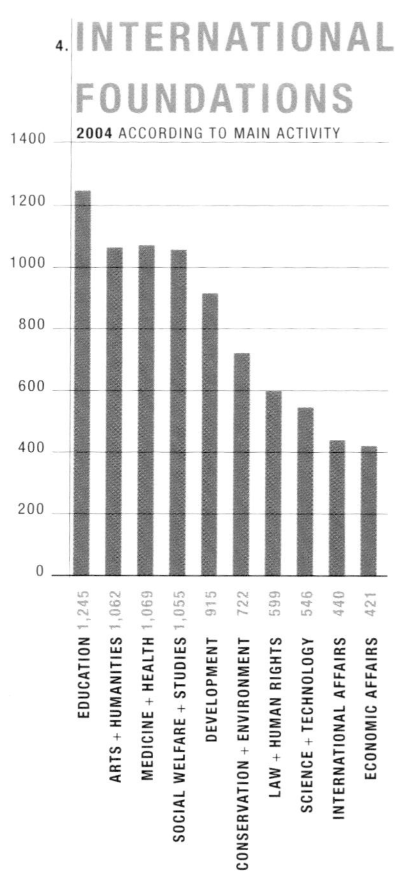
4. INTERNATIONAL FOUNDATIONS
2004 ACCORDING TO MAIN ACTIVITY
1400
1200
1000
800
600
400
200
0
EDUCATION 1,245
ARTS + HUMANITIES 1,062
MEDICINE + HEALTH 1,069
SOCIAL WELFARE + STUDIES 1,055
DEVELOPMENT 915
CONSERVATION + ENVIRONMENT 722
LAW + HUMAN RIGHTS 599
SCIENCE + TECHNOLOGY 546
INTERNATIONAL AFFAIRS 440
ECONOMIC AFFAIRS 421

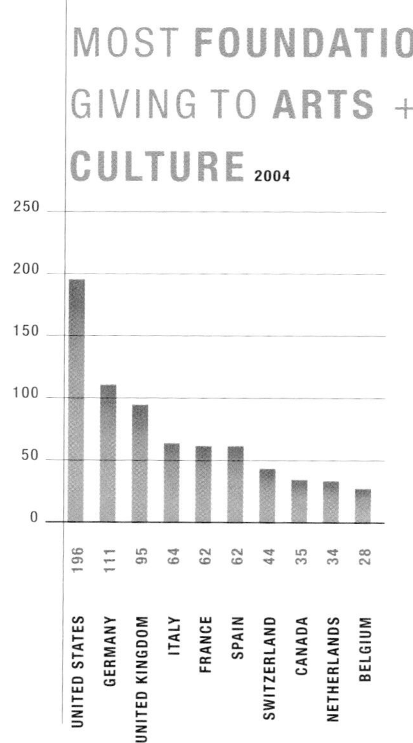
5. COUNTRIES WITH MOST FOUNDATIONS GIVING TO ARTS + CULTURE 2004
250
200
150
100
50
0
UNITED STATES 196
GERMANY 111
UNITED KINGDOM 95
ITALY 64
FRANCE 62
SPAIN 62
SWITZERLAND 44
CANADA 35
NETHERLANDS 34
BELGIUM 28

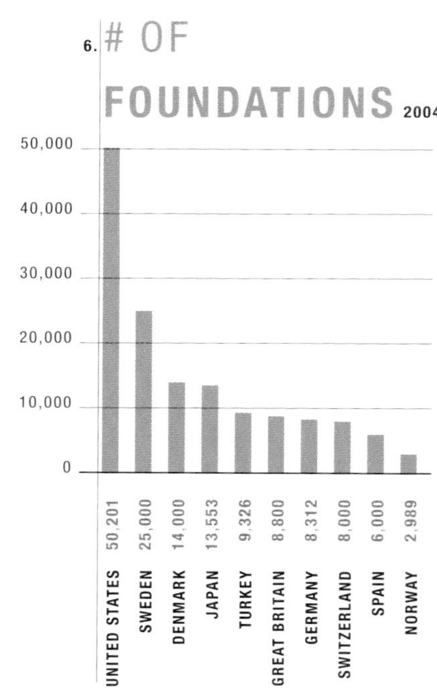
6. # OF FOUNDATIONS 2004
50,000
40,000
30,000
20,000
10,000
0
UNITED STATES 50,201
SWEDEN 25,000
DENMARK 14,000
JAPAN 13,553
TURKEY 9,326
GREAT BRITAIN 8,800
GERMANY 8,312
SWITZERLAND 8,000
SPAIN 6,000
NORWAY 2,989

7. TOP **FOUNDATIONS** IN INTERNATIONAL GIVING

	FOUNDATION NAME	STATE	DOLLAR AMOUNT	# OF GRANTS
1.	**BILL & MELINDA GATES FOUNDATION**	WA	**$188,260,218**	**42**
2.	**THE FORD FOUNDATION**	NY	**$161,511,671**	**997**
3.	**W. K. KELLOGG FOUNDATION**	MI	**$ 44,504,890**	**107**
4.	**THE ROCKEFELLER FOUNDATION**	NY	**$ 43,273,209**	**220**
5.	**JOHN D. AND CATHERINE T. MACARTHUR FOUNDATION**	IL	**$ 38,032,000**	**124**
6.	**THE WILLIAM AND FLORA HEWLETT FOUNDATION**	CA	**$ 22,638,000**	**53**
7.	**CARNEGIE CORPORATION OF NEW YORK**	NY	**$ 22,586,300**	**36**
8.	**THE LINCY FOUNDATION**	CA	**$ 22,277,855**	**1**
9.	**THE ANDREW W. MELLON FOUNDATION**	MI	**$ 17,541,190**	**62**
10.	**THE AVI CHAI FOUNDATION**	NY	**$ 18,379,601**	**7**
11.	**CHARLES STEWART MOTT FOUNDATION**	MI	**$ 17,541,190**	**160**
12.	**DAVID AND LUCILE PACKARD FOUNDATION**	CA	**$ 16,725,702**	**68**
13.	**THE KRESGE FOUNDATION**	MI	**$ 10,200,000**	**13**
14.	**THE PACKARD HUMANITIES INSTITUTE**	CA	**$ 7,342,232**	**15**
15.	**ARTHUR S. DEMOSS FOUNDATION**	FL	**$ 7,084,739**	**4**
		TOTAL	**$637,898,797**	1,903

8. TOP **NON-U.S. RECIPIENTS** OF U.S. FOUNDATION GRANTS

	RECIPIENT NAME	COUNTRY	DOLLAR AMOUNT	# OF GRANTS
1.	**WORLD HEALTH ORGANIZATION**	SWITZERLAND	$ 69,664,245	**24**
2.	**GLOBAL FUND TO FIGHT AIDS, TUBERCULOSIS & MALARIA**	SWITZERLAND	$ 50,000,000	**1**
3.	**GOVERNMENT OF ARMENIA**	ARMENIA	$ 22,418,266	**2**
4.	**AVI CHAI**	ISRAEL	$ 18,115,167	**1**
5.	**VOLUNTARY HEALTH SERVICES**	INDIA	$ 12,978,870	**1**
6.	**MURDOCH UNIVERSITY**	AUSTRALIA	$ 9,792,730	**1**
7.	**MAKERERE UNIVERSITY**	UGANDA	$ 8,106,441	**15**
8.	**INTERNATIONAL COUNCIL OF AIDS SERVICE ORGANIZATIONS**	CANADA	$ 7,148,291	**2**
9.	**SWISS TROPICAL INSTITUTE**	SWITZERLAND	$ 6,672,860	**1**
10.	**NATIONAL COMISSION OF HUMAN DEVELOPMENT**	PAKISTAN	$ 6,568,888	**1**
11.	**PLANNED PARENTHOOD FEDERATION, INTERNATIONAL**	ENGLAND	$ 5,925,000	**5**
12.	**UNIVERSITY OF CAPE TOWN**	SOUTH AFRICA	$ 5,776,890	**23**
13.	**UNIVERSITY OF DAR ES SALAAM**	TANZANIA	$ 5,468,300	**4**
14.	**CHAWTON HOUSE LIBRARY**	ENGLAND	$ 5,260,580	**3**
15.	**LONDON SCHOOL OF HYGIENE & TROPICAL MEDICINE**	ENGLAND	$ 5,129,713	**6**
		TOTAL	$239,026,241	90

9. INTERNATIONAL CULTURAL FOUNDATIONS

LOCATIONS + HEAD QUARTERS

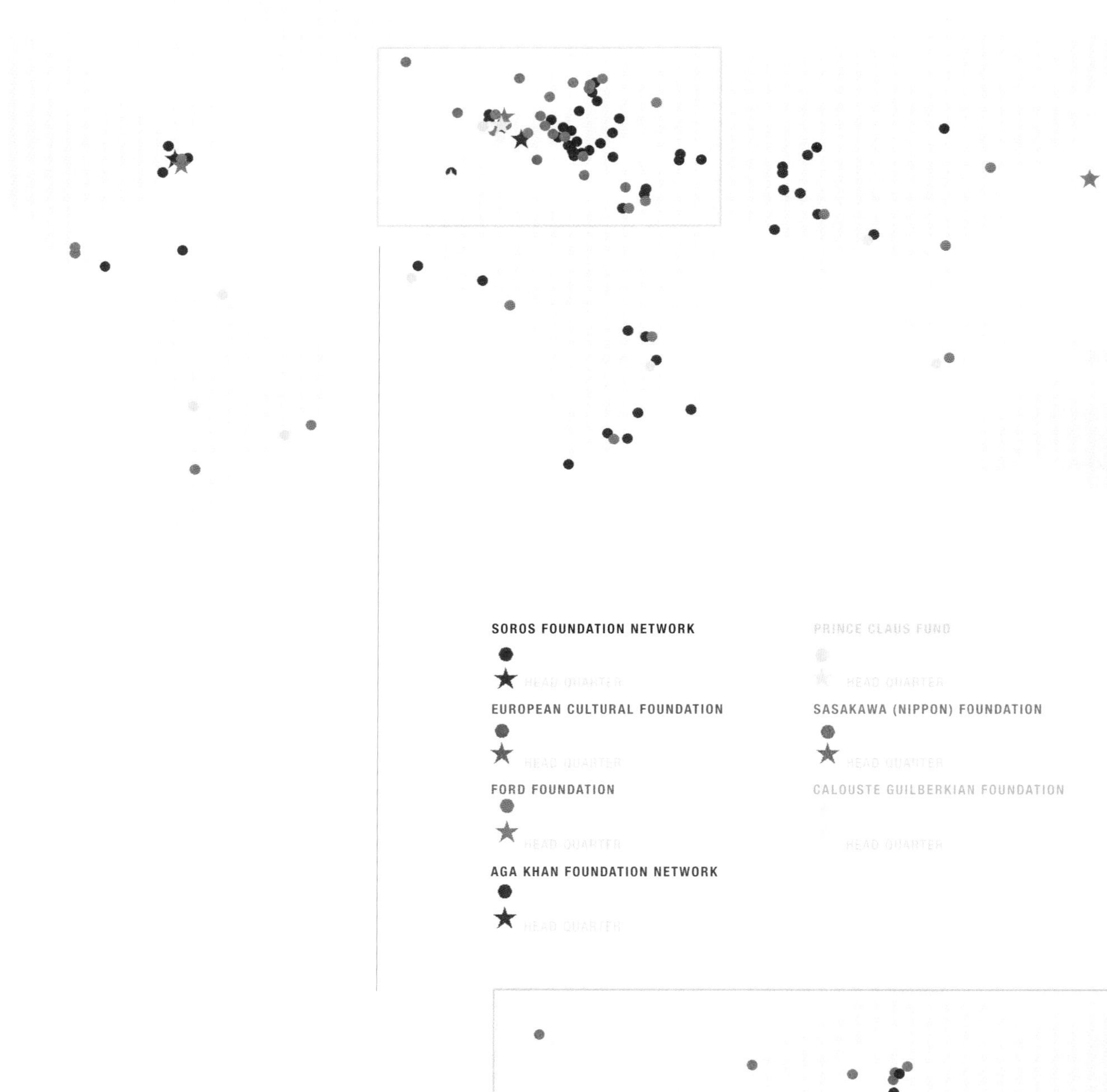

TRANSNATIONAL CULTURAL CORPORATIONS Cultural TNCs include entertainment, media, publishing, and now also web-based conglomerates with a variety of different holdings spanning Internet, publishing, IT, radio, and television mediums. Over the past decade, giant transnational cultural corporations (cultural TNCs) have emerged through considerable consolidation and expansion: today, a relatively small number of corporations, typically as diversified holdings, control the majority of formal cultural industries. For example, 80% of commercial music and films in the world are distributed by a small number of cultural TNCs (IMCA, 2005). These parent companies shape media and entertainment offerings, and influence the promotion of artistic talent and cultural products according to corporate interests.

WHAT DO WE KNOW ABOUT CULTURAL TNCS?

The statistics show that some of the corporations have revenues that exceed those of certain countries. In 2005, News Corporation owned 27 broadcast television stations and had revenues of $24.5 billion USD. Time Warner had revenues of $43.6 billion USD and General Electric, $149.7 billion USD. Clear Channel owns around 1,225 radio stations in 300 cities and dominates the audience share in 100 of 112 major markets in the United States (Perlstein, 2002). CBS and ABC own one-fifth as many stations as Clear Channel (Perlstein, 2002). These media giants are linked internationally, for instance, General Electric owns Telemundo, one of the two largest Spanish broadcasting networks (Khan, 2003). Sony, which made its name through electronics, now has more than 1,000 subsidiaries worldwide.

WHAT ARE THE ISSUES?

The oligopolization of the cultural industries raises questions of diversity, fair competition, and cultural domination. Cultural TNCs have sought to loosen government regulations through lobbying, campaign contributions, and buying intellectual property rights, including hiring artists via contracts that limit their rights to their own creative output. In this way, the ability of corporations to profit from individual creative production is protected by law.

At the local and regional level, some producers and productions may become increasingly marginalized, prompting attempts to promote independent production of culture and to monitor the large cultural TNCs. These include UNESCO's Convention on Cultural Diversity, and also the actions of nongovernmental organizations like Corp Watch, Oligopoly Watch, and Media Alliance.

Accountability and control of information are key issues in the debate surrounding cultural TNCs. In Brazil, by law, foreigners can only acquire 30 percent of a media company and their ability to influence editorial output or management appointments is restricted. In Australia, local productions must account for 55 percent of the content on free-to-air TV and in New Zealand, local content is controlled, but regulators and networks agree on quotas. In France, media ownership and content are tightly regulated. A growing number of countries have taken steps to protect local production of cultural materials, albeit with varying success, raising the specter of protectionism as economic globalization pressures are increasing.

The 1996 Telecommunications Act in the United States removed the requirement for radio and television broadcaster to include public interest programming in their broadcast, and removed controls on corporate media ownership. The Act had huge implications for cultural industries, not only within the US, but internationally because of the domination by US conglomerates of radio and television industries. In terms of television, the US market is the largest in the world, and the US is the largest exporter of broadcast content.

According to the British Television Distributors Association, the US controls more than 60 percent of global trade in television exports. 93 percent of feature films on UK television in 2001 were US owned or co-produced (Financial Times, 2006). In many countries, the US co-produces programs with local companies, making the influence of US broadcasters difficult to fully detect (Financial Times, 2006).

The more developed a TV market, the more investment it directs to domestic productions or to local remakes of imported show formats, rather than strictly imported formats (Financial Times, 2006). In other words, the influence of TNCs reflects inequalities in the globalizing world: developed countries are less susceptible to exposure by foreign, western media and entertainment than poor countries without strong independent and local outlets. This has implications for the development of cultural industries in these countries.

Cultural TNCs are linked closely with the other TNCs such as Ford, GM or Exxon as shareholders and overlapping board memberships (Active Opposition, 2003). Disney and McDonald's had an exclusive marketing partnership for 10 years, and until 2006 when Disney decided to distance itself from the fast food identity, now increasingly linked in the public eye to childhood obesity and diabetes.

Cultural TNCs are now moving into web-based spheres, which will have implications for the flow and control of information and Internet services. The Internet offers an opportunity for more equal access to information and cultural production, and sites that offer blogspots or capabilities to create music and movies, for example, encourage local production. Also, new media are increasingly participatory, which offers huge opportunities for democratic participation and exchange of ideas. However, with the growing presence of cultural TNCs on the Internet, local and independent forms of production may be threatened.

CULTURAL INGOS AND FOUNDATIONS

Globalization shapes an emergent transnational civil society, where international NGOs, foundations and similar organizations are active across national boundaries. While these organizations operate in many areas, they are also present in the field of culture. Some of these organizations have existed for many decades, such the P.E.N Club, an international association for poets, essayists and novelists, the European Cultural Foundation, or Eric Arts, a European association at the intersection of cultural policy, arts and research. Others are more recent, such as the International Federation of Arts and Cultural Agencies, an association of governmental agencies in the field, or the International Network for Cultural Diversity (INCD), which is made up of artists and cultural groups working against cultural homogenization.

Cultural INGOs and foundations refer to civil society organizations that contribute to the ongoing process of cultural exchange and dissemination. These organizations are involved in funding, implementation, facilitating partnerships, and creating collaborative and community initiatives. The Council of Europe (2001) suggests the following roles for cultural INGOs:

- In a democratic framework, civil society is increasingly important in the field of culture for it provides the necessary mechanisms for inciting change
- NGOs play a significant role in the reconstruction of the democratic state and the building of a pluralistic civil society
- Corporate philanthropy and sponsorship are important for the development of a strong third sector, especially in the arts
- NGOs are critical to the process of cultural policy elaboration, necessitating an effective bottom-up communication in this process
- The arts play a significant role in social inclusion

Arts and culture NGOs have been experiencing considerable growth in recent years. Between 1992 and 2001, arts and culture NGOs steadily grew from 984 to 1,138. However by 2002, an exponential growth of cultural NGOs brought these figures closer to two thousand. In 2004, there were 1,423 cultural NGOs, 158 of which are INGOs, and 683 arts NGOs, of which 37 were INGOs.

In the United States, private and community foundation funding for the arts more than doubled between 1995 and 2001, peaking at $4.2 billion in 2001. This dramatic increase in support for the arts occurred during a period of significant cuts in federal, state, and local government funding for the arts. Arts funding as a percent of overall funding is around 12-15% (Table 1). In a 2003 study conducted by the Foundation Center, approximately 8% of foundations allocate at least half of their grant dollars for arts and culture and approximately 21% allocate at least a quarter to the arts. The majority of funding is distributed to museum activities and performing arts. In addition, 25 of the largest funders by arts giving accounted for a smaller share of overall arts support in 2001 compared to earlier years, suggesting that the base of large arts funders has grown and support for arts is growing amongst smaller foundations. Independent foundations provide over three-quarters of arts funding, of which half are family foundations, followed by corporate (11.6%) and community foundations (7.4%).

TABLE 1: **DISTRIBUTION OF US ARTS FUNDING BY FOUNDATIONS** (2001)

Museum Activities	34%	Historical Activities	6%
Performing Arts	30%	Arts-Related Humanities	3%
Media Communications	8%	Other	4%
Multidisciplinary Arts	8%		
Visual Arts	7%	Total dollars	$1.98 billion

Source: the Foundation Center, 2003

Another survey conducted by the Fitzcarraldo Foundation shows that the distribution of arts funding In Europe is a departure from American foundation patterns (Tables 2 and 3). While comparisons are difficult to make due to different methods of measurement, a cursory observation (Table 2) shows that funding discrepancies can be found in the areas such as performing arts (30% vs.17%) and humanities and literature (3% versus 11%).

TABLE 2: **DISTRIBUTION OF EUROPEAN ARTS FUNDING** (2001)

Visual Arts	19%	Audiovisual	9%
Performing Arts	17%	Intangible Heritage	9%
Literature	11%	New Media	7%
Cultural Heritage	11%	Community Arts	6%
Interdisciplinary	11%		

Source: Fitzcarraldo Foundation, 2003

TABLE 3: **CORE EUROPEAN FUNDED ACTIVITIES IN THE ARTS**

(Respondents could make more than one selection, therefore does not add to 100%)

Exhibitions	24%	Mobility	14%
Publications/Preservation/Dissemination	22%	Preservation & Restoration	13%
Training & Professional Development	20%	Art Education	11%
Production	18%	Acquisition	9%
Research & Documentation	17%	Distribution	6%
Networking	16%	Other	4%
Pilot Projects	15%	Residency	3%
Prizes & Awards	14%		

Source: Fitzcarraldo Foundation, 2003

WHAT ARE THE ISSUES?

The Council of Europe has identified three main issues relevant to the needs and demands of arts and culture organizations. First, the need to build successful arts and business partnerships. This can be carried out through the development of education opportunities, capacity building, identification of successful case studies and good practice, increased private sector involvement, utilization of boards and trustees to attract business sponsorship, and building business networks to support the arts.

The second issue is the interface between culture and policy. Cultural organizations can implement a bottom-up approach in cultural policy elaboration by achieving a consensus within the cultural sector about policies, implementation of a communication portal for the efficient transfer of information relevant to culture and policy (i.e. yearly reports), creating a cultural policy think tank, and the mobilization of artists to proactively engage with policy concerns.

The third issue relates to the role of arts and culture in the social inclusion processes. Arts foundations can be further integrated through cross-sectoral cooperation between the state and civil society through the development of formal education programs and training, distribution of literature documenting the arts as a tool for social inclusion, and building a lobby of prominent artists for arts promotion.

GLOBAL SITES + EVENTS

HONG KONG + MUMBAI

NEW YORK CITY

LOS ANGELES

LONDON

GLOBAL EVENTS

SIGNIFICANT CITIES

SYMBOLIC SITES

HONG KONG - population by ethnicity - visiting arrivals - inward + outward movements of aircraft + ocean vessels - international trade

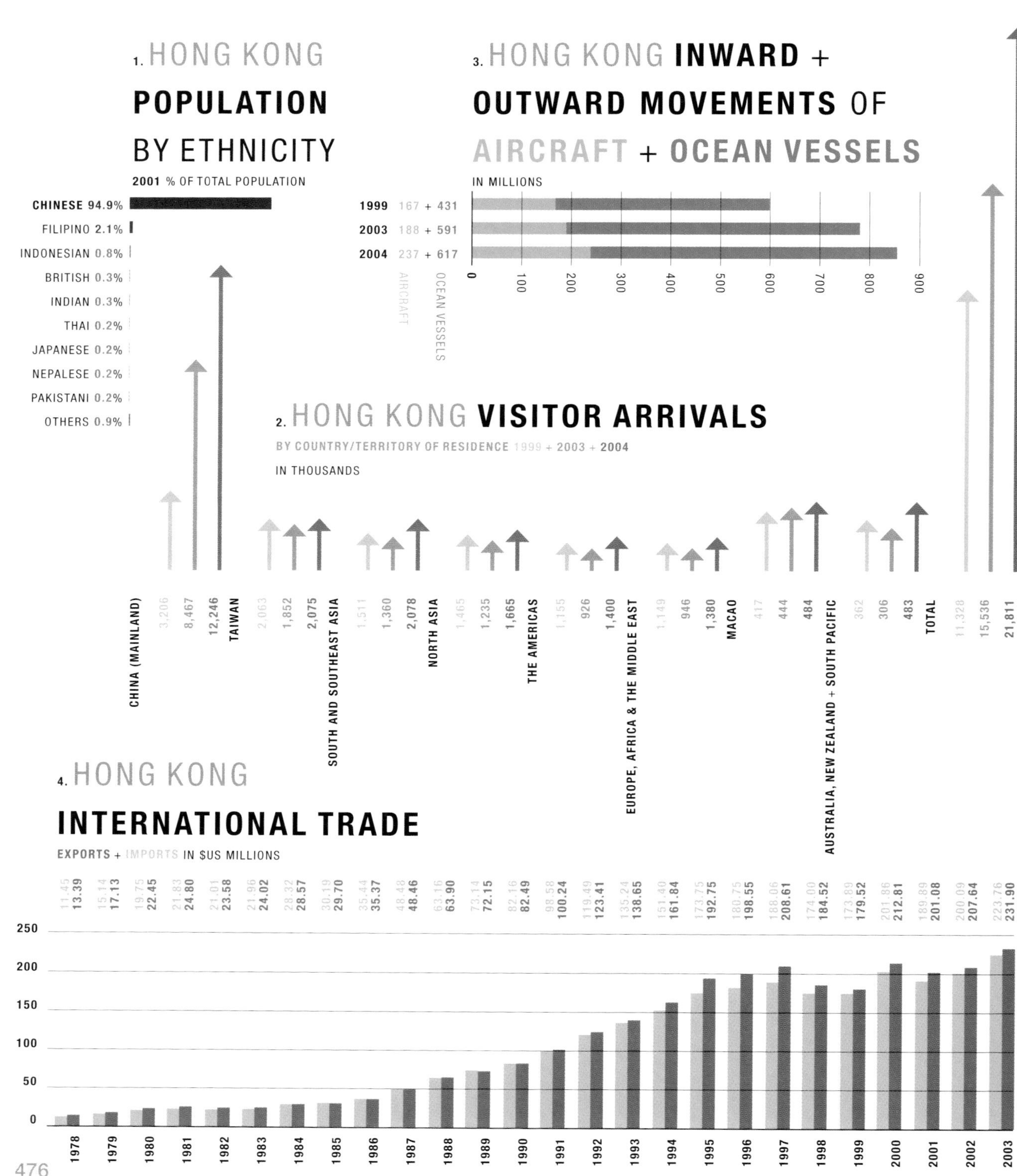

1. HONG KONG
POPULATION BY ETHNICITY
2001 % OF TOTAL POPULATION
CHINESE 94.9%
FILIPINO 2.1%
INDONESIAN 0.8%
BRITISH 0.3%
INDIAN 0.3%
THAI 0.2%
JAPANESE 0.2%
NEPALESE 0.2%
PAKISTANI 0.2%
OTHERS 0.9%
3. HONG KONG INWARD + OUTWARD MOVEMENTS OF AIRCRAFT + OCEAN VESSELS
IN MILLIONS
1999 167 + 431
2003 188 + 591
2004 237 + 617
AIRCRAFT
OCEAN VESSELS
0 100 200 300 400 500 600 700 800 900
2. HONG KONG VISITOR ARRIVALS
BY COUNTRY/TERRITORY OF RESIDENCE 1999 + 2003 + 2004
IN THOUSANDS
CHINA (MAINLAND) 3,206 8,467 12,246
TAIWAN 2,063 1,852 2,075
SOUTH AND SOUTHEAST ASIA 1,511 1,360 2,078
NORTH ASIA 1,465 1,235 1,665
THE AMERICAS 1,155 926 1,400
EUROPE, AFRICA & THE MIDDLE EAST 1,149 946 1,380
MACAO 417 444 484
AUSTRALIA, NEW ZEALAND + SOUTH PACIFIC 362 306 483
TOTAL 11,328 15,536 21,811
4. HONG KONG INTERNATIONAL TRADE
EXPORTS + IMPORTS IN $US MILLIONS
1978 11.45 13.39
1979 15.14 17.13
1980 19.75 22.45
1981 21.83 24.80
1982 21.01 23.58
1983 21.96 24.02
1984 28.32 28.57
1985 30.19 29.70
1986 35.44 35.37
1987 48.48 48.46
1988 63.16 63.90
1989 73.14 72.15
1990 82.16 82.49
1991 98.58 100.24
1992 119.49 123.41
1993 135.24 138.65
1994 151.40 161.84
1995 173.75 192.75
1996 180.75 198.55
1997 188.06 208.61
1998 174.00 184.52
1999 173.89 179.52
2000 201.86 212.81
2001 189.89 201.08
2002 200.09 207.64
2003 223.76 231.90
250
200
150
100
50
0

MUMBAI - population growth - % share religions - % of migrants - population, literacy + work - % of all approved proposals for foreign direct investment + foreign direct investment

1. MUMBAI POPULATION GROWTH

% CHANGE 1950 – 2000 + FORECAST 2015

POPULATION IN MILLIONS

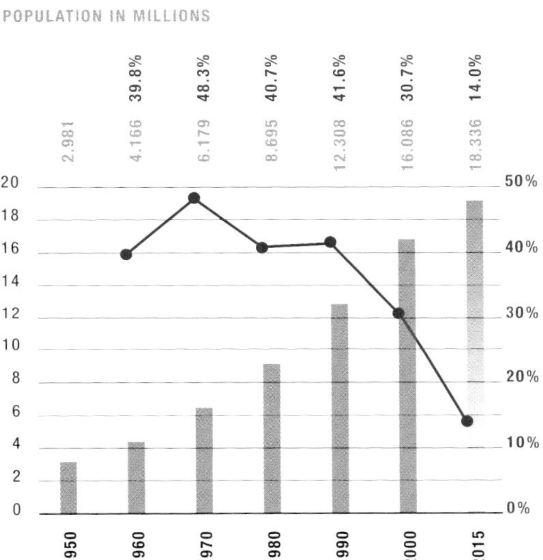

2. MUMBAI % SHARE RELIGIONS

2001

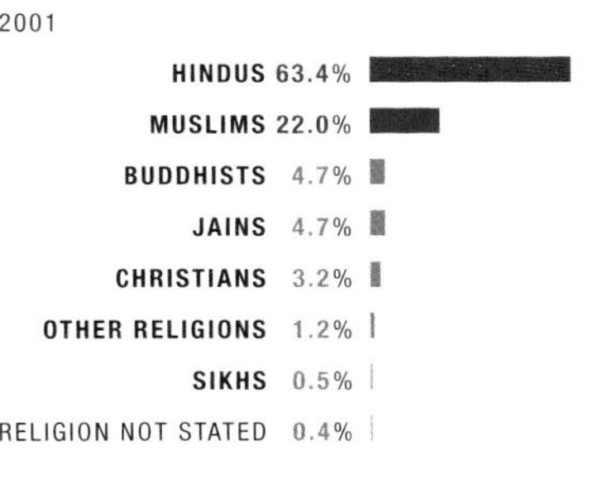

3. MUMBAI % OF MIGRANTS

% OF ALL MIGRANTS IN MUMBAI

% OF TOTAL POPULATION IN MUMBAI

2001 CENSUS

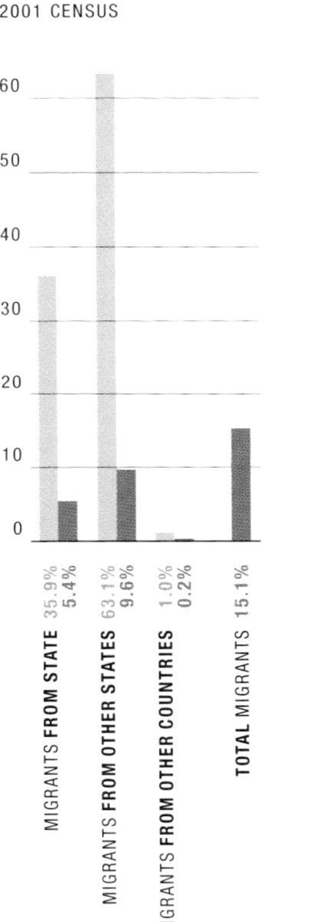

4. MUMBAI POPULATION, LITERACY + WORK

BY GENDER % MALE + FEMALE

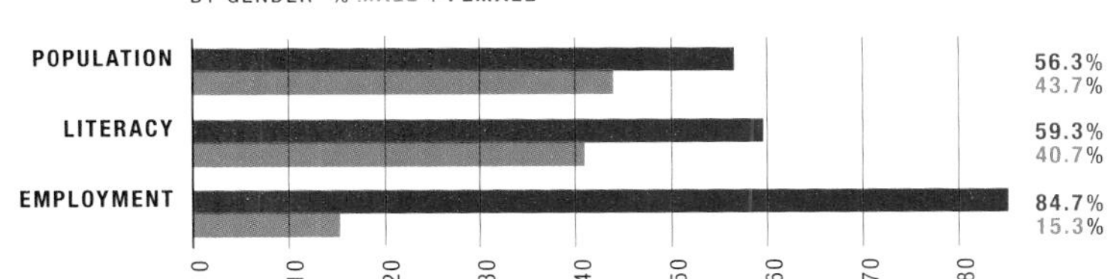

5a. MUMBAI FOREIGN DIRECT INVESTMENT

% OF ALL APPROVED PROPOSALS BY TOP TEN COUNTRIES 2004

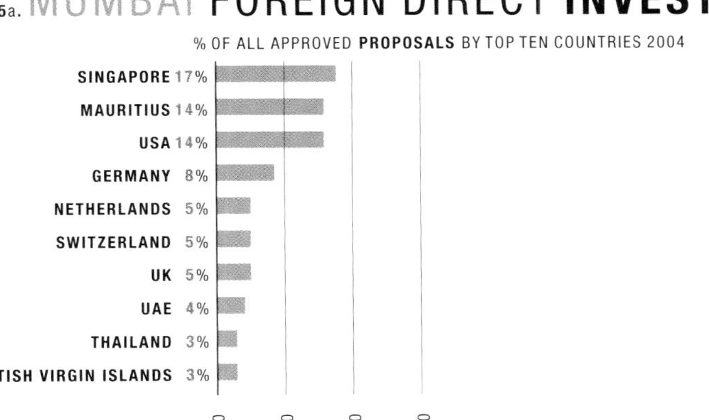

5b. MUMBAI FOREIGN DIRECT INVESTMENT

TOTAL # OF PROPOSALS APPROVED 2005

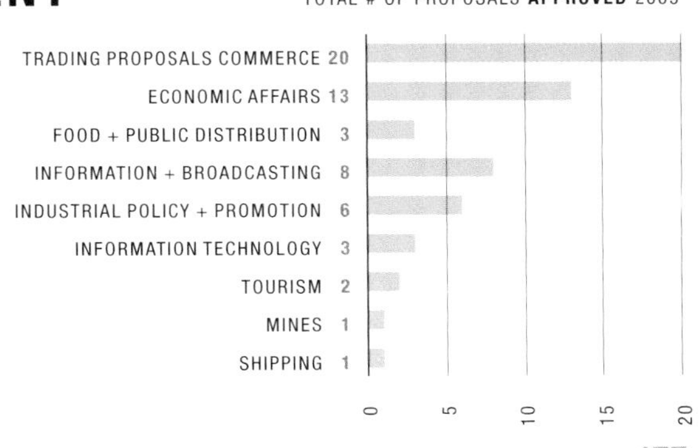

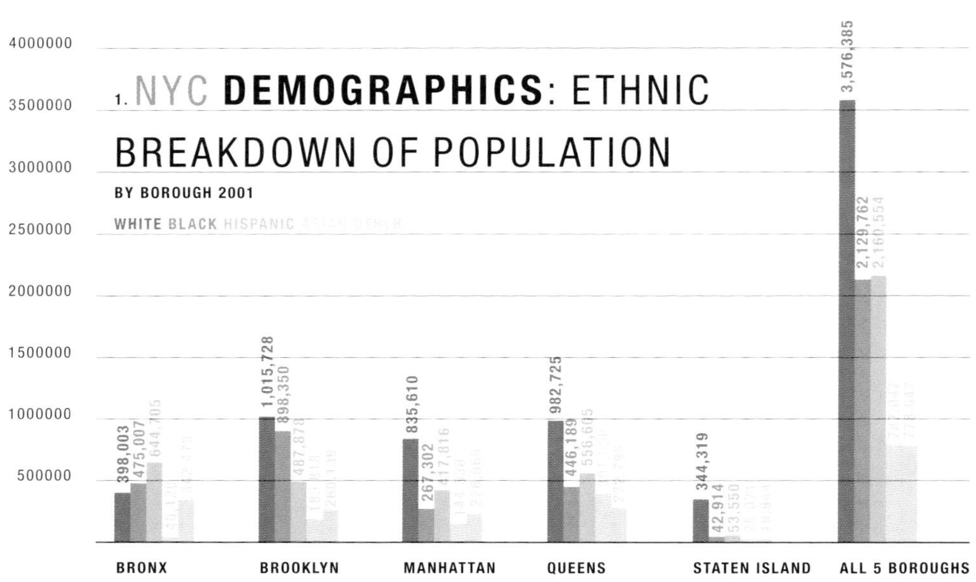

2. NYC TOP 20 COUNTRIES OF ORIGIN FOR **FOREIGN-BORN CITIZENS**

2000 POPULATION

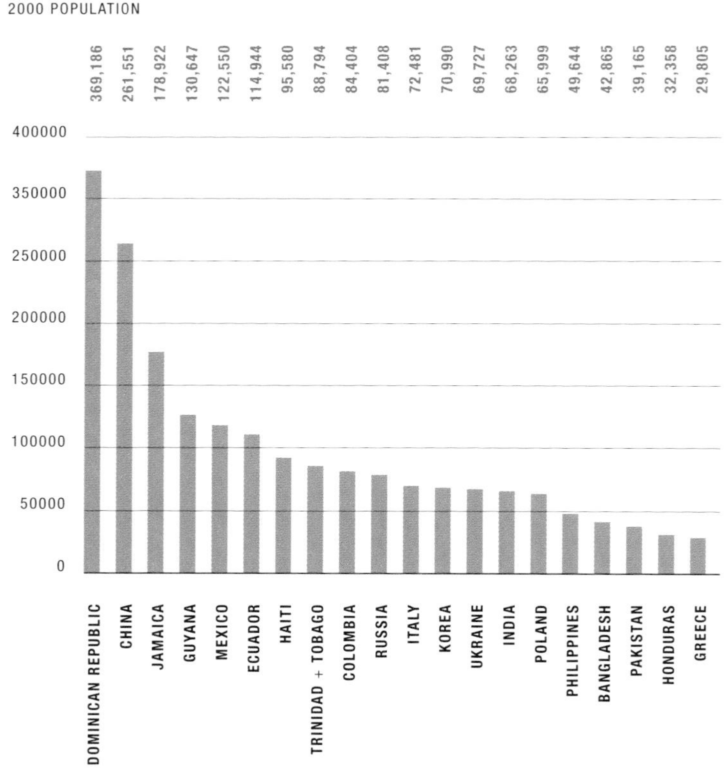

3. NYC **DEMOGRAPHICS**: TOP TEN **LANGUAGES SPOKEN** AT HOME

POPULATION > 5 YRS IN 2000

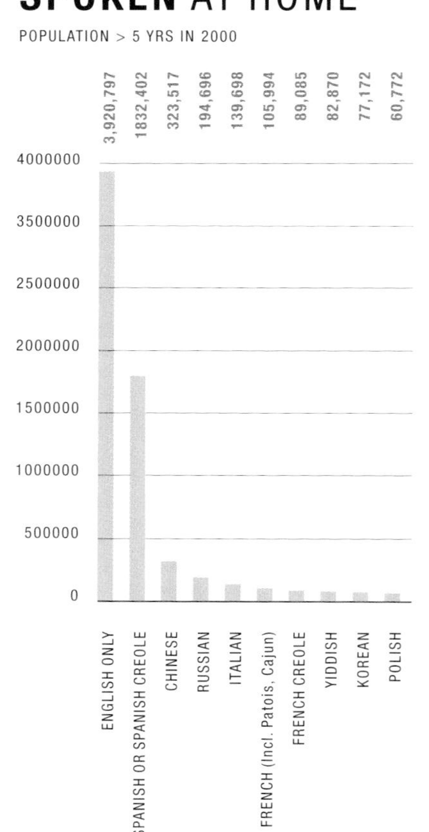

NEW YORK CITY

- demographics: **ethnic breakdown of population** by boroughs 2001
- top 20 countries of **origin for foreign-born** 2000
- demographics: **languages spoken at home** for population > 5 years in 2000
- port of NY + NJ: **value of all cargo imports + exports** 2003 + 2004
- top 20 fortune 500: **companies based in nyc** w/ **yearly revenue over 20 billion dollars** 2003

4. PORT OF **NEW YORK** + **NEW JERSEY**: VALUE OF ALL CARGO IMPORTS AND EXPORTS

2003 + **2004** IN $US THOUSANDS

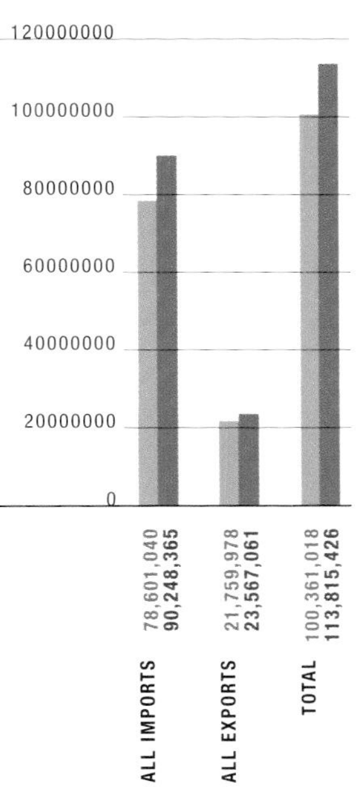

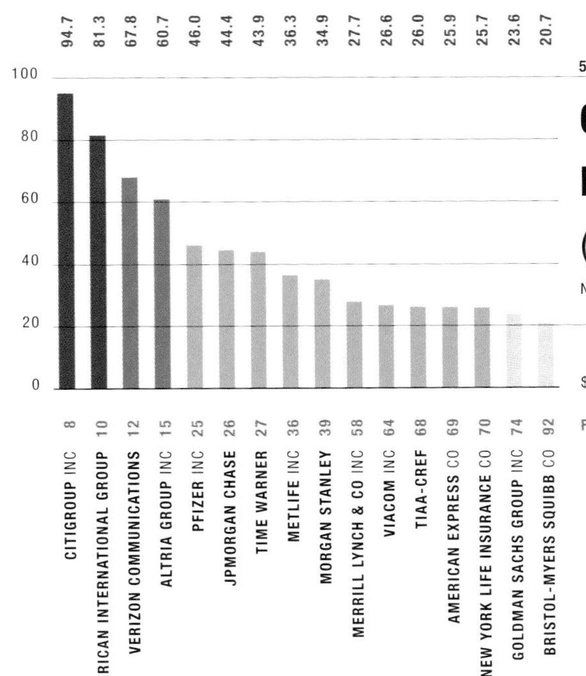

5. NYC: FORTUNE 500 **COMPANIES** WITH A YEARLY **REVENUE** OVER **20 BILLION** (2003)

NYC IS HOME TO MORE FORTUNE 500 COMPANIES THAN ANY OTHER US CITY

$US BILLIONS

FORTUNE 500 RANK

1. L.A. COUNTY: RACIAL POPULATIONS

2005 ESTIMATE % OF LA COUNTY

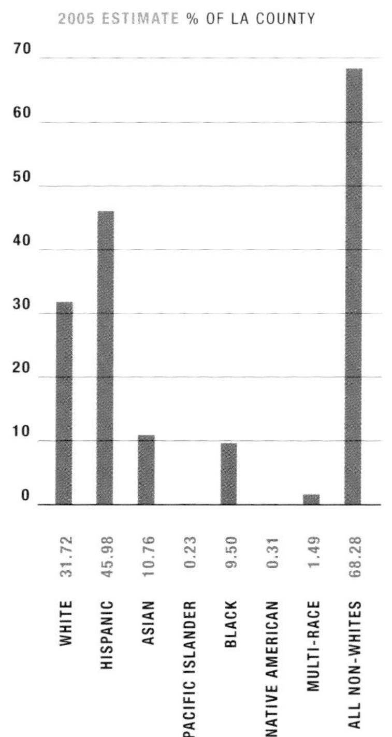

2. L.A. COUNTY: TOP 20 COUNTRIES OF ORIGIN FOR FOREIGN-BORN CITIZENS

% OF ALL FOREIGN-BORN RESIDENTS OF COUNTY

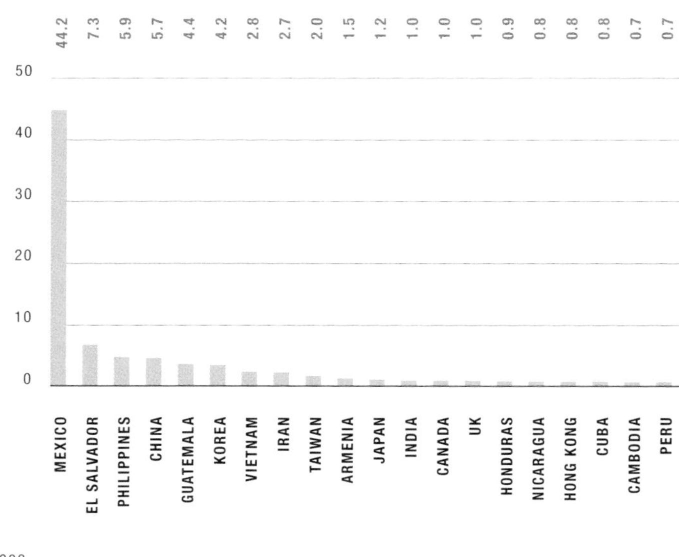

3. LOS ANGELES: TOP US ETHNIC NEWSPAPERS PUBLISHED

ESTIMATED CIRCULATION AS OF NOVEMBER 2001

140000
120000
100000
80000
60000
40000
20000
0

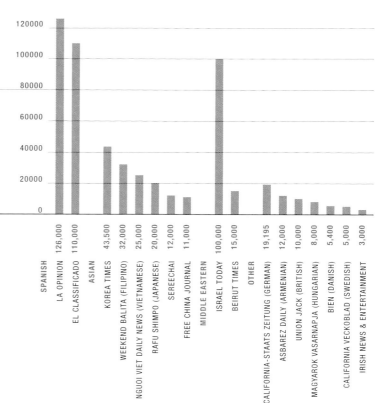

SPANISH	
LA OPINION	126,000
EL CLASSIFICADO	110,000
ASIAN	
KOREA TIMES	43,500
WEEKEND BALITA (FILIPINO)	32,000
NGUOI VIET DAILY NEWS (VIETNAMESE)	25,000
RAFU SHIMPO (JAPANESE)	20,000
SEREECHAI	12,000
FREE CHINA JOURNAL	11,000
MIDDLE EASTERN	
ISRAEL TODAY	100,000
BEIRUT TIMES	15,000
OTHER	
CALIFORNIA-STAATS ZEITUNG (GERMAN)	19,195
ASBAREZ DAILY (ARMENIAN)	12,000
UNION JACK (BRITISH)	10,000
MAGYAROK VASARNAPJA (HUNGARIAN)	8,000
BIEN (DANISH)	5,400
CALIFORNIA VECKOBLAD (SWEDISH)	5,000
IRISH NEWS & ENTERTAINMENT	3,000

LOS ANGELES

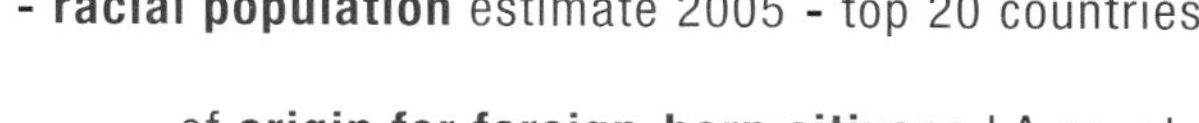

- **racial population** estimate 2005 - top 20 countries of **origin for foreign-born citizens** LA county - top **us-ethnic newspapers published** estimated circulation 2001 - port of LA: **imports + exports** - top 20 fortune 500 **companies based in LA county**

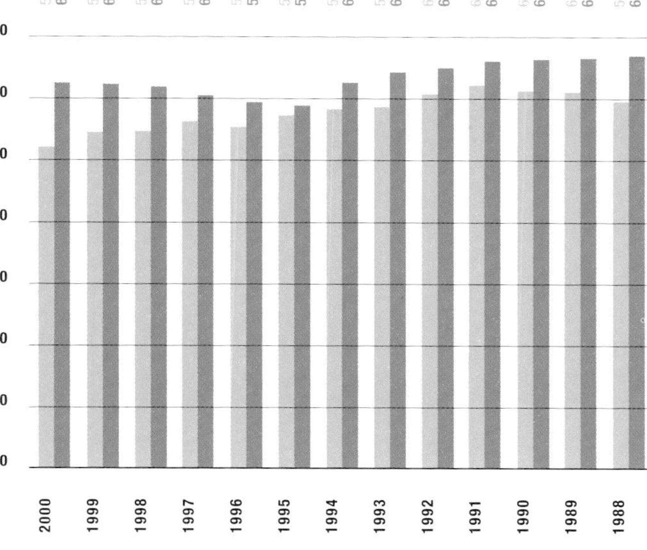

4. LOS ANGELES **PORT:** **EXPORTS + IMPORTS**

% OF ALL EXPORTS IN CA

% OF ALL IMPORTS IN CA

5. LOS ANGELES: **TOP 20** FORTUNE 500 **L.A. COUNTY-BASED COMPANIES**

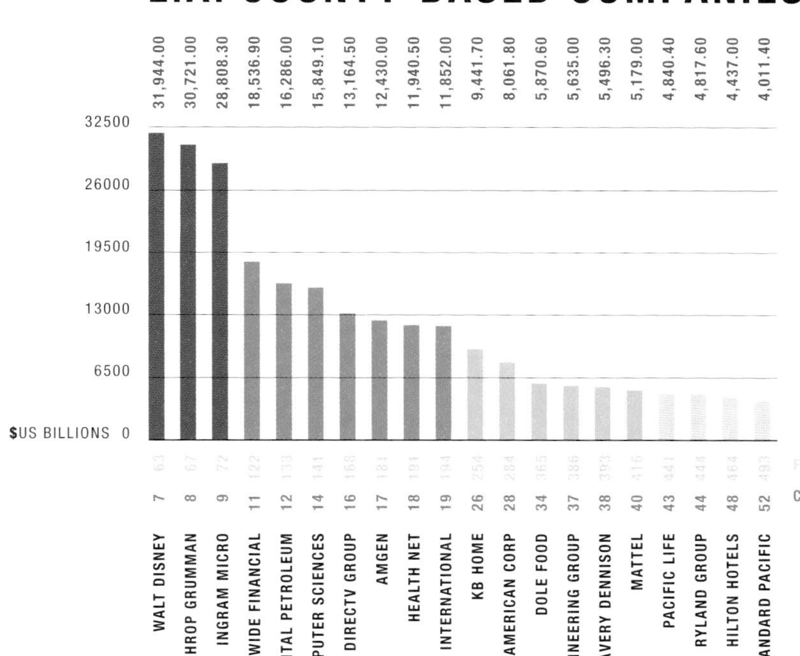

1. LONDON: POPULATION BY ETHNIC GROUP APRIL 2001

WHITE: BRITISH	59.8%
WHITE: IRISH	3.1%
WHITE: OTHER	8.3%
MIXED: WHITE + BLACK CARIBBEAN	1.0%
MIXED: WHITE + BLACK AFRICAN	0.5%
MIXED: WHITE + ASIAN	0.8%
MIXED: OTHER	[illegible]%
ASIAN OR ASIAN BRITISH: INDIAN	6.1%
ASIAN OR ASIAN BRITISH: PAKISTANI	2.0%
ASIAN OR ASIAN BRITISH: BANGLADESHI	2.2%
ASIAN OR ASIAN BRITISH: OTHER	[illegible]%
BLACK + BLACK BRITISH: CARIBBEAN	4.8%
BLACK + BLACK BRITISH: AFRICAN	5.3%
BLACK + BLACK BRITISH: OTHER	0.8%
CHINESE	1.1%
OTHER MINORITY ETHNIC GROUP	1.6%

2. LONDON: RELIGOUS DIVERSITY

CHRISTIAN	58%
BUDDHIST	1%
HINDU	4%
JEWISH	2%
MUSLIM	8%
SIKH	1%
ATHEIST	16%
OTHER	1%
NON RESPONSIVE	9%

4. LONDON: TOP CITY-BASED GLOBAL TNCs

SALES + PROFITS + ASSETS + MARKET VALU
IN US$ BILLIONS

$US BILLIONS 0 50 100 150 200 250 300 350 400 450 500 550

	FORBES RANK	Sales	Profits	Assets	Market value
HSBC GROUP	5	76.38	12.36	1,274.22	193.32
BP	8	249.47	22.63	206.91	225.93
BARCLAYS	20	47.87	5.92	1,587.06	75.99
LLOYDS TSB GROUP	47	52.38	4.28	532.22	54.33
AVIVA	78	75.61	2.03	431.29	33.10
ANGLO AMERICAN	116	27.89	3.34	51.55	55.67
BT GROUP	136	35.20	3.44	50.95	30.16
PRUDENTIAL	166	49.15	0.82	333.06	25.36
ASTRAZENECA	167	22.69	4.46	23.72	72.74
BRITISH AMER TOBACCO	174	20.66	2.11	33.83	49.89

3. LONDON:

MOST DIVERSE BOROUGHS

BASED ON 2001 CENSUS OF THE 32 BOROUGHS, 13 HAD OVER 30% NON-WHITE POPULATION

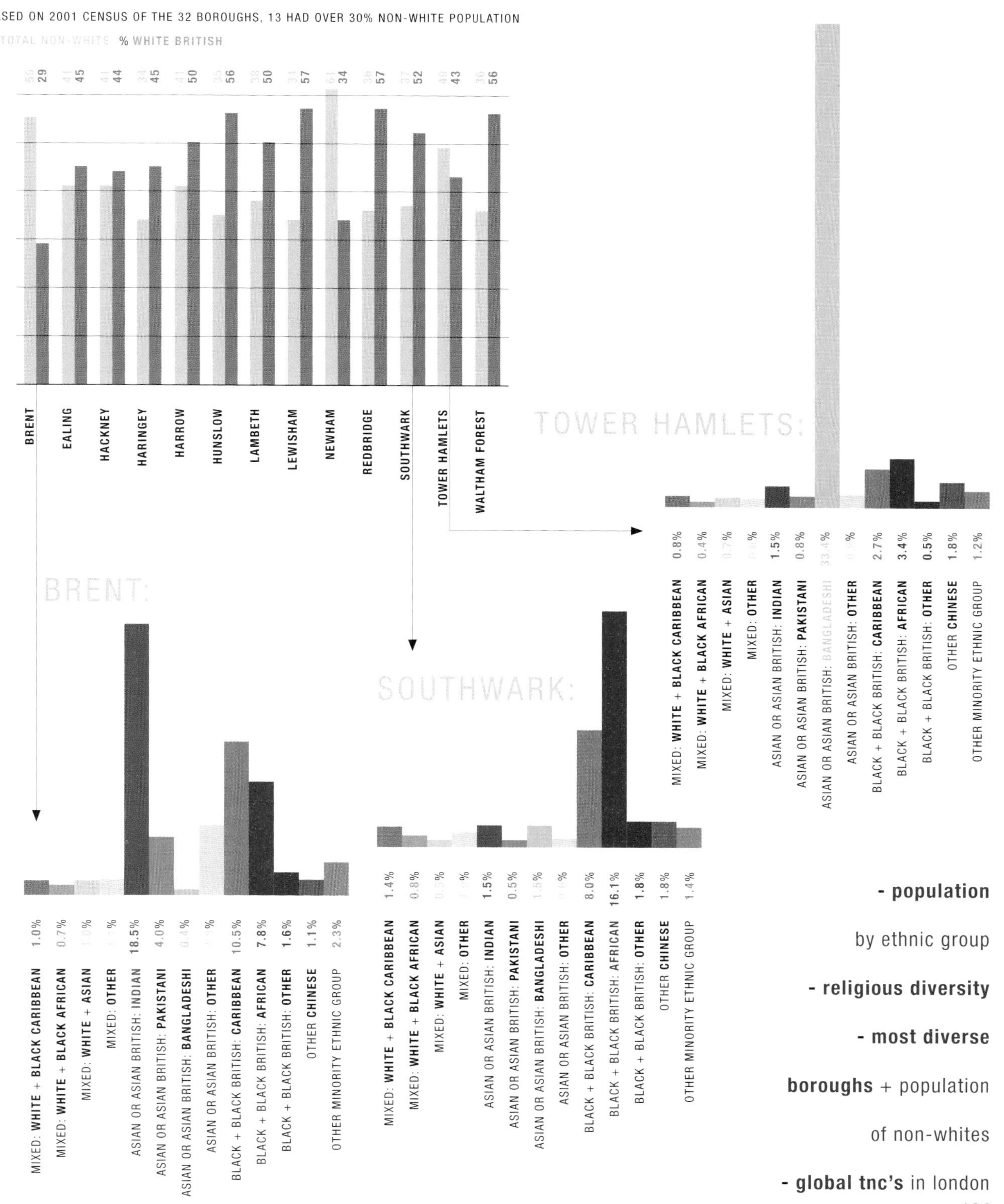

- population by ethnic group

- religious diversity

- most diverse boroughs + population of non-whites

- global tnc's in london

1. RELIGIOUS PILGRIMAGES

ESTIMATED # OF VISITORS OR PILGRIMS

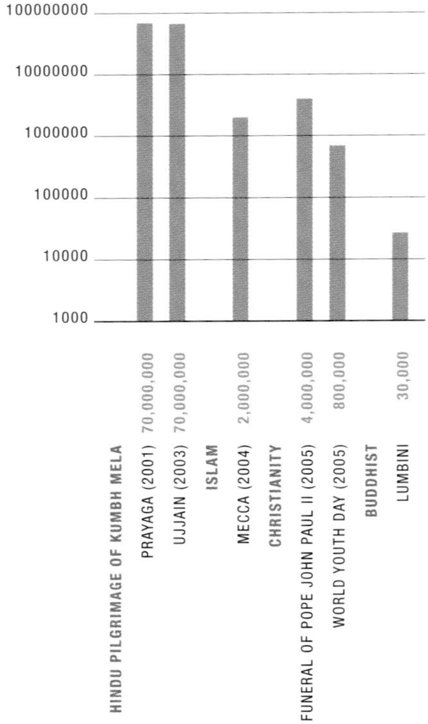

100000000
10000000
1000000
100000
10000
1000

HINDU PILGRIMAGE OF KUMBH MELA	
PRAYAGA (2001)	70,000,000
UJJAIN (2003)	70,000,000
ISLAM	
MECCA (2004)	2,000,000
CHRISTIANITY	
FUNERAL OF POPE JOHN PAUL II (2005)	4,000,000
WORLD YOUTH DAY (2005)	800,000
BUDDHIST	
LUMBINI	30,000

2. POPULAR INTERNATIONAL MUSIC FESTIVAL VENUES

ESTIMATED # PARTICIPANTS ESTIMATED # PERFORMERS/DJS

FESTIVAL IN THE DESERT (MALI) IS WELL-KNOWN, HOWEVER, BECAUSE OF ITS REMOTENESS, NOT AS WIDELY ATTENDED

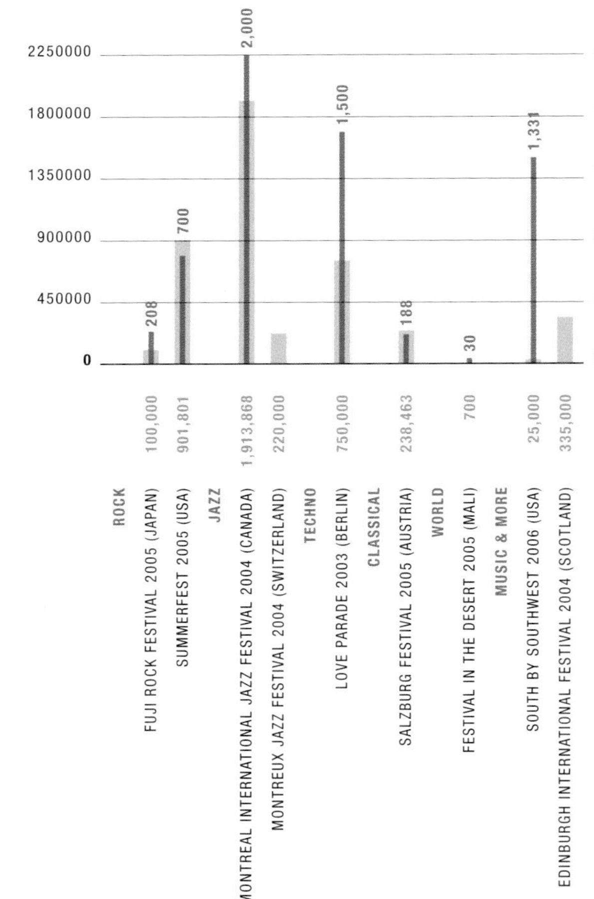

6. WORLD FAIRS

VISITORS IN MILLIONS

PARTICIPATING COUNTRIES

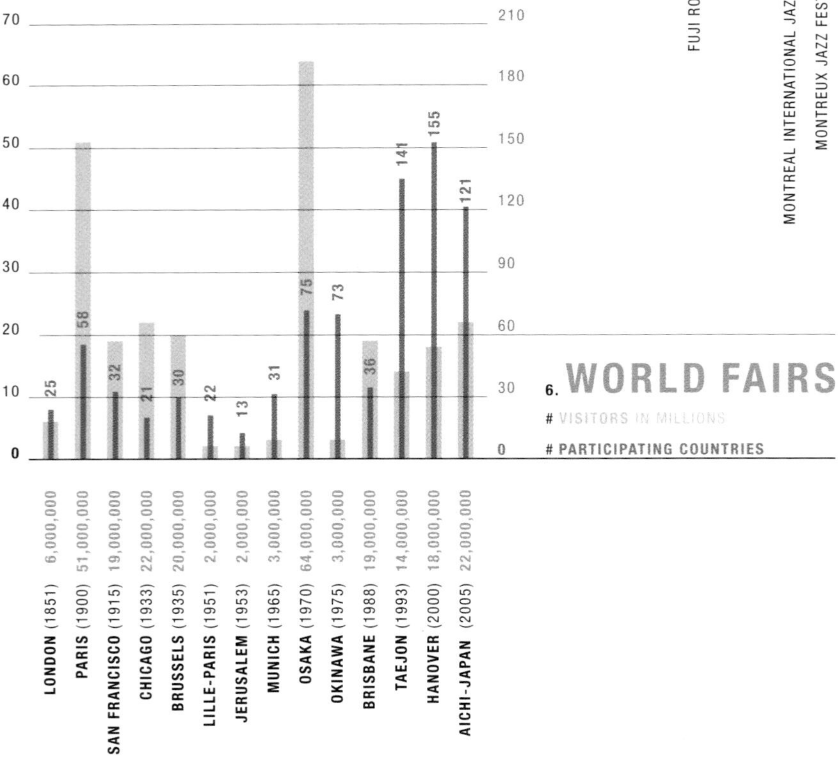

70 210
60 180
50 150
40 120
30 90
20 60
10 30
0 0

	# Visitors	# Participating countries
LONDON (1851)	6,000,000	25
PARIS (1900)	51,000,000	58
SAN FRANCISCO (1915)	19,000,000	32
CHICAGO (1933)	22,000,000	21
BRUSSELS (1935)	20,000,000	30
LILLE-PARIS (1951)	2,000,000	22
JERUSALEM (1953)	2,000,000	13
MUNICH (1965)	3,000,000	31
OSAKA (1970)	64,000,000	75
OKINAWA (1975)	3,000,000	73
BRISBANE (1988)	19,000,000	36
TAEJON (1993)	14,000,000	141
HANOVER (2000)	18,000,000	155
AICHI-JAPAN (2005)	22,000,000	121

- religious pilgrimages
- music festival venues
- film festivals
- book fairs
- documenta exhibit
- world fairs
- burning man

GLOBAL EVENTS

3. INTERNATIONAL FILM FESTIVALS

PARTICIPATION BY ATTENDANCE

OF INTERNATIONAL FILMS SHOWCASED

VENICE FILM FESTIVAL ATTENDANCE FIGURE IS # OF PARTICIPANTS TO ALL EVENTS AT THE VENICE BIENNALE (ART, THEATRE, DANCE, MUSIC, AND FILM

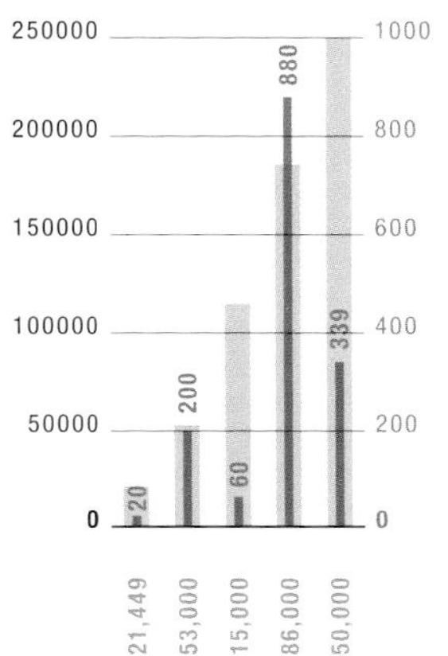

4. NOTABLE INTERNATIONAL BOOK FAIRS

ATTENDEES # OF EXHIBITORS/SELLERS

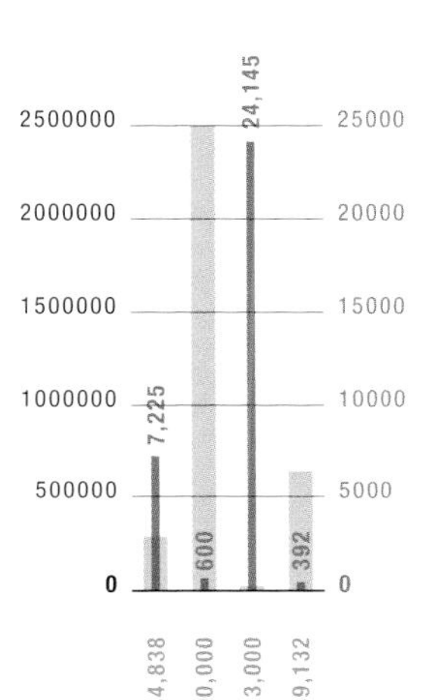

5. DOCUMENTA EXHIBIT 1955-1997

VISITORS # ARTISTS

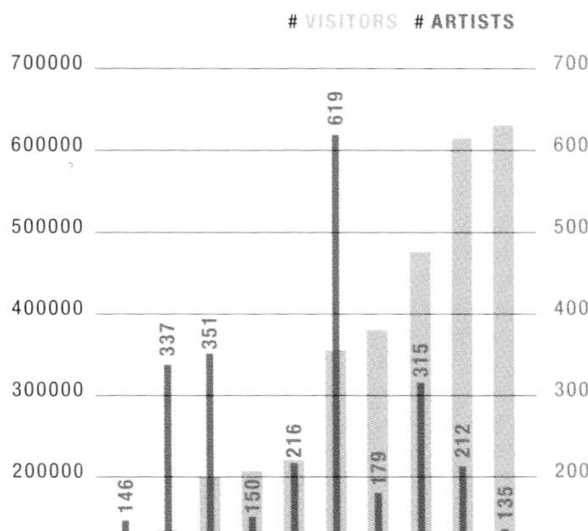

7. BURNING MAN

ALTERNATIVE, INTERACTIVE, + INTERNATIONALLY REKNOWNED ART FESTIVAL

IGHT OF BURNING MAN IN FEET # OF ART INSTALLATIONS # OF THEME CAMPS

OF PARTICIPANTS # OF VOLUNTEERS

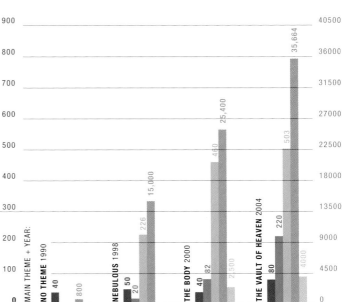

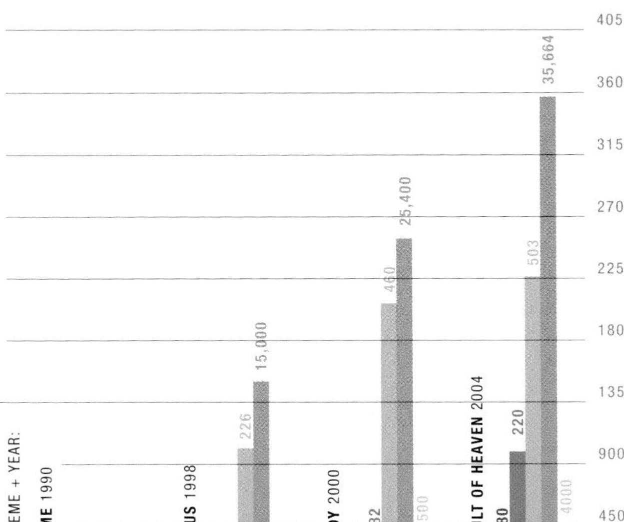

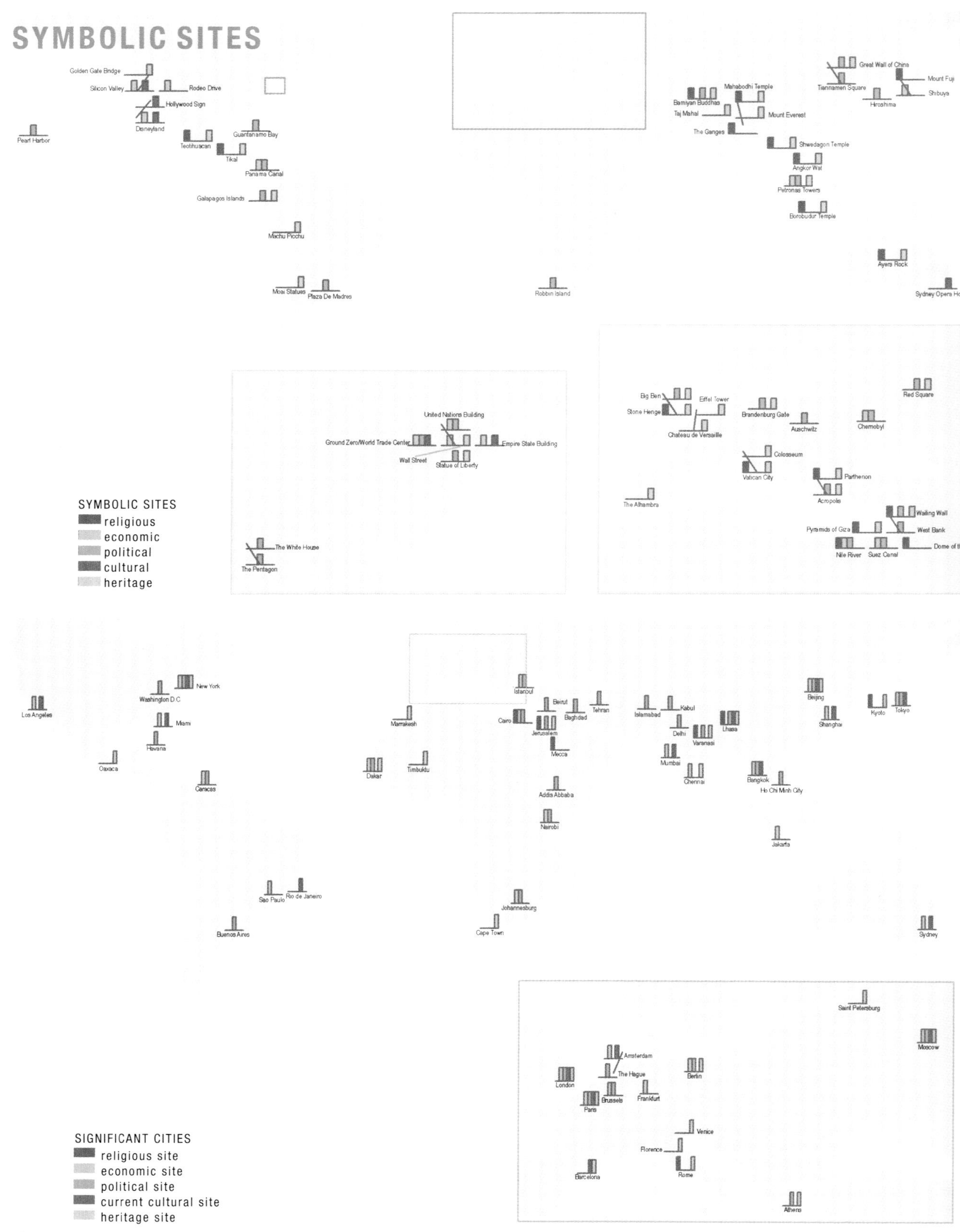
SYMBOLIC SITES
Golden Gate Bridge
Silicon Valley
Rodeo Drive
Hollywood Sign
Disneyland
Pearl Harbor
Teotihuacan
Guantanamo Bay
Tikal
Panama Canal
Galapagos Islands
Machu Picchu
Moai Statues
Plaza De Madres
Robbin Island
Great Wall of China
Mount Fuji
Tiannamen Square
Shibuya
Hiroshima
Mahabodhi Temple
Bamiyan Buddhas
Taj Mahal
Mount Everest
The Ganges
Shwedagon Temple
Angkor Wat
Petronas Towers
Borobudur Temple
Ayers Rock
Sydney Opera Hou
United Nations Building
Ground Zero/World Trade Center
Empire State Building
Wall Street
Statue of Liberty
The White House
The Pentagon
Big Ben
Stone Henge
Eiffel Tower
Chateau de Versaille
Brandenburg Gate
Auschwitz
Chernobyl
Red Square
Colosseum
Vatican City
Parthenon
Acropolis
The Alhambra
Wailing Wall
Pyramids of Giza
West Bank
Dome of the
Nile River
Suez Canal
SYMBOLIC SITES
religious
economic
political
cultural
heritage
Los Angeles
Washington D.C
New York
Miami
Havana
Oaxaca
Caracas
Marrakesh
Dakar
Timbuktu
Istanbul
Beirut
Cairo
Jerusalem
Baghdad
Tehran
Mecca
Addis Abbaba
Nairobi
Islamabad
Kabul
Delhi
Varanasi
Lhasa
Mumbai
Chennai
Bangkok
Ho Chi Minh City
Jakarta
Beijing
Shanghai
Kyoto
Tokyo
Sao Paulo
Rio de Janeiro
Buenos Aires
Johannesburg
Cape Town
Sydney
Saint Petersburg
Moscow
Amsterdam
The Hague
London
Berlin
Paris
Brussels
Frankfurt
Venice
Florence
Rome
Barcelona
Athens
SIGNIFICANT CITIES
religious site
economic site
political site
current cultural site
heritage site

GLOBAL CITIES Every period of modern human history has featured cities as centers of information, communication, economic activities and trade as well as loci of political power and cultural influence. The distinct urban cultures of cities like New York, London, Paris, Berlin, Hong Kong, Tokyo, Shanghai, Buenos Aires, Cairo or Mumbai have long exerted transnational influence, as centers of cultural creativity and innovation.

WHAT DO WE KNOW ABOUT GLOBAL CITIES?

What sets the current period apart from the 19th century, when many of today's global cities became more transnational, is the change in global connectedness. Innovations in technology make it possible for connections to happen at greater speed, with greater volume and frequency, resulting in complex flows of goods, services, capital, people, and information; it also creates greater connectivity among 'bads' such as diseases in the case of epidemics, and crime, for example, drug trafficking, smuggling, and white collar crime.

According to the National Research Council (2003: 82-3), the world's urban population will grow from 2.9 billion in 2000 to nearly 5 billion by 2030. High-income countries will account for only 28 million out of the expected 2.12 billion increase. On average urban areas are growing by about 1 million people a week, and much of this takes place in cities with over 1 million people. In 1950, five of the twenty urban agglomerations were in developing countries; by 2000, 13 were, and projections for 2015 are that all but five cities on the top twenty will be. Tokyo, New York-Newark, Buenos Aires, Los Angeles, and Osaka-Kobe, will be the only top 20 cities outside the developing world (Figure 1). Clearly, such high growth rates in cities like Mumbai or Lagos imply serious challenges in terms of housing, physical infrastructure and the environment, health care, social services, education, etc.

However, it is not the scale of urban agglomerations themselves that matters for global city status. New York was the world's largest city in 1950, with 12.3 million people, followed by Tokyo with 11.1, then London (8.3) and Paris (5.4). Fifty-five years later, all top 20 urban agglomerations have more then 10 million people, and London and Paris are no longer part of the list (Figure 1). Yet cities like London, perhaps the most global of world cities, or Paris, occupy a central role in economic, political and cultural terms. Indeed, it is the multi-functionality of cities as global centers of trade, commerce, politics, and culture that sets them apart from other mega agglomerations (see Scott, 2001).

UN-Habitat (2004: 22) identified major changes in the spatial structure of cities as a result of globalization. These patterns are clearly visible in global cities such as New York, London, Los Angeles, Hong Kong and, to a lesser extent, Mumbai.

- First, driven by economic opportunities and considerations, cities are shifting their attention away from their geographic hinterlands towards external locations. Many decisions affecting the economy and well-being are made outside city or national boundaries. Global cities are therefore outward looking for the sake of maintaining global competitiveness;
- Second, global production patterns are changing from vertical integration of producers, suppliers, finance and distribution within one location to horizontal integration across noncontiguous sites, often involving activities between different countries or continents, operating on '24-7' schedules;
- Third, business locations are less based on access to local markets and consumers than on their centrality in terms of global connectivity, which implies a splintering of economic activities in which physical proximity is not a major consideration.

These changes imply many challenges to global cities: additional functions have had to be found for central business districts, and adjacent areas, many with substandard housing stocks. Cities like Paris (the Centre Pompidou and La Defense) and London (Covent Garden / Southwark and Docklands) have embarked on projects of grand cultural and economic revitalization. The branding of cities as cultural and economic icons has led to greater awareness of cultural heritage and distinctiveness. Successful urban redevelopment has brought gentrification to desirable central locations, and also has attracted migrants who settled in areas at the urban fringe. In this way, the rising globalization of cities has increased social tensions as populations diversify.

WHAT ARE THE ISSUES?

Globalization intensifies diversity and differentiation among populations, producing polymorphous and variegated urban cultures. Such cultures can enrich and strengthen cities, but they can also exclude and be a source of social and cultural divisions. Some communities based on choice and self-interest do not coincide with neighborhood boundaries, and some neighborhoods fail to function as a community in the traditional sense of belonging.

Managing these issues and the potential conflicts they harbor goes beyond the capacity of conventional urban planning. The pluralistic, diverse, outward looking and competitive global city requires a new multi-cultural literacy (UN-Habitat, 2004: 6), with a greater role allocated to civil society as a participating actor, and information technology as a new way of communicating with diverse constituencies to achieve greater social accountability of urban planning and governance.

FIGURE 1: 2005 GLOBAL CITIES POPULATION IN MILLIONS

TOKYO	35.327
MEXICO CITY	19.013
NEW YORK / NEWARK	18.498
MUMBAI	18.336
SAO PAULO	18.333
DELHI	15.334
CALCUTTA	14.299
BUENOS AIRES	13.349
JAKARTA	13.194
SHANGHAI	12.665
DHAKA	12.560
LOS ANGELES / LONG BEACH / SANTA ANA	12.146
KARACHI	11.819
RIO DE JANEIRO	11.469
OSAKA-KOBE	11.286
CAIRO	11.146
LAGOS	11.135
BEIJING	10.849
METRO MANILA	10.677
MOSCOW	10.672

RANK AGGLOMERATION + COUNTRY	2015 POPULATIONS IN MILLIONS
01 TOKYO	36.214
02 MUMBAI	22.645
03 DELHI	20.946
04 MEXICO CITY	20.647
05 SAO PAOLO	19.963
06 NEW YORK / NEWARK	19.717
07 DHAKA	17.907
08 JAKARTA	17.498
09 LAGOS	17.036
10 CALCUTTA	16.798
11 KARACHI	16.155
12 BUENOS AIRES	14.563
13 CAIRO	13.123
14 LOS ANGELES / LONG BEACH / SANTA ANA	12.904
15 SHANGHAI	12.666
16 METRO MANILA	12.637
17 RIO DE JANEIRO	12.364
18 OSAKA /KOBE	11.359
19 ISTANBUL	11.302
20 BEIJING	11.060

GLOBAL EVENTS, SYMBOLIC SITES AND SIGNIFICANT CITIES The growth and spread of festivals and other symbolic events over recent years mirrors trends of globalization, and the simultaneous homogenization and localization of cultures and forms of creativity. They are outlets for expression of the values of a particular society or societies. The cultural significance of celebrations, festivals, and sites lies in their ability to promote unity, share knowledge, to confirm values and beliefs, evoke emotional response, reinforce identity, and to serve as conduits for cross-cultural exchange. Symbolic places are often sites for religious, economic, political, cultural, or heritage-based events.

WHAT DO WE KNOW ABOUT GLOBAL EVENTS, SYMBOLIC SITES + SIGNIFICANT CITIES?
According to the International Festival and Events Association, the special events industry includes approximately 1 million regularly reoccurring events around the world. Global and local festivals and events attract tourists and media, sometimes branding a city or place with a certain identity and often having a significant impact on the local economy. Many global festivals and cultural events around the world surround music, art, cinema and other media, or religion and place specific themes and histories. Four million people were estimated to have made a pilgrimage to witness the funeral of Pope John Paul II in 2005 and 70 million Hindus participated in the Kumbh Mela religious festivals in the holy cities of Prayaga and Ujjain (Wikipedia, 2006 and CNN, 2005)

Symbolic cities and sites around the world are notable because of their religious, economic, political, historical, and/or cultural significance. Most world cities have significance across all of these categories. In the Middle East and Europe many sites and cities are significant for their religious symbolism, such as Lumbini (the birthplace of Gautama Buddha, the founder of Buddhism), Nazareth (the birthplace of Jesus), or Lourdes (the site in France where, in 1958, the Virgin Mary allegedly appeared to a young a girl). Religious pilgrimages are performed within and from/to these key religious sites. The annual Haj to the Muslim holy city of Mecca is among the most prominent religious pilgrimages worldwide.

World Fairs represent another significant global event. While the main goal of the World Fair has been entertainment and representation, since its inception in 1851, the Fair has represented notions of global connectedness, cohesion, and interchange of ideas and innovation. The numbers of visitors at World Fairs have fluctuated greatly, while numbers of participating countries have risen steadily. The most recent world fair in Aichi, Japan drew over 20 million visitors and 121 countries participated (BIE).

World festivals include more traditional and long-standing events along with newer more alternative celebrations that embrace fringe, non-mainstream forms of expression. Both types of festivals are growing in number; the alternative Burning Man Festival for art, for example, which began in 1986 with 20 people, now attracts over 35,000 participants. Numbers of visitors at Documenta, the world's largest show of contemporary art in Kassel, Germany have risen significantly since its inception in the 1950s; almost five times as many people attended the exhibit in 1997 as did in 1955 (Documenta 12). The Venice Biennale, which began in 1893, includes exhibitions of international art, architecture, music, theater, and dance, and now draws 320,000 visitors each year. The Edinburgh Festival Fringe, started in 1947, showcases theater, comedy, music, dance, exhibitions and other events and attracted 1.35 million people from around the world in 2005.

The main international film festivals are all located in North America or Europe, with the oldest and most prestigious festivals in Europe. North America boasts both the largest film festival (Toronto International Film Festival) and the largest independent film festival (Sundance) in the world. Around 4.5 million people attended eight of the most popular international music festivals throughout 2003 to the beginning of 2006 (see suite graphics). World book fairs tend to occur in key global cities, while music and film festivals may be held in more obscure locations, such as the Sundance Film festival in Park City, Utah or the Montreux Jazz Festival in Montreux, Switzerland, at the foot of the Alps in the "Swiss Riviera."

WHAT ARE THE ISSUES?
Large-scale international exhibitions, events, and festivals face the task of organizing and making coherent the great diversity of styles, conceptions, and approaches that exist around the world (Weinberg and Pratt Brown, 2006). Who decides what is worthy of display and celebration in these international festivals is a contentious issue. The Documenta exhibit at the end of the 20th century, for example, was criticized because it excluded work from artists outside of Europe and the Americas.

The question of who can attend and participate in global events highlights the fact that many global festivals and events reinforce art and creativity as the realm of a wealthy elite, while other, usually more local events, provide opportunities for all people in a society to participate in expression and celebration. Thus, global events and festivals highlight issues surrounding cultural diversity. In 2001, UNESCO adopted the Universal Declaration on Cultural Diversity in order to support the "fruitful diversity of... cultures... taking into account the risks of identity-based isolationism and standardization associated with globalization" (UNESCO, 2002). The Convention of the Protection and Promotion of the Diversity of Cultural Expressions adopted subsequently (2005) crystallizes these fears and aspirations.

Some charge that globalization has caused a westernization of world cultures, and a decline of local ceremonies, customs, festivals, and other symbolic traditions. Whether this trend is due simply to forces of modernization or to globalization has yet to be determined. The domination of many large-scale events and festivals by certain western influences may point to commodification and commercialization trends. At the same time that these trends of homogenization are occurring, local and regional cultural realities are being reaffirmed and given global visibility through festivals and like events.

COMMUNICATION + MEDIA

HUMAN LANGUAGES

PRINT MEDIA

BOOKS

MUSIC

TELEPHONES

INTERNET

BLOGS

MOVIES

TV + RADIO

TV + ONLINE NEWS

HUMAN LANGUAGES

top languages - book translations - language of web users - linguistic diversity - illiteracy

1a. TOP 10 LANGUAGES

LEADERS INTERNATIONAL ORGANIZATIONS

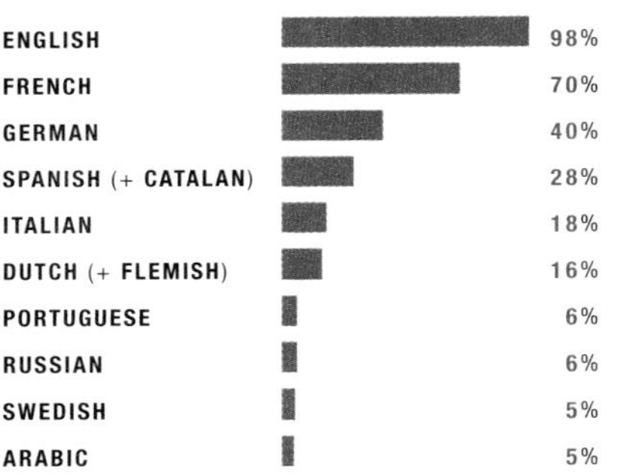

1b. WORLD LANGUAGES

SPEAKERS AS FIRST LANGUAGE

EUROPEAN | MIDDLE EASTERN | ASIAN/PACIFIC

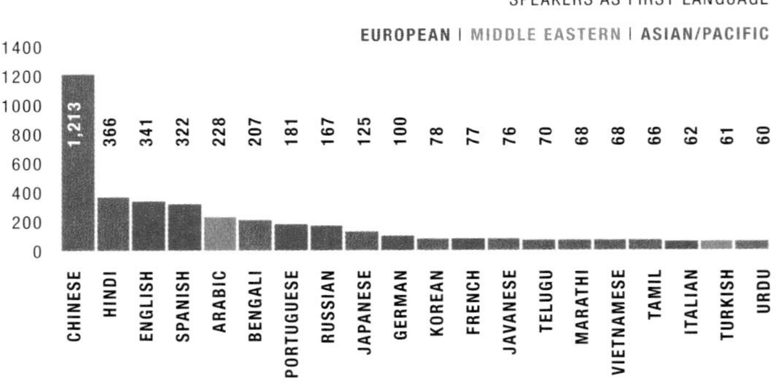

2. BOOK TRANSLATIONS

HIERARCHICAL NETWORK OF BOOK TRANSLATIONS BETWEEN LANGUAGES

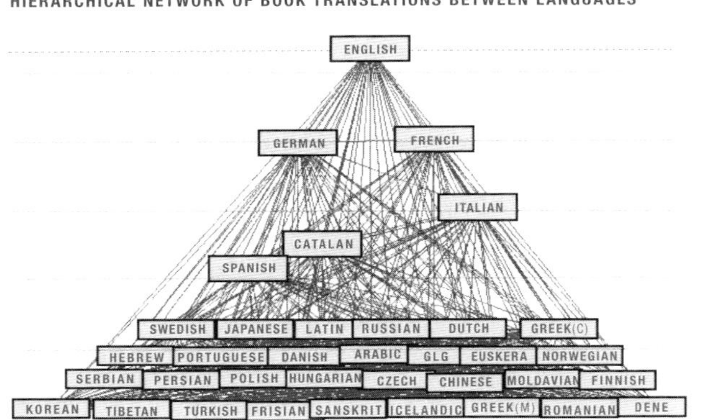

3. LANGUAGES OF THE WEB

	% OF TOTAL USERS	PENETRATION
ENGLISH	35%	26%
CHINESE	13%	8%
JAPANESE	8%	52%
SPANISH	7%	15%
GERMAN	7%	57%
FRENCH	5%	10%
KOREAN	4%	41%
ITALIAN	4%	49%
PORTUGUESE	3%	10%
DUTCH	2%	57%

4. LINGUISTIC DIVERSITY

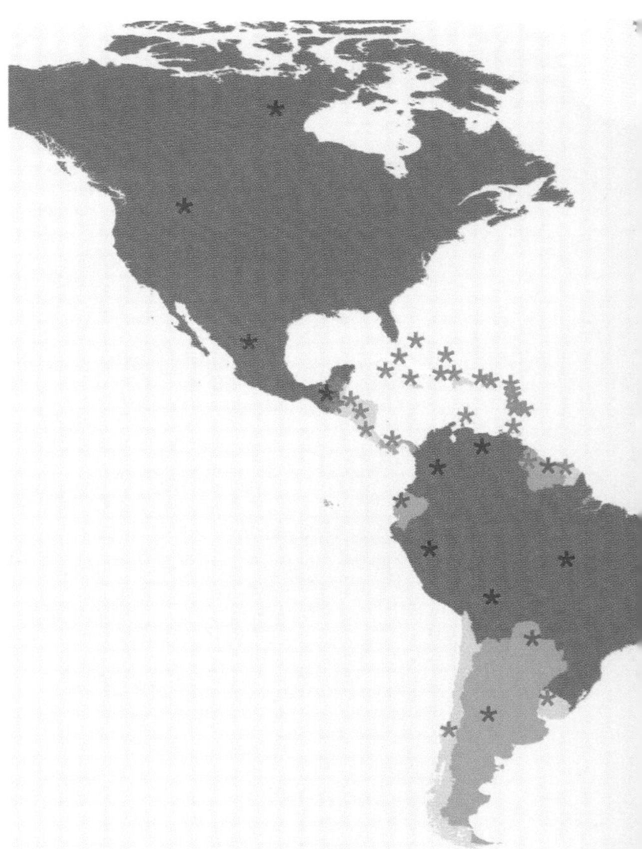

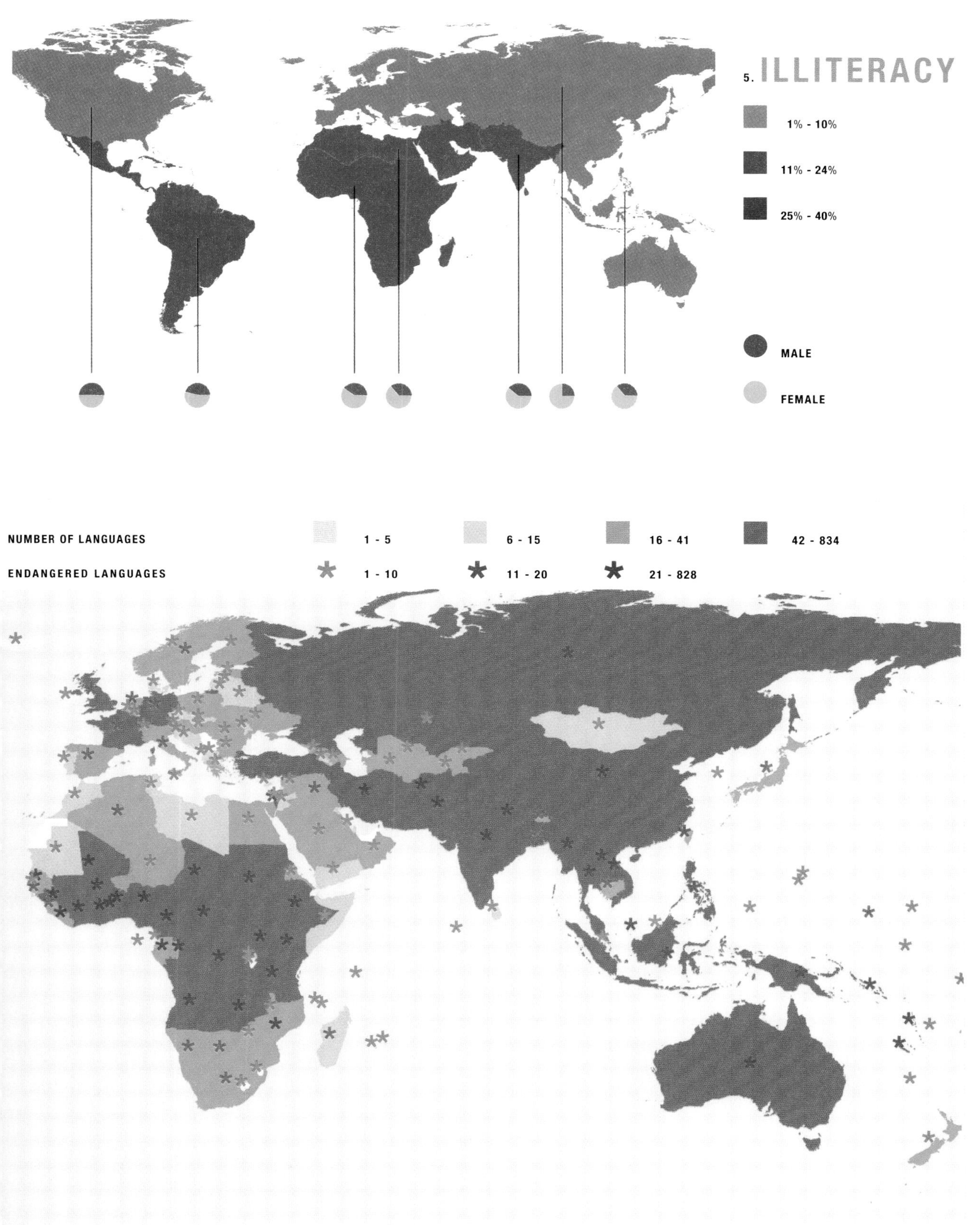
5. ILLITERACY
1% - 10%
11% - 24%
25% - 40%
MALE
FEMALE
NUMBER OF LANGUAGES
1 - 5
6 - 15
16 - 41
42 - 834
ENDANGERED LANGUAGES
1 - 10
11 - 20
21 - 828

PRINT MEDIA

- **top newspapers**
- **top publications by circulation**

+ international herald tribune

+ the economist

- **IHT readership**

1. WORLD'S TOP NEWSPAPERS

BY CIRCULATION (000's) 2005

01.	YOMIURI SHIMBUN JAPAN	14,067
02.	THE ASAHI SHIMBUN JAPAN	12,121
03.	MAINICHI SHIMBUN JAPAN	5,587
04.	NIHON KEIZAI SHIMBUN JAPAN	4,635
05.	CHUNICHI SHIMBUN JAPAN	4,512
06.	BILD GERMANY	3,867
07.	SANKEI SHIMBUN JAPAN	2,757
08.	CANOKO XIAOXI (BEIJING) CHINA	2,627
09.	PEOPLE'S DAILY CHINA	2,509
10.	TOKYO SPORTS JAPAN	2,425
11.	THE SUN UNITED KINGDOM	2,419
12.	THE CHOSUN ILBO SOUTH KOREA	2,378
13.	USA TODAY USA	2,310
14.	THE WALL STREET JOURNAL USA	2,107
15.	DAILY MAIL UNITED KINGDOM	2,093
16.	THE JOONGANG ILBO SOUTH KOREA	2,084
17.	THE DONG-A ILBO SOUTH KOREA	2,052
18.	NIKKAN SPORTS JAPAN	1,965
19.	HOKKAIDO SHIMBUN JAPAN	1,922
20.	DAINIK JAGRAN INDIA	1,911
21.	YANGTSE EVENING POST CHINA	1,715
22.	SPORTS NIPPON JAPAN	1,711
23.	THE NIKKAN GENDAI JAPAN	1,686
24.	TIMES OF INDIA INDIA	1,680
25.	GUANGZHOU DAILY CHINA	1,650
26.	THE MIRROR UNITED KINGDOM	1,597
27.	YUKAN FUJI JAPAN	1,559
28.	SHIZUOKA SHIMBUN JAPAN	1,479
29.	NANFANG CITY NEWS CHINA	1,410
30.	DAINIK BHASKAR INDIA	1,405
31.	SANKEI SPORTS JAPAN	1,368
32.	HOCHI SHIMBUN JAPAN	1,354
33.	YANGCHENG EVENING NEWS CHINA	1,320
34.	MALAYALA MANORAMA INDIA	1,309
35.	LIBERTY TIMES TAIWAN	1,300
36.	THAI RATH THAILAND	1,200
37.	NEW YORK TIMES USA	1,121
38.	HINDUSTAN TIMES INDIA	1,108
39.	CHUTIAN METRO DAILY CHINA	1,084
40.	GUJURAT SAMACHAR INDIA	1,051
41.	ANANDA BAZAR PATRIKA INDIA	1,046
42.	XINMIN EVENING NEWS CHINA	1,045
43.	EENADU INDIA	1,039
44.	NISHI-NIPPON SHIMBUN JAPAN	1,025
45.	KRONEN ZEITUNG AUSTRIA	1,009
46.	WAZ MEDIENGRUPPE GERMANY	1,001
47.	UNITED DAILY NEWS TAIWAN	1,000
48.	CHINA TIMES CHINA	1,000
49.	DAILY SPORTS JAPAN	999
50.	THE HINDU INDIA	989

3. BASIC INFORMATION ON IHT READERSHIP

AVERAGE HOUSEHOLD INCOME	US$ 200,993
AVERAGE NET WORTH*	US$ 1,796,440
COLLEGE GRADUATE	94%
SENIOR MANAGEMENT**	90%
INTERNATIONAL BUSINESS TRIPS, PAST YEAR: +1	70%
INTERNATIONAL BUSINESS TRIPS, PAST YEAR: +7	33%
AVERAGE # OF BUSINESS TRIPS, PAST YEAR:	9
INTERNATIONAL BUSINESS HOTEL NIGHTS, PAST YEAR: +1	96%
INTERNATIONAL BUSINESS HOTEL NIGHTS, PAST YEAR: +15	64%

SOURCE: IHT READER SURVEY 2002. BASE: WORLDWIDE READERSHIP

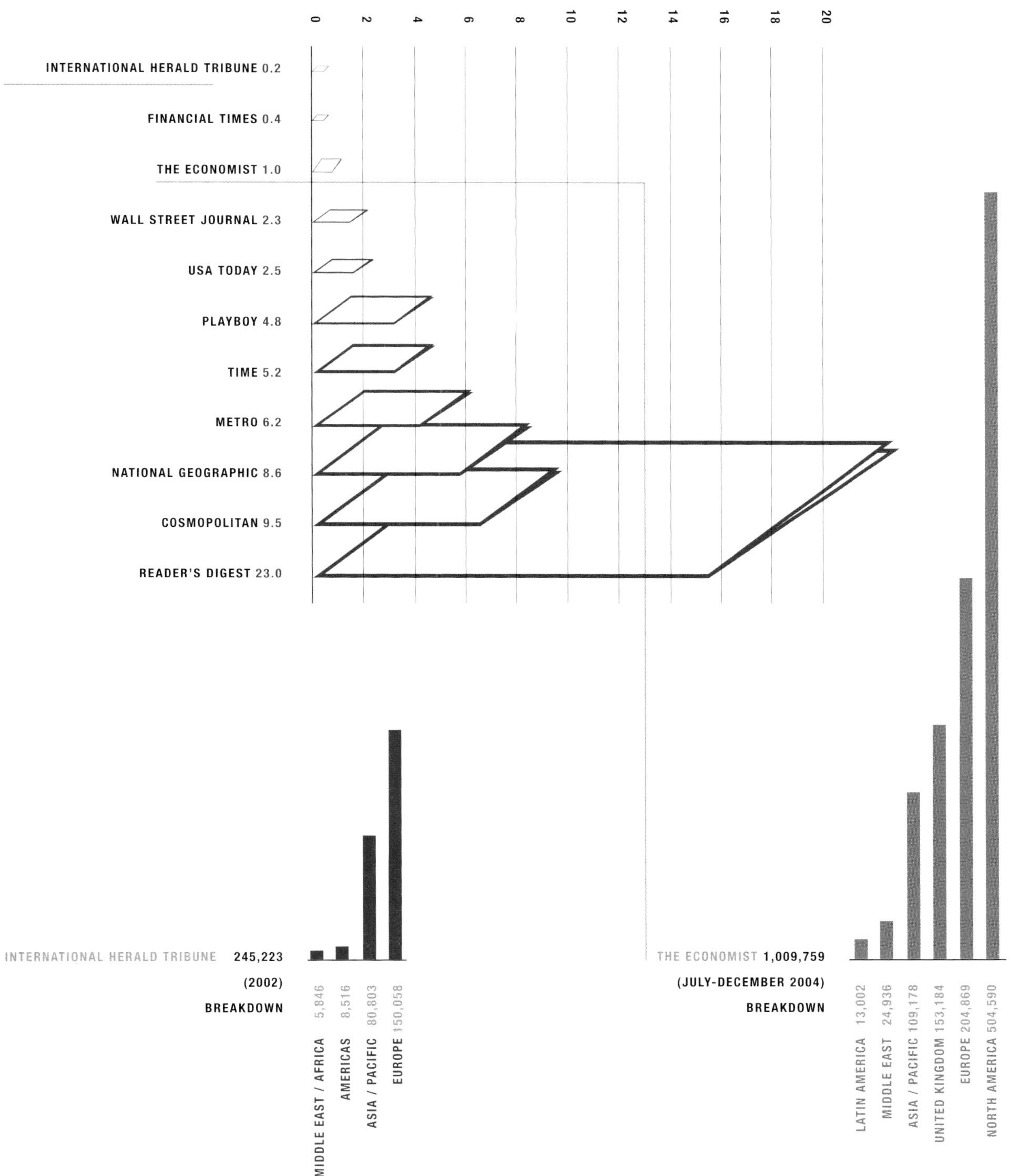
2. TOP 11 PUBLICATIONS BY CIRCULATION
2004 IN MILLIONS
0
2
4
6
8
10
12
14
16
18
20
INTERNATIONAL HERALD TRIBUNE 0.2
FINANCIAL TIMES 0.4
THE ECONOMIST 1.0
WALL STREET JOURNAL 2.3
USA TODAY 2.5
PLAYBOY 4.8
TIME 5.2
METRO 6.2
NATIONAL GEOGRAPHIC 8.6
COSMOPOLITAN 9.5
READER'S DIGEST 23.0
INTERNATIONAL HERALD TRIBUNE 245,223
(2002)
BREAKDOWN
MIDDLE EAST / AFRICA 5,846
AMERICAS 8,516
ASIA / PACIFIC 80,803
EUROPE 150,058
THE ECONOMIST 1,009,759
(JULY-DECEMBER 2004)
BREAKDOWN
LATIN AMERICA 13,002
MIDDLE EAST 24,936
ASIA / PACIFIC 109,178
UNITED KINGDOM 153,184
EUROPE 204,869
NORTH AMERICA 504,590

BOOKS - books published by languages - top book markets - # of publishers - largest publishers - # book imprints

1. BOOKS PUBLISHED BY LANGUAGES:

2a. TOP 10 BOOK MARKETS BY VOLUME

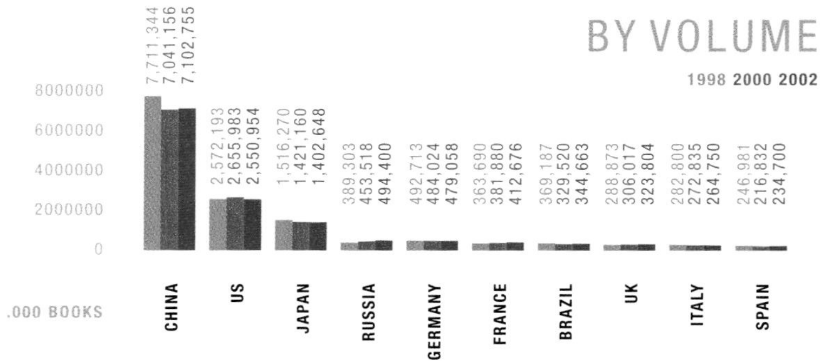

2b. TOP 10 BOOK MARKETS BY VALUE

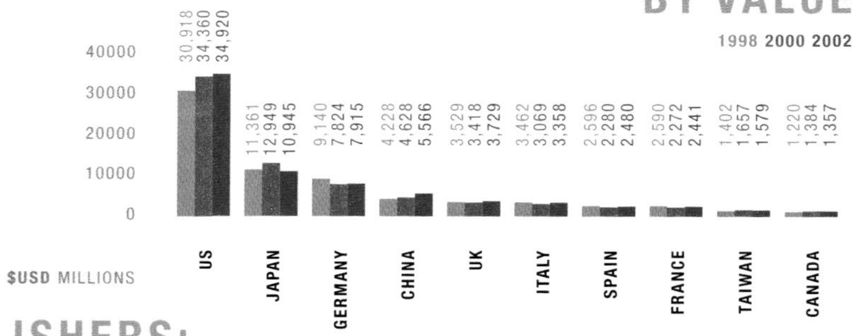

3. ESTIMATED # OF PUBLISHERS:

TOP MARKETS / PER SELECT COUNTRY

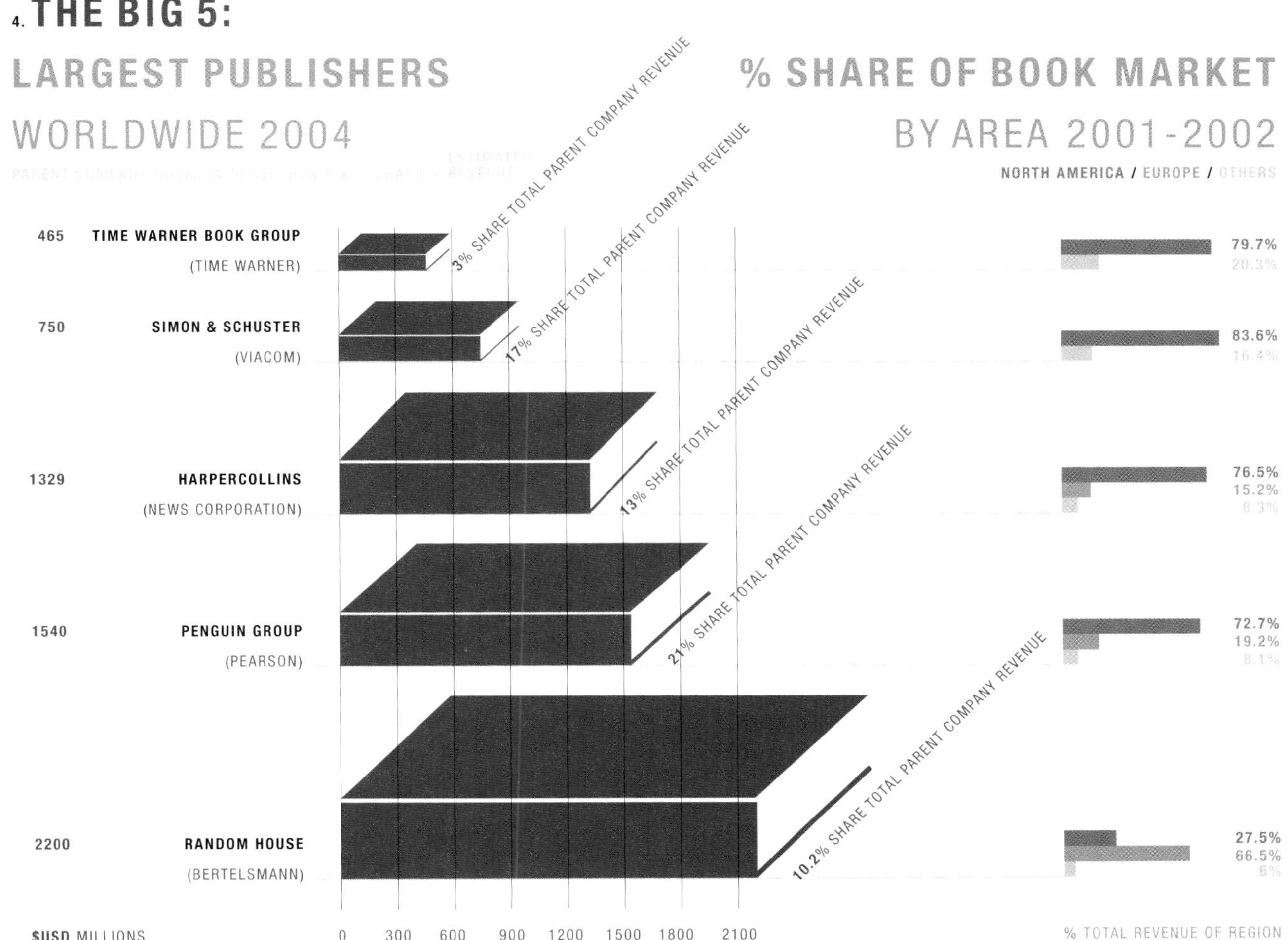

5. # BOOK IMPRINTS

	RANDOM HOUSE	PENGUIN BOOKS	HARPER COLLINS	SIMON & SCHUSTER	TIME WARNER BOOK GROUP
stimated Values	(BERTELSMANN)	(PEARSON)	(NEWS CORPORATION)	(VIACOM)	(TIME WARNER)
# OF IMPRINTS:	250	17	29	20	25
EXAMPLE HOLDINGS:	BANTAM, DELL, DOUBLEDAY, KNOPF, FODORS	PENGUIN, AVERY, DUTTON, PUTNAM, PUFFIN, VIKING, ROUGH GUIDES	HARPERCOLLINS, PERENNIAL, WILLIAM MURROW, AVON	ALL SIMON & SCHUSTER SUBSIDARIES, MTV BOOKS	TIME LIFE BOOKS, LITTLE BROWN, SUNSET
# OF MAIN ARKET COUNTRIES:	10	10	6	3	2
	GERMANY	AUSTRALIA	USA	AUSTRALIA	USA
	USA	CANADA	CANADA	CANADA	UK
	UK	INDIA	UK	UK	
	CANADA	IRELAND	AUSTRALIA		
	CHILE	JAPAN	NEW ZEALAND		
	KOREA	NEW ZEALAND	INDIA		
	INDIA	SINGAPORE			
	AUSTRALIA	AFRICA			
	NEW ZEALAND	UK			
	SOUTH AFRICA	USA			

MUSIC - recorded music retail sales - % change in value of units of recorded music sold - best-selling album - growth - music purchased at us locations - music trends

2. % CHANGE IN VALUE OF UNITS OF RECORDED MUSIC SOLD:

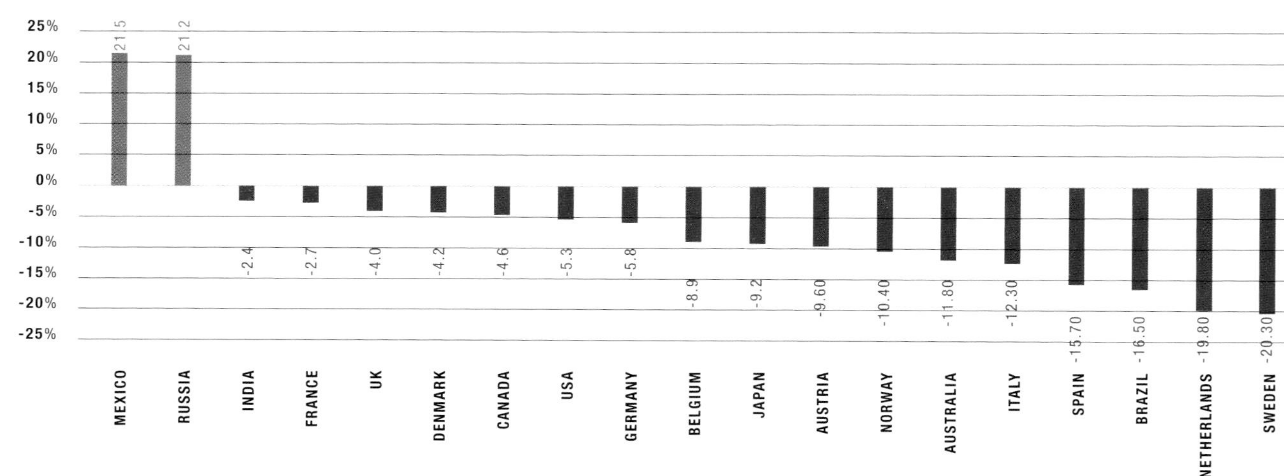

3. MUSICAL ACTS WITH A TOP 3 BEST-SELLING ALBUM IN MORE THAN ONE COUNTRY:

4. GROWTH OF US MUSIC INDUSTR

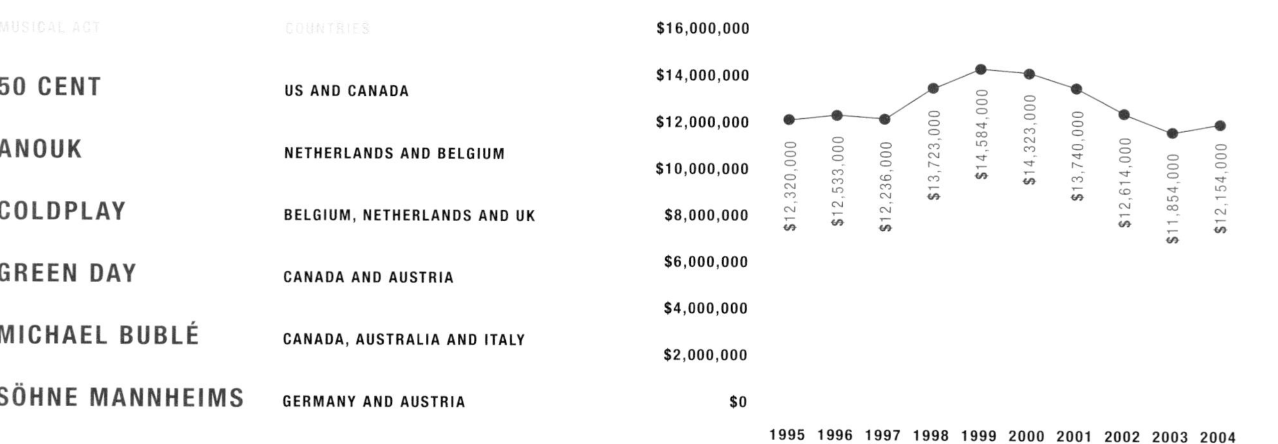

MUSICAL ACT	COUNTRIES
50 CENT	US AND CANADA
ANOUK	NETHERLANDS AND BELGIUM
COLDPLAY	BELGIUM, NETHERLANDS AND UK
GREEN DAY	CANADA AND AUSTRIA
MICHAEL BUBLÉ	CANADA, AUSTRALIA AND ITALY
SÖHNE MANNHEIMS	GERMANY AND AUSTRIA

1. VALUE OF RECORDED MUSIC RETAIL SALES IN US$MILLIONS:

TOP 5:

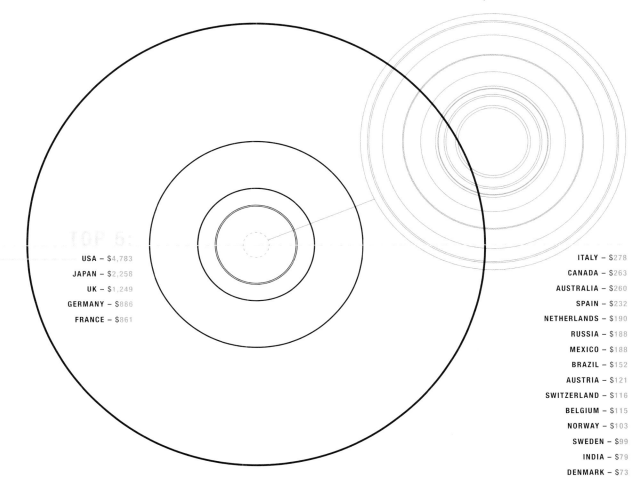

USA – $4,783
JAPAN – $2,258
UK – $1,249
GERMANY – $886
FRANCE – $861

ITALY – $278
CANADA – $263
AUSTRALIA – $260
SPAIN – $232
NETHERLANDS – $190
RUSSIA – $188
MEXICO – $188
BRAZIL – $152
AUSTRIA – $121
SWITZERLAND – $116
BELGIUM – $115
NORWAY – $103
SWEDEN – $99
INDIA – $79
DENMARK – $73

5. % OF MUSIC PURCHASED AT US LOCATIONS:

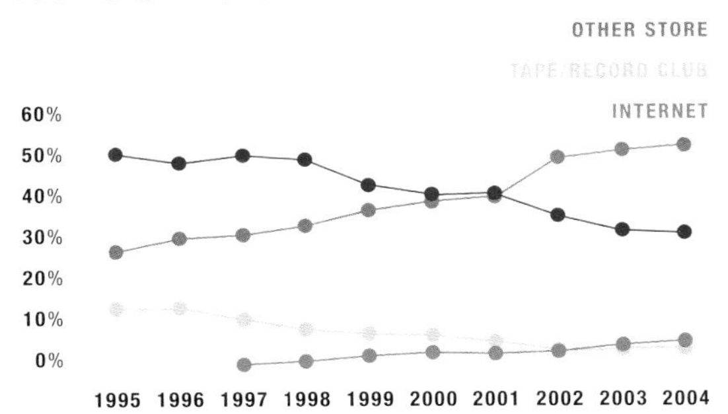

6. % OF TOTAL US SALES BY TYPE OF MUSIC:

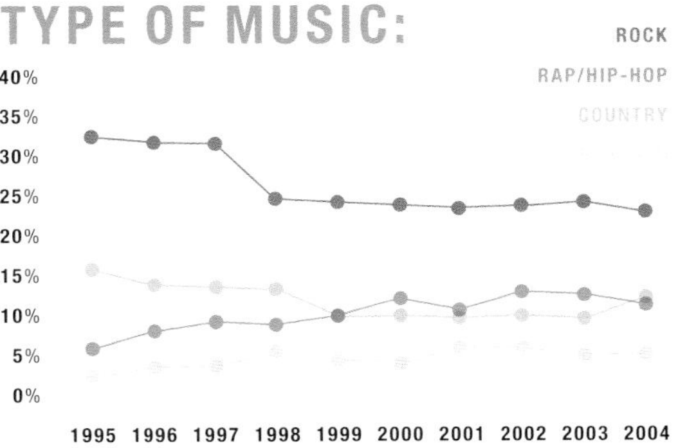

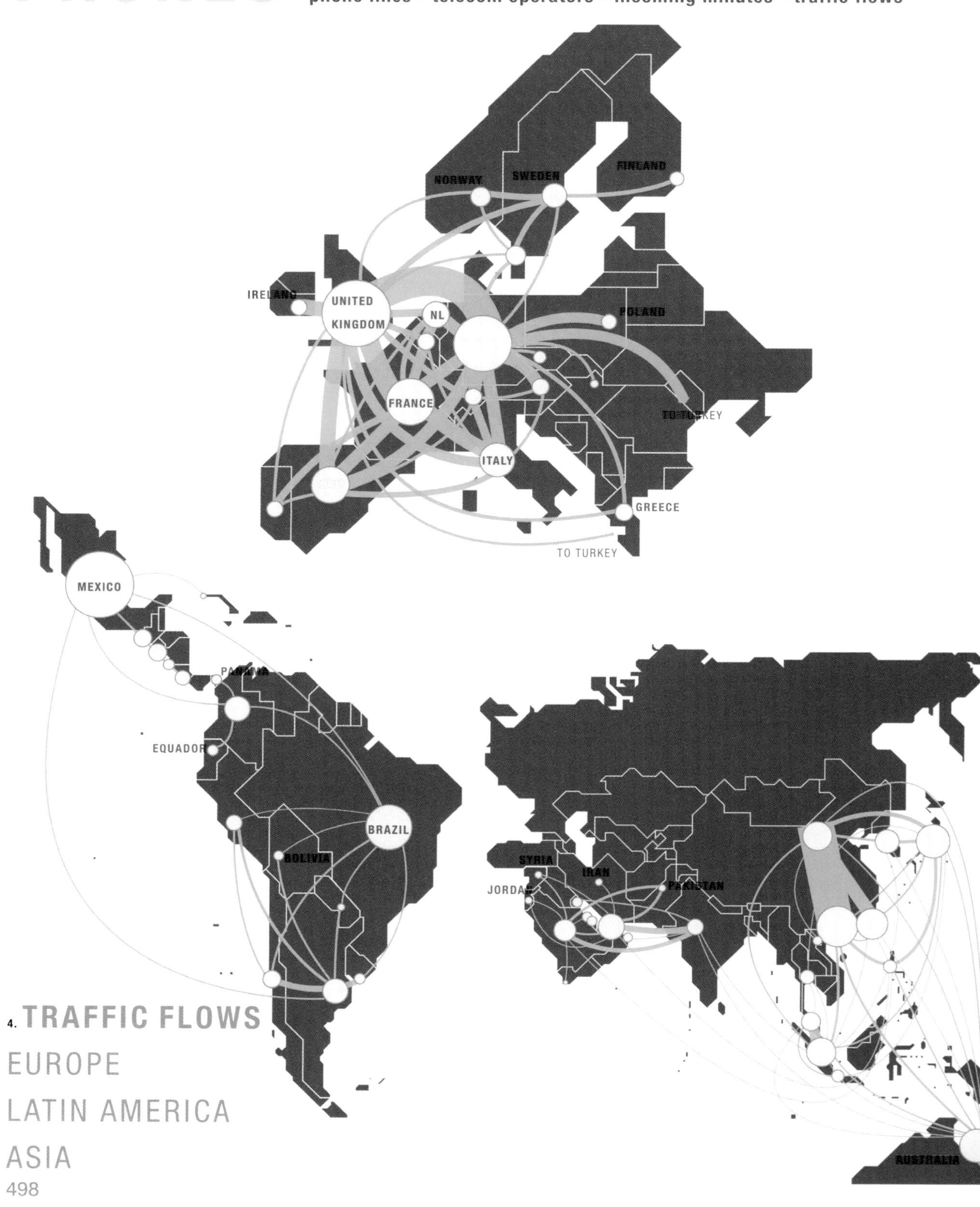

4. **TRAFFIC FLOWS**

EUROPE

LATIN AMERICA

ASIA

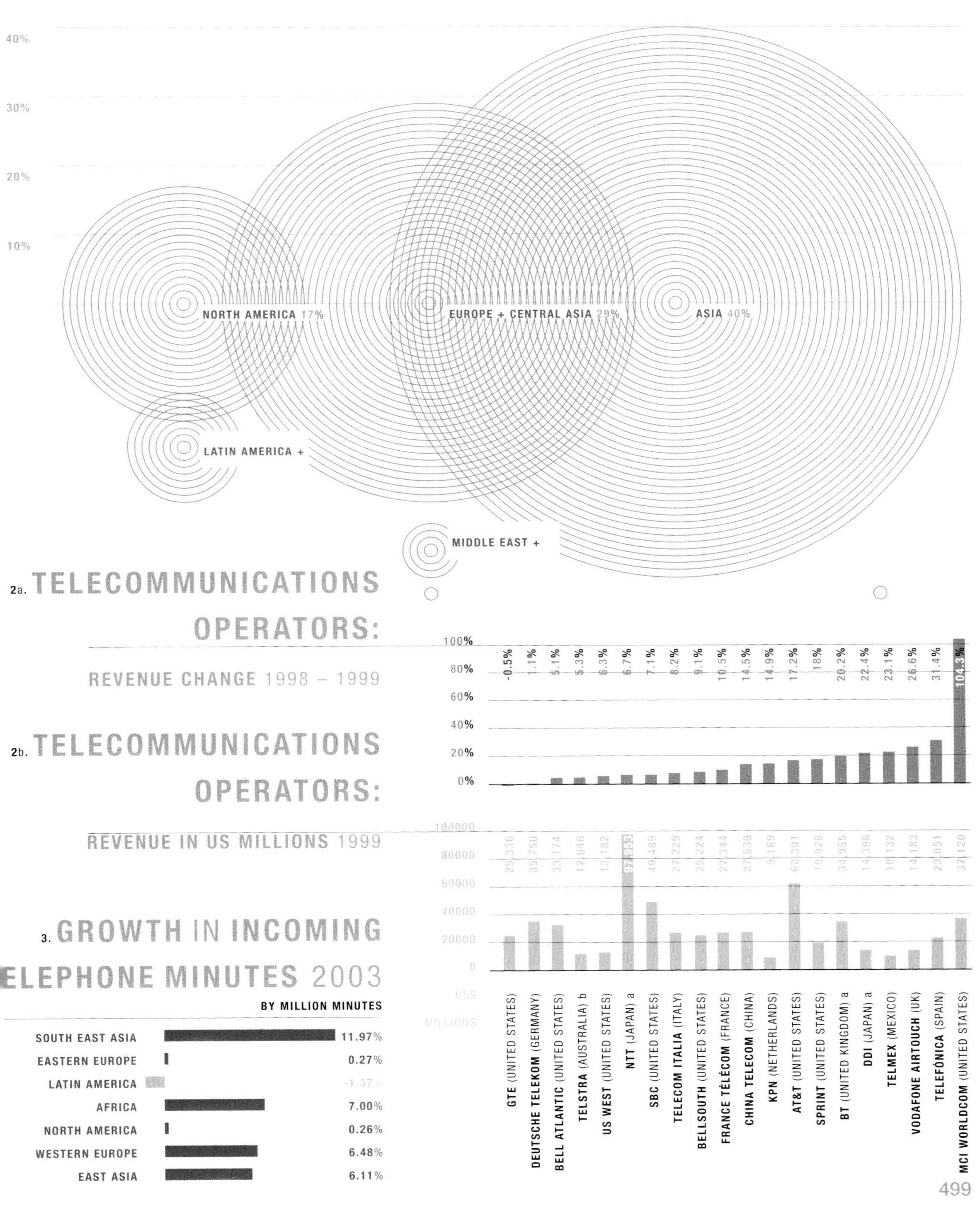
1. % OF TELEPHONE LINES IN USE BY REGION 2002-2003:
40%
30%
20%
10%
NORTH AMERICA 17%
EUROPE + CENTRAL ASIA 29%
ASIA 40%
LATIN AMERICA +
MIDDLE EAST +
2a. TELECOMMUNICATIONS OPERATORS:
REVENUE CHANGE 1998 – 1999
100%
80%
60%
40%
20%
0%
-0.5%
1.1%
5.1%
5.3%
6.3%
6.7%
7.1%
8.2%
9.1%
10.5%
14.5%
14.9%
17.2%
18%
20.2%
22.4%
23.1%
26.6%
31.4%
104.3%
2b. TELECOMMUNICATIONS OPERATORS:
REVENUE IN US MILLIONS 1999
100000
80000
60000
40000
20000
0
US$ MILLIONS
25,336
35,750
33,174
12,046
13,182
97,953
49,489
27,229
25,224
27,344
27,539
9,169
62,391
19,928
34,955
14,396
10,132
14,183
23,051
37,120
GTE (UNITED STATES)
DEUTSCHE TELEKOM (GERMANY)
BELL ATLANTIC (UNITED STATES)
TELSTRA (AUSTRALIA) b
US WEST (UNITED STATES)
NTT (JAPAN) a
SBC (UNITED STATES)
TELECOM ITALIA (ITALY)
BELLSOUTH (UNITED STATES)
FRANCE TÉLÉCOM (FRANCE)
CHINA TELECOM (CHINA)
KPN (NETHERLANDS)
AT&T (UNITED STATES)
SPRINT (UNITED STATES)
BT (UNITED KINGDOM) a
DDI (JAPAN) a
TELMEX (MEXICO)
VODAFONE AIRTOUCH (UK)
TELEFÓNICA (SPAIN)
MCI WORLDCOM (UNITED STATES)
3. GROWTH IN INCOMING TELEPHONE MINUTES 2003
BY MILLION MINUTES
SOUTH EAST ASIA 11.97%
EASTERN EUROPE 0.27%
LATIN AMERICA -1.37%
AFRICA 7.00%
NORTH AMERICA 0.26%
WESTERN EUROPE 6.48%
EAST ASIA 6.11%

INTERNET - countries and wireless access points + cities and wireless access points - world wireless access points - broadband + growth - internet users - google

2. BROADBAND SUBSCRIBERS PER 100 INHABITANT

BY COUNTRIES (DEC 2004)

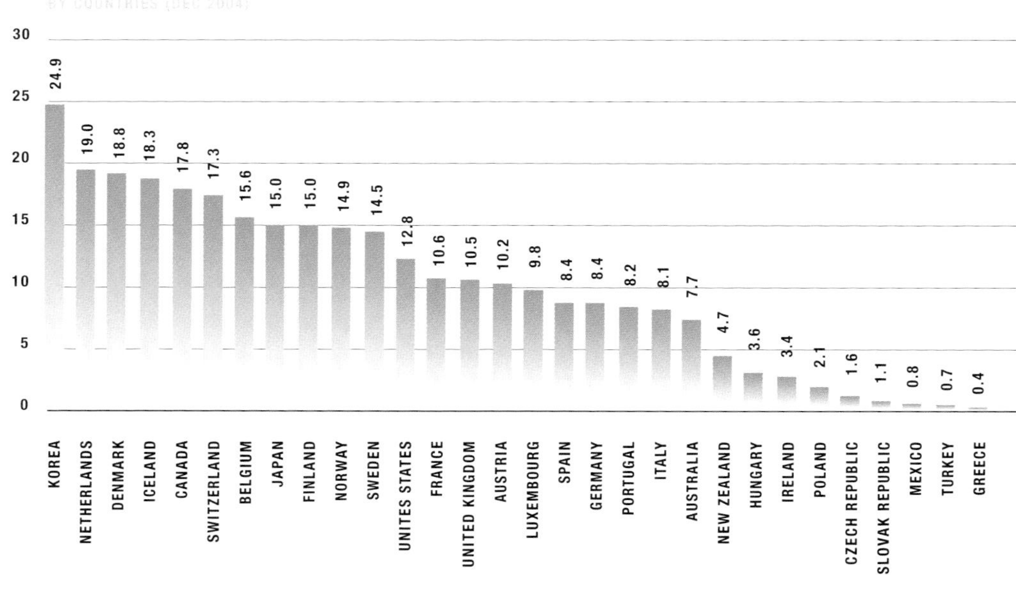

3a. GROWTH IN BROADBAND USE

BY REGION + COUNTRIES WITH MOST GROWTH

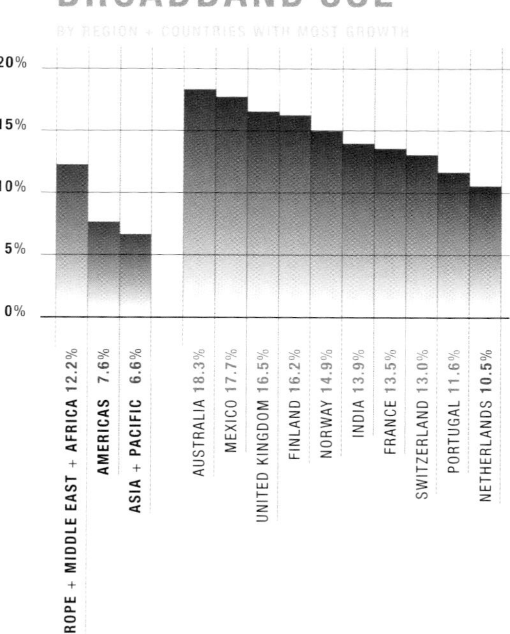

3b. GROWTH IN INTERNET USAGE

2000 – 2005

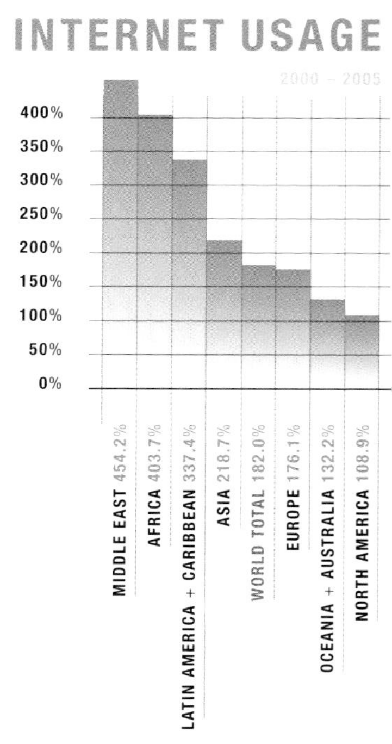

1. % OF WORLD PUBLIC WIRELESS ACCESS POINTS: BY REGION

40%
30%
20%
10%
0%

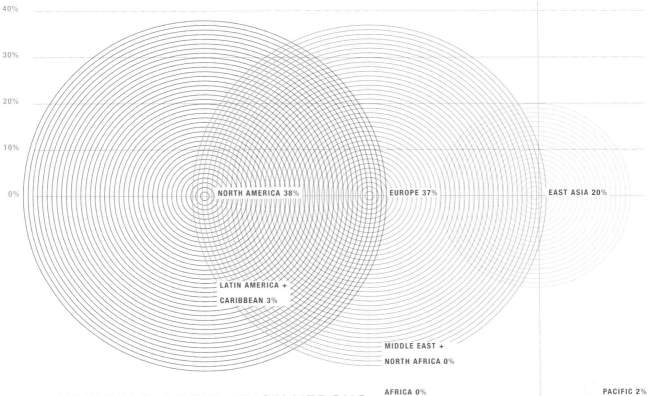

NORTH AMERICA 38%
EUROPE 37%
EAST ASIA 20%
LATIN AMERICA + CARIBBEAN 3%
MIDDLE EAST + NORTH AFRICA 0%
AFRICA 0%
PACIFIC 2%

3c. % OF WORLD POPULATION VERSUS WORLD INTERNET USERS

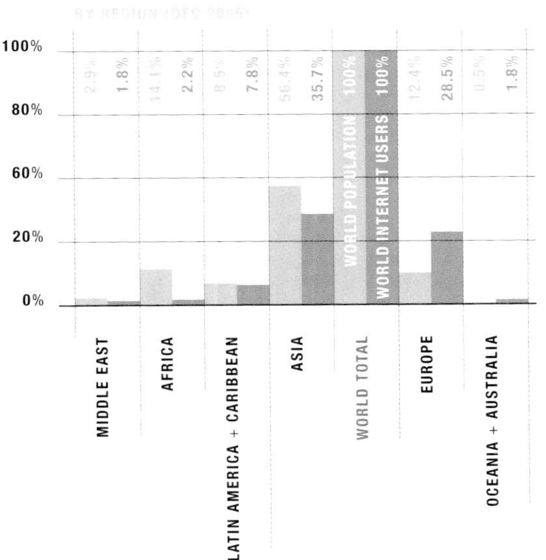

BY COUNTRIES:	
UNITED STATES	37,459
UNITED KINGDOM	12,669
SOUTH KOREA	9,415
GERMANY	8,593
JAPAN	5,978
FRANCE	3,888
ITALY	1,769
NETHERLANDS	1,703
TAIWAN	1,475
CANADA	1,397
SWITZERLAND	1,294
AUSTRALIA	1,283
SPAIN	1,186
BRAZIL	1,167
BELGIUM	977
DENMARK	917
AUSTRIA	853
HONG KONG	761
SINGAPORE	683
SWEDEN	657
MEXICO	566

BY CITIES:	
SEOUL	2,056
TOKYO	1,799
LONDON	1,624
PARIS	895
SAN FRANCISCO	804
DAEGU	787
NEW YORK	643
SINGAPORE	620
BUSAN	617
HONG KONG	605

4. # INTERNET USERS

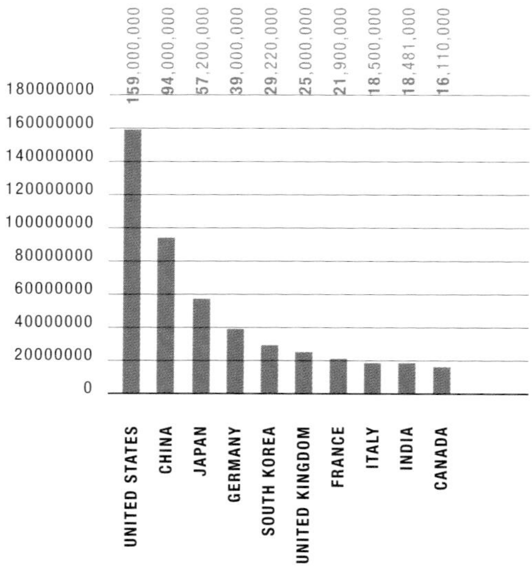

OF INTERNET HOSTS

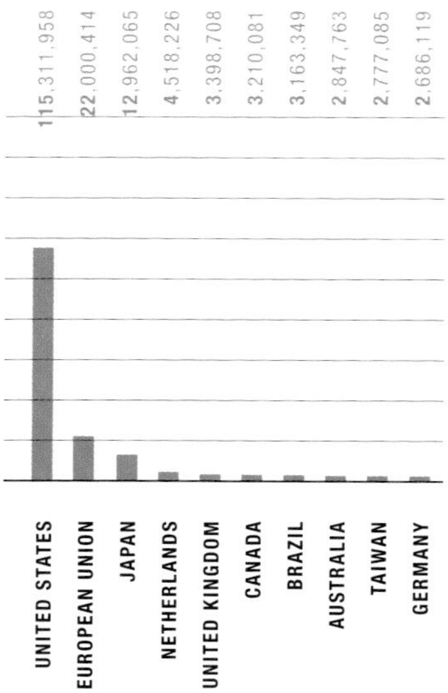

5a. TOP INTERNET GENRES

BY # OF PAGE IMPRESSIONS IN A WEEK (JAN 16 - 22 2006)

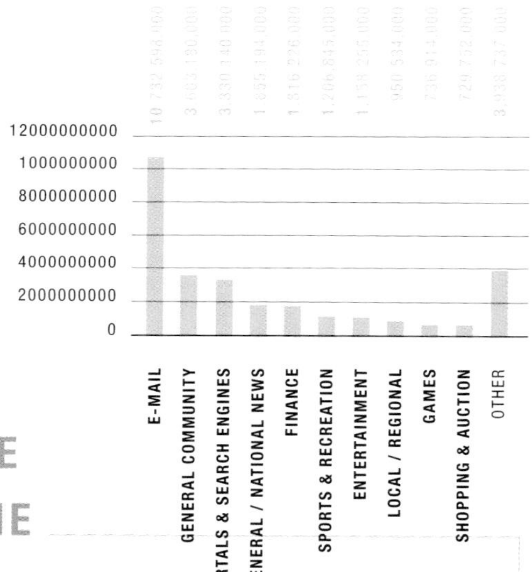

5b. # DOMAIN NAMES

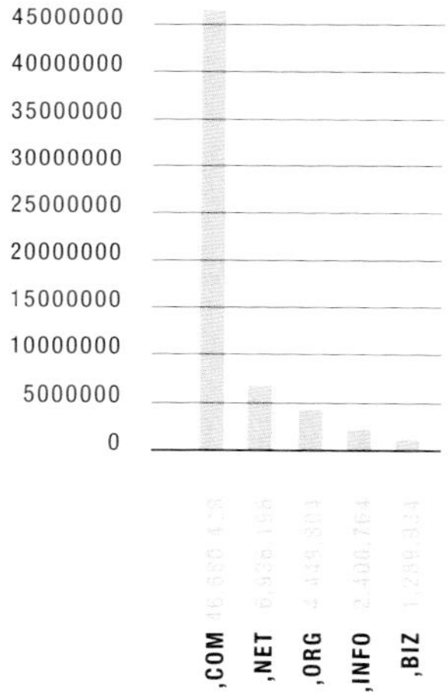

6. GOOGLE TIMELINE

SEPTEMBER 98 GOOGLE OPENS

DECEMBER 98 HAS 10,000 SEARCH QUERIES A DAY AND PC MAGAZINE NAMES THEM ONE OF THE TOP 100 WEBSITES OF THE YEAR

FEBRUARY 99 500,000 QUERIES A DAY

SEPTEMBER 99 3 MILLION QUERIES A DAY AFTER AOL/NETSCAPE SELECT GOOGLE FOR THEIR SEARCH ENGINE

JUNE 00 18 MILLION QUERIES A DAY. PARTNERSHIP WITH YAHOO IS ANNOUNCED

DECEMBER 00 100 MILLION QUERIES A DAY

OCTOBER 01 GOOGLE BECOMES PROFITABLE. USERS CAN NOW LIMIT SEARCHES TO ANY OF 26 DIFFERENT LANGUAGES. PARTNERSHIPS ARE FORMED IN ASIA AND LATIN AMERICA

2001 GOOGLE IMAGE SEARCH AND CATALOG SEARCH ARE LAUNCHED

2002 GOOGLE NEWS AND FROOGLE ARE LAUNCHED

2003 BLOGGER, GOOGLE ADSENSE, TOOLBAR, AND DESKBAR ARE LAUNCHED

FEBRUARY 04 6 BILLION ITEMS ARE IN THE EXPANDED WEB

APRIL 04 LOCAL SEARCH AND GMAIL ARE LAUNCHED

AUGUST 04 GOOGLE BECOMES PUBLIC

OCTOBER 04 GOOGLE ANNOUNCES REVENUES OF $805.9 MILLION, UP 105 PERCENT OVER THE YEAR

2005 GOOGLE VIDEO, MAPS, EARTH AND TALK ARE LAUNCHED

BLOGS - blogs by region - blog writers profile - blog hosting sites - growth of # of blogs

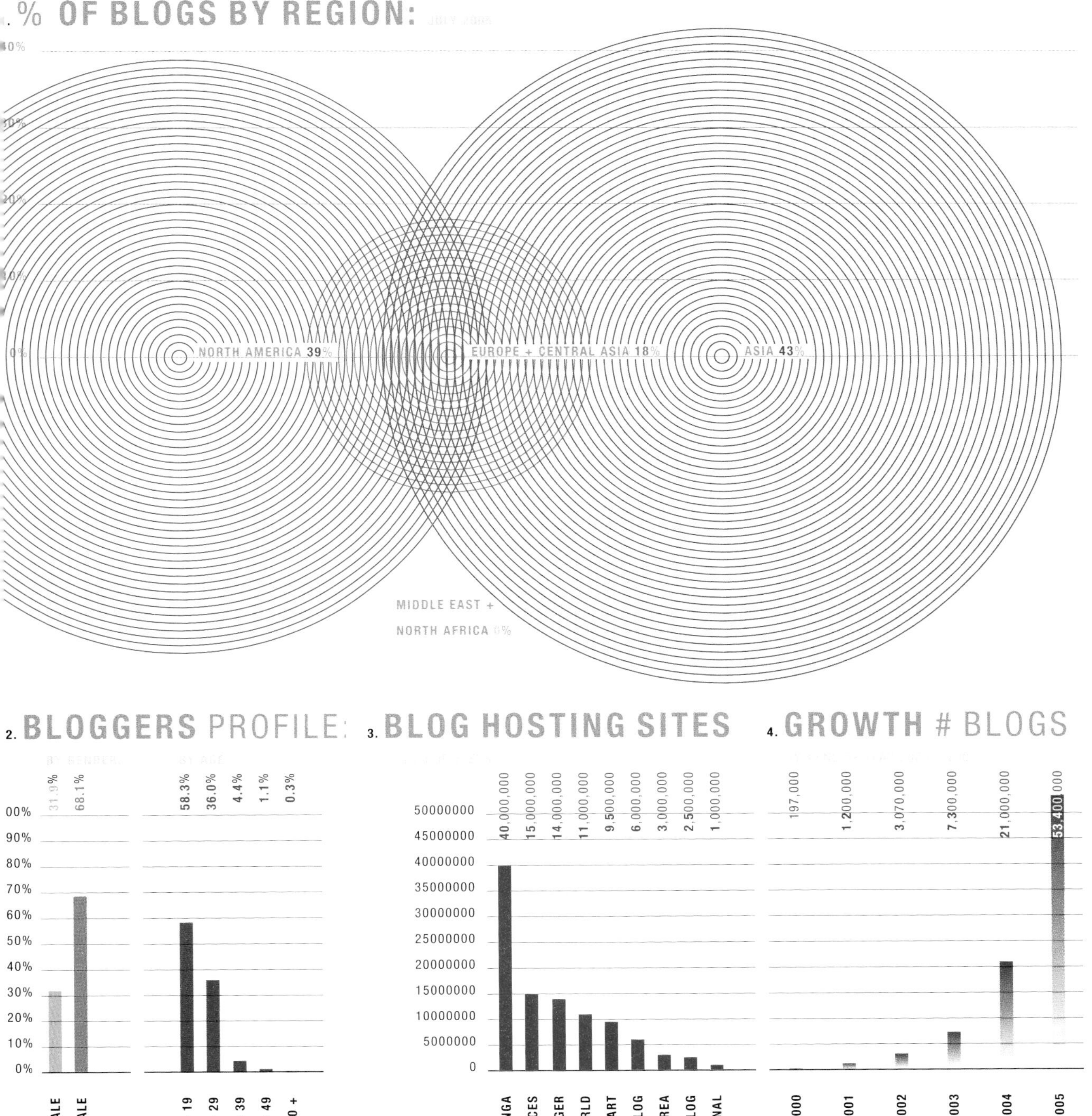

1. GLOBAL TOP 10 COUNTRIES OF MOVIE GOERS

IN MILLIONS 2003–04

01.	INDIA	MOVIE TICKETS SOLD	**2,860** MILLION	FILM INVESTMENT	**192** MILLION [08.]
02.	UNITED STATES	MOVIE TICKETS SOLD	**1,421** MILLION	FILM INVESTMENT	**14,661** MILLION [01.]
03.	INDONESIA	MOVIE TICKETS SOLD	**190** MILLION		
04.	FRANCE	MOVIE TICKETS SOLD	**155** MILLION	FILM INVESTMENT	**813** MILLION [04.]
05.	GERMANY	MOVIE TICKETS SOLD	**149** MILLION	FILM INVESTMENT	**687** MILLION [05.]
06.	JAPAN	MOVIE TICKETS SOLD	**145** MILLION	FILM INVESTMENT	**1,292** MILLION [02.]
07.	UNITED KINGDOM	MOVIE TICKETS SOLD	**139** MILLION	FILM INVESTMENT	**825** MILLION [03.]
08.	SPAIN	MOVIE TICKETS SOLD	**131** MILLION	FILM INVESTMENT	**304** MILLION [06.]
09.	MEXICO	MOVIE TICKETS SOLD	**120** MILLION		
10.	CANADA	MOVIE TICKETS SOLD	**113** MILLION	FILM INVESTMENT	**133** MILLION [10.]
	ITALY			FILM INVESTMENT	**247** MILLION [07.]
	SOUTH KOREA			FILM INVESTMENT	**134** MILLION [09.]

SOLD MOVIE TICKETS 100 MILLION

FILM INVESTMENT 100 MILLION

2. GLOBAL TOP 10 COUNTRIES IN FILM INVESTMENT

IN MILLIONS

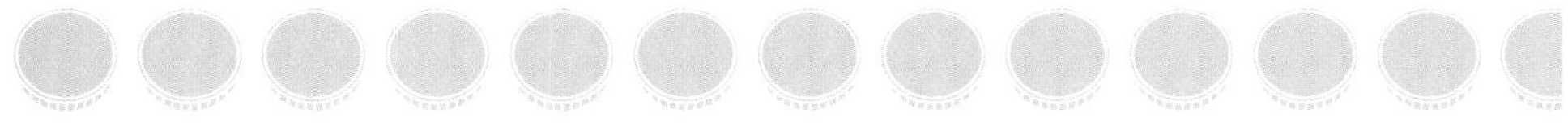

ADMISSION IN THOUSANDS

INDIA	3,296,720
CHINA	2,145,000
USA	1,435,008

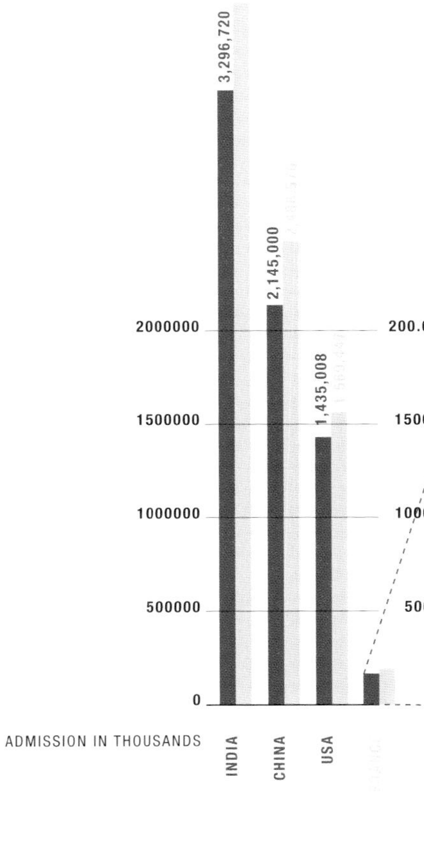

3. TOP 20 COUNTRIES RANKED BY # OF ADMISSIONS

Country	YEAR 2001	FORECAST YEAR 2010
FRANCE	170,048	195,388
GERMANY	156,313	195,213
UK	147,488	179,734
JAPAN	144,478	200,325
MEXICO	137,550	176,806
SPAIN	131,443	143,752
ITALY	113,850	142,877
CANADA	100,331	122,153
AUSTRALIA	92,326	108,403
BRAZIL	72,760	121,307
SOUTH KOREA	66,420	84,052
RUSSIA	44,720	63,651
ARGENTINA	35,422	51,530
SOUTH AFRICA	31,050	42,318
BELGIUM	24,205	30,228
HONG KONG	21,218	25,808
SWITZERLAND	20,800	27,271

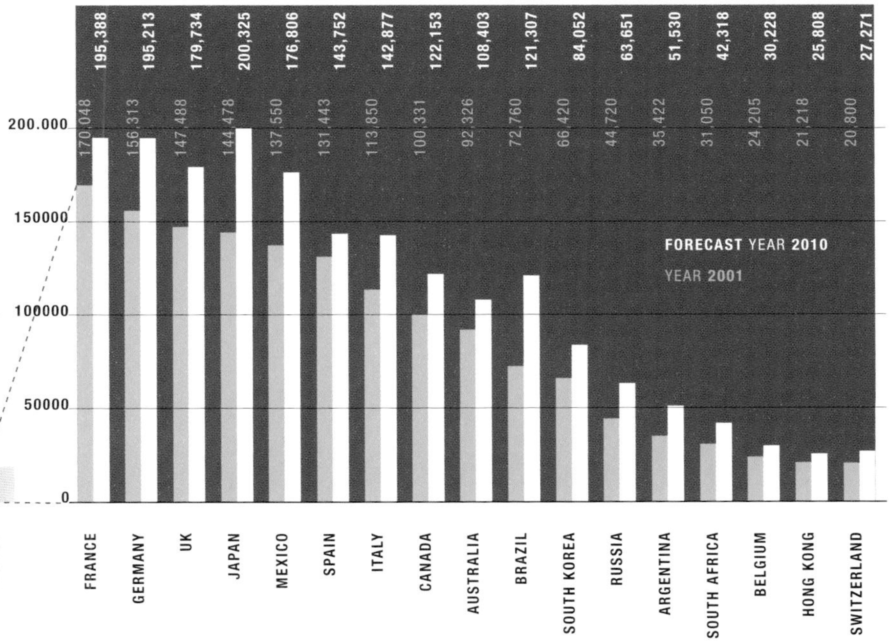

- film production investment + global market share - box office revenues

- top 20 **film entertainment companies**

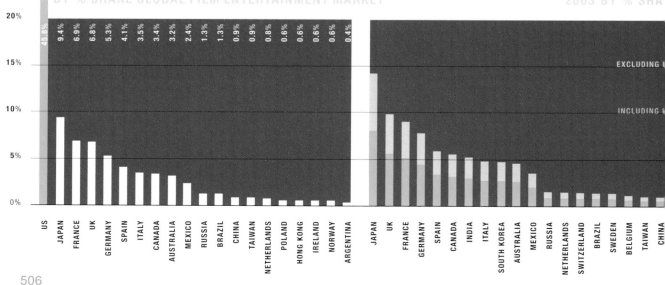

4. 2005 TOP 20 FILM PRODUCTION STUDIOS: % GLOBAL MARKET SHARE

MARKET SHARE	
WARNER BROS.	16.9%
20TH CENTURY FOX	16.5%
PARAMOUNT	11.6%
UNIVERSAL	11.4%
SONY	11.1%
BUENA VISTA	10.4%
DREAMWORKS SKG	5.7%
NEW LINE	4.8%
MIRAMAX / DIMENSION	4.2%
LIONS GATE	3.2%
MGM / UA	2.1%
WEINSTEIN COMPANY	0.5%
IMAX	0.2%
IDP	0.2%
THINKFILM	0.2%
N WAVE	0.1%
MAGNOLIA	0.1%
NEWMARKET	0.1%

Axis: 0%, 5%, 10%, 15%, 20%

5a. % GROWTH BOX OFFICES 2003 – 2004

CHINA	50.0%
ARGENTINA	46.7%
POLAND	42.6%
TAIWAN	38.7%
RUSSIA	28.8%
BRAZIL	18.5%
MEXICO	16.4%
FRANCE	15.0%
ITALY	10.3%
SINGAPORE	9.6%
SPAIN	7.6%
ISRAEL	7.3%
HONG KONG	5.9%
HUNGARY	5.6%
GERMANY	5.0%
AUSTRALIA	4.8%
IRELAND	4.3%
JAPAN	3.8%
UK	3.7%
CZECH REP.	2.0%

Axis: 0%, 50%, 100%

5b. COUNTRY BOX OFFICES BY % SHARE GLOBAL FILM ENTERTAINMENT MARKET

US	45.8%
JAPAN	9.4%
FRANCE	6.9%
UK	6.8%
GERMANY	5.3%
SPAIN	4.1%
ITALY	3.5%
CANADA	3.4%
AUSTRALIA	3.2%
MEXICO	2.4%
RUSSIA	1.3%
BRAZIL	1.3%
CHINA	0.9%
TAIWAN	0.9%
NETHERLANDS	0.8%
POLAND	0.6%
HONG KONG	0.6%
IRELAND	0.6%
NORWAY	0.6%
ARGENTINA	0.4%

Axis: 0%, 5%, 10%, 15%, 20%

5c. GLOBAL BOX OFFICE REVENU

2003 BY % SHA

EXCLUDING

INCLUDING

JAPAN, UK, FRANCE, GERMANY, SPAIN, CANADA, INDIA, ITALY, SOUTH KOREA, AUSTRALIA, MEXICO, RUSSIA, NETHERLANDS, SWITZERLAND, BRAZIL, SWEDEN, BELGIUM, TAIWAN, CHINA

6. TOP 20 FILM ENTERTAINMENT COMPANIES: BY REVENUE IN EUROS (MILLIONS)

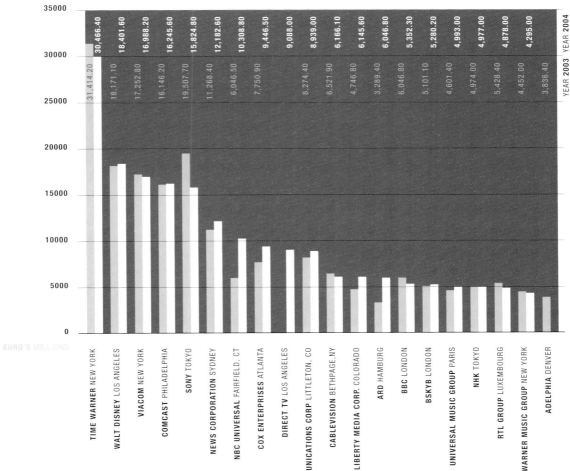

Company	Year 2003	Year 2004
TIME WARNER NEW YORK	31,414.20	30,466.40
WALT DISNEY LOS ANGELES	18,171.10	18,401.60
VIACOM NEW YORK	17,252.80	16,988.20
COMCAST PHILADELPHIA	16,146.20	16,245.60
SONY TOKYO	19,507.70	15,824.80
NEWS CORPORATION SYDNEY	11,268.40	12,182.60
NBC UNIVERSAL FAIRFIELD, CT	6,046.50	10,308.80
COX ENTERPRISES ATLANTA	7,750.90	9,446.50
DIRECT TV LOS ANGELES		9,088.00
ECHOSTAR COMMUNICATIONS CORP LITTLETON, CO	8,274.40	8,939.00
CABLEVISION BETHPAGE, NY	6,521.90	6,166.10
LIBERTY MEDIA CORP. COLORADO	4,746.80	6,145.60
ARD HAMBURG	3,289.40	6,046.80
BBC LONDON	6,046.80	5,352.30
BSKYB LONDON	5,101.10	5,280.20
UNIVERSAL MUSIC GROUP PARIS	4,601.40	4,993.00
NHK TOKYO	4,974.00	4,977.00
RTL GROUP LUXEMBOURG	5,428.40	4,878.00
WARNER MUSIC GROUP NEW YORK	4,452.00	4,295.00
ADELPHIA DENVER	3,836.40	

EURO'S MILLIONS

5d. COUNTRY BOX OFFICES

RANKED BY REVENUE 2004

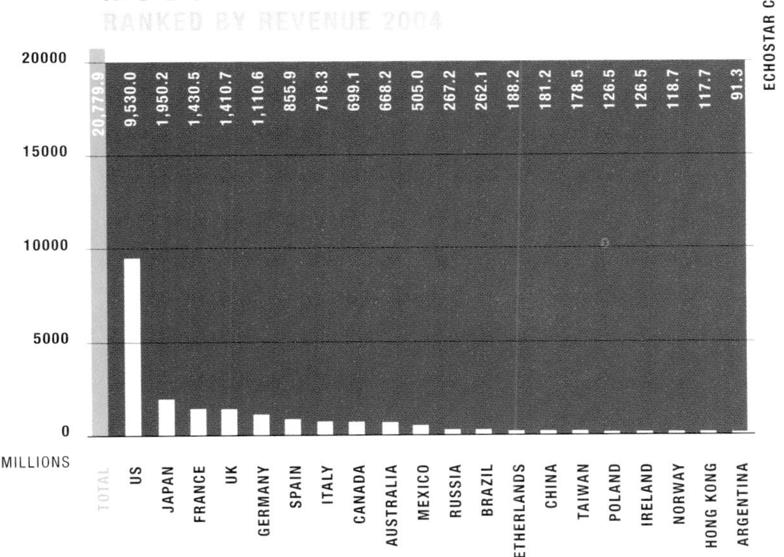

TV + RADIO - television stations - radio stations

- international shortwave listeners - households by radio type - # of listeners - weekly audience BBC radio

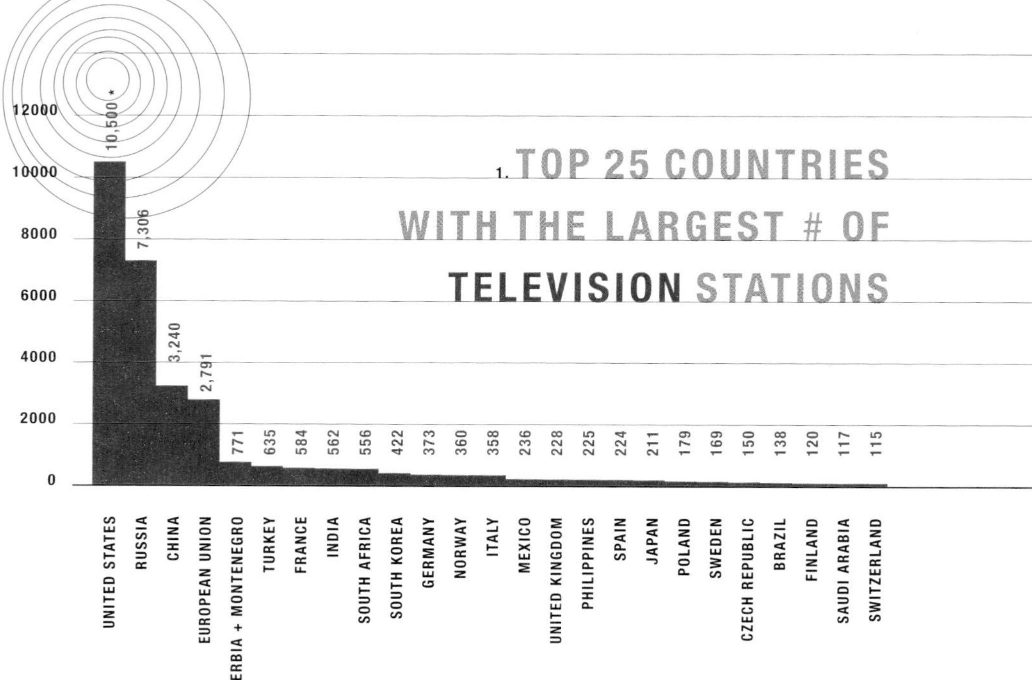

3. % OF INTERNATIONAL SHORTWAVE LISTENERS

VERY LOW	LOW	MODERATE	HIGH	VERY HIGH
LESS THAN 1%	BETWEEN 1–5%	5–10%	10–30%	OVER 30%
JAMAICA	ZIMBABWE	SLOVAKIA	ETHIOPIA	CAMEROON (U)
USA	EGYPT	BARBADOS	IVORY COAST (U)	KENYA
CHINA	JORDAN	ECUADOR	GHANA	NIGERIA
JAPAN	BULGARIA	AZERBAIJAN	MOZAMBIQUE	SUDAN
AUSTRALIA	MACEDONIA	BELARUS	SENEGAL	TANZANIA
MALAYSIA	POLAND	INDIA	ZAMBIA	
THAILAND	ROMANIA	SRI LANKA	ALBANIA	
SINGAPORE	TURKEY	VIETNAM	SERBIA + MONTENEGRO	
PHILIPPINES	MEXICO		GUYANA	
KOREA	PERU		GEORGIA	
TAIWAN	TRINIDAD + TOBAGO		BANGLADESH	
	ESTONIA		PAKISTAN	
	KYRGHYZSTAN		NEPAL	
	LATVIA			
	LITHUANIA			
	UKRAINE			
	UZBEKISTAN			
	RUSSIA			
	INDONESIA			

4. % HOUSEHOLDS BY RADIO TYPE

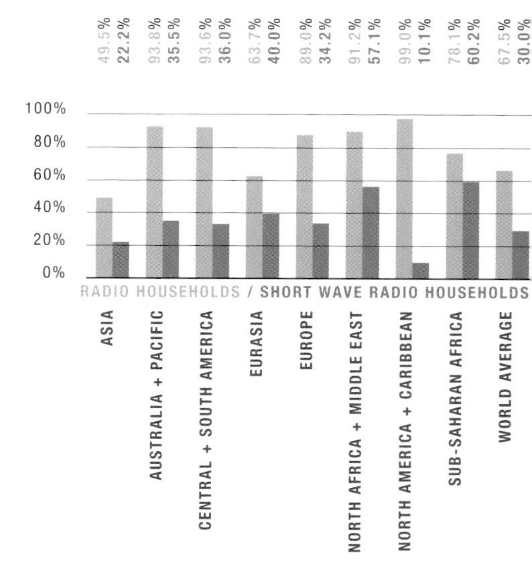

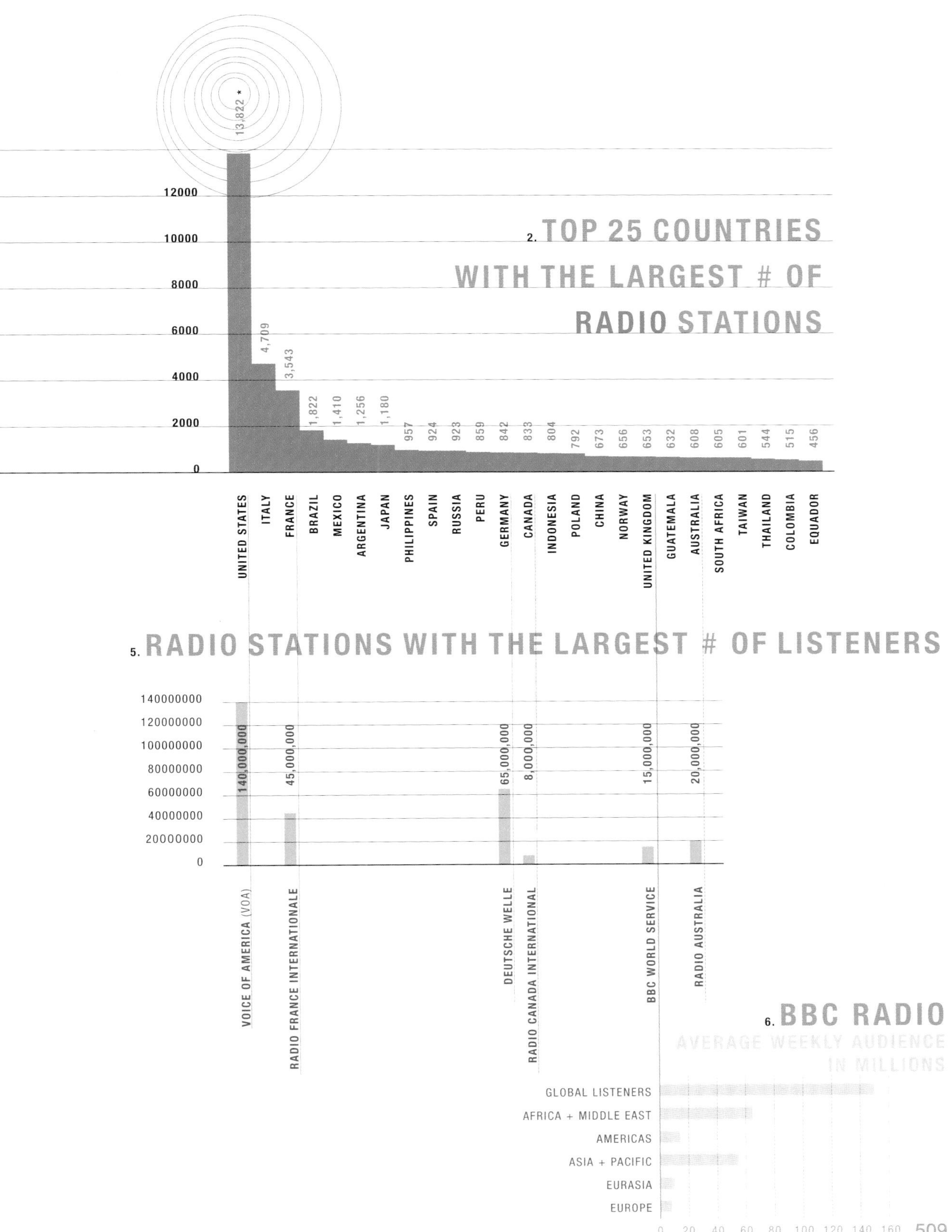

2. TOP 25 COUNTRIES WITH THE LARGEST # OF RADIO STATIONS
12000
10000
8000
6000
4000
2000
0
13,822 *
4,709
3,543
1,822
1,410
1,256
1,180
957
924
923
859
842
833
804
792
673
656
653
632
608
605
601
544
515
456
UNITED STATES
ITALY
FRANCE
BRAZIL
MEXICO
ARGENTINA
JAPAN
PHILIPPINES
SPAIN
RUSSIA
PERU
GERMANY
CANADA
INDONESIA
POLAND
CHINA
NORWAY
UNITED KINGDOM
GUATEMALA
AUSTRALIA
SOUTH AFRICA
TAIWAN
THAILAND
COLOMBIA
EQUADOR
5. RADIO STATIONS WITH THE LARGEST # OF LISTENERS
140000000
120000000
100000000
80000000
60000000
40000000
20000000
0
140,000,000
45,000,000
65,000,000
8,000,000
15,000,000
20,000,000
VOICE OF AMERICA (VOA)
RADIO FRANCE INTERNATIONALE
DEUTSCHE WELLE
RADIO CANADA INTERNATIONAL
BBC WORLD SERVICE
RADIO AUSTRALIA
6. BBC RADIO
AVERAGE WEEKLY AUDIENCE IN MILLIONS
GLOBAL LISTENERS
AFRICA + MIDDLE EAST
AMERICAS
ASIA + PACIFIC
EURASIA
EUROPE
0 20 40 60 80 100 120 140 160

TV + ONLINE NEWS - bbc global - major global news outlet comparisions - online news consumption - al jazeera audience profile

1. BBC GLOBAL (WORLD NEWS TV)

DISTRIBUTION TO HOMES WITH 24-HOUR RECEPTIO

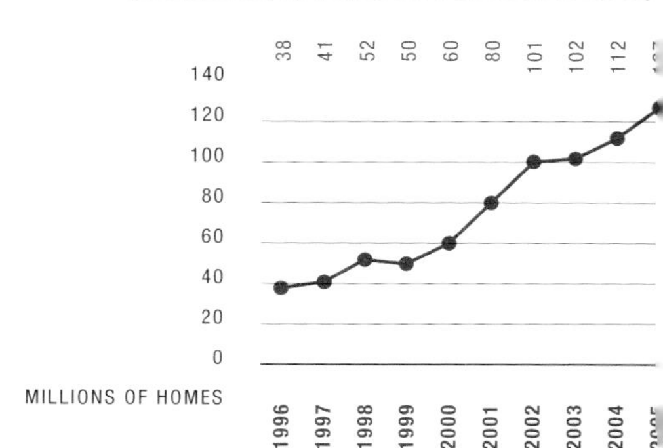

2. MAJOR GLOBAL NEWS OUTLET COMPARISONS

	HEAD QUARTERS	VIEWERSHIP	LANGUAGES
BBC WORLD	UNITED KINGDOM	37.6 MILLION UK ALONE DEC 04	43
AL JAZEERA	QATAR	40.0 MILLION UNKNOWN TIME FRAME	2
CNN		75.6 MILLION NOV 04	4

3. ONLINE NEWS CONSUMPTION UNIQUE MONTHLY USERS

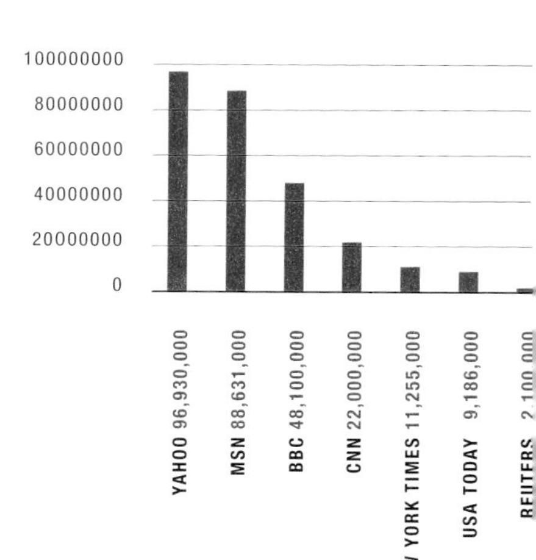

4. AL JAZEERA AUDIENCE PROFILE:

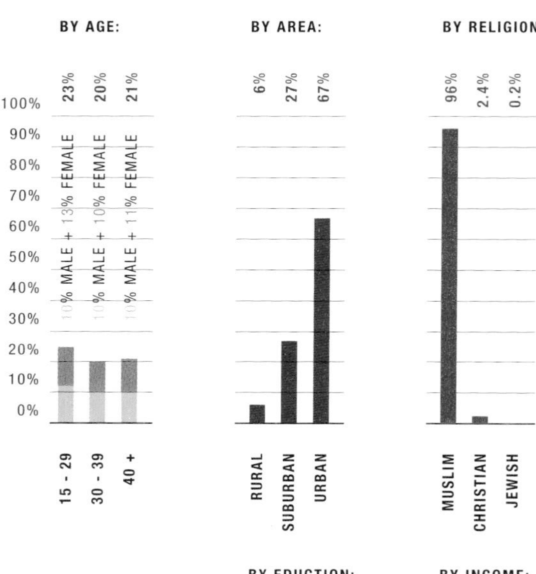

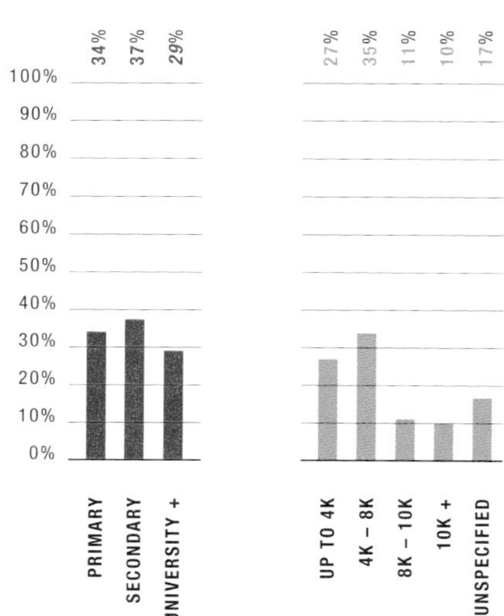

HUMAN LANGUAGES The world's languages make a up a complex and fast-changing mosaic that is becoming more consolidated, with many smaller languages dying out, and differentiated at the same time, as larger languages such as English are undergoing differentiation processes. The graphs in this suite show that:

- About fifteen of the world's languages dominate in terms of number of speakers
- A significantly different set of languages is dominant in terms of international usage
- Illiteracy, underdevelopment and language loss are closely related
- The world's international leadership is polyglot, with English as the central medium.

WHAT IS LANGUAGE?

Human language is unique in being a symbolic communication system that is learned instead of biologically inherited. While many definitions exist, language can formally be defined as a system of finite arbitrary symbols combined according to rules of grammar for the purpose of communication. Individual speakers employ sounds, gestures and other symbols when using languages to represent objects, concepts, emotions, ideas, and thoughts. Languages are rarely discrete units with clearly defined boundaries but typically extend across geographic, cultural and social space. What actually constitutes a language is shaped by social, cultural, or political factors in fundamental ways, and is closely linked to notions of individual as well as collective identity—which is why language is so often part of, or invoked in, communal, regional, national and international conflicts of many kinds. Not surprisingly, the process of globalization is bringing many changes to the world's languages.

WHAT DO WE KNOW ABOUT LANGUAGES?

At first, estimates of the number of languages at 6,000 and 7,000 suggest an image of immense linguistic diversity (see Ethnologue website). However, a relatively small number of languages are dominant in terms of number of speakers. The thirty most spoken languages make up nearly two-thirds of the world's population, and the fifteen most spoken ones about half. Chinese (Mandarin, Cantonese, Wu, Min Nan, Jinyu), Hindi, English, Spanish, Arabic, Bengali, Portuguese, Russian, Japanese, and German are spoken by 100 million speakers as first language. About 97 percent of the world's population speak about four percent of the world's languages; and conversely, about 96 percent of the world's languages are spoken by about three percent of the world's people (Bernard, 1996, p. 142). According Crystal (2001), 500 of the world's languages have less than 100 speakers, and 1,500 have less than 1,000.

Education, nation-building, economic and technological development tends to privilege larger, dominant languages over minority languages, in particular those not codified in written form. The current wave of language concentration is linked to the long-term impact of colonialism and subsequent economic and technological changes. At least 50 percent of the world's languages are losing speakers, and UNESCO estimates that about 90 percent of the languages may be replaced by dominant languages by the end of the 21st century.

Much of the diversity of languages is in the Pacific, the Americas and to a lesser extent, Africa, where languages are relatively numerous and average fewer speakers (Table 1). By contrast, Europe's languages, fewer in numbers, have more speakers.
Additionally, with the exception of North America, there is a close relationship between linguistic diversity and illiteracy, particularly in Africa, South America and Asia-Pacific.

Moreover, there is a divergence between the number of speakers and multiple media usage (spoken, print, broadcasting, electronic), domain uses (tourism, business, diplomacy, academia, etc), and translations. English, German, French, Spanish and Italian are central in the network of translations, with Chinese, Hindi, Arabic, Bengali, and Portuguese much less so. English, Chinese, Japanese, Spanish, German and French dominate the Internet. Smaller languages such as Catalan and Dutch are more visible in print and electronic media than larger languages such as Urdu, Russian or Arabic. In this way, it is seen that economic development and higher average levels of education add clout to languages even though they may have fewer speakers.

Some languages like English, Spanish and French have a greater presence in more countries and media outlets for other reasons, as well. First, a delayed result of colonialism. When these languages were imposed on colonies and adapted by elites, they set in motion a complex process of merging with, and displacement among indigenous languages. Second, political decisions about language use in international diplomacy, aviation, and commerce, privilege dominant languages over others. Consequently, English in particular has achieved a status as the lingua franca of the 21st century, influencing and even infiltrating many languages around the world.

WHAT ARE THE ISSUES?

There is a tension between the economics of communication, which tends to favor fewer languages for reducing transaction costs on the one hand, and the social and cultural identity of those speaking one or more of the world's other thousands of languages on the other. English is clearly on the rise as the world's lingua franca of business, technology and academia, not only among elites but the population at large in many countries, particularly young people. However, this is unlikely to lead to a monolingual world, at least in the short to medium term, as the most globalized regions and cities of the world are also those with the greatest diversity in language use.

Nonetheless, as language use is not only driven by economics but also shaped by political preference, countries have mounted a response to the rise of dominant languages such as English. Some countries, such as France, have tried to use policy measures to stem the influence of English ('Franglais'), while other like Germany, the Netherlands and Mexico have a chosen more laissez-faire attitudes. As a result, mixed use of such languages leads to the rise of 'Spanglish' (Spanish and English) and 'Denglish' (German and English), suggesting the beginning of what could become more profound differentiation processes among dominant languages.

Many countries have some form of language policy in place which is typically tied to domestic rather than international issues, and is often tied to political conflicts, actual and potential, past and present. These language policies range from assimilation policies aiming at greater language homogeneity by trying to reduce the number and influence of minority languages (e.g., Turkey), to policies advocating co-existence of two or more languages inside a state (e.g., Belgium), to valorization policies that favor the official language (France, Italy) to non-intervention (Germany, Argentina). In the process of globalization, domestic language policies are likely to come under pressure, as are the language regulatory agencies and norm setting institutions of many countries that remain closely tied to the notion of the nation state.

TABLE 1. **DISTRIBUTION OF LANGUAGES BY AREA OF ORIGIN**

AREA	LIVING LANGUAGES		NUMBER OF SPEAKERS			
	count	percent	count	percent	mean	median
AFRICA	2,092	30.3	675,887,158	11.8	323,082	25,391
AMERICAS	1,002	14.5	47,559,381	0.8	47,464	2,000
ASIA	2,269	32.8	3,489,897,147	61.0	1,538,077	10,171
EUROPE	239	3.5	1,504,393,183	26.3	6,294,532	220,000
PACIFIC	1,310	19.0	6,124,341	0.1	4,675	800
TOTALS	6,912	100.0	5,732,861,210	100.0	828,105	7,000

PRINT MEDIA The term 'print media' refers to newspapers, periodicals, journals, magazines, printed mail, signs, and other ink-press forms. Today, the realm of print media is experiencing rapid growth, but is recently challenged by emerging web-based news outlets. The expansion of the Internet and growing generations of youth exposed to computer and online technology not only threatens the existence of traditional print media, but also the oligopolies that have enjoyed control of the news print world. The suite on print media illustrates that:

- The top five most circulated world newspapers are Japanese
- 80% of the top 50 circulated world newspapers come from Asia (Japan, China, Korea, India, Taiwan, and Thailand)
- Reader's Digest has the largest global magazine circulation of 23 million, followed by Cosmopolitan, National Geographic, Time Magazine and Playboy
- No newspapers from the Middle East, South America, and Africa are included in the top 50 circulated world newspapers. Al-Ahram, Egypt, is the most circulated Middle Eastern newspaper ranking 57th worldwide

WHAT DO WE KNOW ABOUT PRINT MEDIA?

In recent years, according to UNESCO (2005), international trade in newspapers and periodicals increased by an average of 2.1% annually, with growth rates in high-income countries (between 1.8% and 3.4%) lower than in low-income countries (between 12.3% and 14.3%). Conversely, nearly 93% of all exported newspapers and periodicals come from high-income countries and 67% of all newspapers and periodicals traded worldwide were traded in Europe alone (UNESCO, 2005).

In recent years, the print media industry has grown in many Asian countries, while it has declined in most western countries, especially the US and Germany. In 2002, for example, weekday circulation of US newspapers dropped 11% from levels twelve years ago (Deutsche Presse-Agentur, 2005) and the gross advertising expenditures of German newspapers fell by almost 3% (The Business, 2003). China, India, and Japan are currently the top Asian newspaper markets, while Singapore and Indonesia have been growing significantly over the past five years. Newspaper circulation in India increased approximately 24% (both between 2001 and 2002, and 2003 to 2004) and the readership base increased by 10% (Hindustan Times, 2005).

Despite recent growth in Asian countries, countertrends of slowed growth, even decline are beginning to occur. In Japan, though circulation and advertising sales are on the rise, many young readers increasingly turn to the internet for their news and information. In both Japan and China, the increasing prevalence of free sheets adds pressure on traditional paid newspapers. Russia and Turkey are two other emerging markets; the Russian print media market is expected to double by 2008 (RosBusiness Consulting Database, 2005). Table 1 shows growth and decline by continent between 2000 and 2004.

WHAT ARE THE ISSUES?

Similar to the book industry and traditional publishing in general, the world of print media is facing competition from new electronic sources of information and communication. Digital technologies allow for more immediate, searchable, personalized, and instantaneous news media, and many of these information sources are free, posing further barriers to traditional print media. Equally, the proliferation of technologies that allow for self-publishing, so called "Zines" (small printed booklets that usually contain satire, poetry, rants, ideas, political and social commentaries, etc.) and other independent newspapers and magazines, are quickly gaining popularity.

To attract new advertisers, media companies are 'branding' publications and creating niche products. In order to streamline production, more and more newspapers, such as the New York Times and the Boston Globe, are outsourcing to free-lance journalists, designers, editors and presses. Some critics have complained that outsourcing and commodification of print media have caused a 'tabloidization' of the industry, and reduced its capacity as a watch-dog of public affairs.

Because of the movement towards non-traditional print formats by both readers and advertisers,[1] printers and media companies are crossing over in order to retain and capture new clienteles. By 2003, about 60% of all publishers and printers were involved in some sort of cross-media by maintaining websites, creating PDFs, etc. (Graphic Arts Monthly, 2003). As costs and loses rise, print media companies that cannot compete by changing their services and streamlining their production are at an increased risk of folding.

Newspaper readers tend to be more frequent among older adults (European Report 2005), whereas younger readers choose alternative (internet, television) news sources. This generational effect further contributes to the declining growth in the sector in much of the developed world, and to its growth limits in Africa, Asia and Latin America. Indeed, there is an emerging consensus among experts that future growth will come from the Internet and the electronic advertising options it offers (Middle East Company News Wire, 2005).

The central questions for the print media sector increasingly surround the possible replacement of traditional media products and processes with new technologies, models, outlets, and ways of distribution. This will clearly challenge current business models first and foremost, and with it the oligopolies of print media conglomerates that account for a large share of global newspaper and magazine production and distribution. These questions guide the industry as it moves forward, searching for new and sustainable business model approaches as technologies and reader preferences continue to change.

TABLE 1: **PRINT MEDIA MARKETS BY REGION**

REGION	% CHANGE CIRCULATION 2000-2004	% CHANGE # OF NEW TITLES
ASIA	4.1	4.1
SOUTH AMERICA	6.3	1.1
AFRICA	6	10.4
EUROPE	(-1.4)	1.3
NORTH AMERICA	(-0.2)	(-0.1)
AUSTRALIA + OCEANIA	(-1)	1.4

Source: The World Association of Newspaper's Annual Survey of World Press Trends released in 2005. Includes data from the 215 countries around the world where newspapers are published. www.wan-press.org/article7321.html

BOOKS The international book publishing market is becoming increasingly dominated by a handful of transnational corporations formed through mergers and acquisitions. This process of concentration began in the 1980s, driven by greater economies of scale in publishing and later with the incorporation of other types of media (e.g. music, movies, and television). A process of diversification and decentralization is simultaneously occurring due to innovations in information technology that create new opportunities for self-publishing and public access to various print mediums. These developments have raised questions regarding intellectual property rights and information flows, and have changed understandings and uses of books around the world. The indicator suite shows that:

- Five publishing houses dominate the global book publishing market; in 2003 their combined revenues were approximately $6.3 billion
- Random House, the largest publisher worldwide, accounts for 35% of the total revenue made by the "Big Five" publishers
- The United States dominates the global book market in terms of market value, but comes in second to China in terms of the volume of books sold
- The number of publishers in the United States is over twice the number located in the other six top markets combined (i.e., UK, Australia, Spain, Germany, New Zealand, and France).
- Over half of all books published worldwide are published in English, Chinese or German-in 2004, 375,000 new books were published worldwide by five main English-speaking countries, i.e., US, Canada, UK, Australia, and New Zealand (Bowker, 2005).

WHAT ARE BOOKS, THE BOOK INDUSTRY, AND BOOK PUBLISHING?

A 'book' is traditionally understood as a bound collection of pages that is not a periodical, journal or magazine. Today, books also include e-books, which are electronic versions that can be found on the Web. The term 'publishing' refers to the issuing of copies of printed materials. Today, various self-publishing and print-on-demand technologies are also available on the Web. Globalization has profoundly affected the book industry; beginning in 1891 when international copyright laws were created, authors and printing houses have increasingly become competitors on a global scale.

WHAT DO WE KNOW ABOUT BOOKS?

Books represented approximately 19% of $11.3 billion in trade of cultural goods in 2002, directly behind recorded media, the leading category. Books and other print media grew 3.7% between 1994 and 2002, with slower growth in high-income countries (between 1.8% and 3.4% from 1994 to 2002), and higher rates in low-income countries (12.5% on average). Despite this large increase, the share of low-income countries in the global book trade remains small. About 87% of all book exports in 2002 came from high-income countries, with 53% from Europe alone (UNESCO, 2005).

Book trades occur mainly between Europe and North America, with less involvement by Asia and limited participation by Africa. The top book producers at the end of the 20th century were the UK, Germany, the US, Spain, and Japan with between 111,000 and 56,000 books produced each year; and Burkina Faso, Togo, Ghana, Benin, and Gambia at the other extreme, with between 5 and 10 books produced a year (UNESCO, 2005). Losses due to illegal copying of copyrighted books exceeded $15.8 billion in 2005, with copyright infringements most prevalent in Russia, China, and South Korea (Publishers Weekly, 2006b).

In 2005, US book sales reached $25.1 billion and book publishers spent about $232 million on advertising (Publishers Weekly, 2006a, c). In Japan, approximately 65,500 books were published per year by the end of the 20th century; in China, a rapidly emerging market for books, over 100,000 new titles are published, representing a tenfold increase over the past decade (Goff, 2006). Worldwide, used-books sales increased heavily, thanks in part to the proliferation of websites that sell them (internet sales of used trade books rose 33% in 2004 [The Writer, 2006]).

WHAT ARE THE ISSUES?

The world's book industry is dominated by an oligopoly of five publishing houses-all transnational corporations-that pose challenges to book production, access and dissemination. Some experts fear that the global commodification of books will lead to 'dumbing down' and sensationalist pushing of select bestsellers. However, e-books, print-on-demand, small presses, and independent-publishing options are opening alternatives to authors (and readers).

As information technology grows, attention in the book industry is increasingly focused on the concept of the book's content as private or public property. While e-books have not yet found full acceptance by the reading public, it is an expanding market (Table 1) that offers new opportunities for preserving, updating, and disseminating texts. At the same time, because information in the Web age is tied to a boundless space, it can be easily copied and altered, often without regard to ownership and copyrights. The ongoing Google project to scan millions of books from libraries in the US and the UK in order to increase access to printed materials illustrates this issue. Some view this and similar projects as an expansion of the possibilities of human knowledge, while others see it as an attempt to replace traditional books, which devalues creativity and disrespects ownership.

Similarly, while technologies for transmitting, reproducing, and storing data make access to books easier and often more interactive, issues such as piracy, pose challenges for the book industry where definitions and practices of intellectual property vary across nations. In many developing countries, piracy of books, especially textbooks, is common practice with local presses and individuals. Textbook piracy is most pronounced in Asia where college attendance is increasing, the use of English in education is widespread, and where less expensive and high quality printing services abound. Lower prices in developing countries create flows of illegal copies back into richer nations via the Web.

Many developing countries rely on book imports, which bring with them elements of outside cultures into local contexts. Book shortages, lack of infrastructure, illiteracy, few local publishers and the prevalence of English books exacerbate inequities between developing and developed countries. In this light, books are both tools for cultural enrichment, education and empowerment, and tools for sustaining the global socioeconomic and political hierarchy of nations; thus, ownership and participation in the publishing industry are key social indicators of how books are used and viewed in a broader context.

Banning and censoring of books is perhaps as old as the field of publishing itself. Many countries also have strict control over the publishing process, which limits the types of books being published and distributed. The Beacon for Freedom of Expression project (www.beaconforfreedom.org), sponsored by the Norwegian Government, lists over 500,000 books and newspapers that have been censored through the better half of the last millennium.

The book itself, as the publishing industry at large, is undergoing a revolutionary process that challenges the very definition of what constitutes a book, its purpose, cultural relevance and form. Will the 'book' gradually be replaced by some new form or model for storing and retrieving, presenting and disseminating, as well as selling and buying fiction, information and knowledge?

TABLE 1: **SELECTED E-BOOK INDUSTRY STATISTICS** 2004 / 2005

	AMOUNT 2005	% CHANGE FROM 2004
E-BOOK UNITS SOLD FOR 2ND QUARTER	$ 484,933	36%
E-BOOK REVENUES FOR 2ND QUARTER	$3,182,499	69%
E-BOOK TITLES PUBLISHED FOR 2ND QUARTER	1,024	24%

* Source: International Digital Publishing Forum, March 3, 2006: http://www.idpf.org/doc_library/statistics/Q22005.htm

MUSIC & MOVIES While music is an integral part of human history, reflecting deeply cultural, often religious roots, its modern understanding is much more in line with that of movies-recorded and commercially produced products that are part of a growing cultural economy. Similar to book publishing, the global industry around music and movies is increasingly dominated by a small number of transnational mega-media corporations. This 'entertainment complex' is commonly referred to as 'Hollywood' (Scott, 2005), even though the corporate headquarters of the five largest film entertainment companies are in New York (Time Warner, Viacom), Los Angeles (Walt Disney), Philadelphia (COMCAST) and Tokyo (Sony).

In light of the profound influence of popular music and movies on national and regional cultures, concern over Western, in particular American, dominance in global media is growing. Not surprisingly, the US leads the world in production and revenue generated from film and music. Propelled by financial resources and economies of scale, Hollywood has created a globalizing trend in both movies and music, yet that is increasingly threatened in the era of the Web. The suites on Music and Movies illustrate the following:

- In 2005, six film studios control nearly 80% of global market share, of these five are US companies
- The US alone accounts for 46% of the global film entertainment market
- US feature films are responsible for more than half of domestic box office revenue internationally
- The value of the recorded music retail sales in the US tops the world and is nearly double that of its nearest rival, Japan
- From 2004 to 2005, only Mexico and Russia experienced a positive increase in music sold

WHAT DO WE KNOW ABOUT MUSIC AND MOVIES?

The music industry has experienced rapid concentration in the past 10 years (Oligopoly Watch, www.oligopolywatch.com). Until recently, between 80-90% of the global music market was made up of the 'Big Five' record companies (Vivendi Universal, Time Warner, Sony, EMI Records, and BMG). With the merger between Sony and BMG music (a.k.a., Bertelsmann AG) in 2004, the "Big Five" became the "Big Four" (Table 1). Despite the existence of smaller labels, most are owned by or in contractual agreements with the "Big Four." Overall, the global pop music industry is valued at $30 billion, where 89% of all recorded music is bought in the top 10 markets. In 2005, seven of the top 10 global best-selling albums were produced by US records labels.

Internationally, CD sales have slumped since 1999, which is attributed to the rise of pirated CDs and illegal downloads from file sharing and Peer-2-Peer networks. In 2005, music revenues recovered somewhat with the increase in websites offering legally purchased digital downloads to computers, MP3 players and mobile phones. Similar to the motion picture industry, the global music industry remains dependent on international sales from superstar releases (BBC World Service).

Since 2004, global motion picture revenue has dropped $1.4 billion due to declining admission rates and increasing piracy of DVDs (Informa Telecoms and Media). Rising ticket prices to offset declines in attendance have not yet closed the gap. Although India and China dominate admission rates internationally, low ticket prices indicate that the influence of movie-goers at the box office is not as noticed as in the US, Japan or Europe.

The emergence of digital music, Peer-2-Peer file sharing, and broadband connections make both music and movies easier to access, copy and distribute; thus, challenging the fundamentals of the business models underlying the 'entertainment complex.' What is more, these new technologies have decreased production and distribution costs, opening up opportunities for musicians, singers, composers, directors and actors, locally and internationally. As major media conglomerates compete and struggle to stay afloat, other film and music industries are rising. Today, Bollywood, located in Mumbai, is the most prolific feature film producer in the world, followed by the US, with Japan, China, and France as other major international movie hubs (McLaughlin, 2005). In financial terms, however, the US still out-performs other country markets.

WHAT ARE THE ISSUES?

Digitalization (i.e., the electronic construction of sound and video through binary codes) not only implies profound changes for the entertainment industry, it also changes the way we think about music and video-we now can listen to and watch music and movies on digital players, including computers, mobile telephones and hand-held devices. We are able to access and download music and video files through the internet and broadband connections, changing the nature of music and video from a tangible object (e.g., a record or movie reel) to a stream of information to be accessed and played anywhere and at anytime.

The proliferation of piracy and illegal downloads has created a revenue crisis in recent years for both music and film industries. The music industry has been hit particularly hard by piracy, but is collaborating with national governments to crack down on illegal file sharing. Technological and marketing innovation has also helped to bring the music industry out of near ruin in 2005 through the success of legal purchased downloads. In addition, a number of high profile court cases levied against file sharers have been successful in stemming Peer-2-Peer networks and illegal sharing in the US and much of Western Europe (Table 2). Yet, it remains harder to control piracy in some areas, for instance, in China 90% of all CDs are pirated.

Piracy, illegal reproductions and downloads have adversely affected Hollywood as well. By contrast, Bollywood and Nollywood (Nigeria), though also affected, have chosen to combat falling revenue in different ways. Average production costs and cycles in India and Nigeria are much lower than in the US, requiring smaller absolute revenue to generate a profit and allowing for a constant flooding of local markets. Nollywood films are produced within a month (McLaughlin, 2005), and new movies are available on video or DVD within a week of release (Ruigrok, 2006). Additionally, Bollywood works closely with the music industry to release movies and soundtracks together, generating media hype around a creative audio-visual package for consumers.

France and Canada have been instrumental in sparking international debate over cultural heritage protection as a means to limit and guard against the infiltration of 'foreign,' (i.e. American) music and film. Uganda and Ghana have felt that Nollywood's proliferation into their countries have undermined their own fledging film markets (McLaughlin, 2005). In the music industry the backlash is not quite as strong against US dominance, but many countries have regulations reserving certain percentages of radio and TV airtime for national artists.

TABLE 1: **THE "BIG FOUR" MUSIC INDUSTRY CONGLOMERATES** 2005

	% WORLD SHARE
Universal Music Group	**25.5%**
Sony BMG Music Entertainment	**21.5%**
EMI Group	**13.4%**
Warner Music Group	**11.3%**
Independent Labels	**28.3%**

Source: The International Federation of Phonogram and Videogram Producers, 2005

TABLE 2: **PIRACY GROWTH** 2000-2004

YEAR	MILLION OF UNITS PIRATED	% CHANGE FROM PREVIOUS YEAR
2000	**640**	
2001	**950**	**48.4%**
2002	**1,085**	**14.2%**
2003	**1,130**	**4.1%**
2004	**1,155**	**2.2%**

Source: The International Federation of Phonogram and Videogram Producers, 2005

TELEPHONES, THE INTERNET & BLOGS Communication has evolved since the age of Morse code to today's elaborate networks of analogue and digital cables sending and receiving emails, voice and instant messages over computers and other wireless technology. The Internet, or the "Web," is a complex system of interconnected computer systems, largely via fiber-optic broadband cables. Blogs are public online journals posted by individuals expressing unedited views and opinions. Of particular notice, Blogs have played an important role in evolving the Internet into participatory forms of communication, including news, encyclopedias and social networking.

Telephones and now, the Internet, both spread through globalization as well as facilitate a globalizing process, bringing people, locations, and economies closer. In spite of this, global advancements in communication technology have not spread equally across regions or communities. Today, the infiltration of the Internet in all aspects of communication highlights the tensions of ownership and privacy in a boundless technological space and policy solutions to a growing global digital divide. The suites on Phones, the Internet and Blogs illustrate the following:

- Europe and North America account for almost 80% of all public wireless access points, while Africa and the Middle East have none
- Asia and North America account for more than 80% of all Internet blogs
- Women blog more than twice as often as men
- Over 90% of all blogs are written by people under the age of 30

WHAT DO WE KNOW ABOUT PHONES, THE INTERNET AND BLOGS?

Land-based telephone lines are increasingly replaced by cell phones; for instance, in some countries there are 500% more cell phones in use than traditional landline phones. This is prevalent in middle-income to low-income countries where landline infrastructure is nonexistent and unreliable, or in high-income countries where access and affluence make cell phone ownership attainable to most citizens. Telephone usage remains dominated by flows from North America to Asia and Europe; whereas phone connections to and from Africa are relatively non-existent.

Today, Internet usage reaches nearly 16% of the world population, accounting for a little over 1 billion people worldwide; however, this is unequally spread, with heavy bias in industrialized countries in Asia, Europe and North America. Nearly 80% of global wireless connections are located in North America and Europe. This growing global digital divide is the result of unequal access to computers, Internet network technology, computer literacy, and costs associated with purchasing and owning computers that can connect to the Internet. Worldwide, South Korea has the largest percentage of households with broadband connection (Mueller, 2006). Elsewhere, for the nearly three billion people that live on less than two dollars a day (Shah, 2006), access to the Internet remains illusive.

While blogging is most common in Asia and North America, the global popularity of blogging is spreading, with new blogs entering the Internet everyday. The total number of blogs online is not completely certain, but blog search engines (such as Technorati.com) claim searches through as many 41.4 million sites with 2.4 billion links. Most blogs attract small audiences and focus on local topics; though in contrast, some blogs have audiences upwards of 3,000 readers. Bloggers use the public space of the Internet to rate, write about, or comment on daily journals, original art works, favorite restaurants, music or movies. Additionally blogs are used to share political and social viewpoints. In China, the spread of blogs has been cited as one of the main sources for spreading public news and current events outside the realm of government control. Not only do blogs include the traditional written word, but video blogs or "vlogs" are also increasing for both news related stories and amateur video production (Kluth, 2006).

WHAT ARE THE ISSUES?

Concerns regarding the communications industry center on censorship, ownership, privacy and access. The recent controversy surrounding Google's decision to censor the content of Google-China at the request of the Chinese government provoked heated discussions about censorship on the Internet and the right to control the use of cyberspace (Mills, 2006). Similarly, the recent acquisition of MySpace.com by News Corporation (owned by media tycoon Rupert Murdoch) has raised questions about the ramifications of corporate ownership of the Internet and potential privacy and free-speech infringements. MySpace.com and similar social networking websites are known to target users for commercial advertisement, consumer choice and practice data, and to track trends in fashion and music (Hempel, 2006); thus, highlighting the tension between public access and use of a highly effective form of mass communication to the benefit of corporate media conglomerates unbeknownst to most audiences.

Another facet of the ownership and privacy debate is the origin of dominant Internet technologies. Google and Yahoo remain the top two search engines used worldwide, as is evidenced by their infiltration into quotidian language, such as "do you Yahoo?" and "just Google it". This popularity coupled with the birth of the Internet in the US has lead to concerns about US bias in Internet technology. In response, the EU has announced the creation of a "rival Google" search engine called Quaero, a joint investment between the French and German governments. Plans for Quaero are solely as a government funded project instead of a privately owned business venture. While Quaero is not yet online and functioning, it has sparked widespread discussion about the need for a true public entity search engine based outside of the US (O'Brien, 2006). However, in light of the recent revelation of widespread wire tapping by the United States government on its own citizens, there is also concern for the widespread use of governmentally controlled websites worldwide.

Blogs remain the ultimate space of free speech for the global public at large. Blogs and wiki's, public web-encyclopedias, are allowed to be changed by users and are not monitored by anyone in particular, but the reading population in general; thereby, raising issues of information control. South Korea has the only successful wiki online "newspaper" called Ohmy News, which relies entirely on citizen posts and edits. While this phenomenon of participatory conversations about news and current events has worked to influence South Korea's traditional news sources, Ohmy News is a very rare case. Other large media sources have tried to establish online citizen created participatory 'newspapers' but have been forced to shutdown because of Internet vandalism and misuse as platforms to further biased, inaccurate and, at times, hateful content (Kluth, 2006).

A pressing issue connected to access to the Internet and blogs is the rampant use of cyberspace for pornography. This reflects a growing international governance and law enforcement problem that is often tied to human trafficking and crime.

TABLE 1: **INTERNET USAGE - THE BIG PICTURE**

WORLD REGIONS	% POPULATION OF WORLD	% INTERNET USAGE OF POPULATION	% USAGE OF WORLD	% USAGE GROWTH (2000-2005)
AFRICA	14.1	2.6	2.3	423.9
ASIA	56.4	9.9	35.6	218.7
EUROPE	12.4	36.1	28.5	177.5
MIDDLE EAST	2.9	9.6	1.8	454.2
NORTH AMERICA	5.1	68.6	22.2	110.3
LATIN AMERICA + CARIBBEAN	8.5	14.4	7.8	342.5
OCEANIA + AUSTRALIA	0.5	52.6	1.7	134.6
WORLD TOTAL	100.0	15.7	100.0	183.4

source: Internetworldstats.com

TV + RADIO are major vehicles for the flow of information on a national and transnational scale. To a large extent, these flows, their content, as well as access to them, both reflect and perpetuate global power structures. The result is an amalgamation of perspectives and imbalanced formation that favor the developed world and exclude many voices, viewers and listeners in the Global South. The indicator suite, "TV and Radio" shows that:

• Of all the countries, the US has both the largest number of television stations (10,500) and radio stations (13,822)
• Western radio stations dominate the global market with the largest number of listeners
• Among world regions, North Africa, the Middle East, and Sub-Saharan Africa have the largest percentage of households with short wave radio access-an indicator of limited access to other media
• The 'national' broadcasters (Voice of America, Radio France Internationale, Deutsche Welle and BBC World Service) attract large audiences worldwide

WHAT IS TV AND RADIO?

Television is a system for transmitting, receiving, and reproducing audio and visual information from one place to another via wires and radio waves. Considered the most powerful medium of mass communication and a valued entertainment source, television is a major industry. Prior to the advent of television, radio broadcasting was the primary means for news and communication over long distances. Radio is a system that conveys information between various points by relying on the wireless transmission of electromagnetic waves through space. Short wave radio, operating at frequencies between 3 and 30 MHz, can reach longer distances than AM/FM radio, but vary greatly in regard to quality of sound. International broadcasting typically broadcasts over short wave in a range of frequencies and languages. Not subject to local regulation, short-wave radio can add to political diversity in countries with limited freedom of information; it can also serve as a tool of political propaganda.

WHAT DO WE KNOW ABOUT TV AND RADIO?

The United States currently has the largest share of the world's number of television and radio stations. Europe is also highly represented among the top 25 countries with the largest number of television stations, as is the Asia Pacific region with China (#3), India (#8), South Korea (#10), the Philippines (#16), and Japan (#18) represent. South Africa (9) is the only African nation to place in the top 25, as is Mexico (14) for Latin American. Whereas a greater number of Latin American countries are represented within the top 25 countries with the largest number of radio stations, South Africa remains the only African nation to rank in the top 25.

Western radio stations command the highest volume of listeners around the world. The British Broadcasting Company (BBC) World Service has the largest international audience at 153 million with programs offered in 43 different languages, while Voice of America follows next with an audience of 140 million and a total of 55 languages. Radio Deutsche Welle has less than half the number of listeners at 65 million (in 30 languages), followed by Radio France Internationale with 45 million (in 19 languages), Radio Australia with 20 million (in 6 languages), and Radio Canada Internationale with 8 million (in 5 languages).

While international broadcasting is dominated by the West, its audience largely derives from the remaining parts of the world. Over 44% of BBC Radio's average weekly audience is located in Africa and the Middle East, while Asia Pacific accounts for over 35% of BBC's average weekly listeners, together comprising 80% of BBC's total audience. On the other hand the Americas account for less than 8% of BBC Radio's audience, where as Eurasia make up less than 7%, and Europe around 5%.

Countries with fewer television stations and radio broadcast stations tend to have higher numbers of international short wave radio listeners. The majority of African, Middle Eastern, Eurasian, and South Asian countries have three or less television stations, while Kenya only has eight options as far as radio stations; Nigeria, Sudan, and Tanzania have three; and Cameroon has one. Interestingly, these five countries have the highest percentage of international short wave listeners followed by a dozen African, Middle Eastern, Eurasian, and South Asian countries that also tend to have few television stations. Further, North Africa, the Middle East, and Sub-Saharan Africa are the only regions where the majority of households have short wave radio, compared to the world average of 30%. However, only a few countries in these regions have international broadcasting stations themselves.

Likewise, countries with low television ownership and cable television subscription rates tend to have higher volumes of international short wave radio listeners. Compared to the United States, which has 938 television sets and 255 cable subscriptions per 1000 people, the five African countries with the highest percentage of international short wave listeners average a total of 127 television sets and 0.3 cable subscriptions per 1000 people. The Democratic Republic of Korea has low television and radio ownership and cable television subscription rates along with a high number of radio stations (56 total including an international broadcasting station), perhaps indicating national efforts to control the nature of information available to the public.

WHAT ARE THE ISSUES?

Unequal access and control of content are critical issues. As television and radio programs are developed and aired by networks, they not only provide information, but also inculcate certain viewpoints and opinions. Those located in developing parts of the world have fewer options for information access and largely consume what others produce, thereby perpetuating a culture of hegemony, i.e. typically Western popular culture; thus, television and radio function as a reflection and medium of dominant paradigms and power imbalances. The West dominates world TV and radio with respect to volume of stations and listeners; moreover, in other parts of the globe such as Asia Pacific, Latino America, and Africa, the West commands a large share of television, radio programming and content, thus more or less subtly affecting regional cultures.

Of course, there are notable exceptions to the dominance of Western, (i.e., American and European content) as the popularity of Brazilian TV novellas in South and Central America, Japanese cartoons in Asia, or Nigerian soaps in Sub-Saharan Africa suggest. Moreover, business opportunities rather than cultural sensitivities inform corporate strategies of media giants like MTV (Santana, 2003). Founded and launched in the US in 1977, MTV quickly spread to Europe and first entered Asia via Japan in 1992. In Asia, MTV found that merely bringing American and European pop culture to various reaches of the globe was inadequate and began considering the integration of local culture in its programming to maximize efficiency. Following this experiment, MTV featured indigenous artists and created local programs, sustaining regional broadcasts in some areas (i.e. Malaysia and Singapore) while individualizing stations in other countries (i.e. Philippines, Thailand, and Indonesia). The network additionally highlights new artists on a regional and global scale, thus creating a global music culture.

TV + ONLINE NEWS Television and the Internet are gaining in importance as media sources for news in terms of access and use. Online news is steadily reclaiming a portion of the audience that print media lost to television news, but it is also growing of its own accord via news portals. TV news refers to the broadcast of information regarding current events and happenings through the medium of television. The majority of news stories are pre-recorded reports edited and pieced together by the television networks, while live reports are presented by reporters on the scene, often with the help of a studio reporter. Producers determine what stories are included or excluded, and they thereby influence the outcome of a newscast. Thus, news is shaped by individuals and consequently informed by their culture.

Online news describes the practice of disseminating current events via the Internet and is rooted in the tradition of print media, which monopolized the mass media market before technological advances helped make radio and television the primary media. The advent of the Internet allowed the print media industry to reverse the trend of declining readership because it was able to reach more readers, generate additional revenue through advertisement, and promote the print product. Also, online sites enabled TV news networks to post programs online after broadcasting. While established news providers (print media and television) including the New York Times, CNN, and Business Week were the first to create online news sites, internet-based portals like Yahoo soon followed suit and now see the highest rates of usage by those seeking online news. Today, all major newspapers and weeklies maintain websites, as do many radio and television stations.

The indicator suite shows wide and expanding reach of TV and Online news:

• The Cable News Network (CNN) reaches over 75 million viewers, while Al Jazeera has approximately 40 million, and the British Broadcasting Company (BBC), around 38 million.

• The majority of Al Jazeera's audience comes from urban areas, identifies as Muslim, is male, has at least a high school degree, and earns an annual income of $1,000 USD or more. *

• Over the last decade, BBC Global has experienced a steady increase in distribution to homes with 24-hour reception, growing more than threefold from 38 million households in 1996 to 127 million in 2005.

* Yahoo News has the highest number of unique monthly users, followed by MSN.

WHAT DO WE KNOW ABOUT TV AND ONLINE NEWS?

The Cable News Network (CNN, owned by Time Warner), British Broadcasting Company (BBC), and Al Jazeera currently dominate the share of TV news viewers around the world. Founded in 1980 by Ted Turner, CNN is a private news network based in Atlanta with 42 bureaus and more than 900 affiliates worldwide that presently maintains networks in four different languages. Al Jazeera is an Arabic-language television channel that began broadcasting in 1996 with a $150 million grant from the Emir of Qatar. Perceived as a trustworthy source of information, compared to government or local channels, Al Jazeera is the most frequently viewed news channel in the Middle East, and its exclusive interviews and footage have been rebroadcast by the western media. BBC is a public broadcasting network that aired its first TV bulletin in 1954. Currently, BBC serves 43 countries worldwide.

Another notable media outlet is Germany's Deutsche Welle (DW), a public institution for foreign broadcasting. DW-TV does not charge stations for use of its programming, and as a result, its News Journal and other programs are rebroadcast on numerous public broadcasting stations in several countries such as the United States and Australia (Wikipedia, 2006). Started in 1953 as a short wave radio service, in 1994 Deutsche Welle became the first public broadcaster in Germany with a World Wide Web presence. In 2003, the German government passed the "Deutsche Welle Law", which defined the company as a three-media organization — making DW-WORLD.DE an equal partner with DW-TV and DW-RADIO. The spirit behind the Act is to present German as a cultural and democratic state and to promote intercultural exchange, including presenting points of view from other regions and cultures. In 2005, Deutsche Welle started to provide newscasts anchored by Arabic-speakers, the first European station to do so. Its television programming provides content in German, English, French and Arabic, while its radio and web presence provide content in 30 languages.

Meanwhile, TV5MONDE, which broadcasts several channels of French language programming, is the fourth largest global television network available around the world after MTV, CNN and BBC World (Wikipedia, 2006). TV5MONDE is the only digital, global French language network, broadcasting 24 hours a day, 365 days a year, to more than 160 million households in 200 countries worldwide, making it the second largest global network in terms of subscribers.

Of online news sites, Yahoo News has the highest number of unique monthly users (almost 97 million), followed by MSN (86.5 million), BBC (48 million), CNN, (22 million), the New York Times (over 11 million), USA Today (over 9 million), and Reuters (2.1 million). Yahoo News' monthly users exceed the reported number of CNN viewers (75 million). Over ninety-five percent of BBC's unique users access the TV news site as opposed to the radio news site, and 83% of Reuters users visit their website at least once a day, spending an average of 5 minutes and 16 seconds per visit. In the US, 21 percent of web users consume news through online news sites, where as 7 percent read both online and print news. In addition to the New York Times and USA Today, other American news publications like the Washington Post, the Los Angeles Times, and the San Francisco Chronicle, receive a high volume of unique monthly visits (around 7.4 million, 3.8 million, and 3.4 million respectively).

WHAT ARE THE ISSUES?

CNN, Al Jazeera, and BBC have each received charges of biased reporting in the past. Conservatives have accused CNN's reporting of enforcing a liberal position, whereas international journalists have criticized CNN for leniency in reporting on Bush's War on Terror. In its coverage of the Iraq War, CNN allegedly depicted violent images and focused more on "human interest" stories, with a systematic bias in favor of the US occupation. In 2002, an international Indian network petitioned CNN for an alleged pro-Pakistani bias.

Al Jazeera has been criticized by countries including Algeria, Bahrain, Morocco, and Spain for purported biased reporting and has received accusations of anti-American bias since airing video statements by Osama bin Laden and other Al Qaeda leaders following September 11. With regard to the Iraq War, Al Jazeera has faced allegations of inciting anti-occupation violence and consequent restrictions in reporting. BBC has received both accusations of being against and for the ruling British party, as well as being anti-Israel and also overly sympathetic to the enemy during British military campaigns. In the past, several countries including Uzbekistan, China, Zimbabwe, Sri Lanka, and Pakistan have banned BBC news as a result of reporting that antagonized ruling parties.

The absorption of local TV news outlets into large media companies poses questions regarding the commodification and monopolization of news. In addition, "the burst of all-news channels [is being] ignited by two critical forces: the falling cost of technology and television's power in the international marketplace" (Carvahal, 2006). 24-hour all-news network seem to be emerging in various regions, including France, which hopes to launch its own all news channel with government funding. A Pan African channel–to be presented in English and French–is also in the planning stages.

The 'CNN Effect' argues that expedited news travel (via the Internet and 24 hour international television news) has often resulted in unsound policy, by prompting public figures and governments to act hastily in order put on the appearance of effective leadership. Accordingly, the media functions alternately or simultaneously as (1) a policy agenda setting agent, (2) an impediment to the achievement of desired policy goals, and (3) an accelerant to policy decision making (Livingston, 1997). Aware of the public's instant and easy access to information about current events including strategic decisions and actions, global leaders may act to appease public criticism and response, thereby catering their decisions to the segment of the population who can afford television and Internet access.

While a handful of large companies dominate online news, there are other more informal sources that many argue offer less-biased information because they are free from corporate control and are often contributed to by freelance journalists and volunteers. Because online news production is very cost-effective, it has an economic advantage over more traditional news sources that rely on advertising revenues.

As the Internet grows as a news source in developed countries, traditional print media and TV news viewing have declined. From 1984 to 2005 in the US for example, the audience for television evening news fell by almost 38 percent, and newspaper circulation declined by 15 percent (Ahlers and Hessen, 2005). While these figures suggest a continued loss of importance of traditional and TV news sources, internet news sources may instead be used in tandem with other sources. Furthermore, emerging linkages between traditional and new technologies are creating innovative news sources and outlets, such as online news webcasts. Another noteworthy trend is that younger cohorts are turning to the internet for news and information, compared to older adults, who tend to read newspapers.

* These are rough estimates and inconsistent with respect to time and methodology.

MOVEMENTS + COMMUNITIES

MIGRATION

REFUGEES + ASYLUM SEEKERS

TOURISM

TRANSNATIONAL COMMUNITIES

TRANSNATIONAL MOVEMENTS

TRANSPORTATION AIRPORTS

MIGRATION - international immigrants worldwide by region, distribution

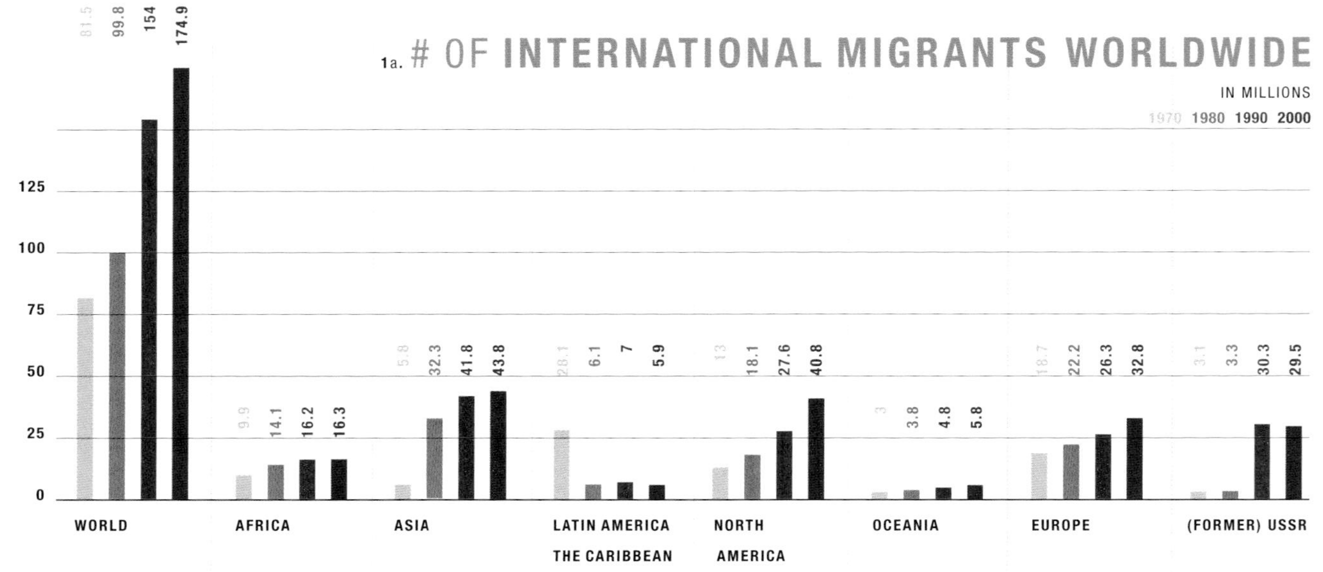

1a. # OF INTERNATIONAL MIGRANTS WORLDWIDE
IN MILLIONS
1970 1980 1990 2000
0
25
50
75
100
125
81.5 99.8 154 174.9
9.9 14.1 16.2 16.3
5.8 32.3 41.8 43.8
28.1 6.1 7 5.9
13 18.1 27.6 40.8
3 3.8 4.8 5.8
18.7 22.2 26.3 32.8
3.1 3.3 30.3 29.5
WORLD
AFRICA
ASIA
LATIN AMERICA THE CARIBBEAN
NORTH AMERICA
OCEANIA
EUROPE
(FORMER) USSR

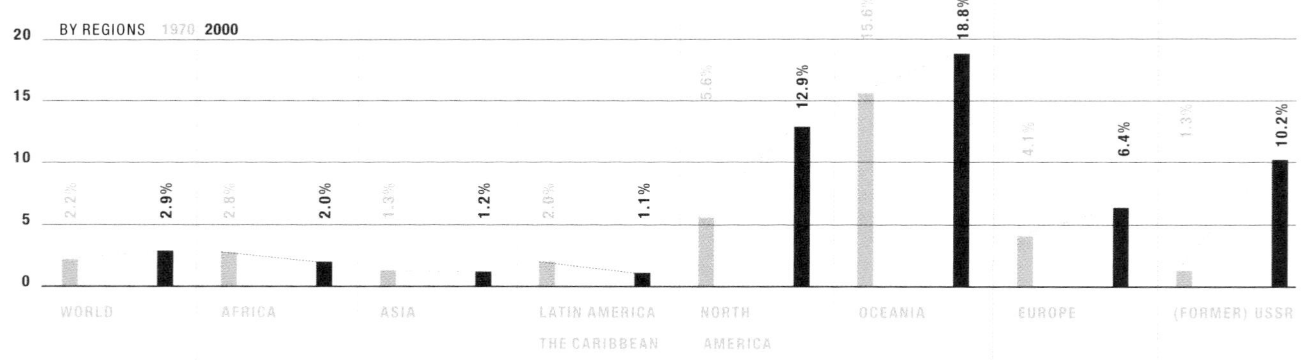

1b. INTERNATIONAL MIGRANTS % OF TOTAL POPULATION
BY REGIONS 1970 2000
0
5
10
15
20
2.2% 2.9%
2.8% 2.0%
1.3% 1.2%
2.0% 1.1%
5.6% 12.9%
15.6% 18.8%
4.1% 6.4%
1.3% 10.2%
WORLD
AFRICA
ASIA
LATIN AMERICA THE CARIBBEAN
NORTH AMERICA
OCEANIA
EUROPE
(FORMER) USSR

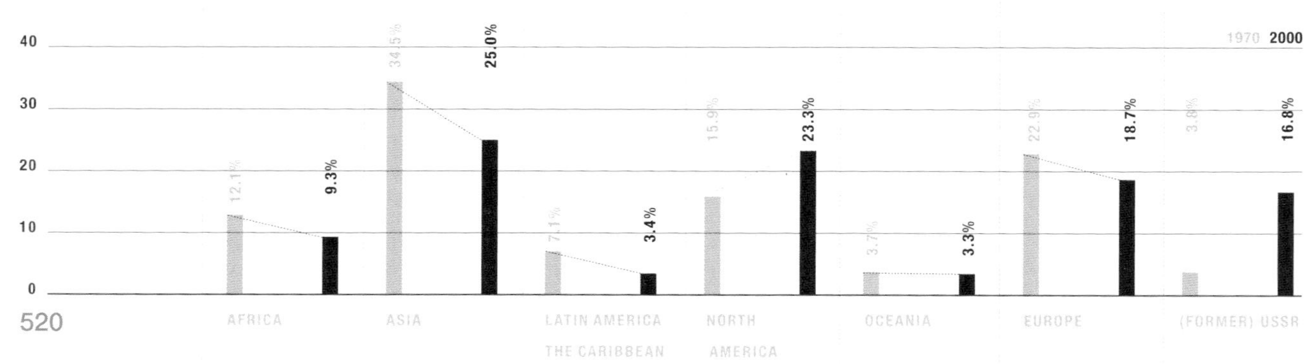

1c. % DISTRIBUTION OF WORLD MIGRANTS BY REGIONS
1970 2000
0
10
20
30
40
12.1% 9.3%
34.5% 25.0%
7.1% 3.4%
15.9% 23.3%
3.7% 3.3%
22.9% 18.7%
3.8% 16.8%
AFRICA
ASIA
LATIN AMERICA THE CARIBBEAN
NORTH AMERICA
OCEANIA
EUROPE
(FORMER) USSR

2. TOP 3 MIGRANT SENDING COUNTRIES

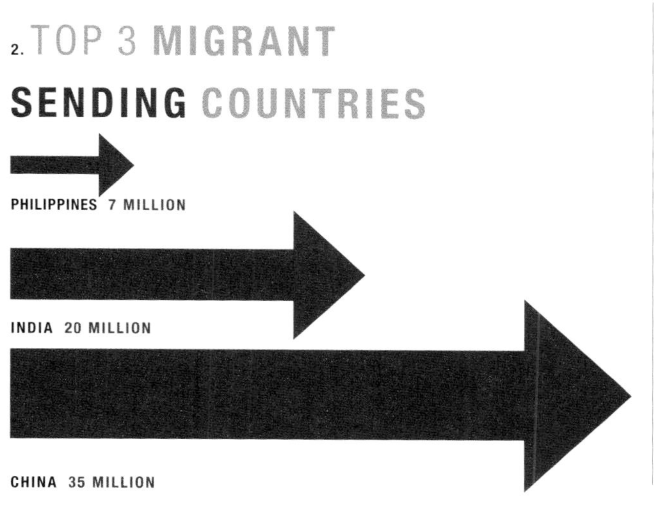

3. WORLD MIGRANT STOCK HOSTED

2004 - 2005 ESTIMATE (POPULATION HOSTED IN MILLIONS)

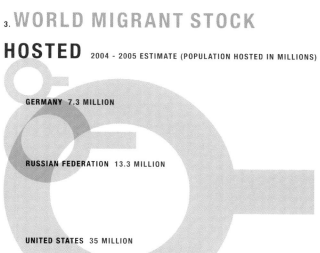

GERMANY 7.3 MILLION

RUSSIAN FEDERATION 13.3 MILLION

UNITED STATES 35 MILLION

4. TOP 20 COUNTRIES HOSTING LARGEST % OF MIGRANTS

2000 + 1970 RANKINGS

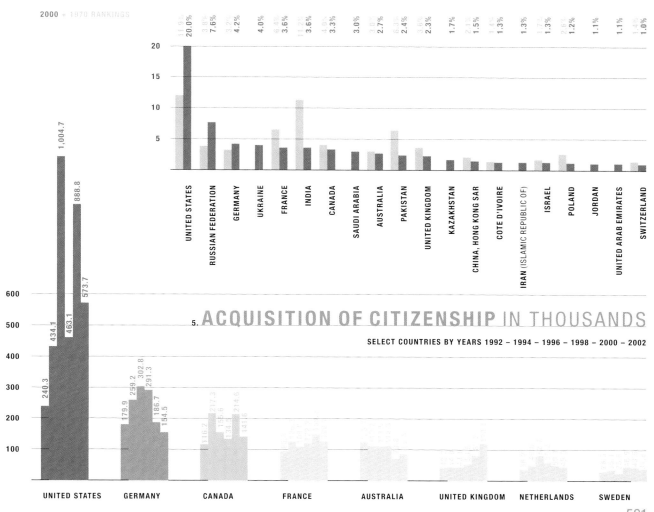

Country	1970	2000
UNITED STATES	11.9%	20.0%
RUSSIAN FEDERATION	3.8%	7.6%
GERMANY	3.2%	4.2%
UKRAINE		4.0%
FRANCE	6.4%	3.6%
INDIA	11.2%	3.6%
CANADA	4.0%	3.3%
SAUDI ARABIA		3.0%
AUSTRALIA	3.0%	2.7%
PAKISTAN	6.3%	2.4%
UNITED KINGDOM	3.6%	2.3%
KAZAKHSTAN		1.7%
CHINA, HONG KONG SAR	2.1%	1.5%
COTE D'IVOIRE	1.4%	1.3%
IRAN (ISLAMIC REPUBLIC OF)		1.3%
ISRAEL	1.7%	1.3%
POLAND	2.6%	1.2%
JORDAN		1.1%
UNITED ARAB EMIRATES		1.1%
SWITZERLAND	1.4%	1.0%

5. ACQUISITION OF CITIZENSHIP IN THOUSANDS

SELECT COUNTRIES BY YEARS 1992 – 1994 – 1996 – 1998 – 2000 – 2002

Country	1992	1994	1996	1998	2000	2002
UNITED STATES	240.3	434.1	1,004.7	463.1	888.8	573.7
GERMANY	179.9	259.2	302.8	291.3	186.7	154.5
CANADA	116.2	217.3	155.6	134.5	214.6	141.6
FRANCE						
AUSTRALIA						
UNITED KINGDOM						
NETHERLANDS						
SWEDEN						

foreign born labor force - income gap top 3 sending & receiving countries - % perspective labor force us

top 20 countries receiving remittance - top 20 countries sending remittance - remittage sent by workers in us

6. FOREIGN BORN LABOR FORCE

IN SELECTED COUNTRIES 2000 (% SHARE OF TOTAL DOMESTIC LABOR FORCE)

AUSTARLIA	24.5%
CANADA	19.2%
FRANCE	6.0%
GERMANY	8.8%
NEW ZEALAND	18.9%
SWEDEN	5.0%
UNITED KINGDOM	4.4%
UNITED STATES	12.4%

7. INCOME GAP MEN & WOMEN

IN TOP 3 SENDING & HOST COUNTRIES 2003

(ESTIMATED AVERAGE EARNED INCOME IN $USD THOUSANDS PPP)

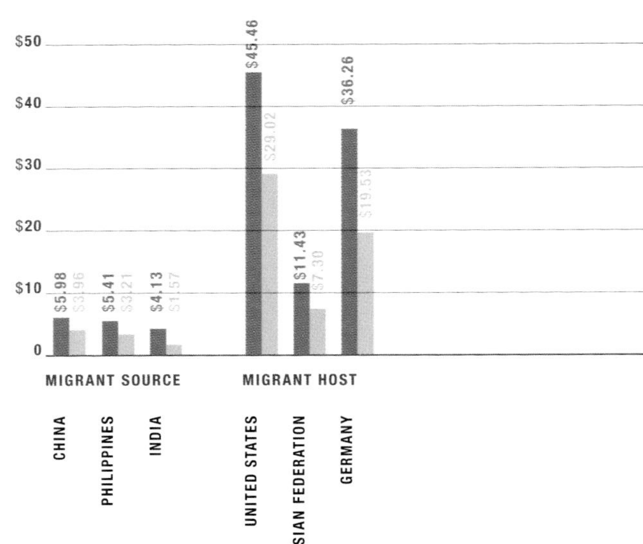

8. % LABOR FORCE IN THE UNITED STATES 2000

NATIVE-BORN AND FOREIGN-BORN BY SECTOR

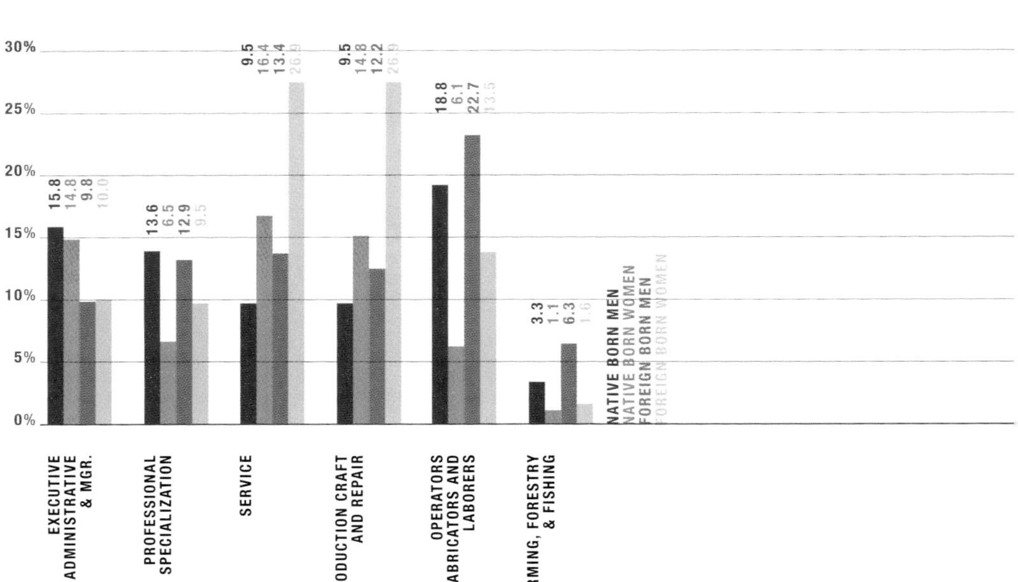

10. TOP 20 COUNTRIES RECEIVING + SENDING REMITTANCE 2001
(BY VALUE IN $USD BILLIONS)
10.0 9.9 6.4 3.3 2.9 2.8 2.3 2.1 2.0 2.0 1.9 1.8 1.5 1.5 1.5 1.4 1.4 1.3 1.2 1.1
INDIA MEXICO PHILIPPINES MOROCCO EGYPT TURKEY LEBANON BANGLADESH JORDAN DOMINICAN REPUBLIC EL SALVADOR COLOMBIA YEMEN PAKISTAN BRAZIL ECUADOR FORMER YUGOSLAVIA THAILAND CHINA SRI LANKA
UNITED STATES SAUDI ARABIA GERMANY BELGIUM SWITZERLAND FRANCE LUXEMBOURG ISRAEL ITALY JAPAN SPAIN KUWAIT OMAN NETHERLANDS BAHRAIN UNITED KINGDOM DENMARK CZECH REPUBLIC VENEZUELA NORWAY
28.4 15.1 8.2 8.1 8.1 3.9 3.1 3 2.6 2.3 2.2 1.8 1.5 1.5 1.3 1.3 0.7 0.7 0.7 0.7
0 5 10 15 20 25 30
11. TOP 20 COUNTRIES RECEIVING REMITTANCE 2001
(BY % OF GROSS DOMESTIC PRODUCT)
37.3 26.5 22.8 17.0 16.2 16.1 15 13.8 13.8 13.6 13.5 12.8 9.7 9.3 8.9 8.9 8.5 8.5 7.9 7.0
TONGA LESOTHO JORDAN ALBANIA NICARAGUA YEMEN MOLDOVA LEBANON EL SALVADOR CAPE VERDE JAMAICA FORMER YUGOSLAVIA MOROCCO DOMINICAN REPUBLIC VANUATU PHILIPPINES HONDURAS UGANDA ECUADOR SRI LANKA
12. AVERAGE REMITTANCES SENT BY MIGRANTS IN THE US
DEC-JAN 2003 ($USD TO MAJOR SELECT RECIPIENT COUNTRIES)
1200 900 600 300 0
1104 790 562 397 385 307 280 203
INDIA PAKISTAN BANGLADESH PHILIPPINES MEXICO EGYPT EL SALVADOR DOMINICAN REPUBLIC
13. REMITTANCES TO SELECT MAJOR RECIPIENT COUNTRIES
2000 (% SHARE WORLDWIDE & REGIONWIDE)
80 70 60 50 40 30 20 10 0
2% 2% 2% 2% 2% 2% 2% 3% 4% 4% 5% 6% 8% 8% 8% 15%
YEMEN NIGERIA GREECE DOMINICAN REPUBLIC EL SALVADOR JORDAN BANGLADESH MOROCCO PORTUGAL SPAIN EGYPT TURKEY CHINA PHILIPPINES MEXICO INDIA

REFUGEES + ASYLUM SEEKERS

- principal source of **refugees** and **internally displaced people** by number and by region
+ **asylum locations**
- **refugees** hosted and per capita income of **host nations**

1. PRINCIPAL SOURCE OF REFUGEES AS OF DEC.31 2004

FORMER **PALESTINE**
AFGHANISTAN
SUDAN
MYANMAR
BURUNDI
CONGO-KINSHASHA
IRAQ
LIBERIA
SOMALIA
VIETNAM
COLOMBIA
ANGOLA
ERITREA
CHINA
BHUTAN
NORTH KOREA
NEPAL
SRI LANKA
CROATIA
PHILIPPINES
RWANDA
TAJIKISTAN
CHAD
ETHIOPIA

AFGHANI ASYLUM LOCATIONS:	
PAKISTAN	960,041
ISLAMIC REPUBLIC OF IRAN	952,802
GERMANY	38,576
THE NETHERLANDS	25,907
UNITED KINGDOM	22,494
CANADA	15,242
UNITED STATES	9,778
INDIA	9,761
AUSTRALIA	8,037
DENMARK	6,437
UZBEKISTAN	5,238

SUDANI ASYLUM LOCATIONS:	
CHAD	224,924
UGANDA	214,673
ETHIOPIA	90,451
KENYA	67,556
DEM. REP. OF THE CONGO	45,226
CENTRAL AFRICAN REPUBLIC	19,470
UNITED STATES	17,994
EGYPT	14,904

CONGOLESE ASYLUM LOCATIONS:	
UNITED REP. OF TANZANIA	153,474
ZAMBIA	66,248
CONGO	58,834
BURUNDI	48,424
RWANDA	45,460
UGANDA	14,982
ANGOLA	13,510
SOUTH AFRICA	9,516
FRANCE	7,665
GERMANY	6,668
UNITED KINGDOM	5,973
CANADA	5,069

3. REFUGEES HOSTED + PER CAPITA INCOME OF HOST NATIONS 2004

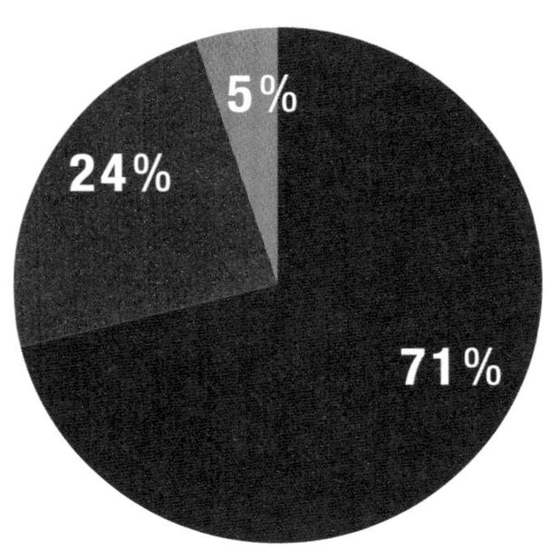

% OF HOST COUNTRIES W/ PER CAPITA INCOME BELOW $2,000 (8,002,900 HOSTED)
% OF HOST COUNTRIES W/ PER CAPITA INCOME BETWEEN $2,000 - $10,000 (2,684,400 HOSTED)
% OF HOST COUNTRIES W/ PER CAPITA INCOME OVER $10,000 (614,400 HOSTED)

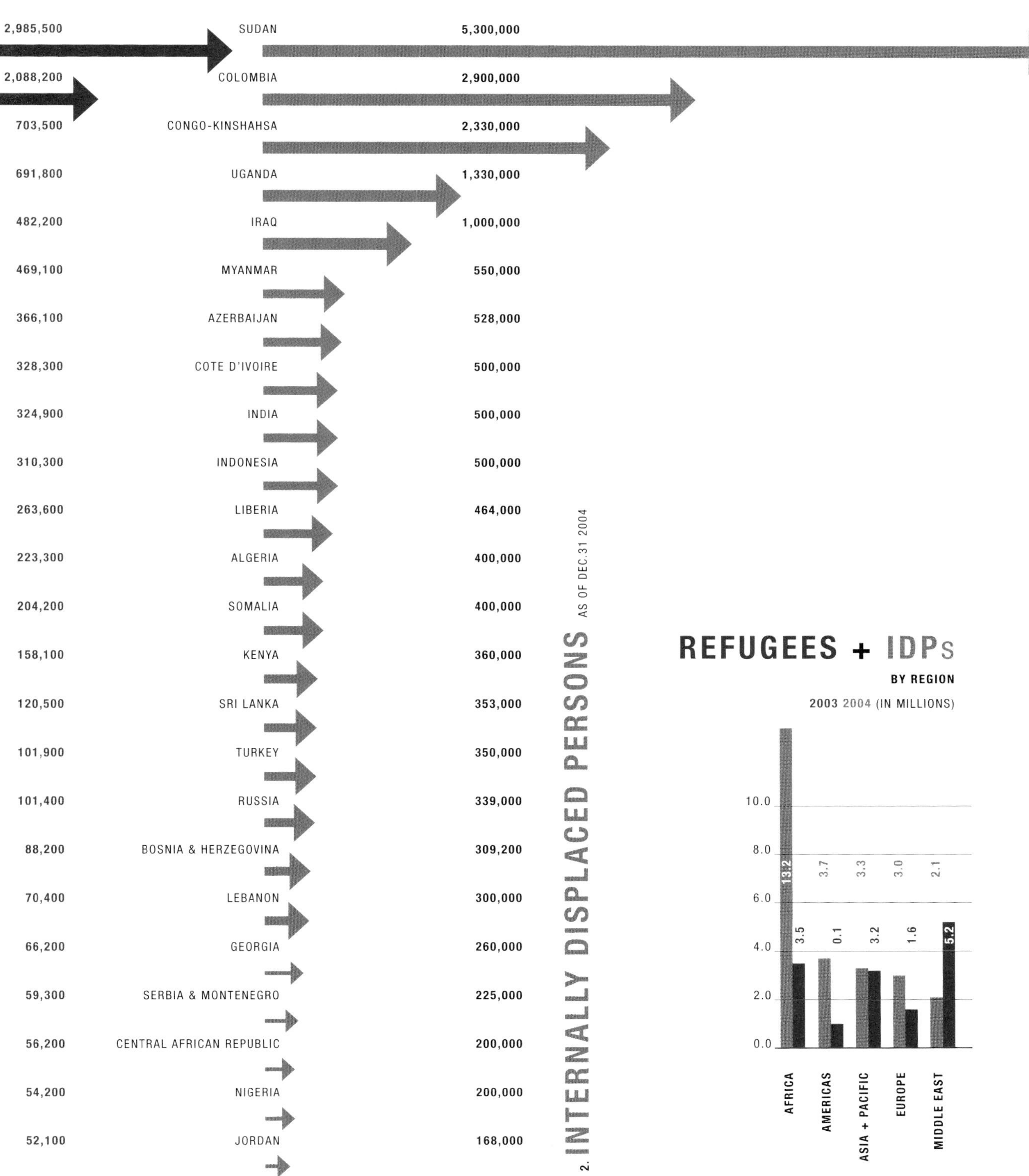

2,985,500
SUDAN
5,300,000
2,088,200
COLOMBIA
2,900,000
703,500
CONGO-KINSHAHSA
2,330,000
691,800
UGANDA
1,330,000
482,200
IRAQ
1,000,000
469,100
MYANMAR
550,000
366,100
AZERBAIJAN
528,000
328,300
COTE D'IVOIRE
500,000
324,900
INDIA
500,000
310,300
INDONESIA
500,000
263,600
LIBERIA
464,000
223,300
ALGERIA
400,000
204,200
SOMALIA
400,000
158,100
KENYA
360,000
120,500
SRI LANKA
353,000
101,900
TURKEY
350,000
101,400
RUSSIA
339,000
88,200
BOSNIA & HERZEGOVINA
309,200
70,400
LEBANON
300,000
66,200
GEORGIA
260,000
59,300
SERBIA & MONTENEGRO
225,000
56,200
CENTRAL AFRICAN REPUBLIC
200,000
54,200
NIGERIA
200,000
52,100
JORDAN
168,000
2. INTERNALLY DISPLACED PERSONS AS OF DEC.31 2004
REFUGEES + IDPs
BY REGION
2003 2004 (IN MILLIONS)
10.0
8.0
6.0
4.0
2.0
0.0
13.2
3.5
3.7
0.1
3.3
3.2
3.0
1.6
2.1
5.2
AFRICA
AMERICAS
ASIA + PACIFIC
EUROPE
MIDDLE EAST

TOURISM - outbound tourism - international tourist arrivals - top 10 international tourist destinations 2004 + 2020 - tourism spenders - tourist receipts - travel & tourism total global demand

1. OUTBOUND TOURISM BY REGION 1990 + 2000 + 2004

DEPARTURES IN MILLIONS

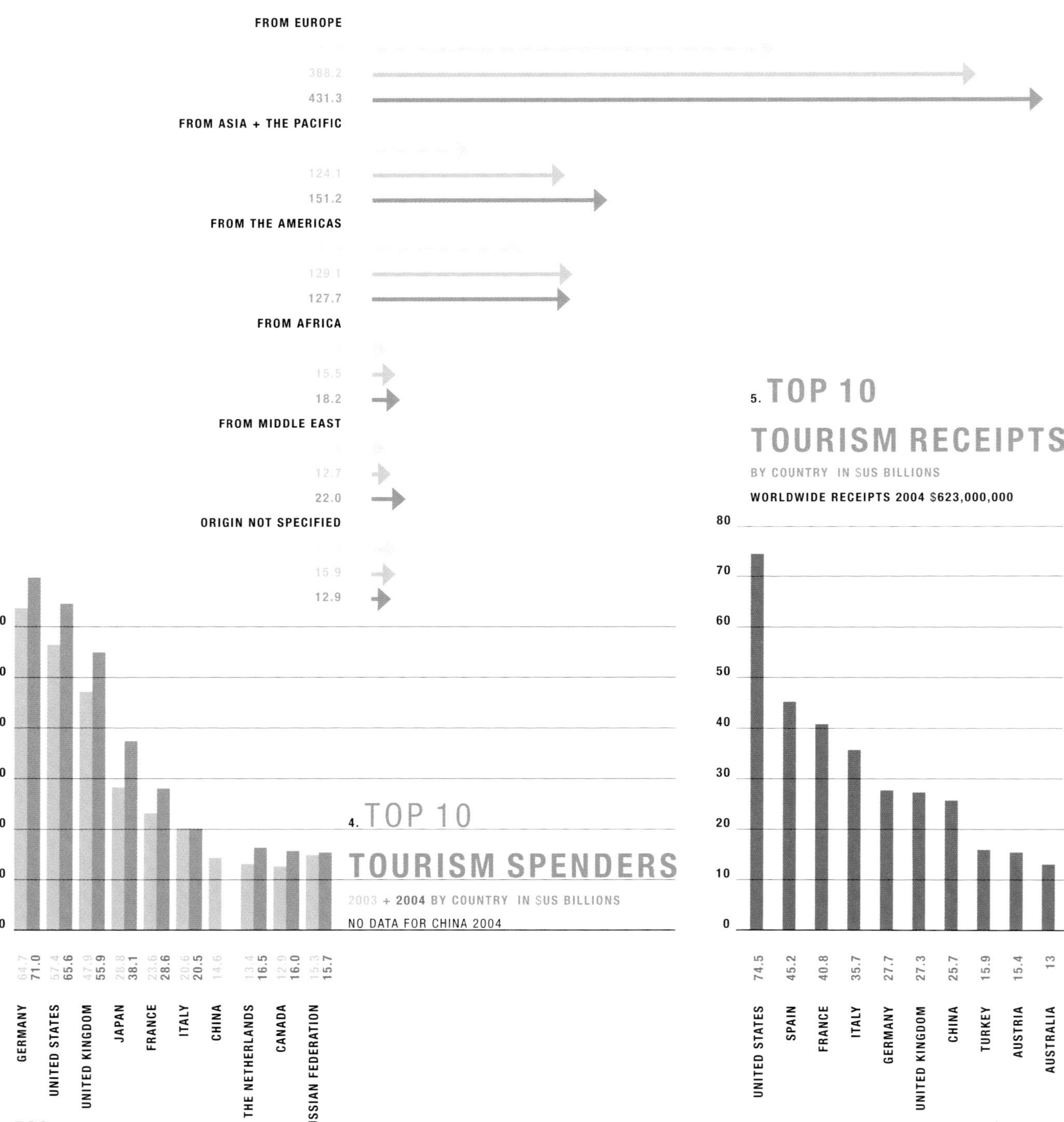

2. INTERNATIONAL TOURIST ARRIVALS BY REGION

ARRIVALS IN MILLIONS

TO EUROPE

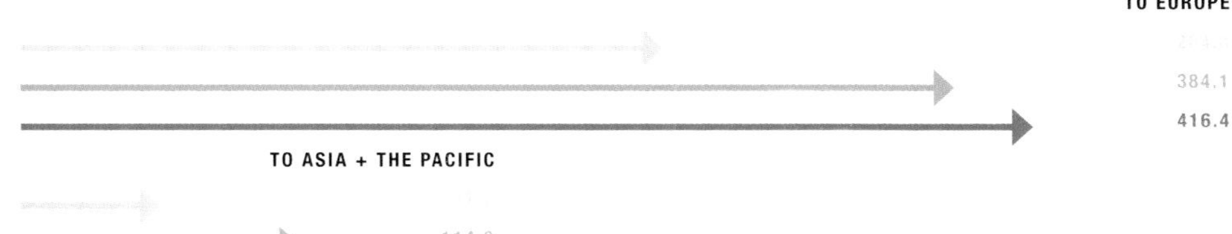

114.9

152.5

TO THE AMERICAS

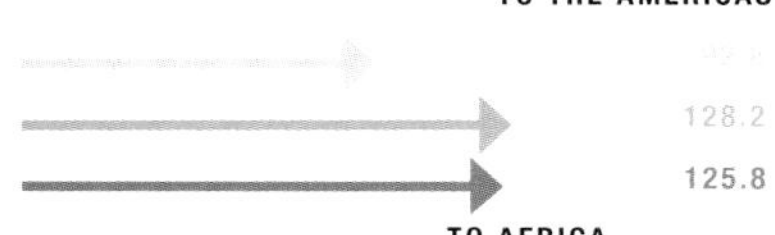

TO AFRICA

3. TOP 10 INTERNATIONAL TOURIST DESTINATIONS 2004 + 2020

ARRIVALS IN MILLIONS

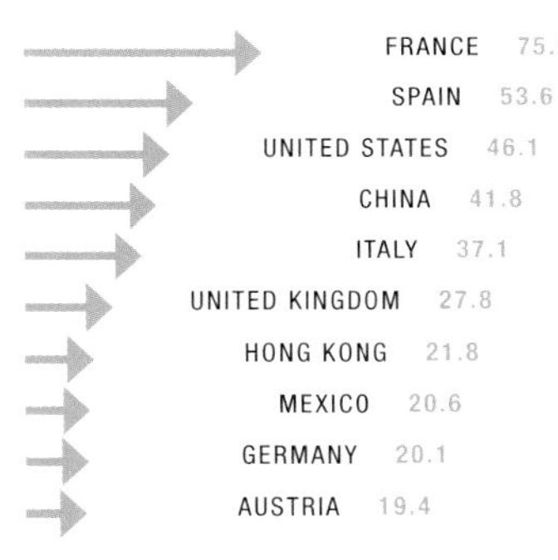

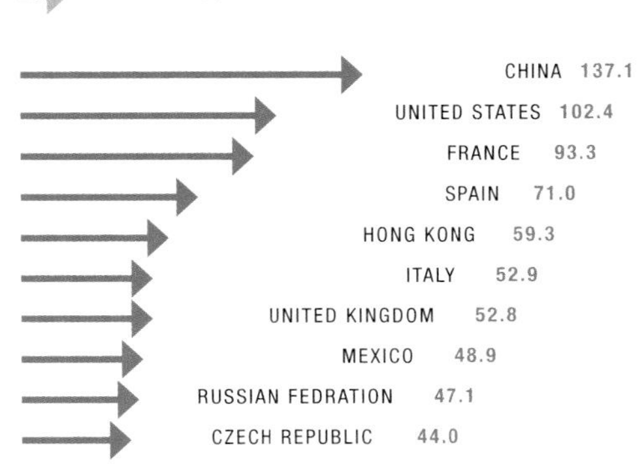

6. 2005 TRAVEL + TOURISM TOTAL GLOBAL DEMAND

IN $US BILLIONS

TOTAL GLOBAL ACTIVITY GENERATED BY TOURISM = $6,201,500,000

EUROPE	2,272.0 $US BILLION
NORTH AMERICA	1,880.2
NORTH EAST ASIA	974.2
SOUTH EAST ASIA	165.5
LATIN AMERICA	133.2
MIDDLE EAST	128.6
SOUTH ASIA	59.3
NORTH AFRICA	47.3
CARIBBEAN	45.5

- international tourist destination **change - asian + pacific tourist market** affected by sars **- tsunami effect** on **passenger travel arrivals** at phuket airport, thailand

1. TOP 10 INTERNATIONAL TOURIST DESTINATIONS

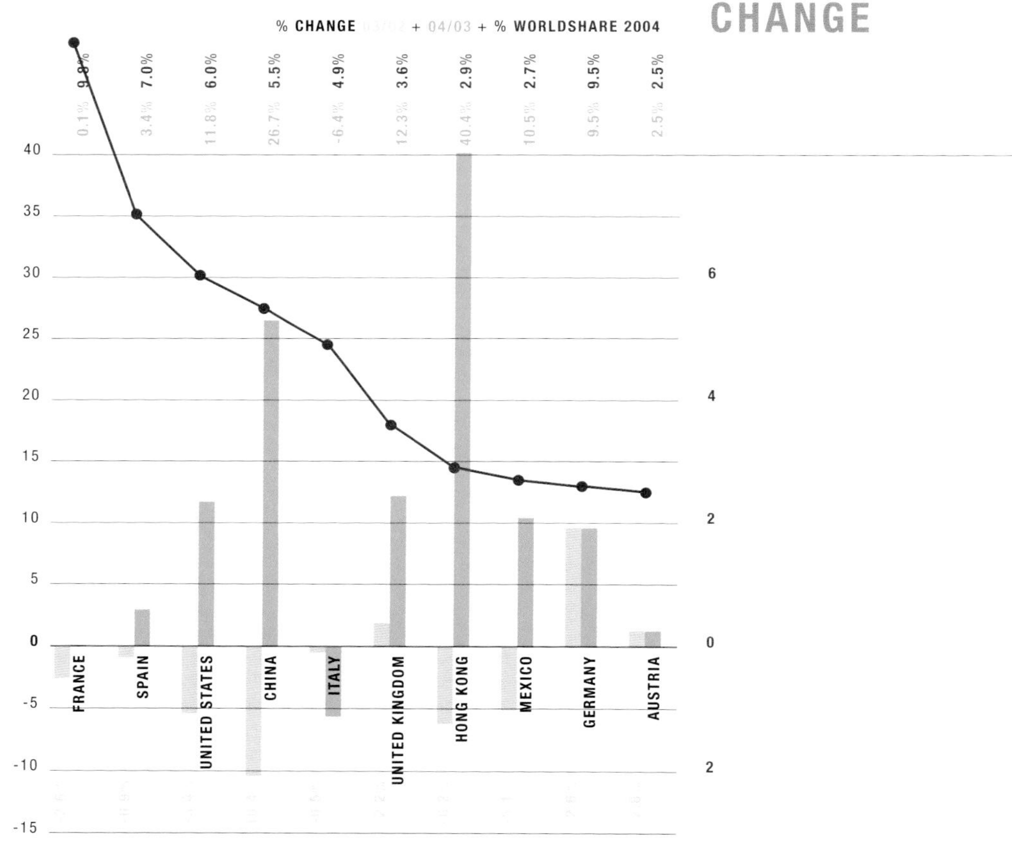

2. ASIAN + PACIFIC **TOURIST MARKET**

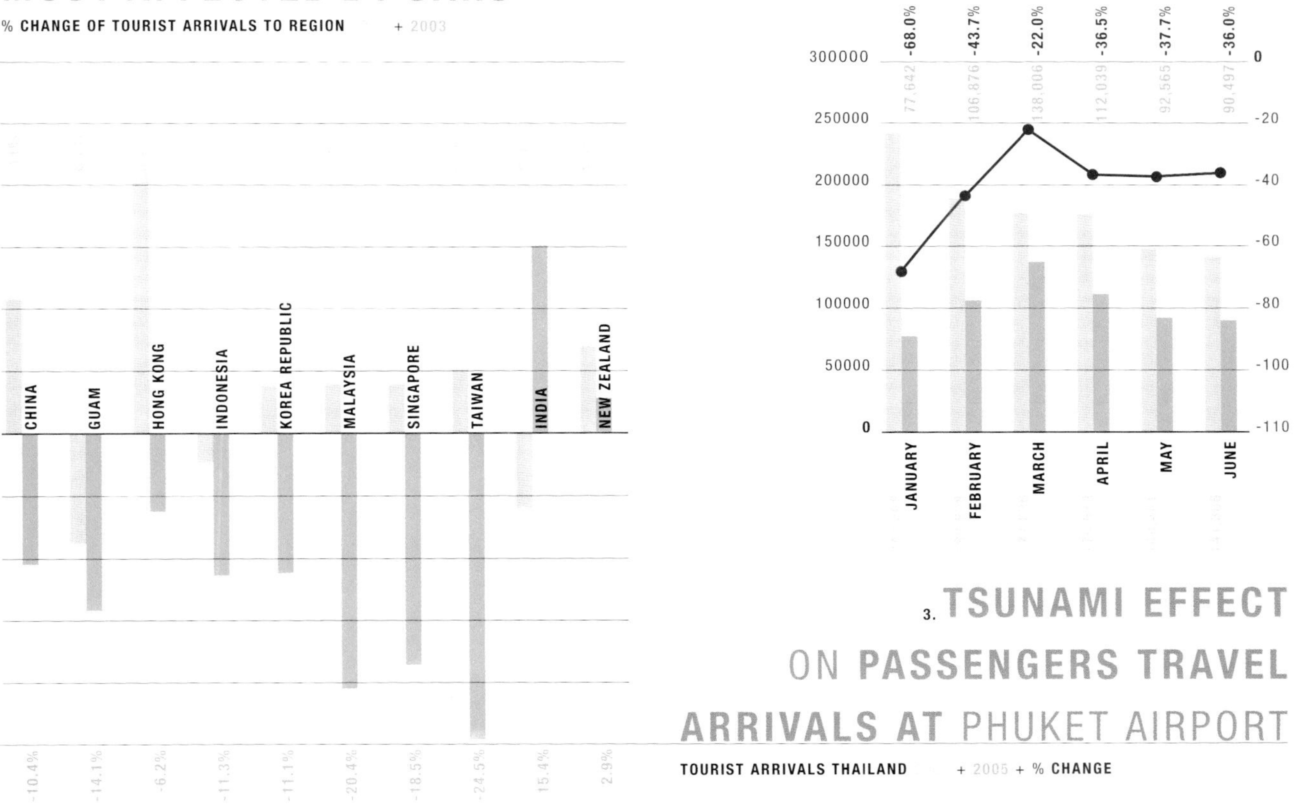

MOST AFFECTED BY SARS
% CHANGE OF TOURIST ARRIVALS TO REGION + 2003
CHINA
GUAM
HONG KONG
INDONESIA
KOREA REPUBLIC
MALAYSIA
SINGAPORE
TAIWAN
INDIA
NEW ZEALAND
-10.4%
-14.1%
-6.2%
-11.3%
-11.1%
-20.4%
-18.5%
-24.5%
15.4%
2.9%
-68.0%
-43.7%
-22.0%
-36.5%
-37.7%
-36.0%
77,642
106,876
138,006
112,039
92,565
90,497
300000
250000
200000
150000
100000
50000
0
0
-20
-40
-60
-80
-100
-110
JANUARY
FEBRUARY
MARCH
APRIL
MAY
JUNE
3. TSUNAMI EFFECT
ON PASSENGERS TRAVEL
ARRIVALS AT PHUKET AIRPORT
TOURIST ARRIVALS THAILAND + 2005 + % CHANGE

TRANSNATIONAL COMMUNITIES

- **people in refugee-like situations** - estimated population of **kurds** - estimated size of **kurdish diaspora** - # of **roma** in europe - estimated **jewish population** - largest # of overseas **filipino worker population**

1. PEOPLE IN REFUGEE LIKE SITUATIONS

ESTIMATED # NOT FORMALLY RECOGNIZED BY GOVERNMENTS AS 'REFUGEES' BUT EXIST IN A 'DIASPORIC' STATE (UNITED STATES COMMITTEE FOR REFUGEES & IMMIGRANTS 2005)

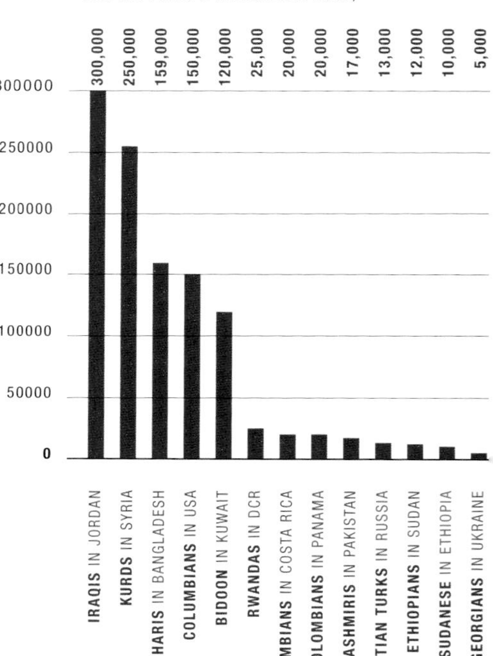

2. ESTIMATED POPULATION OF KURDS WITHIN KURDISH TERRITORY

BY THOUSANDS

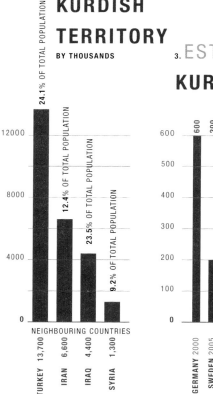

24.1% OF TOTAL POPULATION

12.4% OF TOTAL POPULATION

23.5% OF TOTAL POPULATION

9.2% OF TOTAL POPULATION

12000

8000

4000

0

NEIGHBOURING COUNTRIES

TURKEY 13,700

IRAN 6,600

IRAQ 4,400

SYRIA 1,300

3. ESTIMATED SIZE OF KURDISH DIASPORA

SELECTED COUNTRIES BY THOUSANDS

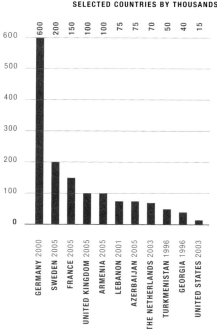

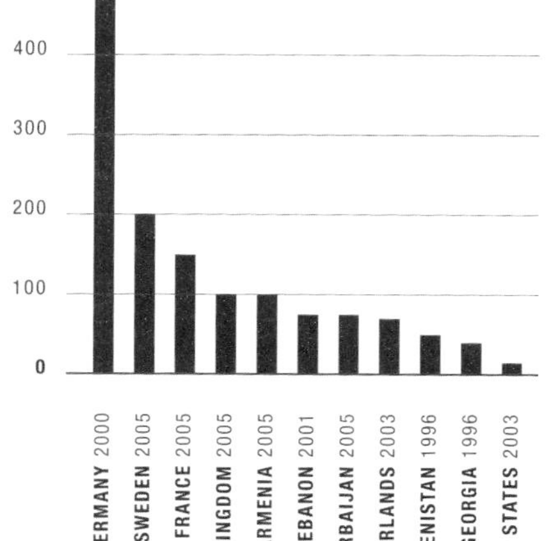

4. COUNTING THE ROMA IN EUROPE

OFFICIAL GOVERNMENT CENSUS

LOCAL NGO/OTHER EXPERT ESTIMATES

IN # AND % OF TOTAL POPULATION

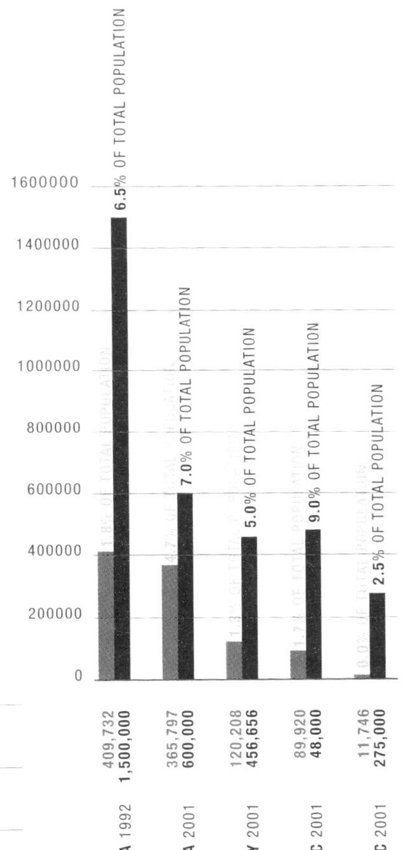

5. ESTIMATED JEWISH POPULATION 2002

IN # WORLD TOTAL DIASPORA SIZE

JEWISH DIASPORA BY REGIONS

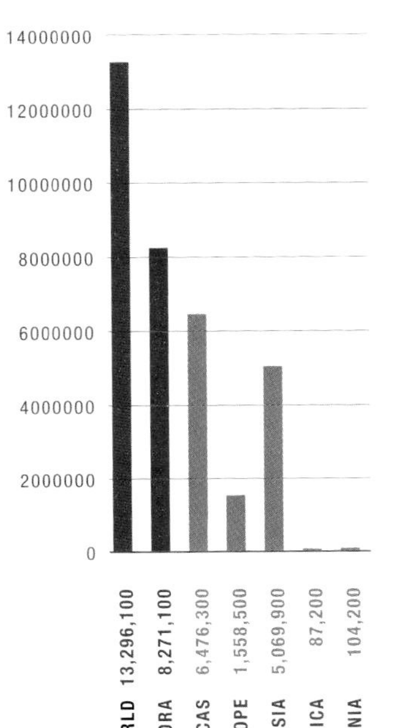

6. LARGEST # OF OVERSEAS FILIPINO WORKER POPULATION

BY COUNTRY AND REGIONS IN #

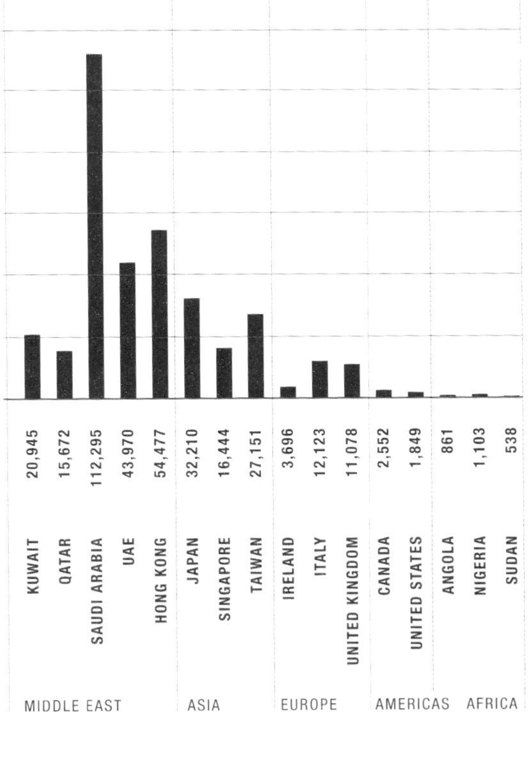

TRANSNATIONAL MOVEMENTS

- the greatest danger facing the world - world social forum events - thoughts on **global consumerism** and **culture -** thoughts on **international financial institutions -** thoughts on **globalization - financial sponsors wsf - growth of social forums**

1. WHAT DO CITIZENS RANK AS THE GREATEST DANGER FACING THE WORLD?

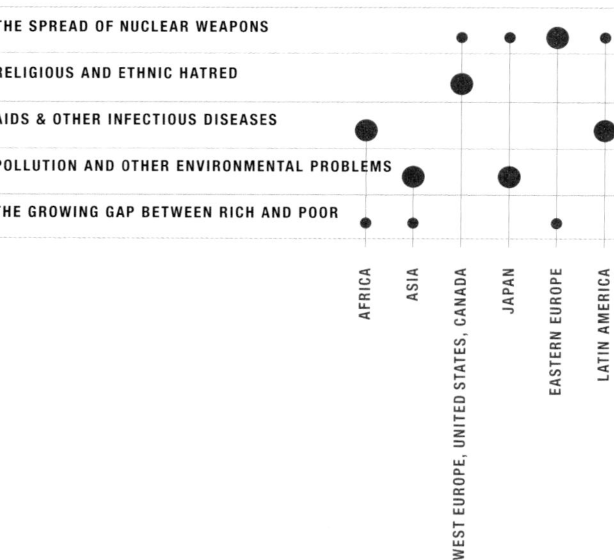

2. WORLD SOCIAL FORUM EVENTS

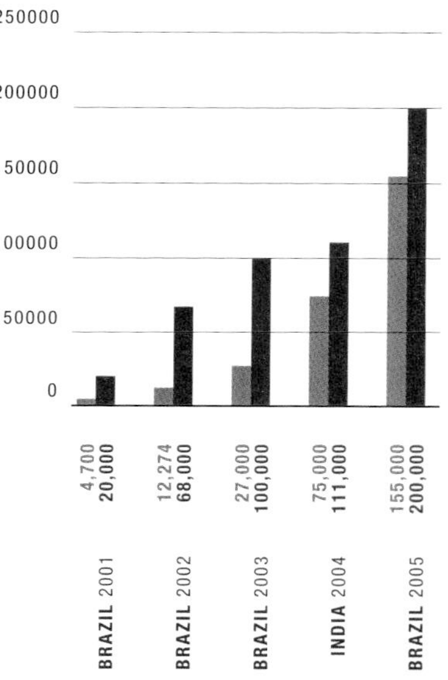

6. FINANCIAL SPONSORS OF THE WORLD SOCIAL FORUM

MUMBAI, INDIA 2004

SPONSORS OF WSF PROCESS

BR PETROBAS
CAIXA DO BRASIL
CORREIOS
FORD FOUNDATION
FUNDACAO BANCO DO BRASIL

SPONSORS OF WSF IN MUMBAI

ACTIONAID
ALTERNATIVES, CANADA
ATTAC, NORWAY
COMITE CATHOLIQUE CONTRE LA FAIM ET POUR LE DEVELOPPEMENT (CCFD)
CHRISTIAN AID
DEVELOPMENT & PEACE
EVANGELISCHER ENTWICKLUNGSDIENST
FUNDERS NETWORK ON TRADE & GLOBALIZATION
HEINRICH BOLL FOUNDATION
HUMANIST INSTITUTE FOR CO-OPERATION W/DEVELOPING COUNTRIES
INTER CHURCH ORGANIZATION FOR DEVELOPMENT COOPERATION
OXFAM INTERNATIONAL
SOLIDAGO FOUNDATION
SOLIDARITES, NORWAY
SWEDISH INTERNATIONAL DEVELOPMENT COOPERATION AGENCY
SWISS AGENCY FOR DEV. & COOPERATION
TIDES FOUNDATION
WORLD COUNCIL OF CHURCHES

*** PORTO ALEGRE, BRAZIL 2005**

SPONSORS OF WSF PROCESS & WSF IN BRAZIL

BANCO DO BRASIL
BRASIL GOVERNO FEDERAL
BR PETROBAS
CAIXA DO BRASIL
CORREIOS
CHRISTIAN AID
CAFOD
COMITE CATHOLIQUE CONTRE LA FAIM ET POUR LE DEVELOPMENT (CCFD)
ELECTROBAS
EVANGELISCHER ENTWICKLUNGSDIENST
FORD FOUNDATION
FUNDACAO BANCO DO BRASIL
FURNAS
GOVERNO DO RIO DE GRANDE DO SOL
INTER CHURCH ORG. FOR DEV. CO-OPERATION
INFRAERO, BRAZILIAN AIRPORTS
MISEREOR INTERNATIONAL
OXFAM NETHERLANDS
PERFEITURA DO MUNICIPIO DE PORTO ALEGRE
ROCKEFELLER BROTHER'S FUND

* Information for 2005 does not distinguish between those who sponsored the process and those who sponsored the forum event

3. WHAT DO CITIZENS THINK ABOUT **GLOBAL CONSUMERISM** AND CULTURE?

QUESTION: IS GLOBAL CONSUMERISM AND COMMERCIALISM A THREAT TO YOUR CULTURE OR NOT A THREAT TO YOUR CULTURE?

% WHO RESPONDED **THREAT TO OUR CULTURE**

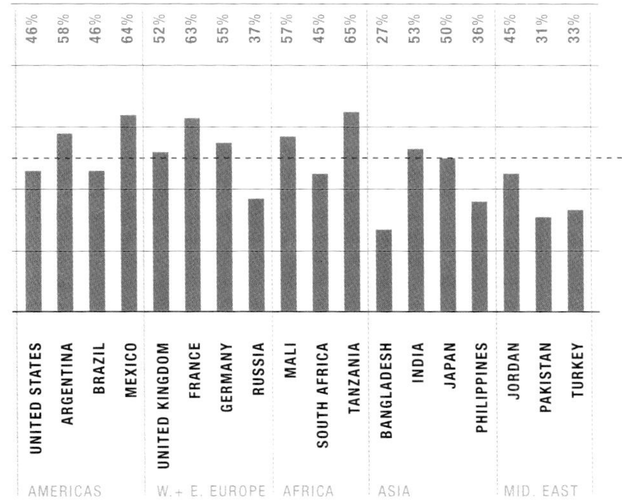

4. WHAT DO CITIZENS THINK ABOUT **INTERNATIONAL FINANCIAL INSTITUTIONS**?

QUESTION: IS THE INFLUENCE OF INTERNATIONAL ORGANIZATIONS LIKE THE WORLD BANK, IMF, AND WORLD TRADE ORGANIZATION VERY GOOD / SOMEWHAT GOOD / SOMEWHAT BAD / VERY BAD?

% **WHO RESPONDED VERY GOOD / SOMEWHAT GOOD**

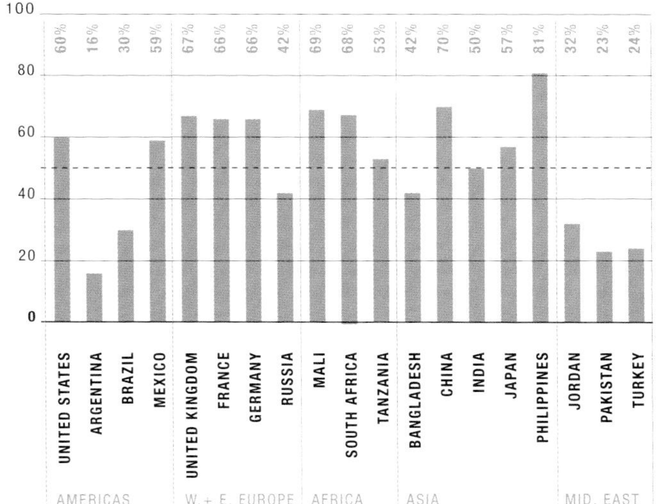

5. WHAT DO CITIZENS THINK ABOUT **GLOBALIZATION**?

QUESTION: DO YOU THINK GLOBALIZATION IS A VERY GOOD THING / SOMEWHAT GOOD THING / SOMEWHAT BAD / VERY BAD THING?

% **WHO RESPONDED VERY GOOD / SOMEWHAT GOOD**

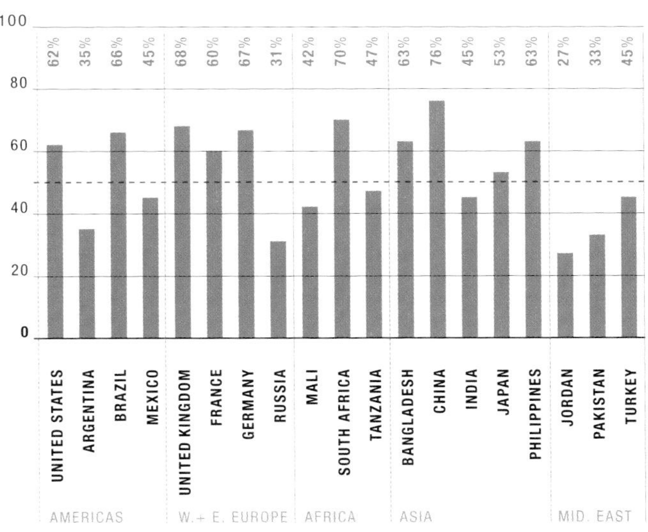

7. GROWTH OF **SOCIAL FORUMS** 2001-2004

REGIONAL/THEMATIC

NATIONAL

LOCAL

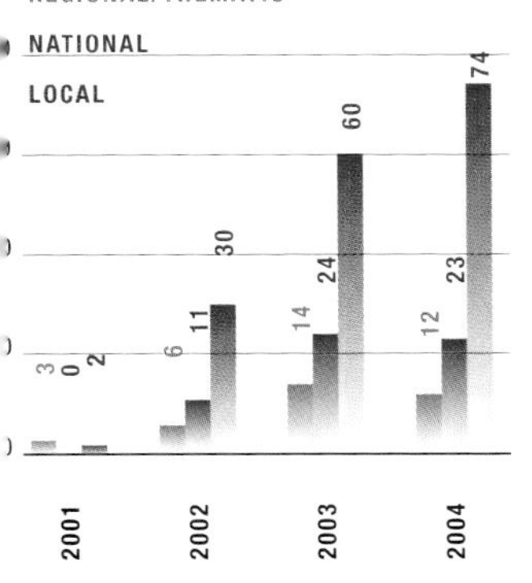

6. PARALLEL EVENTS DURING G8 COLOGNE SUMMIT 1999

J18 INTERNATIONAL DAY OF ACTION

OUR RESISTANCE IS AS TRANSNATIONAL AS CAPITAL

43 COUNTRIES PARTICIPATED IN J18

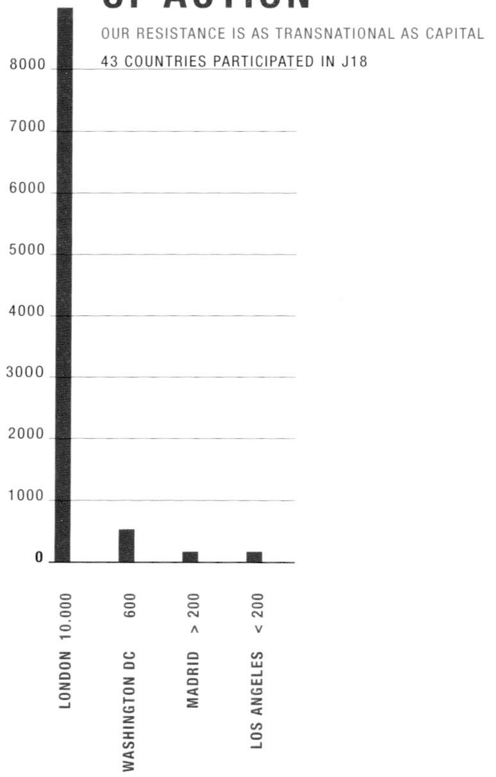

7. FEBRUARY 15 2003 INTERNATIONAL DAY OF PROTEST TO US INVASION OF IRAQ

FOR SELECT CITIES, AN ESTIMATED # OF 800 CITIES PARTICIPATED

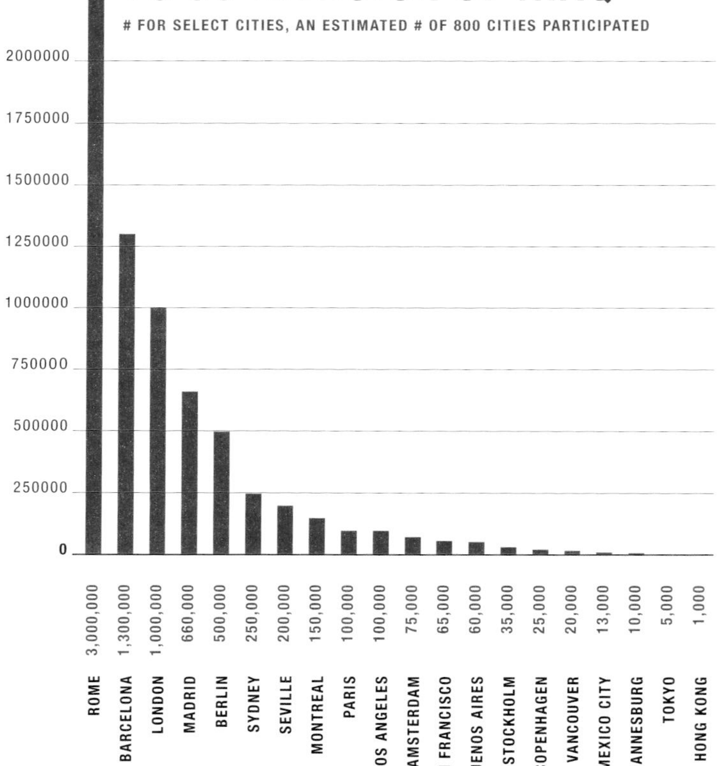

8. GROWTH OF PARALLEL SUMMITS

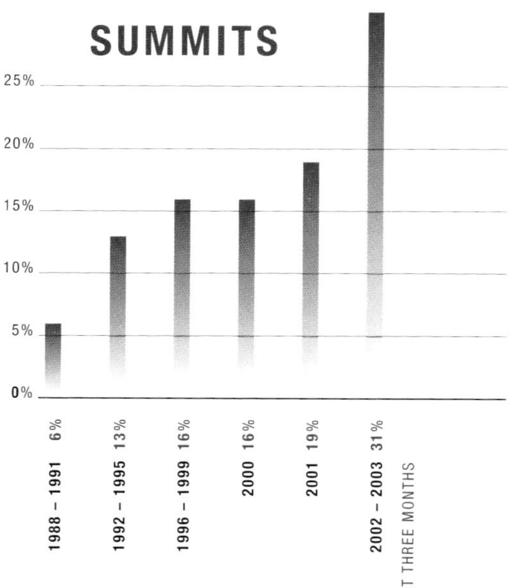

9. US IMAGE BEFORE + AFTER INVASION OF IRAQ

% FAVORABLE VIEW OF US BY SELECTED COUNTRIES

1999 – 2000 SUMMER 2002 MARCH 2003 MARCH 2004

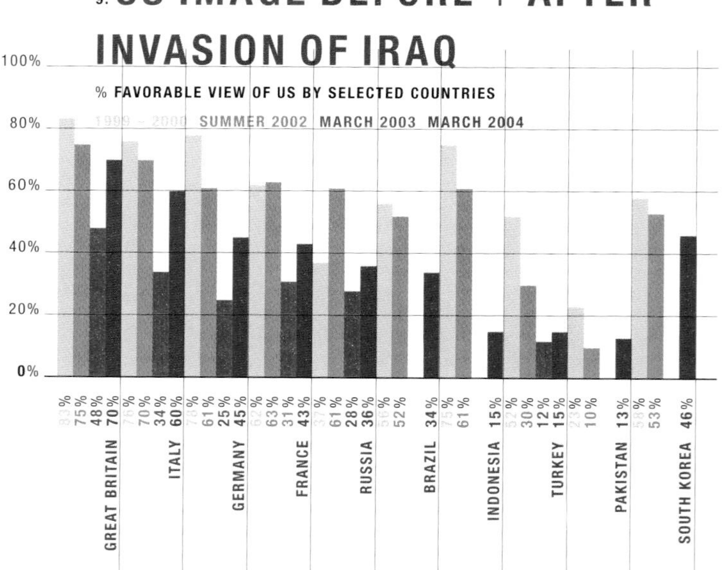

10. GLOBAL GREEN FEDERATION

\# OF PARTIES BY REGION

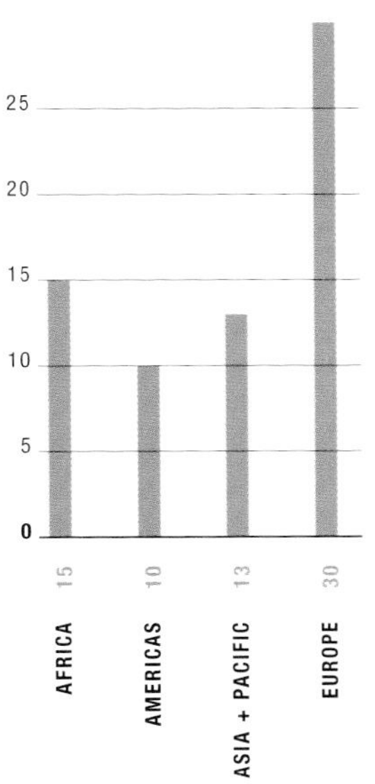

11. GREENPEACE MEMBERSHIP RELATIVE TO GROWTH OF ENVIRONMENTAL NGOs

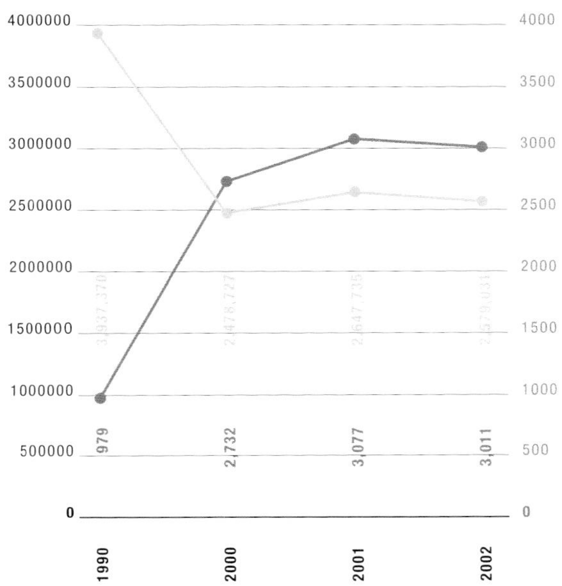

12. TRANSPARENCY INTERNATIONAL:

INCOME IN EUROS NATIONAL CHAPTER GROWTH

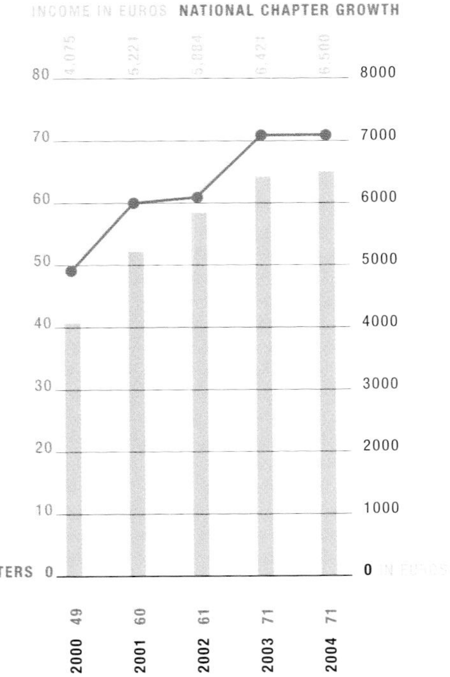

13. INTERNATIONAL COMMITTEE FOR THE RED CROSS:

GROWTH IN OPERATIONS 1995 – 2004

ICRC ACTIVE 3 COUNTRIES TOTAL PERSONNEL

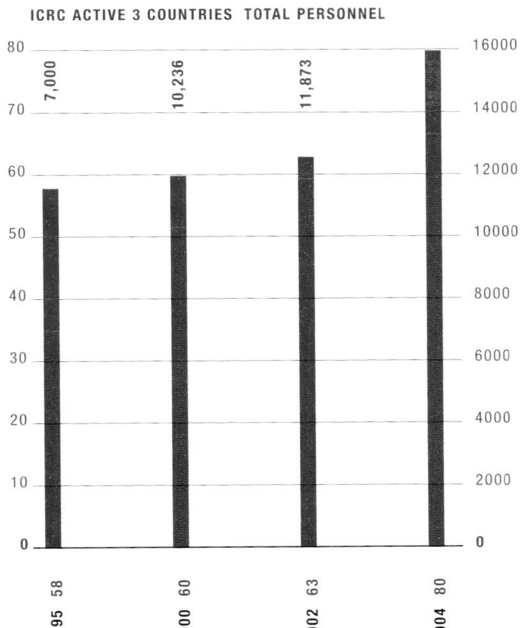

TRANSPORTATION AIRPORTS

- top 50 world airports total passengers - top 10 airports passengers growth - total online travel sales

- inter-region flights - regional trends + monthly passenger load factors

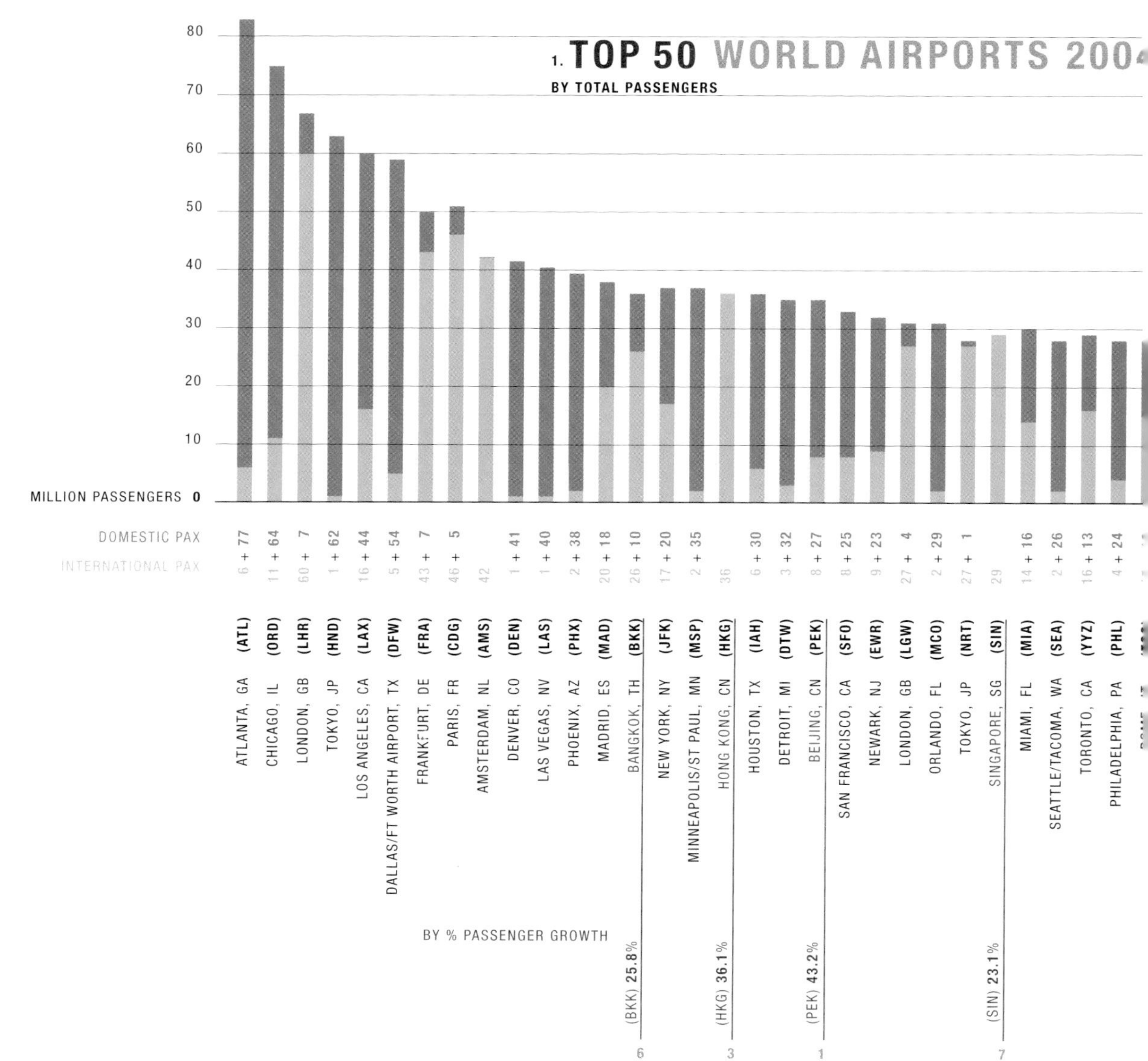

2. TOP 10 WORLD AIRPORT

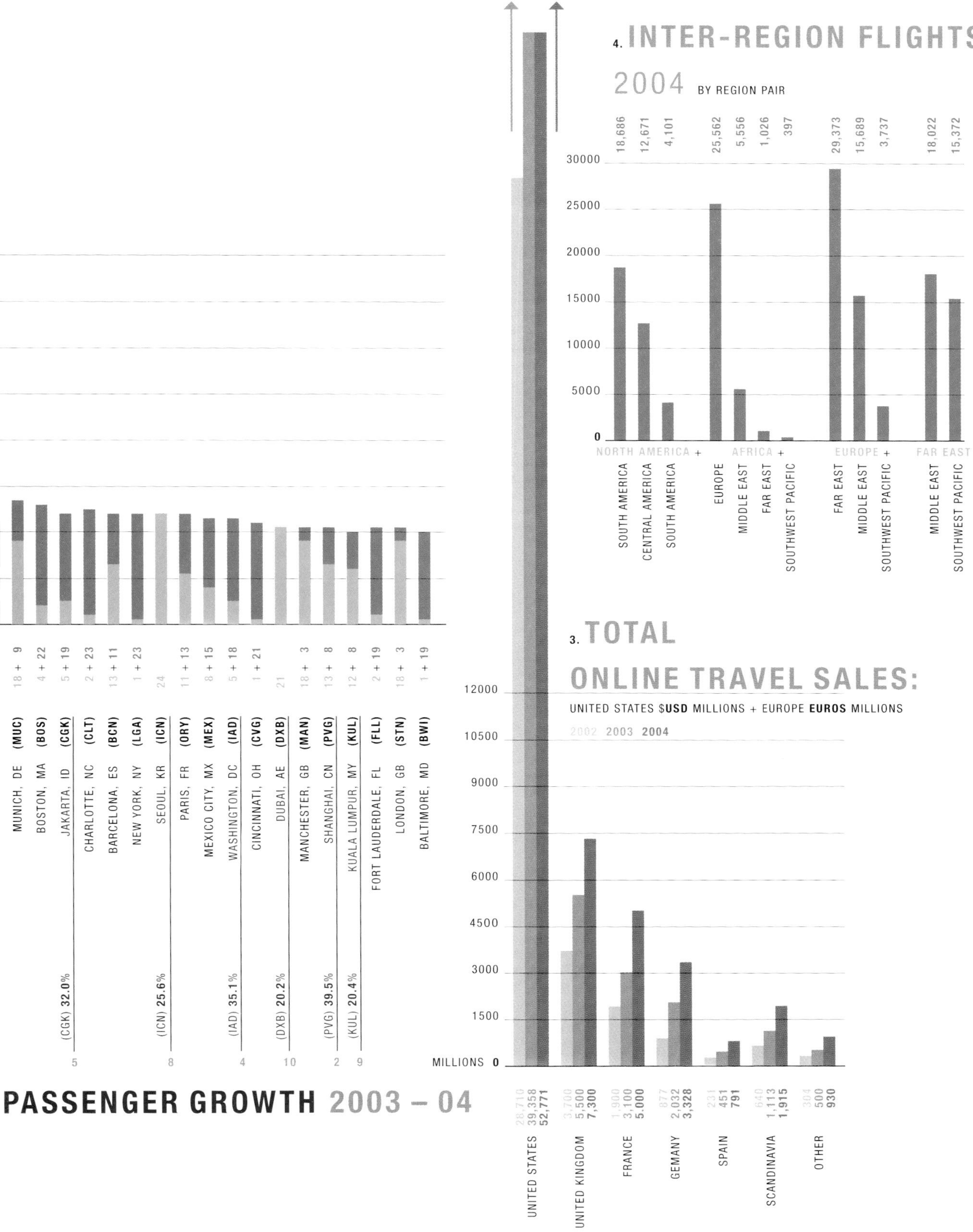

4. INTER-REGION FLIGHTS
2004 BY REGION PAIR
18,686
12,671
4,101
25,562
5,556
1,026
397
29,373
15,689
3,737
18,022
15,372
30000
25000
20000
15000
10000
5000
0
NORTH AMERICA +
SOUTH AMERICA
CENTRAL AMERICA
SOUTH AMERICA
AFRICA +
EUROPE
MIDDLE EAST
FAR EAST
SOUTHWEST PACIFIC
EUROPE +
FAR EAST
MIDDLE EAST
SOUTHWEST PACIFIC
FAR EAST +
MIDDLE EAST
SOUTHWEST PACIFIC
3. TOTAL
ONLINE TRAVEL SALES:
UNITED STATES $USD MILLIONS + EUROPE EUROS MILLIONS
2002 2003 2004
12000
10500
9000
7500
6000
4500
3000
1500
MILLIONS 0
28,710 39,358 52,771 UNITED STATES
3,700 5,500 7,300 UNITED KINGDOM
1,900 3,100 5,000 FRANCE
877 2,032 3,328 GEMANY
231 451 791 SPAIN
640 1,113 1,915 SCANDINAVIA
304 500 930 OTHER
18 + 9 MUNICH, DE (MUC)
4 + 22 BOSTON, MA (BOS)
5 + 19 JAKARTA, ID (CGK)
2 + 23 CHARLOTTE, NC (CLT)
13 + 11 BARCELONA, ES (BCN)
1 + 23 NEW YORK, NY (LGA)
24 SEOUL, KR (ICN)
11 + 13 PARIS, FR (ORY)
8 + 15 MEXICO CITY, MX (MEX)
5 + 18 WASHINGTON, DC (IAD)
1 + 21 CINCINNATI, OH (CVG)
21 DUBAI, AE (DXB)
18 + 3 MANCHESTER, GB (MAN)
13 + 8 SHANGHAI, CN (PVG)
12 + 8 KUALA LUMPUR, MY (KUL)
2 + 19 FORT LAUDERDALE, FL (FLL)
18 + 3 LONDON, GB (STN)
1 + 19 BALTIMORE, MD (BWI)
(CGK) 32.0%
(ICN) 25.6%
(IAD) 35.1%
(DXB) 20.2%
(PVG) 39.5%
(KUL) 20.4%
5
8
4
10
2
9
PASSENGER GROWTH 2003 – 04

5. REGIONAL TRENDS

WITHIN **EUROPE**

PASSENGER # IN THOUSANDS

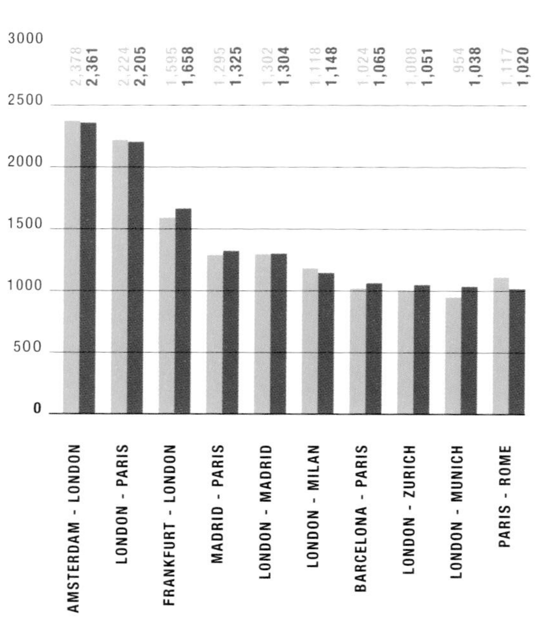

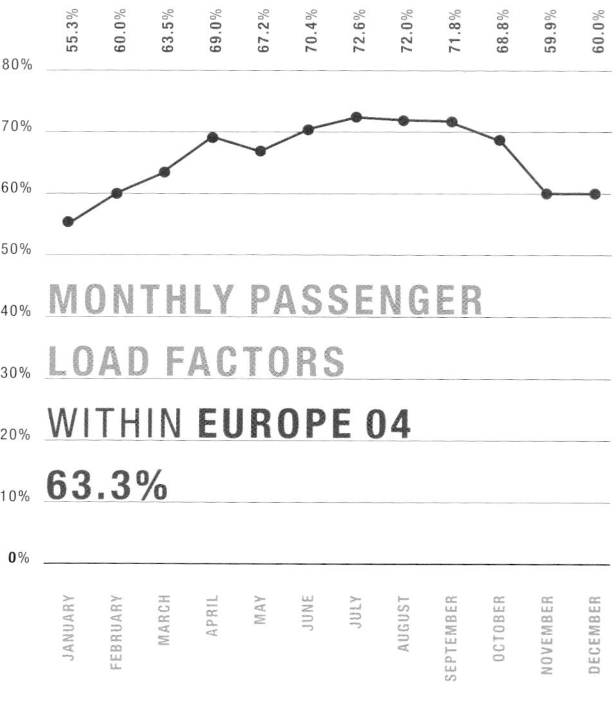

REGIONAL TRENDS

EUROPE - NORTH AMERICA

PASSENGER # IN THOUSANDS

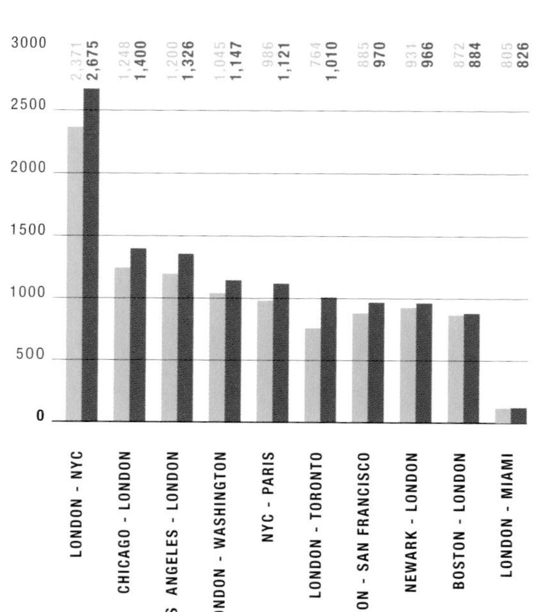

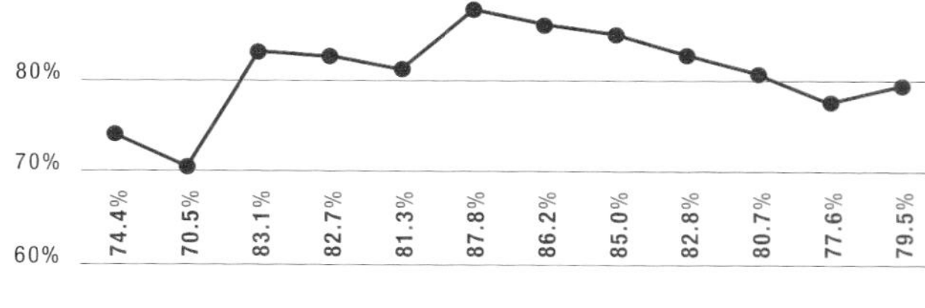

60%
50%
40% **MONTHLY PASSENGER**
30% **LOAD FACTORS**
20% **EUROPE - NORTH AMERICA 04**
10% **81.4%**
0%

JANUARY FEBRUARY MARCH APRIL MAY JUNE JULY AUGUST SEPTEMBER OCTOBER NOVEMBER DECEMBER

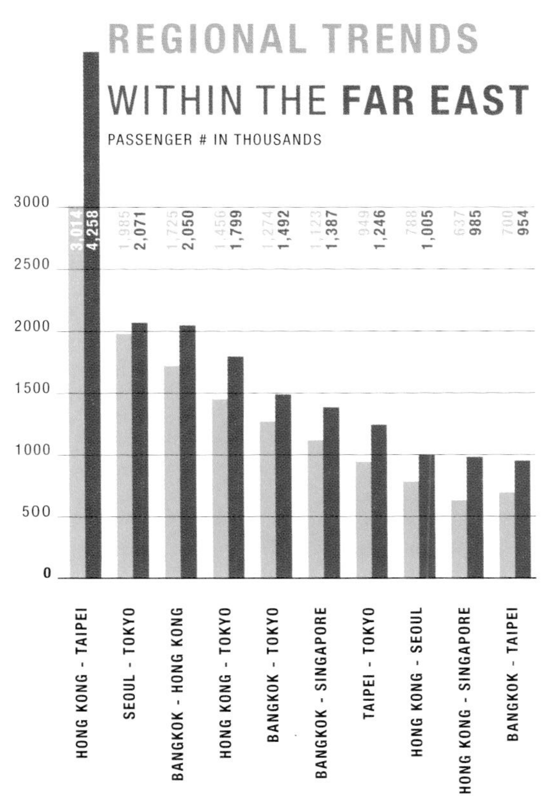
REGIONAL TRENDS
WITHIN THE FAR EAST
PASSENGER # IN THOUSANDS
3000
2500
2000
1500
1000
500
0
3,014
4,258
1,985
2,071
1,725
2,050
1,456
1,799
1,274
1,492
1,123
1,387
949
1,246
788
1,005
637
985
700
954
HONG KONG - TAIPEI
SEOUL - TOKYO
BANGKOK - HONG KONG
HONG KONG - TOKYO
BANGKOK - TOKYO
BANGKOK - SINGAPORE
TAIPEI - TOKYO
HONG KONG - SEOUL
HONG KONG - SINGAPORE
BANGKOK - TAIPEI

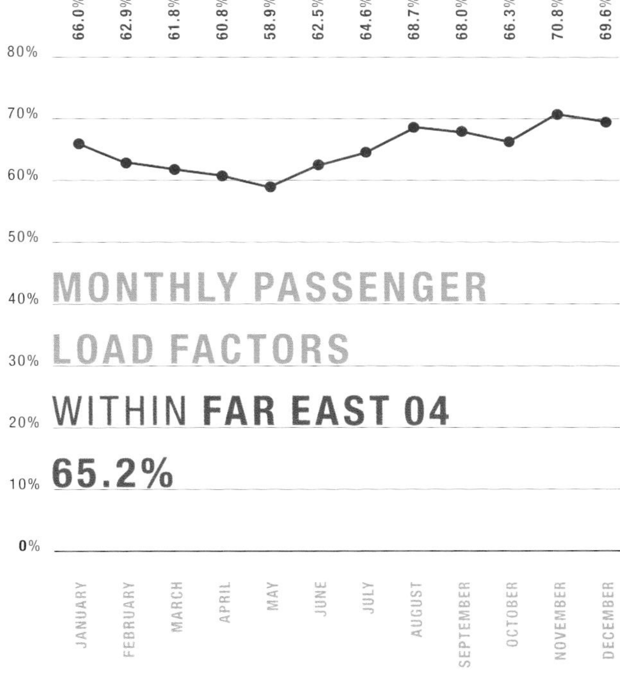
66.0%
62.9%
61.8%
60.8%
58.9%
62.5%
64.6%
68.7%
68.0%
66.3%
70.8%
69.6%
80%
70%
60%
50%
40%
30%
20%
10%
0%
MONTHLY PASSENGER
LOAD FACTORS
WITHIN FAR EAST 04
65.2%
JANUARY
FEBRUARY
MARCH
APRIL
MAY
JUNE
JULY
AUGUST
SEPTEMBER
OCTOBER
NOVEMBER
DECEMBER

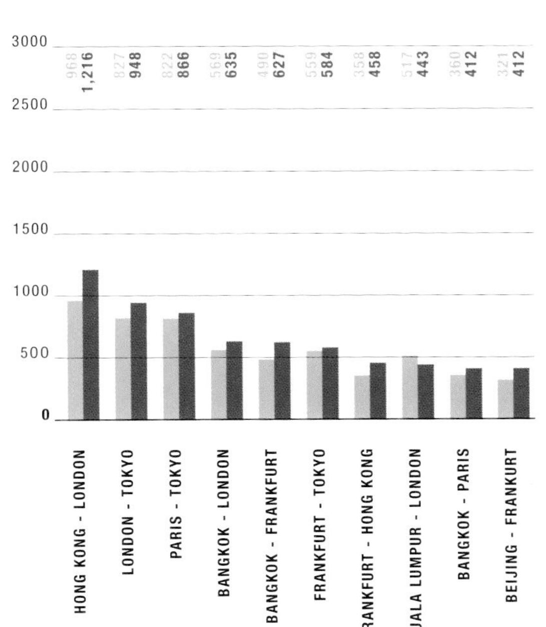
REGIONAL TRENDS
EUROPE - THE FAR EAST
PASSENGER # IN THOUSANDS
3000
2500
2000
1500
1000
500
0
968
1,216
827
948
822
866
569
635
490
627
559
584
358
458
517
443
360
412
321
412
HONG KONG - LONDON
LONDON - TOKYO
PARIS - TOKYO
BANGKOK - LONDON
BANGKOK - FRANKFURT
FRANKFURT - TOKYO
FRANKFURT - HONG KONG
KUALA LUMPUR - LONDON
BANGKOK - PARIS
BEIJING - FRANKURT

80%
70%
75.3%
76.4%
76.5%
74.7%
70.3%
75.3%
79.0%
78.2%
79.8%
79.8%
75.6%
74.3%
60%
50%
40%
30%
20%
10%
0%
MONTHLY PASSENGER
LOAD FACTORS
EUROPE - FAR EAST 04
76.3%
JANUARY
FEBRUARY
MARCH
APRIL
MAY
JUNE
JULY
AUGUST
SEPTEMBER
OCTOBER
NOVEMBER
DECEMBER

TRAVEL Examination of the travel and tourism industry provides key insights into the process of globalization. The transportation sector is one of the world's largest industries and includes the movement of people and materials via airplanes, boats, warehouses, pipelines, trucks, etc., and the logistical services that support this movement. In the US, the transportation industry employs about 16% of all of the nation's workers (Plunkett Research, Ltd, 2005/6) and at the end of the 20th century, it accounted for 10% of all jobs globally (The International Ecotourism Society, 2000). Tourism can be defined as travel for recreational, business, academic or other personal purposes and the provision of services for either type of travel. There are two main bodies that govern, investigate, and monitor global tourism: the World Tourism Organization (WTO), which is part of the United Nations, and the World Travel and Tourism Council (WTTC). The WTO defines a tourist as someone who travels at least 50 miles from their home.

The indicator suites on airports and tourism highlight the following:

• 8 of the 10 fastest growing airports are located in Asia
• Between 2000 and 2004, outbound and inbound tourism increased globally, except in the Americas where both outbound and inbound tourism levels declined slightly
• France, Spain, and the United States were the top three tourist destinations in 2004, though China is expected to surpass France as the number one tourist destination by 2020
• Tourism from the Middle East, Asia, and Africa (73%, 22% and 17%, respectively) surpassed tourism from Europe (11%) between 2000 and 2004

WHAT DO WE KNOW ABOUT TRAVEL AND TOURISM?

In 2004, air transportation accounted for 43% of all arrivals around the world and road/land travel accounted for 45% (World Tourism Organization, 2005b). International tourist arrivals climbed to 808 million in 2005 (Xinhua General News Service, 2006). Most travel purposes were for leisure, holiday and recreation (52%), while 16% of trips were business related (World Tourism Organization, 2005b).

Tourism in Asia and the Pacific, and the Middle East accounted for much of the new growth in the sector since 2004, increasing by 28% and 18% respectively (World Tourism Organization, 2005b). Since the SARS epidemic, Asian destinations have rebounded strongly and continue to expand—an indicator of the region's increasing presence as a global economic and cultural force. The Middle East is witnessing solid growth, partly due to various governmental and investment policies encouraging travel to the region; and travel to northern Africa is also on the rise.

Alternately, North America and Western Europe, traditional leaders in global tourism, showed lower increases of tourism, with popular European destinations (e.g. France, Spain and Italy) declining in numbers of visits. However, it is expected that the proximity of European countries and the Euro will further facilitate travel between nations, and help maintain the region as a top travel destination in the future.

Using UNESCO data, Figure 1 shows a network analysis of global educational exchange, illustrating the extensity of student exchange flows between world regions. 34% of exchange students travel from the US to Europe, and little educational exchanges occurs between South America and Africa (.08% and .01% to and from Africa and South America) (UNESCO Institute for Statistics, 2005). Between 2003 and 2004, the number of students traveling from the US to Asia increased by 90% (Institute of International Exchange, 2005a). Students from India, China, Korea, Japan, and Canada represented the largest demographic of international students in the United States in 2004-2005 (Institute of International Exchange, 2005b).

Natural disasters and international conflicts, such as the Tsunami, SARS, and the US invasion of Iraq have affected tourism and travel drastically, especially where many world regions rely heavily upon tourism industries. At the end of 2005, air service and hotel capacity within tsunami-affected locations, was still approximately 20 percent lower than before the disaster (World Tourism Organization, 2005). Countries that were particularly devastated by this natural disaster were those that relied on the tourism industry for livelihood and income. The Maldives, for example, which received 60% of its GPD from tourism, registered revenue losses from tourism of $255 USD after the Tsunami (Asian Development Bank, 2005a,b).

Similarly, after the SARS epidemic surfaced, tourist arrivals to Taiwan decreased over 2003 by almost 25%, whereas the country had previously been registering an increase of almost 5%. In Malaysia and Singapore, tourist arrivals dropped by 20.4% and 18.5% respectively (World Tourism Organization, 2004). New Zealand and India were the only two countries in Asia and the Pacific to report positive increases in percent change of tourist arrivals, between 2002 and 2003 (World Tourism Organization, 2004).

WHAT ARE THE ISSUES AND DYNAMICS?

Forces of globalization and related world trends are affecting travel and tourism in several ways. First, the industry is experiencing consolidation through mergers and acquisitions. Second, low cost carrier airlines are one of the fastest growing forms of air travel, displacing traditional market carriers. Also, the information age has offered the travel and tourism industry huge perks for tracking travel, outsourcing, and increasing efficiencies. Today, online travel sales are booming. Along with being affected by globalization, travel and transportation networks are facilitating globalization by linking and connecting businesses and individuals. The recent ease of travel facilitates the globalization of culture and/or the displacement of local cultures by tourism. Simultaneously cultures have been commodified and marketed to attract tourists.

Global travel and tourism activity is expected to grow by 4.2% per year in real terms between 2007 and 2016 (World Travel and Tourism Council, 2006). New world dynamics and emerging economies have shifted the focus to Asian countries as both origins and destinations for travelers. Demands for tourism are especially strong and growing in emerging and growing economies, because of increasing levels of disposable income. These trends are expected to increase and increasing flows of travelers bring environmental consequences, which are becoming more and more important to confront. Growing travel consumption means that pollution related to air travel is on the rise.

The fear of terrorism after 9/11 have dramatically affected the travel industry, specifically via massive losses and restructuring, and increases in airport security.

FIGURE 1: **NETWORK ANALYSIS OF EDUCATIONAL EXCHANGE** 2002-2003:

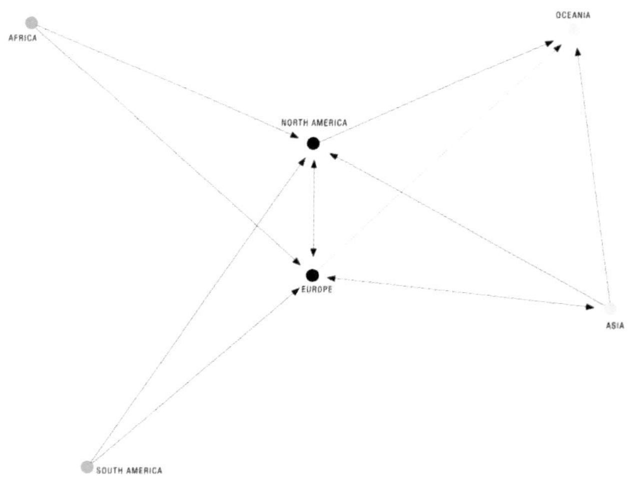

MIGRATION, DIASPORAS & TRANSNATIONAL COMMUNITIES

Migration is a worldwide phenomenon that has long shaped and changed the face of commerce and trade, politics, culture, art and society. The indicator suite on migration, refugees and asylum seekers, and transnational communities, shows that the world's population is increasingly becoming migratory, creating a complex network in terms of people movements, diasporas, transnational communities, and homelands. Specifically:

- At the global level, migration has doubled between 1970 and 2000, affecting all continents, but predominately Europe, Asia and North America
- In 2004, the top three migrant sending countries were the Philippines, India and China
- In 2004, the top three migrant receiving countries were the United States, the Russian Federation, and Germany
- Worldwide, India is the top remittance receiving country of an estimated $10 billion in 2001
- A majority of refugees, asylum seekers and internationally displaced peoples are from Palestine, Afghanistan, Sudan, Congo, and Colombia
- The United States (Jews), Germany (Kurds), and Saudi Arabia (Filipino) host the largest diaspora communities.

WHAT IS DIASPORA?

The term diaspora comes from the Greek meaning "to scatter and to sow." Before the 1960's, the term was primarily used in reference to Jewish communities outside of Palestine, yet today, diaspora continues to resonate as a term used to define the displacement and laying down of roots of modern-day migrants, refugees and asylum seekers (Baumann, 2000). While governments maintain differing definitions of what constitutes "a migrant," "a refugee," or "an asylum seeker," what is clear is that today's usage of "diaspora" encompasses the experiences of persons residing and settling down in foreign lands and contested cultural, economic, and political boundaries in a globalized world, or what anthropologist James Clifford calls, "the contact zones of nations, cultures, and regions" (Clifford, 1994). Because of these "contact zones," diasporic communities are inextricably tied to issues of race, class, gender, religion, language, culture, ethnicity, labor, welfare, nationhood and the transnational; and therefore, often at the center of heated policy debates.

THE MYTHS AND REALITIES OF MIGRATION

- A majority of refugees and asylum seekers do not flee to rich countries; they are mostly hosted in countries with a per capita income below $2,000 (USCRI, 2004)
- Many people exist in "refugee-like" situations, but are not formally recognized by governments as refugees, denying them entry into countries, residency and citizenship (e.g., Kurds in Syria, Iraqis in Jordan, or Biharis in Bangladesh)
- Migration is sometimes cyclical—receiving countries are also sending countries (i.e., in Germany and Australia, for every 3 persons moving into the country, 2 moved out, see IOM, 2005)
- Remittances remain a strong driving force of migration and their importance takes on new dimensions as they rival aid and foreign direct investment into developing countries
- While it remains uncontested that many migrant sending countries must address the factors that push people out of their homelands (i.e., poverty), migrant receiving countries must address their roles in creating the pull factors that lead people in (i.e., NAFTA and Mexican migration to the United States)
- Innovations in communication and information technology facilitate links between home countries and diaspora communities that fill gaps of information and skilled-based knowledge created by the "brain-drain" phenomenon (IOM, 2005)
- Migration is primarily caused by global economic and social inequalities, and driven by formal and informal networks of people and communities

WHAT ARE THE ISSUES?

Migration, especially informal or underground migration, is hard to measure and assess in its consequences. As a phenomenon it involves flows of labor, money, social capital, culture, and knowledge, as well as aspects of identity and identity politics in sending and receiving countries alike. Ongoing issues about how to define legal and illegal migrants, asylum seekers and internationally displaced peoples occur in a context of growing tensions about immigration, citizenship and national security. Countries such as the United States, France, Germany or the United Kingdom have seen heated debates surrounding national identity and migration policies (see chapters on migration).

Scholars such as Huntington (2004) argue that current waves of migration to the US, in particular the influx of Hispanic immigrants, are eroding the underlying Protestant values the country was founded on, gradually changing it to a bilingual, multicultural society. Moreover, the recent protests and rallies held across the US by immigrant, migrant and undocumented workers shed light on the growing influence of migrant and diaspora communities on national politics in most developed countries. While the US case reveals the reliance of modern economies on the cheap labor migrants provide, the riots in France in 2005 brought to the open the failure of including migrants into the labor market.

Growing labor migration has increased the flow of remittances, which for long have played a key role in supporting families and community development in developing countries. A recent Philippine government program allows migrants to donate their money to development projects in local communities. Mexican migrants in the United States use small-town associations to direct their monies into local communities back home. These channels of transferring money avert the high rates charged by banks and private money transfer companies.

Migration of professionals and university-educated specialists from developing to developed regions of the world has created a phenomenon known as the "brain-drain," e.g. nurses from South Africa moving to Britain, from the Philippines to Britain to Norway; Indian programmers working in Germany, or Pakistani physicians practicing in the US. However, the counter-flow against a brain-drain is the "brain-gain" that occurs when students return as professionals after having been educated abroad, bringing with them skills and knowledge.

Among some metropolitan regions, and facilitated by transnational corporations and university alliances, we see the emergence of "brain-exchange" among highly mobile professionals and academics. A related phenomenon is that of the 'corporate nomads,' i.e. highly skilled professionals that move across countries and regions following postings and assignments in transnational corporations. These 'nomads' create networks of exchange of skills and knowledge across corporations and their cultures.

TRANSNATIONAL MOVEMENTS TABLE 1 (SEE NEXT PAGE):
TRANSNATIONAL ADVOCACY NETWORKS—OPPORTUNITIES & THREATS

OPPORTUNITIES	THREATS
Able to respond quickly to recent developments or to organize an urgent action campaign	As networks increase in size, they become less centralized; creating leadership confusion
Facilitate and ease exchanges of information, ideas and resources (funds, facilities, staff, training, and technology)	Framing of ideas and agendas can be difficult across many stakeholders
Bring together numbers of different stakeholders and facilitate cross-cultural communication	International networking is costly
Is diverse and heterogeneous	Legitimacy of larger international networks can be challenged at the local and regional level
Can link local players with key international players	Transnational networks can mirror a North-South hierarchy (i.e., whereby main resources and actors come from the North on behalf of Southern causes)
Cross-networking of related advocacy agendas (e.g., anti-globalization movement with debt relief)	

Source: Adapted from Keck & Sikkink, 1999

TRANSNATIONAL MOVEMENTS The anti-globalization movement (also known as a transnational advocacy network or transnational movement) is at once an umbrella term of many movements along similar goals, agendas or messages (e.g., the uniting of poverty alleviation and debt relief campaigns), as it is part of a new "internationalism," whereby the movement models "being a part of a greater international society" of activists, reformers, politicians and local organizers. It is thus a 'transnational advocacy network' (Keck and Sikkink, 1999).

As globalization and the consolidation of economic and political actors places a larger reliance on international organizations and world governing bodies to address far-reaching policy issues, stakeholders at both the local and regional levels must seek out ways to influence these world governing bodies to further their causes (Smith and Wiest, 2005). Not surprisingly, the rapid succession of globalization and the changes it has brought about have also fomented an increase in transnational movements and the proliferation of international nongovernmental organizations.

The suite on transnational movements illustrates a popular ambivalence about globalization as the formation of an increasingly global forum of organizing:

- More than 50% of citizens in Argentina, Mexico, France, Germany, Mali and Tanzania view global consumerism as a threat to culture
- At the same time, more than 50% of citizens in the US, Brazil, UK, France, Germany, South Africa, Bangladesh, China and the Philippines view globalization as a positive force
- Parallel summits have grown since the late 1980s, the largest growth of 31% seen between 2002 and the first three months of 2003
- Greenpeace membership has declined in direct relation to the growth of environmental NGOs

WHAT DO WE KNOW?

Transnational movements are both hindered and facilitated by the processes and institutions of globalization. These movements are of civil society and movements for civil society; hence, intrinsically linked to civic participation, democracy, public consciousness and knowledge formation within nation states (Smith and Wiest, 2005). Recent surveys, such as the World Values Survey or Pew Global Attitudes Project, highlight some of the opinions and issue awareness worldwide (see Suite). The escalation of parallel summits is further evidence of a growing transnational movement that calls for equal "development" for all mankind.

Awareness and information sharing are essential to issue formation for any social movement, yet for transnational movements, the connection of issues across boundaries and global spheres is imperative. These movements are characterized by overlapping agendas and themes, thereby giving rise to a collective identity and ability to mobilize around an overarching goal (Ghimire, 2005). This was exemplified by the successful turnout of the International Day of Protest on February 15th (or F15), when demonstrators protested worldwide in over 800 cities (see Suite). The attacks of September 11th and the US invasion of Iraq in March 2003, enabled the anti-globalization movement to simultaneously rally against neoliberalism and to what many see as a growing Western or US imperialism of nations and cultures (political and economic).

WHAT ARE THE ISSUES?

The formation of transnational networks and movements does not come easily, nor is it necessarily ensured success (Table 1). While the range of stakeholders is seen as a positive element, this diversity and the horizontal structure of transnational movements can make for an unstable or fragile alliance (Ghimire, 2005). Alliances are also threatened by a North-South structure within the movement that resembles the global economic and political hierarchy organizers seek to change. However, Smith and Wiest (2005) point out that a country's link to global financial institutions is not the only agent of transnational networking, but "ties to the global polity" (common amongst developing countries) are also essential to transnational organizing. In this light, Smith and Wiest argue that transnational movements have both the potential to support "world-system stratification," as well as "help sow the seeds for its transformation."

Despite these challenges, transnational movements have enjoyed some success. Criticisms of the anti-globalization movement as purpose driven and without a plan for action have been undercut by the efforts for debt relief stakeholders to be integrated into important decision-making processes, and the subsequent approval by G8 nations to excuse the debts of some of the most impoverished nations. Yet, the future of the debt relief campaign, among others, remains elusive and the question of whether these transnational movements can overcome the traditional cycle of social movements (whereby they are born, grow, achieve success and then dissolve) remains in question.

The answer appears to lie in the nature of civil society and the inter-dependence between a movement and people. The longevity of a campaign seems predicated on the stability of civil society to maintain a healthy momentum, without imploding or erupting into violence. The protests surrounding the Danish cartoons (Figure 1) exemplifies this delicate relationship and sheds light on the looming uncertainty of transnational movements to prevent and control violence in the face of freedom of speech, ideas and expression.

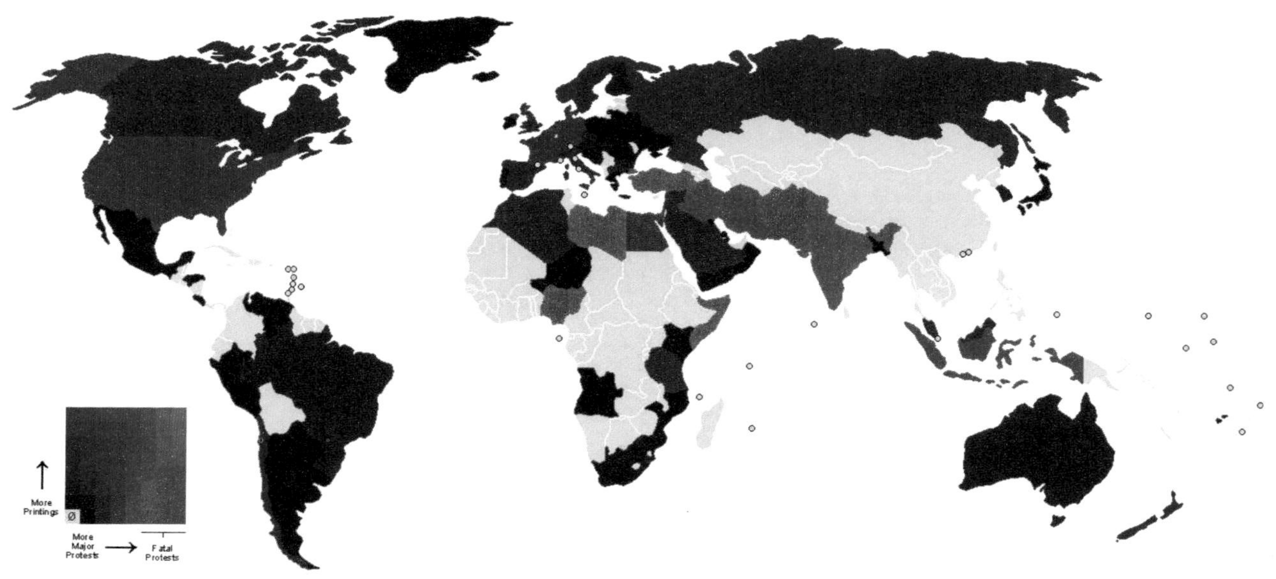

REGULATORY FRAMEWORKS

INTERNATIONAL STANDARDS

- iso: **annual production of international standards** 1998–2005 - iso: **annual production:** # of pages on **international standards** 1998–2005 - **iso production of international standards** by technical sector 2005 - **iso total production** by technical sector 1947–2005 - change of % of **portfolio of iso international standards** 1998–2005

1. ISO: ANNUAL PRODUCTION OF INTERNATIONAL STANDARDS

1998 – 2005

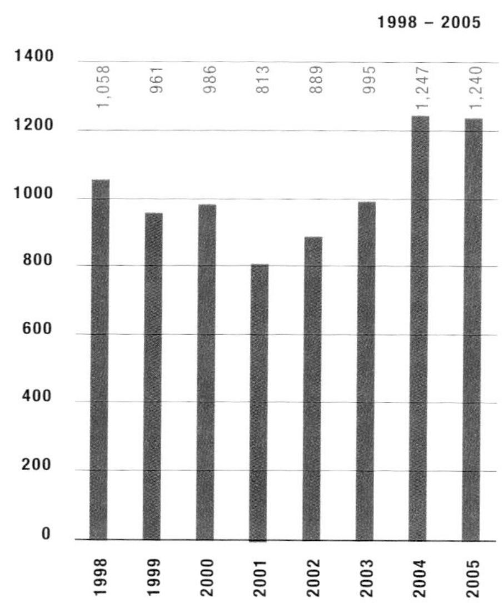

2. ISO: ANNUAL PRODUCTION: # OF NEW PAGES OF INTERNATIONAL STANDARDS

1998 – 2005

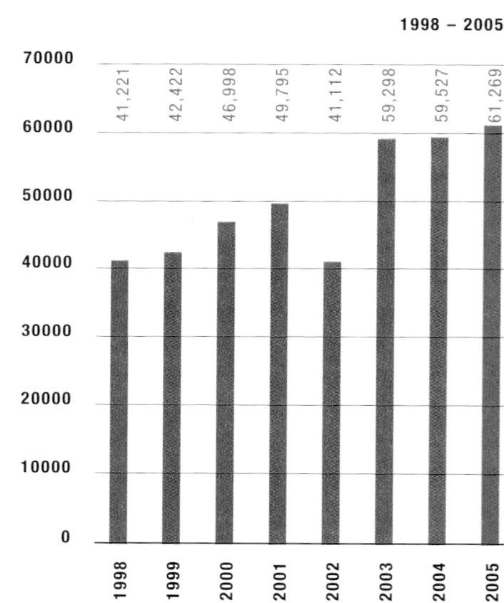

3. ISO TOTAL PRODUCTION BY TECHNICAL SECTOR

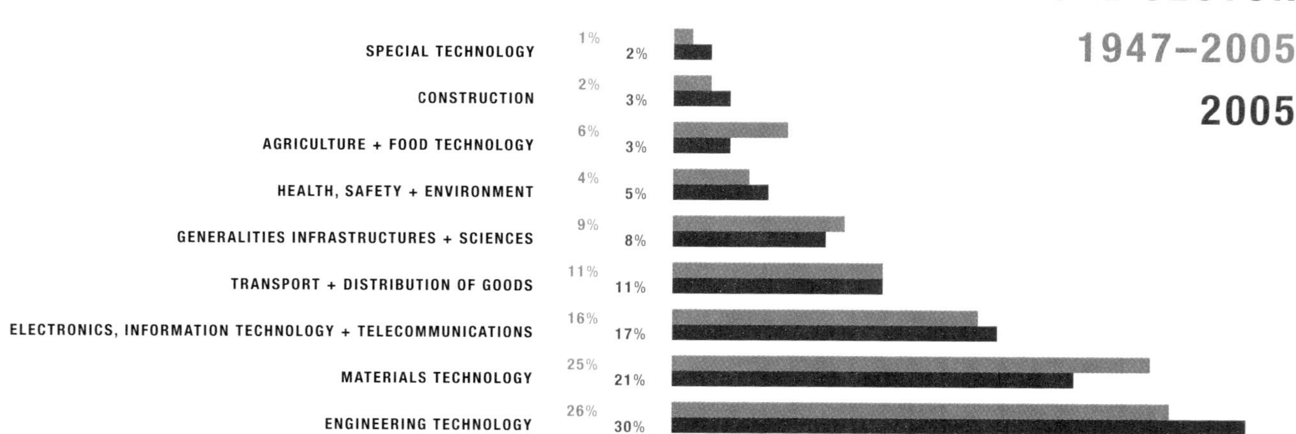

- iso 9001: **2000 quality management systems** - worldwide total of **iso 9001: 2000 certificates** - annual growth of **iso 9001: 2000 certificates** - top 10 countries for **iso 9001: 2000 certificates** - iso 14001: **environmental management sysytems** - worldwide total of **iso 14001 certificates** - annual growth of **iso 14001 certificates** - top 10 countries for **iso 14001 certificates** - **isbn allocated worldwide** until 2005

4. CHANGE IN % OF PORTFOLIO OF ISO INTERNATIONAL STANDARDS

1998 – 2005

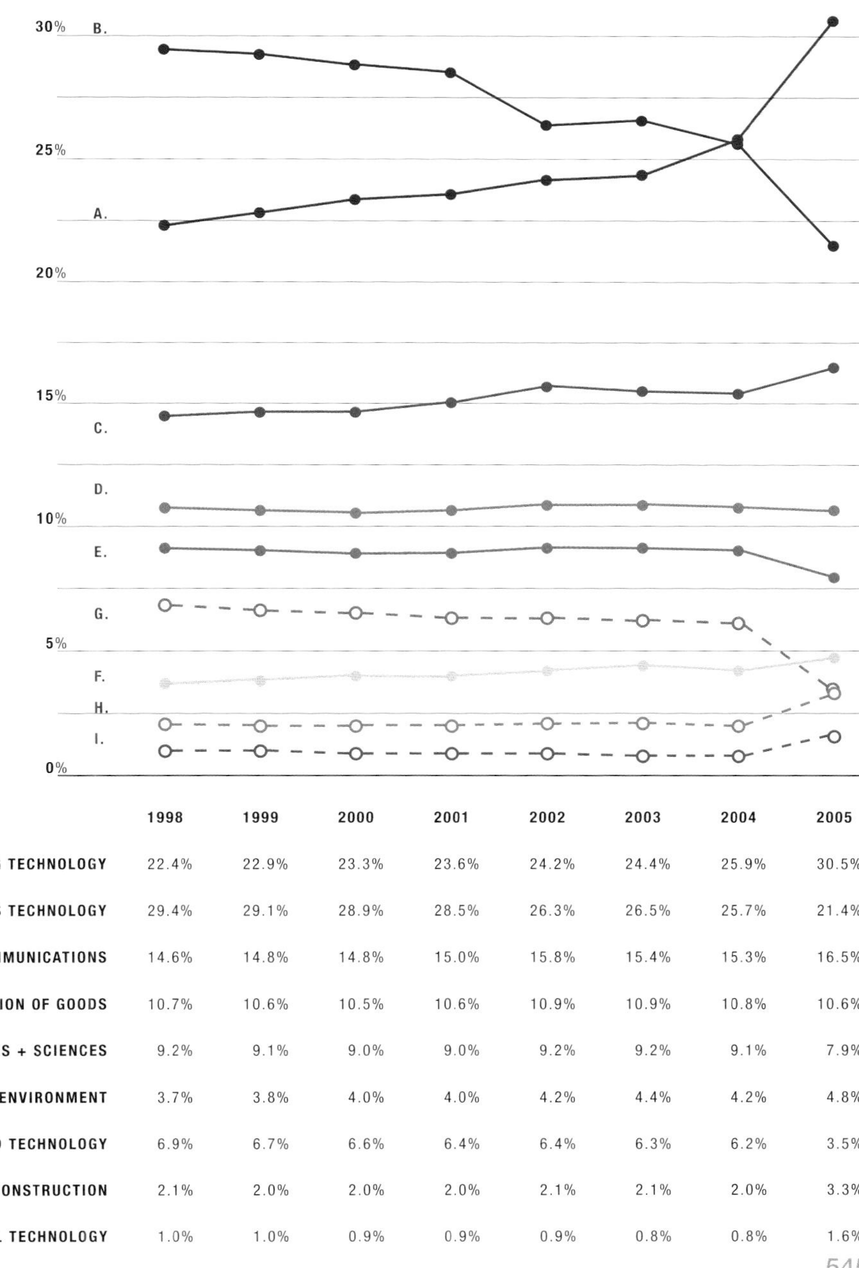

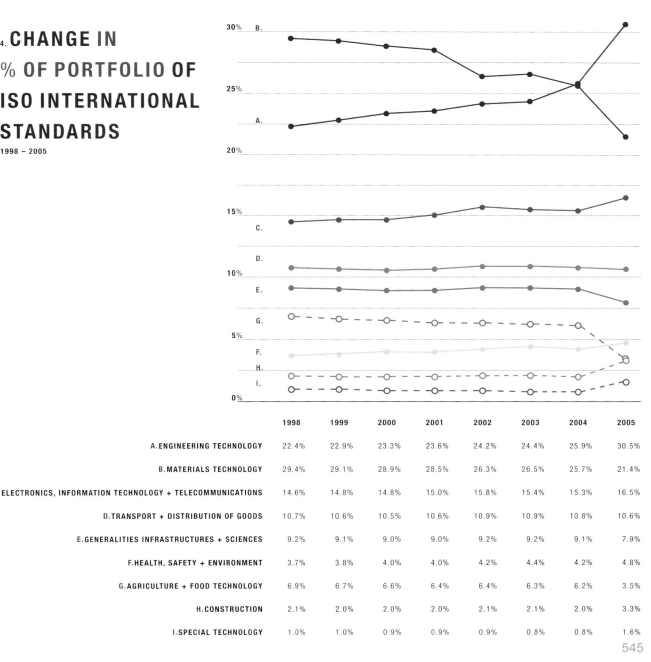

	1998	1999	2000	2001	2002	2003	2004	2005
A.ENGINEERING TECHNOLOGY	22.4%	22.9%	23.3%	23.6%	24.2%	24.4%	25.9%	30.5%
B.MATERIALS TECHNOLOGY	29.4%	29.1%	28.9%	28.5%	26.3%	26.5%	25.7%	21.4%
.ELECTRONICS, INFORMATION TECHNOLOGY + TELECOMMUNICATIONS	14.6%	14.8%	14.8%	15.0%	15.8%	15.4%	15.3%	16.5%
D.TRANSPORT + DISTRIBUTION OF GOODS	10.7%	10.6%	10.5%	10.6%	10.9%	10.9%	10.8%	10.6%
E.GENERALITIES INFRASTRUCTURES + SCIENCES	9.2%	9.1%	9.0%	9.0%	9.2%	9.2%	9.1%	7.9%
F.HEALTH, SAFETY + ENVIRONMENT	3.7%	3.8%	4.0%	4.0%	4.2%	4.4%	4.2%	4.8%
G.AGRICULTURE + FOOD TECHNOLOGY	6.9%	6.7%	6.6%	6.4%	6.4%	6.3%	6.2%	3.5%
H.CONSTRUCTION	2.1%	2.0%	2.0%	2.0%	2.1%	2.1%	2.0%	3.3%
I.SPECIAL TECHNOLOGY	1.0%	1.0%	0.9%	0.9%	0.9%	0.8%	0.8%	1.6%

5a. ISO 9001:2000 QUALITY MANAGEMENT SYSTEMS

UP TO THE END OF DECEMBER 2004, AT LEAST **670,399** ISO 9001:2001 CERTIFICATES WERE USED IN **154** COUNTRIES AND ECONOMIES. THE 2004 TOTAL REPRESENTS AN INCREASE OF **172,480** (+35%) OVER 2003, WHEN THE TOTAL WAS **497,919** IN **149** COUNTRIES AND ECONOMIES.

WORLD RESULTS	DEC.2000	DEC.2001	DEC.2002	DEC.2003	DEC.2004
WORLD TOTAL	408,631	44,388	167,210	497,919	670,399
WORLD GROWTH			122,822	330,709	172,480
# OF COUNTRIES / ECONOMIES		98	134	149	154

5b. WORLDWIDE TOTAL OF ISO 9001:2000 CERTIFICATES

DECEMBER 2000 – DECEMBER 2004

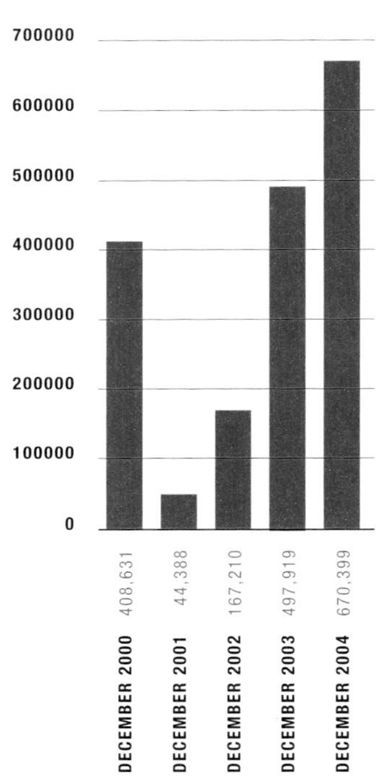

5c. ANNUAL GROWTH OF ISO 9001:2000 CERTIFICATES

DECEMBER 2000 – DECEMBER 2004

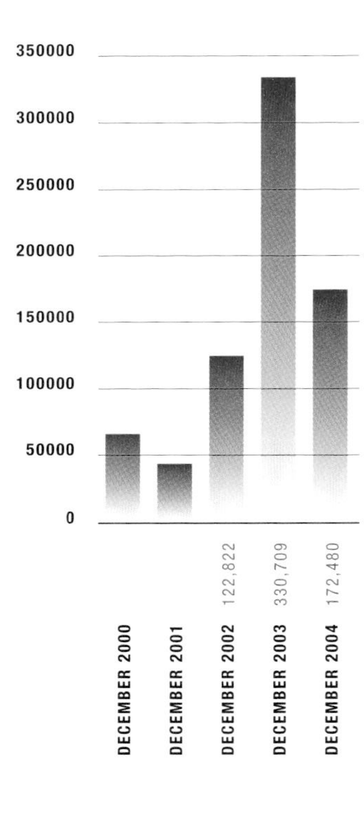

5d. TOP 10 COUNTRIES FOR ISO 9001:2000 CERTIFICATES

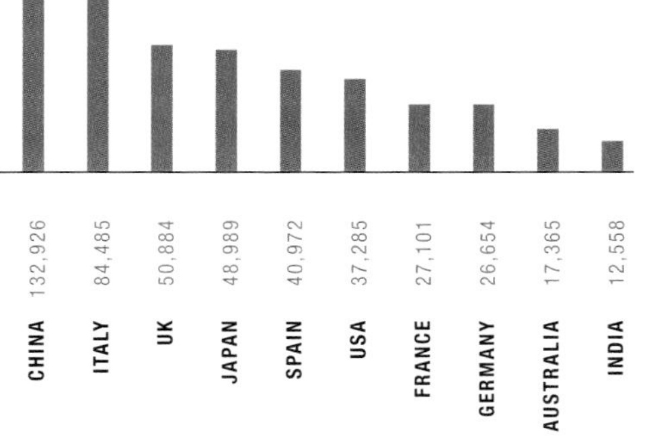

6a. ISO 14001 ENVIRONMENTAL MANAGEMENT SYSTEMS

UP TO THE END OF DECEMBER 2004, AT LEAST **90,569** ISO 14001 CERTIFICATES WERE USED IN **127** COUNTRIES AND ECONOMIES. THE 2004 TOTAL REPRESENTS AN INCREASE OF **24,499** (+37%) OVER 2003, WHEN THE TOTAL WAS **66,070** IN **113** COUNTRIES AND ECONOMIES.

WORLD RESULTS	DEC.1999`	DEC.2000	DEC.2001	DEC.2002	DEC.2003	DEC.2004
WORLD TOTAL	14,106	22,897	36,765	49,449	66,070	90,569
WORLD GROWTH	06,219	08,791	13,868	12,684	16,621	24,499
# OF COUNTRIES / ECONOMIES	84	98	112	117	113	127

6b. WORLDWIDE TOTAL OF ISO 14001 CERTIFICATES

DECEMBER 1999 – DECEMBER 2004

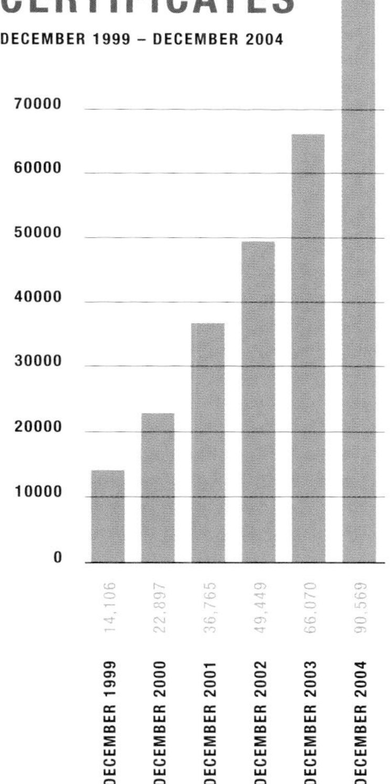

6c. ANNUAL GROWTH OF ISO 14001 CERTIFICATES

DECEMBER 1999 – DECEMBER 2004

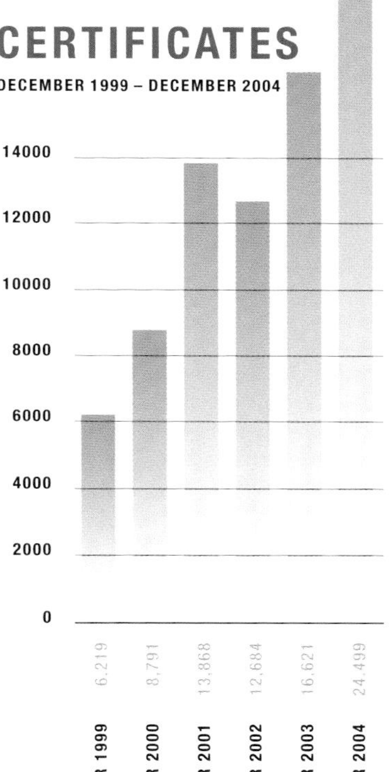

6d. TOP 10 COUNTRIES FOR ISO 14001 CERTIFICATES

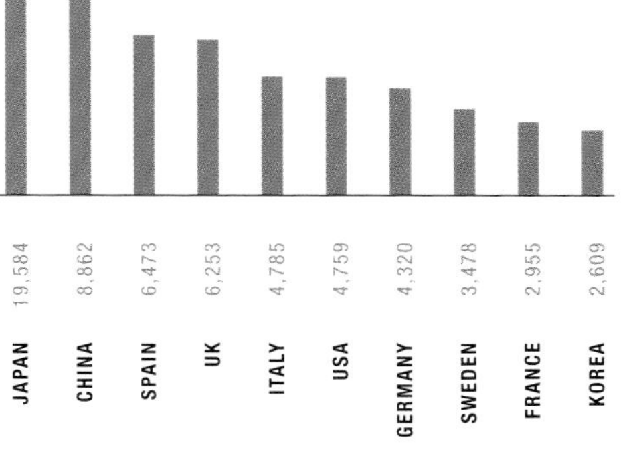

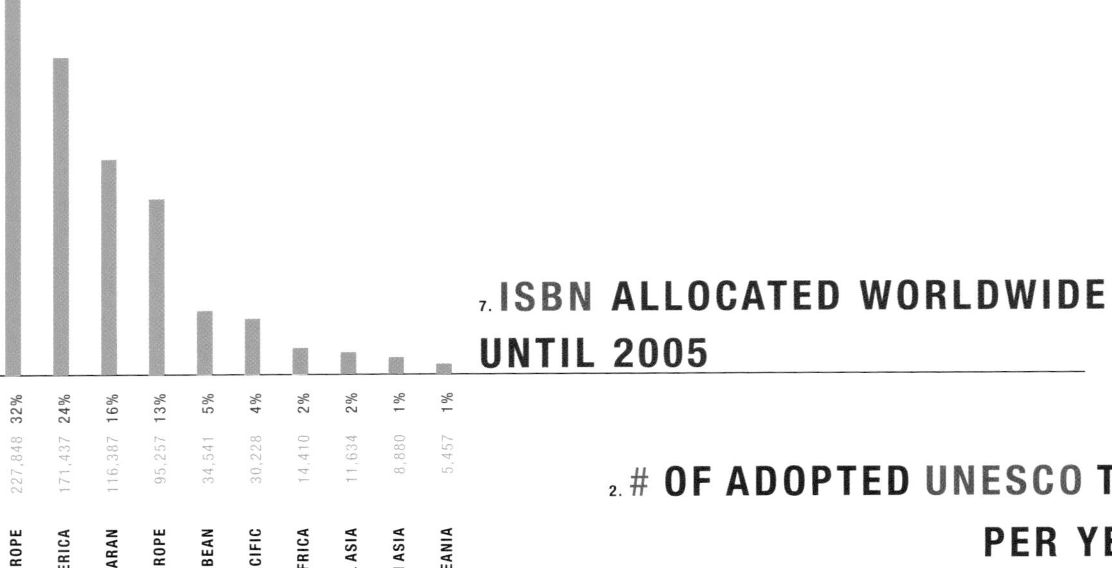

7. ISBN ALLOCATED WORLDWIDE UNTIL 2005

2. # OF ADOPTED UNESCO TREATIES PER YEAR 1984 – 2005

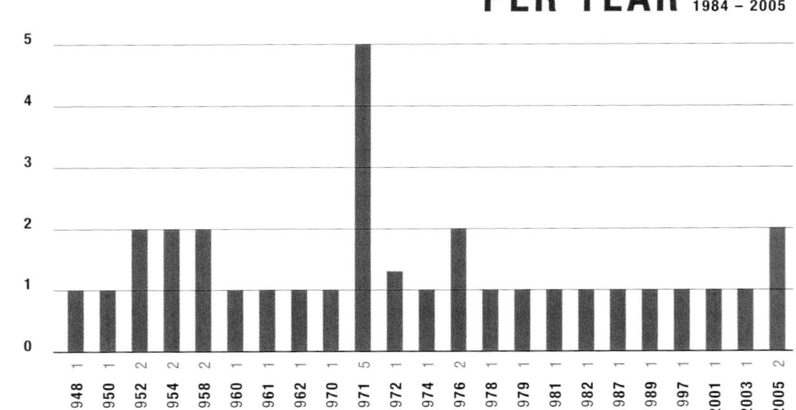

1. UNESCO CONVENTIONS

CODE	RATIFIED CONVENTIONS	YEAR OF ADOPTION
AFI	- Agreement for Facilitating the International Circulation of Visual and Auditory Materials of an Educational, Scientific and Cultural character with Protocol of Signature and model form of certificate provided for in Article IV of the above-mentioned Agreement	1948
AI	- Agreement on the Importation of Educational, Scientific and Cultural Materials, with Annexes A to E and Protocol annexed	1950
P3	- Protocol 3 annexed to the Universal Copyright Convention concerning the effective date of instruments of ratification or acceptance of or accession to that Convention	1952
UCCA	- Universal Copyright Convention, with Appendix Declaration relating to Article XVII and Resolution concerning Article XI	1952
CPC	- Convention for the Protection of Cultural Property in the Event of Armed Conflict with Regulations for the Execution of the Convention	1954
PCP	- Protocol to the Convention for the Protection of Cultural Property in the Event of Armed Conflict	1954
CEO	- Convention concerning the Exchange of Official Publications and Government Documents between States	1958
CIEP	- Convention concerning the International Exchange of Publications	1958
CDE	- Convention against Discrimination in Education	1960
ICP	- International Convention for the Protection of Performers, Producers of Phonograms and Broadcasting Organizations	1961
PIC	- Protocol Instituting a Conciliation and Good Offices Commission to be Responsible for Seeking the Settlement of any Disputes which may Arise between States Parties to the Convention against Discrimination in Education	1962
CMPP	- Convention on the Means of Prohibiting and Preventing the Illicit Import, Export and Transfer of Ownership of Cultural Property	1970
CPPP	- Convention for the Protection of Producers of Phonograms against Unauthorized Duplication of their Phonograms	1971
CWI	- Convention on Wetlands of International Importance especially as Waterfowl Habitat	1971
P1-SR	- Protocol 1 annexed to the Universal Copyright Convention concerning the application of that Convention to the works of stateless persons and refugees	1971
P2	- Protocol 2 annexed to the Universal Copyright Convention concerning the application of that Convention to the works of certain international organizations	1971

INTERNATIONAL REGULATORY FRAMEWORKS

- **unesco conventions** - # of **adopted unesco treaties** per year 1984–2005 - total # of **countries signing** per **unesco treaty** - **timeline of unesco treaties adopted** - frequency of treaty support by enesco members: average # of **countries signing each year since adoption** - frequency of treaty support by unesco members: **proportion** (%) of **unesco membership signing each treaty** - **how many countries ratified how many treaties**

3. TOTAL # OF COUNTRIES SIGNING PER UNESCO TREATY

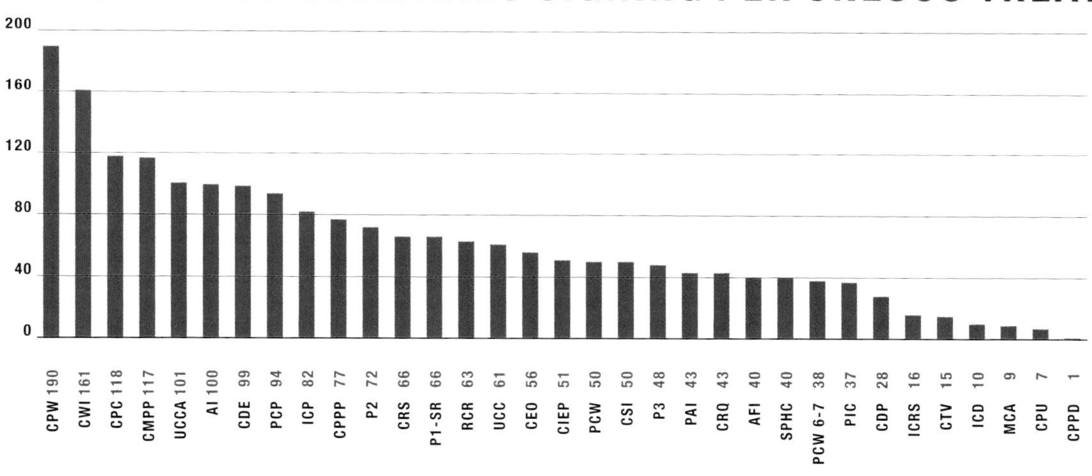

CODE	RATIFIED CONVENTIONS	YEAR OF ADOPTION
UCC	- Universal Copyright Convention as revised on 24 July 1971, with Appendix Declaration relating to Article XVII and Resolution concerning Article XI.	1971
CPW	- Convention concerning the Protection of the World Cultural and Natural Heritage	1972
CDP	- Convention relating to the Distribution of Programme-Carrying Signals Transmitted by Satellite	1974
ICRS	- International Convention on the Recognition of Studies, Diplomas and Degrees in Higher Education in the Arab and European States bordering on the Mediterranean	1976
PAI	- Protocol to the Agreement on the Importation of Educational, Scientific and Cultural Materials, with Annexes A to H	1976
CRS	- Convention on the Recognition of Studies, Diplomas and Degrees in Higher Education in the Arab States	1978
MCA	- Multilateral Convention for the Avoidance of Double Taxation of Copyright Royalties, with model bilateral agreement and additional Protocol	1979
RCR	- Regional Convention on the Recognition of Studies, Certificates, Diplomas, Degrees and other Academic Qualifications in Higher Education in the African States	1981
PCW	- Protocol to amend the Convention on Wetlands of International Importance especially as Waterfowl Habitat	1982
PCW 6-7	- Protocol to amend articles 6 and 7 of the Convention on Wetlands of International Importance especially as Waterfowl Habitat	1987
CTV	- Convention on Technical and Vocational Education	1989
CRQ	- Convention on the Recognition of Qualifications concerning Higher Education in the European Region	1997
SPHC	- Second Protocol to the Hague Convention of 1954 for the Protection of Cultural Property in the Event of Armed Conflict	1999
CPU	- Convention on the Protection of the Underwater Cultural Heritage	2001
CSI	- Convention for the Safeguarding of the Intangible Cultural Heritage	2003
CPPD	- Convention on the Protection and Promotion of the Diversity of Cultural Expressions	2005
ICD	- International Convention against Doping in Sport	2005

4. TIMELINE OF UNESCO TREATIES ADOPTED:

5. FREQUENCY OF TREATY SUPPORT BY UNESCO MEMBERS: AVERAGE # OF COUNTRIES SIGNING EACH YEAR SINCE ADOPTION

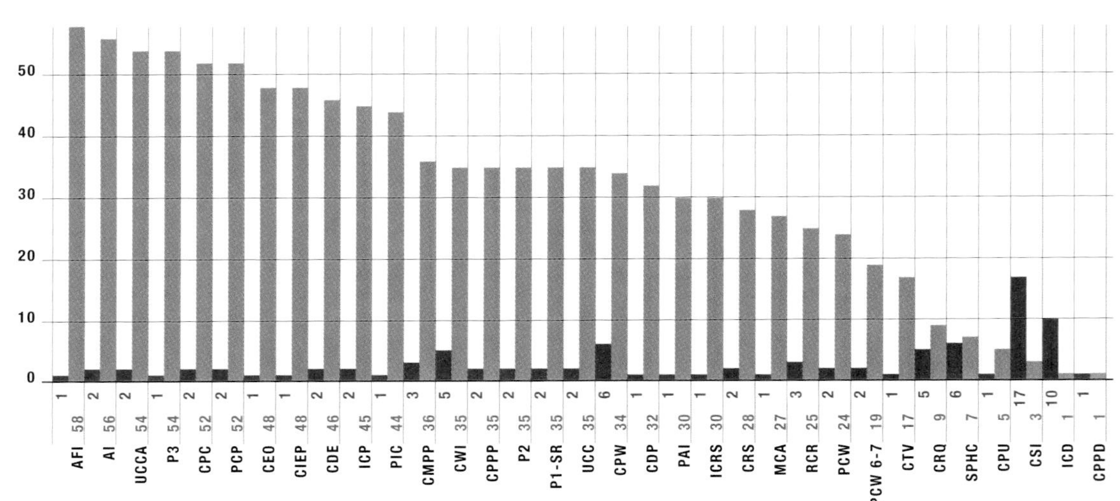

6. FREQUENCY OF TREATY SUPPORT BY UNESCO MEMBERS: PROPORTION (%) OF UNESCO MEMBERSHIP SIGNING EACH TREAT

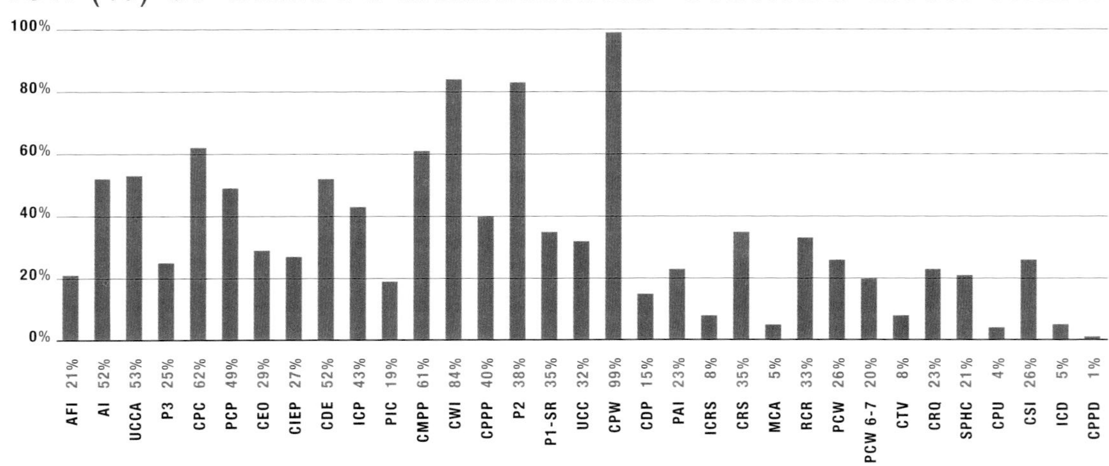

RATIFICATION FREQUENCY PER YEAR SINCE ADOPTION:

Years (axis): 1948 1949 1950 1951 1952 1953 1954 1955 1956 1957 1958 1959 1960 1961 1962 1963 1964 1965 1966 1967 1968 1969 1970 1971 1972 1973 1974 1975 1976 1977 1978 1979 1980 1981 1982 1983 1984 1985 1986 1987 1988 1989 1990 1991 1992 1993 1994 1995 1996 1997 1998 1999 2000 2001 2002 2003 2004 2005 2006

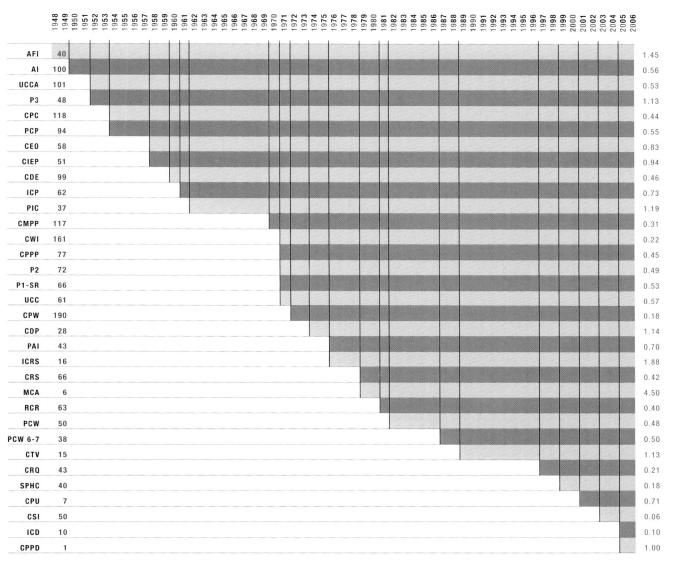

TREATY:	# OF COUNTRIES RATIFIED:	RATIFICATION FREQUENCY PER YEAR SINCE ADOPTION:
AFI	40	1.45
AI	100	0.56
UCCA	101	0.53
P3	48	1.13
CPC	118	0.44
PCP	94	0.55
CEO	58	0.83
CIEP	51	0.94
CDE	99	0.46
ICP	62	0.73
PIC	37	1.19
CMPP	117	0.31
CWI	161	0.22
CPPP	77	0.45
P2	72	0.49
P1-SR	66	0.53
UCC	61	0.57
CPW	190	0.18
CDP	28	1.14
PAI	43	0.70
ICRS	16	1.88
CRS	66	0.42
MCA	6	4.50
RCR	63	0.40
PCW	50	0.48
PCW 6-7	38	0.50
CTV	15	1.13
CRQ	43	0.21
SPHC	40	0.18
CPU	7	0.71
CSI	50	0.06
ICD	10	0.10
CPPD	1	1.00

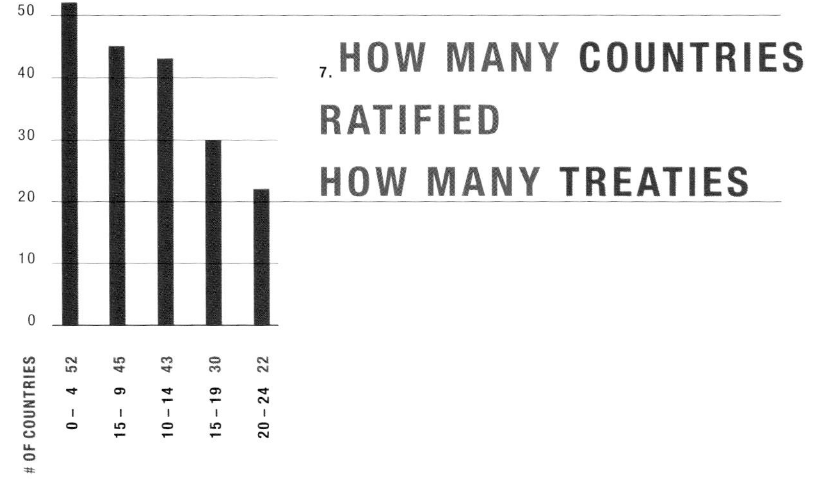

7. HOW MANY COUNTRIES RATIFIED HOW MANY TREATIES

INTERNATIONAL STANDARDS

International Standards are agreements on common technical approaches that are used worldwide. Typical examples are: Internet standards such as HTTP, SMTP, or HTML; units of measure of electrical power; battery sizes; GSM standard for mobile phones; or paper sizes like A4. While, until recently, global standards applied primarily to technical fields and issues, they increasingly consider non-technical aspects as well, with management practices and environmental impact as prominent examples. International standards also include classification systems for books, periodicals, and works of music.

Together, such standards have very profound impacts on human and organizational behavior across cultural and national boundaries. They are often very subtle forces of globalization in the sense that they shape everyday behavior and penetrate virtually all aspects of human endeavor. Standards are therefore part of the increasingly global social organization of rationalized modernity, and contribute, in the name of efficiency and safety, greater similarities across countries (Meyer et al, 1997).

The International Organization for Standardization (ISO) is the major international standard-setting body. Composed of representatives from national bodies, the organization was founded in 1947 to produce and disseminate worldwide industrial and commercial standards, the so-called ISO standards. While ISO is a non-governmental organization (NGO), its ability to set standards makes it a powerful actor as these standards often become accepted internationally through treaties and find their way into national legislation. The ISO works closely with international organizations, national governments, and corporations. For example, ISO cooperates with the International Electrotechnical Commission (IEC), which is responsible for standardization of electrical equipment and major transnational corporations in the field of consumer electronics and communication technology.

WHAT DO WE KNOW?

As the indicator suite on international standards shows, ISO has typically produced between 800 and 1200 standards, most of them in the field of engineering and technology. In terms of output, ISO has issued around 60,000 printed pages of standards annually since 2003. Important non-technical standards are ISO 9000 and ISO 14000:

- ISO 9000 is concerned with the quality of management, customer satisfaction, and applicable regulatory requirements for continually improving performance

- ISO 14000 is primarily concerned with environmental management, the minimization of harmful effects, and the continual improvement of environmental performance

According to ISO, the ISO 9000 and ISO 14000 families have a "worldwide reputation known as 'generic management system standards'. 'Generic' means that the same standards can be applied to any organization, large or small, whatever its product. 'Management system' refers to what the organization does to manage its processes or activities. 'Generic' also signifies that no matter what the organization is or does, if it wants to establish a quality management system or an environmental management system, then such a system has a number of essential features which are spelled out in the relevant standards of the ISO 9000 or ISO 14000 families" (http://www.iso.org/iso/en/aboutiso/introduction/index.html#twelve).

Related to ISO 9000 and ISO 14000 families of standards are the Social Accountability Standards, in particular SA 8000 that ensures just and decent working conditions. The SA 8000 standard covers all core international labor rights contained in the ILO Conventions, the International Declaration of Human Rights and the UN Convention on the Rights of the Child including child labor, forced labor, health and safety, freedom of association and right to collective bargaining, discrimination, discipline, working hours and wages. ISO 8000, ISO 9000 and ISO 14000 establish transnational social and legal expectations about corporate behavior.

Other standard setting organizations include:

The International ISBN Agency is in charge of coordinating, promoting and supervising the worldwide use of the ISBN system. ISBN "is a unique machine-readable identification number, which marks any book unmistakably. This number is defined in ISO Standard 2108. The number has been in use now for 30 years and has revolutionized the international book-trade. 166 countries and territories are officially ISBN members" (http://www.isbn-international.org/en/whatis.html).

The International Standard Music Number Agency promotes, coordinates and supervises the world-wide use of the ISMN system. It acts as the registration authority for this ISO Standard (ISO 10957) as a means of uniquely identifying printed music publications. It standardizes and "promotes internationally" the use of numbers of printed music publications in order that one edition of a title or one separate component of an edition can be distinguished from all other editions or components by means of a unique international standard music number.

REGULATORY FRAMEWORKS The Constitution of UNESCO came into force a year after its signing on November 16, 1945, with the mandate to "contribute to peace and security by promoting collaboration among the nations through education, science and culture in order to further universal respect for justice, for the rule of law and for the human rights and fundamental freedoms which are affirmed for the peoples of the world, without distinction of race, sex, language or religion, by the Charter of the United Nations."

To this end, UNESCO (a) collaborates in the work of advancing the mutual knowledge and understanding of peoples, through all means of mass communication and to that end recommend such international agreements as may be necessary to promote the free flow of ideas by word and image; (b) gives fresh impulse to popular education and to the spread of culture; and (c) maintains, increases and diffuses knowledge (www.unesco.org).

A major part of UNESCO's work is the process of creating, negotiating, implementing and governing international regulatory frameworks for education, science, and culture. Three kinds of instruments are important in furthering UNESCO's activities in this regard:

- International Conventions are subject to ratification, acceptance or accession by States. They define rules with which the States undertake to comply in particular fields such as broadcasting or specified issues such as cultural diversity. The General Conference considers the draft texts submitted to it and, if it sees fit, adopts the instrument after which it is put to member states for ratification.

- Recommendations are instruments that formulate principles and norms for international regulation and invite Member States to take whatever legislative or other steps may be required in conformity with the constitutional practice of each State. Recommendations are not subject to ratification; however, Member States are invited to apply them in policymaking and legislation.

- Declarations are formal and solemn instruments that set forth universal principles and express great and lasting importance, such as the Declaration of Human Rights. Declarations, like recommendations, are not subject to ratification.

The regulatory framework built by UNESCO has achieved great scope and complexity since the 1950s, and now spans a wide range of academic, educational, cultural and artistic aspects – from a Universal Copyright Convention (1952), and the Convention Against Discrimination in Education (1960), to the Convention on the Protection and Promotion of the Diversity of Cultural Expressions (2005).

As the indicator suite shows, this framework continues to expand and 'thicken' in terms of the number of conventions; yet, it does so at a slower pace than in the 1960s and 1970s. Only five treaties were adopted since 1990, as opposed to 12 in the 1970s alone. There is also a slow-down in the way countries become signatories of treaties once negotiated and accepted. Only nine of the over 30 treaties are signed by more than 80 member states; the majority of treaties are signed by between 40 and 80 members, and nine by less than 40. As result, a major problem of the international regulatory framework is its 'patchy' structure and unevenness by which member states become signatories and parties of treaties through ratification and, ultimately, implementation at national levels.

The 2005 Convention on the Protection and Promotion of the Diversity of Cultural Expressions has become one of the most celebrated in the organization's history. It builds upon ideas in the Universal Declaration on Cultural Diversity, which UNESCO adopted in 2001. For example, in Article 8 of the Declaration, fundamental principles are established about the nature of cultural goods:

In the face of present-day economic and technological change, opening up vast prospects for creation and innovation, particular attention must be paid to the diversity of the supply of creative work, to due recognition of the rights of authors and artists and to the specificity of cultural goods and services which, as vectors of identity, values and meaning, must not be treated as mere commodities or consumer goods.

While its adaption was appased by the US government, this new Convention has crystallized many anxieties, hopes and asirations eleswhere countries like Canada or France see the Convention as a 'quantum leap' forward towards a more comprehensive system of global cultural governance based on fundamental principles. The current US administration questions the very assumptions underlying the Convention and voices opposition to full implementation others believe that the Convention, like many that were adopted in the past, may ultimately find only limited real support by governments in terms of policymaking and regulations in the arena of culture.

EXCERPTS FROM THE 2005 CONVENTION ON THE PROTECTION AND PROMOTION OF THE DIVERSITY OF CULTURAL EXPRESSIONS

I. OBJECTIVES AND GUIDING PRINCIPLES

Article 1 – Objectives

The objectives of this Convention are:

a) to protect and promote the diversity of cultural expressions;

b) to create the conditions for cultures to flourish and to freely interact in a mutually beneficial manner;

c) to encourage dialogue among cultures with a view to ensuring wider and balanced cultural exchanges in the world in favour of intercultural respect and a culture of peace;

d) to foster interculturality in order to develop cultural interaction in the spirit of building bridges among peoples;

e) to promote respect for the diversity of cultural expressions and raise awareness of its value at the local, national and international levels;

f) to reaffirm the importance of the link between culture and development for all countries, particularly for developing countries, and to support actions undertaken nationally and internationally to secure recognition of the true value of this link;

g) to give recognition to the distinctive nature of cultural activities, goods and services as vehicles of identity, values and meaning;

h) to reaffirm the sovereign rights of States to maintain, adopt and implement policies and measures that they deem appropriate for the protection and promotion of the diversity of cultural expressions on their territory;

i) to strengthen international cooperation and solidarity in a spirit of partnership with a view, in particular, to enhancing the capacities of developing countries in order to protect and promote the diversity of cultural expressions.

Article 2 – Guiding principles

1. Principle of respect for human rights and fundamental freedoms

Cultural diversity can be protected and promoted only if human rights and fundamental freedoms, such as freedom of expression, information and communication, as well as the ability of individuals to choose cultural expressions, are guaranteed. No one may invoke the provisions of this Convention in order to infringe human rights and fundamental freedoms as enshrined in the Universal Declaration of Human Rights or guaranteed by international law, or to limit the scope thereof.

2. Principle of sovereignty

States have, in accordance with the Charter of the United Nations and the principles of international law, the sovereign right to adopt measures and policies to protect and promote the diversity of cultural expressions within their territory.

3. Principle of equal dignity of and respect for all cultures

The protection and promotion of the diversity of cultural expressions presuppose the recognition of equal dignity of and respect for all cultures, including the cultures of persons belonging to minorities and indigenous peoples.

4. Principle of international solidarity and cooperation

International cooperation and solidarity should be aimed at enabling countries, especially developing countries, to create and strengthen their means of cultural expression, including their cultural industries, whether nascent or established, at the local, national and international levels.

5. Principle of the complementarity of economic and cultural aspects of development

Since culture is one of the mainsprings of development, the cultural aspects of development are as important as its economic aspects, which individuals and peoples have the fundamental right to participate in and enjoy.

6. Principle of sustainable development

Cultural diversity is a rich asset for individuals and societies. The protection, promotion and maintenance of cultural diversity are an essential requirement for sustainable development for the benefit of present and future generations.

7. Principle of equitable access

Equitable access to a rich and diversified range of cultural expressions from all over the world and access of cultures to the means of expressions and dissemination constitute important elements for enhancing cultural diversity and encouraging mutual understanding.

8. Principle of openness and balance

When States adopt measures to support the diversity of cultural expressions, they should seek to promote, in an appropriate manner, openness to other cultures of the world and to ensure that these measures are geared to the objectives pursued under the present Convention.

POLICY

CULTURAL POLICY +

DIPLOMACY ORGANIZATIONS

CULTURAL POLICY + DIPLOMACY ORGANIZATIONS

1. # OF UNESCO GLOBAL ALLIANCE PARTNERS

BY REGION

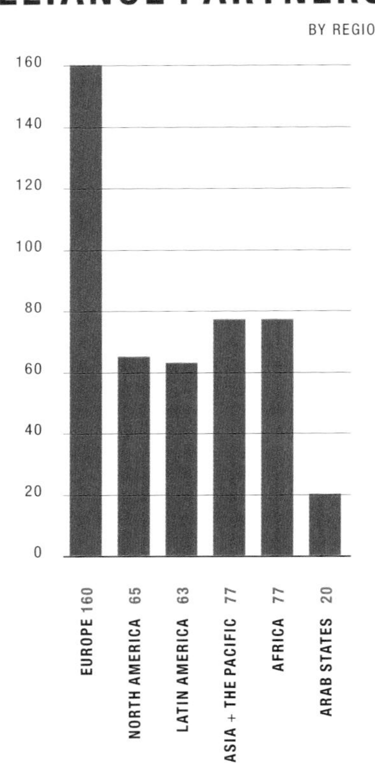

2. # OF IFACCA CURRENT MEMBERS 2006

BY TYPE AND REGION

3. # OF CREATIVE EXCHANGE PARTNERS

BY REGION

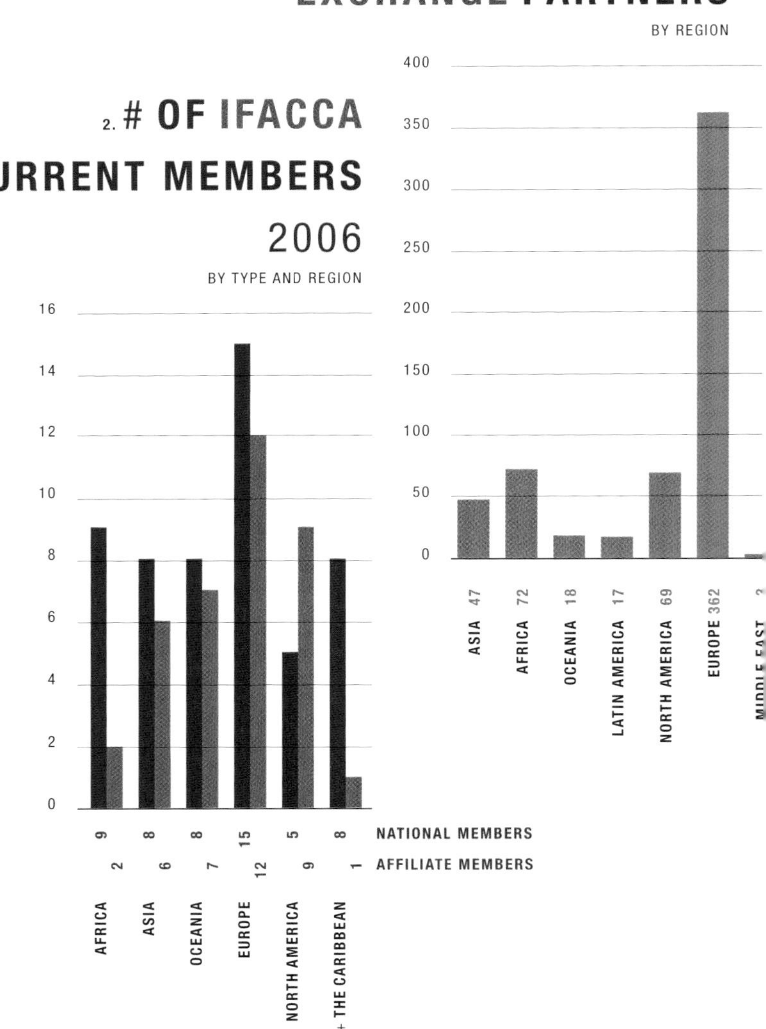

- # of **unesco global alliance partners** by region - # **of international federation of arts councils and culture agencies** (ifacca) **current members** by type and region, 2006 - # **of creative exchange partners** by region - **locations of cultural diplomacy organizations** by region - # **of locations of british council** by region

4. LOCATIONS OF CULTURAL DIPLOMACY ORGANIZATIONS

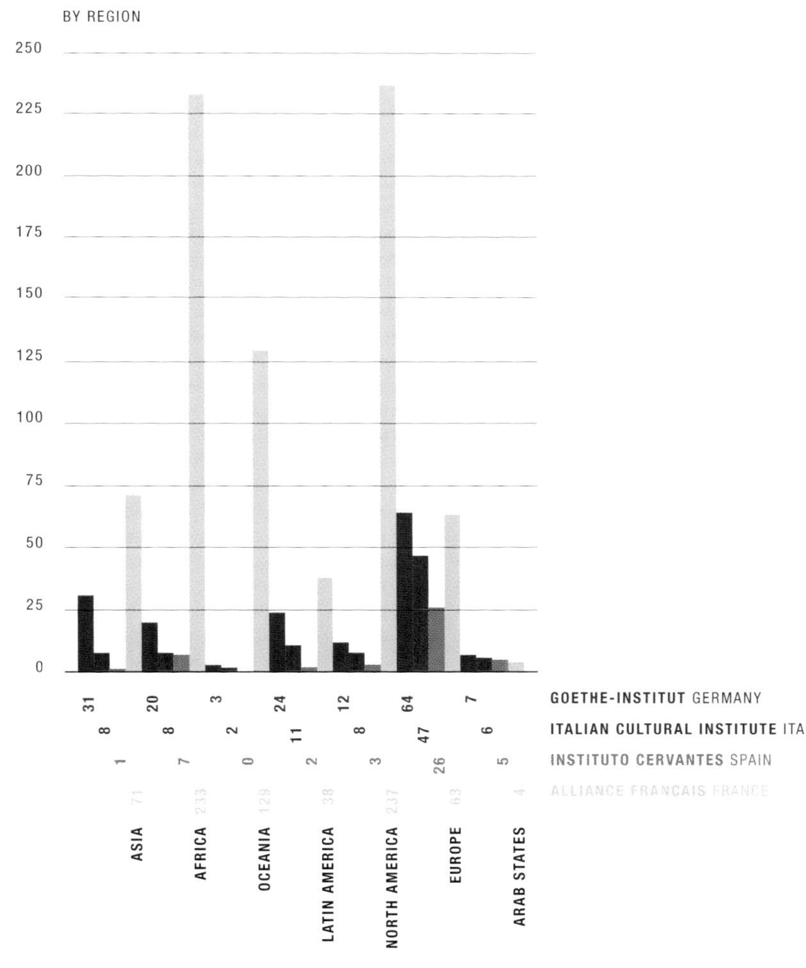

5. # OF LOCATIONS OF BRITISH COUNCIL

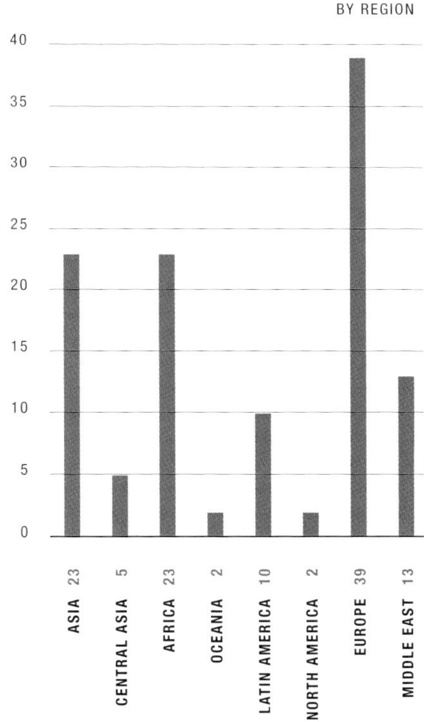

CULTURAL DIPLOMACY + CULTURAL OBSERVATORIES

The field of cultural diplomacy is a growing infrastructure of organizations that includes a system of separate govern-mental departments and refers to the exchange of ideas, information, art, lifestyles, value systems, traditions, beliefs and other aspects of culture between different countries, regions and groups to achieve rapport and understanding. Traditionally, cultural diplomacy involved government agencies with respect to negotiating treaties, alliances, shaping policy, etc., but today it increasingly includes non-governmental organizations (NGOs) and networks. Indeed there has been a proliferation of actors in the field of cultural diplomacy, with expanding networks linking public agencies and private organizations. Cultural diplomacy is seen as a vehicle of 'soft power' that stresses relations among countries by way of culture, art and education, as opposed to the 'hard power' of conventional political diplomacy.

Some countries such as France consider cultural policy to be the third pillar of foreign policy-making alongside the political and economic. Accordingly, French embassies and consulates typically include a specialized cultural affairs office. Above the bilateral governmental system, a new multi-lateral network of inter-governmental cooperation is taking shape. This network includes prominently, not only UNESCO and related organizations, but also the International Federation of Arts Councils and Culture Agencies (IFACCA) which aims to benefit artists, arts organizations and communities worldwide.

IFACCA is a network of mostly governmental agencies in the field of arts and culture. According to the IFACCA website, its vision is a "dynamic network, sharing knowledge and creating understanding to enrich a world of artistic and cultural diversity," in which IFACCA seeks to:

- strengthen the capacity of arts councils and national culture agencies to meet the challenges and opportunities of globalization and technological change;
- consolidate the collective knowledge of arts councils and culture agencies;
- build networks, promote understanding and enhance cooperation between arts councils and national arts agencies;
- encourage support for arts practice and cultural diversity; and
- create and maintain a supple and accountable organization (2006)

In addition to official cultural diplomacy at the ministerial or department levels, there are cultural agencies that are increasingly independent of official policy and diplomatic structures. These agencies not only promote the language and cultural heritage of the country they represent, but should seek greater levels of cooperation to facilitate dialogue and encourage understanding and appreciation of cultural differences. They typically try to present and further the interests of a national culture in an increasingly international and global context. An example is the British Council which works in 110 countries and collaborates in nearly 2,000 arts events annually:

Our purpose is to build mutually beneficial relationships between the people of the UK and other countries and increase appreciation of the UK's creative ideas and achievements. This work is driven by a strong belief in internationalism, a commitment to professionalism and an enthusiasm for creativity (British Council, 2006).

Similarly, the Goethe Institut promotes the study of German people and culture abroad and encourages international cultural exchange. "We draw from the many sections of our cosmopolitan society and culture combining the experience and ideas of our partners with our cross-national experience...We embrace the politico-cultural challenges of globalization" (Goethe Institut, 2006). Like the British Council, the Alliance Francaise, the Instituto Cervantes, or the Italian Cultural Institute, the Goethe Institut maintains a worldwide network of centers. However, these agencies vary in their independence from official government budgets and policies, with the Goethe Institute being the most independent.

Another layer of the growing infrastructure of international cultural diplomacy are alliances between the UN and NGOs organizations, with UNESCO's Global Alliance partners as a prime example, whereby their primary purpose is, "to strengthen cultural industries in developing countries by encouraging knowledge-sharing, capacity building, good practice and mentoring between our members" (UNESCO, 2006).

Another striking trans-national trend is the emergence of cultural 'observatories' that expressly monitor, analyse and act as clearing houses for activities, development and policies in the cultural field (as distinct from organizations whose work includes some such functions). The idea now is that such dedicated bodies can collectively provide an 'information infrastructure' for the purposes of comparison and cooperation not just within nations but also across boundaries. The movement began at the national level with the creation in 1989 of the *Observatoire des Politiques Culturelles* in Grenoble, France, and the term has now spread across the world (see the non-exhaustive list below). While an 'International Network of Observatories on Cultural Policies' planned by UNESCO has not materialized, the latter has an Observatory on the Information Society. In 2002 the Observatory of Cultural Policies in Africa was set up in Mozambique, while in 2003 the Organization of American States began work on an 'Inter-American Cultural Policy Observatory'. A key trans-national development in 2006 was the launch, at the initiative of the European Cultural Foundation, of the *LabforCulture*, an online platform for information, exchange, debate and research on European cultural cooperation.

LIST: **SOME ENTITIES WITH TRANS-NATIONAL OBSERVATORY FUNCTIONS**

Asia-Europe Foundation
http://www.asef.org/

Boekmanstichting
http://www.boekman.nl/

Convenio Andrés Bello
http://www.cab.int.co/

Creative exchange
http://www.creativexchange.org/

Culturelink - the Network of Networks for Research and Cooperation in Cultural Development
http://www.culturelink.org/

ERICArts - European Research Institute for Comparative Cultural Policy and the Arts
http://www.ericarts.org/

EUCLID International
http://www.euclid.co.uk/

INTERARTS – (European Observatory of Regional and Urban Cultural Policies)
http://www.interarts.net/

International Federation of Arts Councils and Culture Agencies (IFACCA) LabforCulture
http://www.labforculture.org/

Observatory of Cultural Policies in Africa
http://www.imo.hr/ocpa/

Pacific Asia Observatory for museums and cultural diversity in sustainable development
http://www.pacificasiaobservatory.org/

Regional Observatory on Financing Culture in East-Central Europe
(The "Budapest Observatory")
http://www.budobs.org/

UNESCO Observatory on the Information Society
http://portal.unesco.org/ci/en/ev.php-URL_ID=7277&URL_DO=DO_TOPIC&URL_SECTION=201.html

CONFLICT + COOPERATION

ARMS

- 15 largest **arms producing companies** by sales 2003 - regional **military expenditure estimates** 1995–2004 - **us companies** with **largest department of defense contract awards for work in iraq 2002–june 2004** in $usd current 2004 millions - 15 countries with the **highest military expenditures by purchasing power parity** 2004 - nations with **highest military expenditures** 25 % of gross domestic product 2004 - 20 nations with **largest total armed forces** 2002 - leading suppliers of **arms transfer agreements with developing nations** 1997–2004 - network analysis: **global trade in arms** - leading **developing nation recipients of arms transfer agreements** 1997–2004

1. 15 LARGEST **ARMS-PRODUCING COMPANIES** BY SALES 2003

IN USD$ MILLIONS

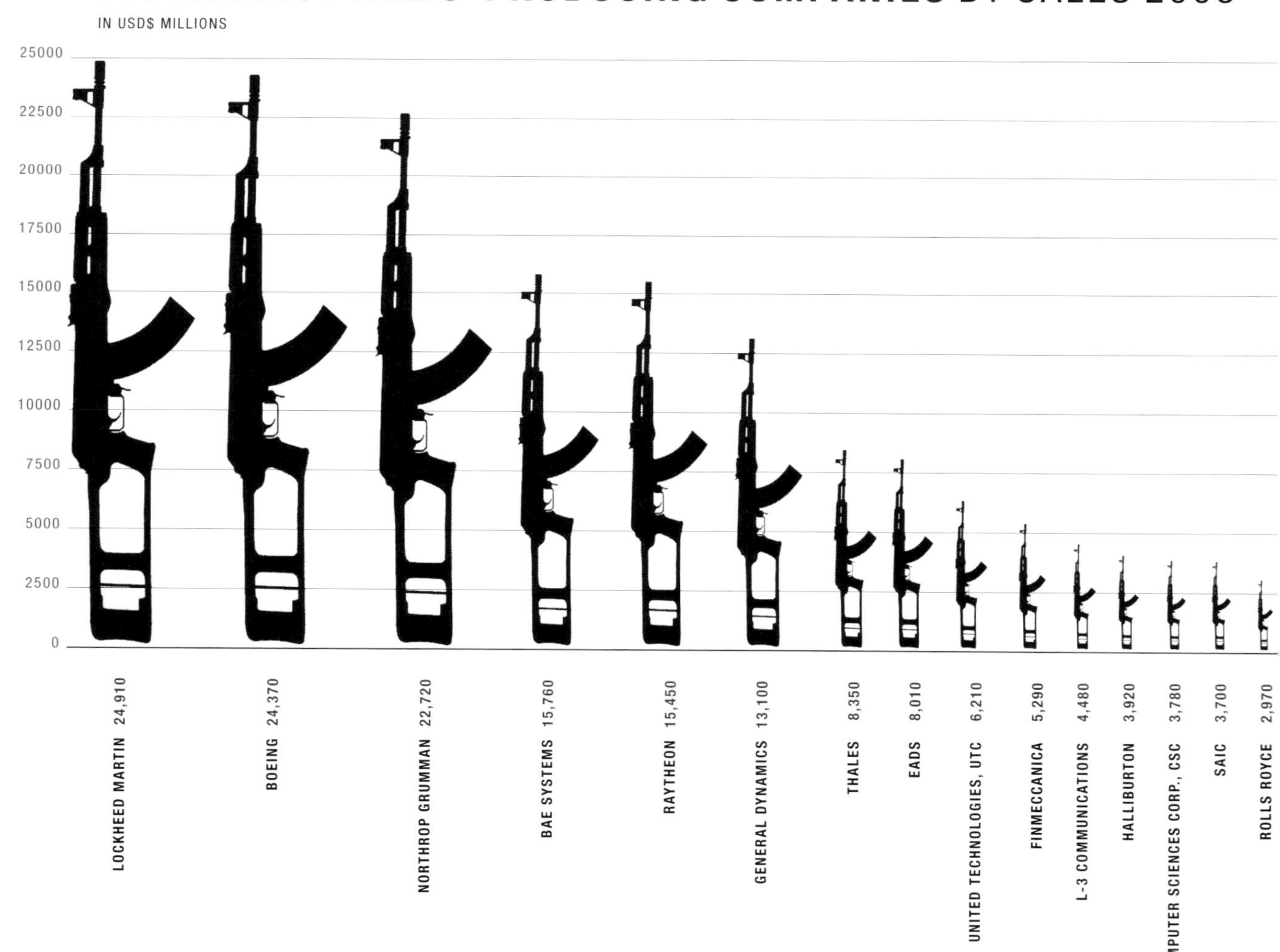

2. MILITARY EXPENDITURE ESTIMATES BY REGION 1995 – 2004

IN CONSTANT 2003 USD$ BILLIONS

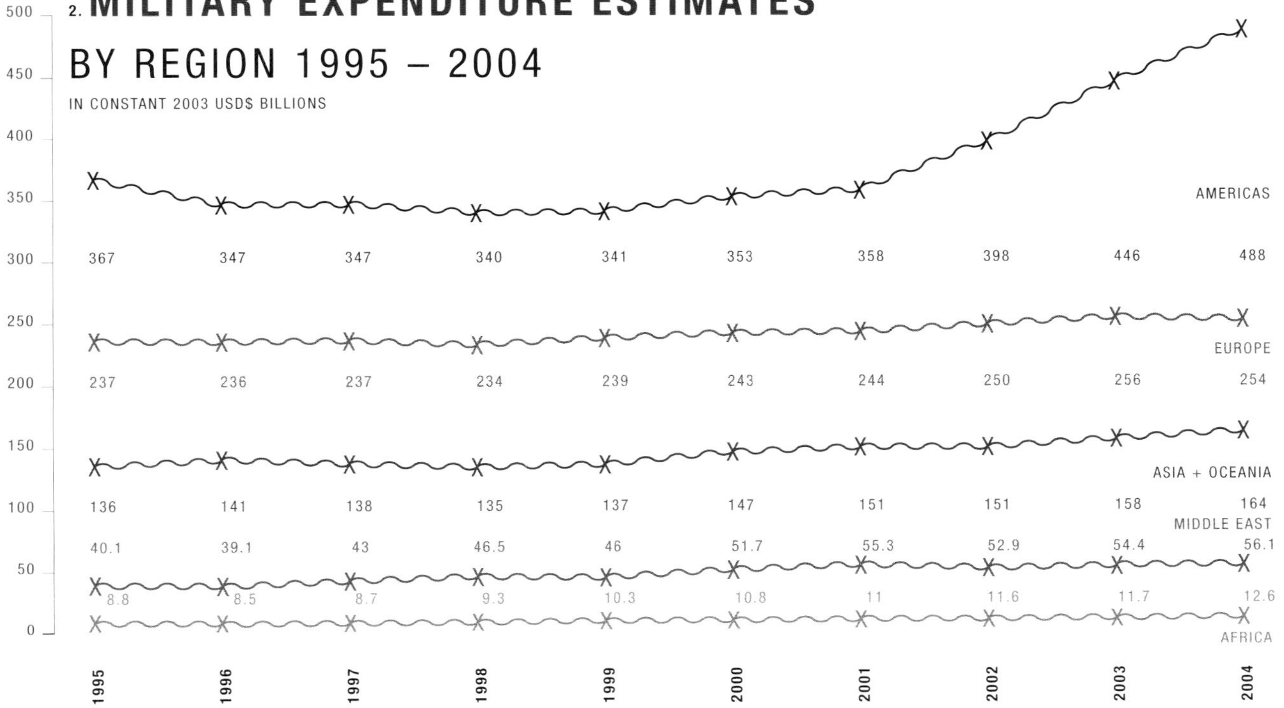

Region	1995	1996	1997	1998	1999	2000	2001	2002	2003	2004
AMERICAS	367	347	347	340	341	353	358	398	446	488
EUROPE	237	236	237	234	239	243	244	250	256	254
ASIA + OCEANIA	136	141	138	135	137	147	151	151	158	164
MIDDLE EAST	40.1	39.1	43	46.5	46	51.7	55.3	52.9	54.4	56.1
AFRICA	8.8	8.5	8.7	9.3	10.3	10.8	11	11.6	11.7	12.6

Axis: 0, 50, 100, 150, 200, 250, 300, 350, 400, 450, 500

3. US COMPANIES WITH LARGEST DEPARMENT OF DEFENSE CONTRACT AWARDS FOR WORK IN IRAQ 2002 – JUNE 2004

CONTRACT IN CURRENT USD$ MILLIONS, 2004

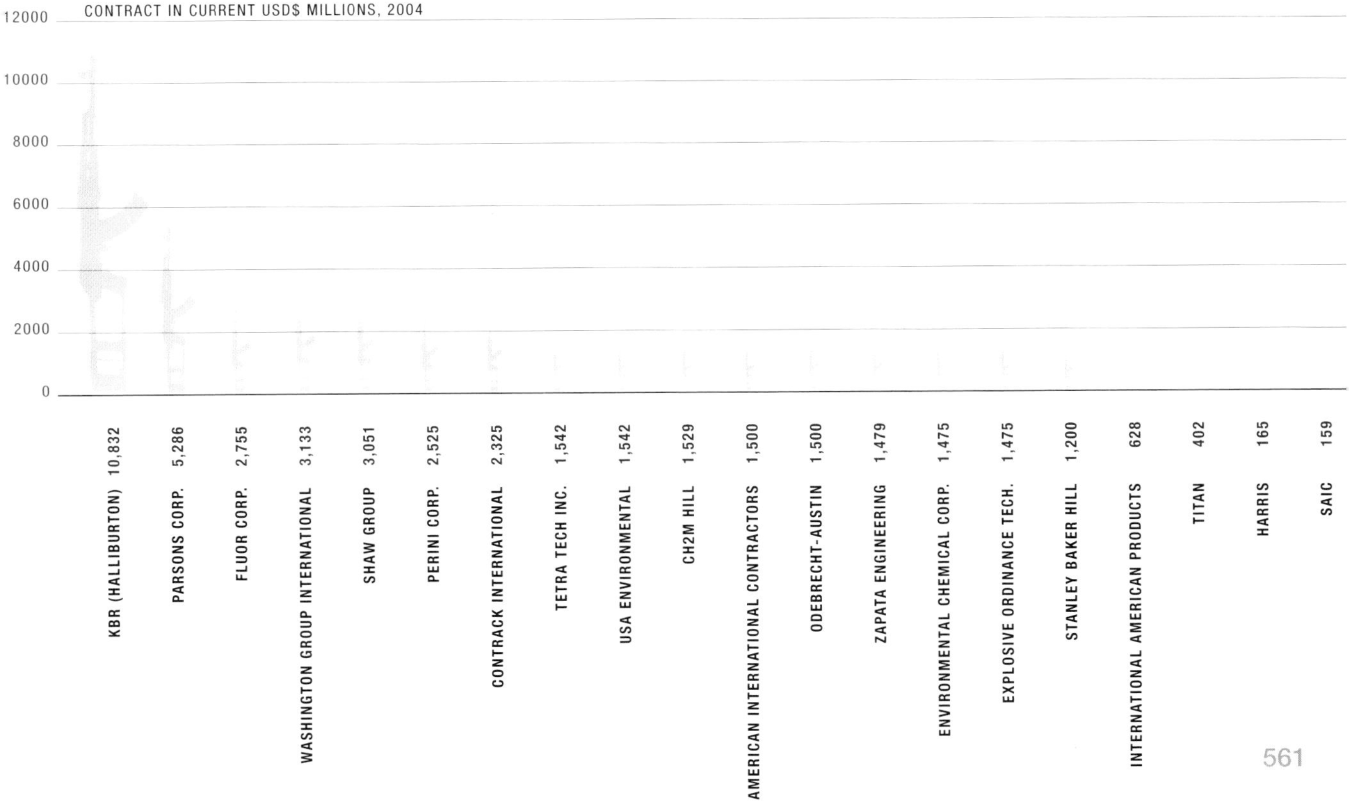

KBR (HALLIBURTON)	10,832
PARSONS CORP.	5,286
FLUOR CORP.	2,755
WASHINGTON GROUP INTERNATIONAL	3,133
SHAW GROUP	3,051
PERINI CORP.	2,525
CONTRACK INTERNATIONAL	2,325
TETRA TECH INC.	1,542
USA ENVIRONMENTAL	1,542
CH2M HILL	1,529
AMERICAN INTERNATIONAL CONTRACTORS	1,500
ODEBRECHT-AUSTIN	1,500
ZAPATA ENGINEERING	1,479
ENVIRONMENTAL CHEMICAL CORP.	1,475
EXPLOSIVE ORDINANCE TECH.	1,475
STANLEY BAKER HILL	1,200
INTERNATIONAL AMERICAN PRODUCTS	628
TITAN	402
HARRIS	165
SAIC	159

Axis: 0, 2000, 4000, 6000, 8000, 10000, 12000

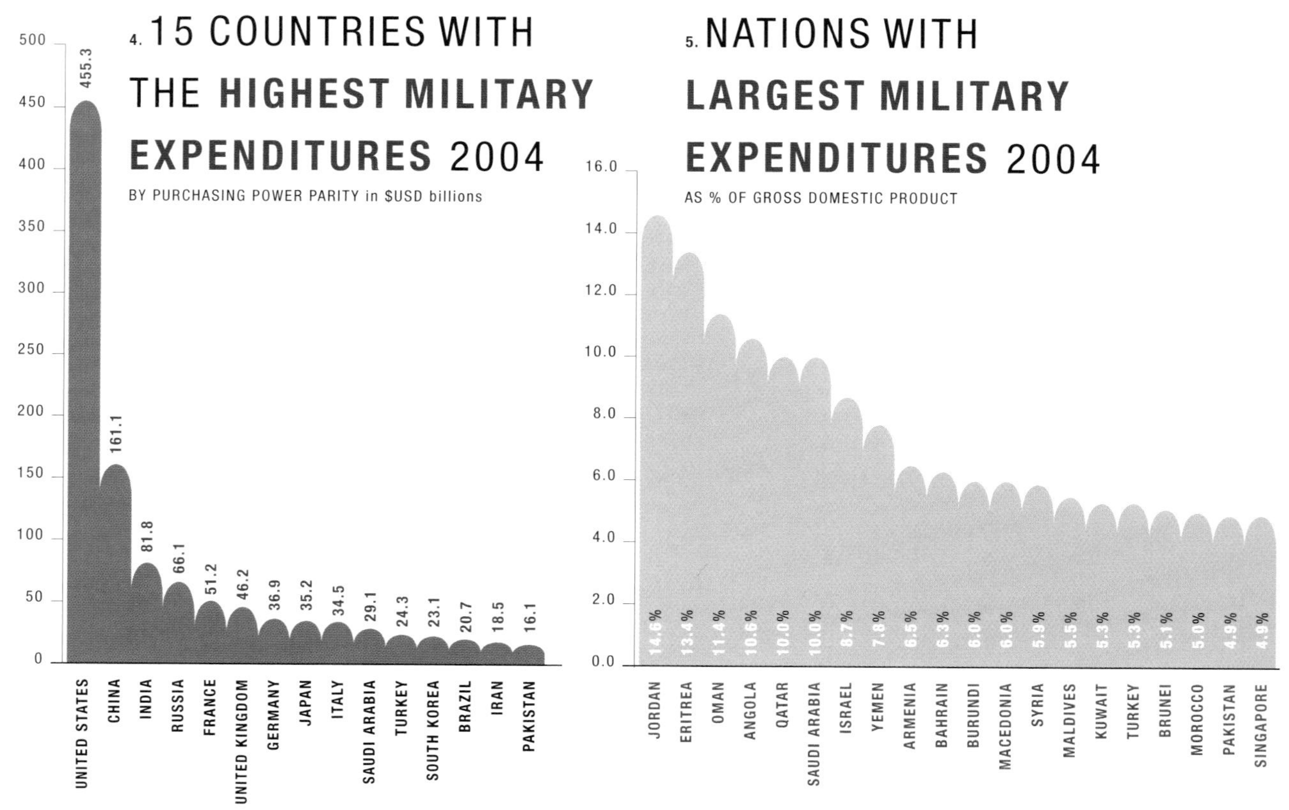

6. 20 NATIONS WITH LARGEST TOTAL ARMED FORCES 2002

★ = 100

CHINA	★★★★★★★★★★★★★★★★★★★★★★ + 70	2,270
UNITED STATES	★★★★★★★★★★★★★★ + 14	1,414
INDIA	★★★★★★★★★★★★ + 98	1,298
REPUBLIC OF KOREA	★★★★★★ + 86	686
PAKISTAN	★★★★★★ + 20	620
IRAN	★★★★★ + 20	520
TURKEY	★★★★★ + 15	515
VIETNAM	★★★★ + 84	484
MYANMAR	★★★★ + 44	444
EGYPT	★★★★ + 43	443
SYRIA	★★★ + 19	319
THAILAND	★★★ + 6	306
UKRAINE	★★★ + 2	302
INDONESIA	★★ + 97	297
GERMANY	★★ + 96	296
BRAZIL	★★ + 88	288
FRANCE	★★ + 60	260
ETHIOPIA	★★ + 53	253
JAPAN	★★ + 40	240
ITALY	★★ + 17	217

7a. LEADING SUPPLIERS OF **ARMS TRANSFER AGREEMENTS** WITH DEVELOPING NATIONS 1997 – 2004

IN CURRENT $USD MILLIONS, 2004

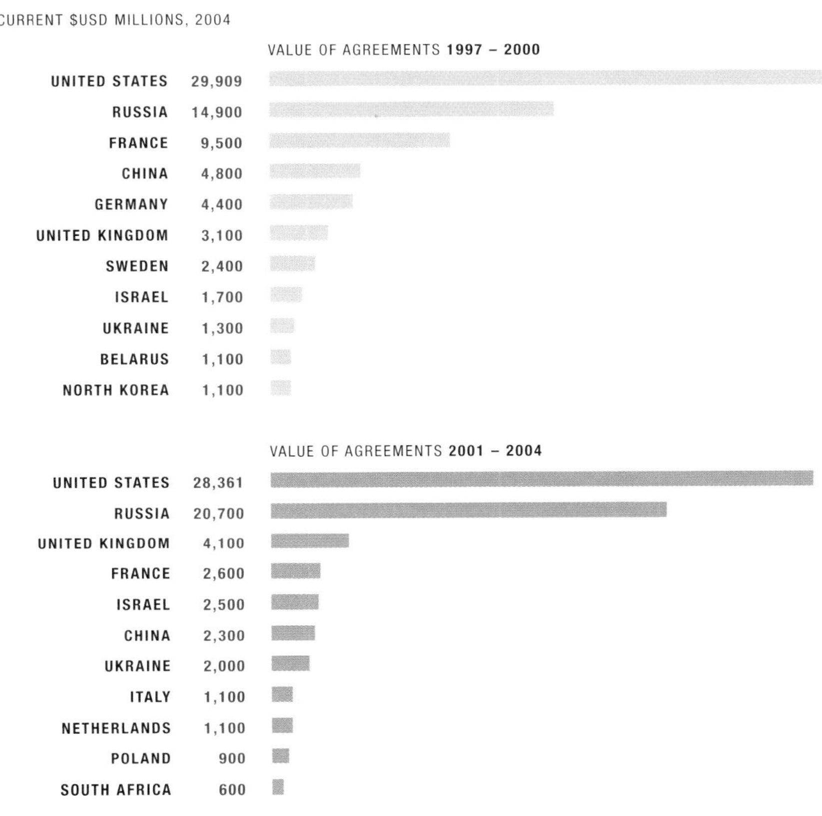

7b. LEADING DEVELOPING NATION RECIPIENTS OF **ARMS TRANSFER AGREEMENTS** 1997 – 2004

IN CURRENT $USD MILLIONS, 2004

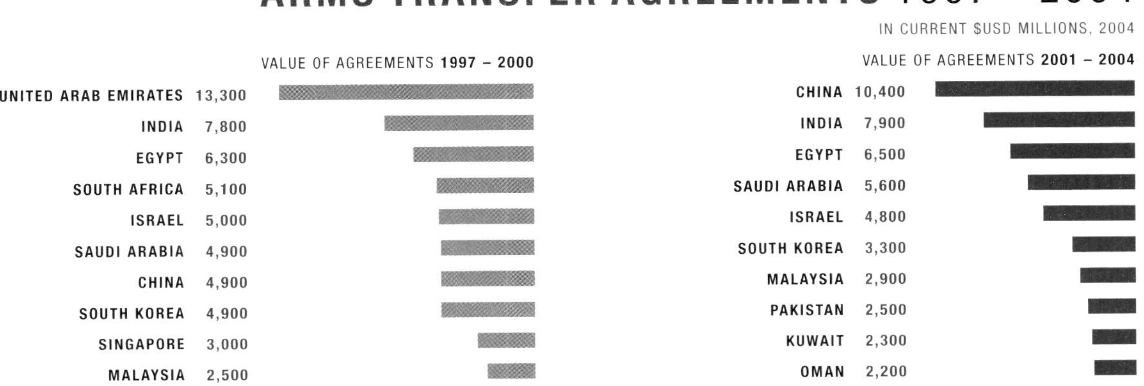

8. NETWORK ANALYSIS: **GLOBAL TRADE IN ARMS**

SIZE OF BUYING OR RECEIVING ARMS IS INDICATED BY THE SIZE OF THE NODE
(THE LARGER THE NODE, THE MORE ARMS ARE SOLD OR BOUGHT BY A COUNTRY OR REGION).

BUYER-SELLER RELATIONSHIPS ARE INDICATED BY PROXIMITY
(THE CLOSER THE COUNTRY—SELLER—IS TO A REGION—BUYER—THE STRONGER
THE TRADE RELATIONSHIP)

AMERICAS
USA
ISRAEL
ASIA
SWEDEN
RUSSIA
OCEANIA
UKRAINE
GERMANY
AFRICA
UK
CHINA
EUROPE
FRANCE
CANADA
MIDDLE EAST

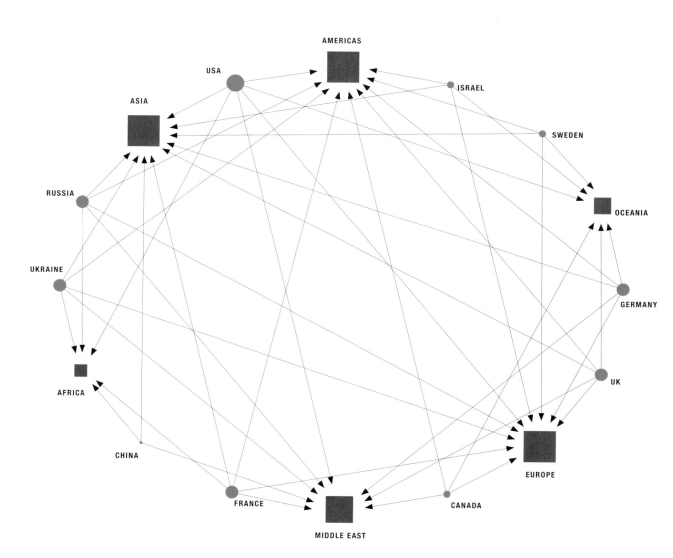

CONFLICT RESOLUTION + PEACEKEEPING

- # of **conflict resolution** by typology of conflict - # of **organizations** by area of concern - # of **peace missions** by type of organization 1995–2004 - **multilateral peace missions** by region 2004 - comparison of **active peace-keeping ingo's** by revenue 2002–2004 - **food for peace:** top 10 **recipients** 1995 + 2004 - total **troop strength of un peacekeeping operations** 1995–2004 - leading **troop contributors to un peacekeeping missions** 2004 - current **un peacekeeping operations** 2004

1. # OF **CONFLICT RESOLUTIONS** BY TYPOLOGY OF CONFLICT

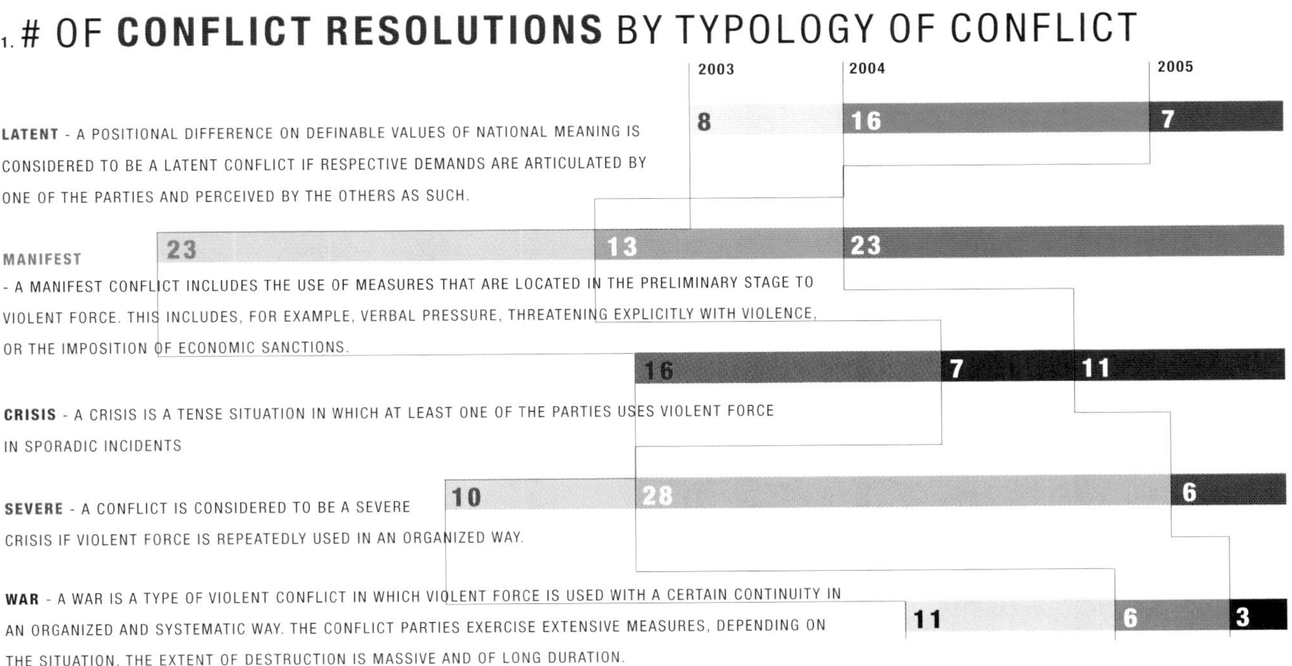

2003
2004
2005
LATENT - A POSITIONAL DIFFERENCE ON DEFINABLE VALUES OF NATIONAL MEANING IS CONSIDERED TO BE A LATENT CONFLICT IF RESPECTIVE DEMANDS ARE ARTICULATED BY ONE OF THE PARTIES AND PERCEIVED BY THE OTHERS AS SUCH.
8
16
7
MANIFEST - A MANIFEST CONFLICT INCLUDES THE USE OF MEASURES THAT ARE LOCATED IN THE PRELIMINARY STAGE TO VIOLENT FORCE. THIS INCLUDES, FOR EXAMPLE, VERBAL PRESSURE, THREATENING EXPLICITLY WITH VIOLENCE, OR THE IMPOSITION OF ECONOMIC SANCTIONS.
23
13
23
CRISIS - A CRISIS IS A TENSE SITUATION IN WHICH AT LEAST ONE OF THE PARTIES USES VIOLENT FORCE IN SPORADIC INCIDENTS
16
7
11
SEVERE - A CONFLICT IS CONSIDERED TO BE A SEVERE CRISIS IF VIOLENT FORCE IS REPEATEDLY USED IN AN ORGANIZED WAY.
10
28
6
WAR - A WAR IS A TYPE OF VIOLENT CONFLICT IN WHICH VIOLENT FORCE IS USED WITH A CERTAIN CONTINUITY IN AN ORGANIZED AND SYSTEMATIC WAY. THE CONFLICT PARTIES EXERCISE EXTENSIVE MEASURES, DEPENDING ON THE SITUATION. THE EXTENT OF DESTRUCTION IS MASSIVE AND OF LONG DURATION.
11
6
3

2. # OF **ORGANIZATIONS** BY AREA OF CONCERN

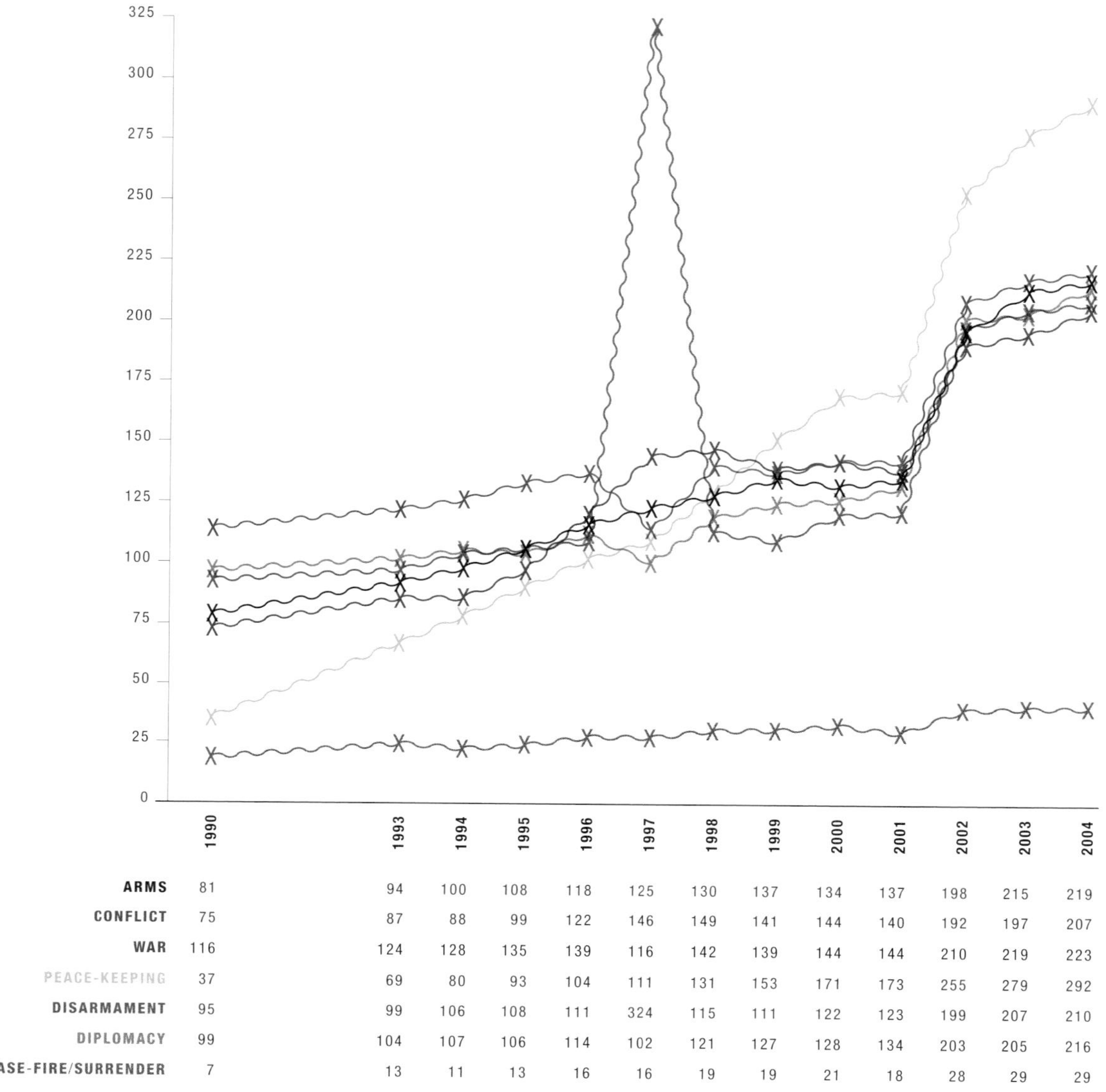

	1990	1993	1994	1995	1996	1997	1998	1999	2000	2001	2002	2003	2004
ARMS	81	94	100	108	118	125	130	137	134	137	198	215	219
CONFLICT	75	87	88	99	122	146	149	141	144	140	192	197	207
WAR	116	124	128	135	139	116	142	139	144	144	210	219	223
PEACE-KEEPING	37	69	80	93	104	111	131	153	171	173	255	279	292
DISARMAMENT	95	99	106	108	111	324	115	111	122	123	199	207	210
DIPLOMACY	99	104	107	106	114	102	121	127	128	134	203	205	216
CEASE-FIRE/SURRENDER	7	13	11	13	16	16	19	19	21	18	28	29	29

3. # OF **PEACE MISSIONS**

BY TYPE OF ORGANIZATION 1995 – 2004

	UNITED NATIONS	**REGIONAL ORGANIZATIONS OR ALLIANCES**	**NON-STANDING COALITIONS**
1995	26	16	6
1996	24	18	4
1997	23	22	7
1998	21	26	8
1999	24	30	7
2000	22	25	7
2001	18	26	7
2002	20	21	7
2003	18	26	8
2004	21	29	6

4. **MULTILATERAL PEACE MISSIONS 2004**

BY REGION 2004

CENTRAL AMERICA + CARIBBEAN	3
SOUTH AMERICA	1
NORTH AFRICA	14
SOUTH AFRICA	2
MIDDLE EAST	8
ASIA	5
SOUTH CENTRAL ASIA	2
WEST EUROPE	5
EAST EUROPE	4
SOUTH EUROPE	11
OCEANIA	1

5. COMPARISON OF ACTIVE PEACEKEEPING INGOs

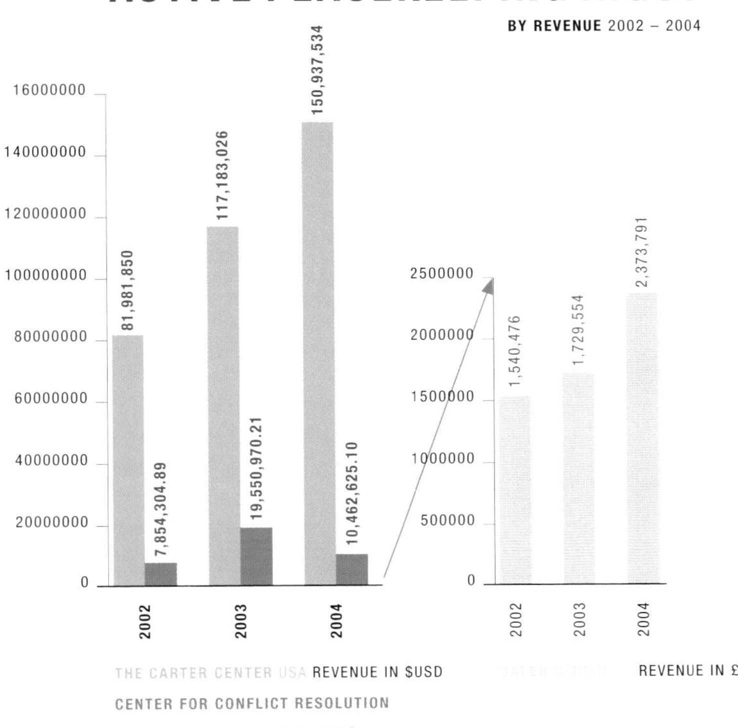

6. FOOD FOR PEACE: TOP 10 RECIPIENTS

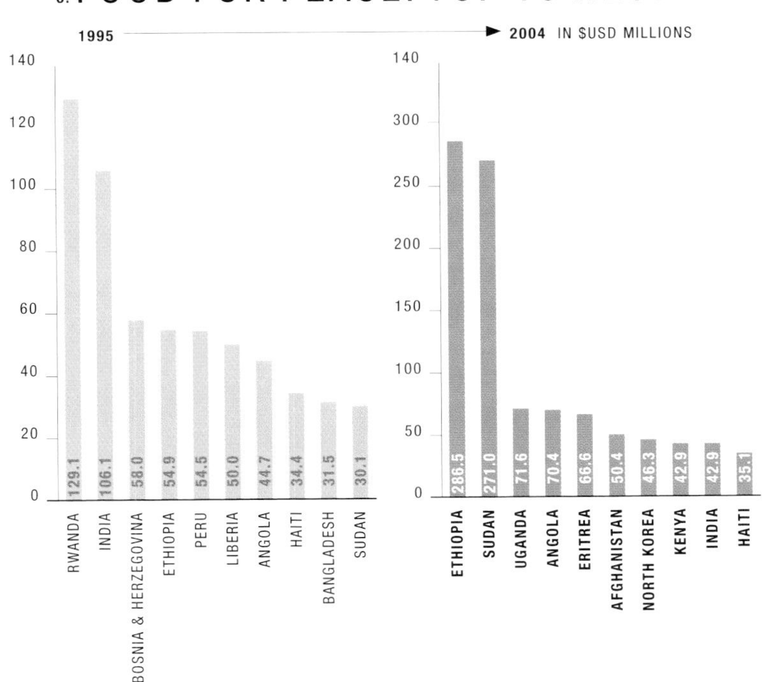

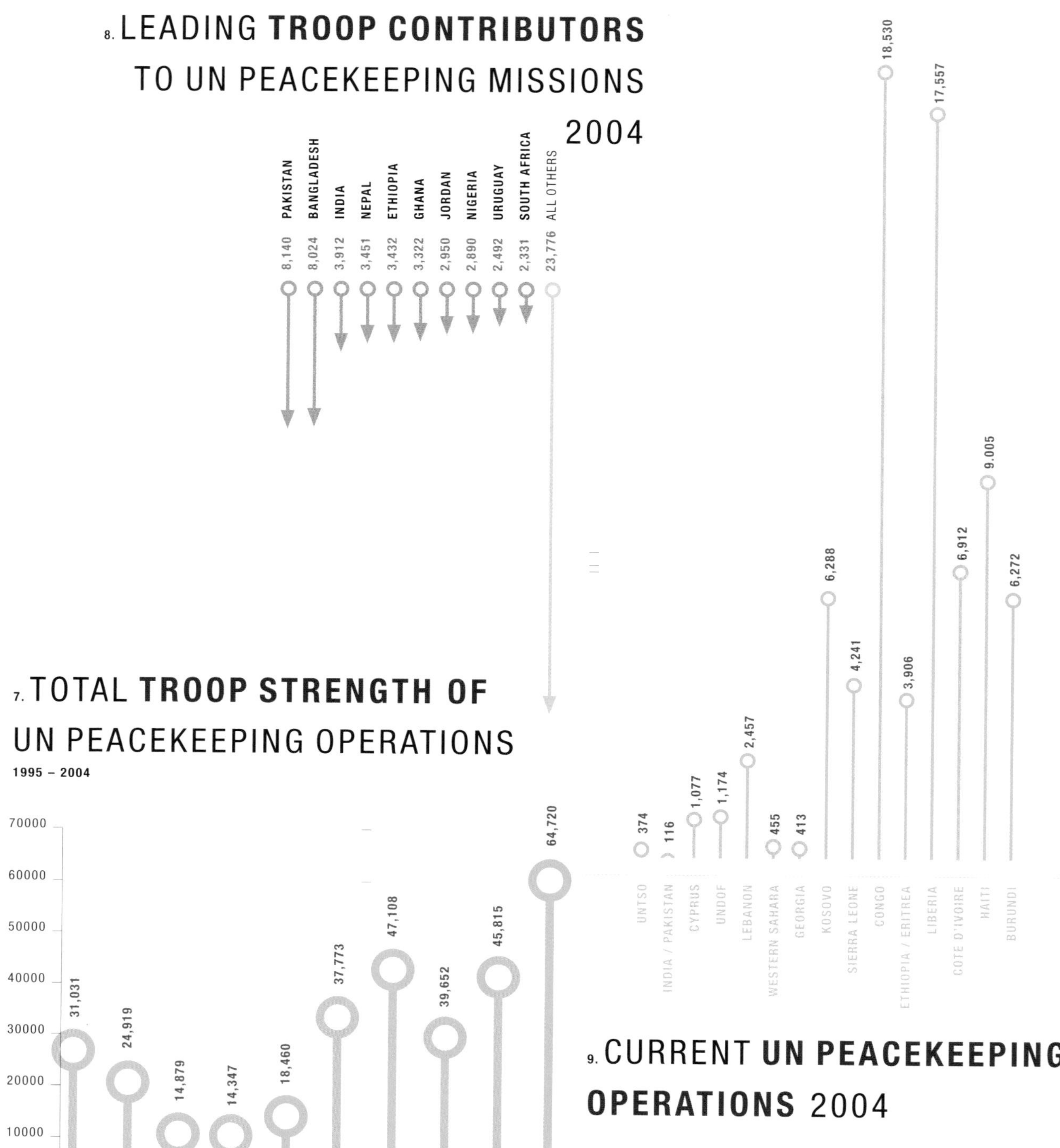

8. LEADING TROOP CONTRIBUTORS TO UN PEACEKEEPING MISSIONS 2004
PAKISTAN 8,140
BANGLADESH 8,024
INDIA 3,912
NEPAL 3,451
ETHIOPIA 3,432
GHANA 3,322
JORDAN 2,950
NIGERIA 2,890
URUGUAY 2,492
SOUTH AFRICA 2,331
ALL OTHERS 23,776
7. TOTAL TROOP STRENGTH OF UN PEACEKEEPING OPERATIONS
1995 – 2004
70000
60000
50000
40000
30000
20000
10000
0
1995 31,031
1996 24,919
1997 14,879
1998 14,347
1999 18,460
2000 37,773
2001 47,108
2002 39,652
2003 45,815
2004 64,720
9. CURRENT UN PEACEKEEPING OPERATIONS 2004
UNTSO 374
INDIA / PAKISTAN 116
CYPRUS 1,077
UNDOF 1,174
LEBANON 2,457
WESTERN SAHARA 455
GEORGIA 413
KOSOVO 6,288
SIERRA LEONE 4,241
CONGO 18,530
ETHIOPIA / ERITREA 3,906
LIBERIA 17,557
COTE D'IVOIRE 6,912
HAITI 9,005
BURUNDI 6,272

CURRENT CONFLICTS + ISSUES / TENSIONS

- **the peace and conflict ledger** 2005 - global trends in **political discrimination** 1950–2003 - global trends in **economic discrimination** 1950–2003 - global trends in **political discrimination of minorities** 1950–2003 - global trends in **violent conflicts** 1946–2004 - type of **armed conflict worldwide** 1946–2004 - **evolution** of different types of **armed conflicts** from 1964 to 2004 - levels of internationalized **internal armed conflict** 1946–2004 - # of **deaths current ongoing conflict** through 2005 - top 15 conflicts: **average # of casualties** per year through 2005

1. THE **PEACE + CONFLICT LEDGER** 2005

The Peace and Conflict Ledger lists the 161 larger countries in the world—all those with populations greater than 500,000 in 2005—and rates each country on seven indicators of capacity for building peace and managing potentially destabilizing political crises. We rate a country's peace-building capacity high insofar as it has managed to avoid outbreaks of armed conflicts while providing reasonable levels of human security, shows no active policies of political or economic discrimination against minorities, successfully managed movements for self-determination, maintained stable democratic institutions, attained substantial human and material resources, and is free of serious threats from its neighboring countries. Countries are listed by world region and, within each region, first, according to countries with current or recent episodes of armed conflict and, second, from lowest (red) to highest (green) peace-building capacity. Because many global trends in the qualities of peace have steadily improved since the early 1990s, some minor changes have been made to the Ledger to increase our ability to report differences among countries on certain indicators. These changes do not affect comparison of the current Ledger with previous editions of Peace and Conflict.

COLUMN 1: **PEACE-BUILDING CAPACITY**
The summary indicator of peace-building capacity is located on the far left side of the ledger. It summarizes the seven component indicators listed on the right side of the ledger and described below. The ranking is used to classify the countries in each geographical region according to a single global standard. The armed conflict indicator, also located on the left side of the ledger, is not used in the calculations but is used to highlight countries with major armed conflicts in recent years. Red and yellow icons on the seven component indicators are evidence of problems whereas green icons signal a capacity for managing conflict without resorting to serious armed conflict. Weighted values are assigned to each of the seven indicators (-2 for red, -1 for yellow, +1.5 for green) and averaged for the number of icons listed (a blank indicator value is not used in the calculation). Countries with an average less than -1 have red icons on the summary indicator of capacity and yellow icons signal an average score between -1 and 0. Countries with an average greater than 0 are given green icons.

COLUMN 2: **ARMED CONFLICT**
The icons in this column are used to highlight countries with the very real threat of major armed conflicts being fought in early-2005, as summarized in Appendix figure 11.1 and described in Appendix table 11.1; these icons are not used in calculating the indicators of peace-building capacity red icon highlights countries with an ongoing (low, medium, or high intensity) major armed conflict in early 2005; a yellow icon identifies countries with either a sporadic or low-intensity armed conflict in early 2005 or an armed conflict that was suspended or repressed between early 2001 and early 2005. Episodes of political violence must have reached a minimum threshold of 1,000 battle related deaths to be considered major armed conflicts. New episodes of political violence that have emerged in the past two years, in which there have been substantial numbers killed but, which have not yet reached the 1,000 death threshold, are identified by an orange icon.

COLUMN 3: **HUMAN SECURITY**
The icons in this column indicate the general quality of human security in the country over the past ten-year period, 1991-2000. The Human Security indicator incorporates information on armed conflicts and rebellions, inter-communal fighting, refugee and internally displaced populations, state repression, terrorism, and, in a few cases, genocide. Red icons indicate countries that have had a generally high level of human security problems in several of the categories over a substantial period of time.
A yellow icon indicates a country that has had problems of somewhat lower magnitude over a more limited span of time. Countries that have had some human security problems but not at the higher levels noted above are left blank on this indicator (a neutral value). Green icons indicate countries that have performed well and experienced little or no human security problems during the previous ten-year period.

COLUMN 4: **SELF-DETERMINATION**
The icons in this column take into account the success or failure of governments in settling self-determination conflicts from 1985 through 2004 based on information summarized in Appendix tables 11.2 and 11.3. Red icons signify countries challenged by violent conflicts over self-determination in early 2005. Yellow icons flag countries with one of these two patterns: either (a) non-violent self-determination movements in early 2005 but no track record of accommodating such movements in the past 20 years; or (b) violent self determination movements in early 2005 and a track record of accommodating other such movements in the past 20 years. Green icons signify countries that have successfully managed one or more self-determination conflicts since 1985, including countries with current non-violent self-determination movements. Countries with no self-determination movements since 1985 are blank in this column.

COLUMN 5: **DISCRIMINATION**
Active government policies or social practices of political or economic discrimination against minority identity groups are strongly associated with divided societies, con-

NORTH ATLANTIC

PEACE-BUILDING CAPACITY	ARMED CONFLICT		HUMAN SECURITY	SELF-DETERMINATION	DISCRIMINATION	REGIME TYPE	DURABILITY	SOCIETAL CAPACITY	NEIGHBORHOOD
□	■	UNITED STATES	○	○	○	○	○	○	○
□		AUSTRIA	○			○	○	○	○
□		BELGIUM	○	○		○	○	○	○
□		CANADA	○	○	○	○	○	○	○
□		DENMARK	○			○	○	○	○
□		FINLAND	○	○		○	○	○	○
□		FRANCE	○			○	○	○	○
□		GERMANY	○			○	○	○	○
□		GREECE	○			○	○	○	○
□		IRELAND	○			○	○	○	○
□		ITALY	○	○		○	○	○	○
□		NETHERLANDS	○			○	○	○	○
□		NORWAY	○	○		○	○	○	○
□		PORTUGAL	○			○	○	○	○
□		SPAIN				○	○	○	○
□		SWEDEN	○	○		○	○	○	○
□		SWITZERLAND	○	○	●	○	○	○	○
□		UNITED KINGDOM	○	○	○	○	○	○	○

FORMER SOCIALIST BLOC

PEACE-BUILDING CAPACITY	ARMED CONFLICT		HUMAN SECURITY	SELF-DETERMINATION	DISCRIMINATION	REGIME TYPE	DURABILITY	SOCIETAL CAPACITY	NEIGHBORHOOD
	■	RUSSIA	●			○	●	○	○
■		ARMENIA				●			
■		AZERBAIJAN							
■		TAJIKISTAN				●		●	●
		BOSNIA				●	●		○
		GEORGIA				○	○		
		KYRGYZSTAN	○	○		●	○		●
		SERBIA + MONTENEGRO				○	●		○
		TURKMENISTAN	○				○		●
		UZBEKISTAN		○			○		●
□		ALBANIA				○			○
□		BELARUS	○					○	○
□		BULGARIA	○			○	○	○	○
□		CROATIA				○	●	○	○
□		CZECH REPUBLIC	○			○	○	○	○
□		ESTONIA	○		○	○	○	○	○
□		HUNGARY	○		○	○	○	○	○
□		KAZAKHSTAN	○	○			○		●
□		LATVIA	○			○	○	○	○
□		LITHUANIA	○			○	○	○	○
□		MACEDONIA		○		○	●	○	○
□		MOLDOVA	○			○	○		○
□		POLAND	○			○	○	○	○
□		ROMANIA	○	○	○	○			○
□		SLOVAK REPUBLIC	○	○		○	○	○	○
□		SLOVENIA	○			○	○	○	○
□		UKRAINE	○			○	○		○

LATIN AMERICA + THE CARRIBBEAN

PEACE-BUILDING CAPACITY	ARMED CONFLICT		HUMAN SECURITY	SELF-DETERMINATION	DISCRIMINATION	REGIME TYPE	DURABILITY	SOCIETAL CAPACITY	NEIGHBORHOOD
□	■	COLOMBIA	●	○		○	○		○
■	□	HAITI				●	●	●	○
		ECUADOR			●	○	●		○
		GUATEMALA				○			○
		PERU				○	●		○
□		ARGENTINA	○			○	○	○	○
□		BOLIVIA	○		○	○	○		○
□		BRAZIL				○	○	○	○
□		CHILE	○			○	○	○	○
□		COSTA RICA	○			○	○		○
□		CUBA					○		○
□		DOMINICAN REPUBLIC	○		●	○			○
□		EL SALVADOR				○	○		○
□		GUYANA	○		●	○	○		○
□		HONDURAS	○			○	○		○
□		JAMAICA	○			○	○	○	○
□		MEXICO				○		○	○
□		NICARAGUA	○	○		○	○		○
□		PANAMA	○			○	○		○
□		PARAGUAY	○			○	○		○
□		TRINIDAD & TOBAGO	○	○		○	○	○	○
□		URUGUAY	○			○	○	○	○
□		VENEZUELA	○			○	○	○	○

ASIA + THE PACIFIC

PEACE-BUILDING CAPACITY	ARMED CONFLICT		HUMAN SECURITY	SELF-DETERMINATION	DISCRIMINATION	REGIME TYPE	DURABILITY	SOCIETAL CAPACITY	NEIGHBORHOOD
■	■	NEPAL					●	●	●
	■	INDIA	●			○	○		●
	■	INDONESIA	●	●		○			
■		AFGHANISTAN	●		○	●	●	●	●
■		MYANMAR (BURMA)	●	●	●		○	●	
■	□	PAKISTAN		●		●			●
■		SOLOMON ISLANDS				●	●		
		SRI LANKA	●		●	○	○		●
□		PHILIPPINES			○	○	○		
■		CAMBODIA				●		●	
		BANGLADESH		○	●	○	○	●	
		BHUTAN	○		●		○	●	
		CHINA					○		
		EAST TIMOR				○	●	●	
		FIJI	○			○	●		
		NORTH KOREA					○		
		LAOS	○	●			○	●	
	□	THAILAND		●		○	○		
		VIETNAM					○	●	
□		AUSTRALIA	○	○		○	○	○	
□		JAPAN	○			○	○	○	
□		SOUTH KOREA	○			○	○	○	
□		MALAYSIA	○			●	○	○	
□		MONGOLIA	○			○	○		
□		NEW ZEALAND	○		○	○	○	○	
□		PAPUA NEW GUINEA		○		○	○		
□		SINGAPORE	○			●	○	○	
□		TAIWAN	○	○		○	○	○	

NORTH AFRICA + THE MIDDLE EA

PEACE-BUILDING CAPACITY	ARMED CONFLICT		HUMAN SECURITY	SELF-DETERMINATION	DISCRIMINATION	REGIME TYPE	DURABILITY	SOCIETAL CAPACITY
■	■	ALGERIA	●		●	●		
■	■	IRAQ	●		○	●	●	
	■	ISRAEL		●	●	○	○	○
■		IRAN			●		●	
■		LEBANON			●	●	●	○
		EGYPT					○	
		JORDAN				●	○	
		LIBYA					○	○
		MOROCCO					○	
	□	SAUDI ARABIA			●		○	○
		SYRIA					○	
		TUNISIA	○			●	○	
	□	TURKEY	●	●	●	○	○	
	□	YEMEN				●	○	●
□		BAHRAIN	○		○		○	○
□		CYPRUS	○			○	○	○
□		KUWAIT	○				○	○
□		OMAN	○				○	○
□		QATAR	○				○	○
□		UNITED ARAB EMIRATES	○				○	○

AFRICA SOUTH OF THE SAHARA

ARMED CONFLICT		HUMAN SECURITY	SELF-DETERMINATION	DISCRIMINATION	REGIME TYPE	DURABILITY	SOCIETAL CAPACITY	NEIGHBORHOOD	PEACE-BUILDING CAPACITY
■	BURUNDI	●			●	●	●	●	
■	D.R. CONGO	●	○		●	●	●	●	
■	NIGERIA		●		●		●		
■	SUDAN	●		●		○	●	●	
■	UGANDA				●	○	●	●	
	ANGOLA	●	●		●				
	CENTRAL AFRICAN REPUBLIC				●	●	●		
	REPUBLIC OF CONGO			●	●		●		
	ETHIOPIA		●	○	●		●	●	
	COTE D'IVOIRE				●	●			
	LIBERIA				●	●	●		
	RWANDA	●			●	○	●	●	
	SIERRA LEONE	●		○	●	●	●		
	SOMALIA	●			●	●	●	●	
	BURKINA FASO	○			●	●	●		
	GUINEA BISSAU				●	●	●		
	GUINEA				●		●		
	CAMEROON			●	●	○			
	CHAD		○	○	●	○	●		
	COMOROS	○	○		●	●	●		
	DJIBOUTI	○	○		●			●	
	EQUATORIAL GUINEA				●	○			
	ERITREA			○		○	●	●	
	GABON	○			●	○			
	GAMBIA	○			●		●		
	GHANA	○			○	●	●		
	KENYA			○	○	●	●	●	
	LESOTHO	○			○	●			
	MADAGASCAR	○			○		●		
	MAURITANIA	○		●		○			
	MOZAMBIQUE				○	○	●		
	NIGER		○		●		●		
	SENEGAL		○		○	●			
	TANZANIA	○	○		●	●	●	●	
	TOGO	○			●	○	●		
	ZAMBIA	○			●				
	BENIN	○			○	○	●		
	BOTSWANA	○			○	○	○		
	MALAWI	○			○	○	●		
	MALI	○	○	○	○	○	●		
	MAURITIUS	○			○	○	○		
	NAMIBIA	○			○	○			
	SOUTH AFRICA		○	○	○	○	○		
	SWAZILAND	○				○			
	ZIMBABWE		○	○		○			

tentious politics, and self-determination grievances. They are also indicative of strategies of exclusion by dominant groups. This indicator looks at general levels of both political and economic discrimination against minorities at the end of 2003. Red icons denote countries with active government policies of political and/or economic discrimination against minorities comprising at least ten percent of the population in 2003. Yellow icons identify countries where there are active social practices of discrimination by dominant groups against minority groups that comprise at least ten percent of the population but no official sanctions. Green icons are assigned to countries with little or no active discrimination and government policies designed to help remedy or alleviate the effects of past discriminatory policies and practices for groups constituting at least five percent of the population. Countries with little or no active discrimination against minorities are blank in this column.

COLUMN 6: **REGIME TYPE**

The icons in this column show the nature of a country's political institutions in early 2005. Red icons are anocracies (see section 4, following), that is, countries with governments in the mixed or transitional zone between autocracy and democracy. Yellow icons represent full autocratic regimes. Green icons are full democracies.

COLUMN 7: **DURABILITY**

The icons in this column take into account the maturity of a country's system of government and, as such, its conflict management capabilities. New political systems have not yet consolidated central authority nor established effective institutions and, so, are vulnerable to challenges and further change, especially during their first five years. So are the governments of newly-independent countries. Red icons highlight countries whose political institutions in early 2005 were less than five years old, that is, they were established between 2000 and 2004. Yellow icons register countries whose polities were less than ten years old; established between 1995 and 1999. Green icons are used for countries whose polities were established before 1995.

COLUMN 8: **SOCIETAL CAPACITY**

The governments of rich societies are better able to maintain peace and security than are governments of poor societies. We use an indicator that combines information on both GDP per capita (income) and societal energy consumption per capita (capitalization) over the past five-year period to rate countries on this indicator. Red icons signify countries in the lowest quintile (the bottom 20%) of societal capacity. Yellow icons flag countries in the second quintile. Countries in the third quintile are left blank. Green icons identify countries in the top two quintiles (the upper 40%) in societal capacity.

COLUMN 9: **NEIGHBORHOOD**

We define ten politically relevant "neighborhoods": West Africa, North Africa, East Africa, South Africa, Middle East, South Asia, East Asia, South America, Central America, and Europe/North America. For each region we gauge the extent of armed conflicts in early 2005 and the prevailing types of regimes, either democratic, anocratic, or autocratic. Countries with green icons are in regions with relatively low armed conflict and mostly democratic governments. Countries with red icons are in "neighborhoods" with high armed conflict and many anocratic, or transitional, regimes. Countries with yellow icons are in regions with middling levels of armed conflict and mostly autocratic regimes. For countries that straddle regions, or are situated in regions with mixed traits, a final determination was made by reference to armed conflicts in bordering countries. For example, countries with two or more bordering countries engaged in armed conflicts are coded red on this indicator. Island states without close, "politically-relevant" neighboring states are blank on this indicator.

[1] Interstate wars are included with this indicator but are not used in evaluating a country's general quality of human security (column 3). The only current situations of major interstate war are the armed conflicts between the United States and insurgents and al Qaeda operatives in Iraq and Afghanistan. Countries that have contributed peacekeeping troops to various locations of past and continuing violence are not considered to be "at war."

2. GLOBAL TRENDS IN **POLITICAL DISCRIMINATION** 1950 – 2003

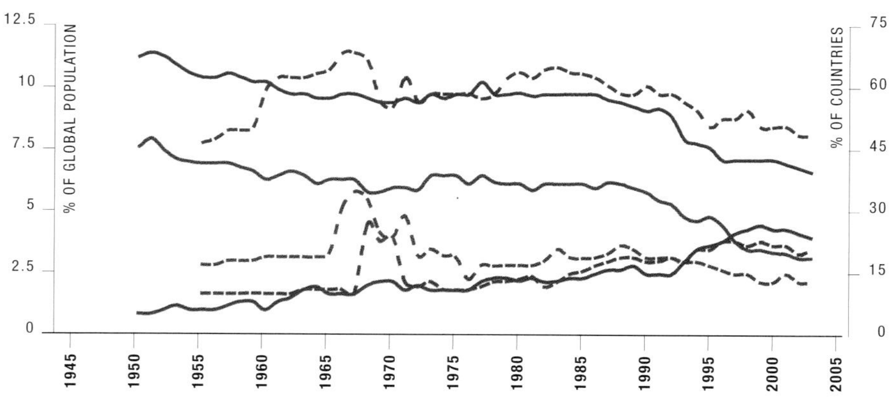

3. GLOBAL TRENDS IN **ECONOMIC DISCRIMINATION** 1950 – 2003

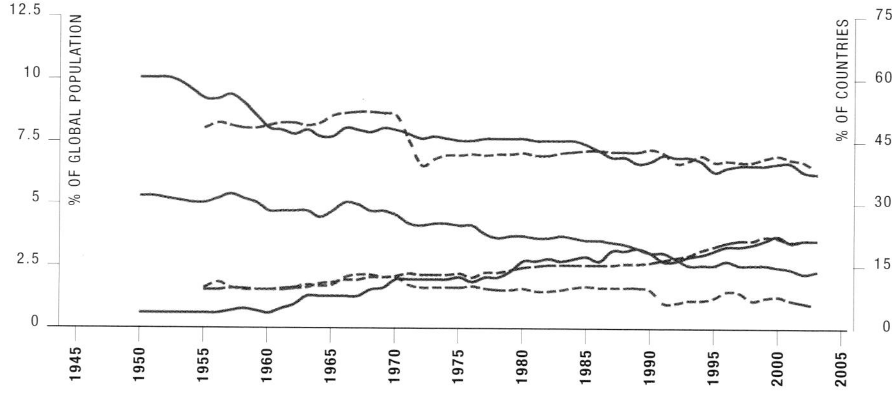

2. GLOBAL TRENDS IN **POLITICAL DISCRIMINATION** OF MINORITIES 1950 – 2003

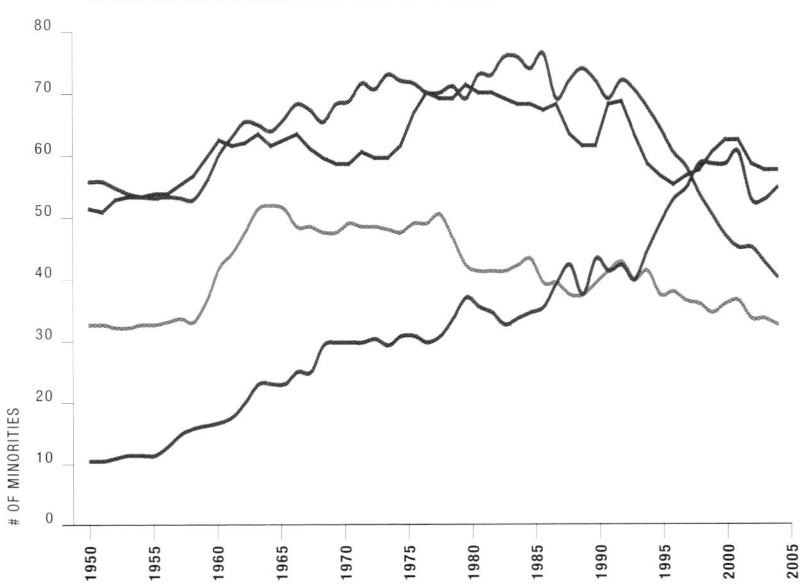

2. GLOBAL TRENDS IN **VIOLENT CONFLICTS** 1946 – 2000

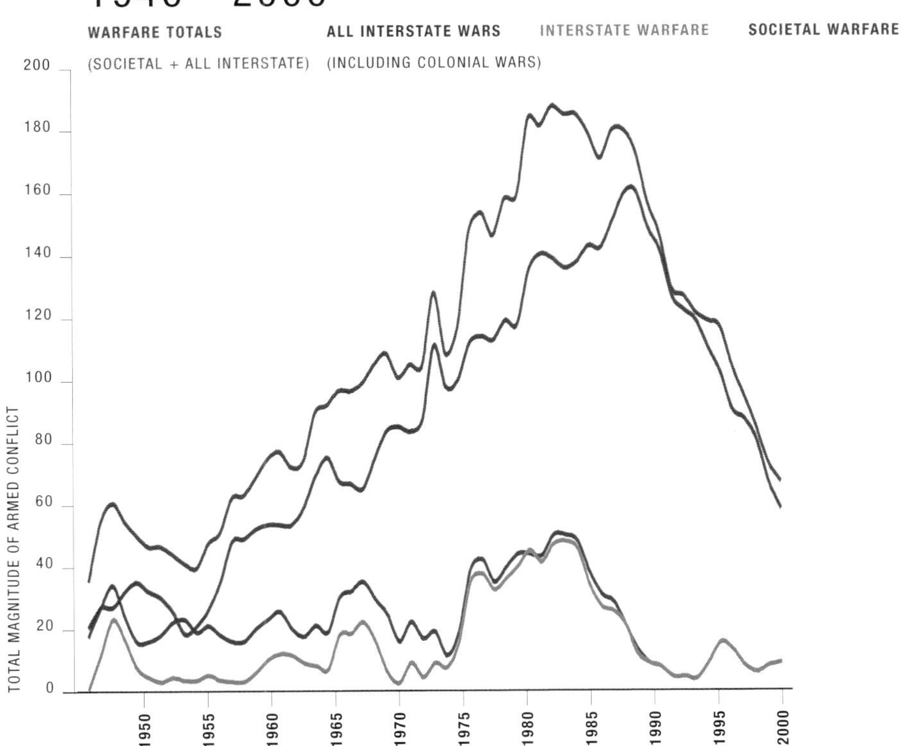

6. TYPE OF **ARMED CONFLICT WORLDWIDE** 1946 – 2004

76	481	1289	585
3%	20%	53%	24%

1. EXTRASYSTEMIC ARMED CONFLICT
OCCURS BETWEEN A STATE AND A NON-STATE GROUP OUTSIDE ITS OWN TERRITORY.
(IN THE COW PROJECT, EXTRASYSTEMIC WAR IS SUBDIVIDED BETWEEN COLONIAL WAR AND IMPERIAL WAR, BUT THIS DIVISION IS NOT USED HERE.)

2. INTERSTATE ARMED CONFLICT
OCCURS BETWEEN TWO OR MORE STATES.

3. INTERNAL ARMED CONFLICT
OCCURS BETWEEN THE GOVERNMENT OF A STATE AND INTERNAL OPPOSITION GROUPS WITHOUT INTERVENTION FROM OTHER STATES.

4. INTERNATIONALIZED INTERNAL ARMED CONFLICT
OCCURS BETWEEN THE GOVERNMENT OF A STATE AND INTERNAL OPPOSITION GROUPS WITH INTERVENTION FROM OTHER STATES.

7. EVOLUTION OF DIFFERENT TYPES OF **ARMED CONFLICTS** FROM 1946 TO 2004

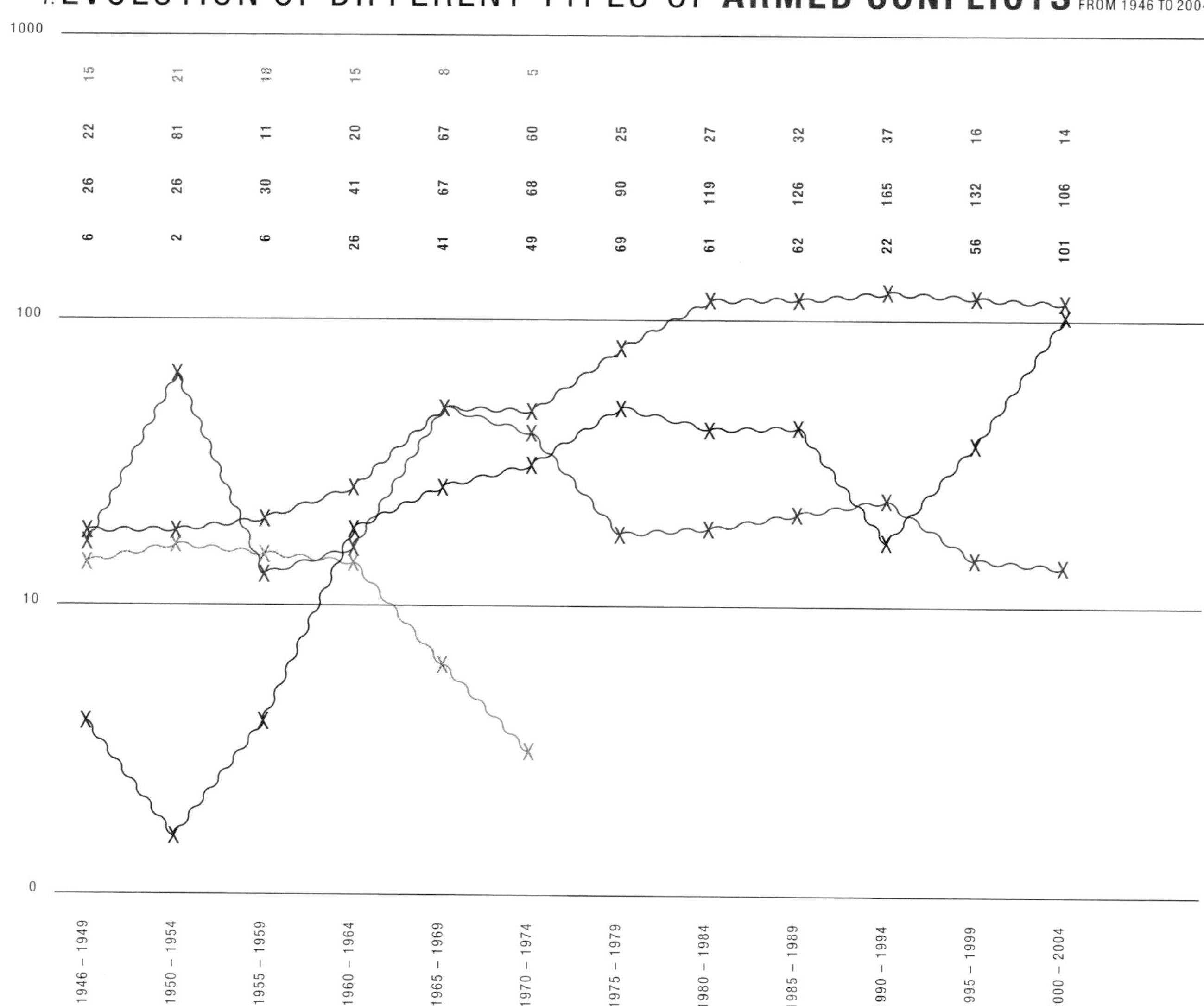

8. LEVELS OF INTERNATIONALIZED INTERNAL ARMED CONFLICT 1946 – 2004

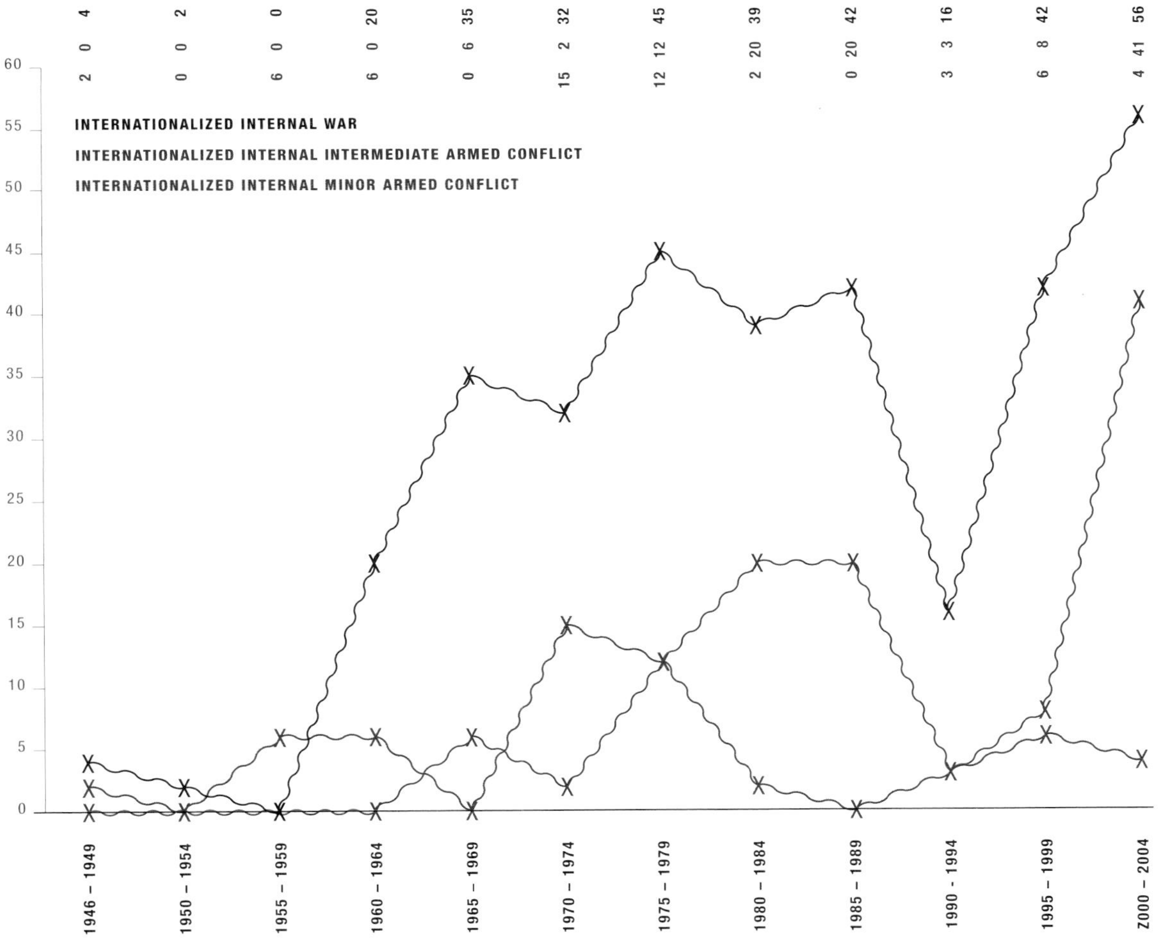

INTERNATIONALIZED INTERNAL WAR

INTERNATIONALIZED INTERNAL INTERMEDIATE ARMED CONFLICT

INTERNATIONALIZED INTERNAL MINOR ARMED CONFLICT

1946 – 1949	2	0	4
1950 – 1954	0	0	2
1955 – 1959	6	0	0
1960 – 1964	6	0	20
1965 – 1969	0	6	35
1970 – 1974	15	2	32
1975 – 1979	12	12	45
1980 – 1984	2	20	39
1985 – 1989	0	20	42
1990 – 1994	3	3	16
1995 – 1999	6	8	42
2000 – 2004	4	41	56

60 55 50 45 40 35 30 25 20 15 10 5 0

9. # OF **DEATHS** FROM CURRENT ONGOING **CONFLICTS** THROUGH 2005

† = 500 DEATHS

SOLOMON ISLANDS	500
CONGO-BRAZZAVILLE	500
SAUDI ARABIA	700 (+ 200)
CENTRAL AFRICAN REUBLIC	1,000
LIBERIA	1,000
TURKEY	1,000
YEMEN	1,000
THAILAND	1,200 (+ 200)
PAKISTAN	1,500
INDIA	1,500
NIGERIA	1,500
HAITI	2,000
PAKISTAN	2,000
THAILAND	2,500
COTE D'IVOIRE	3,000
INDONESIA	3,000
ANGOLA	3,500
NEPAL	8,000
UGANDA	12,000
AFGHANISTAN	15,000
ISRAEL	20,000
INDIA	25,000
RUSSIA	30,000
INDIA	35,000
IRAQ	40,000
PHILIPPINES	50,000
COLOMBIA	50,000
NIGERIA	55,000
ALGERIA	60,000
SUDAN	60,000
SOMALIA	100,000
BURUNDI	100,000
MYANMAR	100,000
D.R.C (ZAIRE)	1,500,000

10. TOP 15 CONFLICTS: AVERAGE # OF **CASUALTIES** PER YEAR THROUGH 2005

PHILIPPINES	1,515
MYANMAR	1,754
HAITI	2,000
INDIA	2,333
COLOMBIA	2,380
THAILAND	2,500
AFGHANISTAN	3,750
ALGERIA	4,615
RUSSIA	5,000
SOMALIA	5,882
BURUNDI	8,333
NIGERIA	18,333
IRAQ	20,000
SUDAN	30,000
D.R.C (ZAIRE)	166,666

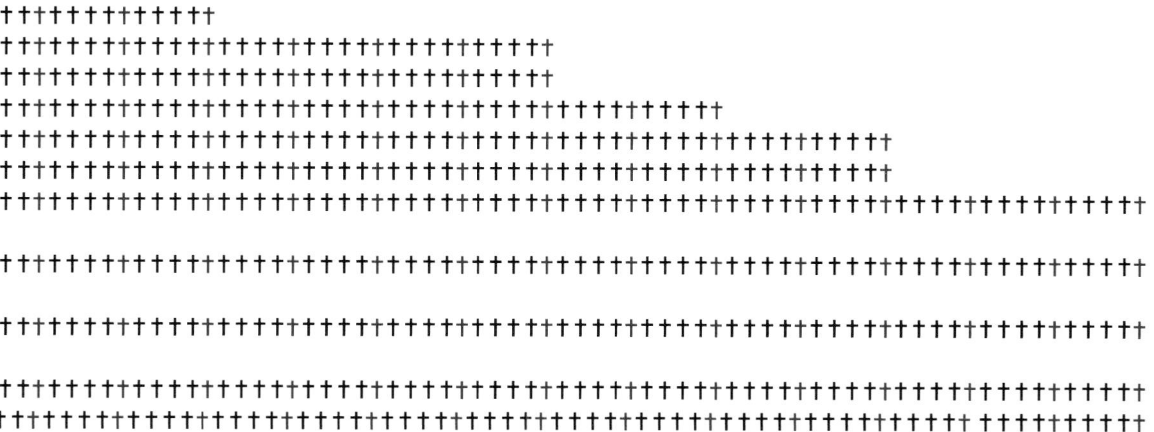

HUMAN RIGHTS - regional overview 2005: **human rights issues** by region - average **physical integrity rights** index - average **empowerments rights** index - average scores of **disappearance, extrajudicial killings** + **torture** - average scores of **freedom-related rights** - average scores of **political imprisonment** + **participation** - types of **women's rights** by region and average - # of **civil society organizations** by select human rights issues + region, 2006

1. REGIONAL OVERVIEW 2005

HUMAN RIGHTS ISSUES	AFRICA	AMERICAS	ASIA + THE PACIFIC	EUROPE	CENTRAL ASIA	MIDDLE EAST + NORTH AFRICA
ABUSES BY OFFICIALS AND IMPUNITY				●	●	
ARMED CONFLICT	●		●			●
CONFLICT, CRIME, AND INSTABILITY		●				
DEATH PENALTY	●	●	●	●		●
ECONOMIC, SOCIAL, AND CULTURAL RIGHTS	●	●				
INTERNATIONAL JUSTICE	●					●
NATIONAL SECURITY		●				
REGIONAL INITIATIVES	●					●
RACISM AND DISCRIMINATION				●	●	
REPRESSION OF DISSENT				●	●	
"WAR ON TERROR"		●	●	●		●
HUMAN RIGHTS						
HUMAN RIGHTS DEFENDERS	●	●	●			●
ACTION FOR HUMAN RIGHTS				●	●	
IMPUNITY FOR HUMAN RIGHTS VIOLATORS		●				●
THE ARAB CHARTER ON HUMAN RIGHTS						●
POLITICS						
POLITICAL REPRESSION	●					
ELECTIONS AND DENIAL OF CIVIL AND POLITICAL RIGHTS			●			
POLITICAL VIOLENCE						●
REFUGEES						
REFUGEES, INTERNALLY DISPLACED PEOPLE AND MIGRANTS			●			
REFUGEES AND ASYLUM-SEEKERS				●		
REFUGEES AND MIGRANTS						●
WOMEN						
VIOLENCE AGAINST WOMEN	●	●	●	●		●
WOMEN'S RIGHTS						●

NOTE: DOT INDICATES REPORTED ABUSES, IN SOME COUNTRIES IN EACH REGION, AS IDENTIFIED BY AMNESTY INTERNATIONAL 2005

2. AVERAGE **PHYSICAL INTEGRITY RIGHTS** INDEX

BY REGION AND YEAR

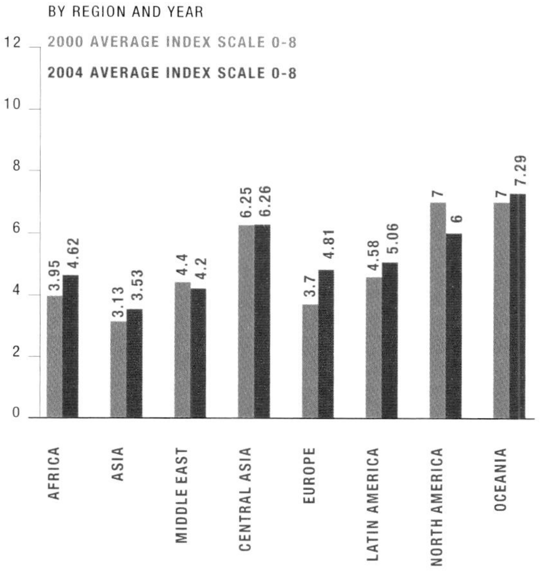

3. AVERAGE **EMPOWERMENT RIGHTS** INDEX

BY REGION AND YEAR

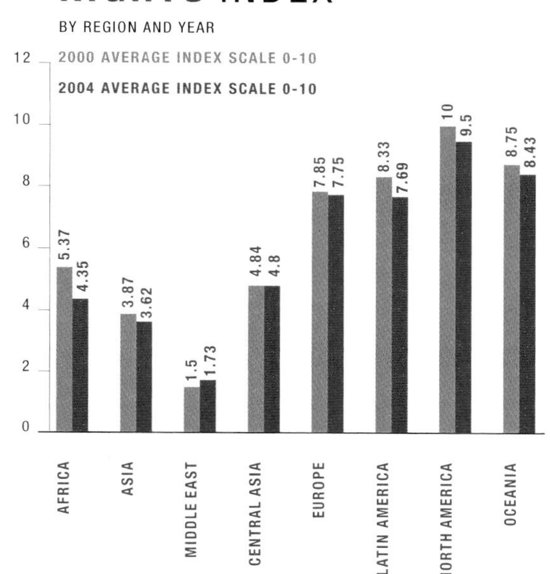

4. AVERAGE SCORES OF **DISAPPEARANCE EXTRAJUDICIAL KILLING + TORTURE**

BY REGION 2004

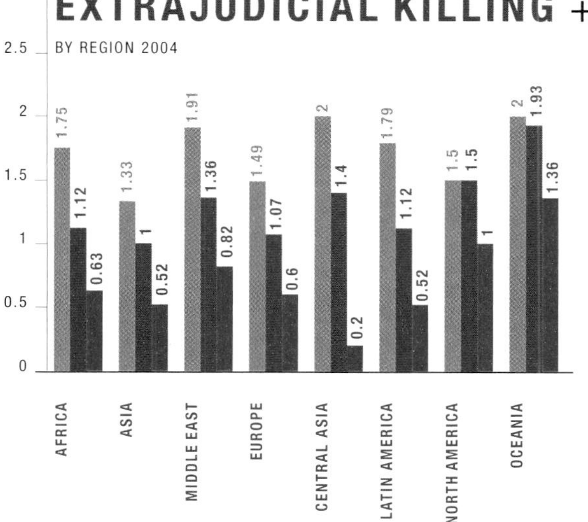

5. AVERAGE SCORES OF **FREEDOM-RELATED RIGHTS**

BY REGION 2004

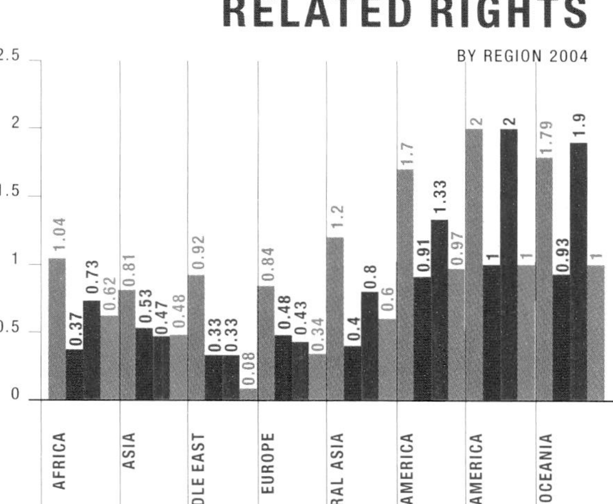

6. AVERAGE SCORES OF POLITICAL IMPRISONMENT + PARTICIPATION

BY REGION 2004

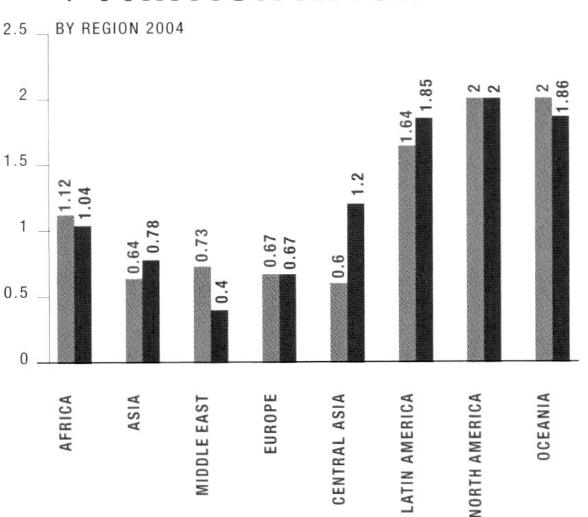

7. TYPES OF WOMEN'S RIGHTS

BY REGION + AVERAGE 2004

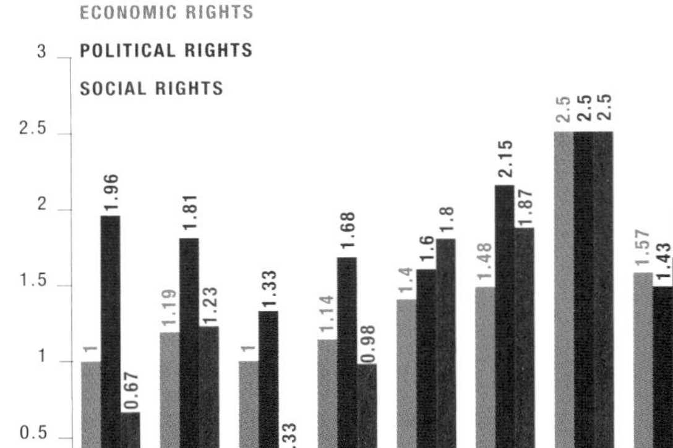

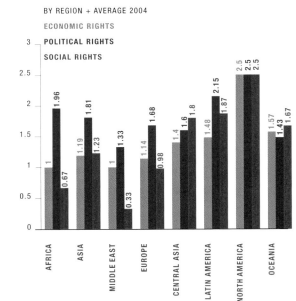

8a. # OF CIVIL SOCIETY ORGANIZATIONS

BY SELECT HUMAN RIGHTS ISUES + REGION 2006

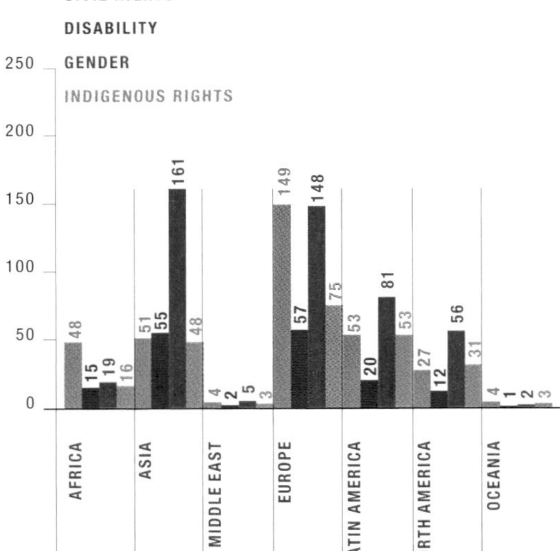

8b. # OF CIVIL SOCIETY ORGANIZATIONS

BY SELECT HUMAN RIGHTS ISUES + REGION 2006

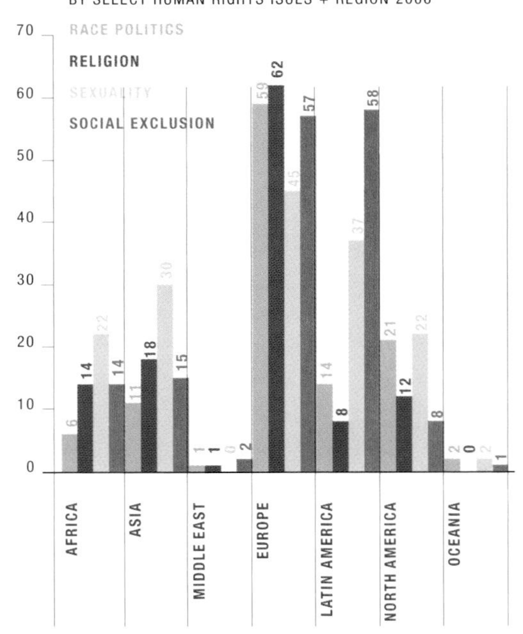

TERRORISM

- international terrorism **incidents by tactic** worldwide 1970–2005 - international terrorism **injuries by tactic** worldwide 1970–2005 - international terrorism **fatalities by tactic** worldwide 1970–2005 - international terrorism **incidents by region** worldwide 1970–2005 - international terrorism **injuries by region** worldwide 1970–2005 - international terrorism **fatalities by region** worldwide 1970–2005 - international terrorism **incidents by target** worldwide 1970–2005 - international terrorism **injuries by target** worldwide 1970–2005 - international terrorism **fatalities by target** worldwide 1970–2005 - international terrorism **incidents by group classification** worldwide 1970–2005 - international terrorism **injuries by group classification** worldwide 1970–2005 - international terrorism **fatalities by group classification** worldwide 1970–2005 - international and domestic terrorism **incidents by target** 2005 (includes domestic + international accidents) - top 20 **religious terrorist groups by fatalities & injuries** 1968–2006

1a. INTERNATIONAL TERRORISM INCIDENTS

BY TACTIC WORLDWIDE 1970 – 2005

INTERNATIONAL INCIDENTS ARE THOSE IN WHICH TERRORISTS GO ABROAD TO STRIKE THE TARGETS

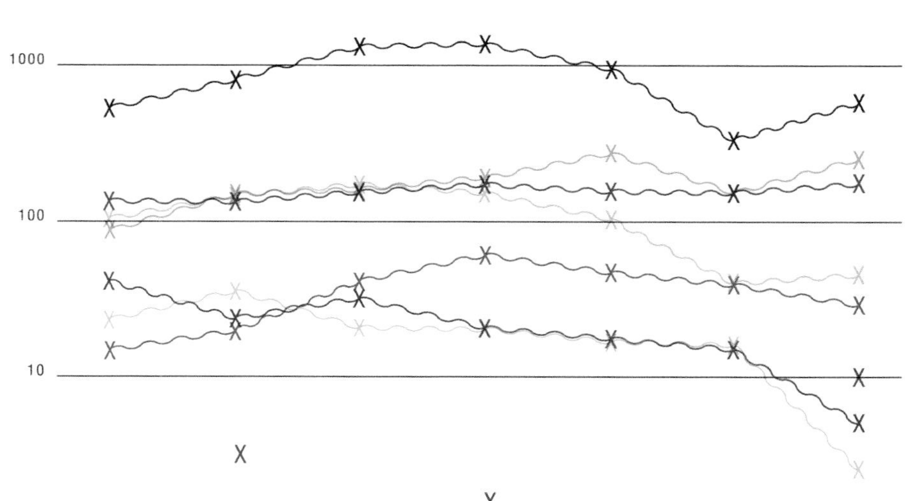

	1970–1975	1975–1980	1980–1985	1985–1990	1990–1995	1995–2000	2000–2005
ARMED ATTACK	94	180	200	280	440	190	397
ARSON	17	29	61	78	68	59	46
ASSASSINATION	101	158	232	178	104	62	67
BARRICADE/HOSTAGE	36	55	31	30	22	20	4
BOMBING	726	904	1195	1362	974	522	764
HIJACKING	61	37	50	31	24	17	7
KIDNAPPING	126	123	184	235	191	180	244
UNCONVENTIONAL ATTACK	0	5	0	2	0	1	10

2a. INTERNATIONAL **TERRORISM INJURIES**

BY **TACTIC WORLDWIDE** 1970 – 2005

INTERNATIONAL INCIDENTS ARE THOSE IN WHICH TERRORISTS GO ABROAD TO STRIKE THE TARGETS

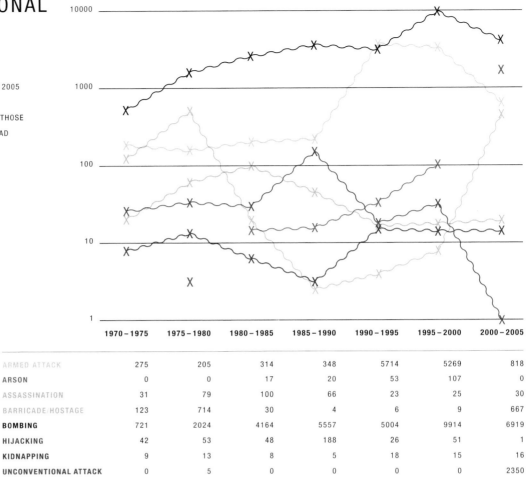

	1970–1975	1975–1980	1980–1985	1985–1990	1990–1995	1995–2000	2000–2005
ARMED ATTACK	275	205	314	348	5714	5269	818
ARSON	0	0	17	20	53	107	0
ASSASSINATION	31	79	100	66	23	25	30
BARRICADE/HOSTAGE	123	714	30	4	6	9	667
BOMBING	721	2024	4164	5557	5004	9914	6919
HIJACKING	42	53	48	188	26	51	1
KIDNAPPING	9	13	8	5	18	15	16
UNCONVENTIONAL ATTACK	0	5	0	0	0	0	2350

1b. INTERNATIONAL **TERRORISM INCIDENTS**

BY **REGION WORLDWIDE** 1970 – 2005

INTERNATIONAL INCIDENTS ARE THOSE IN WHICH TERRORISTS GO ABROAD TO STRIKE THE TARGETS

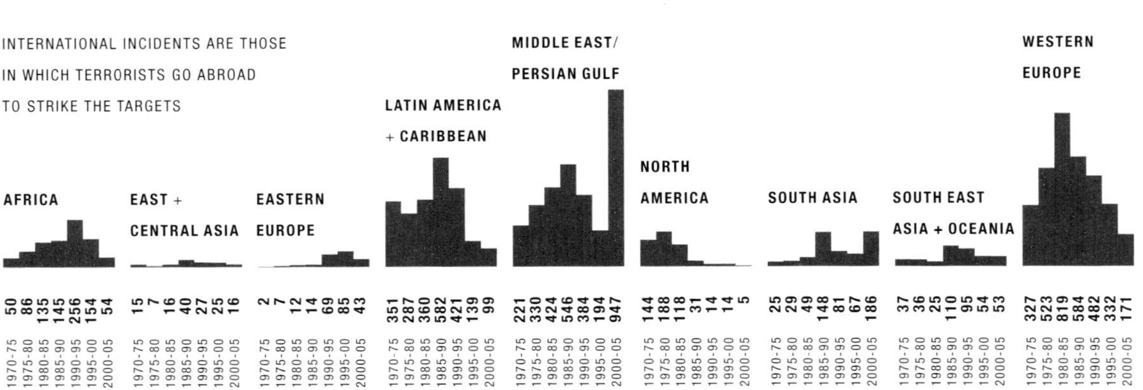

2b. INTERNATIONAL **TERRORISM INJURIES**

BY **REGION WORLDWIDE** 1970 – 2005

INTERNATIONAL INCIDENTS ARE THOSE
IN WHICH TERRORISTS GO ABROAD
TO STRIKE THE TARGETS

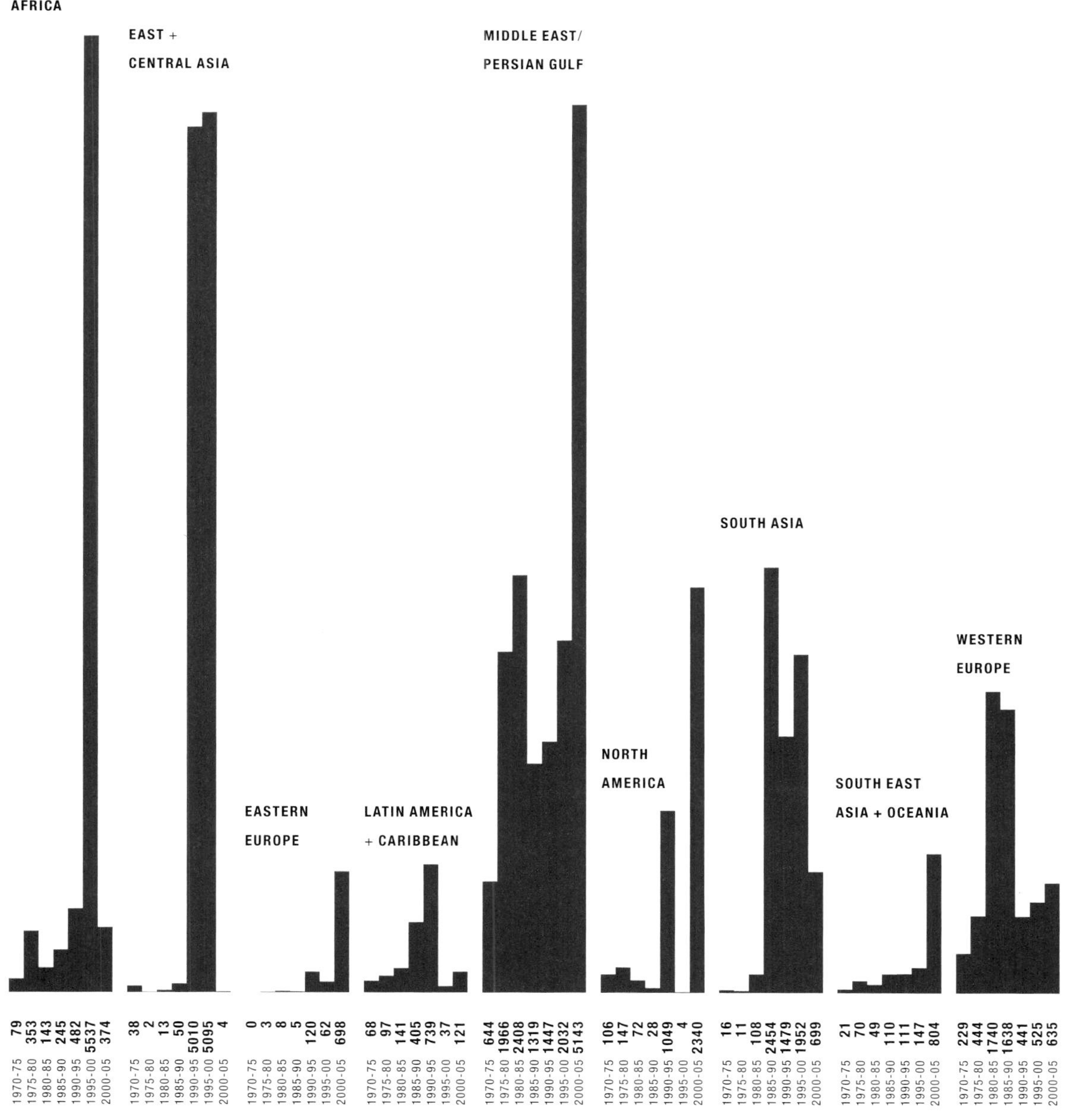

3a. INTERNATIONAL TERRORISM FATALITIES

BY TACTIC WORLDWIDE 1970 – 2005

INTERNATIONAL INCIDENTS ARE THOSE IN WHICH TERRORISTS GO ABROAD TO STRIKE THE TARGETS

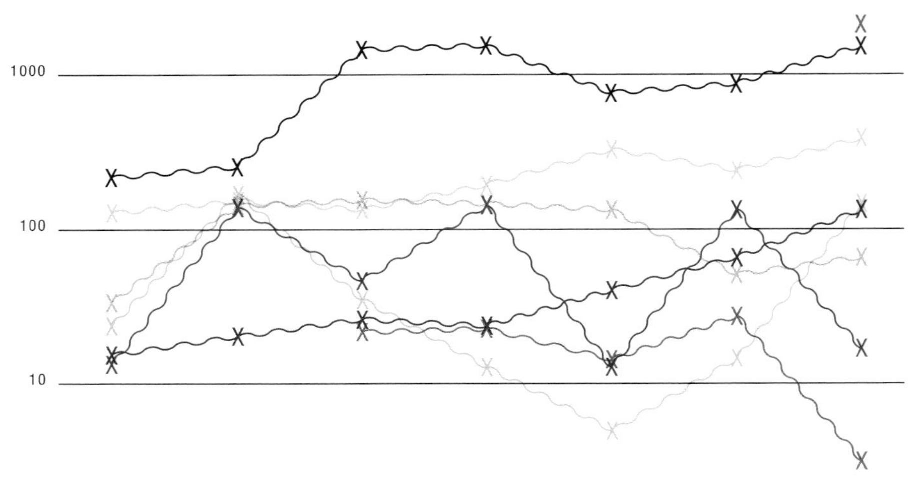

	1970–1975	1975–1980	1980–1985	1985–1990	1990–1995	1995–2000	2000–2005
ARMED ATTACK	115	188	132	290	518	382	590
ARSON	0	0	34	36	16	44	5
ASSASSINATION	53	157	191	167	129	71	82
BARRICADE/HOSTAGE	38	234	55	11	7	17	171
BOMBING	338	406	1648	1936	881	941	1866
HIJACKING	13	142	67	159	11	129	23
KIDNAPPING	19	31	42	38	61	82	127
UNCONVENTIONAL ATTACK	0	0	0	0	0	0	2982

3b. INTERNATIONAL TERRORISM FATALITIES

BY REGION WORLDWIDE 1970 – 2005

INTERNATIONAL INCIDENTS ARE THOSE IN WHICH TERRORISTS GO ABROAD TO STRIKE THE TARGETS

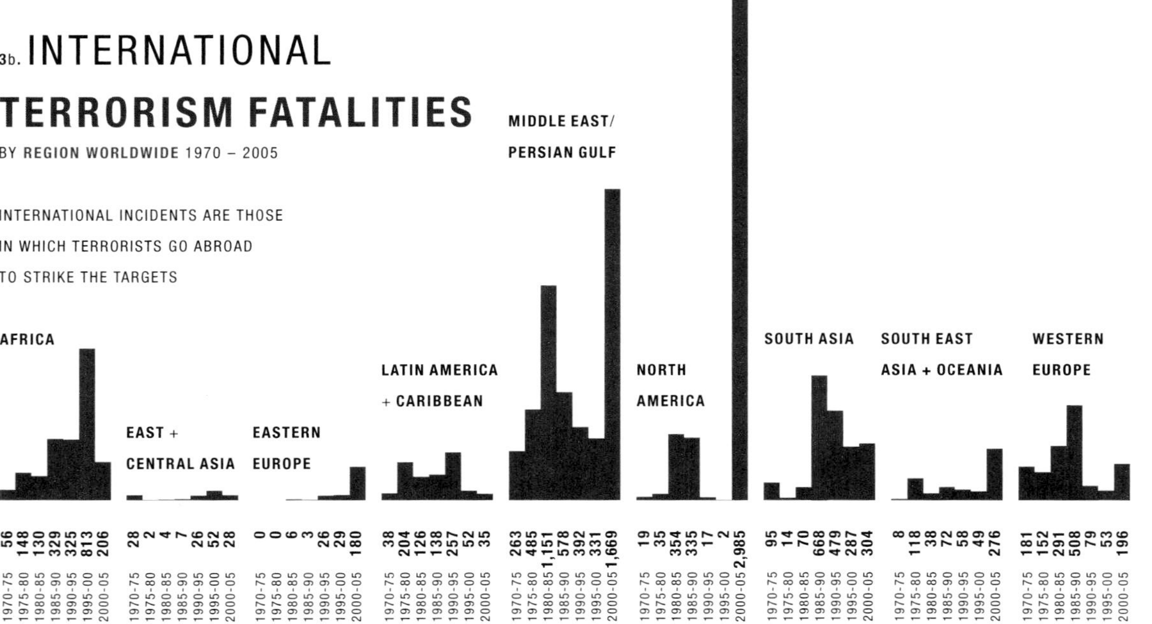

1c. INTERNATIONAL **TERRORISM INCIDENTS**

BY **TARGET WORLDWIDE** 1970 – 2005

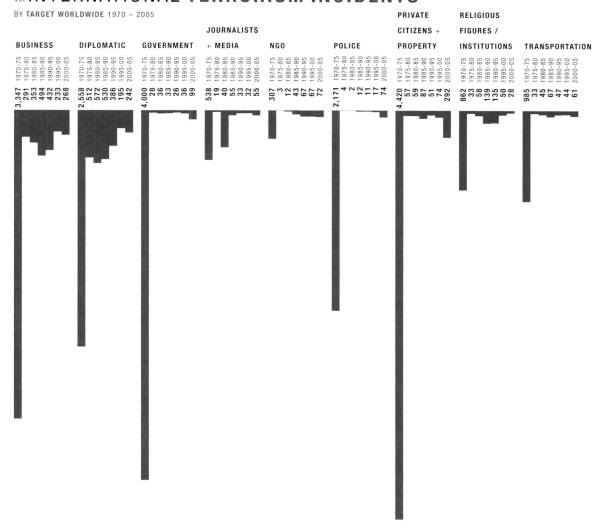

Target	1970-75	1975-80	1980-85	1985-90	1990-95	1995-00	2000-05
BUSINESS	3,347	291	353	494	432	233	268
DIPLOMATIC	2,558	512	572	530	386	195	242
GOVERNMENT	4,000	28	36	33	26	36	99
JOURNALISTS + MEDIA	538	19	40	55	33	32	55
NGO	307	3	12	43	67	67	72
POLICE	2,171	4	2	12	11	17	74
PRIVATE CITIZENS + PROPERTY	4,420	57	59	87	51	74	292
RELIGIOUS FIGURES / INSTITUTIONS	862	33	58	139	135	50	28
TRANSPORTATION	985	33	45	67	47	44	61

1d. INTERNATIONAL **TERRORISM INCIDENTS**

BY **GROUP CLASSIFICATION WORLDWIDE** 1970 – 2005

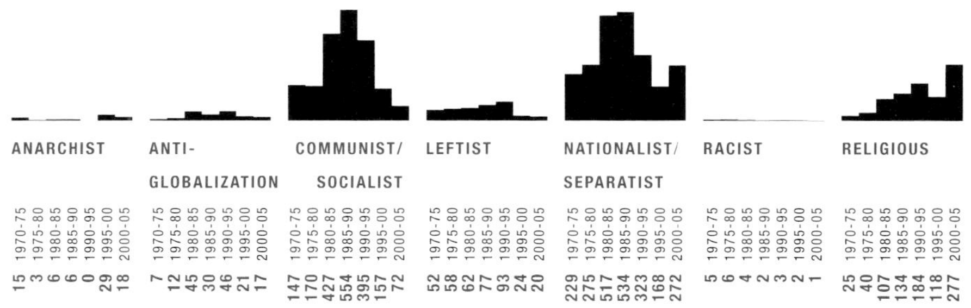

Group	1970-75	1975-80	1980-85	1985-90	1990-95	1995-00	2000-05
ANARCHIST	15	3	6	6	0	29	18
ANTI-GLOBALIZATION	7	12	45	30	46	21	17
COMMUNIST/ SOCIALIST	147	170	427	554	395	157	72
LEFTIST	52	58	62	77	93	24	20
NATIONALIST/ SEPARATIST	229	275	517	534	323	168	272
RACIST	5	6	4	2	3	2	1
RELIGIOUS	25	40	107	134	184	118	277

2c. INTERNATIONAL **TERRORISM INJURIES**

BY **TARGET WORLDWIDE** 1970 – 2005

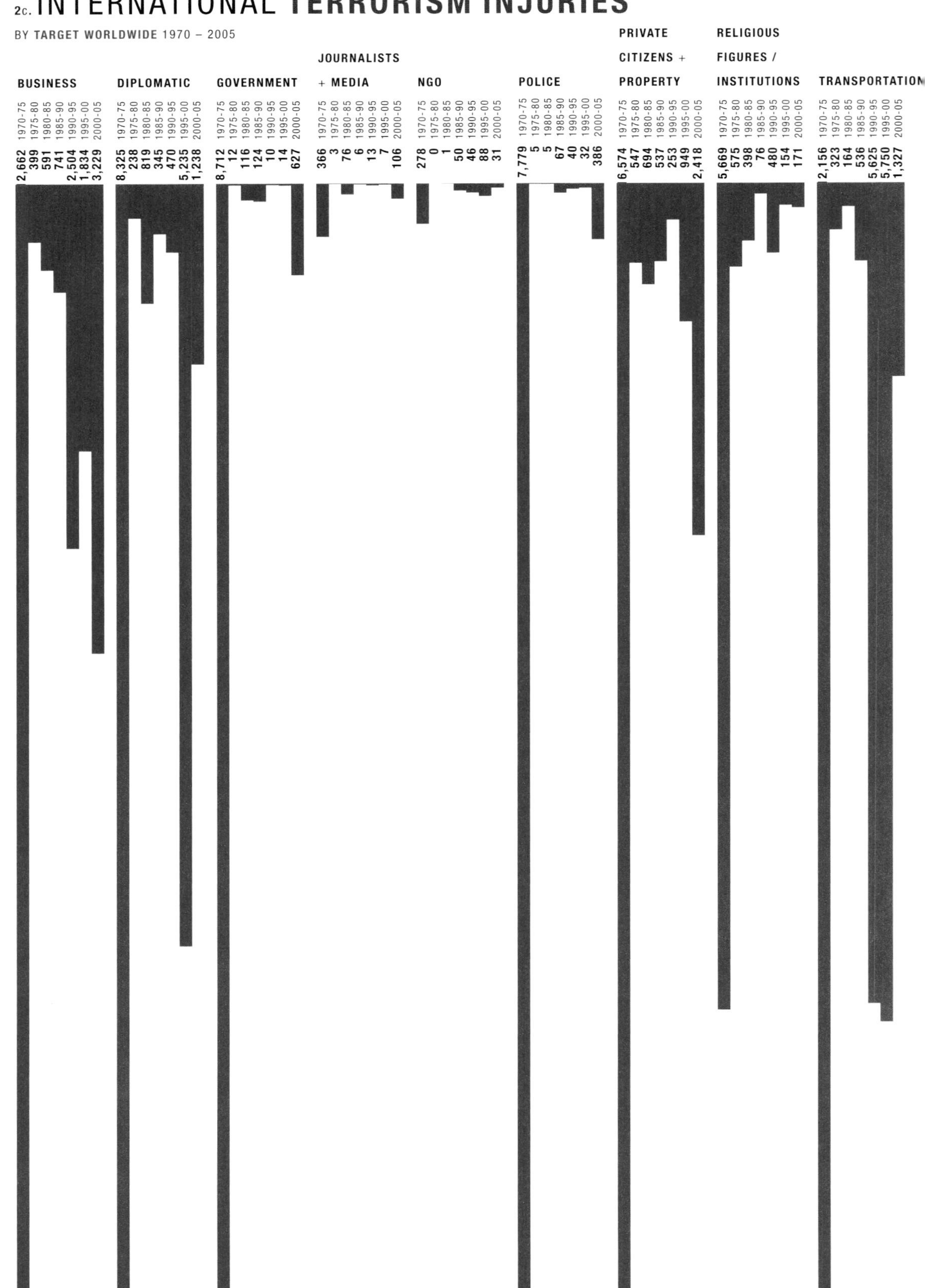

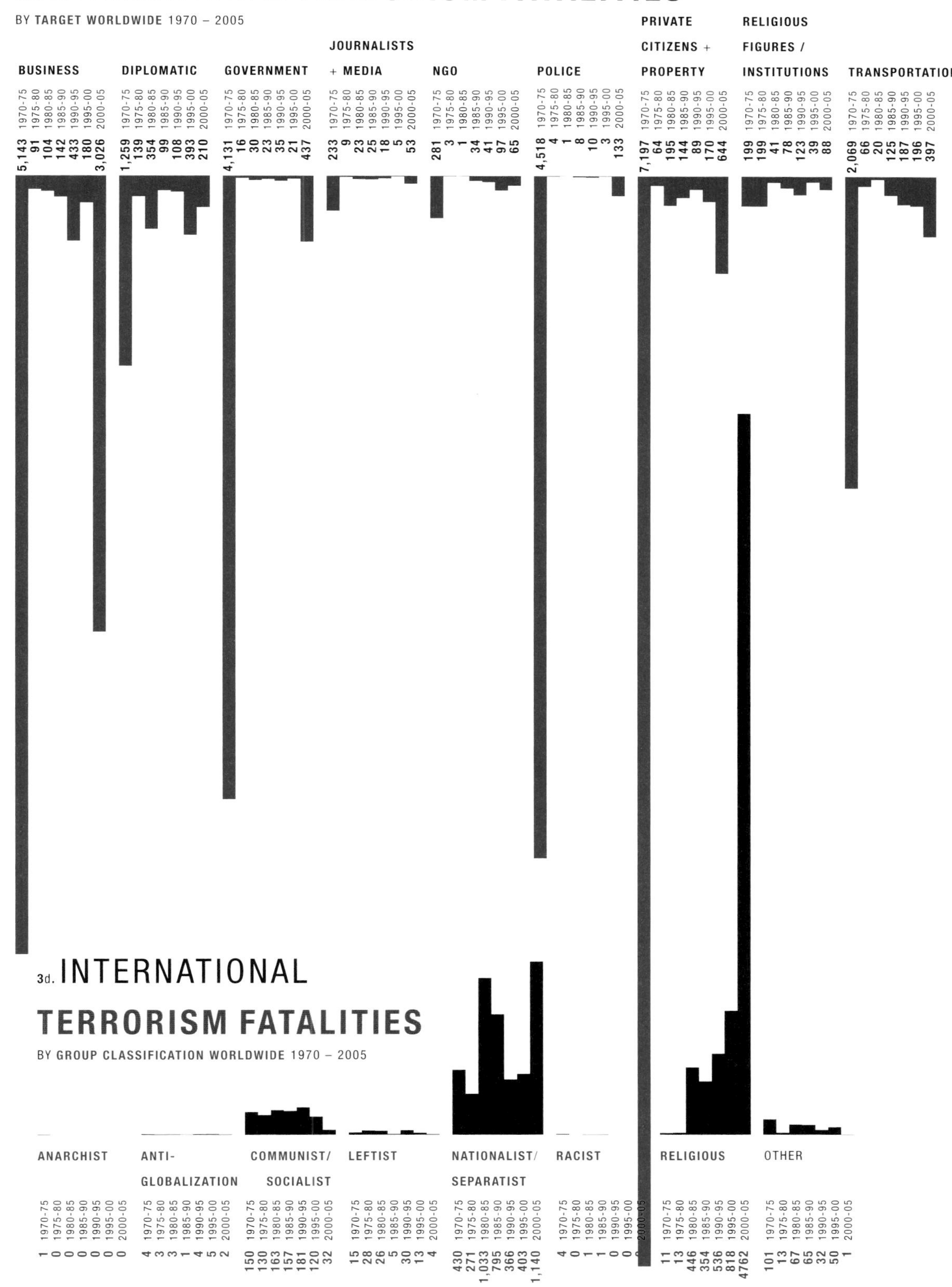
3c. INTERNATIONAL TERRORISM FATALITIES
BY TARGET WORLDWIDE 1970 – 2005
BUSINESS
5,143 1970-75
91 1975-80
104 1980-85
142 1985-90
433 1990-95
180 1995-00
3,026 2000-05
DIPLOMATIC
1,259 1970-75
139 1975-80
354 1980-85
99 1985-90
108 1990-95
393 1995-00
210 2000-05
GOVERNMENT
4,131 1970-75
16 1975-80
30 1980-85
23 1985-90
35 1990-95
21 1995-00
437 2000-05
JOURNALISTS + MEDIA
233 1970-75
9 1975-80
23 1980-85
25 1985-90
18 1990-95
5 1995-00
53 2000-05
NGO
281 1970-75
3 1975-80
1 1980-85
34 1985-90
41 1990-95
97 1995-00
65 2000-05
POLICE
4,518 1970-75
4 1975-80
1 1980-85
8 1985-90
10 1990-95
3 1995-00
133 2000-05
PRIVATE CITIZENS + PROPERTY
7,197 1970-75
64 1975-80
195 1980-85
144 1985-90
89 1990-95
170 1995-00
644 2000-05
RELIGIOUS FIGURES / INSTITUTIONS
199 1970-75
199 1975-80
41 1980-85
78 1985-90
123 1990-95
39 1995-00
88 2000-05
TRANSPORTATION
2,069 1970-75
66 1975-80
20 1980-85
125 1985-90
187 1990-95
196 1995-00
397 2000-05
3d. INTERNATIONAL TERRORISM FATALITIES
BY GROUP CLASSIFICATION WORLDWIDE 1970 – 2005
ANARCHIST
1 1970-75
0 1975-80
0 1980-85
0 1985-90
0 1990-95
0 1995-00
0 2000-05
ANTI-GLOBALIZATION
4 1970-75
3 1975-80
3 1980-85
1 1985-90
4 1990-95
5 1995-00
2 2000-05
COMMUNIST/ SOCIALIST
150 1970-75
130 1975-80
163 1980-85
157 1985-90
181 1990-95
120 1995-00
32 2000-05
LEFTIST
15 1970-75
28 1975-80
26 1980-85
5 1985-90
30 1990-95
13 1995-00
4 2000-05
NATIONALIST/ SEPARATIST
430 1970-75
271 1975-80
1,033 1980-85
795 1985-90
366 1990-95
403 1995-00
1,140 2000-05
RACIST
4 1970-75
0 1975-80
1 1980-85
1 1985-90
0 1990-95
0 1995-00
0 2000-05
RELIGIOUS
11 1970-75
13 1975-80
446 1980-85
354 1985-90
536 1990-95
818 1995-00
4762 2000-05
OTHER
101 1970-75
13 1975-80
67 1980-85
65 1985-90
32 1990-95
50 1995-00
1 2000-05

2d. INTERNATIONAL **TERRORISM INJURIES**

BY **GROUP CLASSIFICATION WORLDWIDE** 1970 – 2005

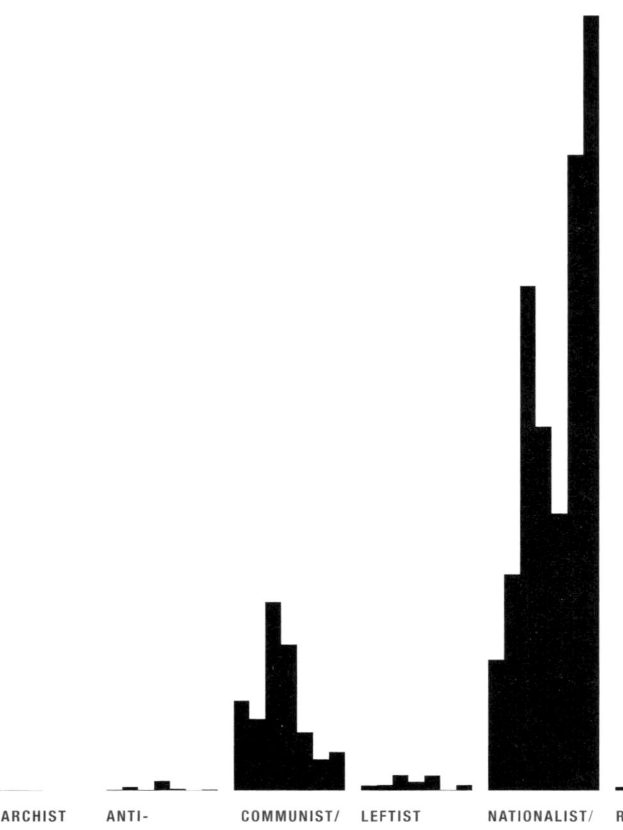

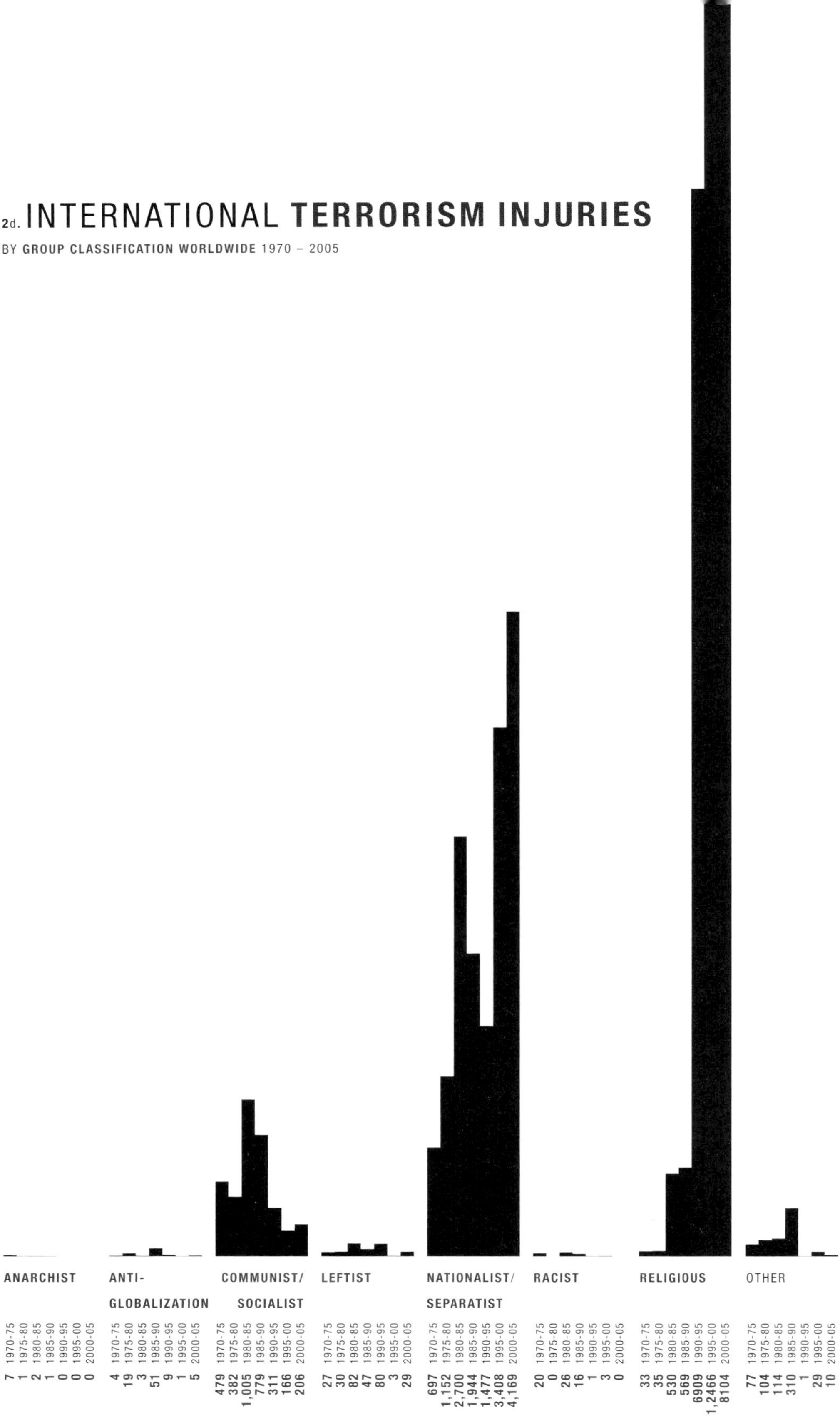

4. INTERNATIONAL + DOMESTIC **TERRORISM INCIDENTS**

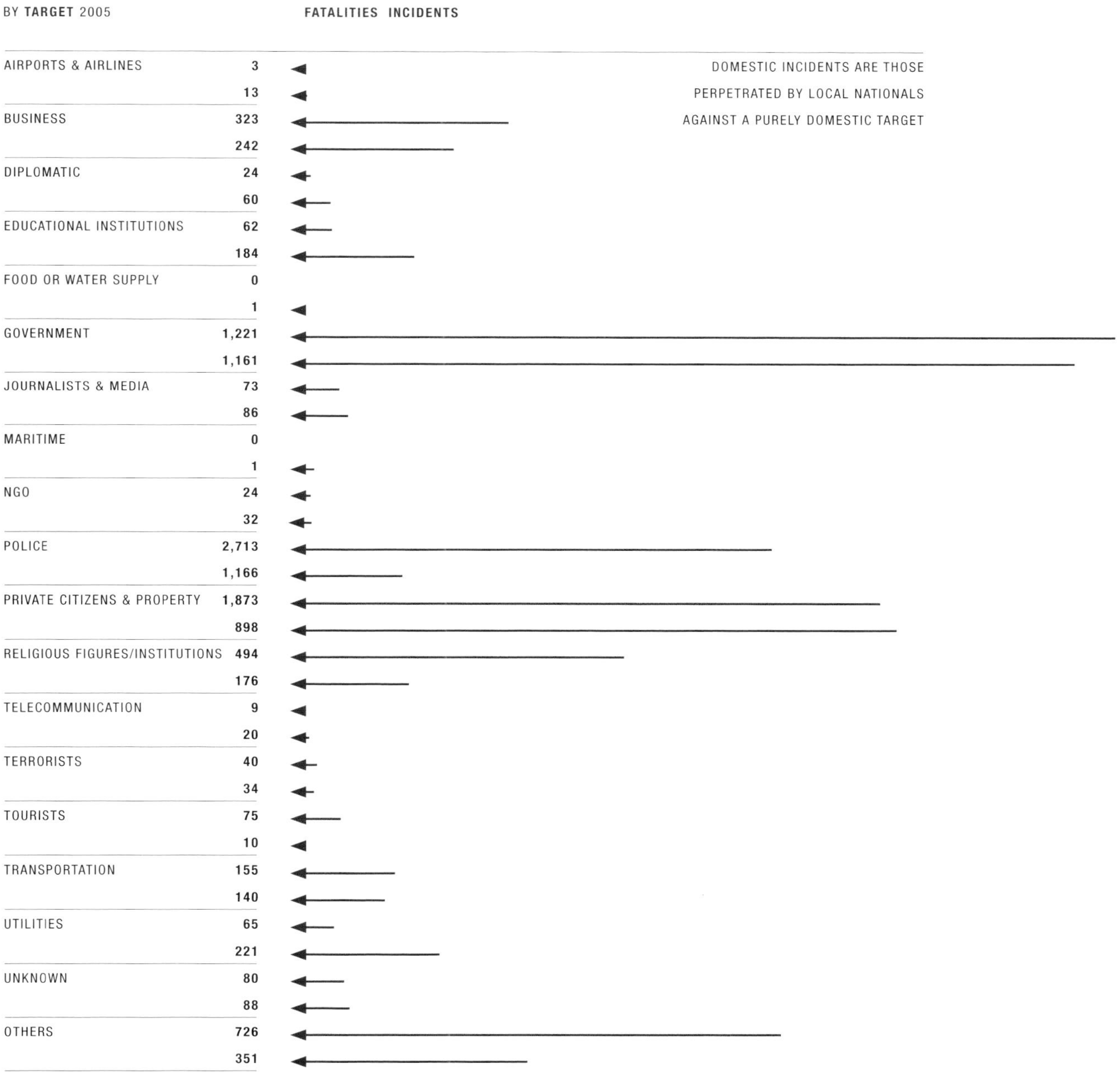
BY TARGET 2005
FATALITIES INCIDENTS
DOMESTIC INCIDENTS ARE THOSE PERPETRATED BY LOCAL NATIONALS AGAINST A PURELY DOMESTIC TARGET
AIRPORTS & AIRLINES 3
13
BUSINESS 323
242
DIPLOMATIC 24
60
EDUCATIONAL INSTITUTIONS 62
184
FOOD OR WATER SUPPLY 0
1
GOVERNMENT 1,221
1,161
JOURNALISTS & MEDIA 73
86
MARITIME 0
1
NGO 24
32
POLICE 2,713
1,166
PRIVATE CITIZENS & PROPERTY 1,873
898
RELIGIOUS FIGURES/INSTITUTIONS 494
176
TELECOMMUNICATION 9
20
TERRORISTS 40
34
TOURISTS 75
10
TRANSPORTATION 155
140
UTILITIES 65
221
UNKNOWN 80
88
OTHERS 726
351

5. TOP 20 TERRORIST GROUPS

BY FATALITIES + INCIDENTS 2005

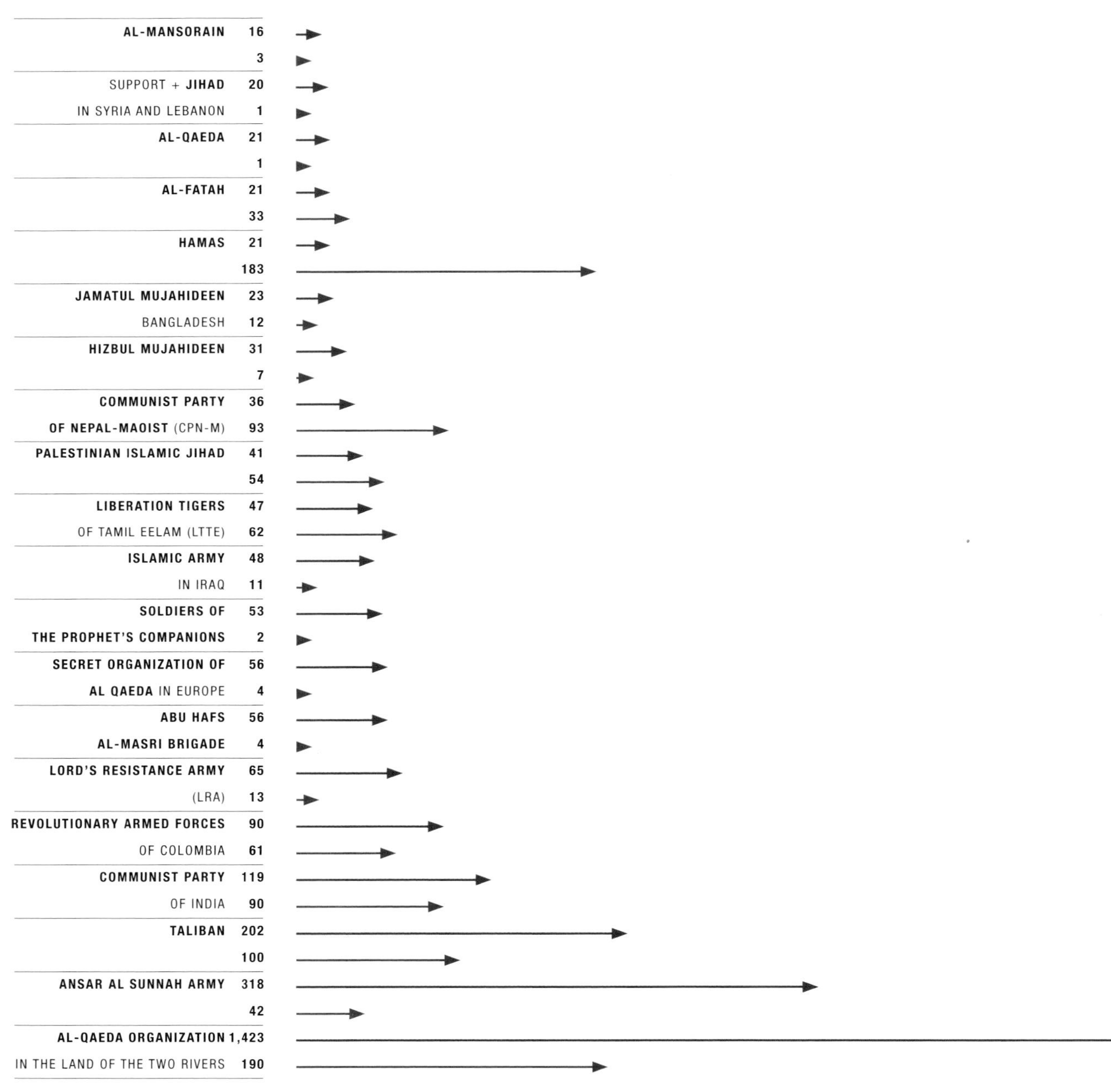

AL-MANSORAIN 16
3
SUPPORT + JIHAD 20
IN SYRIA AND LEBANON 1
AL-QAEDA 21
1
AL-FATAH 21
33
HAMAS 21
183
JAMATUL MUJAHIDEEN 23
BANGLADESH 12
HIZBUL MUJAHIDEEN 31
7
COMMUNIST PARTY 36
OF NEPAL-MAOIST (CPN-M) 93
PALESTINIAN ISLAMIC JIHAD 41
54
LIBERATION TIGERS 47
OF TAMIL EELAM (LTTE) 62
ISLAMIC ARMY 48
IN IRAQ 11
SOLDIERS OF 53
THE PROPHET'S COMPANIONS 2
SECRET ORGANIZATION OF 56
AL QAEDA IN EUROPE 4
ABU HAFS 56
AL-MASRI BRIGADE 4
LORD'S RESISTANCE ARMY 65
(LRA) 13
REVOLUTIONARY ARMED FORCES 90
OF COLOMBIA 61
COMMUNIST PARTY 119
OF INDIA 90
TALIBAN 202
100
ANSAR AL SUNNAH ARMY 318
42
AL-QAEDA ORGANIZATION 1,423
IN THE LAND OF THE TWO RIVERS 190

6. TOP 20 RELIGIOUS TERRORIST GROUPS

BY FATALITIES + INJURIES 2005

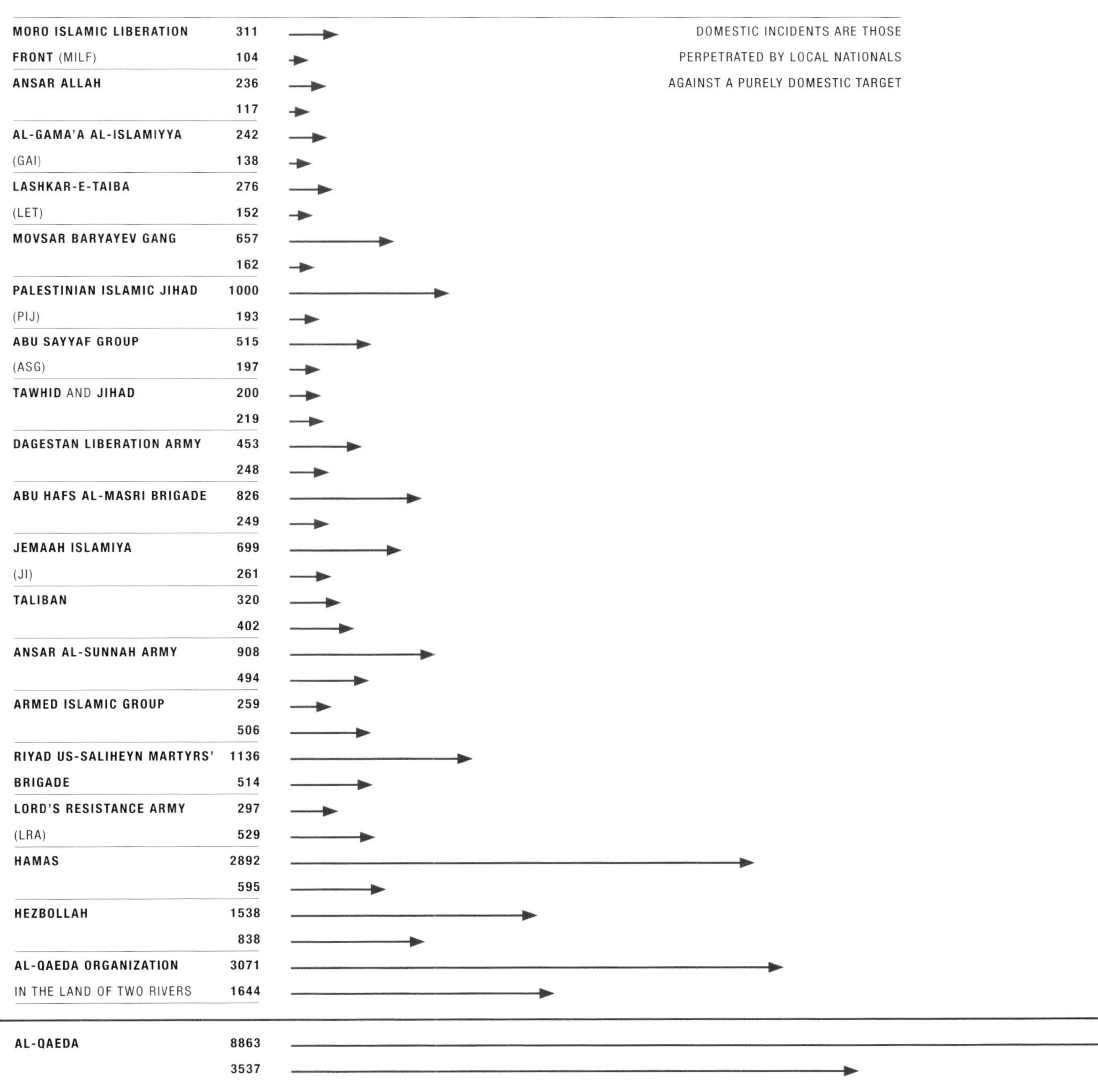
DOMESTIC INCIDENTS ARE THOSE
PERPETRATED BY LOCAL NATIONALS
AGAINST A PURELY DOMESTIC TARGET
MORO ISLAMIC LIBERATION FRONT (MILF) 311 104
ANSAR ALLAH 236 117
AL-GAMA'A AL-ISLAMIYYA (GAI) 242 138
LASHKAR-E-TAIBA (LET) 276 152
MOVSAR BARYAYEV GANG 657 162
PALESTINIAN ISLAMIC JIHAD (PIJ) 1000 193
ABU SAYYAF GROUP (ASG) 515 197
TAWHID AND JIHAD 200 219
DAGESTAN LIBERATION ARMY 453 248
ABU HAFS AL-MASRI BRIGADE 826 249
JEMAAH ISLAMIYA (JI) 699 261
TALIBAN 320 402
ANSAR AL-SUNNAH ARMY 908 494
ARMED ISLAMIC GROUP 259 506
RIYAD US-SALIHEYN MARTYRS' BRIGADE 1136 514
LORD'S RESISTANCE ARMY (LRA) 297 529
HAMAS 2892 595
HEZBOLLAH 1538 838
AL-QAEDA ORGANIZATION IN THE LAND OF TWO RIVERS 3071 1644
AL-QAEDA 8863 3537

TRAFFICKING + CORRUPTION

- total # of **country signatures** per convention - trafficking in persons: # of **source, transit or destination countries** - trafficking in persons: **combination of source, transit or destination countries - the tiers + placement** of countrie - illicit drug production: **opium & cocaine** - illicit drug production: **methamphetamine** - average **corruption perception index** cpi by region + year - top 10 countries of **corruption perception index score** 2005 - top 10 countries of **corruption perception index score** 2005 - bottom top 10 countries of **corruption perception index score** 2005 - world's 10 **most corrupt leaders**

1. TOTAL # OF **COUNTRY SIGNATURES** PER CONVENTION

2a. TRAFFICKING IN PERSONS: # OF **SOURCE**, **TRANSIT** OR **DESTINATION COUNTRIES**

IN TOTAL # OF COUNTRIES

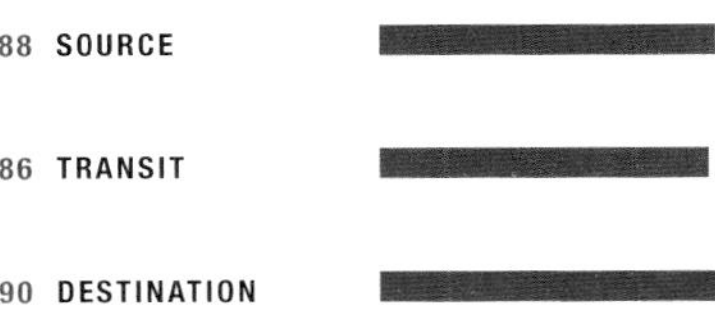

2b. TRAFFICKING IN PERSONS: COMBINATION OF **SOURCE**, **TRANSIT** OR **DESTINATION COUNTRIES**

IN TOTAL # OF COUNTRIES

3. THE **TIERS** + PLACEMENTS

TIER 1: **COUNTRIES WHOSE GOVERNMENTS FULLY COMPLY WITH THE ACT'S MINIMUM STANDARDS.**

TIER 2: **COUNTRIES WHOSE GOVERNMENTS DO NOT FULLY COMPLY WITH THE ACT'S MINIMUM STANDARDS, BUT ARE MAKING SIGNIFICANT EFFORTS TO BRING THEMSELVES IN COMPLIANCE WITH THOSE STANDARDS**

TIER 2 WATCH LIST: **COUNTRIES WHOSE GOVERNMENTS DO NOT FULLY COMPLY WITH THE ACT'S MINIMUN STANDARDS, BUT ARE MAKING SIGNIFICANT EFFORTS TO BRING THEMSELVES IN COMPLIANCE WITH THOSE STANDARDS AND:**

A THE ABSOLUTE NUMBER OF VICTIMS OF SEVERE FORMS OF TRAFFICKING IS VERY SIGNIFICANT OR IS SIGNIFICANTLY INCREASING; **OR**

B THERE IS A FAILURE TO PROVIDE EVIDENCE OF INCREASING EFFORTS TO COMBAT SEVERE FORMS OF TRAFFICKING IN PERSONS FROM THE PREVIOUS YEAR; **OR**

C THE DETERMINATION THAT A COUNTRY IS MAKING SIGNIFICANT EFFORTS TO BRING THEMSELVES INTO COMPLIANCE WITH MINIMUM STANDARDS WAS BASED ON COMMITMENTS BY THE COUNTRY TO TAKE ADDITIONAL FUTURE STEPS OVER THE NEXT YEAR

TIER 3: **COUNTRIES WHOSE GOVERNMENTS DO NOT FULLY COMPLY WITH THE MINIMUM STANDARDS AND ARE NOT MAKING SIGNIFICANT EFFORTS TO DO SO.**

PLACEMENTS **TIER 1**:

AUSTRALIA
AUSTRIA
BELGIUM
CANADA
COLOMBIA
CZECH REPUBLIC
DENMARK
FRANCE
GERMANY
HONG KONG
ITALY
LITHUANIA
LUXEMBOURG
MOROCCO
NEPAL
THE NETHERLANDS
NEW ZEALAND
NORWAY
POLAND
PORTUGAL
SOUTH KOREA
SPAIN
SWEDEN
UNITED KINGDOM

PLACEMENTS **TIER 2**:

AFGHANISTAN
ALBANIA
ALGERIA
ANGOLA
ARGENTINA
BANGLADESH
BELARUS
BOSNIA/HERZEGOVINA
BRAZIL
BULGARIA
BURKINA FASO
BURUNDI
CHAD
CHILE
CONGO (DRC)
COSTA RICA
COTE D'IVOIRE
CROATIA
CYPRUS
EAST TIMOR
EGYPT
EL SALVADOR
EQUATORIAL GUINEA
ESTONIA
ETHIOPIA
FINLAND
GABON
GEORGIA
GHANA
GUATEMALA
GUYANA
HONDURAS
HUNGARY
INDONESIA
IRAN
ISRAEL
JAPAN
KAZAKHSTAN
KENYA
KYRGYZ REPUBLIC
SENEGAL
SERBIA-MONTENEGRO
SINGAPORE
SLOVENIA
SRI LANKA
SWITZERLAND
SYRIA
TAIWAN
TAJIKISTAN
TANZANIA
THAILAND
TURKEY
UGANDA
URUGUAY
VIETNAM
YEMEN
ZAMBIA

4a. ILLICIT DRUG PRODUCTION: OPIUM + COCAINE PRODUCTION LEVELS IN HECTARES

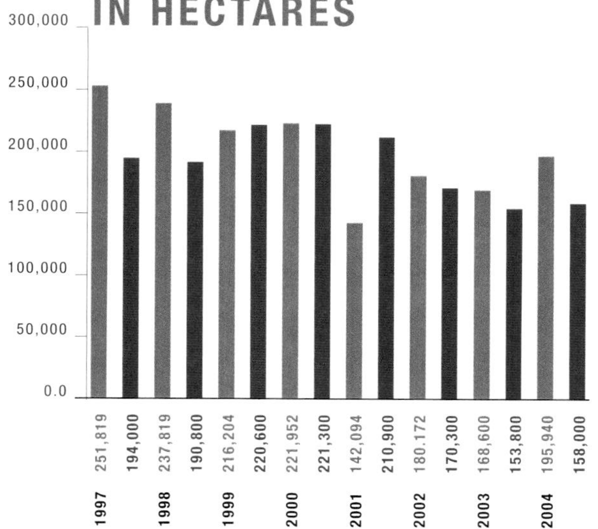

4b. ILLICIT DRUG PRODUCTION: METHAMPHETAMINE + # OF LABS

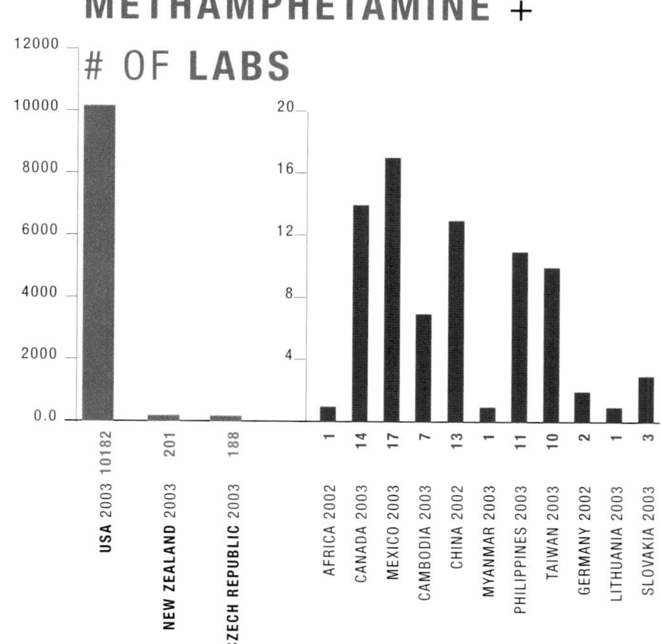

PLACEMENTS **TIER 2**

WATCHLIST:

ARMENIA
AZERBAIJAN
BAHRAIN
BELIZE
BENIN
CAMEROON
CHINA (PRC)
DOMINICAN REPUBLIC
THE GAMBIA
GREECE
GUINEA
HAITI
INDIA
MAURITIUS
MEXICO
NICARAGUA
NIGER
PHILIPPINES
RUSSIA
RWANDA
SIERRA LEONE
SLOVAK REPUBLIC
SOUTH AFRICA
SURINAME
UKRAINE
UZBEKISTAN
ZIMBABWE

PLACEMENTS **TIER 3**:

BOLIVIA
MYANMAR
CAMBODIA
CUBA
ECUADOR
JAMAICA
KUWAIT
NORTH KOREA
QATAR
SAUDI ARABIA
SUDAN
TOGO
UNITED ARAB EMIRATES
VENEZUELA

5. AVERAGE CORRUPTION PERCEPTION INDEX CPI

2000 CPI | 2005 CPI

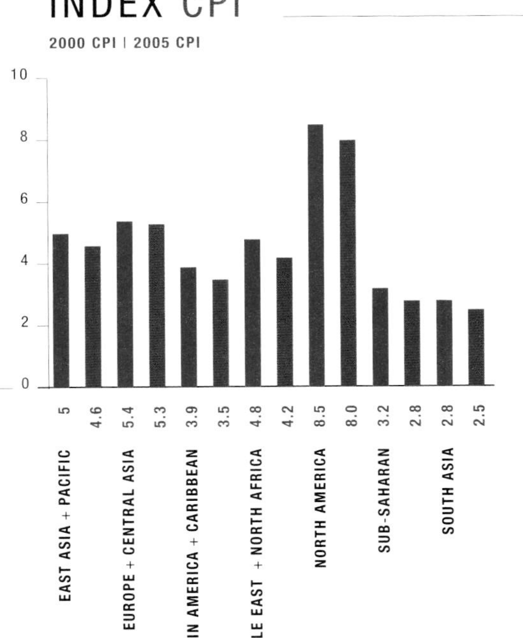

TOP 10 COUNTRIES OF **CORRUPTION PERCEPTION INDEX SCORE** (0-10) 2005

1. ICELAND	9.7
2. FINLAND	9.6
3. NEW ZEALAND	9.6
4. DENMARK	9.5
5. SINGAPORE	9.4
6. SWEDEN	9.2
7. SWITZERLAND	9.1
8. NORWAY	8.9
9. AUSTRALIA	8.8
10. AUSTRIA	8.7

BOTTOM 10 COUNTRIES OF **CORRUPTION PERCEPTION INDEX SCORE** (0-10) 2005

150. TAJIKISTAN	2.1
151. ANGOLA	2.0
152. COTE D'IVOIRE	1.9
153. EQUATORIAL GUINEA	1.9
154. NIGERIA	1.9
155. HAITI	1.8
156. MYANMAR	1.8
157. TURKMENISTAN	1.8
159. BANGLADESH	1.7
160. CHAD	1.7

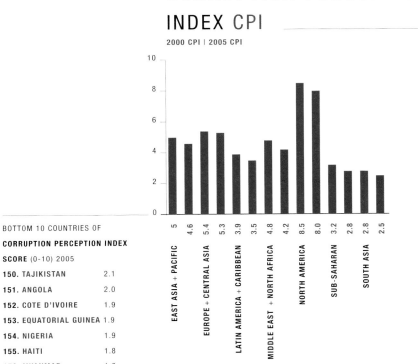

6. WORLD's 10 MOST CORRUPT LEADERS

NAME	POSITION	FUNDS EMBEZZLED[2]
MOHAMED SUHARTO	PRESIDENT OF INDONESIA (1967 – 1998)	**15–35** BILLION
FERDINAND MARCOS	PRESIDENT OF THE PHILIPPINES (1967 – 1998)	**5–10** BILLION
MOBUTU SESE SEKO	PRESIDENT OF ZAIRE (1965 – 1997)	**5** BILLION
SANI ABACHA	PRESIDENT OF NIGERIA (1993 – 1998)	**2–5** BILLION
SLOBODAN MILOSEVIC	PRESIDENT OF SERBIA/YUGOSLAVIA (1989 – 2000)	**1** BILLION
JEAN-CLAUDE DUVALIER	PRESIDENT OF HAITI (1971 – 1986)	**300–800** MILLION
ALBERT FUJIMORI	PRESIDENT OF PERU (1990 – 2000)	**600** MILLION
PAVLO LAZARENKO	PRIME MINISTER OF UKRAINE (1996 – 1997)	**114–200** MILLION
ARNOLOD ALEMÁN	PRESIDENT OF NICARAGUA (1997 – 2002)	**100** MILLION
JOSEPH ESTRADA	PRESIDENT OF THE PHILIPPINES (1998 – 2001)	**78–80** MILLION

PIRACY - anti-piracy actions 2003 - software piracy rates - domestic music piracy levels around the world 2001 - kazaa media desktop application usage (more music piracy) - pirated product containment rates for dvd and home-video markets in select countries

1. ANTI-PIRACY ACTIONS 2003

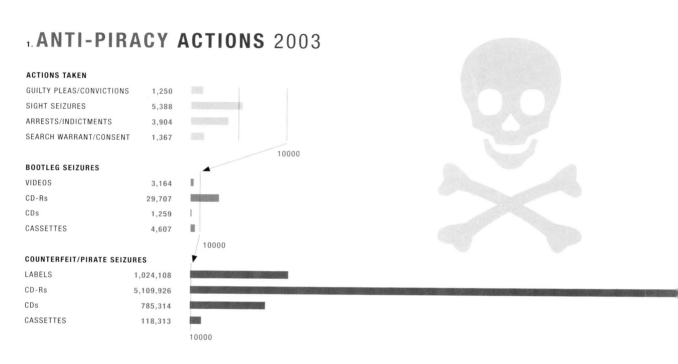

ACTIONS TAKEN	
GUILTY PLEAS/CONVICTIONS	1,250
SIGHT SEIZURES	5,388
ARRESTS/INDICTMENTS	3,904
SEARCH WARRANT/CONSENT	1,367

10000

BOOTLEG SEIZURES	
VIDEOS	3,164
CD-Rs	29,707
CDs	1,259
CASSETTES	4,607

10000

COUNTERFEIT/PIRATE SEIZURES	
LABELS	1,024,108
CD-Rs	5,109,926
CDs	785,314
CASSETTES	118,313

10000

2. SOFTWARE PIRACY RATES

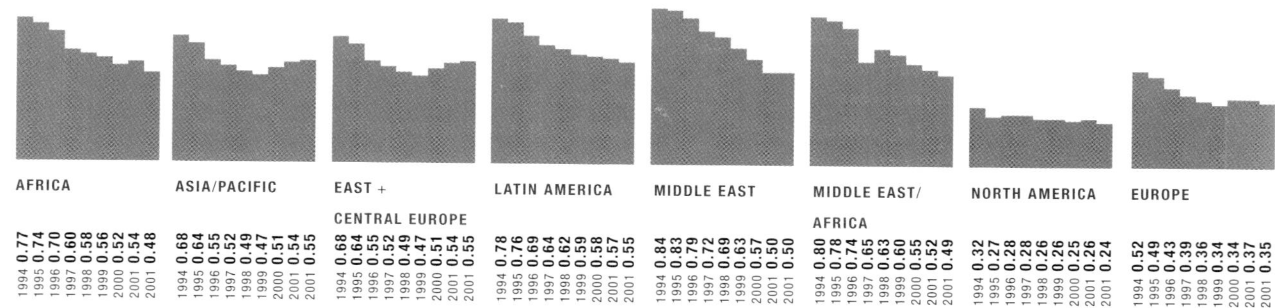

3. DOMESTIC MUSIC PIRACY LEVELS AROUND THE WORLD

2001 IN UNITS

	OVER 50%	25–50%	10–25%	LESS THEN 10%
NORTH AMERICA				CANADA UNITED STATES
EUROPE	BULGARIA CIS (OTHER) ESTONIA GREECE LATVIA LITHUANIA ROMANIA RUSSIA UKRAINE	CYPRUS CZECH REPUBLIC ITALY POLAND SLOVAKIA SPAIN	CROATIA FINLAND HUNGARY NETHERLANDS SLOVENIA TURKEY	AUSTRIA BELGIUM DENMARK FRANCE GERMANY ICELAND IRELAND NORWAY PORTUGAL SWEDEN SWITZERLAND UNITED KINGDOM
ASIA	CHINA INDONESIA MALAYSIA PAKISTAN	INDIA PHILIPPINES TAIWAN THAILAND	HONG KONG SINGAPORE SOUTH KOREA	JAPAN
LATIN AMERICA	BOLIVIA BRAZIL CENTRAL AMERICA COLOMBIA ECUADOR MEXICO PARAGUAY PERU VENEZUELA	ARGENTINA CHILE URUGUAY		
AUSTRALIA				AUSTRALIA NEW ZEALAND
MIDDLE EAST	EGYPT	ISRAEL KUWAIT LEBANON SAUDI ARABIA	BAHRAIN OMAN QATAR	UNITED ARAB EMIRATES
AFRICA	KENYA NIGERIA		GHANA SOUTH AFRICA ZIMBABWE	

WORLD

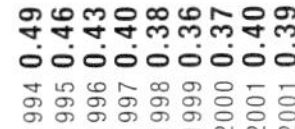

4. KAZAA MEDIA DESKTOP APPLICATION USAGE

IN # OF UNIQUE USERS

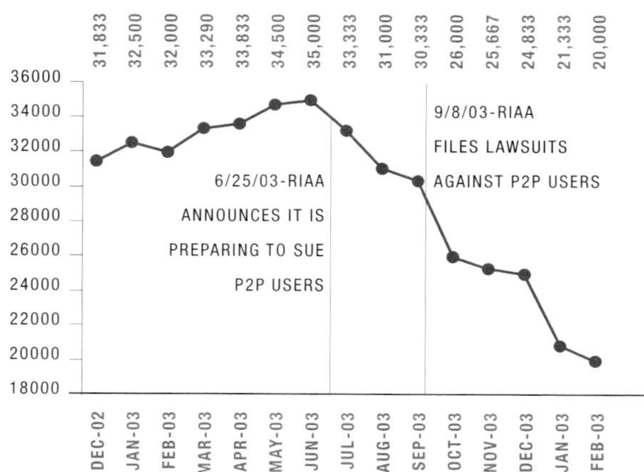

5. PIRATED PRODUCT CONTAINMENT RATES FOR DVD + HOME-VIDEO MARKETS

IN SELECT COUNTRIES AS OF MARCH 2003

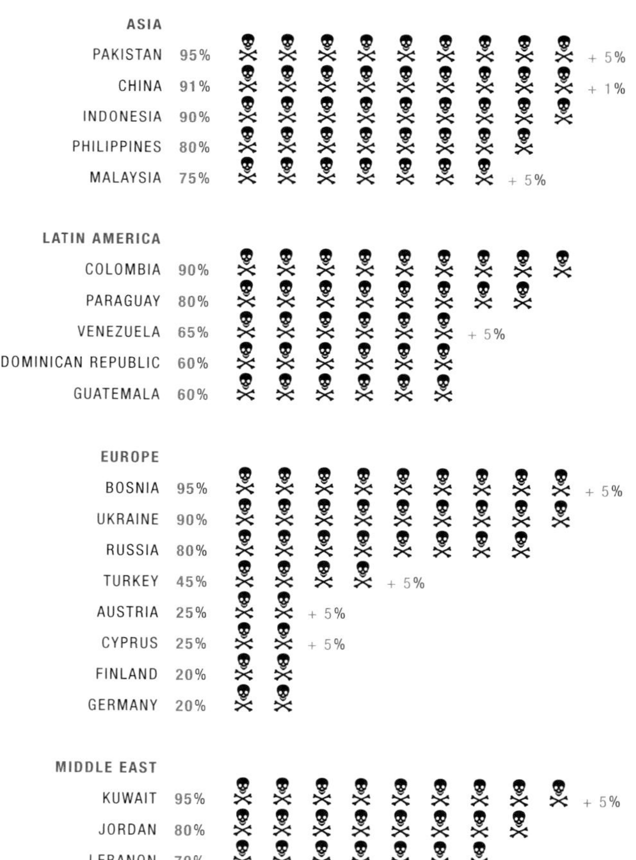

ARMS As personal instruments and military hardware of offense or defense, arms refer to small portable weapons, such as rifles, carbines, pistols, etc., or larger equipment such as tanks, helicopters, and ships. Today, the arms trade permeates national borders, linking distant economies in tight association, all the while functioning as a major worldwide business currently estimated at more than $25 billion each year (Acton, 2006). The proliferation of arms does not necessarily cause conflict, but it makes conflict more likely and can exacerbate already violent situations.

WHAT DO WE KNOW ABOUT ARMS AND WHAT ARE THE ISSUES?

The sales of arms are dominated by a handful of large companies. In 2003, Lockheed Martin, Boeing, and Northrop Grumman were the top three arms-producing companies (measured in terms of non-black market production) with combined revenues of $72,000 million. Halliburton was the 12th largest arms-producing company and had the largest US Department of Defense contract in Iraq from 2002 through 2004 of over $10,830 million (SIPRI, 2005).

The US and Russia supply the majority of arms transfer agreements (or export licenses) to developing nations. While Russia is growing as a provider of such agreements, Germany and China decreased their agreements drastically from the periods between 1997-2000 and 2001-2004. China, India, Egypt, Saudi Arabia, and Israel are the nations that receive the most agreements in terms of value (Grimmett, 2005). As a region, Asia alone received 41% of worldwide arms transfers between 2001 and 2004, and Europe received about 26.6% (Grimmett, 2005). Between 1997 and 2000, the United Arab Emirates received the most arms transfer agreements and from 2001 and 2004, China was the main recipient. Despite the fact that the United States' military expenditure was over two and a half times that of China in 2004, the size of Chinese armed forces was over one and a half times larger than that of the US (IISS, 2003).

The arms trade is lucrative and associated with the persistence of regional and global power relations on the one hand, and patterns of poverty and underdevelopment on the other. Approximately 7 to 8 million pieces of arms are produced each year worldwide, most of which are made in the US, Russia, and China (UNDP, 2005). A majority of small arms enter the market legally, and most foreign arms sales are targeted to developing nations. The developing world spends approximately $20 billion USD a year on arms (Acton, 2006). In 2004, the value of arms deliveries to developing nations was close to $22.5 billion (Grimmett, 2005). The US and Russia accounted for over 58% of all arms transfer agreements with developing nations from 1997 to 2004 (Grimmett, 2005). The US primarily has its arms agreements with the Near East and Asia; Russia has most number of agreements (82%) with Asia (Grimmett, 2005). From 1997 to 2004, the US, Russia and France were the three countries with the most arms transfer agreements with developing nations; and India, China and the United Arab Emirates were the leading developing nation recipients of arms transfer agreements (Grimmett, 2005).

For areas in persistent conflict, small wars have become income generators, ways to provide "employment" for individuals (many of whom are children) who have few options for making money. In these conflicts today, small arms, such as machine guns, handguns, and assault rifles are increasingly used and it is estimated that they kill half a million people a year on average (one person per minute) (UNDP, 2005). Small arms are the weapons of choice for new conflicts and are responsible for the ballooning death rates, especially amongst civilian non-combatants, commonly associated with current conflicts. It is estimated that light weapons were the only arms used in 46 out of 49 major conflicts globally during the 1990s, and that civilian deaths accounted for 80 to 90% of parties killed in conflicts (compared with the 5% rate of civilian death during World War I) (Klare, 1999).

Some governments have recently begun monitoring the small arms trade. For instance, in 1998, many arms importing countries in Sub-Saharan Africa signed the Moratorium on the Import, Export and Manufacture of Small Arms and Light Weapons in West Africa, which was the world's first regional moratorium on small arms. Other regions have also initiated monitoring and control programs, but these established agreements are often not legally binding and inconsistent across regions.

While arms sales are monitored by exporting countries, arms often end up in the hands of brutal and oppressive regimes. For example, in 2003, 20 of the top 25 U.S. arms clients in the developing world (80%) were either undemocratic regimes or governments with records of major human rights abuses (Berrigan, Hartung, Heffel, 2005).

Levels of military expenditures vary by region depending on ability to spend and the political priorities of governments. In 2004, military expenditures by the US ($488 billion USD) almost doubled those of Europe, and almost tripled those of Asia and Oceana (SIPRI, 2005). Military expenditures in the Middle East and Africa were the lowest: $56.1 billion and $12.6 billion respectively (SIPRI, 2005). However, if military expenditures are measured in relation to gross domestic product (GDP), Middle Eastern countries, such as Jordan and Oman, and Eritrea in North Africa, spend the most proportionately on their militaries. In fact, all of the top 15 countries that spend the highest percentage of their GDP on the military are located in the Middle East or Africa (CIA, 2004). The inflated expenditure on military in these regions correlates to a high prevalence of inter-national and national conflicts there.

The debate surrounding the proliferation of nuclear and biological technologies exacerbate tensions and suspicions between countries in the West, the Middle East and Asia. Similarly, the expansion of military presence by the US in regions such as the Middle East and Latin America under the auspices of spreading hope, freedom, democracy, and peace fuel, hatred and widen divides.

CONFLICT RESOLUTION & UN PEACEKEEPING

Conflict resolution, peacekeeping, and conflict settlement rest on a moral obligation or code that emphasizes collective responsibility for a world of peace and prosperity. This link is expressed clearly in the Universal Declaration of Human Rights, and more recently in the 2005 United Nations' Human Development Report, which focused on the role of the international community in times of conflict and war: "The rights violated by conflict are universal human rights that the entire international community has a moral and legal duty to uphold" (UNDP, 2005: 151).

This statement, however, overlooks the longstanding tension between upholding universal principles while honoring national sovereignty in terms of non-interference. In fact, governments and other stakeholders disagree on how to balance both principles, and on just how much and in what capacity intervention is warranted and appropriate. Some argue that too much intervention represents imposition of outside culture, values, and norms on specific countries or regions that are typically poor and often struggling. By contrast, too little engagement could amount to willful neglect in the face of more conflict and violence than could be the case otherwise, with Rwanda in the 1990s and Darfur currently as prime examples.

WHAT ARE CONFLICT RESOLUTION AND PEACEKEEPING?

Conflict resolution is broadly understood as the process by which disputes or conflicts are resolved. A successful and lasting resolution satisfies each party's and stakeholder's interests, and addresses their needs as well as underlying concerns and grievances. Conflict resolution can be accomplished through mediation, conciliation, arbitration, or litigation. All methods require third party intervention, but each arrives at a resolution differently. For example, while litigation involves decision-making by a third party, mediation signifies an attempt by the parties to reach some common agreement with the guidance, but not the decision-making, by a third party. Negotiation is resolution in the traditional bargaining sense. Conflict management recognizes conflict as a social and organizational tool, which can be managed for more beneficial and progressive outcomes.

The UN was established in 1945 to promote international peace and security. The organization's mission is to "maintain international peace and security; to develop friendly relations among nations; to cooperate in solving international economic, social, cultural and humanitarian problems and in promoting respect for human rights and fundamental freedoms; and to be a centre for harmonizing the actions of nations in attaining these ends." (http://www.un.org/aboutun/basicfacts/unorg.htm). Since the initiation of the UN collective security system, established after the Second World War, the intensity, magnitude, and scope of interstate wars has declined. What is more, after the Cold War, the role of the UN as a peacekeeper increased, albeit frequently without adequate material and human resources commensurate to the typically complex tasks involved.

WHAT DO WE KNOW ABOUT CONFLICT RESOLUTION AND PEACEKEEPING?

There has been a slow growth in peacekeeping efforts and numbers of peacekeeping organizations since 2000. As noted in the Current Conflicts, Issues, and Tensions suite, conventional wars have decreased over the past years, whereas other types of conflicts have increased in prevalence. The numbers of different types of peacekeeping and building organizations have been steadily increasing and have fluctuated since 1990 based on this global need. Between 1996 and 1998, for example, there was a spike in organizations that focused on disarmament. During this time, the numbers of UN troops dropped from about 25,000 to about 14,300 (United Nations Peace Operations). Between 2001 and 2002, all peacekeeping and building organizations saw an increase in numbers—whereas there were 37 peacekeeping organizations in 1990, there were close to 300 in 2004.

Since the middle of the 1990s, when the UN carried out the majority of peace missions globally, the number of UN missions has been decreasing, and regional organizations and alliances now account for most of the peace missions executed worldwide (29 missions compared to the UN's 21) (SIPRI, 2005).

In 2004, UN peacekeeping operations were focused in the Congo and Liberia, as African countries typically have very low peace-building capacity, with over 18,500 and 17,500 operations respectively in each. Other operations occurred at that time in nations such as Haiti, Ivory Coast, Kosovo, Burundi and East Timor, among others. In 2004, UN troop strength reached an all time high of 64,720 people. In 2005, most UN peacekeeping missions were located in Africa, followed by the Middle East.

WHAT ARE THE ISSUES?

A primary lesson learned is that post-conflict peace-building requires sustained engagement and adequate resources for building and strengthening state and civil society institutions. When peace settlements are reached, there are traditionally short-term surges of humanitarian aid, which then disappear and are rarely replenished. Conflict resolution, aid, and post-conflict reconstruction work contributed by outside donor countries can exacerbate conflicts if they favor one party or are insensitive to cultural intricacies and histories (see the relevant chapters by Viejo Rose; Nelson, Carver and Kaboolian; and Thompson). Furthermore, the work of outside and local civil society organizations are hindered by limited capacity and resources. While there has been a growth of INGOs and NGOs that organize peacekeeping activities, very few actually go into war-torn or conflicted areas.[1]

More at issue in recent years is that the one agency charged with monitoring and upholding peace-processes worldwide, the United Nations, is hindered by a growing divide of conservatives and reformists amongst member states who believe the institution itself is a liability for peacekeeping around the world (Falk, 2006). The legitimacy of the UN is further questioned when it fails to penalize members states that violate its conventions or fail to pay their dues (i.e., as is the case with the United States). The public generally sees the UN's successes and failures mainly in relation to peace and security issues (Falk, 2002); thus, the ability of the UN to adequately provide peace monitoring and promotion can be further crippled when public opinion views UN efforts as failures, as seen throughout the 1990s with Bosnia and Rwanda, and more recently in Darfur.

Although the number of conflicts worldwide has decreased, the intensity has increased, as demonstrated in the Current Conflicts suite. Newer weaponry, greater availability of small arms, and the use of communication technology in financing armed conflict endanger the livelihoods and rights of civilians caught by violence. Such situations are cause for reform to bring the international system of conflict prevention, management and resolution closer to the demands of the 21st century.

[1] The Carter Center, the Center for Conflict Resolution, and Safer World are three examples of organizations that do travel into conflict areas.

CURRENT CONFLICTS, ISSUES, AND TENSIONS

Recent positive trends in global conflict have been counter-balanced by negative trends that pose obstacles for peace. While major armed conflicts have decreased in prevalence, other types of violence are rising, in particular the so-called 'New Wars' (Kaldor, 1999) that include complex civil wars and conflicts associated with the trauma and legacy of weak states.

Armed conflict remains one of the largest obstacles to human development; it violates the right of people to both life and security (UNDP, 2005). Border disputes, competition, ethnic and religious tensions, economic inequalities, intervention, natural resources, demographic changes and migrations, historically entrenched values, identity conflicts, and economic and political shifts—all contribute to the prevalence of violent and prolonged conflict within nations. The lack of stable institutions, corruption, and other structural and cultural factors exacerbate tensions and pose challenges to poor countries struggling to emerge from prolonged periods of conflict.

Almost three times as many conflict-related deaths occurred in the 20th century than in the previous four centuries combined (UNDP, 2005). Since the end of the Cold War, however, there has been an overall decline in armed conflict, including ethno-national wars for independence, interstate wars, and repression of ethnic minorities (Peace and Conflict, 2005). By 2004, the general magnitude of global welfare decreased by over 60 percent since it reached a high in the mid-1980s (Marshall and Gurr, 2005).

Although the number of conflicts has declined, recent conflicts have yielded larger numbers of fatalities and more prolonged fighting; for instance, in the Western Sudan region of Darfur and Rwanda (UNDP, 2005). Moreover, internal conflicts have become more prevalent than interstate conflicts. In fact, there were over four times as many internal conflicts in 2004 than there were in 1946, whereas, interstate conflict decreased by almost half during this time (PRIO, 2005).

Globally, since 1990, more than 3 million people have died in armed conflicts, and most of these deaths have occurred in the world's poorest countries in Africa and Asia (UNDP, 2005). Between 1990 and 2003, almost 40% of the world's conflicts were in Africa (UNDP, 2005). In Zaire/Congo alone, 1.5 million deaths were tallied in ongoing conflicts between 1990 and 2005 (Marshall, 2006).

WHAT ARE THE ISSUES?

Failed states are characterized by both active violent internal conflict and vulnerability to conflict. The "Failed States Index" (The Fund for Peace and the Carnegie Endowment for International Peace, 2006) identified many African nations as unstable: Sudan, the Democratic Republic of the Congo, the Ivory Coast, Iraq, Zimbabwe, Chad, Somalia, Haiti, Afghanistan, and Guinea are some of the most critical regions worldwide.

These and other countries at risk are struggling to create stable governance structures. Strong institutions are key for lasting peace and stability (see Beverly Crawford's chapter in the volume), and violent conflict most often occurs in regions with weak institutions, persistent poverty, and intense polarization (UNDP, 2005). In fact, nine out of the ten countries with the lowest Human Development Indicator scores have experienced conflict some time after 1990; suggesting that countries that suffer from violent conflict are the furthest from achieving the Millennium Development Goals (UNDP, 2005).

Violent conflict exacerbates historically entrenched biases, tensions and perceptions; and perpetuates cycles of mistrust, hatred, and fear. It also reverses gains in human rights and development and destroys traditional forms of mediation and other institutions and structures. For example, Angola, Burundi, and Nepal, three countries that have experienced some of the longest periods of conflict, rank high on the Human Poverty Index, have higher mortality rates for children under-five years, and have debt rates greater than their GDP. Not only are the costs and effects of conflict felt more heavily in poorer nations, but within a nation the costs of violent conflict are borne more heavily by the country's poor and marginalized populations.

In the years following the Cold War, official discriminatory policies have been declining, a trend first seen within Western democracies in the late 1960s and with the end of colonialism and the universal recognition of principles of human rights and self-determination (Marshall and Gurr, 2005). These developments have encouraged minorities to seek political, human, and social rights from their countries and have perhaps contributed to the decline in instances of conflict over recent years. In 2005, almost half as many states had official policies of political discrimination against specific ethnic groups as did in 1950 (over 44 percent of states). Rates of economic discrimination declined from over 31% of states to 13.7% (Marshall and Gurr, 2005). Remedial policies to confront entrenched discrimination have also increased substantially around the world since 1955 (Marshall and Gurr, 2005). In places like North Africa and the Middle East, however, there has been little movement towards remedial policies or actions for marginalized groups.

As the world becomes increasingly violent conflicts, once local, are becoming transnational. Increased movements of assets and people, the flow of communication, global diasporas, and other forms of interconnectedness have created situations in which conflicts are played out on a global stage. Migration, in particular, can potentially create conflict that can be exploited by political entrepreneurs and instrumentalized—which poses both opportunities for resolution and barriers that further fragment communities and cultures (see chapters on migration).

Whereas globalization is seen by some as a powerful tool for unity, progress and development, others see it as a hegemonic process that promotes a single cultural and economic model (see chapter by Achugar). In this view, tensions based on unequal distribution of economic and cultural production fuel conflicts (between the "North" and the "South", or the Arab and Western worlds for instance). Economic and political inequities resulting from globalization can cause cultural conflict. As Crawford explains in her chapter, liberal democracies can lessen cultural conflict through certain institutions and electoral systems, whereas illiberal democracies make cultural conflict worse.

Ideological and perceptual schisms exist on global levels, based on identities, histories, values, and emotions. Global media sources and academia highlight these divisions, perhaps exacerbating and entrenching them in different regions' cultural psyches. Governments can actively oppose the influx of outside culture and influence. Mega identities (see chapter by Corm) link politics with religion and cultural values, and promote mistrust and misunderstanding.

HUMAN RIGHTS

At the most fundamental level, human rights are inalienable rights closely intertwined with the rule of law. More concretely, human rights are linked to issues of corruption versus transparency; violence versus peace; terror versus justice; and thus, inextricably tied to instances of political, economic and socio-cultural conflict. The juxtaposition of these issues highlights the delicate balance necessary in a globalizing world to maintain and protect rights in the name of human dignity, equality and preservation.

What are currently known as human rights have undergone years of elaboration to create meaningful standards to be followed by governments, and enjoyed by people, around the world. Today, there are seven core UN treaties and six supplementals that signatory countries must abide by. Together, these treaties define human rights as based on the following principles (United Nations, 1948):

- All humans are born free and equal in dignity and rights
- Human rights bare no "distinction of any kind, such as race, colour, sex, language, religion, political or other opinion, national or social origin, property, birth or other status".
- The right to life, liberty and security of person is a right essential to the enjoyment of all other rights
- The right to economic, social and cultural rights are indispensable for human dignity and the free development of personality

Ever since the struggle for human rights began, there has been widespread growth of related "rights" movements that prominently include the workers' and women's movement, and also movements protecting the rights of children, migrants and refugees, indigenous peoples, religions, cultural heritage and traditions, the elderly and disabled, and more recently, the rights for those living with HIV/AIDS. These movements have gained momentum and significance through the identification of human rights (i.e., "women's rights as human rights") thus leading to further action by international governing bodies like the UN or the EU to enact conventions that address these individual issues.

WHAT DO WE KNOW ABOUT HUMAN RIGHTS?

A recent study as part of the Cingranelli-Richards Human Rights Dataset, which compared levels and types of rights among regions, found that Oceania leads the world in providing physical integrity rights to their populations, based on rights surrounding torture, extrajudicial killing, political imprisonment, and disappearances (CIRI, 2004). Asia, Africa, the Middle East, and Latin America offer the least physical integrity rights, but have scored higher ranks in recent years, compared to the past (CIRI, 2004). Between 2000 and 2004, rights in North America decreased (CIRI, 2004). The Middle East was the only region that saw an increase in empowerment rights of movement, speech, workers rights, religion, and political participation, between 2000 and 2004; all other regions registered declines in such freedoms (CIRI, 2004). According to the study, the US had the highest score (10 or a possible 10) on the empowerment rights index in 2000, but fell to 9.5 in 2004 (CIRI, 2004).

In terms of women's economic, social, and political rights, North America and Latin America were some of the freest regions, while the Middle East, followed by Africa and then Europe registered lower degrees of women's rights (CIRI, 2004). Importantly, 183 nations have signed the Convention on the Elimination of all Forms of Discrimination against Women (Division for the Advancement of Women http://www.un.org/womenwatch/daw/cedaw/states.htm).

A variety of civil society organizations (CSOs) worldwide address human rights issues, with Amnesty International and Human Rights Watch among the most prominent and vocal; many other CSOs focus on gender issues and civil rights in local and regional contexts, e.g., the situation of Sinti and Roma in Central and Eastern Europe. Overall, Europe has the highest numbers of human rights CSOs, and the Middle East and Oceania have the lowest (One World Partners, 2004).

WHAT ARE THE ISSUES?

In light of current conflicts in Iraq and Afghanistan, and ongoing conflicts in many developing nations (i.e., Sudan, Nepal, the Congo and Zimbabwe), the most salient issue today is the abuse of powers and human rights injustices by governments in the name of national security. The 2006 Annual Report by Amnesty International sees the "broken promises and failures of [world] leadership" (Amnesty International, 2006) as a leading cause of human rights abuses today. Similarly, in its 2006 report, Human Rights Watch critically points to the "hypocrisy factor" (Human Rights Watch, 2006) of the US government and some of its allies in de facto undermining efforts to improve the human rights situations in conflict areas. So long as the US government maintains a somewhat ambiguous stance towards torture, interrogation, and imprisonment without due process, other governments may well feel encouraged to engage in actions that themselves violate the Convention on Human Rights and the Geneva Convention.

The competing priorities of governments underscore the reality that human rights often are secondary to political and economic interests. Yet no one country or government, especially those in positions of great power and influence, can afford to bend the rules and still maintain a peaceful and respectful presence in the world or in the processes that foster democracy and justice. In this light, the diminishing credibility of leading nations could become a growing hindrance to the promotion of human rights in the world today.

What is more, the capacity of international governing bodies to enforce human rights conventions has come into question over the last few years. Many CSOs are calling for a reform of the UN system to increase international oversight of human rights, and enhance the legal capacity for implementing and enforcing human rights legislation. The establishment of the International Court of Criminal Justice is a prime example of this process. CSOs are also demanding that, in a globalizing world, attention should shift from an exclusive focus on state actors to private actors as violators of human rights, in particular corporations, but also religious and political groups.

TERRORISM is one of the major security concerns of the 21st century, although in terms of a global average, the probability of being killed in a terrorist attack is very low. Much of the power of terrorism lies in its ability to evoke fear, causing not only economic and political problems, but also cultural, social and psychological ones. Indeed, while terrorism may not cause numerous deaths at one time (unless perpetrated by larger state actors), it is associated with significant psychological trauma that imprints itself on the social fabric and collective consciousness of society.

Terrorism based on, or evoking, religion has increased in recent years, as have attacks involving anti-globalization and nationalist or separatist sentiments. While some believe that recent terrorism attacks signify the existence of a great global divide, or "clash of civilizations" to use Huntington's term, others see the acts as representative of ingrained structural problems and deep-seated conflicts in individual societies or regions.

WHAT IS TERRORISM?

According to Marshall and Gurr (2005), terrorism is a type of political violence that targets civilian, non-combatant populations, which includes both repressive and expressive forms. Repressive terrorism is employed by authorities to enforce order from above, whereas expressive terrorism is used by constituents against authority or symbols of authority. Terrorism is a personalized, one-sided application of violent force, which is unique because of its huge perceptual impact.

WHAT DO WE KNOW ABOUT TERRORISM?

From 2003 to 2005, terrorism accounted for approximately 20,000 deaths (mostly civilian) worldwide (UNDP, 2005). According to the Terrorism Knowledge Base (2006), on which the data in the balance of this section are based, terrorism is concentrated in the Middle East, South Asia, Europe, and parts of Latin America. Developed countries are more likely to be targets of terrorism, but are less likely to experience great numbers of deaths from each incident. North America saw a decline in terrorism between the 1970s and 2000, and spikes in the mid 1990s, and in 2001, as evident by the events of September 11, 2001, and other recent attacks. Rates of terrorism and related injuries and deaths have increased in Eastern Europe and the Middle East since the 1970s. In 2005, al-Qaeda, the Taliban, and the Revolutionary Armed Forces of Colombia were the terrorist groups that caused the most fatalities.

International terrorism, a highly visible form of terrorism, has increased since the 1970's with the Bader-Meinhof Gang in Germany (attack on the West German embassy in Stockholm), the IRA (attacks in London), and Middle Eastern groups (e.g., hijacking of airplanes) as early prime examples of terrorists crossing national boundaries to further their cause. Terrorism by religious, nationalist, separatist and anti-globalization groups has increased significantly since 1970, whereas violence by groups based around issues of race, communism or socialist ideals has decreased significantly.

Bombings, armed attacks and kidnappings are the leading forms of international terrorism; and account for the most injuries and fatalities caused by terrorism worldwide. By contrast, local assassinations, barricading, hostage taking, and hijackings have declined in recent years. Most international terrorism is directed towards businesses, diplomatic targets, or private citizens and property.

WHAT ARE THE ISSUES?

International terrorism has traditionally represented only a small portion of global terrorism. In fact, over 90 percent of terror incidents before September 11, 2001 were carried out nationally (Marshall and Gurr, 2005). Despite the relatively low frequency of international terrorist acts, their visibility and salience on the world stage suggest that they represent focal events crystallizing larger underlying issues, divisions, and trends. Both international and other acts of terrorism are often used as statements about perceived injustice in terms of poverty, underdevelopment, unequal resource distribution, cultural and political oppression, or weak and absent governance institutions (Marshall and Gurr, 2005). International terrorism can also be understood as a specific reaction against globalization that may be perceived as an imposition of a dominant Western system on local cultures.

Thanks to the recent penetration and expansion of communication technologies, terrorism is broadcast around the world, making its power exponential by instilling fear in its targets and their allies, and making individuals unsure about their personal safety. In public opinion polls from developed countries, it is evident that most people feel that the world is less safe than during the Cold War, due primarily to threat of terrorist attacks (UNDP, 2005). While some of these fears are founded, a distinct culture of fear has evolved around safety and terrorism that perpetuates cultural misconceptions and misunderstanding.

In 2001, the United States launched its official 'war on terrorism' in response to the Al Qaeda attacks of September 11th. It represents a statist approach to eradicate terrorism that emphasizes a focus on the organization of terrorist groups rather than attacking the causes of terror itself. The 'war' so far includes: the Afghan war of 2001; the Iraq war of 2003; a search for weapons of mass destruction; a massive shift in spending priorities and increases in military budgets; questionable treatment of prisoners in Guantanamo Bay and human rights practices such as rendition flights; torture of prisoners; and surveillance of phone calls and Internet traffic.

TRANSNATIONAL CRIME–including corruption, humans trafficking, drug smuggling, and piracy–is greatly advanced by globalization and developments in communication technology. At the same time, however, improved transnational cooperation among law enforcement agencies, better surveillance tools, and the emergence of civil society institutions have facilitated detection and prosecution.

• Broadly defined, corruption is the "abuse of entrusted power for private gain" (Transparency International, 2006) and refers to a variety of activities such as falsification of documents, theft, embezzlement, demands, extorting, cronyism, and giving/receiving bribes.
• Piracy today is generally understood as the unauthorized duplication of goods, which are protected by intellectual property rights such as software, music, books, and videos, even information. We mainly refer to it here in its software and music incarnations.
• Human Trafficking refers to the smuggling of migrants and the trafficking of human beings for prostitution and slave labor.

WHAT WE KNOW ABOUT TRANSNATIONAL CRIME

Transnational crime reflects complex social, political economic phenomena and the growth of these activities threaten the safety of individuals and hamper countries in their social, economic and cultural development (Crime Prevention and Criminal Justice, 2006). Corruption in particular places power in the hands of a few, thereby harming the most poor and vulnerable. Not surprisingly, we see on the trafficking & corruption suite that corruption is more prevalent in countries with less effective legal institutions, civil service codes, and accountability mechanisms, and without free media or vital civil society. Data from the "Failed States Index," compiled by Foreign Policy, the Fund for Peace, and the Carnegie Endowment for International Peace indicate a strong correlation between corruption and instability: eight out of the ten most stable countries are the 10 least corrupt. Furthermore, Transparency International, a leading non-governmental organization devoted to combating corruption, publishes an annual Global Corruption Report. In 2005, Scandinavian countries in general, New Zealand and Singapore ranked at the top of Transparency International's Corruption Perception Index, while nations in South Asia, Sub-Saharan Africa, and the Caribbean had the lowest scores (Transparency International, 2005).

Almost every country in the world is affected by human trafficking, according to the United Nations Office on Drugs and Crime (UNODC). The UN reports that victims of human trafficking came from 127 countries, passed through some 98 others on their way to their destination in 137 countries (Deutsche Presse-Agentur, 2006). Global efforts to confront human trafficking are hindered by a lack of accurate empirical data, and some countries' unwillingness to acknowledge the prevalence of the problem. Out of the approximately 192 nations worldwide, only 89 nations have signed the Optional Protocol to the Convention of the Rights of the Child on the Sale of Children, Child Prostitution and Child Pornography. Only 94 nations have signed the Protocol to Prevent, Suppress and Punish Trafficking in Persons (US Department of State, 2004). It is estimated that worldwide, there are 250,000 child soldiers (UNDP, 2005) but just 97 nations have signed the Optional Protocol to the Convention on the Rights of the Child in Armed Conflict.

The piracy suite reveals that global technology has facilitated easy access to information and goods and has sparked a heated debate regarding the circulation and use of texts, music, movies, and software. Piracy of music via the internet has been linked by some with the decline in music sales over the last years, and thus with great losses for the recording industry. Data show that most music downloads and uploads are to and from the United States (Oberholzer, F. & Strumpf, K. 2004). While overall worldwide software piracy rates have been declining, rates in Central and Eastern Europe rose sharply from 2000-2002 and in the Middle East, to a lesser extent, from 2001-2002 (IPR, 2003). North America, Western Europe and Latin America have the lowest rates of piracy, while countries in East and Central Europe, such as Bulgaria, Latvia, Russia, and Greece, have the highest rates. Accordingly, North America and Latin America have ratified the most treaties protecting property rights, while Eastern and Central European countries have passed a much lower number of treaties.

WHAT ARE THE ISSUES?

The main challenge in combating transnational crime is developing effective legal systems that can help build democratic societies based on the rule of law-and to do so in a way that promotes collaboration. Standards and norms, however, vary widely. The crime of piracy, for example, reveals the challenges to existing legal systems. Litigation surrounding online music share pages has curbed usage. In the first nine months after the Recording Industry Association of America (RIAA) announced its 2003 lawsuit against the peer-to-peer file sharing application KaZaa, the numbers of unique users of the site dropped by 43 percent (Pew Internet Project & comScore, 2004). Nevertheless, while recording associations, software companies, and individuals have sued some illegal copiers and disseminators, mounting a comprehensive and permeating aggressive legal campaign in all countries around the world is next to impossible. What is more, countries have different conceptions of intellectual property and property rights. Therefore, controlling piracy is not simply a matter of deciding whether to use incentives or reprimands or how to adapt to new technologies. Rather, it involves the fundamental debate surrounding intellectual property, property rights, and freedom of the individual.

Human trafficking is a global issue, but a lack of reliable data that would allow comparative analyses and the design of policies and countermeasures is scarce (Trafficking in Persons: Global Patterns, 2006). There is a need to strengthen the criminal justice response to trafficking through legislative reform, awareness-raising and training, as well as through national and international cooperation. Currently, it appears that prosecutions depend heavily on victim testimony. This is especially problematic since traffickers play on the fear and ignorance of their victims.

A large part of the approach to addressing corruption is a push by civil society, the public, and other stakeholders, for greater transparency and accountability from governments and business. Transparency includes more open reporting and auditing mechanisms, and participation by stakeholders in decision-making processes. Other methods to address issues of corruption include: establishment of codes of conduct, protection for 'whistle-blowers,' reduction of incentives for corruption, making rules about conflicts of interest, integrity pacts, and consistent prosecution for perpetrators (Transparency International, 2006). Governments can indicate that they are practicing legitimate processes by signing agreements and initiatives. The Extractive Industries Transparency Initiative (EITI), for example, was recently established as a system whereby governments that have extractive industries can report that they are not corrupt; The 20 countries below-most of them still rated in the bottom third of Transparency International's 2005 Corruption Perceptions Index-have committed to the EITI since a Lancaster House Conference in June 2003.

Africa
• Angola
• Cameroon
• Chad
• Congo, Democratic Republic of
• Congo, Republic of
• Equatorial Guinea
• Gabon
• Ghana
• Guinea
• Mauritania
• Niger
• Nigeria
• Sao Tome and Principe
• Sierra Leone

Europe and Central Asia
• Azerbaijan
• Kazakhstan
• Kyrgyz Republic

East Asia and Pacific
• Mongolia
• East Timor

Latin America and the Caribbean
• Bolivia
• Peru
• Trinidad & Tobago

(EITI, 2005)

REFERENCES

Numerals refer to chapter sections, and tables or graphs within each section

THE CONTEXT OF CULTURE

1.A ECONOMIC GLOBALIZATION

1a.-1b. Anheier, H.K., Glasius, M. and Kaldor, M. (2006) Global Civil Society 2006/7, London: Sage Publications.

2a.-2b. World Bank Development Indicators. (2005) Regional Trade Blocs. Available at http://devdata.worldbank.org/wdi2005/Section6.htm (accessed 4/3/06).

3a.-3b. United Nations Conference on Trade and Development. (UNCTAD) World Investment Report 2005.
Available at http://www.unctad.org/en/docs/wir2005_en.pdf. (accessed 4/3/06).

4. United Nations Conference on Trade and Development. (UNCTAD) World Investment Report 2005.
Available at http://www.unctad.org/en/docs/wir2005_en.pdf. (accessed 4/3/06).

1.B GLOBAL CIVIL SOCIETY

1. Anheier, H.K., Glasius, M. and Kaldor, M. (2006) Global Civil Society 2005/6, London: Sage Publications.

2. Anheier, H.K., Glasius, M. and Kaldor, M. (2005) Global Civil Society 2004/5, London: Sage Publications.

Union of International Associations. Yearbook of International Organizations: Guide to Civil Society Networks, 2003 and 2004.

3. Union of International Associations. (2004) Yearbook of International Organizations: Guide to Civil Society Networks.

4a.-4c. Anheier, H.K., Glasius, M. and Kaldor, M. (2005) Global Civil Society 2004/5, London: Sage Publications.

5. Council of Europe. Available at http://www.coe.int/T/E/NGO/public/Participatory_status/. (accessed 4/3/06).

World Bank, (forthcoming). World Bank-Civil Society, Review of Fiscal Years 2002 - 2004 Engagement, Annex I: Civil Society Consultation Efforts in Country Assistance Strategies (CASs); Annex II - Society Civil Society Involvement Efforts in Poverty Reduction Strategy Papers (PRSPs).

World Trade Organization. (WTO)
Available at http://www.wto.org/english/forums_e/ngo_e/ngo_e.htm.
(accessed 4/6/06).

1.C POLITICAL & LEGAL GLOBALIZATION

1. - 4. Office of the United Nations High Commissioner for Human Rights. Available at http://www.ohchr.org/english/law/index.htm. (accessed 4/6/06)

International Labor Organization. (ILO)
Available at http://www.ilo.org/ilolex/cgi-lex/ratifce.pl?C087. (accessed 4/6/06).

United Nations Treaties. Available at http://untreaty.un.org/ENGLISH/bible/englishinternetbible/Bible.asp#partI. (accessed 4/6/06)

5. - 6. Elkington, J. "What should be on the World Economic Forum-or whatever replaces it-a decade from now?" Value News Network. Issue 1, Volume 1. Available at http://www.valuenewsnetwork.com/articlepdfs/14_pdf_VALUE_davos_p16-23.qxd.pdf. (accessed 4/19/06).

7. The World Bank Group. (2005) Governance Indicators: 1996-2004. Available at http://www.worldbank.org/wbi/governance/govdata/. (accessed 4/6/06).

8.-9. Global Policy Forum. Peacekeeping Operations Expenditures. Available at http://www.globalpolicy.org/finance/tables/pko/expend.htm. (accessed 4/19/06).

Global Policy Forum. Appropriations and Assessments for Peacekeeping Operations (2001/2002). Available at http://www.globalpolicy.org/finance/tables/pko/assess02.htm. (accessed 4/19/06).

Global Policy Forum. UN Regular Budget Expenditures in Current vs. Real Terms (1971-2003). Available at http://www.globalpolicy.org/finance/tables/reg-budget/currentreal.htm. (accessed 4/19/06).

10. International Court of Justice. Available at http://www.icj-cij.org/icjwww/igeneralinformation/ibbook/Bbookframepage.htm. (accessed 4/19/06).

11.-12. Interpol. (2004) Annual Activity Report. Available at http://www.interpol.int/Public/ICPO/InterpolAtWork/iaw2004.pdf. (accessed 4/19/06).

Interpol. (2003) Annual Activity Report. Available at http://www.interpol.int/Public/ICPO/GeneralAssembly/AGN73/Reports/agn73r01.pdf.
(accessed 4/19/06).

Interpol. (2002) Annual Activity Report. Available at http://www.interpol.int/Public/ICPO/GeneralAssembly/AGN72/Reports/agn72r01.pdf.
(accessed 4/19/06).

Interpol. (2001) Annual Activity Report. Available at http://www.interpol.int/Public/ICPO/GeneralAssembly/AGN71/Reports/agn71r01.pdf.
(accessed 4/19/06).

digest: globalization

Beck, U. (2000) *What is Globalization?* Cambridge, UK, Malden, MA: Polity Press.

Berger, P. L. (1997) "Four Faces of Global Culture", *The National Interest* (49): 23(7).

Held, D. and McGrew, A. G. (2000) *The Global Transformations Reader: An Introduction to the Globalization Debate.* Malden, MA: Polity Press.

Kaldor, M., Anheier, H., and Glasius, M. (2003) "Global Civil Society in an Era of Regressive Globalization", in Kaldor M., Anheier, H., and Glasius, M. (eds), *Global Civil Society 2003.* Oxford: Oxford University Press.

SOCIAL ASPECTS OF CULTURE

2.A VALUES

IDENTITIES

1a.-3. World Values Survey. 1999-2004. Available at www.worldvaluessurvey.org. (accessed 2/2/06).

ECONOMIC VALUES

1.-8. World Values Survey. 1999-2004. Available at www.worldvaluessurvey.org. (accessed 2/2/06).

SOCIAL VALUES

1.-4. World Values Survey. 1999-2004. Available at www.worldvaluessurvey.org. (accessed 2/2/06).

POLITICAL VALUES

1.-2. World Values Survey. 1999-2004. Available at www.worldvaluessurvey.org. (accessed 2/2/06).

RELIGIOUS VALUES

1.-6. The Pew Research Center for the People and the Press. (2002) "What the world thinks in 2002. How Global Publics View: Their Lives, Their Countries, The World, America."
Available at http://people-press.org/reports/display.php3?ReportID=165. (accessed 2/2/06).

The Pew Research Center for the People and the Press. (2002) "What the world thinks in 2002. Summer 2002. 44 Nation Survey."
Available at http://people-press.org/dataarchive/signup.php3?DocID=168. (accessed 2/2/06).

World Values Survey. 1999-2004. Available at www.worldvaluessurvey.org (accessed 2/2/06).

GENDER VALUES

1.-2. United Nations Development Program (UNDP). Human Development Report 2005 (HDR). Available at http://hdr.undp.org/reports/global/2005/pdf/HDR05_HDI.pdf. (accessed 1/5/06).

World Health Organization (WHO). World Health Statistics 2005. Available at http://www.who.int/healthinfo/statistics/en/ (accessed 1/5/06)

3. World Bank (WB). World Bank Development Indicators 2005. Available at http://web.worldbank.org/WBSITE/EXTERNAL/DATASTATISTICS/0,,contentMDK:20523710~hlPK:1365919~menuPK:64133159~pagePK:64133150~piPK:64133175~theSitePK:239419,00.html (accessed 1/5/06)

4. United Nations Education, Scientific, and Cultural Organization (UNESCO) Statistics Division. Available at http://www.uis.unesco.org/ev_en.php?ID=2867_201&ID2=DO_TOPIC (accessed 1/5/06)

5.-8. Pew Research Center. Pew Global Attitudes Project. Available at http://pewglobal.org/commentary/display.php?AnalysisID=90 (accessed 1/5/06)

RELIGIOUS INSTITUTIONS

1. CIA World Factbook 2005. Available at https://www.cia.gov/cia/publications/factbook/geos/xx.html (accessed 2/10/06)

2.-4. The Interactive Bible. Available at http://www.bible.ca/catholic-church-hierarchy-organization.htm (accessed 2/10/06)

Catholic-Pages.Com. Available at http://www.catholic-pages.com/hierarchy/cardinals_list.asp (accessed 8/1/06)

Wikipedia.com. Available at http://en.wikipedia.org/wiki/List_of_Roman_Catholic_archdioceses (accessed 8/1/06)

5. Adapted from Global Mapping International (2005). Available at http://www.gmi.org/ (accessed 2/10/06)

6. World Christian Encyclopedia. Available at http://www.wnrf.org/cms/next200.shtml (accessed 2/10/06)

7.-11. World Evangelization Research Center. Available at http://www.gordonconwell.edu/ockenga/globalchristianity/gd/gd.htm (accessed 2/10/06)

12.-14. Adapted from Global Mapping International (2005). Available at http://www.gmi.org/ (accessed 2/10/06)

digest: identities

Appadurai, Arjun. (1990). "Disjuncture and Difference in the Global Cultural Economy", *Public Culture* 2:2 (Spring).

Appadurai, Arjun. (1996) *Modernity at Large: Cultural Dimensions of Globalization.* Minneapolis: University of Minnesota Press.

Beck, Ulrich. (2000) *What is Globalization?* Cambridge, UK: Polity Press.

Held, D. and McCrew, A. (eds) (2000) *The Global Transformation Reader.* London: Polity Press.

Huntington, S.P. (2004) *Who are We?* New York: Simon and Schuster.

Sen, Amartya. (2006) *Identity and Violence: The Illusion of Destiny.* New York: Norton.

digest: values

Inglehart, R., Basáñez, M., and Moreno, A.M. (1998) *Human Values and Beliefs: A Cross-Cultural Sourcebook Political, Religious, Sexual, and Economic Norms in 43 Societies: Findings from the 1990-1993 World Value Survey.* Ann Arbor, MI: University of Michigan Press.

Inglehart, Ronald, et al. (2000) "World Values Surveys and European Values Surveys, 1981-1984, 1990-1993, and 1995-1997", ICPSR 2790, Ann Arbor, MI: University of Michigan.

Van Deth, J. W. and Scarbrough, E. (eds) (1995) *The Impact of Values.* New York: Oxford University Press.

digest: attitudes on globalization

Garrett, G. (1999). *Trade, capital Mobility and Government Spending around the World.* New Haven, CT: Yale University, Department of Political Science.

Guillen, M. F. (2001). "Is Globalization Civilizing, Destructive or Feeble? A Critique of Five Key Debates in the Social Science Literature", *Annual Review of Sociology*, 2001 p. 235-60.

Meyer, J.W., Boli J, Ramirez, F.O., and Thomas G. M. (1997). 'World Society and the Nation-State', *American Journal of Sociology*, 103(1) p. 144-81.

Pew Charitable Trust-2002 Global Attitudes Survey. Available at www.people-press.org/reports/display.php3?ReportID=185. (accessed 2/22/06).

digest: religious institutions

Barnett, D. (2001) *World Christian Encyclopedia: A Comparative Survey of Churches and Religions in the Modern World.* Oxford: Oxford University Press.

Bunting, M. (2005) *Where Faith is a Healer: The answer to Africa's problems increasingly lie with spirituality rather than politics.* The Guardian, 28 March.

Chadwick, O. (1990) *The Secularization of the European Mind in the Nineteenth Century.* Cambridge University Press.

Pew Research Center. (2002) "Among Wealthy Nations...U.S. Stands Alone in Its Embrace of Religion." The Pew Research Center for the People and the Press, 19 December.

Prokopy, J. and Smith, C. (1999) *Latin America Religion in Motion.* London Routledge.

Robinson, S. (2000) The Lord's Business. *Time Europe.* 7 February, Vol. 155(5).

2.B KNOWLEDGE

CREATION

1.-2. National Institute for Research Advancement. (NIRA) World Directory of Think Tanks 2005. Available at http://www.nira.go.jp/ice/nwdtt/. (accessed 9/1/05).

3.-4. National Institute for Research Advancement. (NIRA) World Directory of Think Tanks 2005. Available at http://www.nira.go.jp/ice/nwdtt/. (accessed 9/1/05).

Brookings Institution. Annual Report 2005. Available at http://www.brookings.edu/admin/2005annualreport/AnnualReport2005.pdf. (accessed 1/11/06).

Aspen Institute. Annual Report 2004. Available at http://www.aspeninstitute.org/atf/cf/{DEB6F227-659B-4EC8-8F84-8DF23CA704F5}/2004AnnRprt.pdf. (accessed 1/11/06).

Cato Institute. Annual Report 2004. Available at http://www.cato.org/about/reports/annual_report_2004.pdf (accessed 1/11/06)

Council on Foreign Relations. Annual Report 2005. Available at http://www.cfr.org/about/annual_report/ (accessed 1/11/06)

Heritage Foundation. Annual Report. Available at http://www.heritage.org/About/loader.cfm?url=/commonspot/security/getfile.cfm&PageID=79003 (accessed 1/11/06)

Rand Corporation. Annual Report 2004. Available at http://www.rand.org/about/annual_report/2004/RAND_2004_Annual_Report.pdf. (accessed 1/11/06).

Institute for Employment Studies. Annual Review 2005. Available at http://www.employment-studies.co.uk/ies/ies_review_05.pdf (accessed 1/11/06)

Institute for Development Studies. Annual Report 2004-05. Available at http://www.ide.go.jp/English/index4.html. (accessed 1/11/06).

International Institute for Strategic Studies. Available at http://www.iiss.org/about-us. (accessed 1/11/06).

Overseas Development Institute. Available at http://www.odi.org.uk/about.html. (accessed 1/11/06).

DIW Berlin, German Institute for Economic Research. Available at http://www.diw.de/english/produkte/publikationen/taetigkeitsbericht/index.html. (accessed 1/11/06).

Institute for Economic Research at the University of Munich. Annual Report 2004. Available at http://www.cesifo-group.de/pls/portal/docs/PAGE/IFOCONTENT/NEUESEITEN/ABOUT/ABOUTIFO/IFOJAHRESBERICHT/IFO_ANNUAL_REPORT_2004/JB_2004_ENGLISCH.PDF. (accessed 1/11/06).

Kiel Institute for World Economics. Annual Report 2004. Available at http://www.ifw-kiel.de/pub/bericht/ar04.pdf. (accessed 1/11/06).

Institute for Developing Economies. Japan External Trade Organization. Available at http://www.ide.go.jp/English/index4.html. (accessed 1/11/06).

Mitsubishi Research Institute, Inc. Available at http://www.mri.co.jp/E/index.html. (accessed 1/11/06).

Mizuho Information and Research Institute, Inc. Available at http://www.mizuho-ir.

co.jp/english/about/profile.html. (accessed 1/11/06).

5.-8. United Nations Educational, Scientific, and Cultural Organization. (UNESCO) EFA Global Monitoring Report. Available at http://portal.unesco.org/education/en/file_download.php/f92a40287666c9dee65e9528ac75b495table9_tertiaryed.pdf. (accessed 9/30/05).

9.-12. Institute of Higher Education, Shanghai Jiao Tong University. Available at http://ed.sjtu.edu.cn/rank/2005/ARWU2005Main.htm. (accessed 8/23/05).

Academic Ranking of World Universities. Top 500 World Universities. Available at http://ed.sjtu.edu.cn/rank/2005/ARWU2005_Top100.htm. (accessed 1/11/06).

13.-14. Stanford University, 2006 Facts. Available at http://www.stanford.edu/home/stanford/facts/. (accessed 1/11/06).

University of California, Statistical Summary of Students and Staff. (2004) Available at http://www.ucop.edu/ucophome/uwnews/stat/statsum/fall2004/statsumm2004.pdf. (accessed 1/11/06).

Cambridge University Reporter. Available at http://www.admin.cam.ac.uk/reporter/2005-06/special/08/b_finance2006.pdf. (accessed 1/11/06).

Massachusetts Institute of Technology. (MIT) Available at http://web.mit.edu/facts/focus.shtml. (accessed 1/11/06).

Harvard University Fact Book 2004-2005. Available at http://vpf-web.harvard.edu/budget/factbook/current_facts/Online_Harvard_Fact_Book_05.pdf. (accessed 1/11/06).

15. United Nations Educational, Scientific, and Cultural Organization. (UNESCO) Available at http://stats.uis.unesco.org. (accessed 10/10/05).

DISSEMINATION

1.-5. Ulrich's Periodical Database website. Available at http://www.ulrichsweb.com/ulrichsweb/ (accessed 2/20/06)

STORAGE

1a.-1b. Library Technology Guides. Available at http://www.librarytechnology.org/. (accessed 10/3/05).

United Nations Educational, Scientific, and Cultural Organization. (UNESCO) Available at http://publishing.unesco.org/depositories.aspx#MACAO. (accessed 10/3/05).

2.-4. Harvard University website. "Harvard University Library Annual Report 2003-2004." Available at http://hul.harvard.edu/publications/ar04.pdf (accessed 10/3/05)

Cambridge University website. "Cambridge University Library Annual Report for the Year 2004-2005." Available at http://www.lib.cam.ac.uk/About/annual_report_2004-5.pdf (accessed 10/3/05)

Associate of Research Libraries. Available at http://www.arl.org/index.html (accessed 10/3/05)

University of California website. "University of California Library Statistics, July 2005." Available at http://www.slp.ucop.edu/stats/04-05.pdf (accessed 10/3/05)

California Digital Library website. "California Digital Library: Key Indicators for Collections and Use July 2001 to June 2002." Available at http://www.cdlib.org/news/pdf/fy01-02cdl_statsprofile.pdf (accessed 10/3/05)

CALTECH Library website. Available at http://library.caltech.edu/ (accessed 10/3/05)

Columbia University Library website. Available at http://www.columbia.edu/cu/lweb/about/facts.html (accessed 10/3/05)
Princeton University Library website. Available at http://library.princeton.edu/libraries/ (accessed 10/3/05)
University of Chicago Library website. Available at http://www.lib.uchicago.edu/e/about/ (accessed 10/3/05)

Oxford Universities Library website. Available at http://www.lib.ox.ac.uk/ (accessed 10/3/05)

Institute of Higher Education, Shanghai Jiao Tong University. (2005)

5. Encyclopedia Britannica. Available at www.britannica.com. (accessed 3/22/06).

Wikipedia. (2006) Available at www.wikipedia.org. (accessed 3/22/06).

6. Veronis, J. "A comparitive study of six search engines." Universite de Provence. Available at http://www.up.univ-mrs.fr/veronis/pdf/2006-comparative-study.pdf. (accessed 3/22/06).

7.-8. Search Engine Watch. Available at http://searchenginewatch.com/reports/article.php/215646. (accessed 3/22/06).

9.-11. Wikipedia. (2006) Available at http://meta.wikimedia.org/wiki/List_of_Wikipedias#All_Wikipedias_ordered_by_number_of_articles, (accessed 3/22/06).

Wikipedia. (2005) Available at http://stats.wikimedia.org/EN/TablesUsageVisits.htm. (accessed 3/22/06).

12. United Nations Educational, Scientific, and Cultural Organization. (UNESCO) (2005) Available at http://publishing.unesco.org/depositories.aspx#MACAO. (accessed 10/3/05).

13.-14. United Nations Educational, Scientific, and Cultural Organization. (UNESCO) (2005) Available at www.unesco.org (accessed 3/22/06).

European Group on Museum Statistics. (EGMUS) Available at http://www.digital-sepia.de/egmusqua/. (accessed 3/22/06).

The British Museum. Available at http://www.thebritishmuseum.ac.uk/aboutus/faqs/faqs1_4.html#. (accessed 3/22/06).

INNOVATION AND PROTECTION

1.-2. World Intellectual Property Organization. (WIPO) (2004) Available at www.wipo.org. (accessed 2/2/06).

3.-4. World Intellectual Property Organization. (WIPO) (2004) Available at www.wipo.org. (accessed 2/2/06).

Fortune Global 500. Available at http://money.cnn.com/magazines/fortune/global500/industries/, (accessed 2/2/06).

5. World Intellectual Property Organization Statistics. Patent Cooperation Treaty (PCT) Statistical Indicators Report, Annual Statistics (2004).

6.-7. World Intellectual Property Organization. (WIPO) (2004) Available at http://www.wipo.int/ipstats/en/statistics/patents/top_applicants.html. (accessed 2/2/06).

U.S. Census Bureau. International Programs Center, International Data Base.

8.-9. World Intellectual Property Organization. (WIPO) (2004) Available at http://www.wipo.int/ipstats/en/statistics/patents/top_applicants.html. (accessed 2/2/06).

10.-11. European Innovation Scoreboard (2005). Available at http://www.trendchart.org/scoreboards/scoreboard2005/key_dimensions.cfm. (accessed 2/28/06).

digest: knowledge

Bellman, Eric. (2005) "India to WTO: Help US Protect Herbs, Tea and Yoga." *Wall Street Journal*, 19 December.

Brown, Michael F. (1998) 'Can Culture be Copyrighted?,' *Current Anthropology*, 39(2): 193-222.

Ulrich's Periodicals Directory. Available at http://library.dialog.com/bluesheets/html/bl0480.html. (accessed 5/11/06).

United Nations Educational, Scientific and Cultural Organization. (UNESCO) "UNESCO Publishing." Available at http://publishing.unesco.org/depositories.aspx#MACAO. (accessed 5/10/06).

World Intellectual Property Organization. (WIPO) (2004) "Intergovernmental Committee on Intellectual Property and Genetic Resources, Traditional Knowledge and Folklore: The protection of traditional knowledge", presented at seventh session, Geneva Nov 1-5, 2004.

World Intellectual Property Organization. (WIPO) "Patents and PCT." Available at http://www.wipo.int/ipstats/en/statistics/patents. (accessed 5/10/06).

Youngfeng, Zheng. "China's Patent Protection of Traditional Medicine." *South Centre: an intergovernmental organization of developing countries.* Available at http://www.southcentre.org/info/southbulletin/bulletin39/bulletin39-03.htm. (accessed 5/11/06).

2.C PRACTICES AND HERITAGE

HERITAGE PRESERVATION AND DESTRUCTION

1.-4. United Nations Educational, Scientific, and Cultural Organization. (UNESCO) Available at http://whc.unesco.org/en/list/. (accessed 4/25/06).

5. - 6. United Nations Educational, Scientific, and Cultural Organization. (UNESCO) Available at http://www.unesco.org/culture/intangible-heritage/masterpiece.php?lg=en. (accessed 5/12/06).

7. Riedlmayer, A. J. (2002) Destruction of Cultural Heritage in Bosnia-Herzegovina, 1992-1996: A Post-war Survey of Selected Municipalities. Available at http://www.savingantiquities.org/pdf/BosHeritageReport-AR.pdf. (accessed 5/15/06).

8. United Nations Educational, Scientific, and Cultural Organization. (UNESCO) Available at http://whc.unesco.org/en/danger/. (accessed 4/25/06).

ENVIRONMENT

1.-2. International Energy Agency. (IEA) (2005) CO2 Emissions from Fuel Combustion: 1971/2003. IEA, Paris.

3.-5. Yale University. Center for Environmental Law and Policy, Et. Al. 2005. " Environmental Sustainability Index Report." Available at http://sedac.ciesin.columbia.edu/es/esi/ESI2005.pdf. (accessed 2/11/06).

6. World Economic Forum. Global Risk Network 2006. Available at http://www.weforum.org/site/homepublic.nsf/Content/Global+Risk+Programme%5CGlobal+Risks+Resources. (accessed 2/11/06).

7. Transboundary Freshwater Dispute Database, Oregon State University. Available at http://www.transboundarywaters.orst.edu/projects/events/. (accessed 2/11/06).

PARTICIPATION

1. World Values Survey. Available at http://www.jdsurvey.net:8080/bdasepjds/wvsevs/PrinAnalize.jsp. (accessed 2/13/06).

2. Eurostat. (2002) "Europeans Participation in Cultural Activities, a Eurobarometer Study..." Available at http://europa.eu.int/comm/public_opinion/archives/ebs/ebs_158_en.pdf. Figure 5.1, pg. 9. (accessed 2/13/06).

3. World Values Survey. Available at http://www.jdsurvey.net:8080/bdasepjds/wvsevs/PrinAnalize.jsp. (accessed 2/13/06).

4. Eurostat. (2002) "Europeans Participation in Cultural Activities, a Eurobarometer Study..." Available at http://europa.eu.int/comm/public_opinion/archives/ebs/ebs_158_en.pdf. Figure 6.1, pg. 11. (accessed 2/13/06).

5.-7. National Endowment for the Arts. (NEA) (2004) Available at http://www.nea.gov/pub/NEASurvey2004.pdf. (accessed 2/13/06).

8.-12. European Commission. (2004) "How Europeans spend their time." Available at http://epp.eurostat.cec.eu.int/cache/ITY_OFFPUB/KS-58-04-998/EN/KS -58-04-998-EN.PDF. (accessed 2/13/06).

Japan Statistics Bureau. (2001) Survey on Time Use and Leisure Activity. Available at http://www.stat.go.jp/english/data/shakai/2001/tokeihyo.htm. (accessed 2/13/06).

Statistics New Zealand. Time Use Statistics. (1999) Available at http://www.stats.govt.nz/tables/time-use-statistics-1999.htm. (accessed 2/13/06).

Statistics Canada. (1998) Average Time Spent of Activities, by Sex. Available at http://www.statcan.ca/english/Pgdb/famil36a.htm. (accessed 2/13/06).

SPORTS

1. Forbes. (2006) Available at http://www.forbes.com/lists/2006/03/28/soccer-manchester-madrid_cz_pm_06soccerland.html. (accessed 4/21/05).

2. Federation Internationale de Football Association. (FIFA) 2002 World Cup Review. Available at http://www.fifa.com/documents/static/development/FWC_Korea_japan_2002_A_part1.pdf. (accessed 2/22/06).

3.-5. Federation Internationale de Football Association. (FIFA) FIFA Annual Review. Available at http://www.fifa.com/documents/fifa/publication/2005_FIFA_financial_report_EN.pdf. (accessed 2/22/06).

6.-10. International Olympic Committee. (IOC) (2006) Revenue Fact Sheet. Available at http://multimedia.olympic.org/pdf/en_report_845.pdf. (accessed 5/5/06).

11. ATP Tournaments & Tennis Grand Slams. (2004) Available at http://www.atptennis.com/en/newsandscores/news/2005/attendance_records.asp. (accessed 5/22/06).

PGA Tour. (2004) Available at http://en.wikipedia.org/wiki/Sports_league_attendances. (accessed 5/5/06).

Tour de France. (2005) Available at http://www.letour.fr/2005/presentationus/chiffres.html. (accessed 5/22/06).

digest: heritage preservation and destruction

Daniel, Lucy. (2006) "Landmarks lost in the rubble of war", *Financial Times.*

United Nations Educational, Scientific, and Cultural Organization, (UNESCO) World Heritage. Available at http://whc.unesco.org/. (accessed 6/1/06).

digest: environment

Goddard Institute for Space Studies, Carbon Dioxide Information Analysis Center (2006). Available at http://www.giss.nasa.gov/. (accessed 6/15/06).

International Energy Agency. (IEA) (2005) *CO2 Emissions from Fuel Combustion: 1971-2003.* Paris: IEA

Transboundary Freshwater Dispute Database. (2005) A project of the Oregon State University, Department of Geosciences.
Available at http://www.transboundarywaters.orst.edu/. (accessed 3/23/06).
World Values Survey, (1999-2004). Available at: http://www.worldvaluessurvey.com/. (accessed 3/23/06).
Yale Center for Environmental Law and Policy. (2005) Environmental Sustainability Index: *Benchmarking National Environmental Stewardship.*
Connecticut: Yale University.

digest: cultural participation

Bourdiieu, Pierre (1984). Distinction: A Social Critique of the Judgment of Taste. Harvard University Press, Cambridge.

Bourdieu, Pierre and Passeron, Jean-Claude (1977). Reproduction Education, Society and Culture. Sage, Beverly Hills, CA.

DiMaggio, Paul and Mukhtar, Toqir (2004). "Arts Participation as Cultural Capital in the United States, 1982-2002: Signs of Decline?" in Poetics Vol. 32 (pp. 169-194)

Environics Research Group, Ltd. Prepared for the Department of Canadian Heritage, "Arts & Heritage Participation Survey." (2000)

Lewis, J. and Miller, T. (2003). Critical Cultural Policy Studies: A reader. Oxford: Blackwell. United Nations Development Programme, Volunteering, Accessed http://et.undp.org/unv/un_volunteers.htm, 5/18/2006

UNESCO World Heritage Site, Scientific and Cultural Organizations, Accessed http://portal.unesco.org/en/ev.php-URL_ID=32734&URL_DO=DO_TOPIC&URL_SECTION=201.html, 5/19/2006

digest: sports & recreation

Goldblatt, David. (2004) *Football Yearbook: 2004/5.* London: Dorling Kindersley Ltd.

International Working Group on Women in Sports. (IWG) Available at http://www.canada2002.org/e/progress/index.htm. (accessed 5/18/06).

National Geographic Society. (2006) "Soccer United the World" Map.

ECONOMIC ASPECTS OF CULTURE

3.A ECONOMY

CULTURAL INDUSTRIES

1. UNESCO. (2006) available at http://portal.unesco.org/culture (accessed 7/13/06).

2.-3. Canadian Heritage. (2005) Argentina: Cultural Industries Sector Profile. Available at http://www.canadianheritage.gc.ca/progs/ac-ca/progs/rc-tr/progs/eccc-ttcc/market/index_e.cfm. (accessed 4/21/06).

Government of Western Australia. Department of Culture and Arts. (2003) Available at http://www.artswa.wa.gov.au/documents/2003VitalStats FactSheetsCh5.pdf. (accessed 4/22/06).

World Intellectual Property Organization. (2006) Available at http://www.wipo.int/about-wipo/en/en. (accessed 7/13/06).

Statistics Canada. (2006) Available at http://www40.statcan.ca/l01/cst01/gdps04a.htm. (accessed 4/22/06).

Ping, Y. (2005) "Creative industries to be developed." China Daily. Available at http://www.chinadaily.com.cn/english/doc/2005-12/05/content_500399.htm. (accessed 4/22/06).

Hong Kong Trade Development Council. (2002) "Creative industries in Hong Kong." Available at http://www.tdctrade.com/econforum/tdc/tdc020902.htm. (accessed 4/22/06).

New Zealand Institute of Economic Research. (2002). Creative Industries in New Zealand, as reported to the New Zealand Economic Development Agency. Available at http://www.nzte.govt.nz/common/files/nzier-mapping-ci.pdf. (accessed 4/22/06).

Singapore Government Ministry of Information, Communication, and the Arts. "Creative industries take center stage in November 2005." Available at http://www.mica.gov.sg/pressroom/press_0510051.html. (accessed 4/22/06).

South African Department of Arts & Culture. (1998) In Short: South African Cultural Industries. Available at http://www.dac.gov.za/reports/reports.htm. (accessed 4/22/06).

Bureau of Economic Analysis. http://www.bea.gov/bea/industry/gpotables/gpo_action.cfm?anon=101&table_id=12753&format_type=0. (accessed 4/26/06).

4. Eurostat Data Shop Network. Available at http://europa.eu.int/rapid/pressReleasesAction.do?reference=STAT/04/68&format=HTML&aged=1&language=EN&guiLanguage=en. (accessed 04/06/2006).

5. Fortune Global 500. Available at http://money.cnn.com/magazines/fortune/global500/industries/, (accessed 03/10/06).

Forbes Global 2000. Available at http://www.forbes.com/2005/03/30/05f2000land.html. (accessed 03/10/06).

GLOBAL ARTS MARKET

1. Art Basel. Available at http://www.artbasel.com/ca/bt/kh/. (accessed 4/26/06).

2. The Armory Show. (2005)

3. Art Cologne. (2005)

4. Sotheby's. (2000-2005) "Annual Reports." Available at http://www.shareholder.com/bid/EdgarSearch.cfm?keywords=%22annual+report%22 (accessed 4/26/06).

5.-12. Art Sales Index. (2005) Available at http://www.art-sales-index.com/system/ (accessed 4/26/06).

CULTURAL CONSUMPTION & EXPENDITURES

1.-2. United Nations. (2004) National Account Statistics.

3. US Department of Commerce. Bureau of Economic Analysis. Available at http://www.bea.gov/bea/dn/nipaweb/nipa_underlying/SelectTable.asp?Benchmark=P#S2 and http://www.bea.gov/bea/dn/nipaweb/SelectTable.asp?Selected=N#S3 (accessed 4/21/06).

4. National Endowment for the Arts (NEA). (2000) Available at http://www.nea.gov/pub/Notes/74.pdf (accessed 4/21/06)

5.-7. Hill Strategies Research Inc. "Consumer spending on culture in Canada, the provinces and 15 metropolitan areas 2003."

TRADE IN GOODS AND SERVICES

1.-4. UNESCO Institute for Statistics. International Flows of Selected Cultural Goods and Services, 1994-2003. Available at http://www.uis.unesco.org/template/pdf/cscl/IntlFlows_EN.pdf. (accessed 1/7/05).

5. Financial Times. (04/03/06) Special Report: Global Brands.

digest: culture and the economy

Adorno, Theodor W. and Max Horkheimer (1947) Dialektik der Aufklärung. Amsterdam: Querido.

Americans for the Arts, March 2005 "Creative Industries 2005: the Congressional Report" Washington, DC.

Hesmondhalgh, David and Pratt, Andy (2005). Cultural Industries and Cultural Policy. International Journal of Cultural Policy, Vol. 11., No. 1, 2005

Raboy, Marc., (et.al), (1994). Cultural Development and the Open Economy: A Democratic Issue and a Challenge to Public Policy. Canadian Journal of Communication [online], 19(3) Available at:www.cjc-online.ca/ (Accessed 6/27/06)

"How the BrandZ Top 100 Global Ranking was Created", Andy Farr, Millward Brown Optimor, Financial Times, Special Report: Global Brands, Monday April 3, 2006

"A Focal Point for Culture in the Future", UNESCO Division of Arts and Cultural Enterprise, Culture; Accessed on 6/3/2006, http://portal.unesco.org/culture/en/ev.php-URL ID=2461&URL DO=DO TOPIC&URL SECTION=201.html

3B.PROFESSIONS

ARTISTIC & CULTURAL PROFESSIONS

1. EUROSTAT Labour Force Survey. Available at http://epp.eurostat.cec.eu.int/cache/ITY_PUBLIC/3-26052004-BP/EN/3-26052004-BP-EN.HTML. (accessed 4/16/06).

2. International Labor Organization, Labor Statistics Database, Segregat Data. Available at http://laborsta.ilo.org/. (accessed 4/16/06).

3. Eurostat Data Shop Network. Available at http://europa.eu.int/rapid/pressReleasesAction.do?reference=STAT/04/68&format=HTML&aged=1&language=EN&guiLanguage=en. (accessed 4/16/2006).

4. U.S. Department of Labor. Bureau of Labor Statistics. Available at http://www.bls.gov/data/home.htm. (accessed 4/16/06).

5. Davies, R. and Lindley, R. (2003) "Artists in figures: a statistical portrait of cultural occupations." Arts Council England Research Report 31.

6. Eurostat Data Shop Network. Available at http://europa.eu.int/rapid/pressReleasesAction.do?reference=STAT/04/68&format=HTML&aged=1&language=EN&guiLanguage=en. (accessed 4/16/2006).

7.-8. United Nations Education, Scientific, and Cultural Organization (UNESCO) Institute for Statistics. (2002-03). Available at http://stats.uis.unesco.org/ReportFolders/reportfolders.aspx (4/16/06)

digest: cultural professions

Danish Ministry of Culture. (2002) "Multi-annual Accord on the Ministry of Culture's Study Programmes." Available at http://www.kum.dk/sw10006.asp. (accessed 5/26/06).

Davies, Rhys and Lindley, Robert. (2003) "Artists in figures: a statistical portrait of cultural occupations." Arts Council England Research Report 31.

European Commission. (2001) "Exploitation and development of the job potential in the cultural sector." Munich: MKW Wirtschaftsforschung GmbH.

Florida, Richard. (2003) "The Rise of the Creative Class: And How It's Transforming Work, Leisure, Community and Everyday." New York: Basic Books.

Florida, Richard (2005) "The Flight of the Creative Class: The New Global Competition for Talent." New York: Harper Collins Publishers, Inc.

Gottschall, Karin and Betzelt, Sigrid. (2001) "Self-Employment in Cultural Professions: Between De-Gendered Work and Re-Gendered Work and Life-Arrangements?", paper presented at the Gender Conference on "Changing Work and Life Patterns in Western Industrial Countries", WZB Berlin, Sept. 20-21, 2001. Available at www.zes.uni-bremen.de/~kgs/WZB9-01.doc. (accessed 5/25/06).

Milohnic, Aldo. 2005. "On 'Flexible' Employment in Culture." In N. Syob-Dokic (ed.), *The Emerging Creative Industries in Southeastern Europe*, Culturelink Joint Publications Series 8, pages 57-64. Zagreb: Institute for International Relations.

Statistics Canada. "Profile of the Culture Sector in Atlantic Canada." Available at http://www.apeca-acoa.gc.ca/e/library/reports/cultural/section2.shtml. (accessed 5/26/06).

3C. CORPORATIONS AND ORGANIZATIONS

TRANSNATIONAL CORPORATIONS-DISNEY

1a. Walt Disney Company website. Available at http://corporate.disney.go.com/index.html. (accessed 11/04/04).

1b. Walt Disney Company website. Annual Report 2005. Available at http://corporate.disney.go.com/investors/annual_reports/2005/index.html (accessed 6/28/06)

2. Wasko, J., Phillips, M., and Meehan, E.R. (2001) Dazzled by Disney?: the global Disney audiences project. London; New York: Leicester University Press.

3. Disney online. Available at http://corporate.disney.go.com/index.html. (accessed 6/28/06).

TRANSNATIONAL CORPORATIONS-OTHER MAJOR MEDIA CORPORATIONS

1. Third World Traveler. Available at http://www.thirdworldtraveler.com/Global_Media/Global_Media_book.html. (accessed 3/12/06).

2. News Corporation. Available at www.newscorp.com. (accessed 3/12/06).

3. The Nation. (2002) The Big Ten. Available at http://www.thenation.com/special/bigten.html (accessed 3/12/06).

Time Warner website. Available at http://www.timewarner.com/corp/ (accessed 3/12/06)

General Electric (GE) website. Available at http://www.ge.com/en/ (accessed 3/12/06)

Sony website. Available at http://www.sony.com/index.php?pref=noflash (accessed 3/12/06)

Vivendi website. Available at http://www.vivendi.com/ (accessed 3/12/06)

CULTURAL INGO'S & FOUNDATIONS

1.-3. The Union of International Associations. (UIA) (2005) Yearbook of International Organizations 2005-06. Vol. 5, Ed. 42. Munchen, Germany: K.G. Saur.

4.-6. Hartley, Cathy (ed) (2004). International Foundations Directory 2004. Ed. 13. London: Europa Publications Ltd.

7.-8. The Foundation Center. Available at http://fdncenter.org/. (accessed 3/12/06).

9. Aga Khan Foundation Network. Available at http://www.akdn.org/agency/akf.html. (accessed 1/22/06).

Calouste Gulbenkian Foundation. Available at http://www.gulbenkian.org.uk/main_f.htm. (accessed 1/22/06).

European Cultural Foundation. Available at http://www.eurocult.org/. (accessed 1/22/06).

Ford Foundation. Available at http://www.fordfound.org/. (accessed 1/22/06).

Prince Claus Fund. Available at http://www.princeclausfund.org/en/index.html. (accessed 1/22/06).

Sasakawa (Nippon) Foundation. Available at http://www.nippon-foundation.or.jp/eng/link/index.html. (accessed 1/22/06).

Soros Foundation Network. Available at http://www.soros.org/. (accessed 1/22/06).

digest: transnational cultural corporations

Active Opposition. (2003) *Media Consolidation and Corporate Power: An Interview with Walter Cronkite and Others.*

Chester, Jeffery. (2006) "US: The End of the Internet," *The Nation.*

Financial Times. (2006) "What sort of revolution? Among the Audience, A Survey of New Media."

Gonsalves, Antone. (2006) "US: Diverse Coalition Battles AOL's Email Tax." *TechWeb*

Hellweg, Eric. "US: The Net Effect of Neutrality," *Technology Review.*

Independent Music Companies Association. (IMCA) (2005) "Say YES to Creativity and NO to Concentration."

Johnson, Jo. (2000) "The United States of Television," *Financial Times.*

Khan, Mafruza. (2003) *Media Diversity at Risk*, Corporate Research Project.

Perlstein, Jeff. (2002) *Clear Channel: the Media Mammoth that Stole the Airwaves*, CorpWatch.

digest: cultural NGO's and foundations

Council of Europe. (2001) Culture & Civil Society: A Promising Relationship or a Missed Opportunity? Conference Report, November 9-10, 2001. Sofia, Bulgaria.

Fitzcarraldo Foundation. (2003) Cultural Cooperation in Europe: What role for Foundations? Report prepared for the Network of European Foundations for Innovative Cooperation. Available at http://www.fitzcarraldo.it/ricerca/pdf/CulturalCooperation_Final%20Report.pdf. (accessed 5/02/06).

Foundation Center. (2003) Arts Funding IV: Highlights of the Foundation Center's 2003 study. Available at fdncenter.org/gainknowledge/research/pdf/03arthl.pdf. (accessed 5/01/06).

SITES, EVENTS, + FLOWS

4.A GLOBAL SITES AND EVENTS

GLOBAL CITIES-LOS ANGELES

1. Los Angeles County Economic Development Corp. (LAEDC) (2005) L.A. Stats. Available at http://www.laedc.org/economicinformation/lastats/LAStats-2005.pdf. (accessed 4/12/06).

2. Los Angeles Almanac. Foreign Born Persons Residing in Los Angeles County - By Birthplace, 2000 Census. Available at http://www.laalmanac.com/immigration/im06.htm. (accessed 5/9/06).

3. Primedia Business Magazine & Media. (2001) "American Demographics," 23 (11): 26. Available via UCLA Library e-resources.

4. Los Angeles Almanac. Foreign Born Persons Residing in Los Angeles County - By Birthplace, 2000 Census. Available at http://www.laalmanac.com/immigration/im06.htm. (accessed 5/9/06).

5. Fortune. Available at http://money.cnn.com/magazines/fortune/fortune500/states/C.html (accessed 5/9/06).

GLOBAL CITIES-NEW YORK

1. New York City Official Tourism Website. Available at http://www.nycvisit.com/content/index.cfm?pagePkey=57. (accessed 5/11/06).

2. New York City Department of Planning. Population Division. Available at http://home.nyc.gov/html/dcp/html/census/popcur.shtml. (accessed 5/11/06).

3. US Census. (2003) Available at http://www.census.gov/acs/www/Products/Profiles/Single/2003/ACS/Tabular/160/16000US36510002.htm. (accessed 5/11/06).

4. Port Authority of New York and New Jersey. (2004) Available at http://www.panynj.gov/DoingBusinessWith/seaport/html/trade_statistics.html. (accessed 5/11/06).

5. Fortune. (2004) Available at http://money.cnn.com/magazines/fortune/. (accessed 5/11/06).

GLOBAL CITIES-LONDON

1. Office for National Statistics. Focus On London 2003. Available at http://www.statistics.gov.uk/statbase/product.asp?vlnk=10527 (accessed 5/3/06).
2. UK Census 2001.

3. Government Office for London.
Available at http://www.go-london.gov.uk/boroughinfo/. (accessed 5/8/06).

4. Forbes. (2006) Global 2000 List. Available at http://www.forbes.com/2006/03/29/06f2k_worlds-largest-public-companies_land.html. (accessed 5/8/06).

GLOBAL CITIES-HONG KONG AND MUMBAI

1. Government of Hong Kong Special Administration Region of the People's Republic of China. Demographic Statistics Section, Census and Statistics Department. (Inquiry telephone no. : 2716 8345)

2.-3. Hong Kong Special Administrative Region of The People's Republic of China - Government Information Centre. Available at http://www.censtatd.gov.hk/eng/hkstat/hkinf/transport_index.html. (accessed 5/11/06).

4. Asia-Pacific Economic Cooperation (APEC) Study Center. Hong Kong Statistics. Available at http://fbweb.cityu.edu.hk/hkapec/APEC-pages/APEC-Data-HongKong.htm. (accessed 5/11/06).

1. United Nations Department of Economic and Social Affairs/Population Division: World Urbanized Prospects: The 2003 Revision (P. 270) Available at http://www.un.org/esa/population/publications/wup2003/WUP2003Report.pdf. (accessed 5/16/06).

2.-4. Census of India. Available at http://www.censusindiamaps.net/page/Religion_WhizMap1/housemap.htm. (accessed 5/18/06).

5a.-5b. Government of India: Ministry of Finance. Available at http://finmin.nic.in/the_ministry/dept_eco_affairs/fipb/fipb_index.htm. (accessed 5/9/06).

SYMBOLIC SITES & SIGNIFICANT CITIES

Note: The map generated for this suite was created through the collaboration of project researchers

GLOBAL EVENTS

1. BBC News. Muslim Pilgrimage reaches climax. Available at http://news.bbc.co.uk/2/hi/middle_east/3446823.stm. (accessed 5/11/06).

CNN.com. Transcripts. Available at http://transcripts.cnn.com/TRANSCRIPTS/0504/05/lol.01.html. (accessed 5/11/06).

Deutsche Welle. Available at http://www.dw-world.de/dw/article/0,1564,1672843,00.html. (accessed 5/11/06).

Ministry of the Government of Nepal. Available at http://www.mope.gov.np/environment/pdf/state2004/world6.pdf. (accessed 5/11/06).

Wikipedia.com. Kumbh Mela. Available at http://en.wikipedia.org/wiki/Kumbh_Mela. (accessed 5/11/06).

2. Curiel, J. (2003) 'Music miles from nowhere Mali's Festival of the Desert is a truly tough ticket.' The San Francisco Chronicle, January 11. Available at http://www.sfgate.com/cgi-bin/article.cgi?file=/chronicle/archive/2003/01/11/DD160397.DTL. (accessed 5/8/06).

Edinburgh International Festival. (EIF) Available at http://www.eif.co.uk/. (accessed 5/8/06).

Edinburgh International Festival. (EIF) Annual Review 2004.
Available at http://www.eif.co.uk/pdfs/2004_ar.pdf. (accessed 5/8/06).

Festival au desert. Available at http://www.festival-au-desert.org/. (accessed 5/8/06).

Love Fest. (2006) Available at http://www.loveparadesf.org/. (accessed 5/8/06).

Love Parade. (2006) Available at http://www.2camels.com/destination11.php3. (accessed 5/8/06).

Love Parade. (2006) Available at http://www.loveparade.net/. (accessed 5/8/06).

Milwaukee's Summerfest. (2005) Summerfest 2005 "The World's Largest Music Festival" - Overview & Fact Sheet. Available at http://www.summerfest.com/media/newsrelease_detail.php?id=159. (accessed 5/8/06).

Montreal Jazz Festival. Available at http://www.montrealjazzfest.com/fijm2005/presse_en.asp. (accessed 5/11/06).

Salzburg Festival. Available at http://www.salzburgfestival.at/in_eckdaten_e.html. (accessed 5/8/06).

South by Southwest Music and Media Conference. (SXSW) Available at http://2006.sxsw.com/about/. (accessed 5/11/06)

South by Southwest Music and Media Conference. (SXSW) Sponsorship, Exhibition, Events, Marketing. Available at http://2006.sxsw.com/pdf/sxswmktgbroch06.pdf. (accessed 5/11/06)

3. Berlinale Talent Campus. Facts and Figures. Available at http://www.berlinale.de/en/das_festival/festivalprofil/berlinale_in_zahlen/index.html. (accessed 5/8/06).

Festival de Cannes. Figures and Statistics. Available at http://www.festival-cannes.com/organisation/chiffres_stats.php?langue=6002. (accessed 5/8/06).

La Biennale di Venezia. Available at http://www.labiennale.org/en/cinema/. (accessed 5/8/06).

Sundance Film Festival. Available at http://festival.sundance.org/2006/festival/press.aspx. (accessed 5/8/06).

Toronto International Film Festival Group.
Available at http://www.tiffg.ca/content/divisions/tiff.asp. (accessed 5/8/06).

Toronto International Film Festival Group. Available at http://www.tiffg.ca/content/aboutus/annualreport.asp. (accessed 5/8/06).

4. Frankfurt Book Fair. Facts and Figures. Available at http://www.book-fair.com/en/index.php?content=/en/presse_pr/zahlen_fakten/tlp.html. (accessed 5/11/06).

Frankfurt Book Fair. (2005) Facts and Figures. Available at http://www.book-fair.com/imperia/md/content/pdf/unternehmen/factsfigures/factsandfigures2005/facts_figures_korettura.pdf. (accessed 5/11/06).

Hong Kong Book Fair. Available at http://www.hkbookfair.com/previous/summary.htm. (accessed 5/11/06).

Kolkata Book Fair. Available at http://www.kolkatabookfaironline.com/highlights.htm. (accessed 5/11/06).

London Book Fair. Available at http://www.lbf-virtual.com/. (accessed 5/11/06).

5. Documenta. Available at http://www.documenta12.de/archiv/d11/data/english/index.html. (accessed 5/8/06).

6. Bureau International des Expositions. (BIE) Available at http://www.bie-paris.org/main/index.php?p=-100&m2=144. (accessed 5/8/06).

7. Burning Man. Available at http://afterburn.burningman.com/04/history.html. (accessed 4/11/06).

Burning Man. Available at http://www.burningman.com/whatisburningman/about_burningman/bm_timeline.html. (accessed 5/8/06).

digest: global cities

National Research Council. (2003). *Cities Transformed: Demographic Change and Its Implications in the Developing World.* Panel on Urban Population Dynamics. Washington, D.C.: National Academies Press.

Scott, A.J. (ed.) (2001). *Global City Regions: Trends, Theory, Policy.* Oxford: Oxford University Press.

UN-Habitat (2004). *The State of the World's Cities 2004/2005.* London: Earthscan.

digest: global sites and events

Bureau International des Expositions. (BIE) "Exhibitions Information." Available at http://www.bie-paris.org/main/index.php?p=-132&m2=292. (accessed 5/11/06).

CNN Transcript: "Pilgrims Wait in Line Hours to See Pope; Burial of Pope Steeped in Traditions...," aired April 5, 2005. Available at http://transcripts.cnn.com/TRANSCRIPTS/0504/05/lol.01.html. (accessed 5/2/06).

Documenta12. Available at http://www.documenta12.de/archiv/d11/data/english/index.html. (accessed 4/26/06).
Edinburgh Festival Fringe. Available at http://www.edfringe.com. (accessed 6/10/06).

International Festival and Events Association. (IFEA) "About IFEA." Available at http://www.ifea.com/about/. (accessed 5/22/06).

La Biennale di Venezia. Available at http://www.labiennale.org/en/index.html. (accessed 6/12/06).
United Nations Educational, Scientific, and Cultural Organization. (UNESCO) Cultural Diversity. Available at http://portal.unesco.org/culture/en/ev.php-URL_ID=2450&URL_DO=DO_TOPIC&URL_SECTION=201.html. (accessed 6/2/06).

Weinberg, Adam D. and Pratt Brown, Alice. (2006) "Whitney Biennial 2006: Foreword." Available at http://www.whitney.org/www/2006biennial/overview_forward.php. (accessed 6/1/06).

Wikipedia. "Kumbh Mela." Available at http://en.wikipedia.org/wiki/Kumbh_Mela. (accessed 5/25/06).

4.B COMMUNICATION & MEDIA

LANGUAGES

1a.-1b. Grimes, B.F. (2000) Ethnologue, Dallas, Texas: SIL International. 14th edition.

Union of International Associations. (2003) Yearbook of International Organizations: Guide to Civil Society Networks, 2002-2003. Ed. 39, Vol. 5 Munich: K.G. Saur

2. United Nations Educational, Scientific, and Cultural Organization (UNESCO) Translatorum. Available at http://databases.unesco.org/xtrans/stat/xTransStat.html. (accessed 11/4/05).

3. Nielsen Net Ratings and International Telecommunications Union. Available at http://www.internetworldstats.com/stats7.htm. (accessed 9/16/05).

4. Grimes, B.F. (2000) Ethnologue, Dallas, Texas: SIL International. 14th edition.

5. United Nations Development Program (UNDP). Human Development Report (HDR). Available at http://hdr.undp.org/reports/global/2005/pdf/HDR05_HDI.pdf. (accessed 9/16/05).

PRINT MEDIA

1. The World Association of Newspapers. (2005) "Worlds 100 Largest Newspapers." Available at http://www.wan-press.org/article2825.html?var_recherche=100+largest. (accessed 7/28/05).

2. "Global Advertising: Reach the World." (2005) Campaign 27, May 2005. London: Haymarket Business Publications Ltd.

International Herald Tribune. (IHT) (2004) "IHT Reader Survey 2002." Available at http://www.nytco.com/pdf/IHT-Media-Kit-2-2004.pdf. (accessed 7/28/05).

Economist, The. "2005 Annual Report." Available at http://www.economistgroup.com/pdf/Annual_report2005.pdf. (accessed 7/30/05).
New York Times Company. "2004 Annual Report." Available at http://www.nytco.com/pdf-reports/2004NYTannual.pdf. (accessed 7/30/05).

3. International Herald Tribune. (IHT) (2004) "IHT Reader Survey 2002." Available at http://www.nytco.com/pdf/IHT-Media-Kit-2-2004.pdf. (accessed 7/30/05).

BOOKS

1. Booksellers Association (BA) (2005) BA Reports Library. Available at http://www.booksellers.org.uk/ (accessed 1/27/06).

2a.-2b. Euromonitor. Available at http://www.euromonitor.com/mrm/default.asp (accessed 2/3/06).

3. Bokwer. "Global Books in Print Database." Available at http://www.globalbooksinprint.com/GlobalBooksInPrint/. (accessed 2/1/06).

Feldman, G. and Milliot, J. (2004) "Looking again at China." Publishers Weekly. Available at http://www.publishersweekly.com/article/CA485210.html?pubdate=12%2F6%2F2004&display=archive. (accessed 2/1/06).

Goethe-Institut. (2004) Available at http://www.goethe.de/kug/mui/buv/prj/prj/bbd/mrk/boe/en122071.htm. (accessed 2/1/06).

4.-5. Booksellers Association (BA) (2005) BA Reports Library. Available at http://www.booksellers.org.uk/industry/display_report.asp?id=422. (accessed 1/31/06).

Bertelsmann. (2004) "Annual Report 2004." Available at http://www.investis.com/reports/btg_ar_2004_en/report.php?type=1&zoom=1&page=13. (accessed 1/31/06).

Power Financial Corporation. http://www.powerfinancial.com/index.php?lang=eng&comp=pargesa&page=bertelsmann (accessed 1/31/06)

Bertelsmann. (2004) "Annual Report 2004." Available at http://www.investis.com/reports/btg_ar_2004_en/report.php?type=1&zoom=1&page=13. (accessed 1/31/06).

Ketupa.net. "Media Profiles: Pearson." Available at http://www.ketupa.net/bertelsmann1.htm. (accessed 1/31/06).

Pearson. "The Penguin Group: 2005 Performance." Available at http://www.pearson.com/about/peng/perform.htm. (accessed 1/31/06).

Pearson. (2004) "Annual Review and Financial Statements 2004." Available at http://www.pearson.com/investor/ar2004/pdfs/summary_report_2004.pdf. (accessed 1/31/06).

News Corporation. "Earnings release for the quarter and fiscal year ended June 30, 2005." Available at http://www.newscorp.com/investor/download/Usg4q05.pdf. (accessed 1/31/06).

Harper Collins. (2005) "Company Profile." Available at http://www.harpercollins.com/templates.asp?page=companyprofile. (accessed 1/31/06).

Simon & Schuster, Inc. "About S&S: Overview." Available at http://www.simonsays.com/content/feature.cfm?sid=33&feature_id=1625. (accessed 1/31/06).

Viacom. "March 2005 10K." Available at http://www.viacom.com/pdf/form10KMar2005.pdf. (accessed 1/31/06).

Time Warner. (2004) "Annual Review 2004." Available at ftp://ftp.timeinc.net/pub/corp/2004_Annual_Review.pdf. (accessed 1/31/06).

Yahoo Finance. (2006) "Time Warner Group Inc. Company Profile." Available at http://biz.yahoo.com/ic/103/103158.html. (accessed 1/31/06).

Euromonitor Report. (2003) "World Market for Books and Publishing." Available at http://www.gmid.euromonitor.com/Reports.aspx. (accessed 1/31/06)

Millot, Jim. (2005) "Top Five Pubs Take Half of Sales." Available at http://www.publishersweekly.com/article/CA527260.html?text=largest+publishers. (accessed 1/27/06).

MUSIC

1.-3. The International Federation of the Phonographic Industry. (IFPI) (2005) "Digital sales triple to 6% of industry retail revenues as global music market falls 1.9%." Available at http://www.ifpi.org/site-content/press/20051003.html. (accessed 2/2/06).

4.-6. The Recording Industry Association of America. (RIAA) "2004 Consumer Profile." Available at http://www.riaa.com/news/marketingdata/pdf/2004consumerprofile.pdf. (accessed 2/2/06).

MOVIES

1.-2. Mapsoftheworld.com. Available at http://www.mapsofworld.com/world-top-ten/world-top-ten-movie-ticket-sold-countries-map.html. (accessed 1/31/06).

Mapsoftheworld.com. Available at http://www.mapsofworld.com/world-top-ten/world-top-ten-countries-film-investment-map.html. (accessed 1/31/06).

3. xInforma Media Group. (2001) "Global Film Exhibition and Distribution" Available at http://rdsweb2.rdsinc.com/texis/rds/suite2?Session=444fb9460ITBL&isCached=y&ipCnt=0. (accessed 2/6/06).

4. Box Office Mojo. "2005 Studio Market Share." Available at http://www.boxofficemojo.com/studio/?view=company&view2=yearly&yr=2005&p=.htm. (accessed 1/31/06).

5a.-5c. Screen Digest. (2005) "International box office surges: China is the world's fastest growing theatrical market." Screen Digest Limited. Available at http://rdsweb2.rdsinc.com/texis/rds/suite2?Session=444fb9460ITBL&isCached=y&ipCnt=0. (accessed 2/10/06)

Screen Digest. (2004) "West Europe has half non-US B.O.: but the U.S. accounts for almost half the world box office total." Screen Digest Limited. Available at http://rdsweb2.rdsinc.com/texis/rds/suite2?Session=444fb9460ITBL&isCached=y&ipCnt=0. (accessed 2/4/06).

6. Screen Digest. (2005) "Top 50 entertainment companies: top 10 companies account for nearly half the top 50's turnover." Screen Digest Limited. Available at http://www.screendigest.com/reports/mini/2005/top_50/2005-07-01_f3-n/view.html. (accessed 3/4/06).

TV & RADIO

1. 2. CIA World Fact Book 2005. Available at http://www.cia.gov/cia/publications/factbook/fields/2015.html. (accessed 7/28/05)

3. H.K. Diocesan Audio-Visual Centre. "The Future of Radio Veritas." Available at http://www.hkdavc.com/yy/v2-yy-radio3.html. (accessed 7/28/05).

4. Mytton, Graham. CIBAR Annual Conference, London November 2004. "International Radio Continues to Depend on Shortwave." Available at http://www.shortwave.org/graham/depend%20on%20shortwave.pdf. (accessed 7/28/05).

5. Voice of America. Available at http://www.voanews.com/english/portal.cfm. (accessed 7/28/05).

BBC World Service. Available at http://www.bbc.co.uk/worldservice/. (accessed 7/28/05).

Deutsche Welle. Available at http://www.dw-world.de/. (accessed 7/28/05).

Radio Australia. Available at http://www.abc.net.au/ra/. (accessed 7/28/05).

Radio Canada International. Available at http://www.rcinet.ca/. (accessed 7/28/05).

Radio France Internationale. Available at http://www.rfi.fr/. (accessed 7/28/05).

6. BBC World Service. Available at http://www.bbc.co.uk/worldservice/. (accessed 7/28/05).

TV AND ONLINE NEWS

1. British Broadcasting Corporation (BBC) (2005) Annual Report 2004-2005, London: BBC.

2. British Broadcasting Corporation (BBC) (2005) Annual Report 2004-2005, London: BBC. Al Jazeera. Available at http://english.aljazeera.net/HomePage (accessed 1/23/06).

CNN. Available at CNN.com. (accessed 1/24/06).

Allied Media Corp. Available at http://www.allied-media.com/aljazeera/JAZdemog.html. (accessed 1/23/06).

3. Nielsen Net Ratings. (2005) Available at http://www.nielsen-netratings.com/pr/pr_050616.pdf. (accessed 1/24/06).

4. Journalism.org State of the Media Report Available at http://www.stateofthemedia.org/2005/chartland.asp?id=222&ct=line&dir=&sort=&col1_box=1&col2_box=1&col1_isPercent=0&col2_isPercent=0&col3_isPercent=0&col4_isPercent=99&col5_isPercent=99&col6_isPercent=99&col7_isPercent=99&col8_isPercent=99&col9_isPercent=99&col10_isPercent=99 (accessed 1/24/06).

British Broadcasting Corporation (BBC) (2005) Annual Report 2004-2005, London: BBC.

INTERNET

1. J-Wire. "Hot spot Wi-Fi Hotspot Directory." Available at http://www.jiwire.com/hotspot-hot-spot-directory-browse-by-country.htm. (accessed 1/31/06)

2. Organization for Economic Co-operation and Development. (2004) "Information and Communication Technology: OECD Broadband Statistics, December 2004." Available at http://www.oecd.org/document/60/0,2340,en_2825_495656_2496764_1_1_1_1,00.html. (accessed 1/31/06).

3a. Point Topic. (2005) "World Broadband Statistics Q1." Available at http://www.point-topic.com/home/freeforyou/default.asp. (accessed 1/31/06).

3b.-3c. Internet World Stats. "Internet Usage Statistics-The Big Picture." Available at http://www.internetworldstats.com/stats.htm. (accessed 1/31/06)

Internet World Stats. "Internet Usage Statistics-The Big Picture." Available at http://www.internetworldstats.com/stats.htm. (accessed 1/31/06)

4. CIA World Factbook 2005. Available at http://www.cia.gov/cia/publications/factbook/rankorder/2153rank.html. (accessed 1/31/06).

CIA World Factbook 2005. Available at http://www.cia.gov/cia/publications/factbook/rankorder/2184rank.html (accessed 1/31/06).

5a-5b. Nielson Net Ratings. Available at http://www.nielsen-netratings.com/. (accessed 1/15/06).

Internet Corporation for Assigned Names and Numbers (ICANN). Available at www.icann.org (accessed 1/15/066).

6. Google.com. Available at http://www.google.com/corporate/history.html. (accessed 1/19/06).

BLOGS

1. The Blog Herald. Available at http://www.blogherald.com/2005/07/19/blog-count-for-july-70-million-blogs/. (accessed 1/19/06).

2.-4. Perseus. (2005) "The Blogging Geyser." Available at http://www.perseus.com/blogsurvey/geyser.html. (accessed 1/19/06).

TELEPHONES

1. CIA World Factbook. Available at http://www.cia.gov/cia/publications/factbook/

fields/2150.html. (accessed 1/31/06).

2a.-3. International Telecommunications Union. Yearbook of Statistics 2000.

4. PriMetrica, Inc. (2004) Telegeography Research.
Available at www.telegeography.com. (accessed 1/31/06)

digest: languages

Bernard, H. R. (1996) "Language Preservation and Publishing", in Hornberger, N.H., *Indigenous Literacies in the Americas: Language Planning from the Bottom up*. Berlin: Mouton de Gruyter, 139-156.

Crystal, D. (2001) *The Cambridge Encyclopedia of the English Language*. Cambridge: Cambridge University Press.

Ethnologue. "The Languages of the World." Available at http://www.ethnologue.com/. (accessed 5/2/06).

Leclerc, J. (2003) "*Index par politiques linguistiques*", in *L'aménagement linguistique dans le monde*, Québec, TLFQ, Laval University. Available at http://www.tlfq.ulaval.ca/axl/monde/index_politique-lng.htm.
(accessed 5/12/06).

digest: print media

AME Info FX, LLC. (2005) "What is the future of Middle East publishing?" Middle East Company News Wire, 17 January.

Core, Erin. (2003) "Crossing into cross-media: printers looking to expand and retain their clientele are learning to manage and reformat content for a variety of media beyond the printed page", *Graphic Arts Monthly* 75.4, 46(3).

Deutsche Presse-Agentur. (2005) "Japanese newspapers cling to power against Internet", *Deutsche Presse-Agentur*, Finance, 6 July.

Europe Information Service. (2005) "Publishing Commission opens consultation on digital challenges", *European Report*, No. 2990, 21 September.

HT Media Ltd, Assam Tribune. (2005) "Print Media Steadily Fighting Back", Provided Through HT Syndication, Guwahati, India, *Hindustan Times*, 17 July 17.

RBC Network Corp. (2005) "Russian print media market expanding and improving", RosBusiness Consulting Database, 4 July.

Sunday Business Group. (2003) "More bad news as German papers slide into the red", *The Business*, 26 January.

United Nations Educational, Scientific, and Cultural Organization (UNESCO) Sector for Culture, Institute for Statistics. (2005) International Flows of Selected Cultural Goods and Services, 1994-2003. Defining and capturing the flows of global cultural trade.
The World Association of Newspaper's Annual Survey of World Press Trends. (2005) Available at www.wan-press.org/article7321.html. (accessed 6/10/06).

digest: books

Bakkum, Beth. (2006) "'Pre-owned' books gain popularity (used books sales and forecast) (Brief Article)," *The Writer*, 9 March.

"Book ad spending up (Brief Article)." *Publishers Weekly* 253.10, March 6, 2006(a), 15(1).

"English-Speaking Countries Published 375,000 New Books Worldwide in 2004." (2005) *Bowkers*, 12 October.

Goff, Peter. (2006) "A New Chapter for Literature", *South China Morning Post*, 8 February.

"Piracy losses top $600 million (International Intellectual Property Alliance) (Brief Article)," *Publishers Weekly*, 253.8, Feb 20, 2006(b), 3(2).

United Nations Educational, Scientific, and Cultural Organization (UNESCO) Sector for Culture. (2005) International Flows of Selected Cultural Goods and Services, 1994-2003. Defining and capturing the flows of global cultural trade. Montreal: UNESCO Institute for Statistics. Available at http://www.uis.unesco.org/template/pdf/cscl/IntlFlows_EN.pdf. (accessed 11/5/05).

"US book sales hit $25.1b (Brief article)," *Publishers Weekly*, 253.11, March 13, 2006(c), 4(1).

digest: music and movies

BBC Worldservice. "Global Music Machine." Available at www.bbc.co.uk/worldservice. (accessed 4/28/06).

Global Information, Inc. (2006) "Quality to Drive Movie Industry Rebound." January Press Release of "Global Film: Exhibition & Distribution (8th Edition)" published by Informa Telecoms & Media. Available at www.the-infoshop.com/press/itm33329_en.shtml. (accessed 4/29/06).

International Federation of Phonogram and Videogram Producers. (IFPI) "Global Top 10 Albums of 2005." Available at www.ifpi.com. (accessed 5/2/06).

International Federation of Phonogram and Videogram Producers. (IFPI) "Recording Industry in Numbers, 2005" Available at www.ifpi.com. (accessed 4/26/06).
McLaughlin, Abraham. (2005) "Africans, Camera, Action: 'Nollywood' catches world's eye.", *The Christian Science Monitor*, 20 December 20. Available at www.csmonitor.com. (accessed 4/28/06).

Ruigrok, Inge. (2006) "Under the Spell of Nollywood." *The Power of Culture*, Current Affairs. Available at www.krachtvanvulture.nl/uk/current/2006/february/nollywood.html. (accessed 4/28/06).

Scott, A. (2005) On Hollywood. Princeton: Princeton University Press.

digest: tv & radio

Santana, Kenny. (2003) "MTV Goes to Asia", *Yale Global*, 12 August. Available at http://www.globalpolicy.org/globaliz/cultural/2003/0812mtv.htm. (accessed 2/12/06).

digest: tv and online news

Steven Livingston, Clarifying the CNN Effect: An Examination of Media Effects According to Type of Military Intervention. (Harvard University Kennedy School of Government Joan Shorenstein Center for Press and Politics, 1997).

digest: telephone, the internet and blogs

Hempel, Jessi and Lehman, Paula. (2005) "The MySpace Generation: They live online. They buy online. They play online. Their power is growing." *Business Week Online*, 12 December 12. Available at http://businessweek.com/print/magazine/content/05_50/b3963001.htm?chan=gl. (accessed 5/23/06).

Internet World Stats. "World Internet Usage Statistics and Population Stats." Available at http://www.Internetworldstats.com/stats.htm. (accessed 5/26/06).

Kluth, Andreas. (2006) "A Survey of New Media", *The Economist*, April 22-28, 3-20.

Mills, Elinor. (2006) "Google to Censor China Web Searches.", CNET News.com, 24 January. Available at http://news.com.com/Google+to+censor+China+Web+searches/2100-1028_3-6030784.html. (accessed 5/26/06).

Mueller, Katja. (2006) "World Broadband Statistics: Q2005." Point Topic Ltd., London.

O'Brien, Kevin J. (2006) "Europeans Weigh Plan on Google Challenge", *International Herald Tribune*, 18 January.

Shah, Anup. "Poverty Facts and Statistics." Available at http://www.globalissues.org/TradeRelated/Facts.asp. (accessed 5/26/06).

Technorati.com. "About Technorati." Available at http://www.technorati.com/about/. (accessed 5/26/06).

4.C MOVEMENTS AND COMMUNITIES

MIGRATION

1a.-1c. International Organization for Migration. (2005) World Migration 2005 Report. Available at http://www.iom.int//DOCUMENTS/PUBLICATION/wmr_sec03.pdf. (accessed 8/30/05).

2.-4. International Organization for Migration. 2005 International Migration Facts and Figures. Available at http://www.iom.int/en/pdf%5Ffiles/wmr2005%5Fpresskit/wmr%5Ffacts%5Fand%5Ffigures/wmr%5Ffacts%5Fand%5Ffigures.pdf. (accessed 8/30/05).

International Organization for Migration. World Migration 2005 Report. Available at http://www.iom.int//DOCUMENTS/PUBLICATION/wmr_sec03.pdf. (accessed 8/30/05).

5. Systeme d'Observation Permanente des Migrations (SOPEMI) (2001) "Trends in International Migration.

U.S. Immigration and Naturalization Service. (2000) Statistical Yearbook of the Immigration and Naturalization Service. U.S. Government Printing Office. Washington, D.C.

6. - 7. United Nations. "World Economic & Social Survey 2004." Available at http://www.un.org/esa/policy/wess/index.html. (accessed 8/30/05).

8. Mosisa, A. T., "The Role of Foreign-born Workers in the US Economy," Monthly Labor Review, vol.125,no.5. Available at http://www.bls.gov/opub/mlr/2002/05/art1full.pdf. (accessed 8/30/05).

9. International Organization for Migration. World Migration 2005 Report. Available at http://www.iom.int//DOCUMENTS/PUBLICATION/wmr_sec03.pdf. (accessed 8/30/05).

10.-12. International Organization for Migration. (2004) "Development Dimensions of Remittances." Available at http://www.iom.int/documents/publication/en/remittances%5Fdevelopment%5Fdimensions.pdf. (accessed 8/30/05).

REFUGEES & ASYLUM SEEKERS

1. US Committee for Refugees and Immigrants. Available at http://www.refugees.org/. (accessed 2/8/06).

UN Refugee Agency. "2004 Global Refugee Trends." http://www.unhcr.ch/cgi-bin/texis/vtx/statistics/opendoc.pdf?tbl=STATISTICS&id=42b283744. (accessed 2/8/06).

2.-3. Internal Displacement Monitoring Centre. (2004) Global Overview Report. Available at http://www.internal-displacement.org/. (accessed 2/8/06).

US Committee for Refugees and Immigrants. Available at http://www.refugees.org/. (accessed 2/8/06).

TOURISM

1.-5. World Tourism Organization. "Tourism Highlights Edition 2005." Available at http://www.world-tourism.org/facts/menu.html. (accessed 2/10/06).

World Tourism Organization. "Tourism Highlights Edition 2004." Available at http://www.world-tourism.org/facts/menu.html. (accessed 2/10/06).

6. World Travel & Tourism Council. (2005) "2005 World Travel & Economic Research" Available at http://www.wttc.org/2005tsa/pdf/World.pdf. (accessed 2/10/06).

7. World Tourism Organization. "Tourism Highlights Edition 2005." Available at http://www.world-tourism.org/facts/menu.html. (accessed 2/10/06).

8.-9. World Tourism Organization. "Tourism Highlights Edition 2004." Available at http://www.world-tourism.org/facts/menu.html. (accessed 2/10/06).

World Tourism Organization. (2005) "Post-Tsunami Re-Assessment" Available at http://www.world-tourism.org/tsunami/eng.html. (accessed 2/10/06).

TRANSNATIONAL COMMUNITIES

1. United States Committee for Refugees & Immigrants. (2005) World Refugee Survey.

2.-3. Hassanpour, A. and Mojab, S. (2004) Encyclopedia of diasporas: immigrant and refugee cultures around the world. New York: Kluwer Academic/Plenum. Volume 1 (214).

Kurdish Human Rights Project. Available at www.khrp.org (accessed 10/11/05)

4. UNDP Roma Website. (2002). "Avoiding the Dependency Trap." (pages 20-29) Available at http://roma.undp.sk/. (accessed 2/25/06).

5. Department for Jewish Zionist Education. Available at http://www.jafi.org.il/education/100/concepts/demography/demtables.html. (accessed 2/25/06).

6. Philippine Overseas Employment Administration. Available at http://www.poea.gov.ph/docs/2005%20Jan_Jun%20deployment.xls. (accessed 10/11/05).

TRANSNATIONAL SOCIAL MOVEMENTS

1. Pew Research Trust. (2002) Pew Global Attitudes Project. Available at http://pewglobal.org/reports/display.php?ReportID=165. (accessed 10/11/05).

2. World Social Forum. Available at http://www.forumsocialmundial.org.br/dinamic.php?pagina=memoria_numeros_ing. (accessed 10/11/05).

World Social Forum. Available at http://www.forumsocialmundial.org.br/noticias_01.php?cd_news=1709&cd_language=2. (accessed 10/11/05).

Anheier, H.K., Glasius, M. and Kaldor, M. (2006) Global Civil Society 2005/6, London: Sage Publications.

Anheier, H.K., Glasius, M. and Kaldor, M. (2006) Global Civil Society 2005/6, London: Sage Publications.

3.-5. The Pew Research Center for the People and the Press. (2003) Pew Global Attitudes Project, "Views of a Changing World." Available at http://people-press.org/reports/display.php3?ReportID=185. (accessed 10/22/05).

6.-7. Anheier, H.K., Glasius, M. and Kaldor, M. (2006) Global Civil Society 2005/6, London: Sage Publications.

8. BBC News. (1999) Available at http://news.bbc.co.uk/1/hi/uk/370060.stm. (accessed 10/20/05); People's Global Action Network. Available at http://pga.org. (accessed 10/20/05); CNN. (1999) Available at http://www.cnn.com/US/9906/19/g8.protest.01/. (accessed 10/20/05)

Global Action Days. Available at http://www.bak.spc.org/j18/ (accessed 10/20/05)

9. Wikipedia. "February 13, 2003 Anti-war protest." Available at http://en.wikipedia.org/wiki/February_15%2C_2003_global_anti-war_protest#Full_list. (accessed 10/24/05)

wikipedia sites the Associated Press, CNN, Znet, and the Globe and Mail as its sources for these numbers

10. Anheier, H.K., Glasius, M. and Kaldor, M. (2003) Global Civil Society 2003, New York: Oxford University Press.

11. The Pew Research Center for the People and the Press. (2003) Pew Global Attitudes Project, "Views of a Changing World." Available at http://people-press.org/reports/display.php3?ReportID=185. (accessed 10/20/05).

12. Global Green Party. Available at http://www.globalgreens.info/. (accessed 10/25/05).

13. Eden, Sally (2004). "Global Monitor: Greenpeace," New Political Economy, Vol. 9, No. 4, December 2004: pp.598

Anheier, H.K., Glasius, M. and Kaldor, M. (2006) Global Civil Society 2005/6, London: Sage Publications.

Anheier, H.K., Glasius, M. and Kaldor, M. (2005) Global Civil Society 2004/5, London: Sage Publications.

Anheier, H.K., Glasius, M. and Kaldor, M. (2003) Global Civil Society 2003, New York: Oxford University Press.

Anheier, H.K., Glasius, M. and Kaldor, M. (2002) Global Civil Society 2002, New York: Oxford University Press.

Anheier, H.K., Glasius, M. and Kaldor, M. (2001) Global Civil Society 2001, New York: Oxford University Press.

14. Transparency International. (2004) Annual Report. Available at http://www.transparency.org/about_ti/annual_rep/ar_2004/TI%20Annual%20Report%202004.pdf. (accessed 11/14/05).

Transparency International. (2003) Annual Report. Available at http://www.transparency.org/about_ti/annual_rep/ar_2003/annual_report_2003.pdf. (accessed 11/14/05).

Transparency International. (2002) Annual Report. Available at http://www.transparency.org/about_ti/annual_rep/ar_2002/tiar2002.pdf. (accessed 11/14/05).

Transparency International. (2001) Annual Report. Available at http://www.transparency.org/about_ti/annual_rep/ar_2001/annual_report2001.pdf. (accessed 11/14/05).

Transparency International. (2000) Annual Report. Available at http://www.transparency.org/about_ti/annual_rep/ar_2000/ti2000.pdf. (accessed 11/14/05).

Transparency International. (1999) Annual Report. Available at http://www.transparency.org/about_ti/annual_rep/ar_99/pages/contents.htm. (accessed 11/14/05).

15. International Committee for the Red Cross. (2004) Annual Report. Available at http://www.icrc.org/Web/Eng/siteeng0.nsf/htmlall/6CYL6Z/$FILE/icrc_ar_04_operations.pdf?OpenElement. (accessed 11/15/05).

International Committee for the Red Cross. (2002) Annual Report. Available at http://www.icrc.org/Web/Eng/siteeng0.nsf/htmlall/5NFC9B/$FILE/icrc_ar_02_part2.pdf?OpenElement. (accessed 11/15/05).

International Committee for the Red Cross. (2000) Annual Report. Available at http://www.icrc.org/Web/eng/siteeng0.nsf/htmlall/section_annual_report_2000/$File/AN2000_Operational_Support.pdf. (accessed 11/15/05).

International Committee for the Red Cross. (1995) Annual Report. Available at http://www.icrc.org/Web/Eng/siteeng0.nsf/htmlall/section_annual_report_1995?OpenDocument. (accessed 11/15/05).

TRANSPORTATION-AIRPORTS

1.-2. Airports Council International. Available at http://www.airports.org. (accessed 11/23/05).

3. PhocusWright Inc. via IATA

4.-5. IATA, On-Flight Origin-Destination Statistics (ODS)

World Air Transport Statistics. (WATS) (2004) Regional Flow Statistics.

digest: travel

Asian Development Bank. (2005a) "Damage & Needs Assessment of Maldives" Available at http://www.adb.org/Documents/Reports/Tsunami/joint-needs-annex8.pdf. (accessed 4/22/06).

Asian Development Bank. (2005b) "Damage & Needs Assessment of Sri Lanka." Available at http://www.adb.org/Documents/Reports/Tsunami/sri-lanka-annex14.pdf. (accessed 4/26/06).

Electronic Data Systems Corporation. (2006) "Transportation: The Transportation Top 10 Trends. What Trends are Affecting the Travel Industry in 2006." Available at http://www.eds.com/industries/transportation/trends.aspx. (accessed 4/28/06).

Institute of International Exchange. (2005a) "Study Abroad: Leading destinations." Available at http://opendoors.iienetwork.org/?p=69703. (accessed 1/24/06).

Institute of International Exchange. (2005b) "Leading Places of Origin." Available at http://opendoors.iienetwork.org/?p=69691. (accessed 1/24/06).

The International Ecotourism Society. (2000) "Ecotourism Statistical Fact Sheet."

Plunkett Research, Ltd. (2005/6) "Overview of Plunkett's Travel, Airline, Hotel & Tourism Industry coverage." Available at http://www.plunkettresearch.com/Industries/TravelAirlineHotelTourism/tabid/213/Default.aspx. (accessed 4/26/06).

United Nations Educational, Scientific, and Cultural Organization (UNESCO) Institute for Statistics. (2005) "Education- Foreign Students." Available at http://www.uis.unesco.org/ev.php?URL_ID=5187&URL_DO=DO_TOPIC&URL_SECTION=201. (accessed 4/20/06).

World Tourism Organization. (2004) "Tourism Highlights, 2004 Edition."

World Tourism Organization. (2005) "Tourism Highlights, 2005 Edition."

World Travel and Tourism Council. (2006) "World Travel and Tourism Climbing to New Heights."

Xinhua News Agency. (2006) "International tourism sets new record in 2005", in Xinhua General News Service, World News, 20 April.

digest: migration

Baumann, Martin. (2000) "Diaspora: Genealogies of Semantics and Transcultural Comparison." 47(3): 313-337.

Clifford, James. (1994) "Diaspora in Further Inflections: Towards Ethnographies of the Future", Cultural Anthropology, 9(3): 302-338.

Huntington, Samuel. (2004) How are We? The Challenges to America's National Identity. New York: Simon and Schuster.

International Organization for Migration. (IOM) (2005) "International Migration: Facts & Figures." Available at http://www.iom.int/en/PDF_Files/wmr2005_presskit/wmr_facts_and_figures/WMR_Facts_and_Figures.pdf. (accessed 6/1/06).

digest: transnational movements

Ghimire, Kléber B. (2005) "The Contemporary Global Social Movements: Emergent Proposals, Connectivity and Development Implications." No.19, Civil Society and Social Movements Programme, New York: United Nations Research Institute for Social Development.

Keck, M.E. and Sikkink, K. (1999) Transnational Advocacy Networks in International and Regional Politics. New York: United Nations Educational, Scientific, and Cultural Organization (UNESCO).

Smith, J. and Wiest, D. (2005) "The Uneven Geography of Global Civil Society: National and Global Influences on Transnational Association", Social Forces, 84(2): 621-652.

** The Danish cartoon map was adapted from the original version found on Wikipedia.com, whereby the creator drew upon articles from over 20 different news sources to assess the magnitude and spread of protests, and the subsequent violence that ensued.

POLITICAL SYSTEMS + CULTURE

5.A REGULATORY FRAMEWORKS

INTERNATIONAL STANDARDS

1.-4. International Organization for Standardization. (ISO) Annual Reports. Available at http://www.iso.org/iso/en/aboutiso/annualreports/index.html. (accessed 4/20/06).
International Organization for Standardization. (ISO) ISO in figures for the year 2005. Available at http://www.iso.org/iso/en/aboutiso/isoinfigures/archives/January2006.pdf. (accessed 4/20/06).

5a.-6d. International Organization for Standardization. (ISO) The ISO Survey 2004. Available at http://www.iso.org/iso/en/prodsservices/otherpubs/pdf/survey2004.pdf. (accessed 1/22/06).

7. International ISBN Agency. Available at http://www.isbn-international.org/en/agencies.html. (accessed 4/12/06).

INTERNATIONAL REGULATORY FRAMEWORKS

1.-7. United Nations Educational, Scientific, and Cultural Organization. (UNESCO) Africa. Available at http://portal.unesco.org/en/ev.php-URL_ID=23044&URL_DO=DO_TOPIC&URL_SECTION=201.html. (accessed 4/25/06).

digest: global standards

Abbot, K.W. and D. Snidai, 2001. 'International "standards" and international governance', Journal of European Public Policy, 8, 345-70.

Aoki, R., Prusa, T.J., 1993. International standards for intellectual property protection and R&D incentives. Journal of International Economics 35, 251-273.

Garver, Roger C. and Pagliarulo, Michael A. What Are the ISO Series Standards? Industrial Engineering 25:14-15 Sep '93

International Organization for Standardization.
Available at: Http://www.iso.org/iso/en/ISOOnline.Frontpage (Accessed 6/27/06)

Marquardt, Donald. ISO 9000: A Universal Standard of Quality.
Management Review 81:50-52 Jan '92.

Meyer, John W., Boli John, Thomas George M. and Ramirez, Francisco O. (1997). 'World Society and the Nation-State', American Journal of Sociology, 103(1) p.144-81.

digest: regulatory frameworks

United Nations Educational, Scientific, and Cultural Organization. (UNESCO) "Convention on the Protection and Promotion of the Diversity of Cultural Expressions." Complete text available at: http://portal.unesco.org/culture/en/ev.php-URL_ID=29388&URL_DO=DO_TOPIC&URL_SECTION=201.html (accessed 6/27/06)

5.B POLICY

CULTURAL POLICY & DIPLOMACY ORGANIZATIONS

1. United Nations Educational, Scientific, and Cultural Organization. (UNESCO) Global Alliance for Cultural Diversity Partners. Available at http://www.unesco.org/culture/pga/index.php?fnc=consult&lng=en_GB®ion=ALL. (accessed 4/26/06).

2. International Federation of Arts Councils and Culture Agencies. (IFACCA) Current members. Available at http://www.ifacca.org/ifacca2/en/about/page04_CurrentMembers.asp. (accessed 4/28/06).

3. Creative Exchange. Available at http://www8.rapidhost.co.uk:591/creativeex/ro/html/vrc/FMPro?-DB=web_international&-Format=internatsearchbycountry.html&-lay=SearchCountry&-View. (accessed 4/28/06).

4. Alliance Francaise. (AF) Available at http://www.alliancefr.org/. (accessed 4/28/06).

Instituto Cervantes. "Spanish, a language for dialog." Available at http://www.cervantes.es/docs/guias/GuialCIngles.pdf. (accessed 4/28/06).

Italian Cultural Institute in Washington. Available at http://www.iicwashington.esteri.it/IIC_Washington. (accessed 4/28/06).

Goethe-Institut. Goethe Instituts Worldwide: Countries. Available at http://www.goethe.de/ins/wwt/sta/enindex.htm. (accessed 4/28/06).

Google Translator. Available at http://translate.google.com/translate?hl=en&sl=fr&u=http://www.mfe.org/&prev=/search%3Fq%3Dmaisons%2Bfrancaise%26hl%3Den%26lr%3D%26rls%3DSUNA,SUNA:2005-51,SUNA:en. (accessed 4/28/06).

5. British Council. Available at http://www.britishcouncil.org/home. (accessed 4/28/06).

digest: cultural diplomacy; cultural observatories

British Council (2006) Available at www.britishcouncil.org (Accessed 6/23/06)

Goethe Institute (2006), Available at www.goethe-institute.org (Accessed 6/23/06).

INCP (2002), "New and Emerging issues: Concept of Interculturality and the Creation of Cultural Observatories, "Available at http://incp-ripc.org/meetings/2002/newissues_e.shtml (Accessed on 6/23/06).

International Federation of Arts Councils and Culture Agencies (2006), Available at www.ifacca.org (accessed 6/23/06).

Schuster, M.J. (2002), Informing Cultural Policy: the Research and Information Infrastructure. Rutgers University.

UNESCO (2006), "The Global Alliance for Cultural Diversity," Available at: http://portal.unesco.org/culture/en/ev.php-URL_ID-24478&URL_DO=DO_TOPIC&URL_SECTION=201.html (Accessed 6/23/06)

5C. CONFLICT AND COOPERATION

CURRENT CONFLICTS & TENSION LINES

1.-5. Marshall, M. and Gurr, T. (2005) Peace and Conflict 2005. Center for International Development and Conflict Management (CIDCM), University of Maryland, College Park, MD, USA. Available at http://www.cidcm.umd.edu/inscr/PC05print.pdf. (accessed 4/28/06).

6.-8. International Peace Research Institute. (PRIO) Armed Conflict Dataset. (Version 3-2005) Monadic dataset. Available at http://www.prio.no/cscw/armedconflict. (accessed 4/28/06).

9.-10. Monty, M. G. Center for Systemic Peace. Available at http://members.aol.com/cspmgm/warlist.htm. (accessed 2/22/06).

TERRORISM

1a.-6. Terrorism Knowledge Base. Available at www.tkb.org. (accessed 3/14/06).

CONFLICT RESOLUTION & UN PEACEKEEPING

1. Heidelberg Institute on International Conflict Research. Available at http://www.hiik.de/en/index_e.htm. (accessed 3/3/06).

2. Union of International Associations. "Yearbook of International Organizations, 2002-2003." pages 214-222.

3.-4. Stockholm International Peace Research Institute. (SIPRI) (2005) SIPRI Yearbook 2005. Oxford University Press, page 140.

Stockholm International Peace Research Institute. (SIPRI) (2005) SIPRI Yearbook 2005. Oxford University Press, page 169-181.

5. The Carter Center. Annual Report 2002-2003. Available at http://www.cartercenter.org/documents/1625.pdf. (accessed 3/6/06).

The Carter Center. Annual Report 2003-2004. Available at http://www.cartercenter.org/documents/2087.pdf. (accessed 3/6/06).

The Centre for Conflict Resolution. Available at http://ccrweb.ccr.uct.ac.za/index.php?id=4. (accessed 5/7/06).

The Centre for Conflict Resolution. 2003-2004 Annual Report. Available at http://ccrweb.ccr.uct.ac.za/fileadmin/template/ccr/pdf/CCAR_230305.pdf. (accessed 5/7/06).

Saferworld. Annual Report 2002-2003. Available at http://www.saferworld.org.uk/images/pubdocs/Ann%20rpt%2002-03.pdf. (accessed 5/7/06).

Saferworld. Annual Report 2003-2004. Available at http://www.saferworld.org.uk/images/pubdocs/Annual%20report%2003-04.pdf. (accessed 5/7/06).

6. U.S. Agency of International Development. "Celebrating 50 years of food for peace." Available at http://www.usaid.gov/our_work/humanitarian_assistance/ffp/50th/FFP_50thAv_Brochure.pdf. (accessed 5/8/06).

U.S. Agency of International Development. U.S. Oversees Loans and Grants. Available at http://qesdb.usaid.gov/cgi-bin/broker.exe?_program=gbkprogs.program_list.sas&_service=default&unit=N. (accessed 5/8/06).

7.-9. United Nations Peacekeeping Operations. Available at http://www.un.org/Depts/dpko/dpko/bnote.htm. (accessed 5/8/06).

United Nations. "Monthly summary of contributors of military and civilian police personnel." Available at http://www.un.org/Depts/dpko/dpko/contributors/. (accessed 5/8/06).

United Nations. "Peacekeeping 2004 in a snap shot." Available at http://www.un.org/Depts/dpko/dpko/pub/year_review04/snap.pdf. (accessed 5/8/06).

United Nations Peace Operations. Year in Review 2004. Available at http://www.un.org/Depts/dpko/dpko/pub/year_review04/. (accessed 5/8/06).

HUMAN RIGHTS

1. Amnesty International Report. (2005) Africa. Available at http://web.amnesty.org/report2005/2af-index-eng. (accessed 5/5/06).

Amnesty International Report. (2005) Americas. Available at http://web.amnesty.org/report2005/2am-index-eng. (accessed 5/5/06).

Amnesty International Report. (2005) Europe and Central Asia. Available at http://web.amnesty.org/report2005/2eu-index-eng. (accessed 5/5/06).

Amnesty International Report. (2005) Asia and the Pacific. Available at http://web.amnesty.org/report2005/2as-index-eng. (accessed 5/5/06).

Amnesty International Report. (2005) Middle East and North Africa. Available at http://web.amnesty.org/report2005/2md-index-eng. (accessed 5/5/06).

2.-7. Cingranelli, D. L. and Richards, D. L. The Cingranelli-Richards (CIRI) Human Rights Dataset. Available at http://www.humanrightsdata.org. (accessed 5/5/06).

8a.-8b. One World Partners. Global Partner Database. Available at http://www.oneworld.net/section/partners. (accessed 5/5/06).

ARMS

1. Stockholm International Peace Research Institute. (SIPRI) (2005) SIPRI Yearbook 2005. Available at http://www.sipri.org/contents/milap/milex/aprod/top100/SIPRI_TOP100.pdf. (accessed 5/5/06).

2.-3. Stockholm International Peace Research Institute. (SIPRI) (2005) SIPRI Yearbook 2005. Oxford University Press, page 392.

Stockholm International Peace Research Institute. (SIPRI) (2005) SIPRI Yearbook 2005. Available at http://yearbook2005.sipri.org/. (accessed 5/5/06).

4. Stockholm International Peace Research Institute. (SIPRI) The 15 Major Spenders in 2004. Available at http://www.sipri.org/contents/milap/milex/mex_major_spenders.pdf. (accessed 5/5/06).

5. Central Intelligence Agency. (CIA) The World Factbook. Available at http://www.cia.gov/cia/publications/factbook/rankorder/2034rank.html. (accessed 5/5/06).

6. International Institute for Strategic Studies. (IISS) Available at http://www.iiss.org/. (accessed 5/5/06).

7a.-7b. Congressional Research Reports for the people. "Conventional Arms Transfers to Developing Nations, 1997-2004." CRS Report 33051. Available at http://www.fas.org/sgp/crs/natsec/RL33051.pdf. (accessed 5/5/06).

8. Stockholm International Peace Research Institute. (SIPRI) (2005) SIPRI Yearbook 2005. Available at http://yearbook2005.sipri.org/. (accessed 5/5/06).

TRANSNATIONAL CRIME-TRAFFICKING & CORRUPTION

1.-3. U.S. Department of State. 2005 Trafficking in Person Report. Available at http://www.state.gov/documents/organization/47255.pdf. (accessed 5/5/06).

4a.-4b. United Nations Office on Drug and Crime. (UNODC) World Drug Report 2005. Available at http://www.unodc.org/unodc/en/world_drug_report.html. (accessed 5/5/06).

5. Transparency International. 2000 Corruption Perceptions Index. Available at http://www.transparency.org/policy_research/surveys_indices/cpi. (accessed 5/6/06).

6. Transparency International. 2004 Corruption Perceptions Index. Available at http://www.globalcorruptionreport.org/download.html. (accessed 5/6/06).

Transparency International. 2004 Global Corruption Report 2006. Available at http://psdblog.worldbank.org/psdblog/2006/02/global_corrupti.html. (accessed 5/6/06).

TRANSNATIONAL CRIME-PIRACY

1. Recording Industry Association of America. (RIAA) Year End Anti-Piracy Report.

2. Business Software Alliance. (BSA) Eight Annual BSA Global Software Piracy Study: Trends in Software Piracy 1994-2002. Available at http://download.microsoft.com/download/f/5/c/f5cabee0-4ed8-4f0b-a58c-45c377280ca8/BSA_Global_Piracy_Study.pdf. (accessed 5/5/06).

3. International Federation of the Phonographic Industry. (IFPI) (2002) Music Piracy Report. Available at http://www.ifpi.org/site-content/library/piracy2002.pdf. (accessed 5/5/06).

4. ComScore Media Metrix, as it appears on the Pew Internet Project & Comscore Media Metrix Data Memo. (2004) Available at http://www.pewinternet.org/pdfs/PIP_File_Swapping_Memo_0104.pdf (Accessed 7/5/06).

5. Daily Variety. Reed Business Information. 278 (42): A5, March 04, 2003. ISSN: 0011-5509

digest: issues and conflicts

Charlotte, D. and Wellington (eds) (2005) Human Development Report 2005, Published for the United Nations Development Program (UNDP), New York.

The Fund for Peace and the Carnegie Endowment for International Peace. (2006) "The Failed States Index." Foreign Policy.

International Peace Research Institute, Oslo (PRIO) (2005) Armed Conflict Dataset, Version 3. Available at www prio.no/cscw/armedconflict. (accessed 2/12/06).

Kaldor, Mary. (1999) New and Old Wars: Organized Violence in a Global Era. Cambridge: Polity Press.

Marshall, Monty G., and Gurr, Ted R. (2005) Peace and Conflict. Center for International Development and Conflict Management (CIDCM) University of Maryland, MD.

Marshall, Monty G. (2006) Major Episodes of Political Violence 1946-2005. Center for Systematic Peace. Available at http://members.aol.com/cspmgm/warlist.htm. (accessed 2/12/06).

The Uppsala Conflict Data Program. Available at http://www.pcr.uu.se/research/UCDP/graphs/region_only.pdf. (accessed 2/22/06).

digest: terrorism

Charlotte, D. and Wellington (eds.) (2005) Human Development Report 2005, Published for the United Nations Development Program (UNDP), New York.

Foreign Policy in Focus and the Center for Defense Information. (2004) Task Force on a Unified Budget for the United States, Washington, DC.

Marshall, Monty G., and Gurr, Ted R. (2005) Peace and Conflict. Center for International Development and Conflict Management.

Terrorism Knowledge Base. (2006) Available at www.tkb.org. (accessed 5/18/06).

digest: conflict resolution and UN peacekeeping

Falk, Richard. (2002) "The United Nations System: Prospects for Renewal", an article for the Transnational Foundation for Peace and Future Research. Available at http://www.transnational.org/forum/meet/2002/Falk_UNRenewal.html. (accessed 6/23/06).

Falk, Richard. (2006) "Reforming the United Nations: Global Civil Society Perspective and Initiatives", in Global Civil Society Yearbook: 150-186.

Heidelberg Institute of International Conflict Research. (HIIK)

Available at http://www.hiik.de/en/index_e.htm. (accessed 3/3/06).

Stockholm International Peace Research Institute. (SIPRI) (2005) SIPRI Yearbook 2005. Oxford: Oxford University Press. Available at http://www.sipri.org/contents/milap/milex/aprod/top100/SIPRI_TOP100.pdf. (accessed 5/30/06).

United Nations Development Program. (UNDP) Human Development Report 2005. Oxford and New York: Oxford University Press.

United Nations. "United Nations Peacekeeping Operations." Available at http://www.un.org/Depts/dpko/dpko/bnote.htm. (accessed 6/2/06).

United Nations Peace Operations. Available at http://www.un.org/Depts/dpko/dpko/pub/year_review04/. (accessed 6/8/06).

US Agency for International Development. (USAID) (2004) Celebrating Food for Peace. Available at http://www.usaid.gov/our_work/humanitarian_assistance/ffp/50th/FFP_50thAv_Brochure.pdf. (accessed 6/8/06).

digest: human rights

Amnesty International (2006), Annual Report 2006. Available at: http://web.amnesty.org/report2006/index-eng (Accessed 6/23/06)

The Cingranelli-Richards (CIRI) Human Rights Dataset, 2004. Available at: http://www.humanrightsdata.org

Human Rights Watch (2006), World Report 2006. Available at: http://hrw.org/wr2k6/ (Accessed 6/23/06)

One World Partners, http://www.oneworld.net/section/partners.

United Nations (1948), Universal Declaration of Human Rights. Available at: http://www.un.org/Overview/rights.html (Accessed 6/23/06)

digest: arms and military

Acton, James. (2006) "Arms Trade, role of the United Nations and US interests," International Debate Education Association. Available at http://www.idebate.org/debatabase/topic_details.php?topicID=442. (accessed 2/28/06).

Berrigan, F., Hartung, W. D., and Heffel, L. (2005) US Weapons at War 2005: Promoting Freedom or Fueling Conflict? U.S. Military Aid and Arms Transfers since September 11. World Policy Institute Special Report.

Charlotte, D. and Wellington. (eds) (2005) Human Development Report 2005. Published for the United Nations Development Program (UNDP), New York.

CIA Factbook. Available at http://www.cia.gov/cia/publications/factbook/rankorder/2034rank.html. Information is updated constantly. (accessed 2/26/06).

Grimmett, Richard F. (2005) Conventional Arms Transfers to Developing Nations, 1997-2004. CRS Report for Congress # 33051, Congressional Research Service, Library of Congress: August 29, 2005.

International Institute for Strategic Studies. (IISS) (2003) The Military Balance 2003-2004. Oxford: Oxford University Press. Available at http://hdr.undp.org/statistics/data/indic/indic_215_1_1.html. (accessed 2/22/06).

Klare, Michael. (1999) "The Kalashnikov Age", Bulletin of the Atomic Scientists, January/February, p. 19.

Stockholm International Peace Research Institute. (SIPRI) (2005) SIPRI Yearbook 2005. Oxford: Oxford University Press. Available at http://www.sipri.org/contents/milap/milex/aprod/top100/SIPRI_TOP100.pdf. (accessed 3/21/06).

digest: transnational crime and corruption

Charlotte, Denny and Wellington (eds) (2005) Human Development Report 2005, Published for the United Nations Development Program (UNDP), New York.

ComScore Media Metrix, as it appears on the Pew Internet Project & Comscore Media Metrix Data Memo. (2004) Available at http://www.pewinternet.org/pdfs/PIP_File_Swapping_Memo_0104.pdf (Accessed 7/5/06).

Deutche Presse-Agentur. (2006) "Nearly All countries affected by human trafficking, says UN report"

Extractive Industries Transparency Initiative. (EITI) (2006) "EITI Countries" Available at http://www.eitransparency.org/section/countries. (accessed 7/5/06).

International Planning and Research Corporation (IPR) (2003) Eighth Annual BSA GLOBAL Software Piracy Study 1994-2002.
Available at http://download.microsoft.com/download//f/5/c/f5cabee0-4ed8-4f0b-a58c-45c377280ca8/BSA_Global_Piracy_Study.pdf. (accessed 7/5/06).

Oberholzer, F. & Strumpf, K. (2004) The Effect of File Sharing on Record Sales, An Empirical Analysis
Available at http://www.unc.edu/~cigar/papers/FileSharing_March2004.pdf

Recording Industry Association of America. 2003 Year-End Anti-Piracy Report. Available at http://www.riaa.com/news/newsletter/pdf/2004yrEndAPstats.pdf. (accessed 7/5/06)

Transparency International. (2000) Corruption Perceptions Index. Available at www.Transparency.org/cpi/2000/cpi2000.html (accessed 7/5/06)

Transparency international. (2005) Corruption Perceptions Index. 2005 edition available at http://www.transparency.org/policy_research/surveys_indices/cpi/2005. (accessed 7/5/06).

Transparency International. (2006) Global Corruption Report 2006. Available at http://transparency.org/publications/gcr. (accessed 7/5/06).

United Nations Office on Drugs and Crime. (UNODC) (2006) Crime Prevention and Criminal Justice. Available at http://www.unodc.org/unodc/en/

crime_prevention.html. (accessed 6/30/06).

United Nations Office on Drugs and Crime. (UNODC) (2006) Trafficking in Persons: Global Patterns. Available at http://www.unodc.org/pdf/traffickinginpersons_report_2006ver2.pdf. (accessed 6/30/06).

US Department of State. (2004) Victims of Trafficking and Violence Protection Act of 2000: Trafficking in Persons Report. Available at http://www.state.gov/g/tip/rls/tiprpt/2004/. (accessed 7/5/06).

INDEX